How to Pin Down Smoke:
ruangrupa since 2000

Exhibition Histories

Afterall's *Exhibition Histories* book series, published since 2010, addresses what happens when art becomes public. Research led, it is committed to presenting a plurality of voices and critical perspectives, while bringing archival and other primary materials to bear on current and future practice. The series to date has focussed on curatorial experimentation; exhibitionary activity led by artists; and contested articulations of the 'global' and the 'located'. Complementing the books are online publications at afterall.org, discussion events and a research-based masters course in Exhibition Studies at Central Saint Martins, University of the Arts London. As researchers, publishers and teachers at Afterall, we will continue to explore situations that productively challenge and refine our understandings of 'art', 'exhibition' and 'history', mindful of what those terms might mean for the present. This would not be possible without the collaboration of our project partners: Asia Art Archive, based in Hong Kong; the Center for Curatorial Studies at Bard College, New York; documenta Institut, Kassel; and the Faculty of Fine, Applied and Performing Arts, University of Gothenburg.

How to Pin Down Smoke: ruangrupa since 2000

Edited by Wing Chan, Arianna Mercado and David Morris

With contributions by Ronny Agustinus, Leonhard Bartolomeus, Melani Budianta, Wing Chan, chitarum, Ade Darmawan, Özge Ersoy, Charles Esche, Nuraini Juliastuti, Abidin Kusno, Umi Lestari, Arianna Mercado, Ugeng T. Moetidjo, David Morris, farid rakun, Gesyada Siregar, Ibrahim Soetomo, Enin Supriyanto, David Teh, The Secret Agents, Mahardika Yudha and Ardi Yunanto

Exhibition Histories

Introduction: Happy Birthday 4

Wing Chan, Charles Esche, Arianna Mercado & David Morris

How to Pin Down Smoke: ruangrupa since 2000 is the fifteenth book published in the *Exhibition Histories* series. As the title implies, it seeks to do something that is not only difficult but arguably against the very nature of ruangrupa as an artistic collective.[1] Born in 2000 during Reformasi, a process that overthrew Suharto's three-decade-long authoritarian rule of Indonesia, ruru (the short form ruangrupa often use to describe themselves) are in many ways a product of their time and place. Reformasi was a period of regime change and widening possibility in many areas of Indonesia, yet it was about settling with the past without fully investigating it. This required citizens' critical negotiation, toleration and pragmatism in daily life, forms of engagement which have come to define ruru and how they approach the cultural field internationally. Their activities as a collective cross many borders – both geographic and intellectual – and will often frustrate demands for disciplinary precision, control and order which derive from a once-hegemonic (Western, modernist) world view. Instead, they have developed subtle methods to subvert 'art'; they go against earnestness and are flexible, fun-loving and practical; they are playful about their self-image while also being committed to collective practice and their long-established ways of working amongst themselves and with others.

As a group, they are attuned to archiving themselves and producing narratives both printed and online that highlight aspects of their story without claiming a totalising picture or a dogmatic manifesto. They are rooted in their local economies, and not afraid of using capitalist strategies, marketing, networking, mainstream culture or establishment politics when these paths are useful for their survival. As much as they are a product of their Jakarta environment, they are also fully engaged in transnational solidarity, shaping resource- and knowledge-sharing networks that span Africa, Asia, Europe and the Americas. With these strategies, ruru has survived two and a half decades. Through this book and the research that has shaped it, the *Exhibition Histories* editorial collective has constantly returned to three key questions: What kind of collective activism is ruru evocating? Where did it come from? How has it kept ruru going for decades in Jakarta and beyond?

Outside Indonesia, ruru is perhaps most widely recognised for their role as artistic directors of documenta fifteen – or lumbung I – in Kassel, Germany in 2022. To us, the significance of lumbung I is far reaching, and worthy of a book in itself – indeed, there is a substantial growing literature

1 Many thanks to poet Bhanu Kapil and writer Samanth Subramanian for inspiring this book's title; see B. Kapil, *Ban en Banlieue*, New York: Nightboat Books, 2015, p.23; and S. Subramanian, 'The editing floor – Outtakes from Indonesia', *multi-storied substack*, 19 June 2022, available online.

devoted to the event and its repercussions.[2] But rather than have this one project dominate the book, we have chosen to focus on the wide span of ruru's 25-year history – an approach that will also, we hope, open deeper understandings of their work in Kassel.[3] ruru's project sought above all to change the infrastructural basis of the documenta. They experimented with models of resource-sharing and shared economic prosperity rooted in local knowledges in Java, Sulawesi and elsewhere in Indonesia. They exercised their rights as artistic directors to *not* control artists, instead giving participants the tools to autonomously organise themselves. They avoided the heroic position of the star curators of past documentas in favour of being one collective amongst many artists and groups. In retrospect, the project's radical implications, alongside its geographical scope and what this was taken to represent by the German press and cultured bourgeoisie, may help explain the extremity of reaction it received at the time – which also served to obscure the show's actual content.[4] Yet ruru's call to build knowledge about the value of sustainable collectivity against oppressive regimes and institutions only increases in urgency. In widening the scope of ruru's stories through an engagement with their work since 2000, we hope that this book contributes to an expanded appreciation of their practices and their relation to wider liberation activism and the possibilities of art and culture to address commoning, collectivity and situated knowledges.

2 As well as the many publications developed for documenta fifteen/lumbung I and since by members of the lumbung network (many of which are available at books.lumbung.space) and critical engagement at the time, the exhibition has been the focus of special editions of journals such as *Art Review Oxford* (no.5, Autumn 2022), *OnCurating* (no.54, November 2022), *Grey Room* (no.92, 2023) and *Australian and New Zealand Journal of Art* (vol.24, no.1, 2024); and books such as *The Controversy over documenta fifteen: Background, Interpretation and Analysis*, edited by Martin Köttering and Sabine Boshamer (Hamburg: HFBK, 2023), *Art in A Multipolar World* by Mi You (Berlin and Stuttgart: Hatje Cantz, 2025) and *Decolonial Cultural Practices Towards Pluriversal Cultural Institutions and Policies*, edited by Meike Lettau and Özlem Canyürek (London: Routledge, 2025). ruangrupa are also preparing a forthcoming publication of their own 'harvests' from documenta fifteen.

3 See, for instance, Melani Budianta's detailed genealogy of *lumbung* practice across ruru's 25-year history, in this volume.

4 See, for instance, Hanan Toukan, 'Refusing Epistemic Violence: Guernica-Gaza and the "German Context"', *Afterall*, issue 57, Spring/Summer 2024, pp.122–47; and A. Dirk Moses, 'The German Campaign against Cultural Freedom: Documenta 15 in Context', *Grey Room*, no.92, Summer 2023, pp.74–93.

In developing this research, we have relied as much as possible on first-hand experience in its various forms of dialogue, teaching, field trips, parties and even rest. Like an inwardly rotating spiral, we started by talking to ruru's wider circles of collaborators; then people who had personal connections with ruru and its projects; and lastly, ruru themselves, in Jakarta, Makassar, Amsterdam and Kassel. Moving outside-in is a strategy to enter ruru through its networks of collaboration and friendship, but also a way to ease the burden on them to articulate their histories for themselves. Additionally, we found it necessary to leverage the observations and life experiences of ruru's friends for context, noticing the gaps in our own knowledge and understanding.

During the process of producing this book, Afterall also underwent some major changes, towards a more horizontal collective structure, which held curious parallels with what we observed from ruru. Throughout 2024 we slowed our publishing programme and broke the neat divisions in our actual job titles to explore more transversal ways of working together (think Jakarta). We filled in for our colleagues when new baby members came into the picture (think rurukids). We opened our office to connect with friends and visitors for snacks, casual chats and catch-ups (think 'Lekker Eten Zonder Betalen'). These slow transformations continue to be cultivated within the team, and they feel closer to the spirit of resting than progressing.

We felt compelled to ground our research in life experience and to connect it with our community of writers. chitarum, whose work is presented in this book's first section, 'introducing ruangrupa', belongs to a cohort of twenty young writers and practitioners with whom we have been building friendships and mutual mentorship since 2021.[5] chitarum's hand-drawn comic 'apa kabar' ('how are you?') is based on interviews with long-time friend Julia Sarisetiati (aka Sari) and current ruru members. It is a portal into their heartfelt kinships and what sustains this collective on an intimate, personal level. This is complemented by Melani Budianta's expansive critical analysis of ruangrupa's organisational practice. Budianta, a leading scholar of Indonesian social movements, has observed ruru as a fellow traveller for decades. Theorising *lumbung* practice as a principle of resource sharing, she analyses the implementation of such practice and its funding structure

Wing Chan, Charles Esche, Arianna Mercado & David Morris

5 We first met chitarum and Ibrahim Soetomo, another contributor to the present volume, in the context of a series of online and face-to-face workshops that we co-led since 2021. Initiated as 'Terms and Conditions of Writing and Publishing Art in Southeast Asia', the workshops have been co-facilitated by Wing Chan, Thanavi Chotpradit, Brigitta Isabella, Tram Luong, Adeena Mey, David Morris, Eileen Legaspi-Ramirez, Simon Soon and Vuth Lyno.

in ruru's formative period (2000–16), Gudang Sarinah period (2015–18) and Gudskul period (2018–date). Concluding the introductory section is Abidin Kusno, who addresses the deep connection between ruru as an urban collective and their home city of Jakarta. Reconnecting with his urbanist peers Iswanto Hartono and farid rakun, Kusno traces the material conditions and socio-historical context of the city since the 1950s in order to understand the specificity of ruru's Jakarta, and their collective practice as expressive of the multicultural mega-city's everyday urban ecologies and cultural ecosystems.

The expansive middle section of the book is devoted to an extended archive of ruangrupa. It gathers primary materials including photographic documentation, press releases, posters and flyers spanning a quarter century, up to the present. We have organised it with the intention of highlighting the range and diversity of ruru's activities over the years, and as complement to ongoing plans for a free online resource of all these materials and more, to be hosted by lumbung.space in the future.[6] These materials are diverse and sometimes idiosyncratic, reflecting ruru's own practices of archiving, where apparently random snapshots of gatherings and interactions can carry important insights into the longevity of the collective's daily practice. In a sense, ruru is a hoarder. Across many, many projects, they have repeated their core repertoire of creative strategies, refining or elaborating them.[7] ruru hold onto what they created in the 2000s, and they continue to develop their programmes with new generations of members and friends.

This book's archive of ruangrupa also doubles as a gathering point: fresh contributions from over thirty ruru members, friends and observers are placed in dialogue with primary documents, alongside selected historical texts, by Ade Darmawan, Ronny Agustinus, Ugeng T. Moetidjo, David Teh and farid rakun, which in different ways reflect significant moments in ruru's history. These perspectives are complemented by the case studies gathered in the book's third part, with newly commissioned essays

6 The process of assembling a comprehensive archive of ruangrupa continues as a major undertaking, towards which the present publication hopes to contribute (as also detailed in Özge Ersoy's contribution). The selection here reflects the current status of ruangrupa's digital archive-in-progress, where the first decade or so is better represented in the digital folders than the subsequent period. We have balanced this with supplementary research, while also welcoming the opportunity to highlight ruru's formative years – which are also the activities and projects that may be least known to a wider readership beyond Jakarta.

7 For instance, as Melani Budianta notes in her essay, the *lumbung* ethos has characterised ruru's practice from its early days, although its articulation as such has been much more recent.

highlighting particular key projects and areas of concern. Ardi Yunanto, in conversation with Ibrahim Soetomo, details the development of *Karbon*, ruangrupa's publishing platform since 2000. Arianna Mercado considers ruru's formative 2003 solo exhibition 'Lekker Eten Zonder Betalen' ('Tasty Meal Without Paying'), when ruru threw an all-night party at Cemeti Art House in Yogyakarta and exhibited the remnants, including leftover food; the event's imagery has since been circulated as a kind of collective self-portrait. Umi Lestari and Mahardika Yudha explore the history of OK.Video, the international video and media arts biennial organised by ruru since 2003, in the context of social, political and technological shifts in Indonesia since the 1990s. Gesyada Siregar and Leonhard Bartolomeus, as long-time facilitators at Gudskul and RURU Gallery respectively, represent two different generations of practitioners growing up within ruru; their contributions reveal what it is like to work with and live amongst ruru and friends, offering us ways to understand collectivity with concrete examples and insiders' learning. And as soundtrack to this archive-gathering, we have a 'DJ set' insert by The Secret Agents celebrating 25 years with ruru and friends.

The final section of the book expands on key critical, historical and practical questions that will emerge for anyone spending time in the company of ruru's archives. Arianna Mercado and Wing Chan begin with a self-reflexive exploration of the research experience of trying to 'pin down smoke'. Their analysis develops through close encounters with ruru's internal workings, including its membership, financial resources and collaborative processes. Özge Ersoy shares the work of Asia Art Archive as it scopes the archives of ruru for cataloguing, which has developed alongside the research and development of the present publication; Ersoy reflects on the potentials and limitations of archiving a collective as long-lived, complex and playful as ruru. Enin Supriyanto offers a personal view on the Indonesian history leading up to Reformasi (and ruru), guiding us through Gerakan Seni Rupa Baru (New Art Movement), study groups, field research, imprisonment, press freedom and cultural policy. Finally, Nuraini Juliastuti returns us to the practice of *lumbung* – as explored in detail by Melani Budianta at the outset of the book – to develop an expanded repertoire of commoning via the concept of jamming, with examples from ruru's contemporaries and beyond.

Wing Chan, Charles Esche, Arianna Mercado & David Morris

We give our heartfelt thanks to all the contributors to this publication, as well as ruru and Gudskul friends for their generosity throughout the project. As our copy editor Deirdre O'Dwyer asked during the editorial process: 'Are the people working on this ruru book the most kind and generous-spirited group you've worked with?' The openness, trust and companionship of our collaborators added much meaning and warmth to the making of this book. We thank our steadfast partners in *Exhibition Histories*: Sneha Ragavan and Anthony Yung at Asia Art Archive; Lauren Cornell and Tom Eccles at the Center for Curatorial Studies, Bard College; Mick Wilson at the Faculty of Fine, Applied and Performing Arts, University of Gothenburg; and Felix Vogel and Mi You at documenta Institut. This book coincides with ruru's 25th birthday. We wish them a very happy birthday. The research has been a challenging yet enjoyable endeavour. We hope our readers and fellow researchers, writers and cultural workers will connect with ruru in new and unexpected ways. They remain an endlessly surprising and inventive collective, providing a wealth of material to explore fresh ways of imagining art and life together. We hope this book does a little justice to their magnanimous multiplicity.

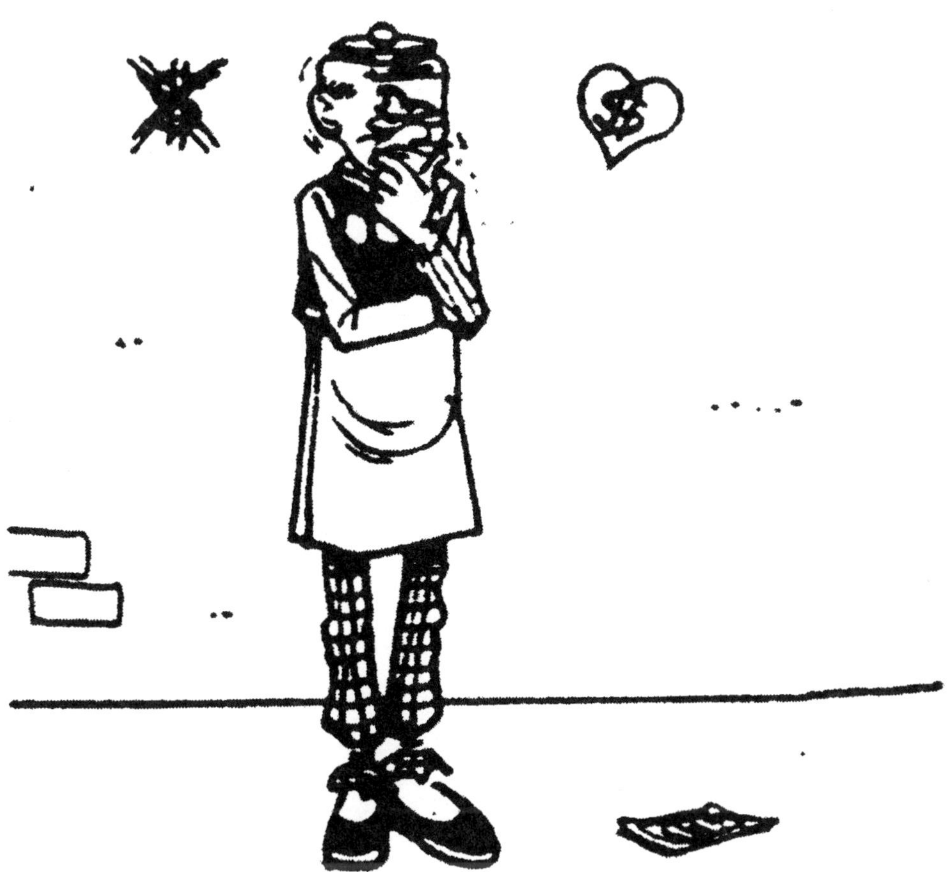

Make space, but more importantly, make time.

This section is a general introduction to ruangrupa from three perspectives. We will follow the historical development of ruru since 2000 in terms of *lumbung* practice; hear from current ruru members about their roles and relationships to the collective; and situate ruru as an expression of Jakarta's complex urban ecology.

Political Economy and Aesthetics of Space: Genealogy of ruangrupa's *Lumbung* Practice

12

Melani Budianta

It was a hot and humid day in mid-October 2024. Inside an auditorium that used to be a futsal hall, I sat with representatives of arts collectives from Papua, Sulawesi, Lombok, Jakarta and Central Java. For three hours plus a half-hour lunch break, in an air-conditioned hall filled with cigarette smoke, we sat in a circle on the floor and discussed the work and challenges faced by the various collectives in their respective localities.

The activists, who were mostly in their twenties and thirties, shared stories of finding space for their creative and critical aspirations in urban and rural environments that see the arts as mere commodities, often for tourists. Neither the arts academy nor the local government nor the private sector understood artists' needs. The common narrative that the young activists shared was one of like-minded young artists forming a collective to work together, share resources and occupy a space in nurturance of their vision in a specific locality. As such, it resembles the path of ruangrupa (often abbreviated as ruru), the Indonesian arts collective founded in Jakarta in 2000.

Indeed, it is no coincidence that ruangrupa's name combines the keywords *ruang*, meaning 'space', and *rupa*, from *seni rupa*, or 'visual arts'. Two co-founders of ruangrupa, Ade Darmawan and Hafiz Rancajale, have recounted their experience as the director and the main curator, respectively, of the 2013 Jakarta Biennale, for example, in terms of the difficulty in finding a venue for the arts exhibition.[1] The Taman Ismail Marzuki (TIM) cultural centre, where international arts and cultural events are usually hosted in Jakarta, was booked, as were other formal venues. In the end they 'activated' heterogenous spaces in the capital city for the whole event, spreading the international in the local level:

> The 2013 Jakarta Biennale tried to expand artistic experiences in areas that had not been touched by contemporary art activities, such as the east, west and north [of the city]. Artists, both individuals and collectives, from within and outside the country, were challenged to process their artistic ideas in public spaces, which in this year's event were manifested in markets, parks, city walls, schools and settlements. At the next level, it was very important to see the art practices that involved themselves with social issues as part of daily struggles, so that these were not only celebrated but also questioned, criticized and optimized. Therefore, the focus this time was on project-based works, research, interdisciplinary work and joint works that involved citizens' participation.[2]

1 Ade Darmawan, interviewed by the author, Jakarta, 2 October 2024; Hafiz Rancajale, interviewed by the author, Jakarta, 19 January 2025.

2 'Jakarta Biennale 2013', https://2021.jakartabiennale.id/jakarta-biennale-2013-2.

Nearly a decade later, ruru would pursue this strategy again, but in Germany, as the main curators of documenta fifteen in 2022. They occupied and transformed the city of Kassel through the artistic experimentation of dozens more collectives from all over the world, but mostly from the Global South. In ruru's hands, documenta was not an exhibition of Art, but of perhaps mundane activities such as cooking in a shared kitchen, playing soccer and beating tiles with bamboo sticks to make music. The public was invited to participate in the 'performance' of these activities, showing how spaces of interaction can, potentially, direct one's perspective towards what might otherwise be taken for granted in daily life.

Such intervention prompts questions about how one defines art, especially in societies that locate art in the confines of world-class galleries. It should be no surprise that responses to documenta fifteen were mixed. Critics variously considered ruru's project to be a 'missed [crosscultural] encounter'; problematic collective arts management that 'bracketed' spectators; and an 'unfulfilled promise' for actual global socio-political transformation.[3] Discussion continues to this day as to whether it was 'the first exhibition of the twenty-first century', or its 'last gasp'.[4]

At the heart of the heated debate was *lumbung*, a concept and practice named after the Indonesian for 'rice barn', where the agricultural harvest is stored in rural villages, enabling food safety and sharing to be organised and managed collectively. The term was chosen by ruru to imagine documenta fifteen, which ruru and the collaborators have since preferred to call 'Lumbung I'.[5] The concept was defined as:

3 A. Dirk Moses, 'The German Campaign Against Cultural Freedom: Documenta 15 in Context', *Grey Room*, no.92, Summer 2023, pp.74–93; Monica Juneja and Jo Ziebritzki, 'Learning with Documenta 15: Principles, Practices, Problems', *Grey Room*, no.92, Summer 2023, pp.94–105; Marina Vishmidt, 'Nothing to See Here: On the Bracketing of the Spectator in a Hyperrelational Exhibition', *Grey Room*, no.92, Summer 2023, pp.117–23.

4 See Charles Esche, 'The First Exhibition of the Twenty-First Century – Lumbung 1 (Documenta Fifteen), What Happened, and What It Might Mean Two Years On', *Australian and New Zealand Journal of Art*, 2024, pp.1–10; and T. Heffernan, N. Farro, N. Papastergiadis, D. Butt, T. McDowell and V. Lynn, 'Responses to Charles Esche', *Australian and New Zealand Journal of Art*, 2024, pp.1–14.

5 In discussions of documenta fifteen, the term 'Lumbung I' is often preferred, not only 'to bypass precisely those demands that the traditions of contemporary art loaded on to it before ruru arrived on the scene, but to refer to the new practice that is expected to continue in the future'. C. Esche, 'The First Exhibition of the Twenty-First Century', op. cit., p.1.

a collective resource pot, operating under the logics of the commons. It is an agglomeration of ideas, stories, (wo)manpower, time, and other shareable resources. Central to *lumbung* is the imagination and the building of these collective, shared resources into new models of sustainable ideas and cultural practices.[6]

Thus, ruru reorganised the existing curatorial system into layers of decision-making by independent artist collectives, which were called 'lumbung members'. Each was given the responsibility of curating their own artistic activities within the space and time of documenta fifteen. The whole management process was shared in democratic, bottom-up meetings called *majelis* before, during and after the exhibition. What was important, therefore, was not the artistic product per se, but the whole process of intervening in the space, as well as of crafting social relations and interactions to make art happen. Thus, aesthetics blended with the economics and politics of space.

A crucial feature of *lumbung*-style organisation is that it is 'locally anchored', that is, grounded in the diverse localities of the lumbung members. The use of non-English terms such as *majelis* (from Arabic) and *nongkrong* (Jakartan youth slang for 'informal gathering') reflects this move away from the homogenising tendency of modernist art. While the decolonialising novelty of *lumbung* practice, as well as its problematic reception, has been widely discussed, the orientalist tendency of generalising *lumbung* has escaped scrutiny. In documenta fifteen, *lumbung* stood as an alternative to neoliberal, individualistic, market-oriented global arts management. In this positioning, it was taken for granted that the term represented local arts practices in the places from which the lumbung members had come.

However, physical agrarian barns are almost non-existent in today's Indonesia, where the rural has been colonialised by both capitalism and urban modernity – the very juncture at which ruangrupa is located. By problematising locality, this essay traces the genealogy of *lumbung* practice in the organisational history of ruru, contextualising it in the political economy of Indonesia as it relates to the national and international arts scene since in the early 2000s. The discussion here will examine the collective imagination in the formative period of ruru and their experimentation with *lumbung* practice as the collective has occupied different spaces of cohabitation, from a house to an abandoned warehouse. The essay will then focus on the Gudskul collective, a merger between ruru and two other collectives, Grafis Huru Hara and Serrum. The research informing this essay draws from print and social media publications of and on ruru and Gudskul, as well as interviews

6 'Lumbung: Short Concept by ruangrupa for documenta 15' (from press information by documenta), *Universe in Universe*, https://universes.art/en/documenta/2022/short-concept.

with Ade Darmawan, co-founder and leader of ruru; Ronny Agustinus and Hafiz Rancajale, also co-founders; farid rakun and Julia Sarisetiati, ruru artists; Grafis Huru Hara and Serrum artists; and participating collectives in the 2024 Gudskul Collective Study programme.

What follows is a history that identifies distinct periods of growth in ruru's exploration and management of various spaces in the arts ecosystem: the formative period (2000–16); the Gudang Sarinah period (2015–18); and the Gudskul period (2018–24). This periodisation stages how ruru has negotiated and rearranged the fluid realms of the private and the public in their 'survival' strategies, which all the while has engaged with *lumbung* as a continuously evolving managerial and aesthetic practice. *Lumbung*, in ruru's case, is a long process of discovery and experimentation. I contend that up to the present, *lumbung* practice has stood out as an empowering imagining of translocal commoning initiatives. As such, it is a contested terrain that ruru and similarly inspired artist collectives struggle to occupy – locally as well as globally.

Lumbung *as Commoning Practice*

The loss of rice barns in Indonesia's villages reflects the country's massive urbanisation rate – which reached 59 per cent by 2023, based on World Bank data.[7] This trend is supported by its 'current spatial policy', which 'tends to facilitate more massive urbanisation than the existing historical trend' and will cause an estimated decrease in rice fields from 26 per cent in 2019 to 24 per cent in 2032.[8] Similarly, the escalation of deforestation since 2001 had caused the loss of 24 million hectares of forest by 2017.[9]

Rapid urban development in Indonesia has not reduced poverty. Instead, with the disempowerment of rural farmers and the expansion of uneducated rural migration to cities, Indonesia is the world's sixth-highest-ranking country in terms of wealth inequality.[10] With more than half of the population living in cities, urban development has been geared towards providing gentrified residential areas as well as recreational and consumption facilities for

7 'Urban Population (% of total population) – Indonesia', World Bank Group website.

8 A.E. Pravitasari, G.S. Indraprahasta, E. Rustiadi, V.B. Rosandi, Y.A. Stanny, S. Wulandari and A. Murtadho, 'Dynamics and Predictions of Urban Expansion in Java, Indonesia: Continuity and Change in Mega-Urbanization', *ISPRS International Journal of Geo-Information*, vol.13, no.3, 2024, p.102.

9 'When We Lost the Forest, We Lost Everything: Oil Plam Plantations and Rights Violations in Indonesia', Human Rights Watch website.

10 'Inequality in Indonesia: Millions Kept in Poverty', Oxfam International website.

the rich and the middle classes. As public and social spaces are turned into commercial areas, the individualised lifestyle becomes normalised.

While there are NGOs working to address the social problems of the urban poor and others in rural or urban areas, since the Cold War era, and specifically the communist cleansing of 1965, leftist critique of the political economy and state governance has been deemed politically off point. The capitalist hegemony that served as the backbone of the New Order (1966–98) has continued to solidify into the present. The Reformasi era, which pushed decentralisation and democratisation beginning in 1998, did not limit this trend; and since 1999, the post-Reformasi era has in fact seen the spread of global capitalism to remote areas.

In seeming contradiction to the Reformasi principles of decentralisation and democratisation, the state in the 2020s has enforced top-down policies including the creation of massive food estates, referred to, ironically enough, as *lumbung pangan*. Enforced rice cultivation on islands where populations formerly sustained themselves with other crops has taken away the food sovereignty of local communities. Extractive industries purchase farmlands from rural families and aggressively evict indigenous communities from their tribal lands.

And all the while, school children are to believe that the traditional collective values of *gotong-royong* (working collectively to help one another) hold Indonesian society together. Actually, the collective and communal spirit did prove handy during the global economic crisis that accompanied the Covid-19 pandemic from 2020 to 2022. What helped the majority of the Indonesian population in surviving the pandemic, including vulnerable populations, was not the state's top-down policy but rather community-based initiatives to pool resources and protect people in their local neighbourhoods.

Globally, the grave impact of capitalist greed – spanning climate change, global warming and extreme poverty – has brought urgency to the call for open-source, non-privatised resource sharing. Commons give an alternative to the neoliberal paradigm of 'growth, competition and extraction' that dominates not only the arts ecosystem but the local-global economy. Implied is a reference to Elinor Ostrom's rebuttal of Garrett Hardin's theory that supports the privatisation of open spaces for sustainability by showing instead the critical role of the collective governance of common resources as a solution.[11] In recent studies, cultural commons are seen as an antidote to state or capital privatisation: '[M]any current campaigns to resist

11 V. Fournier, 'Commoning: On the Social Organisation of the Commons', *M@n@gement*, vol.16, no.4, 2013, pp.433–53.

incorporation into the widening circuits of capitalism are grounded in a shared commitment to keeping alive "the commons" and the collective practices around them that create and sustain community and its ecological bases.'[12] In cultural studies scholarship, the term 'commons' has often been replaced by the verb 'commoning' to suggest the action, or collective everyday practice, of resource sharing as a strategy to create an alternative space and support system within the hegemonic capitalistic world.[13]

Nuraini Juliastuti has used the term 'commons museum' as a conceptual framework 'to examine counter-authoritative cultural institutions, as well as a set of strategies for "worlding" modelled on alternative spaces and community organisations'. Examining the communal practices of the artist collectives Pagesangan and Lakoat.Kujawas, Juliastuti highlights 'creative attempts to reset the lives of their communities by tuning into different realities of progress, while simultaneously allowing space for ancestral worldviews to guide their process'. She continues: 'This involves developing strategies to create public learning spaces that also function as cultural institutions for the well-being of the community. It transforms these spaces into alternative infrastructures for contextual education, archiving and community economies.'[14] Community arts movements, as discussed by Juliastuti, mushroomed in the post-Reformasi period, which was marked by a process of democratisation.

At the same time, they were a critical reaction to the existing arts ecosystem, which, according to Ade Darmawan, in a 2022 cultural oration to the Jakarta Arts Council, was 'elitist, bureaucratic and commercial'.[15] During which, Darmawan mentioned several agents in the arts ecosystem that failed to bring arts to the public: the state, the arts councils, the private sector (the art market, including galleries) and the arts education system. Commoning is especially needed when the state is not there to provide sufficient support for the arts. Standard-setting arts councils are elitist and bureaucratic in their approach, and the market and commercial

12 Vinay Gidwani and Amita Baviskar, 'Urban Commons', *Economic and Political Weekly*, vol.46, no.50, 2011, pp.42–43.

13 S. Gruber, V. Miller, M. Verlič, H.K. Wang, J. Wieger, A. Baldauf and A. Krauss, *Spaces of Commoning: Artistic Research and the Utopia of the Everyday*, London: Sternberg Press, 2016, p.275.

14 Nuraini Juliastuti, *Commons Museum: Pedagogies for Taking Ownership of What is Lost*, Berlin: ICI Berlin Press, 2024, p.2.

15 Ade Darmawan, 'Berakar dan Menjalar: Lumbung Sebagai Model Ekonomi dan Estetika Organisasi Seni' (Taking Root and Spreading Out: Lumbung as an Economic and Aesthetic Model of Art Organisation), Jakarta Arts Council Annual Cultural Speech conference, 10 November 2022.

galleries groom artists for work in the arts as a commodity-based investment. Arts education, in the meantime, struggles to keep up with the fast-changing world of digital, ecological and social transformation. The options individual artists had before the Reformasi era to promote their work were, as Ronny Agustinus has pointed out, the arts gallery and the *sanggar* (arts studio) where attendees studied under the mentorship of an individual artist. A result of the ecosystem's elitist orientation has been a disparity of access and exposure for artists living on the peripheries.[16]

Commoning and community arts initiatives, then, can be seen as efforts to find collective support in a cut-throat, neoliberal and individualistic world, and as offering the possibility for voicing and practicing artistic and critical interventions. While acts of commoning share a similar motivation, they are contextualised in different localities and can be explained using local terms. *Lumbung*, as 'rice barn', refers to a familiar entity among agricultural societies in Southeast Asia but also worldwide. For example, Koji Sato considers the architectural shape of the rice barn as relating to the model of the pile dwelling in the Asia Pacific region.[17] Among diverse ethnic groups, tier-shaped rice barns have variations that include the Sundanese *leuit*, the Minangese *rangkiang* and the Dayak Kenyah *lepubung*.

Sundanese *leuit* (rice barn) from Kasepuhan Cipta Gelar, Sukabumi. Photo: Komaruddin Ibnu Mikam

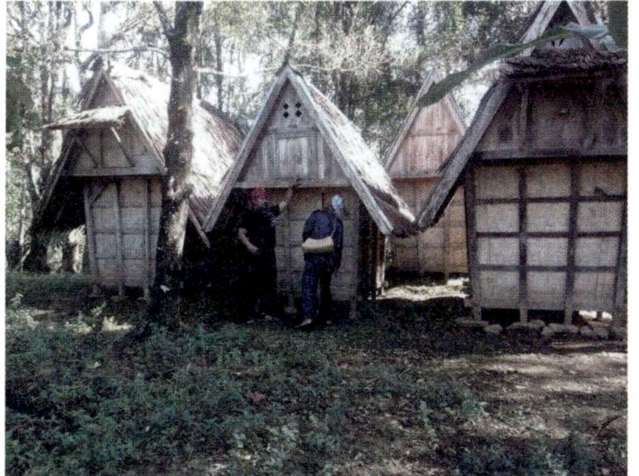

Dayak Kenyah *lepubung*, a village barn in Lung Anai village in East Kalimantan. Photo: Lucas Nay

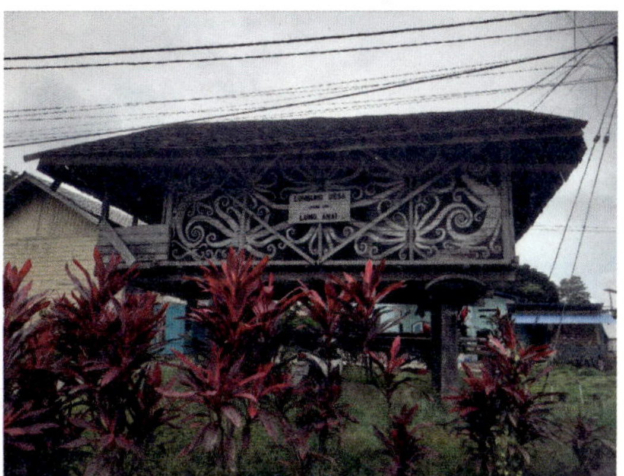

16 Ronny Agustinus, interviewed by the author, Jakarta, 1 October 2024.

17 Koji Sato, 'Menghuni Lumbung; Beberapa Pertimbangan Mengenai Asal-Usul Konstruksi Rumah Panggung di Kepulauan Pasifik' (Inhabiting Lumbung: Several Considerations about the Origin of Stilt Housing Construction in Pacific Archipelago), *Antropologi*, no.49, 2014, pp.31–47.

As a rural space for storing the harvest, the rice barn offers food security and resilience, ensuring that villagers will have resources in times of scarcity or drought. The rice barn's storage, maintenance and sharing are organised collectively through the village assembly. Not merely a space for storage, *lumbung* is related to a village's collective identity – the daily social life of the agrarian community circulates around the rice barn. Its philosophy affirms the commitment of community members to working together for the well-being of the whole.

However, as mentioned earlier, in twenty-first-century Indonesia, the use of village rice barns became almost obsolete due to agricultural land conversion, massive urbanisation and industrialisation, and a state policy of importing rice. Urban consumption, and its attendant lifestyle, has come to permeate the rural economy and lifestyle. In urban modernity, not only the architectural design of *lumbung* but the word itself has been co-opted into commercial resorts, in an exotic commodification devoid of social values.

In the 2010s, however, the communal spirit of *lumbung* was revived by a number of civil society groups and cultural, arts and traditional communities. By using *lumbung* as a symbol, they positioned themselves against the hegemonic marginalisation of communal, rural and traditional indigenous practices. The Japung Nusantara logo, for example, features a rice barn form and is used by an informal network of collaborating urban *kampungs* and rural village cultural activists. The *lumbung* symbol is also used by indigenous, tribal communities like the Dayak Kenyah in East Kalimantan, who still preserve and practice rural traditions and rituals. When *lumbung* is culturally and geographically anchored in a specific location, the use of *lumbung* as logo underscores values of collaboration and collective care otherwise lost in the hustle and bustle of a competitive, individualised world.[18]

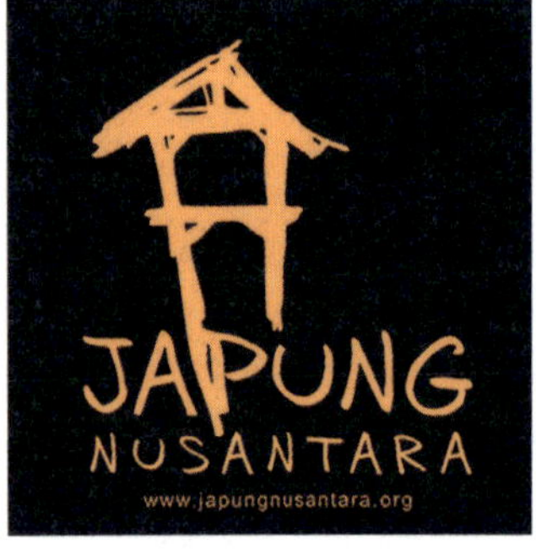

Logo of Japung Nusantara (Network of Nusantara Kampung), designed by Toni Masdiono. Courtesy Japung Nusantara.

18 M. Budianta, 'Lumbung Commoning', UNITAS 100: *Where Scholarship Stands the Test of Time*, vol.95, no.2, 2022, p.348; N. Juliastuti, *Commons Museum*, *op. cit.*

Iswanto Hartono, sketch of *lumbung*, 2020. Courtesy the artist

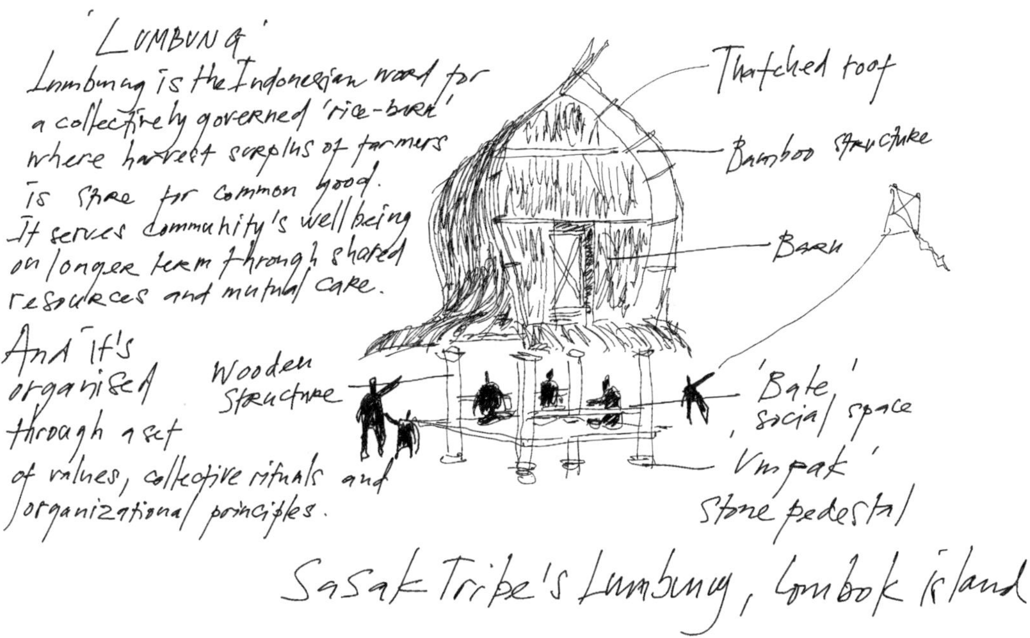

The visual representation of *lumbung* shows that, as a signifier, it is imbued with contested meanings. ruangrupa, located as they are in an urban setting, has adopted *lumbung* in reflection of a nostalgic turn to the rural past. At the same time, the decision to engage *lumbung* as an organisational model reaffirms alternative values against the neoliberal paradigm. In contrast to competition and capitalistic accumulation, this involves key terms of collective sharing: through references to 'common good', 'community well-being' and 'mutual care', 'organisational principles' are highlighted.

How *lumbung* values are implemented into organisational management is a different matter. A tribal/indigenous *lumbung*'s members are families living in a village community. How each family contributes and divides the tasks of keeping and sharing resources is conducted via tribal and village assembly processes. The JAPUNG Nusantara network, for example, has a system of inter-*kampung* solidarity that can be activated whenever necessary. Different phases of ruru's development as an artist collective have necessitated different kinds of *lumbung* management. The subsequent sections of this essay will map ruru's processes of experimentation with *lumbung*, which have dealt not only with organising commoning but also with crafting and occupying different kinds of space, both public and private.

Ade Darmawan's banner of Haji Mohamed Suharto in the artist's studio at the Rijksakademie, Amsterdam; and during a protest against Suharto regime, Dam Square, Amsterdam, 1998. Courtesy the artist

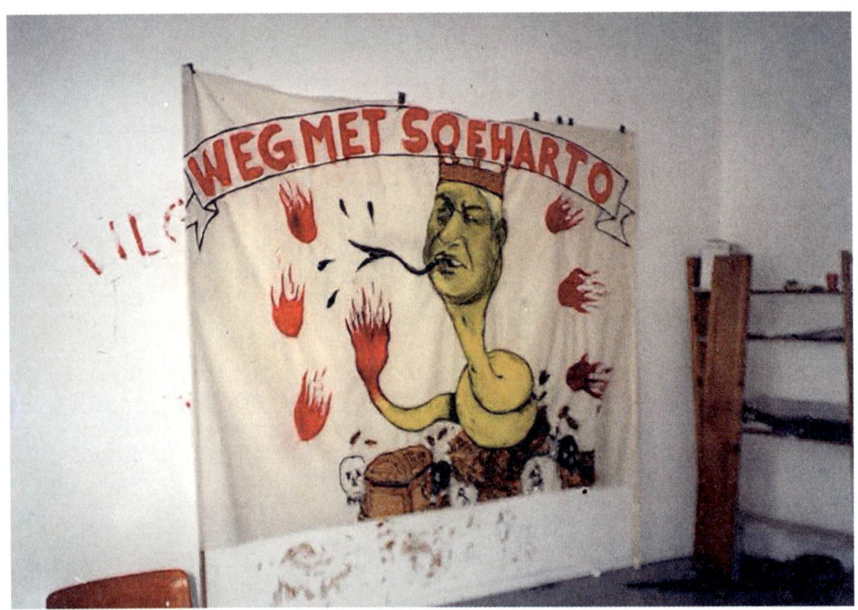

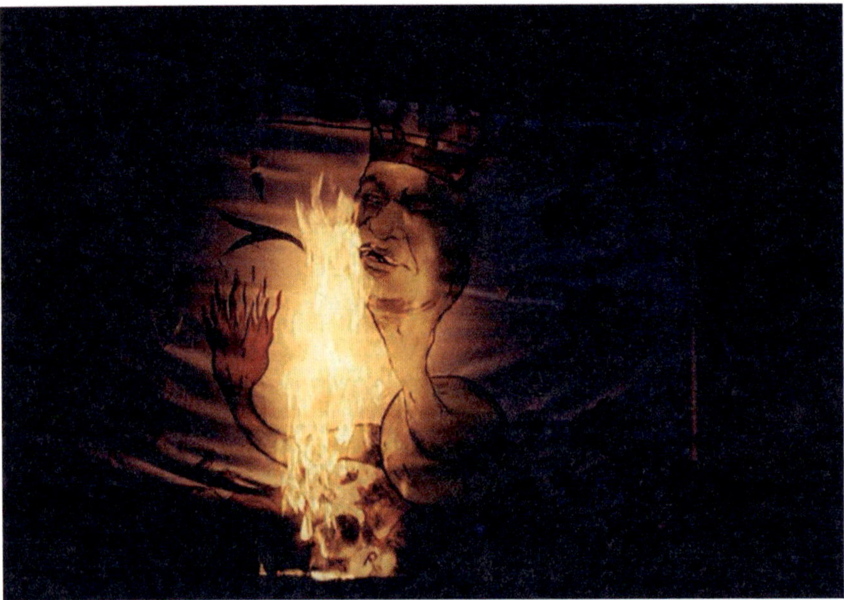

The Formative Period: Finding and Sharing Home (2000–16)

The formative period of ruangrupa was spent moving from one place to the next as the group turned private spaces, specifically various rented houses, into homes shared by continuously coming-and-going 'family' members. During this sixteen-year period, ruru was also developing their artistic and critical intervention into urban space by positioning themselves within the contemporary arts ecosystem of post-Reformasi Jakarta. In crafting various forms of 'collective economy' and 'artistic strategies for the public', ruru was experimenting with 'institutional aesthetics'.[19]

Although ruru was formally established as an artist collective in 2000, the 'embryo' of the entity started earlier, in the mid-1990s. The need to form a collective came from the interactions and friendship of arts students mostly from Jakarta and Yogyakarta. In 1995, students from the Institut Kesenian Jakarta (Jakarta Arts Institute, IKJ) and the Institut Seni Indonesia Yogyakarta (Indonesia Arts Institute in Yogyakarta, ISI) held a forum called 'Dialog Dua Kota' (Dialogue between Two Cities), and the bonding continued to develop afterwards. As Reza Afisina has explained, arts students shared an 'experience of precarity' that entailed not only facilities and funding but also a community that provided a home base for collaborative work.[20]

The period from 1995 to 2000 coincided with the declining power of the New Order. Mounting criticism of the Suharto government, which had held power since the communist cleansing of 1965, was reciprocated by the state's repression of students and intellectuals. Jakarta, as the capital city, became a hotbed. In 1997, there was a violent take-over of the headquarters of the opposition party, Partai Demokrasi Indonesia (PDI), in Jalan Diponegoro, about two kilometres from the IKJ. In May 1998, a national economic crisis accompanied the Asian Financial Crisis and led to riots in a number of shopping centres with concentrated Chinese communities; accompanying the violent events was the orchestrated mass rape of Chinese women. Student protesters who gathered at several campuses, including Trisakti in West Jakarta and Atmajaya University in Central Jakarta, were crushed by the military. Some were killed. Ade Darmawan, who was then in Amsterdam doing a fellowship at the Rjiksakademie, painted Suharto's figure on a banner and burned it at a protest march.

Having emerged from this context, those who co-founded ruru to this day find aesthetics and the arts inseparable from politics. Indeed, their artistic expression cohered as a politics formed within and tied to the urban context

19 A. Darmawan, 'Berakar dan Menjalar', *op. cit.*

20 Sophie Goltz in conversation with Reza Afisina, Ade Darmawan and Iswanto Hartono, 'Collective Crafting in Post-Suharto Indonesia: A Journey with ruangrupa from the Jakarta Institute of the Arts to Documenta Fifteen in Kassel', *Cultural Politics*, vol.18, no.3, 2022, p.434.

of Jakarta. David Teh sees the group as 'bound to Jakarta in every sense, physically, spiritually and conceptually'.[21] Iswanto Hartono, an architect and member of the Chinese-Indonesian minority population who was working close to the scene of the Ketapang riots in West Jakarta in November 1998, has acknowledged that joining ruru afterwards gave him a sense of political identity and a feeling of being embraced as a part of a family.[22]

As Darmawan was returning from The Netherlands in 2000, the initiators of ruru took the opportunity to form the collective. Thomas J. Berghuis marks a fundraising exhibition of 25 Jakarta-, Bandung- and Yogyakarta-based artists' work, held in April 2000 at the Cemara 6 Gallery in Central Jakarta, as the public debut of ruangrupa as an artist collective.[23] The co-founders were Ronny Agustinus, Ade Darmawan, Oky Arfie Hutabarat, Lilia Nursita, Hafiz Rancajale and Rithmi Widanarko, with Darmawan acting as director. The list may grow and shrink in the individual memories of the co-founders, and certainly there were many 'unofficial' members during ruru's formative period. Membership has continued to be informal and 'fluid'. Some join with intensity for a period of time, then leave to attend to other matters; and while most members have an institutional arts education, other professional backgrounds include writer/journalist, researcher, architect and community activist.

The founders of ruru rented their first house in Pasar Minggu, South Jakarta (2000–01). From there, they moved on to three rented houses in the Tebet area, South Jakarta: Tebet Barat (2001–03), Tebet Barat Dalam IX (2004–06) and Tebet Timur Dalam Raya (2006–16). For Jakarta's residents and other urban dwellers in Indonesia, the common necessity to frequently move is often due to increases in rent, the expanding or shrinking needs of a household, or strategic access to perhaps a school or workplace. Affordability was the main issue for members of ruru from the start – as students and recent graduates, they had to make ends meet, and everyone chipped in to rent the houses.

Tebet, as an urban area made up of alleys and main streets, offered a mixture of planned commercial housing and informal *kampung* settlements. In the early 2000s, rooms and houses in Tebet were inexpensive to rent. Living and working in a rented house within an urban area, according to Darmawan in his 2022 cultural oration to the Jakarta Arts Council, helped embed the artist collective in the neighbourhood:

21 David Teh, 'Who Cares a Lot? ruangrupa as Curatorship', *Afterall*, issue 30, 2012, pp.108–17, and reprinted in this volume.

22 S. Goltz, R. Afisina, A. Darmawan and I. Hartono, 'Collective Crafting in Post-Suharto Indonesia', *op. cit.*, p.437.

23 Thomas J. Berghuis, 'ruangrupa: What Could Be "Art to Come"', *Third Text*, vol.25, no.4, 2011, pp.395–407.

> Those occupying the space could imagine living with the neighbours. The living room serves as a space to form initiatives in order to be financially independent. Renters need to negotiate and engage in dialogue with the values of the given society. Side by side with the neighbours, this is an explorative strategy rooted in a specific locality.[24]

Such 'negotiation' with neighbours in Tebet was necessary, for example, when ruru held public bazaars or festivals directly on the street. They welcomed neighbours' participation in the merrymaking, although not everyone shared their same interests. Darmawan has elsewhere remembered that the street was also used by some 'right-wing' neighbours for religious prayer, blocking access to ruru. Yet, *tahu sama tahu* (tacit understanding of different values) has proven key to living in close-knit neighbourhoods.[25]

According to Darmawan, the act of inhabiting a rented house 'was a representation of the working middle class, where ... artists grow'. In his cultural oration, he recalled curating with Rifky Effendy an exhibition of alternative spaces and artist groups in Indonesia, titled 'Fixer' (2010), related to the phenomenon of artist collectives all over Indonesia 'using [the] rented house as [the] centre of activity', to thus make the private and the public inseparable:

> The living room – which is usually the largest – is used as the meeting place. ... The domestic space is turned into a place to welcome guests and other public. The living room also serves as a space for exhibition. The bedrooms are also turned into exhibition space and working space. The toilet becomes the office (*laughter*).[26]

Making a home in a neighbourhood and organising their artist collective like a family within the given urban context of Jakarta is ruru's primary 'survival' strategy, theorised as a working principle:

> A house shows how society perceive[s] space, body and how they organise themselves in small scales. [Occupying the rented house] also shows the practice of managing arts independently. It teaches the lesson of how arts can be organised – imagined, designed and followed.[27]

Although the word *lumbung* was not used in the early years of ruru, they were already experimenting in pooling and coming into agreement about how to share them. 'Small *lumbung* is created from the living room.'[28] The living

24 A. Darmawan, 'Berakar dan Menjalar', *op. cit.*
25 A. Darmawan, interviewed by the author, 2 October 2024.
26 A. Darmawan, 'Berakar dan Menjalar', *op. cit.*
27 *Ibid.*
28 *Ibid.*

room was the space where the collective discussed and initiated projects; it could showcase a single member's work or the collaborative expressions of several; and related activities within it could generate income for the collective. Some portion of whatever income came in from individual or group projects would be saved in the collective pot.

Besides the initial fundraising that was used to rent a house, during their formative period ruru managed to get Hivos, an 'international development organisation guided by humanist values', to sponsor their various programmes, such as street bazaars and urban festivals, workshops and trainings, film screenings, an arts lab, research and documentation, and publications. The Hivos funding lasted ten years (2003–13), and by the eighth year ruru had managed to negotiate a deal to use a portion of the final two years' funds to create a sustainable business model:

> Some of our members are used to [doing] artistic service, like art handling, artistic production, design, festival ... then we start to do *lumbung* commoning, gathering the resources (and capacities) we have, and then managing it as a business unit. Any saving we get from the initiatives, we put in the collective pot.[29]

Importantly, for ruru *lumbung* is not related merely to economic sustenance but to political as well as aesthetic practice. Their first project in 2000 invited two arts groups known for their critical mural work, Taring Padi and Apotik Komik, to respond to the urban environment. However, Ronny Agustinus has mentioned that questions were raised as to the role of ruru, and whether the collective would be simply the 'event organiser' or also have also have its own artistic voice. The artistic voice turned out to be a 'complex' mix, focussing on the very nature of collectivity and public engagement in defining the arts in grounded localities.[30] From the start, ruru has reckoned with the commoning concept, experimenting with how to organise collectivity, invite participation, and foster a sense of belonging and shared responsibility in contributing arts for the public. Grounding itself in Jakarta, ruru has reached out to similar local initiatives, in a practice since conceptualised as 'translokal' networking.

In 2001, ruru served as curator and facilitator for the '1st Jakarta International Art Festival (JakArt@2001) – Habitus Publik'; since 2004, ruru has held this regular programme under the title Jakarta 32°C to engage college students in a 'dialogue and networking forum all over Jakarta and its vicinity for contemporary art and culture'. Relatedly, to tap into students' creativity

29 A. Darmawan, interviewed by the author, 2 October 2024.
30 R. Agustinus, interviewed by the author, 1 October 2024.

in video production, the biannual programme OK.Video was designed to provide space for 'small narratives' done by unknown young artists.[31]

Just as the group is, in David Teh's words, 'through and through a creature of the capital', from the very onset ruru has been wired into an international network. In fact, amongst their earliest activities in 2000, ruru joined the first physical meeting of Rijksakademie Artist Initiative Network (RAIN) in Amsterdam, with six other artist collectives from Asia, Latin America and Africa. In the first formative period, ruru additionally participated in, for example, events for the Gwangju Biennale (2002), the Istanbul Biennial (2005), the Bienal de São Paulo (2014) and the Seoul Museum of Art (2014), and served as the curator of the international contemporary art exhibition Sonsbeek 16 in Arnhem (2016).

The Gudang Sarinah Experiment: Occupying Public Space (2015–18)

By 2015, ruangrupa had established itself as a major hub for arts groups and artist collectives, extending into translocal projects and networks around the globe. Since the 2010 'Fixer' series, it has continuously mapped and showcased various artist collectives in Indonesia and connected them with others from abroad.[32] The collective's co-founders and individual members have been entrusted as artists and curators for reputable international and national collaborations, and their consultation as judges likewise pursued.

In Jakarta in August 2015, Ade Darmawan served among the judges for that year's 'Go Ahead Challenge Artwarding Night', an event celebrating the winners of a competition for youth creative media production, sponsored by the Putera Sampoerna Foundation (formed by a cigarette company). It took place at the Gudang Sarinah warehouse, and ruru's aura – its embrace of indie music and the arts of everyday life – permeated the space, located in Pancoran, South Jakarta.

Darmawan was engaged at Gudang Sarinah again in 2015, as the executive director of the Jakarta Biennale. He had initially approached Ira Puspadewi, CEO of Sarinah Department Store, with the proposal to use the shopping centre itself (fourteen storeys plus a basement) as a venue. The first of its kind in Indonesia, the Sarinah Department Store's historical legacy is complex – President Soekarno was behind its conception, and he named the building after his childhood nanny (after whom he also titled a memoir). Puspadewi

31 M. Andan, 'All for Jakarta: A Note on the Tenth Anniversary of ruangrupa: Decompression# 10, Expanding the Space and Public', *Inter-Asia Cultural Studies*, vol.12, no.4, 2011, pp.591–602.

32 Ade Darmawan and Rifky Effendy co-curated the exhibition 'Fixer: Exhibition of Alternative Spaces and Art Groups in Indonesia' at North Art Space, Jakarta in 2010.

instead offered the 3,000-square-metre space of Gudang Sarinah, across three halls. The Jakarta Biennale, on view from 15 November 2015 to 16 January 2016, displayed works by 70 artists and a handful of arts groups from Indonesia and abroad. It also accommodated public discussions, workshops, music performances and a bazaar. The title of this edition of the Biennale, 'Maju Kena Mundur Kena' (Neither Forward nor Back), alluded to a film, a popular Indonesian comedy from 1983. It also captured the catch-22 of its global-local condition via the tag line 'bertindak sekarang' (act now) – a playful and critical twist in the spirit of the edition's activism.

ruru's experimentation at Gudang Sarinah opened up a new vista. Following the Jakarta Biennale, they decided to occupy Gudang Sarinah's 6,000-square-metre space as their new live-work space. They were not alone. Joining them were three artist collectives and previous collaborators: Serrum, Grafis Huru Hara and Forum Lenteng. According to Darmawan, 'the large space allowed for a bigger "market" (bazaar for the public), inviting middle, small, micro enterprises to participate, and wider forums and network'.[33] It was a daring move, as the cost to run the whole space was 250 million rupiah per month (around 16,000 US dollars). To cover it, the four collectives formed a business unit called RRC (RURU Corps.) and Darmawan designed a complex and layered *lumbung* management.

As shown in a mind-mapping schematic by Darmawan, each artist collective (*setiap organisasi*) within the RRC had the responsibility to share (*berbagi*) in an open-management programme system of resource allocation. Contributions to the *lumbung* pot were voluntary (*sukarela*) and could be 'minimal' so as not to 'endanger' (*membahayakan*) the existence of the larger collective. Everyone received support (*bantuan*) that included a share of *lumbung* profits, resources and space. The financial management was done by building a business ecosystem according to two different routes: commercial and non-commercial programmes.

The collective *lumbung* system did not prove as smooth in operation as on paper. As a merger of one collective (ruru) with three others – each with unique internal and external dynamics – the financial management of the four collectives was the sensitive area. At the end of the Gudang Sarinah period, Forum Lenteng, which had been an important player in various programmes, among them OK.Video and Jakarta 32C, decided to leave. As Darmawan acknowledges, 'It is easy as friends to share idea, time, work and space, but sharing money is something else. ... The problem is if the *lumbung* is seen as an investment, while it is not. *Lumbung* is sharing, and what is gained

33 A. Darmawan, interviewed by the author, 2 October 2024.

Ade Darmawan, mind map of ruangrupa's *lumbung* management, 2015. Courtesy the artist

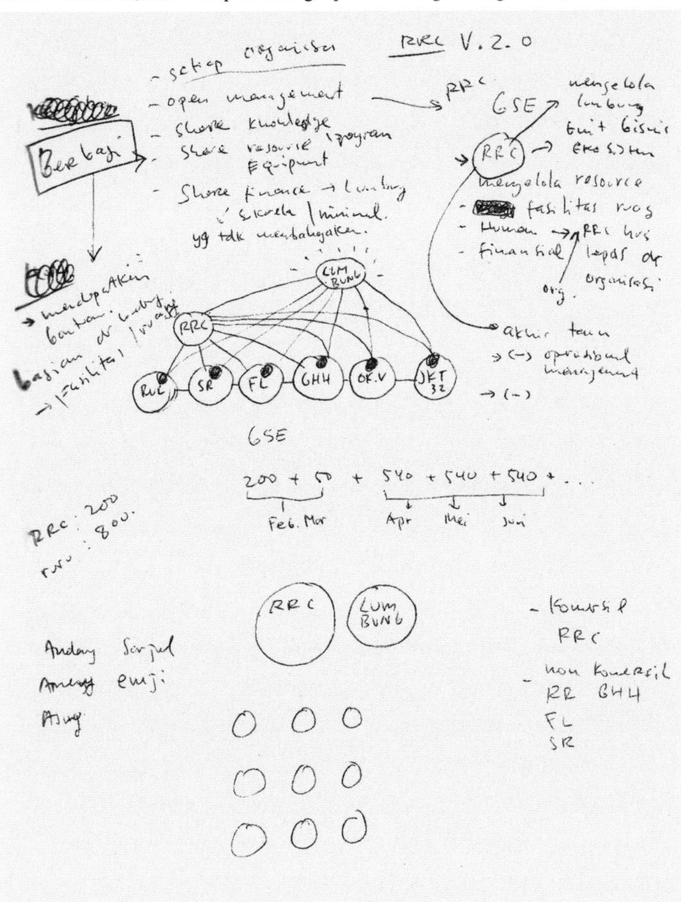

at certain level might be non-monetary.'[34] Additionally, the move from a house to a warehouse was a culture shock to many. Instead of transforming a domestic space for public interaction, the groups now had to domesticate a large public space. Sigit, a member of Serrum, admits that it took him months to move his work space into Gudang Sarinah, where he felt he lost his intimate home environment: 'I am not used to being greeted by the security guard before entering the area.'[35] With the 'family' and 'domestic' aura of the house now gone, members of the collectives were at a loss to 'bump into' one another in the large warehouse.

The *lumbung* experiment in Gudang Sarinah lasted two years, with two biennales and 'wild nights of live music performance, forums and meetings with new artist collectives'. Many lessons were learnt.[36] At the end of 2018, the Gudang Sarinah chapter closed. The collective pot 'was bleeding', but ruru had a new, more viable opportunity.

34 *Ibid.*
35 Gudskul Studi Ekosistem (GSK), interviewed by the author, Jakarta, 11 October 2024.
36 A. Darmawan, interviewed by the author, 2 October 2024.

By the time ruangrupa left their rented house to occupy the Gudang Sarinah, their old Tebet neighbourhood had lost its flavour due to gentrification. After the Gudang Sarinah phase, ruru and the collectives Serrum and Grafis Huru Hara decided to look for a space in a mixed urban *kampung* area in South Jakarta, near its border with the satellite city of Depok. The three collectives created a new entity, called simply Gudskul, with a focus on education through the arts and the activation of networks and cultural resources to create participatory public learning space. The term Gudskul (pronounced as 'good school') is a playful combination of *gudang* (meaning 'storage', a reminder of their previous experiment at Gudang Sarinah) and *skul* (condensing *sekolah*, or 'school').

This time the venture was not based on monthly rent but rather land ownership. In 2018, ruru managed to secure a five-year grant from the Ford Foundation's BUILD (Building Institutions and Network) programme, with flexibility for the grantee to develop strategies of sustainability. The merged collectives, minus Forum Lenteng, managed to convince the Ford Foundation to let them allocate a portion of the funds towards buying 700 square metres of land in Jagakarsa. They made use of an existing building – the futsal sports hall that is the setting of this essay's opening – as a main meeting area, while an adjacent area became the rurushop, kitchen, 'hang-out' place, offices and work/exhibition space. Across the main hall was a stretch of 1,100 square metres, rented in partnership with Haji Endang, their neighbour and the ex-owner of the futsal hall, which they sublet to individuals and collectives involved in the arts, architecture and activism who were formally or informally interested in engaging with Gudskul. This tenants' area is called Gudside. Together, Gudskul and Gudside are called Gudskul Ekosistem:

> Gudskul Ekosistem consists of many elements: artists, curators, art writers, managers, researchers, musicians, directors, architects, cooks, artistic designers, designers, fashion designers, street artists and individuals with various other expertise. This variety makes Gudskul an affluent and dynamic ecosystem. Gudskul also houses a multitude of collectives with differing practices and artistic mediums: installation, archive, video, sound, performance, media art, public participation, printmaking, graphic design, education, etc. This variegated bunch also enrich the issues and involved parties in many collaborative projects, socially, politically, culturally, economically, environmentally or even educationally.[37]

37 See Gudskul website at https://gudskul.art/tentang. My translation.

Different from Gudang Sarinah – a confined space with security guards – the Gudskul Ekosistem blends in with its neighbouring communities, and this has resulted in more intimate public engagement and the bridging of class barriers. Women, youth groups and children access the facilities, for instance through the arts activities programme RURU Kids. As Ronny Agustinus has noted, 'neighbouring women [have done] embroidery together, and their works exhibited in the Gudskul gallery'.[38] Gudside tenants have included Agustinus (now a former ruru member); advisory board member Mirwan Andan, who commutes back and forth between Jakarta to Makassar; and artist collectives such as Makmur Djaya. They contribute to paid and unpaid workshops and training for the public, such as discussions about books and literacy. Non-Indonesian artists also come to Gudskul to mingle with the community. In this way, Gudskul Ekosistem brings arts to the public and gives public exposure to critical thinking and aesthetics.[39]

The financial management of the Gudskul Ekosistem is similar in spirit to the *lumbung* schematic for Gudang Sarinah:

> As an ecosystem, we create *lumbung* system to pool our resources and then share proportionally, according to the need of each collective. The resources of each collective differ in kinds: funding, programme, facilities and books. We pool all the above so that they can be accessed and shared to all collectives.[40]

What is greatly improved is the transparency and collective monitoring. At Jagakarsa, the collectives have started monthly *majelis*, that is, accountability meetings to report on finances and the activities of each constitutive collective as well as Gudskul as a merged entity. What makes the process more complicated is the formalisation of business entities, given that each collective has its own tax and reporting obligations to donors and stakeholders. The Gudsul Ekosistem consists of two companies, Serrum LLC and Rimpang Digital LLC, plus two foundations, Gudskul and Ruang Rupa Foundation, and one association, Serrum Association. Each of the business and organisational entities does its own accounting and reporting, and the Gudskul Foundation is the umbrella for the whole group. Collaboration with international organisations is often done with additional entities. In 2024, for example, ruru secured a collaboration with Tokyo Gedai, Tokyo University of the Arts. They also sent representatives to participate in the DEFOAMAT festival in Tokyo's Daikanyama District. Gudskul, on the other hand, has sent members to the Lumbung Sumida: Sharing Garden programme in Sumida-ku, Tokyo. Such projects have different schemes,

38 R. Agustinus, interviewed by the author, 1 October 2024.
39 *Ibid.*
40 See https://gudskul.art/tentang.

in terms of budget and income reported, and collaboration is evaluated during *majelis*, at which one finance unit oversees the activities of all entities in the *lumbung* commoning process.

At one critical juncture, it is worth noting, the finance unit – with the support of the *majelis* – made a complete change to the *lumbung*: during the pandemic period of 2020 to 2022, all arts and public activities were halted. Gudskul used its space to produce face masks, hand sanitiser and other personal protective equipment for distribution to neighbourhood families. It was a way to be of service during a time of crisis. However, the programme freeze meant no income for the collectives and nothing to take home for individual artists. It was then decided that Gudskul Ekosistem would provide salaries to individual members of the collectives, to help them make ends meet. Fifty individuals altogether were on payroll from 2020 to 2022. When the pandemic emergency ended, the flexibility of the *lumbung* management allowed it to return to how it had previously operated. The *majelis* and the finance unit thus proved adaptive to the changing needs of Gudskul.

Gudskul Studi Kolektif (GSK) and Lumbung *Practice: Filling the Void*

Though organising *lumbung* can be complicated, outreach has nonetheless widened locally and globally, in particular with emerging artist collectives. In October 2024, at the time of the aforementioned gathering at the futsal hall, I met with members of artist collectives from various parts of Indonesia at the Gudskul Ekosistem. They were participating in GSK (Gudskul Studi Kolektif), a two-year programme begun in 2018 for participants to study artist collectives and the arts ecosystem. Amongst them were activists from Makmur Djaya (Jakarta), Riwanua (Makassar, South Sulawesi), the Indonesia Arts Movement (IAM, Papua), Simpasio (Larantuka, East Nusa Tenggara) and Pasir Putih (North Lombok, West Nusa Tenggara). In its first two years, the programme was advertised through an open call, and it recruited around ten individuals interested in collectives, who were themselves artists, journalists, researchers or students. Participants shared the cost of the programme in different categories; depending on their financial ability, they received full or partial scholarships.

Initially, the participants spent up to nine months participating in lectures, workshops and internships, with the target of founding or managing their own collectives. Since its third year, however, the programme has recruited not individuals but collectives. The reason for this shift was that 'it was too challenging to change artists' orientation towards collective activism, as they are more eager to promote their career[s] as artists, and it was too demanding for individual artist[s] to form a collective on his or her own'.[41] As of 2020, the programme involved five to six collectives from different parts of Indonesia, widening to include transnational collectives in 2021 and 2022, from Australia, Taiwan and Kyrgyzstan. During the Covid-19 pandemic, the programme was conducted online, which cut much of its cost. The participants from 2020 to 2022 were invited to join documenta fifteen for one to two months, and to stay in the Fridericianum boarding house in Kassel.

The five GSK 2024 collectives, while locally grounded in different cultural contexts, were all born from the same needs that were not being facilitated by campuses, the city, the job market or the state. Makmur Djaya, like ruru, was created by students of IKJ who craved a critical and creative space for interdisciplinary collaboration. Riwanua, similarly, has served as a learning hub for cultural studies and critical thinking amongst the younger generation, with participants from various backgrounds. Simpasio and IAM were also brought into existence by students or alumni from arts institutions, and they have based their activism in local cultures on the brink of erasure by urban expansion. Simpasio works on archiving, activating and transferring collective memory – oral, written, visual, spatial, tactile, culinary – through various activities in public space and multimedia production by young people and children. Simpasio and IAM reinvent culinary practices using food staples that have been threatened by the government through rice-based food estate policies (the ironic *lumbung pangan*).[42] Simpasio has experimented with sorghum porridge kitchens to reorient young people's taste buds away from the fast food of international franchises. IAM works closely with the local community, doing the collective cooking of *bakar batu* (stone burning) and using locally grown sweet potatoes and non-pork meats (acceptable to a wider audience).

Pasir Putih is the only collective involved that was not initiated by arts students. Their activists include school teachers and students from various disciplines who are motivated by the urgency to fill the void caused by neoliberal policies in terms of inequality and the loss of cultural diversity. Similar to the other collectives, Pasir Putih had difficulty securing a working space until the local rural community gave them permission to use a piece of their land. Pasir Putih then held literacy activities with them, studied local manuscripts and shared traditional farming knowledge and plant-based pharmacology workshops. Like the other collectives, Pasir Putih gives special attention to youth and children, with whom they do various multi-

41 farid rakun, interviewed by the author, Jakarta, 15 November 2024.

42 This irony is noted in Elly Kent, 'The History of Conscious Collectivity Behind ruangrupa', *ArtReview*, 6 July 2022.

media projects, from uploading the harvest schedule via TikTok, to digitising local knowledge, to producing community cinema and theatre.

It has not been easy for the collectives to start engaging with local communities, who may have had disappointing experiences with NGOs and researchers who treated them as objects for research. Pasir Putih, for example, gained trust only after two years working with and in the community. At the end of a project, they return what they have learnt to the community; for example, during exhibitions, the public might take photographs, publications and other such materials home with them. This approach creates a strong sense of belonging amongst local communities.

'We do not use the term empowerment. It is the government that needs to be empowered': this statement from the GSK addresses its overall approach to the political apparatus of the state.[43] Some of the GSK 2024 collectives have had negative brushes with political parties and the government. Pasir Putih's relations with the local government have been strained, apparently due to the group's decision to not be involved in local practical politics in order to achieve political gains, whether in winning an election or passing legislation, lobbying or campaigning. The local government, backed up by a certain political party, was upset that the collective decided to take this distance, and Pasir Putih was asked to vacate the base camp initially provided to them by the local government.

State and local governments' investment in building arts infrastructure such as *taman budaya* (local cultural centres) and *gedung kesenian* (art, buildings) can be considered ineffective and supportive of unsustainable programmes.[44] Thus, like the journey of ruru and Gudskul Ekosistem, the emergence of local arts and cultural collectives is intended to fill in the need for spaces of engaged transdisciplinary cultural activism.

Towards Transnational Lumbung?

In 2024, the GSK was held in tandem with a temporary master's degree programme called Lumbung Practice at the Sandberg Instituut in Amsterdam, in collaboration with De Appel and Gudskul. Designed by Lara Khaldi and Gertrude Flentge, who were members of the artistic

43 GSK, interviewed by the author, 11 October 2024.

44 A member of the Indonesia Arts Movement, named Julio, noted that the formal cultural spaces established by the local government in Papua rarely gave opportunities for youth and student participation, and even arts festivals were limited. GSK, interviewed by the author, 11 October 2024. On other occasions there were discussions about the limited space available for performance and exhibition. The *taman budaya* built 1980s in the provinces were considered mismanaged, neglected or provided at high cost to artists.

team of documenta fifteen, this was clearly an extension of that event.[45] In other words, having been lambasted by the German mainstream media and right-wing politicians, documenta fifteen responded with a defiant collective yell: 'Let there be *lumbung*!'

The new programme has two aspects. The first is practice, in the form of reconnecting with the *lumbung* network developed during documenta fifteen to freshly build *lumbung* to 'reinforce the local'. Second is theory, which entails

> further study of cosmologies of diverse commoning approaches and their application in contemporary artistic practice. Participants will also learn about and experiment with how commons-based approaches like *lumbung* can operate next to a market economy, and how to 'transvest' value from the market to the commons and specifically the tensions this caused in the political, institutional, and media realm.[46]

The question remains: How far has *lumbung*, as 'globally negotiated roots', managed to transvest the other way around, from the commons to the market and the arts ecosystem in diverse locations?[47] Interviewed by Nuraini Juliastuti in 2012, Ade Darmawan voiced ruru's disillusionment with 'failed modernism', 'illusive nationalism' and commodification.[48] In 2024, looking back at the formative phase in which ruru conceptualised the commoning space, Darmawan said that today these challenges have not decreased but rather multiplied in full force: 'commercialisation and bureaucratisation of arts' have 'crazily' solidified more powerfully than ever before.[49]

Especially with ever-rising global capitalism, *lumbung* attracts attention. The Japanese DEFOAMAT festival, for example, considers alternative practices in East Asia and Southeast Asia as sources for new ways of doing things:

> [The] neoliberal economy, which is driving Western-centric globalization, has emphasised economic rationality to the extent that it has created and exacerbated disparities and divisions even within the West, ultimately perpetuating the same essential system that

45 Gertrude Flentge was also the coordinator for RAIN and co-initiator of the Arts Collaboratory ecosystem. ruangrupa has been a member of both networks.

46 See Sandberg Lumbung Practice website at https://open.sandberg.nl/lumbung-practice.

47 C. König, 'documenta fifteen: Awaiting ruangrupa. A Performative Walk through Kassel, September 2021', *Southeast of Now: Directions in Contemporary and Modern Art in Asia*, vol.6, no.1, 2021, pp.211–20.

48 Nuraini Juliastuti, 'ruangrupa: A Conversation on Horizontal Organisation', *Afterall*, issue 30, 2012, pp.118–25.

49 A. Darmawan, interviewed by the author, 2 October 2024.

> existed during the era of imperialism. While there may have been successful development in society up until now, it is also evident that there are numerous challenges that need to be addressed. As we enter the twenty-first century, contemporary Asian culture has been gaining global attention. The era in which Asia and other non-Western regions were regarded as 'peripheral' or 'marginal' is also coming to an end. Post-war Japan has achieved economic development at a faster pace than other Asian countries, but this may also mean that it has reached a dead end sooner. In any case, if things are not going well with the current approach, perhaps it would be a good idea to shift our perspective and return to Asia. By demonstrating solidarity on a common cultural foundation, we can encounter the unique and interesting aspects of Asia that we may have overlooked or not previously recognized. We can explore alternative ways of organizing society.[50]

In a way, the DEFOAMAT festival celebrates the foregrounding of an alternative praxis from the undermined peripheries to cure the ills of the neoliberal, Western hegemony. It is interesting to contrast this framework of postcolonial resistance with Galit Eilat's colonial reading.[51] Eilat looks at the role played by Gertrude Flentge as the coordinator for RAIN and co-initiator of the Arts Collaboratory ecosystem, and at the sponsorship of Dutch organisations such as DOEN and Hivos, to argue that 'the Dutch presence at d15 [documenta fifteen] opened a new gateway between the former empire and its subjects', using ruangrupa, specifically Darmawan, as 'an ally or an agent of its policy'. If, from the DEFOAMAT perspective, the margins offer solutions to the centre, in Eilat's view, this happens in a Westward-movement of cultures and creative industries 'from the peripheries of developing countries to the core of institutions in the developed ones'.

Critical Reflection

Whichever perspective is preferred, the world is mired in similar predicaments. Southeast Asian countries in 2024 have seen the return of totalitarianism, the rise of right-wing conservativism, the strengthened power of oligarchic capitalism and extractive industries, and the marginalisation of indigenous communities. In academia, critical voices not only face political repression and censure from the right wing, but also fall under

50 'Overview', DEFOAMAT website, https://defoamat.com (accessed 13 January 2024).

51 Galit Eilat, 'Ruangrupa: Contemporary Art or Friendship Industry?', *TripleAmpersand Journal (&&&)*, 24 March 2024.

the grip of bureaucratic colonialism, with ranked accreditation systems and key performance indexes to measure their worth – under the hegemonic neoliberalism.

What is left, then, to offer as alternatives? This article shows that the genealogy of *lumbung* in ruru's journey, from Tebet to documenta fifteen and transnational *lumbung* practice, is an organic journey of survival within the neoliberal clutch of arts ecosystems locally in day-to-day reality. While the neoliberal system is a colonial legacy, the dream of carving collective space for artistic collaboration is not dictated from outside. Such collective space is understood to be the existential, locally grounded need of art collectives across Indonesia.

In order to operate, the *lumbung* has to negotiate with governments, international organisations, local organisations and the private sector, including cigarette companies. The *lumbung* is not a space outside but inside the very system it seeks to transform.

One existing problem that arts collectives face is the gender bias described by Yvonne Low: 'Scholars and members of the intellectual and cultural circuit were ... convinced that the Indonesian art world was irrevocably male-dominated, and there existed a mainstream masculine language that excluded female subjectivities.'[52] In spite of this, two of ruru's co-founders are women. And, if the ratio of women's representation in activities is less than that of men, this problem reflects the bias of the larger society. Women managers claim that in each project, they always try to involve women participants, even as the choice is limited.[53] Workshops in curatorial and arts criticism have aimed to (slowly) change the patriarchal, gender-based job division that assigns women to administrative, managerial and archivist work, while promoting men as main players and curators. Julia Sarisetiati, who developed RURU Corps as a business unit, and who at present serves as the coordinator of Gudskul curriculum on strategies of collective sustainability, recognises gender in her discussion of efforts to transform *lumbung* work:

> The care work provides basic knowledge for artistic work and it is a challenge to take turns doing the care work or sharing the burden together, so that everybody can experience and appreciate its significance. In facing pressure of time and output, however, such learning process is not always prioritised as it can slow down the work, due to unequal competence and difficulty in coordination.

52 Yvonne Low, 'Becoming professional: Feminisms and the rise of women-centred exhibitions in Indonesia', *Australian and New Zealand Journal of Art*, vol. 15, no.2, 2015, p.211.

53 Julia Sarisetiati and an anonymous member, correspondences with the author, 20 January 2025.

> The challenge is to make sure that ideas and knowledge is passed from one generation to the next, and that the care work is not dominantly women's sphere.[54]

Some women artists outside of the ruru circle jokingly call them 'the *nongkrong* boys', referring to ruru's informal hang-outs, which usually last from evening until dawn. The designation implies that the timing (unplanned and organic) can alienate women with family obligations, and also that ruru's smoking culture can be inconvenient for nonsmokers.[55]

Another subject of negotiation is the spatiality and governance of *lumbung*. For instance, as discussed earlier, the Gudang Sarinah Ekosistem introduced various tensions, leading some to feel that each collective needs to have its own independent space to create a healthy dynamic. Indeed, a mega city like Jakarta needs as many arts spaces as possible, because spreading and decentralising arts activities is the best thing to do – just as ruru did with the 2013 Jakarta Biennale and at documenta fifteen in Kassel.

Maintaining *lumbung* as a collective financial pot as well as a space organised democratically and transparently for the sustainability of multiple collectives as a whole requires delicately balanced negotiation. *Lumbung* cannot be seen romantically or in an orientalising way as an ideal utopia. Yet, it does enable viable community-based interventions to make the planet a better space for living. *Lumbung* offers transdisciplinary subject-to-subject relations with local communities as important stakeholders in the arts.[56] A collective learning space for the public and members of the collective that engages diverse local experimentation, *lumbung* is continuously shifting to adjust to contextual changes. Today, the urgency to keep *lumbung* is not just alive but thriving – locally. Globally, it is necessary, too, given the escalation of multidimensional crises, from war to climate change. Crucially, *lumbung* must proceed at a rapid pace, so that transformation towards a more humane world does not breathe its 'last gasp'.

54 J. Sarisetiati, correspondence with the author, 20 January 2025.

55 Personal conversation with the author, confidential.

56 GSK, interviewed by the author, 11 Ocotber 2024.

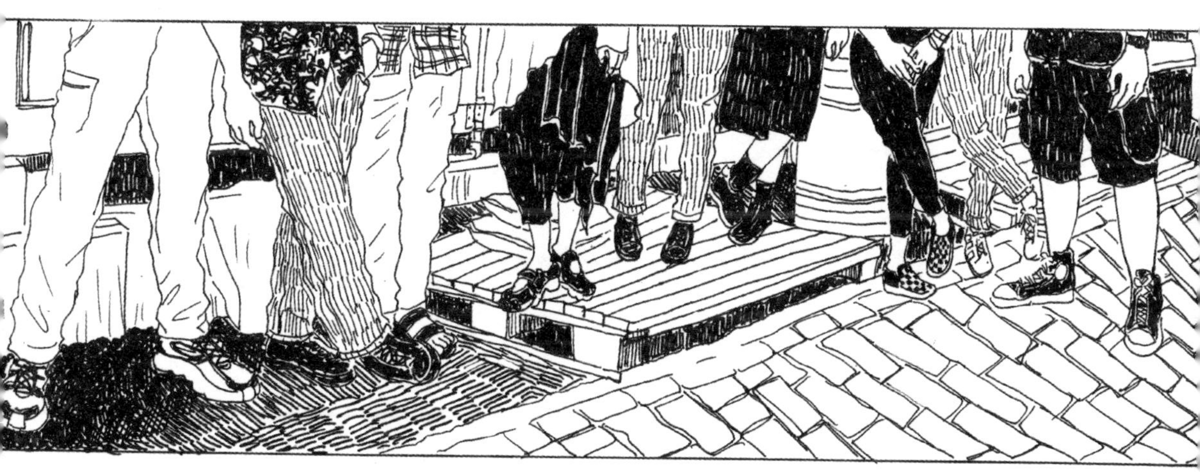

Apa kabar: conversations with ruru

A comic by chitarum

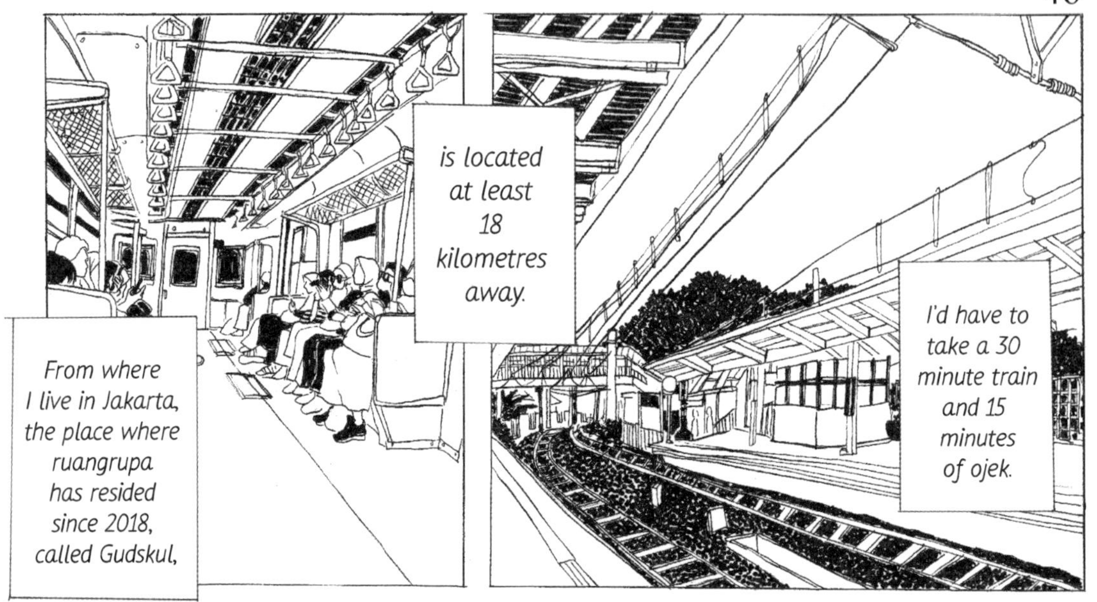
From where
I live in Jakarta,
the place where
ruangrupa
has resided
since 2018,
called Gudskul,
is located
at least
18
kilometres
away.
I'd have to
take a 30
minute train
and 15
minutes
of ojek.

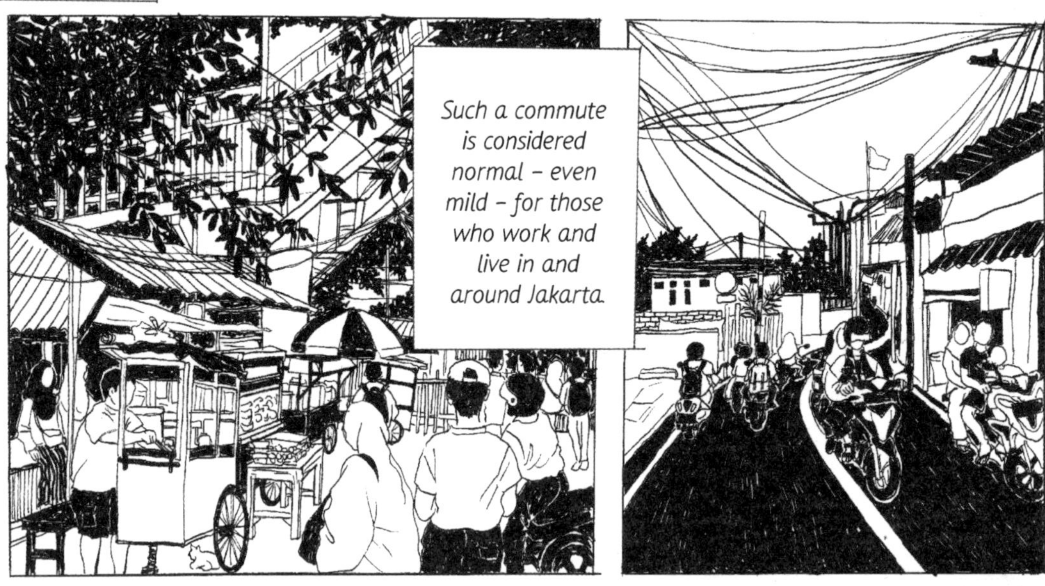
Such a commute
is considered
normal – even
mild – for those
who work and
live in and
around Jakarta.

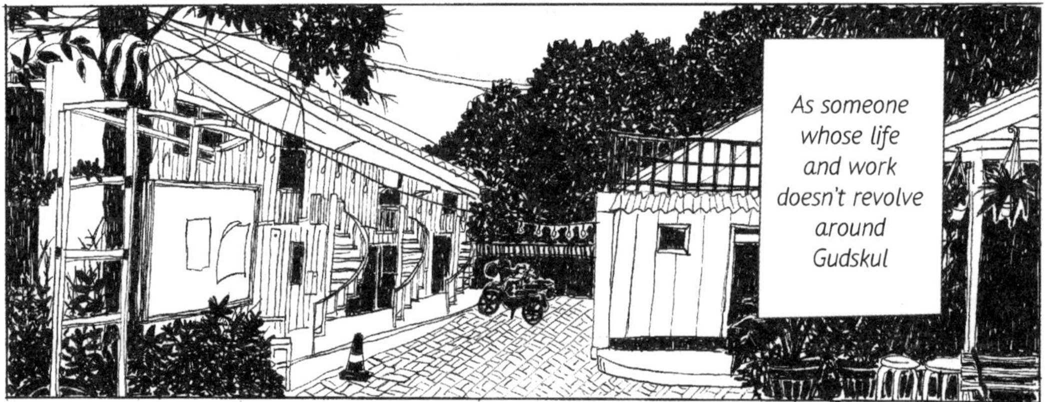
As someone
whose life
and work
doesn't revolve
around
Gudskul

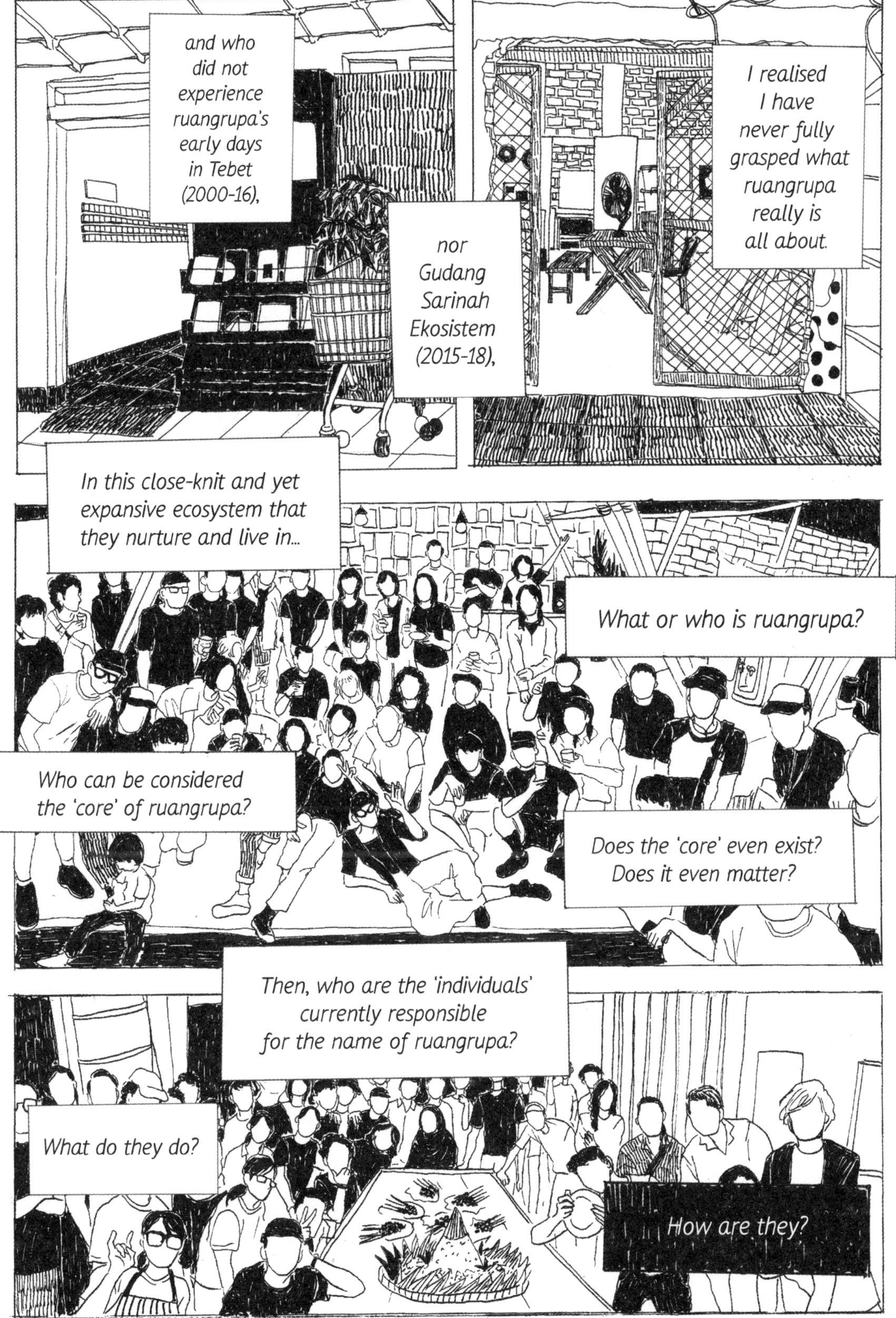
and who did not experience ruangrupa's early days in Tebet (2000-16),
nor Gudang Sarinah Ekosistem (2015-18),
I realised I have never fully grasped what ruangrupa really is all about.
In this close-knit and yet expansive ecosystem that they nurture and live in...
What or who is ruangrupa?
Who can be considered the 'core' of ruangrupa?
Does the 'core' even exist? Does it even matter?
Then, who are the 'individuals' currently responsible for the name of ruangrupa?
What do they do?
How are they?

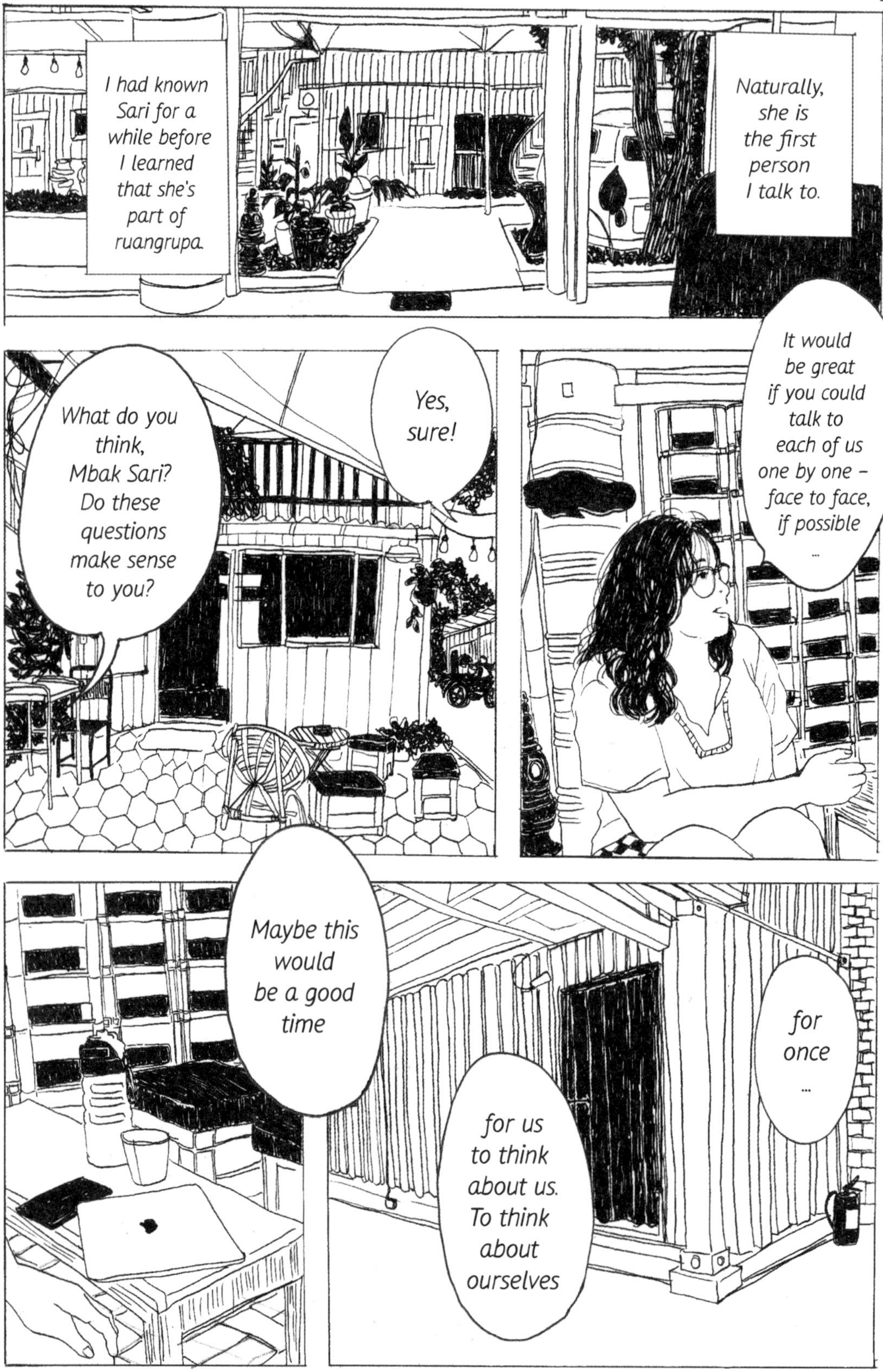

I had known Sari for a while before I learned that she's part of ruangrupa.

Naturally, she is the first person I talk to.

What do you think, Mbak Sari? Do these questions make sense to you?

Yes, sure!

It would be great if you could talk to each of us one by one – face to face, if possible ...

Maybe this would be a good time

for once ...

for us to think about us. To think about ourselves

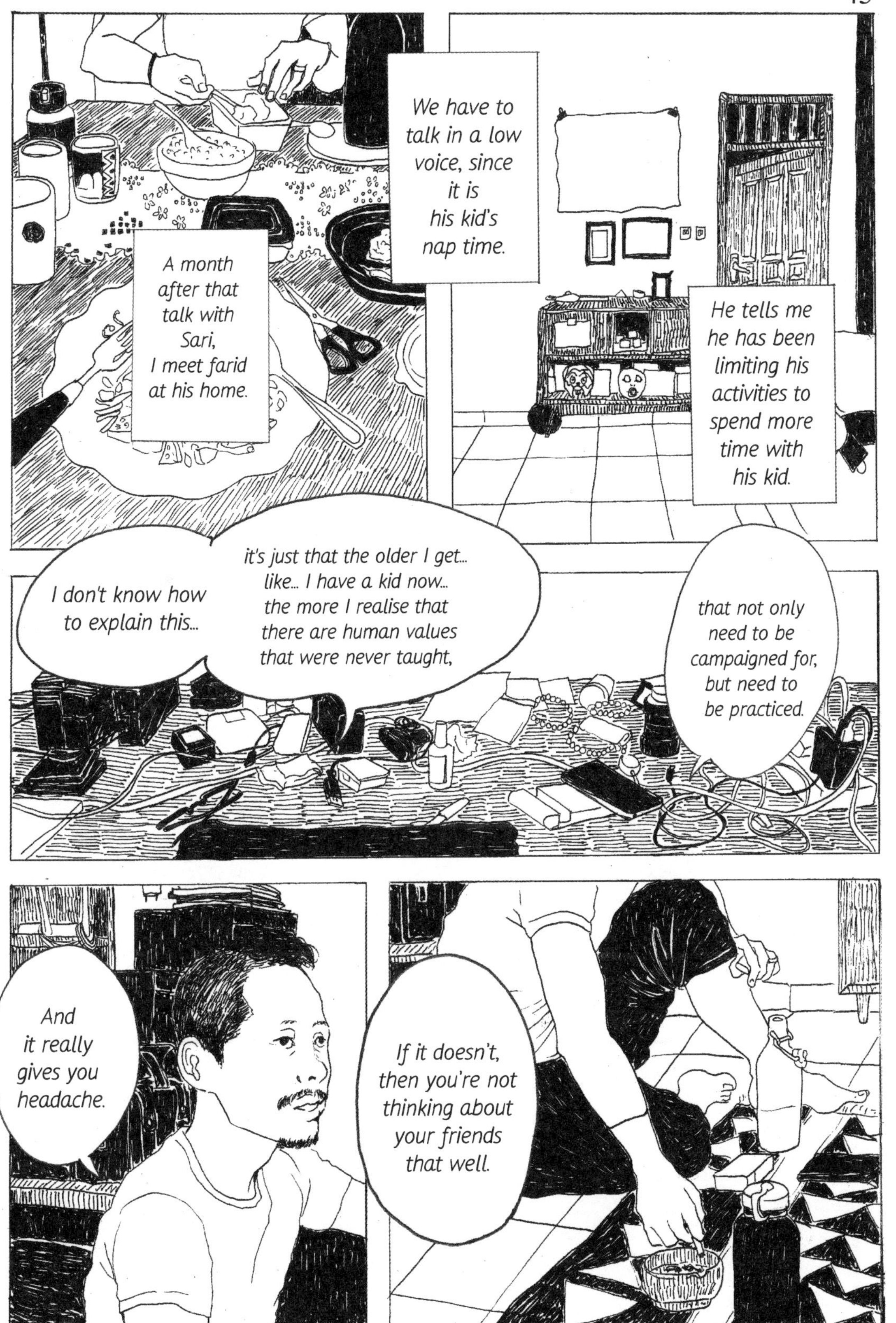
A month after that talk with Sari, I meet farid at his home.
We have to talk in a low voice, since it is his kid's nap time.
He tells me he has been limiting his activities to spend more time with his kid.
I don't know how to explain this...
it's just that the older I get... like... I have a kid now... the more I realise that there are human values that were never taught,
that not only need to be campaigned for, but need to be practiced.
And it really gives you headache.
If it doesn't, then you're not thinking about your friends that well.

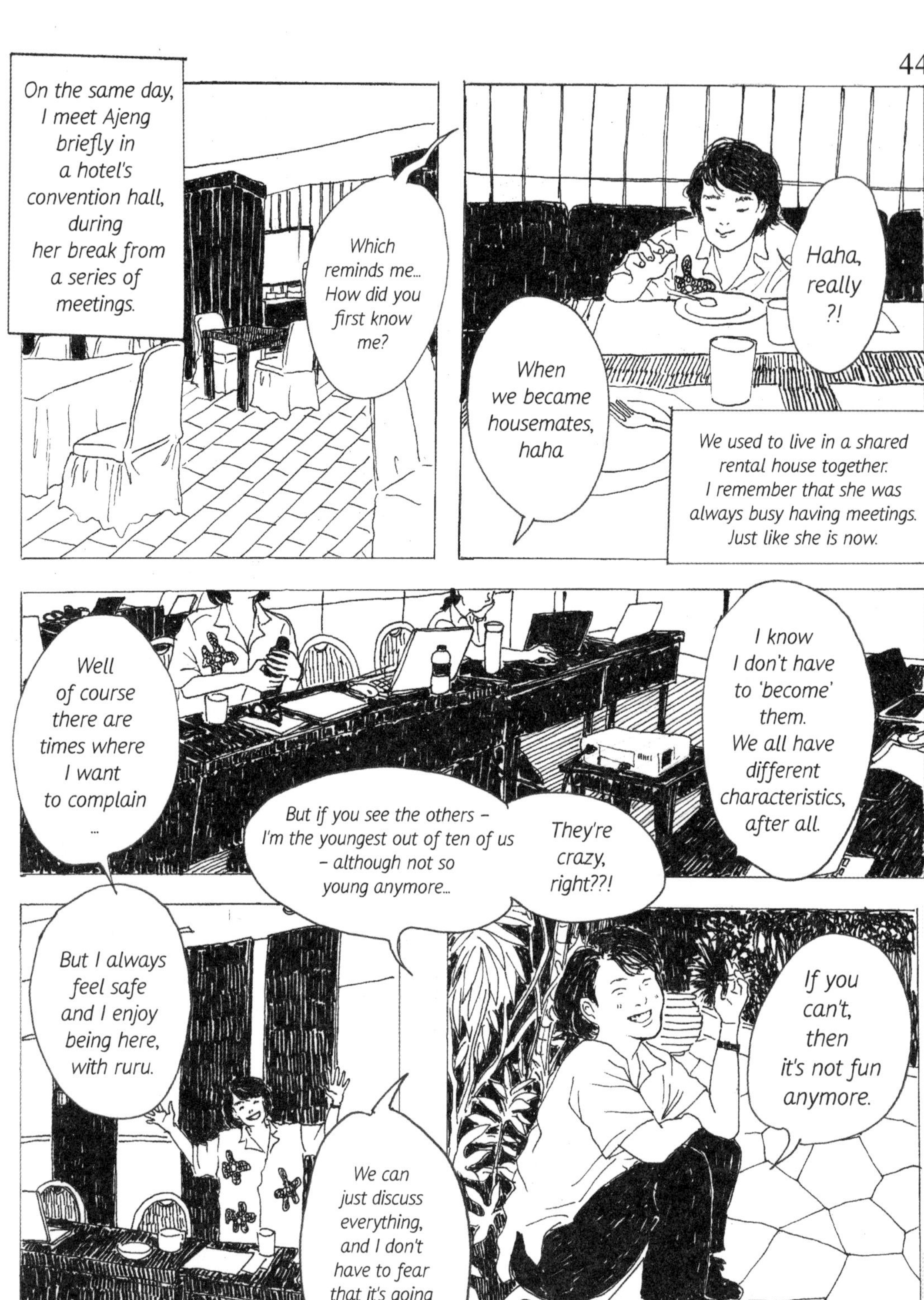
On the same day, I meet Ajeng briefly in a hotel's convention hall, during her break from a series of meetings.
Which reminds me... How did you first know me?
Haha, really ?!
When we became housemates, haha
We used to live in a shared rental house together. I remember that she was always busy having meetings. Just like she is now.
Well of course there are times where I want to complain ...
I know I don't have to 'become' them. We all have different characteristics, after all.
But if you see the others – I'm the youngest out of ten of us – although not so young anymore...
They're crazy, right??!
But I always feel safe and I enjoy being here, with ruru.
If you can't, then it's not fun anymore.
We can just discuss everything, and I don't have to fear that it's going to cause any conflict.

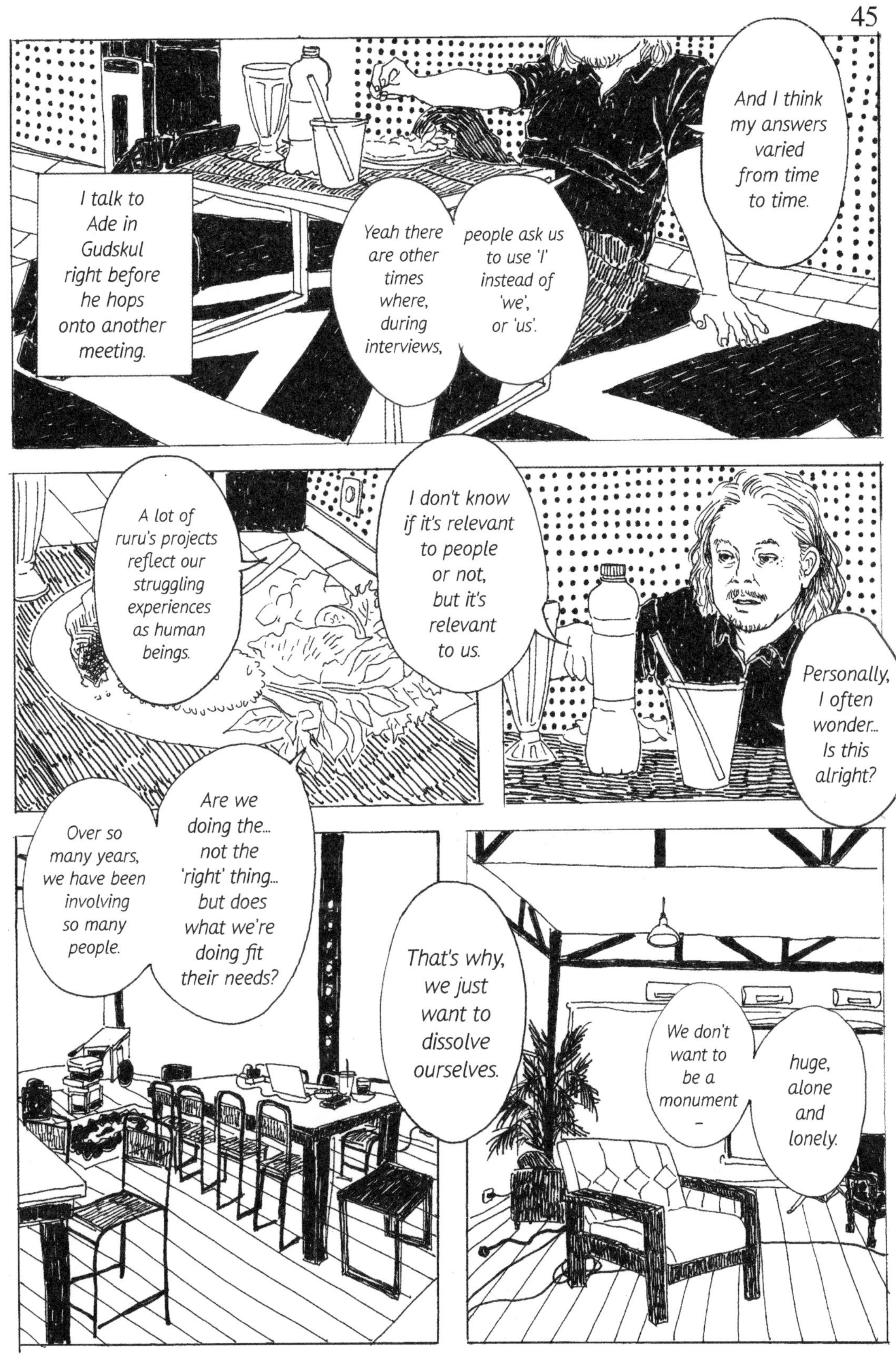

I talk to Ade in Gudskul right before he hops onto another meeting.
Yeah there are other times where, during interviews,
people ask us to use 'I' instead of 'we', or 'us'.
And I think my answers varied from time to time.
A lot of ruru's projects reflect our struggling experiences as human beings.
I don't know if it's relevant to people or not, but it's relevant to us.
Personally, I often wonder... Is this alright?
Over so many years, we have been involving so many people.
Are we doing the... not the 'right' thing... but does what we're doing fit their needs?
That's why, we just want to dissolve ourselves.
We don't want to be a monument –
huge, alone and lonely.

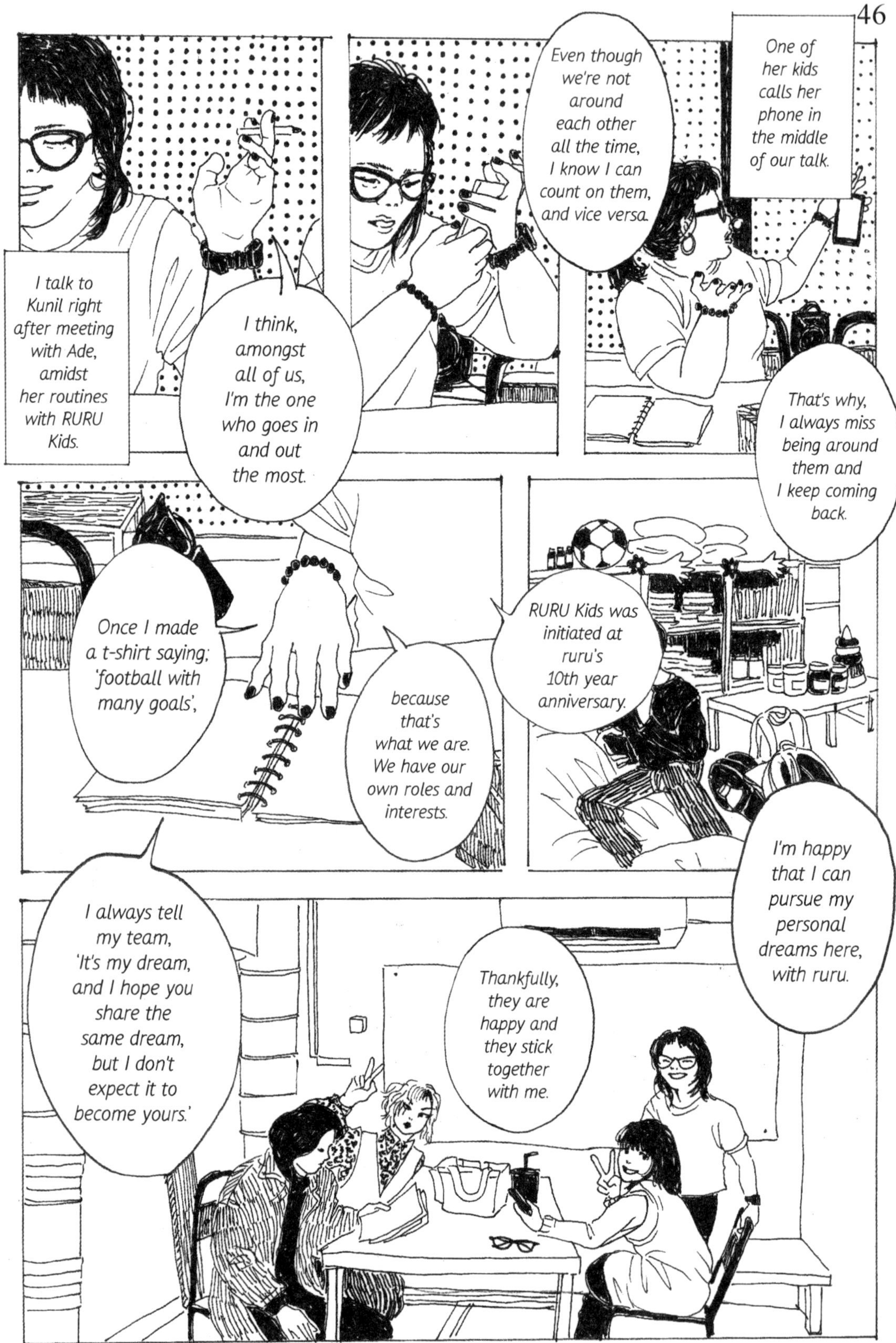
I talk to Kunil right after meeting with Ade, amidst her routines with RURU Kids.
I think, amongst all of us, I'm the one who goes in and out the most.
Even though we're not around each other all the time, I know I can count on them, and vice versa.
One of her kids calls her phone in the middle of our talk.
That's why, I always miss being around them and I keep coming back.
Once I made a t-shirt saying; 'football with many goals',
because that's what we are. We have our own roles and interests.
RURU Kids was initiated at ruru's 10th year anniversary.
I'm happy that I can pursue my personal dreams here, with ruru.
I always tell my team, 'It's my dream, and I hope you share the same dream, but I don't expect it to become yours.'
Thankfully, they are happy and they stick together with me.

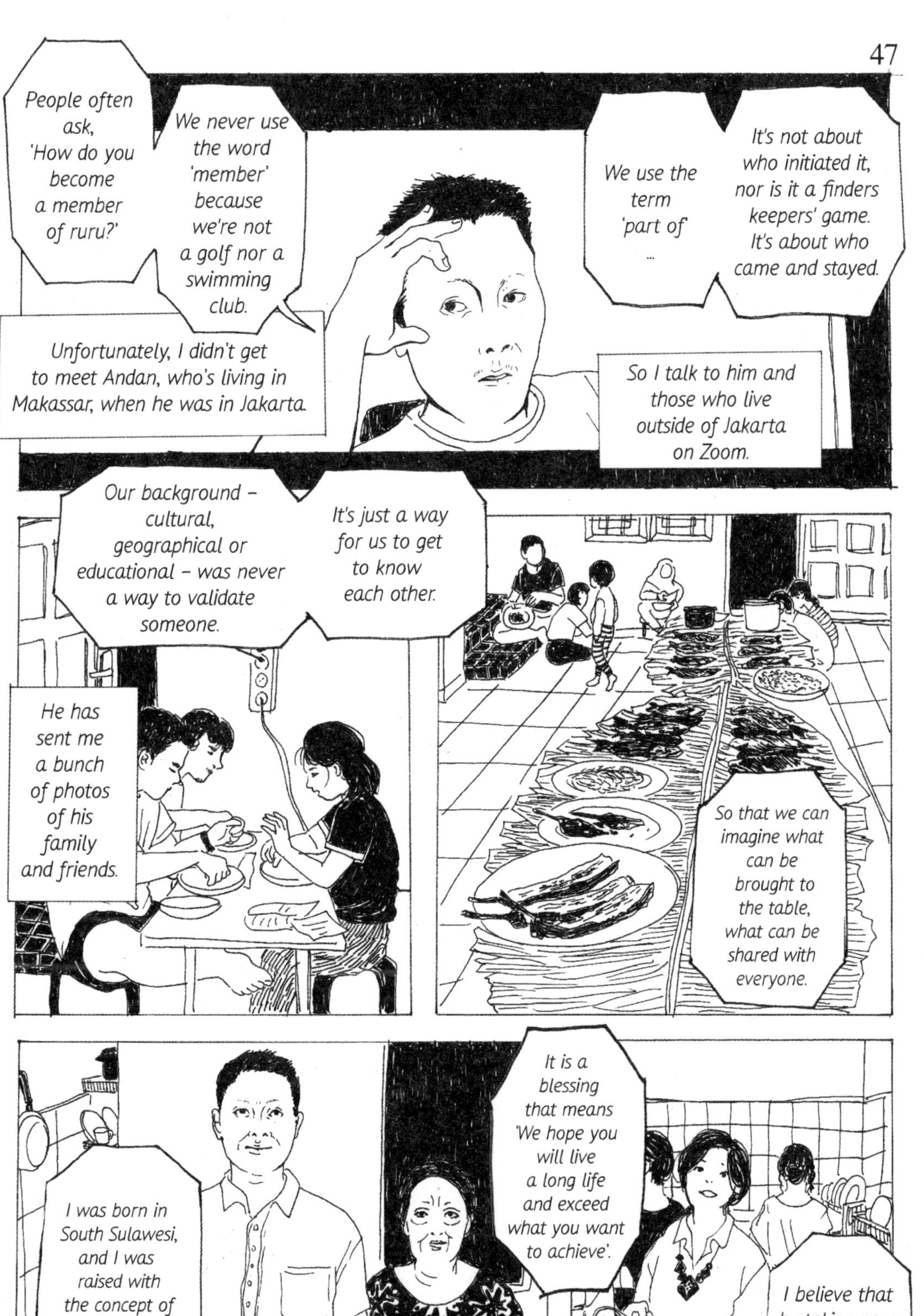
People often ask, 'How do you become a member of ruru?'
We never use the word 'member' because we're not a golf nor a swimming club.
Unfortunately, I didn't get to meet Andan, who's living in Makassar, when he was in Jakarta.
We use the term 'part of' ...
It's not about who initiated it, nor is it a finders keepers' game. It's about who came and stayed.
So I talk to him and those who live outside of Jakarta on Zoom.
Our background – cultural, geographical or educational – was never a way to validate someone.
It's just a way for us to get to know each other.
He has sent me a bunch of photos of his family and friends.
So that we can imagine what can be brought to the table, what can be shared with everyone.
I was born in South Sulawesi, and I was raised with the concept of 'Mattola palallo'.
It is a blessing that means 'We hope you will live a long life and exceed what you want to achieve'.
I believe that by taking care of people, we're also taking care of ourselves.

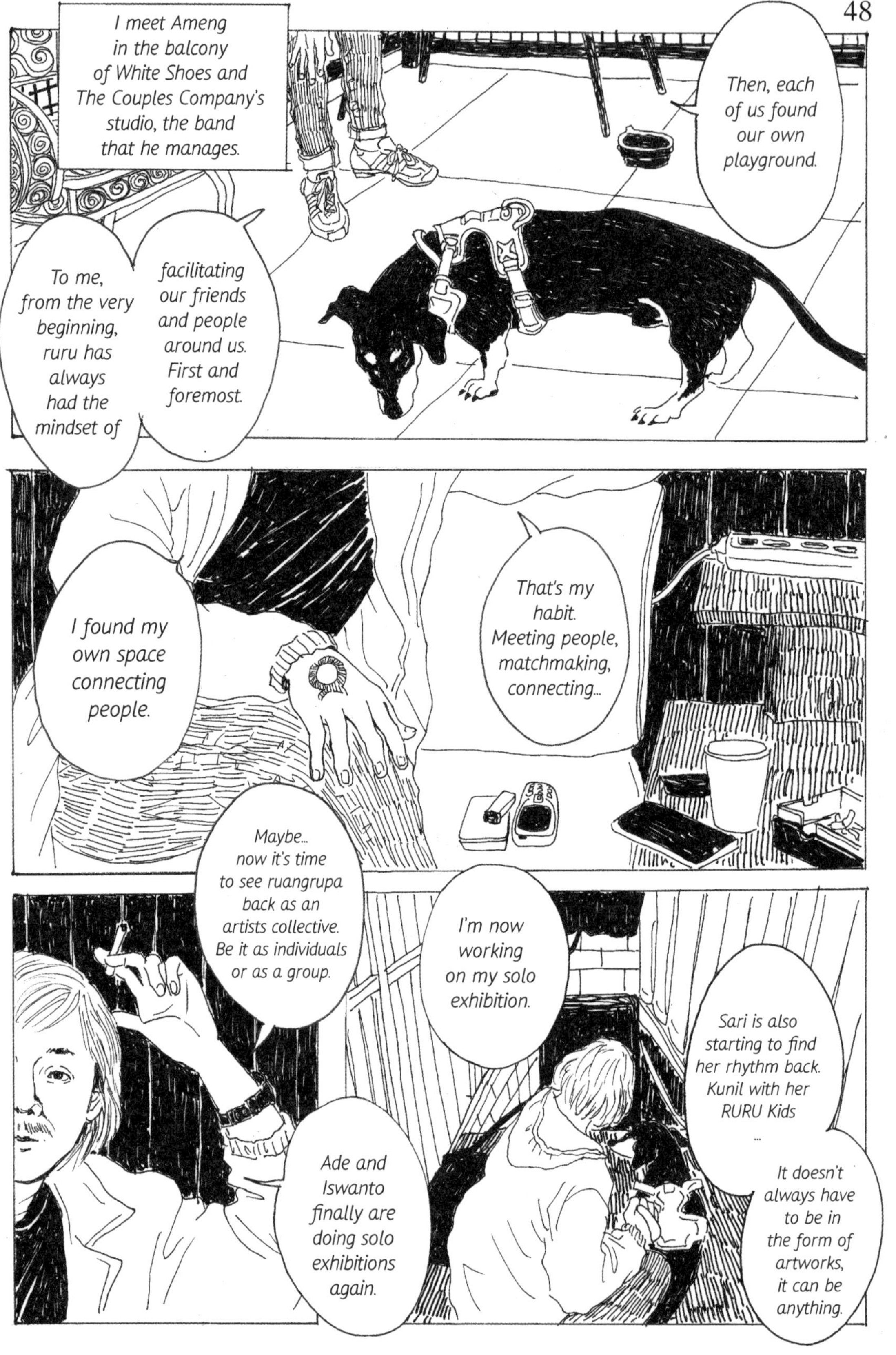
I meet Ameng in the balcony of White Shoes and The Couples Company's studio, the band that he manages.
Then, each of us found our own playground.
To me, from the very beginning, ruru has always had the mindset of
facilitating our friends and people around us. First and foremost.
I found my own space connecting people.
That's my habit. Meeting people, matchmaking, connecting...
Maybe... now it's time to see ruangrupa back as an artists collective. Be it as individuals or as a group.
I'm now working on my solo exhibition.
Ade and Iswanto finally are doing solo exhibitions again.
Sari is also starting to find her rhythm back. Kunil with her RURU Kids ...
It doesn't always have to be in the form of artworks, it can be anything.

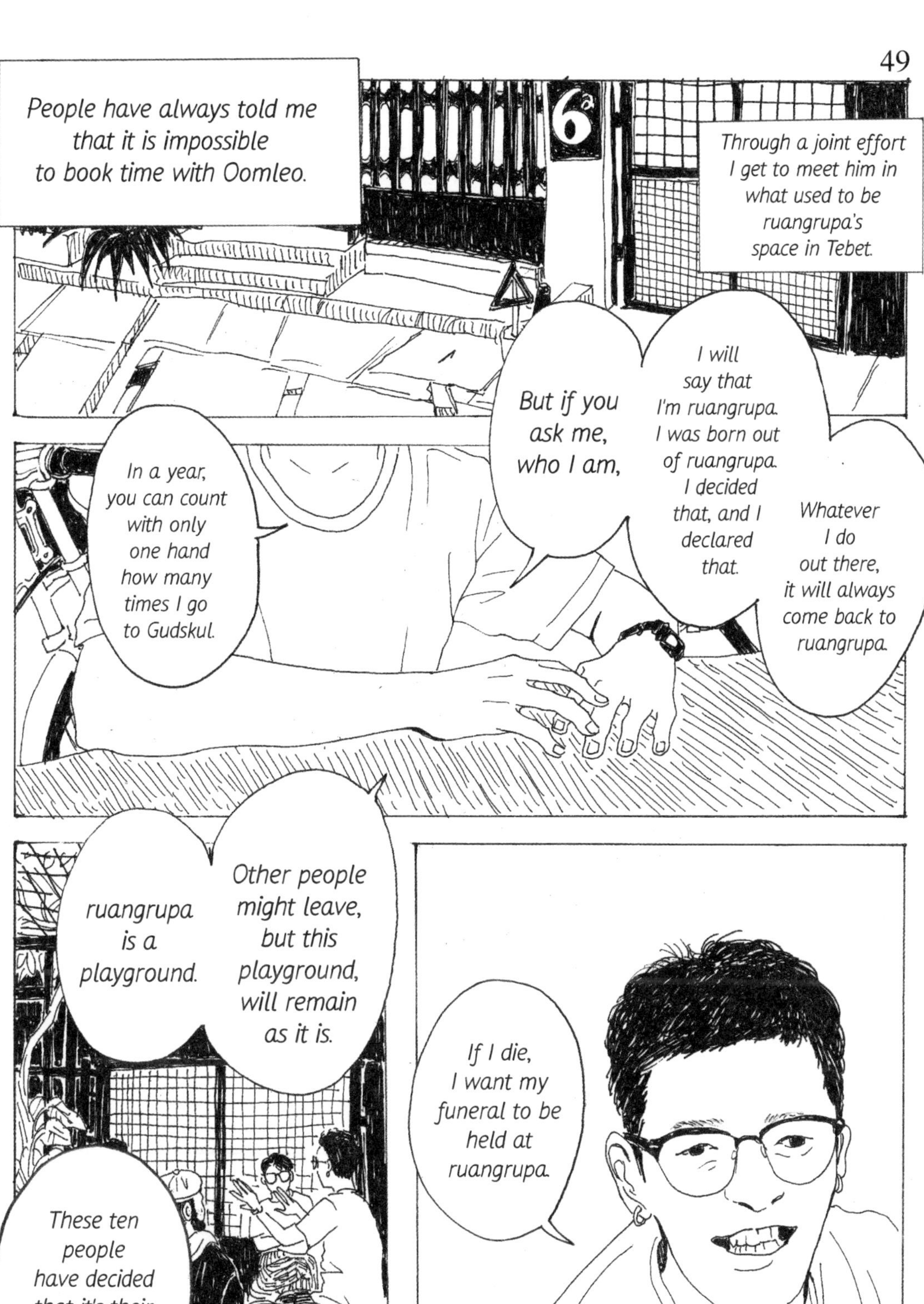
People have always told me that it is impossible to book time with Oomleo.
Through a joint effort I get to meet him in what used to be ruangrupa's space in Tebet.
In a year, you can count with only one hand how many times I go to Gudskul.
But if you ask me, who I am,
I will say that I'm ruangrupa. I was born out of ruangrupa. I decided that, and I declared that.
Whatever I do out there, it will always come back to ruangrupa.
ruangrupa is a playground.
Other people might leave, but this playground, will remain as it is.
These ten people have decided that it's their fate to stay. Including me.
If I die, I want my funeral to be held at ruangrupa.

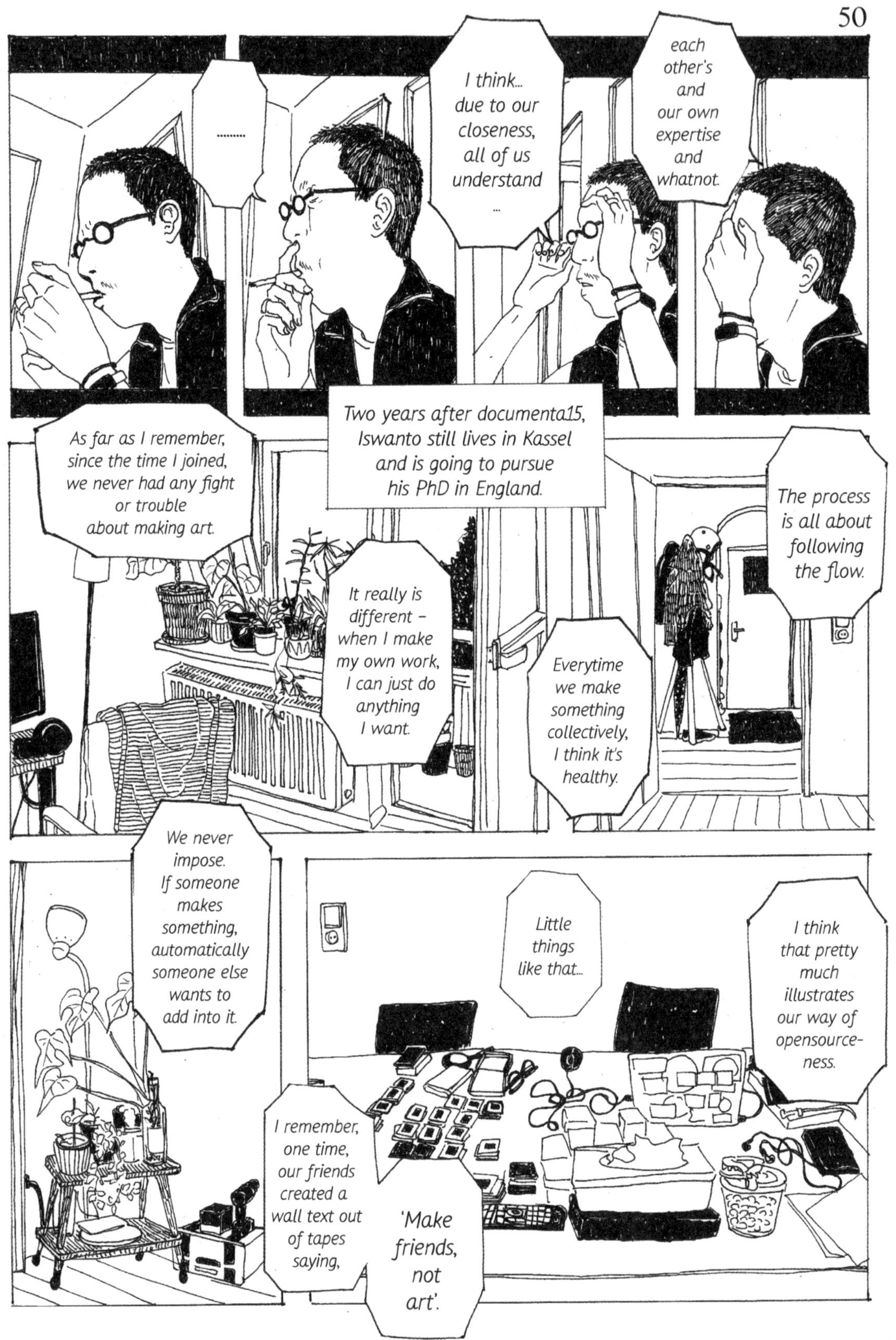
....
I think... due to our closeness, all of us understand ...
each other's and our own expertise and whatnot.
As far as I remember, since the time I joined, we never had any fight or trouble about making art.
Two years after documenta15, Iswanto still lives in Kassel and is going to pursue his PhD in England.
It really is different – when I make my own work, I can just do anything I want.
Everytime we make something collectively, I think it's healthy.
The process is all about following the flow.
We never impose. If someone makes something, automatically someone else wants to add into it.
Little things like that...
I think that pretty much illustrates our way of opensource-ness.
I remember, one time, our friends created a wall text out of tapes saying,
'Make friends, not art'.

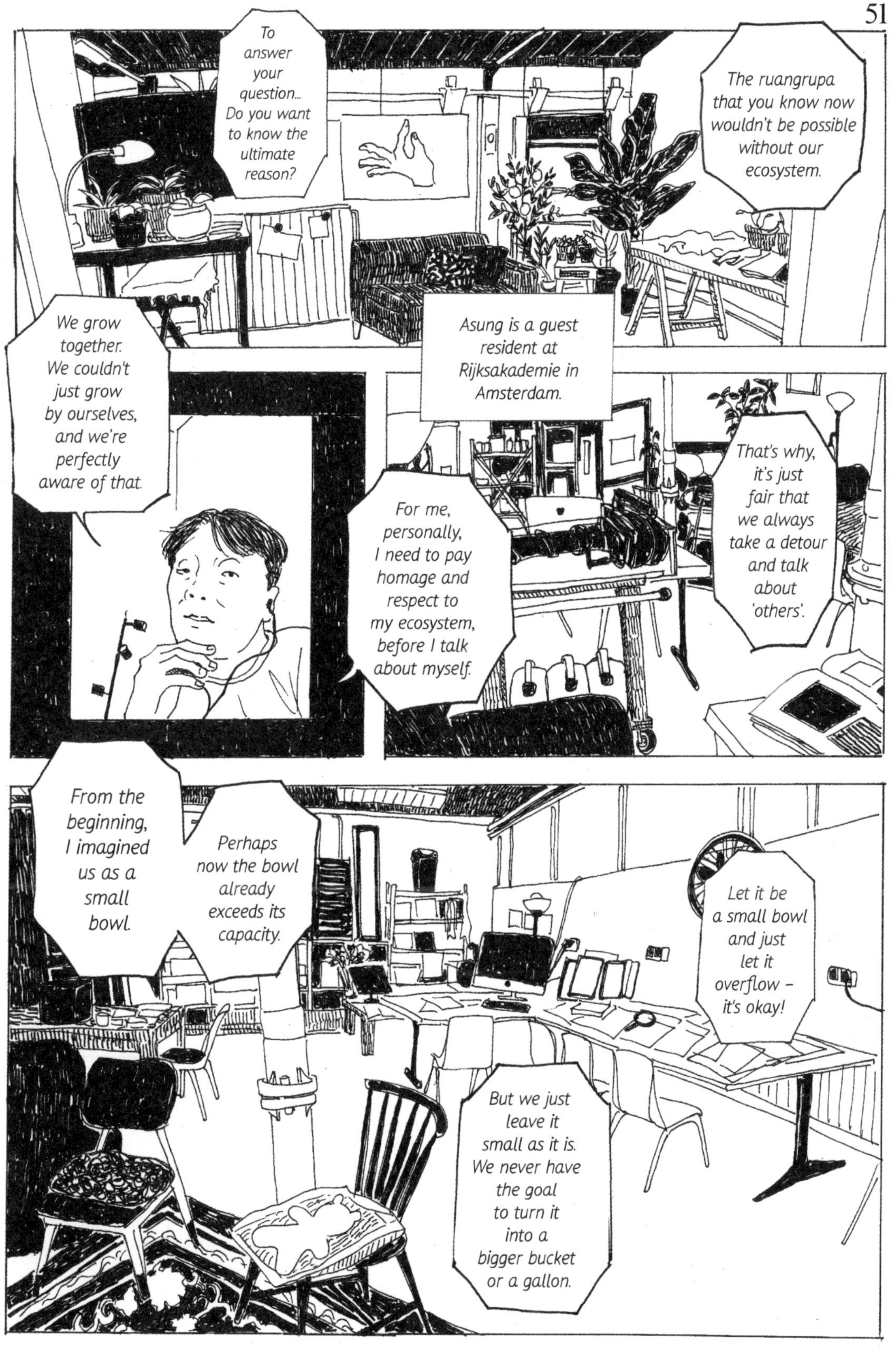
To answer your question... Do you want to know the ultimate reason?
The ruangrupa that you know now wouldn't be possible without our ecosystem.
We grow together. We couldn't just grow by ourselves, and we're perfectly aware of that.
Asung is a guest resident at Rijksakademie in Amsterdam.
For me, personally, I need to pay homage and respect to my ecosystem, before I talk about myself.
That's why, it's just fair that we always take a detour and talk about 'others'.
From the beginning, I imagined us as a small bowl.
Perhaps now the bowl already exceeds its capacity.
Let it be a small bowl and just let it overflow – it's okay!
But we just leave it small as it is. We never have the goal to turn it into a bigger bucket or a gallon.

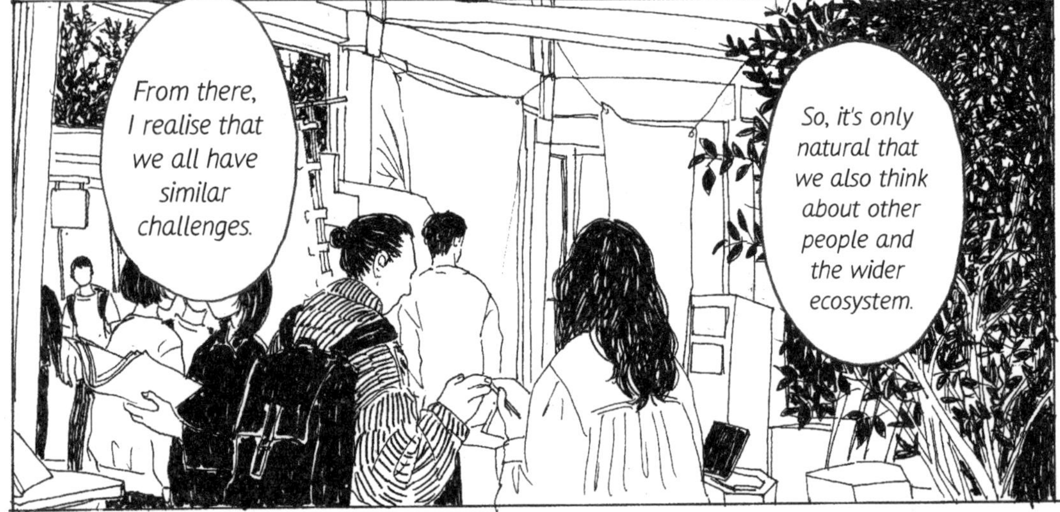
There are always multiple occurences where Sari and I cross paths,
but it's only after I meet her during an OK Pangan project in Tokyo that I get to ask her the questions I asked the others.
For me, ruangrupa is not just a place to work or create programmes
— it's part of the way I think and see things.
Through various interactions, we come to understand that in other places,
there are lots of initiatives that are equally trying to make something relevant
in their respective contexts.
From there, I realise that we all have similar challenges.
So, it's only natural that we also think about other people and the wider ecosystem.

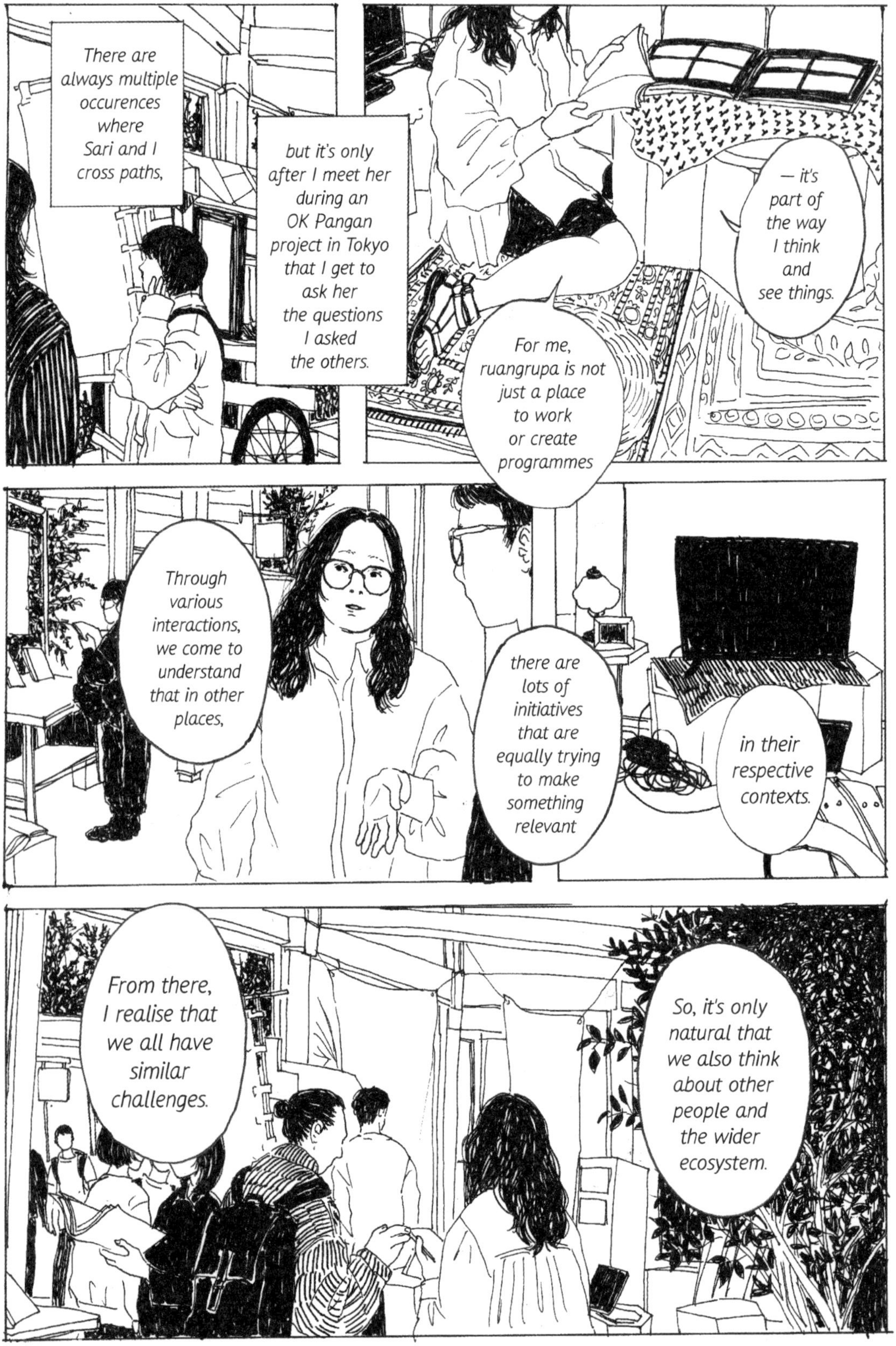

As for where the 'me' is—even though we work collectively, there's still room for personal growth.

I can still make my own work, I can collaborate with many other people, I can even go on residencies elsewhere,

and when I come back to ruangrupa, I'm still welcomed home.

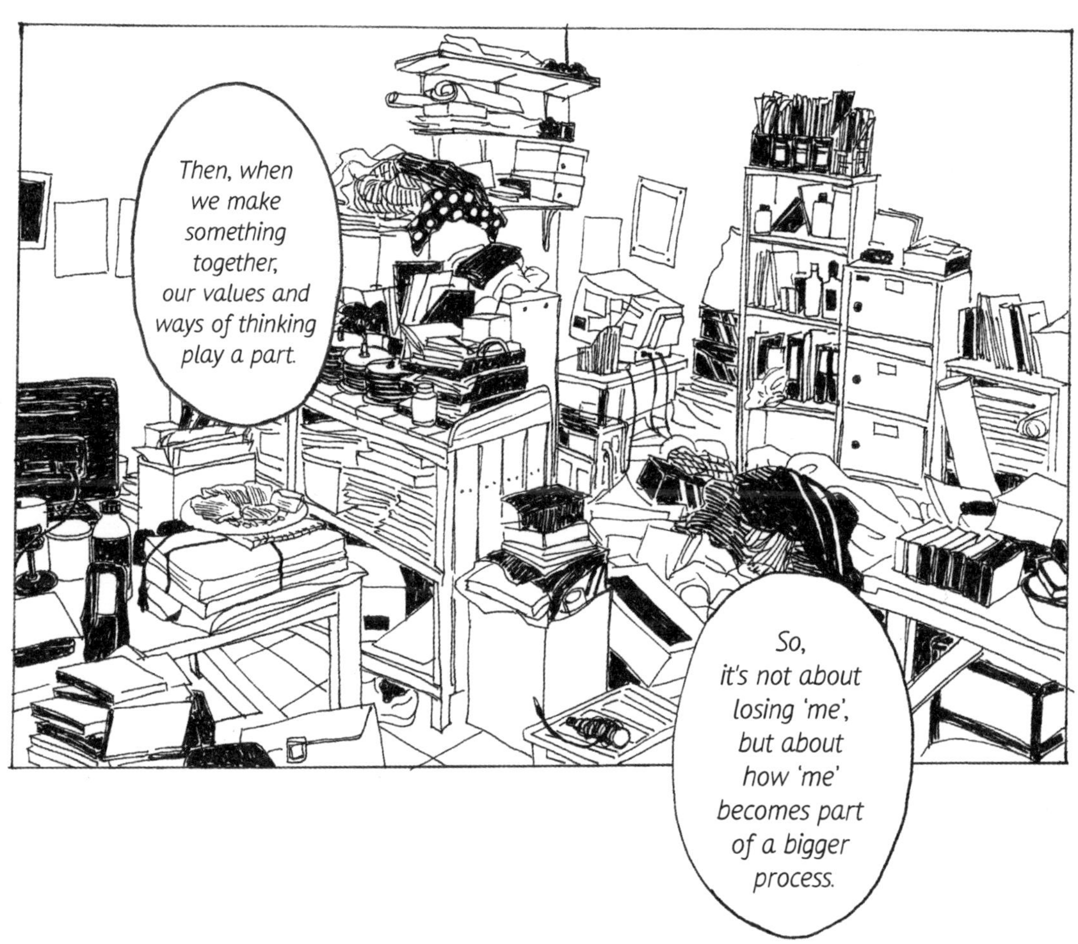

fin

ruangrupa’s direction guide, featured in RURU Corps fact sheet, c.2015. Courtesy ruangrupa

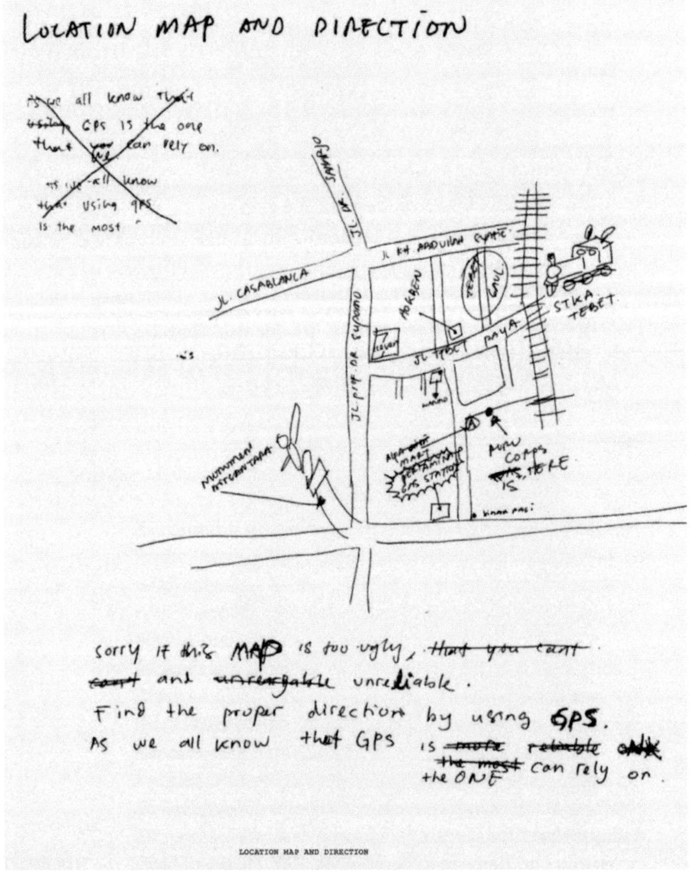

That Jakarta is the intrinsic ecosystem of ruangrupa is obvious, yet still underdiscussed. The following essay attempts to tease out the materiality and socio-historical context of Jakarta in shaping the formation of ruru as an urban collective. But first I must stress that artists are not only creative people, they are also members of a particular social order. They are not unlike me: I am an academic and also a member of a social-cultural milieu. Our work tells us not only who we are, but also the kind of cultural ecosystem within which we are embedded. Let me start, then, by quoting myself from my book *Jakarta* (2023):

> In 1988, towards the end of my architectural training in Surabaya, East Java, my friend and I set up an informal construction firm (informal means without a licence). We renovated houses, designed the interiors of small offices and showrooms, and built garages mostly for our relatives and friends. In Indonesian we were called *pemborong* (a wholesale service in construction). We went to the construction sites and worked with a *mandor* (head of construction workers). Little did I realise that in the two-three years spent running my own construction enterprise, we were engaged in the whole circuit (or should I say circus) of what we in the academic world today called practices of 'informality'. First of all, we were still students, we had no licence, so we never paid any tax. And our relationships with clients and workers were based on mutual understanding. Except for drawings to communicate ideas, nothing was presented on paper. There were no contracts for any work in any of our construction projects. We never applied for any building permits partly because it was expected that we should 'go ahead' so that the field officer (*pengawas lapangan*) from the district or municipality would come and we would settle the account on the site (again without paper). I also learned how to pay local thugs to unload building materials; I learned how to 'donate' bricks, cement and tiles to a local headman or district officer as a 'social contribution' (to upgrade his private residence). Especially, I learned how to ensure the security of the construction site. I did not learn all this from my architectural school. They are all acquired in the field.[1]

Thus reads my confession of my days as a cowboy builder, before I moved to Jakarta to live with my family in 1990. In Jakarta, I would come to realise, such informal and adaptive ways of working are amplified, as are the social contracts they cherish. They form the solid basis of the city's urban ecology

1 Abidin Kusno, *Jakarta: The City of a Thousand Dimensions*, Singapore: NUS Press, 2023, p.2.

and cultural ecosystem, which ruangrupa has been a part of since 2000. Indeed, ruru might well be described as a cowboy collective, engaging in the whole urban circuit/circus of Jakarta. This essay seeks to locate ruru in the ecosystems of Jakarta, mostly spatially and, hence (inevitably), politically. It also asks what the city and ruru have done to each other.

The Centre

Several members of ruru met for the first time as students at the Institut Kesenian Jakarta (IKJ), a formal art school located in the cultural complex of Taman Ismail Marzuki (TIM).[2] Their relations with TIM were marked by ambiguity. It was perhaps Jakarta that attracted them to IKJ more than the school itself. What would prove transformational for them was the urbanity of TIM. Located at the centre of Jakarta, TIM was a crossroads for witnessing turmoil in the political realms of the city and of the nation. However tangentially, a brief history of TIM is useful to understanding ruru and the houses they would later adapt for themselves and friends as they developed an affinity for Jakarta's *kampung* (urban-village) settlements, distinct from TIM.

During Indonesia's early decolonisation era in the 1950s, artists in Jakarta did not have 'houses'. Instead, they were associated with the street. They moved from one place to another in Central Jakarta, from Sawah Besar southward to Senen, passing their time in various *warung kopi* (street cafes) and developing the aura of artists. They seemed to be fine with appearing *lusuh*, *dekil* and *kotor* (in other words, shabby, scruffy and filthy),[3] and made themselves, according to some of their fellow artists, indistinguishable from *kaum jembel* (riff-raff). When their favoured gathering place in Senen began to be developed into a modern shopping complex, they moved to Menteng and convened around Balai Budaya, a cultural hall.[4] Into the 1960s, there continued to be no permanent place for these artists to *nongkrong* (hang out).

In 1968, Ajib Rosidi's writing on the homelessness of Jakarta's artists caught the attention of Ali Sadikin, Governor of Jakarta from 1966 to 1977, who invited Rosidi to his home.[5] The writer suggested to the Governor that

2 The Institute Kesenian Jakarta started as Lembaga Pendidikan Kesenian Jakarta (LPKJ), set up in 1970 by Governor Ali Sadikin and based on the initiative of artists. Sadikin wanted LPKJ to be above the art schools in Bandung and Yogyakarta. See Ramadhan K.H., *Bang Ali: Demi Jakarta, 1966–1977*, Jakarta: Pustaka Sinar Harapan, 1995, p.187.

3 Hendaru Tri Hanggoro, 'Cerita awal Taman Ismail Marzuki', *Historia.id*, 7 February 2020.

4 *Ibid.*

5 Ajib Rosidi, 'Senen: Wajah Yang Lama', *Intisari*, February 1968. See also 'Poros Budaya Cikini 73', *Tempo*, 21 August 2022, pp.88–91.

a place be provided for artists to mingle, and he proposed for consideration *Gelanggang Kesenian Jakarta* (Arena for art), as sketched by the painter Oesman Effendi. In Rosidi's recollection, Sadikin confessed that although he knew nothing about art other than that artists are difficult to handle, he nonetheless believed that Jakarta needed to become the centre of Indonesian culture, because 'a modern city must have an advanced art (*kesenian yang maju*)'.[6]

TIM thus was built, and Sadikin throughout his term continued to raise funds to cover its operational costs.[7] As he intended, TIM was run by artists without political intervention by the government, and it became a barometer for new artistic expression in Indonesia, with IKJ attracting students from different parts of the country.[8] Later, and paradoxically, Sadikin's intention to free art from politics, which stemmed from the post-1965 climate of anti-communism, became a tool of the Suharto regime (aka the Orde Baru, or New Order, 1966–98) to control political and critical expression. As soon as Sadikin stepped down from his position, TIM started to decline in all aspects of its life – the government became involved in the management of the centre, including its arts programming, while funding decreased.

In the same years that the sense of artistic freedom at TIM eroded due to government intervention, the city of Jakarta never failed to offer uncertain opportunities to everyone, notably through its relatively autonomous *kampung* neighborhoods, which continued to grow beneath high-rises and flyovers. Over time, the narrowing space for criticality shifted from TIM as the 'centre' of artistic creation to discursive locales ranging from *kampungs* to the middle-class houses that increasingly provided space for individual studios and *bengkel-bengkel* (local workshops) as well as small private galleries. Pushing critical artists underground, the repressive regime of Suharto ironically contributed to the decentralisation of artistic practices. In other words, it provided a context for the proliferation of independent art collectives in various formal and informal housing complexes, all of which stood out in sharp relief after the collapse of the Suharto regime in 1998.

Middling Urbanism

Jakarta has long been described as a big urban village. One very obvious reason for this is the predominance of *kampungs* throughout the city – mostly

6 Hendaru Tri Hanggoro, 'Cerita awal Taman Ismail Marzuki', *op. cit.*

7 But it was not based on Effendi's sketch. Instead Sadikin instructed his staff architect, Wastu Pragantha Tjong, to design TIM. See 'Poros Budaya Cikini 73', *op. cit.*

8 'Government must not get involved. Let artists be free, so that they can create. Let them grow and dream the unimaginable.' See See Ramadhan K.H., *Bang Ali*, *op. cit.*, p.181. See also 'Poros Budaya Cikini 73', *op. cit.*

unplanned, typically low-income residential areas which have been gradually built and serviced by their inhabitants with sporadic (if any) support from the government. These many *kampungs* are not well integrated into Jakarta's administrative structure.

During the Suharto era, Indonesia, and by extension Jakarta, was run by a corporatist state consisting of the central government and submissive local governments (led by a governor, always with a military background) and a consortium of domestic and foreign business partners, called the 'strategic group' by sociologists Manasse Malo and Peter J.M. Nas. Far below, a multitude of *rakyat* (common people) 'were not organised and did not promote common plans'.[9] The *rakyat* had lived together apart from the strategic group since the colonial era, and while many gradually became integrated into urban society, they were not fully assimilated.[10] Their role within the city of Jakarta as the urban poor living in *kampung* settlements became beneficially problematic. To this day, these pockets of irregular settlement within the city almost always rely on spontaneous communal practices of *gotong royong* (helping one another). *Rakyat* render mutual assistance through the sharing of resources for self-preservation, filling in Jakarta's 'in-between' spaces.

Since colonial times, Indonesia's various governments provided little in terms of knowledge or financial investment in administering *kampung* settlements. One could argue that this neglect was economically and politically motivated. It stemmed from the indirect politics of the colonial regime, which demonstrated an attitude of 'non-interference' to diminish the risk of rebellion and obscure the government's unwillingness to build infrastructure or distribute resources for the welfare of the full population. This form of statecraft 'enabled' *rakyat* to build houses for themselves throughout the colonial era.

Kampung settlements developed in tandem with the formal city, constituting a mutually constitutive as well as antagonistic duality of Jakarta's urban form. I have conceptualised the *kampung* in terms of 'middling urbanism', that is, as a form of urbanism that is tied to the city in mutual apprehension and reciprocation.[11] The relationship between the city and the *kampung* is both symbiotic and pathological. *Kampung* people often view

9 See Manasse Malo and Peter J.M. Nas, 'Queen City of the East and Symbol of the Nation: The Administration and Management of Jakarta', in Jurgen Ruland (ed.), *The Dynamics of Metropolitan Management in Southeast Asia*, Singapore: ISEAS-Yusof Ishak Institute, 1996, p.130.

10 Abidin Kusno, 'Shifting Modalities of Urban Governance: Indonesian Cities over the Long Term', in Edward Aspinall and Amalinda Savirani (ed)., *Governing Urban Indonesia*, Singapore: ISEAS-Yusof Ishak Institute, 2024, pp.24–45.

11 Abidin Kusno, *Jakarta, op. cit.*, chapter 1.

the local government with distrust and fear, as they do its backers – the police, business groups and development agencies. Throughout the New Order period, *kampung* were either under-resourced or opened up for development and land speculation (which continues into the present). Under the pretext of *pembangunan* (development), residents could be evicted. Under the ideology of a 'clean environment' erased of communist threat, *kampung* could be controlled. Overall, the New Order transformed Jakarta through a series of politically and economically motivated flexible regulations, weak environmental controls and manipulable planning. And, over time in Indonesia, lack of planning became an art of governing.

Our ruru lives in an urban ecology of incomplete, inherited infrastructure, where there is always room to maneuver and rearrange the order of things from the middle. While there is no formula for how to govern from the gap, people seem to know how to relate, formulate and stay creative in what Indonesian writer Seno Gumira Ajidarma calls 'the city of a thousand dimensions'.[12] In short, Jakarta is sustained by the everyday assemblage of things that make it work even as it is essentially broken. The city continues to operate and people carry on fixing things their own way. So, we can understand why, two decades into their existence as a collective, ruru continues to be obsessed with the term 'fixer'.[13]

Looseness at the Centre

During ruru's early years, in the aftermath of Suharto's fall from power, major transformations were taking place on the streets of Jakarta. As the manufacturing and construction industries scaled down in activity, their former workers took up any job available, sometimes inventing new professions under the broad category of *kaki lima*, referring to the five-foot distance between a building and the street. In this space, vendors came to operate on almost every street in Jakarta. A newspaper at the time reported: 'The presence of *kaki lima* (vendors) in the capital city is not surprising. However, today their presences have been extremely *marak* (ignited). They do not just display their merchandises on pushcarts or under plastic or canvas tents. Instead, they set up their places with permanent stalls, which they also use as their dwellings.'[14]

12 Seno Gumira Ajidarma, *Tiada Ojek di Paris*, Jakarta: Mizan Publishing, 2015.

13 ruru held the exhibition 'Fixer: Exhibition of Alternative Spaces and Art Groups in Indonesia' at North Art Space, Jakarta in 2010. In 2021, Gudskul revisited 'Fixer' and produced the publication *Articulating Fixer 2021: An Appraisal of Indonesian Art Collectives in the Last Decade* (Jakarta: Yayasan Gudskul Studi Kolektif, 2021).

14 'Jakarta mirip kota kaki lima', *Kompas*, 12 June 2000.

Sutiyoso, Governor of Jakarta from 1997 to 2007, described a 'multi-dimensional crisis' that was causing a 'change in people's behaviour'. In 2002, at the end of his first term, he recalled that, '4,538 demonstrations were staged by Jakartans against me [during that five-year term] ... from small scale rallies to one that led to anarchy'.[15] Some have called this era the beginning of the Reformasi, defined by a 'democratic transition'. Be that as it may, it was caused by a sense of '"looseness" at the center'. One of my own notes on the period reads:

> Post-1998 Indonesia has witnessed an unprecedented 'looseness' at the center..., which generates a feeling that (as reported by a media) 'we seem to be a nation that is just beginning to learn about everything'. ... More than before, the press is free to speak, and critical voices of the 'people' can be heard; political parties are allowed to organise freely; and public protests are tolerated, generating an impression that (quoting a newspaper report) 'today's Jakarta cannot be separated from protest expressing feeling (*unjuk rasa*) in public'. ... This sense that the centre is falling apart has created various civilian groups formed either loosely or tightly around identities 'below' as well as 'above' the nation; familiar groupings include those of class, professional, religious, ethnic, political, as well as moral affiliations. They are all linked to each other by a sense that the nation-state no longer commands any power to protect or rule, or at best, the political elites safeguard only their own interests and completely disregard the rest of the citizens who are left on their own to survive in the worsening realities of urban lives.[16]

In this context of so-called multidimensional crisis, ruru was born and brought up. Indeed, in Jakarta around the turn of the century, the unparalleled rate of change driven by political decentralisation and extended multi-dimensional crisis opened a space for art collectives to engage more openly with the city. Jakarta's looseness at the centre, and its long history of self-reliant urban fixers, perhaps accounts for ruru researcher Mirwan Andan's reflection that ruru gets to its way of working because of Jakarta.[17]

With all its history of power, domination and hierarchy, Jakarta remains a city of loose ends, many contradictory. Perhaps these disjointed pieces

15 'Sutiyoso: Most Maligned Governor?', *Jakarta Post*, 19 July 2002.

16 Abidin Kusno, *The Appearances of Memory: Mnemonic Practices of Architecture and Urban Form in Indonesia*, Durham, NC: Duke University Press, 2010, pp.36–37.

17 See Mirwan Andan, 'All for Jakarta – A Note on the Tenth Anniversary of ruangrupa: Decompression #10, Expanding the Space and Public' (trans. Intan Paramaditha), *Inter-Asia Cultural Studies*, vol.12, no.4, 2011, pp.591–602.

are not so much waiting to be tightened securely, but rather to be continuously fixed and refixed. The city itself grows through the loose ends that have multiplied since the collapse of Suharto's authoritarianism.

The House

The first house, and subsequent houses, that ruru rented to build its community were in a district in South Jakarta that was among the city's first planned neighbourhoods: Tebet.[18] It was developed following the decision of Indonesia's first President, Sukarno, to host the 1962 Asian Games and the 1963 Games of the Newly Emerging Forces (GANEFO). Sukarno saw both events as opportunity to showcase solidarity among newly independent countries in the face of the Tokyo Olympic Games' mostly Western alliance. After Sukarno designated the Senayan area of Jakarta as the main venue for the Asian Games and GANEFO, he carried out the first evictions in the history of postcolonial Indonesia. The largely Betawi population (about 50,000 people) living in Senayan were relocated to several surrounding areas, including Tebet.[19]

The displaced were given the opportunity to own one- and two-bedroom houses of modest size, sited close together on narrow roads that looked more like alleyways. Most of the roads were initially unpaved and single-laned; they were meant for pedestrians, pedicabs and *bajaj* (three-wheel motorised bikes), but certainly not for automobiles. Sustained only by inadequate utilities, with a lack of electricity and water supplied via hand pumps at individual wells, the neighbourhood resembled a dense *kampung* made of brick houses.[20] Nevertheless, over time Tebet received upgrades from private entrepreneurs, who took advantage of its proximity to what had, by the 1980s, become a central area of Jakarta.

As a modestly planned neighbourhood from the 1960s, Tebet is not a *kampung* and instead more like a third space, striking a problematic balance between public and private (job and home) in its engagement with the larger city and its *kampungs*. While in the 1980s, Tebet was known as a place where

18 See Iswanto Hartono and Thomas Berghuis, 'Selatan: Transformation of Urban Cultural Imagery from Melawai to Tebet', in Anthony Gardner (ed.), *Mapping South: Journeys in South-South Cultural Relations*, Victoria, Australia: The South Project Inc., 2013, pp.231–44.

19 See Restu Gunawan, *Gagalnya Sistim Kanal*, Jakarta: Kompas, 2010, p.77. See also Farabi Fakih, *Membayangkan Ibu Kota: Jakarta di Bawah Soekarno*, Yogyakarta: Ombak Press, 2005, p.166.

20 Little research exists on Tebet to date. See Irfan Teguh, 'Penggusuran Kampung untuk Asian Games 1962', *tirto.id*, 17 August 2018. See also Hartono and Berghuis, 'Selatan', *op. cit.*

bapak-bapak (married men with connections) might hide their mistresses, by the 2000s it had become a cultural hot spot for artists and musicians to live and work. In recent years, Tebet has become a popular cultural landscape, especially for young people, in terms of its *nongkrong* spaces – its many cafés, food stalls and shops as well as rental housing. A number of Tebet's streets have been widened to accommodate automobiles, while the cost of housing and rent have gone up.

Fortunately or not, ruru was able to rent a house in Tebet in 2000 due to the 1997–98 *krismon* (monetary crisis) and the rioting that followed, which drove Jakarta's property values down significantly. With many houses nearly destroyed and a good deal abandoned by their owners, proper-size houses became affordable for purchase or to rent. As is often the case in times of crisis, rules became more flexible. Houses were adapted for new functions, and spaces reimagined without the need for permission. A newspaper reported at the time: '[E]specially after the riots of May 1998, many streets are blocked by portals, and behind the blockage, is a phenomenal growth of private enterprises in the housing complex.'[21]

Under the New Order, the street was considered a space of menace, 'the locus of disturbances where the mad, the wanderers and ghosts make appearances', but the new era was marked by street take-overs, whether for protest or cultural production, artistic activities or youth community formation.[22] Indeed, the financial crisis transformed the meaning of the street. In Tebet, the growth of private enterprise spilled across many streets. Since the early 2000s, the streets of a once-private neighborhood have often become public space for diverse cultural activism by the young.[23] The proliferation of informal economic activities and micro-businesses, and the change of mood during the Reformasi era, turned Tebet into a spectacle of cultures and commodities where 'local brands of designer goods have become a kind of guerrilla force against the powerful global brands and logos usually found in Jakarta's posh supermalls'.[24]

Ade Darmawan, a founding member of ruru, has recalled a survey that he conducted in 2009 with co-curator Rifky Effendy for the exhibition 'Fixer': they asked the 21 artist groups participating in the exhibition to send photographs representing the practices of their collectives. Reviewing the submissions, Ade realised that 'almost all the photos representing their organisations showed the houses where they have lived and worked'. Further:

21 A. Matin, 'Bintaro Jaya: Kota taman dan kota toko', *Kompas*, 29 March 2000.

22 For a discussion on the changing meaning of streets, see Abidin Kusno, *Behind the Postcolonial: Architecture, Urban Space and Political Cultures in Indonesia*, London: Routledge, 2000, p.117.

23 See Hartono and Berghuis, 'Selatan', *op. cit.*

24 *Ibid.*, p.235.

Narpati Awangga (aka Oomleo), *Mamah*, 2006, featuring ruangrupa house (greyed out) in Tebet Barat Komp Kejaksaan, Jakarta. Courtesy the artist

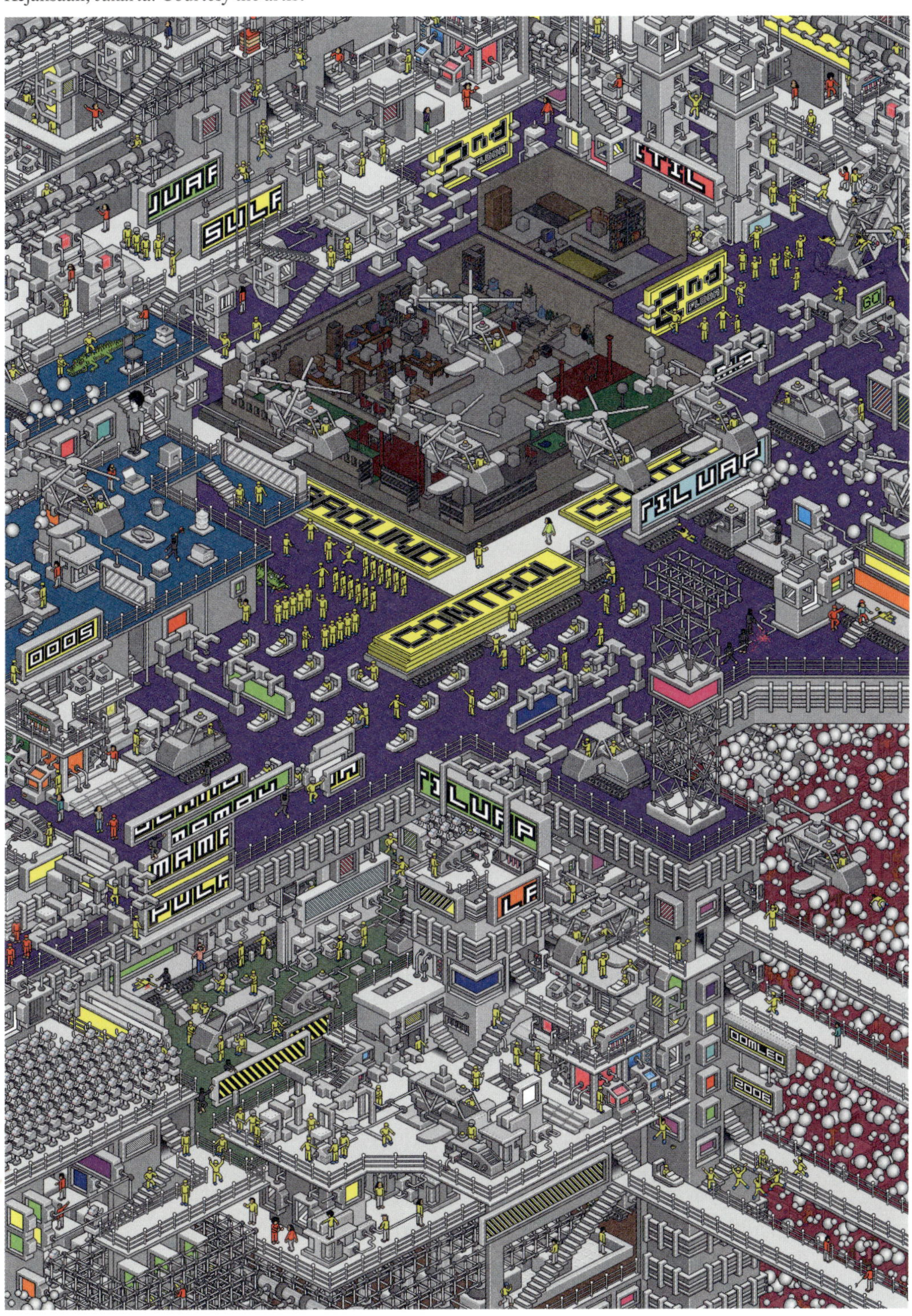

> All the groups ... used a home as the starting point and the centre of their activities, altering and adapting a domestic space into a more public space, converting the living room into a meeting space and exhibition space; and the bedrooms into working spaces or studios, the library, and a space for archives. ... Thus, the house can have two functions: as a space for living and a space for working and gathering.[25]

That the house was a starting point for many emerging collectives was, I think, not only due to the availability and affordability of houses during the *krismon*, but also to general distrust of the state and official art institutions. ruru's relative autonomy seemed to hint at the general gap, or rift, between the government and the urban majority to which most artists belonged. The house offered a retreat from institutional patronage into the anonymous 'private' sphere of commoners. In other words, in a time of uncertainty, the house offered a sense of 'home', or a 'household' to imagine a collective body. Inside the house, it was the living room that served as the bonding domain, and the locus for the exploration of shared interests.

While a borrowed term from the English language, *living room* is quite specific in the Indonesian context. It can refer to the *ruang tamu* (space for guests) that is usually located at the front part of a house. Invented among the middle class to acquire distinction from the lower class, such space is not always available in *kampung* houses. Often decorated to represent the 'outer appearance' of the host, *ruang tamu* can be recognised as staging order, hierarchy and modernity. Saya Shiraishi argues that the *ruang tamu* is a disciplinary space and notes that in a typical middle-class Javanese family's *ruang tamu*, 'the guests of the house are usually offered seats on the red-cloth-covered carved-wood-framed sofas or chairs in the sitting room. The young female manager would sit on a wooden bench and housemaids on the floor steps. The young children of the house were generally found on the floor, playing with the housemen.'[26]

When ruru moved into the house they found to rent in Tebet, it had a *ruang tamu*, but the expected order of the housing complex-style room was soon undone. In the ruru house, as in the houses of other collectives, everyone in the *ruang tamu* sat on the floor or on their feet and there was no distinction between those using the room. With everyone sitting on the floor,

25 Ade Darmawan, 'Curating, Collectives, and Conversation', in Beverly Yong and Furuichi Yasuko (ed.), *Condition Report: Shifting Perspectives in Asia–Curators' Book*, Tokyo: Japan Foundation Asia Centre, 2018, pp.55–56.

26 See Saya Shiraishi, 'Silakan Masuk, Silakan Duduk: Reflections in a Sitting Room in Java', *Indonesia*, vol.41, April 1986, p.110.

chairs and sofas became useless as a medium for establishing hierarchy. Many collectives, including ruru, used their *ruang tamu* as a meeting space. As Darmawan has described it: 'They were sitting down in a circle. Meetings and sharing through conversations had become really important, and a house provided a very comfortable space for allowing these to happen. Such meetings most often took place in the living room (*ruang tamu*), since it is the largest room in most spatial designs of a typical Indonesian home. ... From a simple living room, a group positions itself as a vital part of the supporting infrastructure for art and for the community ... (and) as living among the people.'[27]

In Indonesia, the appropriated term *living room* can also encompass a secondary, more domestic room further into a house, where the television is usually placed. By subverting the English language, ruru has also subverted the divide between inside and outside, and violated any order that is culturally conditioned. In Jakarta, where it can seem hard to divide the public from the private, the living room seems to mediate such an ambiguity. As a space, a situation and a concept, the living room is the inside-out and outside-in of ruru's navigation of Jakarta.

Hacking Objects

By way of ending, let me discuss a project – an amalgam of activist, aesthetic and archivist approaches – that reveals some aspects of what ruru and Jakarta do to each other. Around 2018, as I was trying to navigate Jakarta by carrying out research about *banjir* (flooding), I reached out to my ruru friend farid rakun and members of ruru's ArtLab including Reza Afisina, Rifqi Fajri and Angga Cipta. I wanted to get a sense of how people in Jakarta accommodate the ways of water. We shared the feeling that, as Rudolf Mrázek has put it, 'Jakarta is like a broken flush toilet.'[28] The city is always leaking, which leaves the population no choice but to make friends with flooding,[29] and making friends with the impossible has become a tradition, one that has developed, one could say, out of the state's failure to consistently provide basic, reliable and equitable infrastructure.

Farid and the ArtLab group suggested that we go 'micro', meaning we needed to look at practices of everyday life to reveal the thousand ways in which individuals handle their relations with water and broken infrastructure. The idea was to learn from people in different *kampungs* of Jakarta,

27 Ade Darmawan, 'Curating, Collectives, and Conversation', *op. cit.*, pp.55–56.
28 Rudolf Mrázek, 'Water and the Colonial Imaginary', in *Jakarta: Architecture + Adaptation*, Depok: Universitas Indonesia Press, 2013, p.294.
29 See Abidin Kusno, *Jakarta*, *op. cit.*, pp.71–107.

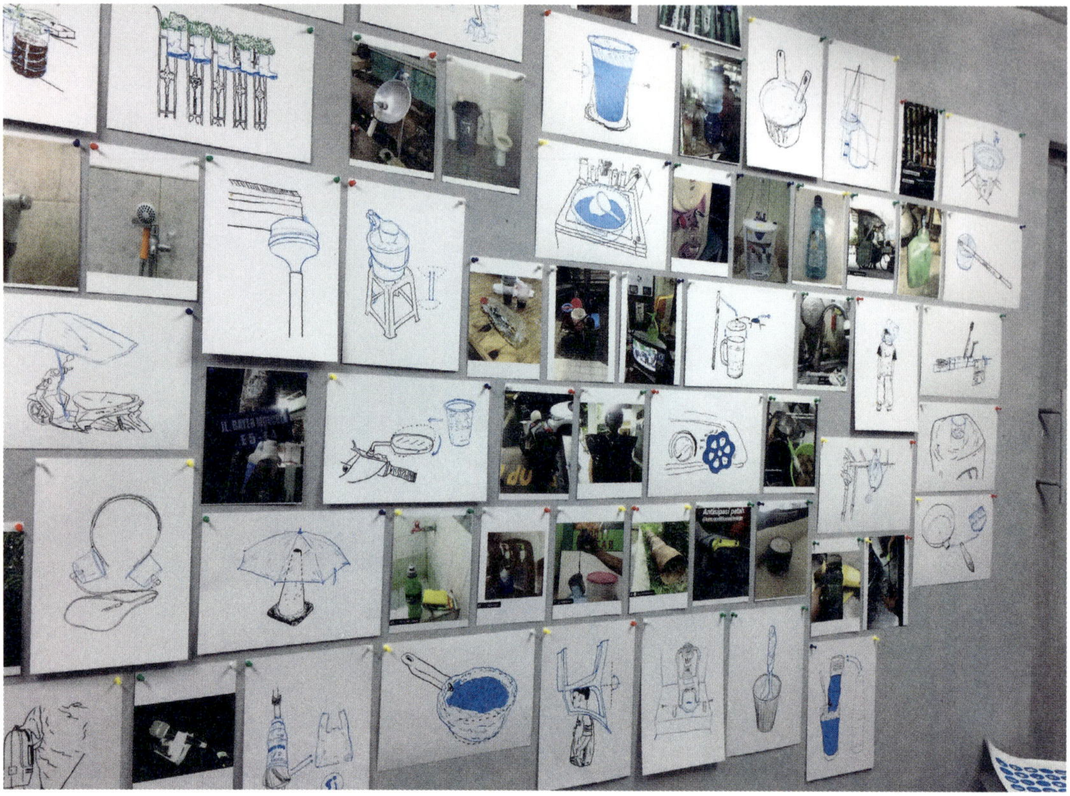

Installation views, 'Water Fleas', exhibition by ArtLab, RURU Gallery, February 2019, with illustrations by Anita Cipta (top) and the ArtLab team (below). Courtesy Angga Cipta

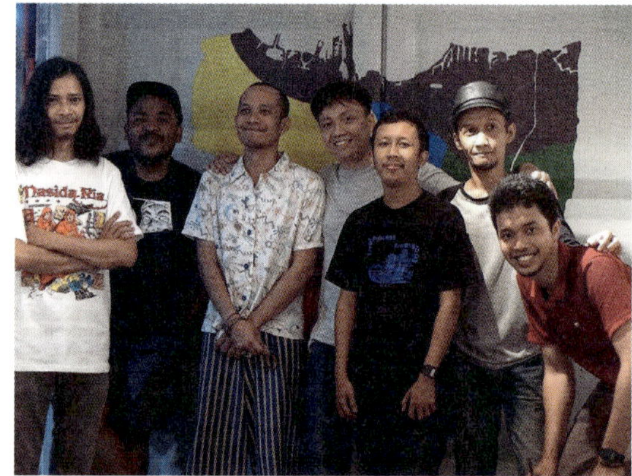

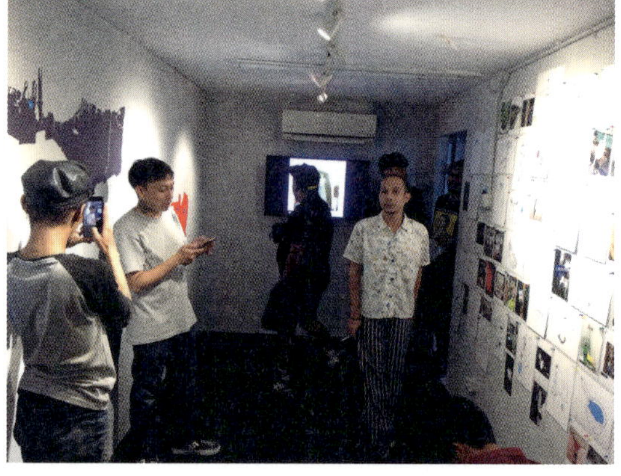

to see how they combine found and sometimes broken objects to hold or move water. The premise was that these practices would be visualised as a display of documentation that might offer an assemblage of the micro-infrastructure that supports the urban majority's everyday survival. In other words, such an assemblage could reveal a method of living in Jakarta.

Farid and ArtLab called the project 'water fleas', associating it with the often unnoticed interconnectedness of the ecosystem within which human exist. Farid uses the word 'hacking' to identify practices that connect unrelated materials to provide alternative infrastructure for everyday life. Conceptually, 'hacking objects' keep the otherwise dysfunctional city running, much like the activities of water fleas maintain an ecological balance. Practically speaking, hacking objects point to the intermingling of formal and informal infrastructures in many *kampung* settlements. In these environments, commodity objects prove their functionality when reused to mend broken infrastructure.

There's more to be said about hacking processes. First, a commodity object, such as a plastic water bottle, goes out of its commodity life when it is reused in a deviation from its original norm. With each hack, or repurposing, there is the issue of where and why this work is being carried out, but we have no idea if those involved in each assemblage have a reflective take on the situation, or if there is a consciousness about how one process could lead to the production of another form. There may be an anticipation of what is yet to come, but the possibilities of deviation from the previous norm and form are perhaps too many to have any certainty. For sure, in Jakarta ephemeral commodities have second lives: the fractured urban infrastructure supplies the ingredients for people to assert their authorial function as the city's 'fixers'.

ruru took photos of different practices of hacking objects in various *kampung* settlements, shortlisting some to give them to Angga Cipta (nicknamed Acip), a gifted illustrator in ArtLab. For Acip, what is important is the techno-artistic aspects of the objects as they are captured through his illustrations, which, when exhibited on the wall, present to viewers an inexhaustible number of commodities as everyday infrastructure. If hacking objects are taking place in locations that are at once near and everywhere in the city, Jakarta could well be understood as a city of incommensurability, 'united' only by an exhibition that brings together fragments. When they are displayed next to one another, we see a commonality in addition to difference. While each fragment is unique, they all appear to share an urban condition: the necessity to mend the broken city from below.

When every use of an object is at once an act of appropriation, the city acquires multiple dimensions with unknown beginnings and endings. Jakarta can be said to lack top-down integrative infrastructure, but the deficiency enables the assemblage of things from below, which is surely precarious and incomplete but sustains the function of everyday life.

ruru's investigations, including 'water fleas' and many others over the years, are based on intensive observations of objects and phenomena in the city – of how one thing gets connected to another in an unexpected way, and how, together, they constitute a new function in different locations, whether in public space or inside houses. They trace the material details of everyday life as recomposed from various sources in extraordinary ways to function as a 'normal' infrastructure. Nothing is straight-forwardly inherited from the past. The craft is immediate, a call to fix now and not later. It is hard to say whether these practices – of hacking objects and of ruru itself – will become recognisable history or disappear into the discarded past. For now, we can take a good walk through Jakarta's streets and alleyways, and we will see what ruru sees and what ruru originates. The details of these practices document the life of ruru's Jakarta.

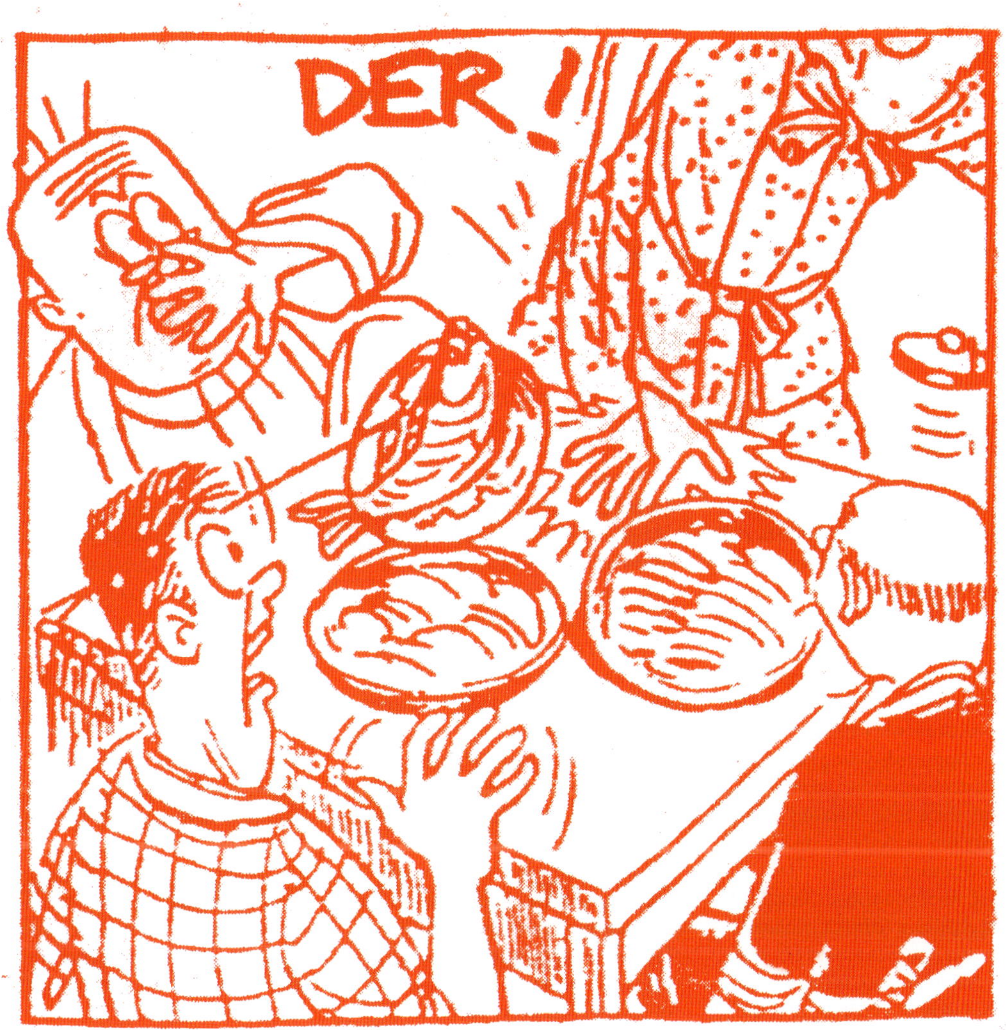

Hang out.

In this section we explore selected ruangrupa projects and exhibitions since 2000. The selection is based on ruru's own archive and available materials – and what has held the most significance for their participants and publics, then and now – alongside key critical perspectives. It offers an extensive (but not comprehensive) document of 25 years of multifarious activity.

Many of ruangrupa's projects correspond to three main 'types':

1. long-term programmes initiated by ruru as producer and organiser;
2. one-off art projects ruru has organised, created or hosted;
3. exhibitions and biennales to which ruru has been invited as 'curator' or 'artist'.

There are plenty of slippages between these types, and they do not account for everything ruru is and does. But they may offer some points of entry into the archive. We may also think of some of ruru's common strategies, such as *living room*, *ekosistem* and *lumbung*, which recur in many variations throughout the pages that follow. In our understanding, strategies for ruru have meant useful, practical ways of survival that reflect their economic realities and their learning from place and people.

1

Most of ruru's long-term programmes were initiated within their first decade and have continued with varying consistency ever since. These programmes were born out of the interests and circumstances of ruru members and friends, including artistic research and collaboration (ruru house residency and exhibition programme, since 2001; ArtLab, since 2008); publishing and visual culture research (*Karbon* journal, since 2000); new media and film practices (OK.Video festival, since 2003); supporting young practitioners and student networks (Jakarta 32°C festival, since 2004; curating and art criticism workshops, since 2008); commerce and exchange (Holy Market, since 2009; RURU Shop, since 2010); childcare (rurukids, since 2010); and music (RRREC Fest, since 2011). In the mid-2010s significant energies were directed towards the co-development and maintenance of shared institutional spaces – Gudang Sarinah Ekosistem (2015–18) and then Gudskul Ekosistem (since 2018) – based on collaboration and resource sharing with like-minded arts initiatives, which also provided the bases for ruru's long-standing programmes and activities.

2

One-off art projects initiated by ruru often take the form of artistic research – usually collaborative, usually including workshops or debates – most often followed by an exhibition-presentation at ruru house (or later RURU Gallery). Many of these derive from ruru's practice of hosting artists in Jakarta, informally and via their artist-in-residence programmes, and draw from long-term interests in aspects of urban life and popular culture; and many of these participants were featured in the 'ruru&friends' and 'ruru.net' exhibitions as part of ruru's tenth anniversary programme 'Decompression #10' (2010–11), signifying their importance as ruru's supporting network. One-off projects often develop from or feed into the long-term programmes described above; for instance, most editions of *Karbon* journal are based on an earlier one-off discussion or workshop hosted by ruru.

3

Since 2001, and with much greater frequency from the 2010s onwards, ruru has been invited to contribute to exhibitions and biennales. They developed diverse approaches to presenting collective work, including celebrating ruru's fun-loving spirit in exhibitions such as 'Lekker Eten Zonder Betalen' ('Tasty Meal Without Paying', 2003); creating site-specific archival fictions, such as *Singapore Fiction* (2011) and *THE KUDA: The Untold Story of Indonesian Underground Music in the 70s* (2012–13); extending their local research on material and popular culture to new contexts, as in *Kaos Project* (for Istanbul Biennial in 2005) and *You're Welcome* (for 'Rethinking Nordic Colonialism Act 3' in 2006); or transplanting ruru space into new places, as seen in their contributions to the Gwangju Biennale (2002), 'The Grand Domestic Revolution' (2009), the 31st Bienal de São Paulo (2014) and Aichi Triennale (2016). Exhibition-making has been present in ruru's practice from the beginning – for instance, 'Jakarta: Habitus Publik', the public art programme ruru curated for JakArt Festival in 2001 – and it is as artistic director of major exhibitions that ruru may be best known internationally. These more recent projects continued the practice of transplanting ruru space, such as ruruhuis in Arnhem a year ahead of Sonsbeek 16: transACTION (2016) and ruruHaus in Kassel two years ahead of documenta fifteen (2022).

'Bersama' ('Together'), Cemara 6 Gallery, Jakarta, 30 March – 8 April 2000

We organised a fundraising exhibition to get financial support for our first project and to bring the ideas about the initiative to the public. The exhibition had a lot of support and involvement from around 25 artists from Jakarta, Bandung and Yogyakarta; part of the sales from this exhibition were donated to ruangrupa. Support from the artists, the gallery, a few foreign countries' cultural centres in Jakarta and from art and cultural NGOs in Jakarta, Bandung and Yogyakarta were the most important thing about this exhibition.

ruangrupa

We didn't really use the word collective when we started. During the 25 years of ruangrupa, people have called us many things – community, group, *sanggar*, collective, or something else. We collaborated to produce things, of course, but in the beginning, we were more focussed on doing things for others, as a kind of supporting space for gathering, discussing, exhibiting – especially for young artists who didn't have space – because there simply weren't enough spaces. In the beginning we borrowed other spaces until we rented a small house – and it was actually very small. From the start, people around us called us *sanggar* – that's how our neighbours referred to us. We never tried to categorise ourselves or define how people should call us. Legally, from the beginning, we've been a foundation (*yayasan*), because we understood early on that we had to navigate the existing system. There's often a tendency to mock formal structures, but in our society people can be quite extreme: either you follow the system fully, or you deconstruct, parody, or subvert it – sometimes with humour, gestures, or even through legitimised forms. Jatiwangi Art Factory and other collectives have done that too. It's like you create an official title just for the authorities – while doing something entirely different underneath.

Ade Darmawan

There are some similarities between ruru and the *sanggar* system. *Sanggar* (guild or workshop) developed during the colonial period, but after independence it really flourished. Some of the *sanggars* became a kind of bureau to spread the government's nationalist sentiment. They had limited resources; they shared space; some of the members lived there. They had painting lessons and made murals, like the early days of ruru.

Agung Jenong

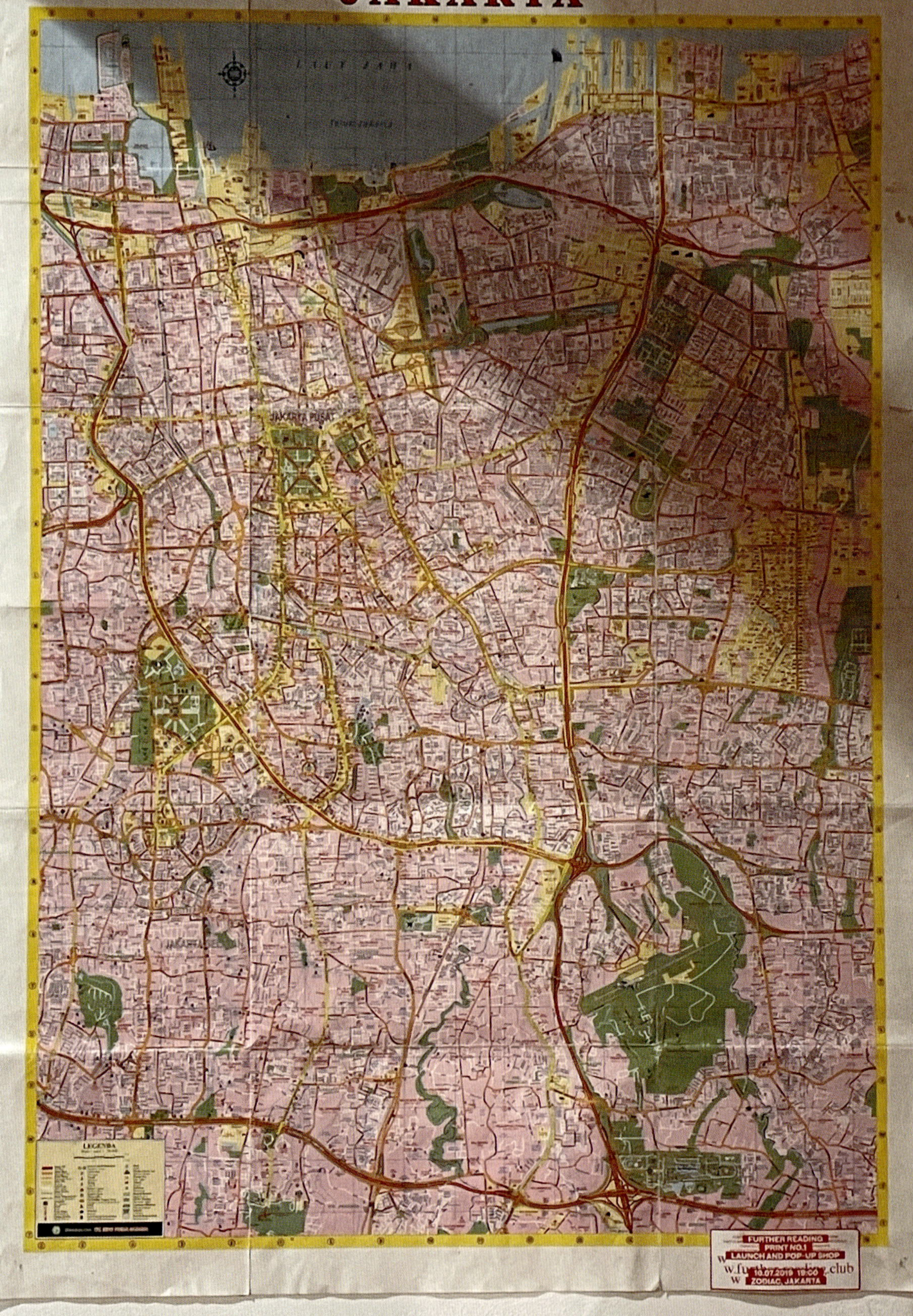
JAKARTA
LAUT JAWA
JAKARTA PUSAT
LEGENDA
FURTHER READING
PRINT NO.1
LAUNCH AND POP-UP SHOP
10.07.2019 19:00
ZODIAC, JAKARTA
.club

Press Release

Ruang Rupa Foundation (Yayasan Ruang Rupa, YRR) is a non-profit organisation founded and managed by several young artists from Jakarta, which provides and organises an art workspace for artists to live and work in a regular programme, with the following missions:

- Tracing and seeking new ideas in art and culture, especially visual arts.
- Allowing creative potentials to move freely by creating an independent and intimate workspace for artists to intensively develop their individual ideas.
- Becoming a place to meet and share ideas from various disciplines of art and fields of study.

The 'Ruang Rupa' workspace programme is divided into four periods per year. In each period, artists will examine certain focus problems determined by the programme coordinator from the Foundation and agreed upon with the artists.

The programme will also be supported by discussion forums, workshops and other things that support the formation of a dialectical and stimulating working atmosphere. At the end of each period, a presentation will be held in the form of an exhibition, publication and discussion.

Ruang Rupa Foundation provides a place to live and work for three months. In addition to technical facilities, there are also library and documentation facilities, internet access, discussion rooms and presentation rooms.

The 'Ruang Rupa' workspace is part of the international art workspace network that is part of RAIN (Rijksakademie International Network).
Founders:
Ade Darmawan
Hafiz
Ronny Agustinus
Lilia Nursita
Oky Arfie Hutabarat
Rithmi

To introduce the activities of this foundation more widely, in addition to fundraising for the foundation's first activities, the following will be held:

'Bersama' ['Together'] fundraising exhibition
With 24 artists from Jakarta, Bandung and Yogyakarta
to be held at Cemara 6 Gallery
Jl. HOS Cokroaminoto No.9–11
Central Jakarta
30 March – 8 April 2000
opening: 30 March 2000 at 19.30 WIB

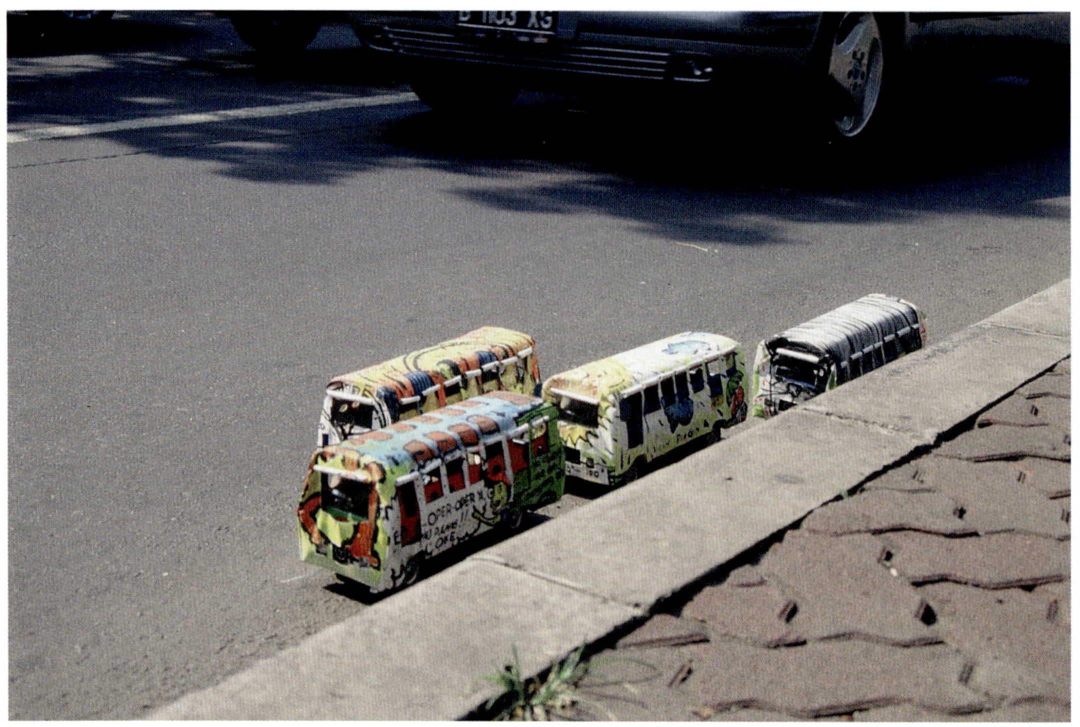

2

In this workshop we invited two groups from Yogyakarta who work intensively in public space – Taring Padi and Apotik Komik – each with different standpoints on public art. The workshop was based at Hanafie Studio (in Depok, a suburb of Jakarta), and the two groups stayed for two weeks together, during which ruangrupa arranged a debate between these groups and two other speakers with different disciplines and perspectives: Marco Kusumawijaya (architect and urban researcher) and FX Harsono (artist and art critic). At the end of the workshop the groups presented and discussed their works in an 'open debate' at the Japan Foundation. During the workshop Taring Padi worked directly with people living around the Ciliwung River, producing large murals inspired by the situation and people who live in that location. The project was supported by the community organisation Komunitas Sanggar Ciliwung, supporting urban and poor people living in the area, organised by Romo Sandyawan. The Apotik Komik project was focused on observation of public transport in Jakarta. They came up with different approaches to the bus system in Jakarta; the idea was to cover the sides of buses with parodic and satirical images of bus users in Jakarta.

ruangrupa

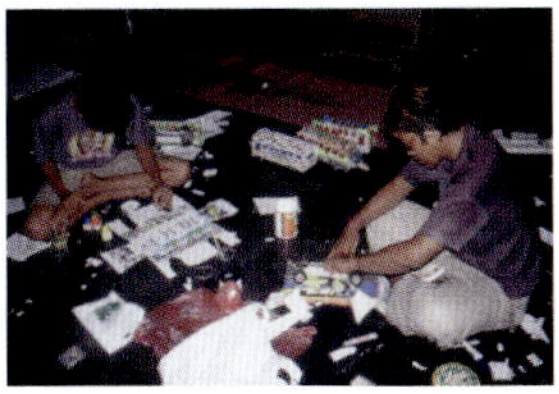

Public art project with Taring Padi and Apotik Komik, Jakarta and Depok, 1–15 June 2000

3

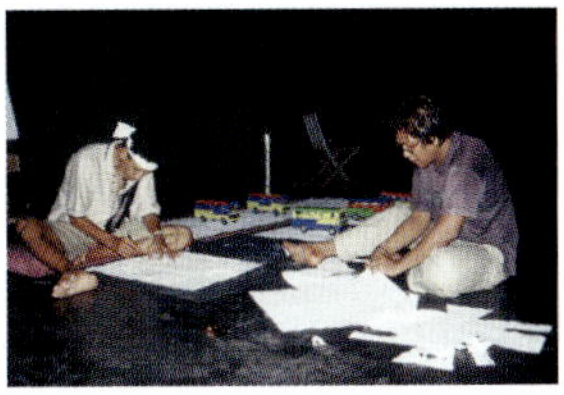

4

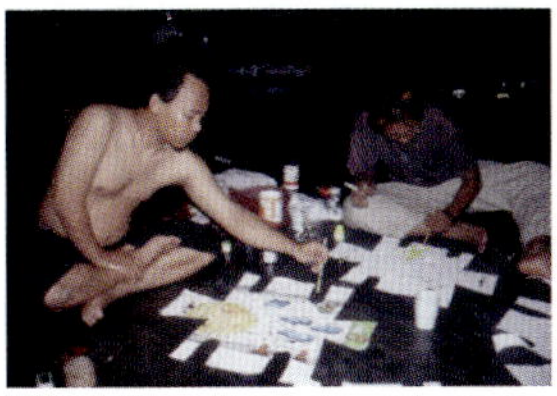

5

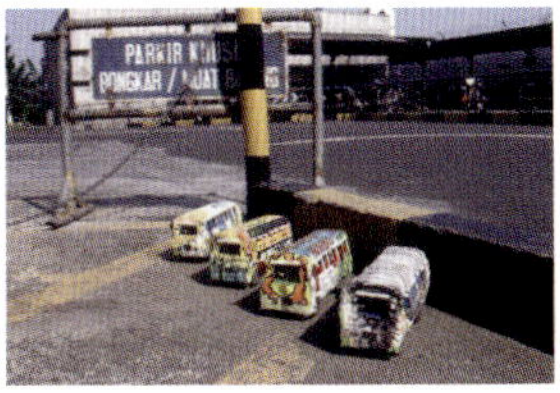

6

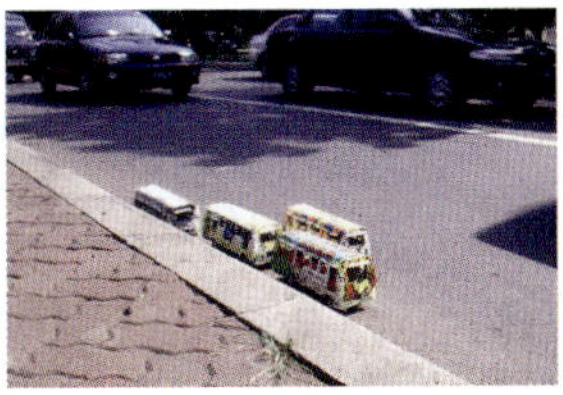

7

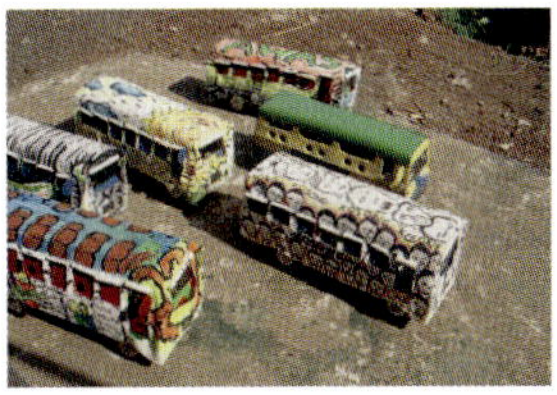

8

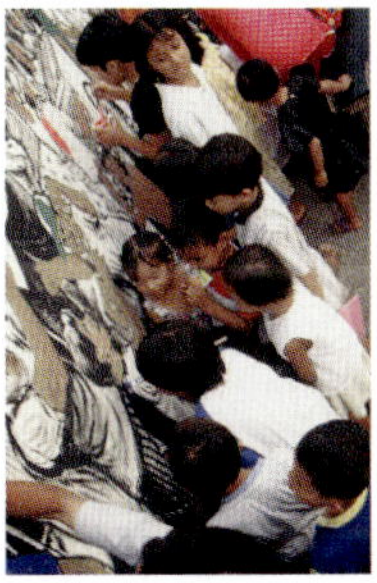

9

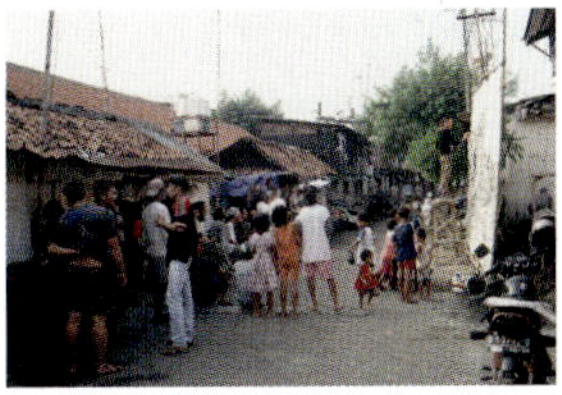

10

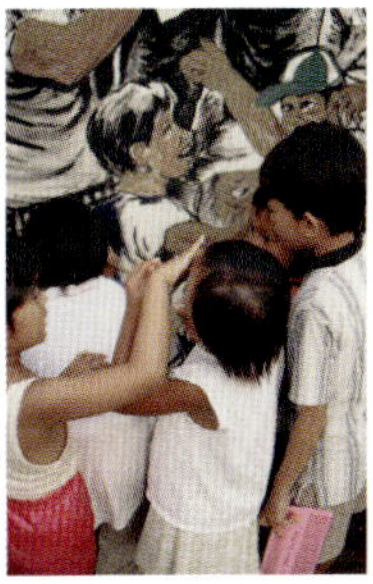

11

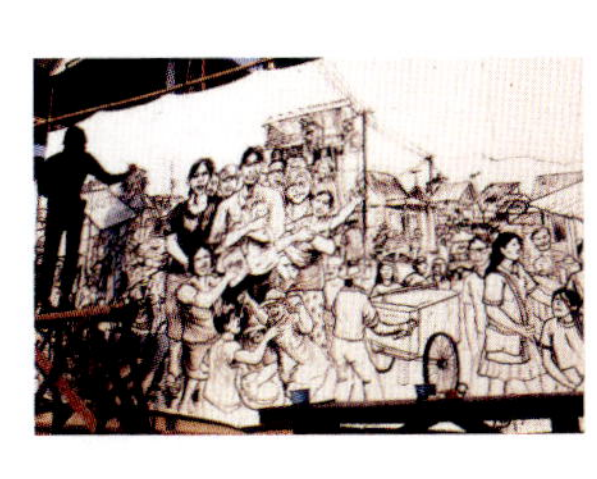

12

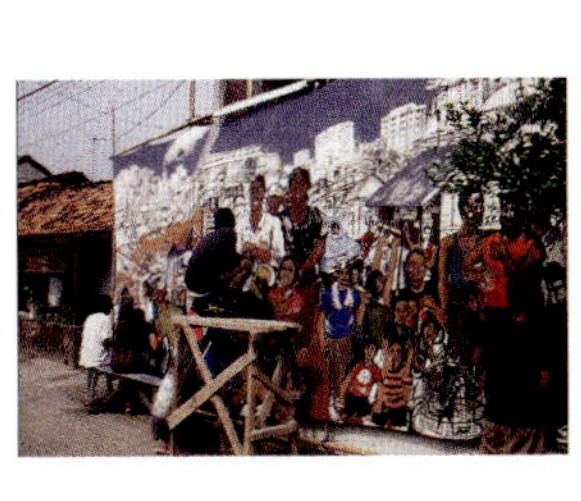

13

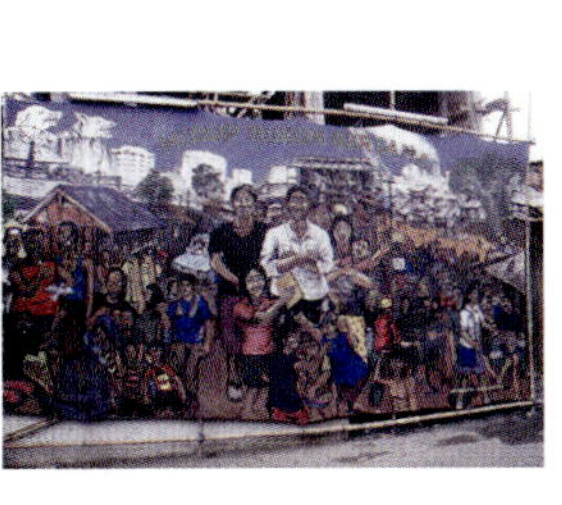

14

Meeting of seven art initiatives in Africa, Asia and Latin America – ruangrupa, Los Mutantes (Mexico City, Mexico), Guias Latinas (Mexico City), Open Circle (Mumbai, India), Centre Soleil d'Afrique (Bamako, Mali), TRAMA (Buenos Aires, Argentina) and PULSE (Durban, South Africa), facilitated by Rijksakademie (Amsterdam, The Netherlands) – which resulted in the formation of the RAIN network, focussing on artist exchange and the global flow of information, publication and documentation.

ruangrupa

During the gathering of RAIN partners in the early 2000s a number of trends emerged. The 'non-Western vs. Western' dichotomy as we then called it, is more complex and entangled than we would formulate it in 2000. Now the 'Global South' is in full attention – great art events like the biennales and documenta are inviting many artists from Africa, Asia and Latin America. A more structural balance in these events, however – instead of a more superficial 'flirt' without wanting to engage in real shifting power dynamics and discussions on what is the meaning of art – is still a long way off. The 'artists' initiative' phenomenon (or, if you will, artists' platform, artists' network, artists' project or artists' organisation) is still gaining strength. Aside from their individual careers, artists are focussing more and more on forms of joint organisation – in order to change something in the local, national or regional environment, to create conditions that are close to the artists' practice or to make joint work. The attention and action of the RAIN partners – at the time – focussing on the socio-political context in which they work is also not an isolated phenomenon in this sense. These three movements, the rise of the artists' initiative, the increased space for art from the global South in the international realm and focussed attention on sociopolitical engaged art appear to be interconnected, and contingent on one another.

Gertrude Flentge

ruangrupa moves into its first house, Pasar Minggu, Jakarta, September 2000

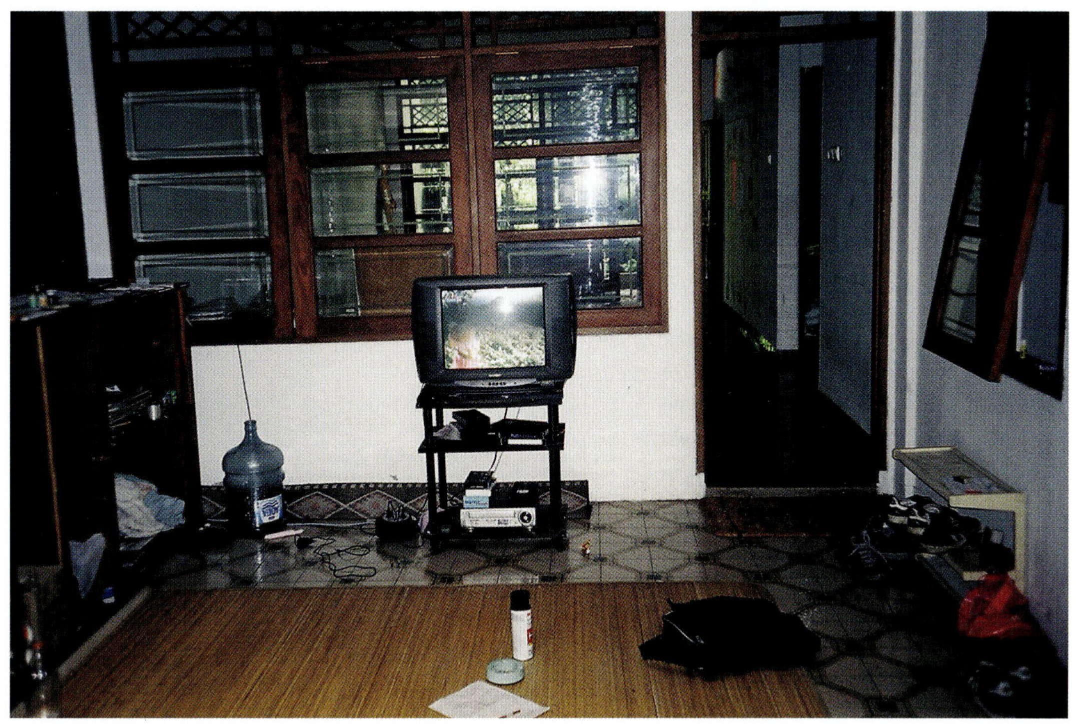

15

Our first rented house was not in Tebet. It was in Pasar Minggu and it lasted for a year. We were at the stage where we just tried to be independent from our family, most of us unemployed. We were all misfits in the art schools. In the house we rented, at night, we competed for a mattress to sleep (*laughs*). My favourite place to sleep is underneath the big table. We were like that for three or four years. After that we had small rented rooms nearby ruangrupa, because we had partners we needed some privacy, and it was time to split (*laughs*). Usually we lived nearby ruangrupa. The houses became like a small workshop, because we had a computer and so on, people stayed there and produced music, films, exhibitions and so on.

Ade Darmawan

ruangrupa is best understood as a label, a grouping of several inter-related intentions. Within the Indonesian art scene, most people know ruangrupa as artist/organisers of international art projects, exhibitions or art festivals. Others understand us as a group of artists whose projects, idioms and style express a specific vision. On the other hand, ruangrupa can also be defined as an art space – a place where various art activities are mediated. Although all members of the collective would never reject a particular categorisation – such as 'artist-run-space' or 'artist-run-initiative' – the fact that the group identifies with different approaches simultaneously, has meant that when it comes to understanding the work and preoccupations of ruangrupa, simple explanations and stereotypic definitions are not adequate.

Agung Jenong

I describe it [ruru] as largely an artist-to-artist coterie, emerging organically to express and to participate, or transform, the scene in the art world and popular culture, reaching out to dispersed, mutating, temporary communities drawn to their convivial, largely masculine ethos of bringing people together. It resonates with global desires for alternative models of assembly and production and new local economies of creative integration, uncomplicated by interest and investment in discursive reflection.

Patrick Flores

ruangrupa is at one hand an inspiration to look at art practice as a non-tangible practice, offering other firm definitions of what art practice stands for and at the other hand is embedded in a European/western language of art. It uses popular culture as a binder to connect people, practitioners, but it is never settling on a clearly conceptual formulated practice. Always open to wonder, challenge, experiment with contexts, accept realities in art and society and continue to test speculations.

reinaart vanhoe

There were several institutions who were movers and shakers of Indonesian arts in post-Reformasi period. In Jakarta, the art ecosystem was dominated by either government institutions (such as Taman Ismail Marzuki), schools (like the Jakarta Arts Institute), or big art spaces with big fundings (such as Komunitas Utan Kayu / Komunitas Salihara). Some smaller organisations exist, of course, but their power and prestige are so limited. These big institutions, with their money and power, wittingly or unwittingly, took the role of gatekeeping, articulating or diminishing certain artistic discourse and tendencies. In Indonesia in general, while Bandung and Yogyakarta have been always seen as the centre of artistic production, Jakarta has occupied the space of commerce and collection. Thus, the emergence of ruangrupa as an organisation, an art space (and other iterations) was truly unique, I think, in terms of its history as a particular product of Indonesia's political reforms (namely the increasing freedom that Indonesian people, including artists felt after the end of the authoritarian regime), its position within the visual art ecosystem in the country (challenging Yogyakarta and Bandung as the centre of visual arts production), and the spirit which is characterised by its affinity with the urban situation (especially Jakarta), the forms of arts/artistic practices (not relying on the old distinction between traditional arts and modern arts exemplified by the distinction between Yogyakarta and Bandung, commerce and non-commerce, arts and non-arts, and its connection with the global arts discourse and practices).

Veronika Kusumaryati

RAIN artist exchange programme, Mali, October 2000

ruangrupa participate in a painting workshop hosted by Centre Soleil d'Afrique in Bamako, with participants from The Netherlands, Senegal, Burkina Faso, Angola and Mali; in the same month ruangrupa participate in a workshop programme hosted by Open Circle (Mumbai) with participants from India, Pakistan, Israel, The Netherlands, Canada, Ecuador and Mexico

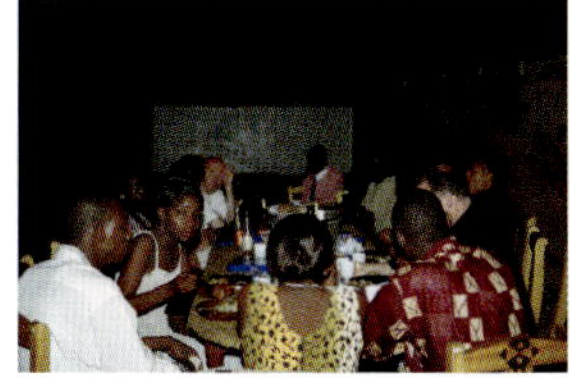

16

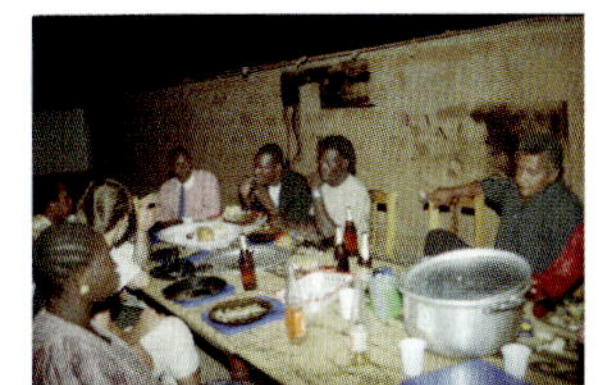

17

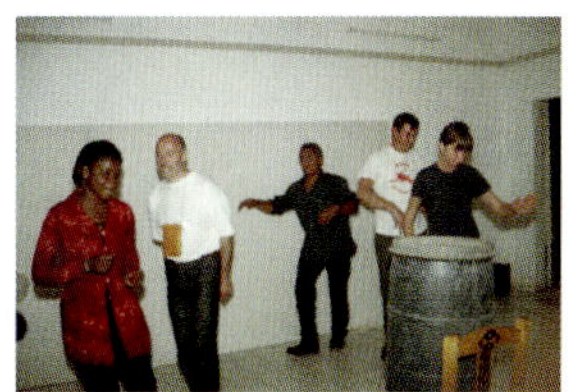

18

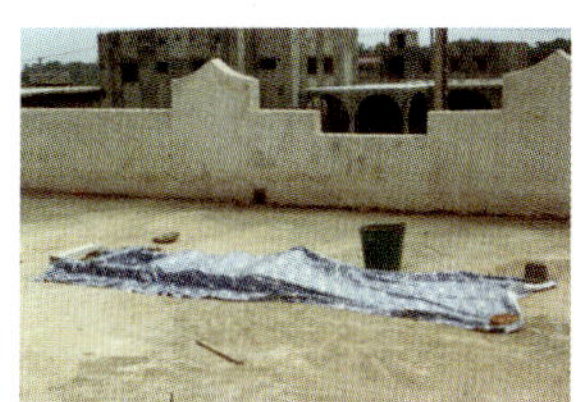

19

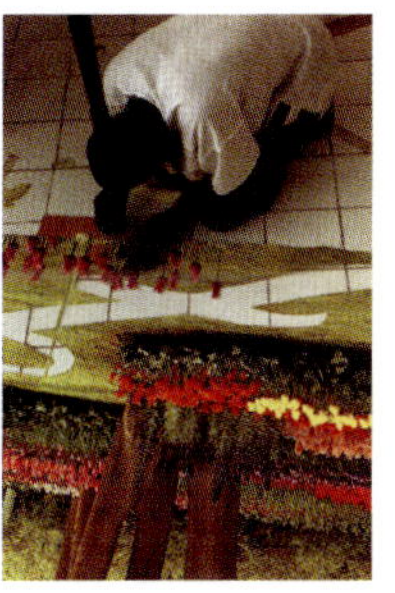

20

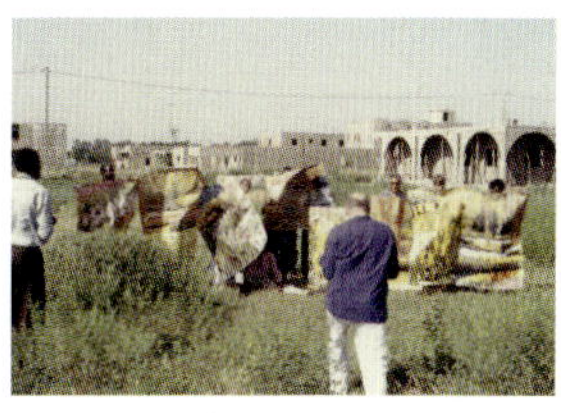

21

'Urban printing workshop', ruru house, 10–24 November 2000

participating artists Hauritsa, Irwan Ahmett, David Tarigan, Syagini Ratnawulan, Alexander Sudheim, Walter von Broekhuizen and reinaart vanhoe; the workshop culminates in a presentation of stickers, t-shirts, publications and other items by the artists on Mikrolet public transport vehicles running from ruru house to Taman Ismail Marzuki (TIM), Jakarta

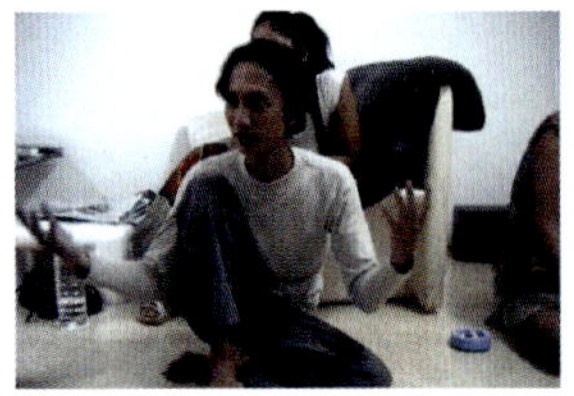

22

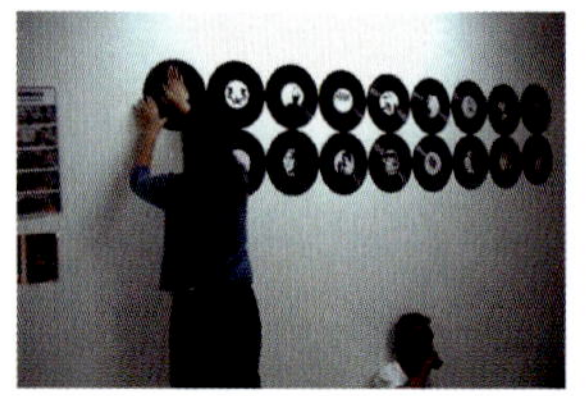

23

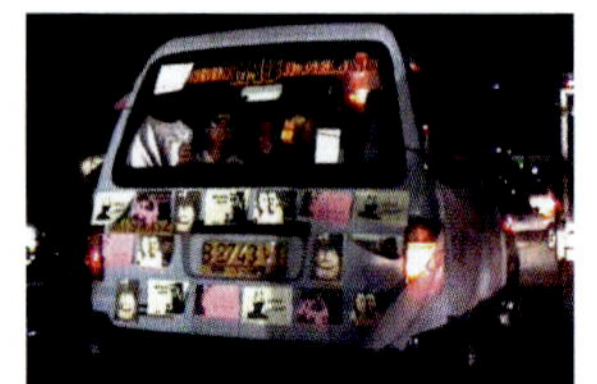

24

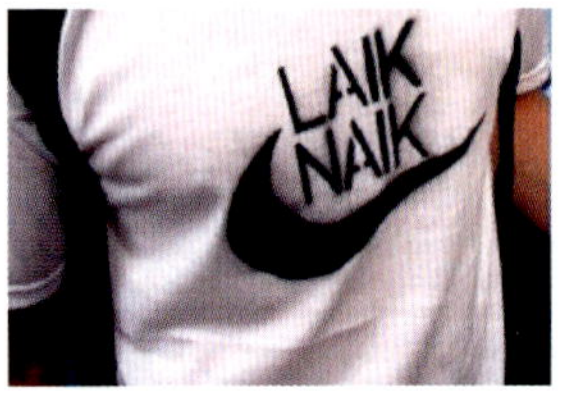

25

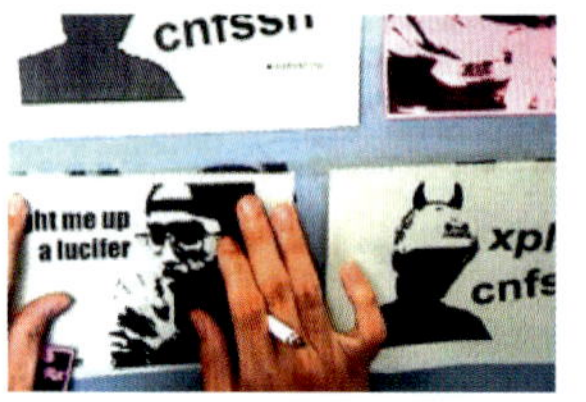

26

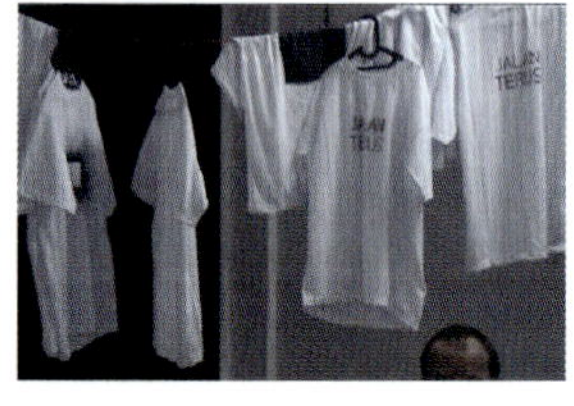

27

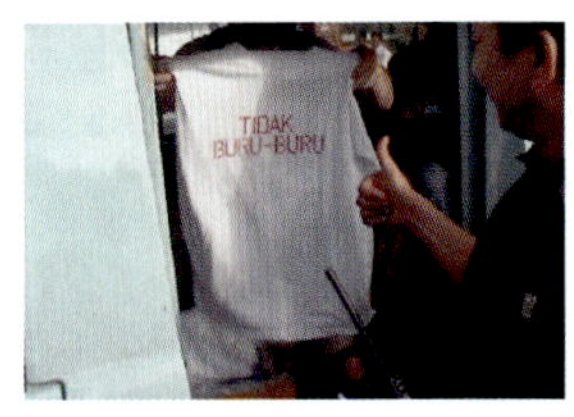

28

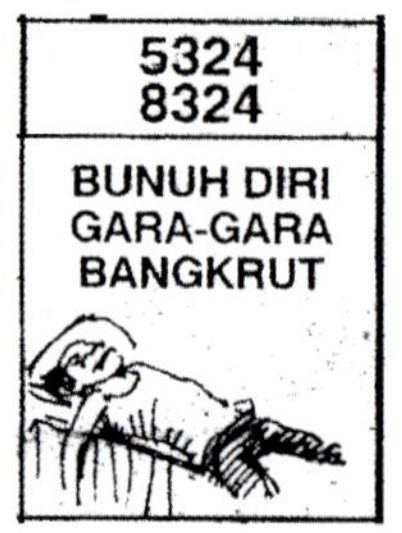

29

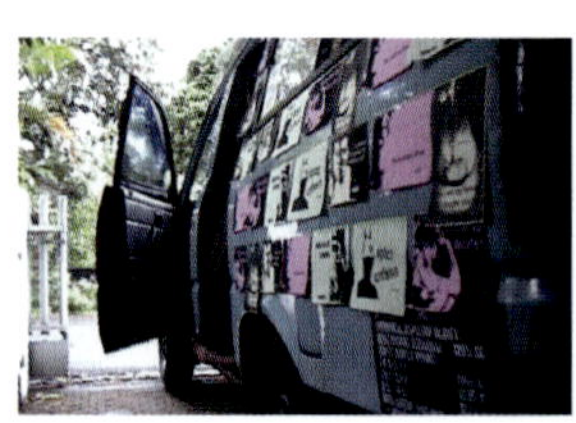

30

Karbon has been a part of ruangrupa's research programme since 2000. Between 2000 and 2006, *Karbon* published seven bilingual (Indonesian and English) editions focussing on contemporary art while reflecting on or expanding upon ruru's art projects. Since 2007, *Karbon* changed its form from print media to an online one, broadening its focus to multidisciplinary views in reading urban spaces and visual culture issues in Indonesia. It also analysed artworks and practices made in (and talked about) urban spaces. It aimed to facilitate the continuity of critical discourse on urban development and visual culture-related issues within Indonesian society.

Ardi Yunanto

In this edition the main subject is 'public art', which is related to ruangrupa's earlier public art project in collaboration with two groups from Yogyakarta, Taring Padi and Apotik Komik. The journal contains essays from artist FX Harsono and architect Marco Kusumawijaya.

ruangrupa

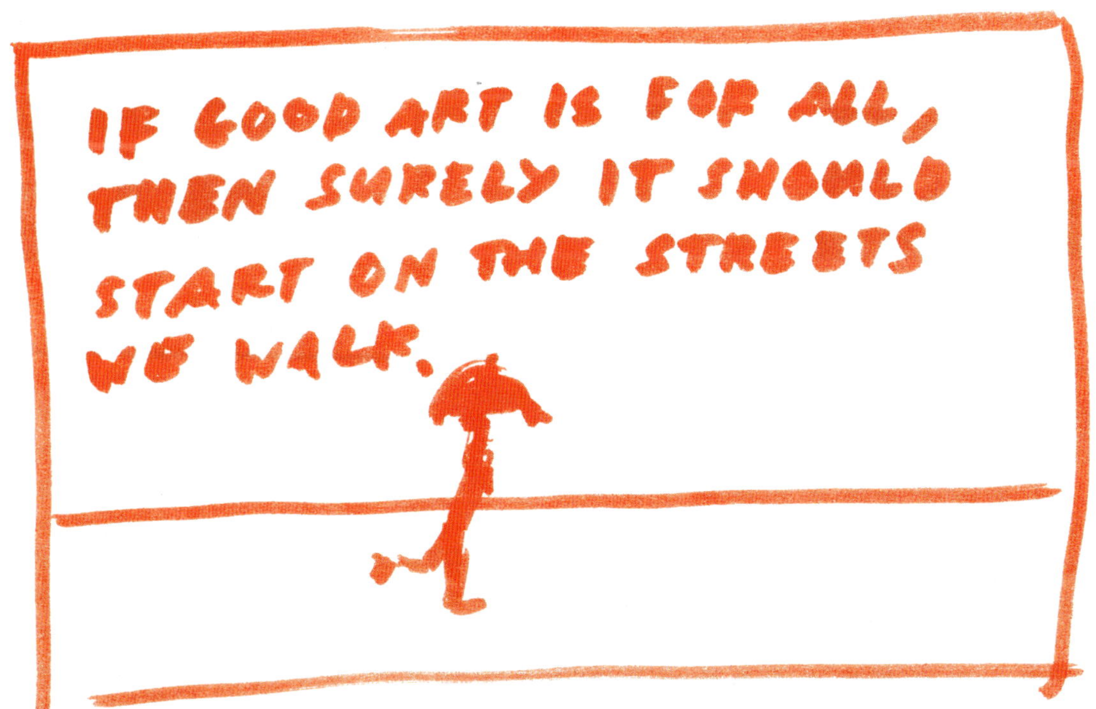

see also pp.366–75

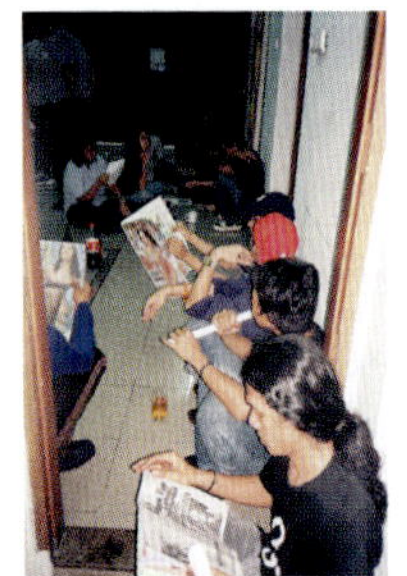

32

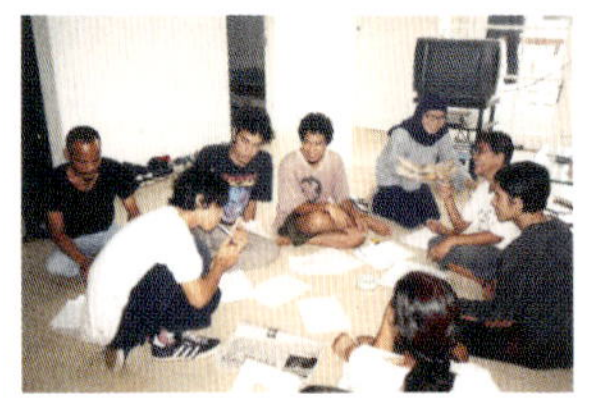

33

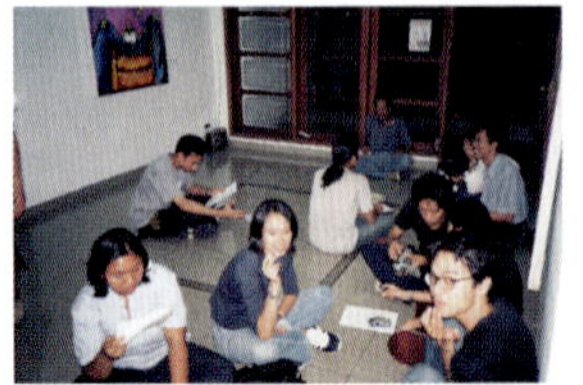

34

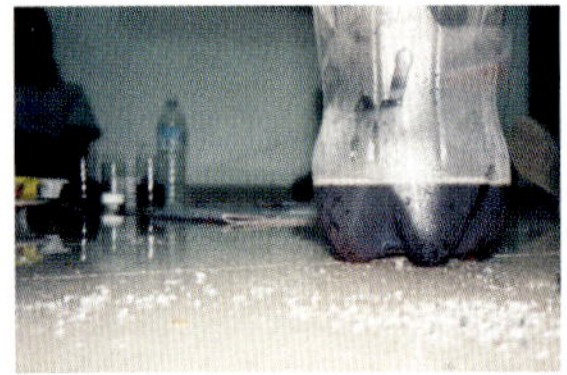

35

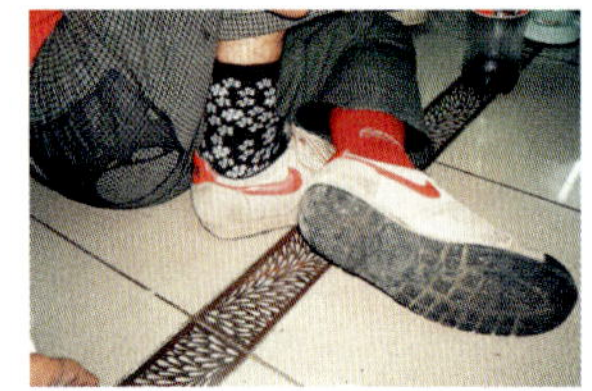

36

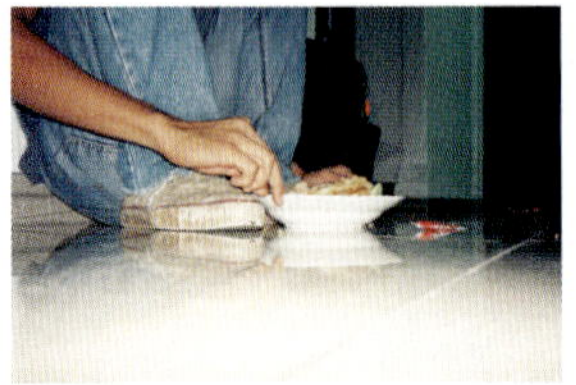

37

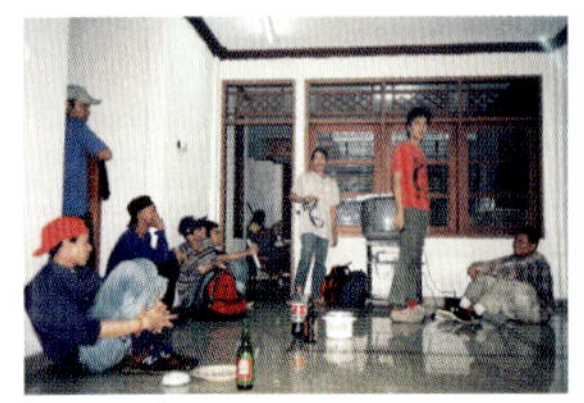

38

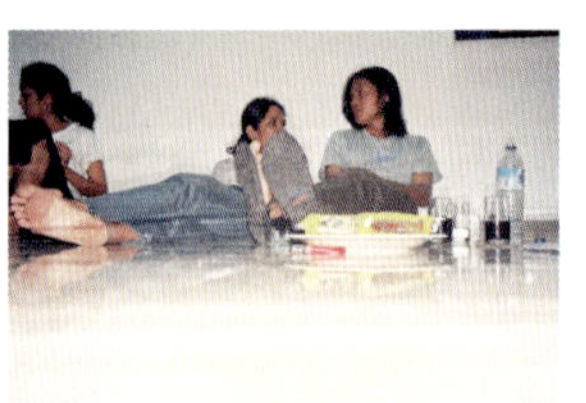

39

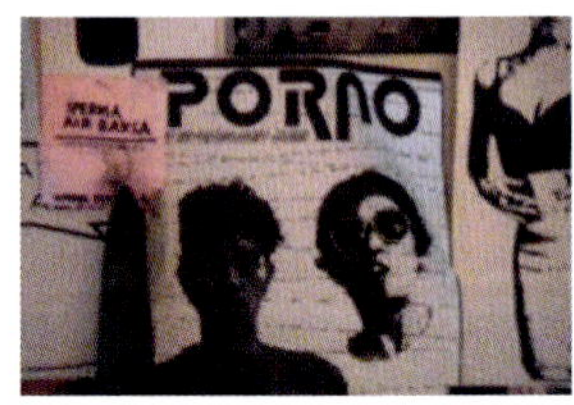

40

'Boy Band Only', artist-in-residence exhibition by Anggun Priambodo and Mateus Bondan, ruru house, April 2001

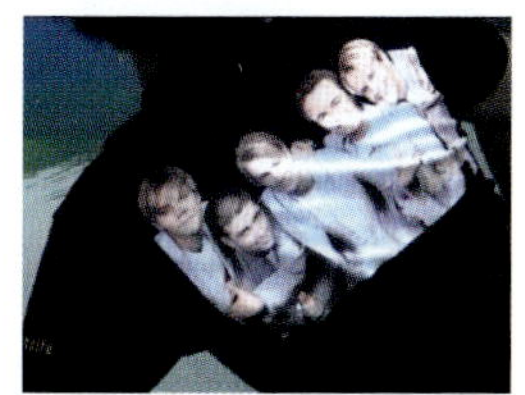

41

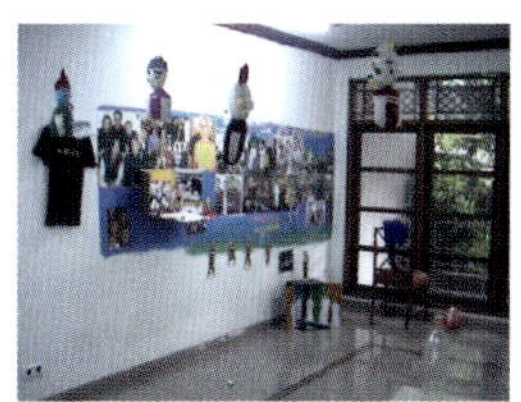

42

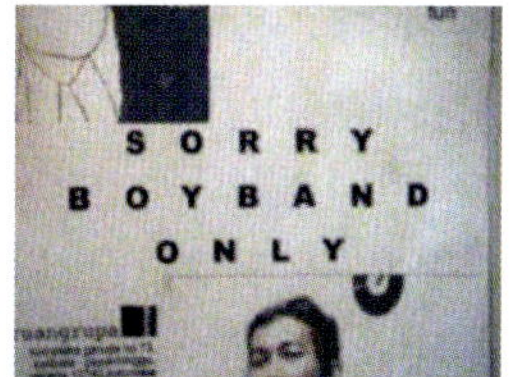

43

The main subject in this edition is the workshop and research on urban printing phenomena in Jakarta. A project on urban printing was done in 2000 with participating artists Hauritsa, Irwan Ahmett, David Tarigan, Syagini Ratnawulan, Alexander Sudheim (RAIN partner), Walter van Broekhuizen and reinaart vanhoe.

ruangrupa

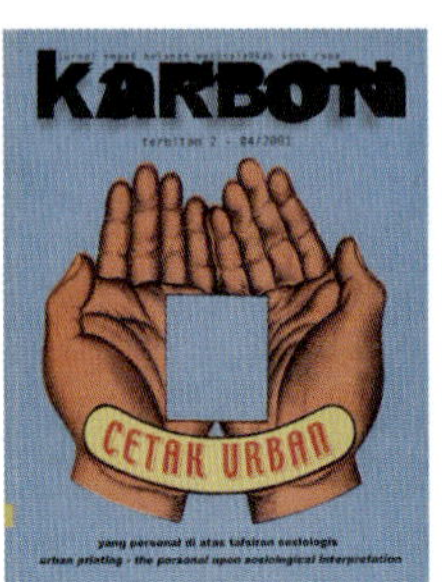

44

'Silent Forces', video art workshop, Japan Foundation, Jakarta, May 2001

with Anne Mie van Kerckhoven, Sebastian Diaz Morales, Aditya Satria and Adrianto Sinaga

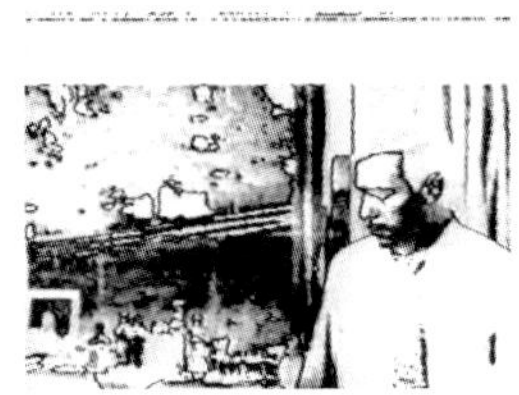

45

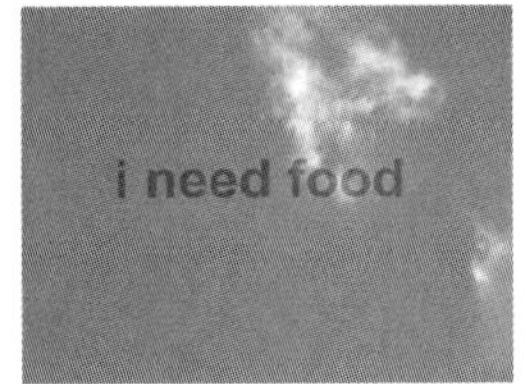

46

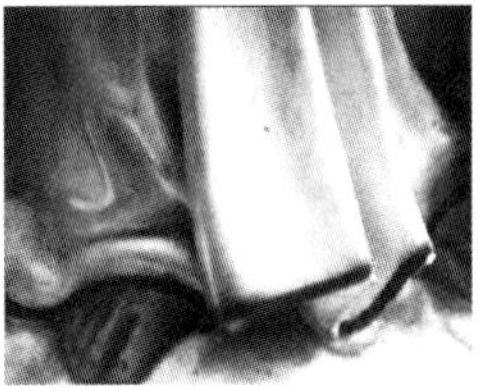

47

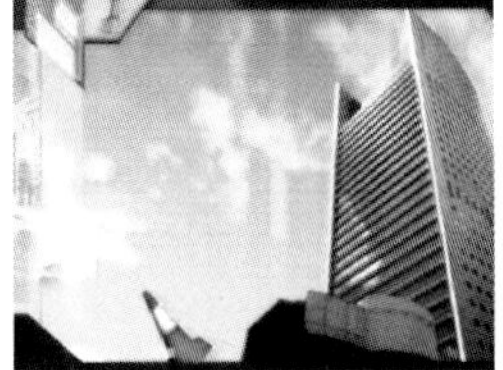

48

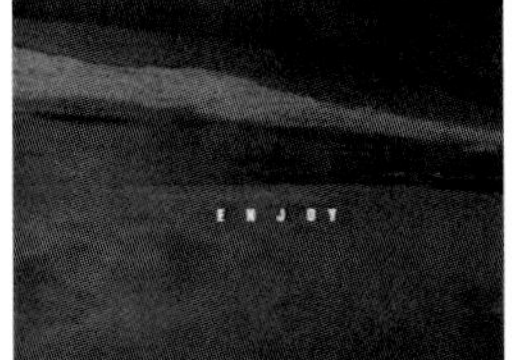

49

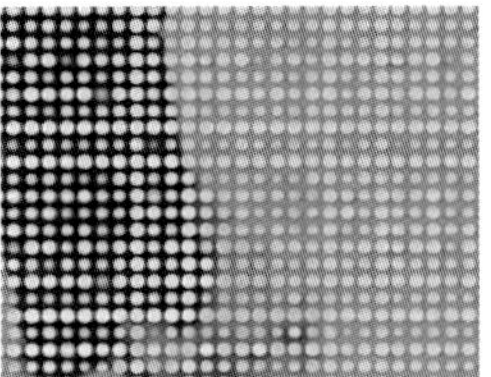

50

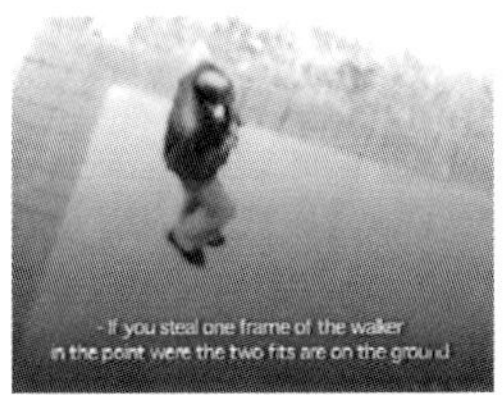

51

'Jakarta Habitus Publik', public art programme, Jakarta, 1 June – 1 July 2001

The main subject for this project is the art activities based on exchange, intervention, negotiation and negation in the public space. The project was divided into four categories: site specific, video art, mural and poster and involved more than fifty artists (individual and group) from Jakarta, Bandung and Yogyakarta. The project took place in June, following two months of research, documentation and preparation. The project raised the issue of the artist's position in society and questioned the public space in the urban environment. During the project we had many problems with the city government over permits. This issue became very important: how art and artists should negotiate in public space like Jakarta, where this space is still 'owned' by the authorities and entails concerns about the inner dynamics of society. There was a very good response, as well as support, from city residents, as well as the media, through publications criticising the city government.

ruangrupa

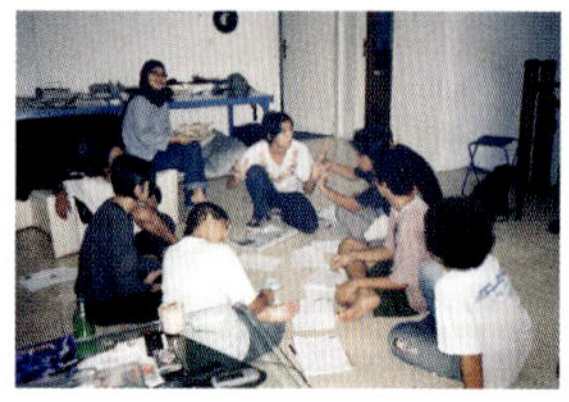

52

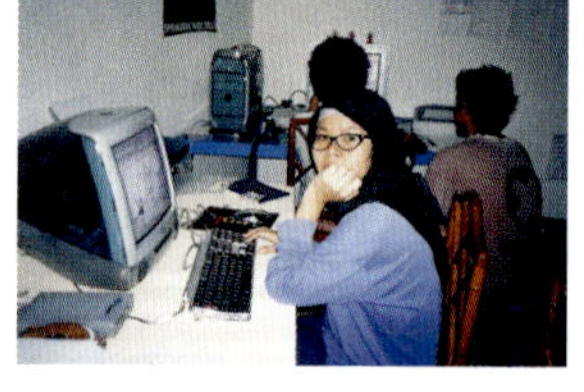

53

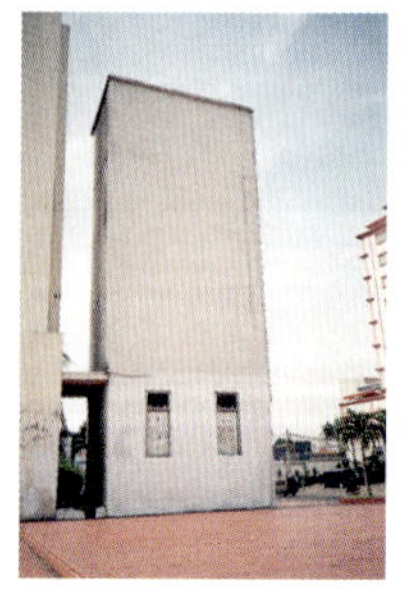

54

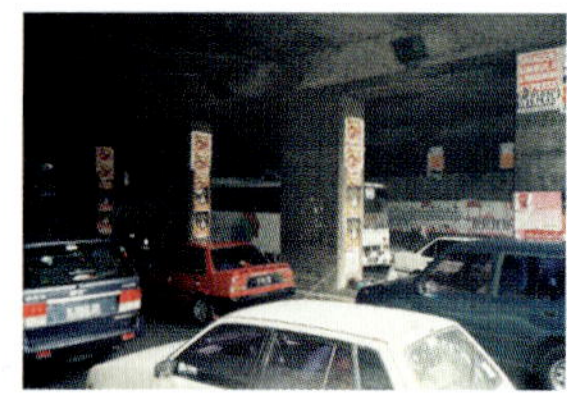

55

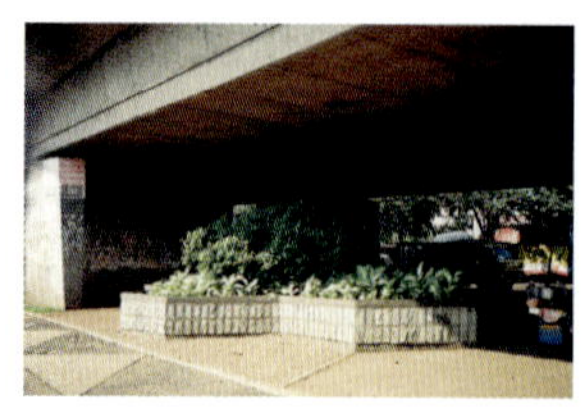

56

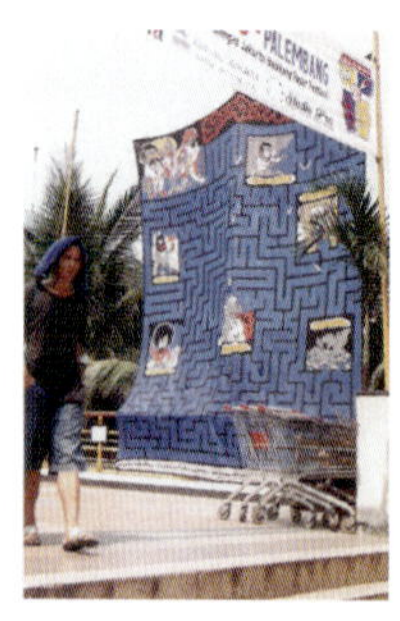

57

'Jakarta Habitus Publik', public art programme, Jakarta, 1 June – 1 July 2001

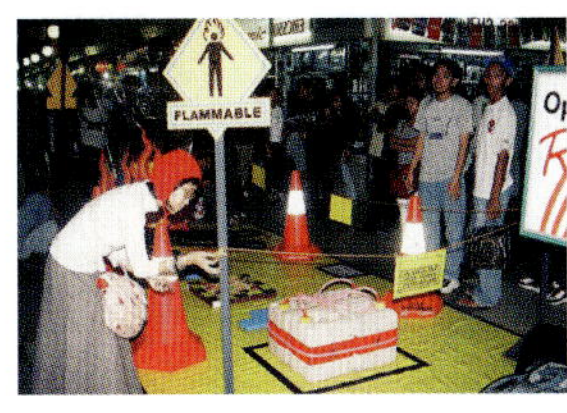

58

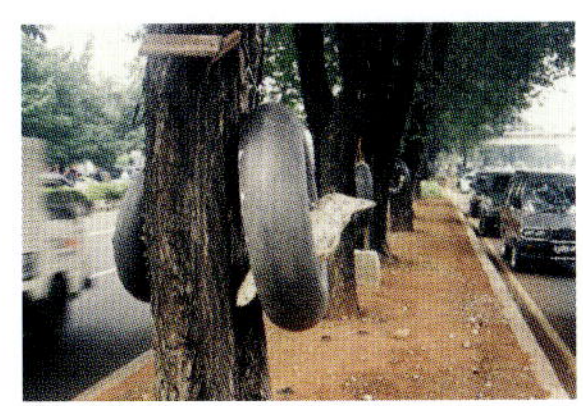

59

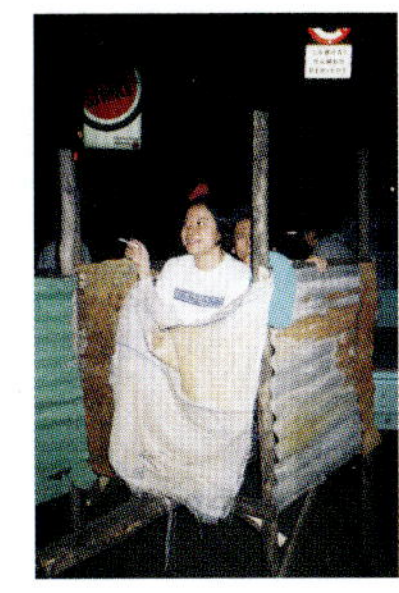

60

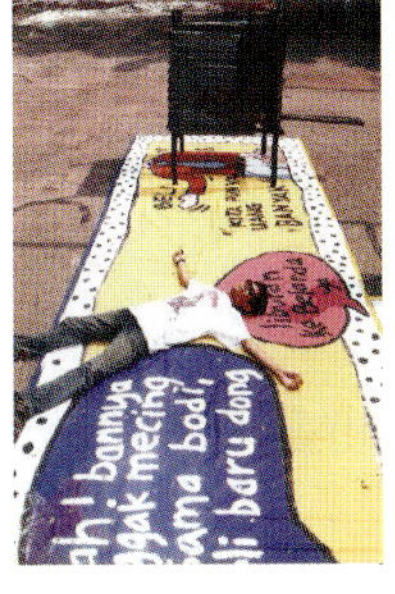

61

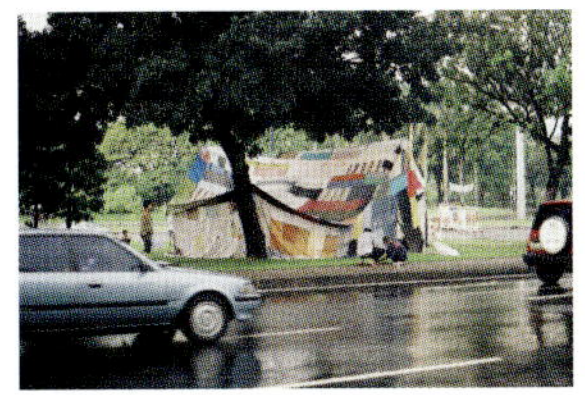

62

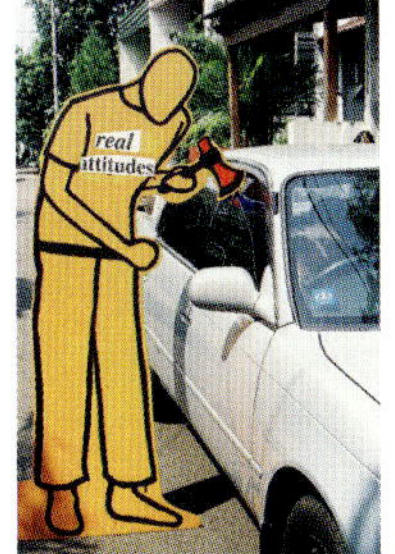

63

ruangrupa was one of the programmers of JakArt. We were both organising and being participating artists. That's the first time I got an artist contract to present something outside of the art school in the public. That's the first time we got funding from the city of Jakarta. Then we started to strategise how to attract bigger funding. In 2003, we started to have an accountant. Kunil was doing the finance but she's also an artist, so extra help was needed.

Reza Afisina

At some point of my early street art research, interviewing graffiti artists, I heard about this thing called JakArt that ruangrupa did in public space in 2001. There were performances, murals, graffiti and all sorts of things. I was curious because a lot of the people whom I interviewed remembered that it was an event that boosted their confidence to not only do graffiti or murals in their family yard or school compound – JakArt gave people confidence to do it on the street. Even though there were some things on the street long ago, they were more like propaganda or gang identification. The graffiti we know now started from the early 2000s, they didn't start like how it would connect to hip-hop elsewhere. I decided I would find out who 'ruangrupa' is. By that time I had already talked to three different street art groups in Jakarta – I think only one is still active now and still working with ruangrupa – but at that time ruru and the artists were not connected yet. Ade suggested I used ruru as a meeting place to hang out with the artists. So every week or two we met in ruru. By the third time I went to ruru, Ade said why don't we make an exhibition. It eventually did become an exhibition of some fifty artists creating graffiti on the site in an old government bank museum in 2005, with no money. But it has a catalogue. It's called *[re]volusi 300cc*.

Grace Samboh

'The Swarm Project', workshop and exhibition, ruru house, Jakarta and Cemeti Art House, Yogyakarta, July 2001

with Tero Nauha, Tina M. Ward and Ade Darmawan

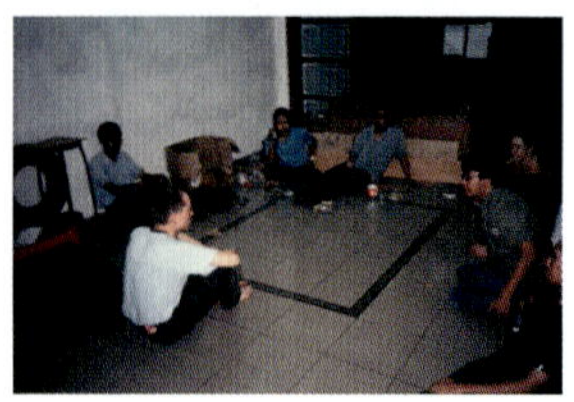

64

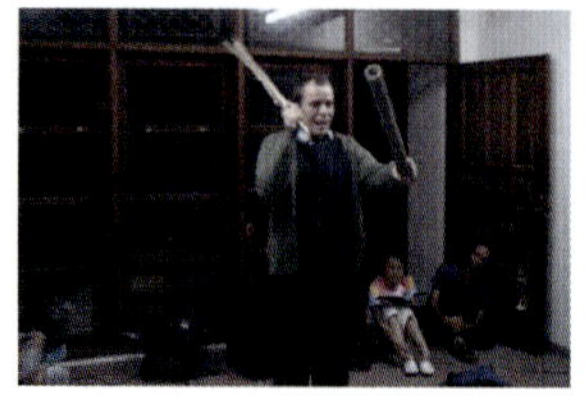

65

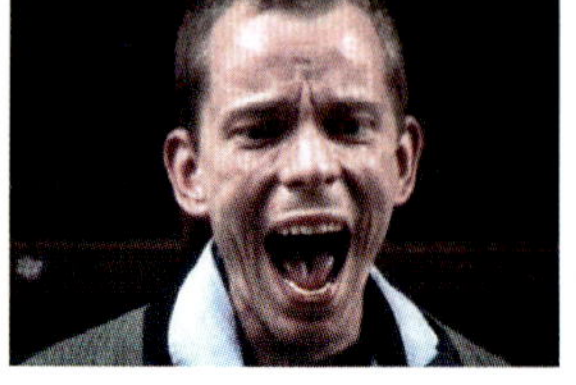

66

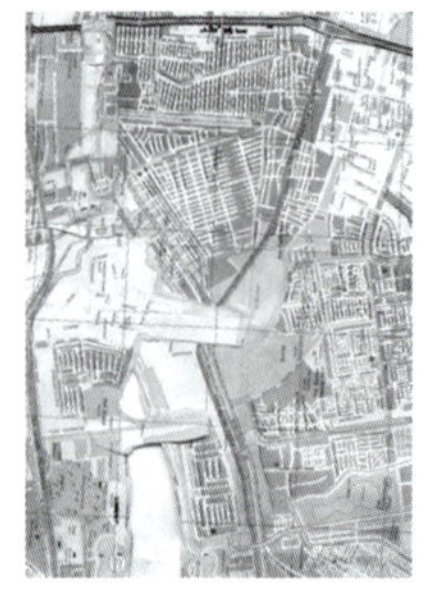

67

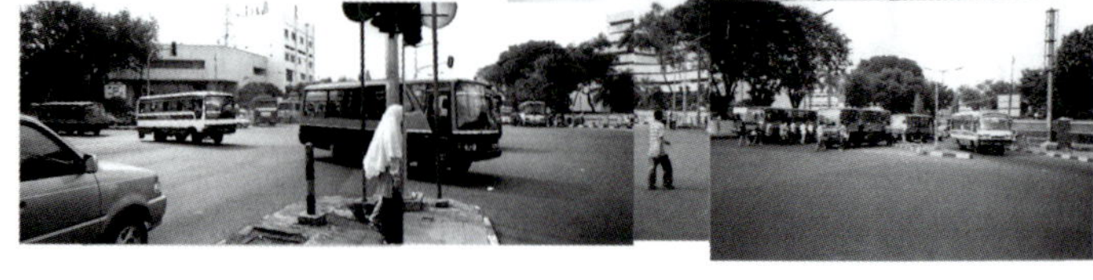

68

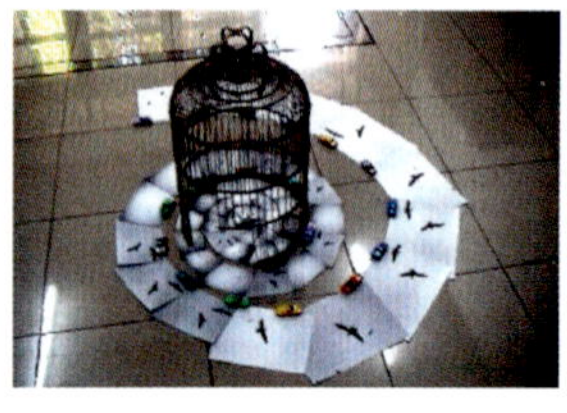

69

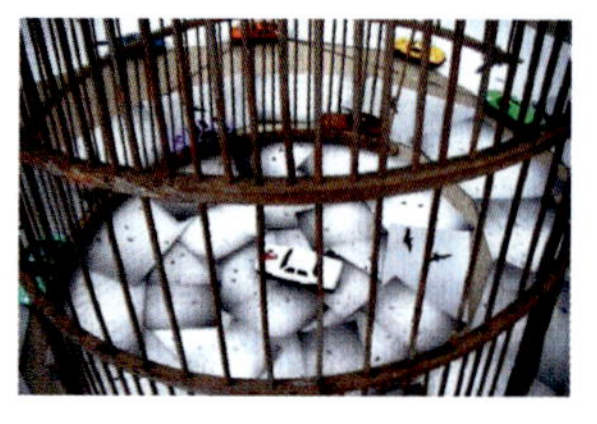

70

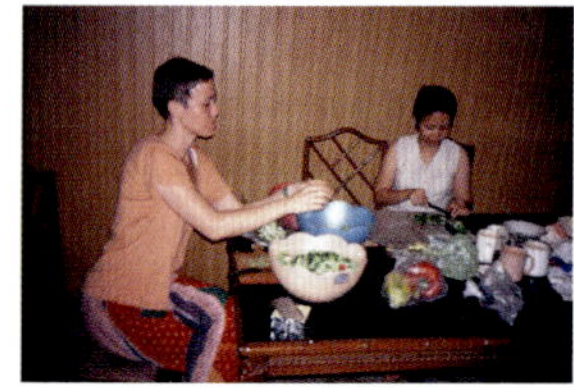

71

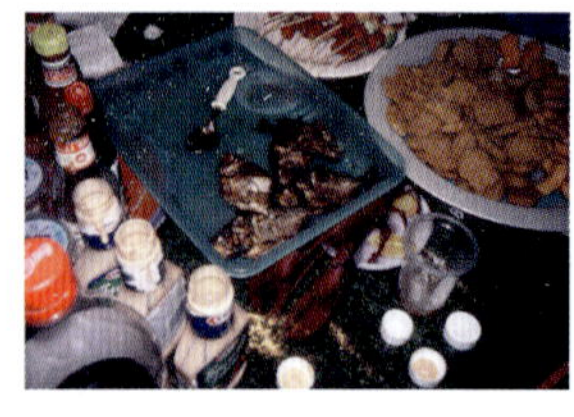

72

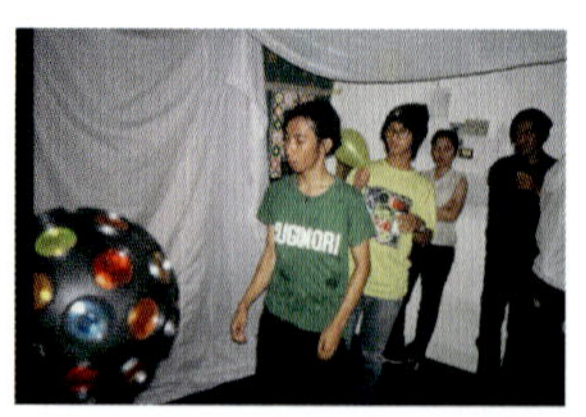

73

'My Sneakers', artist-in-residence exhibition by Michael Blum, ruru house, August 2001

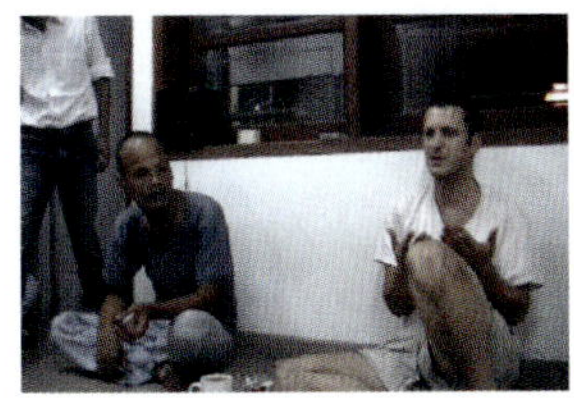

74

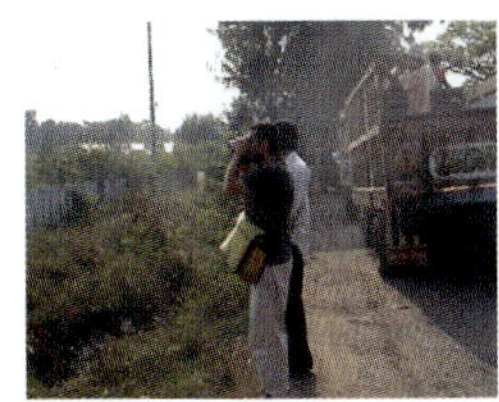

75

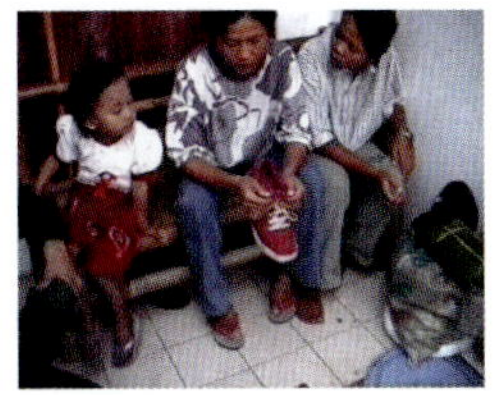

76

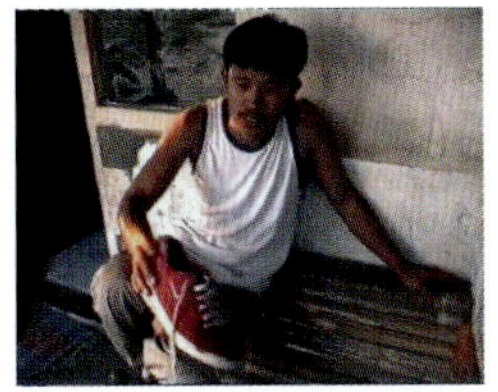

77

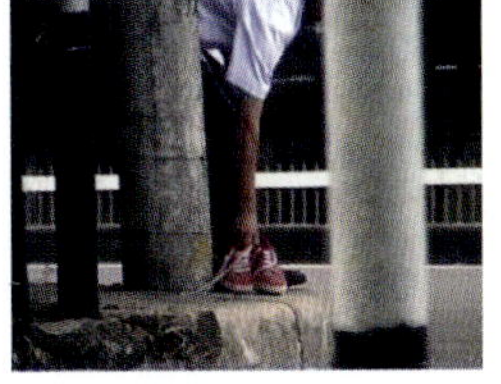

78

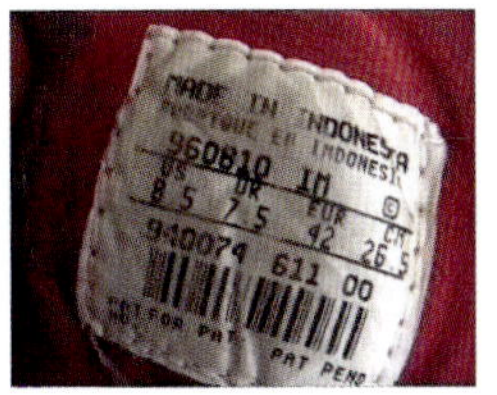

79

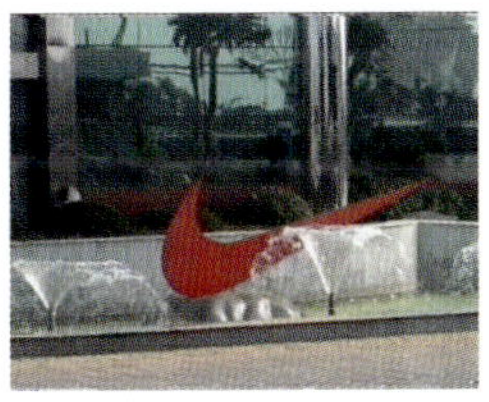

80

ruangrupa moves into its second house, Tebet Barat, Jakarta, October 2001

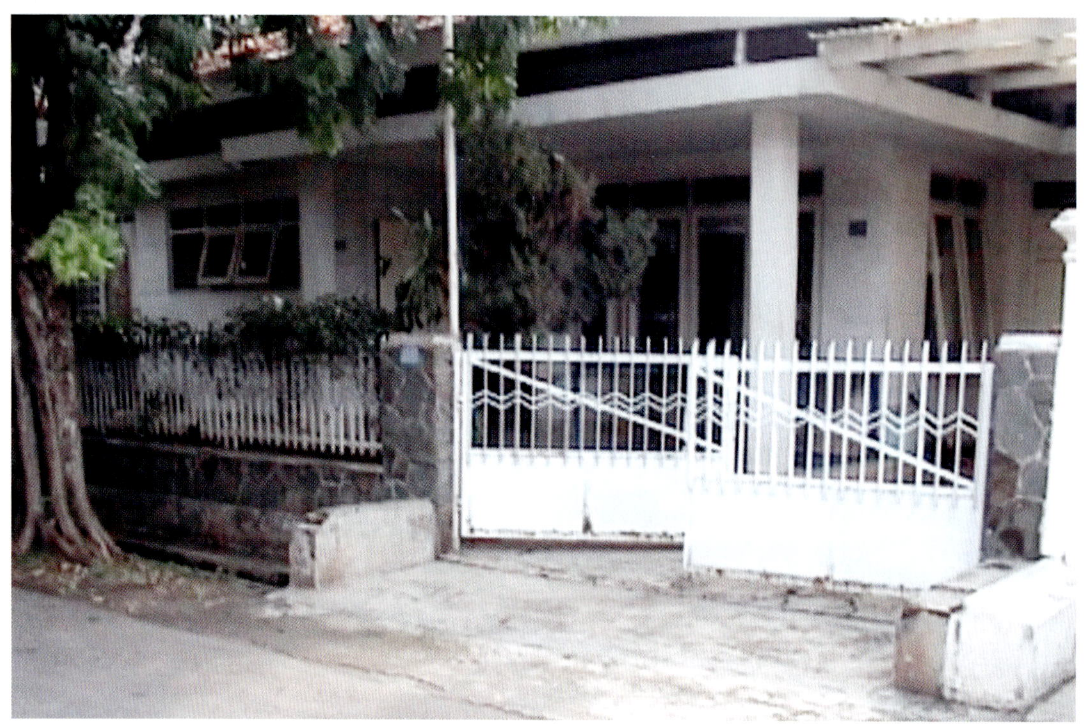

81

Tebet [is] a housing precinct located in the south-eastern part of Jakarta. This area was first developed in the 1960s as a lowrise housing area, part of an urban reconstruction project in the centre of the city. ... Two major factors, of the planned business district and the commuter strip, have made Tebet into a strategic location, transforming it into an area for small businesses and providing a range of services including small offices, restaurants, print shops and so on. These micro businesses rose as a result of the economic crisis that hit Indonesia in 1997.

Iswanto Hartono

Every time we moved, we had a housewarming ritual. We invited people to pray and my mum cooked – *nasi tumpeng*, yellow rice. Then we invited neighbours. We introduced ourselves and explained what we wanted to do .... They couldn't say no, because they were eating the food. It's *nasi tumpeng* diplomacy (*laughs*).

Ade Darmawan

The most important thing about the Living Room is that it has been embedded within our practice since the very beginning, when we moved from one house to another. I think it's because of the nature of Jakarta itself, where we don't have infrastructures for art, so the artists are looking for their own possible space and houses which, in terms of economic sustainability, are more affordable to rent or run. But also, because we grew up during the New Order regime, where public space was controlled, so houses were the safest space where to care for each other. It's a practical paradox, between domestic and public space, and the living room was in the centre of the space, we used it as a common space: everything is common there, people could gather. I remember, in our houses even the bathroom was a working space, things were used as much as we could because we only had a very small space. The ArtLab was in the bedroom and the living room was for meetings, galleries, activations, workshops... It changed during the days, and the people were sleeping there as well. It's the opposite of the bourgeois idea of the living room.

Iswanto Hartono

The subject is video art; most of the content comes from video art and multimedia project 'Silent Forces' – a project by Anne Mie van Kerckhoven (Belgium), Sebastian Diaz Morales (Argentina), Aditya Satria (Jakarta) and Adrianto Sinaga (Jakarta) held at ruangrupa in May 2001.

ruangrupa

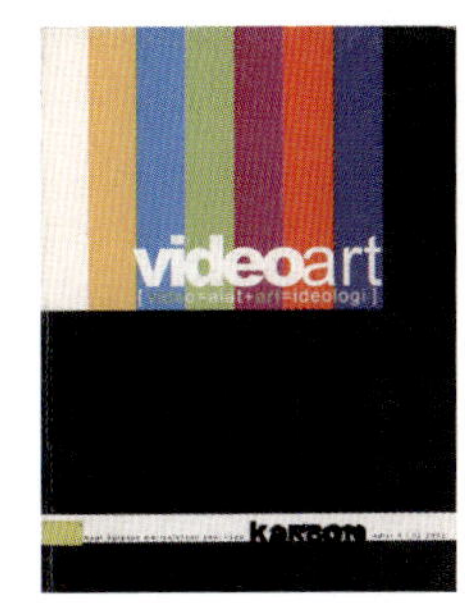

82

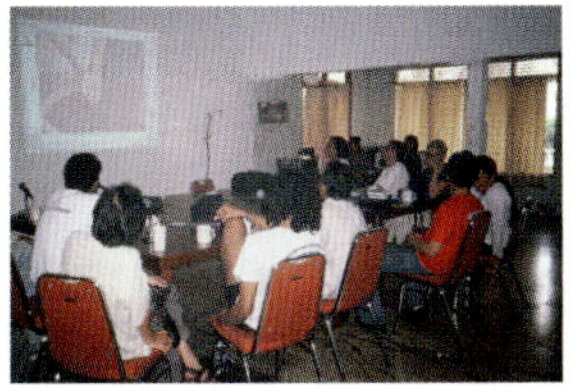

83

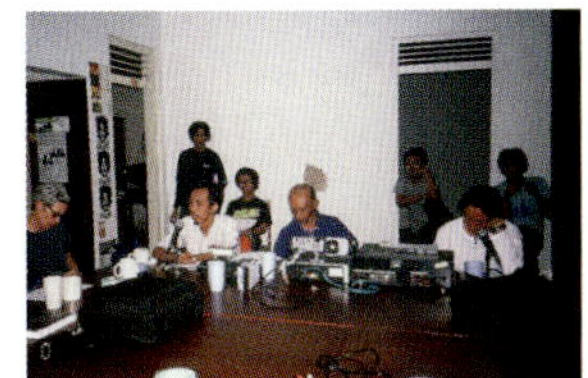

84

politics

observing small narratives politics expanding ideas, space, and the public, in this case, local politics, the politics of space, and strategies of civil society who contribute to the values of contemporary culture

discover some channels to fill in the gaps, speaking from our own position to complete or otherwise enrich the structure by offering more spaces for exploration, without boring attempt to directly oppose whatever establishment.. while at the same time avoiding co-optation.

conducting a set the activities must be taken into great consideration, for to a large degree such activism serves a one-way objective associated with power relations

A place in which various forms of urban activism intersect. This expands the diversity of ideas and the horizon of knowledge that constantly discusses and elaborates.

4th Gwangju Biennale, 'Project 1: P_A_U_S_E', Gwangju, South Korea, 29 March – 29 June 2002

invited to this section of the exhibition alongside a number of art initiatives, ruangrupa presents a reproduction of their Jakarta space featuring works by seven of its members (Ade Darmawan, Aditya Satria, Hafiz Rancajale, Irwan Ahmett, Indra Ameng, Reza Afisina and Ronny Agustinus)

ruangrupa views space not just as a locus for display, made of bricks and white walls, but also as an extension of the body – something connecting to the body. For the current Biennale, the artists present their intentions through performance and screen projection. The first installation, initiated on the opening day, is a display of food left on a table accessible to the public. The remains will be displayed after participants and visitors have finished the food. They will also install a hidden camera in corners of crowded halls; the images of visitors moving throughout the halls will be projected onto a screen hung in their exhibition room. They will also present a film and literature for the viewers, which introduce their activities and works.

4th Gwangju Biennale

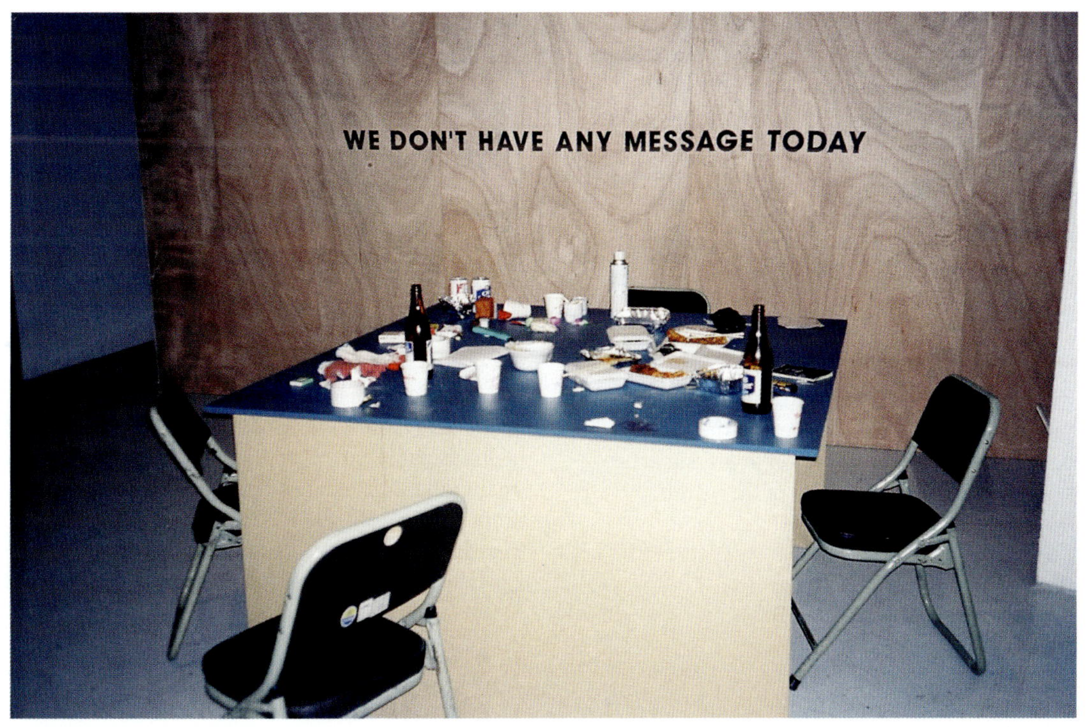

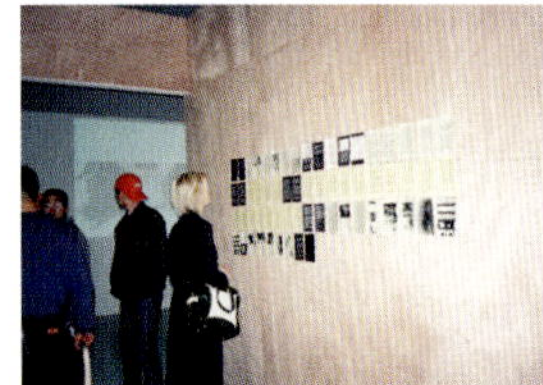

86

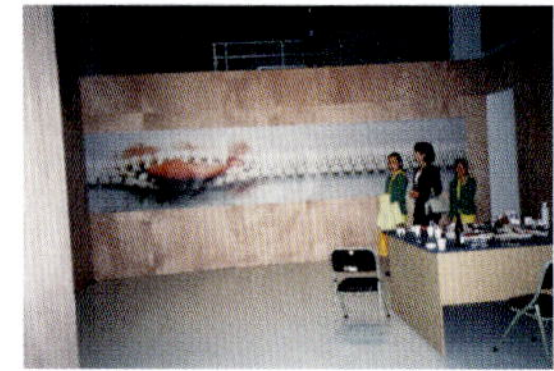

87

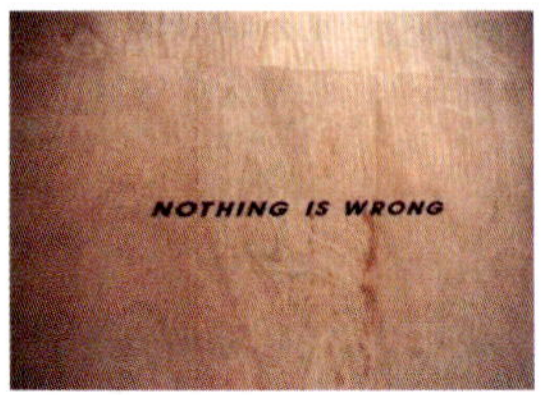

88

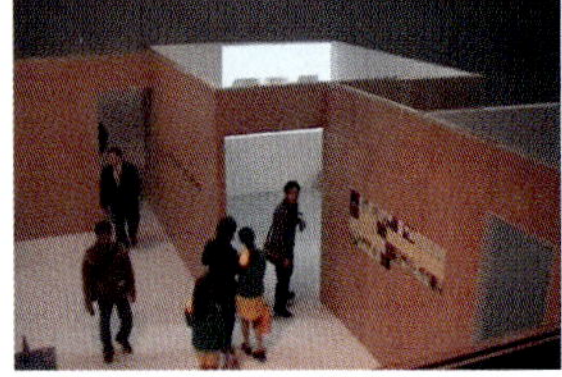

89

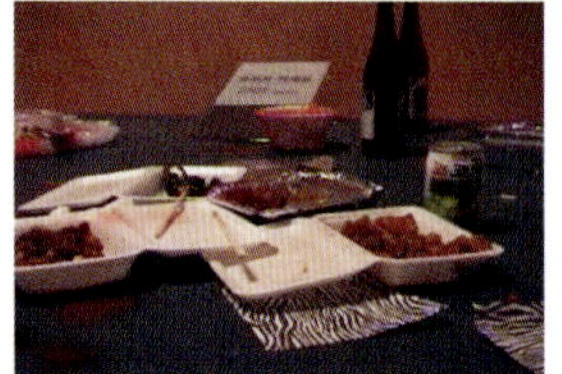

90

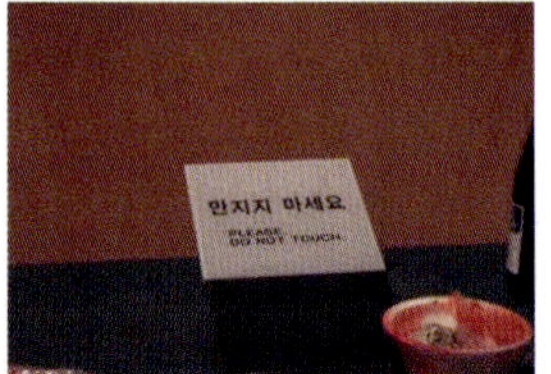

91

I met Ade Darmawan at the Rijksakademie in 1998 when he just arrived in Amsterdam. I visited them in Jakarta before the 2002 Gwangju Biennale. They were a group of very young kids, much younger than the generation around Cemeti in Jogja. The energy was fresh. They focussed much on media art, which was quite new in Indonesia. They discussed so much on the media itself, of the changing language and the shift from propaganda art to something more contemporary. That was a remarkable change I felt at that time. Their setting was interesting too. They lived in a family house, which was perfect. So we (the curators of Gwangju Biennale) decided to invite them to the upcoming biennale as a part of our project to present artists-run spaces from various parts of the world.

Hou Hanru

In 2002, ruangrupa was invited to the Gwangju Biennale. We were awarded an UNESCO award. It was a good moment to receive the prize money, because we had salaries for the first time. Then we started thinking how to make it sustainable; then we started thinking about models of economy, financial systems, educational programmes.

Reza Afisina

The 2002 Gwangju Biennale was an ambitious project. When we [Project 304] arrived, all the technicians had resigned, except the head technician. It was very chaotic. But beautiful in hindsight. That's also where we first met ruangrupa. Ade had just returned to Jakarta from the Rijksakademie, Amsterdam. And ruangrupa got the [UNESCO] award for their participation. It's not fair! Haha.

Gridthiya Gaweewong

ade darmawan

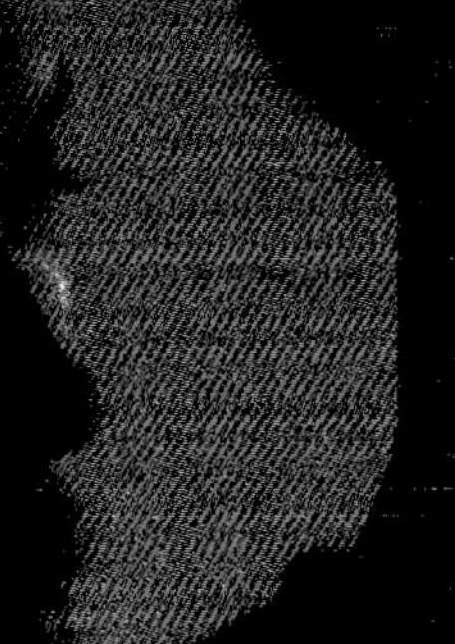

The ground control… dear Bastard…

In every opening at an art space in Jakarta - usually it's a gallery with exotic decoration or a big huge beautiful colonial building - …there is one thing that always so impressed me is when everybody couldn't perform one of the civilized life style called 'standing party' …. After one hour people will just sit down on the floor at some 'cozy' spot , after some boring opening speech, after got a glass of beer, wine or just cup of tea…smoking and drinking, talking and laughing, and they will feel like they are siting in the biggest astray in the world…even its in space with air conditioning …. It's a free country! ….

Garbage and all the dirt in the ground is actually part of the relation between the body and the ground …relation between the body and the object socially, culturally, historically

The relation between the paragraph above and below is just because they are in the same page…

I mean this network is not gonna end up with new imperialism, by sending some artist to other countries...but this consciousness also confronted with the artist' tendencies to go abroad or to become international artist.... It's very important for the carrier, to be an international... even the show its more important than the everyday life experiences ... a new set up have to be made...artist is not an athletes, or underpaid slave of Nike factory...

We are not gonna invite artist from outside Indonesia just to come to Jakarta become an intruder and again rob something in the name of....

money problems for art project always interesting, some artist could survive because they are really good being 'professional artist' - in making a proposal, networking, presenting etc. but some artist they just don't know how to deal with that kind of things or the system doesn't exist, most of the time we should do the 'form follow finances' as well....ha ha ha ...have to be very flexible on money problems...... I start to think to make a manual book for the artist here about getting some money for their projects ..."chicken soup for the artists' soul" ...could be interesting....or to make an exhibition on project proposal made by artists, curators, and organizers....

10

I really agree with my friend Ronny , that artist here should see public as collection of individual with personal history, consciousness, etc , and not as an anonymous entity...so the approach should be more intimate and personal...I think we should learn more from traditional artist here in Indonesia...

...there is no 'center figure' .....try to keep this atmosphere-...and try to be more 'fluid'..

the suggestions sound very interesting, about daily life and try to find the hidden structure the behavior and interactions between the people...

it takes a week for the body and blood to get used to the different climate,

we need your CV as soon as possible for our project proposal...

Back to work, hope to hear from you soon.

Big kiss from Ade Darmawan> 180302

11

published on the occasion of the 4th Gwangju Biennale, this special issue of *Karbon* details the origins of ruangrupa and its vision

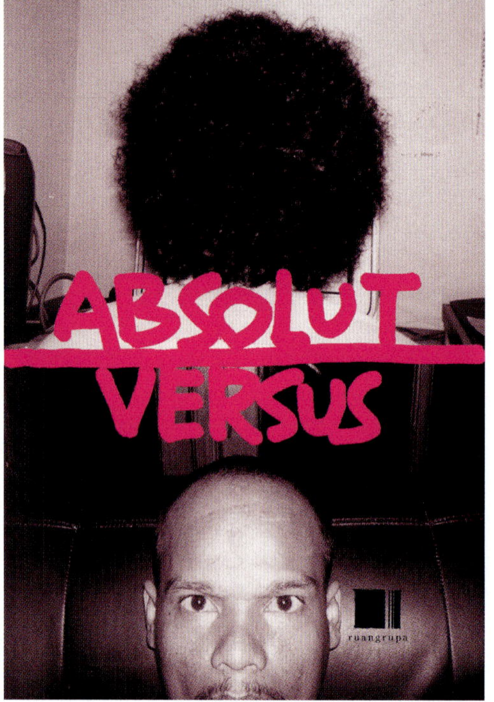

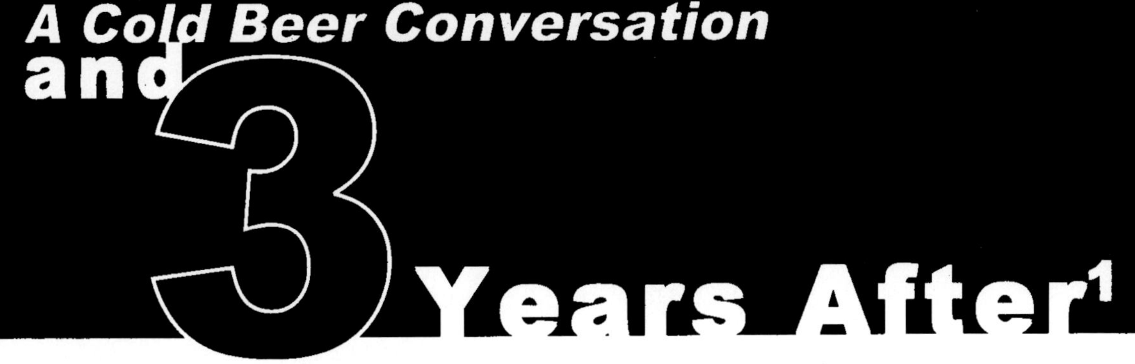

Translated and Edited by Amanda Katherine Rath

"(…) very few artists want to, and are able to, breathe in the "metropolitan air" of Jakarta. For them, Jakarta is merely shelter or a kind of space to be occupied without necessarily knowing about or understanding that space itself. In the end, chaos. Jakarta, as a prime location for developing a broader path for artistic process (not commercial value), is faltering in molding itself (…) Artists in Jakarta form a very heterogeneous community: in their origins, attitudes, character, views, concepts, etc. For me, this is both positive and negative: positive because there is freedom to behave as an individual, negative because, in my view, they [artists] "exploit" Jakarta. The groups in Jakarta (independent, as well as connected) are no more than groups of people who want to take advantage of the situation. (…) For me, this mentality, in effect, makes it difficult for a movement to expand and grow in Jakarta. Almost all of the arts institutions in Jakarta are always in pursuit of status (the artists, art officials, critics, etc.). For me, a painter's mission, as an unconditional responsibility, is to paint and present their work to the public.

(…) Now, if talking about the current rage of consciousness/awareness – raising art (*seni penyadaran*) that most artists now produce, you don't have to believe in it. The problem is not one of belief, but if you understand what I said in my letter, you'll know how to react. They stammer about and then suddenly want to pose as the "spear head" of change in the current atmosphere. All of this masks the real situation. And [artists] are repeatedly trapped within this milieu. Must I speak with them about the issue of believing in it or not? No!!!

(…) Sorry, I don't want to speak so bluntly. And indeed I can't blame the artists 100 %. This can be thought of as being a mutually determining cycle. Our job is to break this vicious cycle."

THE ABOVE LETTER, written by painter Oky Arfie Hutabarat (May 10, 1999), is part of an email discussion between Oky, Ade Darmawan (at that time living in the Netherlands), Hafiz (artist in Jakarta), Ade Tanesia (editor of *Aikon* in Yogyakarta), and myself. The discussion, which eventually included 20 members (mainly passive participants) and covered such topics as iced tea to International Situationism, can be considered a pioneering step in forming a "different" kind of arts organization. At the end of 1999, the same time Ade came back from the Netherlands, the discussion of this illusory space materialized face-to-face over beer and wine, among six "chosen" people. Not long after, the beginning of 2000, Ruang Rupa was established.

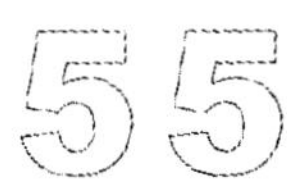

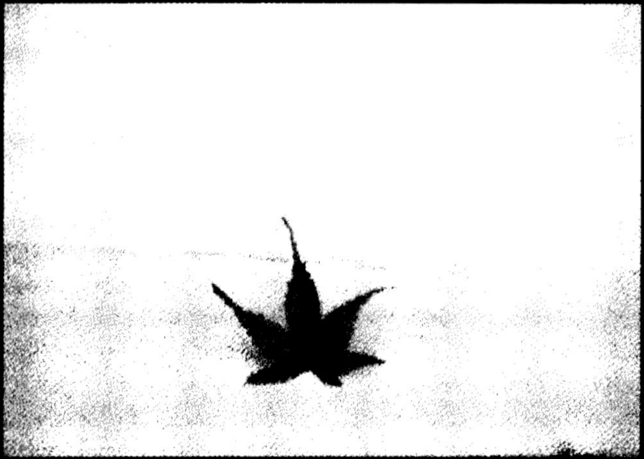

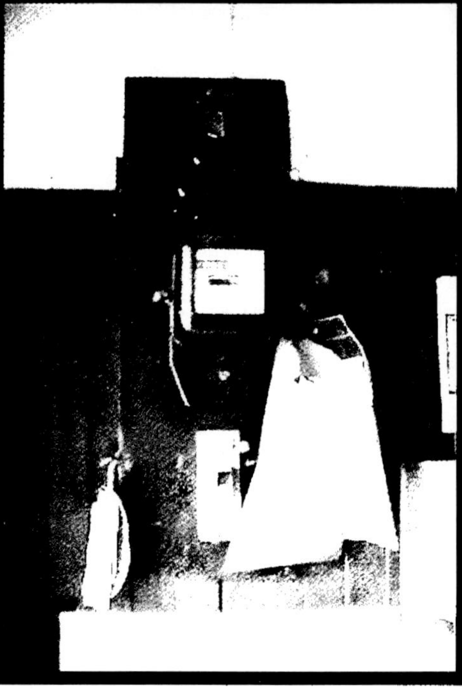

Without direct reference to Oky's letter, Ruang Rupa's principle working platform revolves around the issue of the "urban", particularly that of Jakarta, without "using it as a space to be occupied without knowledge, or understanding, of the space itself"; because "our job is to break the vicious cycle". Although the process of doing so is not as heroic as Oky's concluding sentence, after two years we probably need to reevaluate what we believe that 'space' is, and what the 'job of art' is.

We? Wait a second. That word is actually tricky in summing up what Ruang Rupa is all about. From the beginning, we, ah sorry – 'those of us who founded Ruang Rupa' decided not to combine all of our individual differences into one "communal activity". In fact, I can still remember the initial debates and the quarrels that made for a tense atmosphere in the café where we [the founders of RR] had discussions. Besides the six founding members (at that time some of us worked for an economic-politic magazine that was almost bankrupt –and has since gone bankrupt, an entertainment business, a chicken meat packing plant, and an automotive factory), Ruang Rupa eventually added a writer/painter with the express job of handling the journal [Karbon]. Last year there was a constant revolving door of friends who helped out, whose total working time for Ruang Rupa far exceeded that of the some founding members. For example, I probably show up at Ruang Rupa the least. With all these differences, [the word] "we/us" becomes risky and insufficient. For example, Oky mentioned "the freedom to act as individuals" (email May 10, 1999). Ade added that "we have to be subjective and make an interesting work of art that opens up new levels…" (email May 19, 1999), and Hafiz questioned "imperatives that

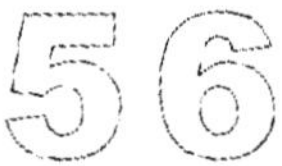

up until now form the public criterion concerning the arts" (email Dec. 23, 1999).

'Public' versus 'individual', 'Us/We' versus 'Me/I': a classic problem yet to be resolved within the debate(s) of Indonesian modern art. But apparently, the people who hang out at Ruang Rupa are oriented toward the 'I' and 'the individual'. Why? I can't speak for the others, but from a philosophical level, I personally don't see 'we' as an immediately effective 'medicine' to cure individualism and the binary opposition of 'self/other' that arrived along with modernism, even if modernism can be viewed as a social pathology. This is because, the hierarchical mentality contained in such a binary cannot yet be directly eradicated by bringing 'the self' into a wider scope: 'I' shifting to the 'we', the individual toward the group, the artist toward the community of art. Even though we are told that we are now in a comprehensive process of democratization, it is as if the hierarchy of superior/inferior is already latent in this country. In fact, it's as if many people feel more secure living within such a hierarchy. For example, two artists once brought an exhibition proposal, complete with financial details, to Ruang Rupa. Hafiz resolutely rejected it (what is Ruang Rupa anyway: gallery, funding, department, or what?), explaining that Ruang Rupa is an organization – he used the words *artist's initiative* – providing work space, materials (not many), that allows 'me' and 'you' as independent individuals and as equals to meet, debate, and work according to our own convictions. If art is meant as a process and an interaction of ideas, then it's the result of which that is exhibited. Hence, the work of art is not the primary aim. Now these two painters seemed uncomfortable with our offer. Apparently they preferred to assume the role of someone looking for work, carrying with them CV's and diplomas, and exhibiting a mentality of an inferior approaching the throne of a gallery owner.

This is just one example [of the latent hierarchy]. An example related to a mentality of superiority can be seen in what actually happens in the practice of 'socially aware art'.[2] The question: who needs to be made aware? Obviously the people, workers, farmers, the poor, the repressed, etc. Who is going bring them to this state of awareness ? This answer is also clear: the artist. Here, the hierarchy of superiority is even more obvious. Certainly 'socially aware art' often inflates complex words such as, 'participation of the masses', 'communal work', etc. Why must artists involve the repressed in artistic projects for the sake of making them 'aware'? On the other hand why not? For example, the farmer compels the artist to abandon their privilege as artist and wake up at dawn to turn and plant the soil. This without it entering the news, without the opportunity to be made into video art, without the Philip Morris Award, Nokia Art Award, Etcetera Award, etc. And this to continue until the harvest season arrives, and the cycle begins again, repeating for say about ten years, for the sake of making the artists 'aware' of the [farmer's] bitter-sweet situation. The hierarchical position of 'aware art' not only considers the artist as 'already enlightened and the farmer as 'not yet enlightened, but at the same time also implies 'art' as a higher level of existence compared to farming. More than likely, the farmer doesn't know anything about social revolution or Rivera's murals of the struggling classes; but on the other hand, what does the artist know about seeds, manure, plant disease, the harvest and the distributors? We should realize the differences and parallels between these two forms of knowledge [farmer's and artist's] if true democratic participation is going to grow. And here is the criticism of art communities that, with a black or white view of modernism, often offering a simplistic solution of 'communal work' versus 'individual work', while ignoring the psychological basis of these two things, as well as confusing the difference between individualism and egoism.

Ruang Rupa's project, included in this Gwangju Bienalle, is thus not a work by 'us' but work by several 'I's or 'selves'. Although, Ruang Rupa is 'I' oriented, it does not immediately follow that Runag Rupa sides with the 'urban' (Sure, in the latest trendy definition, those who support the 'we' are usually identified with 'tradition, village, harmony, art for the people – and because of that...'progressive-proletariat'. The proponents of the 'self' are branded with 'modernity, urban, fragmentation, art-for-art – and thus bourgeois-decadent' [really!]). Ruang Rupa wants to see urban as a space that, like it or not, should be supported while also being critiqued with the same intensity. The urban is neither a sickness – although scarred here and there. Nor is it an angel of salvation – although it constantly draws a yearly migration after *Lebaran* [closure of Ramahdan] of those looking for work. Those who want to curb the flow of urbanization by serving up images of the 'broken city' and the 'peaceful village' are merely toying with standard myths, in no way approaching reality. Repeating what I wrote one year ago in the culture journal *Mitra*: "It is not necessary to deny that our image of the traditional peaceful village and stories of wise indigenous knowledges are romantic compensations for our own cities already in decay..." In art, the intersecting 'skeletons' of concrete and the cowboys of Marlboro-country billboards that fill canvases are only inverted reflections of the structure of the *Mooi Indie's* 3 dictums: mountain, palm tree and rice fields. This framework still exists. The same foolishness from Indonesian films of the 1970's to the primetime soaps of today that always portray Jakarta through: noisy traffic, the national monument, the traffic circle at the Hotel Indonesia, high-rises, street lamps at night, the flicker of the bustling city center, cafes, discothèques, loud music. This portrayal is both the fulfillment of desires and the confession of sins. On the one hand, glamour is the center of depravity that must be reviled, and on the other hand it must continue to be presented without cessation through TV to the remotest corners, while preaching a dream: "this is the real life, come this way...". In this way, stereotypes as well as hypocrisy are strengthened. Efforts to disrupt the hierarchy of center-margins are subverted, thus strengthening its power. The urban, 'the Center', is openly scorned while secretly desired, or as Ade Darmawan has stated:...why are artists more proud of exhibiting outside the country (although in remote countries) rather than exhibiting in Indonesia (in Banjamasin for instance)?"

Clearly, Ruang Rupa does not mean to give into stereotypes or hypocrisy, but [in order to avoid this], the urban should be defined first. Despite the fact that there is no uniform answer, I will say that the urban is "a place where people consume reams of newspapers for the sake of stagnant debates about the discourse of the market and the market discourse of Indonesian art, while at the same time the price of rice in the traditional markets is more expensive than in the supermarkets. Where I can still find a rare Clash CD at a second-hand market, while activists write anti-free-market essays, the stock-market index goes up half a point". Like it or not, the urban is a harsh market, people crowding in on all available capitalism. Yeah, the market: like sex, is often viewed as a type of sin while recognized as the 'greatest human achievement'. We often hear and maybe even express: "The market colonizes! It forces submission! The market alienates!" and at other times we ask ourselves:

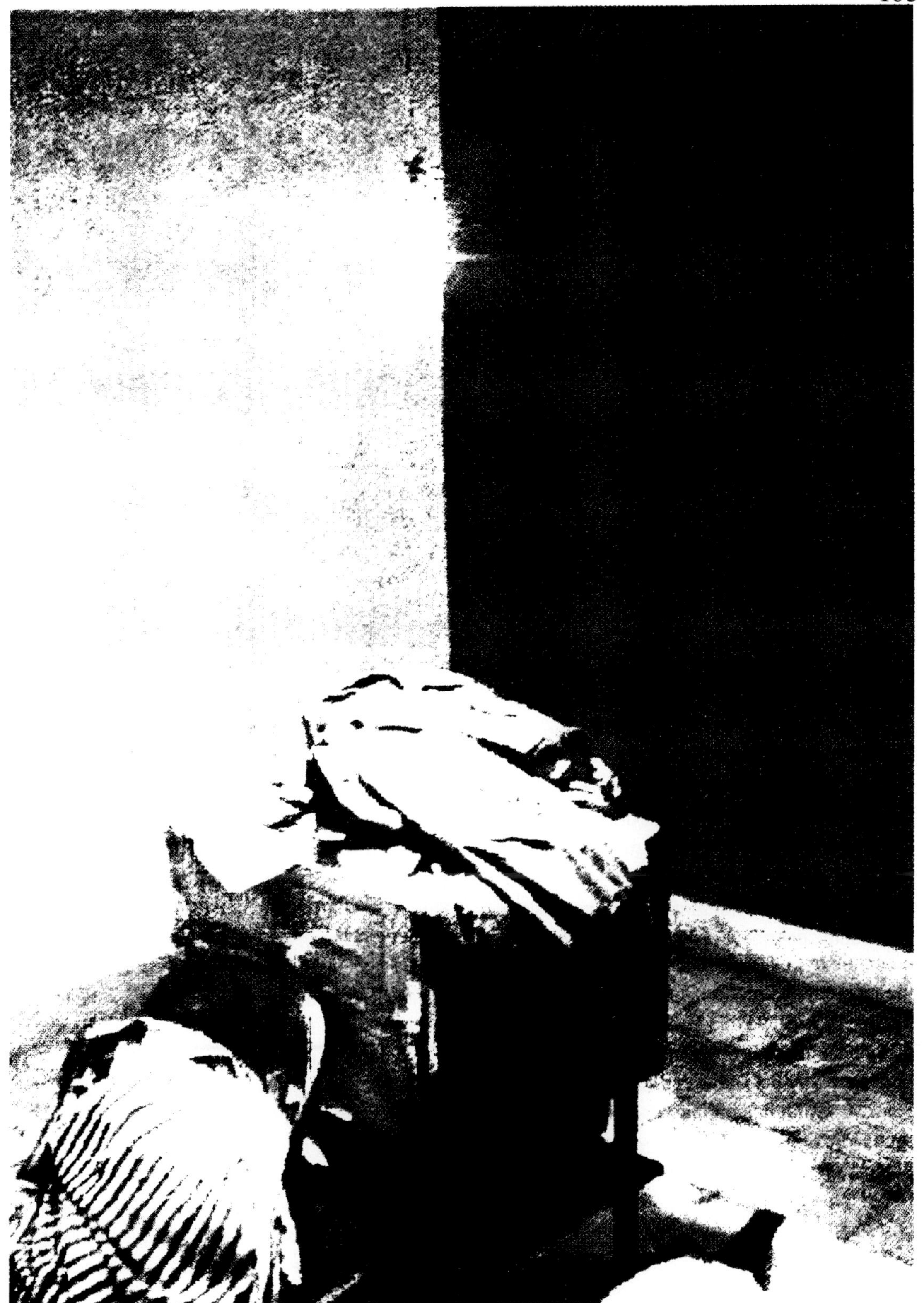

59

"What would we do without the market?". True, the market is full of problems, but to become a romantic ascetic searching for shelter in the clouds, a place that is not-like-a-market, and live there while ridiculing the working public, is not the answer either (in fact, it is through their working experience that people can better understand what actually happens in the world of wage earners).

Surprisingly, in these increasingly feeble times, there are still people bent on dichotomizing the problem of urban as black or white. I think people should watch Wong Kar-Wai's films. In his films, Hong Kong or Kowloon's disordered reality is depicted accurately, but it is not viewed in a sociological or ideological way that objectifies and dichotomizes this reality. The characters in the film view themselves as personal and authentic selves in handling their problems within a urban social milieu, although what they do and say is insignificant and without meaning [in the scope of history]. They don't carry out heroic acts, hunger strikes, or suicidal bombings, but they also don't want to give into a situation that hinders their desires.

Like them, genuine art will always exist in the tension between two constructions: the meta-narrative of social reality and micro-narrative of personal authenticity. Those who delight in criticizing modernism and capitalism in all social, economic and political aspects – devotees of postmodernism – often lose sight of the fact that postmodernism began from within the desire to reveal hidden histories, personal histories, small narratives, that have been sublimated by the linear path of modernism. However, what has happened is merely a repetition. The grand discourse of postmodernism has entered the journals through long and complex quotations, and chalked full of footnotes (and refers to the same scholars: Baudrillard, Foucault, Said, Derrida, etc.). The overarching discipline of cultural studies has become another mainstream just like Developmentalism of the 1980's, as well as anthropological documentary research paid for by international capitalist firms. What then is the distinction between *Terompet Rakyat* and billboards from the New Order?[3] Again, this is a reversed image of the same kind of thinking: political meta-narratives replaced with another political meta-narrative, as if they have forgotten that history consists of physical and intellectual currents that exist on their own; as if they have forgotten what historian Sartono Kartodirdjo asked long ago: where are the histories of those who are not associated with major events? The stories and histories of the ordinary people, the small or 'minor' narratives are missing. This is why Hafiz is concerned about the "hidden things".

I've discussed with Oky our need to re-paint still lifes and flowers, and certainly with a different aim and intention. Ade argued that, quoting a colleague from Eastern Europe, "still lifes and abstraction are political", such that "I believe that a painting of nature and flowers can be seen as a form of resistance, but the one who later buys it is Habibie's wife hahaha…" (email July 21, 1999).[4] I recently attempted to re-paint flowers, a vase of flowers that went against the grain of convention, and showed them in the first exhibition organized by Ruang Rupa (as a fund raising event), at Cemara Gallery in March of 2000. Alongside the works by political satirists Toni Volunteero, Agung Kurniawan, and Alit Ambara, who joined in organizing the exhibition, the works of Ruang Rupa seemed more subjective. For example Hafiz's painting in which a figure of a woman outlined in blue embraces a figure of man depicted in red and black. Within a non-perspectival space, are a white iron bed, bottle, tree, flaming red house, a sketched long bench, a naked couple, dark lines in the background – in short: an intimate landscape, perhaps a landscape of love familiar to both Hafiz and the

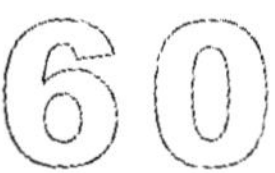

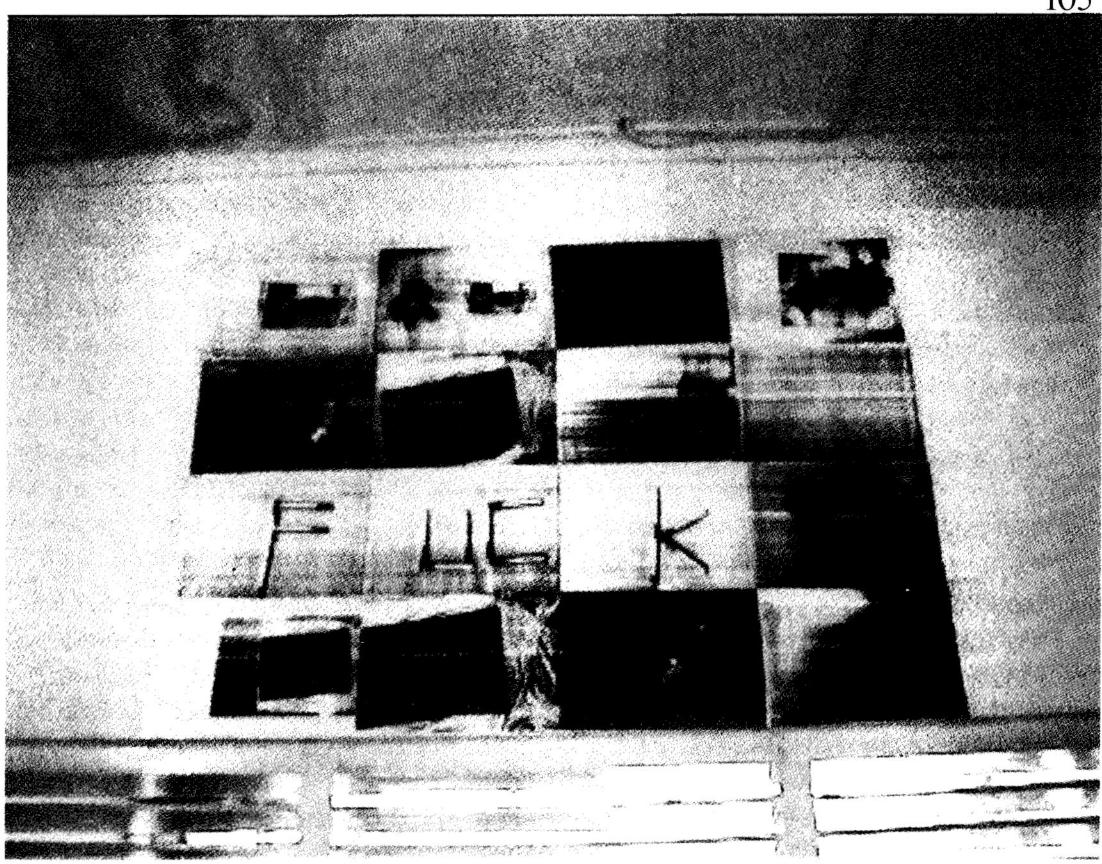

'woman in the painting', without feigning feelings or artificial romanticism.

Since that exhibition, Ruang Rupa has publicly stood on its own. Using a Lilia Nursita's room at Pondok Labu as a base, the artists in residency program was formed. Soon afterwards, [Ruang Rupa] borrowed a space for the first project: a work studio for some "Romantic Rothko" that –without making light of his help to Ruang Rupa – is a prime example of how contemporary architecture can go in the wrong direction (or more precisely, the wrong landscape).

This first project problematized art in public spaces. Ruang Rupa invited and brought together two art communities from Yogyakarta, namely Taring Padi and Apotipk Komik, that at time were known for having a view of art that took an oppositional position as a point of departure in order to work in an aspect of public space in Jakarta of their choosing.[5] To be honest, the choice of these two groups was not based on very deep observation of other communities that also deal with public spaces. The incessant news about them, in addition to being friends with members of the groups, influenced our choice. Recognizing this weakness, this project was fortunately balanced by criticism in Ruang Rupa's own journal *Karbon*. In the inaugural edition of *Karbon*, edited by Ugeng T. Moetisjo (editor of said edition), launched his criticism, the essence of which argued – of course it should be remembered that the sentence that follows is my own interpretation – that 'beauty is divine inspiration and the final reality of a work of art after repression, as deeds of heroism within an age that deviates from human needs". In short Ugeng did not agree with the way these two communities and Ruang Rupa dealt with art in

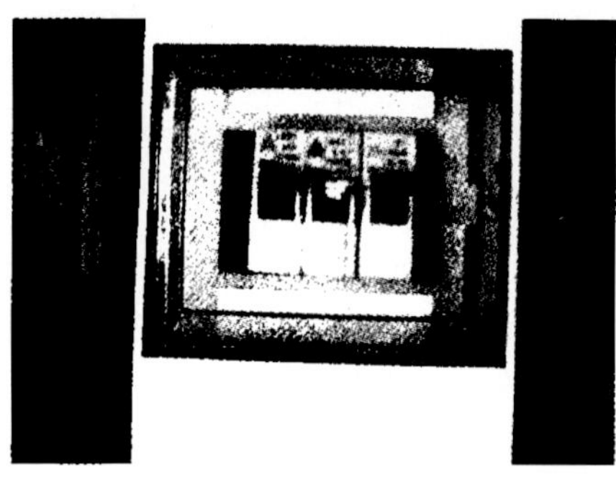

public spaces.

This inaugural edition of *Karbon*'s (November, 2000) got varied reactions from both those with polite praise and those who wanted to subscribe. Most of them criticized Ugeng's use of language not commonly used. Hafiz knows some 'leftist oriented' activists who just threw it away, maybe because of the language, maybe the content. A senior artist sent an email criticizing Ugeng's use of lofty language. However, I often wonder, is *Karbon* really that unintelligible? For example, *Karbon* is a bilingual journal, Indonesian and English. A friend of mine who helps with translations, Theresia Anggraeni, , after skimming the article, understood the essence of UTM's "Case File: Beauty versus the Times" as a first attempt (trying out of ideas). Theresia works as an accountant at an international school and has nothing to do with art theory. Worst case scenario: it is the intention and taste of the self proclaimed learned reader who…

Committed to 'decentralization' per se, *Karbon* is sent to far reaching places [in Indonesia], such as Kutai and Medan (North Sumatra). Who knows how it got there, but *Korban* is also circulated in Bali; several email requests for subscriptions have been sent from there. Due to the Rain Network's channels, it has reached the Netherlands and Belgium. *Karbon* is also read in Barcelona (thanks to Marco Kusumawijaya), and the response by an urban architect from Indonesia – who is currently doing research in the area of Urban Geo-strategy/politics at the Polytechnics University in Cataluna, Barcelona – was included in the second edition. Wherever in the world it may reach, all areas are equally important for the planting of ideas/proposals.

Alright, so that was an egotistically written bit of chronological history, that only wishes to underscore that there is not a unified voice within Ruang Rupa (this can be seen in the publication of the Rijksacademie van Beeldende Kunsten: *Silent Zones: on globalization an cultural interaction* (2001, pp.164-169), where our work was chalked-full with Hafiz's meddling, and you can guess the outcome…a mess!). The similarity among members of Ruang Rupa is found in our differences. But, before this writing becomes too full of self-importance and resembles the slogan 'Unity in Diversity"[6], maybe it's better if I shift to a more theoretical subject. If it's true that Ruang Rupa's unity is in

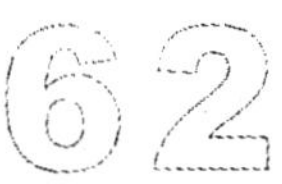

its diversity, what is the thread that binds each person's individual work in Ruang Rupa? How can the "mission of breaking the vicious cycle" bring about something concrete? The answer is actually already within Oky's email: "the mission of a painter is to paint", although it requires clarification as to "what painting is" in a situation that is in complete disarray (because Oky is a conventional painter in terms of technique, therefore the term 'painting' should be understood in wider artistic sense, because as Ade has already witnessed in *Trouble Spot Painting*, the definition of painting has shifted from the problem of 'form' towards the problem of the 'way of thinking').

It's as if the old debate over "art for art's sake" and "art for the people" hasn't been exhausted. What can be done about this conflict that continuously haunts art to this day? I propose that an "art for art's sake" is impossible. Such a principle implies a futile activity. Is it possible that something can be done merely for the sake of doing it? Can we paint only for the sake of painting itself? Can there be such absolute autonomy? Among those who defend the idea of 'art for art's sake', I have never come across someone who paints only for the sake of painting itself. Among other reasons, some paint to articulate a driving energy, some to express ideas and concepts, and others to assist in the fathoming of life; some consider painting as a religious act, others as a way to make money. Not one person has argued that they paint for the sake of painting itself!

Moreover, [Indonesia] really doesn't have a history of 'art for art's sake' that was convincing (and perhaps, along that line, has yet to produce credible works of 'art for the people'). From the beginning, the oldest understanding of art was not just concerned with aesthetics and form[7] but also with function. This to the extent that Prof. Sudjoko once stated that only legitimate art in Indonesia was *seni kriya* or 'applied art or artisan's art'.[8] Although is it not necessary to go to such extremes, I believe that we have never really negated function in creating works of art. And I became really aware of this when I met with Hafiz and Ugeng one afternoon. We were sitting in the shop at the Goethe Institute talking about Ruang Rupa's proposal. After working hours, a young blond girl who hadn't been working there long, came and sat down with us. Hafiz already knew her: a German girl who wanted to know a lot about Indonesian art. The conversation went on about 'Indonesian culture' and took up the whole afternoon. In the middle of the conversation she jotted something down in her notebook and [showing it to us] asked "What's this?" Almost all of us said "a transistor radio". She answered: "No, it's just a circle with a square and three lines". I smiled at hearing that answer. Maybe someone from Europe whose history contains names like Apollonaire or Clive Bell would have an answer like that, but in this country I don't think so. The issue is not a matter of not understanding/misunderstanding art theory, but rather 'mentality', *Weltanschaung*, or world view. An object is rarely neutral, but has associations with something outside of itself, and these associations, more or less lie within the realm of function (or functionality of an object). This is connected to the "absurdity of existence": something that exists without having a purpose outside of itself. The application of such an idea , not based on 'faith' in the notion– historically in Indonesia – often only results in incongruity or nothing if not futility.

Because the nihilism of 'art for art's sake" makes no sense (at least here), art must be for something. It certainly has a purpose. In this regard, "art for the people" is more logical, although not much of a better choice, if we keep in mind the inherent hierarchy contained within "art for the people".

Subsequently, if the one is nonsense, and

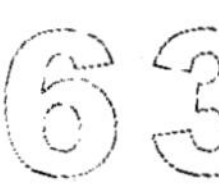

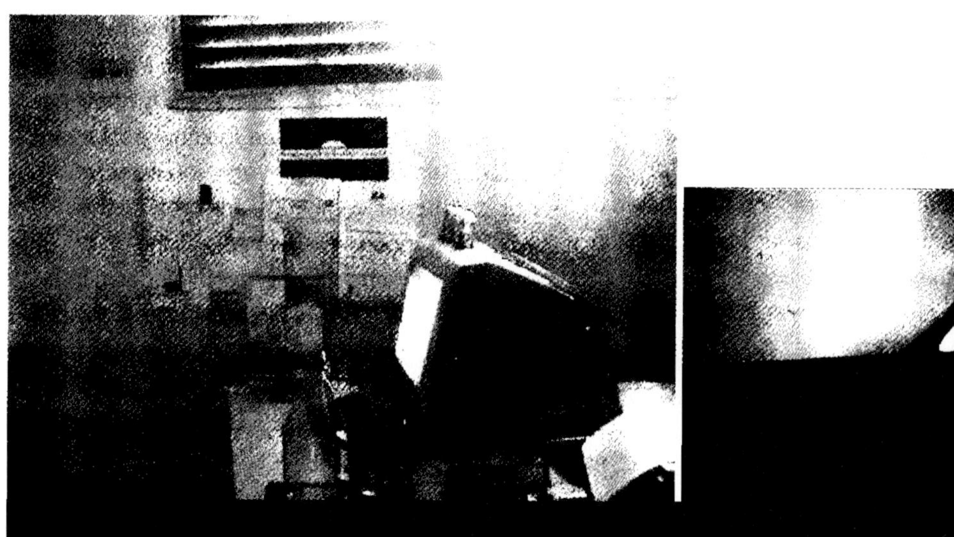

the other adverse, where is art to be located? We have first to look at what are the aims of these two ideas. Both 'art for art's sake' and 'art for the people' imply 'universal communication'. The one is abstract and able to evoke similar feelings in every viewer, both for those who view the color red, for instance, as a violent color, and for those who view it as a sign of good fortune. The other, feels as if it can give voice to the 'universal suffering', as if blind to the fact that, for example, not everyone from one place shares the same concerns as those from another region.

Those who espouse these two ideas concerning art forget that from the first moment language is defective, communication is miscommunication, a picture is a word, and words imply silence, a slippage in every utterance, in every translation there is mistranslation. The *Tower of Babel* is not meant as a curse, but a responsibility. The more 'culture' is pursued, the more diverse the languages become, and art — as one form of language —cannot affect anything except be aware of the defects and miscommunications, acting a small bridge connecting various cultures together without the pretense of joining , much less unifying, them, or — if need be — disrupt these connections.

For this, an aware artist will know that they are always in the middle: the conflict between the 'pleasure of color' and 'human suffering'. Clearly, living in a city and country with so much tyranny forces one to choose sides. Reading the story of an 18 year old woman factory worker, who hasn't eaten in two days (*Kompas*, 12 Dec., 2001), is enough to arouse genuine feelings of anger. The middle ground that I speak of is not the dictum of journalism about 'covering both sides' that tries to remain neutral. One cannot be neutral toward a system that causes a woman to go without food for two

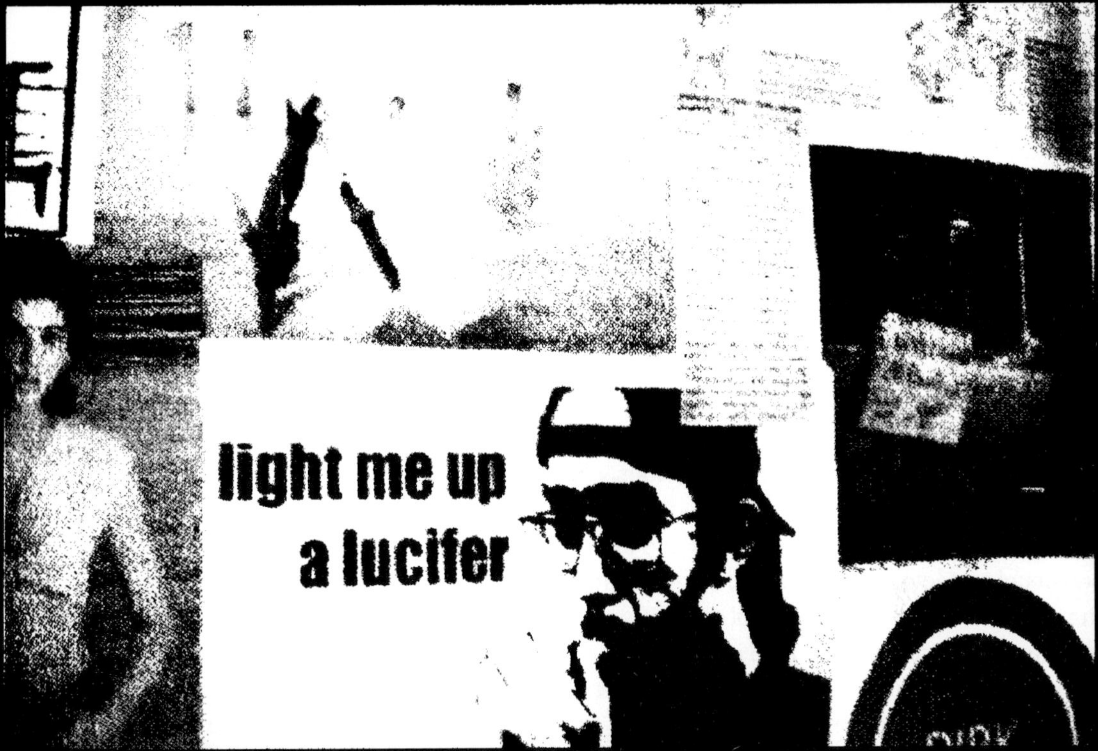

light me up
a lucifer

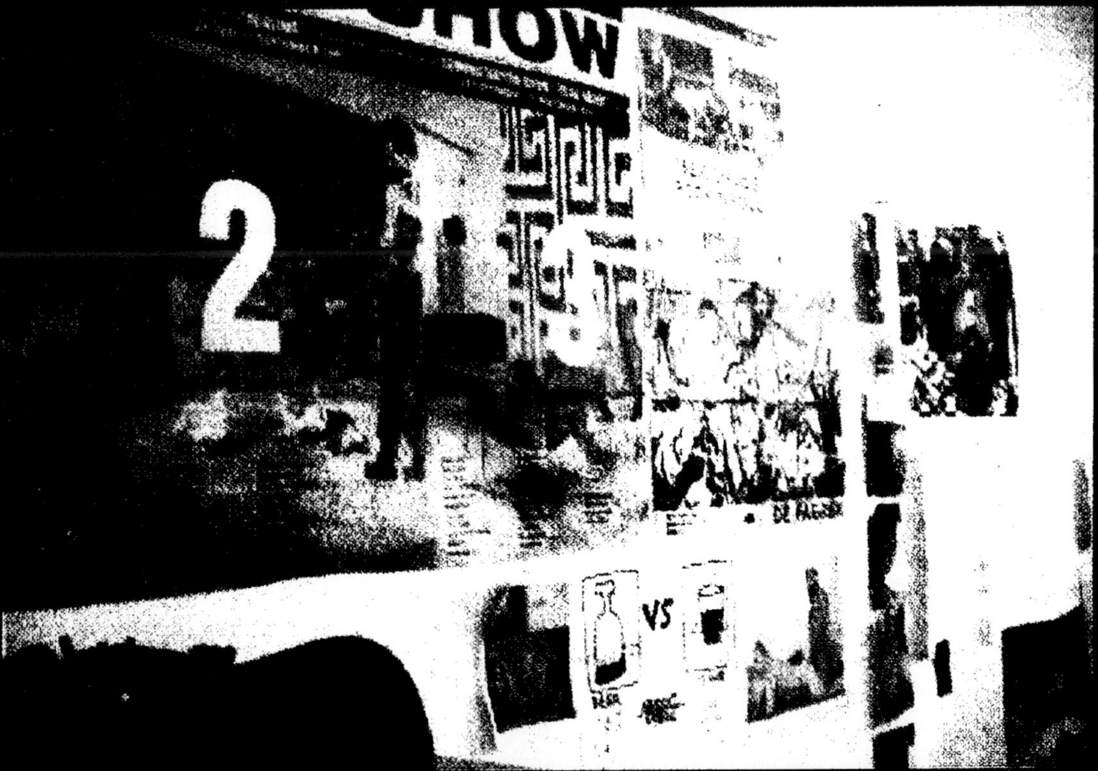

days. Neutrality of this sort is itself nihilism, and should be buried in its grave, along with the philosophy of the ivory tower and romantic artists. The middle that I speak of is the liminal state in which 'anger' becomes 'beauty', 'abuses' become 'inspirations'. A place where we know that art cannot save the world, but that it can inspire people to save the world themselves. The middle as a form of inspiration-transfusion that at least wasn't tertebak. Without this type of 'middle', one can only produce so much window dressing, or 'sloganistic sermons'.

So, have we reached the ideal? Obviously not. Directing Ruang Rupa as a an on-going *artist's initiative* hence has already caused the personnel to decrease their artistic work. Ruang Rupa must be in contact with all of the complexities urban dwellers face in general, from the day to day business like contracting a house, electric and telephone bills. We are in the midst of trying out a new system that enables art work, a journal and administration to proceed without the one interfering with the other.

If there is consistency in Ruang Rupa's work up to this point, it is the attention toward 'urban space' and 'small narratives'. These two points are linked with Ruang Rupa views of *visual culture* and *fine art* itself. *Visual Culture*, broadly speaking, is related to urban space, and usually becomes the main theme of our Artists in Residency projects. At the same time, *fine art* is more related to the small narratives of the artist, their own works of art, albeit going beyond the boundaries of conventional *fine art*. For example, Ruang Rupa's video project that extended for a period of months and involved members from Argentina, Belgium, Germany, and Jakarta. For this project, video was considered as a phenomenon of visual technology of urban space, and the individual artist's video art works as "small narrations". Within the scope of *visual culture*, Ruang Rupa does not view a work of art as immediately becoming *fine art* just because it is art, and from works of applied art (printing, packaging, banners, etc.) as *low art* simply because it is not art. In this case, it is more a matter of intensity and creative energy. The postmodernist zealots – in an effort to depose the domination of "*high art*" – boisterously celebrated the return of "*low art*" from its marginal position, as if without critical consideration. In this regard, we can see in every tradition of *visual culture* various levels of aesthetic, creativity, passion, and tension in each work.

The notion of an urban space is probably already clear. This city is already absurd to the core, from the governor to the singing beggar. On Monday mornings the narrow streets are packed with people leaving for work, as if they are the hardest working people in the world. But come Thursday the traffic flows more easily. There are not so many people. Where are the people that were going to work on Monday? Are they taking a day off? Or have they forgotten that Thursday is a work day too? Quoting from our proposal for the curators of this Biennale, people living in Jakarta have forgotten that plastic is not a banana leaf – it can't be thrown away as easily as a leaf with the hope it will go away on its own. They have also forgotten that, unlike dirt, asphalt and bus floors don't absorb spit.

It can just be amnesia, a critical condition suffered by urban people. The way to healing is none other than one's own process of remembering and memory. In fact, within what is called 'collective memory', each person has their own space that cannot be occupied by another person. Chairil [Anwar] wrote "Solitude is one's own fate" (1946), not just for the sake of writing a love poem (that later became one of the most beloved poems of Indonesian literature), but also to reveal the irony of modernism that was assailing developing countries. The calm and quiet of the sheltered

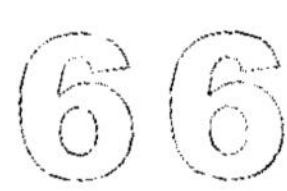

communal life was suddenly thrust into a clamorous world wherein people must *choose* their own path in isolation. Meaning is no longer a given. "There is a new kind of person, and can be called 'I'" (Chairil Anwar, 1948).[9]

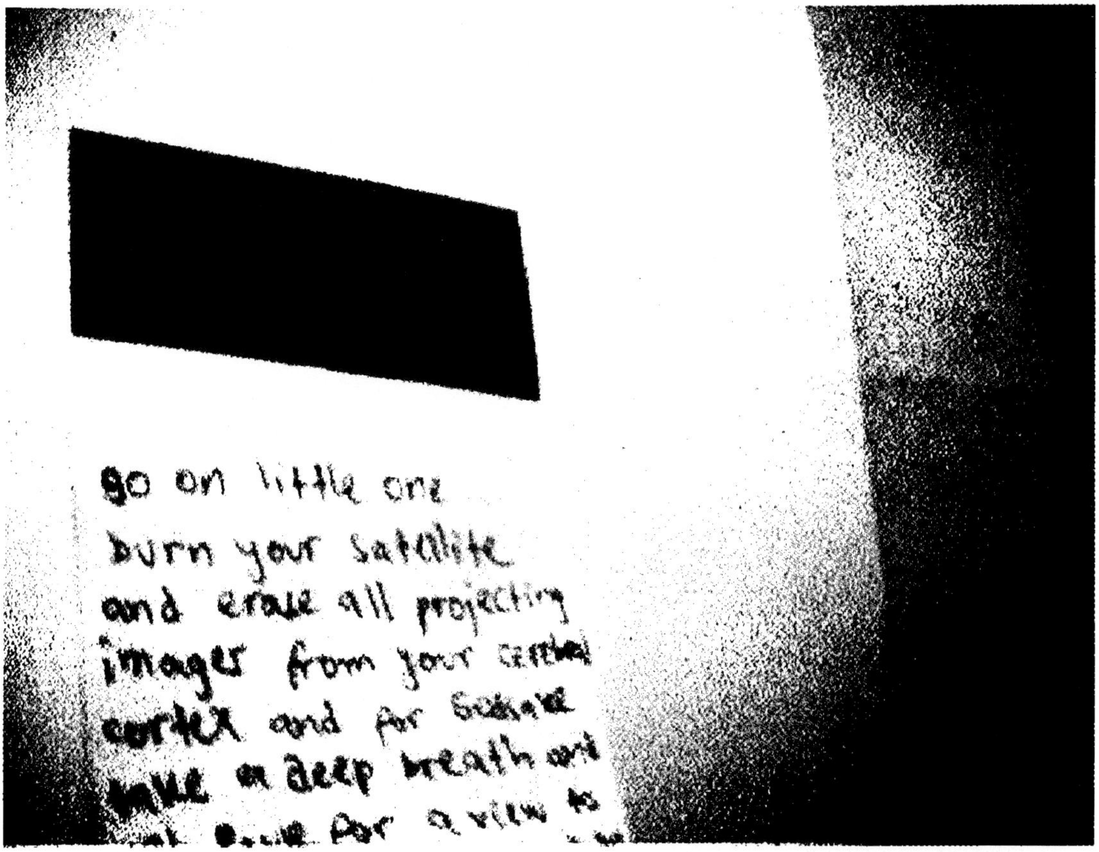

If Ruang Rupa persists with the issue of 'little narratives', this is because of such a realization, a realization that communality cannot stave off the pace of modernism, 'I' is irrevocably present and cannot be taken back. This does not imply that life itself has lost meaning. It is exactly at this moment in time when politics are done with a small 'p' and pragmatism with a 'P', that meaning is lost when it lost its solitary position. It has been drawn into alliances, projects fortified by regulations and laws, echoed in such slogans as "the revolution is not over", "give substance to independence" , and "push on with reformation' . Ruang Rupa, for example, is not a group of people that depicts Jakarta via the contrasts between generalizations of poverty and wealth. Those who are fond of such generalizations, are usually those who give them meaning, and these can be divided into two things: between the side of power (read politics) and the opposition (read activist). Poverty is often stereotyped by the police as the source of criminality, as if they have forgotten the blue collar crimes that have proven detrimental, and carried out by those who cannot claim poverty as their motive. Right now activists regularly support the realm of criminality under the pretext of poverty, as if they too have forgotten that by doing so, they bolster the stereotype created by their competition (police and politics). Generalizations, black and white definitions,

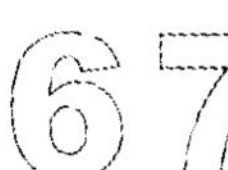

stereotypes – these are not what Ruang Rupa carries out. We are more drawn to the gray jungle of Jakarta, taking from the plethora of bazaar stickers stuck everywhere such as our second project: *Urban printing: The Personal in Sociological Interpretation*. During the process of completing this project, came across a newspaper agency called "Failed Hope" (*Harapan Gagal*) in the area of Kampung Melayu, a district crowded with buses. It was as if the owner of the agency was ridiculing his own failed dreams in a big city. A name like that is not just a name, but holds within it a story, hope, and the confidence to make fun of oneself. What si so important about one agent among 1,000's in Jakarta? But it's places like that that perhaps inspire Ruang Rupa.

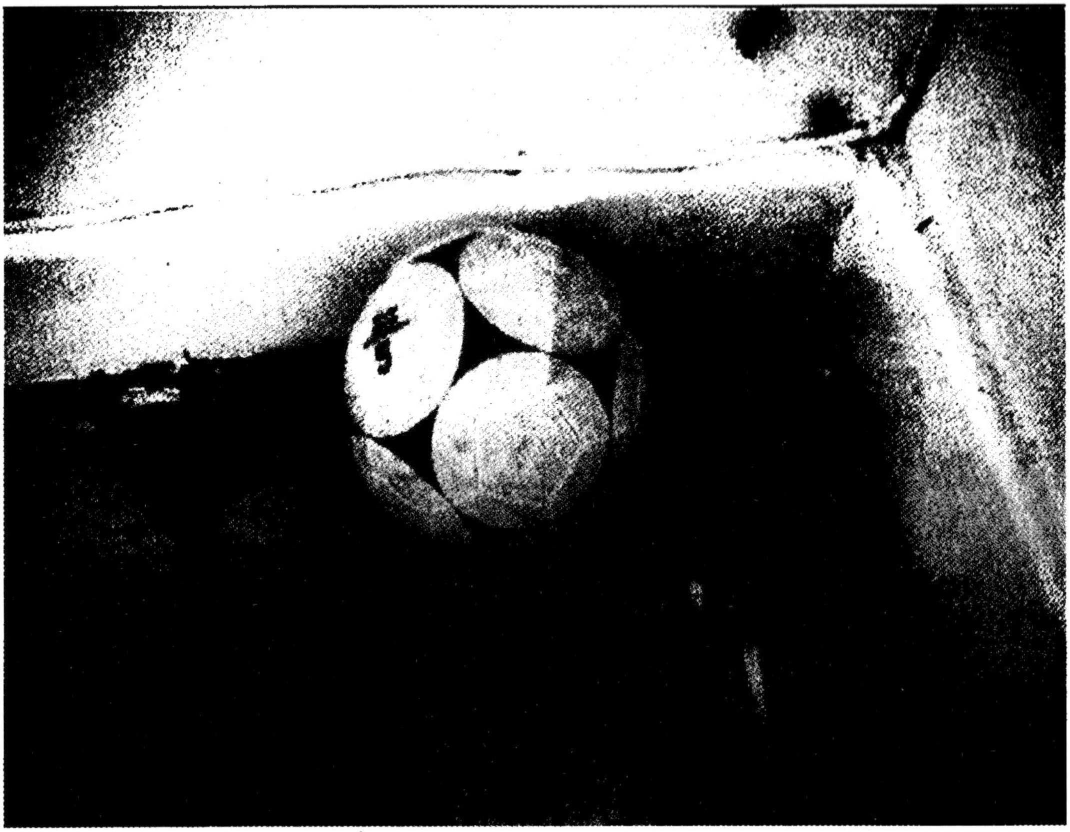

Alexander Sudheim (an artist/musician from South Africa invited to participate in our Urban Printing project), remembering the history of his country overshadowed by institutionalized racism, was taken aback by a sticker "Janitors against Apartheid" which he found in Blok M. Sudheim later commented that it was "The weirdest shit I picked up there" . Concerning the work of Ruang Rupa, he also commented (quoted from within the spirit of narcissism): "I have respect for the initiative spirit and natural abilities of everyone involved to mutually interact in clever and creative way, not like the crazy paranoia of Europeans who are convinced that if you don't force someone to 'work' within the most puritan understanding of work, the project will never be finished.". Regarding the urban he stated: "Space is like water, and in Jakarta we are like a group of fish in a shallow mudhole, each one trying to permeate our brains and bodies. But don't forget, the lack of oxygen can also effect interesting hallucinations...". But I wasn't

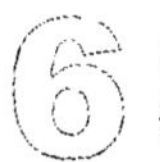
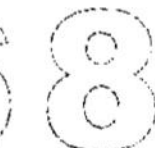

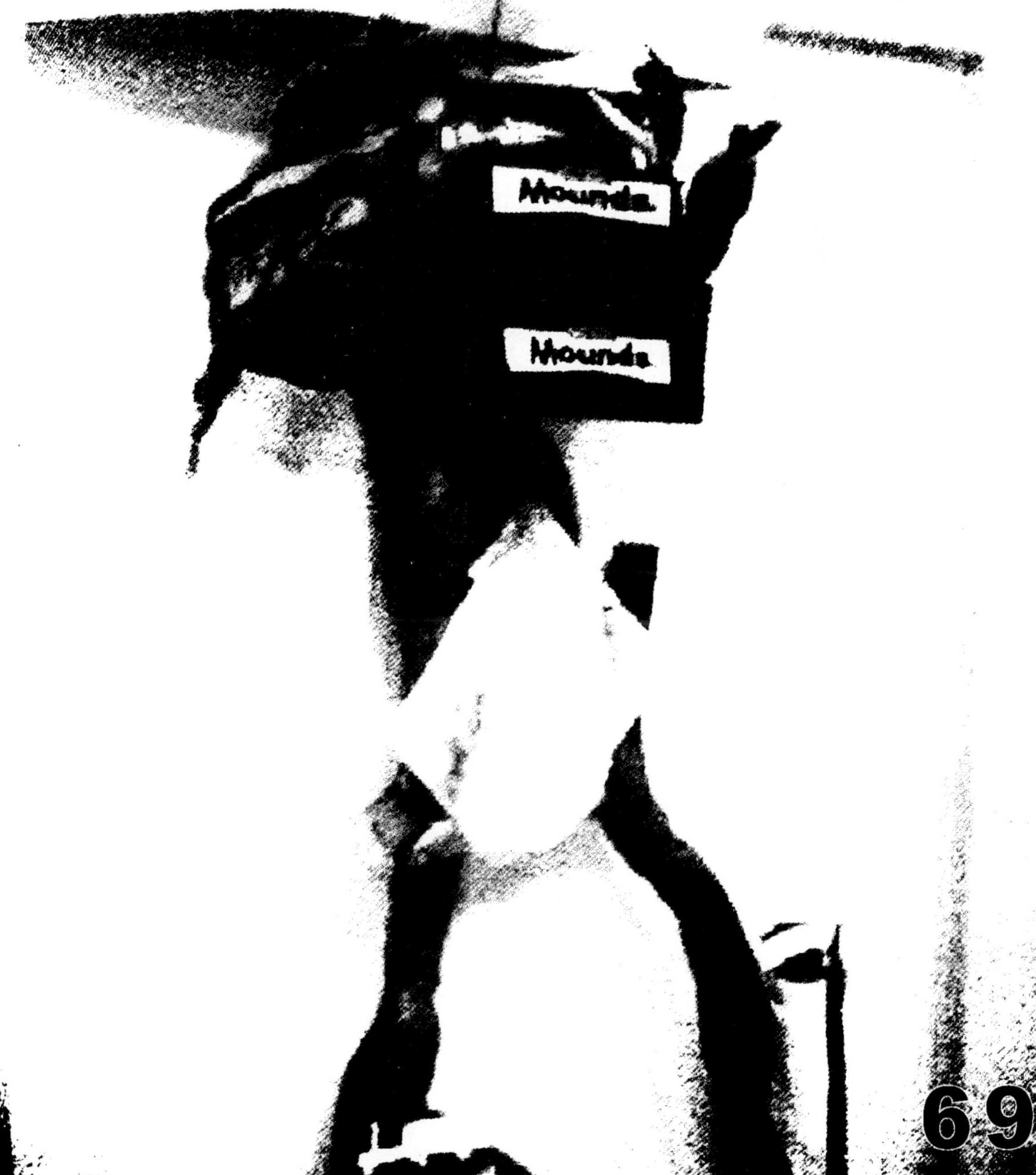
Mounds
Mounds
69

hallucinating when I wrote to Reinaart van Hoe (an artist from Europe): "artists can no longer work in public space for the sake of being aware (*penyadaran*), because social awareness these days is constructed by mass media and NGO's. Artists can no longer offer entertainment, because there are many forms of media more entertaining like yellow journalism and television. Artists can no longer disturb or shock the public, they are already disturbed with everyday economic problems and shocked by oft-changing political policies. Therefore, the only way for artists to enter the public domain is through a more intimate approach, speak about more personal issues. This is because the public is not an anonymous entity, but a group of many people who have names, histories, and feelings of their own" (28 Nov. 2000). Ade relayed our concerns to Gertrude Flentege (Rain coordinator) and added "It's quite strange that people become accustomed to shocking things. This is rather depressing and in fact makes us rethink the position of the artist in this kind of situation".

What is the position of the artist in this state of affairs, and in history. Yes, the history of modern art in Indonesia is truly a vast project, let along the history of 'post-modern' art; the emergence of which was colored by the scandal of the biennial sham that surprisingly has never been seen as an important historical note. People are busy, once again searching for innovation of medium, for the sake – they say – of struggling against the stagnation of form and content. It is as if they have forgotten the 'champion of the revolution' is nothing new, but the inspiration that they convey has never stagnated. Behind all this, behind the inflated facade of history that has never been critiqued – while eliminating all dishonensty that yields only peddlers of ornamental garbage – Ruang Rupa tries to work, as a group of individuals who have their own little narratives, within the confines of a wide, yet narrow space. This without having to be narrowly categorized as this or that. Ruang Rupa tries to be as aware as possible that the dream of an ideal culture is a fantasy, that a living art comes from within memories – small, personal, insignificant, simple, and sometimes ignored, that without these, life has no meaning; and without memories people would eventually die. They would kill themselves.

Ronny Agustinus – Dec. 2001

Notes of the author:

Cold Beer Conversation is the title of Hafiz's email message dated July 15, 1999. On July 22, 1999, Ade argued that the beer *Corona* was marketed in Spain under the sexy label of *Coronita*.

If there are those who feel this writing is longwinded, confusing, ridiculous, narcistic, and doesn't explain anything, this is true. This is because sometimes the activities of Ruang Rupa are also like that. Lie is sometimes like that. Besides that it is raining today and I can't go anywhere, and the only to kill time is to write this long treatise. While listening to the rain fall, I am reminded that *hujan* or rain is synonymous with RAIN in English and with the acronym RAIN (or Rijksakademie Artists Initiative Network in Ruang Rupa slang) that flows over with feelings of postcolonial guilt…he..he…he.

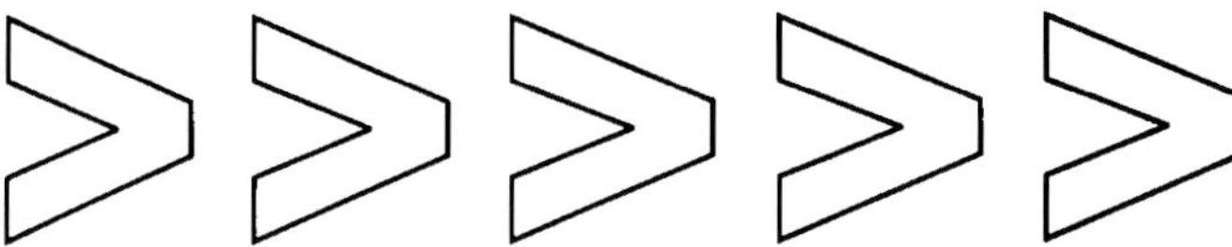

[1] Footnotes have been added by the translator/editor Amanda Katherine Rath.

[2] The original term is seni penyadaran. It roughly translates into awareness art, yet within the context of a type of 'art for the people' meaning artists make art specifically in-tune with real issues of certain groups of people. Penyadaran is difficult to translate as it forms of type of verb such as the 'making of awareness art'.

[3] *Terompet Rakyat* refers to a work created by Taring Padi, one of the many groups of artists/activists that emerged after the fall of Suharto. TP uses mediums of mass communication such as posters and billboards, murals, etc. as a way of making inexpensive art that is also accessible to, and easily understood by, larger segments of the population. TP, as well as some of their colleagues, have been criticized for aestheticizing politics and reconstructing a populist ideal of 'art for the people' that replaces one ideology with another. The use of billboards in this case is ideally in opposition to (among other things) New Order Developmentism that ushered in a rapid growth in multinational advertisements as part (or symptom) of the modernizing process.

[4] Paintings of nature-scapes, or landscapes are often considered a conservative and decorative form of art, favored by the elites and has been associated with Commercial art, Suharto's and later his replacement Habibie's political party which 'ruled' Indonesia for over thirty years. Commercial art is also associated with 'safe' art. In other words, it was supported by and often consumed by not only the 'ordinary' growing middle class, but also by government officials.

[5] Both Taring Padi (sharp tip (spear) of the rice plant) and Apotik Komik (Comic Pharmacy) emerged during the chaos of the fall of Suharto. Members of both groups were previously involved in student activism which helped, in no small part, to bring Suharto down. Their leftist ideological orientation has been compared to that of Lekra (communist cultural organization during the 1950's and 1960's) which was purged along with the Communist Party after Suharto came to power.

[6] "Unity in Diversity" was (and may perhaps still be) the national slogan depicting a national culture consisting of diverse ethnicties, languages and religions. It was used by the state and the military through education indoctrination as a means of disavowing the different needs and concerns of the many for the sake of the center.

[7] The original terms used are *keluhuran* and *kegunan*, two Javanese words concerning expectations about and appearances of forms. These terms cannot be directly translated as they also have spiritual and ethical connotations. The editor has used approximating, and unfortunately too simplistic, English terms.

[8] The first Indonesian to receive a Doctorate in Art. Indonesia has no Dept. of the History of Art.

[9] Chairil Anwar (1922-1949) was a young poet who emerged during the Japanese Occupation and became well known for his work during the war for Independence, while working in Jakarta. He and his group argued the outsider position of the writer/artist, and declared the individuality of the self as the necessary position of that outsider. It was the 'modern self' that Anwar depicted in his many poems entitled 'Aku' or 'I' (1943. Chairil's poem has come to mean both a declaration of the self and the birth of a nation in the throes of modernization and history.

'what do you mean by using another?', ruru house, April 2002

with Yunawantyo, Aditya Satria and Ernest Wang

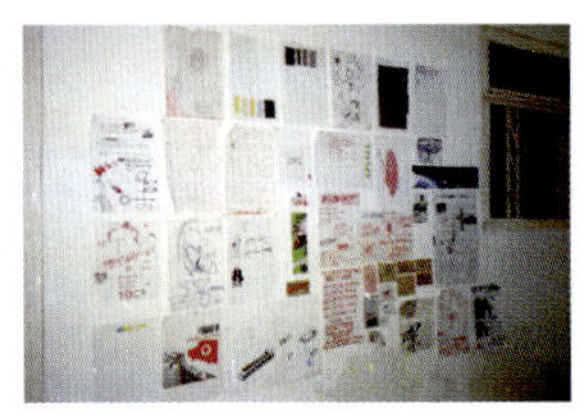

93

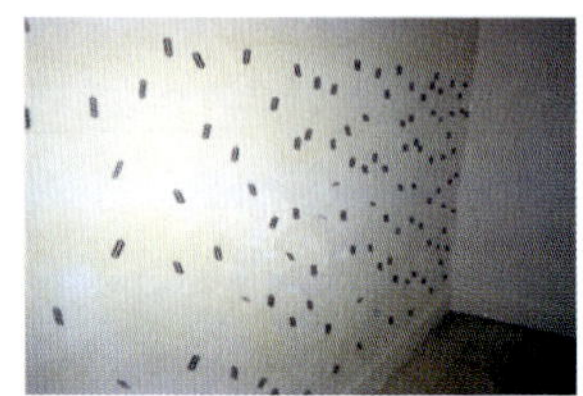

94

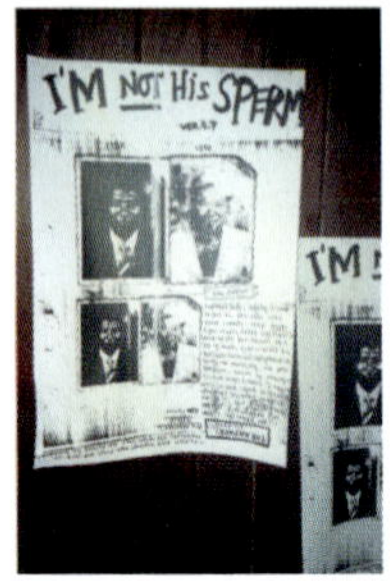

95

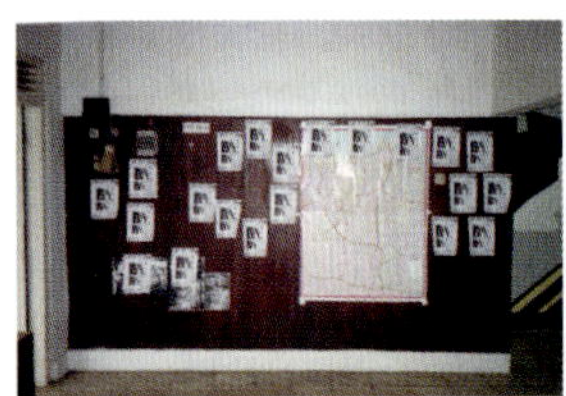

96

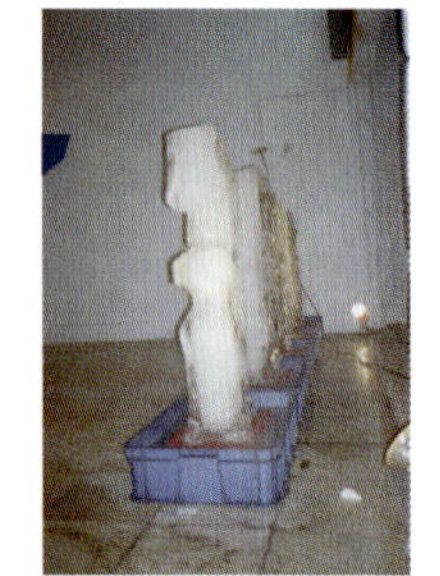

97

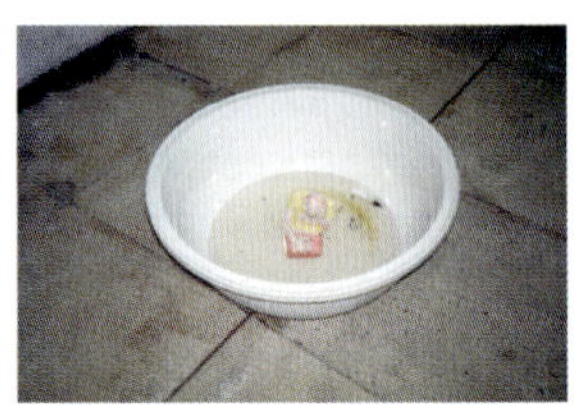

98

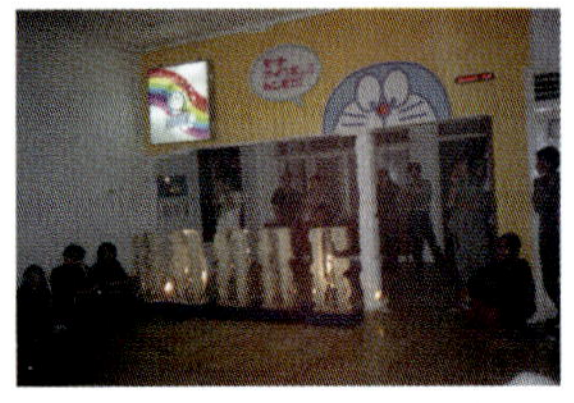

99

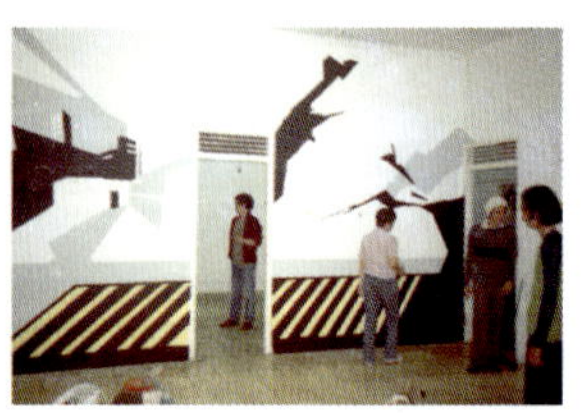

100

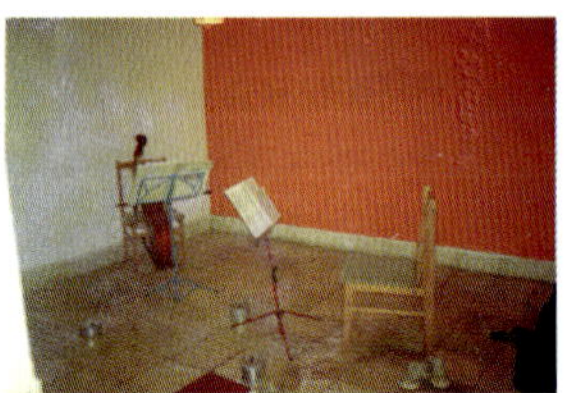

101

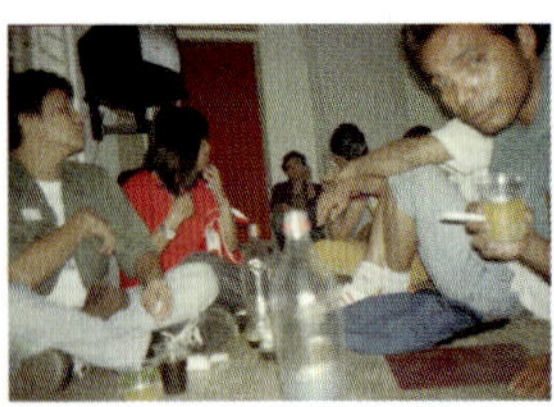

102

In our first three years it was not easy. From the beginning, we were already thinking if we were to depend on a funding body that could support us, then we need to consider what kind of funding we needed or which funding body was suitable and could meet our way of practice or thinking. There was lots of funding after Reformasi, NGOs mostly. We learned about the mapping of alternative spaces in Asia through the book published by Japan Foundation in the 2000s. Suddenly we were part of this, we were not alone (although over 90 per cent of the spaces recorded then are inactive now). We found similarity with other initiatives, such as artist residencies. We had to find something that's quite unique to show to our bigger funders. Within the first three years, we had already exercised our networks – we had lots of exchange with international artists through RAIN and Rijks networks, some of them shared knowledge of what is video art. Then we had the first OK.Video festival in 2003. But festivals and events were only one way that we could use to educate ourselves. That's why we have publications and catalogues, to share our questions.

Reza Afisina

There were commonalities within a certain kind of class we came from ... the precarity, a shared sense of the economic and also personal insecurity of which both Iswanto and Reza are speaking. I saw how, because of this common experience of precarity, the dialogues between students acquired an intensity and how the campus became a space where experimentation could sprout, emerge, in the nineties. A lot of political demonstrations, a lot of artistic experimentation because students were actually living on campus – they were sustained there, materially, which is not the case anymore. To live was actually part of the education; it was the school, the art-school environment.

Ade Darmawan

[W]e created these 'houses' or 'living rooms' for the first time in 2002 at the Gwangju Biennale. We tried to play with how people interact with the capacity of a space. We never really impose that our space needs to be oriented towards the artistic. We need space, that's the most important thing. And we need to know if we could govern, put together the spaces, how interdependent they are, because we need to think about different kinds of structures. Sometimes it could be meant to be like a gallery space, sometimes a housing space, sometimes a market space. This space is changing: sometimes it belongs to students, sometimes to public space, sometimes it's a theatre or performance space. Perhaps ... in Europe you have spaces that have been designated – you have art centres, museums, galleries. But in Indonesia, we don't have a very solid structure we could gain access to until you exhibit there, it's not really accommodating nor supporting our practice, especially in the sense of collective or experimental practices.

Reza Afisina

The art infrastructure in Indonesia is always 'lacking', or incomplete, which makes it fail to accommodate each individual to play his or her role properly the way the Western notion of art infrastructure is supposed to play out, and this fact is heavily related to the power relations mentioned, such as governmental bureaucracy, authority, economical problems and so on. Within this handicap we actually can discover some channels to fill in the gaps, like taking our own position to complete, or in other words enrich the structure by offering more spaces of explorations, without having tendencies to oppose to the establishment of whatsoever but also maintain not to be co-opted with it as well. Part of the efforts involve trying to make the best use of what we have in the infrastructure, at least, which so far has not been taken all the way. Revitalisation of the infrastructure is part of the objective, something to be continuously negotiated and processed.

ruangrupa

‘print 2000+2 project’, Taman Ismail Marzuki (TIM), Jakarta, 27 May – 4 June 2002

with Ade Darmawan, Anggun Priambodo, Hafiz Rancajale, Henry Foundation, Indra Ameng, Irwan Ahmett, Lilia Nursita, Mahesa Almeida, Matheus Bondan, Mushowir Bing, Oscar, Reza Asung, Ronny Agustinus and Tisna Sanjaya

T FOLLOW ME FOR FYOUR FINAN CIAL FREEDOM

103

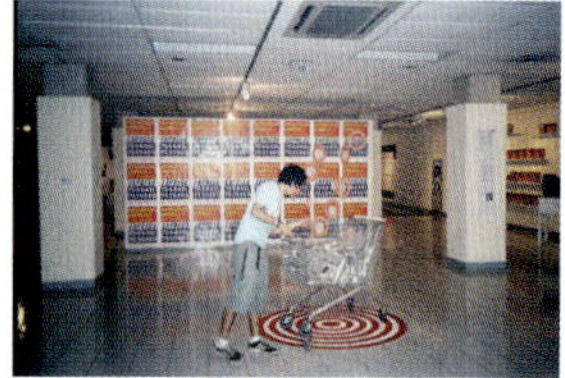

104

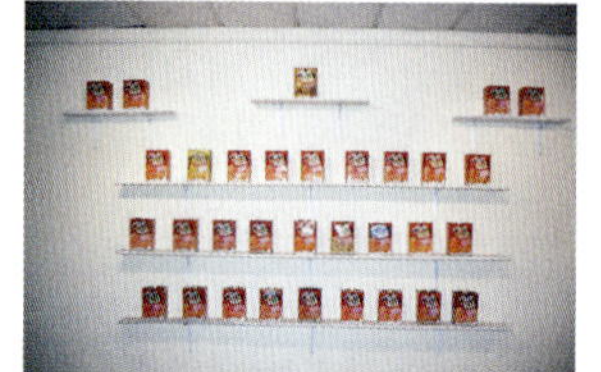

105

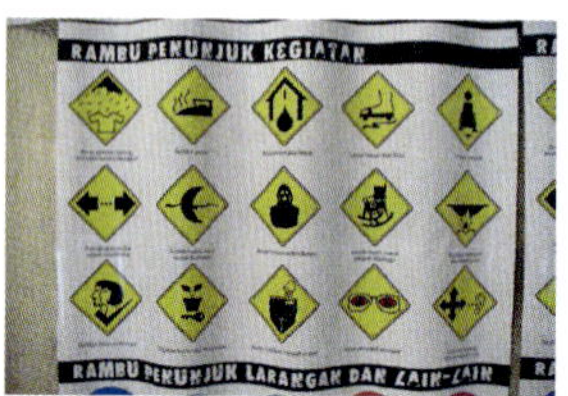

106

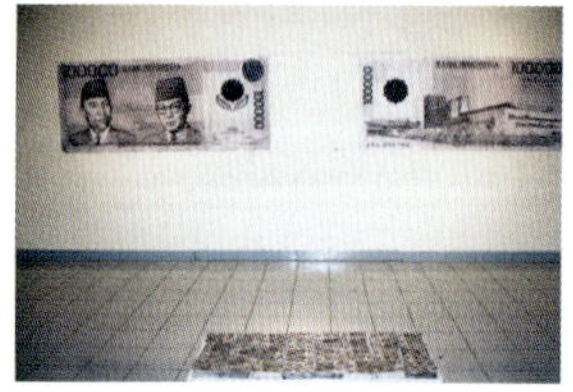

107

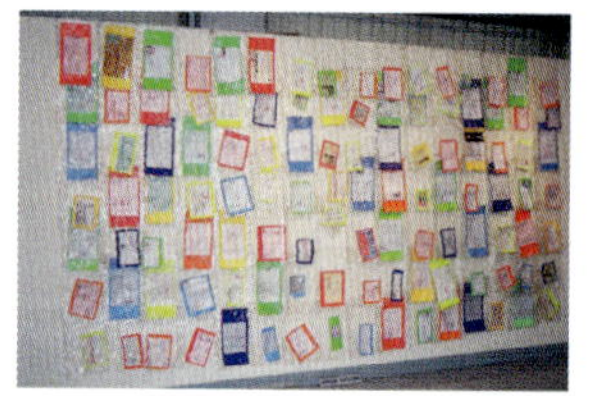

108

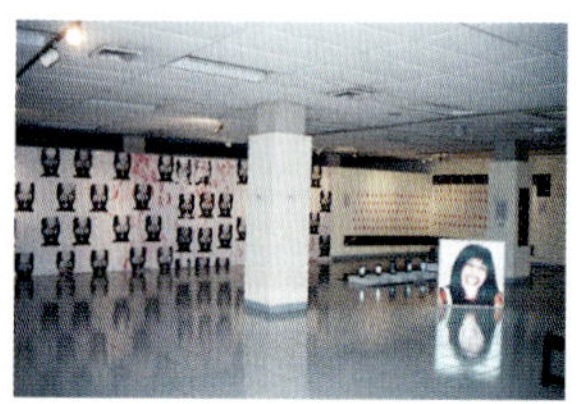

109

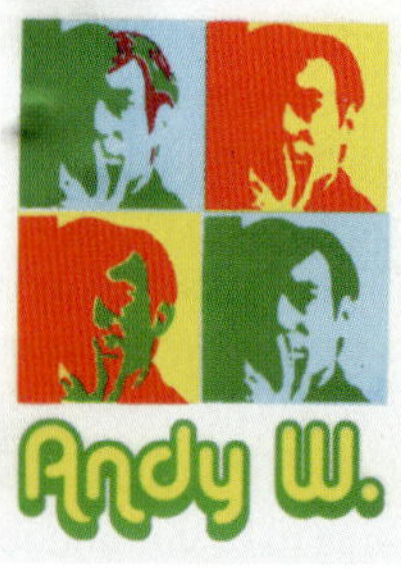

110

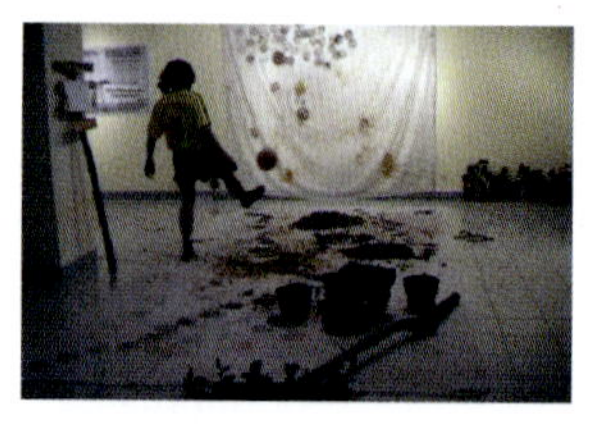

111

with ruangrupa, Los Mutantes, El Despacho, Open Circle, Centre Soleil d'Afrique, TRAMA, PULSE, CEIA and Rijksakademie

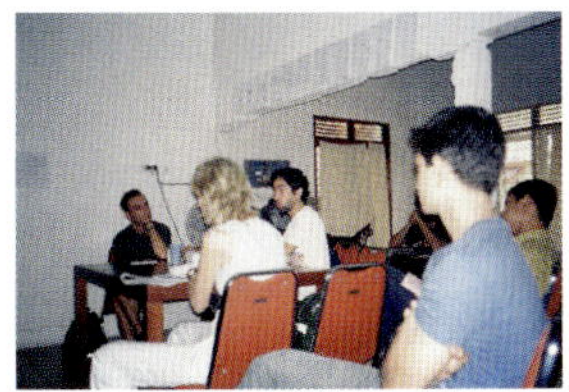

112

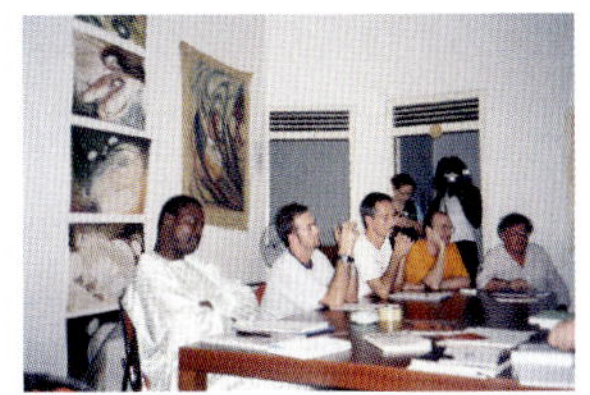

113

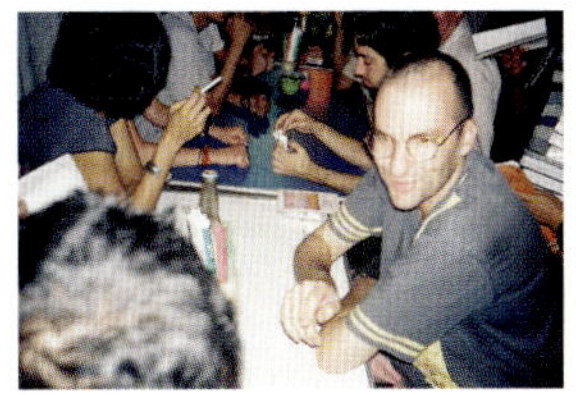

114

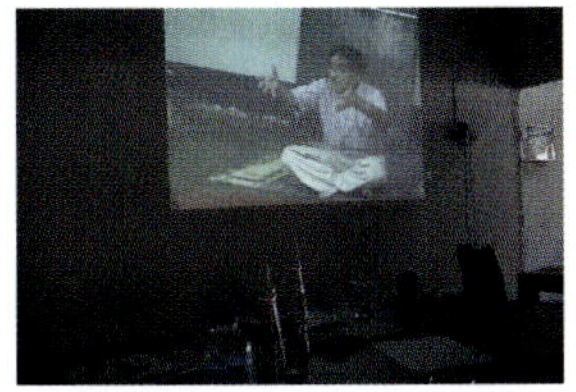

115

I got to know Ade Darmawan when he was a resident at the Rijksadkademie van Beeldende Kunsten in 1999 and I started working there. At the end of that year we had an amazing opportunity by being invited by the Ministry of Foreign Affairs to develop a project based on the work they had supported in engaging artists from Africa, Asia and Latin America at the Rijks. At that time a few had started to develop an artist's initiative after having returned to their own country, and also Ade was just starting something with friends in Jakarta after the fall of Suharto. So that is how we started the RAIN network: a network for artists initiatives in Africa, Asia and Latin America set up by alumni of the Rijks, to support each other's practice and build so called south-south and south-north exchange. In the year 2000 this was quite new and very exciting.

Gertrude Flentge

'SMS – Short Message System', ruru house, 25 July – 15 August 2002

with artist-in-residence Tina Gillen, Jimmi Multhazam, Oscar Firdaus and Ade Darmawan

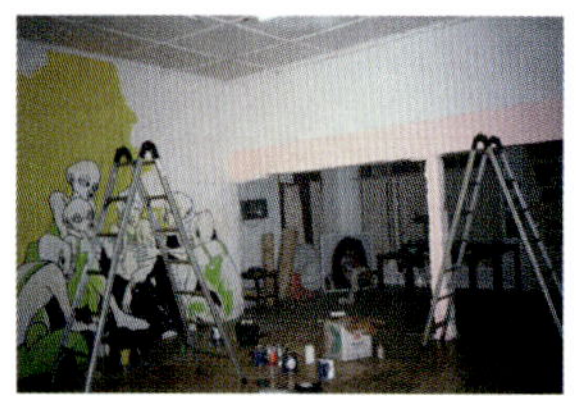

116

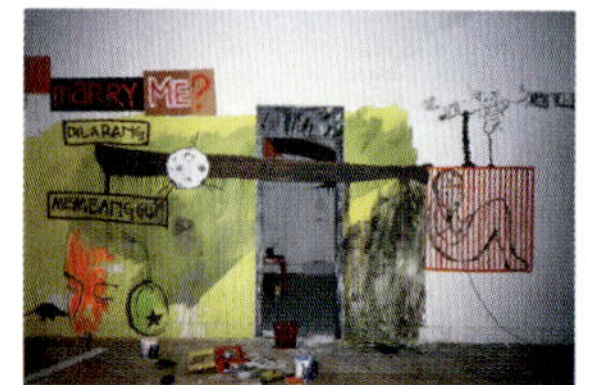

117

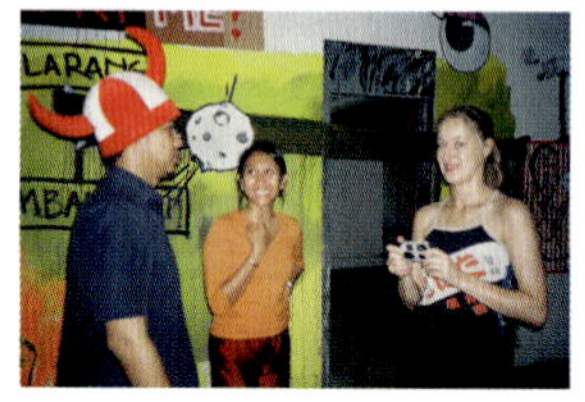

118

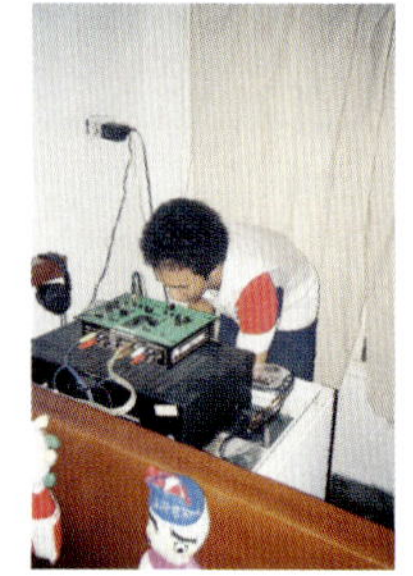

119

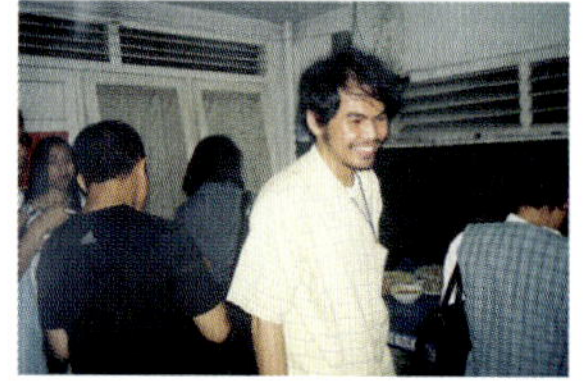

120

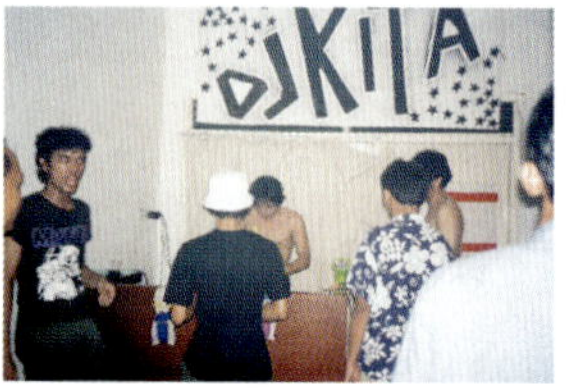

121

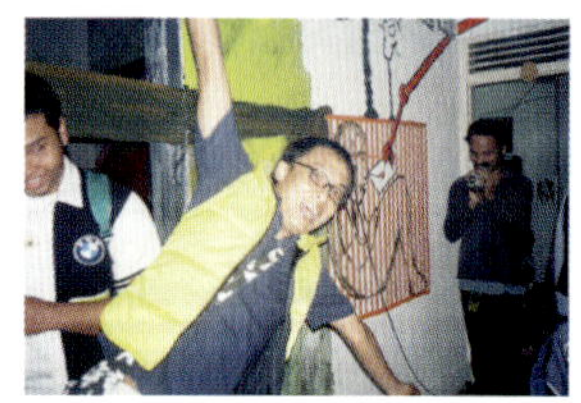

122

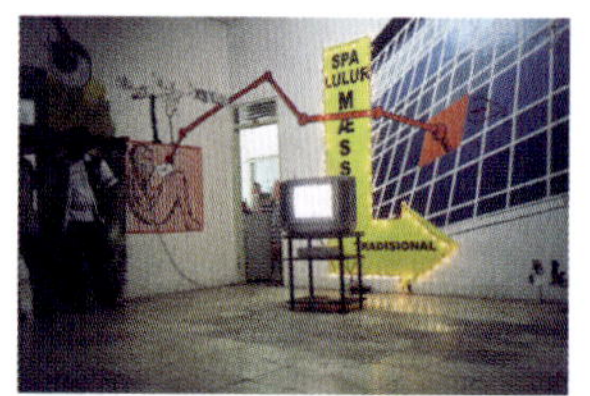

123

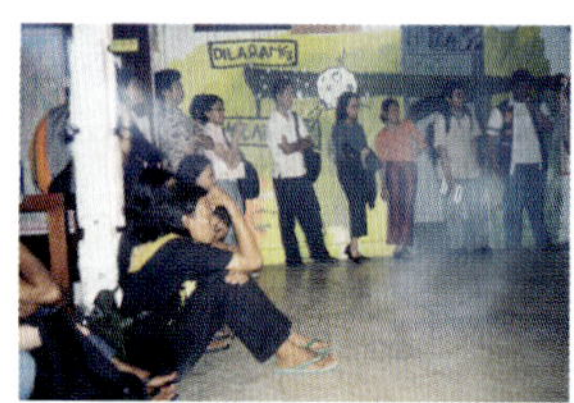

124

The subject of this edition is performance art in Indonesia. Most of the content comes from the transcription of a performance discussion in ruangrupa involving many performance artists and art critics from different cities.

ruangrupa

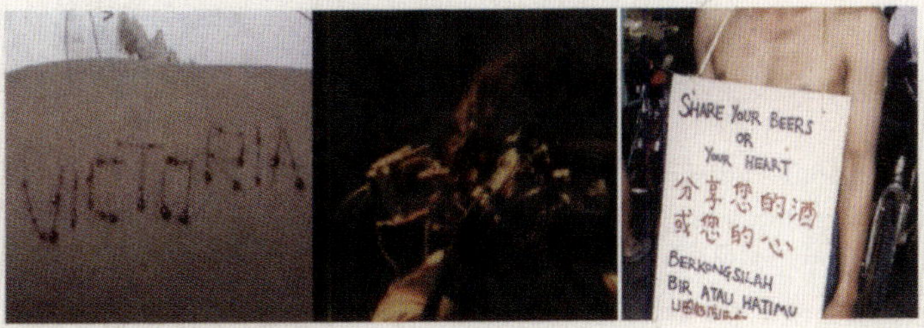

Questioning the Act: Between the Body and the Verb Mempertanyakan Tindakan: Antara Raga dan Verba

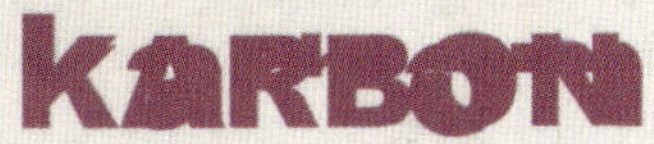

fourmonthly art journal / jurnal seni rupa empat bulanan

Edisi 4 - 0 9/ 2 0 0 2

We're not against something, but we build upon what's not there before. [People and institutions] can be antagonistic to what we do, but we don't just want to be reactive. We just keep on doing what we know, but we're not going to take over what universities or schools do.

farid rakun

Under the Suharto regime, Indonesia was a very segregated society. The ethnic minority populations in Indonesia could not enter the government or the army or state universities or they got prosecuted, and I was part of it even if I was born in Indonesia. Shortly after the regime was toppled down, ruangrupa emerged, and it felt to me like an oasis. It's plural, everything mixed together, without any hierarchy, ignorant of societal norms. I felt very much at home when in ruangrupa. I felt very safe since then.

Iswanto Hartono

In our ecosystem, we like to hang out – it's something we call *nongkrong*. Our space is like a big, warm living room. It's a place where people from different generations, backgrounds and skill sets come together. Our *nongkrong* sessions are free and open. We joke, share life stories, and most often, exchange ideas. Many of those ideas turn into collaborative projects – our version of project-based learning. One of the regular topics we discuss is: how can we stay productive, support each other and strengthen the economy of our ecosystem? It all begins with conversations – sharing ideas, concerns and what we hope to build together.

Daniella F. Praptono

I first learned about ruru from Iswanto Hartono (Wawan), who, in his early career, was a faculty member in the architecture department at Tarumanagara University (Untar), Jakarta, where I taught for about a year (in 1990). For Wawan, architectural education was too restrictive, and what bothered him most was that he found himself uncontainable. He thus created for himself a space for getting lost, at a neglected 'attic' of the school's building. I think he was in the state of self-exile. Every Thursday or Friday afternoon he hosted 'tea-space' for *nongkrong* (hanging out). We talked about all kinds of things from 'what is in your name' to 'kiamat' (the end of the world). Soon, Wawan left his attic and Untar for good. He found his true community in ruru. My subsequent meetings with Wawan were always accompanied by members of ruru. It was easy to connect. In some ways we were all products of Suharto era. While ruru emerged only during the transitional period, much of what they did was inseparable from the past. Or perhaps ruru carries a burden from the past, which after so many years has not become less heavy. This is because they inherited the mess from the Suharto era. Jakarta surely has changed as the city had to go along with time, but somewhere in ruru's work the new and the old coexist as if time has never changed. That is ruru's Jakarta.

Abidin Kusno

'Polygame', performance art programme, ruru house, 3 November 2002

with W. Christiawan, Mimi Fadmi, Hendrawan Riyando and Rahmat Jabaril, organised with Asbestos Art Space, Bandung

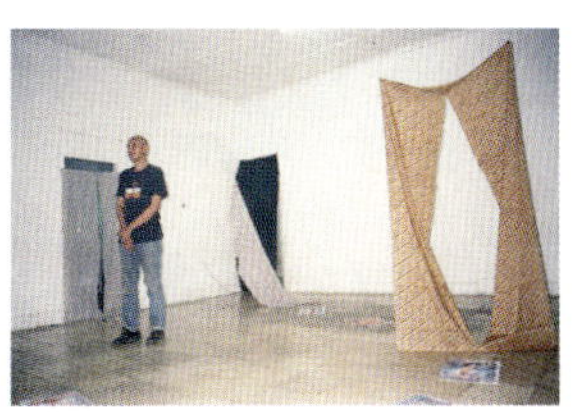

126

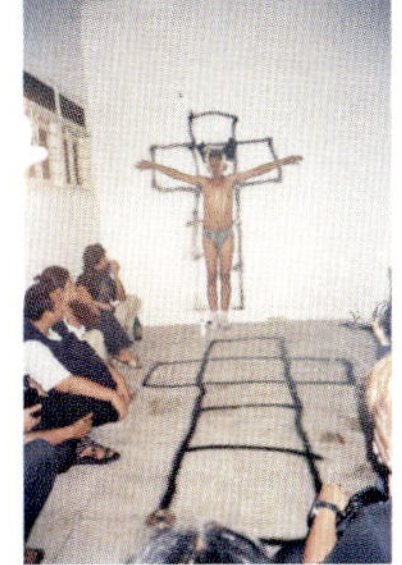

127

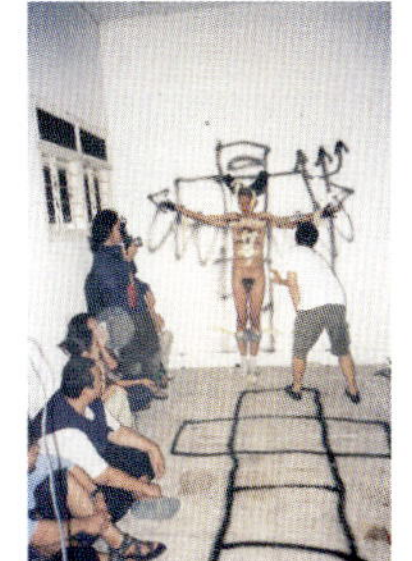

128

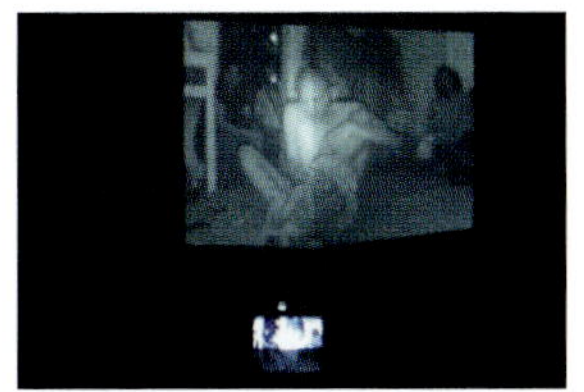

129

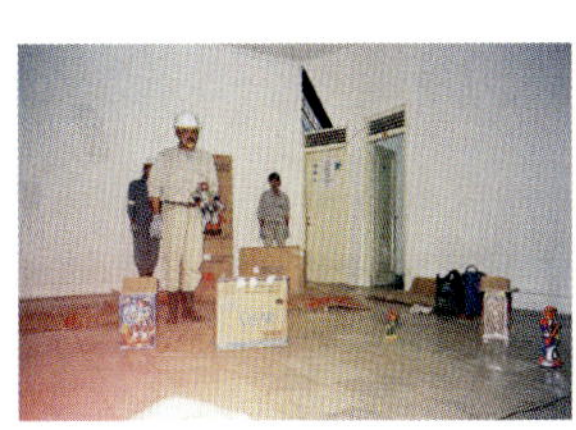

130

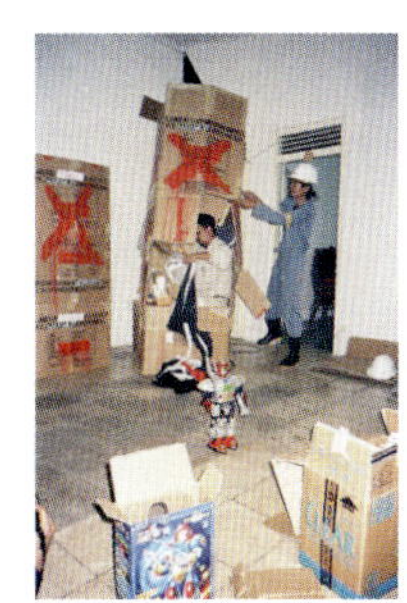

131

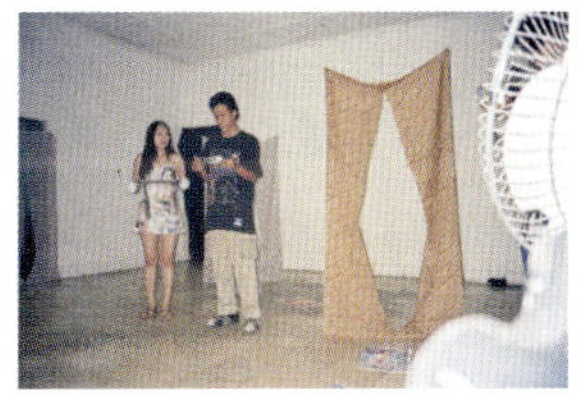

132

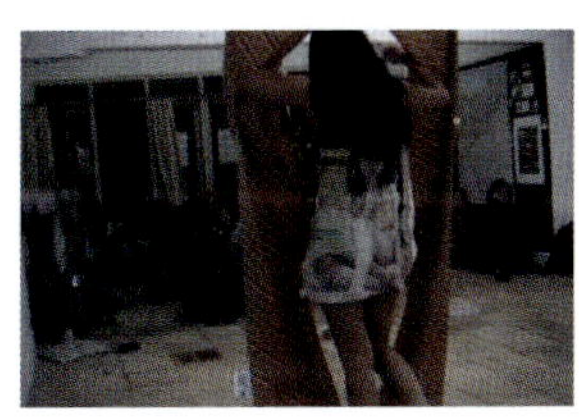

133

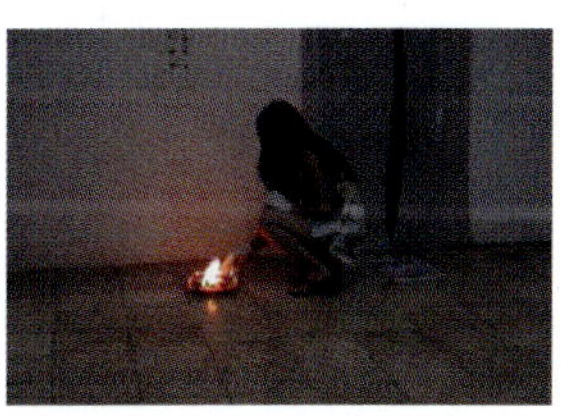

134

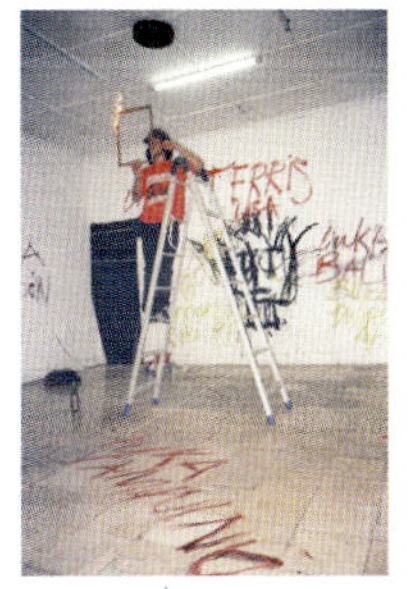

135

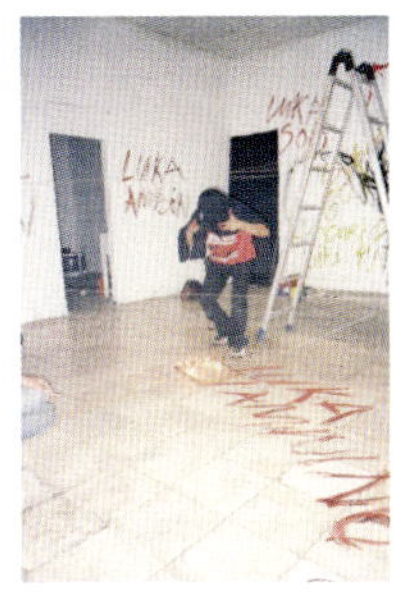

136

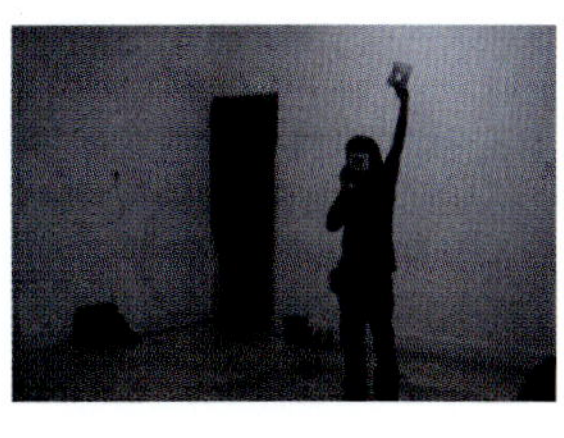

137

'Garbage Sale', ruru house, 26 January – 27 February 2003

an exhibition of artworks, collectibles, second-hand items and 'garbage', with all items offered for sale, organised to raise funds for ruangrupa's activities

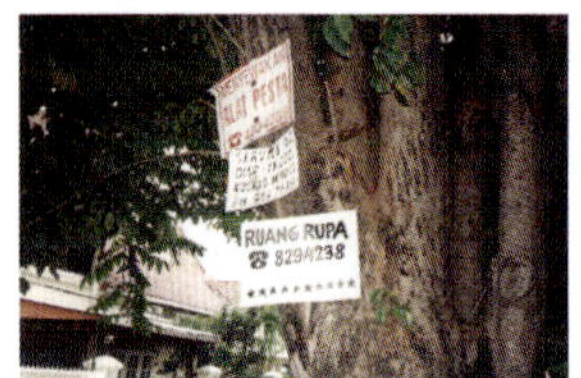

138

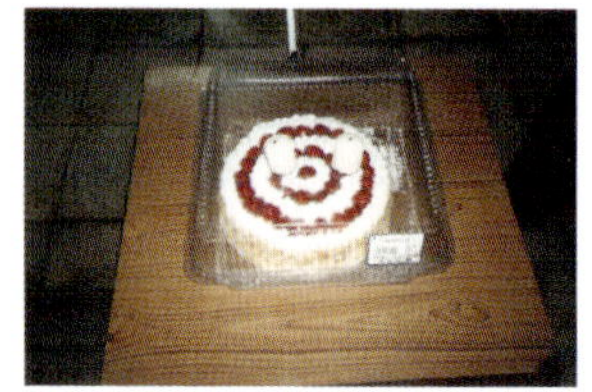

139

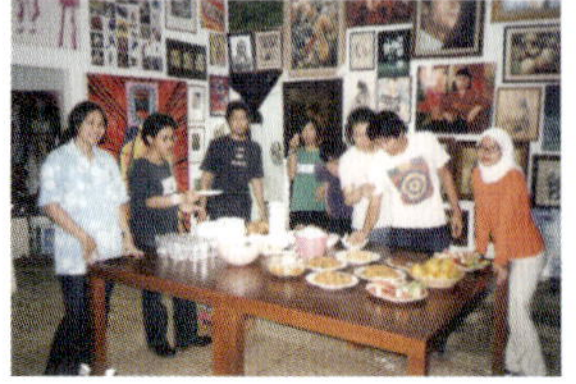

140

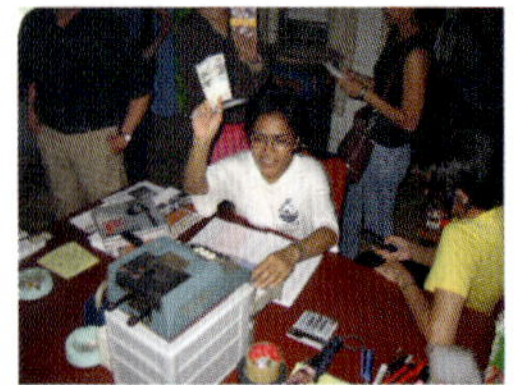

141

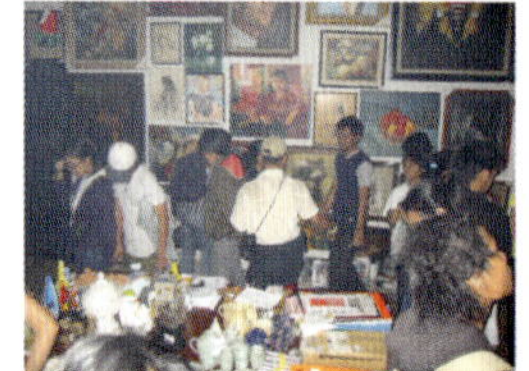

142

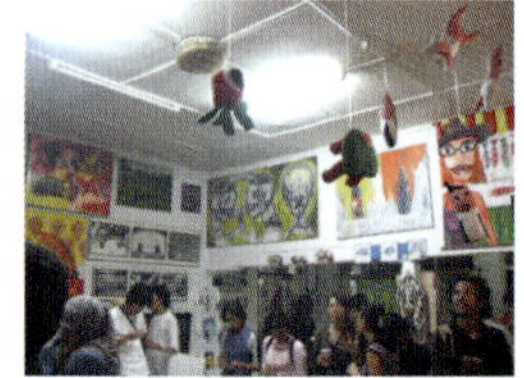

143

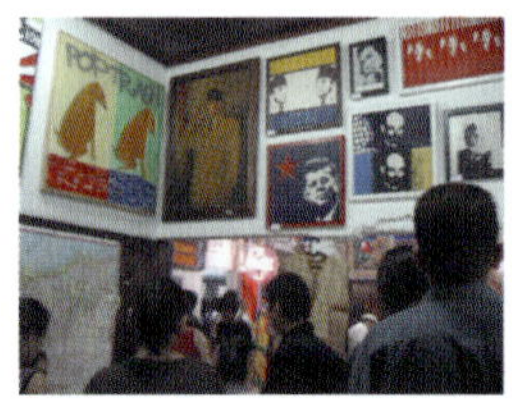

144

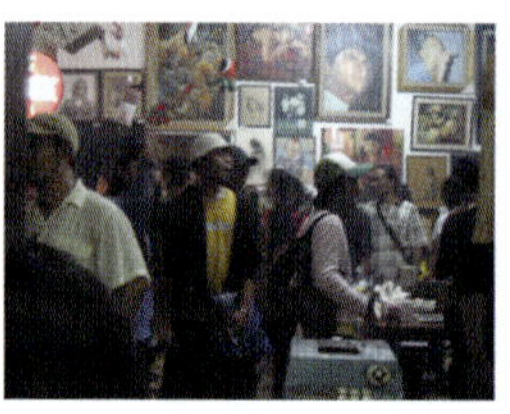

145

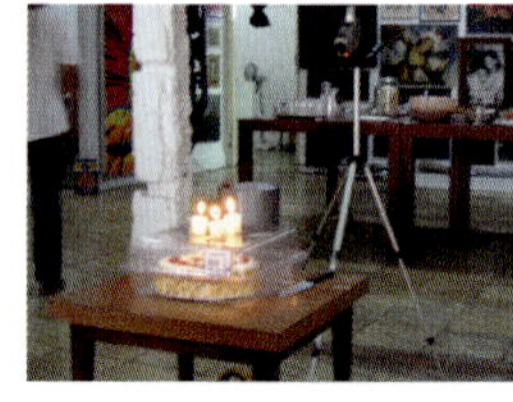

146

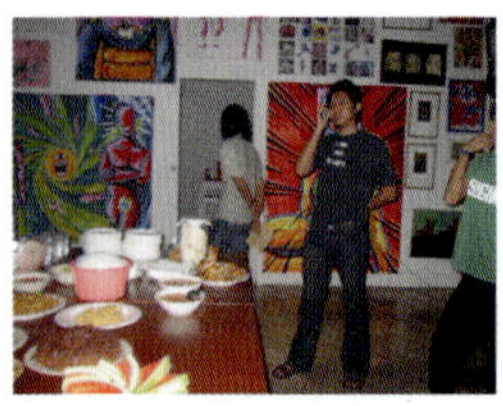

147

'Lekker Eten Zonder Betalen' ('Tasty Meal Without Paying'), Cemeti Art House, Yogyakarta, 2–30 March 2003 125

A group exhibition held in Cemeti Art House, Yogyakarta. In this project we are addressing the intensity as an alternative space in Jakarta. Jakarta, which is specifically associated with the stereotype: fast, aggressive, banal, amoral but pretending to be moralistic, alienated, chaos, sado-masochistic etc. ruangrupa addressing unstructured/undefined and not centralised (no curator, but fourteen artists working together), with all diverse ways and mediums in this project. ruangrupa setting up a platform/space for interaction between people, objects and the specific atmosphere of gallery space through the dinner party and music. All the traces of activities and objects, filled by memory and energy, are left in the gallery space for the exhibition.

ruangrupa

LEKKER ETEN ZONDER BETALEN

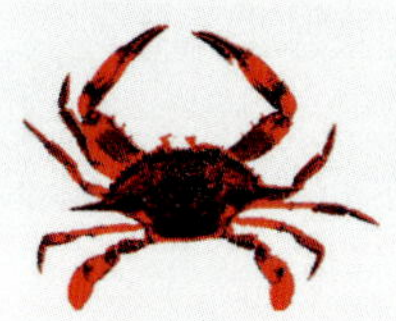

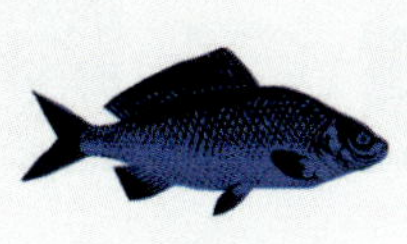

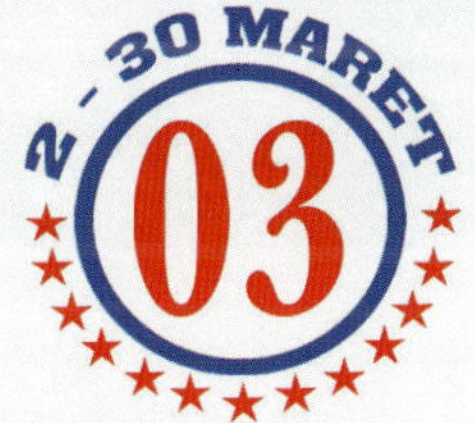

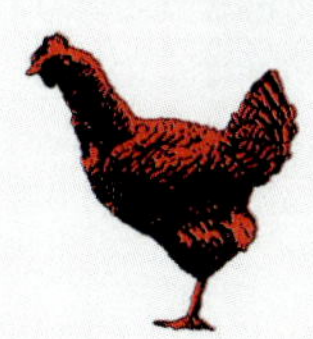

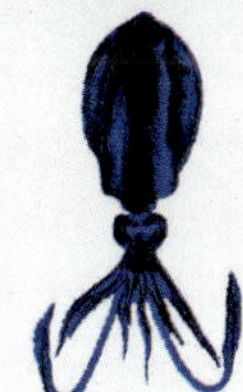

ADE DARMAWAN
ADITYA SATRIA
ANGGUN PRIAMBODO
BONDAN
ELIM
FARAH WARDANI
HAFIZ
HENRY FOUNDATION

INDRA AMENG
IRWAN AHMETT
LILIA NURSITA
MUSHOWIR
OSCART DE KEMANO
REZA ASUNG
RONY AGUSTINUS
TERESA STOK

ruangrupa

Pembukaan
2 Maret 2003
19.00 WIB

Pameran
3 - 30 Maret 2003
09.00 - 16.00 WIB
setiap harinya

Cemeti Art House
Jl. Dl. Panjaitan 41
Yogyakarta 55143
Tel. (62) 274371051

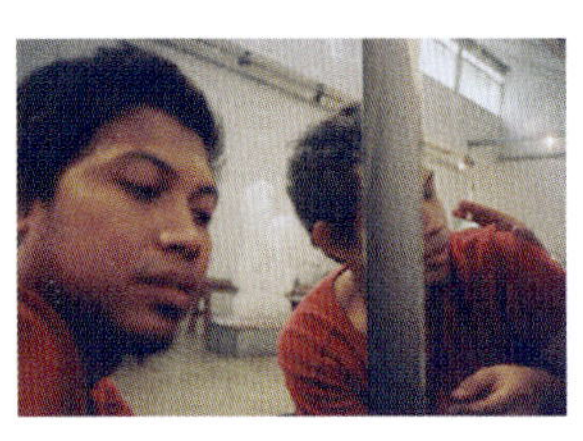

149

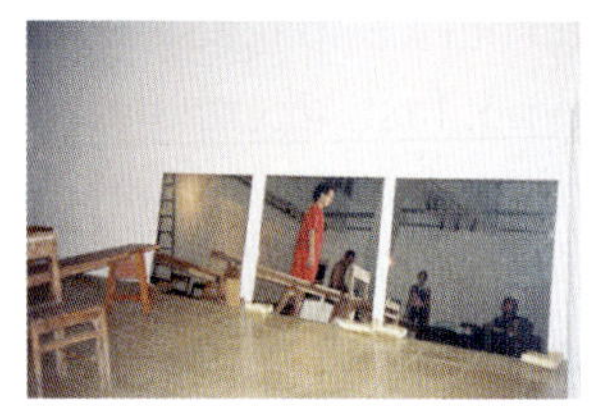

150

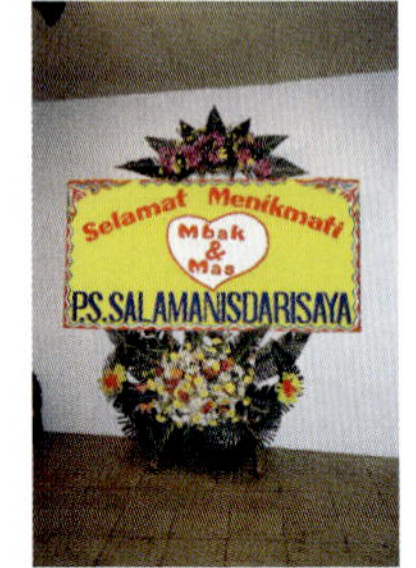

151

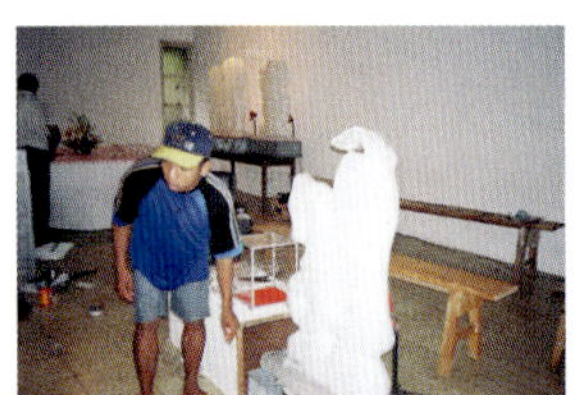

152

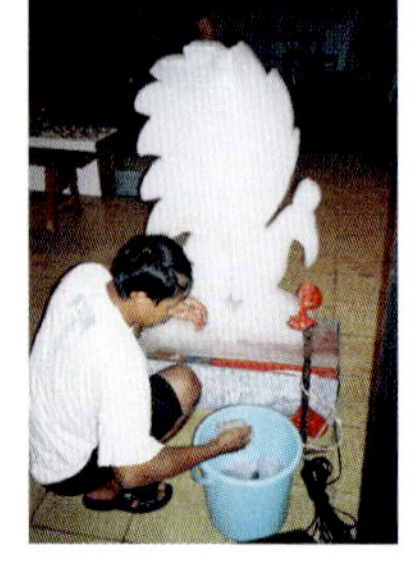

153

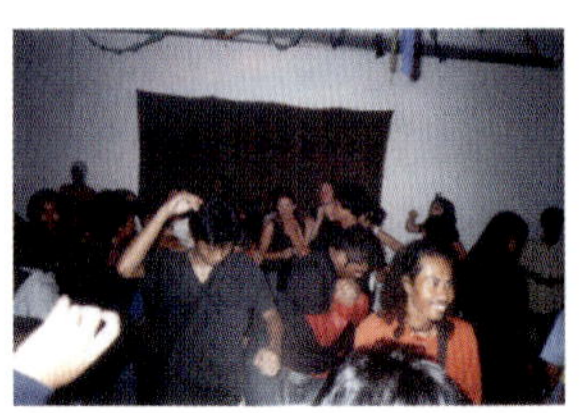

154

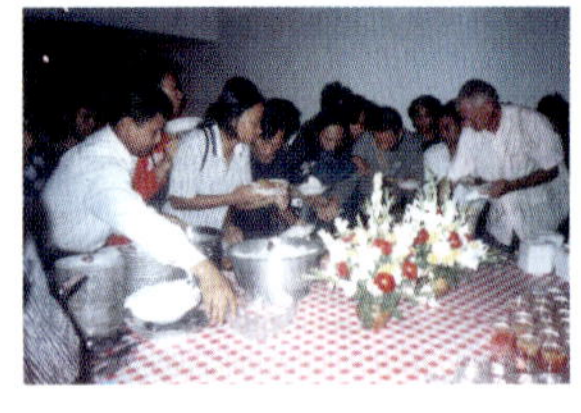

155

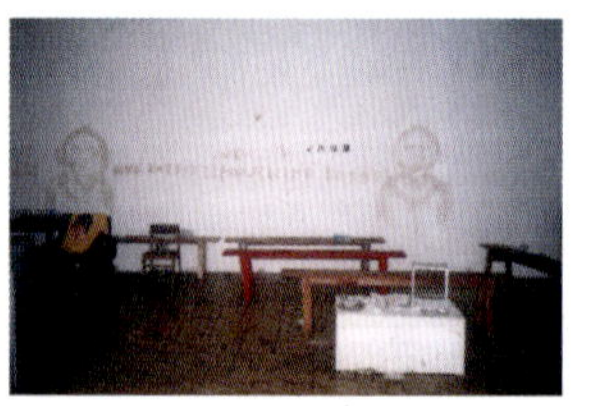

156

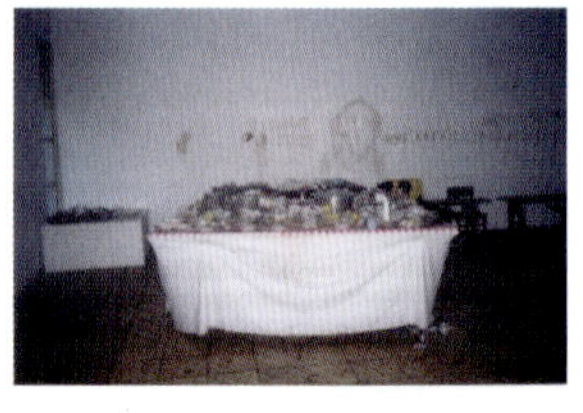

157

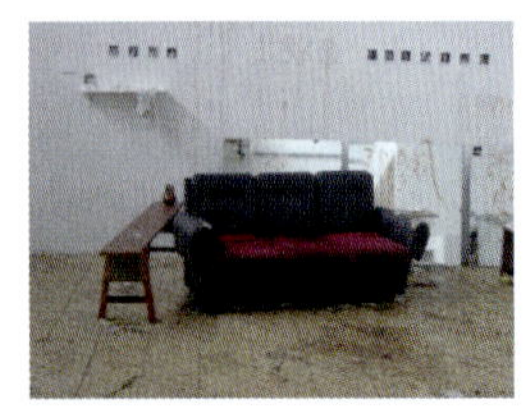

158

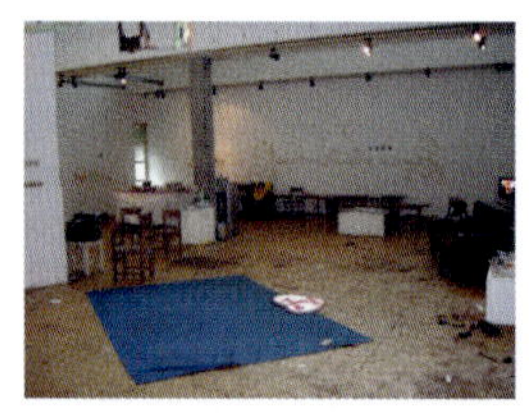

159

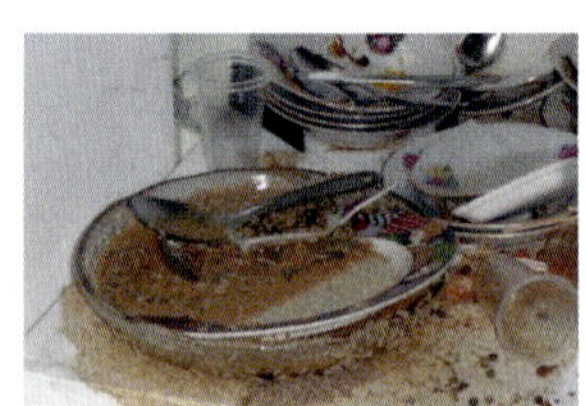

160

Ruang Rupa exhibition invites unique participation

Ade Tanesia
Contributor
Yogyakarta

Many exhibitions place visitors in a passive position: they come, observe and appreciate works of arts on display, and that's it.

But *Lekker Eten Zonder Betalen* (Nice Eating Without Paying), an ongoing exhibition organized by Ruang Rupa at Cemeti Art House, is quite different.

At the exhibition's opening, the visitors were not taken around the exhibition hall to observe the exhibited works. Instead, they came as if attending a party.

Upon arrival, the visitors were greeted with a flower bouquet with an inscription saying, "Have a good time, ladies and gentlemen. P.S. Nice greeting from me". The organizer, Ruang Rupa, is a group of Jakarta-based artists.

The hall was decorated with five ice statues and colorful lighting. A special space was set for the performance, upstairs, of a Jakarta band. A number of 1980s-style sofas were provided for the guests, as well as dinner. Beside the dining table, there was a wash basin and a table where oxygen tubes were placed.

After eating, the guests could enjoy the music performed upstairs and then they could dance, with music accompaniment arranged by a DJ. The longer the visitors had a good time dancing, the more chaotic the situation became as some of them began to throw pieces of cake at each another.

Interestingly, a video camera and a Polaroid camera installed on the wall recorded all these activities. When the party was over, all that was left were dirty plates on the table and floor, empty bottles and glasses, food remnants and chairs all over the place. All of them were left as they were. It's these "leftovers", along with the documentation that are now being exhibited.

Naturally, the exhibition raises question, what does it really offer?

The initial idea for the exhibition came from a different perspective in viewing the arts. In this perspective, artists are no longer the center of creation. They only stimulate things to happen and serve as mediators. Statements that art is noble are questioned and even discarded. Art cannot be expected to solve problems but is enough to inspire people.

Through the exhibition, Ruang Rupa created an interaction between the exhibited works and the viewers, eliminating distance between the viewers and the viewed, thus no longer presenting the final product of an artist's creation.

Ruang Rupa chose a "party" with good reason. In local culture, dining and food have a significant role for people from the cradle to the grave. Eating together does not simply fill an empty stomach, but forges solidarity.

Ruang Rupa understands the value of social relationships, given the fast pace of life in the artists' hometown, Jakarta, where people have become alienated from each other. In busy Jakarta, social life can be found at a cafe or restaurant, at financial expense. Only when they go to a birthday or wedding party are they free from a "paying" commitment.

With this phenomenon in the background, Ruang Rupa presents an exhibition without overtly introducing a specific artistic element. Instead, they have tried to introduce visitors to a particular social experience.

But Jakarta and Yogyakarta are not just far apart in terms of distance. In Jakarta people might be thirsty for relationships but in Yogyakarta, social relationship between people are still close.

Still, it was interesting to observe how the exhibition developed, observing how the visitors showed their true colors. In Yogyakarta, where people prefer to be modest and the very opposite of arrogant, some took their chance to show their true colors when the opportunity knocked.

In a way, if one believes there is nothing original or authentic in artistry, Ruang Rupa has tried to show it at this particular exhibition. This project, however, reminds one of the works of German artist Josep Beuys. In his exhibition in Italy, he invited a number of people to a discussion with him and then all the dirty glasses, cigarette stubs and pieces of paper scattered around during the discussion were later exhibited.

Still, social experience like Beuys' discussion with some of his guests, or the party held by Ruang Rupa, are a creative process in practicing art.

The distance between a work of art that is considered noble and the audience was questioned and consequently led to an idea to create something that would involve the public. In the West, this idea could be traced back to the Dadaist Movement in the 1916-1922 or the Fluxus Movement in 1960s, in which books on the history of art were burned.

The same restlessness has remained a trend in international contemporary fine art today. The artistic ideas and practice that Ruang Rupa is now offering are inseparable from the constellation of ideas in international contemporary fine arts.

Lekker Eten Zonder Betalen (Nice Eating Without Paying) exhibition runs until March 30 at the Cemeti Art House, Jl. DI Panjaitan 41, Yogyakarta. Tel: 0274 371015, e-mail: cemetiah@indosat.net.id; or cemetiarthouse.com

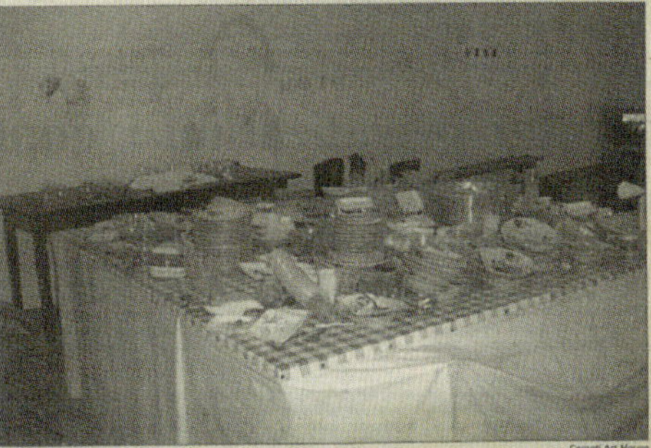

Cemeti Art House

Dirty plates, remnants of food and drink *(photo above)* and scattered chairs on a littered floor *(photo below)* make up an exhibition at the Cemeti Art House in Yogyakarta. The unique exhibition strives to involve visitors, and therefore, it does not present the final product of the artist's creation.

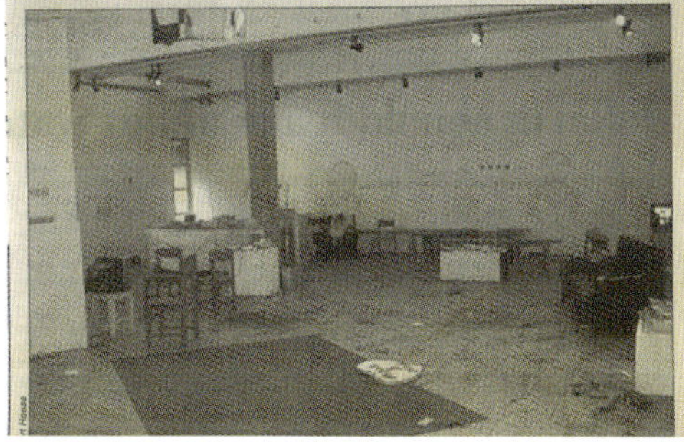

The Jakarta Post, Saturday, March 22, 2003

see also pp.376–87

'Surround', artist-in-residence presentations, ruru house, April 2003

with Reza Afisina, Mushowir, Deddy Perkasa and Chairul Rachman

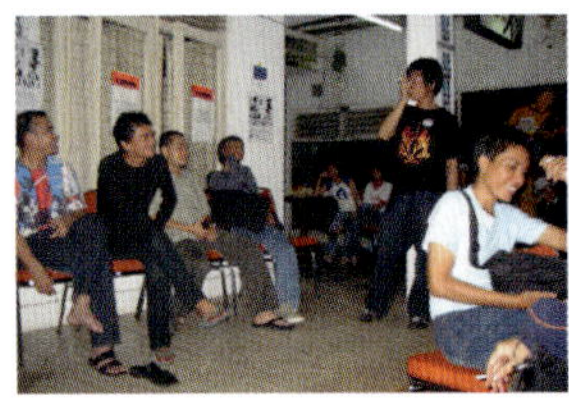

161

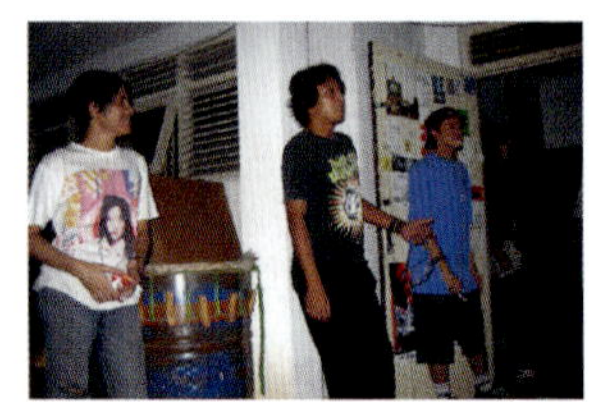

162

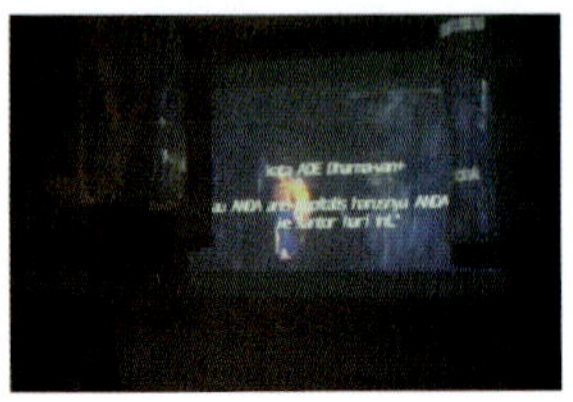

163

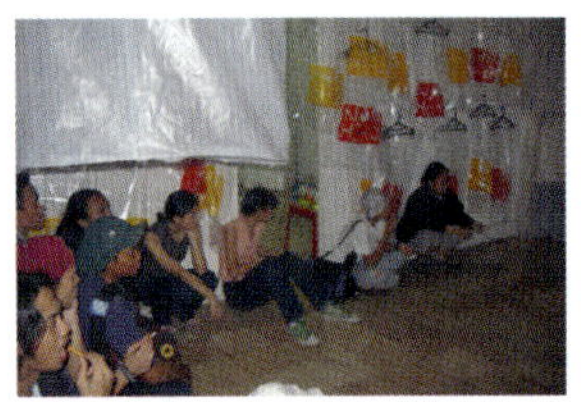

164

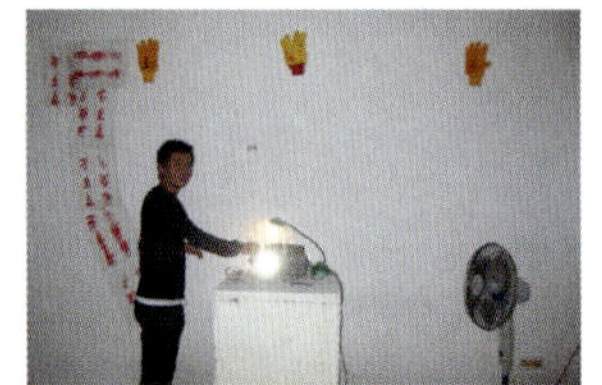

165

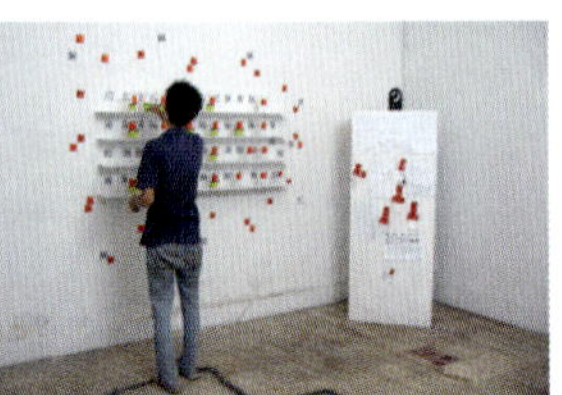

166

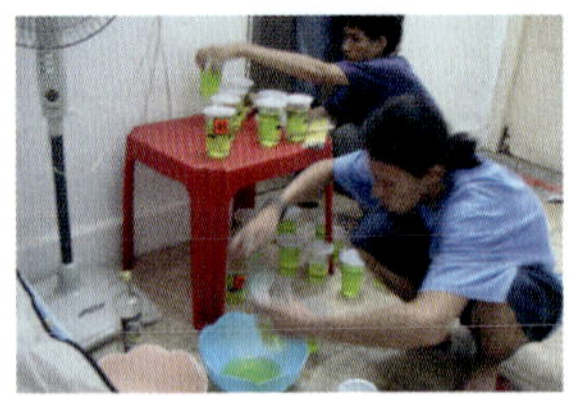

167

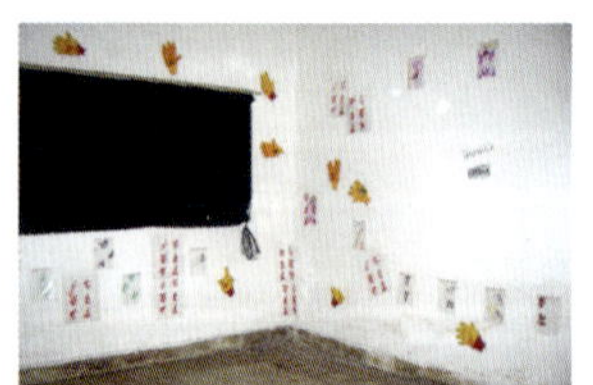

168

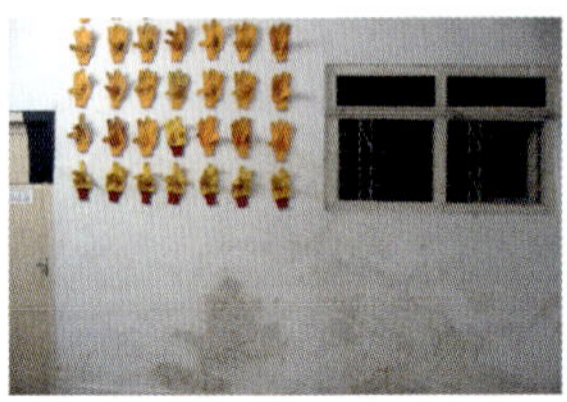

169

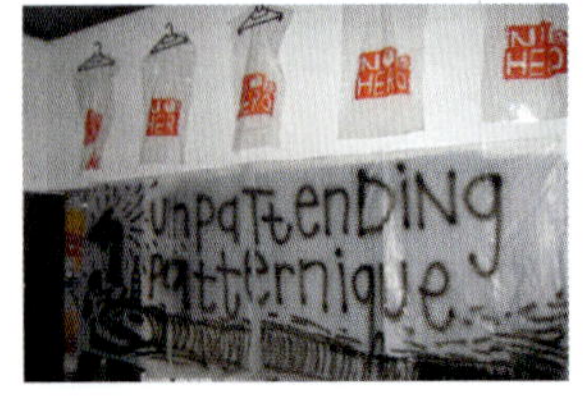

170

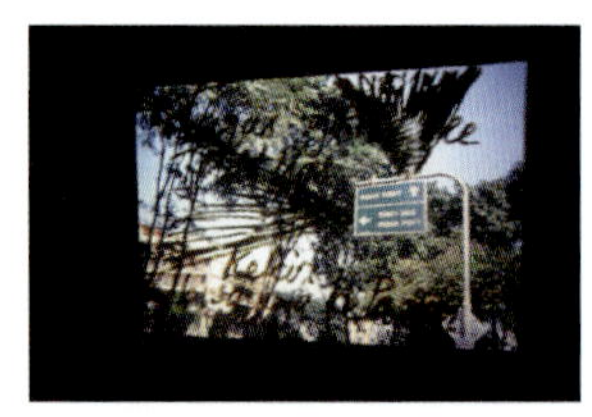

171

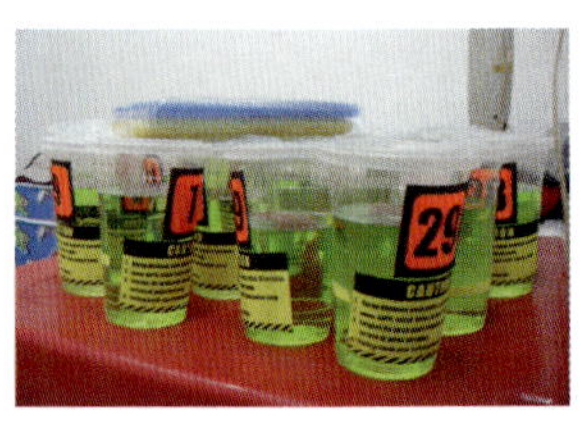

172

‘Seduction (Boys Don’t Cry)’, ruru house, 25 May – 7 June 2003

with young women artists from Bandung: Syagini Ratna Wulan, Prilla Tania, Dewi Aditya, Herra Pahlasari, Ferial Affif and Puji Siswanti; curated by Rifky Effendi

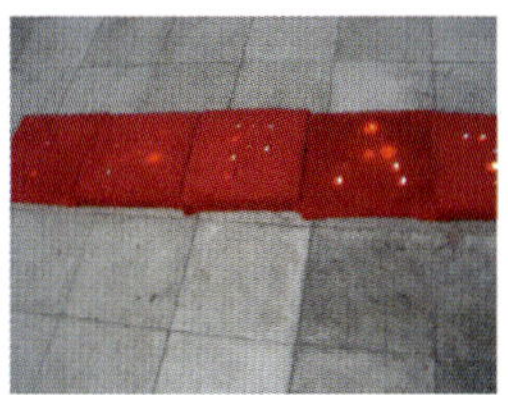

173

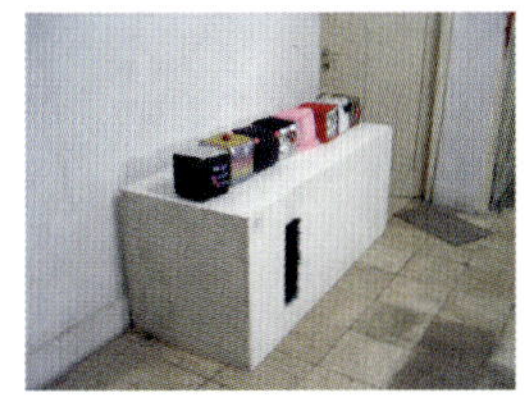

174

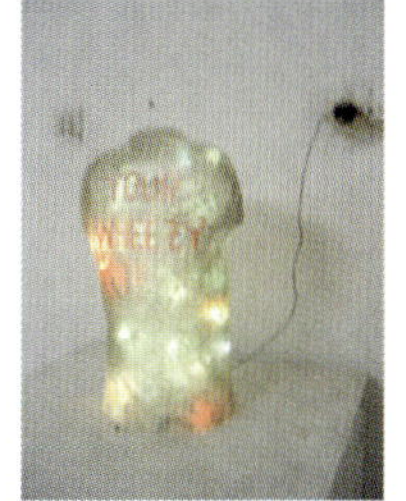

175

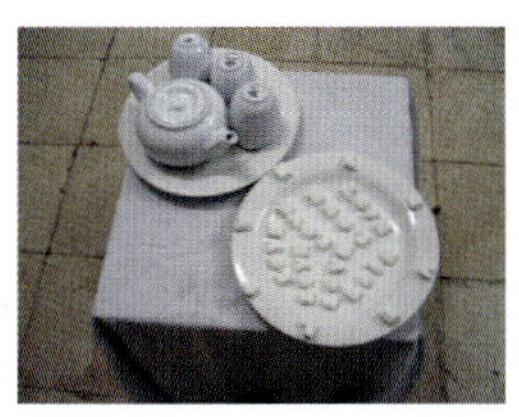

176

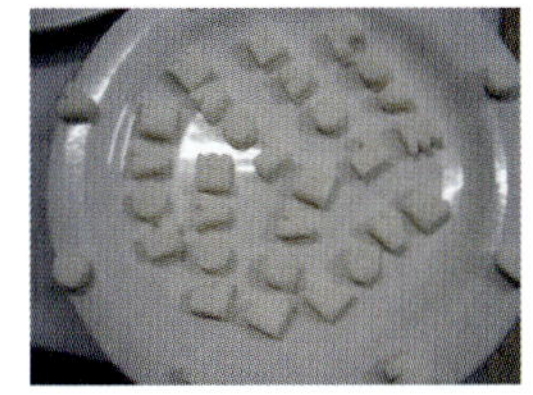

177

178

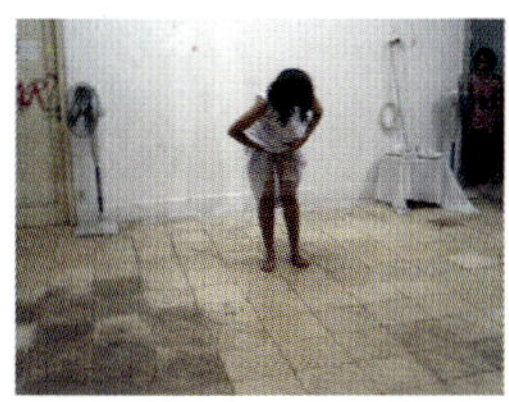

179

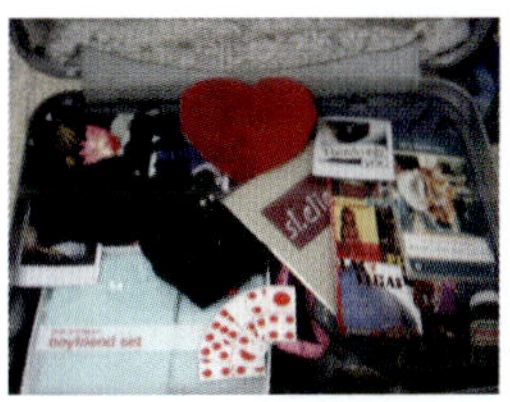

180

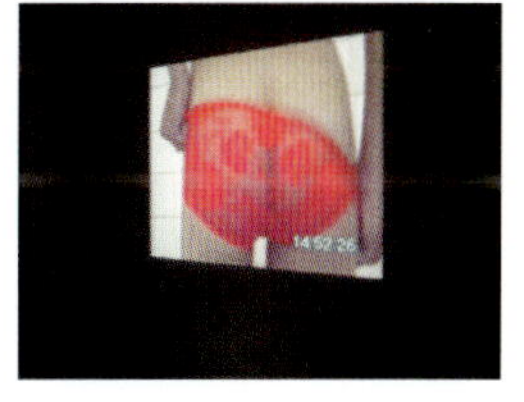

181

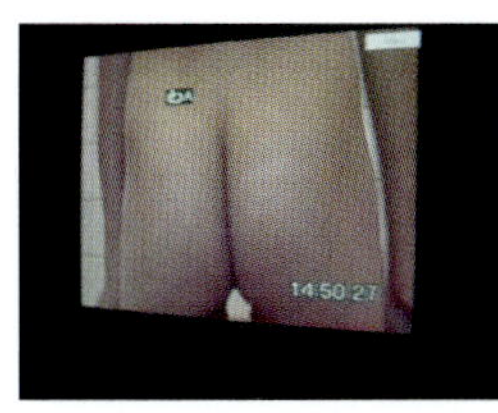

182

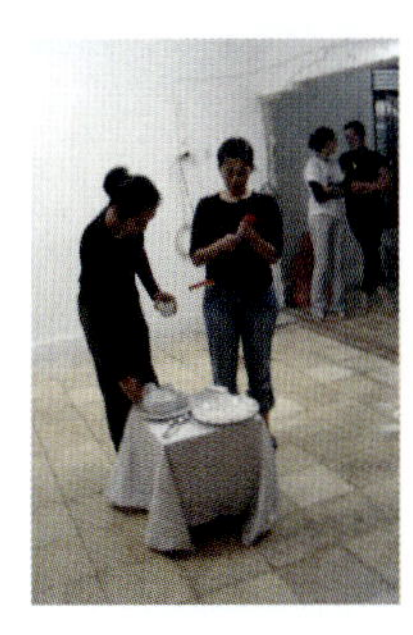

183

Within the last four to five years, we can see a rapid growth of alternative spaces in various places. The development of such spaces is surely related to the condition of art infrastructure in Indonesia. This phenomena also indicates a kind of tension that is happening in our art scene. In this edition, *Karbon* presents the issue of alternative space as its theme, based on such questions as: what kind of tendency has stimulated the emergence of these alternative spaces; to what extent do the spaces function as options for art to obtain more discursive and independent channels; and also the issue of trends, between the 'mainstream' and 'alternative', as well as the application of the term 'alternative' itself.

Karbon

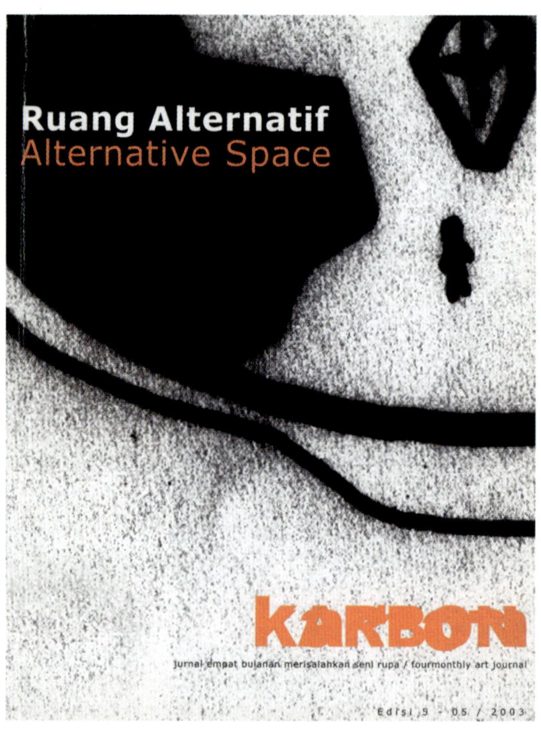

OK.Video – Jakarta Video Art Festival, Galeri Nasional Indonesia, Jakarta, 7–20 July 2003

OK.Video is a biennial media art event [and] a division of ruangrupa. The core purpose of the festival has remained intact since its birth in 2003, that is, to observe, document and examine the developments of technological culture and media that have altered our attitudes and shaped our views of the phenomena in our surroundings. Aside from this biennial festival, OK.Video is also running several other programmes that include work-shops, archives, research, as well as the production, documentation and distribution of media artworks in Indonesia.

ruangrupa

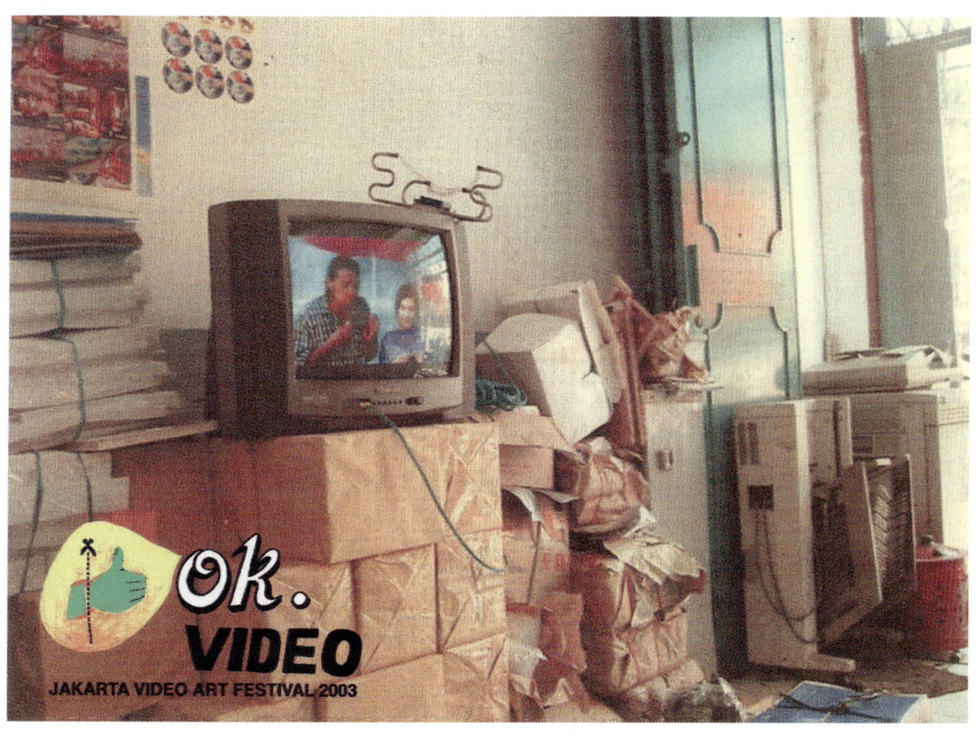

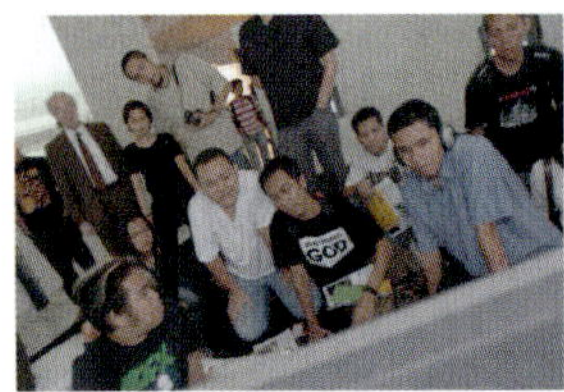

186

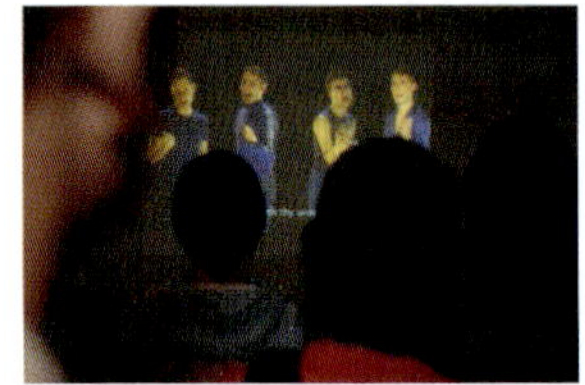

187

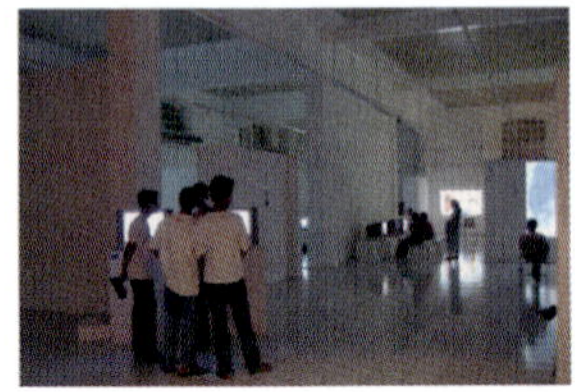

188

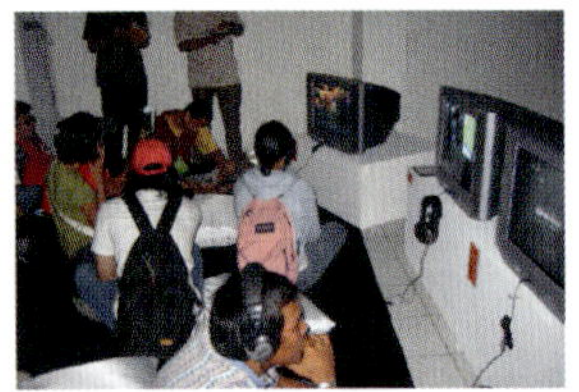

189

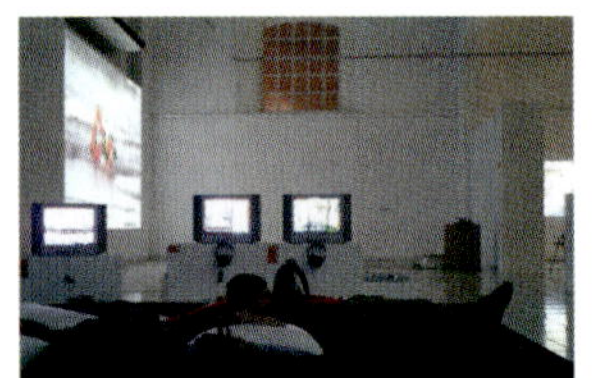

190

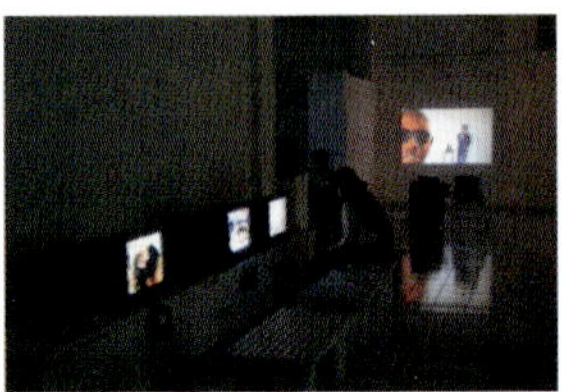

191

JAKARTA VIDEO ART FESTIVAL 2003

Galeri Nasional Indonesia. July 07th - 20th 2003

Exhibition
July 8th - 20th 2003
Monday - Friday:
01.00 - 05.30 pm and 06.30 - 09.00 pm
Saturday and Sunday:
11.00 am - 05.00 pm and 06.30 -11.00 pm

50 videoworks from Indonesia, India, China, Germany, Australia, The Netherlands, France, Sweden, Denmark, USA, Australia, South Africa, Brazil, Argentina, Finland, etc.

Special Presentation
July 8th - 20th 2003
At Main Exhibition Space
Galeri Nasional Indonesia

Videoart Center Tokyo (Japan)
Videotage (Hongkong)
PULSE (South Africa)

"TELEPIDEMIC!"
Video Program by Videoart Center Tokyo
July 10th 2003, 07.30 pm. At ruangrupa

Music Video Screening
July 8th - 20th 2003
Monday - Friday : 01.00 - 05.30 pm and 06.30 - 09.00 pm
Saturday and Sunday: 11.00 am - 05.00 pm and 06.30-11.00 pm

Videoworks by Indonesian artists who work with music as their basis of video exploration.

Workshop
- June 26th - July 3rd 2003
  At ruangrupa
  Conducted by Oliver Zwink, a visual artist from Germany, exploring the theme Urban Space in Jakarta" through video. This workshop will involve participation of young Indonesian video artists.
- July 10th - 17th 2003
  At ruangrupa
  Conducted by Videoart Centre Tokyo, involving students from art academies in Jakarta and other cities
- July 18th - 20th 2003
  At Galeri Nasional Indonesia
  Workshop presentation

Discussion
"Video Art and Contemporary Culture"
July 9th 2003 03.00 pm
At Seminar Room
Galeri Nasional Indonesia

Speakers:
Agung Hujatnikajennong - Indonesian art critic, curator for the OK Video exhibition
Greg Streak - South African artist and curator, founder of PULSE
Stéphanie Moisdon Trembley - French Independent Curator

Artist Talk
July 13th 2003 07.00 pm
At ruangrupa, featuring:
Stani Michiels - Belgian video artist

July 16th 2003 03.00 - 05.00 pm
At Seminar Room Galeri Nasional Indonesia, featuring:
Krisna Murti - Indonesian video artist
Katsuyuki Hattori - Japanese video artist, member of Videoart Center Tokyo, Japan

Exhibition. Workshop. Discussion. Artist Talk. Music Video

Opening / July 07th 2003 / 19.30 WIB / Galeri Nasional Indonesia, Jl. Medan Merdeka Timur 14, Jakarta Pusat

Contact : RUANGRUPA Jl. Tebet Barat Dalam I No. 26 Jakarta 12810, Indonesia T/F. (+62 21) 8294238 email : ruangrupa@cbn.net.id visit us : www.ruangrupa.org

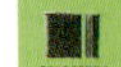
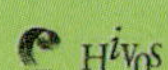
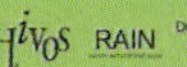
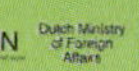
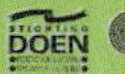
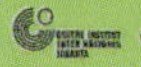
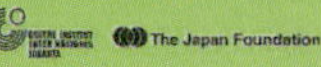
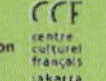
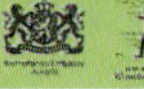
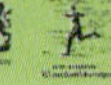
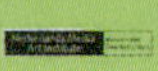
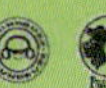

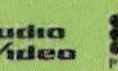
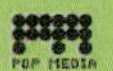

192

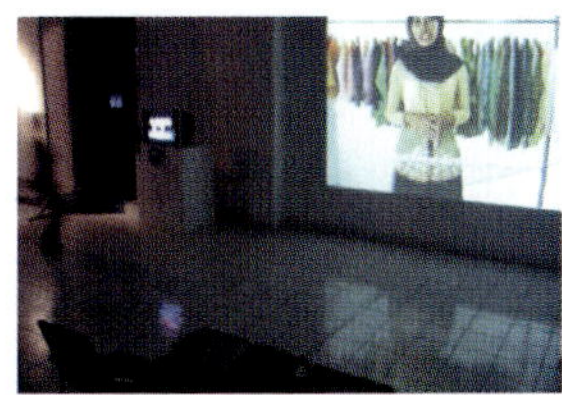

193

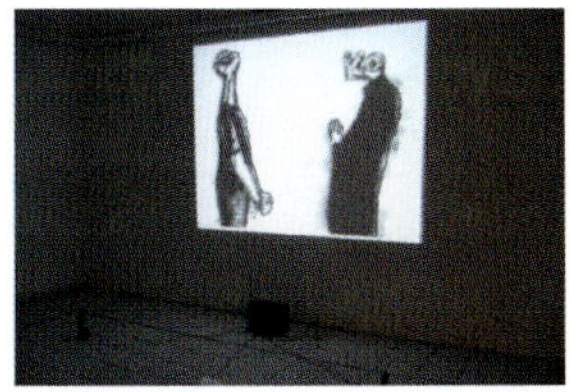

194

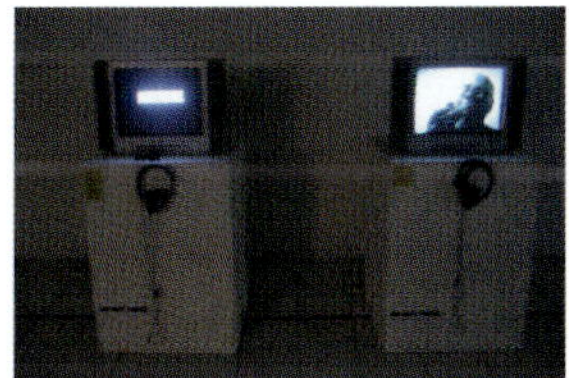

195

We went for a road show early this year [2003] to Bandung, Malang, Purwokerto and Yogyakarta as a sort of a warm-up to the festival. We held some presentations and discussions to measure the enthusiasm for the festival, and we tried to find some video art pieces that we had never seen. The result was quite overwhelming.

Indra Ameng

Organising an event that can be justified conceptually and technically is not an easy task. This festival involves a lot of existing elements, but we needed to do extra work to meet all the different visions from artists, academics, government institutions, the organiser, and public and private institutions.

Ade Darmawan

see also pp.388–409

Participatory art project curated by Farah Wardani, presenting works of Mushowir Bing, as part of a party featuring music by DDV (Club Moral, Belgium), Henry Foundation and DJ Y. Leadbeater. Visitors are invited to record secrets in tapes, creating a time capsule to be buried in the front yard of ruru house.

ruangrupa

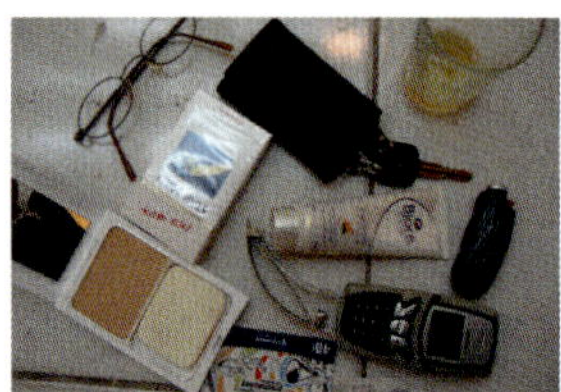

196

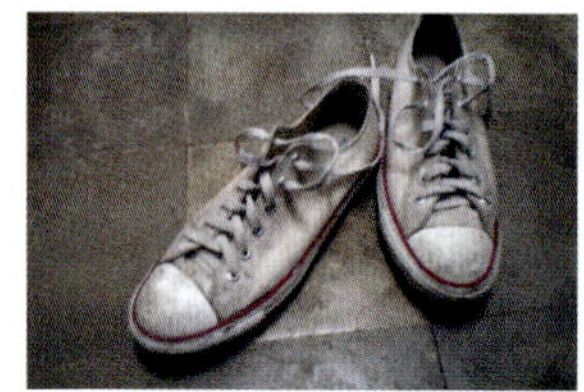

197

Artists' Talk: H.I.R.E. (Reza Afisina and Henry Foundation), ruru house, 13 September 2003

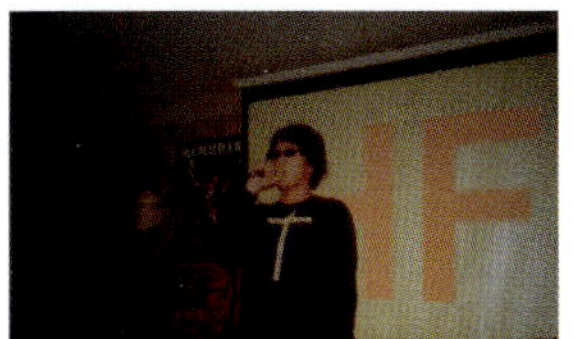

198

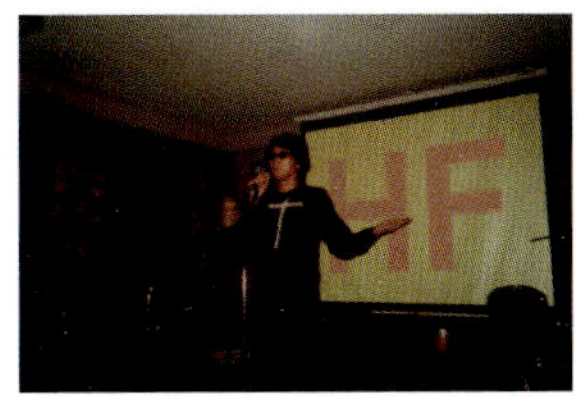

199

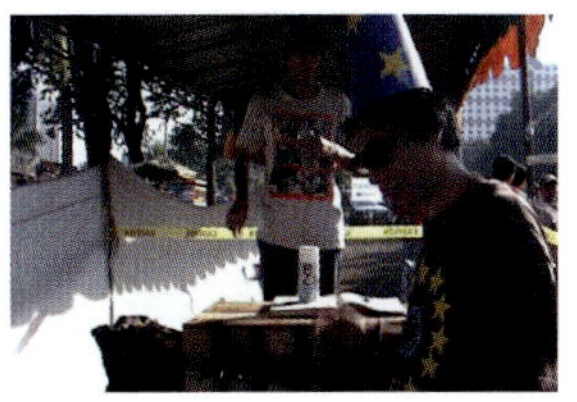

200

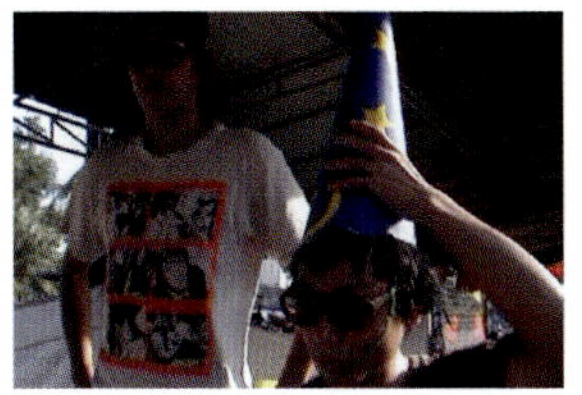

201

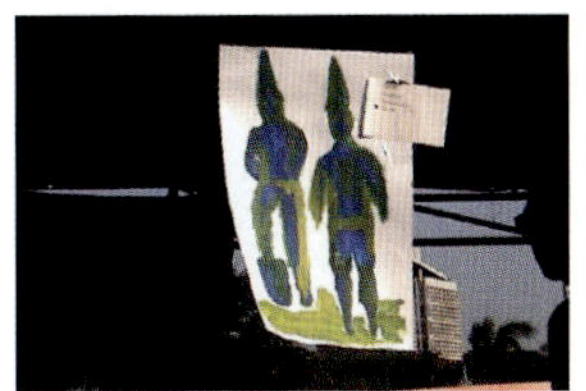

202

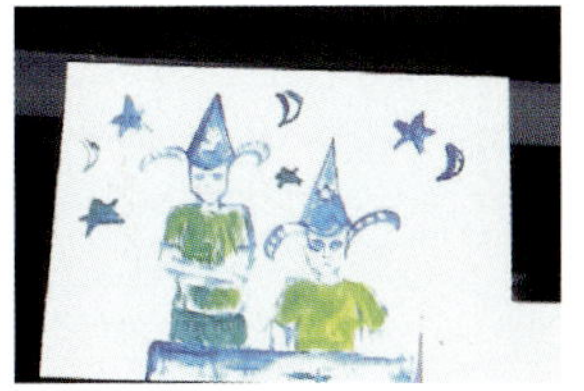

203

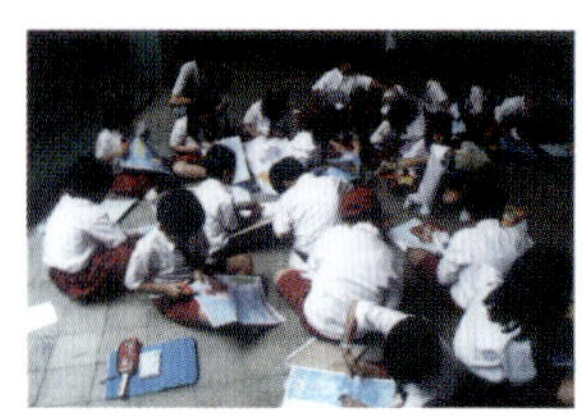

204

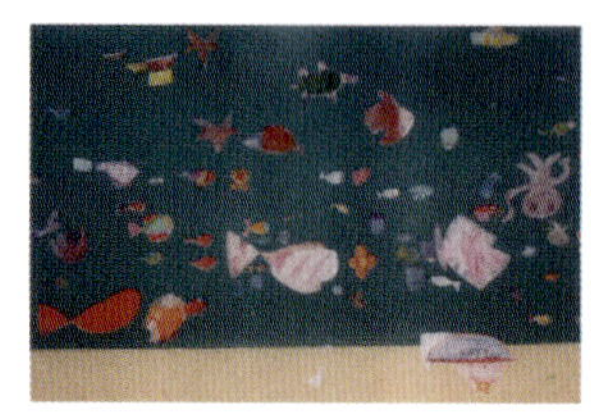

205

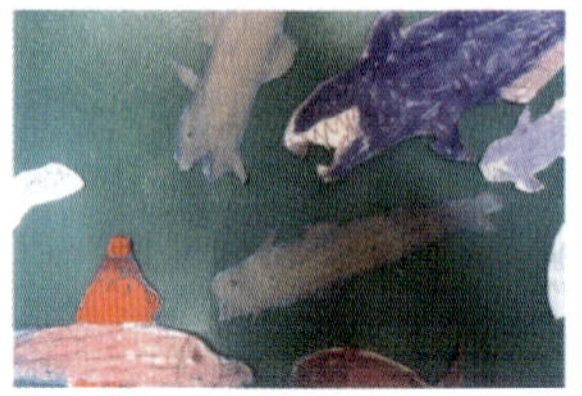

206

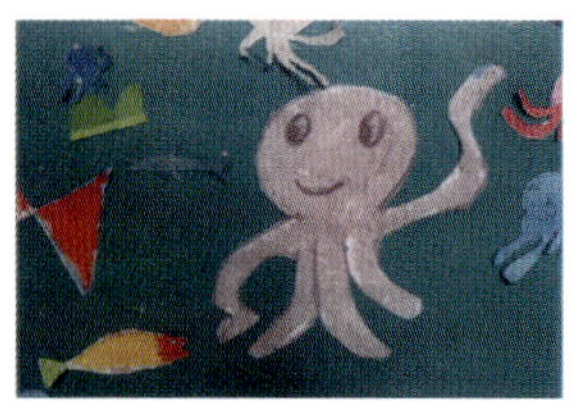

207

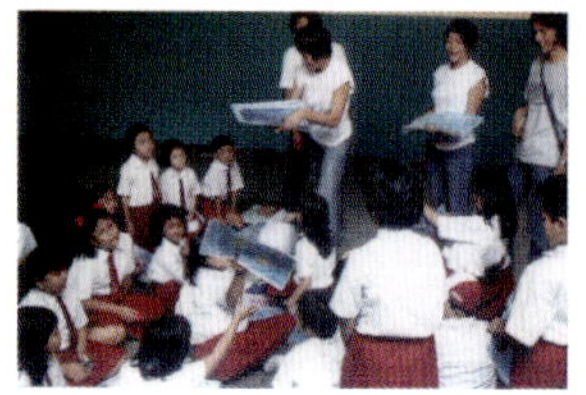

208

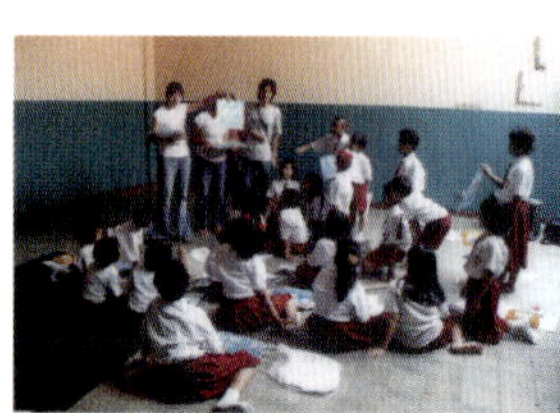

209

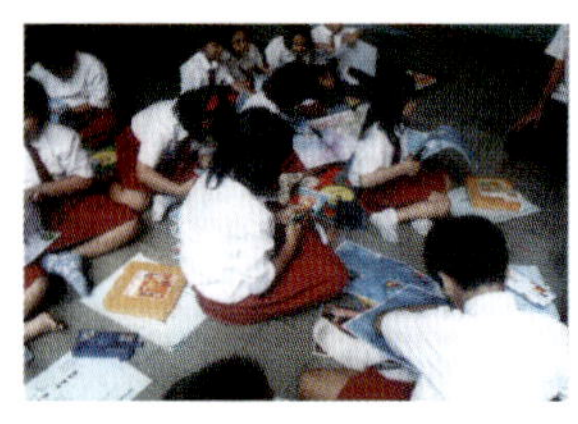

210

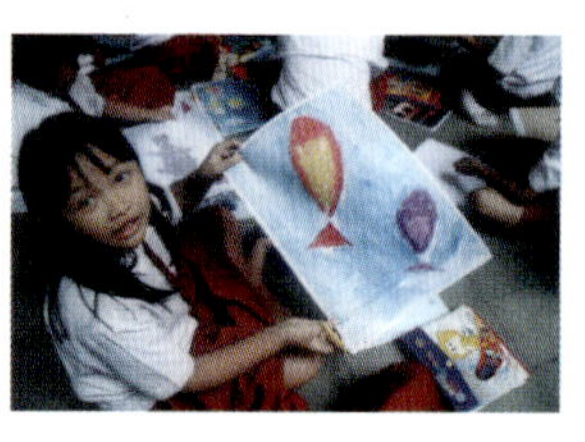

211

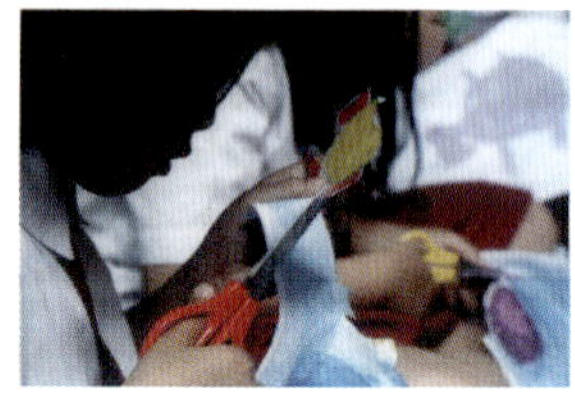

212

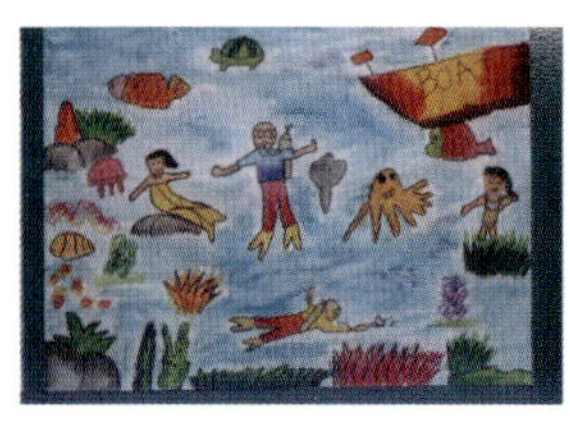

213

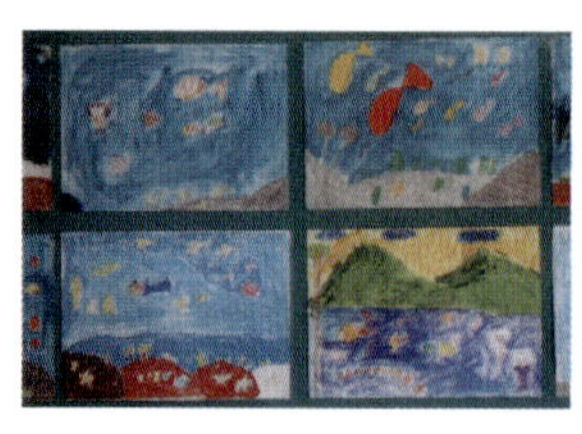

214

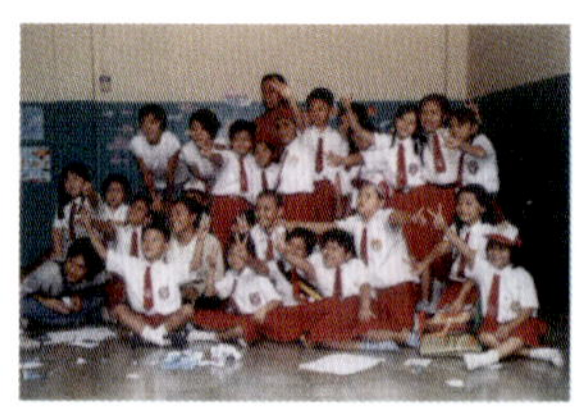

215

We did what we were passionate about and didn't think so much about categorisation, the attempt to define what we were doing at that time. In fact, to be categorised meant that you were visible to the authorities, and they would trap you. As practitioners, to be uncategorised was also a kind of strategy. So we did a lot of different stuff in the beginning, in the mid-1990s. And I remember missing Reza, Indra Ameng, Daniella ... so while there were not necessarily similarities in our practices, we did think about each other, about what kind of space we could create, you know, that could hold us together and that would enable us to support each other – and for that, there was no platform. We had to initiate it. In 2000, when we had our first exhibition and launched ruangrupa, we wrote short texts about how, with growing commercialisation within Indonesia, the arts were also becoming bureaucratic, institutionalised.

Ade Darmawan

In Jakarta in the early 2000s, I saw the kind of practice that I had in mind being done though in a different way, slow and quick at the same time, generous at all times. ruru picked me up at the airport to take me to their rented house. There was always food. There was always somebody available to talk to or take you around. This kind of being available, unconditional, almost 24/7 stuck with me. I think that's something that I still need to learn, that time is fluid. ... At the same time, they were not there to please people. I remember some curators passed by. They were not giving them too much attention either, saying that's the archive if you want to just check. There's a balance and an imbalance of hospitality. They don't really help people. Everything's experienced. The house is always open and you just find out by yourself.

reinaart vanhoe

I think I shared similar attraction and chemistry about ruru with many other post-Reformasi Jakarta aspiring artists at that time, the independent, egalitarian and alternative spirit that we found so refreshing, inspiring and fun. One thing to understand is that around early 2000 the scene was totally not like now, 'contemporary art practice' was still something we treated as a 'discovery' as well all the discourses revolving around it, let alone the market and academy. So what ruru did was opening a gateway and trailblazing a new generation(s). I was seriously thinking of joining ruru structurally – Ade also offered me a position around 2005, as by that time ruru was already at the beginning of shaping up its organisation formally. I was a bit torn because of classic reasons, financial and family, so I decided to stay as a 'productive *nongkrong* friend'; then in 2006 I moved to Jogja to run Indonesian Visual Art Archive. I do think it was the best decision, since we developed collegial working and friendship relations so well, even until now.

Farah Wardani

culture

A cultural space, where dialogues as well as production, distribution and shared of knowledge, could occur.
engaging with the widest landscape of arts and cultural production and involving the public within the arena of production, such as artists, students, the society, multi-disciplinary practitioners, and communities and organizations working in the arts, culture, and social field and their involvement that contributed to the contemporary art discourse

ruangrupa moves into its third house, Tebet Barat Komp Kejaksaan, Jakarta, 2004

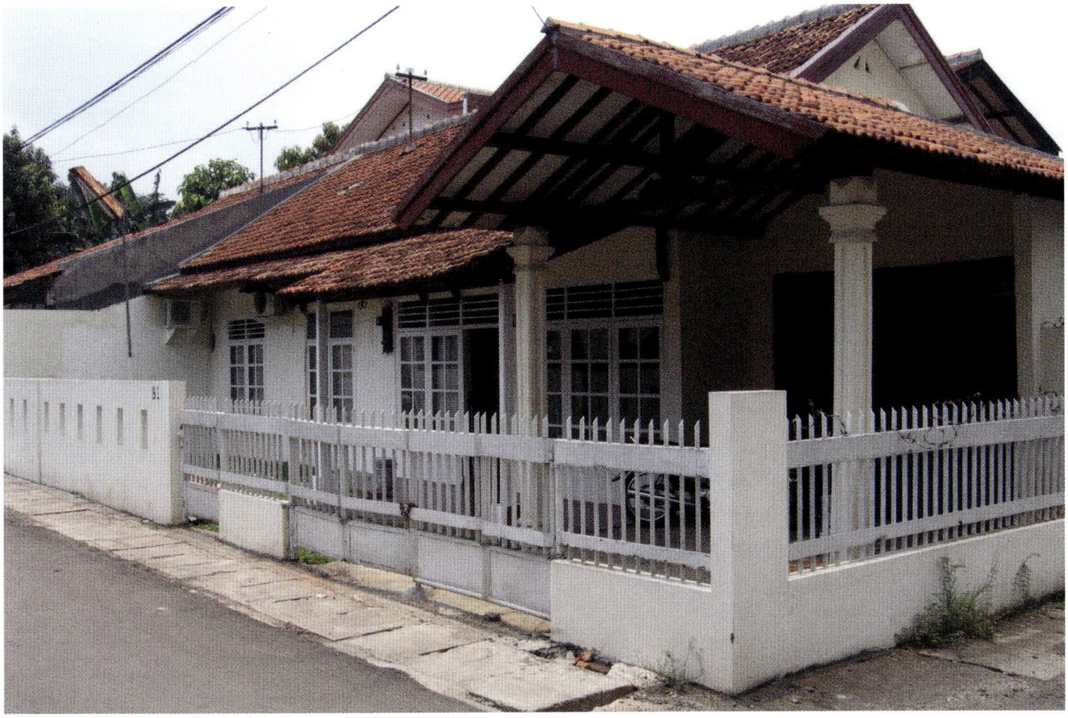

216

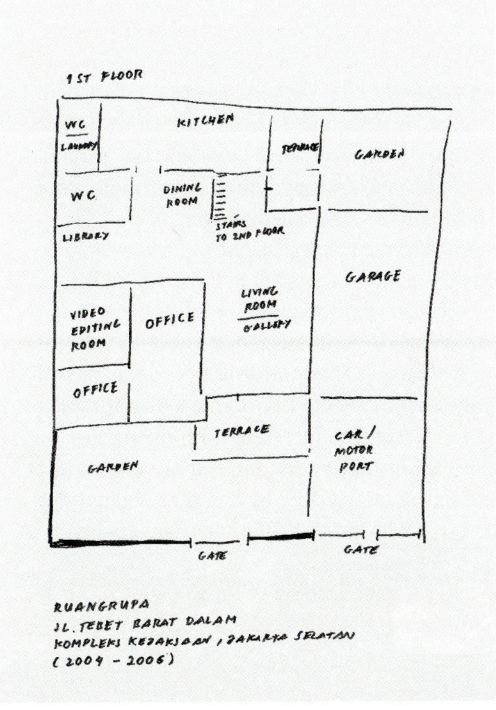

217

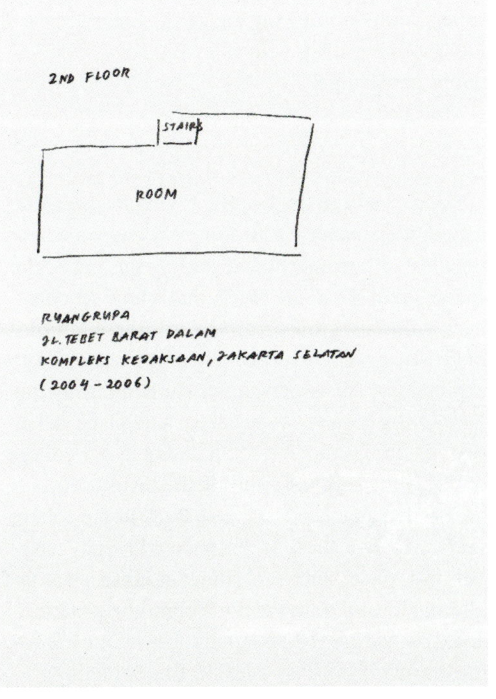

218

ruangrupa moves into its third house, Tebet Barat Komp Kejaksaan, Jakarta, 2004

In 2004, Jalan Tebet Utara Dalam, one of the main streets in Tebet, was transformed into a vibrant shopping street made up of local-brand apparel stores, a skateboarding shop, a designer's shop and a themed café. The shops are well known as 'distro' (short for distribution store). What makes this street different from Jakarta's other shopping precincts is the ambient characteristic of the space created, with diverse cultural activities and events happening within these areas (such as the launch of new indie brands, DJ performances, street music concerts, contemporary art show openings, online radio stations, a vintage clothing Sunday market, writers' workshops and street cinema pilot screenings). All this presents the area with its 'cultural ambience', together with a space for 'youth activism'. If you go there then you will see the vibrancy of these places, and the major cultural transformations that have happened in the post-Suharto era. Something that must be mentioned is the growth in micro business in university cities like Bandung, Yogyakarta and Jakarta. These shops, with their local brands of designer goods, have become a kind of guerrilla force against the powerful global brands and logos usually found in Jakarta's posh supermalls. ... What was previously private space in Tebet has been converted into a vibrant public sphere, transforming the bungalow-lined streets into shopping strips with cafés and spaces for public gathering.

Iswanto Hartono

We don't want to impose the Living Room as a method, because it's always everywhere anyhow: the most important thing regarding this particular space is that it's a safe place, that's how we connect within us, growing up towards these notions of artistic practices, especially in the sense of expressions. As we grew up or studied during the New Order regime, we needed a safe place rather than the things that were happening in our college or inside the campus or inside the institutions. We needed an extended space. Back in the college years, we never thought that we could really have our own space, since everything in Jakarta was not affordable, and that was not a common practice. Later on, we got to know that most of our friends, mostly in Yogyakarta, were starting something from their own houses – like Taring Padi, Cemeti or any group connected to our historical context. So that was the only safe place for us to really stay together, discuss and talk about several things, to make events. Every time every collective organisation or artist group rented a house it was because that's the basic need, so that everyone could live in the same place. Sometimes it's not necessary to form as a collective, like many painters' groups that belong to some local cultural societies, and rent the house together to work together, but for us back in Jakarta, we needed a space that was also meant for living. Since it was difficult for each of us to rent a space, it was better to gather collectively, also because at the same time ruangrupa was forming itself as a collective. So that's why the house is so important for us, and this is not a method: it's the way we see ourselves, based on necessities; it's the place for us to live and work at the same time.

Reza Afisina

I arrived in Jakarta in January 2004. At that time, ruangrupa was in this tiny house in South Jakarta. Everyone was coming in and out. People were living there, working there, doing things together. Everything happened in this house. It was really chaotic but quite organic. We were discussing OK.Video here and there. It was a very slow process, because no one was like, okay, we are going to decide it today. I was used to working in a Japanese way so I was very frustrated, like, who's going to do what and when. But then one day, we went to this market where we could buy pirated DVDS. It's one floor of a small department store where you can find cinemas from all over the world. For me it was like cultural education, because you have access to all films around the world for such cheap prices. We continued discussion and started to be interested in piracy as a cultural study strategy. That's how the concept came initially. So we collected work that uses appropriation as strategy to intervene with the public spaces or history or discourse. It became an international show, because by that time, ruangrupa already had a massive international network.

Che Kyongfa

‘Top Collection’, ruru house, 28 February – 10 March 2004

with Irwan Ahmett, Indra Ameng, Wimo A. Bayang, Henry Foundation, Dimas Jayasrana, Nuraini Juliastuti, Andang Kelana, Angki Purbandono and Farah Wardani

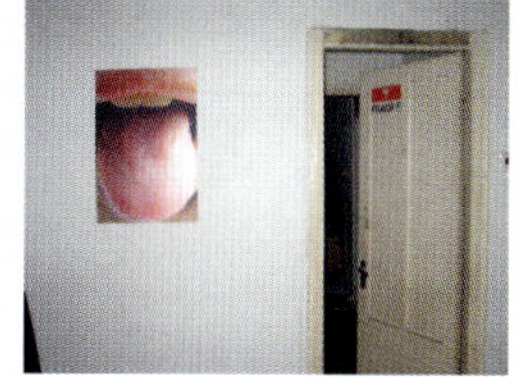

219

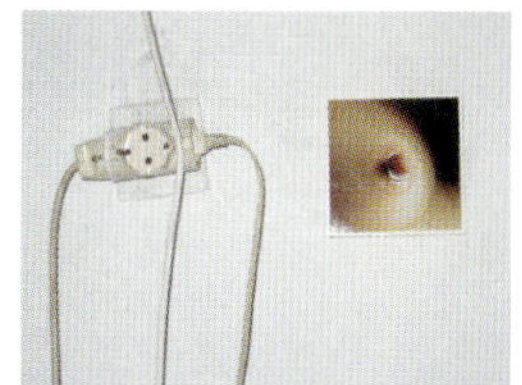

220

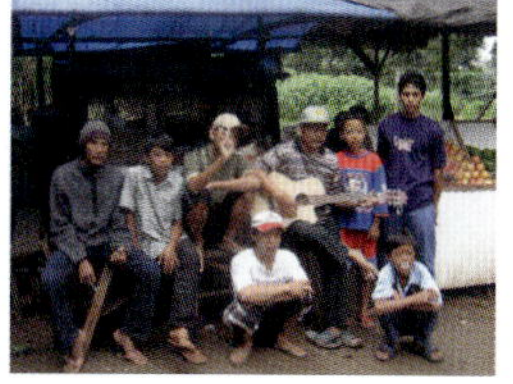

221

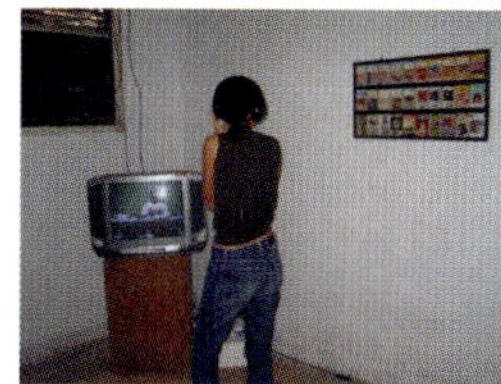

222

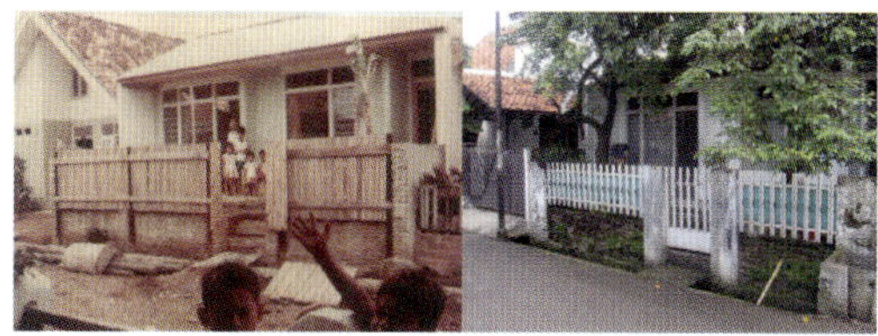

223

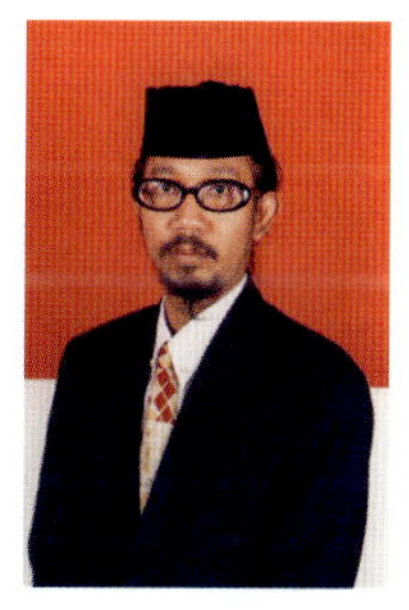

224

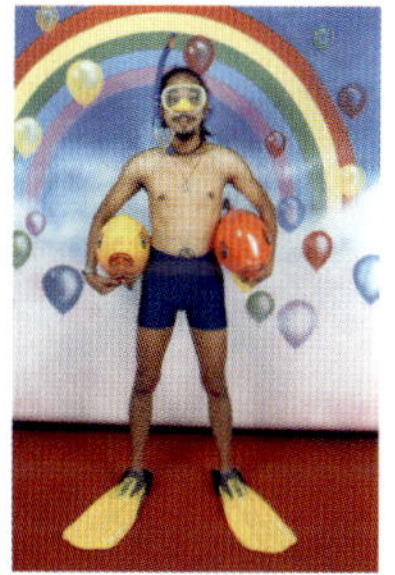

225

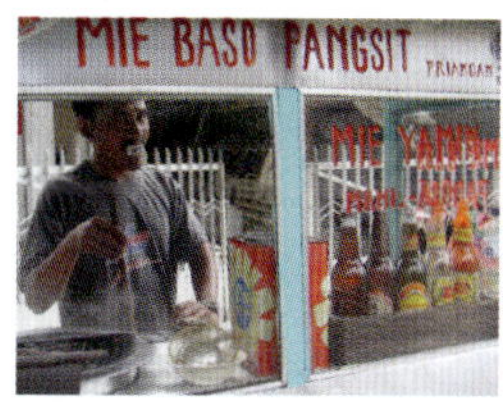

226

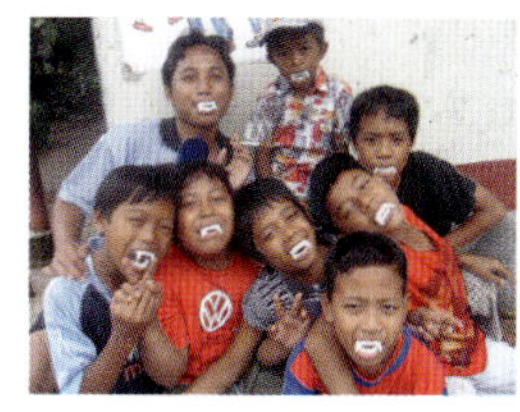

227

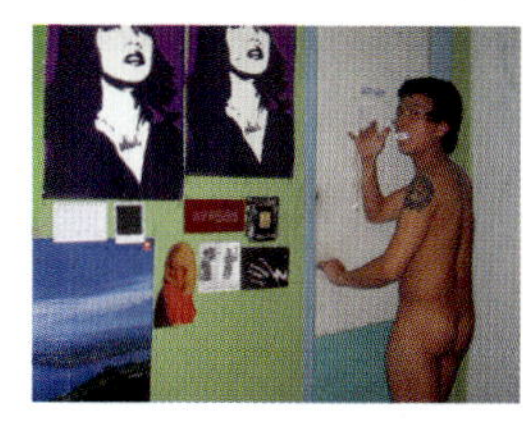

228

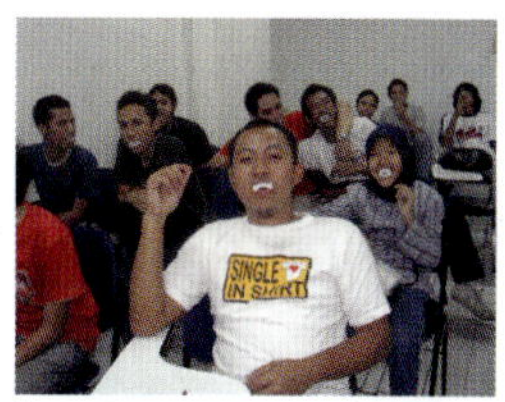

229

'the project #25', artist-in-residence project, March–April 2004

with Aprilia Apsari, Francy Vidriani, Luthfia Ayu Islami and Rebecca Theodora

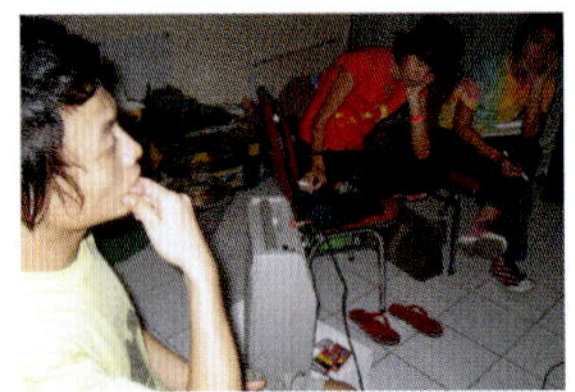

230

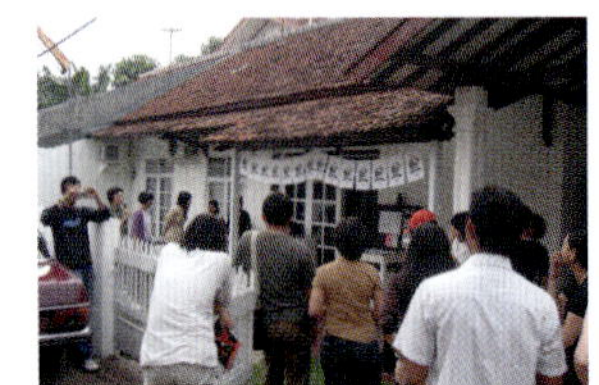

231

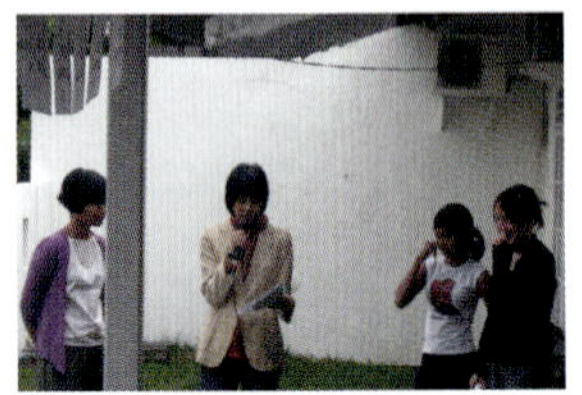

232

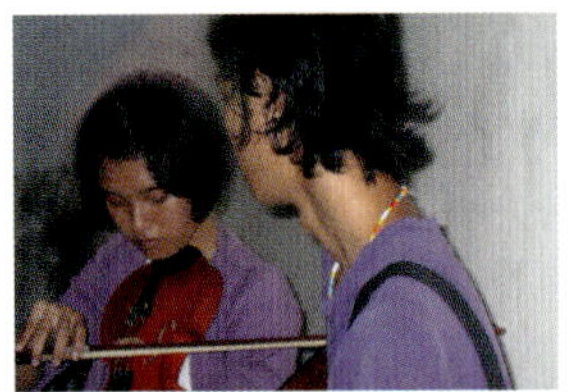

233

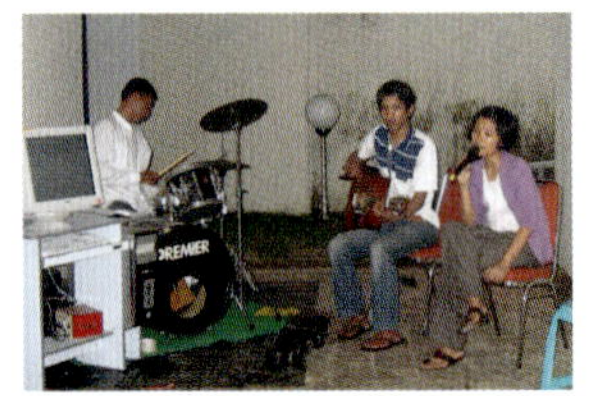

234

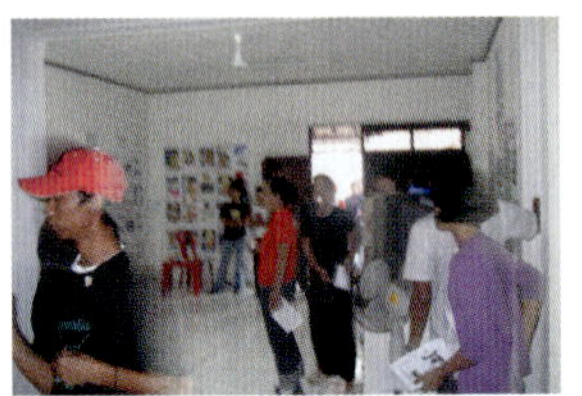

235

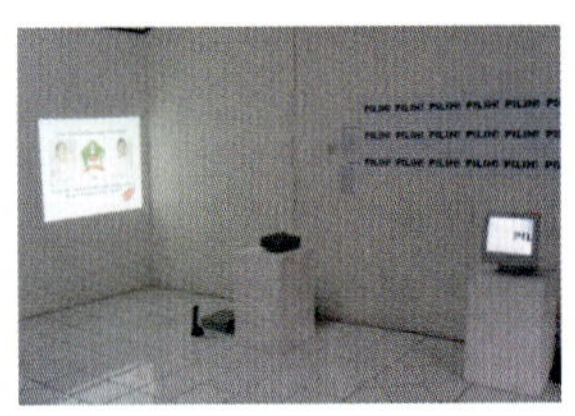

236

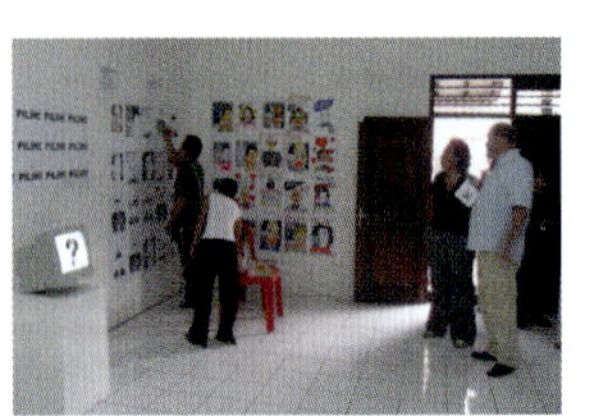

237

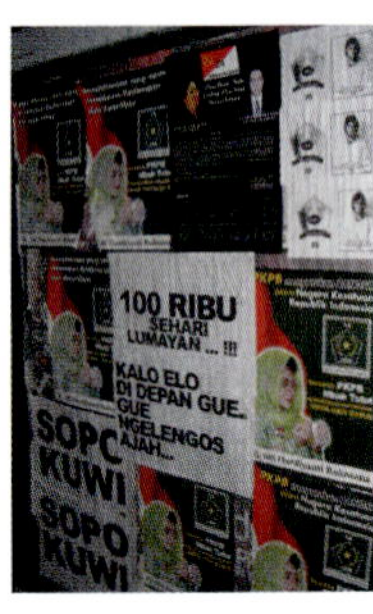

238

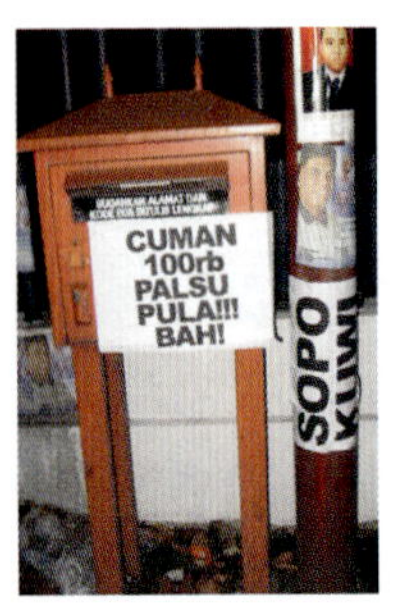

239

Appreciation by the public as art audiences is the end of the whole chains of an art event, delivering a great question of what is expected from this matter in the end. A question of its existence between as an empowering force to support the art development itself, common opinions in everyday basis, or an element which is continuously exploited as sources of artists' creative ideas. The whole issue raises an actual distance, from the weakness of art infrastructure, the lack of attention in reaching the target audiences in art spaces, also the incompetence of the government and academy to functionalise their institutions. In this edition, *Karbon* attempts to detect the shattered pieces of this matter.

Karbon

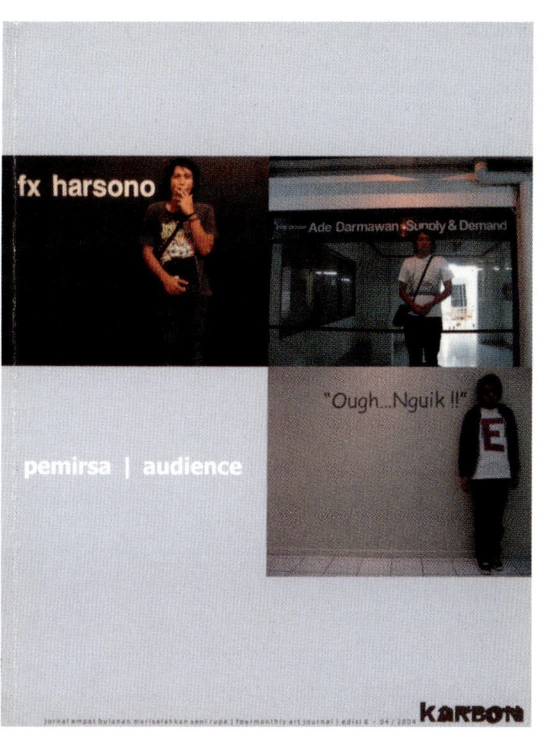

240

collaboration

engaged as a form of collaboration with a number of other disciplines in order to find a formula that can take on and explain the potential of sophisticated products of contemporary art.

collaboration is about giving everyone a remote control

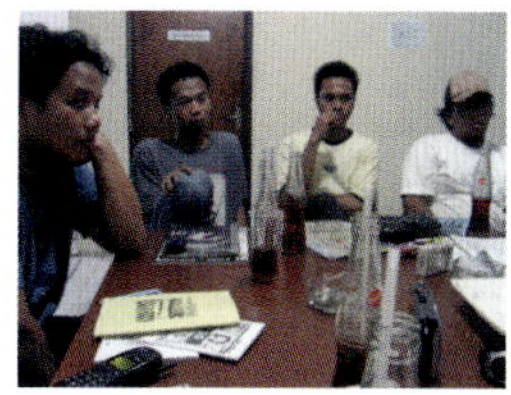

241

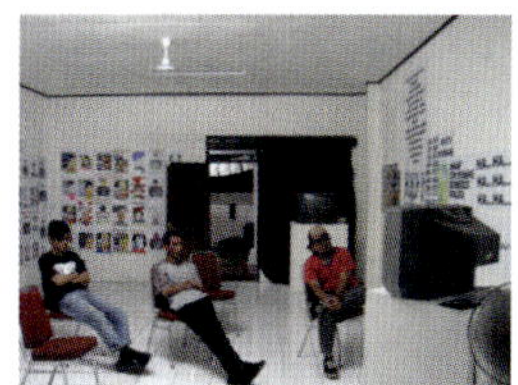

242

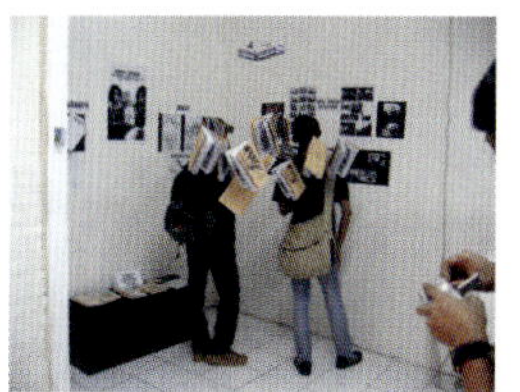

243

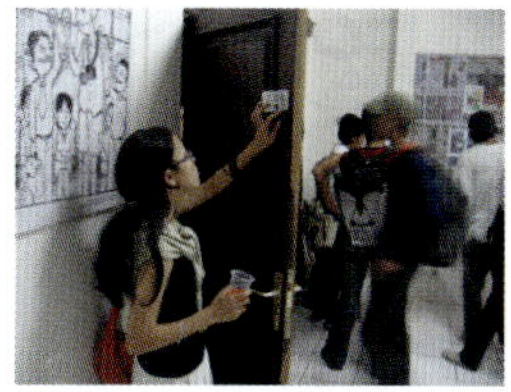

244

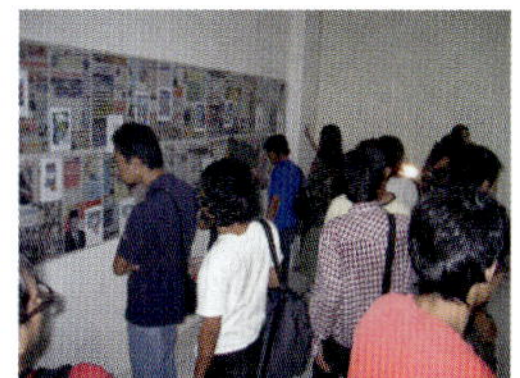

245

'Zero Eye Lution', artist-in-residence exhibition by Andry Moch and M.G. Pringgotono, ruru house, 1–8 October 2004

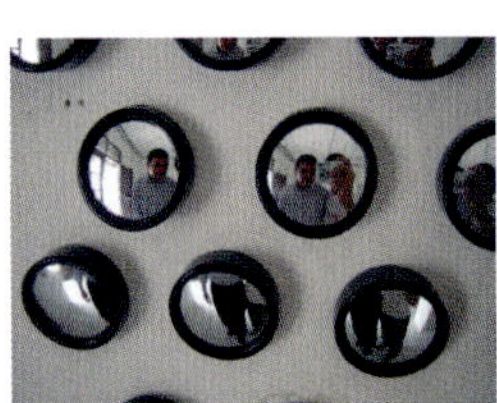

246

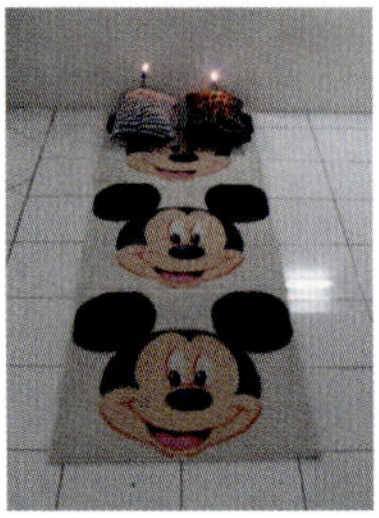

247

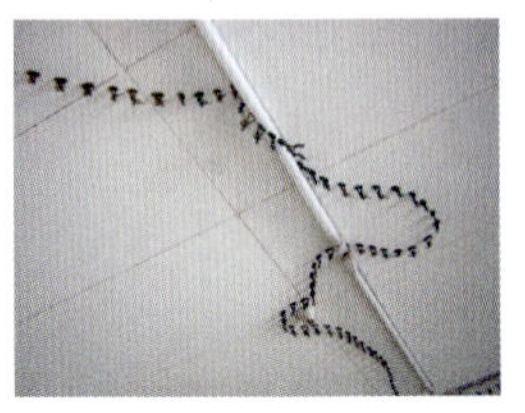

248

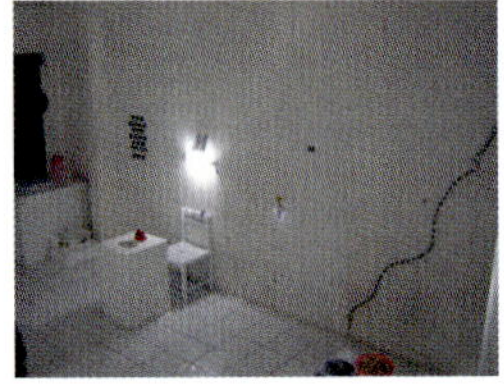

249

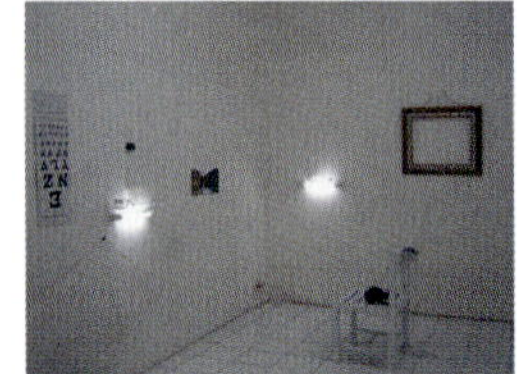

250

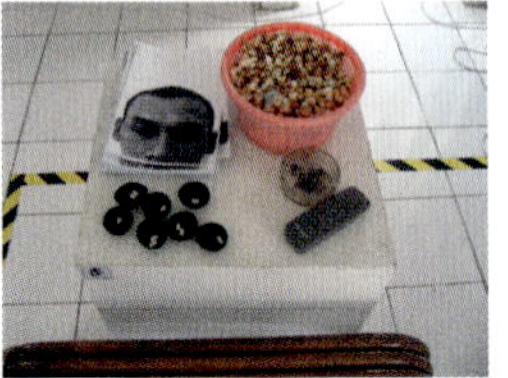

251

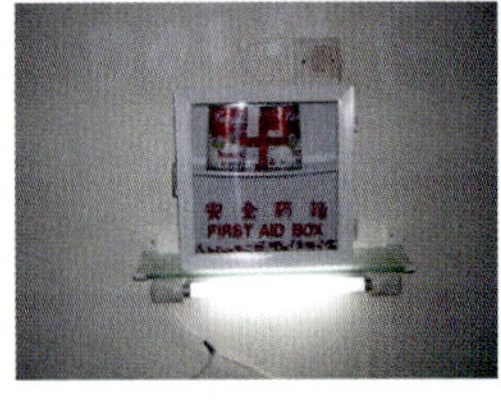

252

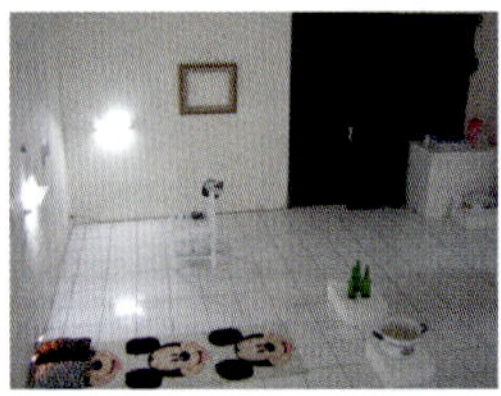

253

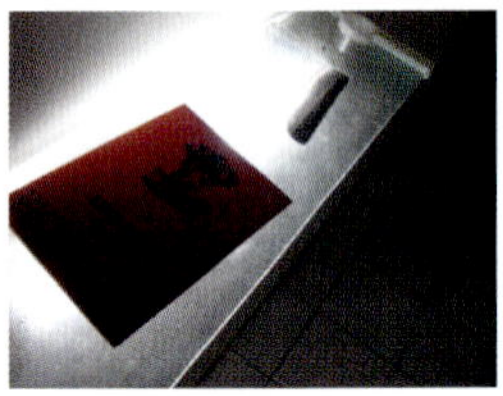

254

Jakarta 32°c is a college students' dialogue and networking forum all over Jakarta and its vicinity for contemporary art and culture. Initiated by ruangrupa since 2004, Jakarta 32°c collects students' ideas and experiments and examines the latest campus issues through exhibition, discussion and writing. Some of Jakarta 32°c programmes are presentation forum and TARKAM discussion and Bicara Tugas Akhir, archiving platform and Sinema Kolekan, a student film screening and periodical radio, Seni Kebut Semalam.

Gudskul Ekosistem

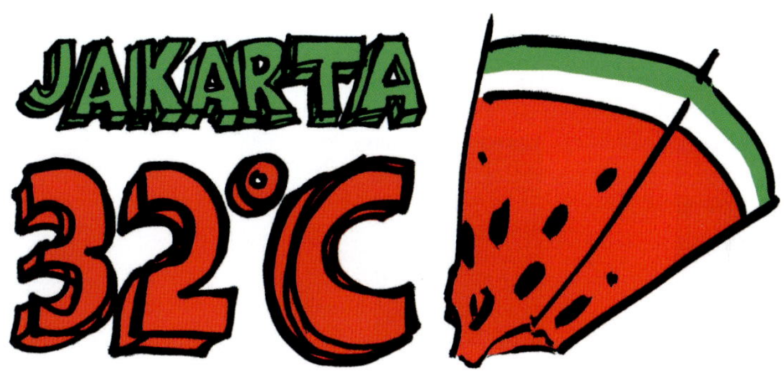

255

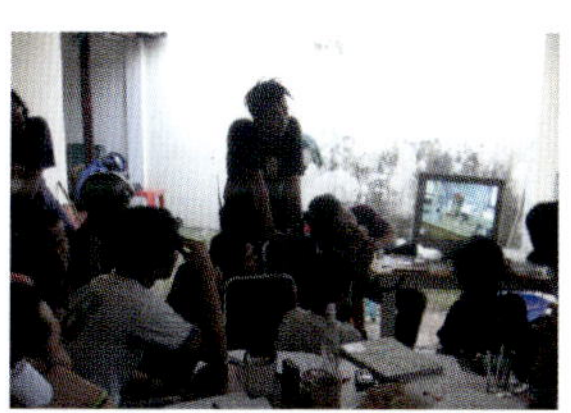

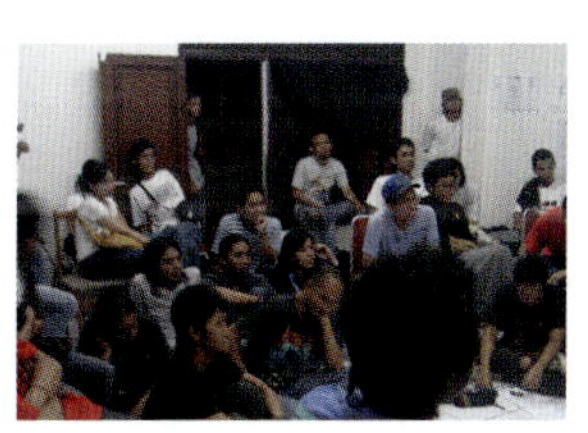

256 257 258

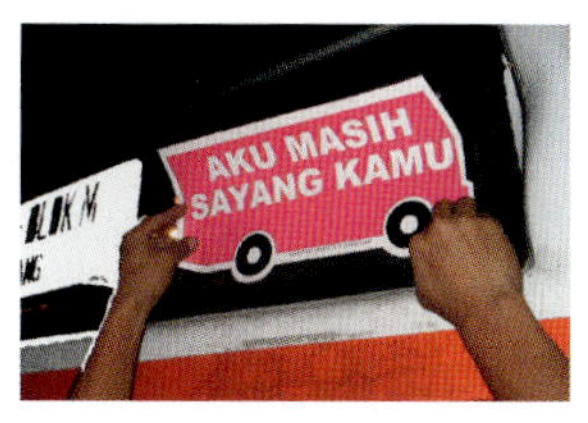

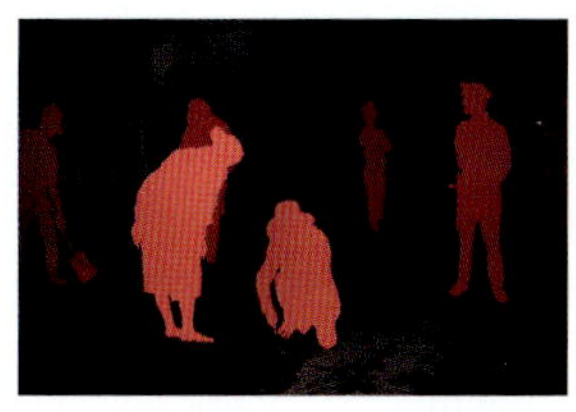

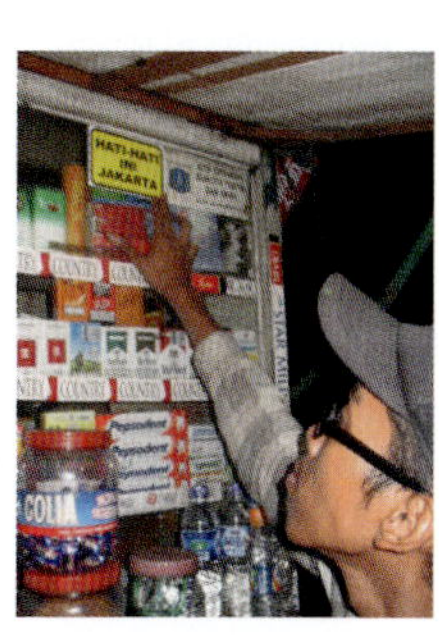

259 260 261

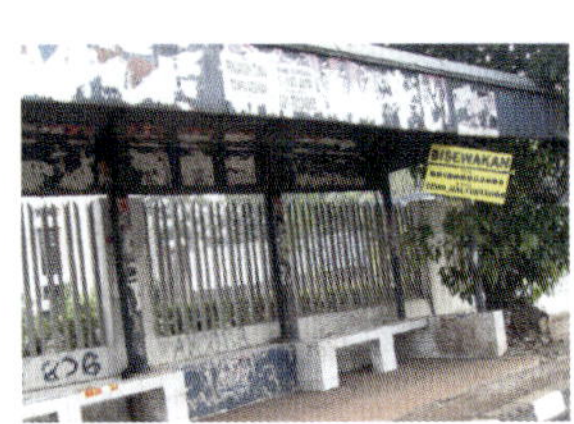

262

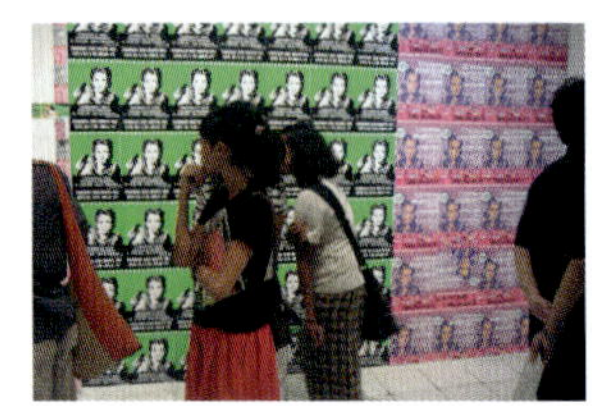

263

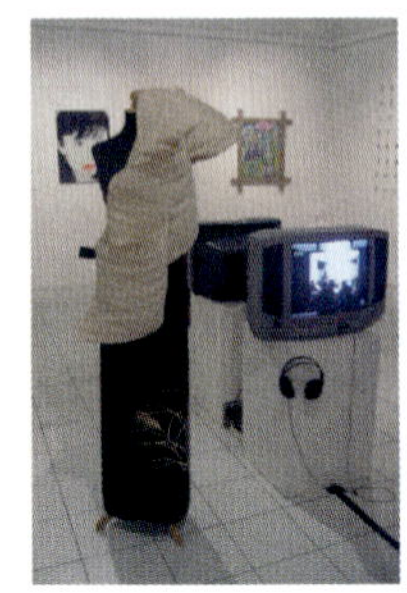

264

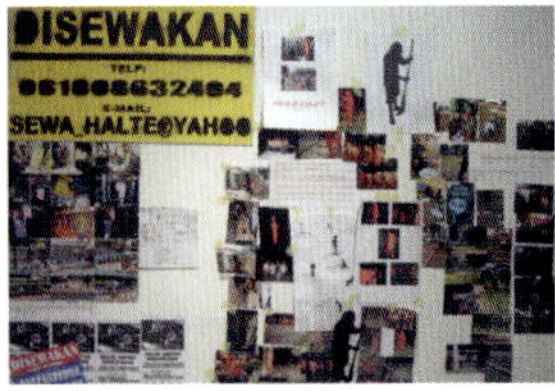

265

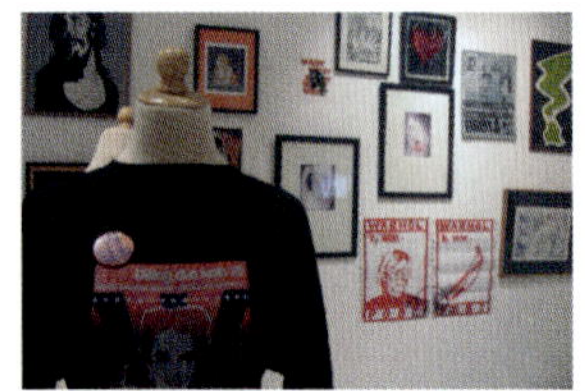

266

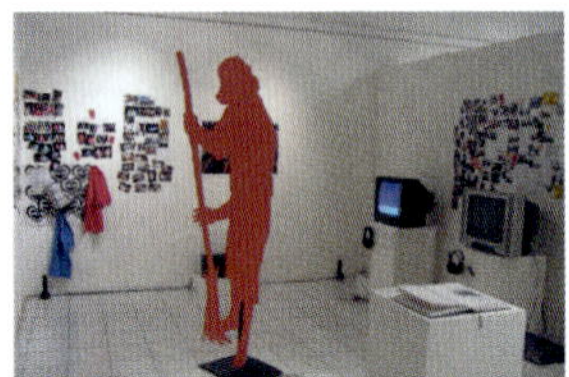

267

The term 'art residency' was very new for me as a first-year university student in 2003. I discussed with my university friends but never quite understood. So we visited ruru house where the art residency lasted for a month with a final exhibition, which we also visited. That's how I got to know ruru. Their house was very surprising. It's more like lifestyle and ambience than art, with the music and so on, plus many posters of international artists and international biennales. ... As a student, it was very very very privileged to have our works be exhibited at the National Gallery during Jakarta 32°C, because it is usually for established artists.

JJ Adibrata

So many of our projects or programmes really came from how we as persons in the city, in the world, evolved. When we did Jakarta 32°C, it's from our reflection that we started from when we were students and we worked a lot with students. It's really because of what we experienced, rather than theory. Many of the programmes started from small talks. RURU Radio, for example, is very simple. Three or four people, including Reza, were talking whether to have a radio. Oomleo then said he knew an application. Soon the Radio was born. We never think big. We always seen us as a collective of smallness. Not expansion. It's always small and medium size, then we connect together.

Ade Darmawan

'Uncensored', artist-in-residence exhibition by Asok and Bayak, ruru house, November 2004

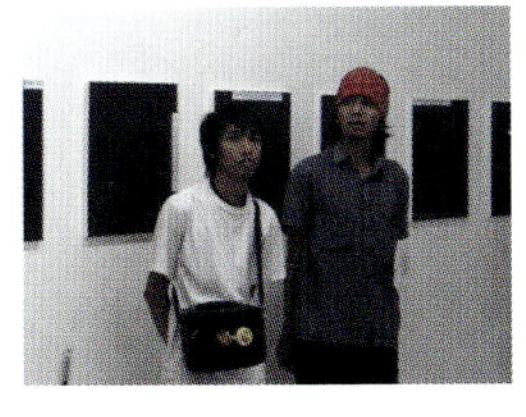

268

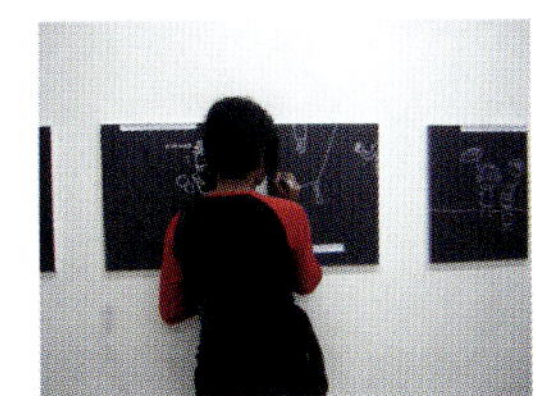

269

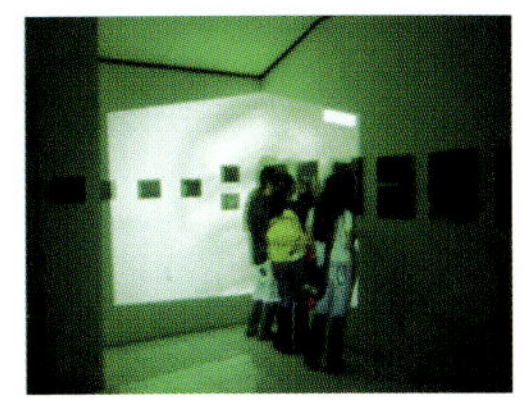

270

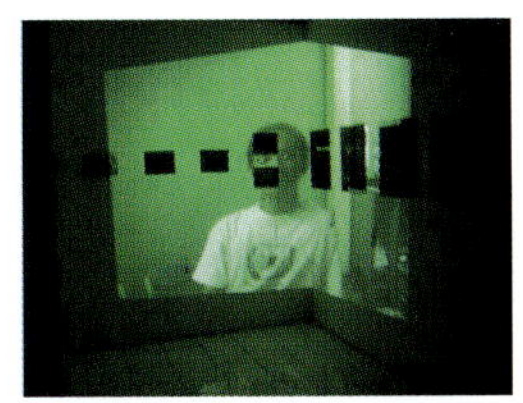

271

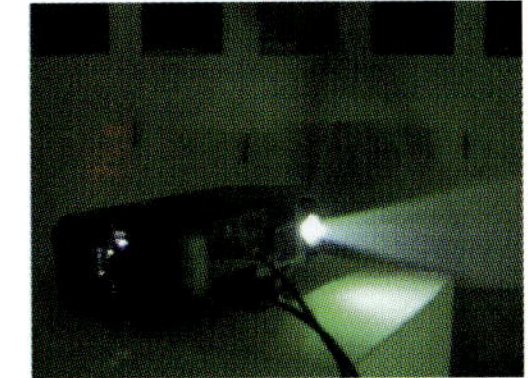

272

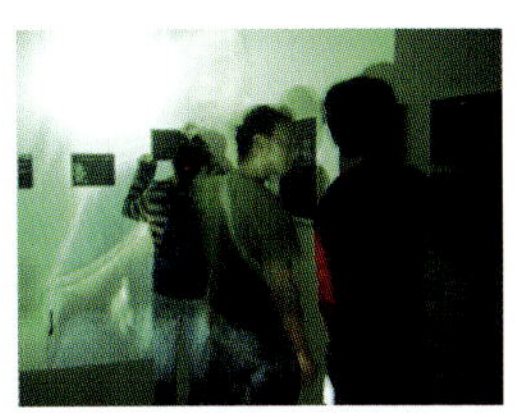

273

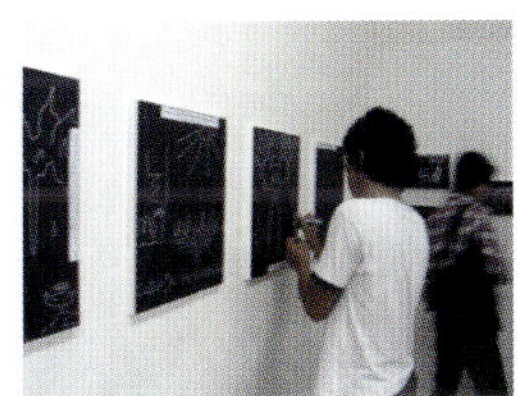

274

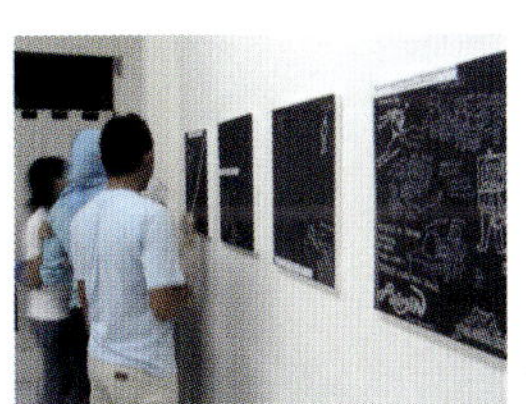

275

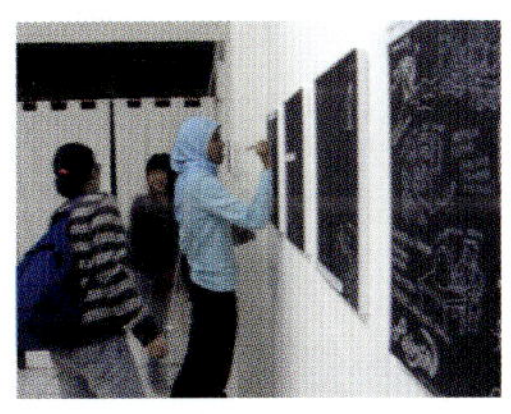

276

'We are the generation that wear too many t-shirt', ruru house, March–May 2005

with Gandung Bagus Amento, Irvine and Wenz Rawk

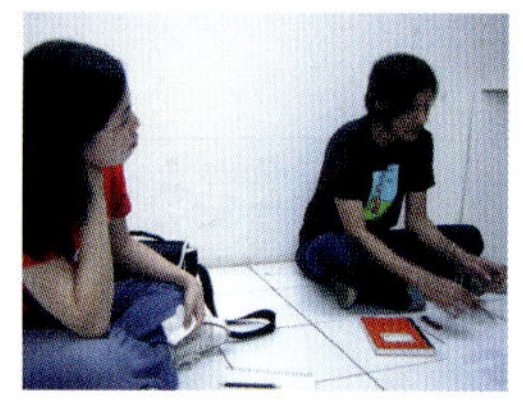

277

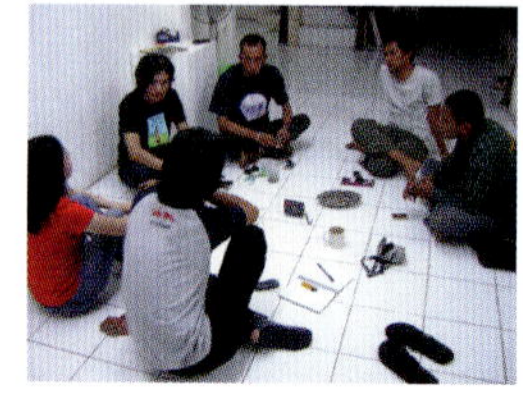

278

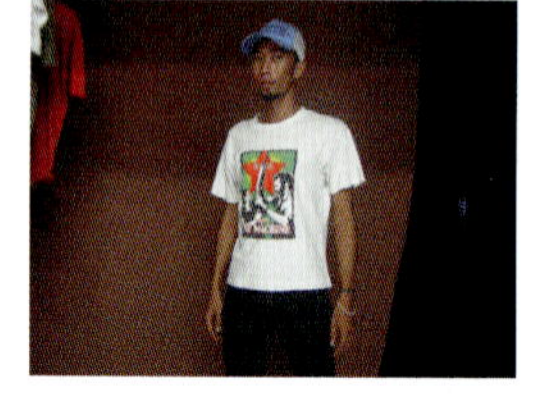

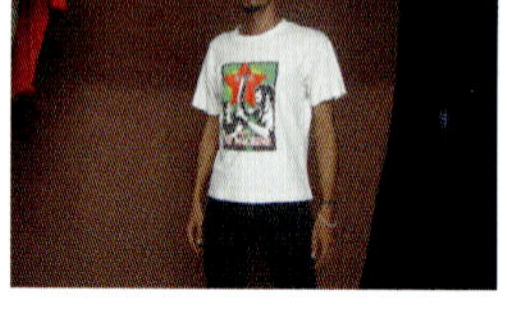

279

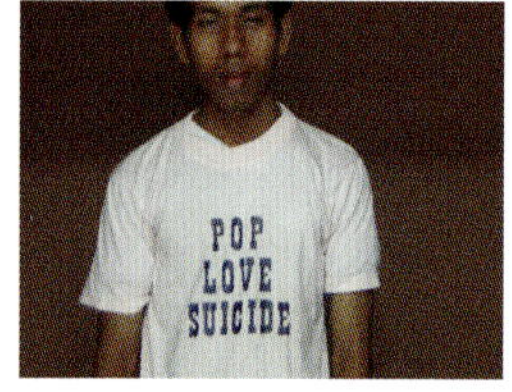

280

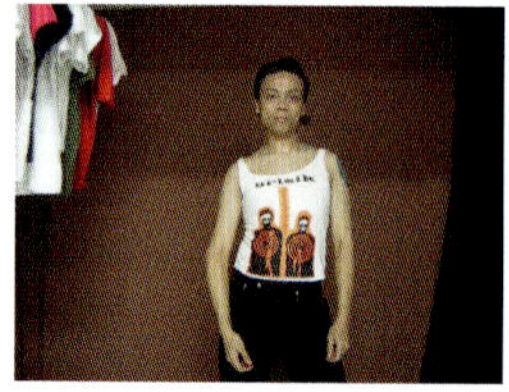

281

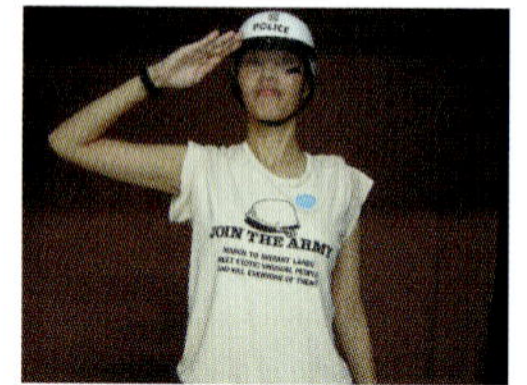

282

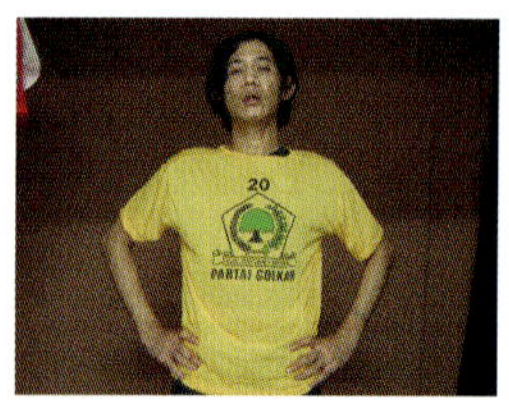

283

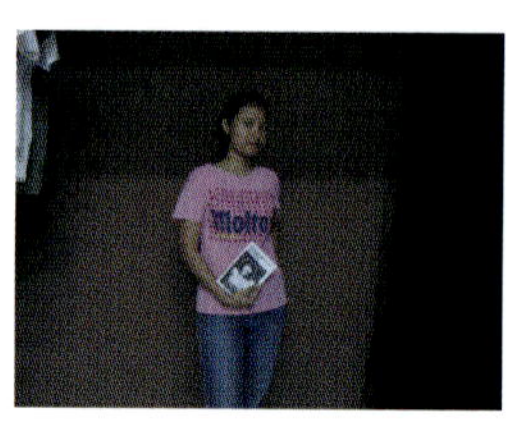

284

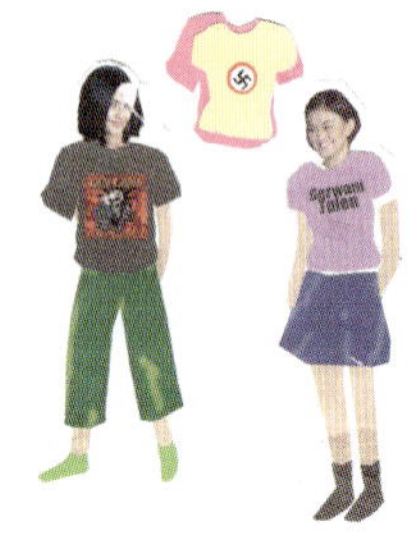

285

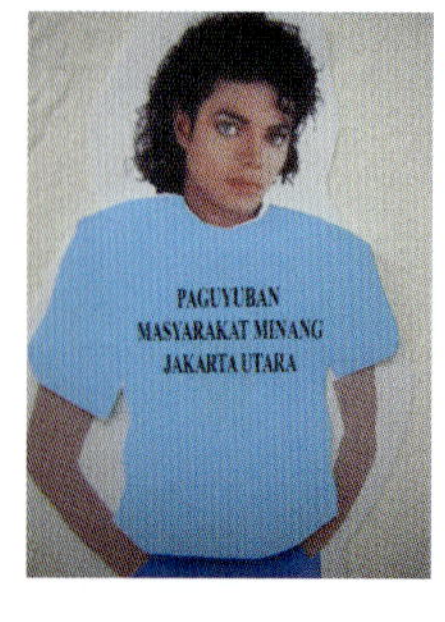

286

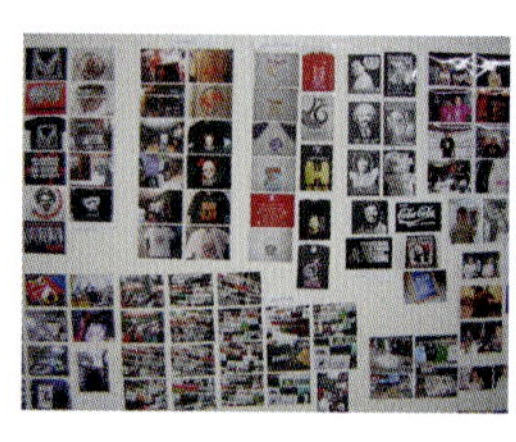

287

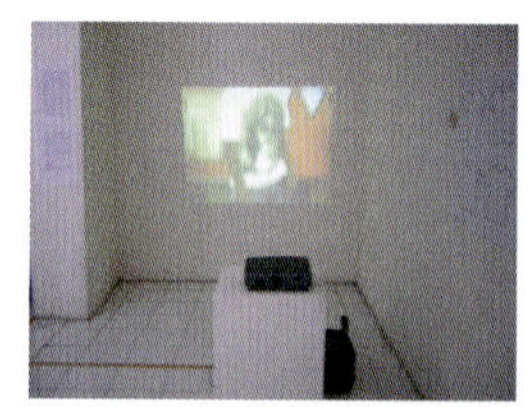

288

OK.Video 'Sub/Version' – 2nd Jakarta Video Festival, Galeri Nasional Indonesia, Jakarta, 17–31 July 2005

At the National Gallery [for OK.Video 2005] there were leaks and they had not enough electricity, they didn't have any equipment. At that time we were in a financial crisis. ruru applied for Hivos and other funding. Some of them didn't come through. ruru borrowed money from friends and families to order monitors and DVD players. After two weeks of the festival they resold all these equipments to pay back people. It was a really ad hoc and DIY exhibition. But it was great for me, I really experienced the horizontal working relationship where there's no director nor curator, we did everything together. The fact that it is possible to work horizontally was really striking for me. It's not that there's no politics, but you have to be very sensitive to see what's going on there. I was only observing. I could be part of it, to be honest, because I was communicating in English. So I was an outsider in every sense, but observing them was quite interesting. Very messy (*laughs*) but was also a really beautiful experience. Without much resource of course. But the sense of freedom was immense as to what we could do. ... The experience really set my work ethics, especially on how to collaborate with people, open up conversations and engage with the audience. I remember the festival was free. Families would spend hours hanging out and looking at the work. ruru made sure visitors were comfortable. So there's no wall texts etc. They put cushions, they brought sofas from somewhere. It was quite a nice memory. And we organised talks funded by Japan Foundation Jakarta office. The discussion was really active. It went on and on. They asked tough questions and had deep discussions. I was already amazed by how engaging these conversations were. And parties, haha. It taught me a lot, about what it is to offer an exhibition to the public. But it was difficult at the same time, because of the lack of infrastructure. I went back to Jakarta this year [2023], my first time in the past ten years. Their effort to keep the OK.Video archive is remarkable. I found the floor plan that I drew at the time.

Che Kyongfa

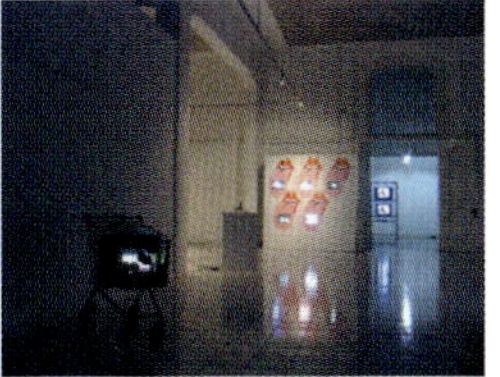

289

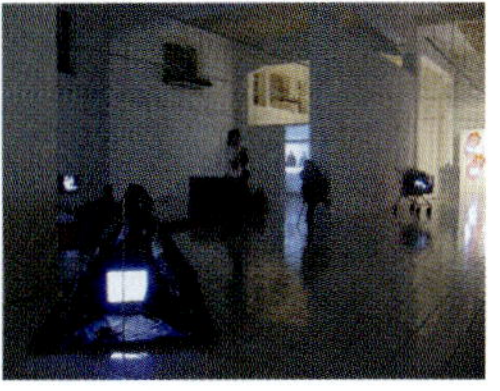

290

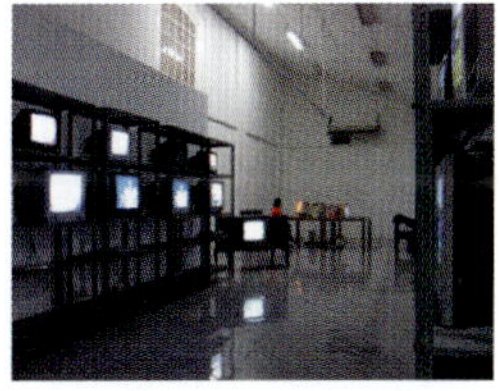

291

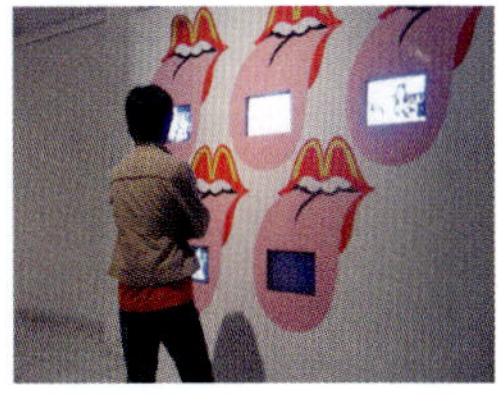

292

'Kaos Project', Istanbul Biennale, Istanbul, Turkey, 16 September – 30 October 2005

[This] project focuses on t-shirts (*kaos* in Indonesian) as a form of popular culture. In Jakarta, t-shirts are used as propaganda, statements or ways to represent an ideology or identity in public space. The wearer might express a collective or personal identity through the t-shirt, or simply be a poser. In particular, many t-shirts in the city used the heads of world famous figures such as Einstein, 'Che' Guevara, Jim Morrison, Superman or Osama Bin Laden and collaged them with the face of Jakarta's local hero, Benyamin Sueb. Benyamin Sueb (1939–95) was a famous singer and film actor from Jakarta. He represented the social reality of Jakartan people in funny, critical, honest and simple ways. His works were very important to Jakartan people of every class and he became a major icon for the city – influencing everything from the language to the local football club. This project reflects on how an iconic figure represents his or her environment. ... The local figure is not only an object of adoration, but can be used by the population to make personal statements or to become a symbol for people that can influence the way they behave on an everyday level. In parallel ruangrupa have researched the status of similar heroes in Istanbul, providing an insight into the different roles and possibilities of popular culture in the two cities.

9th International Istanbul Biennale

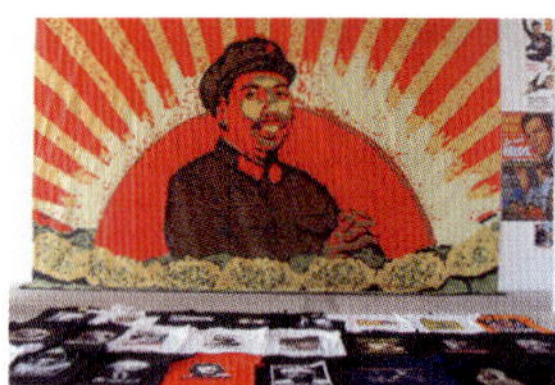

293

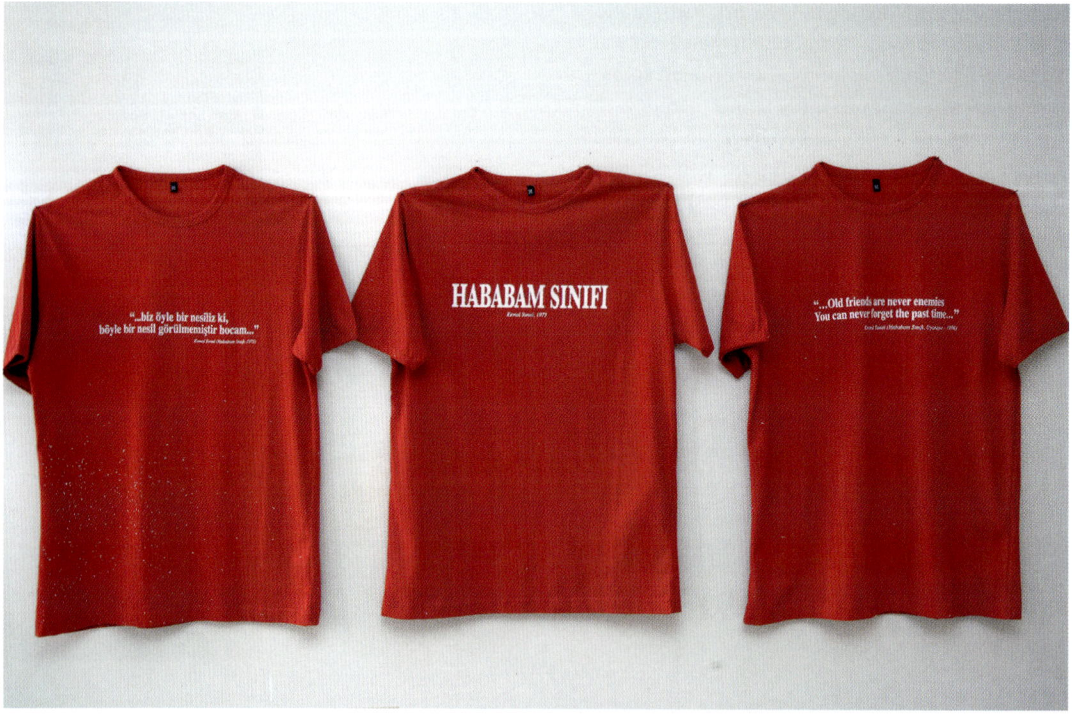

294

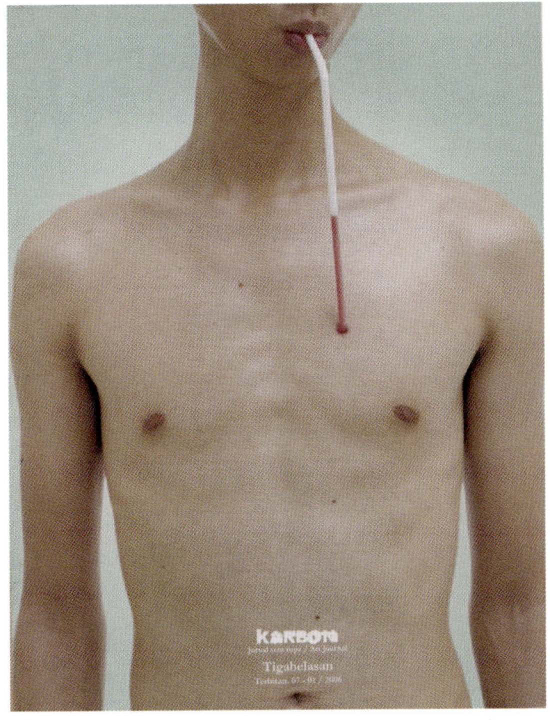

295

Tigabelasan [the basis of this edition of *Karbon*] is a discussion programme held on the 13th of each month. Since the beginning in 2003 until now, Tigabelasan has discussed visual culture in the context of urban culture and environment, and how both influenced the development of art, both directly and indirectly.

Karbon

‘MEN AT WORK: a project about working in the city of Jakarta’, ruru house, 28 March – 24 April 2006

artist-in-residence project and exhibition with Bin Harlan, Godel, Muhammad Ridwan, reinaart vanhoe and RM Herwibowo

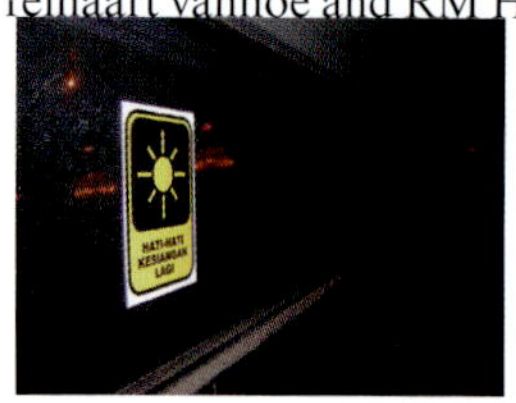

296

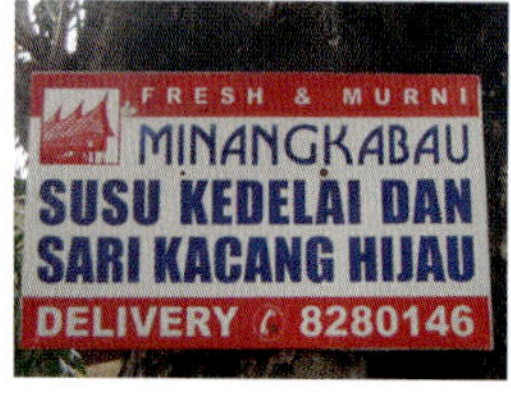

297

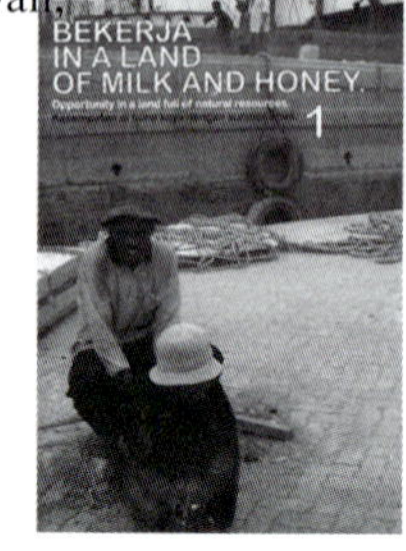

298

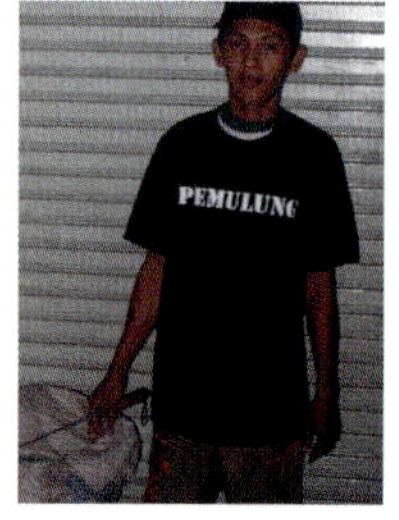

299

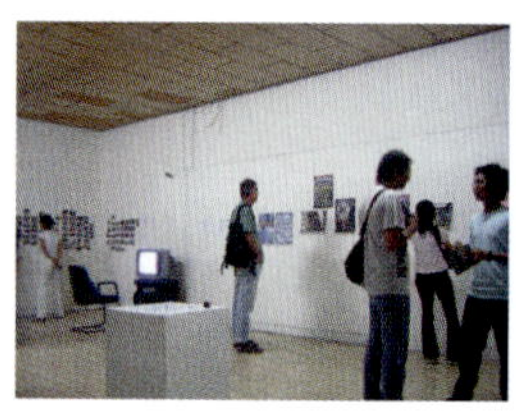

300

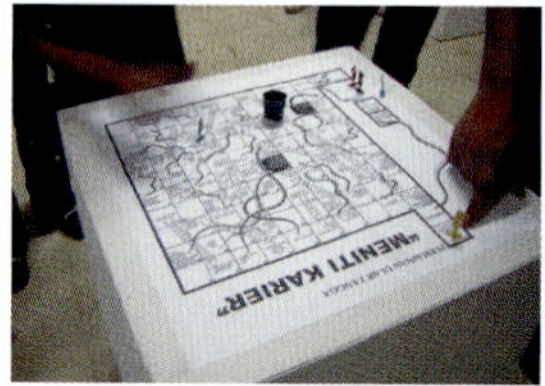

301

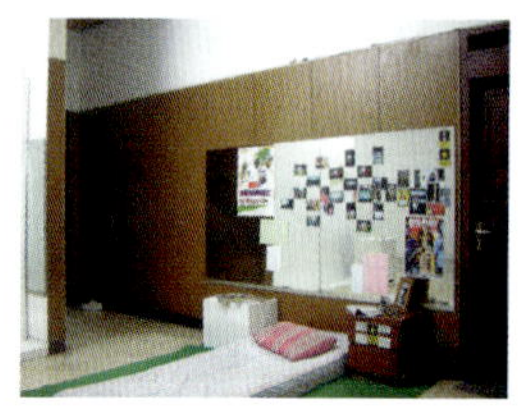

302

303

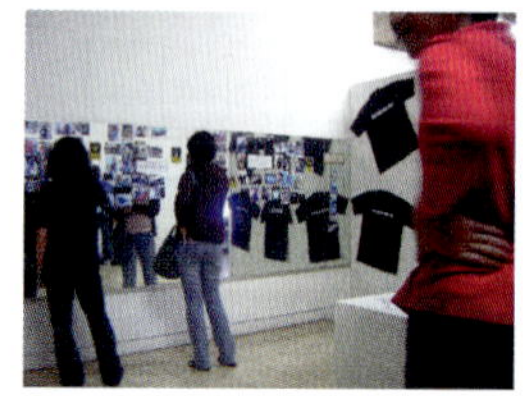

304

'LET THE KIDS PLAY: a workshop about playground in the city of Jakarta', ruru house, May–June 2006

artist-in-residence project and exhibition with MG Pringgotono, Murki Aziz Fikri (Sanggar Anak Akar) and Rene Canales Hayashi

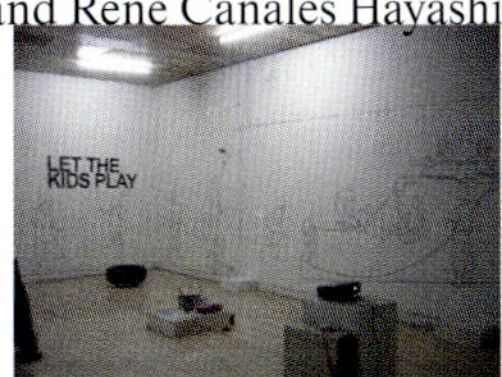

305

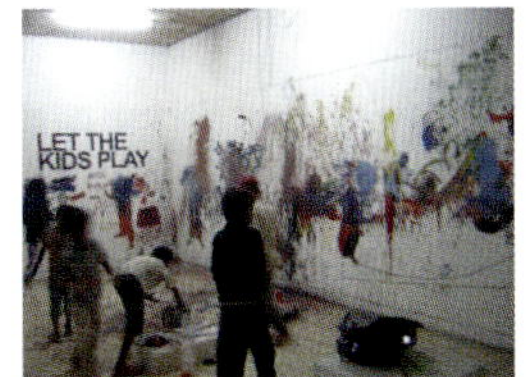

306

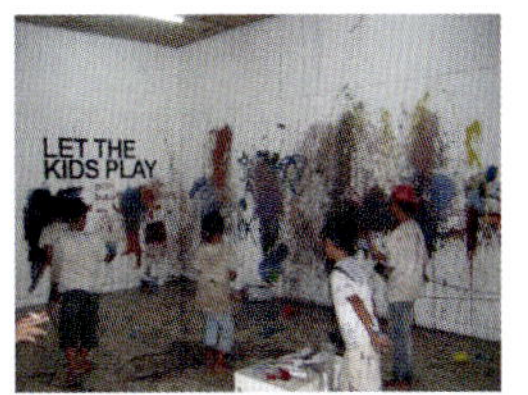

307

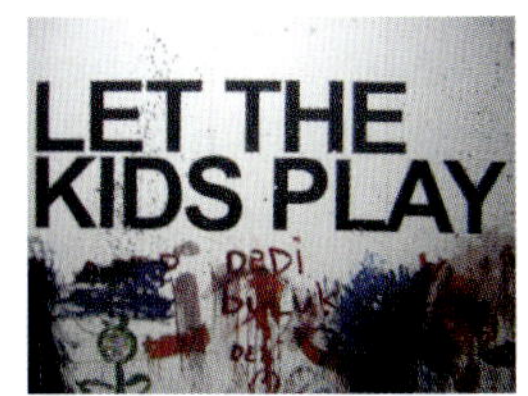

308

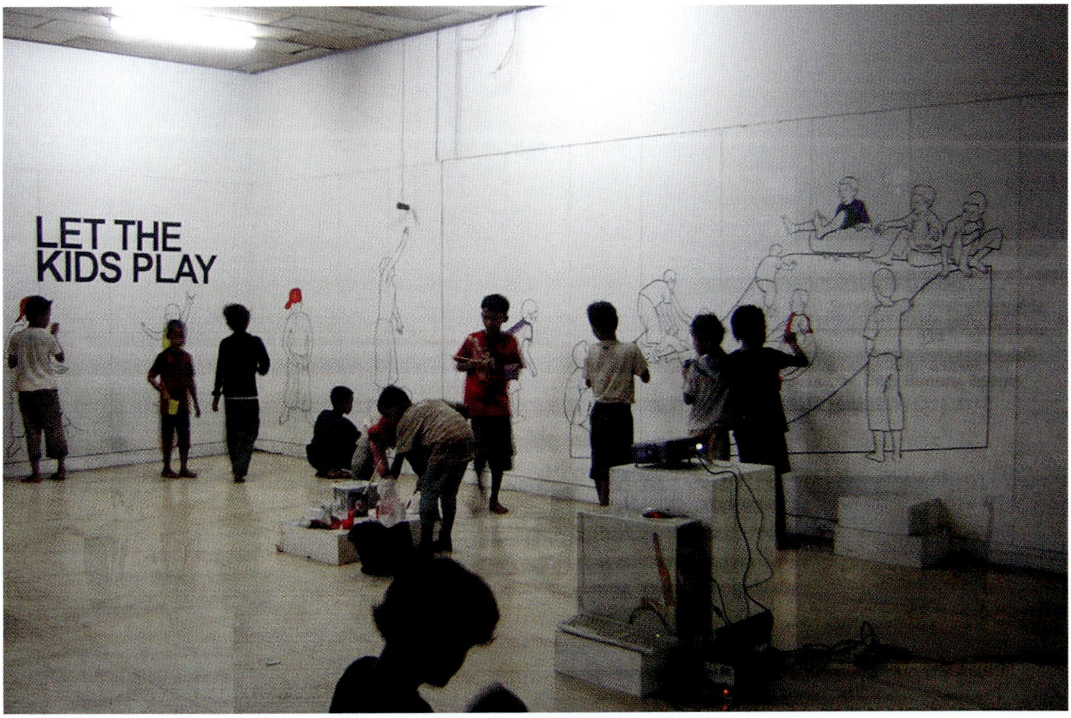

309

Participation in 'Rethinking Nordic Colonialism Act 3: Living (in) the Postcolonial', National Gallery of the Faroe Islands, Tórshavn, 12 May – 4 June 2006

Originally, we wanted to collaborate with different minority communities in the Faroe Islands ... which have been marginalised because of the political/cultural view of the majority, but have somehow managed to survive and are struggling for a more open environment. Although there are indeed minority groups in the Faroe Islands, it turned out to be very difficult to find communities that have organised in associations to improve their rights. As a result of this fact, we decided to introduce ourselves as an Indonesian minority group into Faroese society instead. Posters and postcards representing various Indonesian characters and professions (football players, students, street vendors, soldiers, preachers, artists, etc.) were produced in Jakarta and brought to the Faroe Islands. In addition, we produced a series of t-shirts and pins with short text quotes from the political Faroese authors, Rói Patursson and Kári P., that addressed issues of difference and co-existence. Once we arrived in the Faroe Islands, we collected various news clippings and produced a number of photos that captured our experiences as a minority group there. All this material went into an installation in the Museum Lobby of the Faroe Islands Art Museum along with a PowerPoint presentation of ruangrupa's activities in Jakarta. In addition, the t-shirts, posters and pins were distributed throughout the city of Tórshavn.

ruangrupa

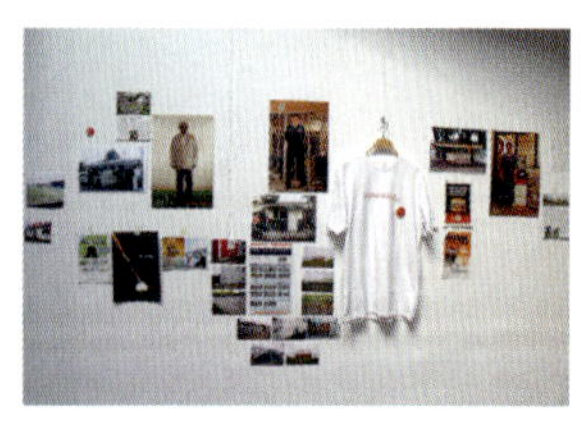

310

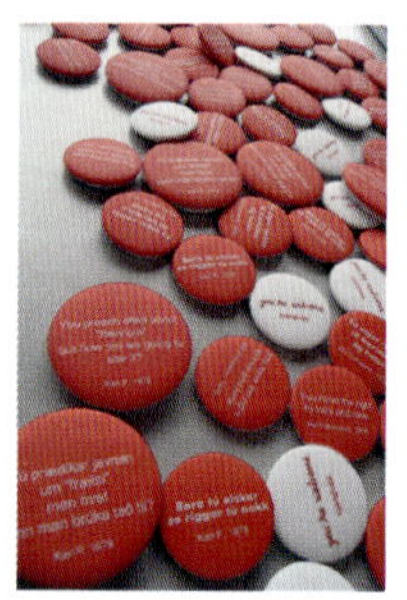

311

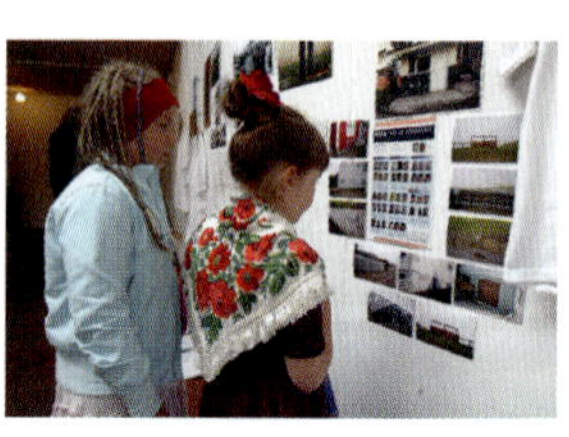

312

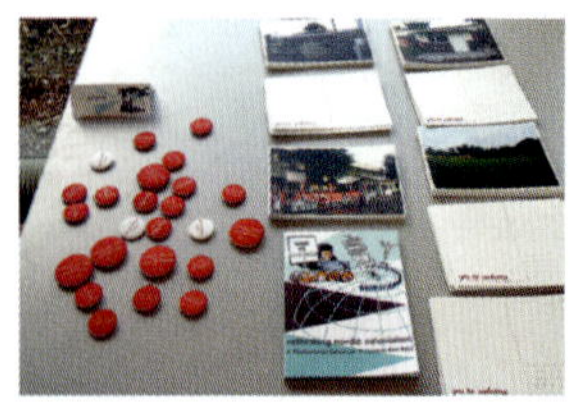

313

Proclaiming themselves as a minority in the Faroes, our Indonesian friends turned the tables on the only seemingly homogenous micronation of 48,000 souls with their project *You're Welcome*, hacking Kuratorisk Aktion's role as hosts for our esteemed artists, performers and activists from all over the globe. By the time we left Tórshavn, all of us were regulars at their Chinese restaurant and fans of their local football team.

Frederikke Hansen

'PICNIC KIT: art project about holiday in the city of Jakarta', ruru house, 24–30 September 2006

with Ari Dina K, Sebastian Friedman and Irayani Queencyputri

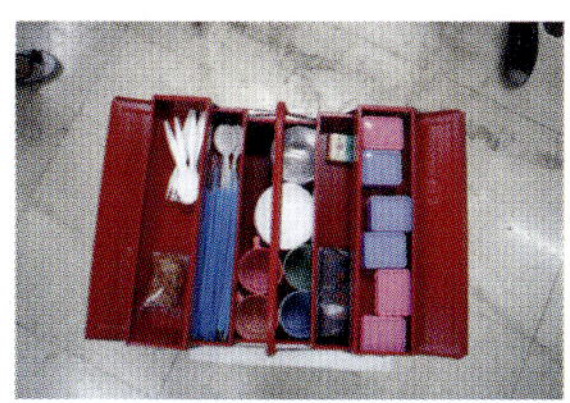

314

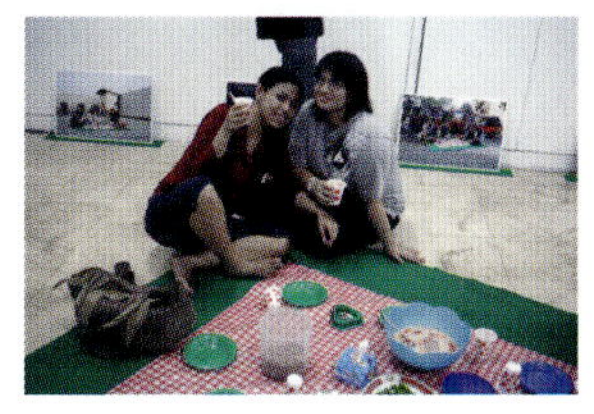

315

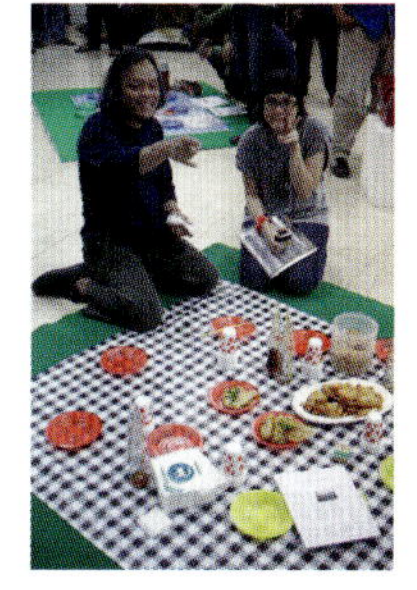

316

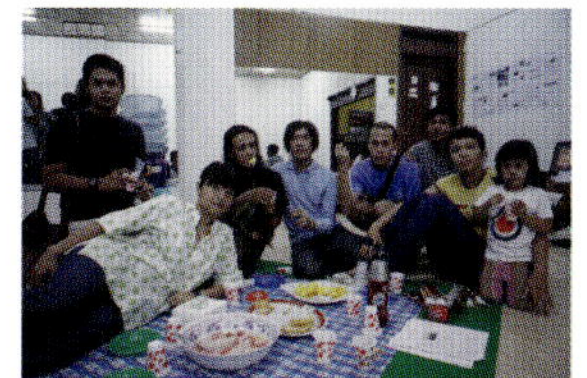

317

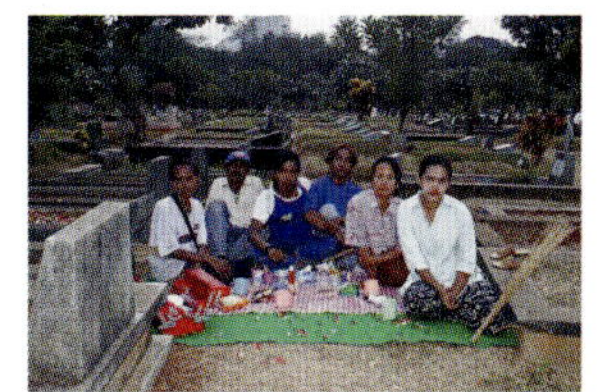

318

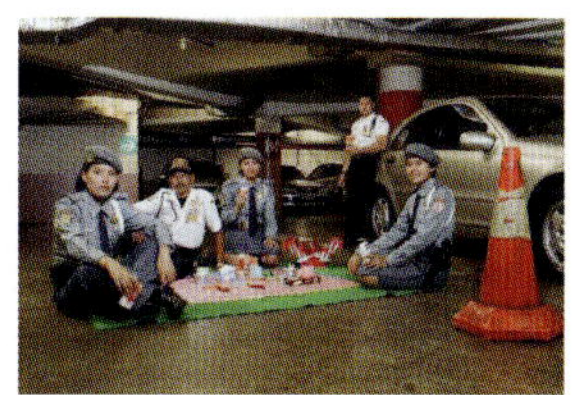

319

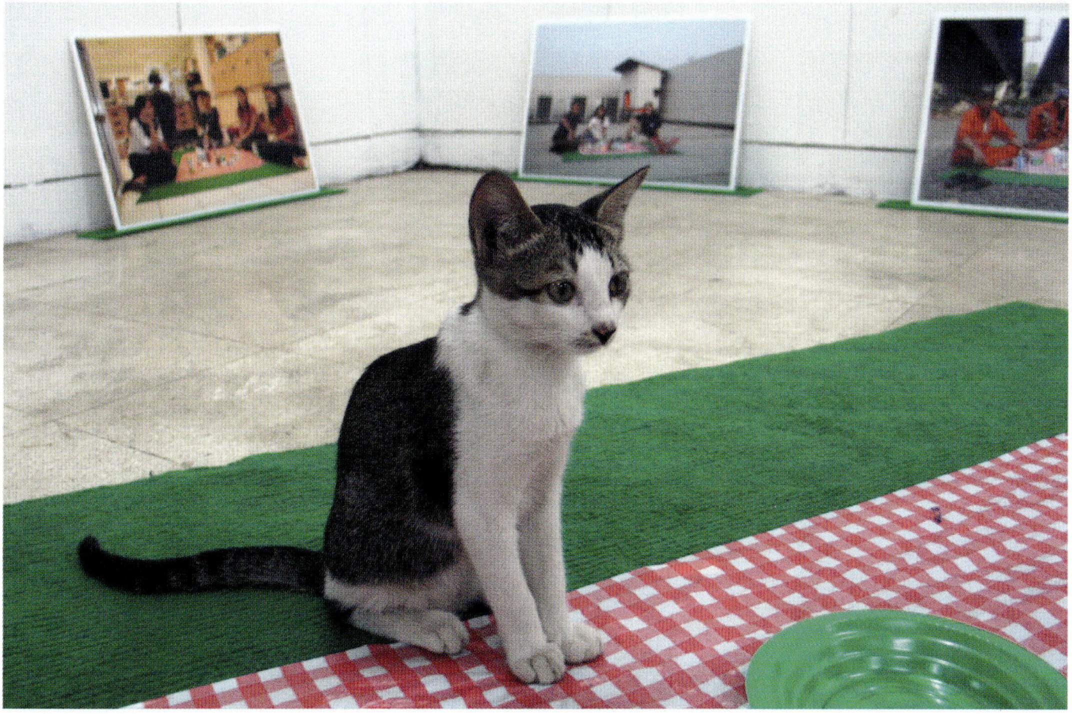

320

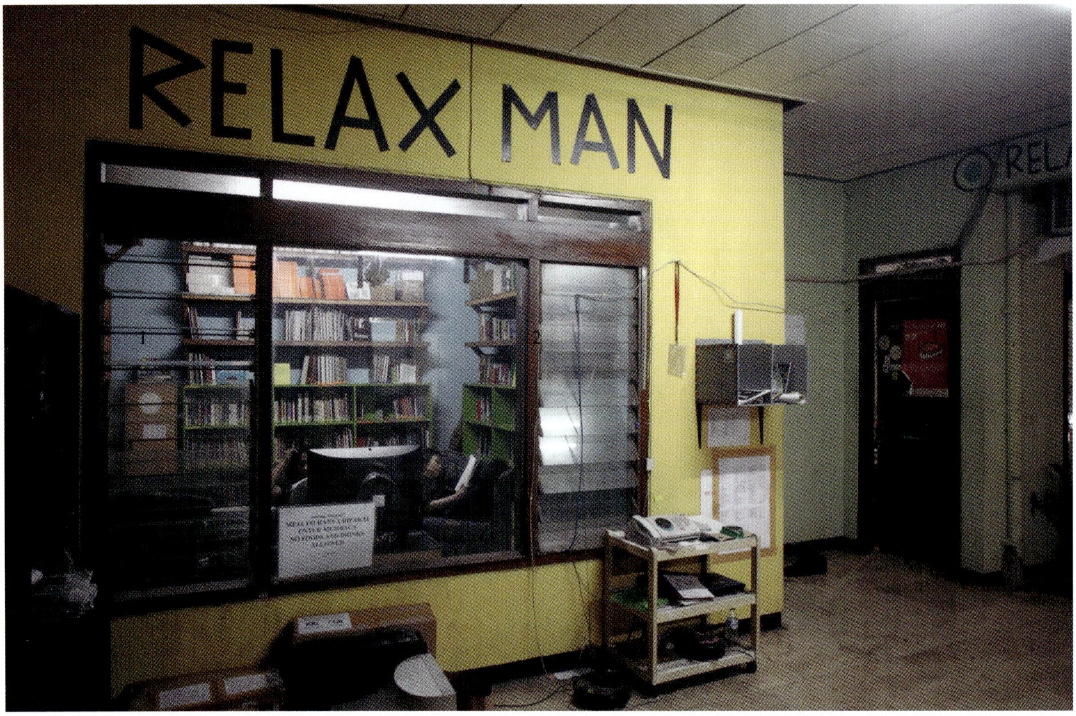

ruangrupa moves into its fourth house, Tebet Timur, Jakarta, 2006

321

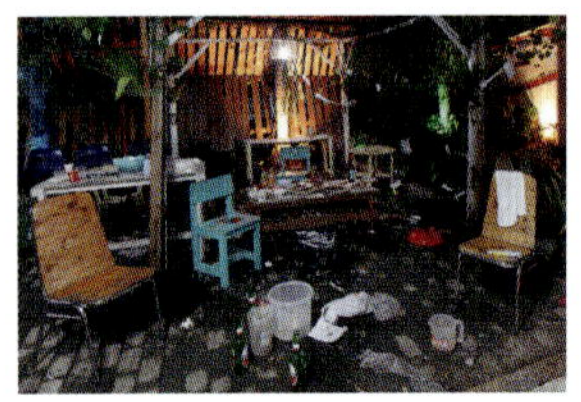

322

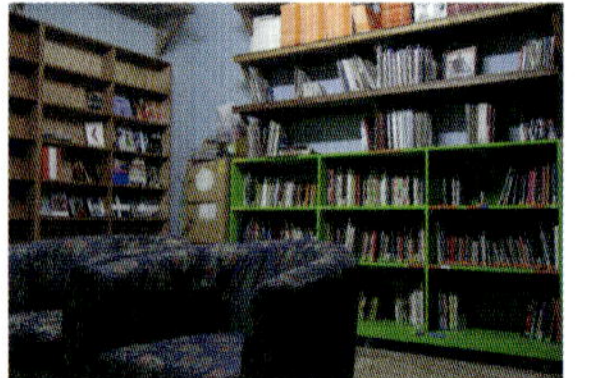

323

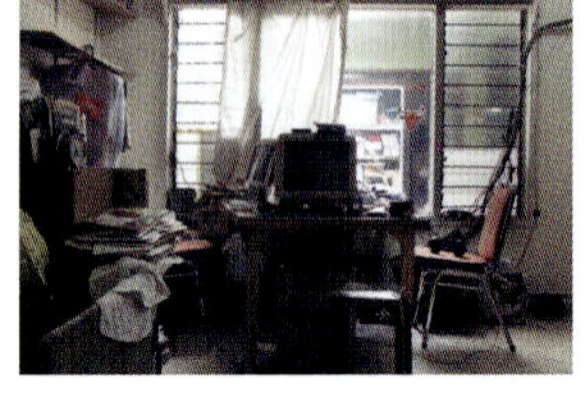

324

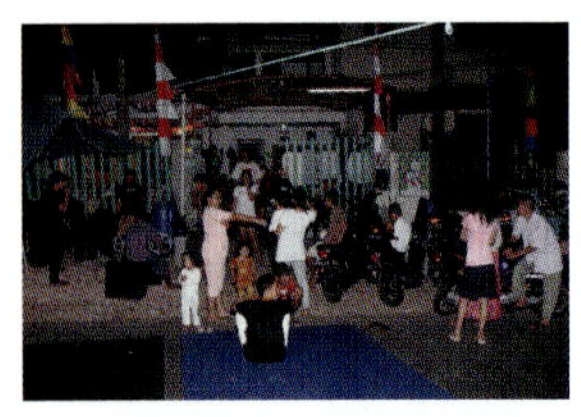

325

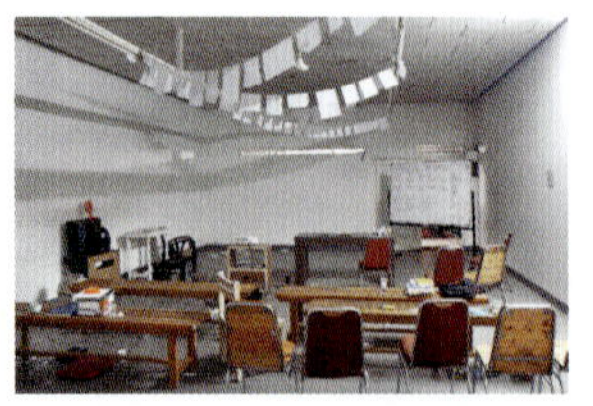

326

'FOR SALE! a project about consume in the city of Jakarta', ruru house, December 2006 – January 2007

with Kautsar Anggakara, Ika Vantiani, Marco Paolo Rolla and Muhammad Thariq

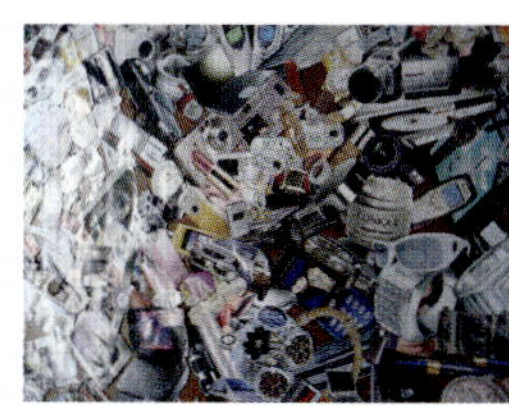

327

328

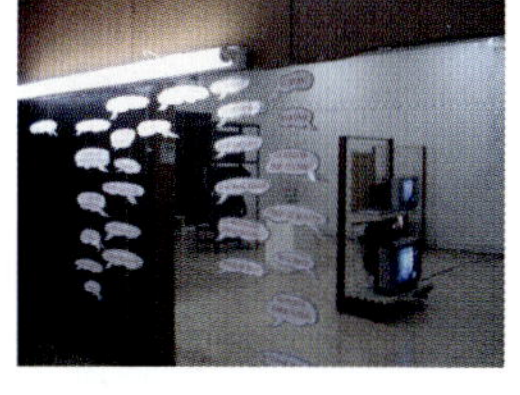

329

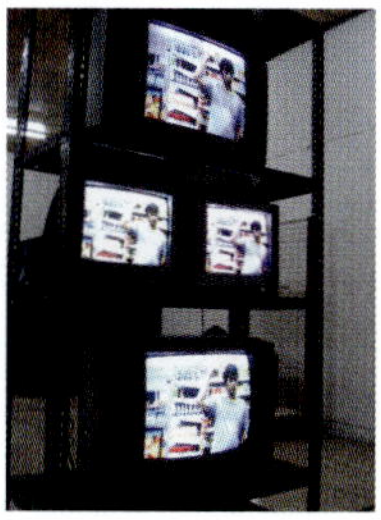

330

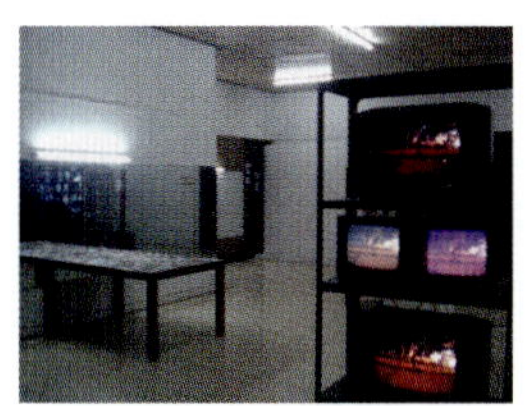

331

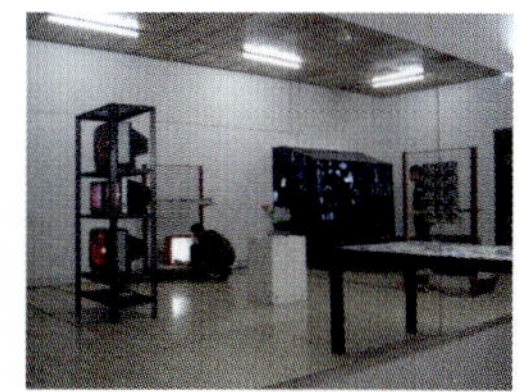

332

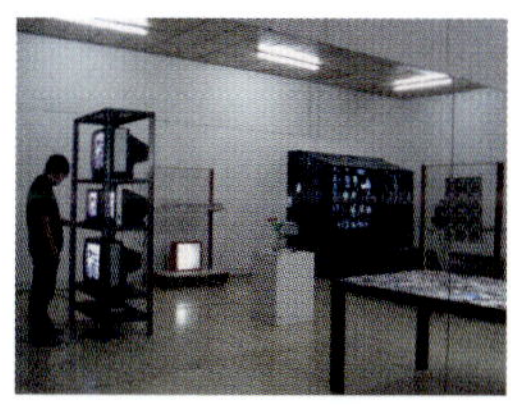

333

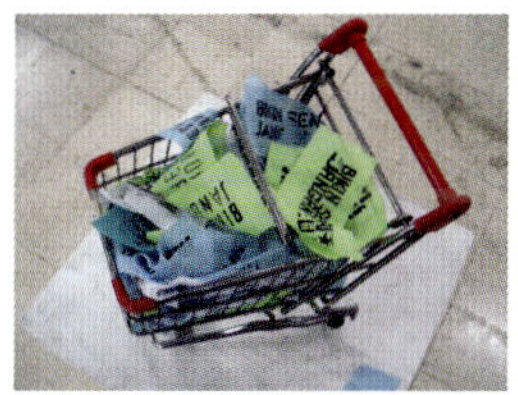

334

ok.Video 'Militia' – 3rd Jakarta International Video Festival, Galeri Nasional Indonesia and other venues, Jakarta, 10–27 July 2007

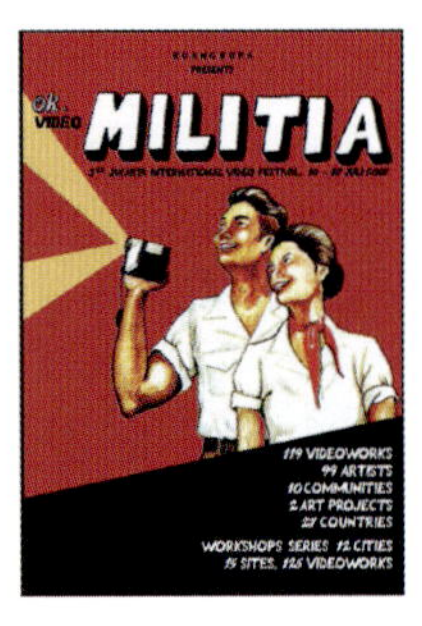

335

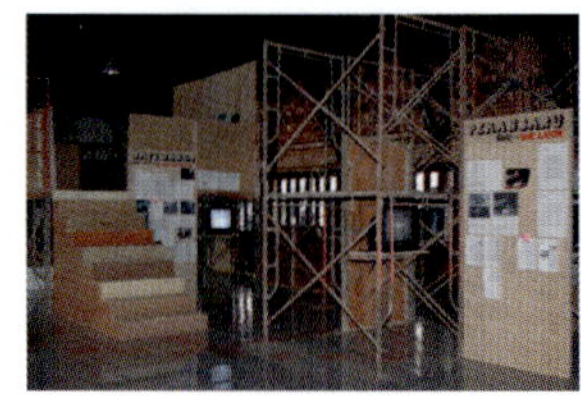

336

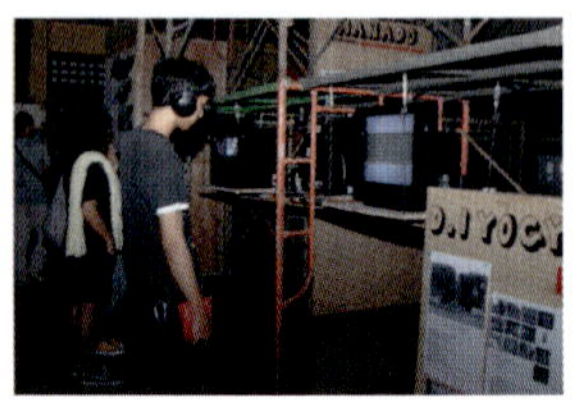

337

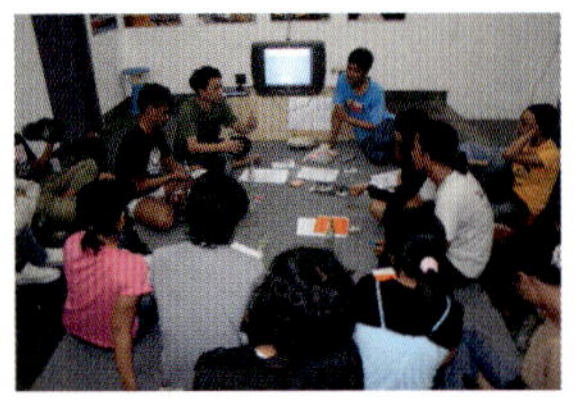

338

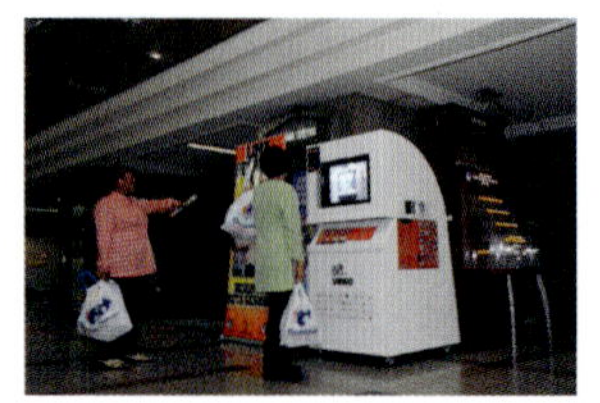

339

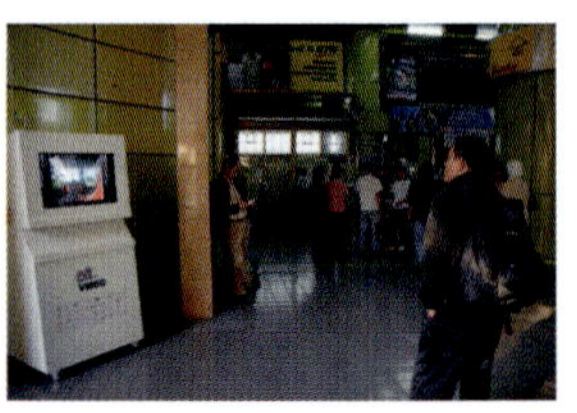

340

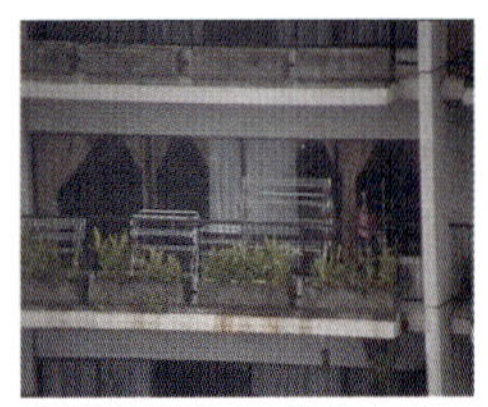

341

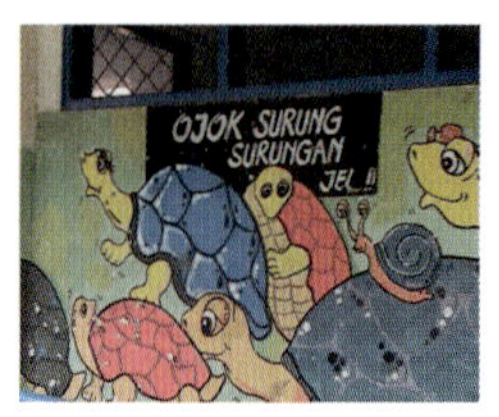

342

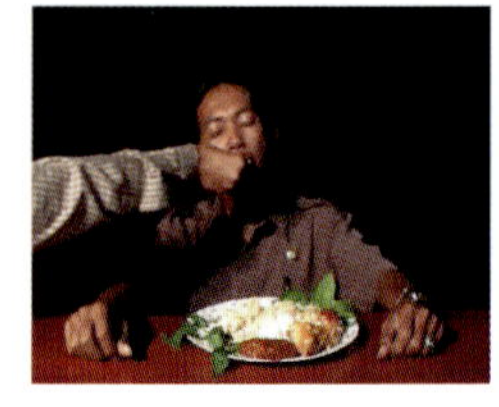

343

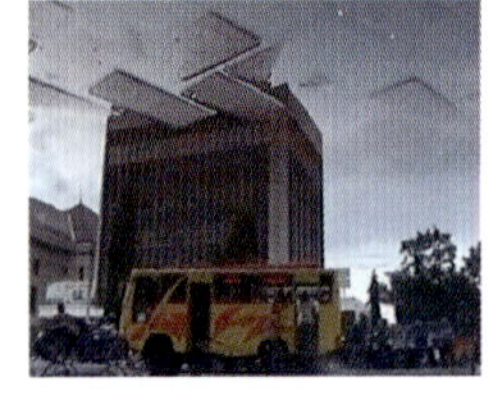

344

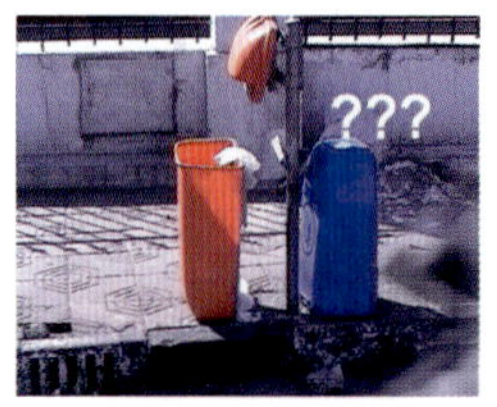

345

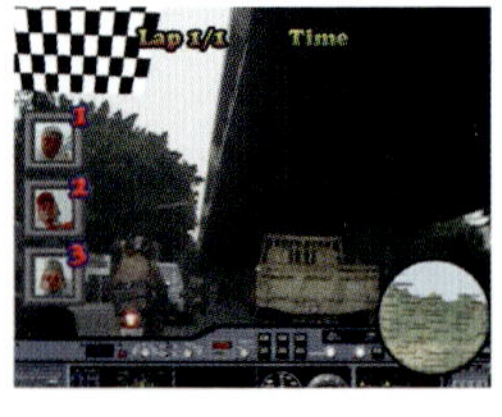

346

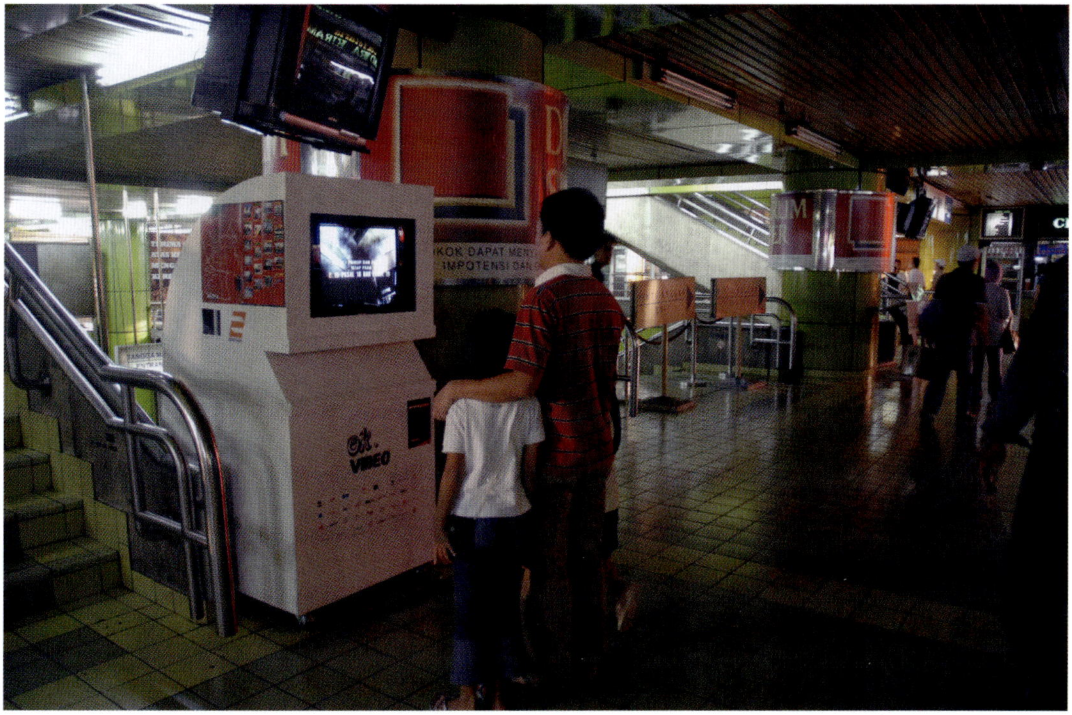

347

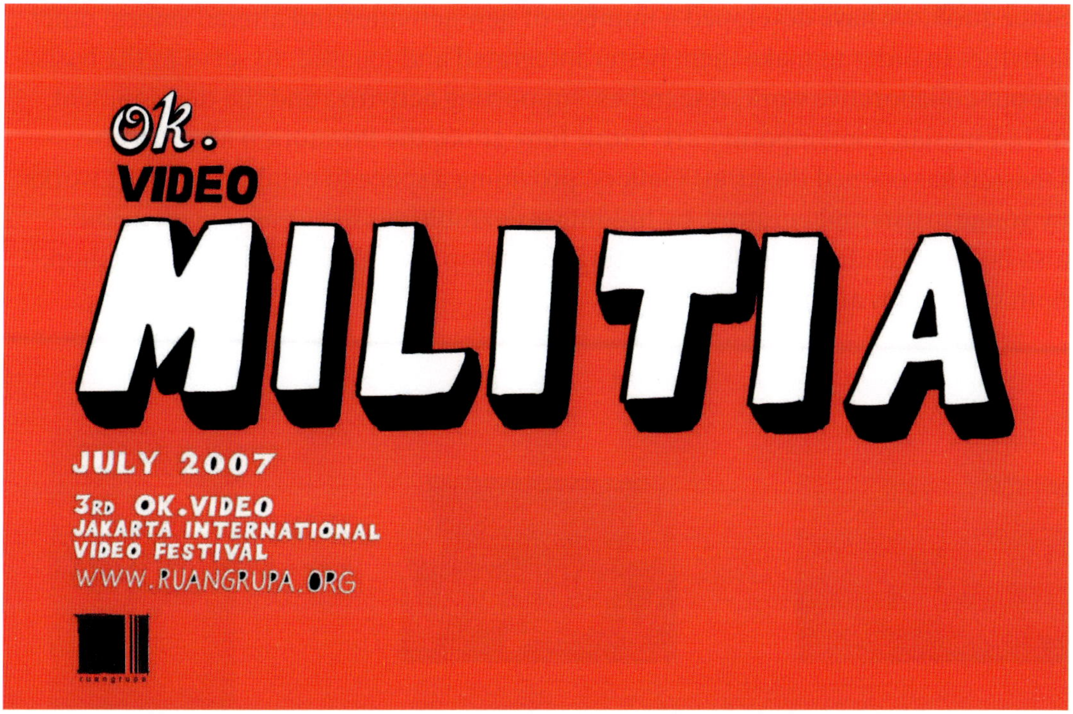

348

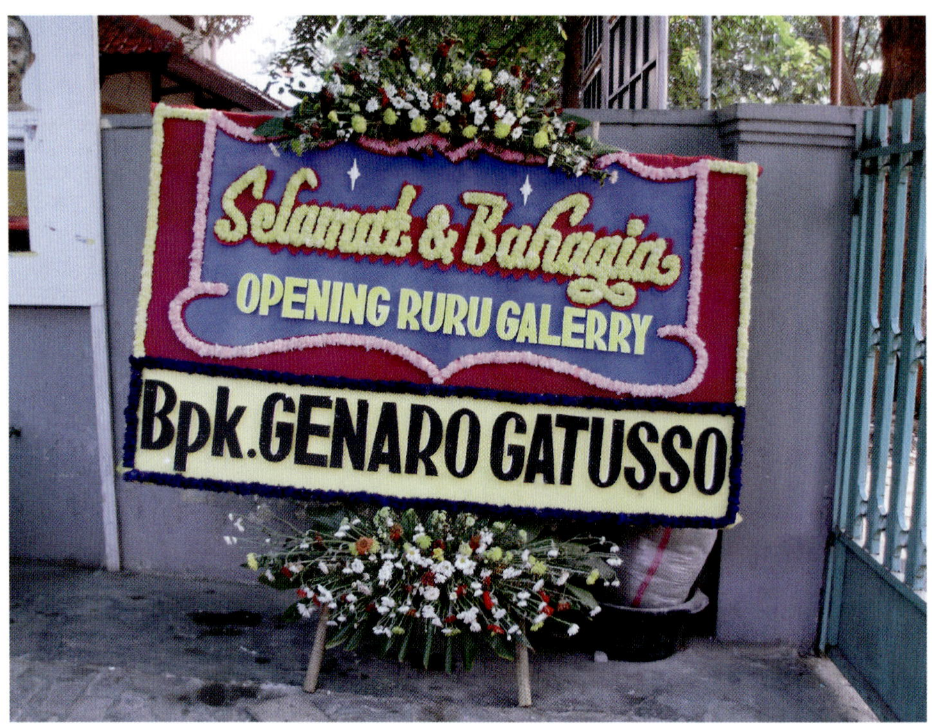

349

Since 2008, we have developed a number of new activities and altered several other activities in order to make them better integrated and focused, to serve as the basis for our collaborative work, researches, supporting activities and the development of Indonesian contemporary art. From June 2008, the Promotion and Support Division has opened the RURU Gallery, providing a space to exhibit visual art works by young artists and curators, by holding six exhibitions in a year. The division also holds art and visual culture writing workshop, as well as curatorial workshop; both workshops are held once a year.

ruangrupa

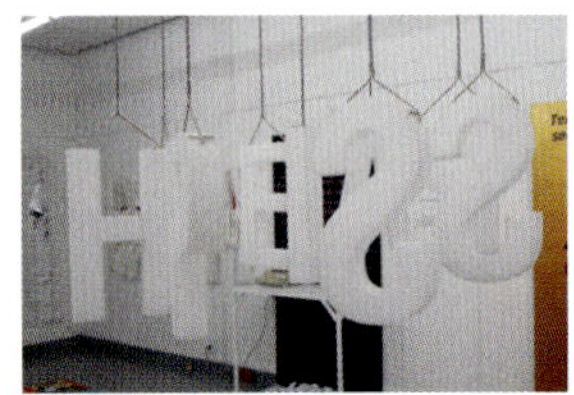

350

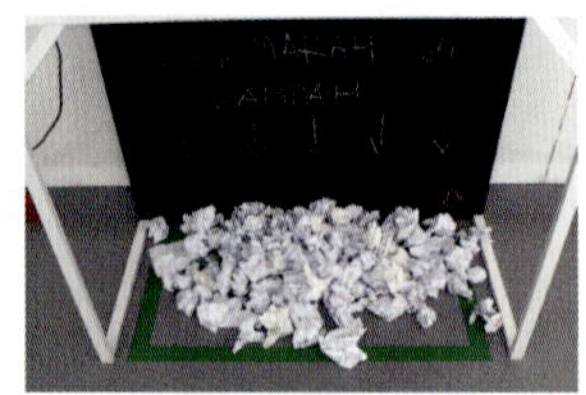

351

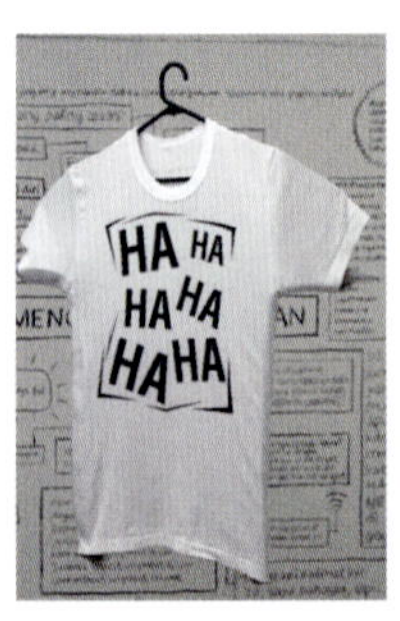

352

'Happiness', exhibition by Irwan Ahmett, RURU Gallery, 14–28 June 2008

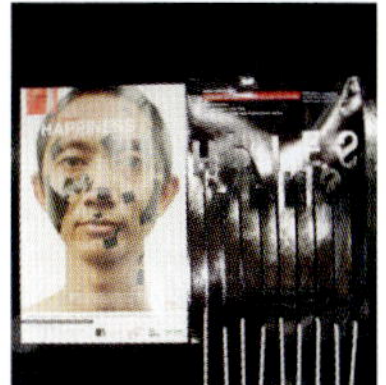

353

I think they asked me whether I'd like to be curator for RURU Gallery. I then realised it was not only curator, but also manager and (sometimes) installer. I said yes, I'd like to see how curating works. Things became more intense: helping Ajeng organise the Arts Collaboratory assembly; or being sent to Taiwan to deliver a ruru presentation with no experience presenting in English. But through that I learned. It's like being thrown into the sea to learn swimming. It can be risky – but I was willing to do it. Perhaps this is also what made some hesitate or even leave ruangrupa.

Leonhard Bartolomeus

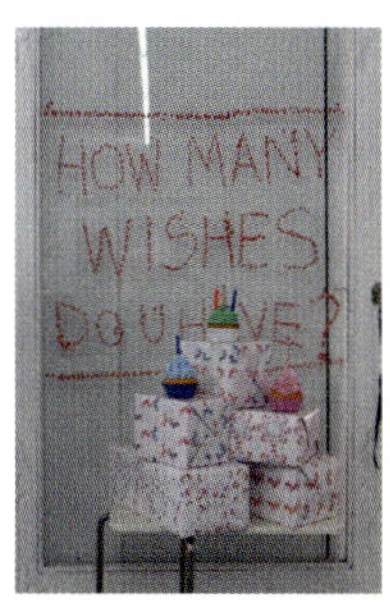

354

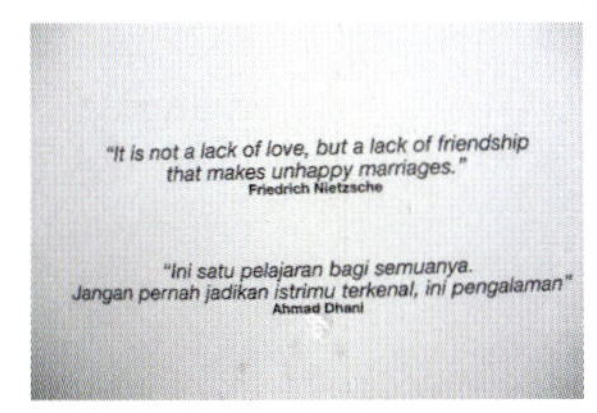

355

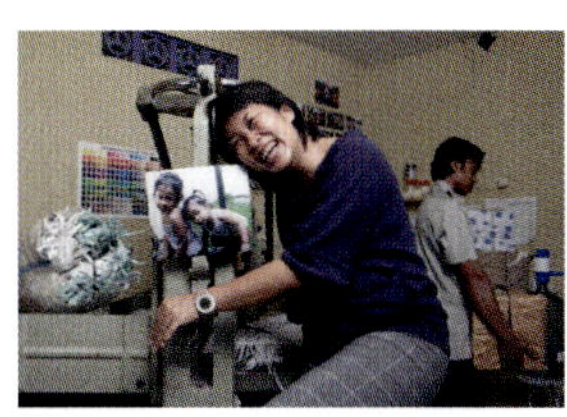

356

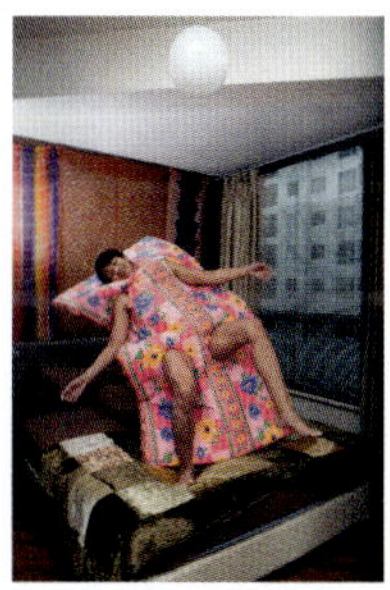

357

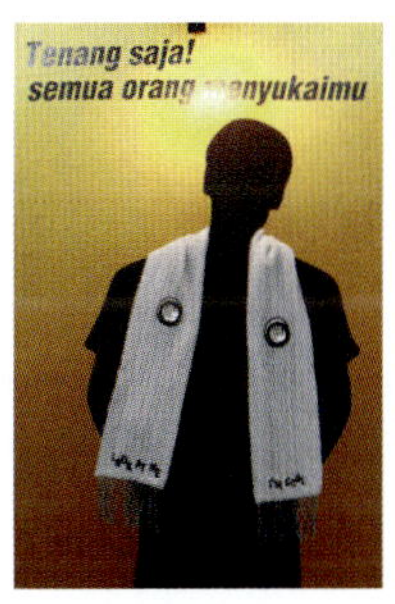

358

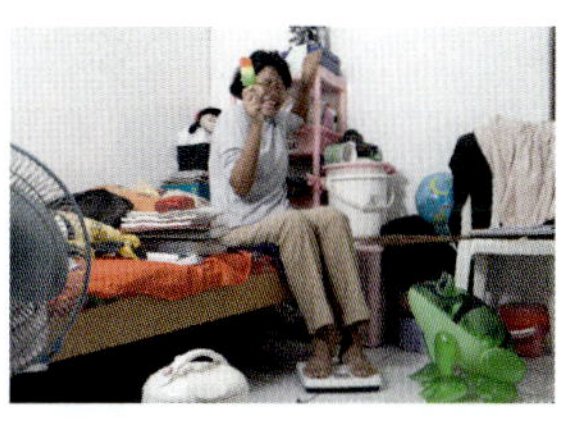

359

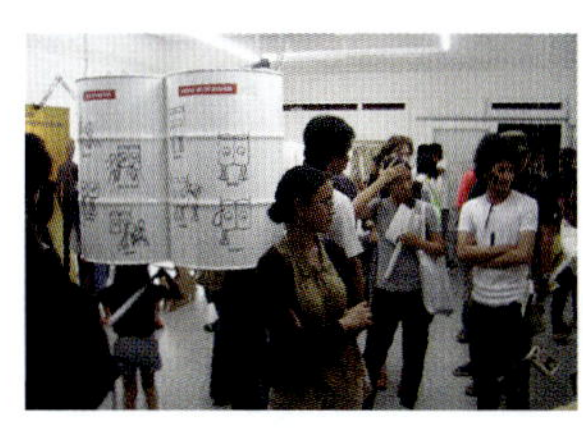

360

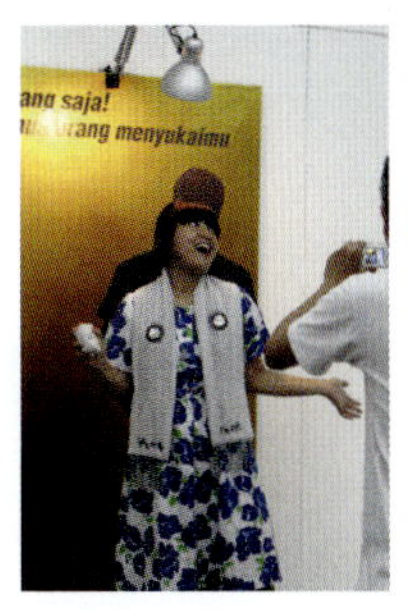

361

see also pp.423–24

Art criticism workshop, ruru house, 16–27 July 2008 164

ruangrupa begins hosting art criticism and curatorial workshops for young practitioners in Indonesia, which take place at RURU Gallery annually until around 2013; www.jarakpandang is created as a publishing outlet co-managed by participants of the art criticism workshops

My interest in joining ruru started to develop after the art criticism workshop. As part of the workshops people could get to know more about ruru, and some of us became members, got involved in ruru's projects, or took part in other projects led by ruru members. I was involved in OK.Video festival, for example. Eventually I heard ruangrupa wanted to have a 're-generation'. Maybe that's why they invited me and Barto and several other young people to get involved. We were paid a sort of commitment fee. We had a joke that the art criticism workshop was like a ruru 'trap'. I think it's a good trap, haha.

Riksa Afiaty

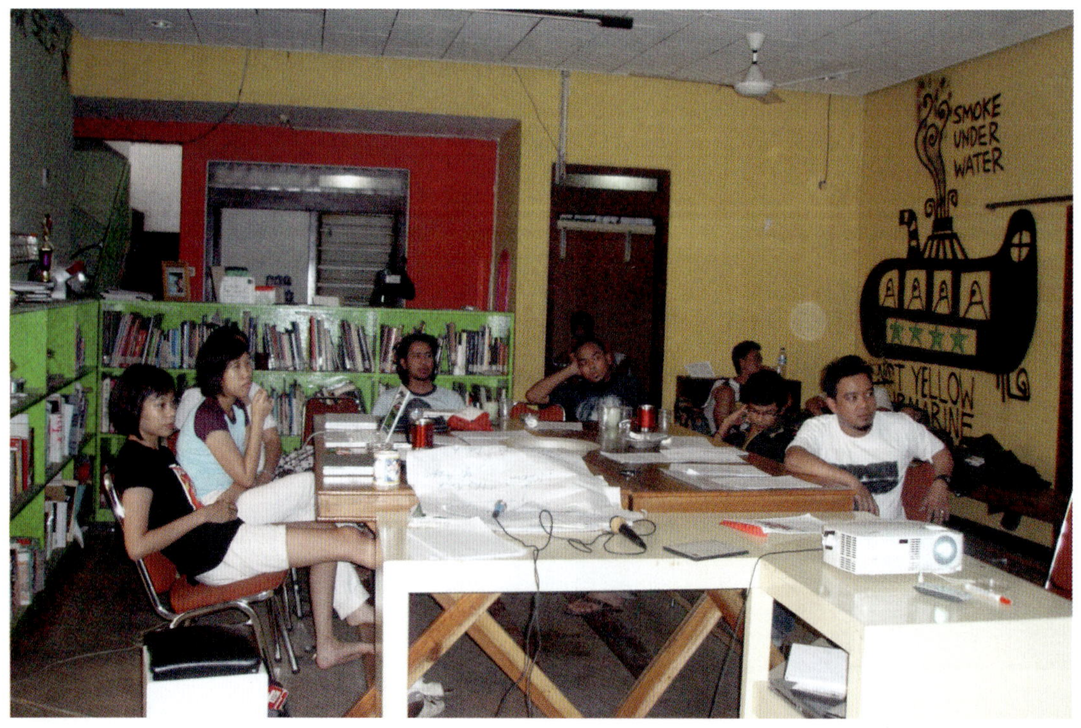

see also p.421

working style

Things to be considered in building up the working style:
think & tank
brainstorming & serial discussion
workshop & criticism
on mediums & other issues
visual studies & models/mock-up
collective & collaboration
support & understanding
love & other demons
jokes & play
music & alcohol & cigarettes

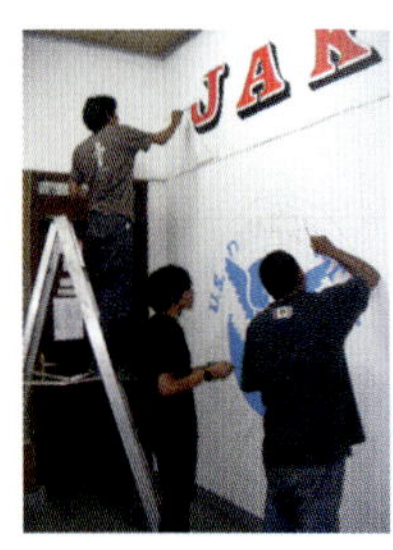

363

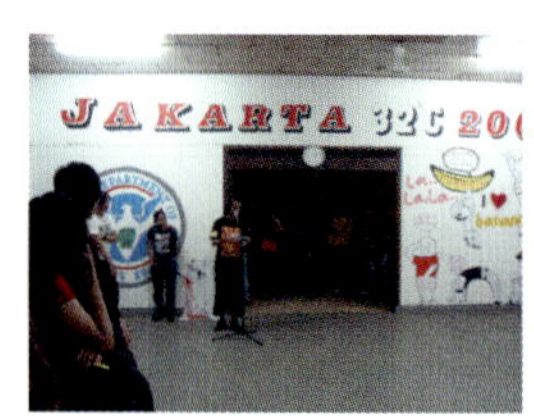

364

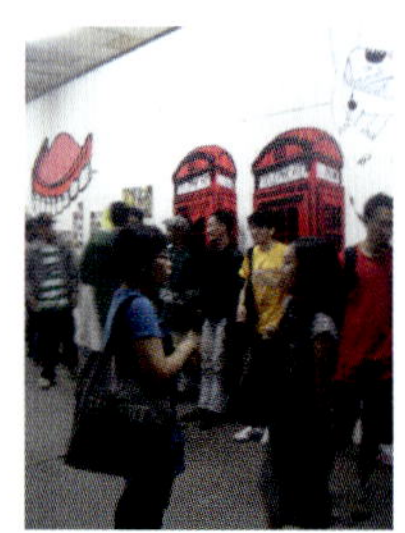

365

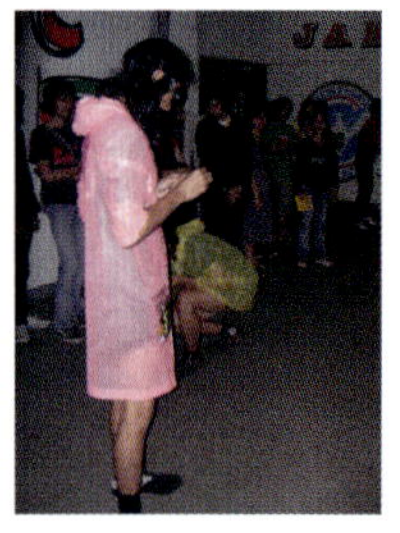

366

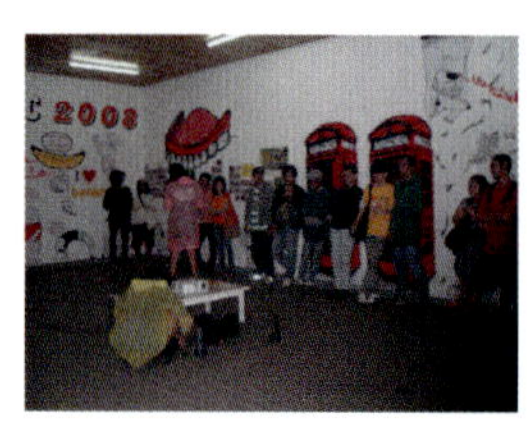

367

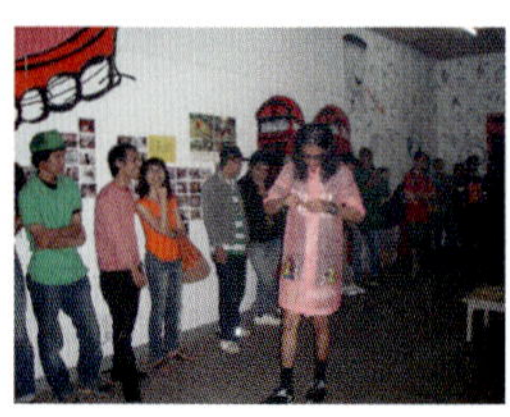

368

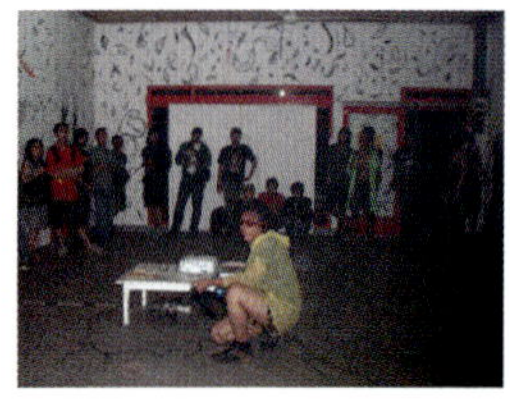

369

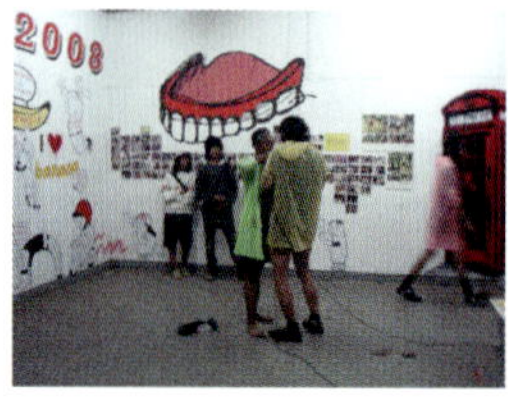

370

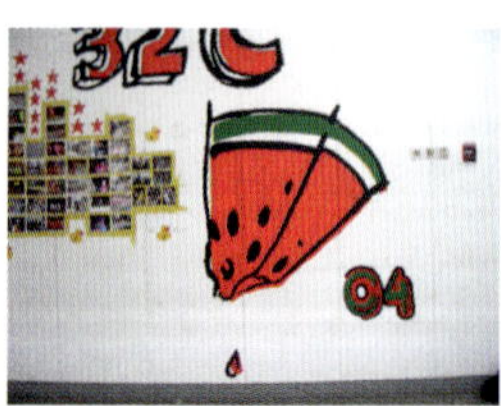

371

ruangrupa has replaced our Artist-in-Residency programme and Art Workshop with the ArtLab programme since 2008, which is designed to conduct research and creative collaborations on urban and media issues. ArtLab's research is thematic. It serves as a collaborative space for individual artists as well as interdisciplinary groups from Indonesia and abroad.

ruangrupa

'HALOMONO 3: paintings, photography, installation, video, graffiti, sticker, live music performance', RURU Gallery, 11–25 October 2008

with Sanchia, Lisza, Heditya, Keke Tumbuan, Aprilia Apsari, Zsou and The Beast Iron, Ludmila Gaffar, Evelyn Pritt, DJ Asung, DJ Yoca and Kudaponi

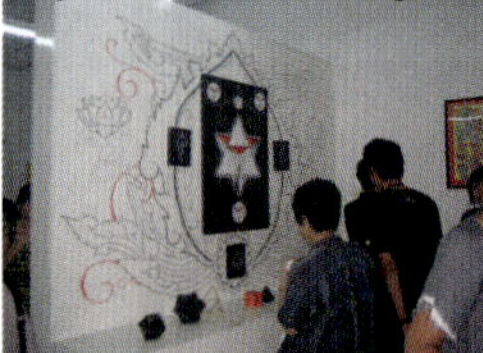

372

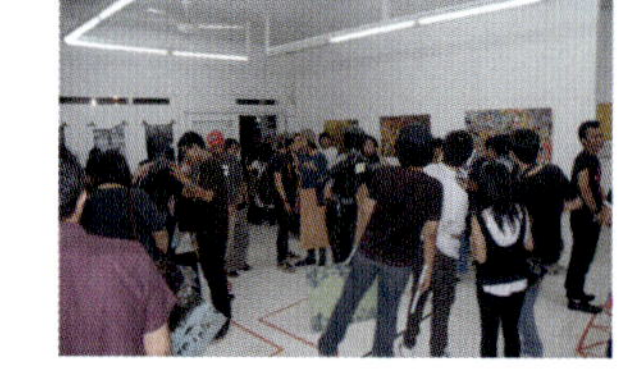

373

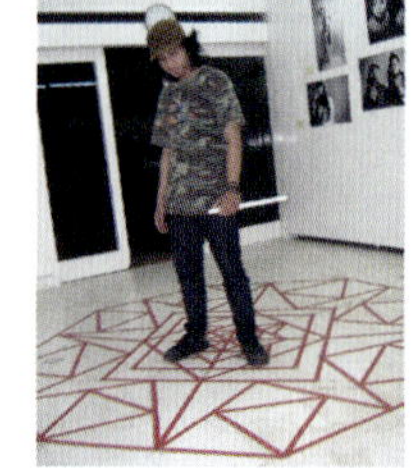

374

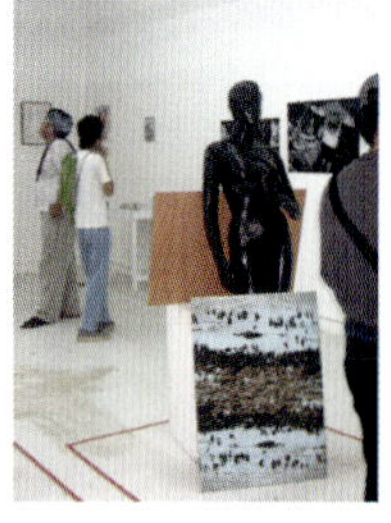

375

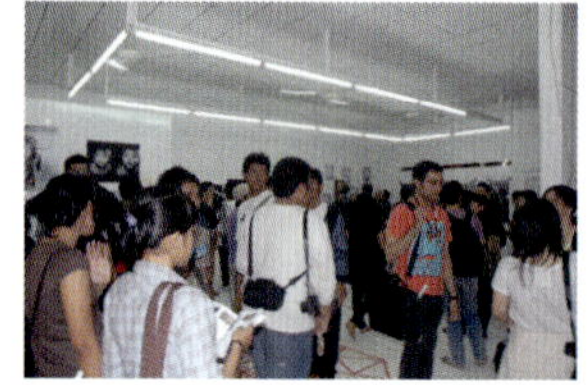

376

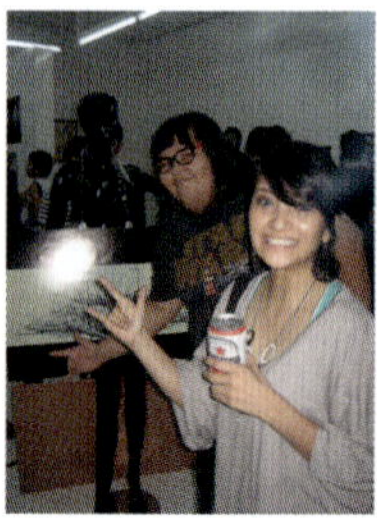

377

‘Siklus’ (‘Cycles’), RURU Gallery, 24 November – 6 December 2008

group exhibition and workshops, with Komunitas Maros

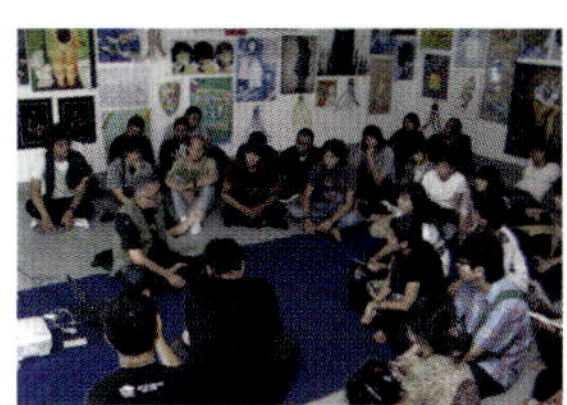

378

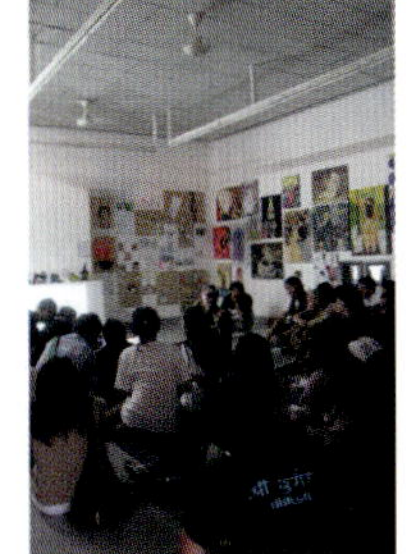

379

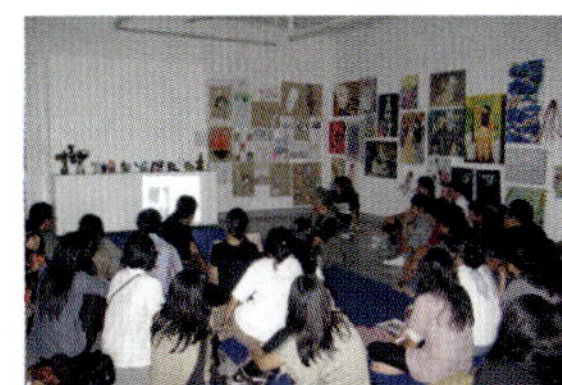

380

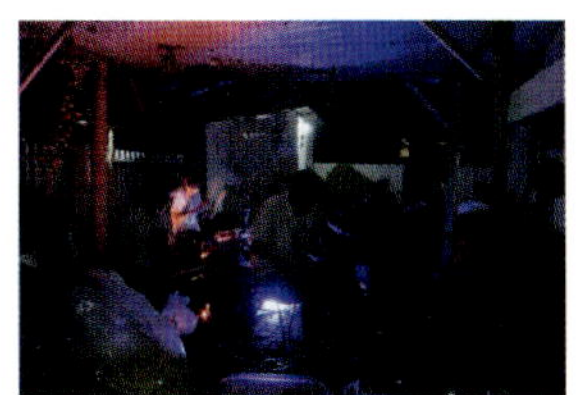

381

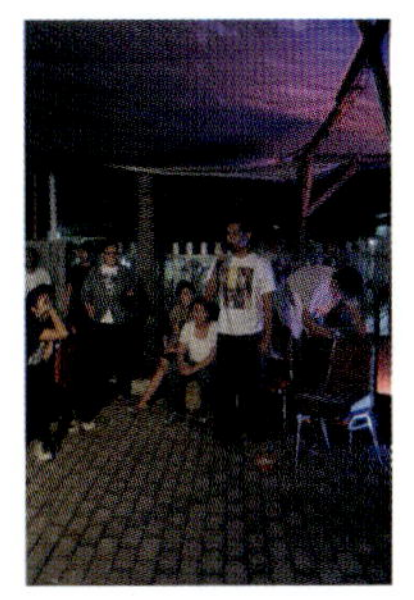

382

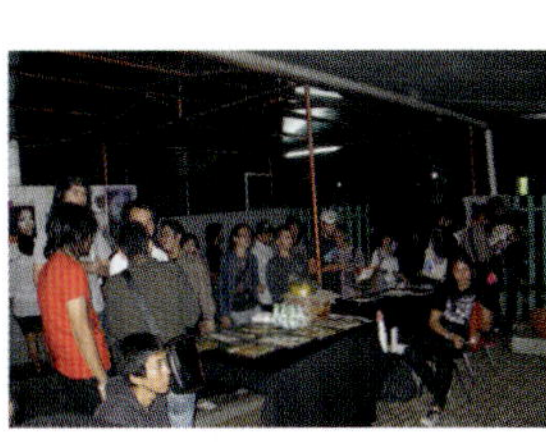

383

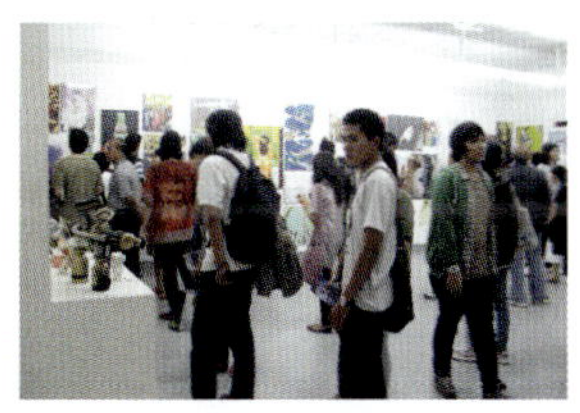

384

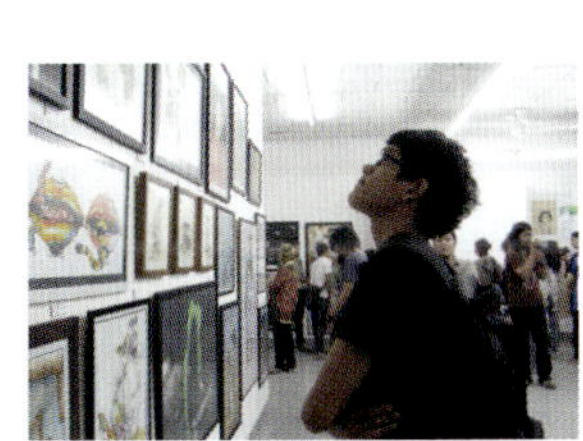

385

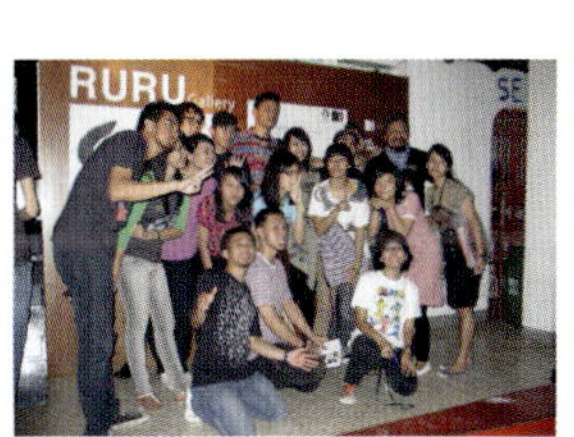

386

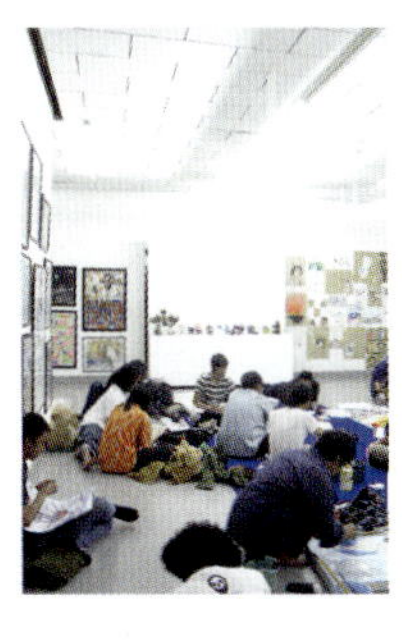

387

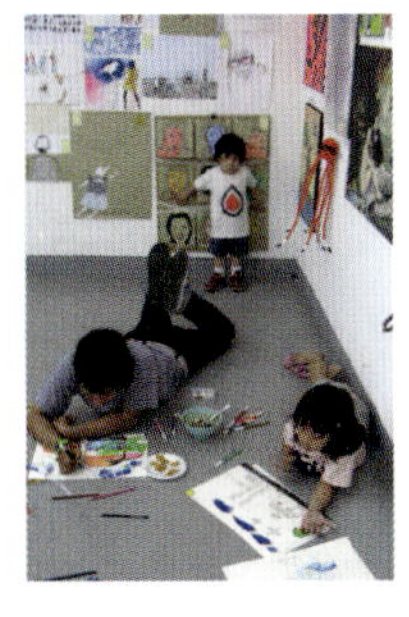

388

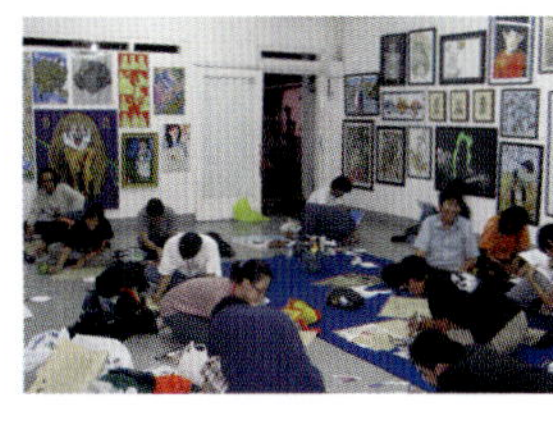

389

'Rayuan Pulau Kelapa' ('The Seduction of Kelapa Island'), exhibition by Aprilia Apsari, RURU Gallery, 13–27 December 2008

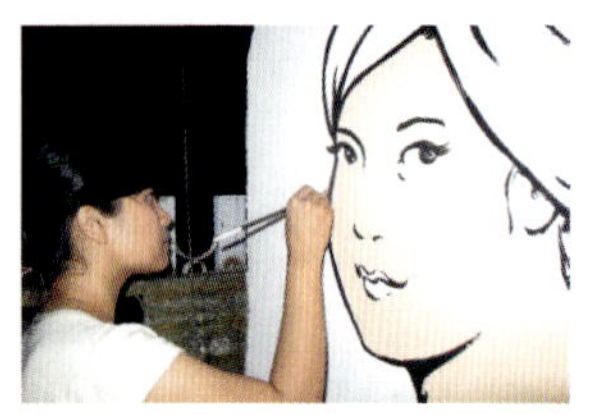

390

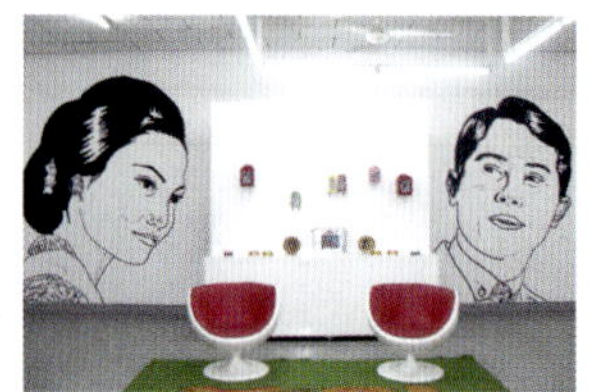

391

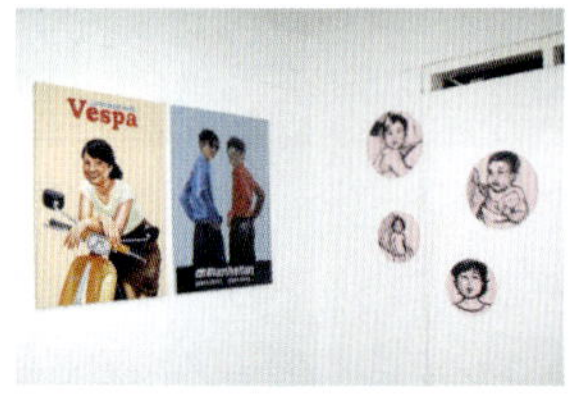

392

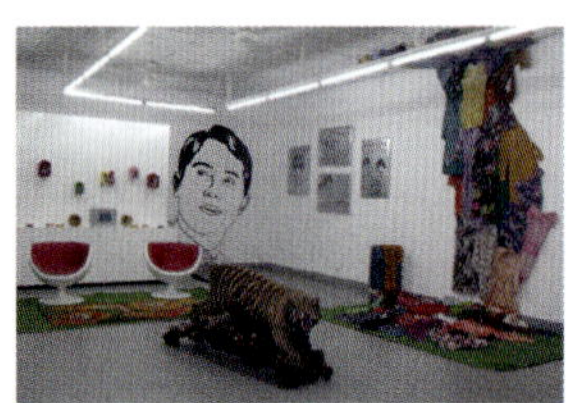

393

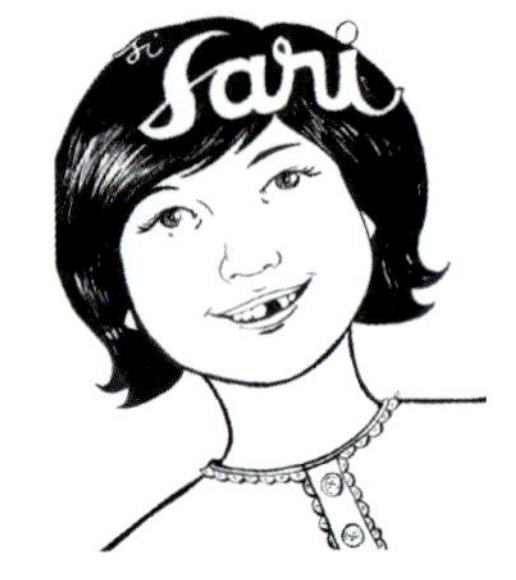

394

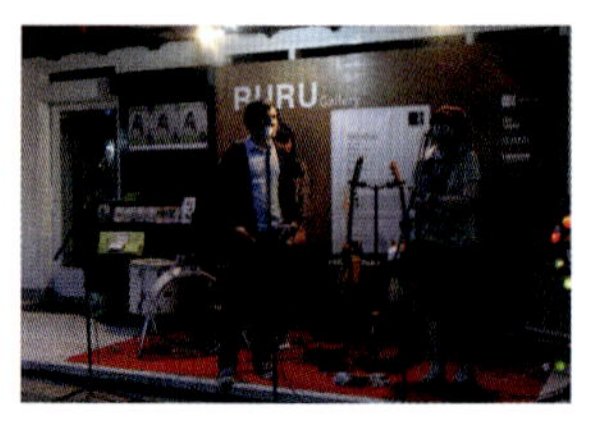

395

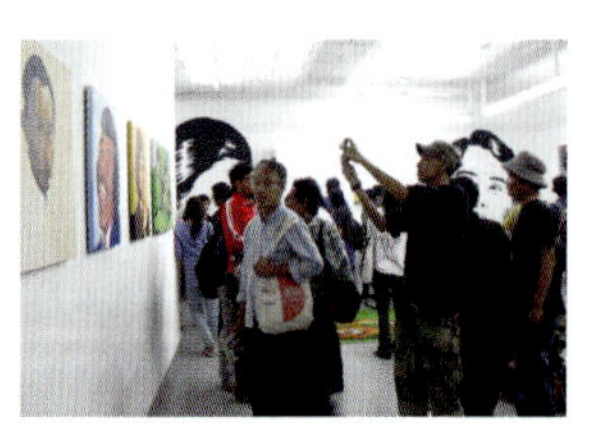

396

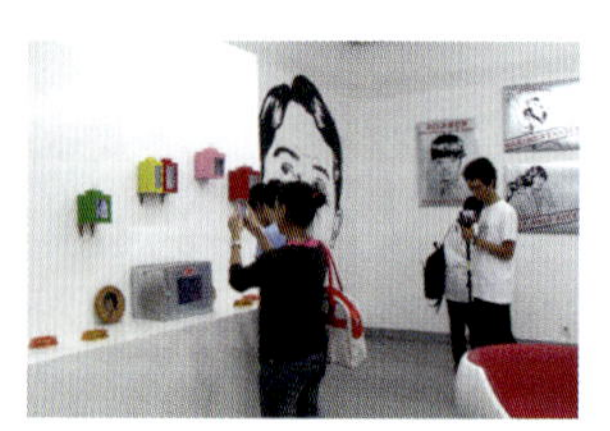

397

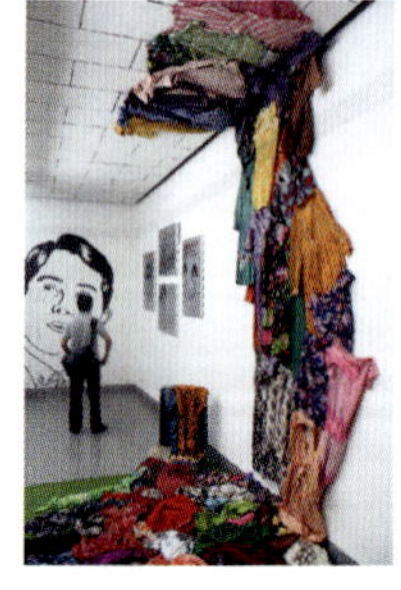

398

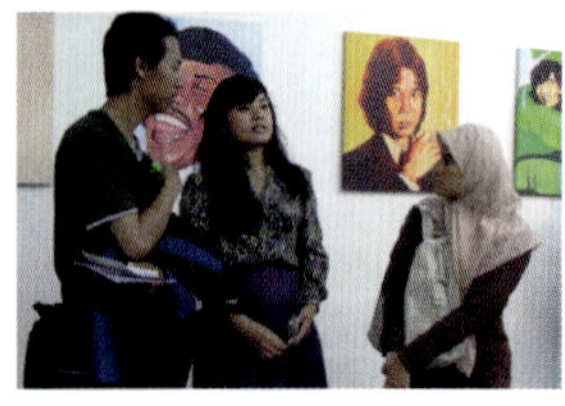

399

ruangrupa is like a band. It's a jam session. There is some order, like a beat, but people are always coming in and out of the session. Maybe not exactly the genre that you're interested in individually, but you're able to play it anyway when we're together.

farid rakun

We cheer our differences; we believe that the group is a collection of different people. We adore each other, we envy each other; we don't read the same stuff, and we don't necessarily watch or listen to things in common. Of course, there is always overlap, intersections between our respective engagements and interests, but we think that the divergences make the collective life of ruangrupa richer. It wasn't always like this – in the beginning, we were, more or less, a group of art school students, sharing a collective life together in such informality – but after some years, we preferred to use the term 'ingredients' – like a kitchen – to construct or represent our identity where one element can actually trigger, accelerate or strengthen the others.

Ade Darmawan

ruru was a boys club and you could tell that they loved each other so much. They would *nongkrong* until 4am in this dingy house and always wanted to be with each other. It would be hard for some women to catch up (due to strict parents, curfews, etc), but I never felt unsafe with them or judged for being a woman. Some other groups were misogynistic, ruangrupa wasn't. They were egalitarian and even feminists.

Farah Wardani

ruru was my first home in Jakarta. I used to hate Jakarta, so it's thanks to them that I went there more often after they invited me to be part of the first OK.Video. Each time, from the airport I'd go straight to ruru, drop my stuff there, then run around working, and come back at night and crash in ruru. And everyone was like, 'How can you do that?' Like, you know, 'It's so messy! Where do you sleep?' It was such a stinky mess, like a boys' den. 'How can you stand it?!' I must've found a corner to camp. If you go to the archive of ruru, you may find, as one of their seasonal greetings images, a picture of their sink. It was absolutely gross (*laughs*). That's my nostalgia of ruru.

Tintin Wulia

In terms of gender, it's a lot better now. But that time [in mid-2000s], it was 98 per cent men. Plus, I was there as a foreigner, an outsider. If there were more women involved, then my experience would have been quite different. Those who were hanging out in ruru house were mostly male. When they hosted students, there were more female students and visitors, but the core members are dominantly male.

Che Kyongfa

To talk about contemporary graphic design in Indonesia, we have to acknowledge the ubiquity of *stiker kota*, or city stickers. *Stiker kota* are small (usually less than 15 centimetres wide), cheap, popular stickers that circulate widely through urban networks. Designers are generally anonymous and work by responding to the popularity of their designs (judged by sales and their appearance on urban surfaces) as well as trends in popular culture. Jakarta-based, artist-run initiative ruangrupa considers stiker kota a visually rich social phenomena and has been researching and archiving them since 2001.

farid rakun

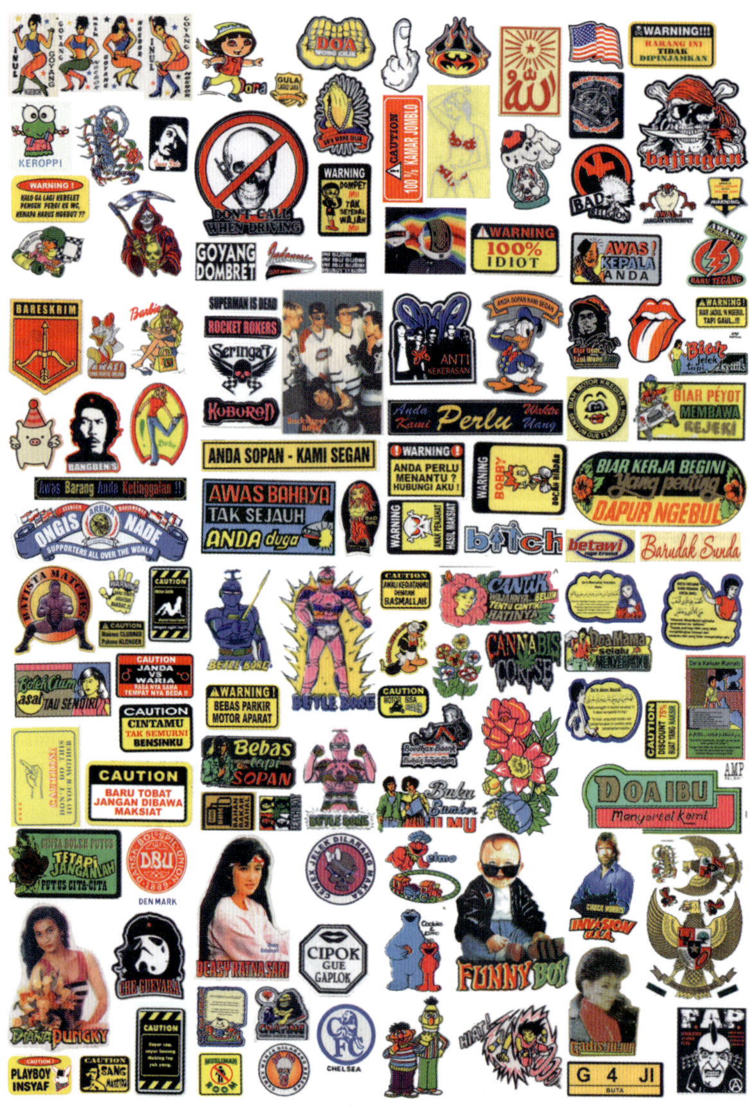

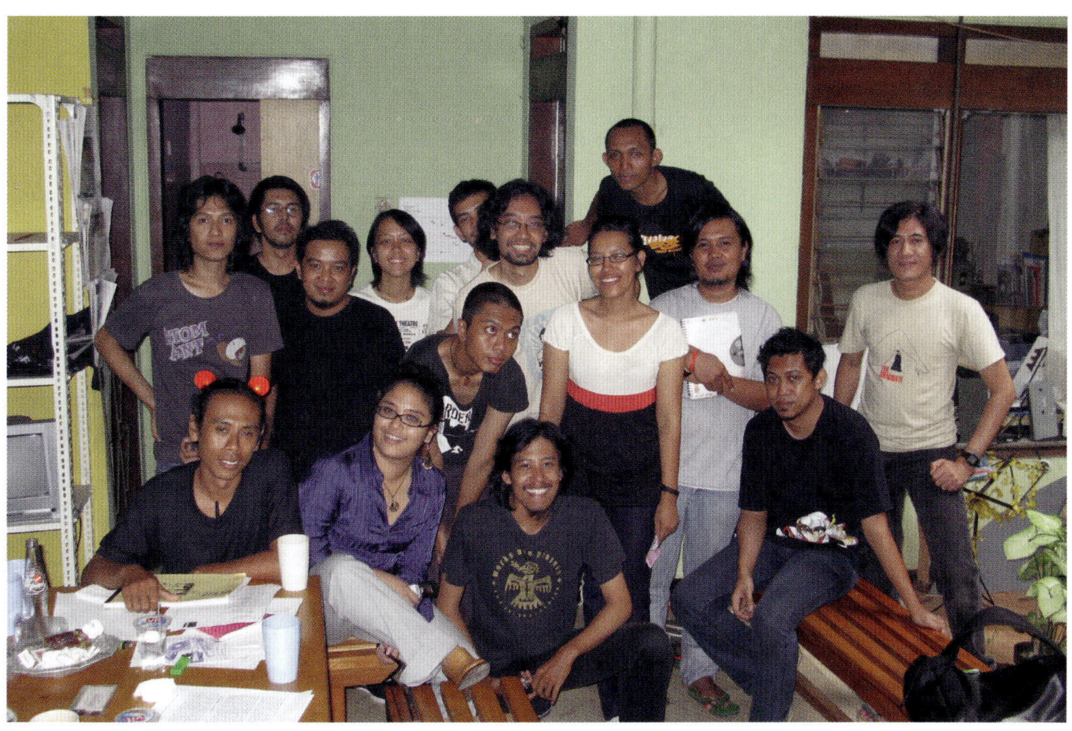

401

We are a very informal network. ruru's informality really fits with what I think is the basis of Indonesian activism. Usually in the West, we think of NGOs or something formal like that. But here, this is more like an organic, fluid space, which serves as an intersection between people. In this atmosphere we always meet with each other in different occasions whether it's in a discussion or other activisms. That is how I got connected with ruru activists.

Melani Budianta

Being mutually supportive is an essential element of the structure and fabric of ruangrupa. As Ade Darmawan, one of ruangrupa's founding members and its current director, once shared, often no one even seems to remember who exactly came up with what idea.

reinaart vanhoe

I do not know any collective whose members are so committed to each other and in which structure is not structured but really embodied. The ultimate host for its members and for anyone that is willing to commit time. The generosity all the members have towards each other. Its passion for the artistic as experimentation combined with its capacity to relativise it.

Gertrude Flentge

It's quite strange in a way. We started ruangrupa as something that is really not for the future. It's the moment we have the same visions between friends who agreed to work together. Each of us just adore each other. When you work together, you would realise, oh you can do this, I really adore you. It's respect, and from that you become also supportive. You understand that it's because of them something works and you cannot do this alone. Then you find the way we did works. We also ignored whose ideas were that. Everything's accumulated and we forgot who started what. It's like filling in for each other. Our ways of working are different, we occupy different space. For example, I'm slow. Reza is very experimental and spontaneous and responsive or adaptive to new situations or conditions. Ade is very sharp. He reads context and mediates things well. Our individual works are also very different. It's also an unsaid agreement that we never have our own exhibitions at ruru.

Indra Ameng

We're often asked: How do we survive? How do we sustain ourselves as a group? Each individual in ruangrupa has their own answer. My most recent reflection is that we've managed to sustain, perhaps even survive, this long precisely because we never gave 100 percent of ourselves to ruangrupa. Instead, we've always practiced this 'in and out' overlapping rhythm – everyone does it - and we celebrate and collectively support each individual. To me, an individual is a whole entity within the collective. And for ruangrupa, the collective becomes stronger when each individual is also strong. That's why this 'in and out' flow is essential – not just as a spatial integration, but as a process that unfolds over time, ideas and resources. And that's what we've done. That's what we continue to do.

Ade Darmawan

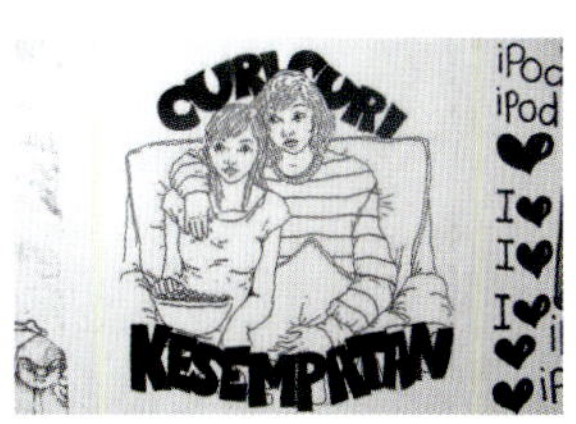

402

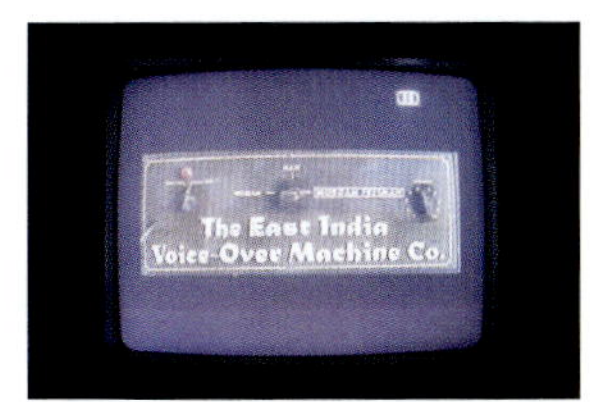

403

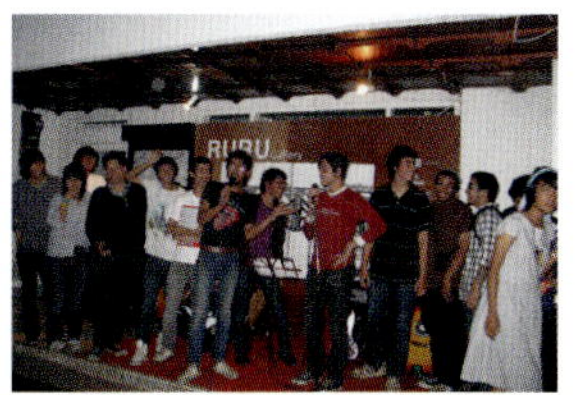

404

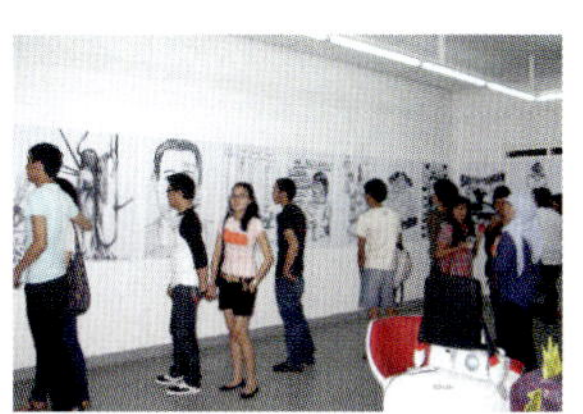

405

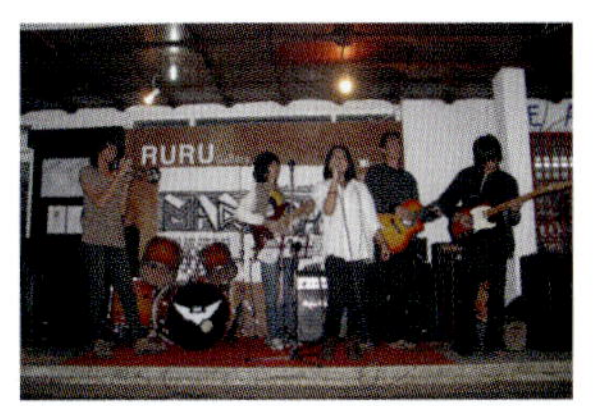

406

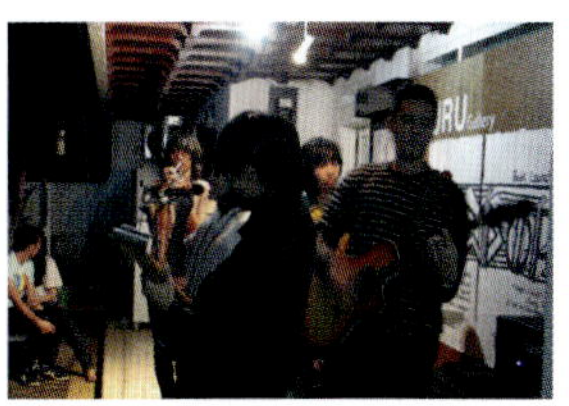

407

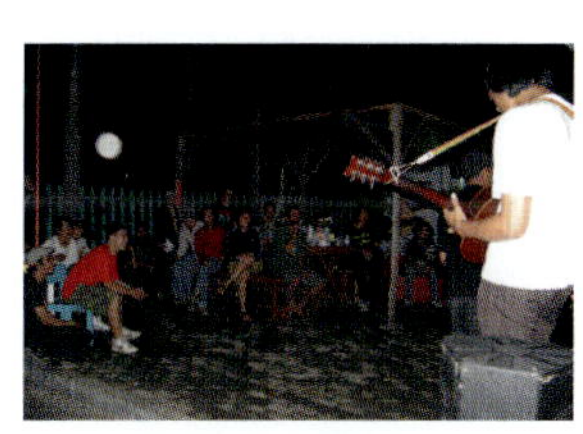

408

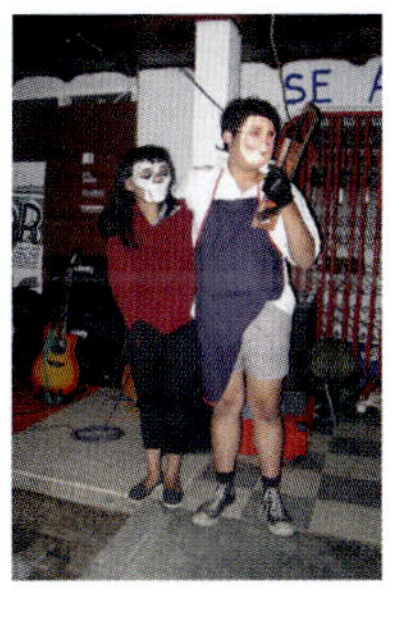

409

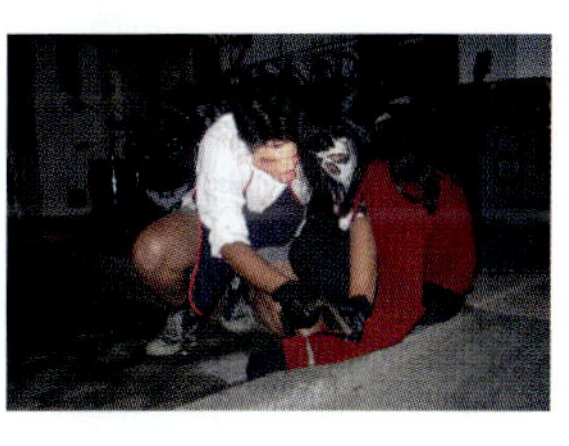

410

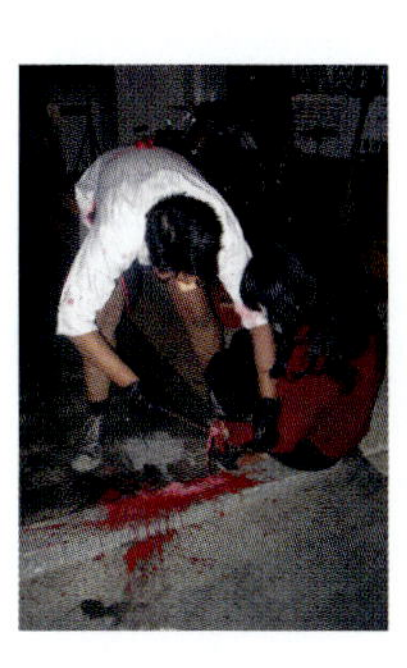

411

Jakarta 32°C Showcase programme at the 13th Jakarta Biennale, Senayan City, Jakarta, 1–7 February 2009

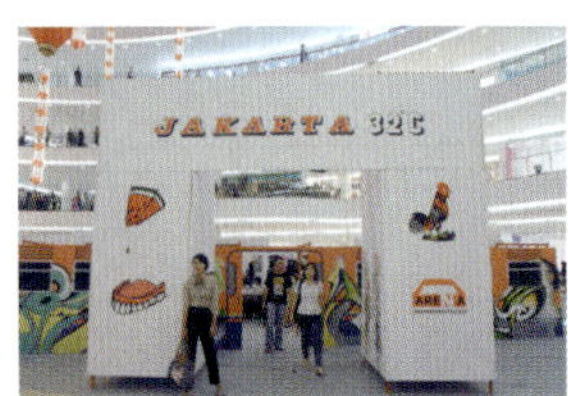

412

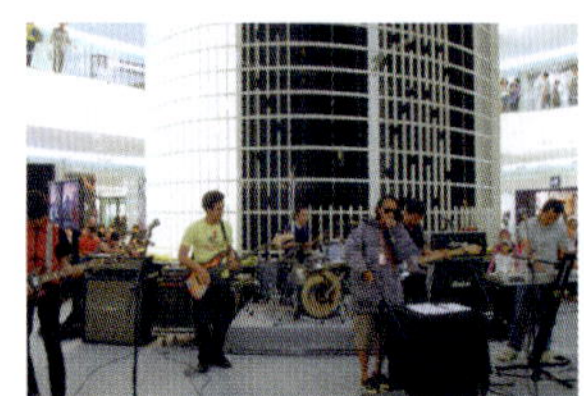

413

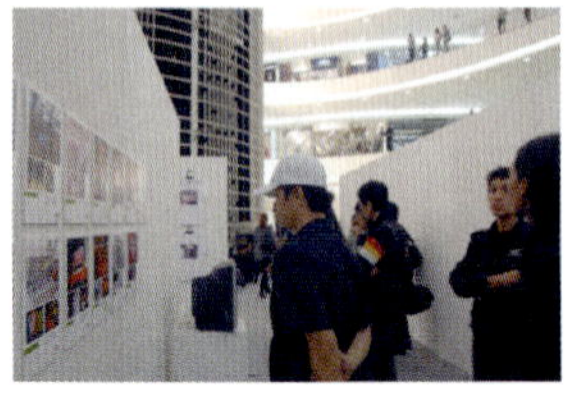

414

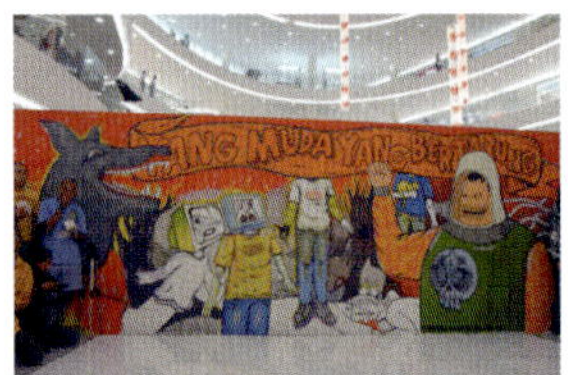

415

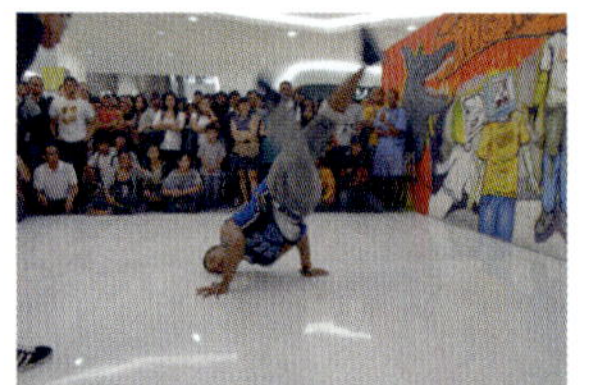

416

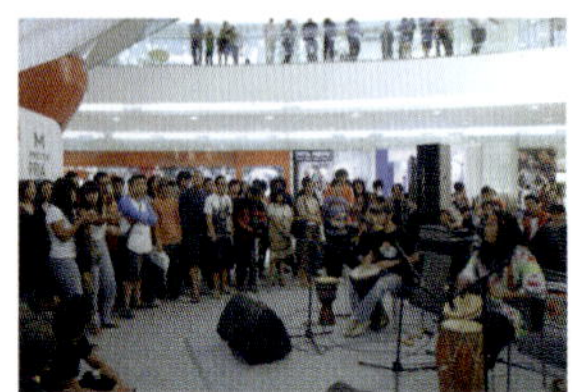

417

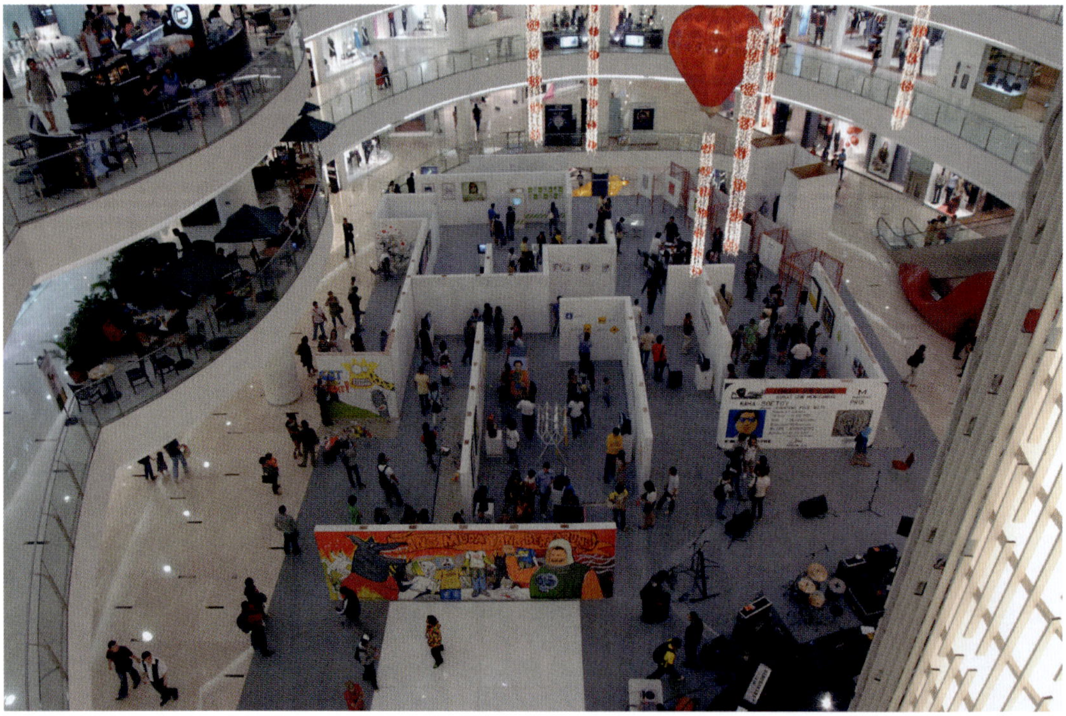

418

Being generous also means on a very simple level being available: the ruangrupa house is open 24/7, you can always sleep there, you can always find someone to talk to, the library is open without restrictions. Spaces that are not currently being used can be claimed by anyone for working, sleeping, holding a meeting, etc. Programmes such as the RURU Gallery or Jakarta 32°C also play a role in sharing knowledge and know-how.

reinaart vanhoe

We shared family connections, too. Back when my mum was still around, ruru friends would come over to my family house for meals and hangouts. Ameng's aunt would ask me how he was doing... I admired Kunil's father... Reza used to exchange Sundanese jokes with my mum. Our bond isn't just about art – it's deeply personal. It's about growing up together. We went through so much in our personal journeys ... marriages, divorces, births, losses. All the things that shape who we are. And to replicate that kind of connection with the younger generation, I think, is not easy. Trust needs time. Our friendship started in the mid 90s so it's about thirty years now. For me, the friendships we have in ruru are more than family – sometimes, even better than family.

Ade Darmawan

The biggest problem for an artist in managing an alternative space is the desire to be bigger, established and famous. An alternative space operator should probably believe that 'institutional death' is the best way out when such desire is becoming irresistible. For when the space has become bigger, it tends to be institutionally rigid, inflexible and given to compromise. Secondly, there is the problem of financial dependence on foreign sponsors. When alternative spaces started to grow here, they were operated in simple ways and on a low budget. However, if it seems one day to have turned into a big, greedy institution with a high budget, financial support from foreign sponsors become the only hope – like father, like son. Moreover, alternative space nowadays has become a new commodity of art scenes everywhere. I regard this present time as a state of emergency, a point of reconsideration.

Agung Kurniawan

'Jendela PM Toh' ('Window PM Toh'), exhibition and workshops by Agus Nur Amal (aka PM Toh), RURU Gallery, 13–28 February 2009

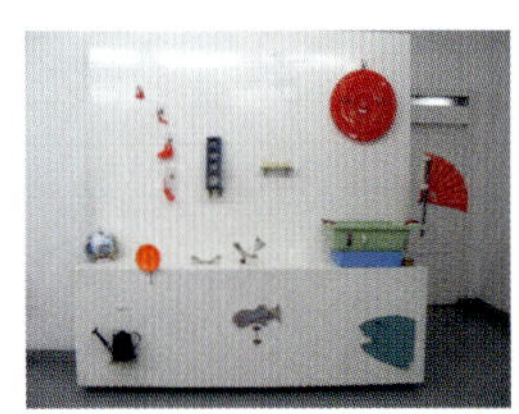

419

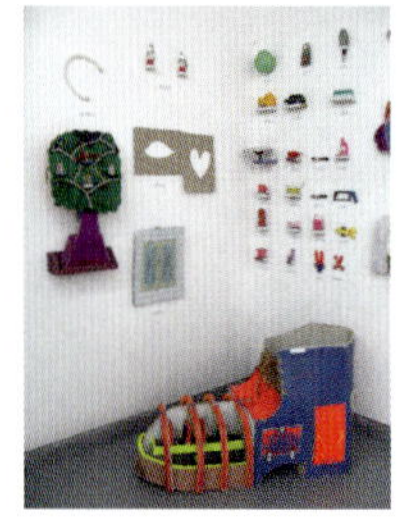

420

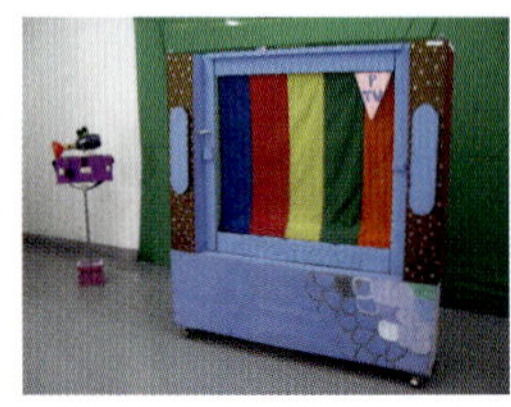

421

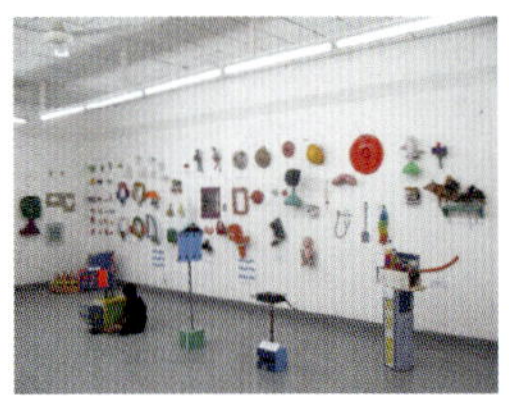

422

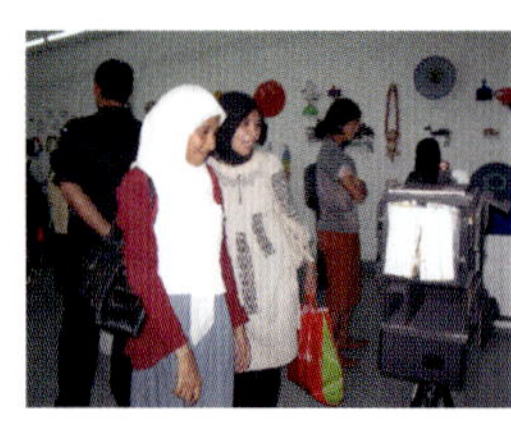

423

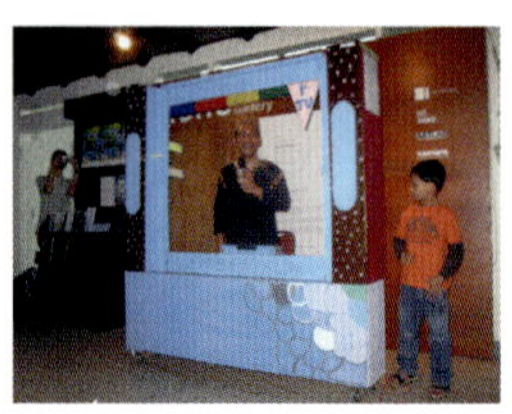

424

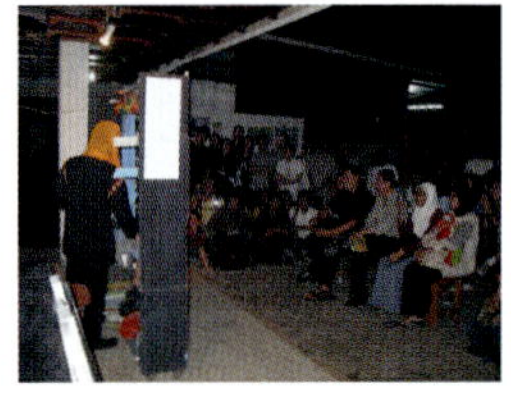

425

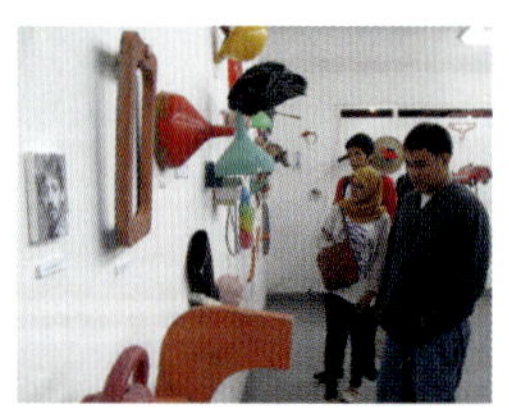

426

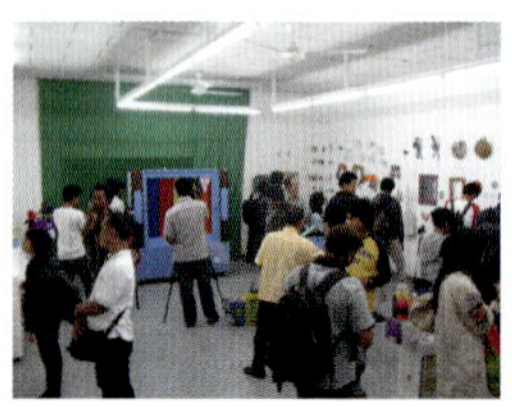

427

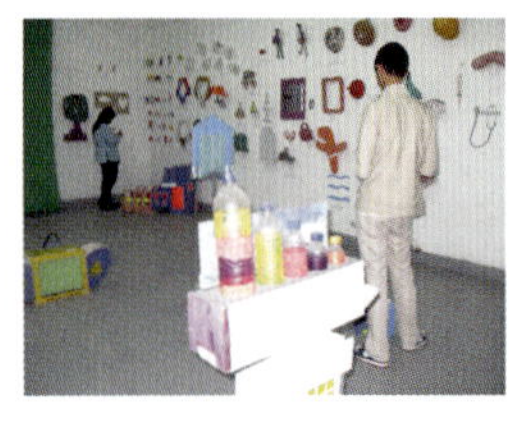

428

429

‘Macro-Micro’, an exhibition of Odile Decq and ODBC architecture firm, RURU Gallery, 6–15 March 2009

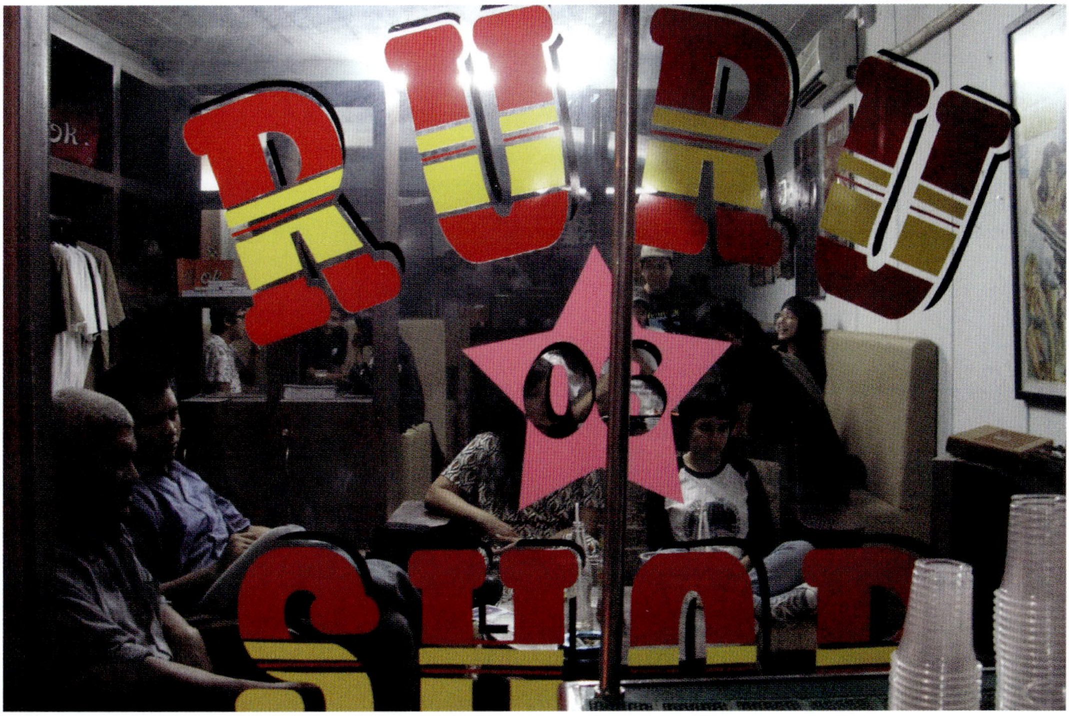

430

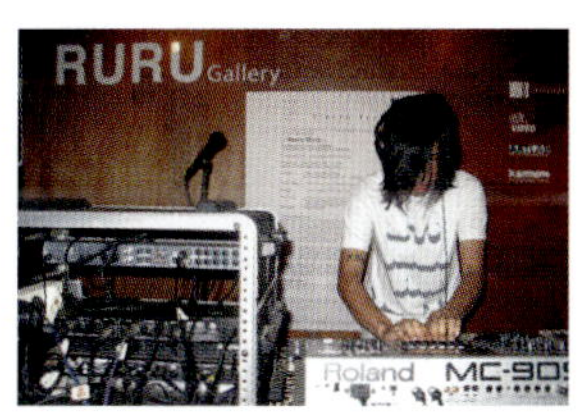

431

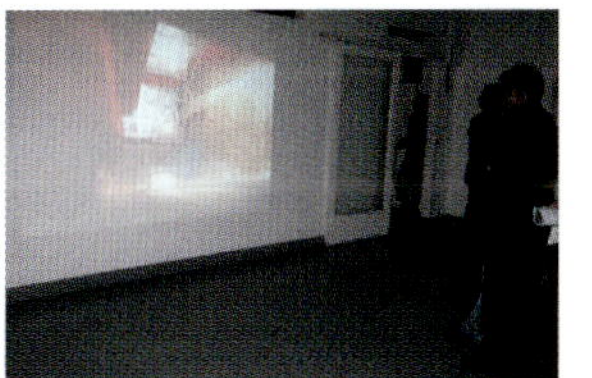

432

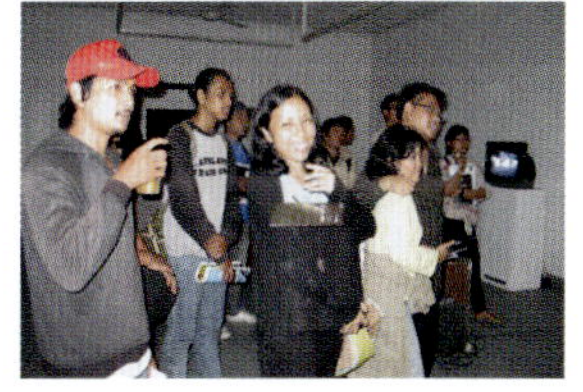

433

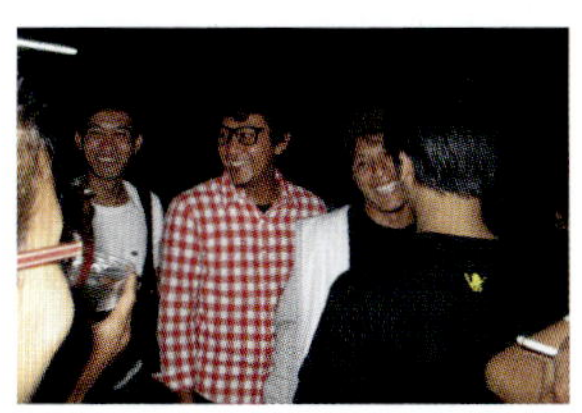

434

'Femme', exhibition and workshops with Stigma Foundation, RURU Gallery, 20–28 March 2009

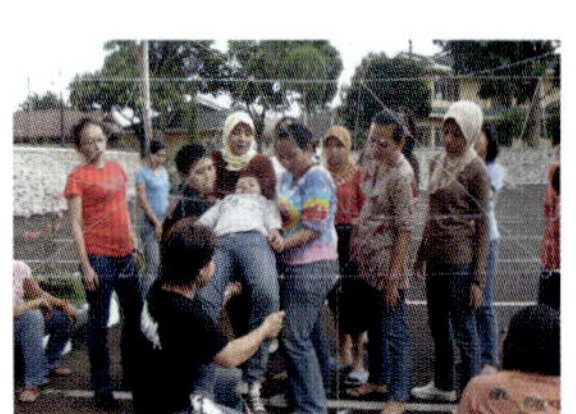

435

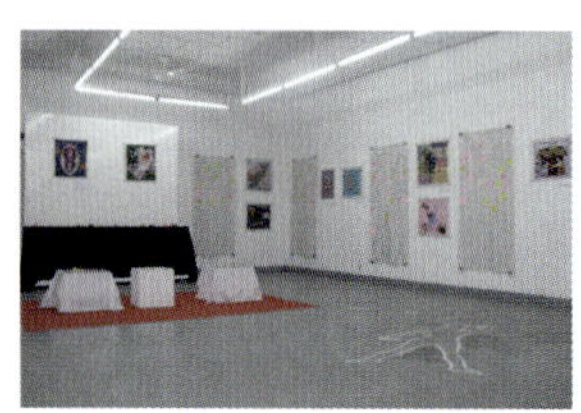

436

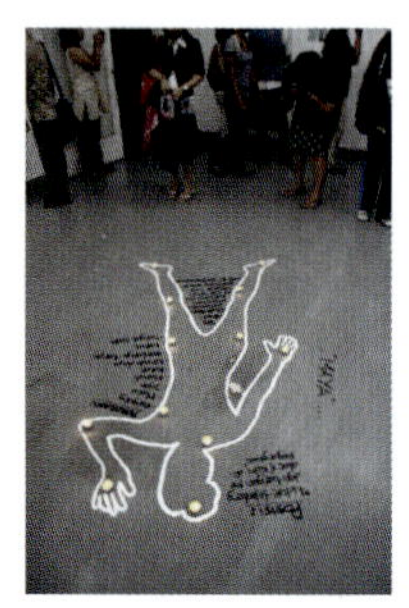

437

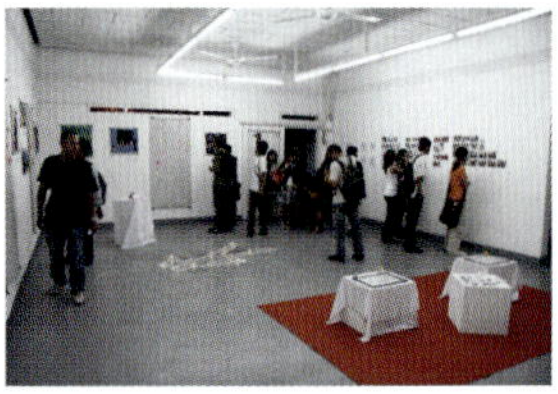

438

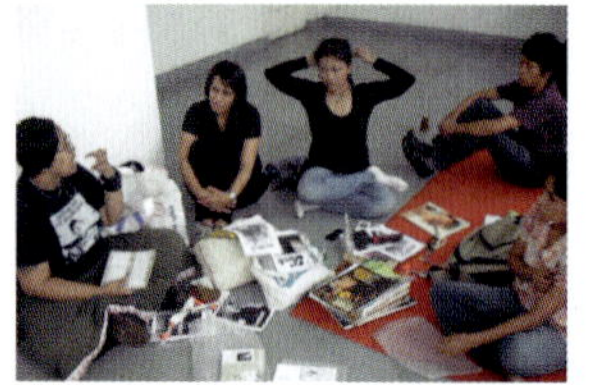

439

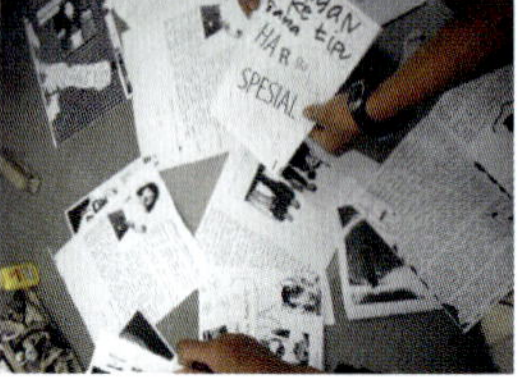

440

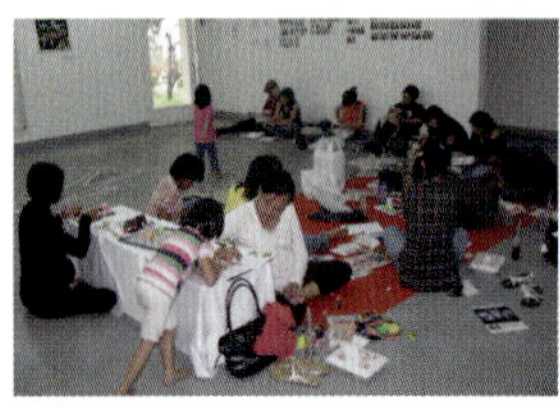

441

'Jimi! Jimi! Jimi!', exhibition by Jimi Multhazam, RURU Gallery, 2–16 May 2009

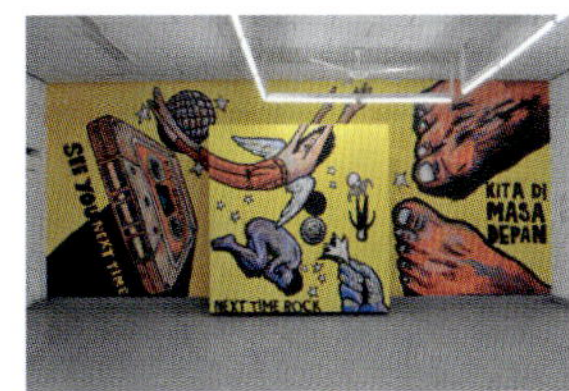

442

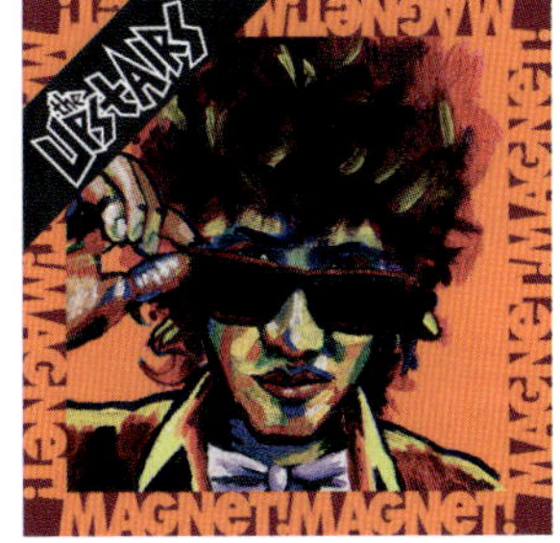

443

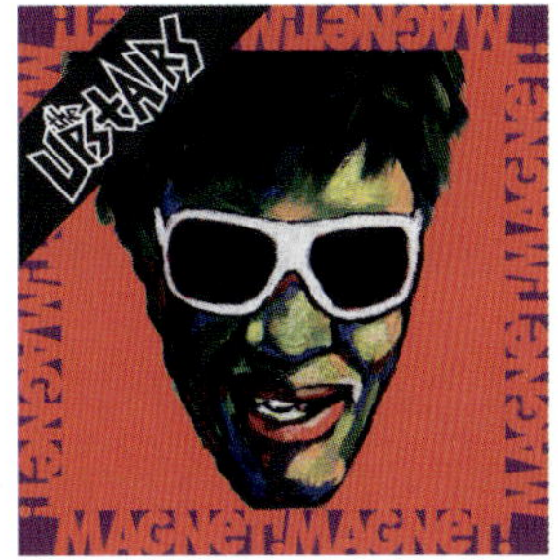

444

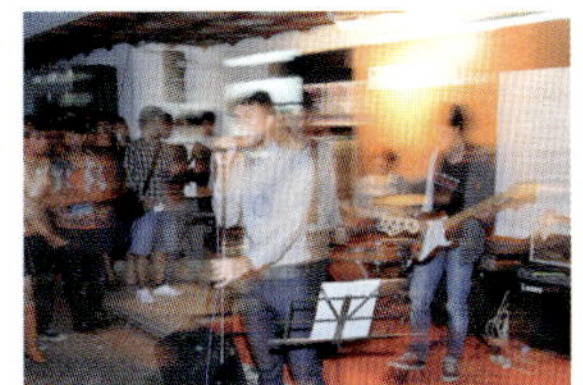

445

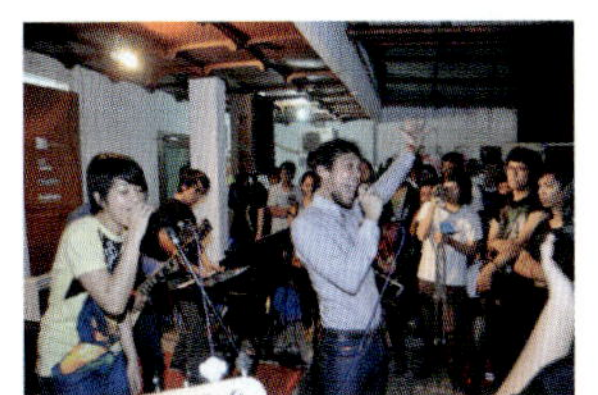

446

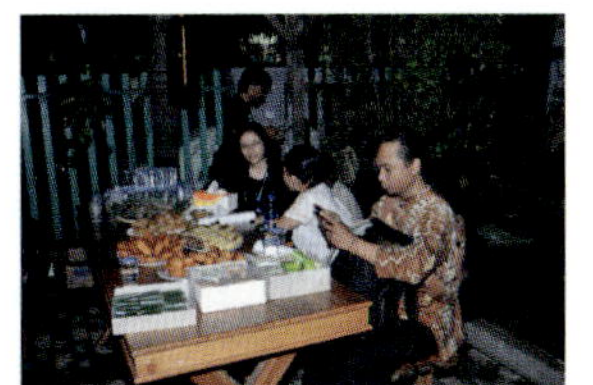

447

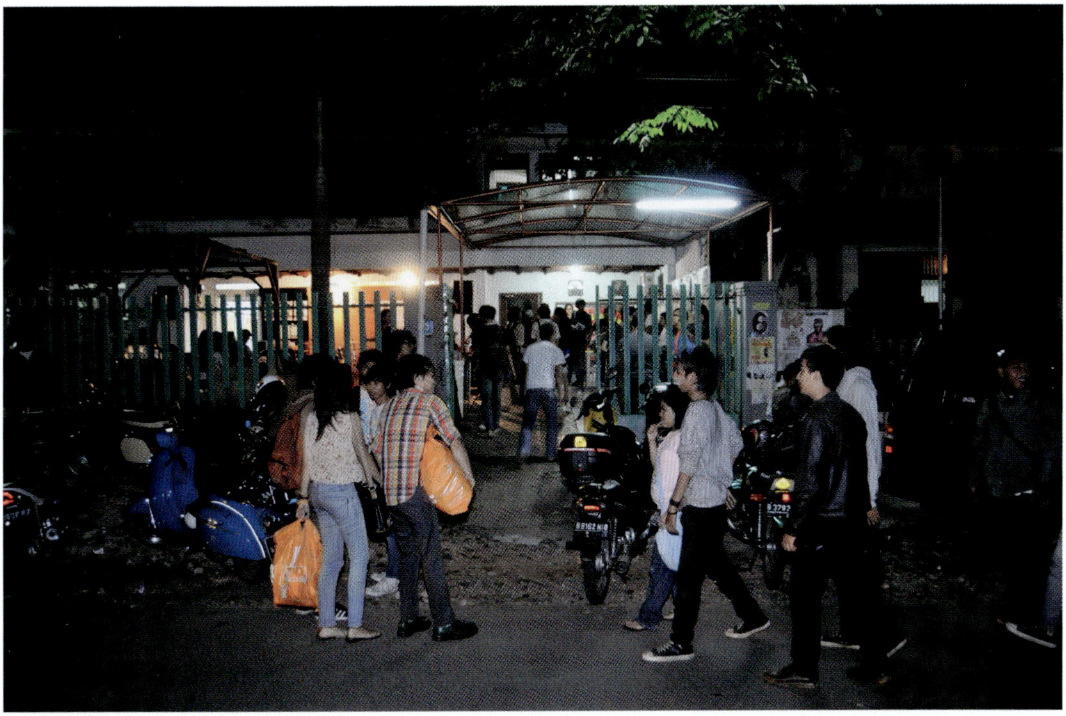

448

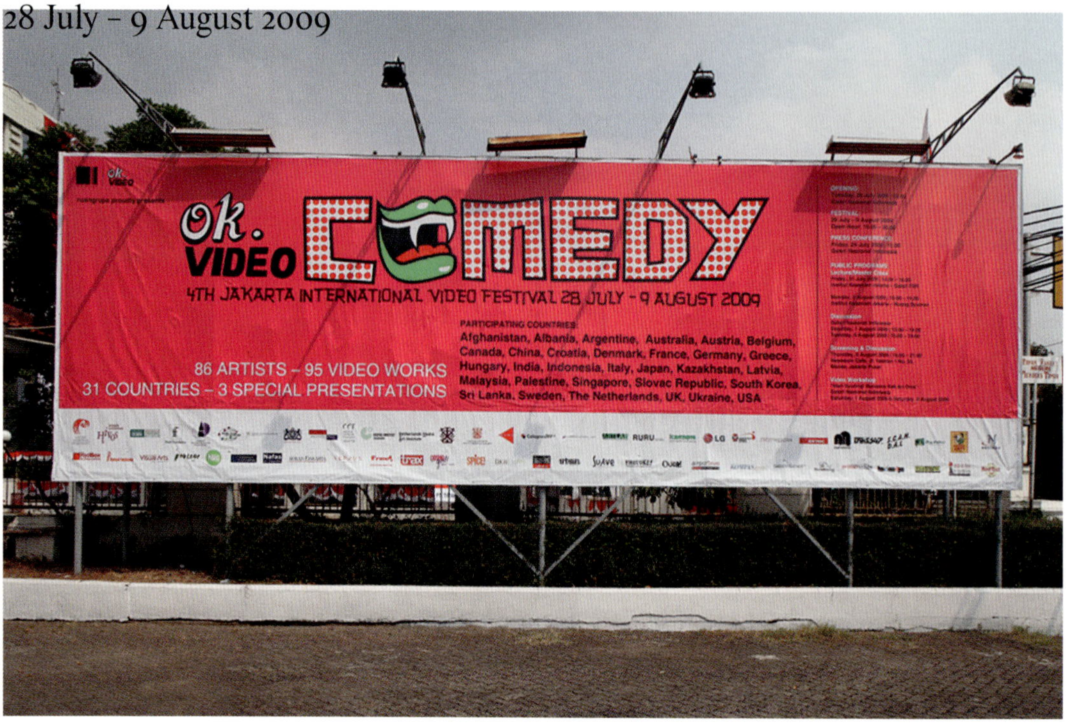

OK.Video 'Comedy' – 4th Jakarta International Video Festival, Galeri Nasional Indonesia and other venues, Jakarta, 28 July – 9 August 2009

449

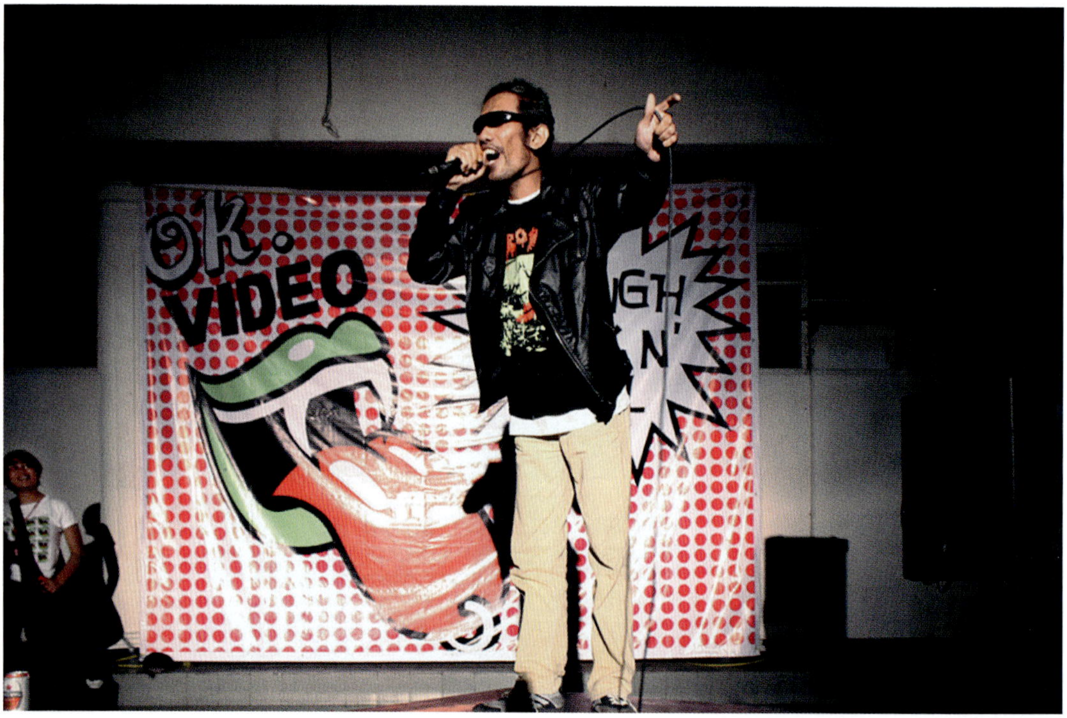

450

ok.Video 'Comedy' – 4th Jakarta International Video Festival, Galeri Nasional Indonesia and other venues, Jakarta, 28 July – 9 August 2009

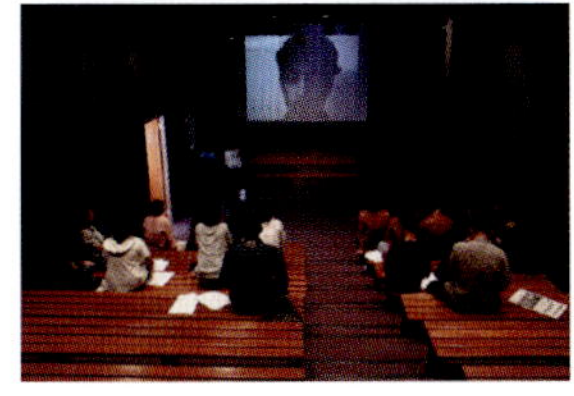

451

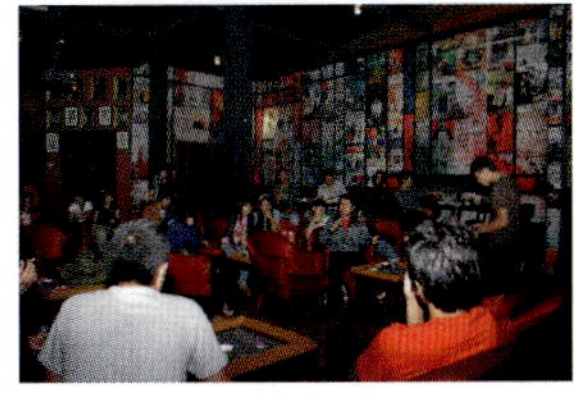

452

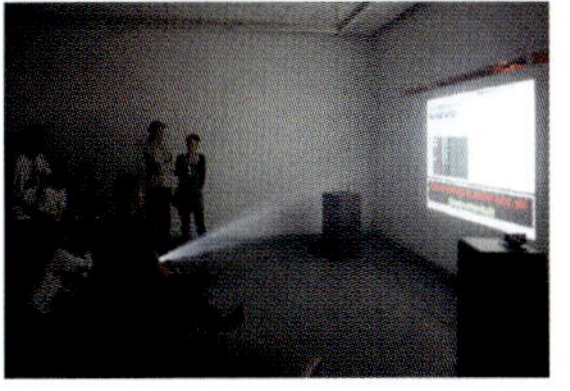

453

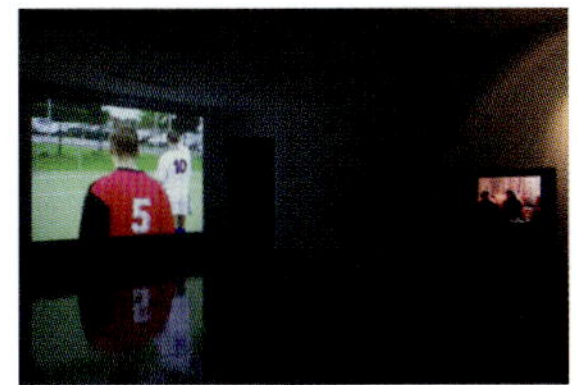

454

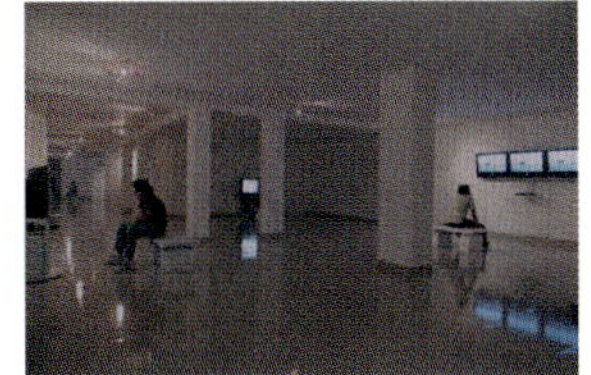

455

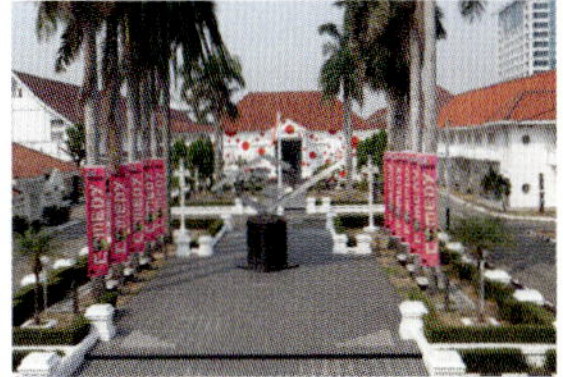

456

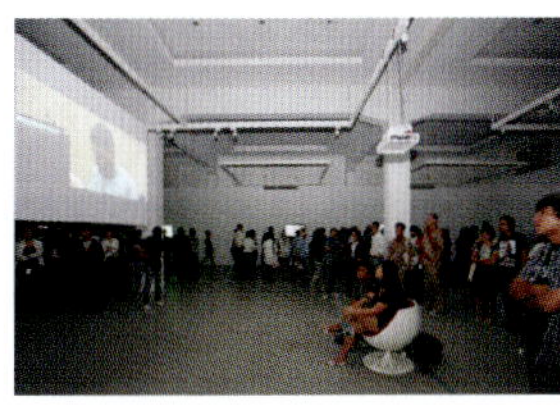

457

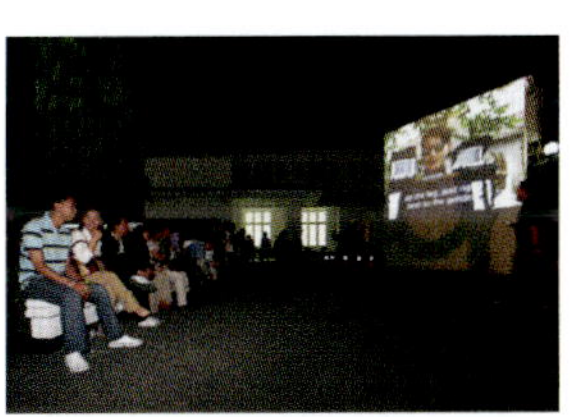

458

'Lonely Market', ArtLab research presentation, ruru house, 15–17 August 2009

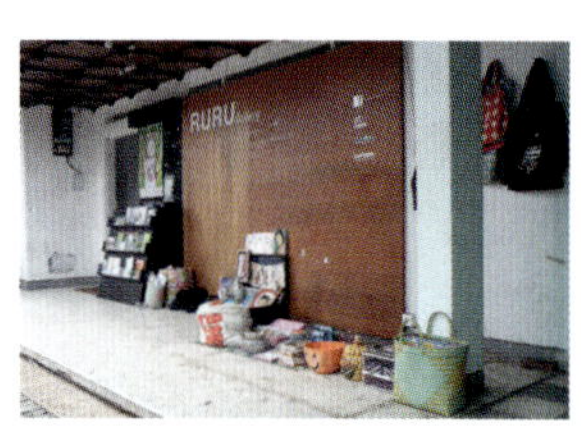

459

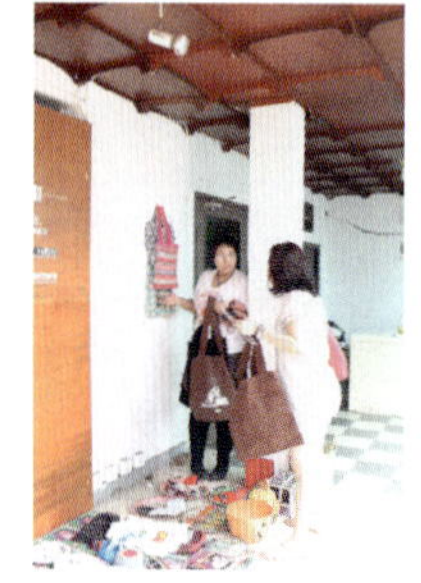

460

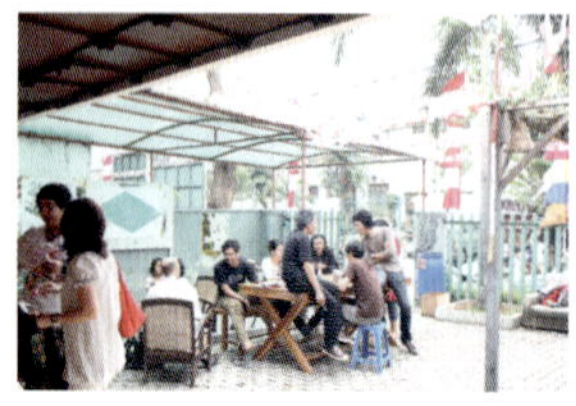

461

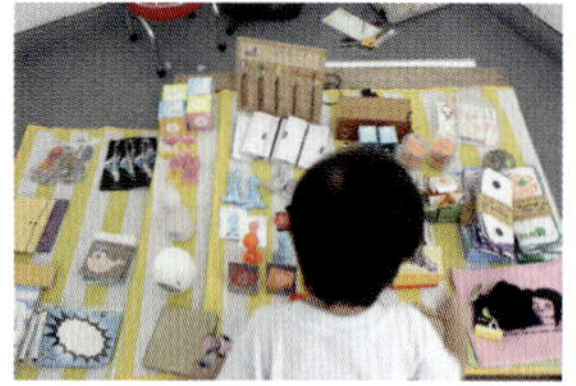

462

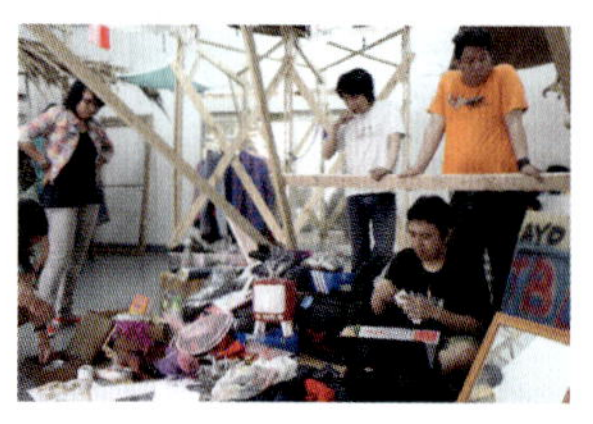

463

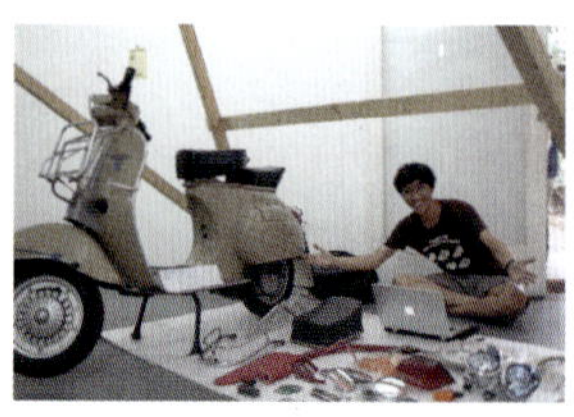

464

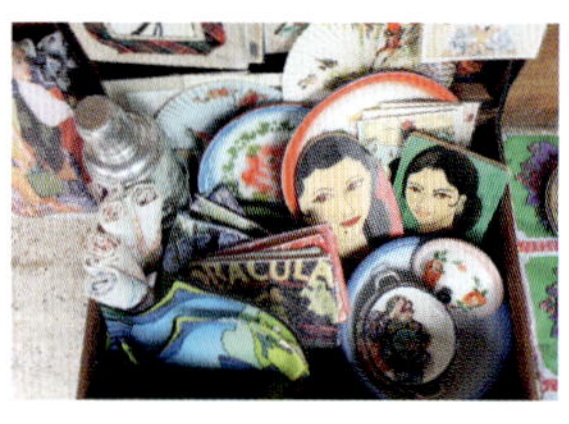

465

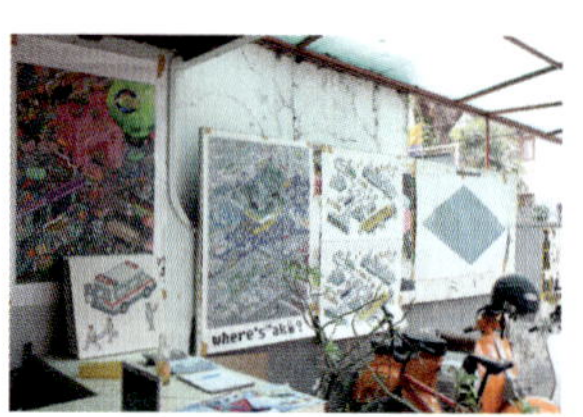

466

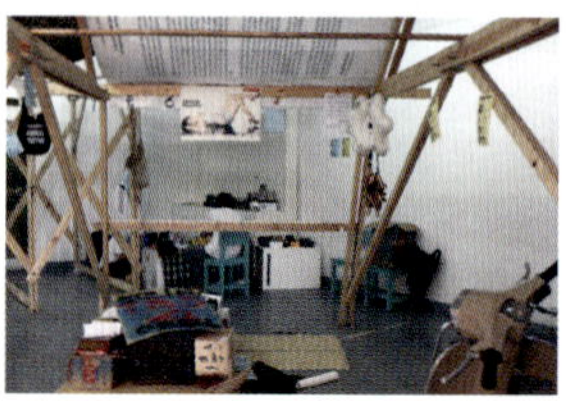

467

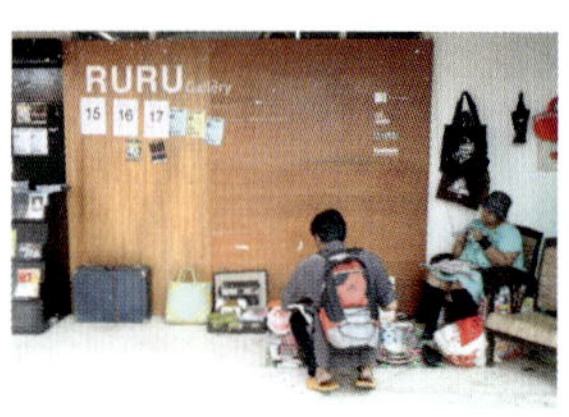

468

'Footage Jive', exhibition by Mahardika Yudha, RURU Gallery, 28 August–13 September 2009

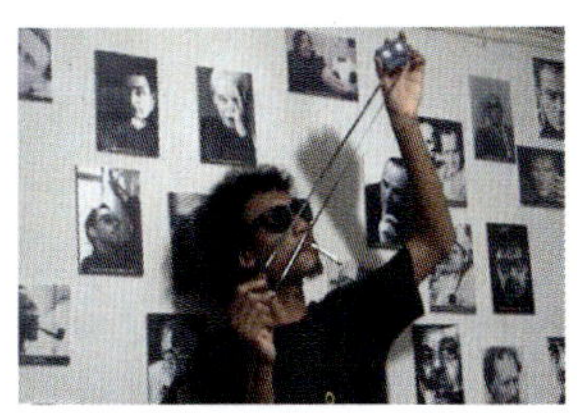

469

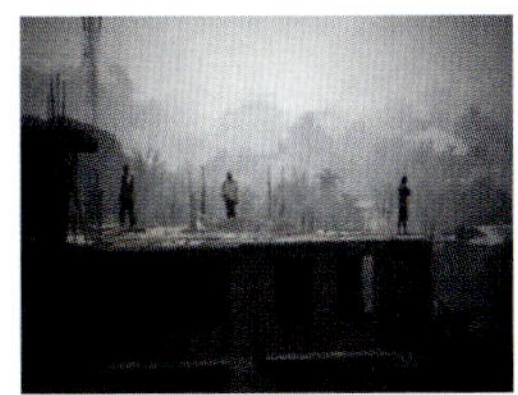

470

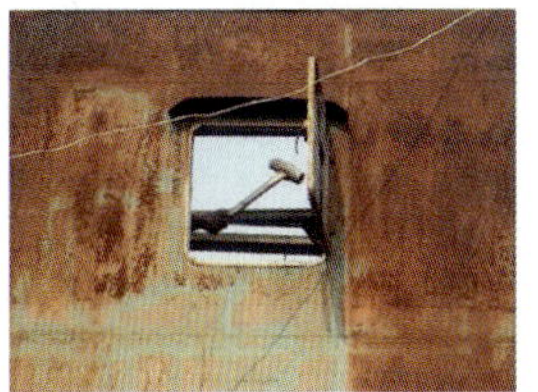

471

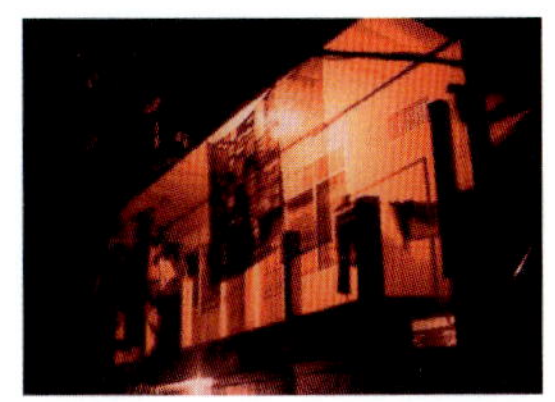

472

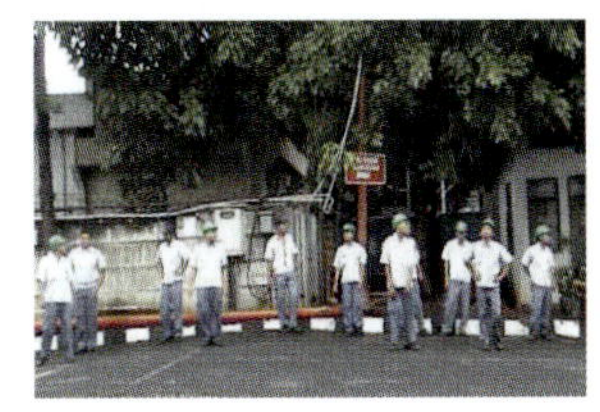

473

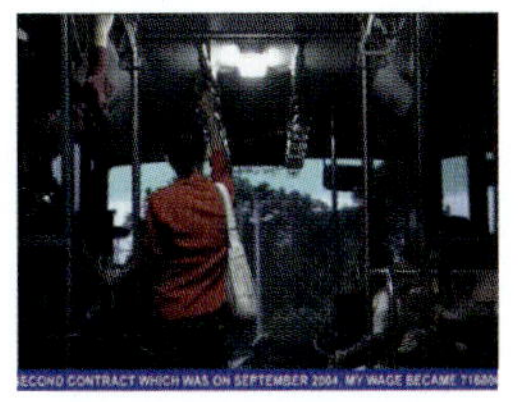

474

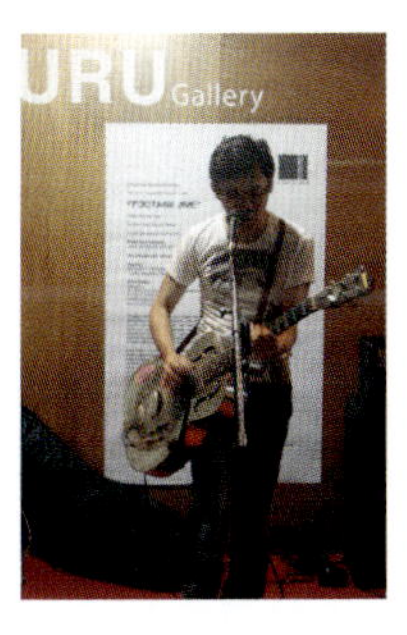

475

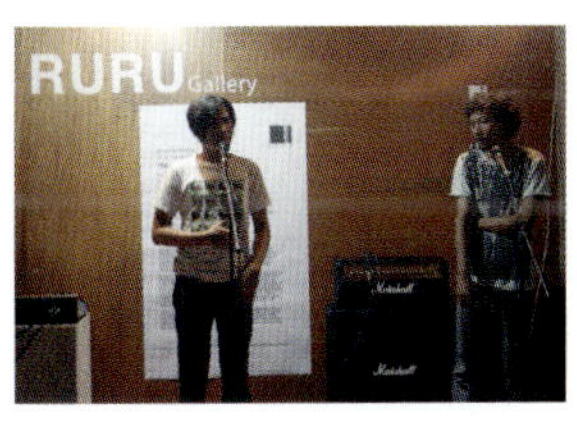

476

Participation in 'Grand Domestic Revolution', Casco Art Institute, Utrecht, The Netherlands, 10–16 October 2009 186

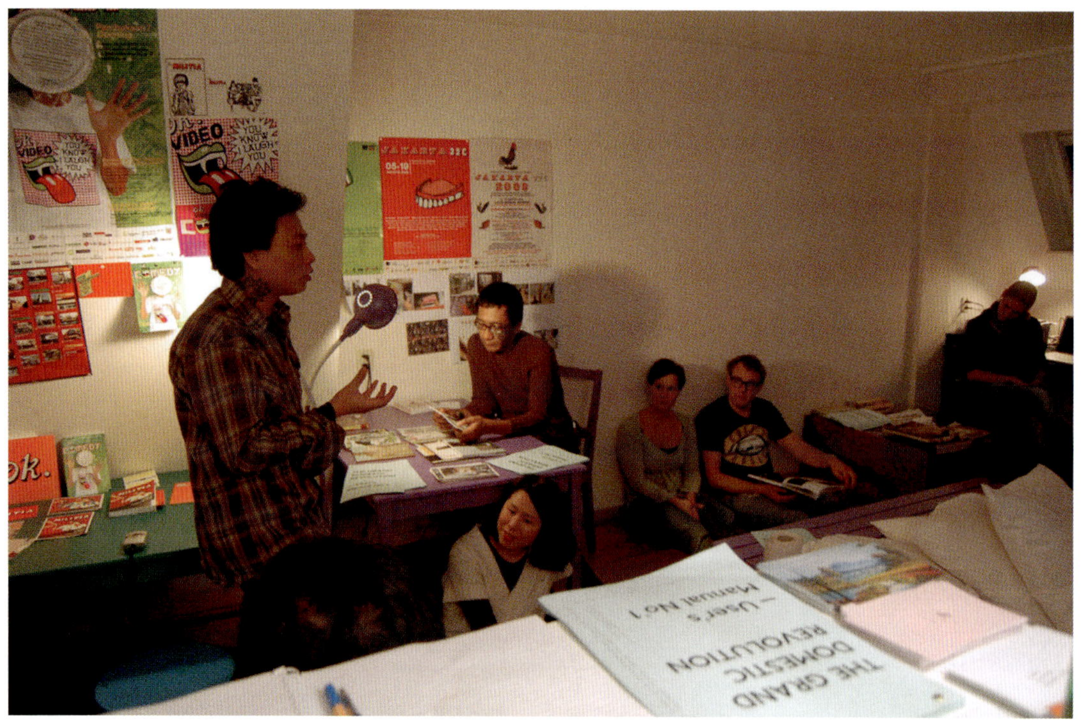

The first ruruhuis was established in 2009 in Utrecht, when ruangrupa was invited to the 'The Grand Domestic Revolution' project. And then ruruhuis was part of our process during the Sonsbeek International Exhibition in Arnhem; and we also had a ruru connected to the space inside a gallery during the São Paulo Biennial together with other collectives, RURU Gakkō as a form of knowledge and creation of our practices before we started. At the time, we called it the ruru institute, and actually it was the first transformation towards the Gudskul collective study. So, the ruruHaus is one of the approaches that we mostly use to have our own space again, a space where everybody could get invited.

Reza Afisina

It was really about ruangrupa's collectivity and their 'living room' culture. This 'Thursday Night Supper' programme by Reza Afisina and Ade Darmawan involved cooking, screening and presentation. It was one of the first projects that I worked on at Casco Art Institute: Working for the Commons, Utrecht, developed with many others including Maiko Tanaka and Yolande van der Heide. Reza and Ade held short-term residency at the apartment we rented as an initial site for the project, Grand Domestic Revolution (2009–12) – which was supported and started as part of Utrecht Manifest Biennale. Many artists, designers, organisers, writers, researchers and neighbours contributed to GDR!

Binna Choi

HOW TO USE THIS HOUSE

1. furniture
- use the furniture that suits your needs, put the rest in storage room
- mixing colors of furniture is better, so you feel multipurpose
- display the furniture as homey as possible for you, be confident the guess will adapt to the situation

2. books
- use the books that suit your needs
- put the books in different places than they are supposed to be, because they are meant to be read
- try to introduce the book that you're reading to your guest

3. kitchen
- you should know how to use *peralatan dapur* and find some of the peralatan dapur which suits your foods
- use all the kitchenware carefully
- always check the foods in storage or in the refrigerator
- put the leftovers in the trash can. for some leftovers, especially decayed foods leaving a bad smell, please do wrap them up before putting in the trash can
- remember the day to collect all the trash and to put it outside to be picked up
- always clean the floor, the sink, the kitchen buffet, and table as

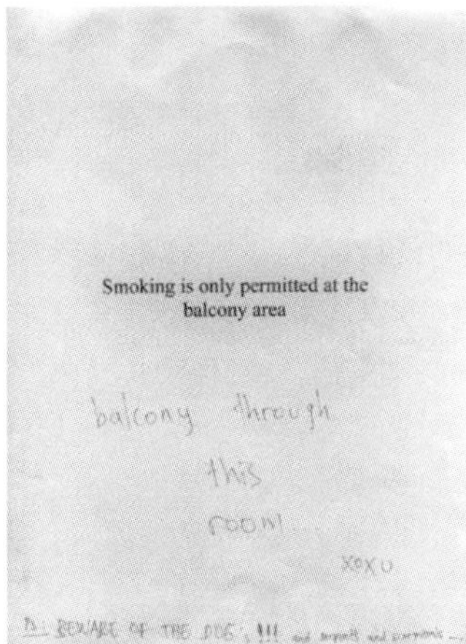

well as the electrical stove
- please use caution if you want to play in the kitchen area
- the electric stove is the worst to cook something with more art in it, that is, with such ingredients as flavor, color, timing, momentum, heat, control, composition, experimentation, etc.

4. living room
- the living room is the room for living
- if you don't have any experience with houses, better start from the living room
- we could do many things in the living room
- the living room also suits someone who lives there or not
- the living room is also a place for gathering around or dining in, it is a very subtle place and here the mixture will be present

5. bedroom
- if you have a guest, make sure to treat them like a king or queen, give them your bedroom, and you stay in the living room ... it's nice in the morning with sunshine, and you can easily prepare breakfast for them

5. storage room
- is not good for art space, better for contemplation

6. walk-in closet
- do not store your weekly garbage here

7. toilet
- if you smoke in here, make sure to use air refresher, and bring your cigarette butt outside and throw it in a trash can
- do not throw your cigarette butt into the toilet (no we never did it)

8. bathroom
- if you come from a tropical country and need a hot shower, make sure it take not more than 10 minutes, otherwise the bathroom will become like a sauna, and it makes everything there wet

9. rooms
- in the winter, do not put the heater on too high, because it expends too much energy and makes your guests uncomfortable

10. balcony
- good for smoking and getting a "power plant"
- very good spot to study dutch house design and dutch couples

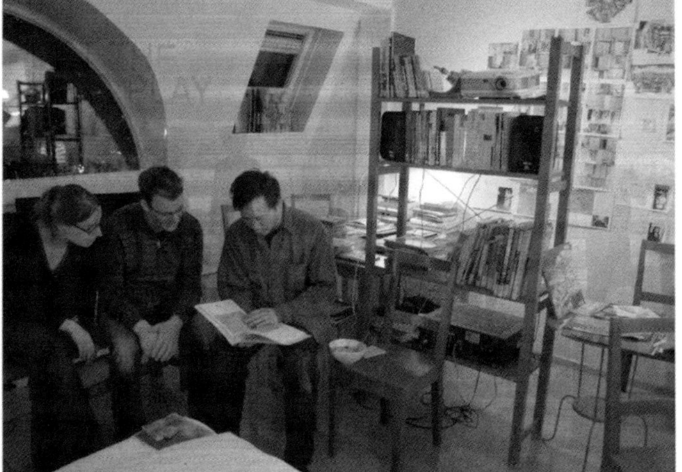

This is a manual for future residents produced in 2009 by Ade Darmawan and Reza Afisina of ruangrupa, the first GDR residents at apartment 18b.

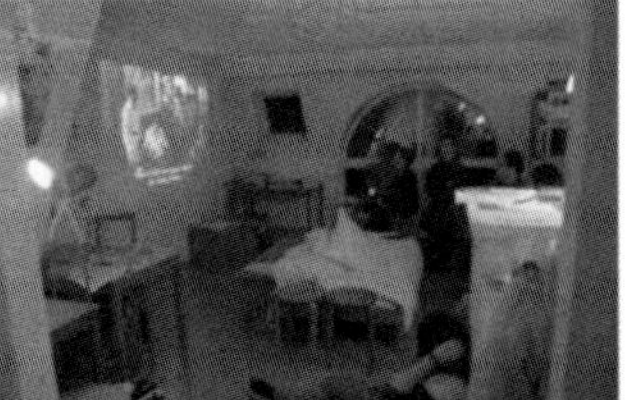

‘copy-paste extraordinaire’, exhibition by Henry Foundation, RURU Gallery, 11–24 October 2009

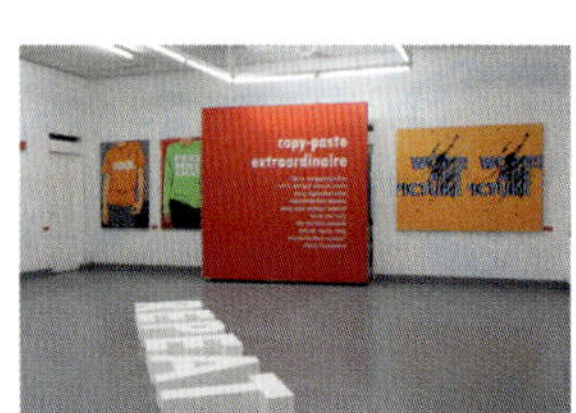

478

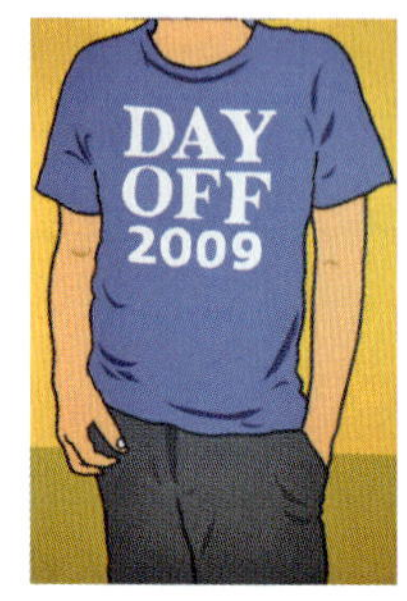

479

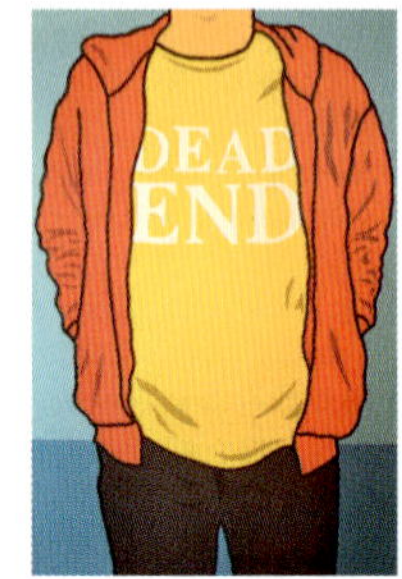

480

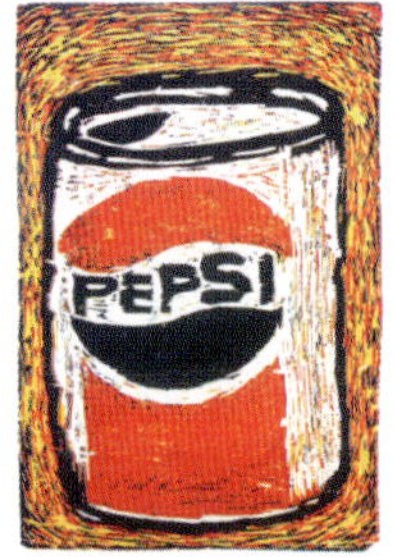

481

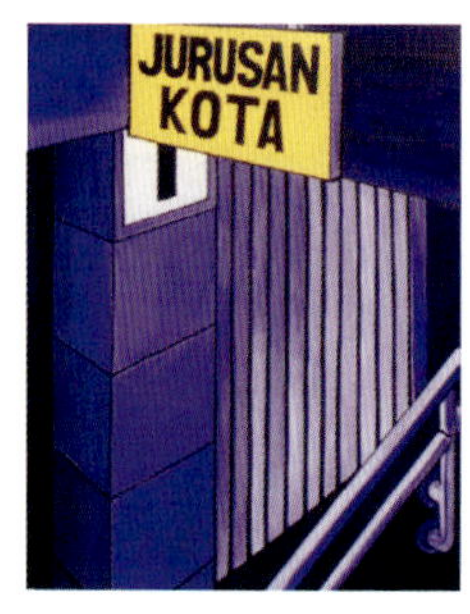

482

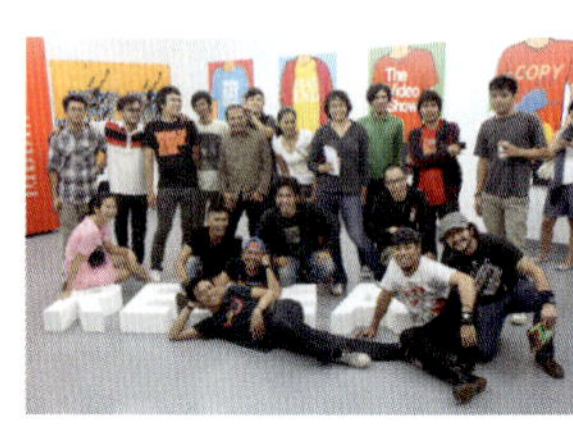

483

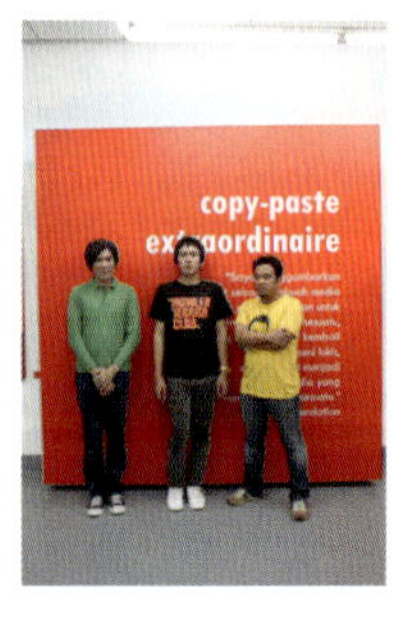

484

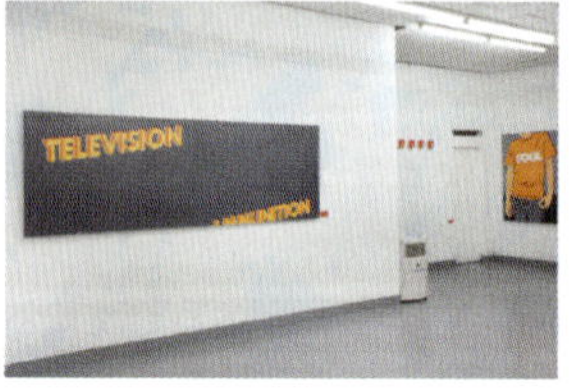

485

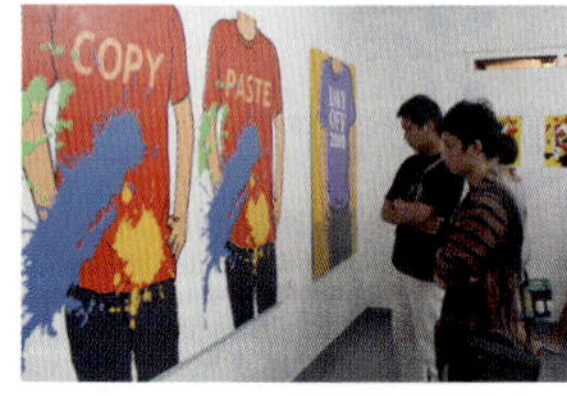

486

'Komik Magnetik: Pameran 10 seniman komik' ('Magnetic Comics: Exhibition of ten comic artists'), RURU Gallery, 13–29 November 2009

with Eko S. Bimantara, Prihatmoko Catur (Moki), Fida Irawanto, Rhoald Marcellius, Azisa Noor, Sulung Widya Prasastya, Aji Prasetyo, Sheila Rooswitha, Erwan Hersi Susanto (Iwank) and Ign. Ade; curated by Ifan Ismail and Yudha Sandy

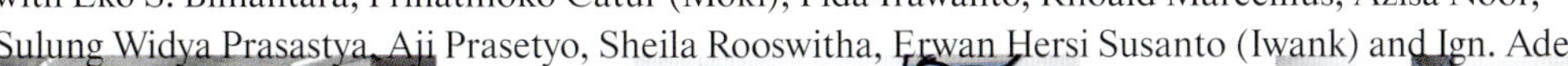

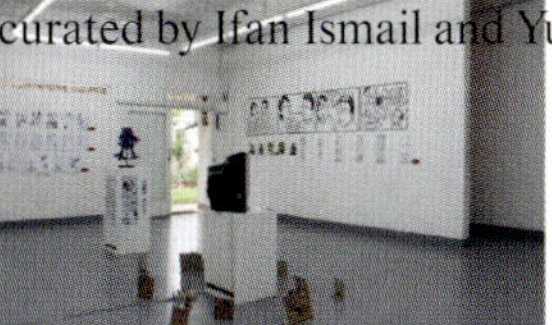

487

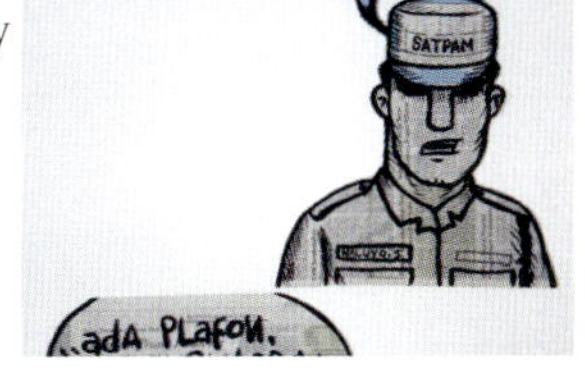

488

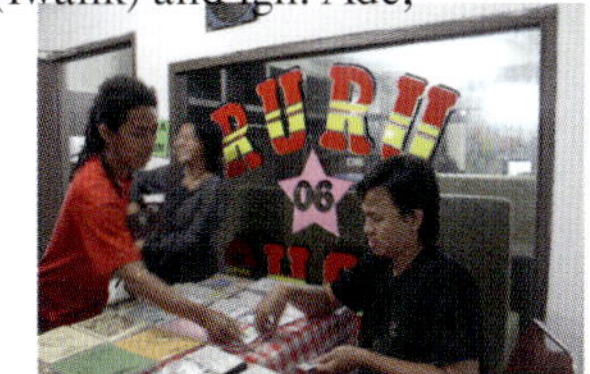

489

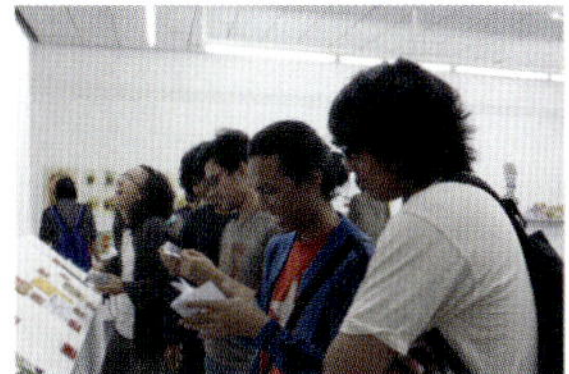

490

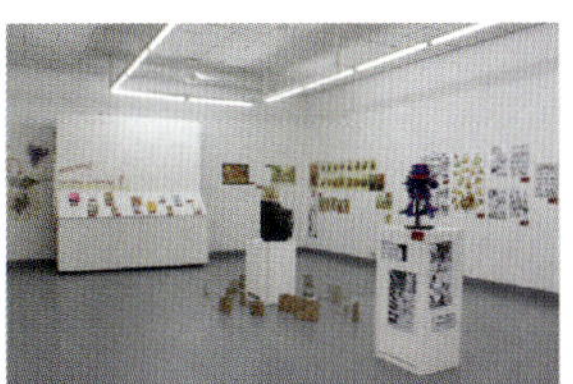

491

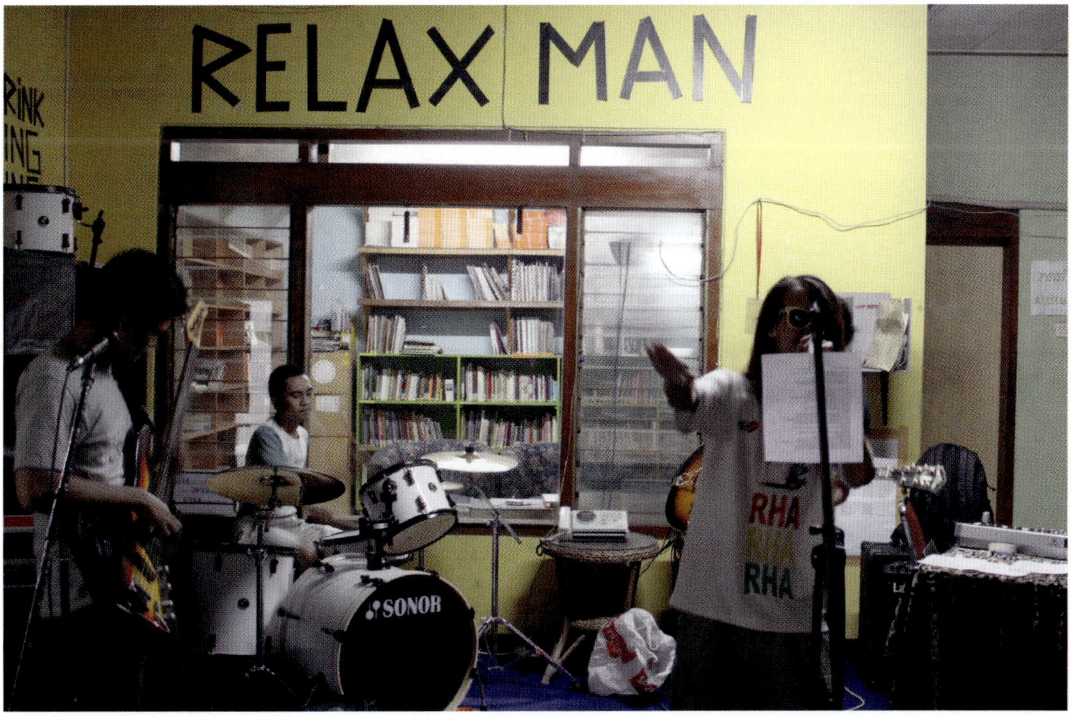

492

Job desc
Job title
structure

it's only an administration function, everyone can be a director

Launch for www.respectastreetartgallery.com, RURU Gallery, 20 February 2010

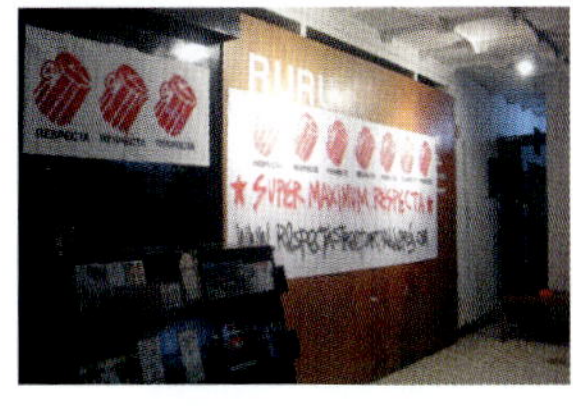

493

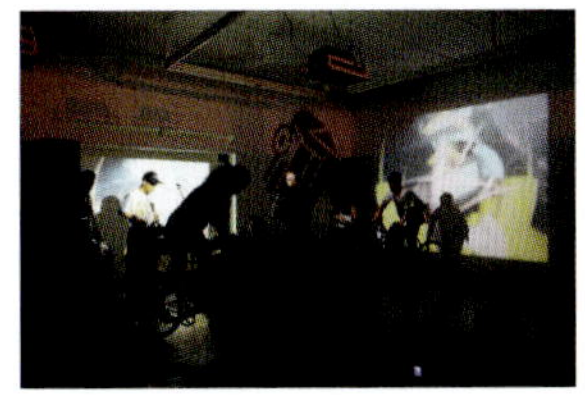

494

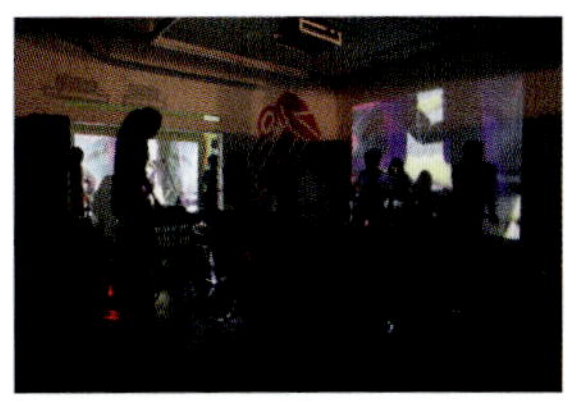

495

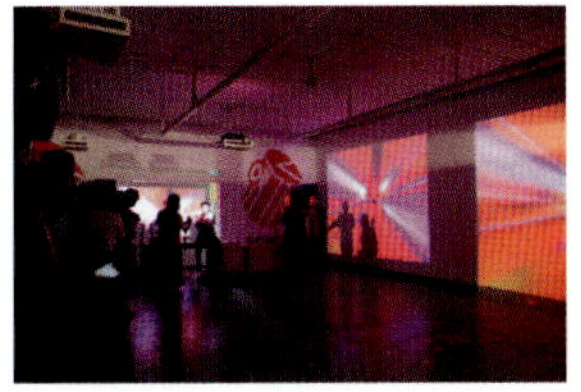

496

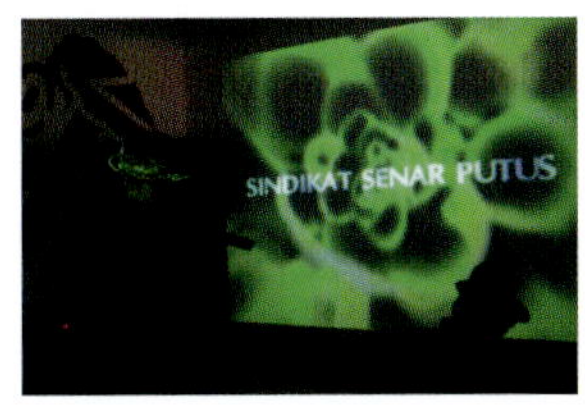

497

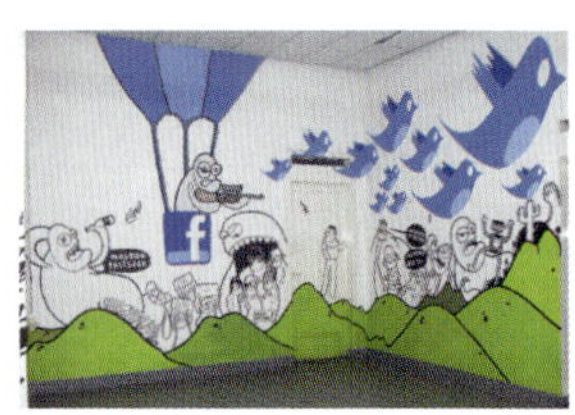

498

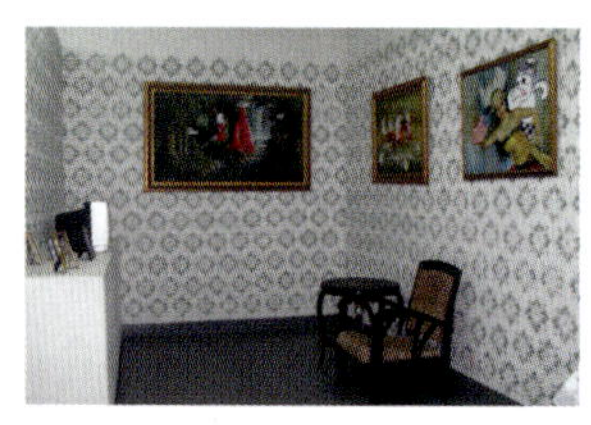

499

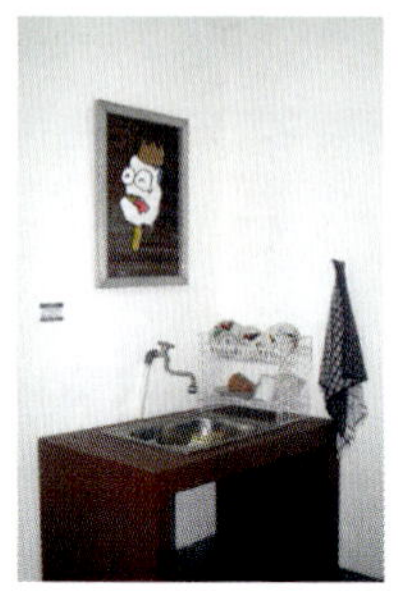

500

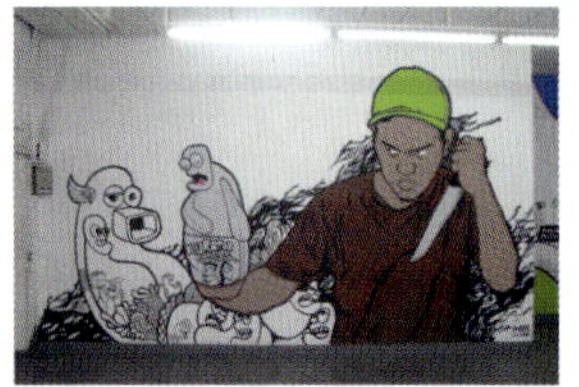

501

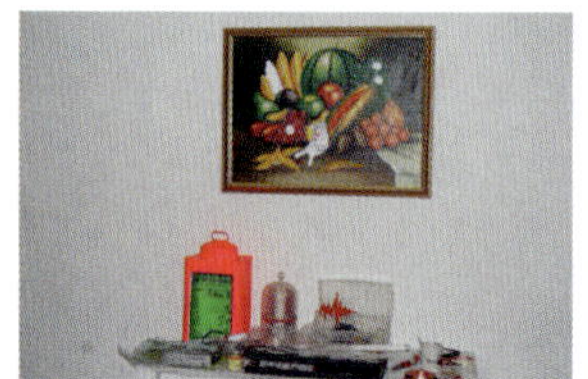

502

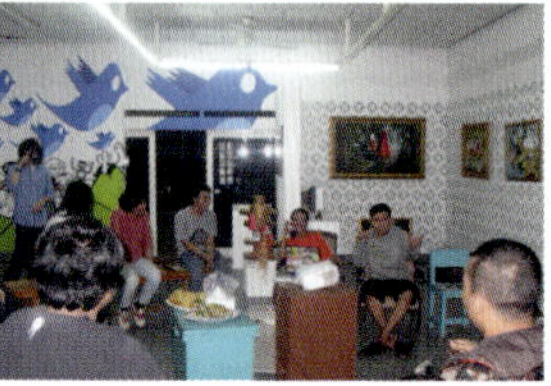

503

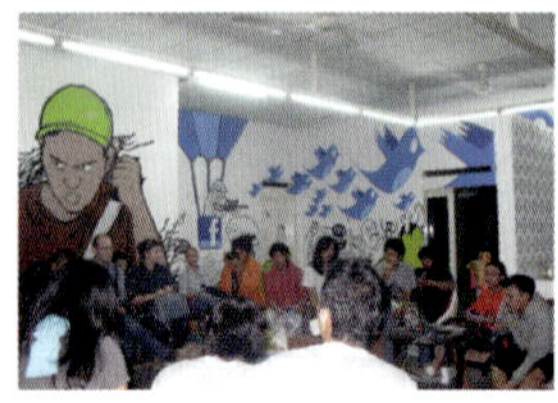

504

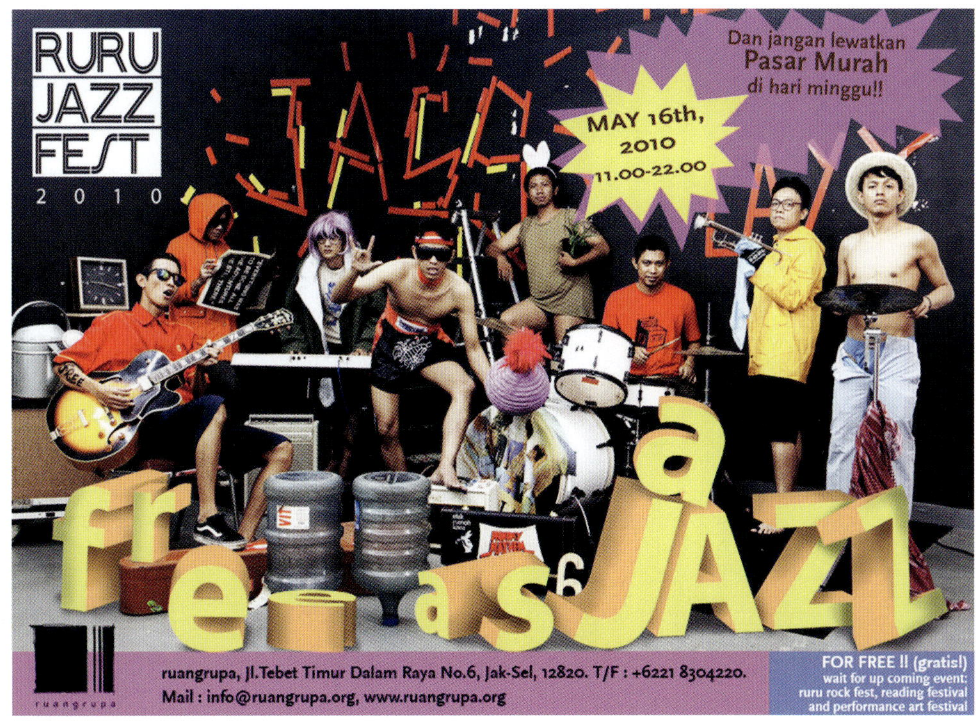
RURU
JAZZ
FEST
2010
Dan jangan lewatkan
Pasar Murah
di hari minggu!!
MAY 16th,
2010
11.00-22.00
free as JAZZ
ruangrupa
ruangrupa, Jl.Tebet Timur Dalam Raya No.6, Jak-Sel, 12820. T/F : +6221 8304220.
Mail : info@ruangrupa.org, www.ruangrupa.org
FOR FREE !! (gratis!)
wait for up coming event:
ruru rock fest, reading festival
and performance art festival

505

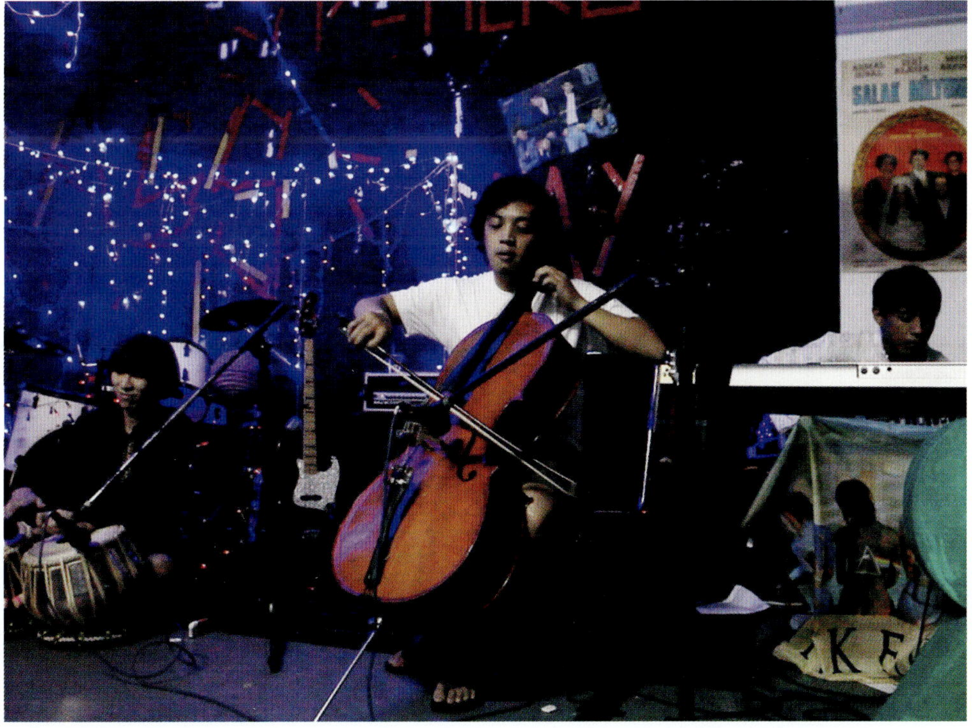

506

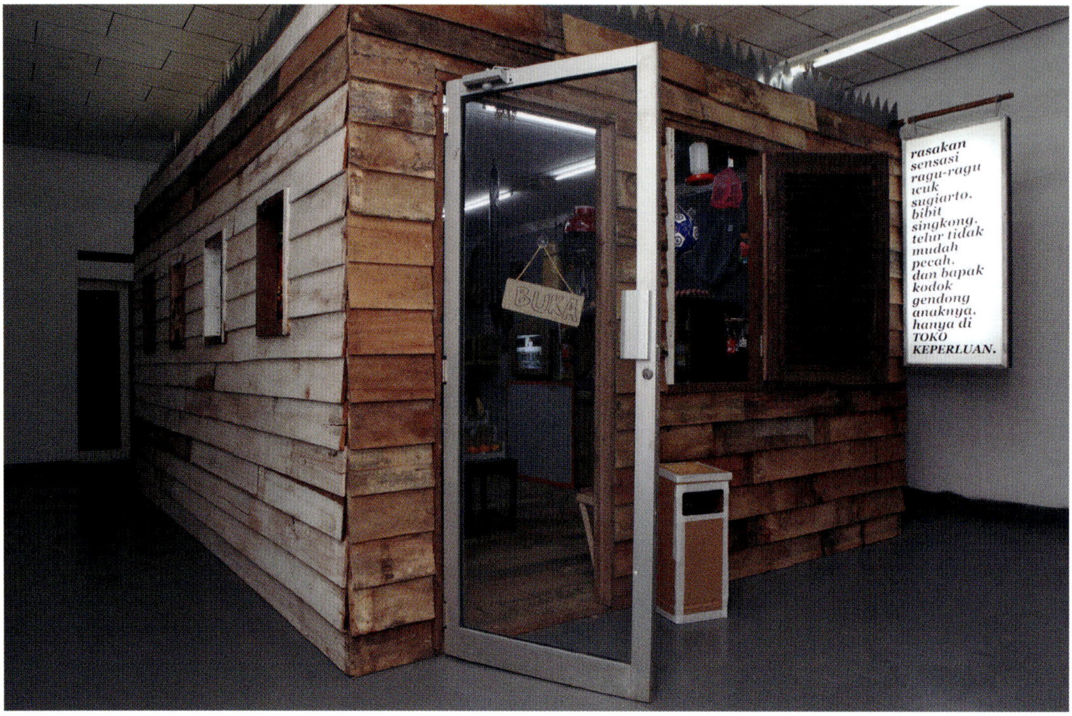

'Toko Keperluan' ('Grocery Shop'), exhibition by Anggun Priambodo, RURU Gallery, 22 May – 5 June 2010

507

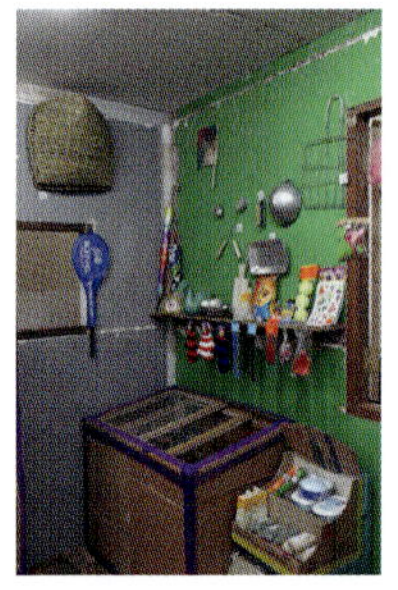

508

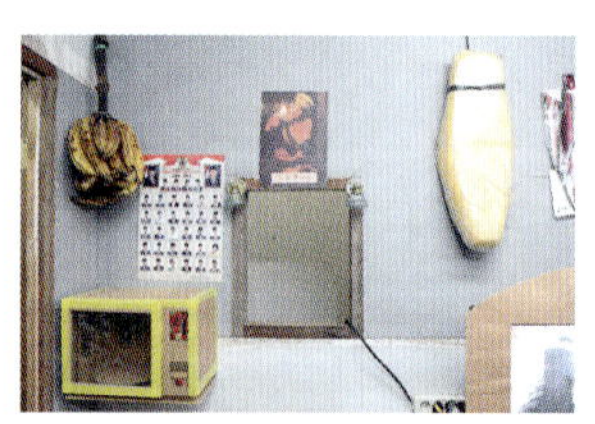

509

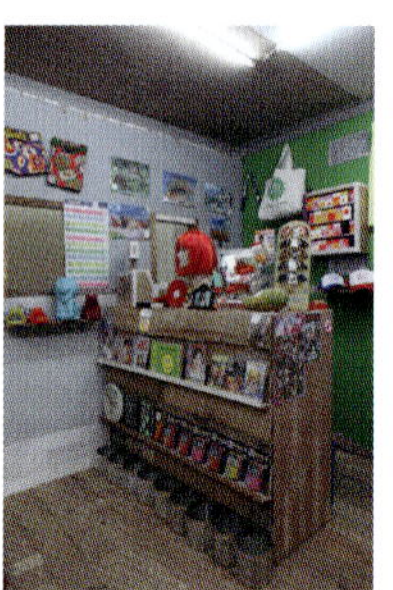

510

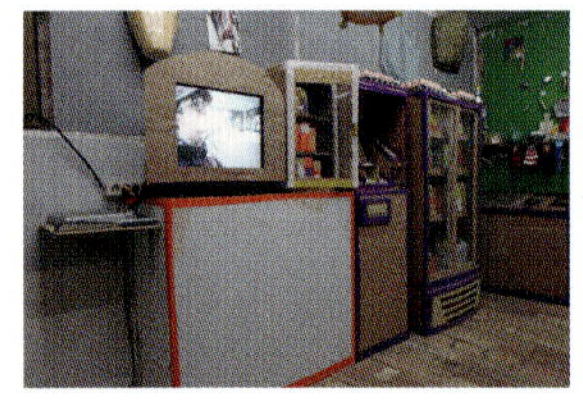

511

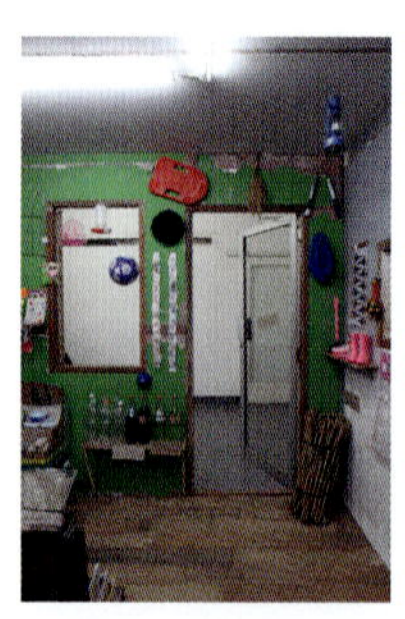

512

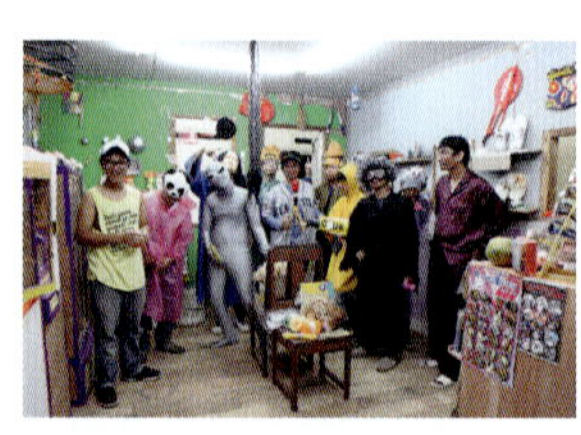

513

'Art on Poskart', RURU Gallery, 9–25 July 2010

featuring postcard-sized works by a range of invited artists; curated by Ika Vantiani

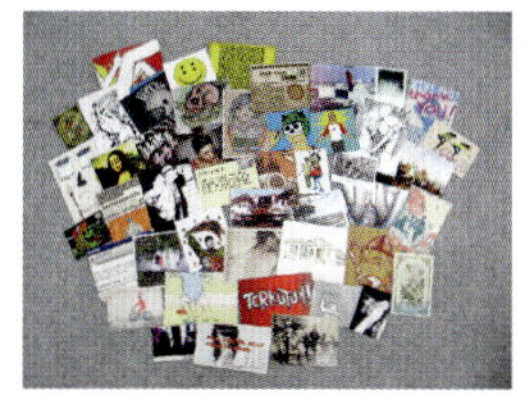

514

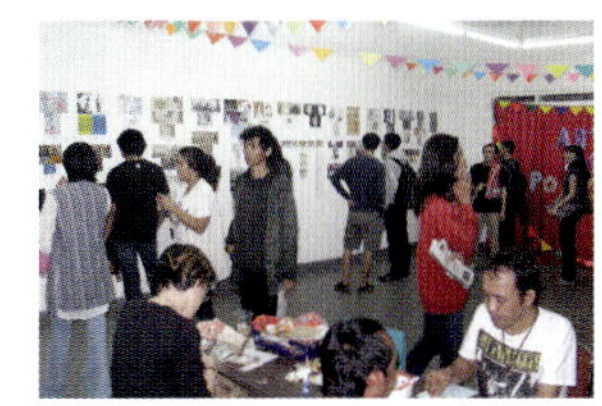

515

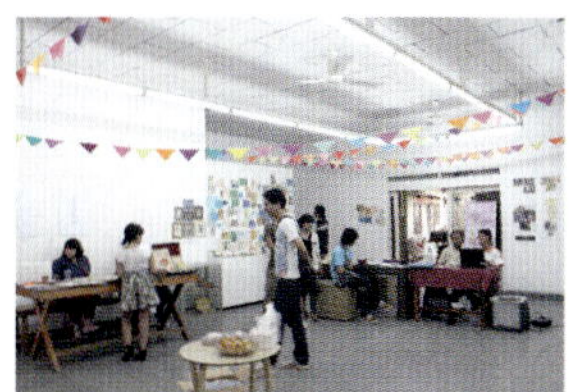

516

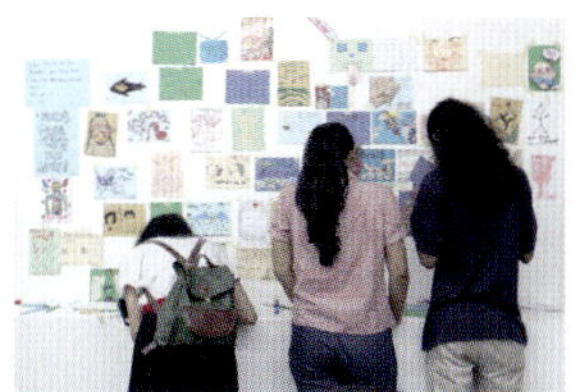

517

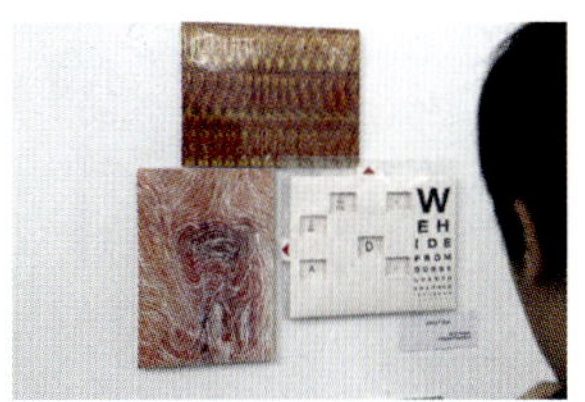

518

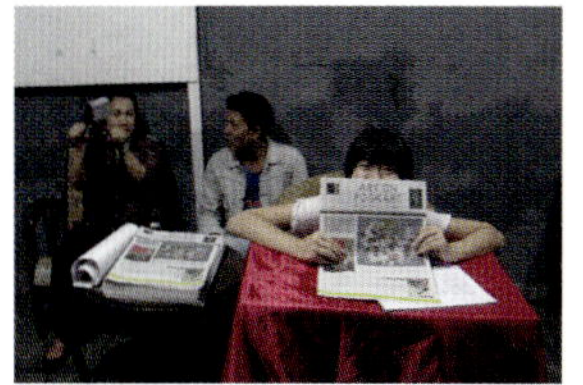

519

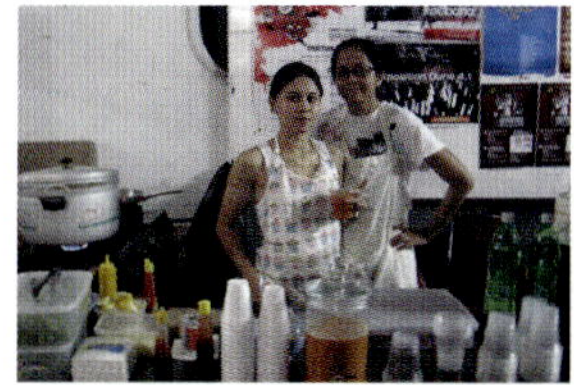

520

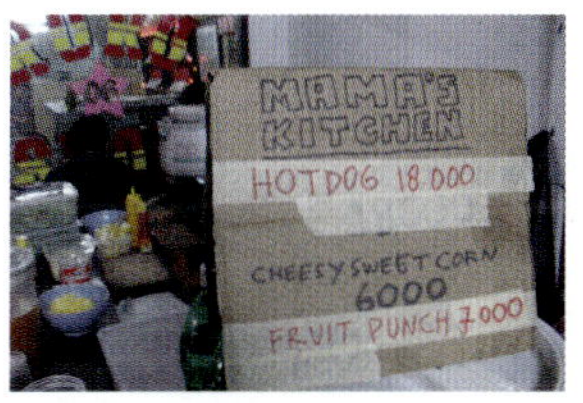

521

'Hanya Memberi Tak Harap Kembali' ('To Give Without Expecting Anything in Return'), Institut Teknologi Bandung, 23–25 July; Kedai Kebun Forum, Yogyakarta, 30 September – 2 October 2010 196

with Ade Darmawan, Andi RhaRhaRha, Anggun Priambodo, Aprilia Apsari, Ardi Yunanto, Ary Sendy, Ari Dina, Bujangan Urban, Daniela Fitria, Hafiz Hauritsa, Henry Foundation, Indra Ameng, Irwan Ahmett, Iswanto Hartono, Isrol Triono, Julia Sarisetiati, Lilia Nursita, Mahardhika Yudha, Mateus Bondan, Mushowir Bing, Oomleo, Oky Arfie, Popo, Reza Asung Afisina, Rio Farabi, Rithmi, Ronny Agustinus, Salah Husein and Ugeng T. Moetidjo; participants and visitors produced and exchanged a variety of print-based works in the gallery space; a third iteration was held at Galeri Nasional Indonesia, Jakarta, as part of the closing events of the 'Decompression #10' programme, for which these were described as 'pre-events'

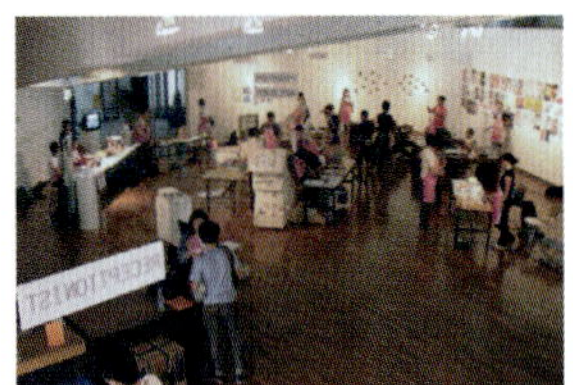

522

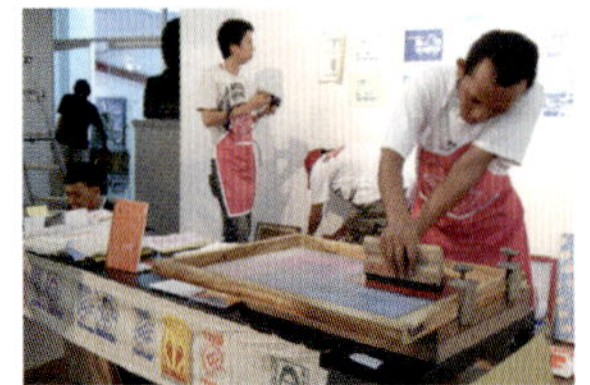

523

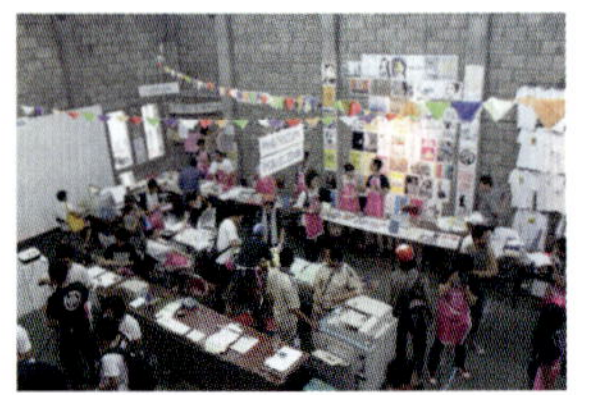

524

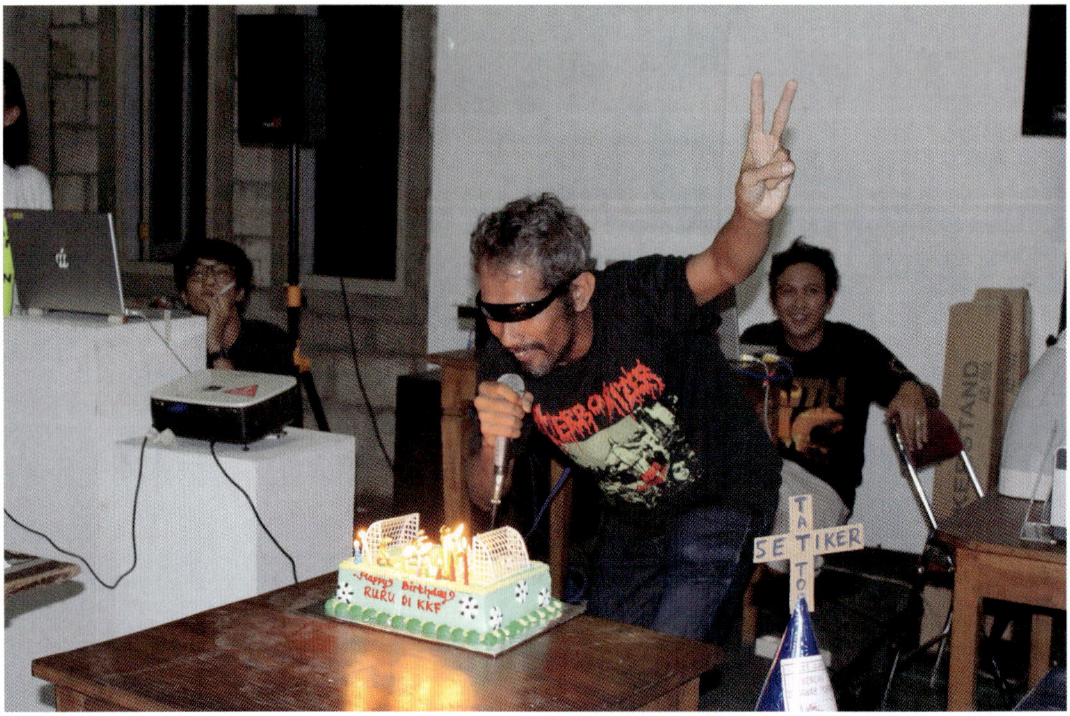

525

rurukids is a space where artists, cross-profession, cross-generation, adults and children of all ages meet as a place to share unlimited knowledge to learn together, create, make friend, and play, in a fun way. Present since 2010, under the auspices of ruangrupa which was then domiciled in Tebet, South Jakarta. It all started when we realised that the conventional education curriculum in Indonesia is one-way, with students as recipients of knowledge and teachers as distributors. In addition, art is not an important subject (each school may vary), so there are fewer opportunities for students to explore themselves, recognise and understand art in their lives. Faced with the existing conditions, as collective artists who are members of an art ecosystem, we have the responsibility to share knowledge through our artistic practices. rurukids provides space for children to act and understand the world in their own way, through collaboration with artists, art practitioners and professional mentors across disciplines to share knowledge and experience in the fields of art and culture in the form of fine arts workshops, music and video performances.

rurukids

One day I said, 'Ade, we have to build a space for children here.' 'Huh? Children? No no no noo,' he replied, we were laughing. We both knew – it's not easy to interact with children. But I convinced Ade that I could handle it. I had experience, and I truly enjoyed spending time with kids. I also told him that, as artists, we have a responsibility to share our knowledge with children. I was disappointed with the arts curriculum in Indonesia – both as a mother and a teacher, I felt we had to do something. So, rurukids was born in 2010, the year ruru celebrated its tenth anniversary. By then, some of our friends in the *ekosistem* had gotten married and had children; some of them joined rurukids. Kids from the neighbourhood joined too. Sometimes, when parents brought their children to work, the kids could play or rest in the rurukids space. In the beginning, it was just the three of us – myself, Mateus Bondan and Rendy. We started small, creating programmes where we invited artists to share their knowledge with children. Now, we've grown. Today, rurukids has seven members – all artists. These days, everyone seems to understand that in our inclusive space, we need to care for children and mothers who visit us. With rurukids, we also advocate for women artists' rights. For example, artist fees are usually discussed, but childcare costs for women artists with children are often overlooked. That needs to change. One of the most memorable moments for me was seeing rurukids featured in documenta fifteen. Children had their own space in the exhibition. They enjoyed the artworks, worked alongside artists from around the world – it was priceless. Another unforgettable moment happened during ruru's birthday this year [2024]. A boy came up to me and called me '*Bu*' ('mother'). I was surprised! He said he used to join rurukids, and now he's in college and still making art. It's just... wonderful. (*laughs*)

Daniella F. Praptono

with Aprilia Apsari, Ariela Kristantina, Bambang Toko Witjaksono, Bujangan Urban, Cahyo Basuki Yopi, Grace Samboh, Henry Foundation, Ican Harem, Ika Vantiani, Irwan Ahmett, Jim Allen Abel, Malaikat, Marishka Soekarna, Muhammad Akbar, Oomleo, Reza Asung Afisina, S.C.A.N.D.A.L., Uji Handoko, Wimo Ambala Bayang, Wiyoga Muhardanto and Wok The Rock; initiated by Wok the Rock and produced by Agung Kurniawan

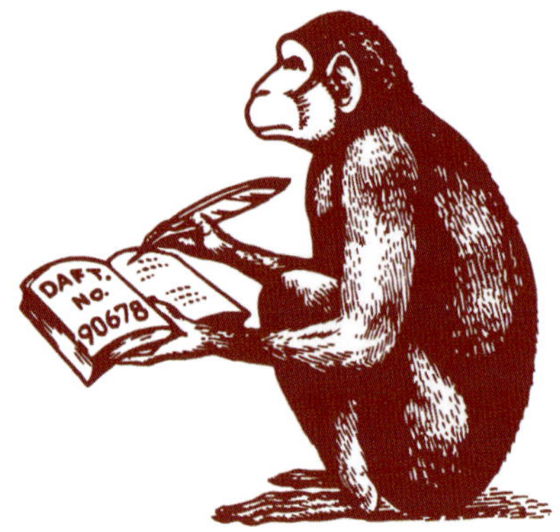

526

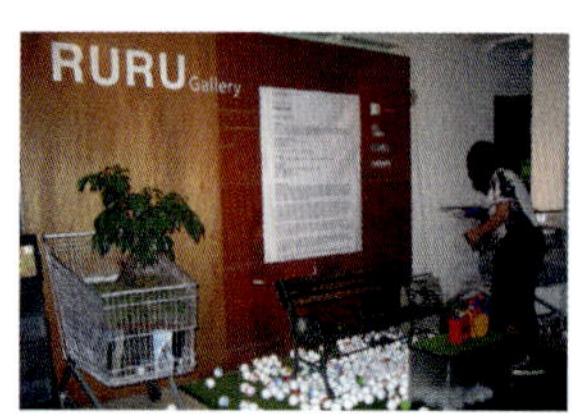

527

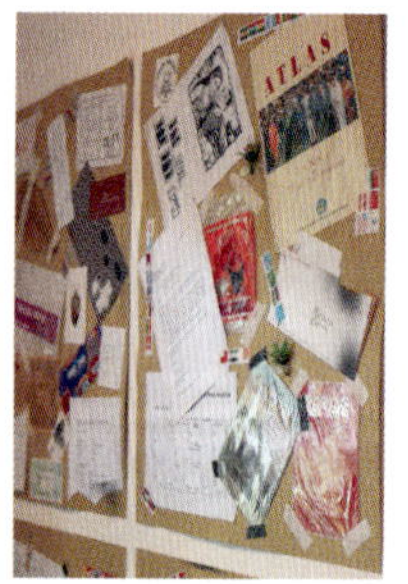

528

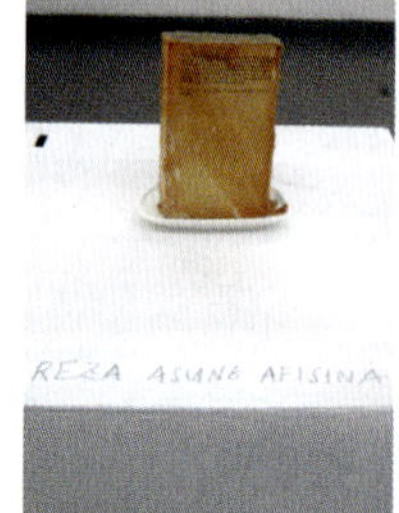

529

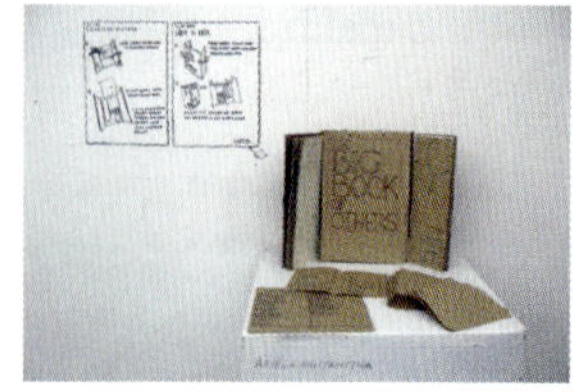

530

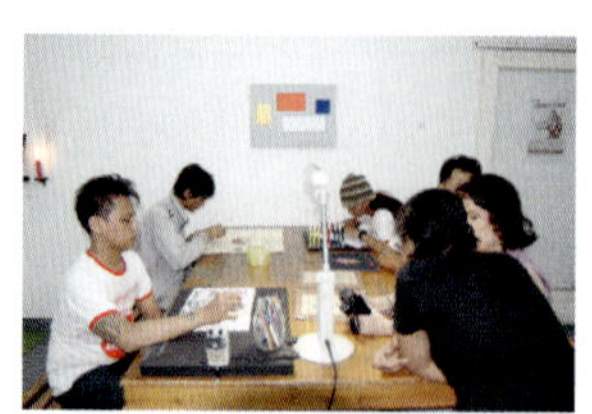

531

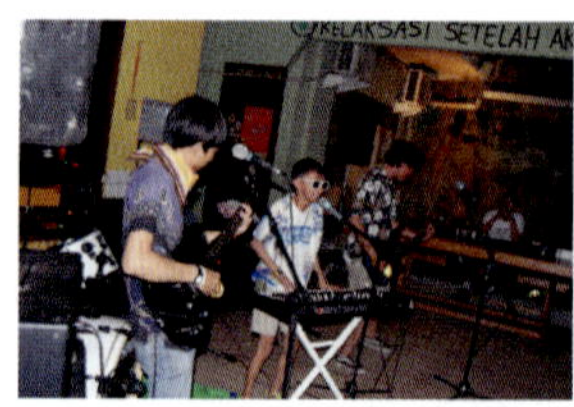

532

When Holy Market happened, I had already moved to Jogja. There were so many previous, impromptu versions of that without the name. Occasionally when someone felt they had too much stuff at home they wanted to get rid of, the market happened. Usually it's an SMS invitation amongst friends. When more people came and were hanging out, so it needed a poster and became official. When there's a poster and there were people who came whom you didn't know and who would inquire where the toilet is, that's when organising needed to come in. Holy Market has always been like this: first the market fills to the front yard, then the domestic space is not enough, something spills out of the house and people occupy the streets. Ade wrote different versions of a text about this private space turned public story since maybe 2010. It's never published but many people have seen very different versions of the text. I would like an update of the text. I think he frames it as a way to be normal in the society: a way for us to be a member of the public so we use the streets the same way other people would use it when they have social occasions like weddings or death, or the mosques do it every Friday.

Grace Samboh

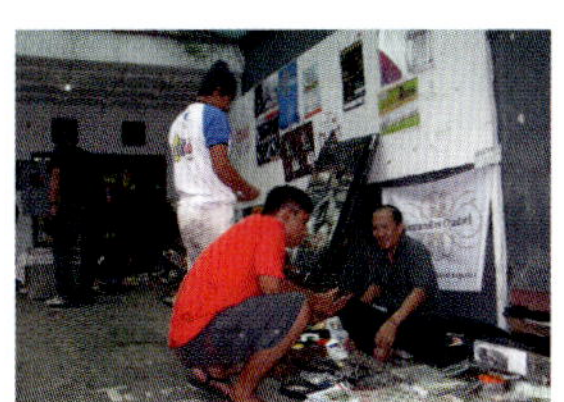

533

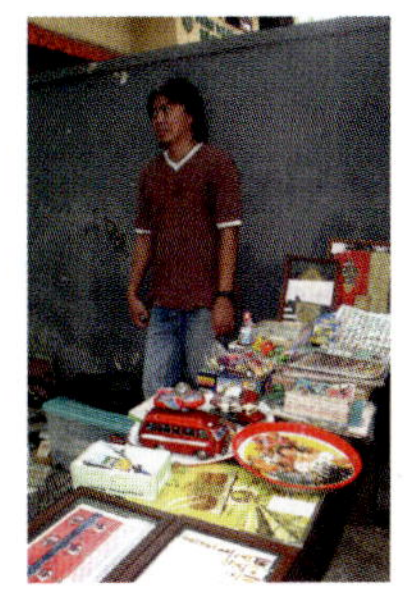

534

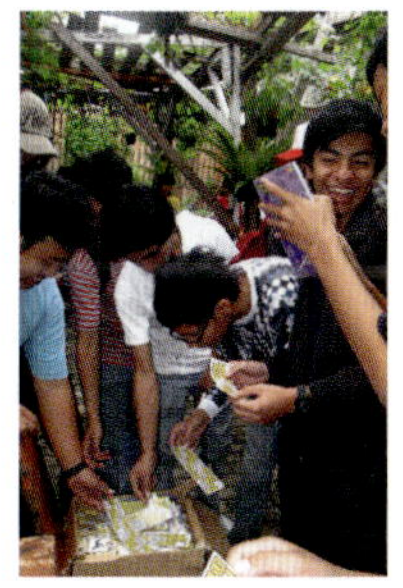

535

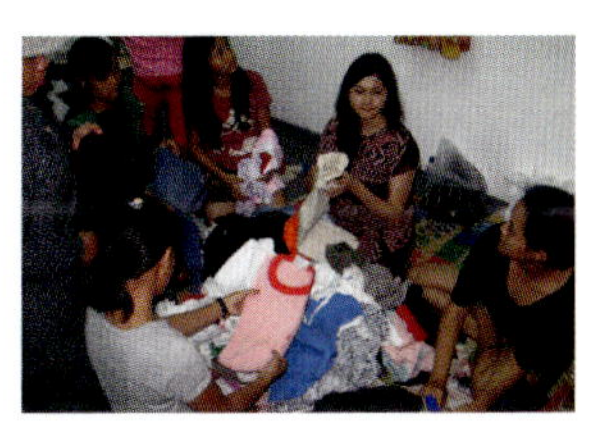

536

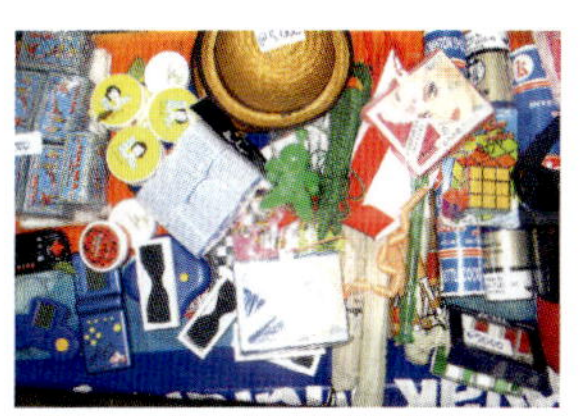

537

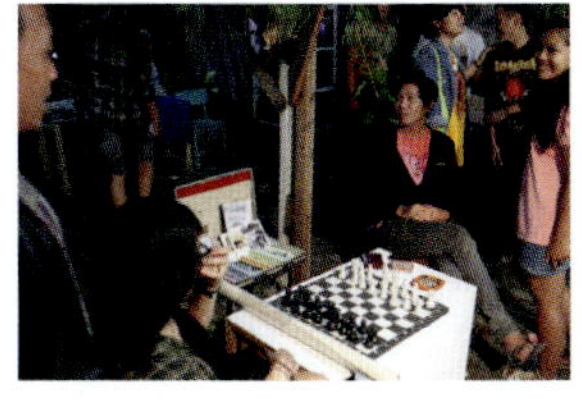

538

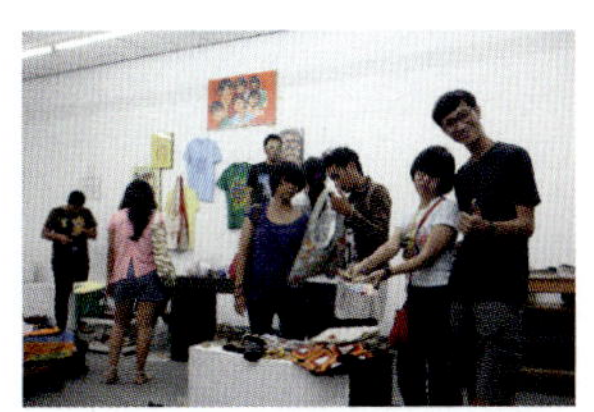

539

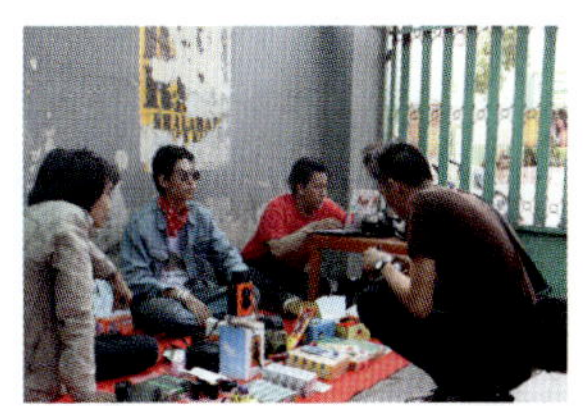

540

'Decompression #10: Expanding the Space and Public', Galeri Nasional Indonesia and other venues, Jakarta, 28 December 2010 – 12 January 2011 200

Expanding the space and public – we think this idea can best represent ruangrupa's work during its ten years of existence. During that time, we have noticed that it was also the most important period in the development of contemporary art stimulated by the acceleration of change in social, cultural and political situations. Not only celebrating the ten years of ruangrupa's journey with all its offerings and ideas so far, we also design this activity to be further used as an instrument to see and examine the development of our ideas as a society about many things in a social and cultural context. ... We involve as many people as possible in the arena of art and cultural production, namely artists, students, communities, cross-disciplinary practitioners and communities and various art, cultural and social organisations whose participation over the past decade has contributed to contemporary art discourse. Furthermore, the events also offer a collective celebration by ruangrupa and various communities in a cultural network that represents the phenomenon of art and culture's involvement in social practices and other disciplines. The event has been prepared for approximately a year, with a snowballing of ideas and plans. ... Plans were constantly in flux and often faced with uncertainties, asking us to always be prepared to adapt, negotiate and strategise.

'ruangrupa's 10th anniversary' consists a series of exhibitions, collaboration projects, seminars, film screening and music festival, workshops, book publication, video and film launches, a number of artistic interventions in public spaces, as well as inter-network and inter-organisational gatherings to share experience and knowledge. The programmes are integrated with one another. All forms of expression are intertwined, just as culture and generation. This will be a wonderful moment to express our gratitude celebrating our fruitful friendship and collaboration throughout the years.

Thank you for your support, trust, passion and intensity ;)

ruangrupa

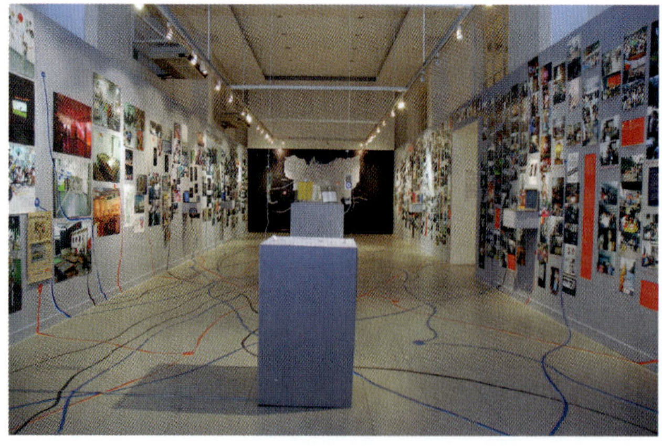

Arsip-Arsip tentang Ruang, Orang dan Gagasan dalam Proses / *Archives on Space, People, and Idea in the Process*

Ugeng T. Moetidjo

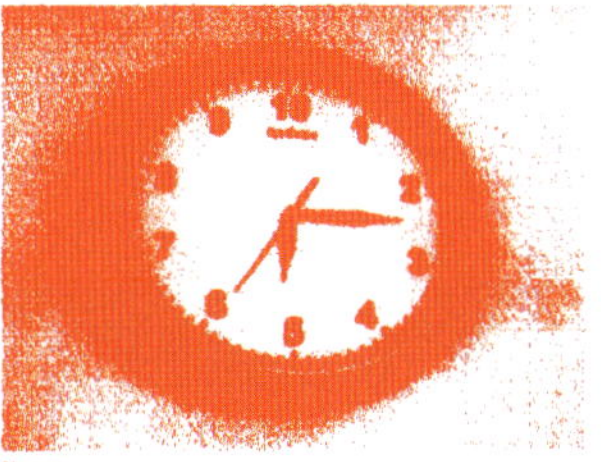

Karya
Andry Mochammad dan MG. Pringgotono,
Zero Eye Lution,
Program Residensi Seniman ruangrupa, 2004.

Future is an idea, since human beings are advancing forward not by their anatomical order to get into a point, but with the idea on how they could get there. What you think about the familiar object today, from language to semiotics is a universal agreement. And it serves as a base for our mistrust against the controlling system behind it: how could part of the majority be so sure with the notion that their perspective towards familiar objects is indeed the normal perception? Maybe materials are indoctrinated reflections, since many begin to literally define them. The project multiplies material personalities into altered and deviant perceptions. And appreciators emotionally enter the perception, with the familiar object normally found in the everyday.

—Andry Mochammad and MG. Pringgotono, Zero Eye Lution, ruangrupa, October 2004

Workshop *Urban Printing*, Proyek Seni ruangrupa, 2000.

Generally speaking, the statement of the two artists above has revealed the most vital part of the reopening process of ruangrupa's documents and archives for this particular exhibition. Their own artistic projects actually did not serve as the beginning of ruangrupa artistic endeavors, based on or utilizing technology in their artistic practices. Four years prior, there had been a video art workshop Silent Forces, followed by audio technology part of Tero Nauha's performance art Swarm (2001), and not to be left out was Urban Printing (2000). But the condition that finally let me closely "re-viewed" and concluded the impressions I acquired from the "existence"—preceding the processes and artistic application

in the Zero Eye Lution project presentation—also let me dwell a little deeper on the process of the works. The process contained three identifications: data, image, and text.
I did not attend the Zero Eye Lution exhibit while it was displayed, and currently the works those two produced could no longer be found. They were not stored. Ruangrupa have never had any storage to archive its artistic works and projects. Not even a part of the exhibition is in existence. Archival works rely solely on the existing documents acquired through visual recording tools. During the early years, documentation was done utilizing negative-positive film tape-based cameras, or mini DVs with their film tape recordings. So, as the case with Zero Eye Lution exhibit, nearly everything from those early artistic events and celebrations could no longer be acquired. A person that attended the exhibit, by the passing of time, would lose a slice of her/his self-narration gained through his attendance in the show. In order to recognize his own part of narration, he needs a coherent picture that could be recognized as a fact. Fortunately, there are one or two things that are still available: exhibition invitation card, and if you're lucky, poster and possibly, the catalogue. These prints for public informational purpose could not do much in rebuilding realities, once experienced by a visitor.
As an archive, the publication materials usually are too heavy on the artistic side and its own visual aspects. The prints function more as data, not facts.
For those who are trying to revisit time, space and people, back to ruangrupa's four relocation processes, could find remembered facts, no matter how small and simple those facts were. For those who want to have another conversation with the needed facts, he could detach himself for a while from the time, space, and interpretations he owns, and enter the archival corridor. The facts are available as photographic images in digital format, through camera captures uploads whose major ability is to represent reality. Today's moment, the one when

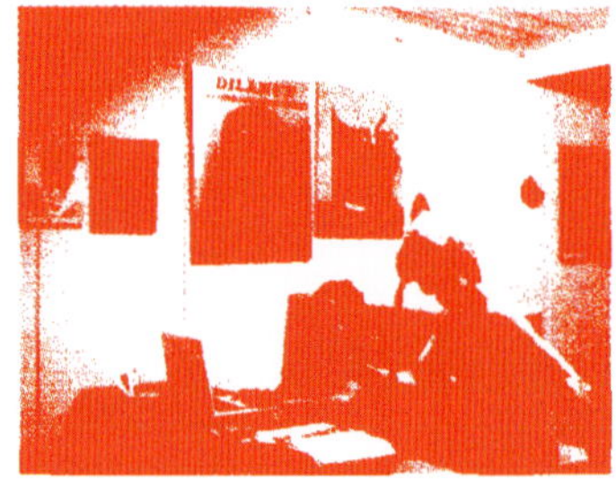

JohnNavid+'Bondi'Bondan_RURU seharihari-24-8-2009 (1).JPG

Arsip undangan *PROJECT #25*, Program Residensi Seniman ruangrupa, 2004.

I "revisit" the processes of the various artistic projects, then is an offer to skip through missed moments in itself. It's one of the cognitive functions of archival. Documents relocate our presence, although we were not there at the exact moment. We might even experience it better, thanks to an interconnection that is determined by our memories in signifying and renaming those material codes.
A similar thing occurred when I spontaneously laughed, seeing a file of picture titled JohnNavid+'Bondi'Bondan_RURUseharihari-24-8-2009 (1).JPG. The scene depicted in the picture was so funny and unimaginable during days that often filled with meetings and discussions on ruangrupa various artistic projects, in the time span of 2000-2010. The scene served as a refreshing short break between the hectic schedule of artistic strategy and work. When I saw the picture, I experienced a condition where I was communicating with a moment, which was once again empty of my presence. This is a temporal matter that completely counted my absence (and everyone else that was not present) to fly the time tunnel through ways, moments, and spaces that could be totally different. Although we believe temporarily in physical presence as the single signifier of our existence, do not forget that time is also constructed in an interlinked digital system. Whoever, by the means of a computer, got hooked into the My Network Places folder in the RURU Shop computer unit could exist exactly on the moment and the point when and where that exact moment was shot. By clicking on 500gbaru (J) on Serfereruru_RUANGRUPA00-10 and landing on the folder called 2009 sub-folder RURU sehari2_folder akhir JohnNavid, the scene that I deemed entertaining before could be opened.
At this stage, the act of clicking is not a single specific case of someone being informed by a computer. It could be applied collectively to the same

single image file. A material file in the analog era needed a physical space with the coexistence of the viewers, or switching if each of them had wanted to see them separately. A material file today can be seen and touched as a print out simultaneously, in the same time on spaces that might be separated physically but coexist in one other shared space: the interlinked digital space. Each of those spaces are communicated via one material file coded digitally and might experience an approximately similar spontaneity, as the case with the JohnNavid+'Bondi'Bondan_RURUseharihari-24-8-2009 (1).JPG image.

The corner space in RURU Shop still exists and could be occupied emitting a similar atmosphere. Maybe the upholstered chairs and tables had been moved around, Aprilia Apsari's metallic zinc painting entitled Dilamun Gelombang Rona Mimpi could be hanged not in the place depicted by the picture, and other stuffs might had been traveling by themselves. Bondi and Navid must be not in the exact same place anymore, but they all could be rearranged one more time, presenting the moment as it was, although it was a depiction of an image file we saw on the computer screen. In other words, we would still be able to reconstruct the circumstances made similar to the origin.

How about many other moments that could not be treated that way—i.e. rooms in the four previous buildings ruangrupa have occupied so far? What could an image file from the year of 2006, depict—being assisted with a sketch of ruangrupa's house plan from 2004, showing in detail the positioning and division, of and in, its every rooms—for example? Maybe the concept of Secrets/No Secrets project (Farah Wardani and Mushowir Bing, ruangrupa, August 2003)—a semifreudian project on technology—could inform us about the state when something we are familiar with exists in a ruang (space) and taking form as a rupa (shape) is put at odds into: Memory records/Memory erases. // Self creates image/Image compresses Self. // Image Produces Reality/ Images Reduces Reality. // Time heals/Time conceals. // Things remain/Things are hidden. // Things are left behind. // Life i realities in transient. // It needs a moment of suspension. // A Space to Reveal.

Based on that kind of reality, this was the time when, "everyone and every activity in every room is being recorded through a mini DV handheld camera", but at the same time, "every recordings are being buried, so no one knows what actually happened inside the room." (Secrets/No Secrets, 2003). At that time, ruangrupa occupied their second rented house on Tebet Barat Dalam I, behind McDonald's. Only two left-over materials, from moments back then, have survived: the public invitation, asking for their participation in the interactive project, as well as a softcopy file on the concept sketch of the Secrets/No Secrets project. The original file couldn't be found. If one demanded the file to be printed, it could serve as no original. If it was printed as a sheet that was so similar to the original, could it function to reproduce its public on its given moment? In popular culture, every reproduction is targeted to also reproduce its public. For this sample case of Secrets/ No Secrets concept material, the reproduction most probably happened only to the file material, without its moment n its actors. Public reproduction could not happen, for its semifreudian moments can not be retraced.

Printing out a softcopy file, and transforming it into a tangible hardcopy should have sufficed reproducing a specific presence and its public. At this point, archive could be understood as a reflection of a sort of location on a selected specific duration. An archival file on a table was thing that had restrictions in its representational material fram be it texts or images. Its functi would experience retrieval und a particular time and space. That's the reason why, at the time Farah Wardani was desiri the original poster of the Lekk Eten Zonder Betalen (2003) to serve as an exhibition materi in the ruru.zip exhibit, she actually wished to be in a time

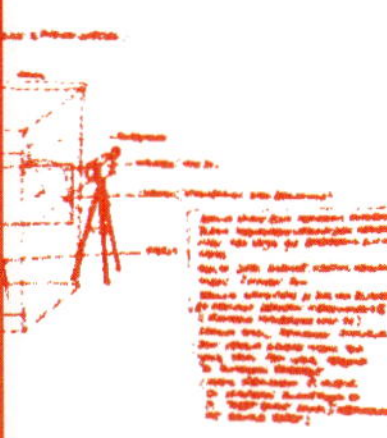

dari *Secrets / No Secrets*, Proyek karya kolaborasi Mushowir Bing dan 03.

and space located outside of the selection. A location considered intact, as it was originally. She wished to go through the tunnel of time and to scale every second of its existence via every points the hand of the clock had pointed out. Not similar to a place where time progresses digitally nowadays. Analogue time was manually sequenced, while digital time is sequenced through a click of a code. A work by Eadweard J. Muybridge, The Horse in Motion (1872) could still be removed from its plot by the use of scissors and manual editing, rendering time relative while its plot justification and duration stood the same (Samuel A. Goudsmit & Robert Claibourne, Time, Time-Life Science Library, 1966, Indonesian trans. 1981: 166). But a video like Mahesa Almeida's Fish Market (OK.Video 2003) could only be rearranged by "replacing" its pictorial code with the risk of changing the plot. Why? The frame counts, by which the plot was constituted, were no longer situated in the normative 24 frames per second, but in its 25 counterpart, with a frame shape that could no longer function as a unity. The same scenario is happening to the time sequence of these documented 2000-2010 ruangrupa's archive materials. In the database, identification made to each document could be changed just a click away, although the main coding stays intact. It was not the case with identification alteration made to archive material posted on the original document. It would have to be removed and would certainly leave a mark. The operation of digital documentary archive signifies a reality outside of its bearer's body.

A person, who scours every chronicle detail of a particular time frame in her/his research effort, would eventually meet one or two unexpected materials that could serve as a form of entertainment in the middle of her/his data looking endeavor. When s/he summons every effort in her/his observation, and makes specific interpretation towards every thing s/he finds, s/he would stop for a moment

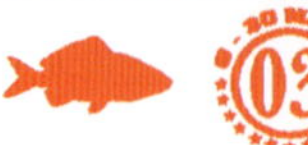
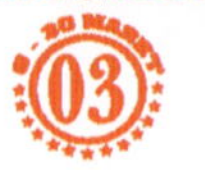
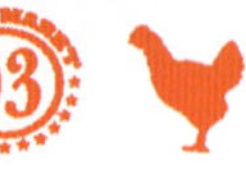
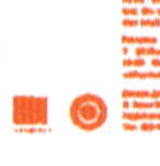

Poster dari *Lekker Eten Zonder Betalen*, Proyek Seni ruangrupa, Rumah Seni Cemeti, 2003.

in a spontaneous pleasure by the discovering of a newfound existence. For instance, I would never have imagined that I could discover, so suddenly, an alternative path taken by the Yogyakarta art modernism in 1949. The sensation was felt through S. Sudjojono's two-page piece, Jogjakarta 1949 that contained a picture: Kartono Yudhokusumo and Nurnaningsih, his wife, in the middle of taking out their first baby son from a charcoal basket box on their bike (Pantja Sila, 1949: 5-6). The knowledge would change my point of view towards the Indonesian modern art situation during the period of revolution. According to Sudjojono, the main difference between modern fine art/painting (of course he reffered to Persagi in making this statement) with its predecessors, Mooi Indie, was the shift of creative workspace from rural (Mooi Indie) to urban (Persagi) (Sudjojono, Seni Loekis, Kesenian dan Seniman, 1946: 48). Although in reality of that particular situation, was only replacing the position of the photographer who took the picture in the first place. Through his camera lens, the photographer had given the transformation of the moment in order for many to review by opening the file.

In similar cases, there have been numerous episodes with similar level of sensitivities and emotional motives. Rendering the image file to be just one of the thousands of image file saved in the directory //serferruru/500gbaru(j)/_. It exists between collection of materials that are so serious in nature: ones that map, as well serve as a sophisticated mapping result on space, time, and interpretation.

The photographic camera on Sudjojono-Yudhokusumo tale, depicted above, had only been a fairly new modern tool. Our painters, through their paintings, had not even touched the issue of representational distortion, made possible by the very obvervatory apparatus. Indonesian modern paintings had not been complicated by a device that would change their every representational symptoms. The artists back then could be said to be very skilfull in depicting realities and transforming them into realism. It's only in the seventies a new realism emerged to contest the representation of brushstrokes. Dede Eri Supria starte

utilizing it to present Jakarta urbanity.
The similar technological representation resulting in comparable effect also exists in other media and projects documented using digital camera. Culture stated that devil was in the (daily) details. It steers us clear from the elusive grand pompousness at times. This serves as the scheme for art projects in the electronic digital century, as warned by MG and Andry Moch. through their Zero Eye Lution project.
In the end, the archives being exhibited here are intended for a wider public. It can't be denied that part of the archives during the year of 2000-2010 could give sufficient narration on public in its double meaning: public as sympathizers and public as residents in a number of location ruangrupa has been housed in and artistically located. When ruangrupa only had one or two artistic projects under its wing, its archival door might have been subconsciously directed to the time tunnel ended up with its various public audience. The objects, the projects are no longer with us. Even space has been relocated four times. With the relocation, brought in also the change of public. The files avoid realities to be repeated unnoticed. Although it must be admitted that to a [certain extent memorabilia has an inevitable sensation.]

Ugeng T. Moetidjo

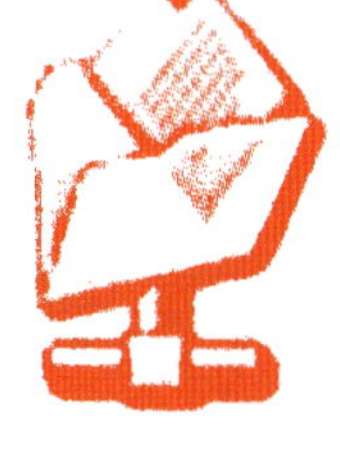

500gbaru (J) on Serferuru

Jakarta 32°c, Galeri Nasional Indonesia, Jakarta, 28 December 2010 – 12 January 2011, part of 'Decompression #10' programme

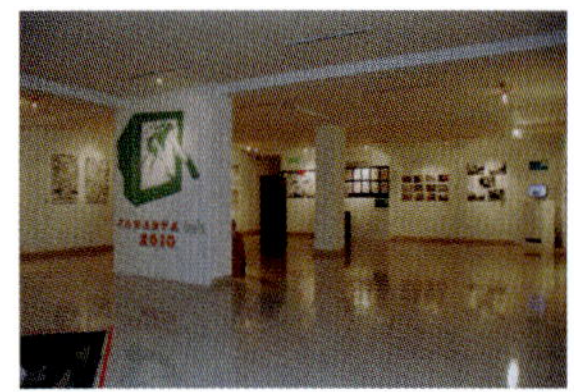

542

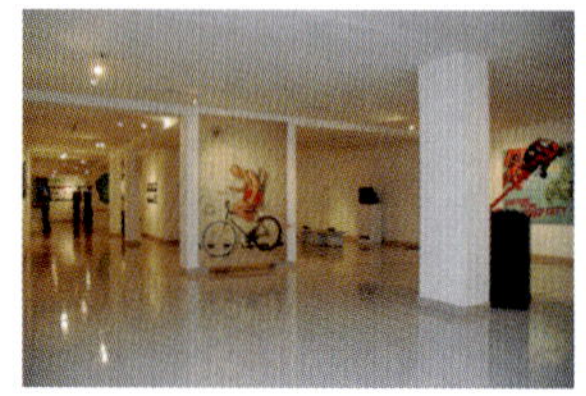

543

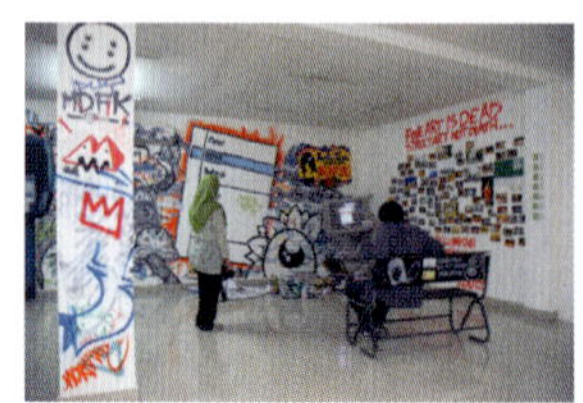

544

JAKARTA 32°C 2010

KAMI MENERIMA PENDAFTARAN UNTUK SEGALA KARYA SENI
DARI SEGALA INSTANSI PERGURUAN TINGGI DI JAKARTA

KARYA BERUPA :
*VIDEO
*LUKISAN
*PATUNG
*DESAIN GRAFIS
*FILM
*INSTALASI
*PROYEK SENI
*SOUND ART
*FASHION
*ARSITEKTUR
*FOTOGRAFI, DLL.

PENDAFTARAN DIBUKA MULAI 1 SEPTEMBER – 1 NOVEMBER 2010
UNTUK INFORMASI LANJUT HUBUNGI KAMI

JL. TEBET TIMUR DALAM RAYA NO.6
JAKARTA SELATAN 12820

(021) 8304220

email : jakarta32c@ruangrupa.org

www.jakarta32c.org
www.ruangrupa.org

KARYA AKAN DIPAMERKAN DI GALERI NASIONAL INDONESIA
PADA TANGGAL : 28 DESEMBER 2010 – 12 JANUARI 2011

KAMI JUGA MEMBUKA WORKSHOP SENI RUPA : BONGKAR JAKARTA
Workshop Video bersama Forum Lenteng
Workshop Ilustrasi bersama Komunitas Maros
Workshop Street Art bersama Artcoholic
Workshop Komunikasi Visual bersama Kampung Segart
Workshop Komik bersama Akademi Samali
Workshop Multimedia bersama sakitkuningcollectivo
Workshop Public Art bersama Serrum
Workshop Performance Art bersama Rewind Art
Workshop Fotografi bersama ruangrupa

ARTS COLLABORATORY
STICHTING DOEN
NATIONALE POSTCODE LOTERIJ
Hivos people unlimited
ARTLAB
RURU Gallery
KARBON www.karbonjournal.org
ok. VIDEO
trax
101.4 trax fm
DAILY WHATNOT
KAMENGSKI
serrum
ARTCO STREET TERROR
REWIND Art
forum lenteng

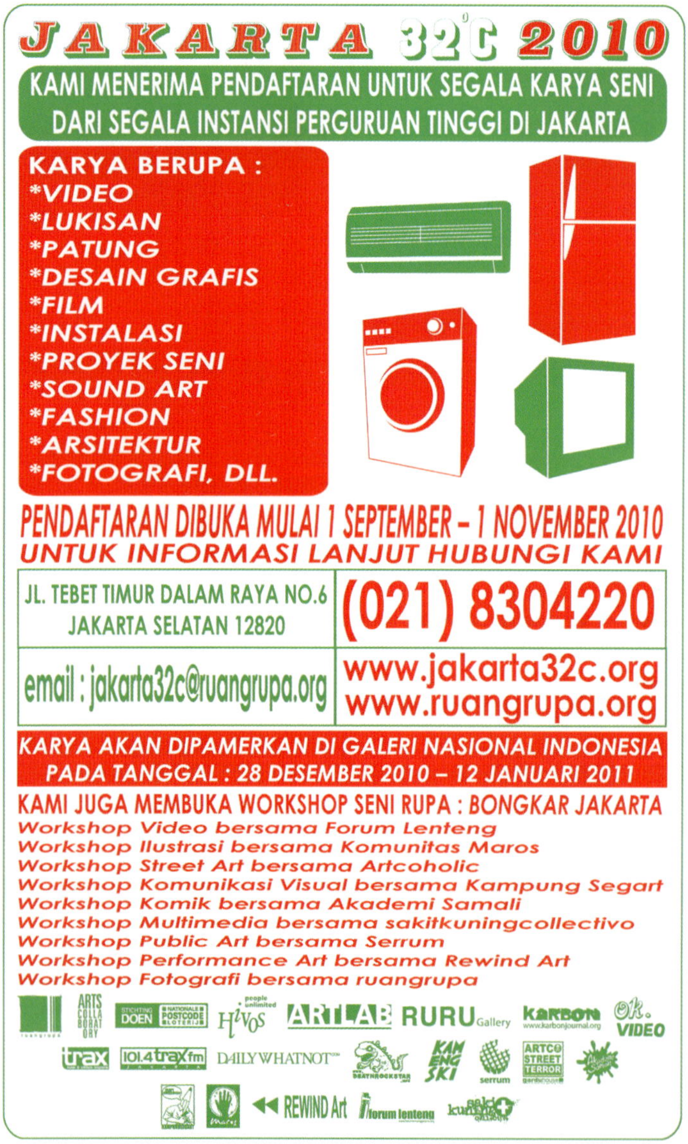

547

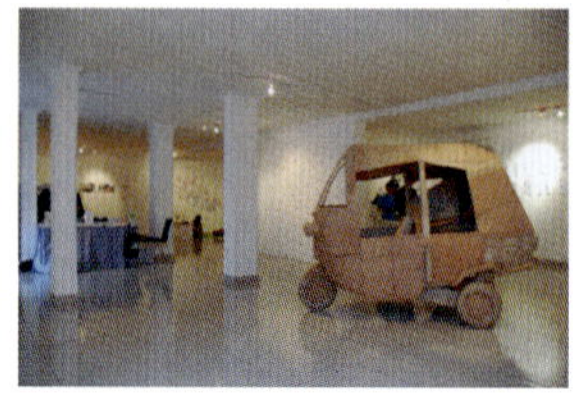

545

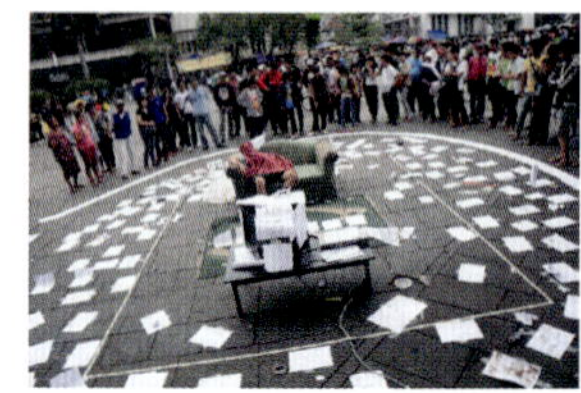

546

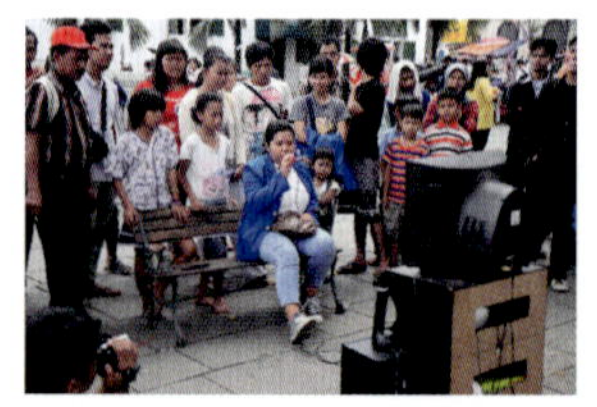

548

RRREC Fest, Galeri Nasional Indonesia, Jakarta, 8–9 January 2011, part of 'Decompression #10' 207

RRREC Fest is an annual programme which takes place since 2010. A music festival, RRREC Fest showcases and unites various artist groups, communities, musicians and music organisers from many places around the world. RRREC Fest is ruangrupa's effort together with young artists to put forth fresh, innovative and inspiring ideas for the music-loving young generation and citizens of Jakarta in general.

RRREC Fest is a statement on the importance of alternative spirit, not only imperative in music world, but also in many facets of cultural practice. RRREC Fest is a place of meeting for music lovers while serving the function of creating new network with musicians, bands, performers, independent music festival organisations, especially those coming from Asia and its surrounding region, enabling dialogue for new collaborative works in the future.

Gudskul Ekosistem

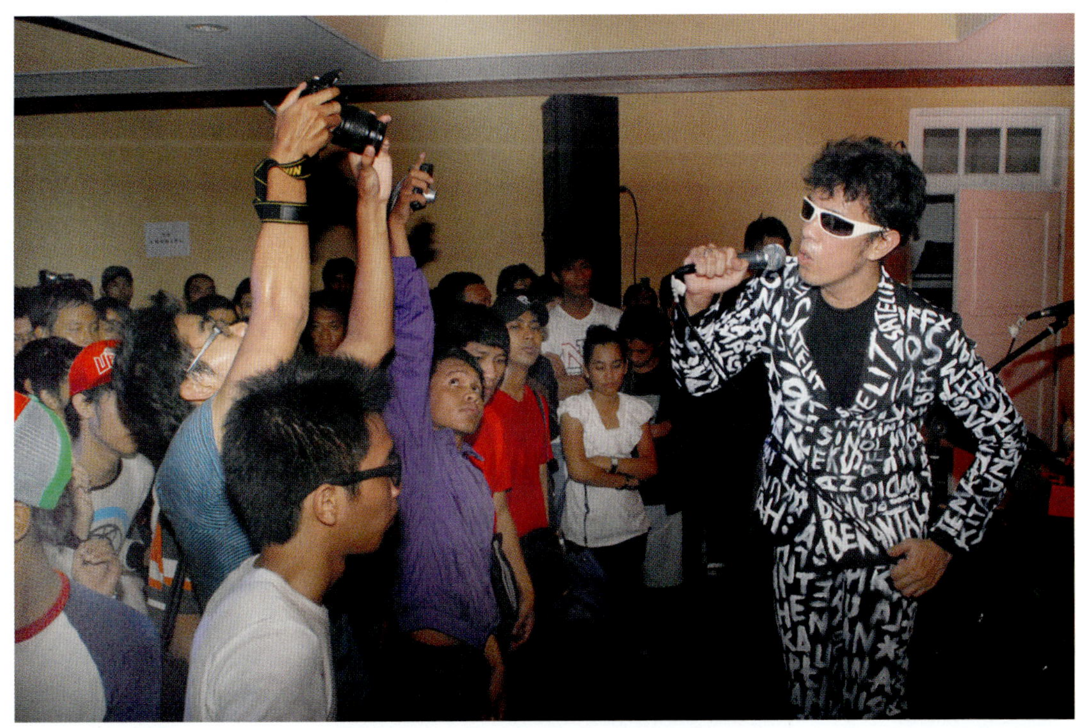

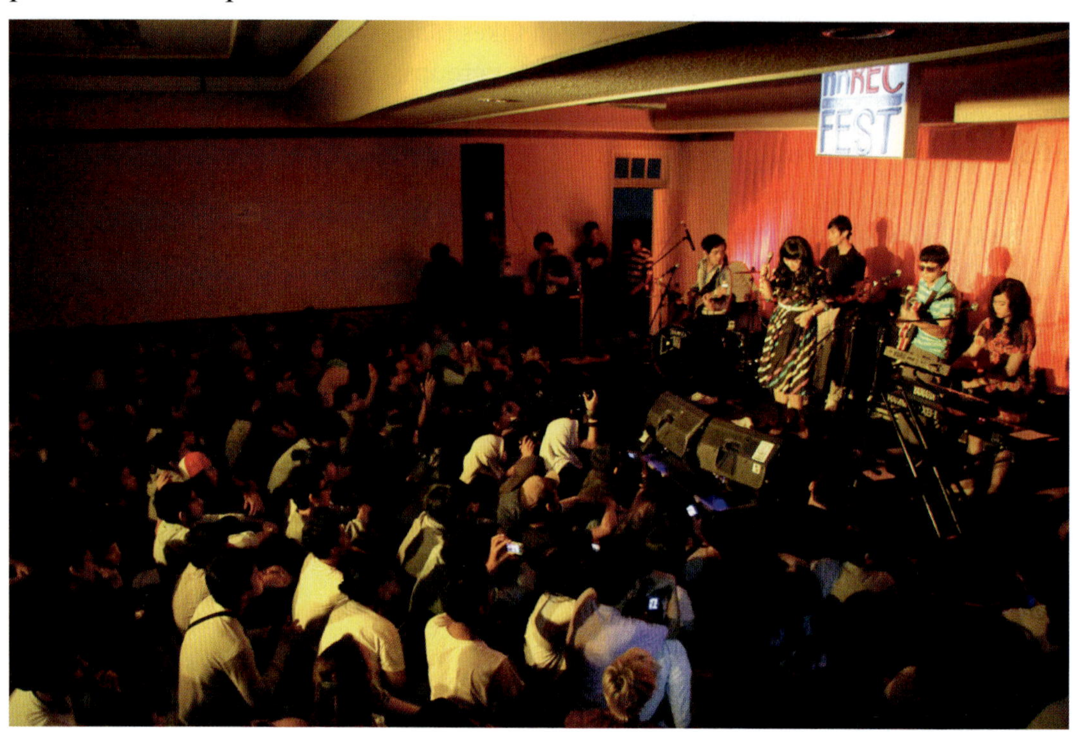

550

RRREC Fest started when ruangrupa had our 10th anniversary. We have a connection with the music scene. We thought it's good to have music programmed in the exhibition at the National Gallery. It made many of us happy but we just continued it as an annual music festival. It's not like building a brand nor to attract a big crowd. Instead, it's something that we like to do. After the fourth time, we discussed whether it's for profit or for fun. We made a conclusion that it's for fun. For me personally, ruru creates this space for us to experiment and invent prototypes, meaning models for small things that can be developed. I think that's what's interesting for us. Seeing a programme as a prototype, we also have less expectation. Even if the model might fail, it's like an addition to experiment. It's always fun in the process.

Indra Ameng

Before RRREC Fest, there's always been SUPERBAD!, which Ameng and Keke do in different venues. The main place was Jaya Pub. Some other people in their generation also did Monday Mayhem in different venues. So the gigs have always been there. It's just that in 2010 it became the brand RRREC Fest.

Grace Samboh

'Decompression #10: Expanding the Space and Public', 28 December 2010 – 12 January 2011

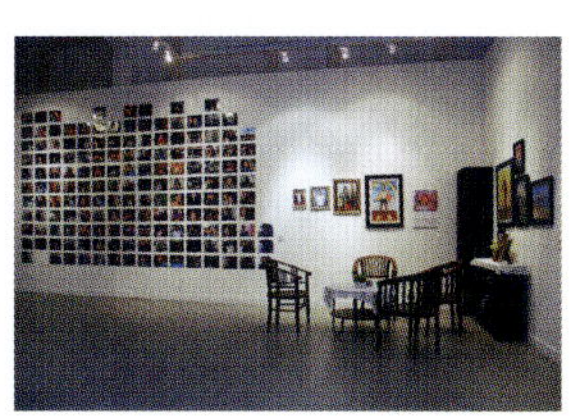

551

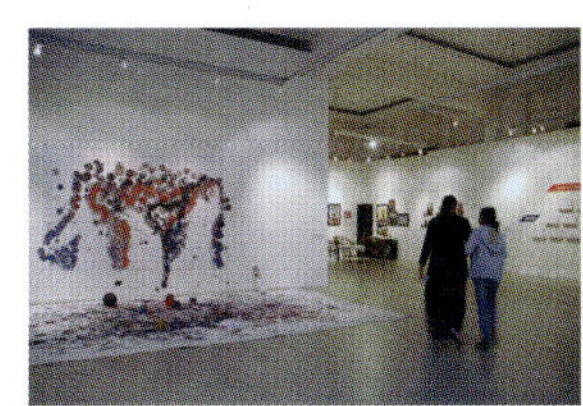

552

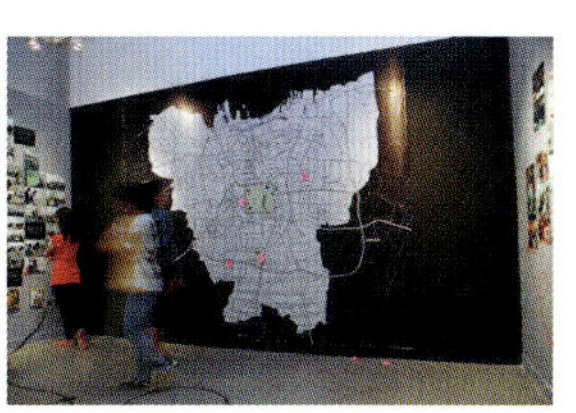

553

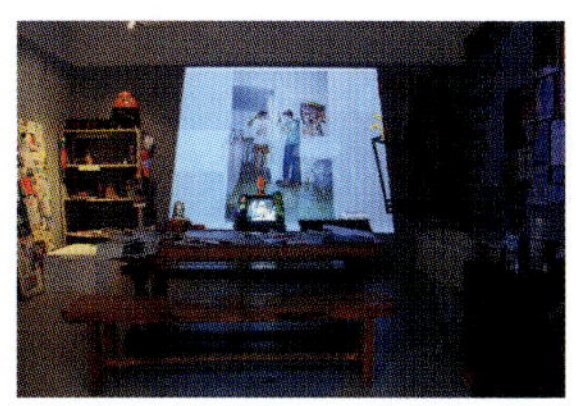

554

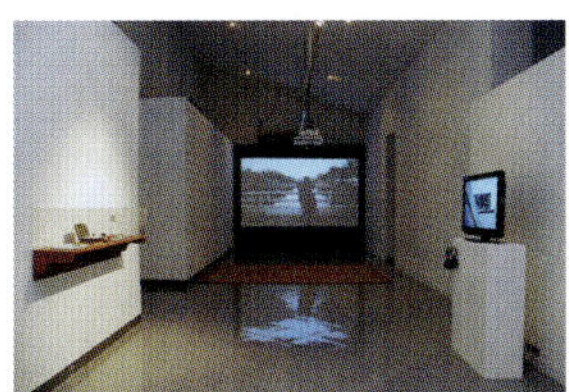

555

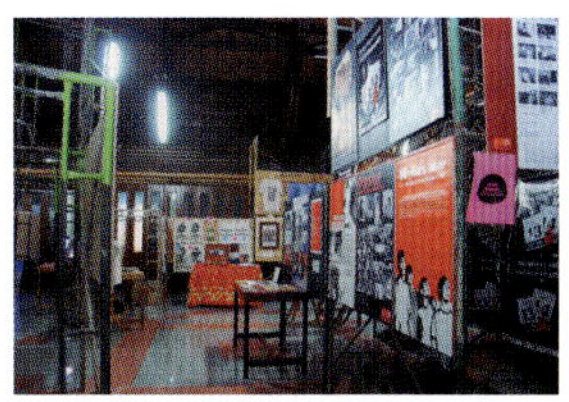

556

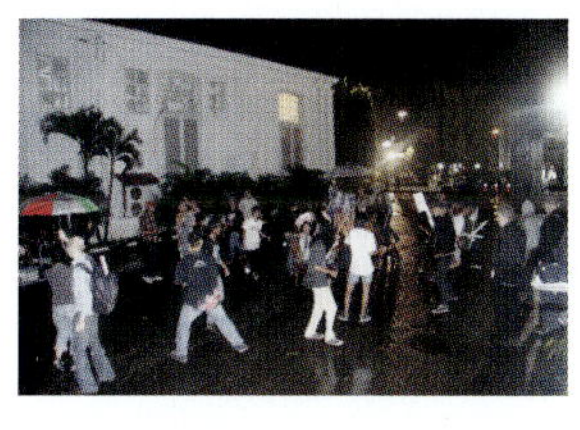

557

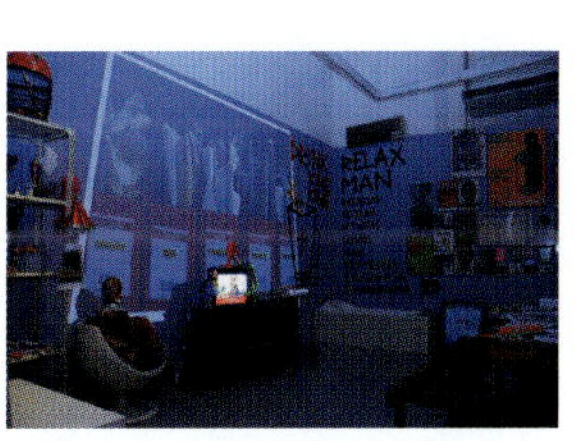

558

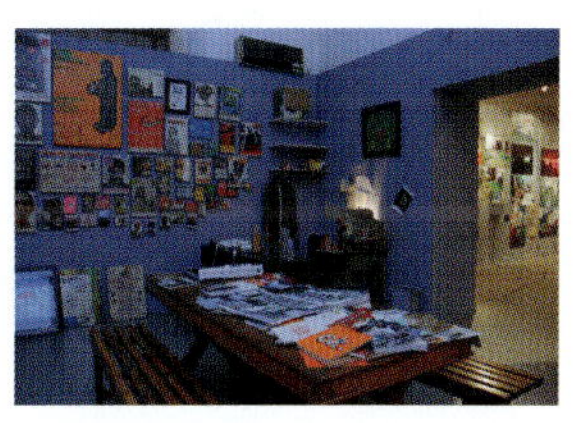

559

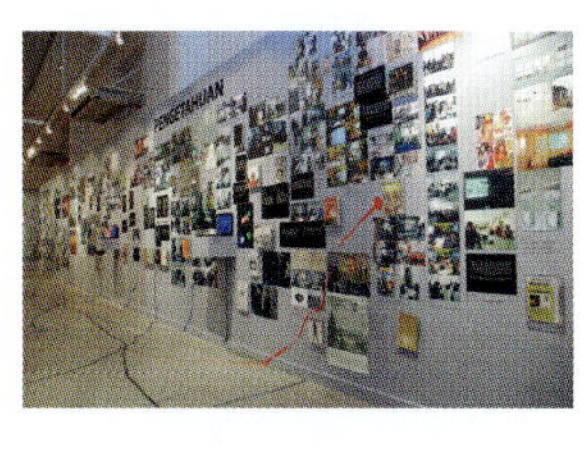

560

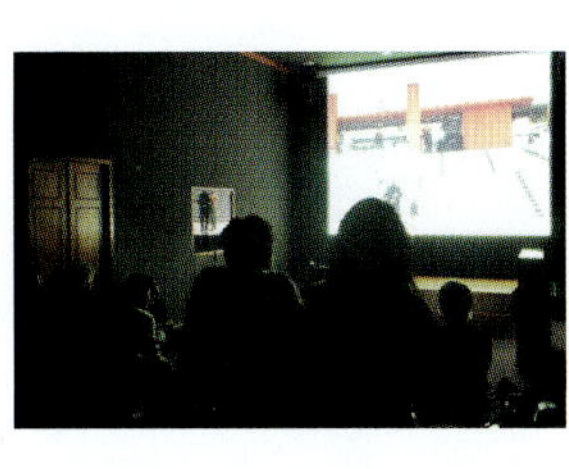

561

'Decompression #10: Expanding the Space and Public', 28 December 2010 – 12 January 2011

ruru's 10th anniversary at the National Gallery was one of my turning points in understanding curatorial practice. I was involved in the ruru.net exhibition as part of Kunci Study Forum & Collective with my two other colleagues, Ferdi Thajib and Nuraini Juliastuti. The ruru.net exhibition consisted of small booths of alter-native spaces, built with interconnected steel structures and not at all like the clean cube of art fairs. These mini showcases were not located in the main hall of the National Gallery of Jakarta; they were in a smaller space in the back of the main hall. Each alternative space had one square where they could put everything related to their organisational practice. Each day there were different programmes. We filled Kunci's space with bits and pieces from our office in Yogyakarta, including our library books and a life-size sticker of our dog, Chepas. If you look at the documentation, you will see a photograph taken from above. You can see all these different collectives and the metal structures that hold their spaces. It struck me that there's a network of alternative spaces from across Indonesia, such as Jatiwangi, Bandung, Surabaya, etc. They were not only artist collectives, but also research centres, libraries, design bureaus. Two years earlier, I joined ruangrupa's workshop on curating but I didn't really find what I was looking for as someone who is interested in collective and curatorial practices. To my surprise, ruru.net gave me a new perspective as to what an exhibition could be. I think this presentation structure of ruru.net – looking at the sociality of people, ideas and things – continued in other ruru projects, such as the Holy Market, and even documenta.

Syafiatudina

Decompression 2010: 10th anniversary ruangrupa. Was it too much, didn't it force the network to put too much energy in it? Perhaps it was the first time to work with scale on a bigger level. (Scale was already in the practice through the reality of the city and the different platforms OK.Video, Jakarta 32°C, Jakarta Biennial 2009) but this time it was pushing limits, I think interesting to understand.

reinaart vanhoe

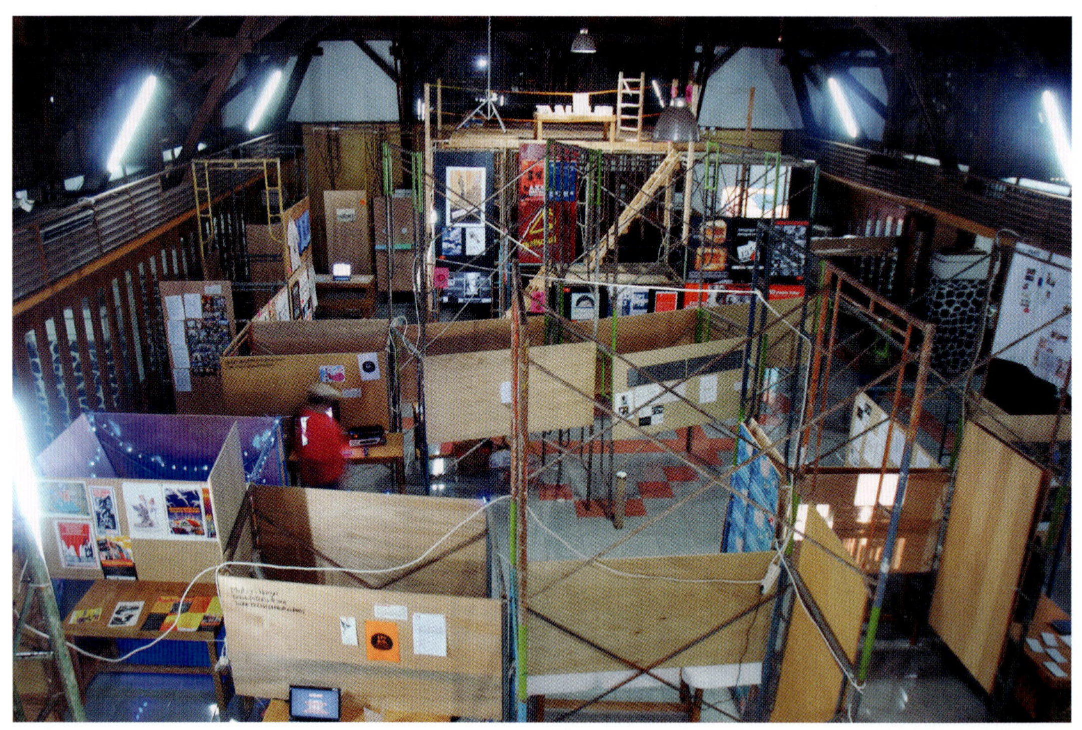

human resource

try to match and negotiate the personal dream to collective dream

passionate people is always better

good sense of humor and multi skills and multi tasking

The question now is whether artists in Java of today, born in the end of the 70s and early 80s, also face a common enemy? I will illustrate a bit the condition of the enemy (the Indonesian state via its apparatus) nowadays: bankrupt economy, intensified crime, racial riots and ethnic cleansing, which are caused by economical reasons but wrapped up in the guise of religious conflicts, and also massive corruption, untouched by law. Yet, what seems quite paradoxical is that there is also an emergence of freedom in many aspects: thought, speech, press, political practice and many others ... ruangrupa, for instance, is quite intensively introducing public art. Its main purpose is to reclaim the public space that has been controlled by bureaucracy, authority and anarchical urban infrastructure (a web of power relations that for me is very typical of Jakarta and other big cities in Indonesia).

Agung Kurniawan

The artist profession is not one that distances itself from the public and social reality. We believe, for example, that there are many ways to deal with global capitalism. One can try to grasp global capitalism in the other continent and transform it on canvas through abstract painting. One can also deal with it by expressing it through mundane, day-to-day expressions, which can surprise and inspire people to think critically at the way things are. ruangrupa is not unconscious that global capitalism has long been an octopus lurking in the bedroom, but one needs to deal with it not only by grand projects, but rather, once again, with small narratives with more frequency. Jakarta, as a locus where all surprises are possible, has to be engaged with according to its context, because many practices – whether conducted by the state or corporations – are not in conjunction with what is needed.

Mirwan Andan

ruangrupa was the go-to place for arts-minded students/youths in Jakarta during the period I got to know them (I would say between 2006–14). ruangrupa was a place, a community, a group of artists, a 'brand', a name that connotes 'artistic practice', 'freedom', 'hip', 'fashionable', 'open', 'urban' and 'trailblazing'. ruangrupa could also be a way of life. ... We went to their parties because they hosted great parties. We came to their talks because their talks addressed topics that were rarely addressed by government arts institutions or large art spaces, such as Komunitas Utan Kayu (now Salihara). I would say that students / youth who went to ruangrupa's events and space in 2006–14 (like me) were equally interested in their ideas, which were a bit unconventional at that time, their spirit/ways of life, and their space (you could just be there and meet interesting people) and it was free! In a big city where everything has to be bought or where money occupies such an important role, the freeness of ruangrupa's space and events speak, perhaps, to the importance of a free and civic public space, which in the case of Jakarta is rare! Jakarta has more shopping malls than parks.

Veronika Kusumaryati

Time is the currency. When we were together for ten years, we knew that we would continue for a lifetime.

Simon Danang Anggoro

'1001 Doors: Reinterpreting the Tradition', Ciputra Marketing Gallery, Jakarta, 26 January – 6 February 2011

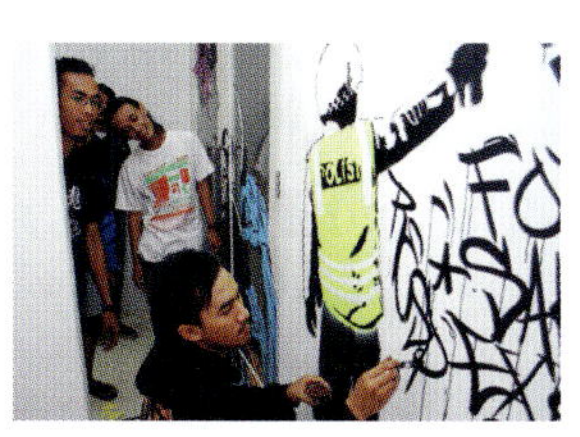

563

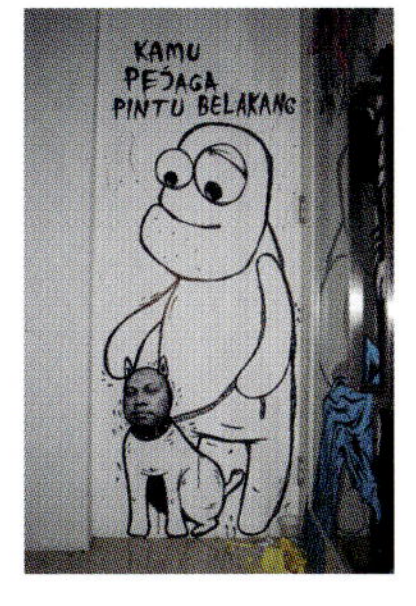

564

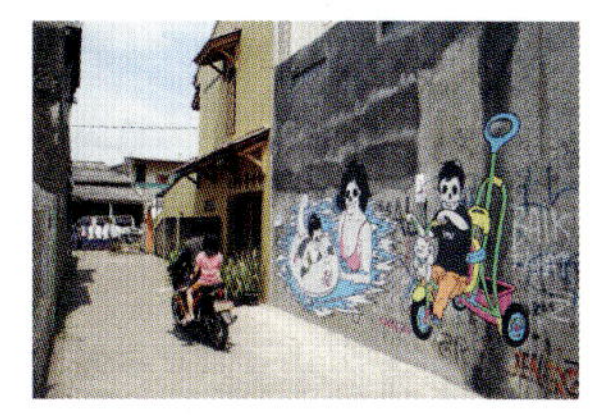

565

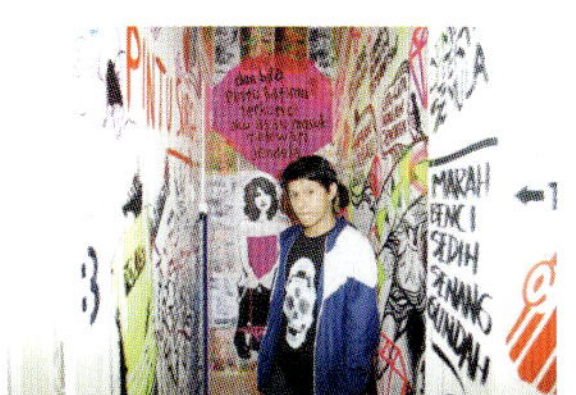

566

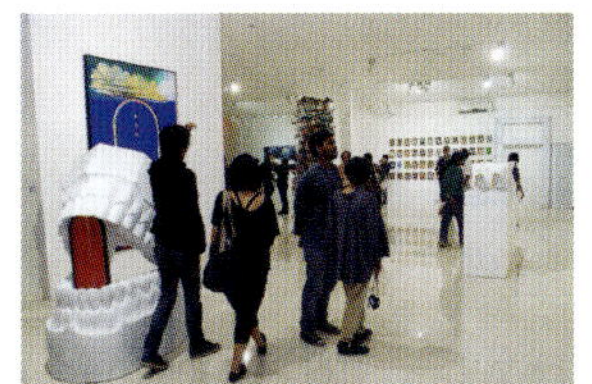

567

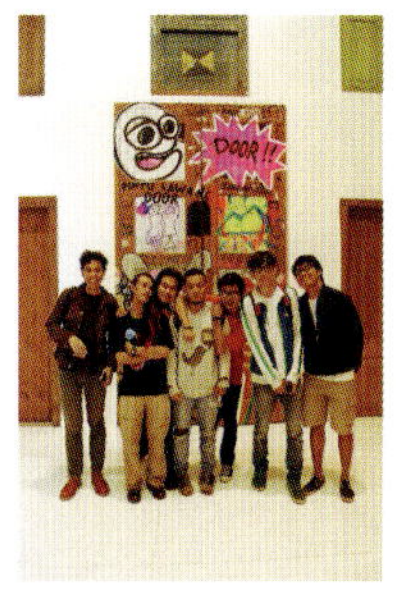

568

Singapore Fiction, installation for the Singapore Biennale, National Museum of Singapore, 13 March – 15 May 2011

In this project we create and recreate the fictional story about Singapore. We collect true and fiction stories from people we meet to reveal the people's personal idea and imagination about their experiences, memories, event, space and history. We use found and used objects that contained by anonymous stories and memories from the several flea markets and second-hand shop to inspire, and also illustrate these fictional stories. ... The *Singapore Fiction* installation will develop and grow by everyday findings, and it will shown in the National Museum of Singapore for the Singapore Biennale 2011.

ruangrupa

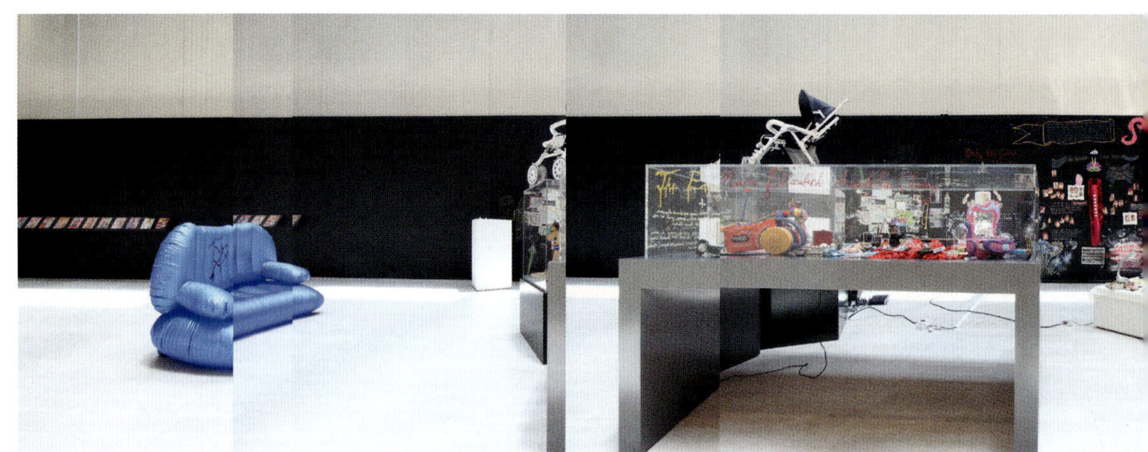

570

Fictifiction
ruangrupa
新加坡寓言
SINGAPORE BIENNALE 2011
OPEN HOUSE

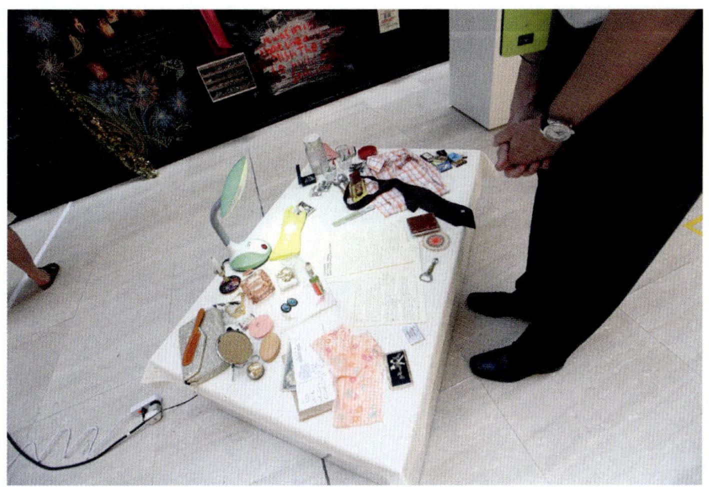

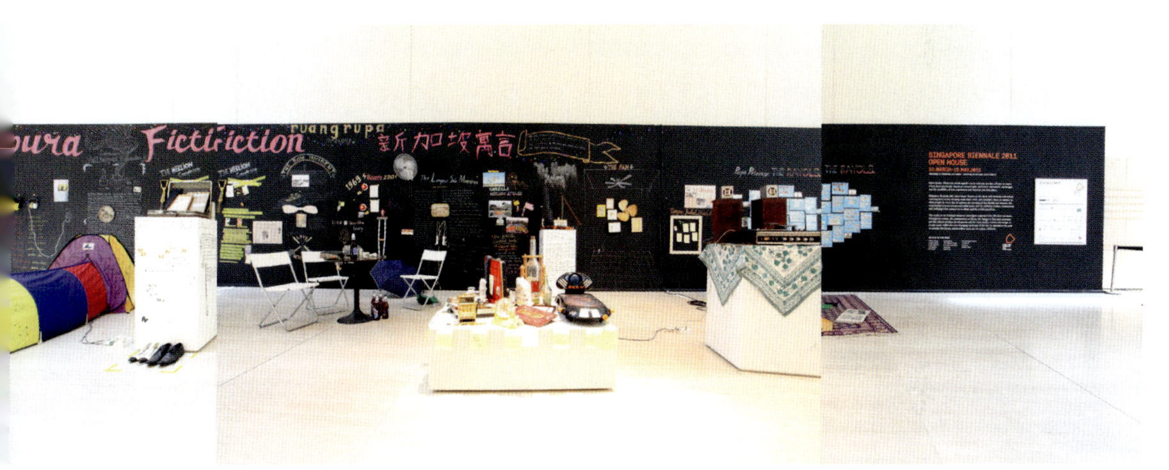

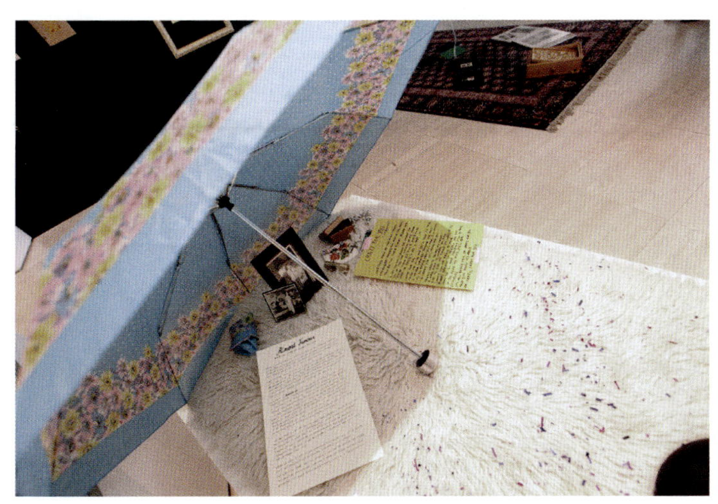

571

Mini OK.*Video Festival*, installation at Art Dubai, Dubai, United Arab Emirates, 16–19 March 2011

Etemad Gallery, Tehran/Dubai
Experimenter, Kolkata
Frey Norris Gallery, San Francisco
Galerie Bertrand & Gruner, Geneva
Galerie Caprice Horn, Berlin
Galerie Chantal Crousel, Paris
Galerie Christian Hosp, Berlin
Galerie El Marsa, Tunis
Galerie Janine Rubeiz, Beirut
Galerie Kashya Hildebrand, Zurich
Galerie Krinzinger, Vienna
Galerie Mario Mauroner Contemporary Art, Vienna/Salzburg
Galerie L.J., Paris
Galerie Michael Janssen, Berlin
Galerie Nathalie Obadia, Paris/Brussels
Marianne Boesky Gallery, New Y
October Gallery, London
Paradise Row, London
Pi Artworks, Istanbul
Pilar Corrias, London
Priska C. Juschka Fine Art, New
Rodeo, Istanbul
Rose Issa Projects, London
Ruangrupa, Jakarta
Salwa Zeidan Gallery, Abu Dhab
Selma Feriani Gallery, London
Sutton Gallery, Melbourne
The Guild Art Gallery, New York/
Traffic, Dubai

572

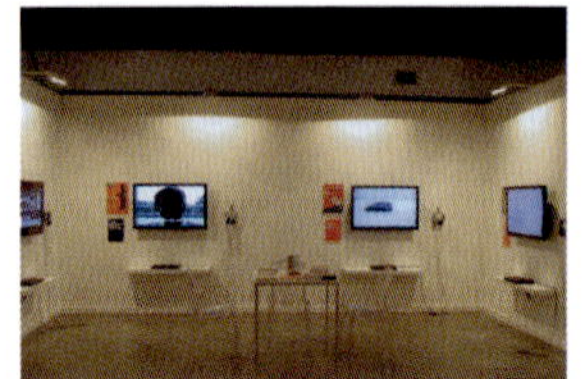

573

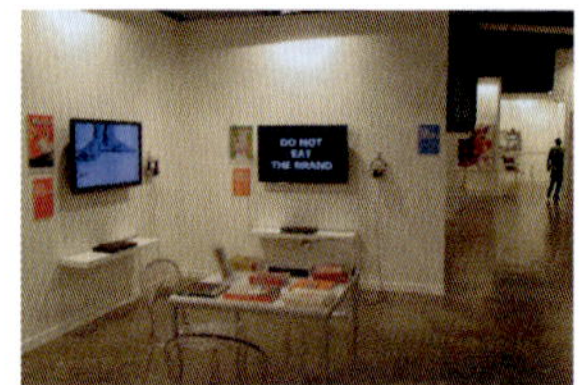

574

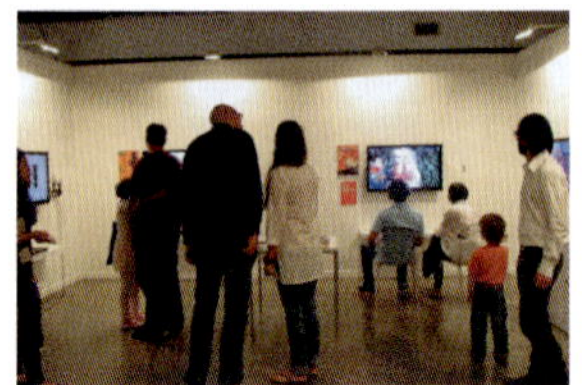

575

Participation in 'Berbeda dan Merdeka 100%' ('Different and Independent 100%'), multiple venues, 13 January & 17 April 2011

Respecta Street Art Gallery (RSAG) and several other street art groups [and ruru] took part in Jakarta Sunday Street Art Movement, held simultaneously in twenty Indonesian cities and in Singapore. The event, now better known as 'Berbeda dan Merdeka 100%' movement, is dedicated to fighting for national human rights and diversity, and has had an enormous impact ... RSAG has supported the establishment of the Indonesian Street Art Database (ISAD), a network of independently managed, community-based efforts toward a more effective historicisation of Indonesian street art for researchers.

Leonhard Bartolomeus

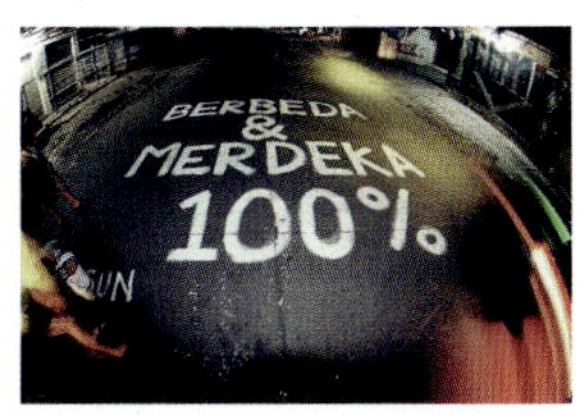

576

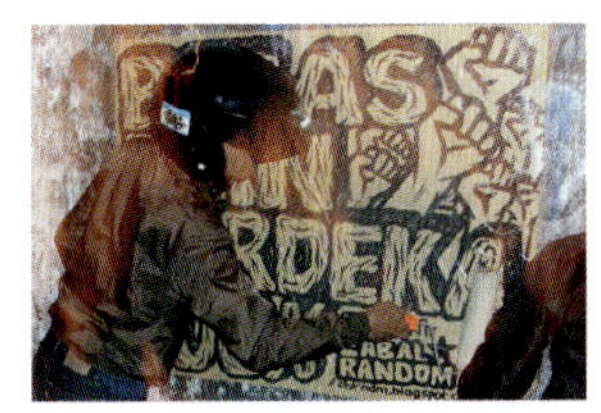

577

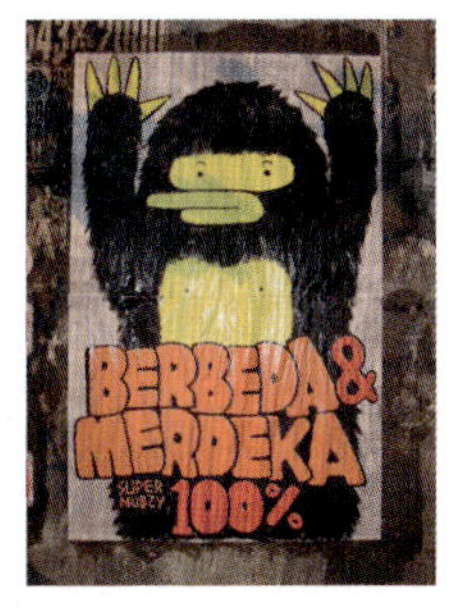

578

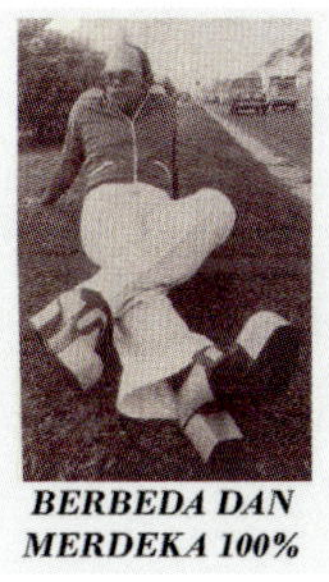

579

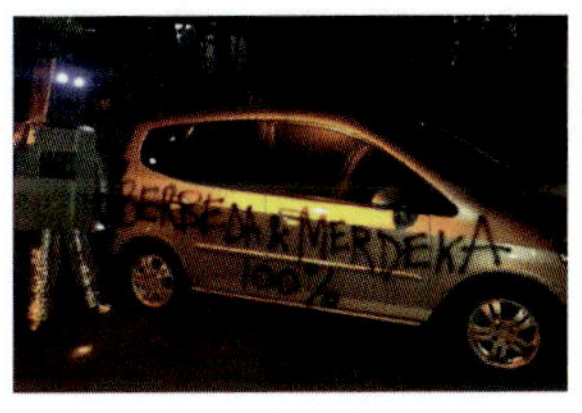

580

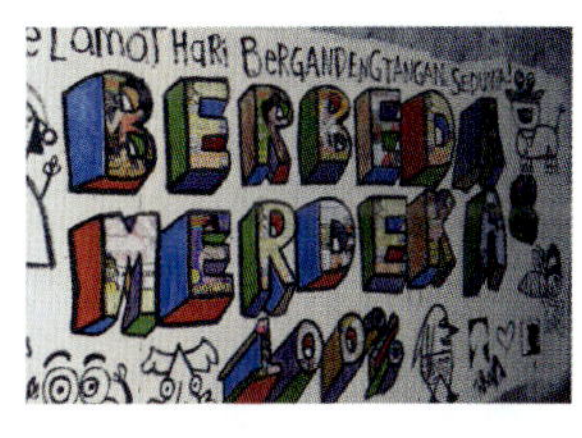

581

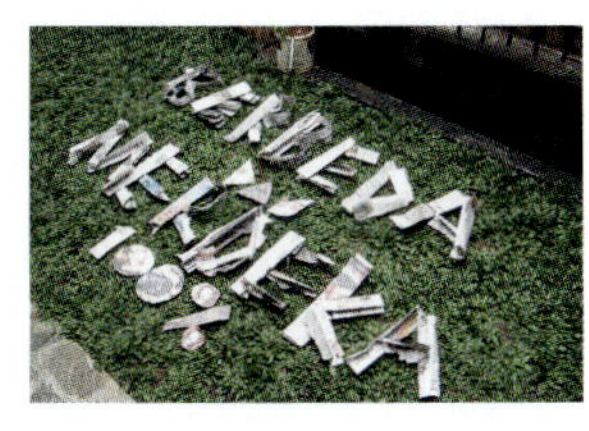

582

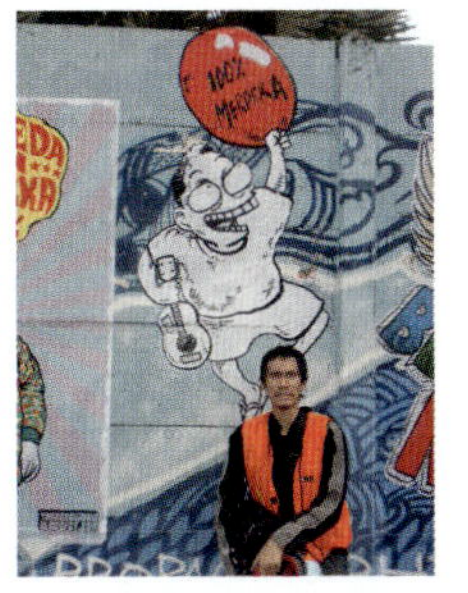

583

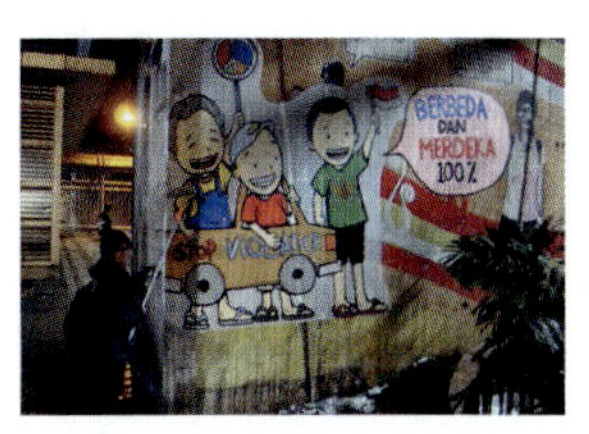

584

ruangrupa present

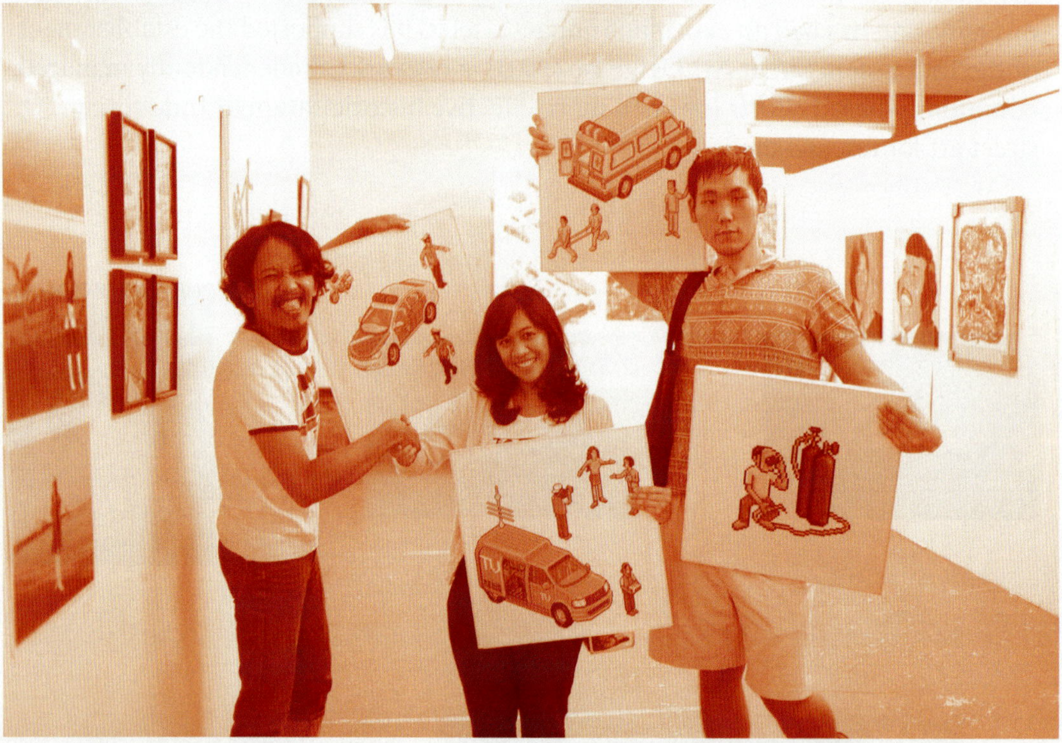

LONELY MARKET

ARTIST' ARTWORKS EDITION

30 APRIL - 1 MAY 2011

from 1 pm - 8 pm at ruangrupa

FEATURING : **GARDU HOUSE. SERRUM. JAKARTA WASTED ARTISTS. OOMLEO. MARISHKA SOEKARNA. APRILIA APSARI. MONICA HAPSARI. HAVE A NICE DAY. IKA VANTIANI. KOMUNITAS PECINTA KERTAS. GALAXY. KAMENGSKI. ASHTWO. ADE DARMAWAN. HENRY FOUNDATION. MATEUS BONDAN. ISROL TRIONO. POPO. KOMIK MAJEMUK. NEEDLE N'BITCH. JAH IPUL. ABIRAMA. RIO FARABI. JOHAN ARDIKA. KEKE TUMBUAN. JIMI MULTHAZAM. INDRA AMENG. BAYBAY. and many more.**

RUANGRUPA. JL. TEBET TIMUR DALAM RAYA NO.6. JAKARTA SELATAN. T: 021 8304220.

presentation of eight t-shirt related projects which ruangrupa and friends did between 2005 and 2011, including 'Kaos Project', as part of The French Cultural Centre's 'Dysfashional #6' art festival

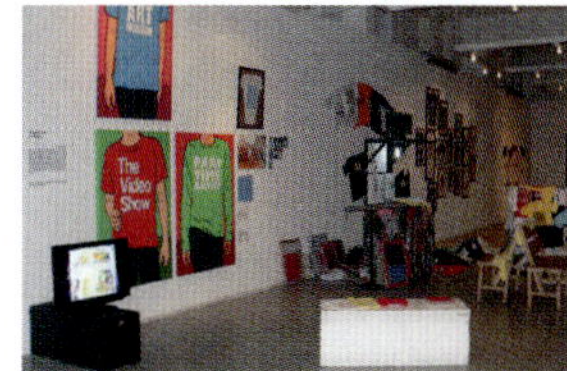

586

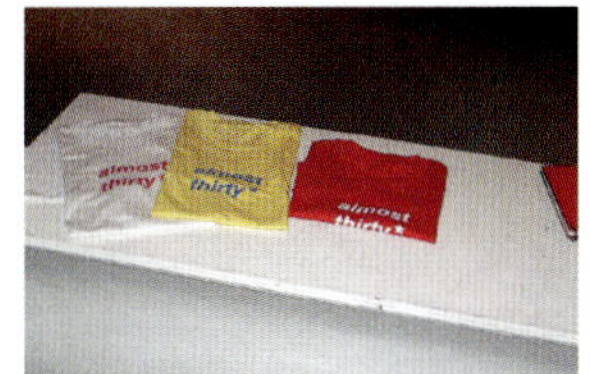

587

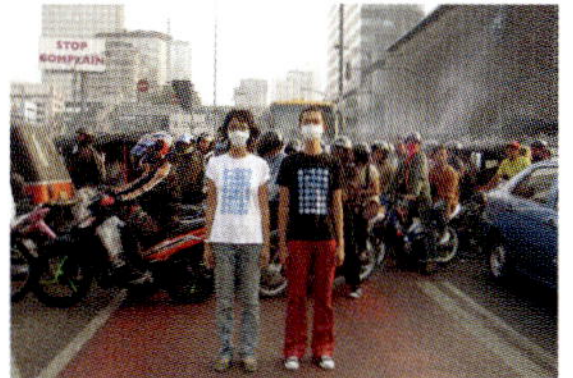

588

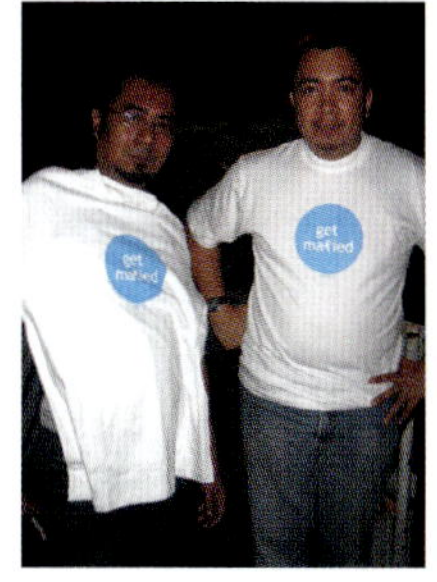

589

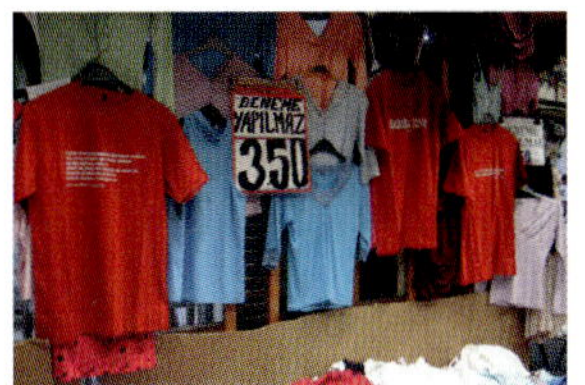

590

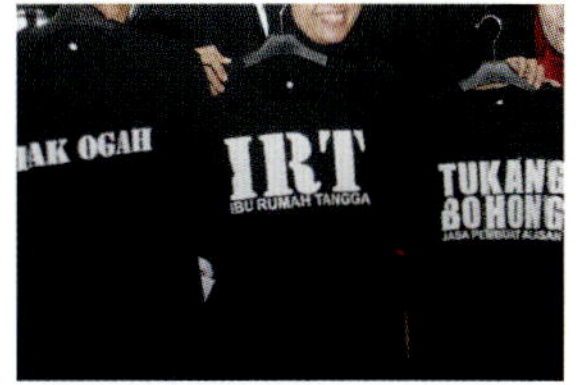

591

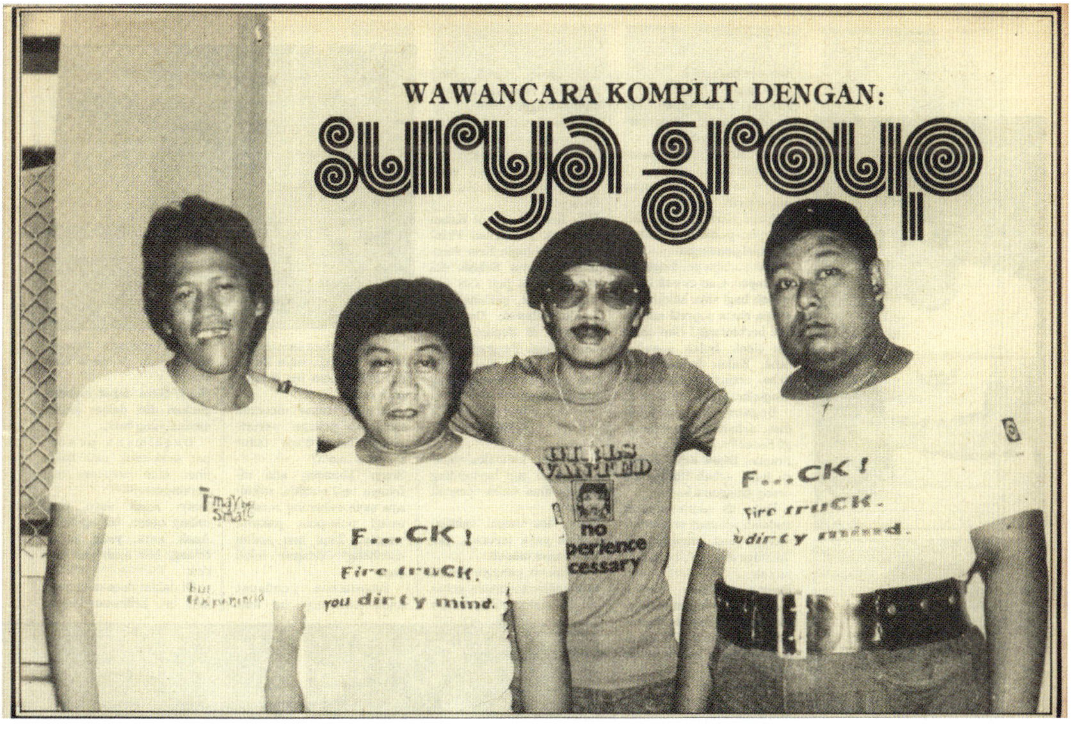

WAWANCARA KOMPLIT DENGAN:

surya group

F...CK!
Fire truCK.
you dirty mind.

no
perience
cessary

592

'The Best of the Beast', Cemeti Art House, Yogyakarta, 7–30 July 2011

with Restu Ratnaningtyas, Bowo Adi Utomo, Beatrix Hendriani Kaswara, Octora, Wimo Ambala Bayang, Dona Prawira Arrisuta, Carolina Rikka Winata, Laksmi Shitaresmi, S. Teddy D, Theresia Agustina Sitompul, Agung Kurniawan, Arya Panjalu, Sara Nuitemans, Popok Triwahyudi, Abdi Setyawan, Jumadi Alfi, Pauhrizi, Ade Darmawan, ruangrupa, Angky Purbandono, Syagini Ratnawulan, Moelyono, FX Harsono, Agan Harahab, Iswanto Hartono, Ugo Untoro, Eko Nugroho, Terra Bajraghosa, Mella Jaarsma, Nindityo Adipurnomo, Maryanto, Gintani Nur Apresia Swastika, Uji Handoko, Dian Ariyani; a later iteration of the exhibition was presented at Salihara Gallery, Jakarta

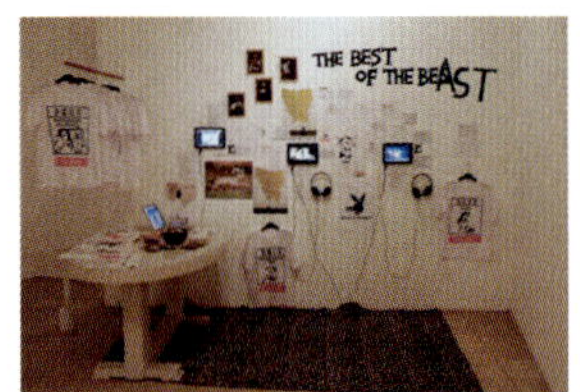

593

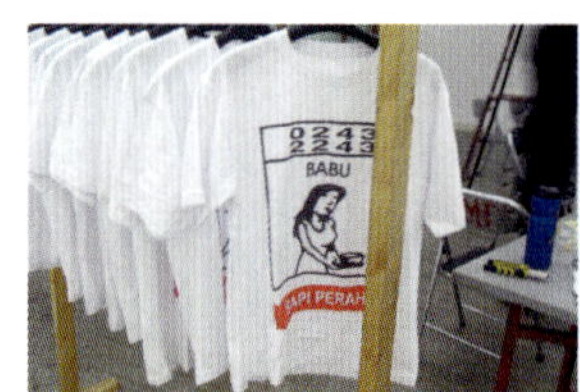

594

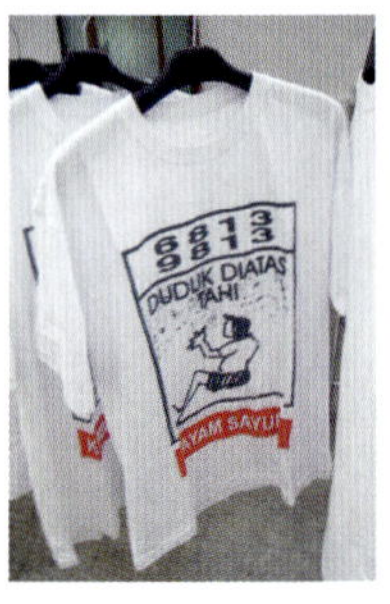

595

Participation in 'City_net Asia 2011', Seoul Museum of Art, 16 September – 20 November 2011

ruangrupa, representing Jakarta, was featured in the biennale with three other participating cities, namely Kanazawa (The 21st Century Contemporary Art Museum), Bangkok (Jim Thompson Art Center) and Seoul (Seoul Museum of Art); ruru presented an installation of ArtLab's projects, 'Cinema Wagon' (2010–11) and 'Lonely Market' (2009)

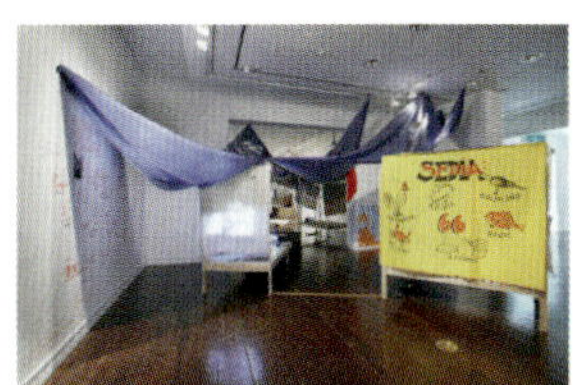

596

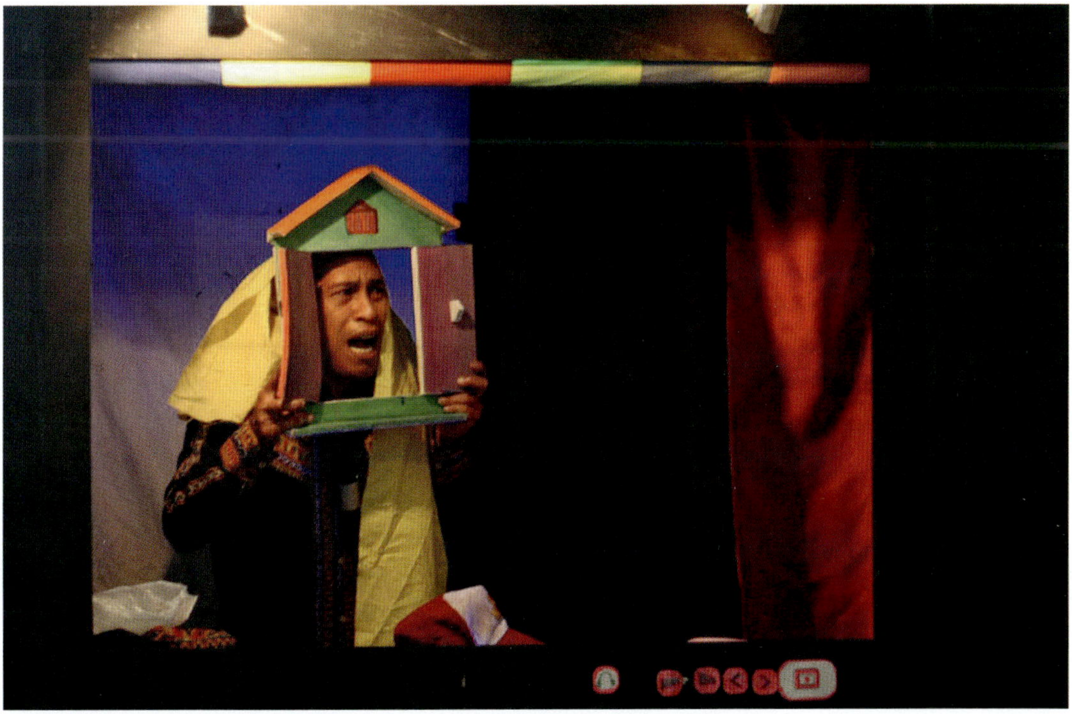

597

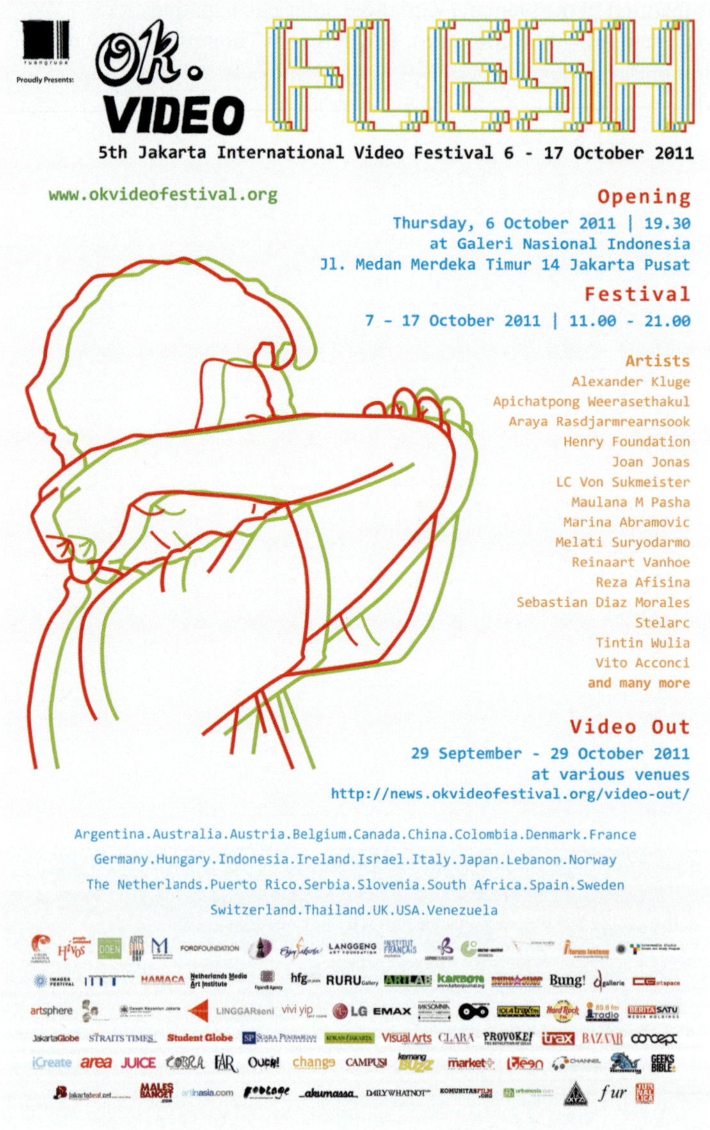

ruangrupa
Proudly Presents:

ok. VIDEO FLESH

5th Jakarta International Video Festival 6 - 17 October 2011

www.okvideofestival.org

Opening
Thursday, 6 October 2011 | 19.30
at Galeri Nasional Indonesia
Jl. Medan Merdeka Timur 14 Jakarta Pusat

Festival
7 - 17 October 2011 | 11.00 - 21.00

Artists
Alexander Kluge
Apichatpong Weerasethakul
Araya Rasdjarmrearnsook
Henry Foundation
Joan Jonas
LC Von Sukmeister
Maulana M Pasha
Marina Abramovic
Melati Suryodarmo
Reinaart Vanhoe
Reza Afisina
Sebastian Diaz Morales
Stelarc
Tintin Wulia
Vito Acconci
and many more

Video Out
29 September - 29 October 2011
at various venues
http://news.okvideofestival.org/video-out/

Argentina.Australia.Austria.Belgium.Canada.China.Colombia.Denmark.France
Germany.Hungary.Indonesia.Ireland.Israel.Italy.Japan.Lebanon.Norway
The Netherlands.Puerto Rico.Serbia.Slovenia.South Africa.Spain.Sweden
Switzerland.Thailand.UK.USA.Venezuela

598

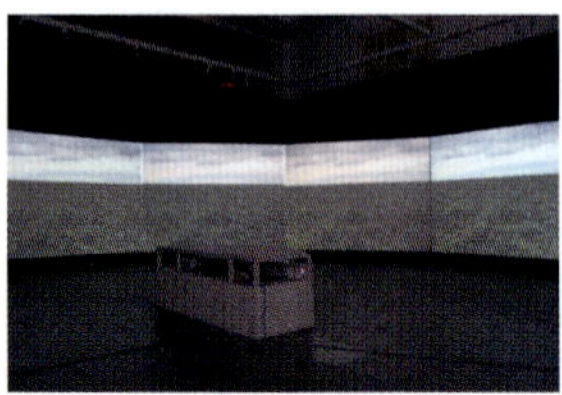

599

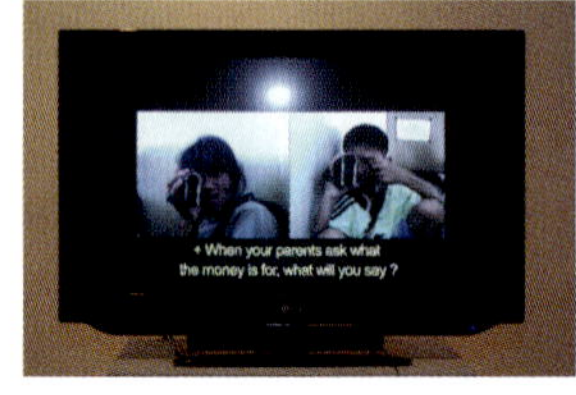

600

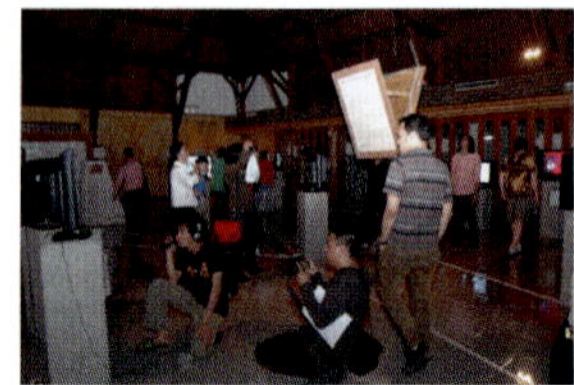

601

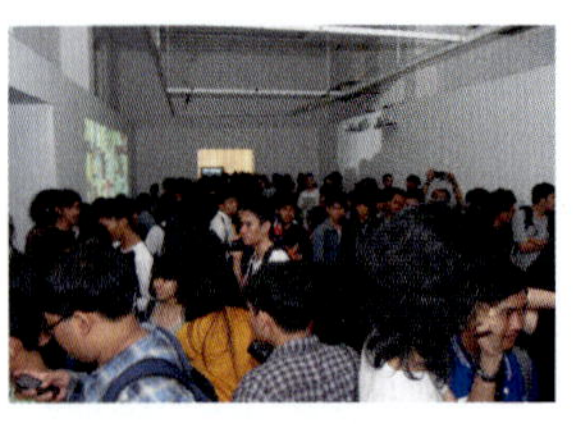

602

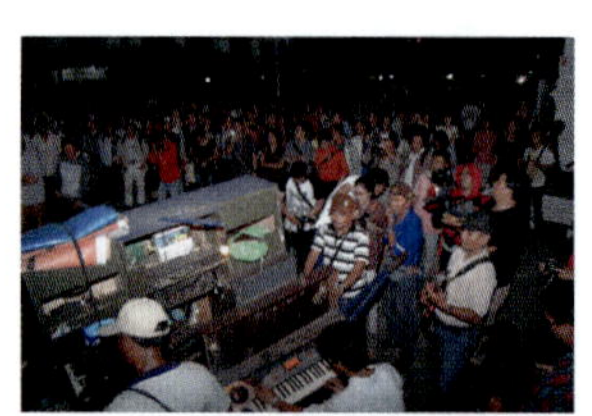

603

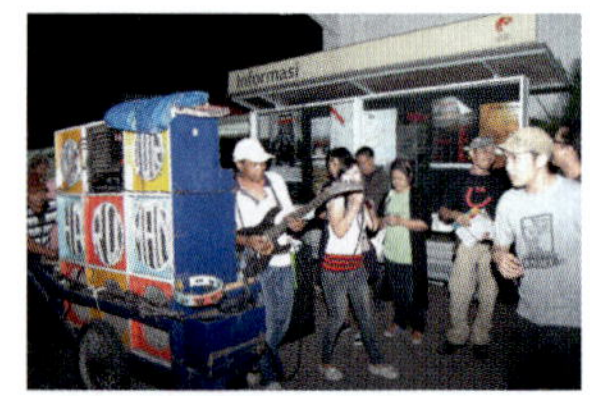

604

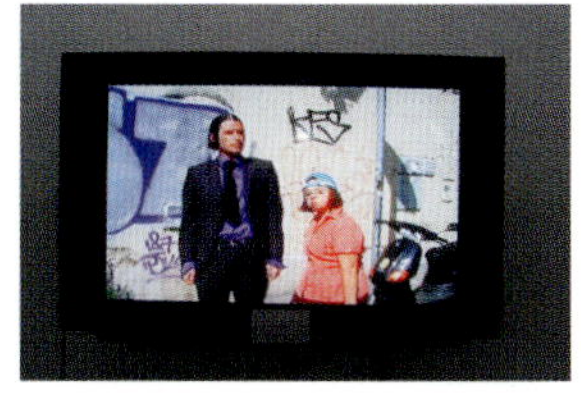

605

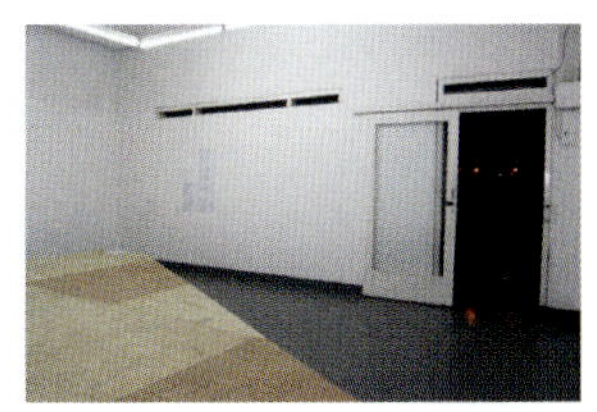

606

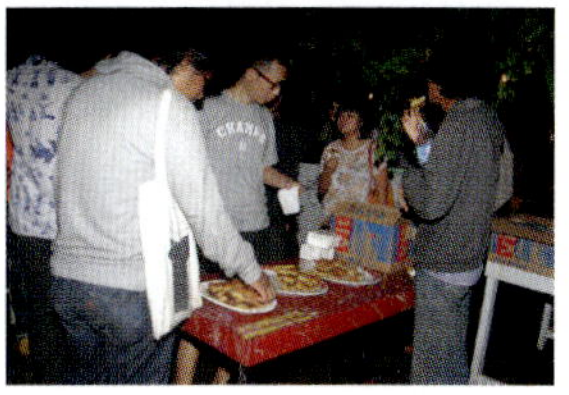

607

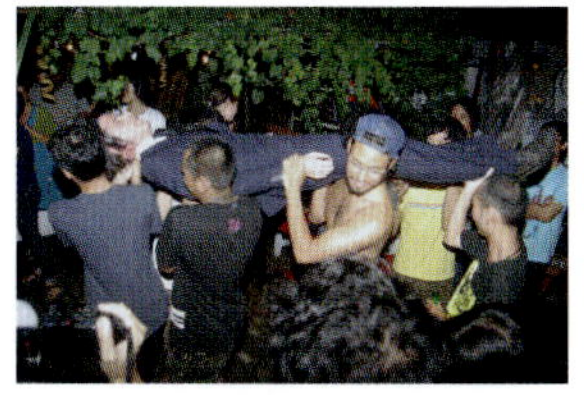

608

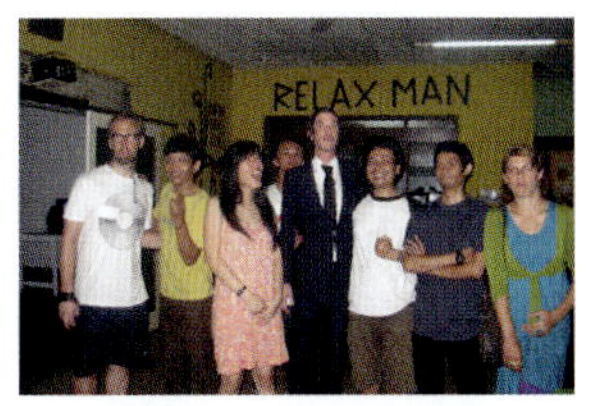

609

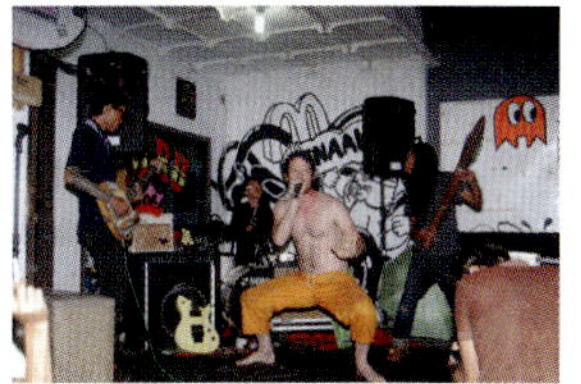

610

'Tanda Mata: Jakarta Merchandise Project', RURU Gallery, 29 March – 14 April 2012

with Cuba Tees, Gardu House, Ika Vantiani, Jah Ipul, Kamengski, Komunitas Pecinta Kertas (KPK), P.A.L.U. and Recycle Experience

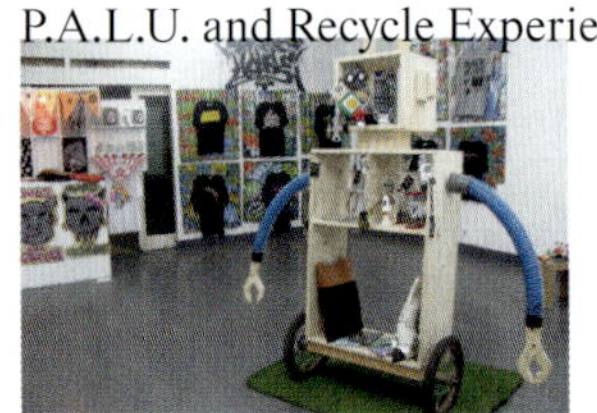

611

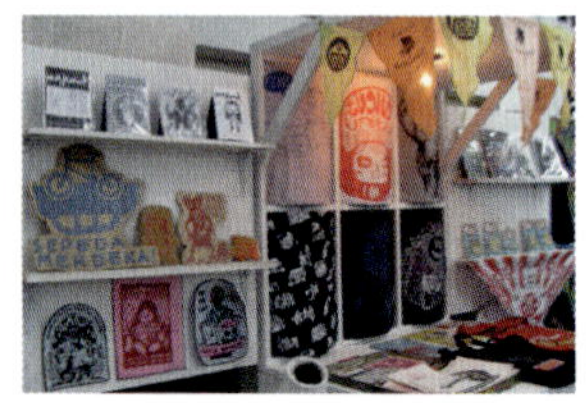

612

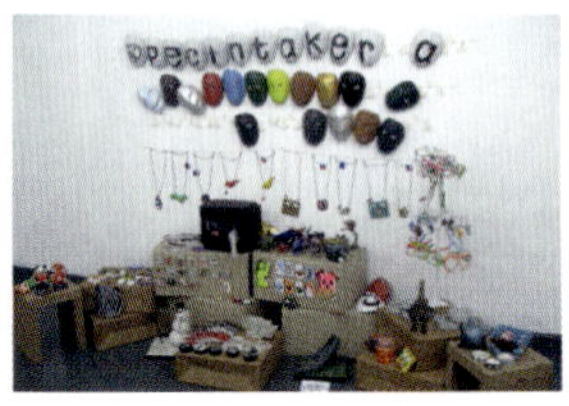

613

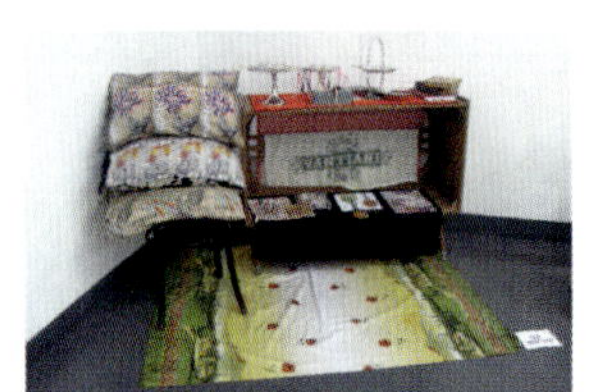

614

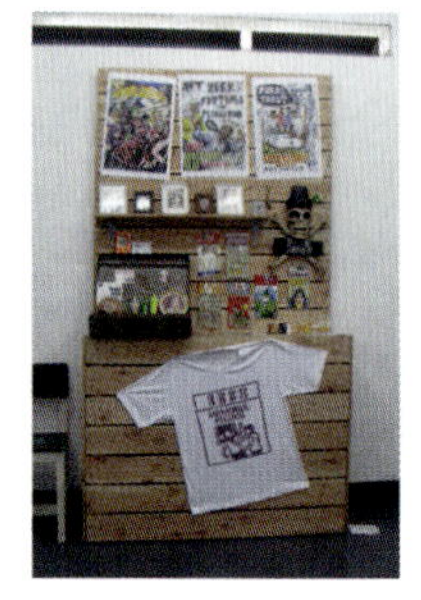

615

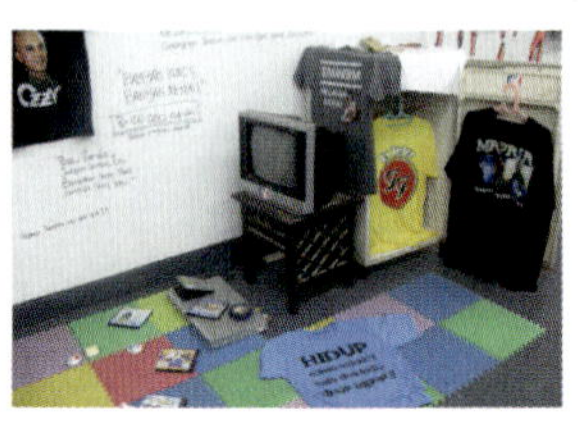

616

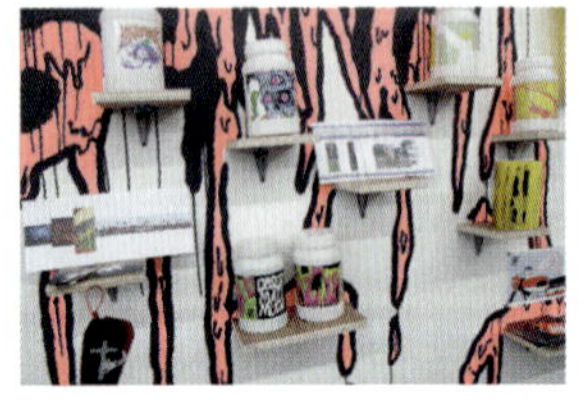

617

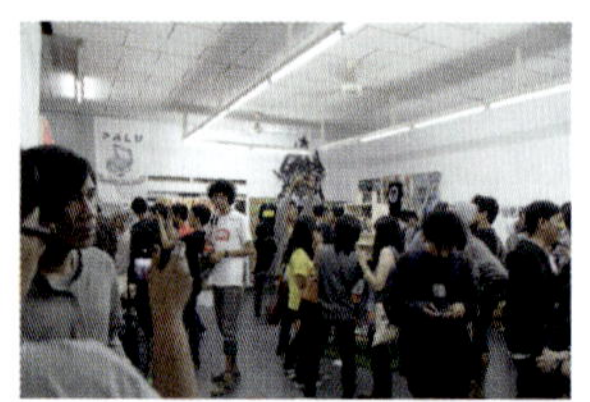

618

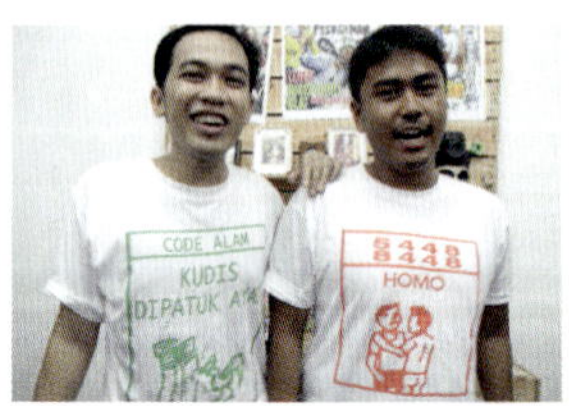

619

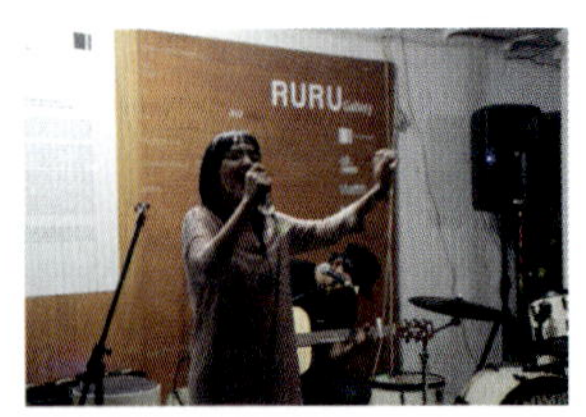

620

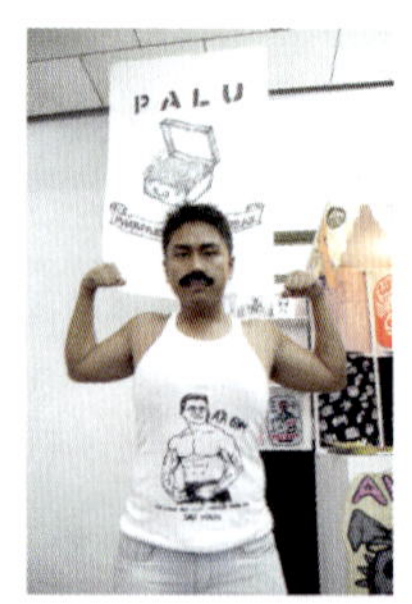

621

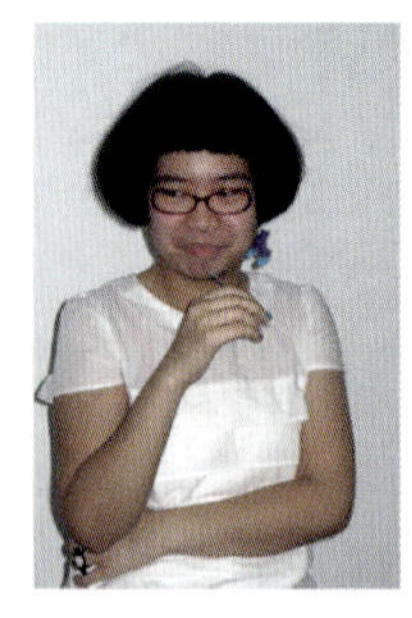

622

local/international partnershit

Develop the regional network project is almost impossible without seeing the local network in each countries, that surely have been developed in other way formal and informally. The regional network should play important role to support and mediate the local network in each country.

Imagine the regional network is an extension network of the local network.

The regional network should developed and set with in the consideration to support the local network. By this constellation both network will find its important role, position, relate and relevant to each other

Build an uncentralized network, based on collaboration and horizontal partnerships, all this would have a lot of forms of cooperation carried out between institutions that will also involve formal infrastructure of various disciplines.

In the end it can form a network that consists of small units that moves and vibrant in every local and intensively interconnected.

Provide sufficient content or issues to share that each network members can relate and relevant to each local context. It makes each member have strong reason to share or discuss a certain issues.

The network should become a platform that conducting a mapping of what is relevant and important issue regionally and furthermore develop it into a bigger discourse by produce, share and distributing the knowledge as an important contribution in the region.

Mapping on partner and sharing data as well as the achievement on working cross and inter discipline with other personal, professional, group, community and in the organizational level

strategically cross platform/organizational;

silaturahmi

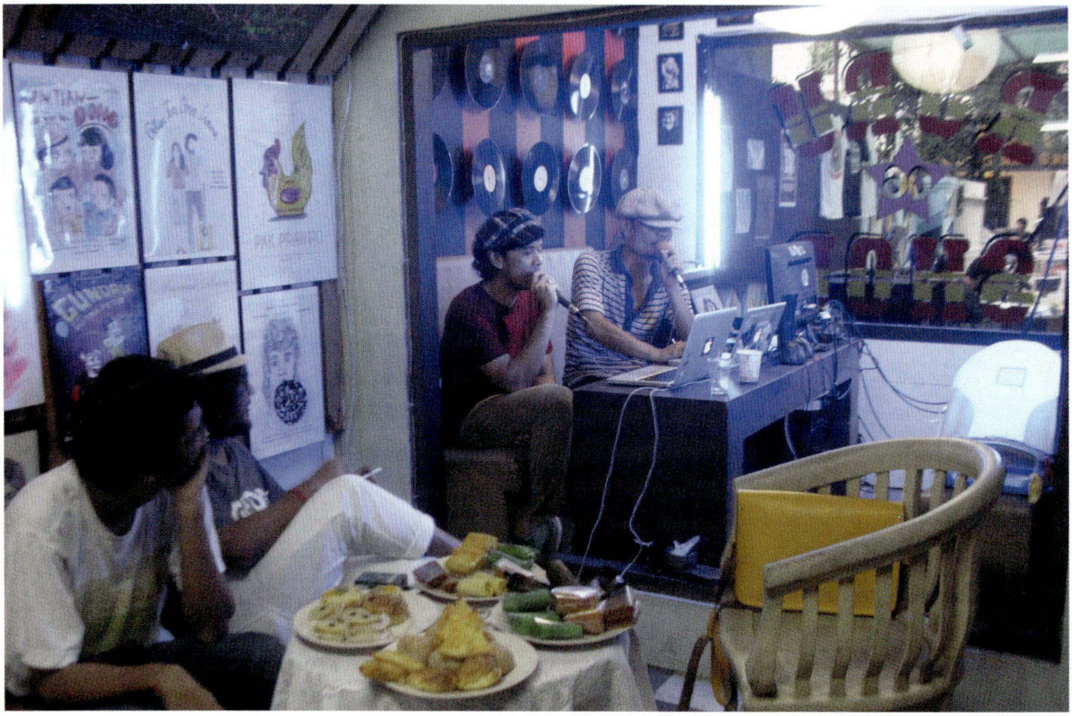

623

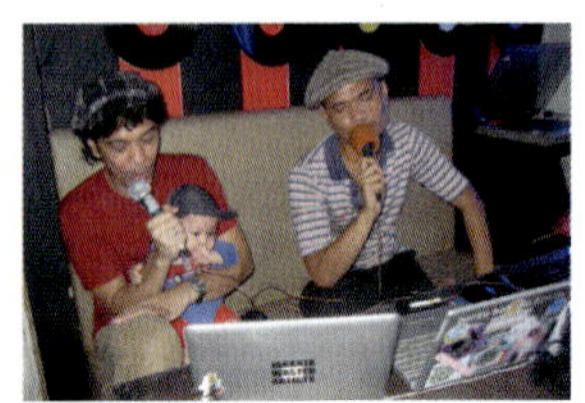

624

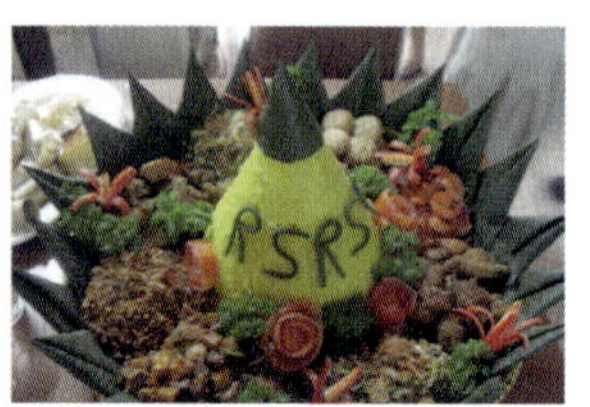

625

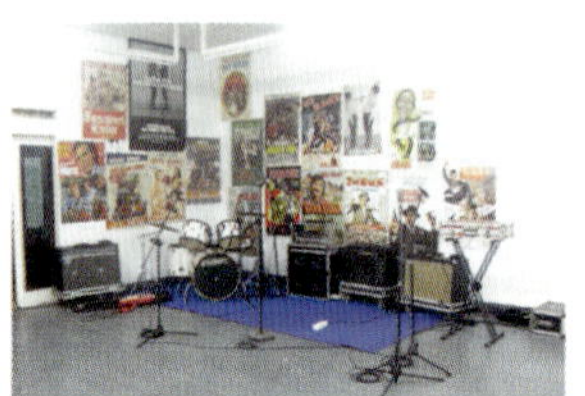

626

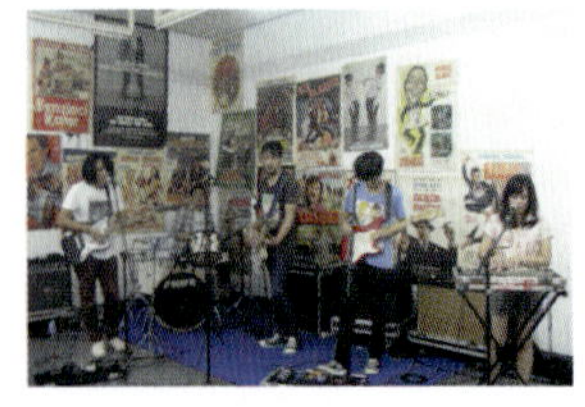

627

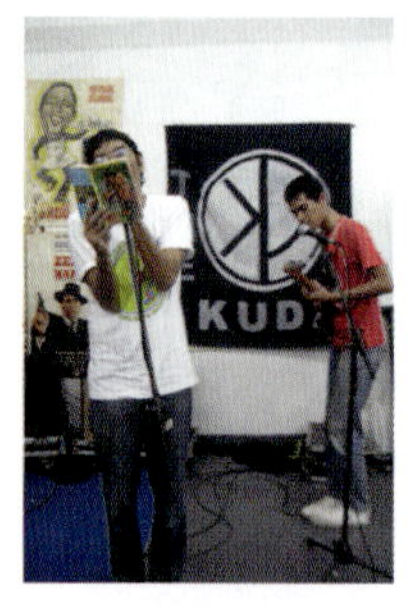

628

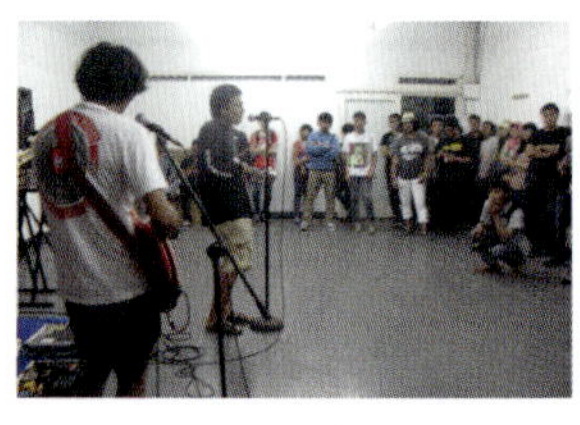

629

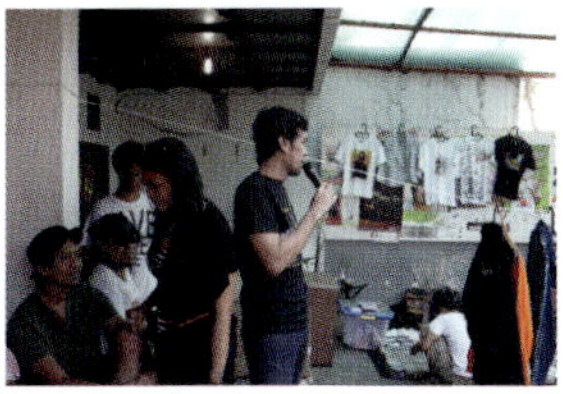

630

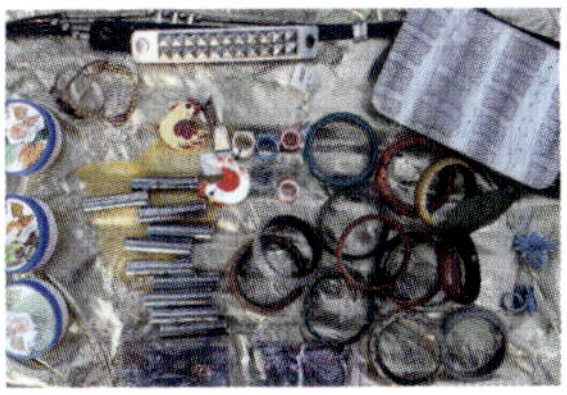

631

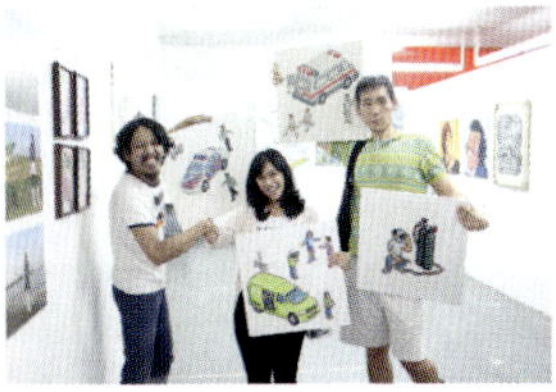

632

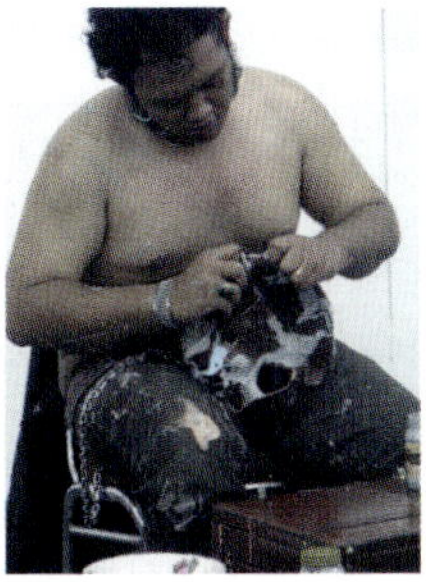

633

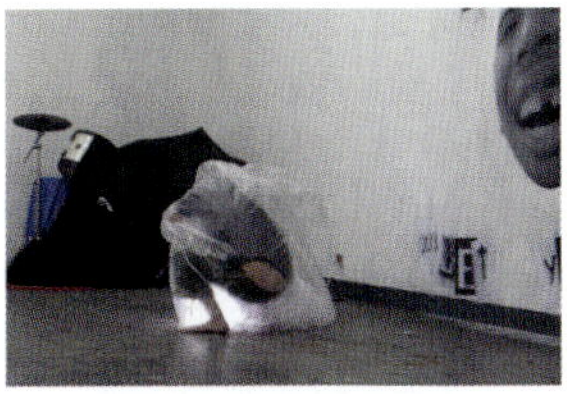

634

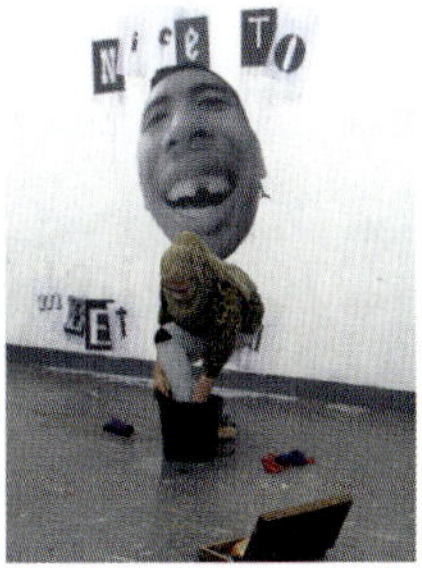

635

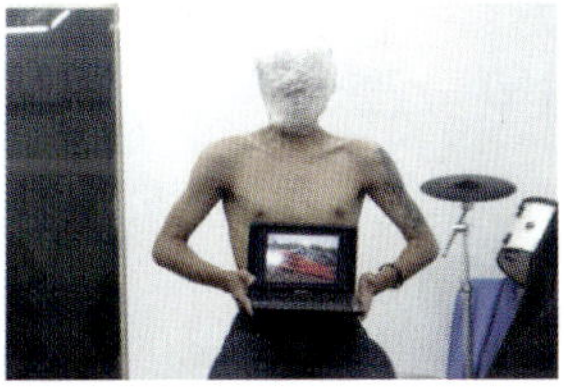

636

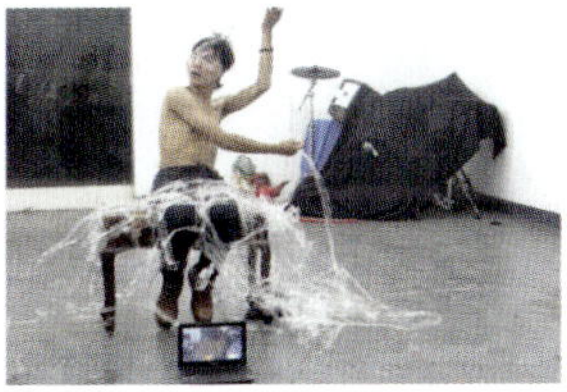

637

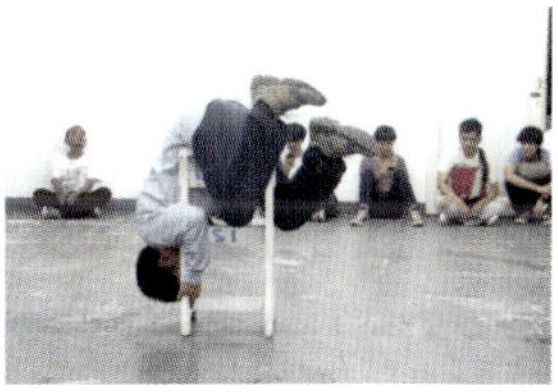

638

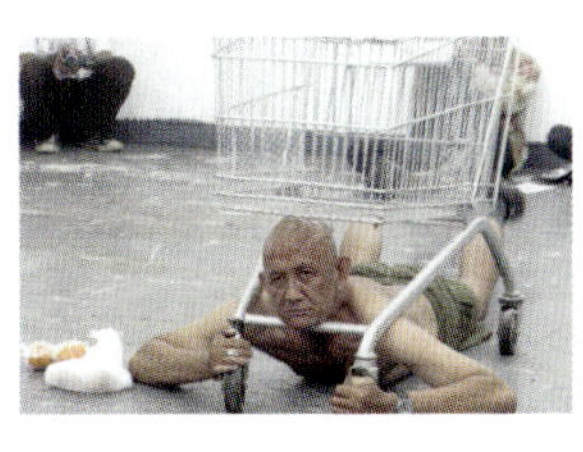

639

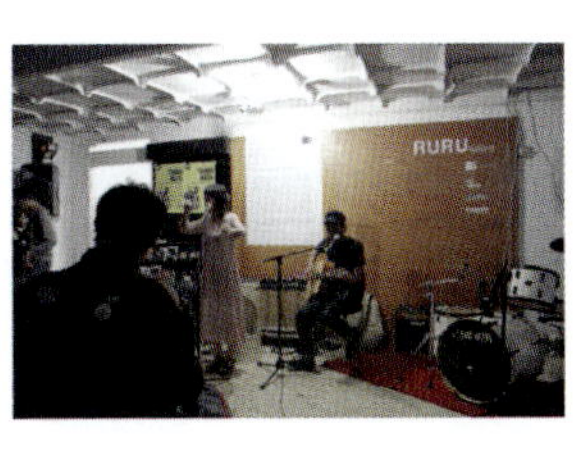

640

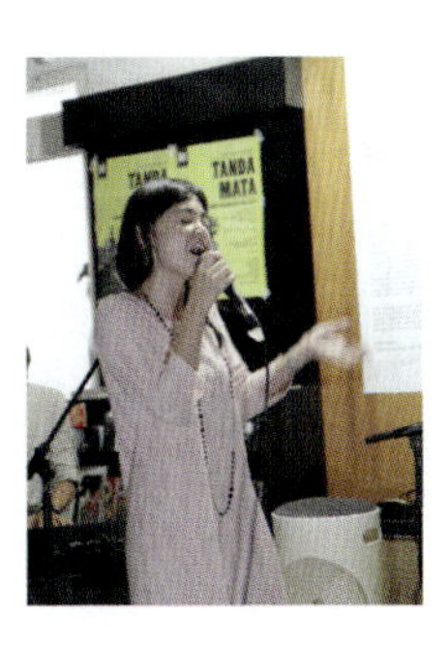

641

‘DRIFT: Pameran Seni Multimedia’ (DRIFT: Multimedia Art Exhibition), RURU Gallery, 7–16 June 2012

with Prilla Tania, Bagaswaro Aryaningtyas and Ricky Janitra

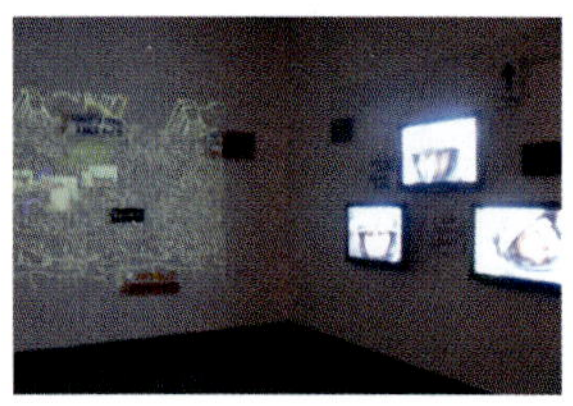

642

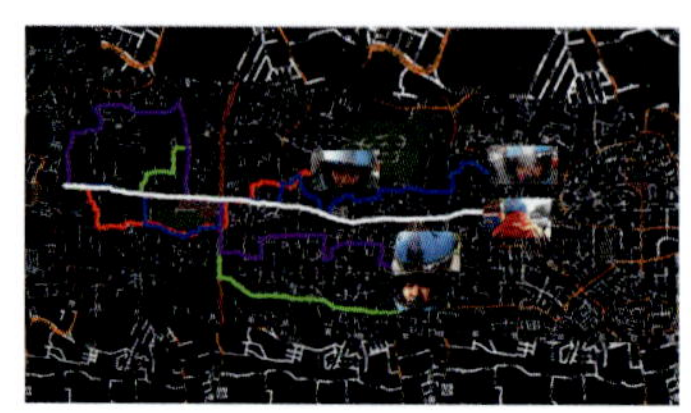

643

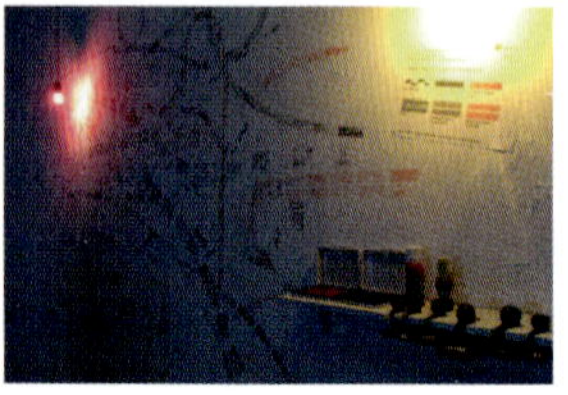

644

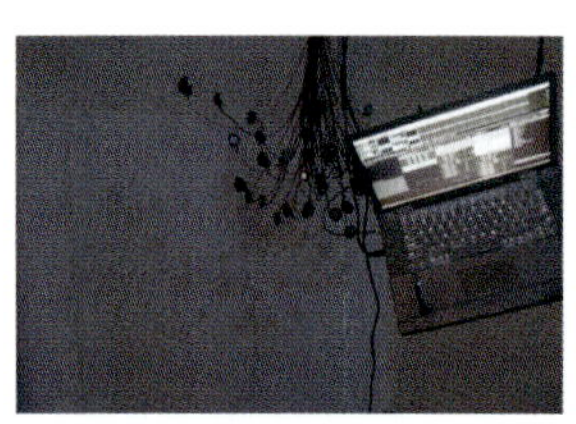

645

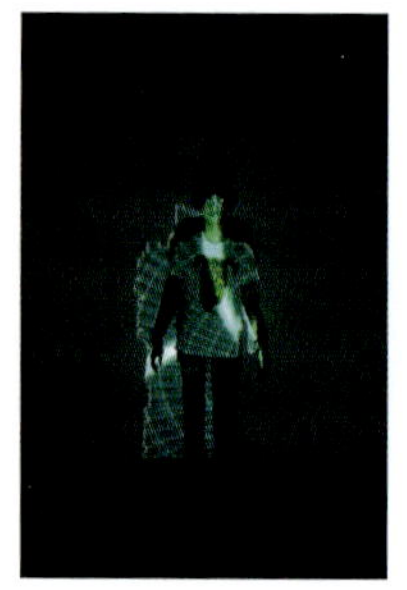

646

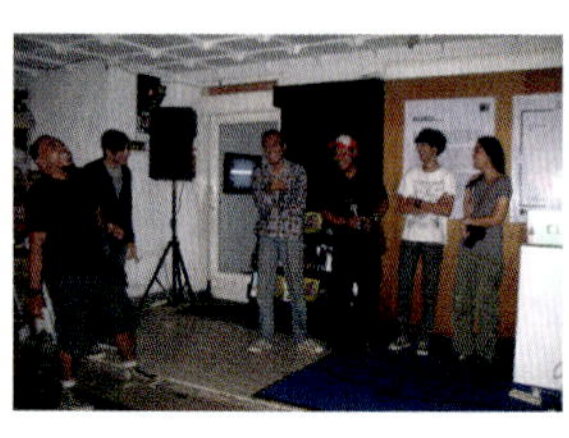

647

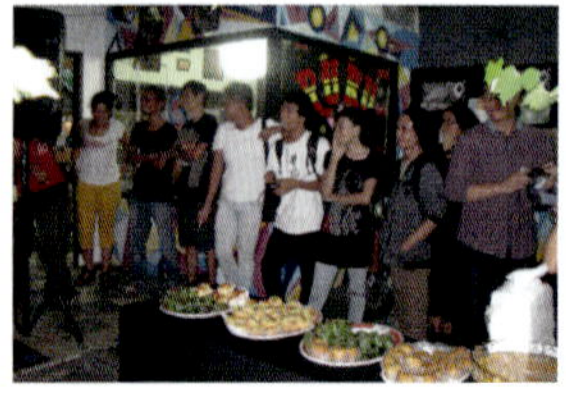

648

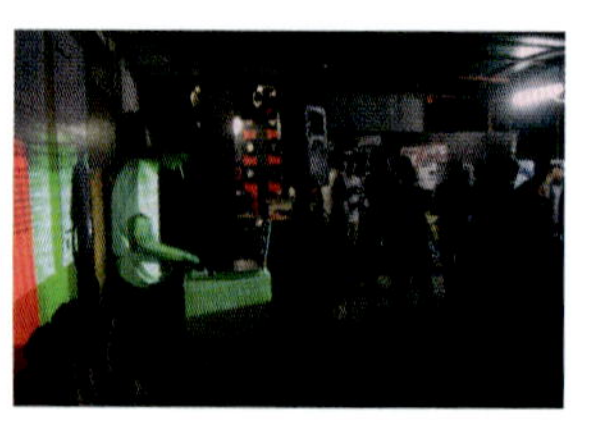

649

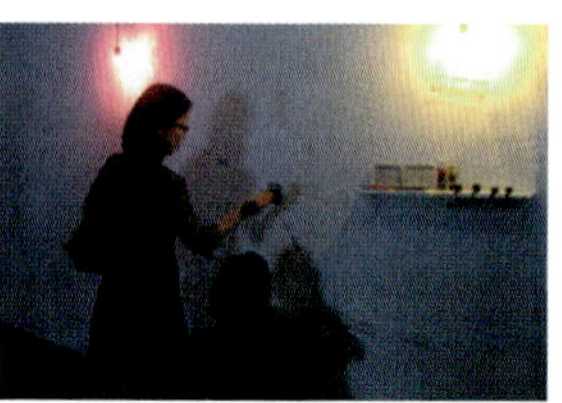

650

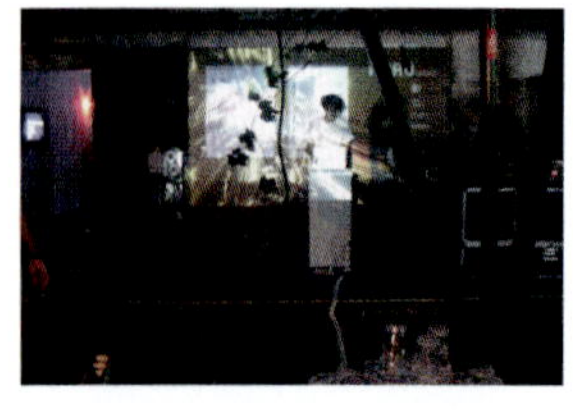

651

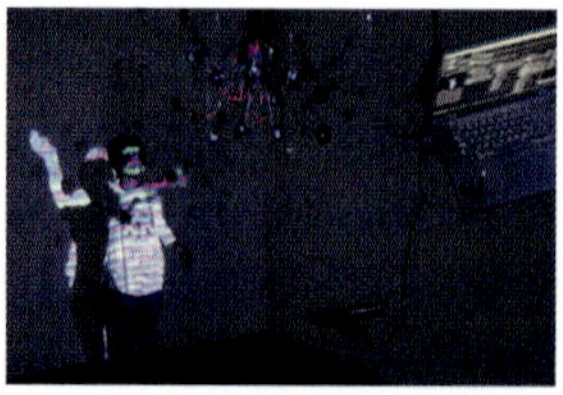

652

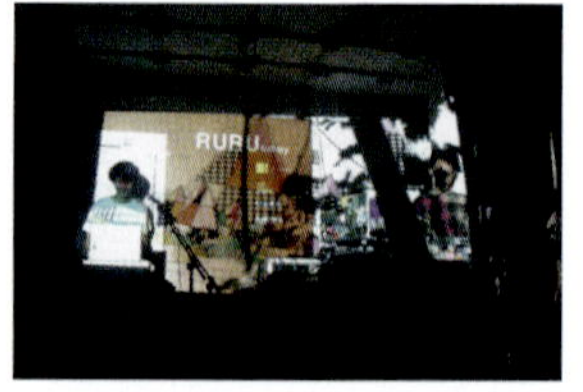

653

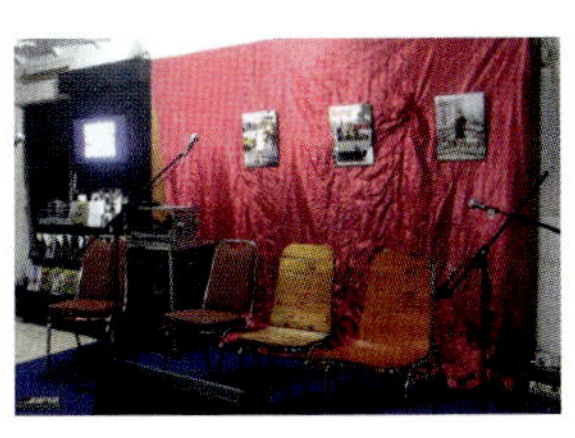

654

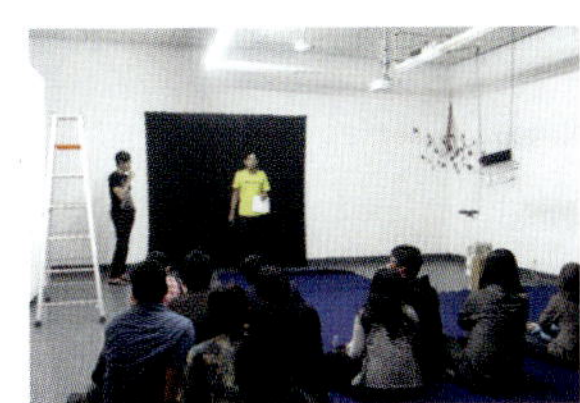

655

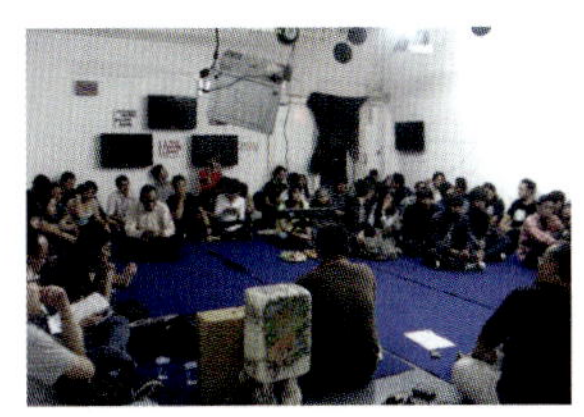

656

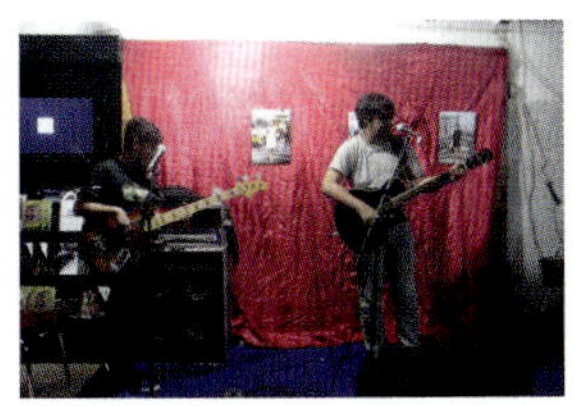

657

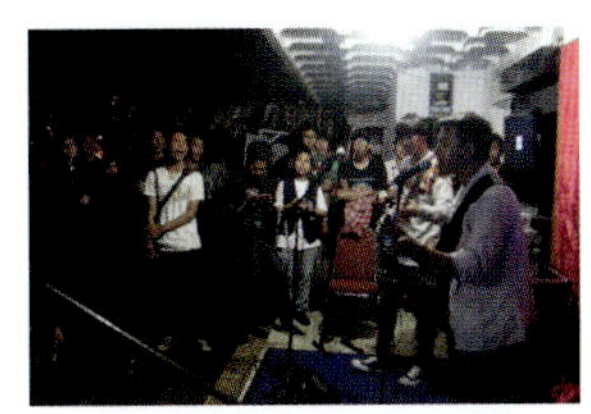

658

'Top Collection #3', RURU Gallery, 21 July – 4 August 2012

with Agan Harahap, Nissal Nur Afryansyah, Reza Afisina, Reza Mustar and The House is Black (Mahardhika Yuda and Mira Febri Mellya); curated by Julia Sarisetiati

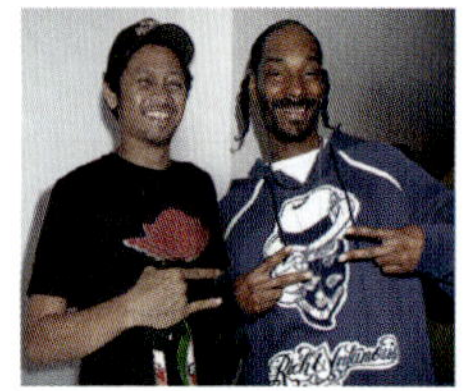

659

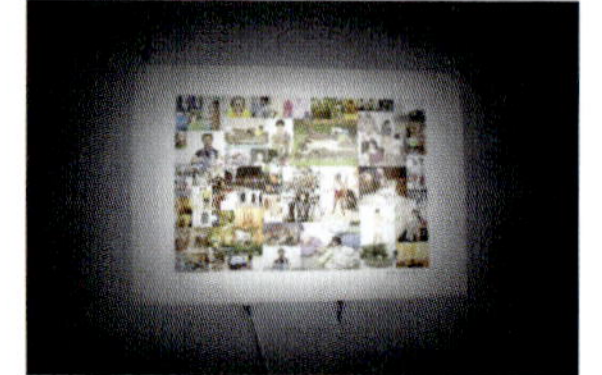

660

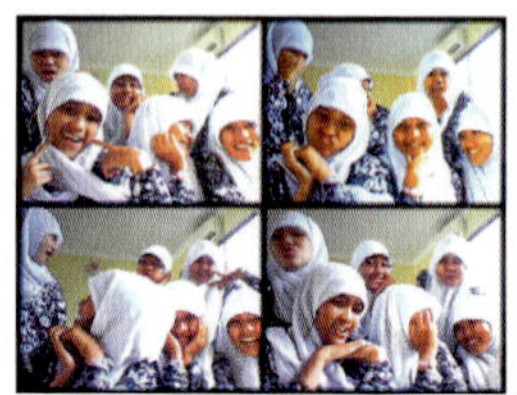

661

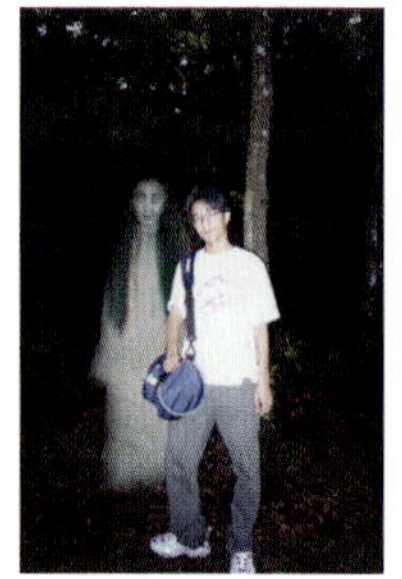

662

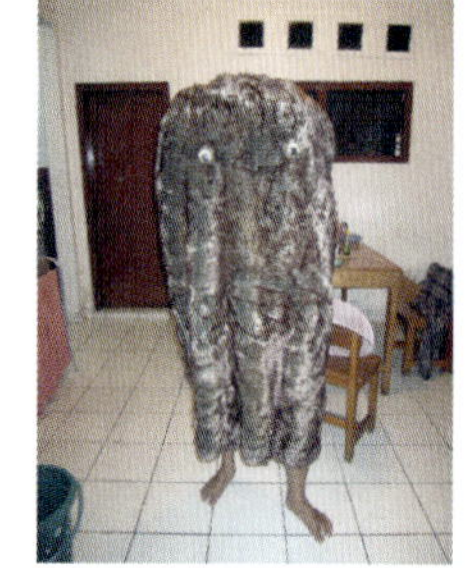

663

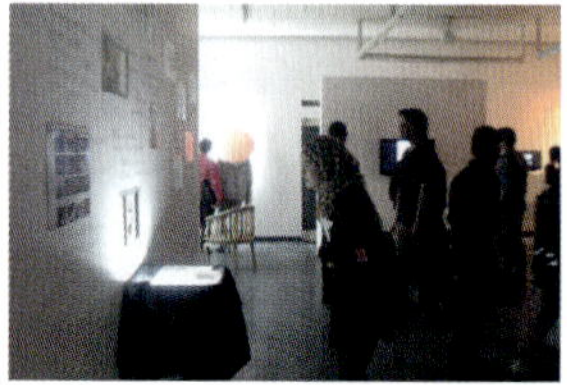

664

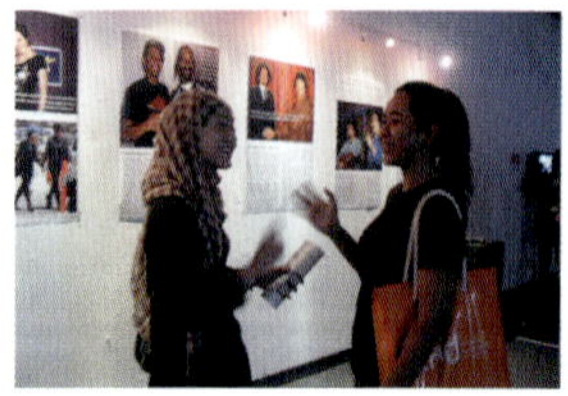

665

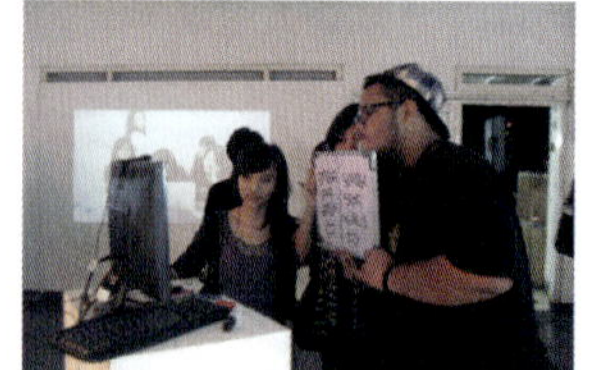

666

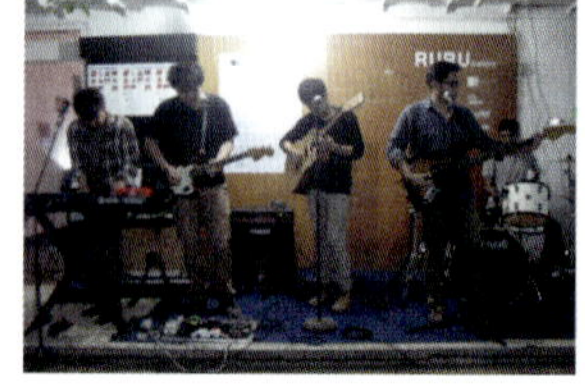

667

Participation in Bazaar Art Jakarta, multiple venues, 26–29 July 2012 233

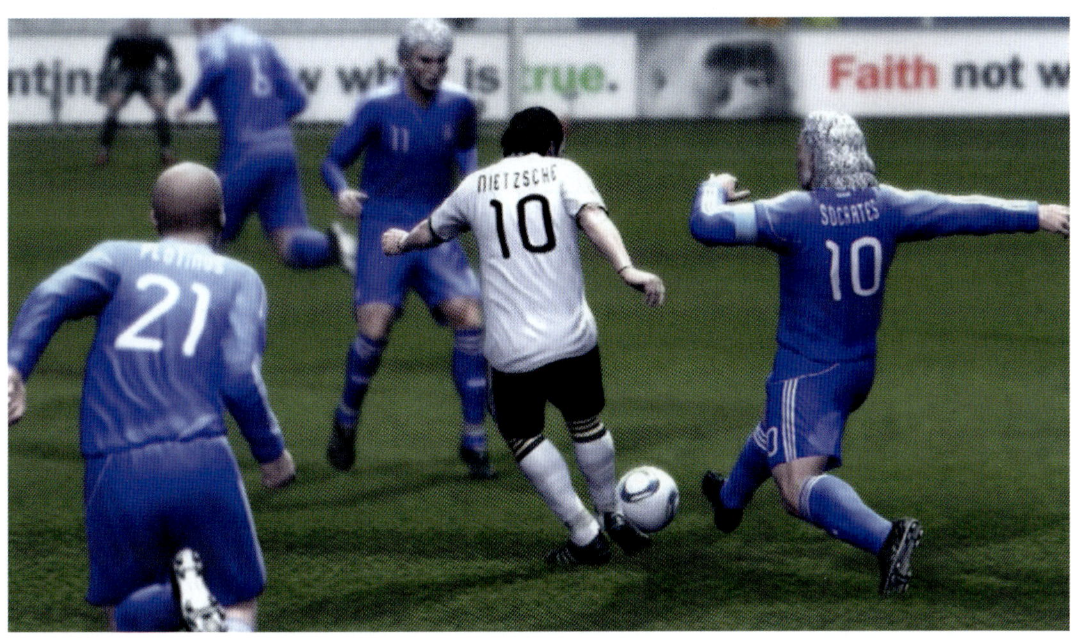

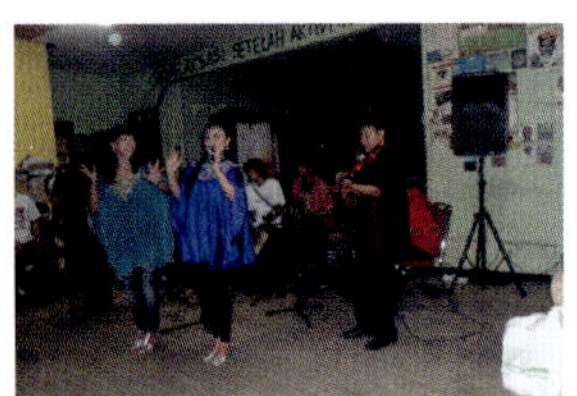

669

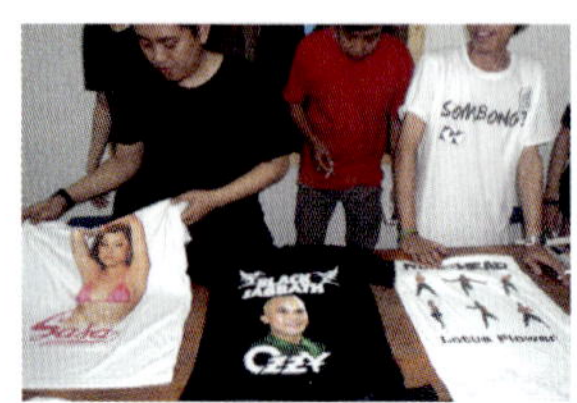

670

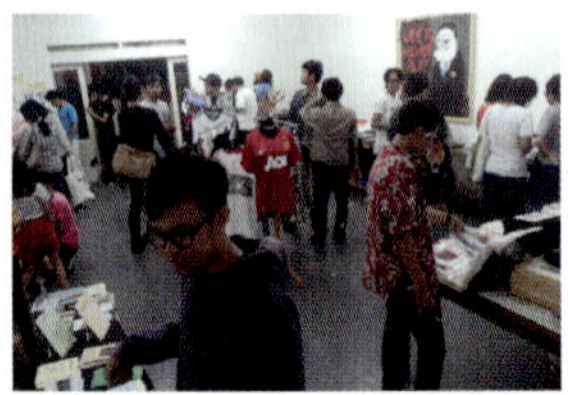

671

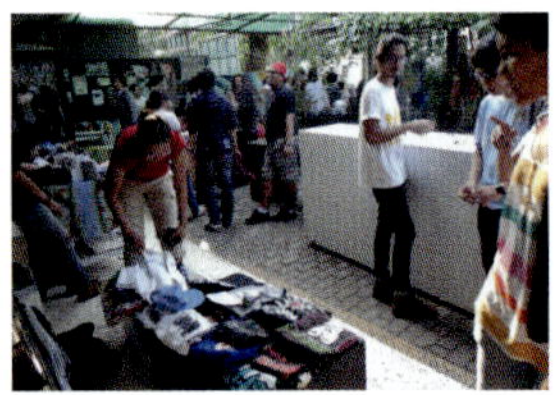

672

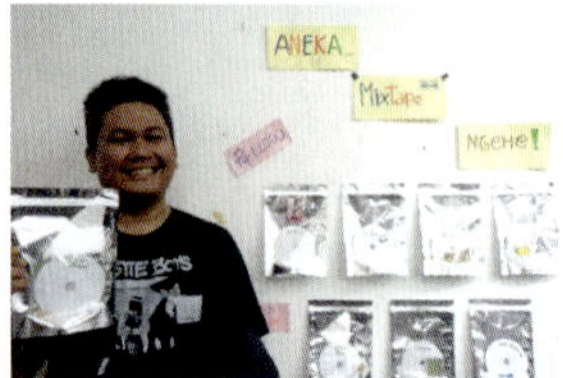

673

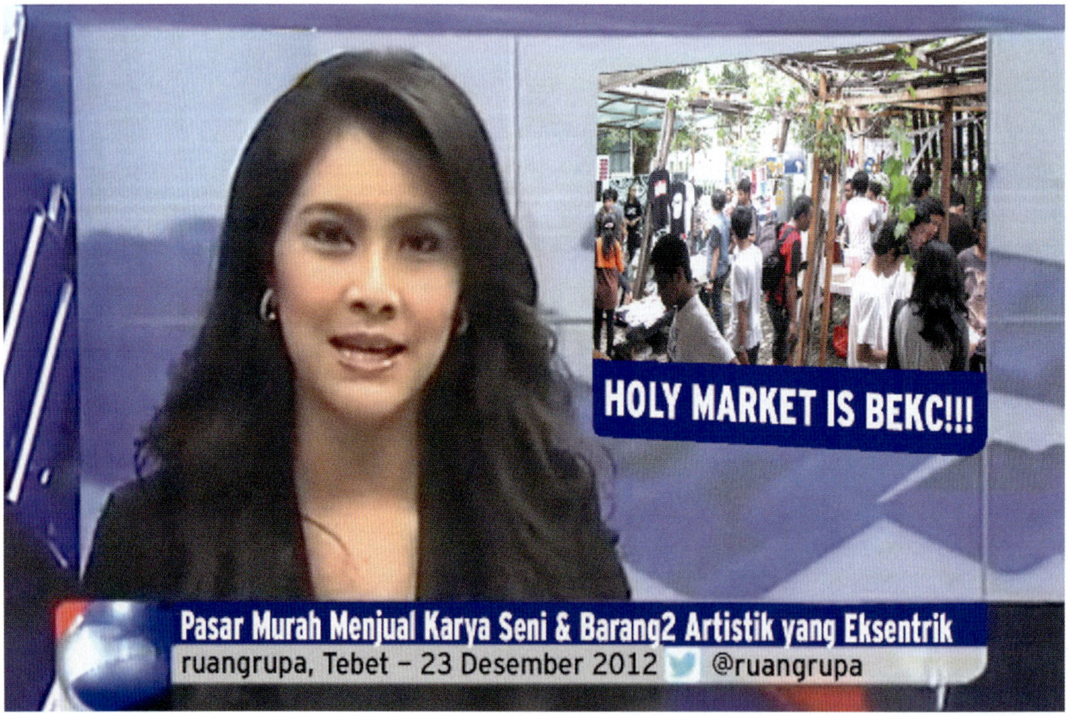

674

conflict

it's overrated

Participation in Busan Biennale, Busan, South Korea, 22 September – 24 November 2012

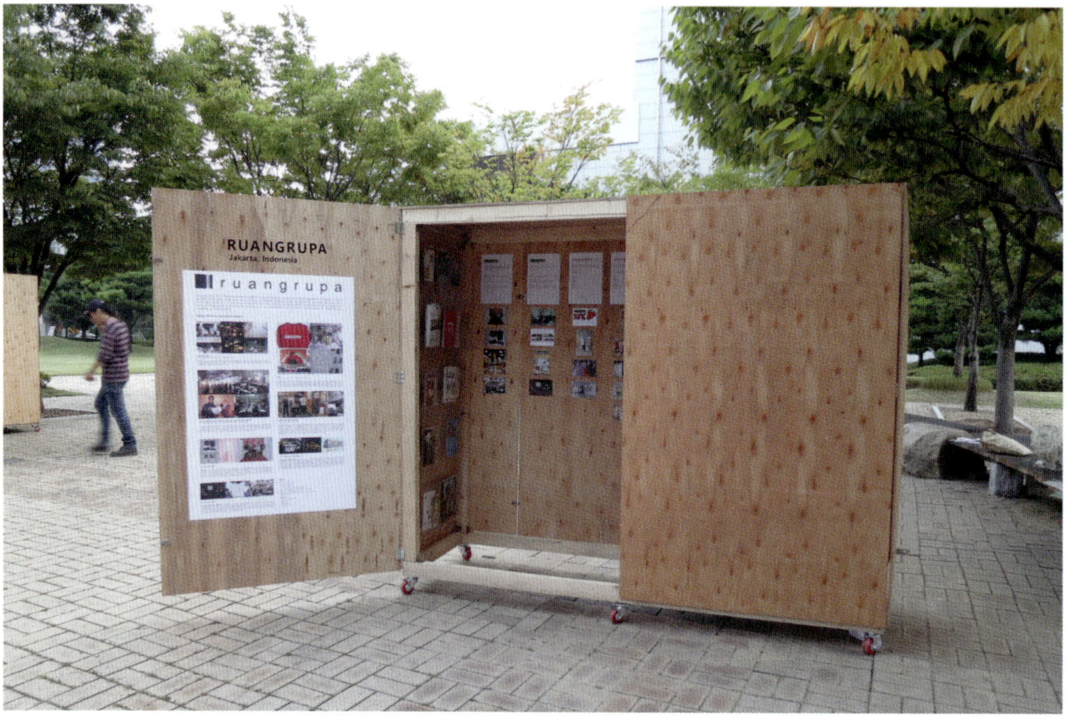

675

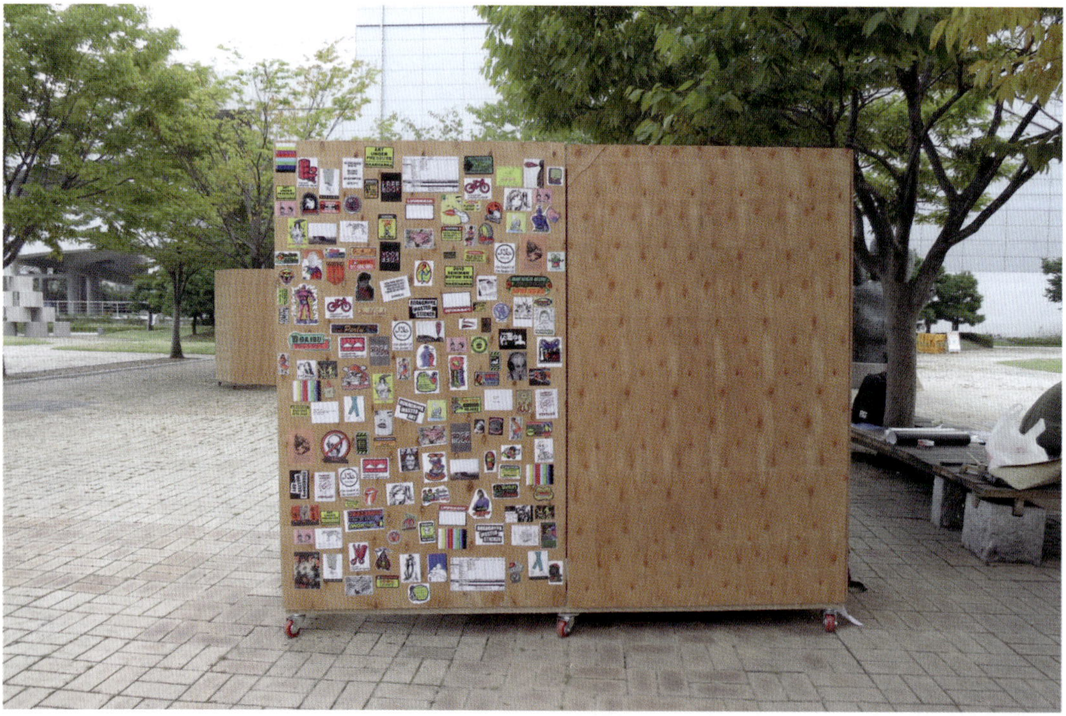

676

Jakarta 32°C, Galeri Nasional Indonesia, Jakarta, 23 September – 8 October 2012

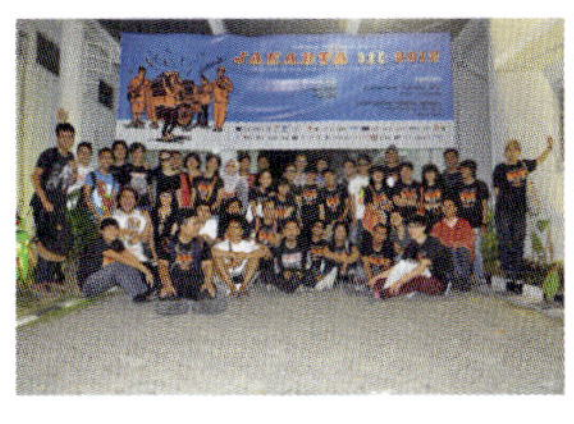

677

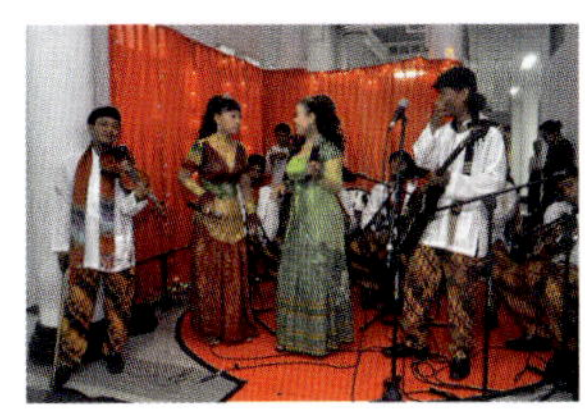

678

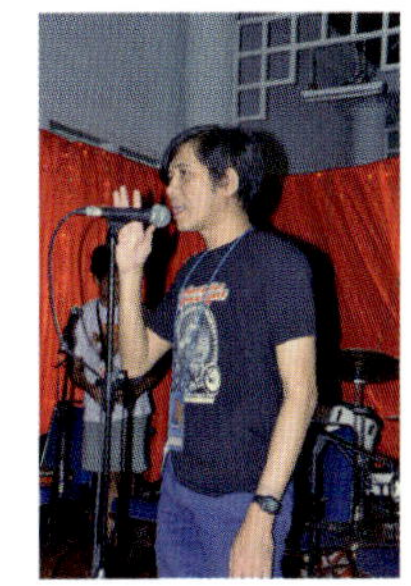

679

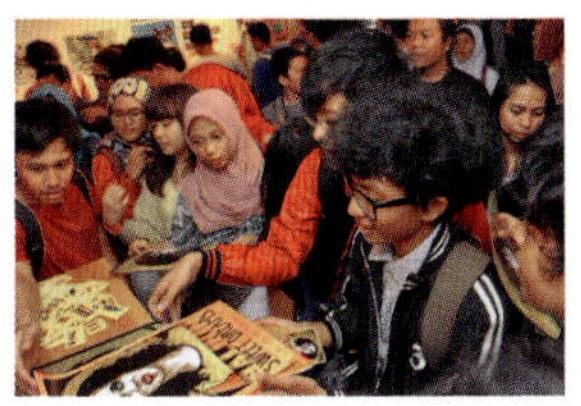

680

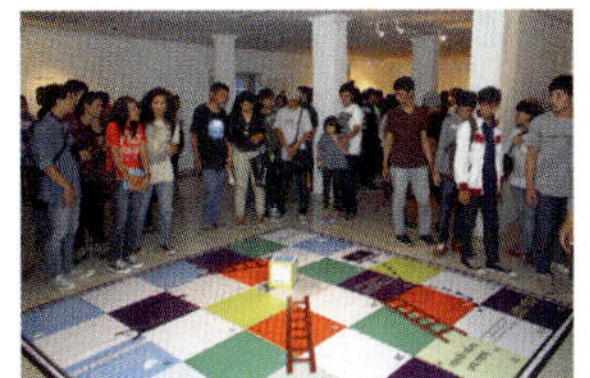

681

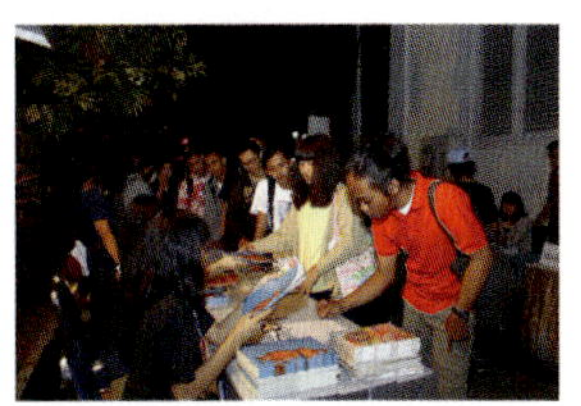

682

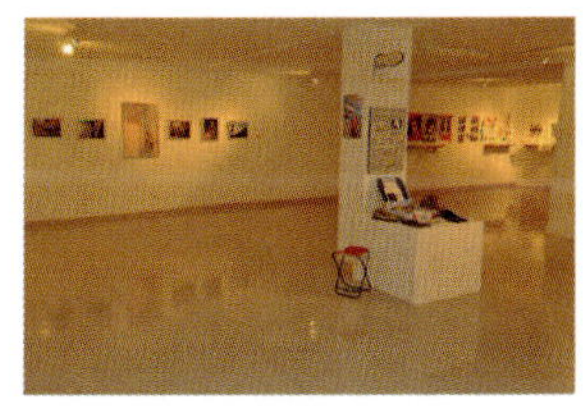

683

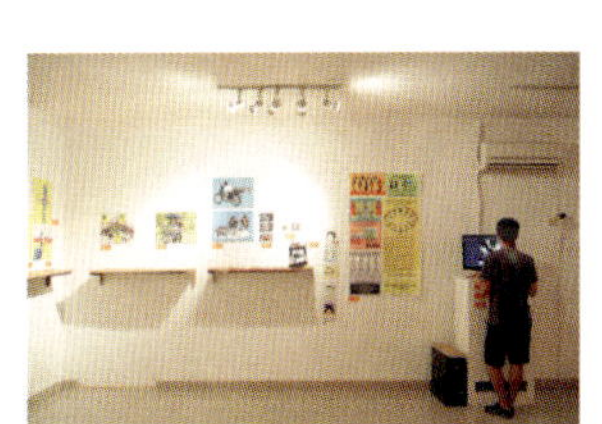

684

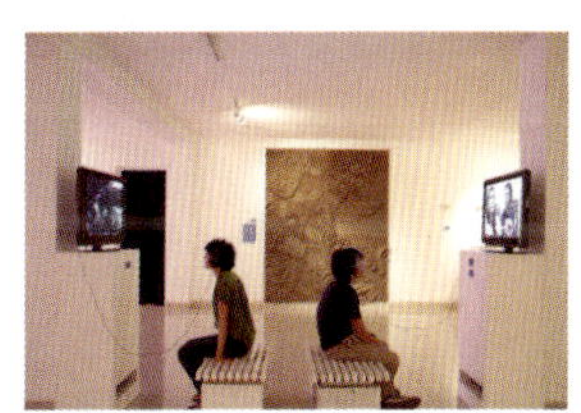

685

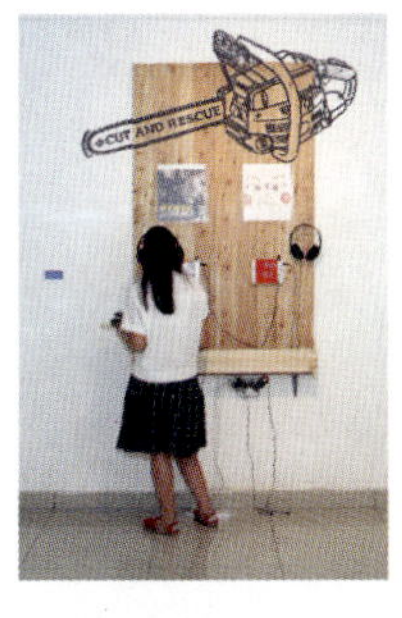

686

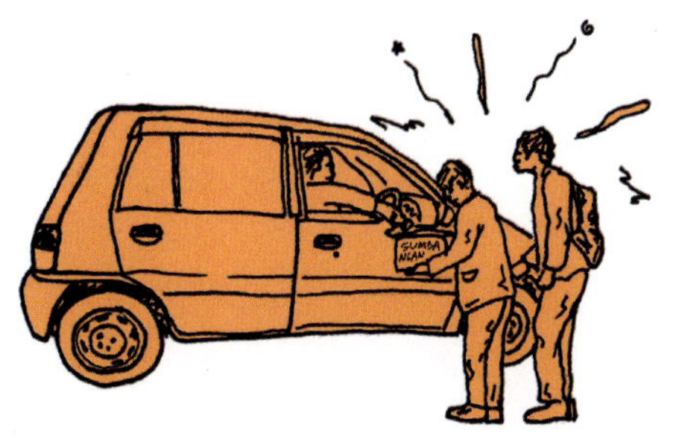

687

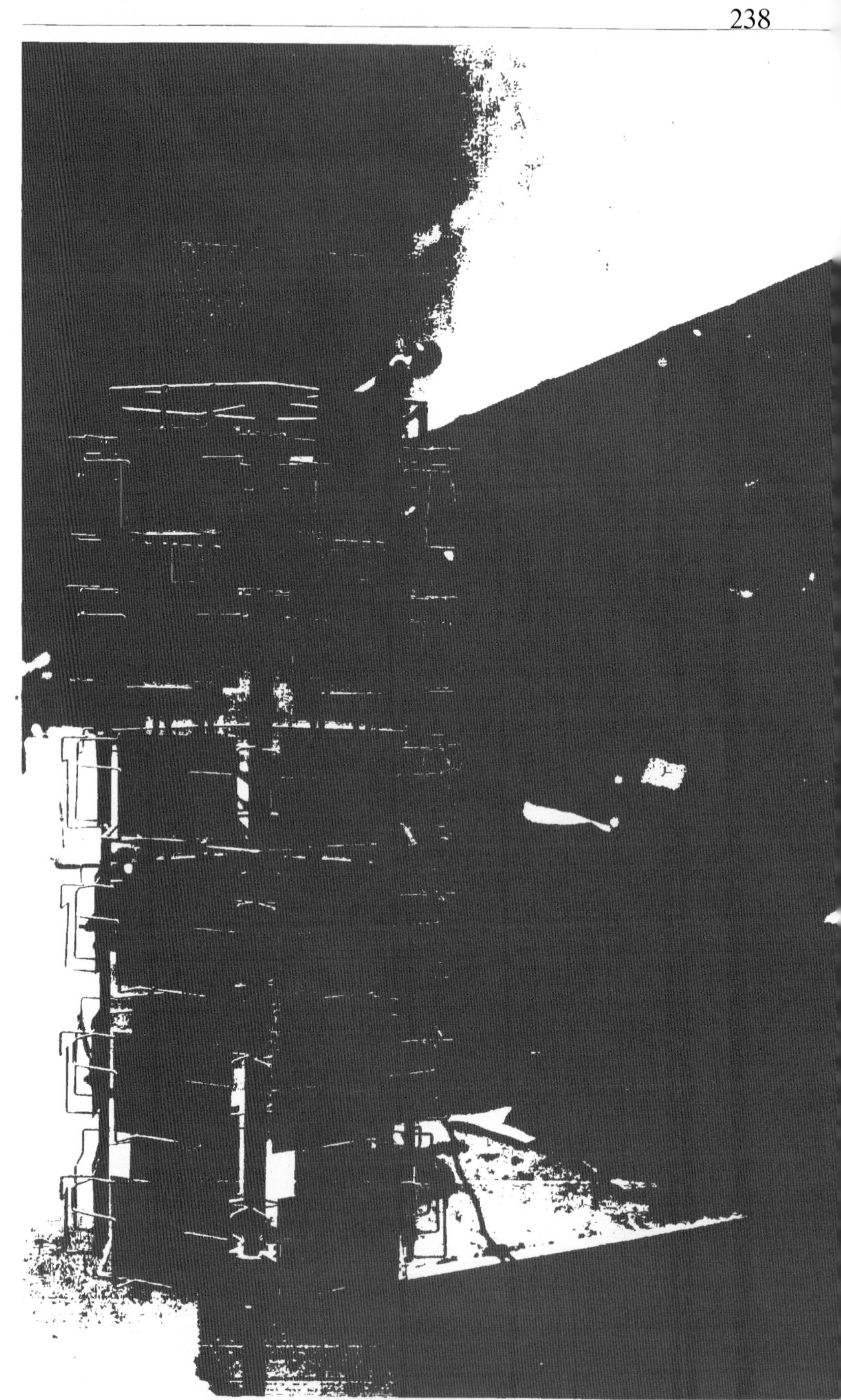

ruangrupa, *Singapore Fiction*, 2011, installation with radio, documentation material, prints and video. Installation view, Singapore Biennial. Photograph: Han. Courtesy the artists and Singapore Art Museum

Previous spread: ruangrupa (ArtLab division), *Lonely Market*, 2009, Jakarta. Courtesy the artists

Who Cares a Lot? Ruangrupa as Curatorship

– David Teh

Amidst the rapidly changing art landscape of Southeast Asia, David Teh sees the Indonesian collective ruangrupa as an intersection of subcultures and artistic currents that defies easy institutionalisation.

Last year Southeast Asia hosted two significant media art shows, both daring to juxtapose recent work from the region with seminal collections from the First World. In 'Video, an Art, a History 1965–2010', the Singapore Art Museum (SAM) tentatively aired its nascent Southeast Asian collection alongside a roving blockbuster from the Centre Pompidou in Paris. At the National Gallery of Indonesia (Galnas), the Jakarta artists' collective ruangrupa held the fifth instalment of their video art biennial, OK Video, featuring a curated selection from the catalogue of Electronic Arts Intermix in New York.[1] Both exhibitions were rare treats, featuring contemporary video works from Indonesia, Thailand and Vietnam, side by side with works by Western artists including Bill Viola, Dan Graham, VALIE EXPORT and Vito Acconci – the first time this canon had alighted on the region en masse. In both exhibitions worlds came together, but they were worlds apart.

I found myself wondering what it would be like if these two worlds were swapped, if SAM were to take over the ageing halls of Galnas, and ruangrupa the colonial nooks and crannies of SAM. For a start, we would see OK Video with fewer mosquitoes, and comfortable seats; with an injection of Singaporean efficiency, Galnas would get a much needed overhaul. SAM would meanwhile be unrecognisable, revived by a shot of the spontaneity and personality it lacks. Alas, it was wishful thinking. One can only dream of a day when the region's resources are effectively shared.

It could be objected that I am not comparing apples with apples. SAM is a well-funded public museum, with its own collection, but, like all of Singapore's institutions, it suffers from the overweening attentions of its bureaucratic parents. Galnas, meanwhile, is a criminally neglected child – a 'national' space for hire – and ruangrupa, while by now a de facto institution, is an autonomous artists' collective, with no collection and largely free from bureaucracy. Yet the comparison was telling: SAM baulked at the task of integrating their works (either spatially or intellectually) with the visiting ones, leaving Southeast Asia a peripheral plug-in for the touring Euro-American canon. At OK Video, the foreign material was not the main event; carefully selected to feed and challenge Indonesia's thriving video communities, it was circumscribed architecturally in its own pavilion, but nested within a locally curated smorgasbord. The contrast was a stark demonstration of the raw value of curatorial vision, a value not proportional to budgets.

Context certainly helps. In Singapore's slick matrix of consumption, small curatorial fumbles will stick out like sore thumbs, while amidst the humming disorder of Jakarta – a city of some ten million souls, with a metropolitan population three times that – a little direction goes a long way. Yet the integration of local and international work was an important achievement, not least because the former draws upon, and critiques, the latter, but also because

1 'Video, an Art, a History 1965—2010', co-curated by Christine van Assche and Patricia Levasseur de la Motte, Singapore Art Museum, 10 June—18 September 2011; and OK Video FLESH: 5th Jakarta International Video Festival, curated by Hafiz, Agung Hujatnikajennong, Farah Wardani, Mahardhika Yudha and Rizki Lazuardi, National Gallery of Indonesia, 6—17 October 2011.

they are connected, whether consciously or unconsciously, through the history of the video medium itself, with shared formal parameters and shared referents in the world beyond the gallery. When it comes to exhibiting media art, it bears remembering that the museum itself is a medium, one to which a lot of media art is not native. The task of domesticating it is therefore fraught, especially in locations where institutions and curatorial practice are relatively young. So how is it that Jakarta, a chaotic mega-city with little infrastructure for contemporary art, has given rise to this sort of curatorial assuredness?

Site and Sound: Jakarta Calling (or, Karaoke as Method)

By far the most developed of Indonesia's 922 inhabited islands, Java is about half the size of the UK, with roughly twice the population. It dominates the national economy, and in creative industries increasingly casts a shadow over its richer neighbours. Of its three artistic hubs, Bandung and Yogyakarta (Jogja) are the established centres of learning and production. Jakarta has long been the business hub, with the most commercial galleries. Given its strong non-commercial agenda, ruangrupa might seem out of place in Jakarta – an hour's flight to the south-east, Jogja's cheap rents and slower pace make it an obvious base for collectives. But ruangrupa is bound to Jakarta in every sense: physically, spiritually and conceptually, it is through and through a creature of the capital. This speaks volumes about the group's significance and the unique path it has taken in Indonesia's current contemporary art boom.

The collective was founded in 2000 by a group of young artists in a city then devoid of platforms for contemporary practice and collaboration. Their workshops and exhibitions fast became magnets for artists, designers and researchers, eliciting broad-based community participation, distinguished by the group's knack for critical exploration of their urban surroundings. This urbanism has been their most consistent refrain. Though they have consistently worked with artists from elsewhere, ruangrupa has made a profound commitment to Jakarta as both site and subject, to its people as both audience and authors. Since day one the group has taken the city itself – a noisy engine room of commerce and administration, not traditionally seen as a font of culture – as the primary protagonist of an epic adventure in collective storytelling. Heuristic as their approach may be, it is not without a certain realism, focused by an insistence upon the vitality of Jakarta's contemporary culture, as rooted not in some timeless past, but in a dense demographic and cultural stew of diverse and inextricable ingredients.

A pre-modern cosmopolitanism was forged here during the Srivijaya maritime empire that dominated the Malay world until the thirteenth century. Sunda Kelapa, as Jakarta was then known, had already long been a melting pot of regional and diasporic trading communities when the Dutch arrived in 1619. Renamed Batavia, the city was colonised and modernised, then nationalised as Jakarta. It is now being globalised, but this doesn't mean homogenisation – rapid economic growth has come with an equally rapid dilation of the public sphere, and for a porous organisation, the city's syncretic soil is fertile indeed. Such an environment puts a premium on openness, a trait ruangrupa exhibits inside and out. While the founders may worry that a new crop of decision-makers has been slow to emerge, a strong DIY ethos and a lack of hierarchy have been key to the group's sustainability. Their suburban headquarters in the south of the city boast a well-used exhibition space, but it's more like a clubhouse: always open, always peopled – a studio, a library, a research lab and a party venue, all in one. It would be lazy to call their collaborative house style 'inclusive'. Ruangrupa is shareware, their partnering indiscriminate – witness the soup of logos on their sponsor rolls. They tap every level of the institutional food chain, with a reach only possible in the last decade or so: from foreign NGOs and municipal and national governments, down to the humblest grassroots initiatives – a big tobacco company here, a national media network there, a small business around the corner.

According to Bandung-based curator Agung Hujatnikajennong, Indonesian contemporary art has seen two distinct phases. The first reflected civil society's atrophy under the authoritarian New Order (1965–98) of the country's second president, Soeharto. The second, which is ongoing, reflects its flourishing and democratisation since the wave of popular

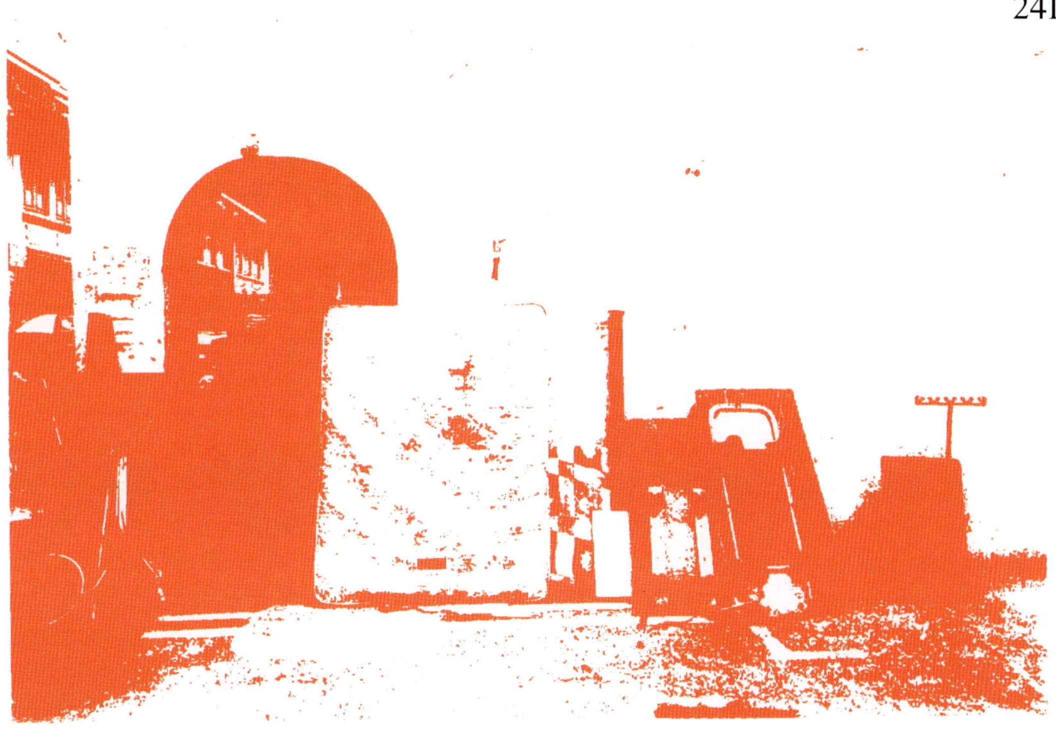

ruangrupa, documentation photograph of the flea markets in Barang Guru, Singapore during research for *Singapore Fiction*, 2011. Courtesy the artists

disgust (*reformasi*) that finally unseated that regime amidst regional financial crisis in 1998.[2] In the earlier period, the social conscience that had long been a cornerstone of national aesthetics – modern art's *sine qua non* since the independence struggle against the Dutch – found expression in a figurative modernism still loosely social realist in its scope. Its story remained that of nationhood, of the people (as, or against, nation), seasoned here and there with the 'local' or the 'traditional'. Artists emerging since *reformasi*, however, are more playful and individualistic, enjoying the latitude of a liberalised public sphere, and the fruits of the country's steady rise in the global neoliberal pecking order. But while exemplary of this new generation, ruangrupa strives to retain something of the representational logic of the old.

The result is a remarkably stable compound of activism and populism. The group's early embrace of lo-fi copy cultures and digital and open publishing models dovetailed with a neo-Situationism that was de rigueur at the couch-surfing stratum of global art in the early 2000s. Since 2000, ruangrupa has published *Karbon*, a journal devoted to urban visual culture, which promotes criticism but also favours plain language. The biennial Jakarta 32°C, which they have organised since 2004, brings students' work into the museum under the group's curatorial umbrella, democratising the first steps to exhibition-making. Jakarta-based festivals like OK Video, meanwhile, become launch pads for nationwide tours and workshops, as did their tenth anniversary festivities in 2010, held under the project banner 'Decompression #10'. And while in an earlier phase workshops were more hands-on and skills-based, as contemporary art production has flourished ruangrupa's educational focus has sharpened around the critical faculties of writing and curatorship. The collective's prodigious capacity for outreach makes for an unruly aesthetic, encompassing everything from punk and street cultures, through documentary and ethnographic research, to conceptual and process-oriented experiments. Binding it all together is a firm conviction that the participants are agents in a living social history, one that is fundamentally urban and modern.

To profile ruangrupa is to describe an *event*: time-based, immediate and loosely

2 Agung Hujatnikajennong, 'Everything Melts onto the Screen: Video and Media Art in Indonesia', presentation at 'Video Vortex #7', Kedai Kebun Forum, Yogyakarta, July 2011. See also his 'The State and the Market: Two Decades of Indonesian Contemporary Art', in *Biennale Jogja XI – Equator #1* (exh. cat.), Yogyakarta: Yayasan Biennale Yogyakarta, 2011, pp.180–89.

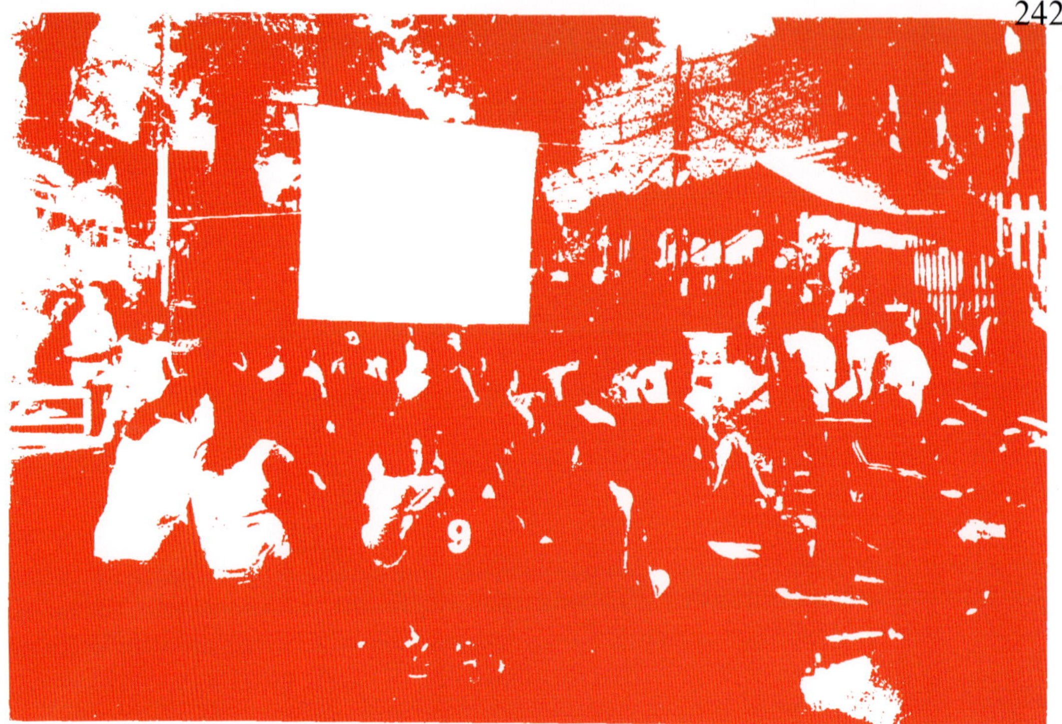

ruangrupa (ArtLab division), *Lonely Market*, 2009, outdoor screening, Jakarta. Courtesy the artists

structured; with a sense of purpose, yet more celebratory than agonistic. If one had to choose a single medium to characterise it, that medium would be karaoke. Indonesians love to sing, and a rich musical patchwork is an ever-present accompaniment to daily life. The refrains of old folk songs segue into distinctive modern genres like the racy *dangdut*, a hybrid of Malay, Indo-Arabic and 1970s rock sounds. A vivid medley of subcultures jostles with local and global pop, especially in the streets, where chronic traffic jams create a captive audience for wandering *ngamen* (buskers). It is no accident that live music and a certain chaotic, mob-karaoke ritual have become trademarks of the ruangrupa experience. Indeed, this carnivalesque sonic profile betrays something of the group's curatorial programme – it is prophetic in the sense Jacques Attali reserved for *composition*, presaging a new regime of cultural production that is live, open source and, above all, poly-vocal.[3]

In his compelling account of Javanese modernity, anthropologist John Pemberton describes an extraordinary process whereby the island's eighteenth-century aristocracy, whose role was rapidly becoming ceremonial, re-encoded the technologies and trappings of Dutch colonial might.[4] The once terrifying sound of cannon fire, for instance, came to announce official diplomatic correspondence, or to mark a royal birthday or wedding; a hybrid pageantry was improvised, retrofitted and elaborately codified. Pyrotechnics made for a spectacle of new order, distracting attention from the drastic defeat of the old. Pemberton also recalls how Soeharto, going through the motions of electoral democracy during the Cold War, took these vestiges of contest and refurbished them once again, as tradition, in the name of another 'new order'. Ruangrupa, we might say, represents the opposite aural evolution. It is a stethoscope held to the rattling yet still growing chest of the metropolis, amplifying the hum of a popular sovereignty – long suppressed by colonialism and authoritarianism – over the ceaseless urban din.

Ruangrupa as Curatorship?

In a recent essay on ruangrupa, art historian Thomas Berghuis takes up some topical vocabularies for lassoing contemporary art's vast diversity of

3 See Jacques Attali, *Noise: The Political Economy of Music* (trans. Brian Massumi), Minneapolis: University of Minnesota Press, 1985.

4 See John Pemberton, *On the Subject of 'Java'*, Ithaca, NY: Cornell University Press, 1994.

practices and newly integrated territories.[5] With nods to Nicolas Bourriaud's relational aesthetics and Terry Smith's reckoning with contemporaneity, he casts the group in the uncertain light of 'the global', as a laboratory for an *art to come*. In the clamour of the Jakarta art world, many would say a breath of speculative air is just what the doctor ordered. But what is missing from this picture is a sense of the intense struggle – in this region, quite peculiar to Indonesia – over creative and intellectual labour. In this struggle the curatorial faculty is crucial, not only because curators are pivotal in capturing talent, but also because curatorial functions have long preoccupied many of the most talented. Some of ruangrupa's core members exemplify this bind, but they stand out for having maintained both their independence from the market and their standing with respect to the curatorial cartel that serves it. They are not the only collective to have thrived since *reformasi*

They are not the only collective to have thrived since* reformasi*, but their endurance and success, at home and abroad, prompts the question: has it been by appropriating the function of curatorship that this independence has been secured?

– there are dozens – but their endurance and success, at home and abroad, prompts the question: has it perhaps been by appropriating the function of curatorship that this independence has been secured?

As a vocation, curatorship in Southeast Asia is tenuous. But in Indonesia, where a bullish market has the profession in its clutches, it is the craft that is tenuous, not the worker. One much sought-after Jogja painter makes enough from the sale of a single picture to buy a large house. Curators have not missed out on the bonanza. This newly struck professional mould, still setting, is guarded by a small band of entrenched taste-makers. In a country where an ample meal can be had street-side for a dollar, they are well rewarded – an anomaly in the region – especially a senior cohort whose number may be counted on one hand. But most of the throughput is handled by a younger generation who came of age during *reformasi*.

At worst, their job entails the perfunctory anointment of new product for the market. For some, the whole process may be done on a smart-phone: syncing calendars, browsing and selecting images, cutting and pasting together a recycled curatorial 'essay', before parachuting into town for the opening reception. It's a well-oiled assembly line, by far the region's most efficient. The conscientious few will manage some conversation with the artist, maybe even write something new, but a backlog of shows leaves little time for research; the typical project-window lasts weeks, not months. It's a pity, for most were trained as artists and have a good grasp on matters of process; they speak persuasively of aesthetic currents, and artists' places within them. But for all their mobility, their horizons as curators are limited by a parochial market, and a lack of credible institutional systems of validation and power.

If Asian modern art history has seldom ventured beyond national framings, this is not without reason. Rarely the product of organic urban fermentation, modern art has more often been a state-sanctioned project. But the unravelling of the Cold War has set the stage for a new mode of circulation and a new currency for the visual – a currency now called the contemporary. Gaining new patrons and markets, artists have filtered out certain modernist strains, and spun what's left in the direction of international trends. But curatorship, by contrast – at least, curatorship as we *now* know it, unhinged from the collection that once grounded the role – has more or less had to invent itself from scratch. In the first proper regional study on the subject, Patrick Flores confirms that the role has always been the province of discursively inclined artists, and not defined around collections. He identifies pioneers such as Apinan Poshyananda (a Thai) and Jim Supangkat (an Indonesian), who plugged Southeast Asian art into international circuits in the 1990s, as the key midwives of this contemporary. Not incidentally, both were trained as artists; no less significantly, neither has ever taught curating, nor trained worthy successors. Entangled by bureaucratic and market

5 Thomas J. Berghuis, 'ruangrupa', *Third Text*, vol.25, issue 4, 2011, pp.395–407.

strictures respectively, they seem to have accrued powers too precious to be handed down. Today's curators have inherited an invisible suit from these pathfinders, with little sense of professional continuity. And the corollary of this failure of professional memory is a failure to historicise exhibition-making *per se*. Ruangrupa and its collaborators stand out here for having kept alive a parallel world for historically informed – if not always art historically informed – ways of working.

Getting Modernity

I recently asked an Indonesian curator – trained and still practicing as an artist – what he thought of the curatorial studies programmes sprouting up around the world. If he were younger, where would he go to study this craft? His answer was revealing: 'The Netherlands. And Japan.' For an emerging leader from the global periphery, the prospect of acquiring curatorial expertise in emerging territories remains dim. And it is more than ironic that he should nominate both of his country's former colonial masters, both wealthy nations with developed infrastructures for art, both steady fonts of the aid that has helped shape professional horizons in Indonesia. The pairing also serves to dramatise a certain historical polarity, perhaps collapsing now, between two very different demographic orders, as the vanguard cosmopolitanism of the Netherlands shrinks into something more akin to Japan's insular nationalism. But my friend was answering, I suspected, with an eye on the past, not the future, which his explanation confirmed: 'Because these two places *really got modernity*.' The emphasis is his, and richly ambivalent – they 'got it' in the sense of understanding it, but perhaps also in the sense of *copping it*, of being on the receiving end of some painful but irrevocable gift. 'Getting' this most 'contemporary' métier would thus entail getting a certain modernity first. Clearly we were no longer talking about modern art, about this or that modernism, but about a *lived* modernity. The key knowledge for curating in Indonesia would be found where an antecedent modernity had taken root, whence Indonesia's own modernity was grafted.

Upon reflection, this insistence on a source modernity also runs counter to the romantic nomadism that still pervades the curatorial discourse of a would-be 'global' field.[7] Against the tide of this globalisation wades the stubborn figure of the modern nation – nation as product of modernity and modernity as the flagship product of nation – a structure that seems almost archaeological amidst the recent vogue for fallen utopias.[8] But decaying though it may be, this concrete modernity in Indonesia's cities is by no means the picturesque relic of a bygone internationalism. It is the everyday built environment, still being refurbished, still humming with life. Thus are Bandung's colonial bungalows repurposed as factory outlets. The weary framework of Jakarta's Taman Ismail Marzuki, a public facility for modern culture inaugurated in 1968, is the subject neither of fond portraits nor of ideological ghost stories – it still functions as a rare and valued piece of public infrastructure.[9]

This unfinished modernity has done nothing to limit ruangrupa's contemporary currency. For the dematerialisation of art, too, is an incomplete project, and the 'relational' turn, far from transcending it, has only upped the ante. As the artwork becomes activity (participation, social engagement, conviviality) the market moves to outflank it, at once celebrating the

6 Patrick D. Flores, *Past Peripheral: Curation in Southeast Asia*, Singapore: NUS Museum, 2008. Apinan, who left the biggest international footprint, was in fact the youngest of a regional cohort that included also Redza Piyadasa in Malaysia and Raymundo Albano in the Philippines. In the Indonesian context, it is worth noting the exceptional case of artist-couple Mella Jaarsma and Nindityo Adipurnomo, who founded the country's first contemporary art space, Cemeti Art House, in Jogja in 1988. Committed to artists' professional development and anything but parochial, Cemeti's legacy – art historical and curatorial – is hard to overstate.

7 I would not be the first to observe that this nomadism is often a smoke screen for the industrial and economic transmigration it quite faithfully maps. See Pascal Gielen, 'Curating with Love, or a Plea for Inflexibility', *Manifesta Journal*, issue 10, 2010, pp.14–15.

8 See, for example, Guy Tillim's *Avenue Patrice Lumumba* (2007–08), or Cyprien Gaillard's *Desniansky Raion* (2007). Louidgi Beltrame's film *Brasilia/Chandigarh* (2008) even made it to Singapore with the Pompidou show. The appeal of this genre is apparently universal, although it might be interesting to compare the respective geographies of production and consumption.

9 The cultural centre was built on the site of a public park established by Raden Saleh, Indonesia's first modern artist, during the Dutch East Indies era. In using this space for exhibitions and concerts, ruangrupa continues a tradition of diverting art's resources towards the provision of public space. Patrick Flores deals specifically with the matter of incomplete modernities in 'The Curatorial Turn in Southeast Asia and the Afterlife of the Modern' (2008), in Melissa Chiu and Benjamin Genocchio (ed.), *Contemporary Art in Asia: A Critical Reader*, Cambridge, MA and London: The MIT Press, 2011, pp.197–210.

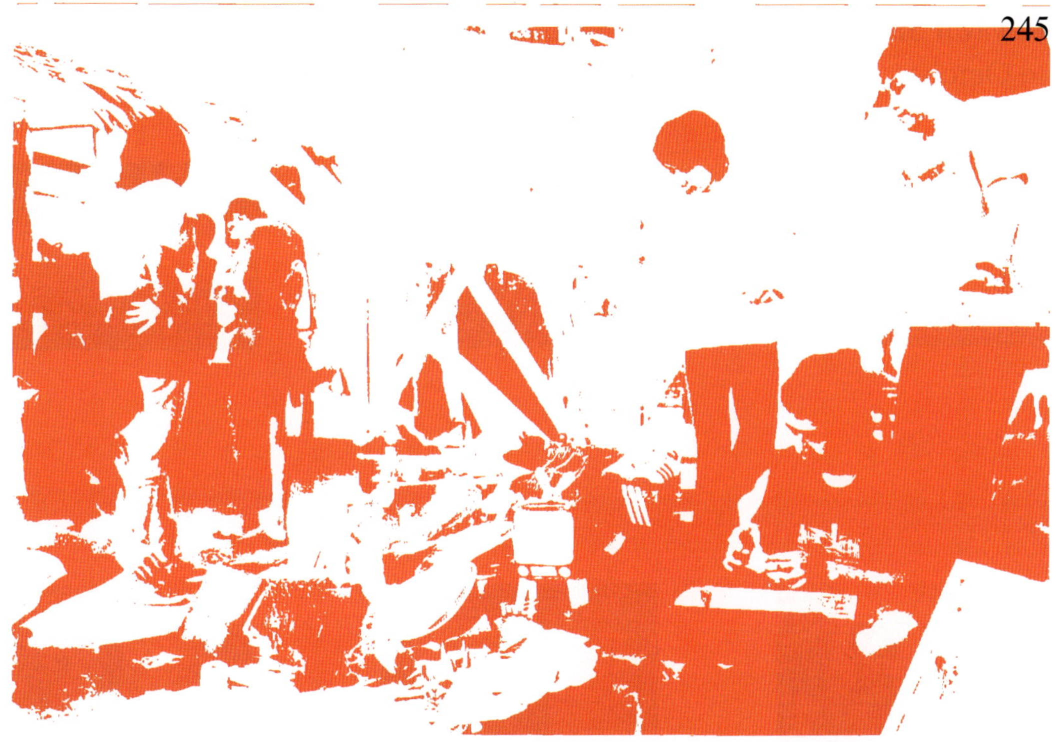

ruangrupa (ArtLab division), *Lonely Market*, 2009, Jakarta. Courtesy the artists

ephemeral and unreified spirit of the work, whilst perfecting its titration into parallel currencies. As a collective exhibiting internationally, whose core activity is the production and dissemination of knowledge rather than things, ruangrupa is hardly immune. Indeed, the collective seems to exemplify that merger of artist and curator so often mooted in the ballooning discourse on exhibition-making. In a recent edition of *Manifesta Journal* devoted to this subject, positions are staked around Walter Benjamin's 1934 lecture 'The Author as Producer'. We can hardly doubt the enduring relevance of this text in the post-industrial world, where museum may be likened to factory, and the mere prospect of collectivisation, as John Roberts points out, no longer distinguishes artist from curator.[10] But these conditions are far from universal, and are by no means the manifest destiny of contemporary art in Asia. For Roberts, the curator unprepared to be an artist should step back into the wings and make way for those truly committed to thwarting art's instrumentalisation. Such a synthesis has the whiff of an undead Hegelianism about it: the 'artist-curator as producer' must finally take responsibility for his own philosophy of production, as Arthur Danto might have put it. But if anything, Southeast Asian artist-curatorship ought to be read against the grain of this *telos*. Even for the region's most conspicuous trailblazers (Apinan and Supangkat), the outcome was precisely the opposite: a renewed separation of roles.

However ruangrupa might seem to embody the disciplinary merger, then, in attributing to the group the form of a curatorship *to come*, with or without the italics, we run the risk of mistaking tactical moves for a strategic programme. And however appealing the image of their 'contemporaneity', the group should first be seen in another light, a light in which modernity and nation still matter, and instrumentality is not (yet) the arch-enemy of art; a light in which artists make artworks and curators curate, and it is possible to do both. Perhaps ruangrupa is more a *spirit* of curatorship — not limited to a single body, yet somehow tied to a place — that would defend the autonomy of artists, singular or plural, but not necessarily that of the artwork. For this spirit the audience, rather than the work of art, may be the ultimate object of curatorial care.

10 John Roberts, 'The Curator as Producer: Aesthetic Reason, Nonaesthetic Reason, and Infinite Ideation', *Manifesta Journal*, issue 10, 2010, pp.51—57. See also Hito Steyerl, 'Is a Museum a Factory?', *e-flux Journal* [online journal], issue 7, 2009, http://www.e-flux.com/journal/is-a-museum-a-factory/ (last accessed on 23 April 2012).

‘Riwayat Saudagar’, exhibition by Saleh Husein, RURU Gallery, 19 October – 2 November 2012

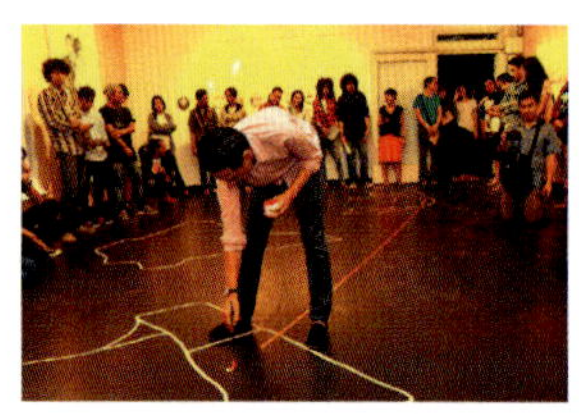

688

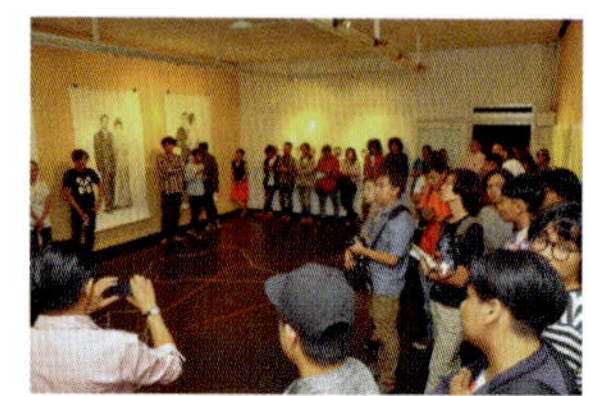

689

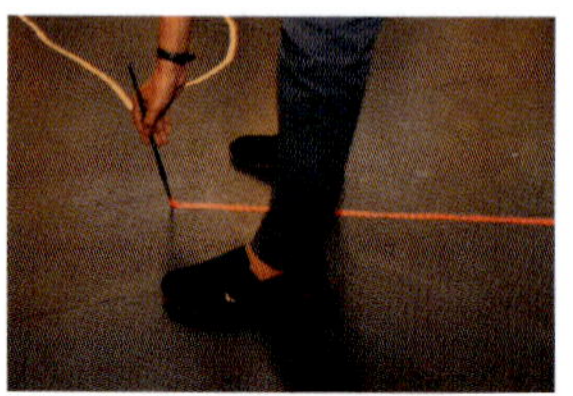

690

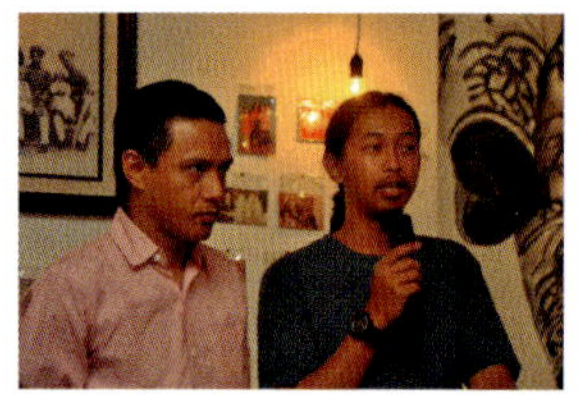

691

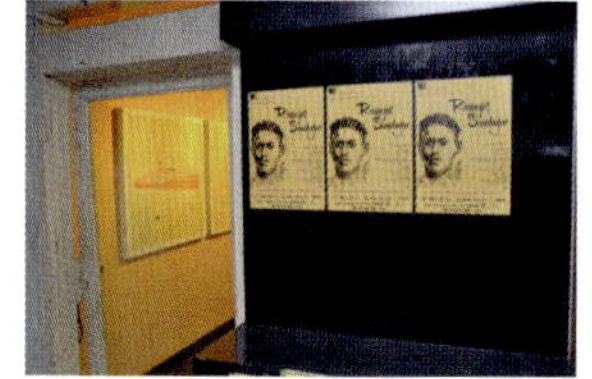

692

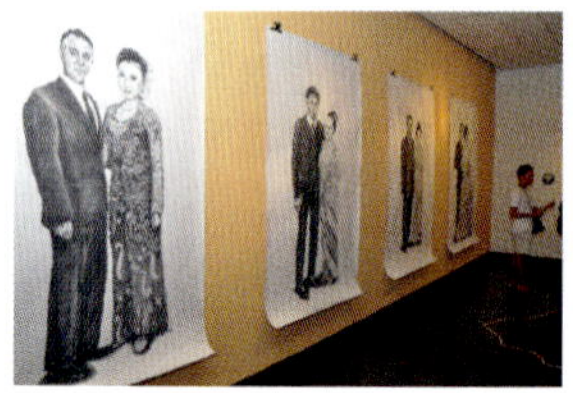

693

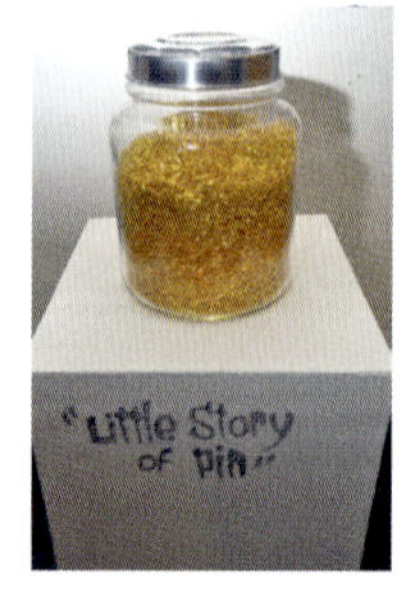

694

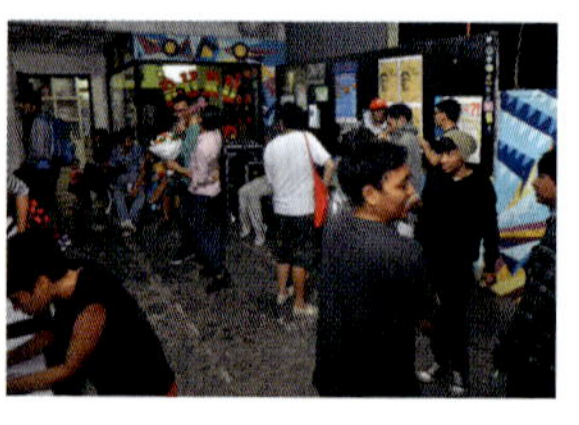

695

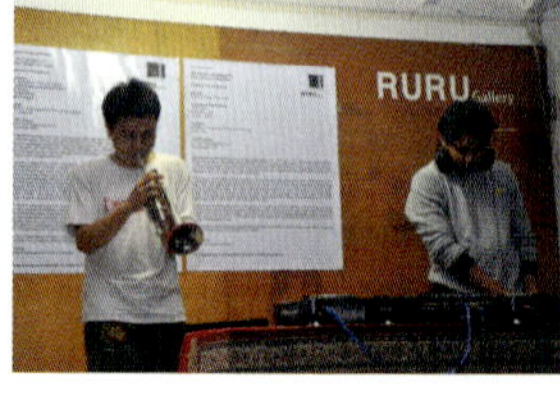

696

'The Sweet and Sour Story of Sugar', Galeri Seni Kunstkring, Jakarta, 23 November – 14 December 2012

ruangrupa developed an exhibition, a video workshop and a discussion responding to Noorderlicht's collection of documentary photography capturing the conditions of sugar industries in The Netherlands, Brazil, Indonesia and Suriname; curated by Indra Ameng and Julia Sarisetiati

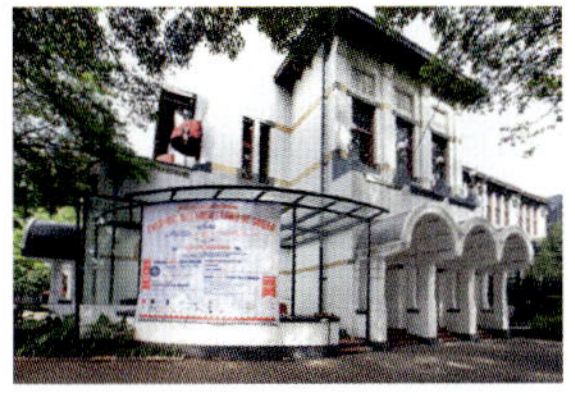

697

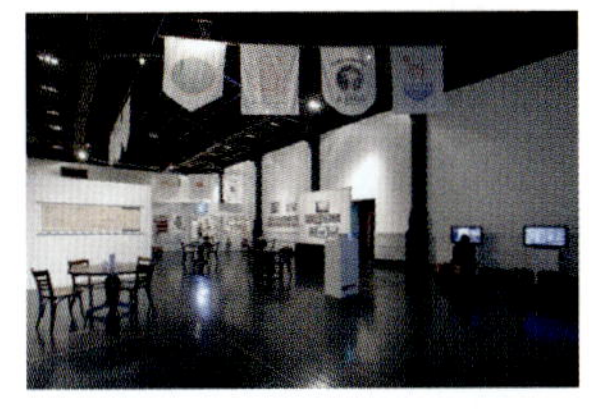

698

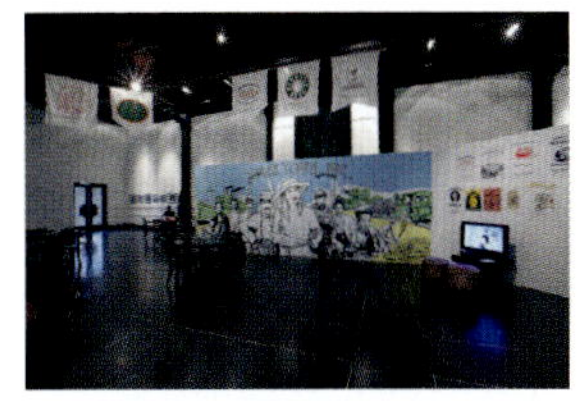

699

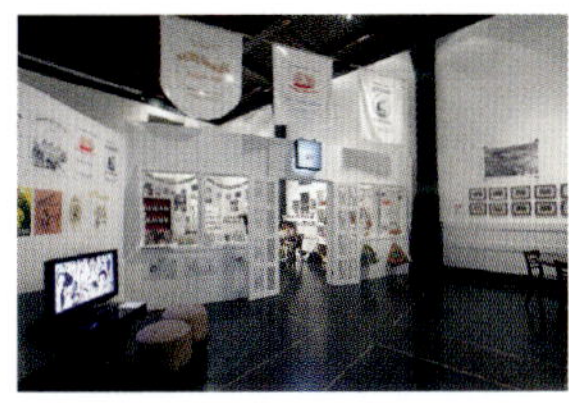

700

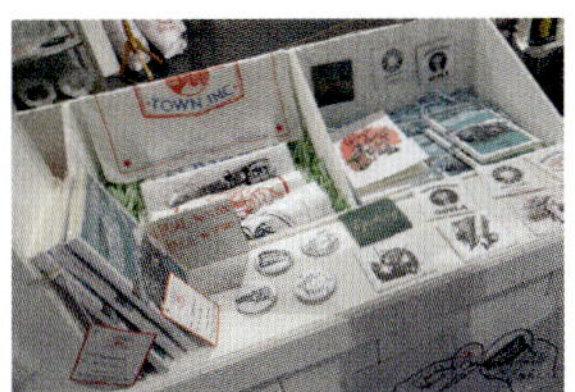

701

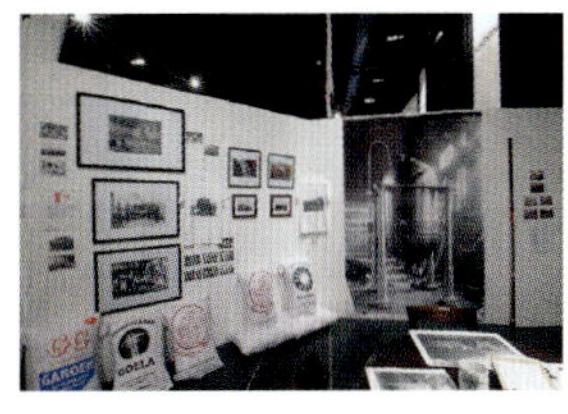

702

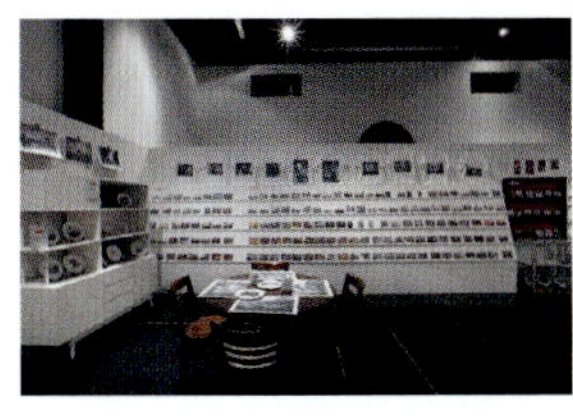

703

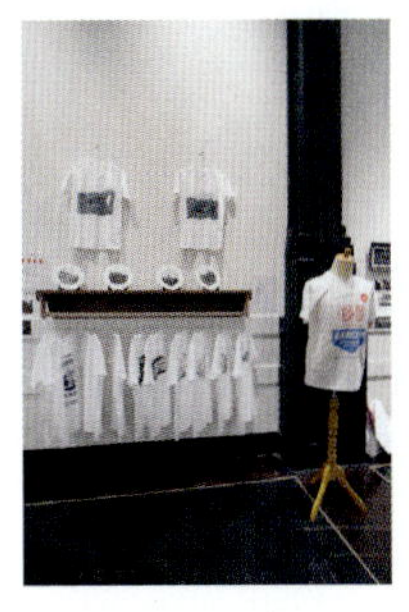

704

THE KUDA: *The Untold Story of Indonesian Underground Music in the 70s*, installation for Asia Pacific Triennale, Queensland Art Gallery, Brisbane, Australia, 8 December 2012 – 14 April 2013 248

To narrate the story of the ties between Jakarta and Brisbane, ruangrupa made up The Kuda, an underground punk rock band that purportedly played in Indonesia in the 1970s. In the myth, an Australian journalist visited Jakarta and returned home with copies of The Kuda's music, touching off a punk revolution in Brisbane's music scene. For their show, ruangrupa created a small museum of artefacts supposedly from that time: the band's instruments; vitrines full of fake books and magazines about The Kuda, aged to look as if they'd survived the 1970s; band t-shirts; a Vespa; black-and-white films of the rockers ambling around in all their slouchy cool. Musicians in Jakarta composed an entire album of songs 'by' The Kuda, which a Brisbane cover band played during the festival. ruangrupa convinced old Brisbane rockers to appear on radio programmes, testifying to the electric influence that The Kuda had on their music. ruangrupa's work isn't ordinarily this high-concept, but the show was prime ruangrupa in many other ways: in its street-urban edge, its impudence, its affection for multimedia exhibits and the so-called lowbrow, and its elliptical take on politics. It delighted them, in particular, that the fiction leaked out of the museum and into real life.

Samanth Subramanian

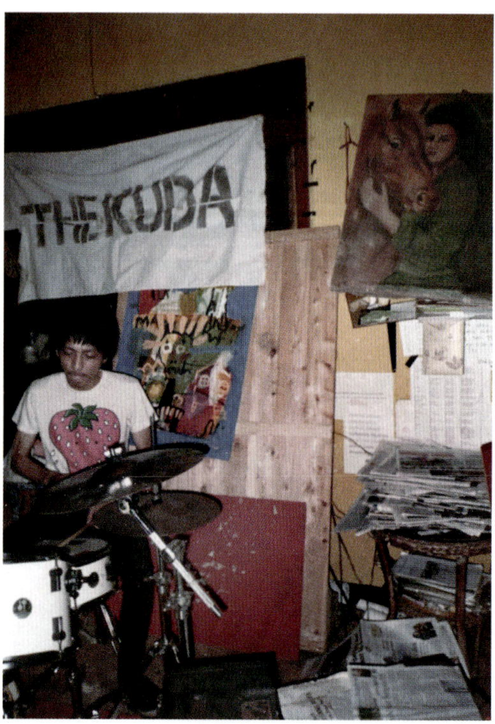

THE KUDA: *The Untold Story of Indonesian Underground Music in the 70s*, installation for Asia Pacific Triennale, Queensland Art Gallery, Brisbane, Australia, 8 December 2012 – 14 April 2013

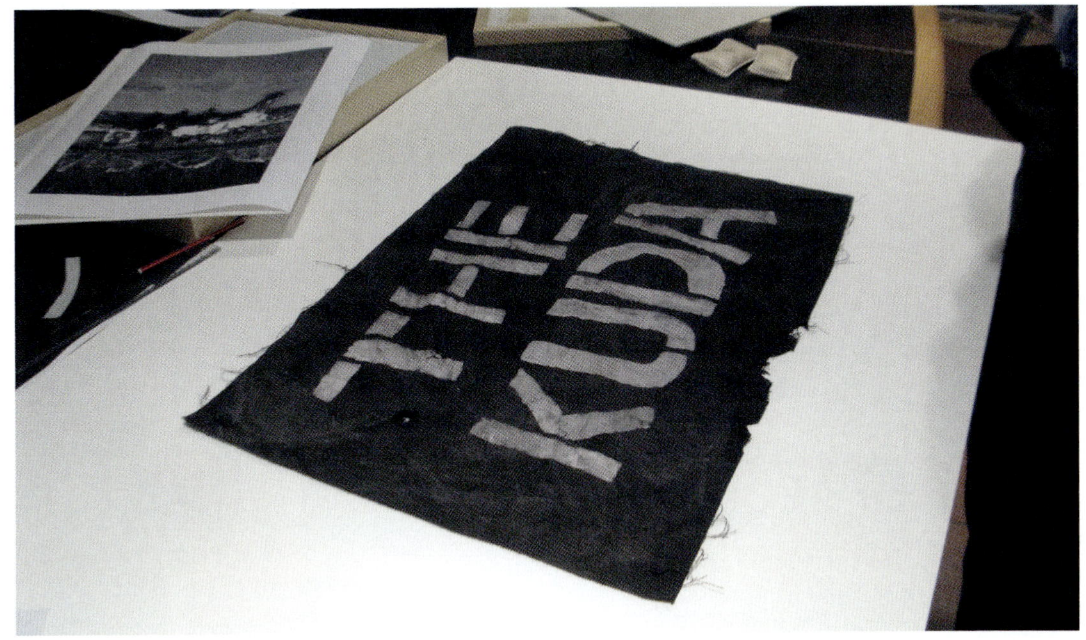

706

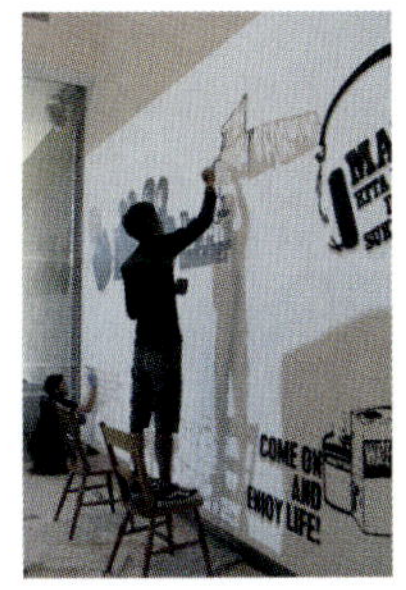

707

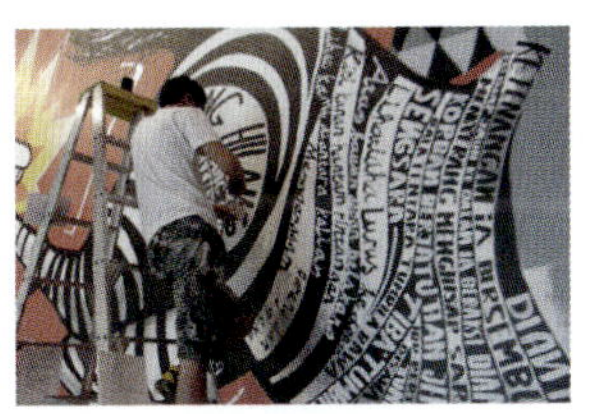

708

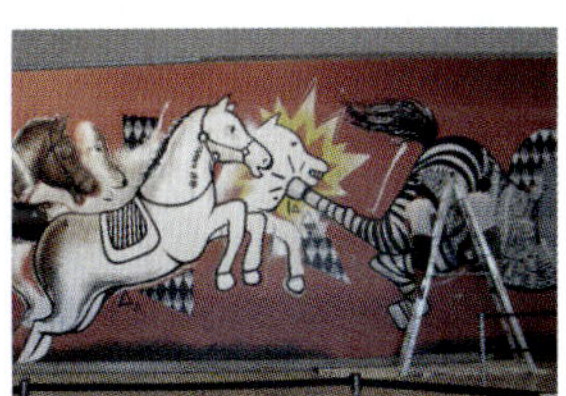

709

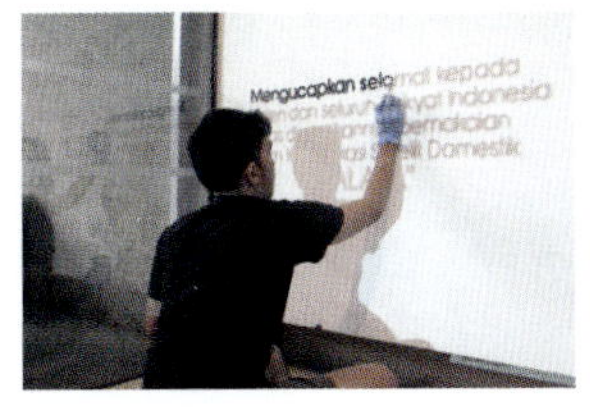

710

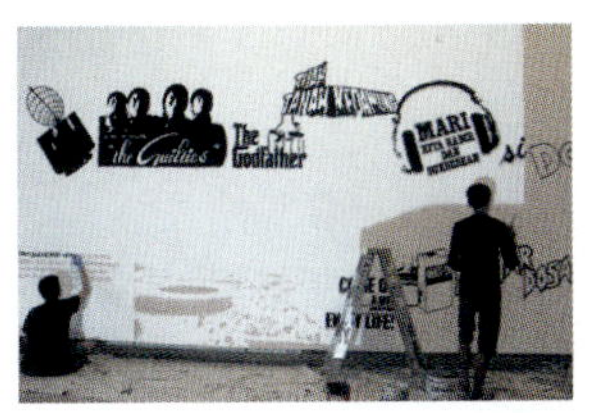

711

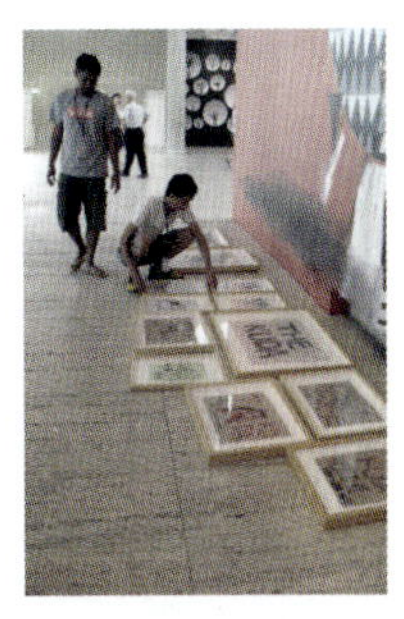

712

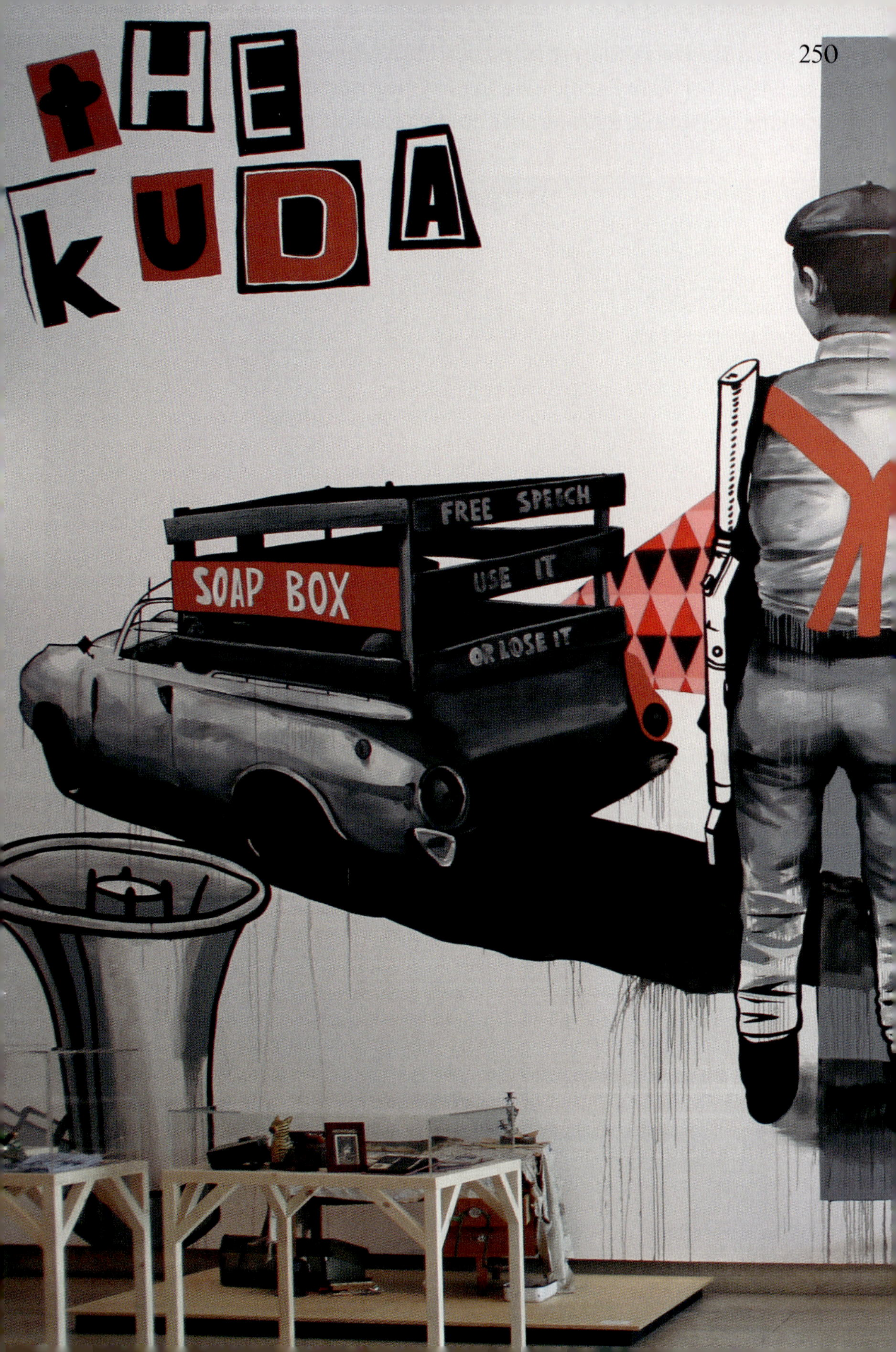
THE KUDA
SOAP BOX
FREE SPEECH
USE IT
OR LOSE IT

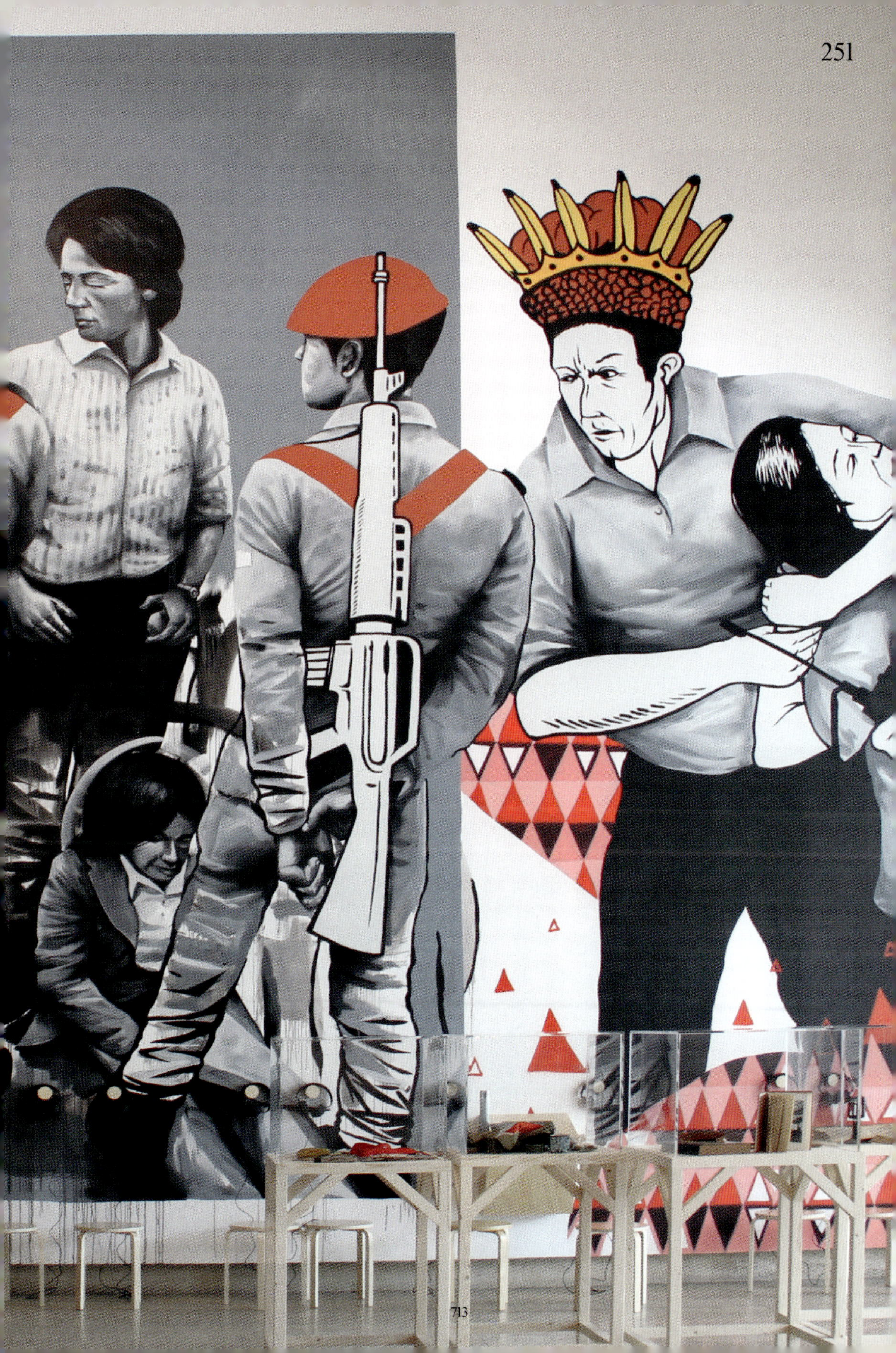
713

THE KUDA: *The Untold Story of Indonesian Underground Music in the 70s*, installation for Asia Pacific Triennale, Queensland Art Gallery, Brisbane, Australia, 8 December 2012 – 14 April 2013

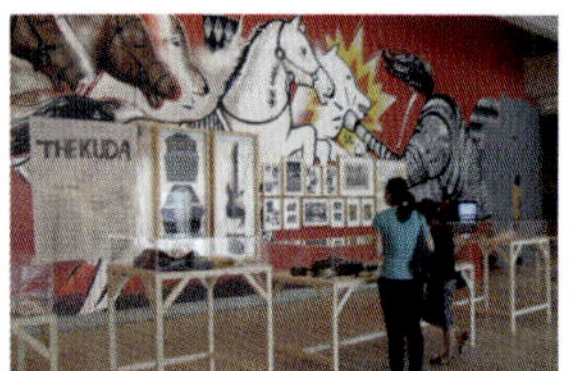

714

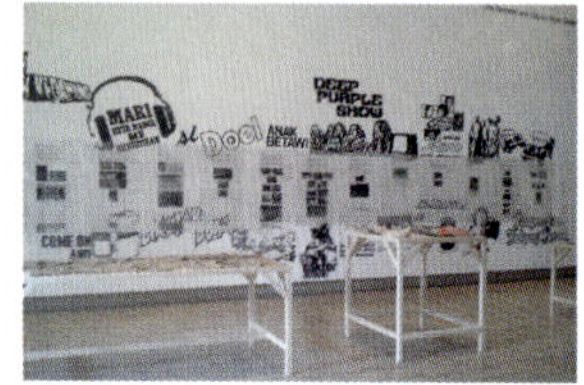

715

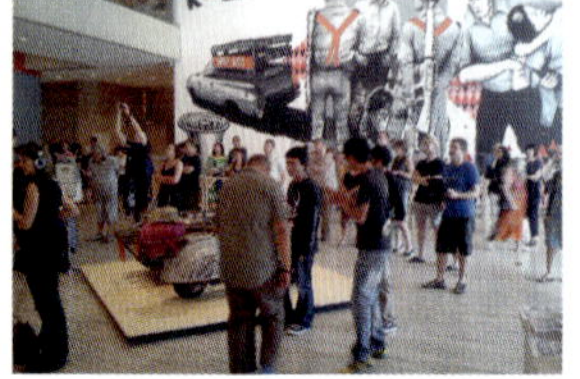

716

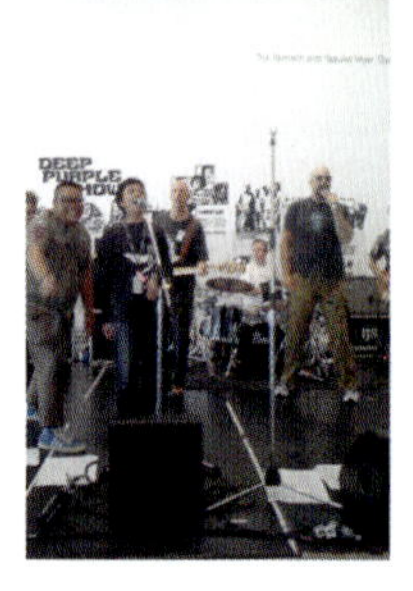

717

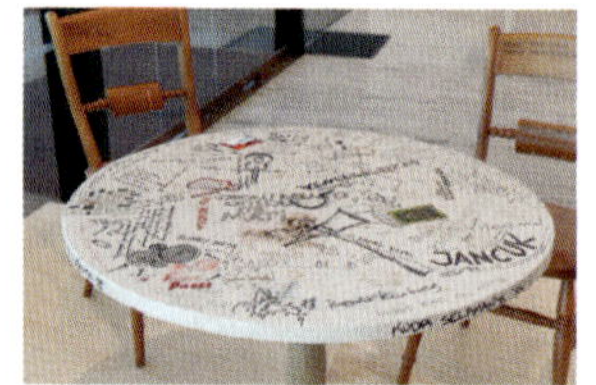

718

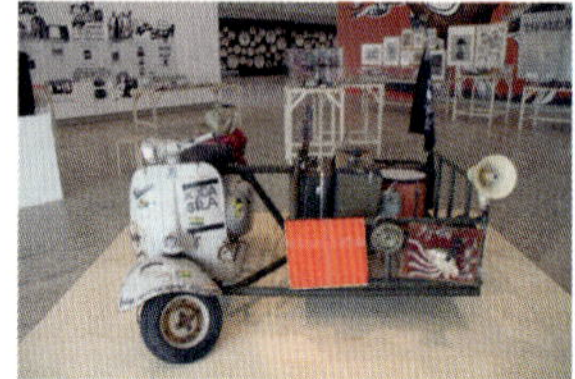

719

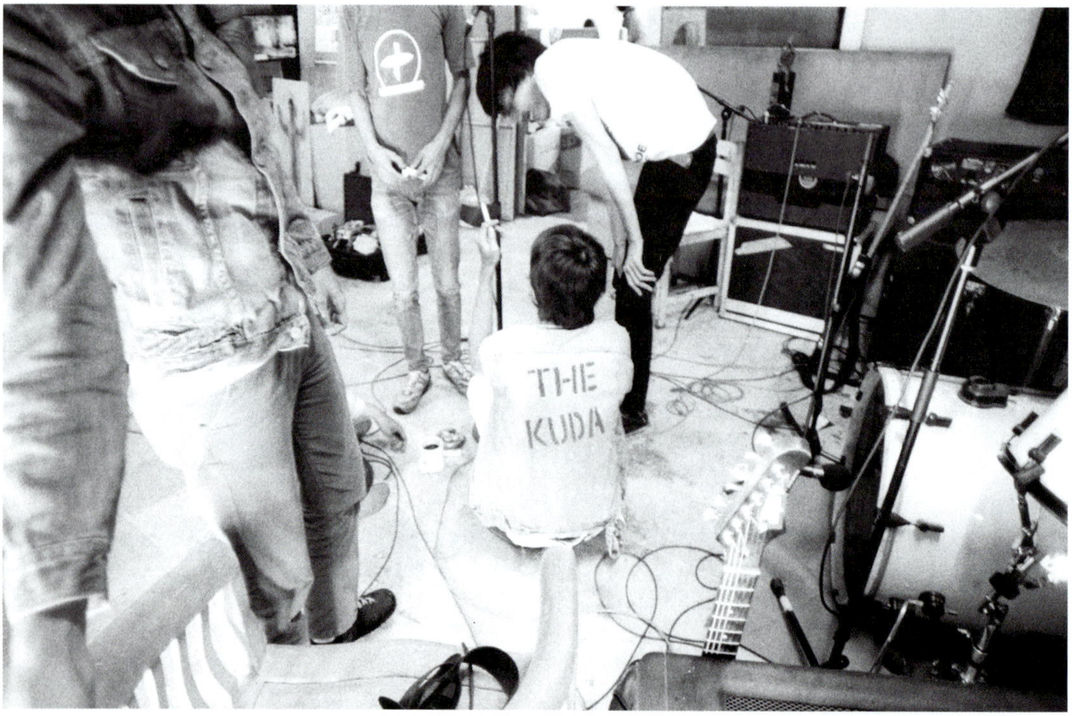

720

THE KUDA: *The Untold Story of Indonesian Underground Music in the 70s*, installation for Asia Pacific Triennale, Queensland Art Gallery, Brisbane, Australia, 8 December 2012 – 14 April 2013

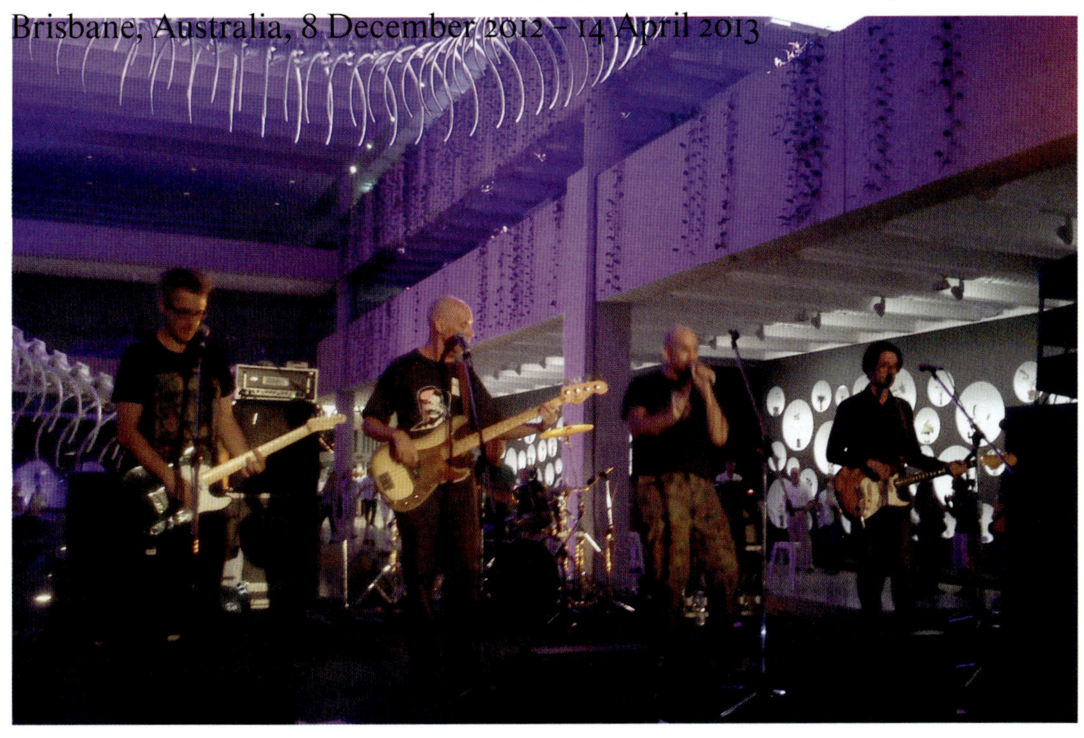

721

Years after that, someone showed us a blog post talking about The Kuda, and I think they didn't know it was actually fiction, because it was very serious writing, talking about how the Indonesian punk scene influenced the Brisbane punk scene.

Ade Darmawan

For the opening night, Ruang Rupa invited legendary Brisbane band The Family Butcher to perform. Inspired by punk music in Brisbane in the '70s, when bands like the Saints, the Go-Betweens and radio stations like 4ZZZ were active, Ruang Rupa linked the Brisbane music scene to the history of an imaginary Indonesian band called The Kuda.

At first sight, visitors wouldn't even realise that The Kuda is a fictional story, as Ruang Rupa has done an amazing job to create the fictional band displaying artifacts as proof of their existence. Through the imaginary band, Ruang Rupa investigates what happened in Indonesia during the 70s, in particular examining popular culture and its social political context. The invented Kuda band was presented as significant to Jakarta's music scene and becoming part of the young people's movement in the early days of Suharto's regime. ruangrupa shows how The Kuda lived through a period of transition in Indonesia and how they built a strong connection with the people in the city. Video documentaries, interviews and research on the development of pop-culture in Indonesia stand side by side with make-believe interviews of prominent figures who talk about the band's importance. Working in collaboration with local artist Fintan Magee, Ruang Rupa have created a huge mural installed in the lobby of the museum. Also on display are items considered historically important: cassette tapes, song notes, clothes, posters, magazines, archival footage – anything a rock group living in the 70s may have collected over the years. The most visible object is the Vespa scooter 'used' by the group during that time. To give a better context of the Indonesian music scene, the artist collective also set up music stations where visitors can hear rock music from the 1970s. Rather than talking only about music, Ruang Rupa's main focus in this project is the subject of history. They explore the thin line between reality and fake, how history can be traced through daily phenomenon and how the history also influenced the life of common people.

Alia Swastika

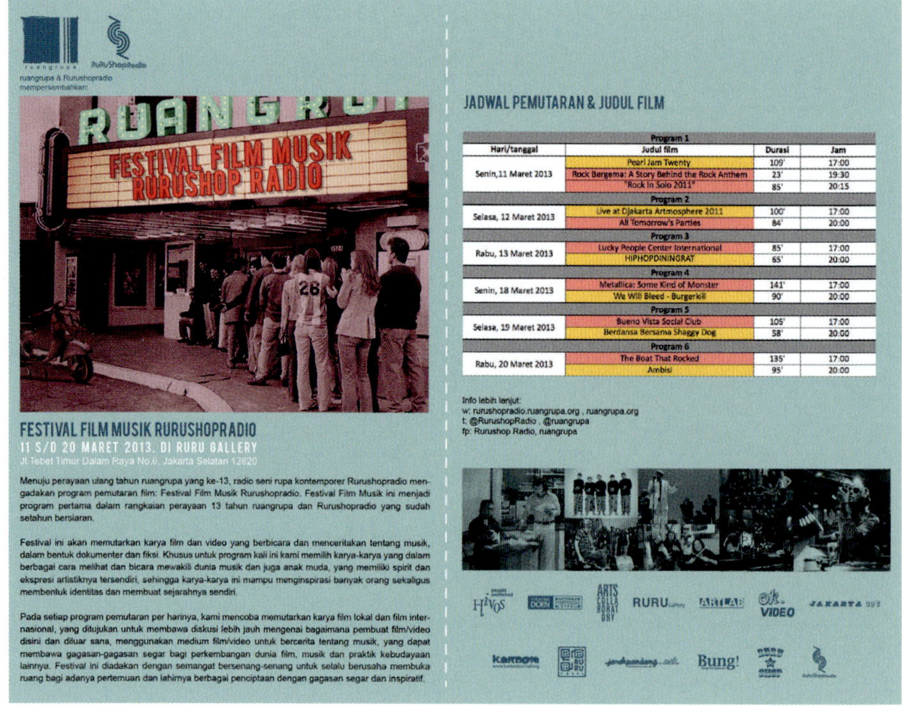

ruangrupa & Rurushopradio mempersembahkan:

FESTIVAL FILM MUSIK RURUSHOP RADIO

FESTIVAL FILM MUSIK RURUSHOPRADIO

11 S/D 20 MARET 2013, DI RURU GALLERY

Jl.Tebet Timur Dalam Raya No.6, Jakarta Selatan 12820

Menuju perayaan ulang tahun ruangrupa yang ke-13, radio seni rupa kontemporer Rurushopradio mengadakan program pemutaran film: Festival Film Musik Rurushopradio. Festival Film Musik ini menjadi program pertama dalam rangkaian perayaan 13 tahun ruangrupa dan Rurushopradio yang sudah setahun bersiaran.

Festival ini akan memutarkan karya film dan video yang berbicara dan menceritakan tentang musik, dalam bentuk dokumenter dan fiksi. Khusus untuk program kali ini kami memilih karya-karya yang dalam berbagai cara melihat dan bicara mewakili dunia musik dan juga anak muda, yang memiliki spirit dan ekspresi artistiknya tersendiri, sehingga karya-karya ini mampu menginspirasi banyak orang sekaligus membentuk identitas dan membuat sejarahnya sendiri.

Pada setiap program pemutaran per harinya, kami mencoba memutarkan karya film lokal dan film internasional, yang ditujukan untuk membawa diskusi lebih jauh mengenai bagaimana pembuat film/video disini dan diluar sana, menggunakan medium film/video untuk bercerita tentang musik, yang dapat membawa gagasan-gagasan segar bagi perkembangan dunia film, musik dan praktik kebudayaan lainnya. Festival ini diadakan dengan semangat bersenang-senang untuk selalu berusaha membuka ruang bagi adanya pertemuan dan lahirnya berbagai penciptaan dengan gagasan segar dan inspiratif.

JADWAL PEMUTARAN & JUDUL FILM

Hari/tanggal	Judul film	Durasi	Jam
Program 1			
Senin,11 Maret 2013	Pearl Jam Twenty	109'	17:00
	Rock Bergema: A Story Behind the Rock Anthem	23'	19:30
	"Rock In Solo 2011"	85'	20:15
Program 2			
Selasa, 12 Maret 2013	Live at Djakarta Artmosphere 2011	100'	17:00
	All Tomorrow's Parties	84'	20:00
Program 3			
Rabu, 13 Maret 2013	Lucky People Center International	85'	17:00
	HIPHOPDININGRAT	65'	20:00
Program 4			
Senin, 18 Maret 2013	Metallica: Some Kind of Monster	141'	17:00
	We Will Bleed - Burgerkill	90'	20:00
Program 5			
Selasa, 19 Maret 2013	Bueno Vista Social Club	105'	17:00
	Berdansa Bersama Shaggy Dog	58'	20:00
Program 6			
Rabu, 20 Maret 2013	The Boat That Rocked	135'	17:00
	Ambisi	95'	20:00

Info lebih lanjut:
w: rurushopradio.ruangrupa.org , ruangrupa.org
t: @RurushopRadio , @ruangrupa
fp: Rurushop Radio, ruangrupa

Artist-in-residence talk with Penny Demertzi, RURU Gallery, 11 April 2013

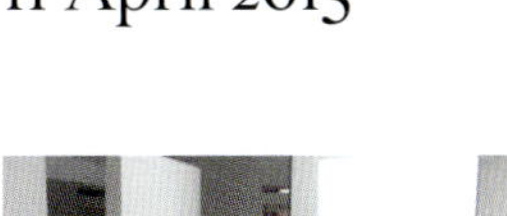

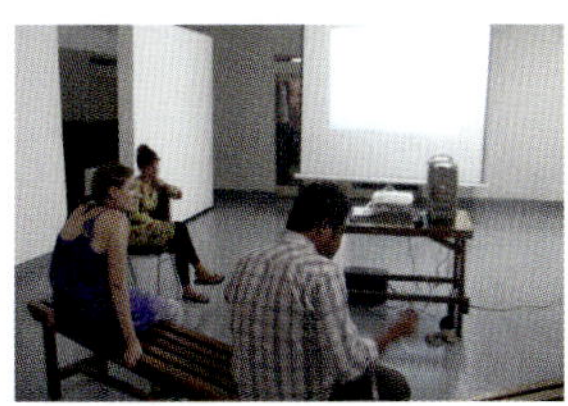

723

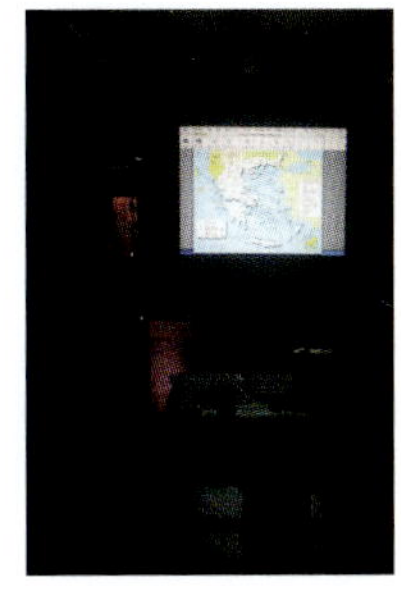

724

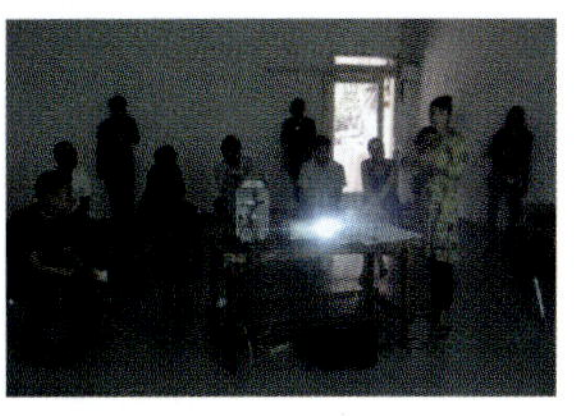

725

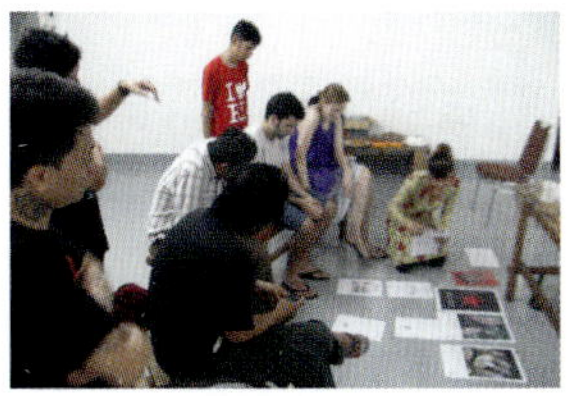

726

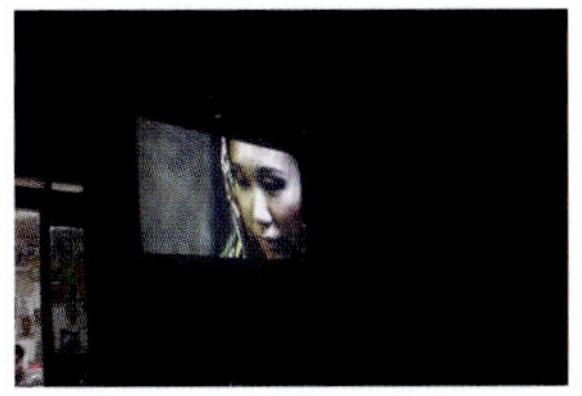

727

with Syaiful Ardianto, Putri Ayu Lestari, Taring Babi, Refreshink Printmaking and Grafis Huru Hara; curated by Asep Topan

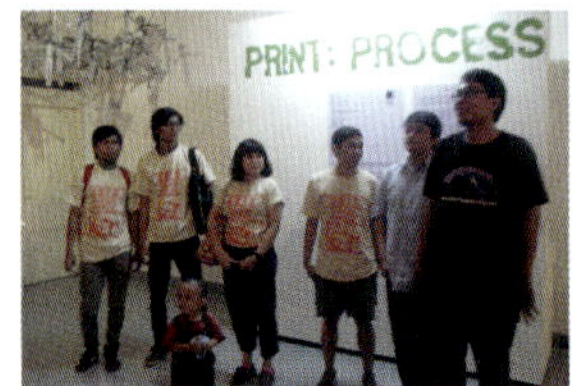

728

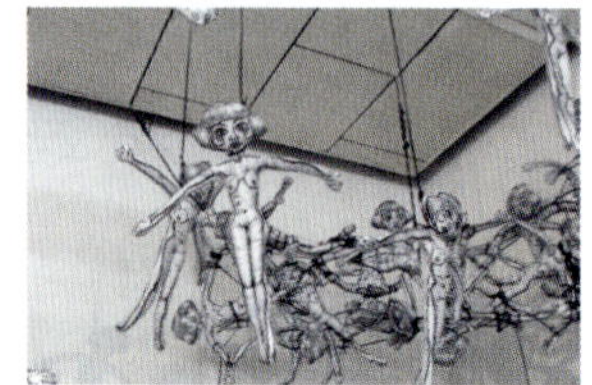

729

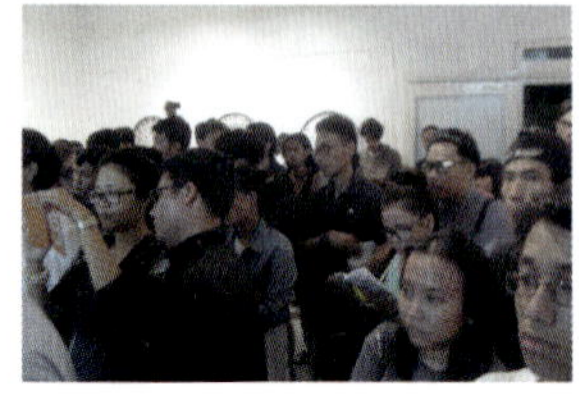

730

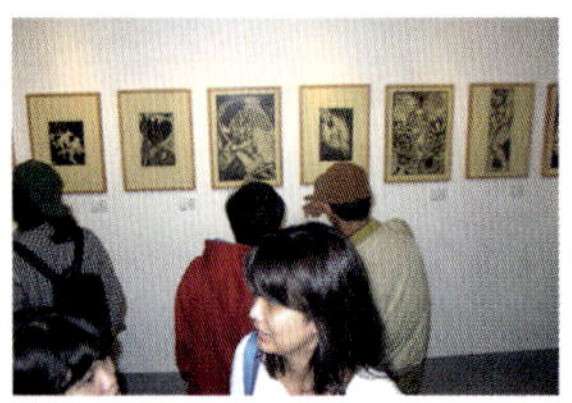

731

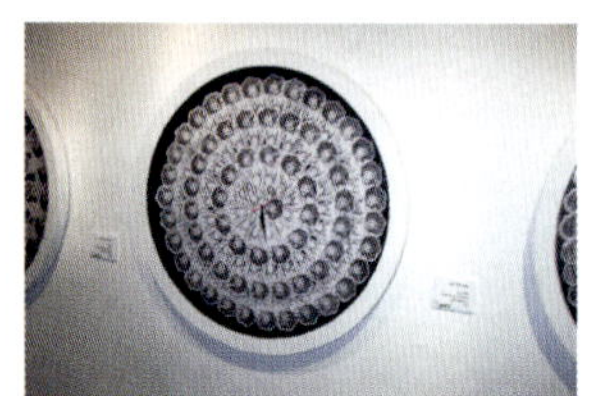

732

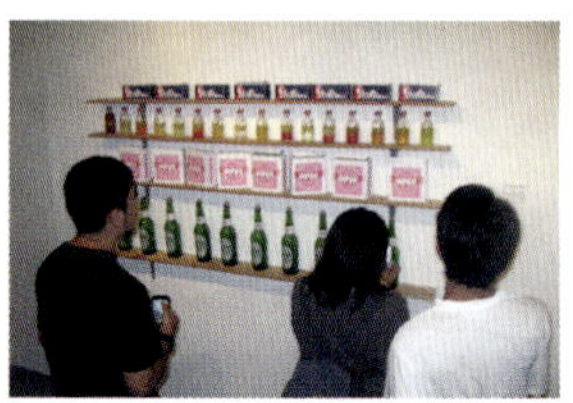

733

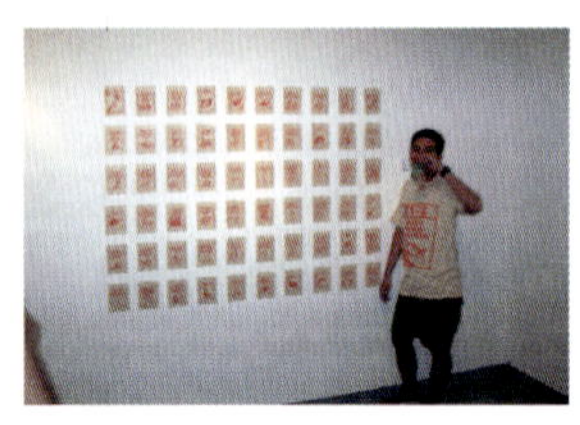

734

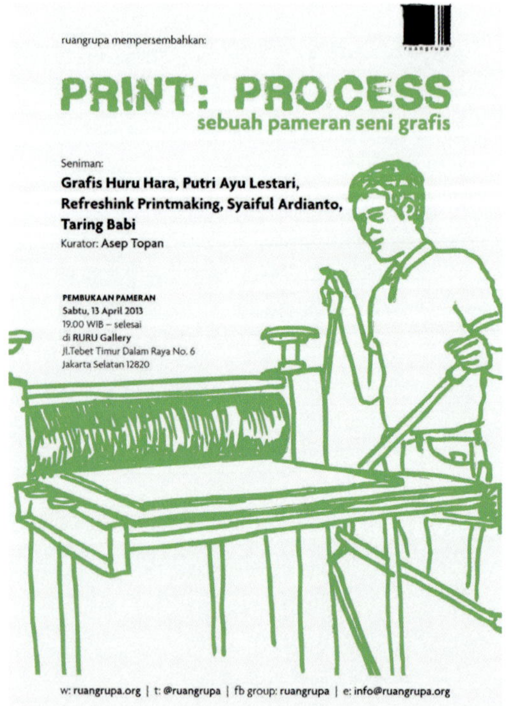

735

'Sarimin is Lost in the Market', ArtLab workshop and talk with Anja Dornieden and Juan David González Monroy, 26 April 2013

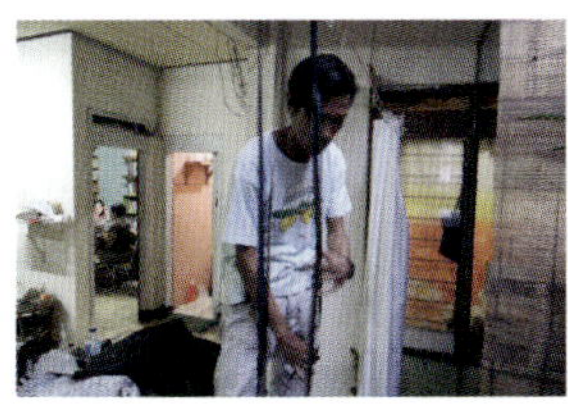

736

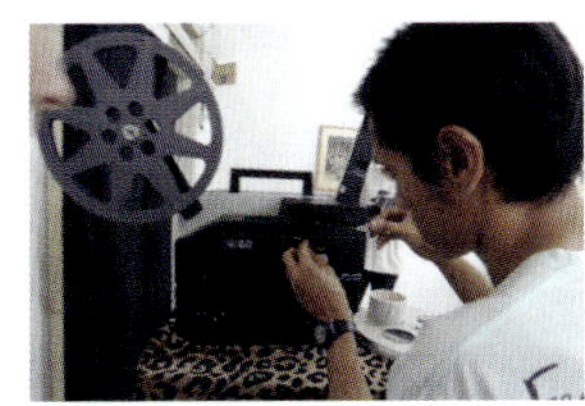

737

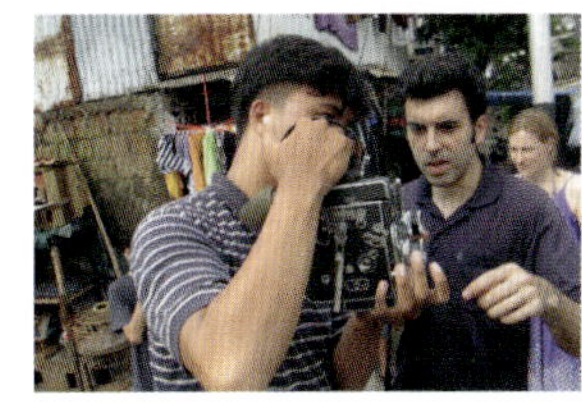

738

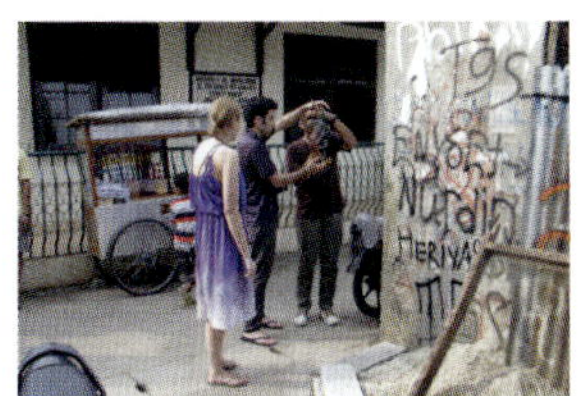

739

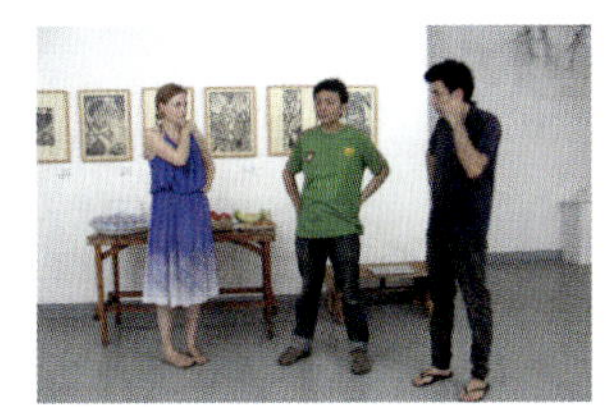

740

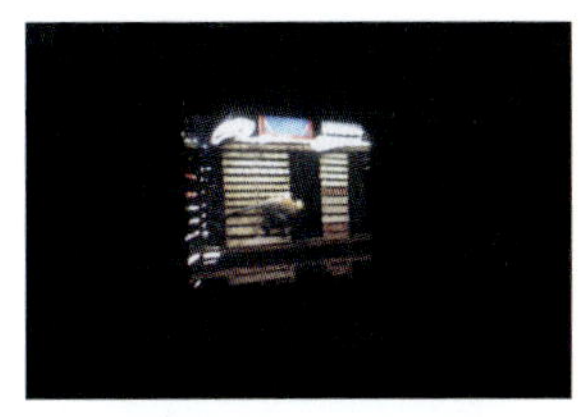

741

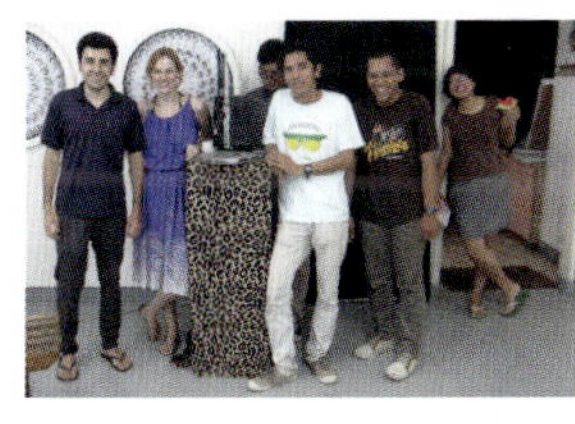

742

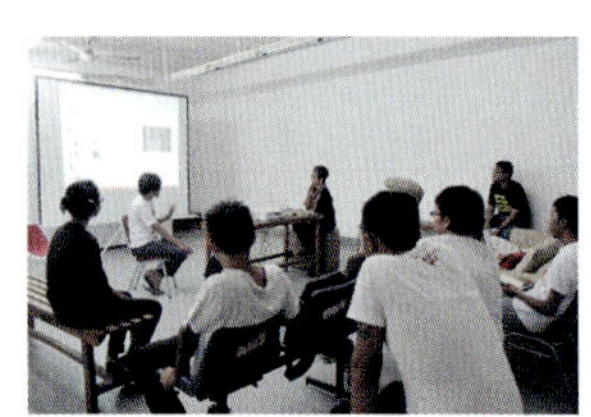

743

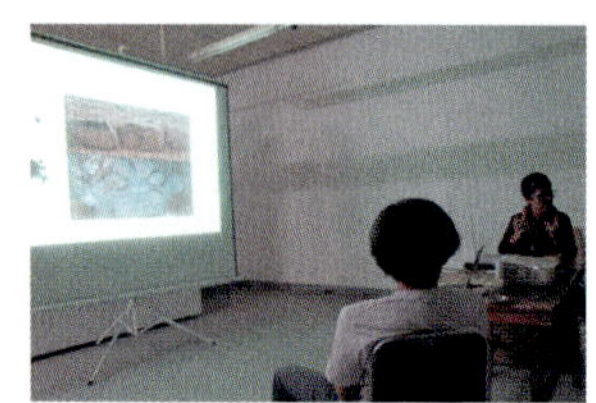

744

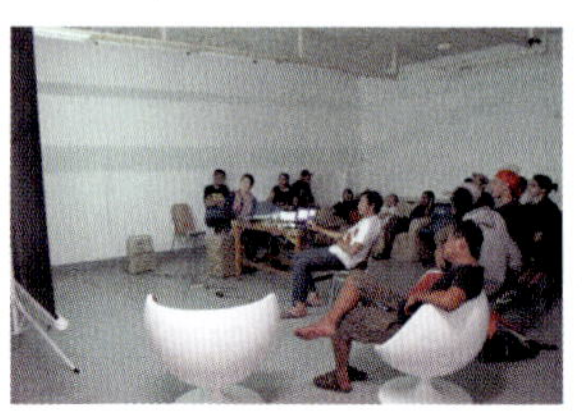

745

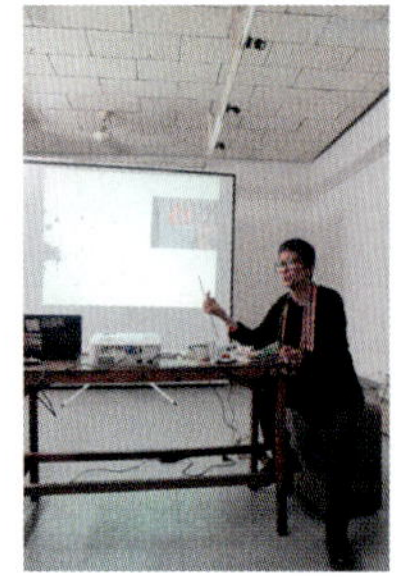

746

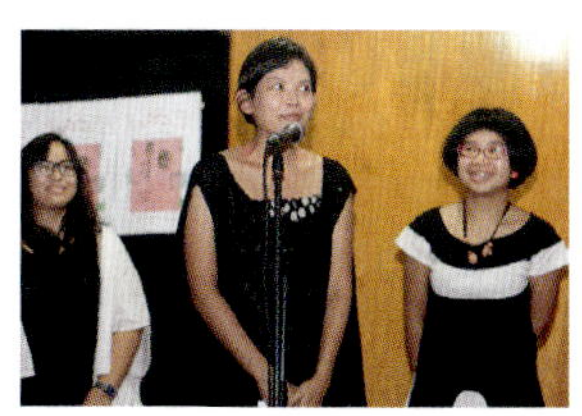
747

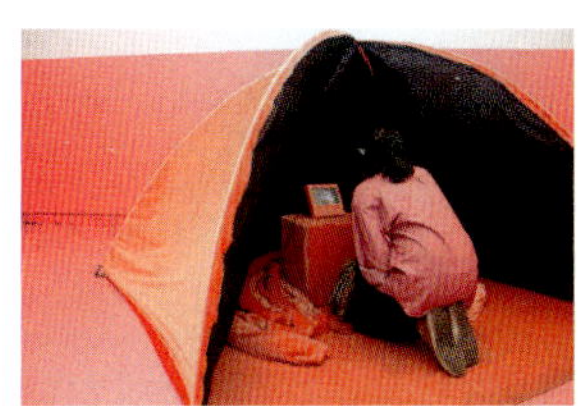
748

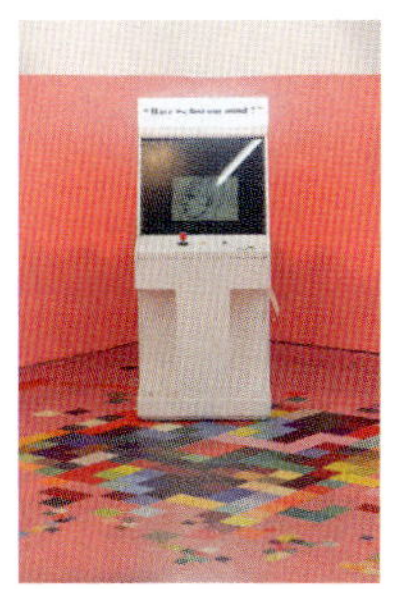
749

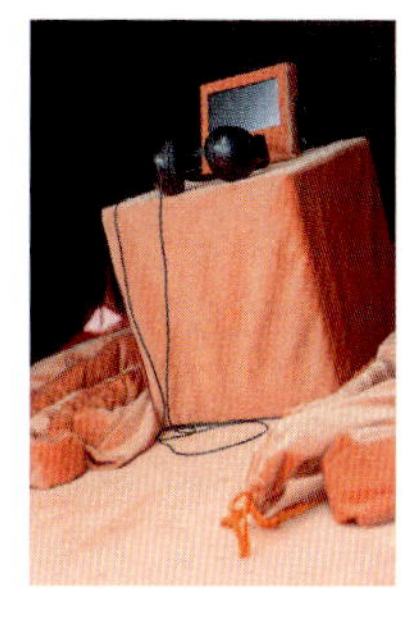
750

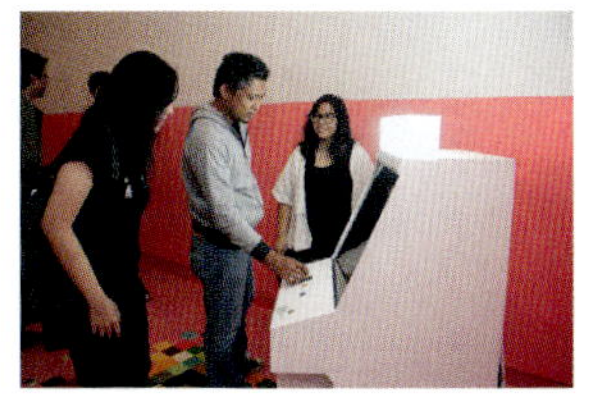
751

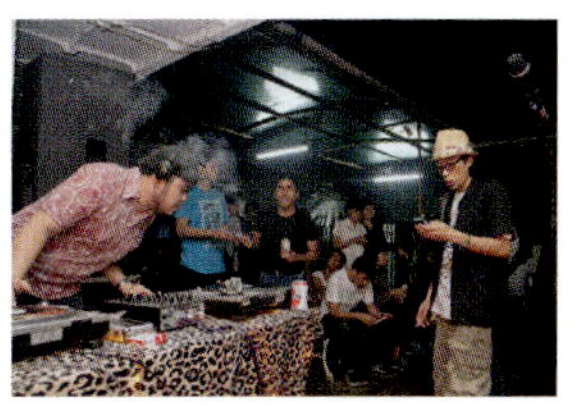
752

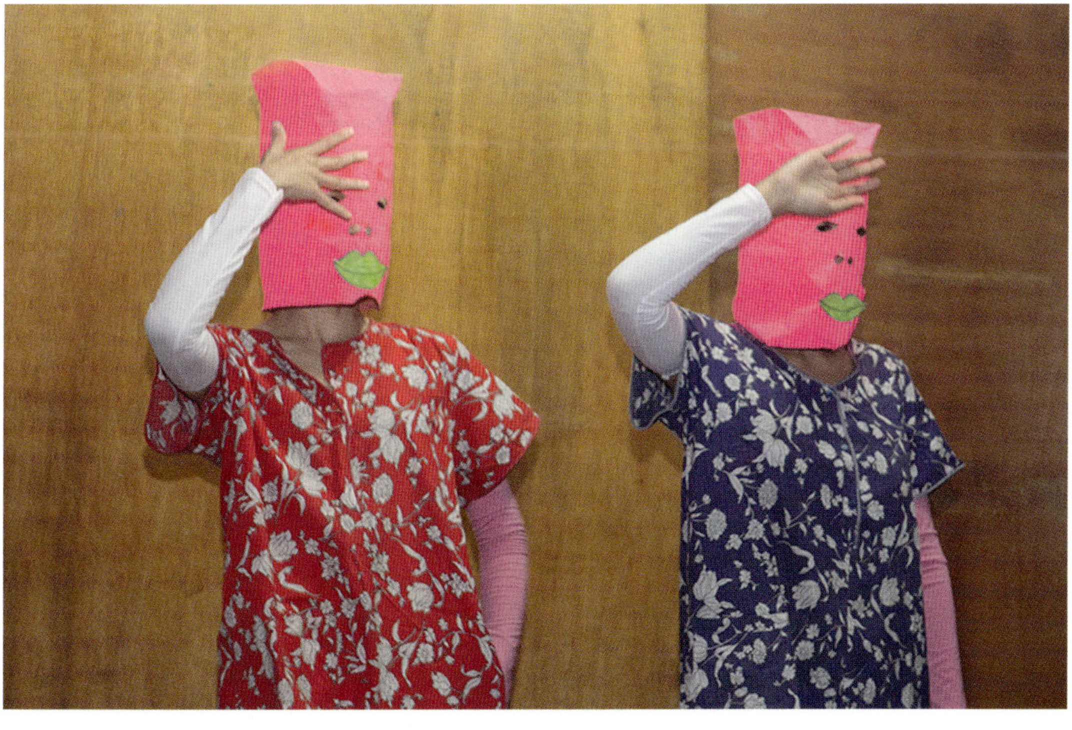

753

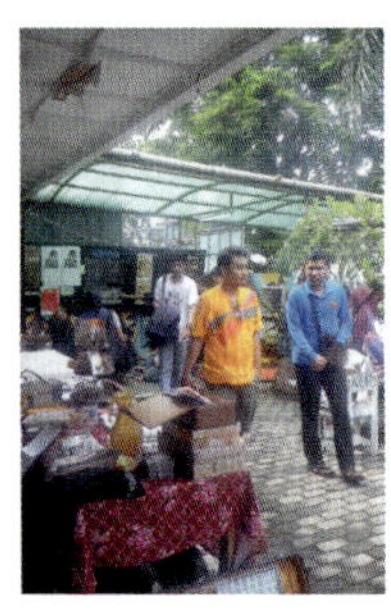

754

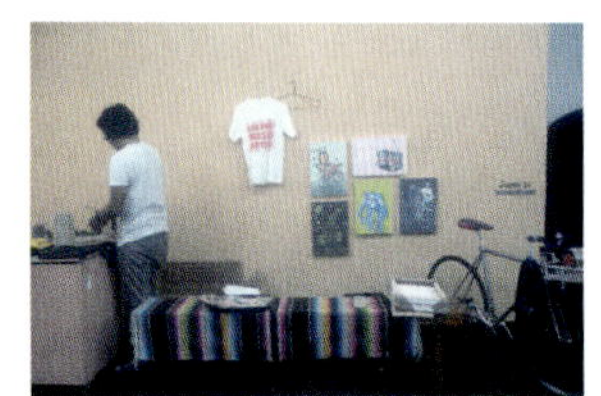

755

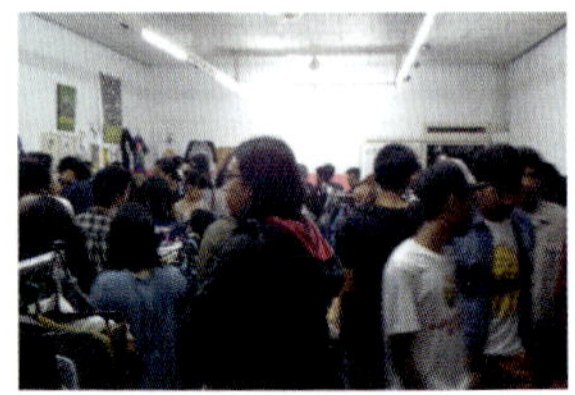

756

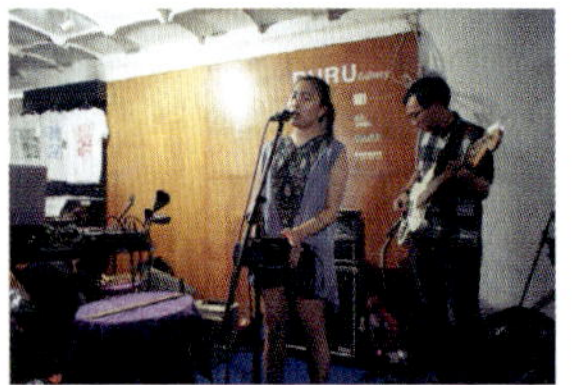

757

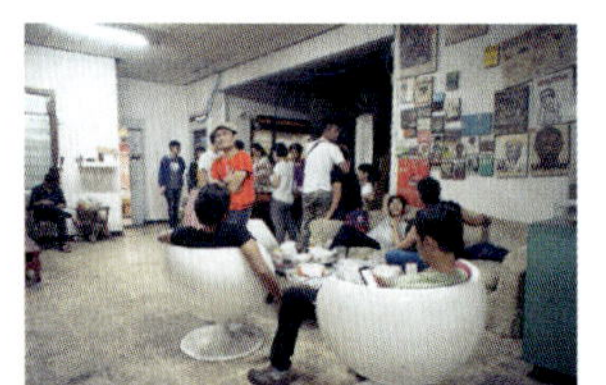

758

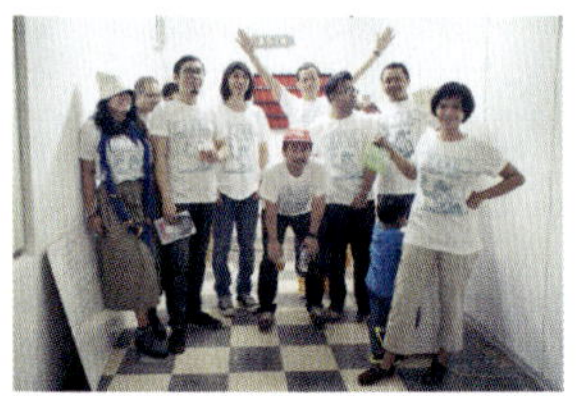

759

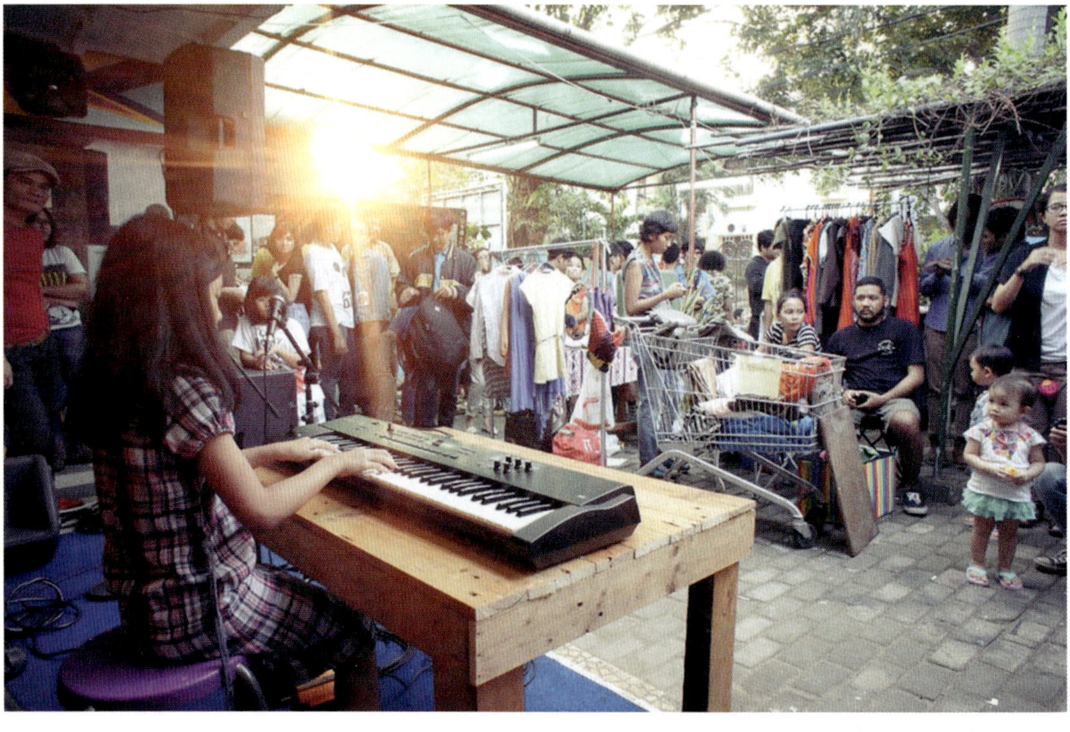

760

261

‘Vertical Villages’, ArtLab exhibition with Keg de Souza, 4A Centre for Contemporary Art, Sydney, Australia, 6 September – 26 October 2013

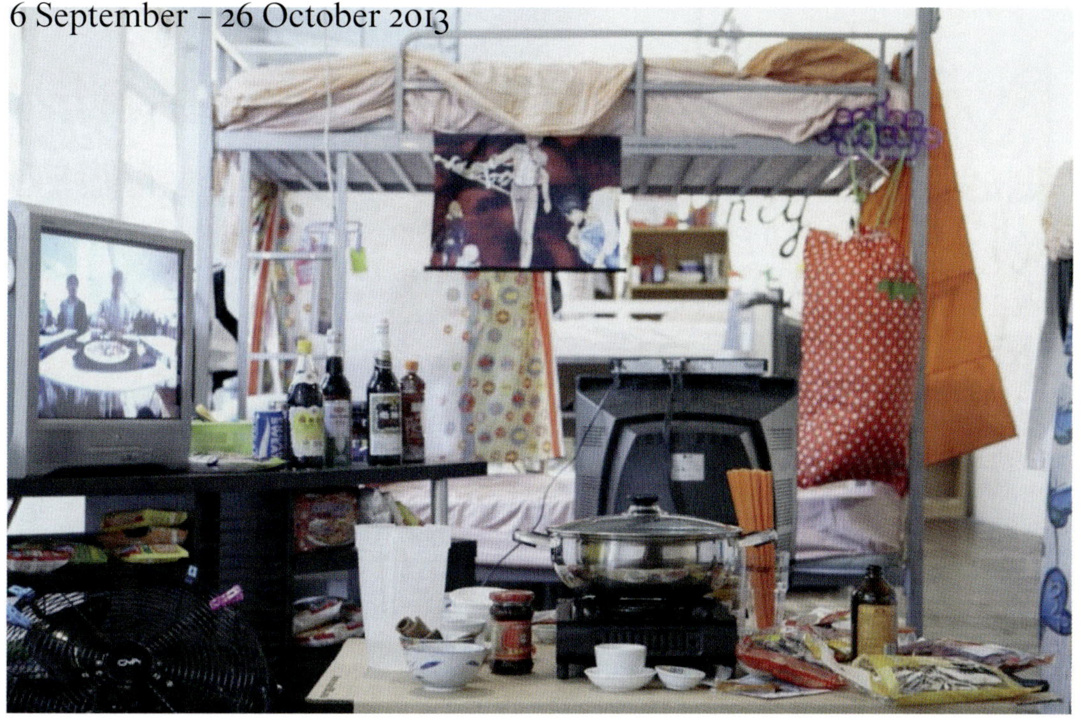

ok.Video 'Muslihat' - 6th Jakarta International Video Festival, Nasional Galeri Indonesia and other venues, Jakarta, 4–15 September 2013

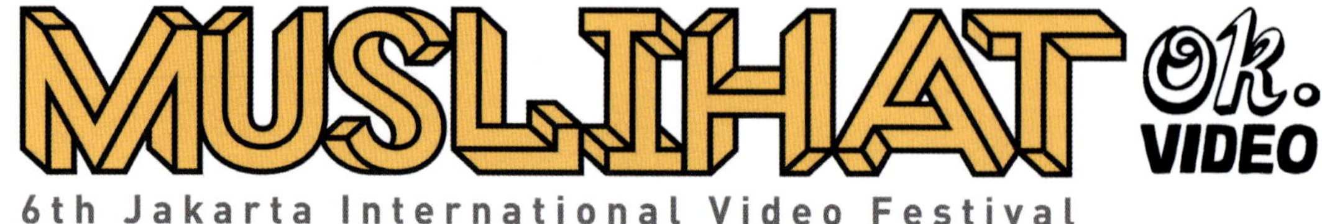

762

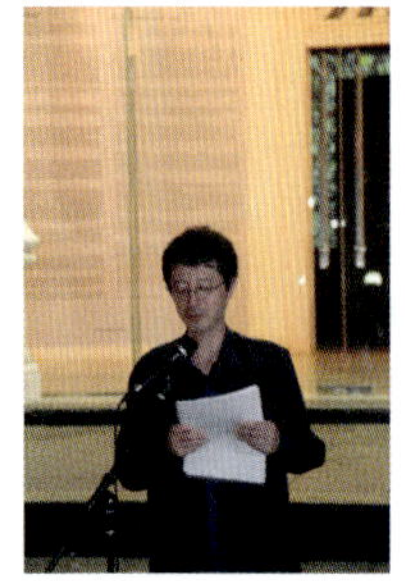

763

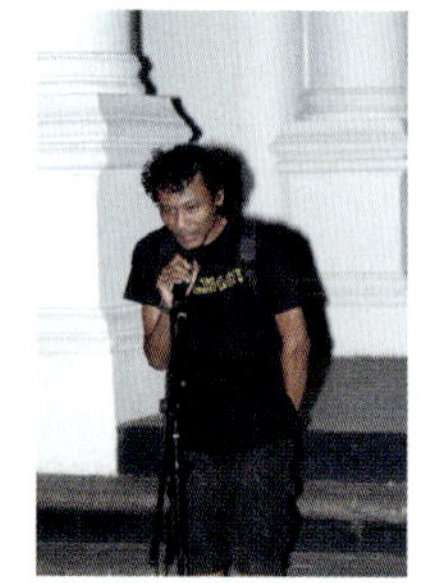

764

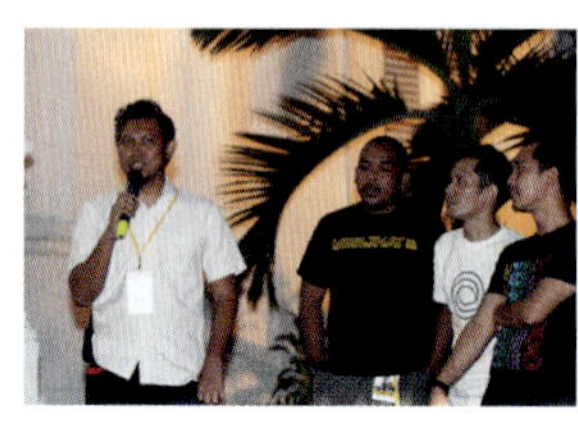

765

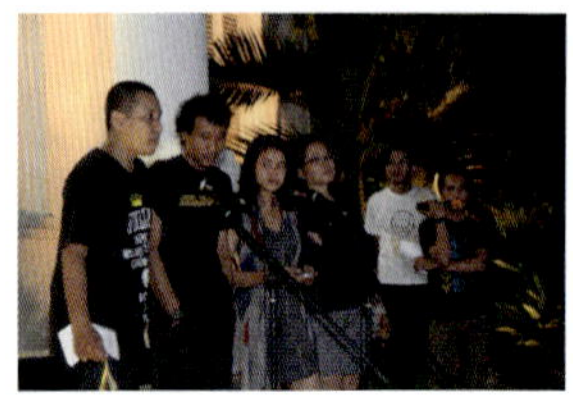

766

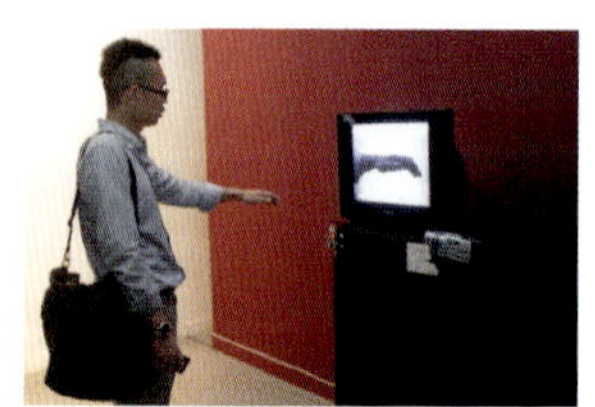

767

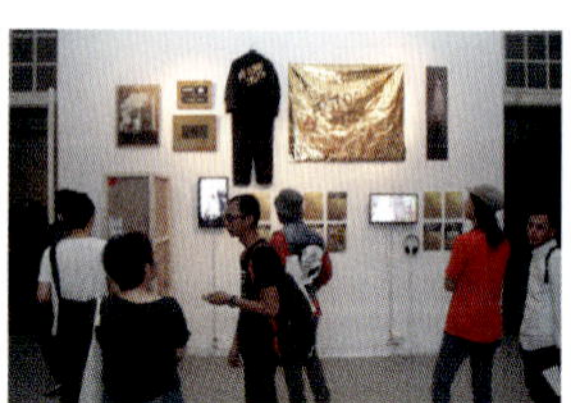

768

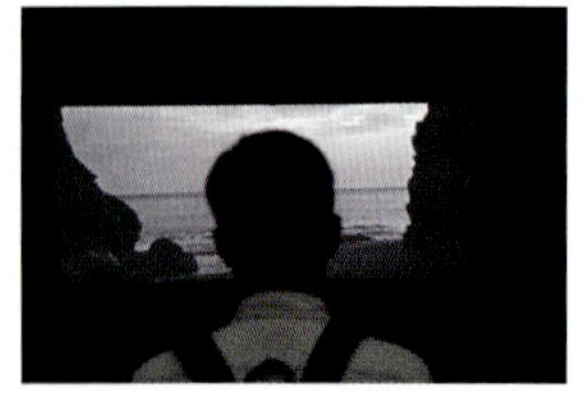

769

770

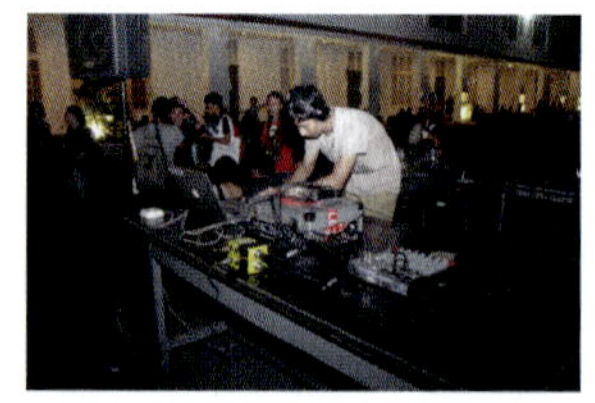

771

'JAF (Jatiwangi Art Factory) vs KINETIK-WAFT', RURU Gallery, 13–27 September 2013

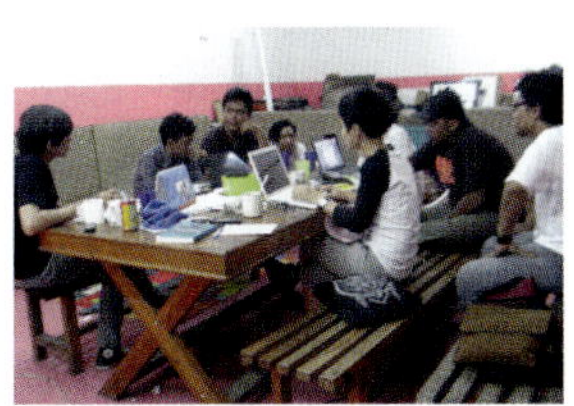

772

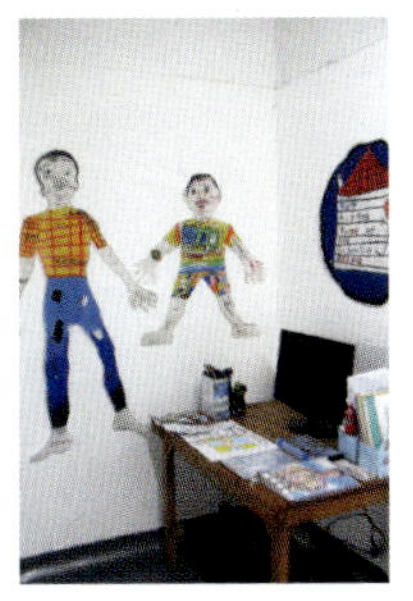

773

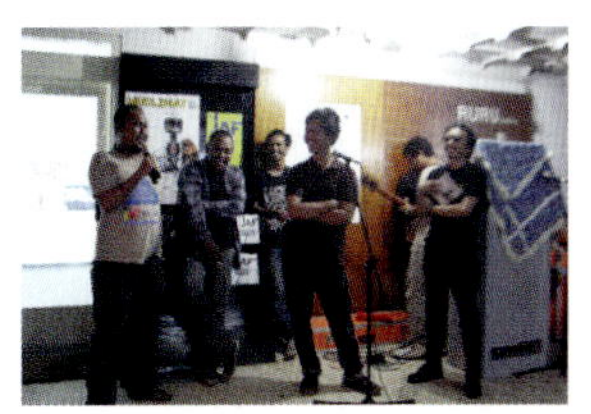

774

‘Begadang Neng?’, RURU Gallery, 25–27 October 2013

with Dila Aku, Ika Vantiani, Keke Tumbuan, Lala Bohang, Marishka Soekarna, Marina Tasha, Monica Hapsari, Nastasha Abigail, Natasha Gabriella Tontey, Neng Iren, Nuri Fatima, Sari Sartje, Sanchia Hamidjaja, Tisa Granicia and Ykha Amelz

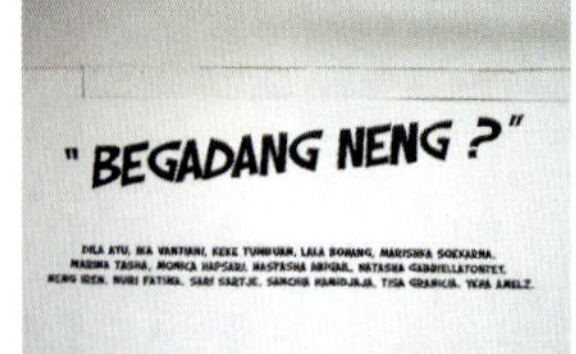

775

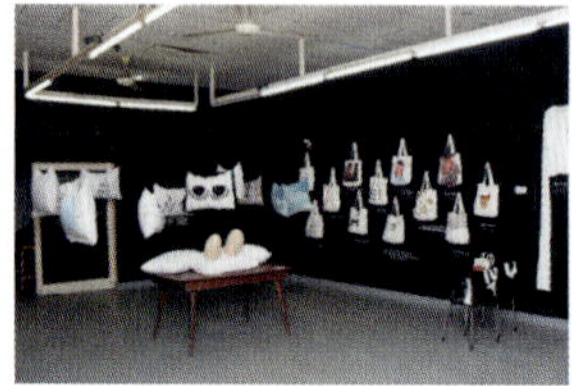

776

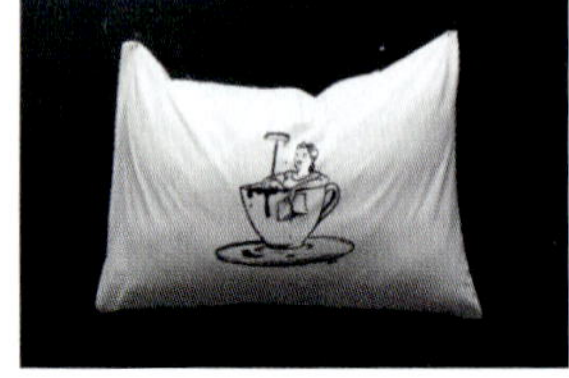

777

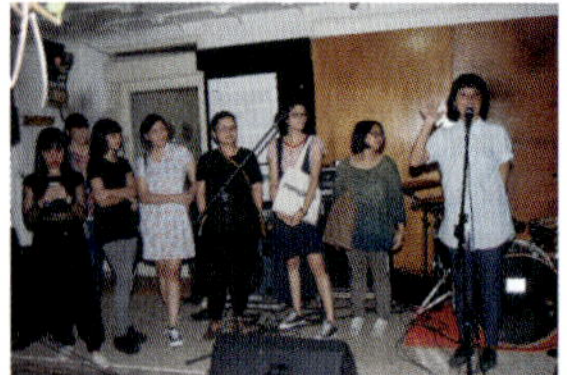

778

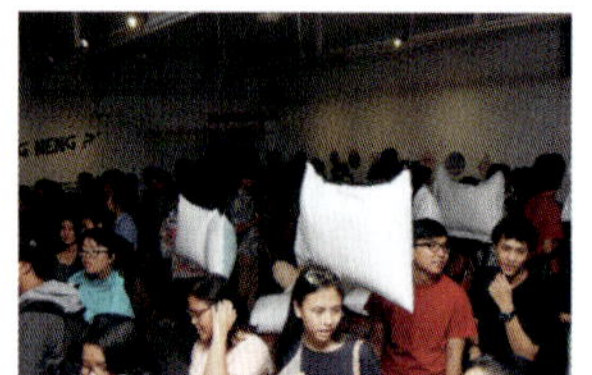

779

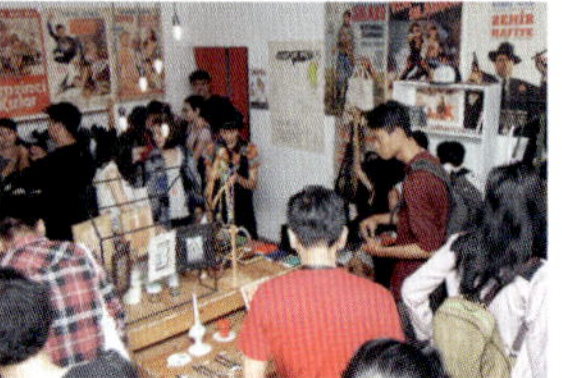

780

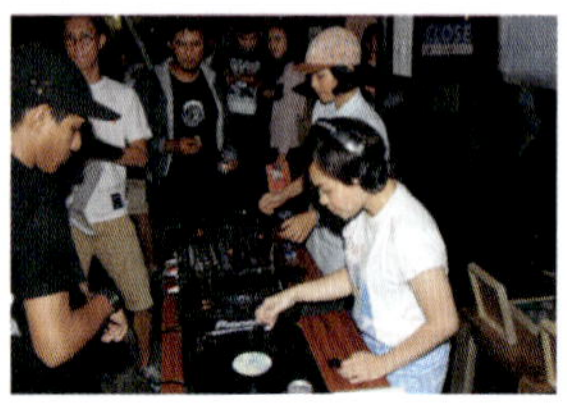

781

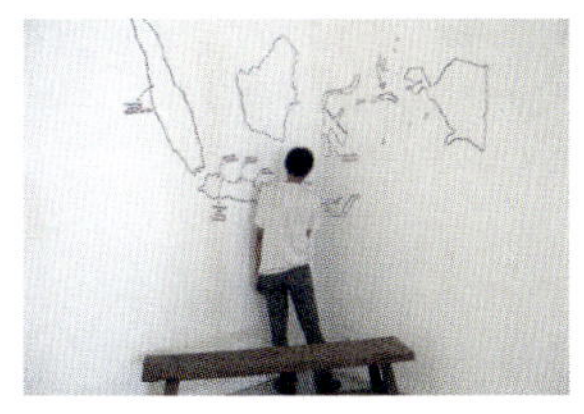

782

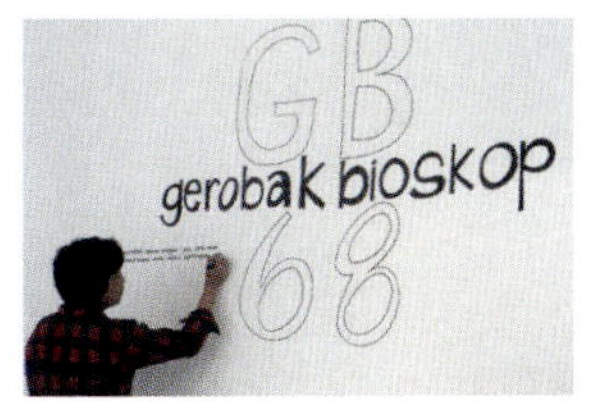

783

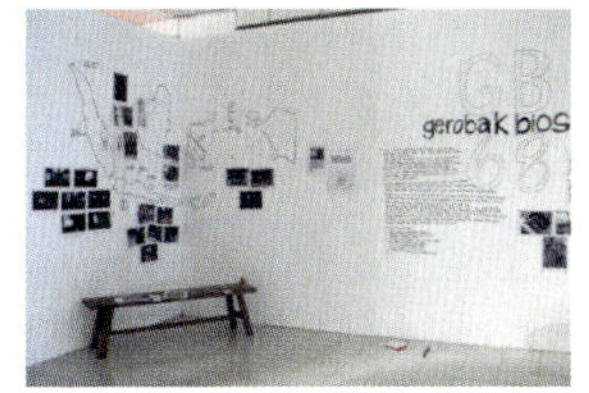

784

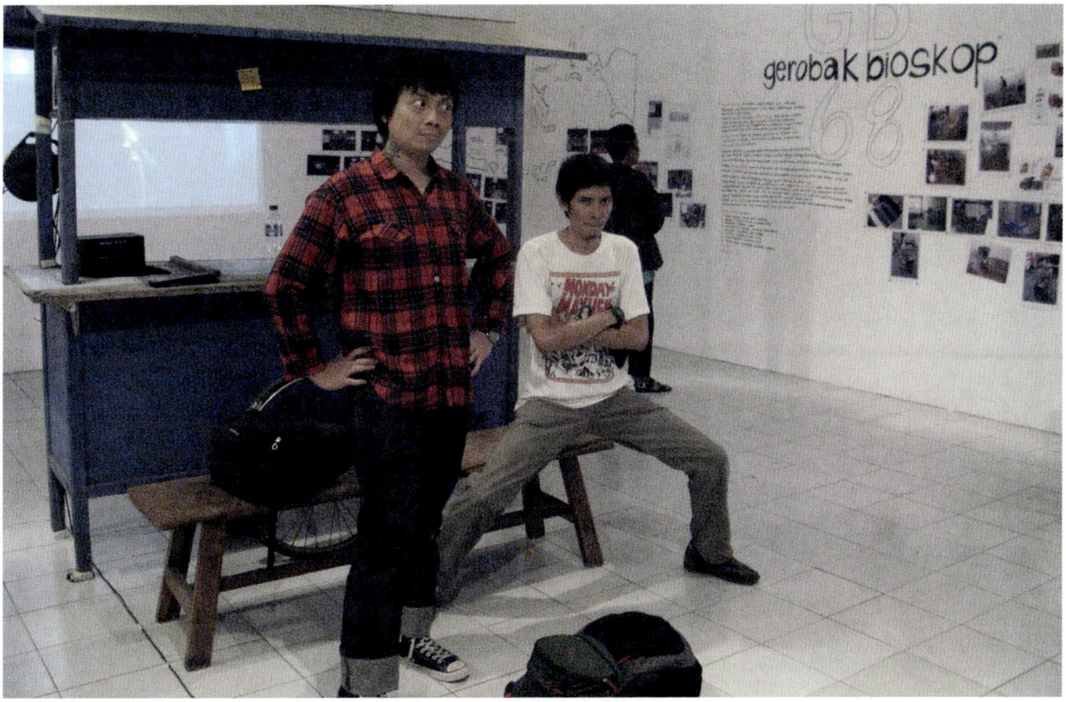

785

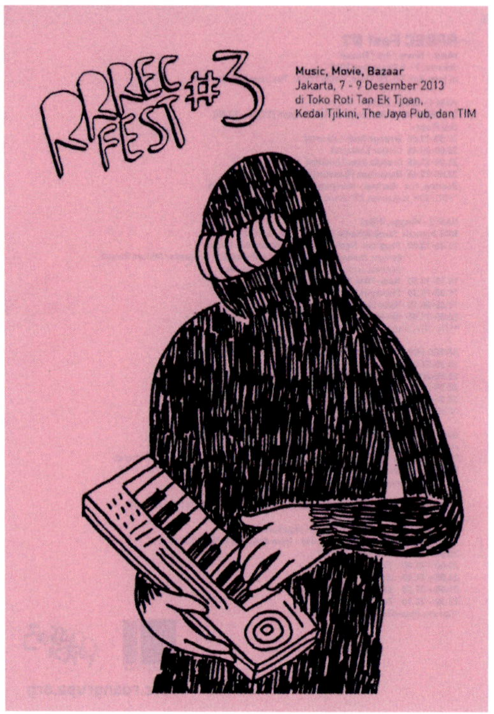

786

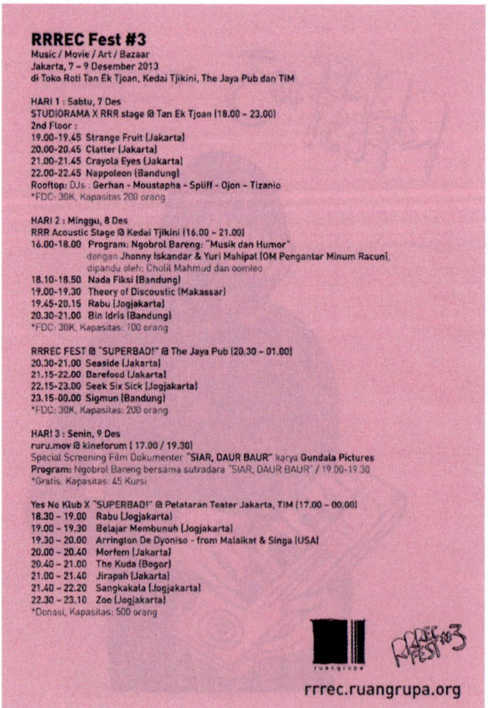

RRREC Fest #3
Music / Movie / Art / Bazaar
Jakarta, 7 – 9 Desember 2013
di Toko Roti Tan Ek Tjoan, Kedai Tjikini, The Jaya Pub dan TIM

HARI 1 : Sabtu, 7 Des
STUDIORAMA X RRR stage @ Tan Ek Tjoan (18.00 – 23.00)
2nd Floor :
19.00-19.45 Strange Fruit (Jakarta)
20.00-20.45 Clatter (Jakarta)
21.00-21.45 Crayola Eyes (Jakarta)
22.00-22.45 Nappoleon (Bandung)
Rooftop: DJs : Gerhan - Moustapha - Spliff - Ojon – Tizanio
*FDC: 30K, Kapasitas 200 orang

HARI 2 : Minggu, 8 Des
RRR Acoustic Stage @ Kedai Tjikini (16.00 – 21.00)
16.00-18.00 Program: Ngobrol Bareng: "Musik dan Humor"
dengan Jhonny Iskandar & Yuri Mahipal (OM Pengantar Minum Racun),
dipandu oleh: Cholil Mahmud dan oomleo
18.10-18.50 Nada Fiksi (Bandung)
19.00-19.30 Theory of Discoustic (Makassar)
19.45-20.15 Rabu (Jogjakarta)
20.30-21.00 Bin Idris (Bandung)
*FDC: 30K, Kapasitas: 100 orang

RRREC FEST @ "SUPERBAD!" @ The Jaya Pub (20.30 – 01.00)
20.30-21.00 Seaside (Jakarta)
21.15-22.00 Barefood (Jakarta)
22.15-23.00 Seek Six Sick (Jogjakarta)
23.15-00.00 Sigmun (Bandung)
*FDC: 30K, Kapasitas: 200 orang

HARI 3 : Senin, 9 Des
ruru.mov @ kineforum (17.00 / 19.30)
Special Screening Film Dokumenter "SIAR, DAUR BAUR" karya Gundala Pictures
Program: Ngobrol Bareng bersama sutradara "SIAR, DAUR BAUR" / 19.00-19.30
*Gratis, Kapasitas: 45 Kursi

Yes No Klub X "SUPERBAD!" @ Pelataran Teater Jakarta, TIM (17.00 – 00.00)
18.30 – 19.00 Rabu (Jogjakarta)
19.00 – 19.30 Belajar Membunuh (Jogjakarta)
19.30 – 20.00 Arrington De Dyoniso - from Malaikat & Singa (USA)
20.00 – 20.40 Morfem (Jakarta)
20.40 – 21.00 The Kuda (Bogor)
21.00 – 21.40 Jirapah (Jakarta)
21.40 – 22.20 Sangkakala (Jogjakarta)
22.30 – 23.10 Zoo (Jogjakarta)
*Donasi, Kapasitas: 500 orang

ruangrupa
RRREC FEST #3
rrrec.ruangrupa.org

787

'In Delta Flux', RURU Gallery, 19–25 December 2013

with Guido van de Werve, Melanie Bonajo, Jeroen Eisinga, Erik Wesselo, Jacobine van Hellemond, Henk Otte, Jan Hoek and Tim Leyendekker; curated by Arjon Dunnewind

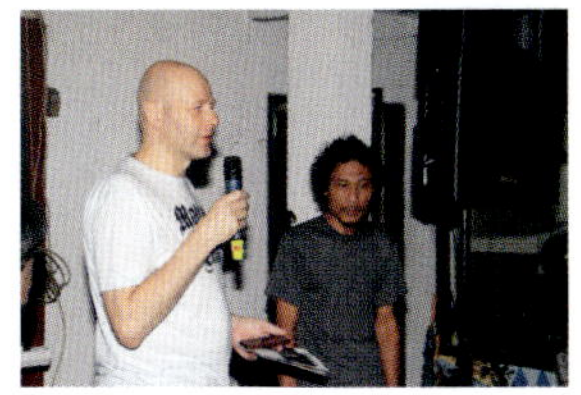

788

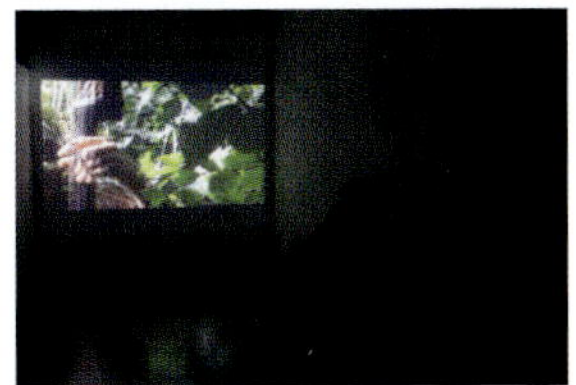

789

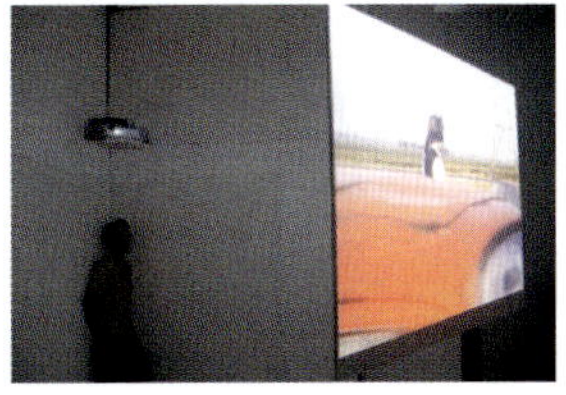

790

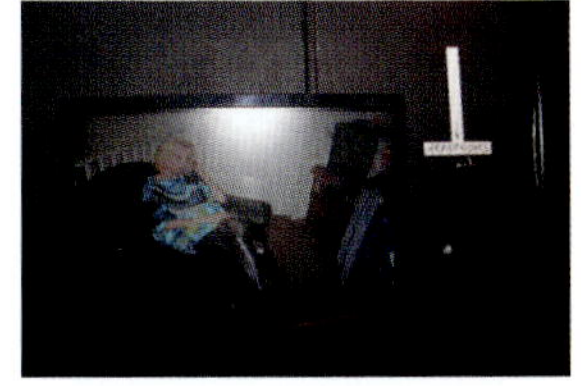

791

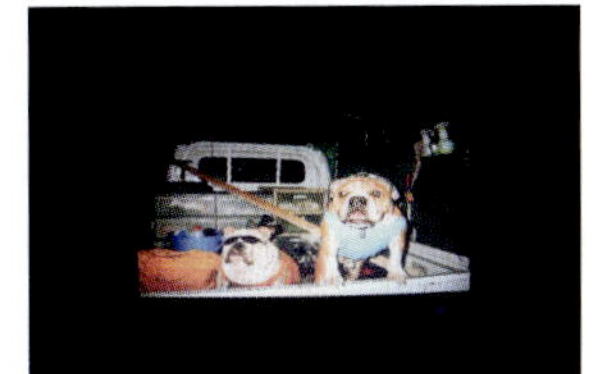

792

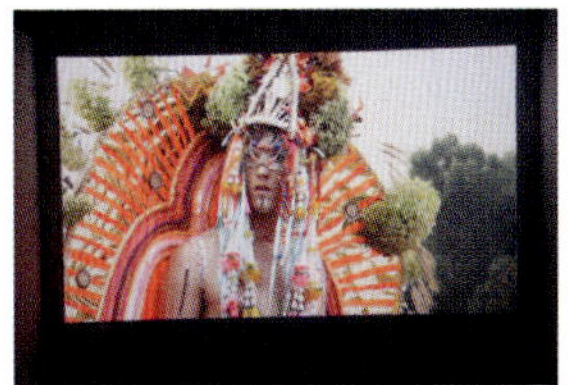

793

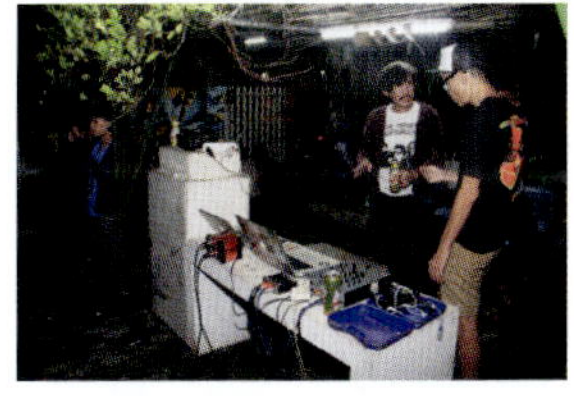

794

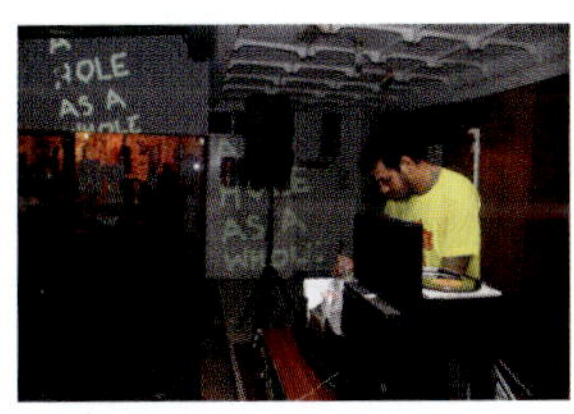

795

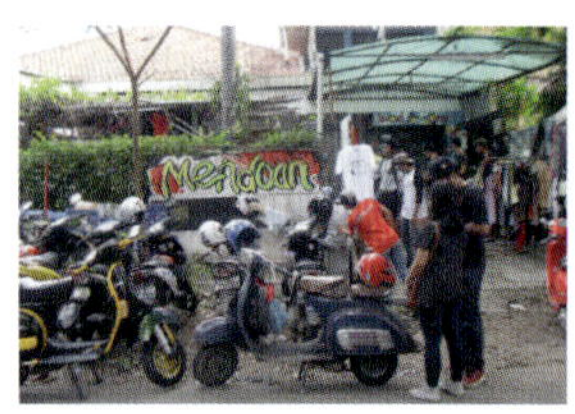

796

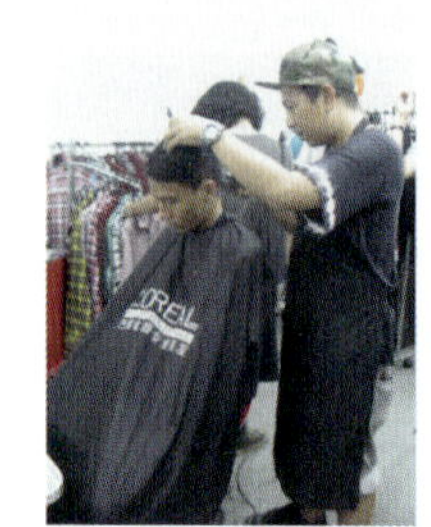

797

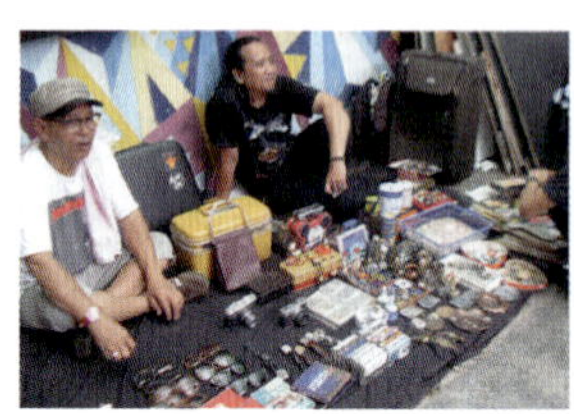

798

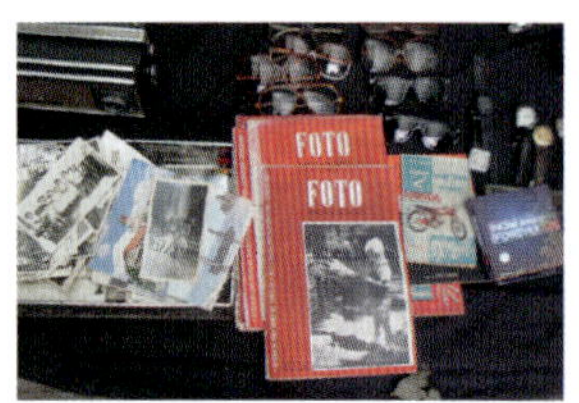

799

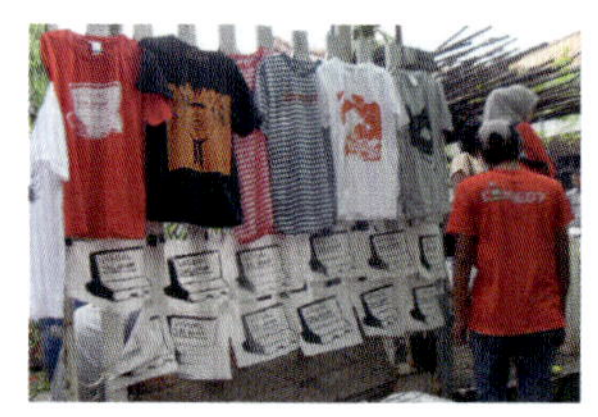

800

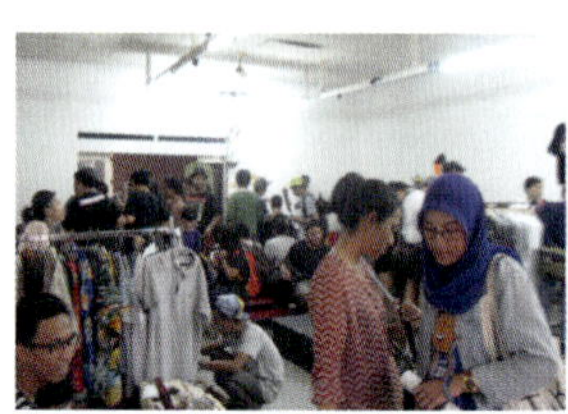

801

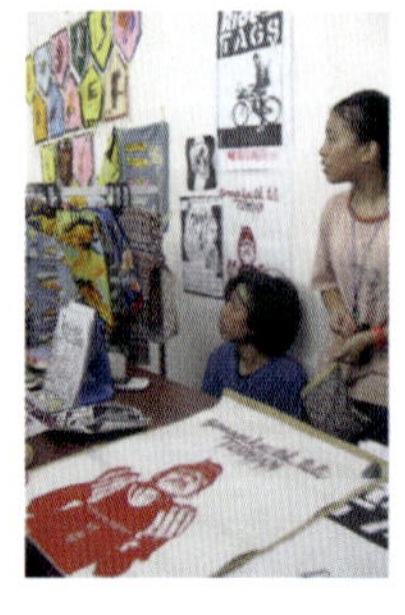

802

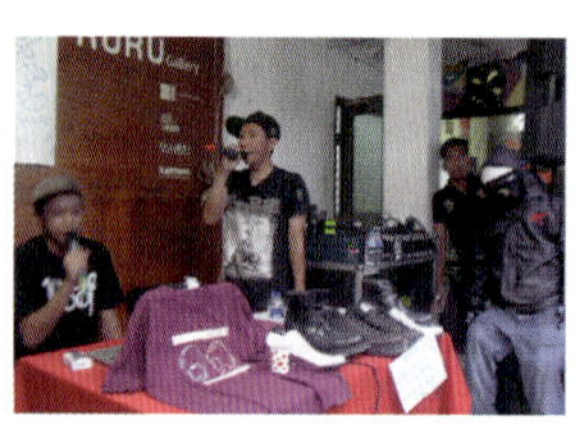

803

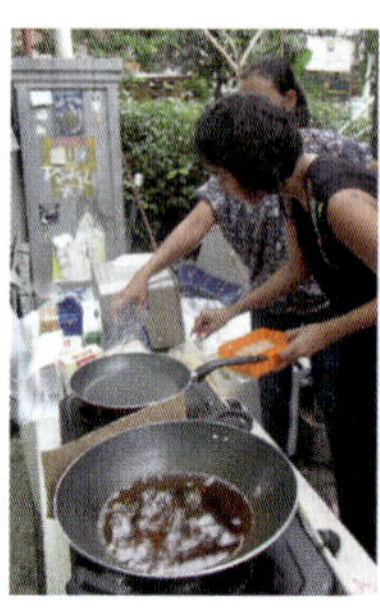

804

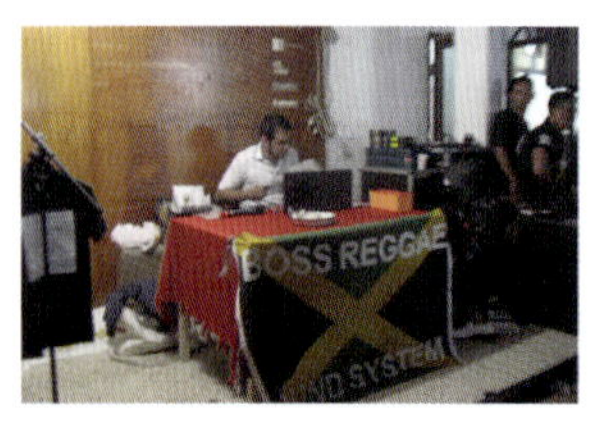

805

806

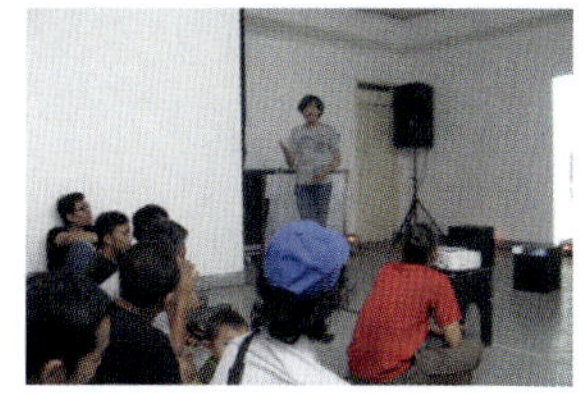

807

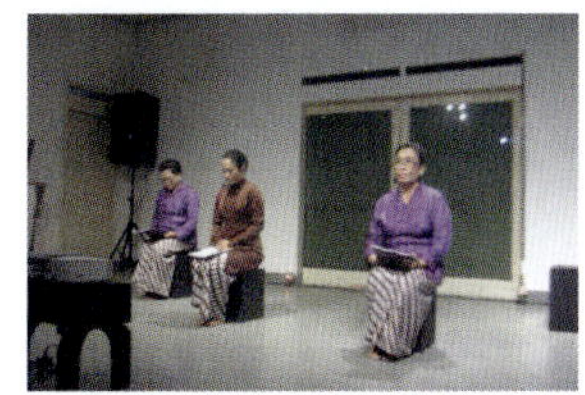

808

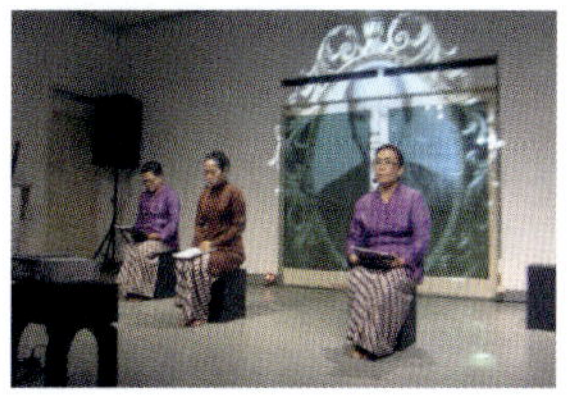

809

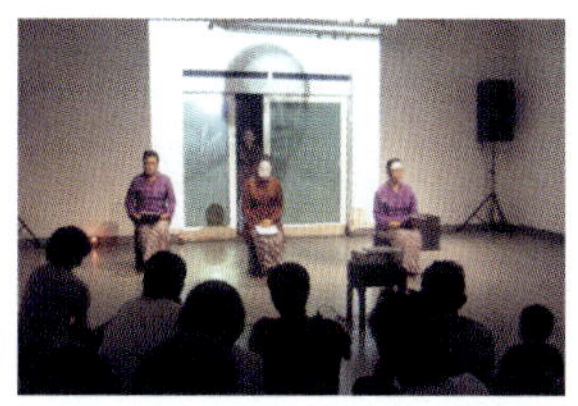

810

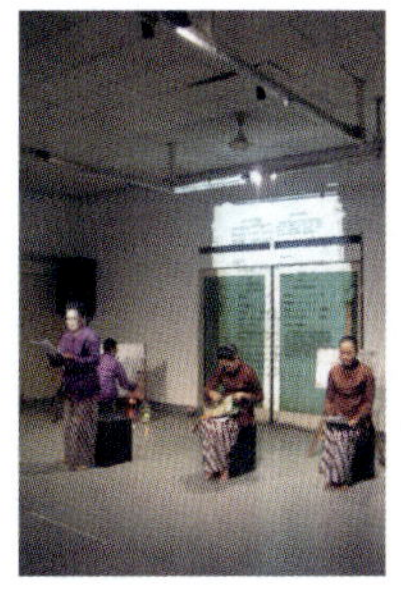

811

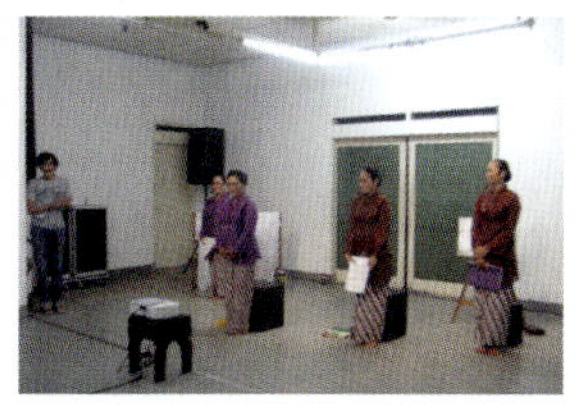

812

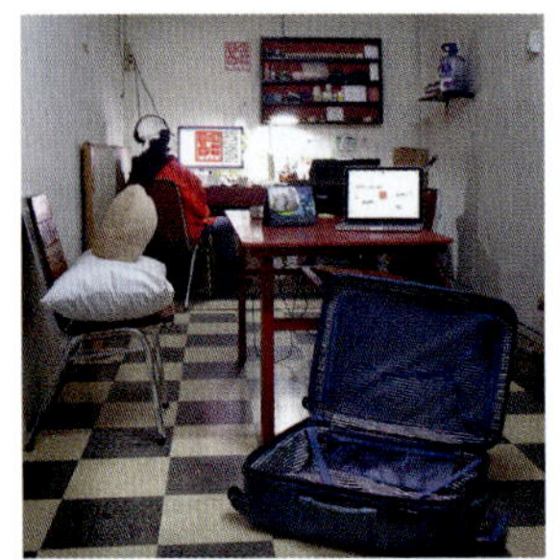

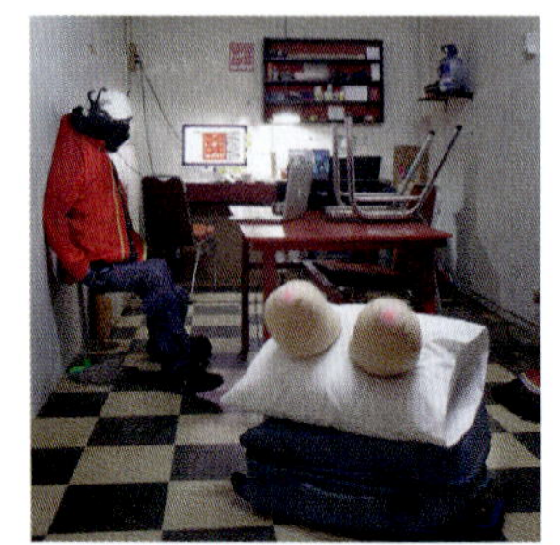

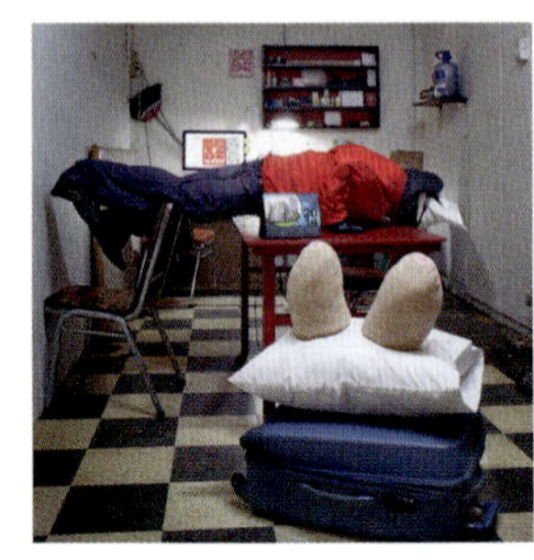

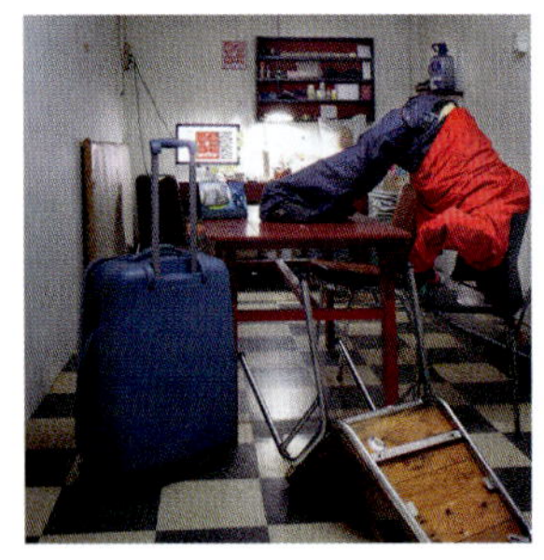

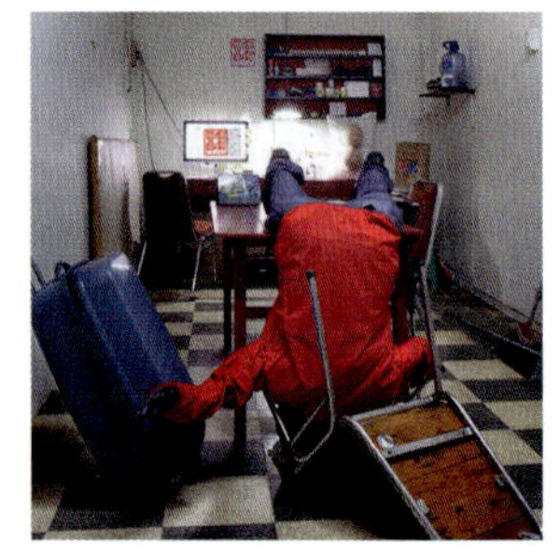

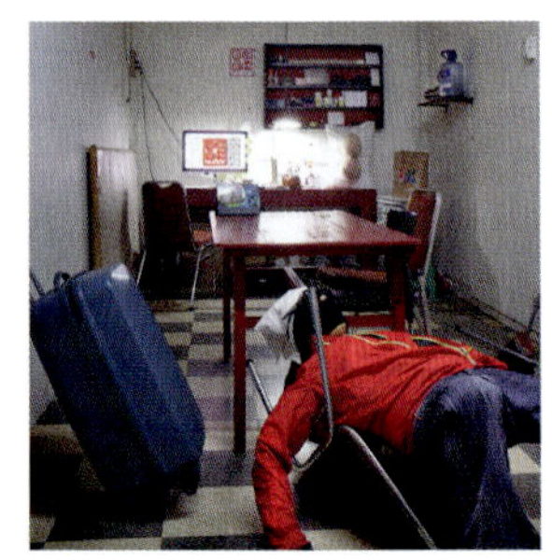

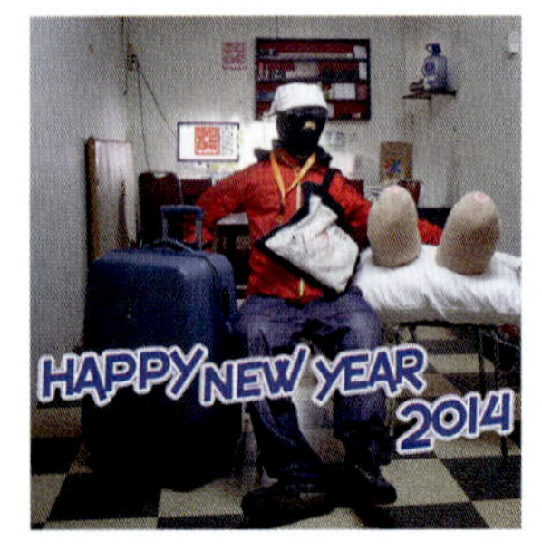

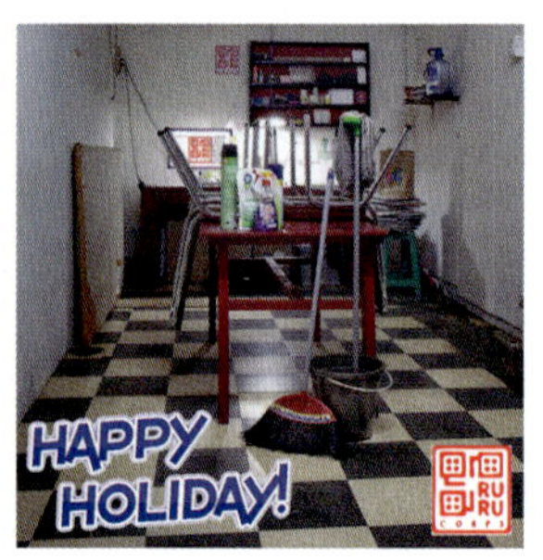

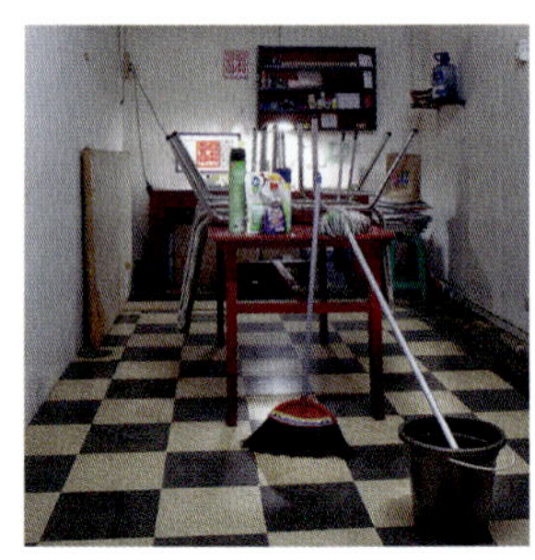

www.rurucorps.com

Regardless of gender, I think everyone has both their masculine and feminine energy. Sometimes, you know, we have some, let's say, cis male members, but they have very feminine ways of thinking, feminine ways of structure. And then sometimes others tease me like 'you behave like a guy', in a hang out. And I think in collective settings, there's always been tensions; how can we balance that feminine and masculine energy as a group? Because there can be moments where we need to become more empathetic and 'motherly'. Like, we'd feel too bad to laugh at this member for messing things up and need to protect their feelings. But sometimes you have to be practical and cold, like, 'we have to get this done'. No matter what they are going through. And for me, let's say, especially with the older generation, sometimes I see them like an uncle, a kind of funky eccentric uncle... Or like the brother who always annoys, or you have to take care of. That familial, that kinship perspective – but not to romanticise that either, since we also have to work together in a professional sense. There are moments where you have to realise, you are my friends, regardless of our genders and age; like, I really hate you for thinking differently than me, but I trust that you will understand my position, and then we will find a time for us to talk about it... It all goes back again to the idea of being friends.

Gesyada Siregar

Now I feel the best way to learn about ruru's collective practice is by doing something or working with them. Although there's also a limit to this because in a working relation, our way of speaking is around coordination and practicalities. But I really enjoy speaking with ruru members who are part of the administration and practically organising things – we can talk more clearly about our shared challenges and why we do what we do.

Syafiatudina

If you have a foreign funder, they always ask in the end for a report about gender equality and so on. But in practice it's a bit challenging and difficult. Because in Indonesia we have a different culture, and patriarchy still. It's still difficult to have more female roles in art collectives. Not everyone can work in such a loose way, for example. Female friends want to have more of a structure – I work from this time to this time – whereas my male friends want to hang out until morning, and so on. ... There's also the stereotype, that most art managers are women, and males are more in the artistic work. But what I feel in ruangrupa is that we push ourselves to always do what we want; and the structure is a way to make this easier. In the structure, I'm a manager, but in real life it's not only me - actually farid also does the function of manager, sometimes Ameng also does. And we are always learning from each other as well.

Ajeng Nurul Aini

an evening dedicated to the memory of late ruru member Ibnu Rizal A (1988–2014)

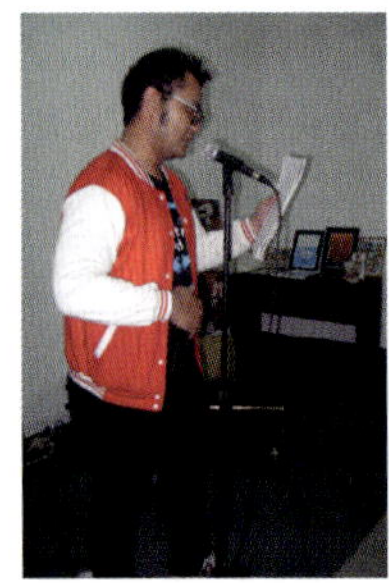

814

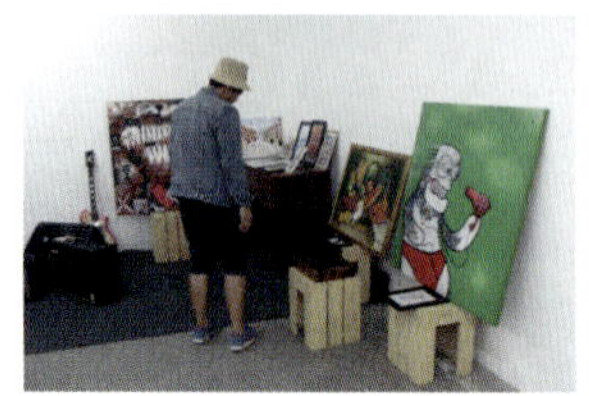

815

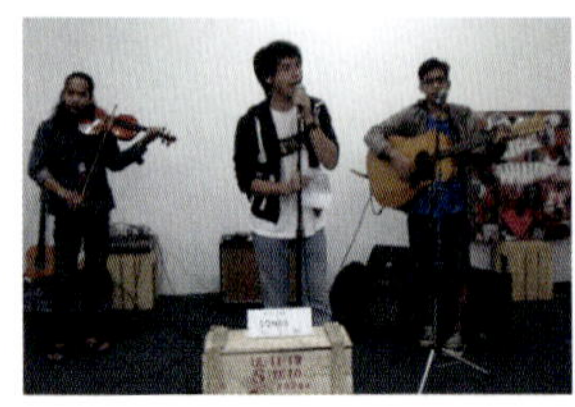

816

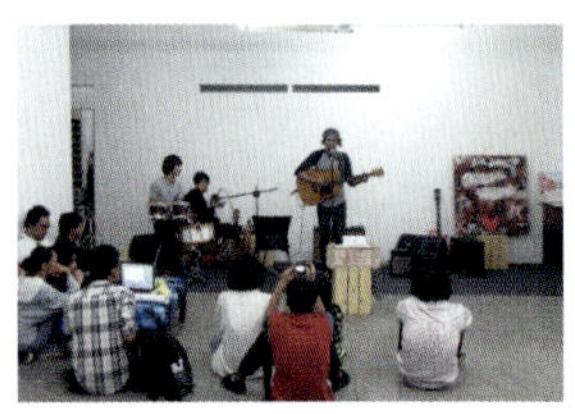

817

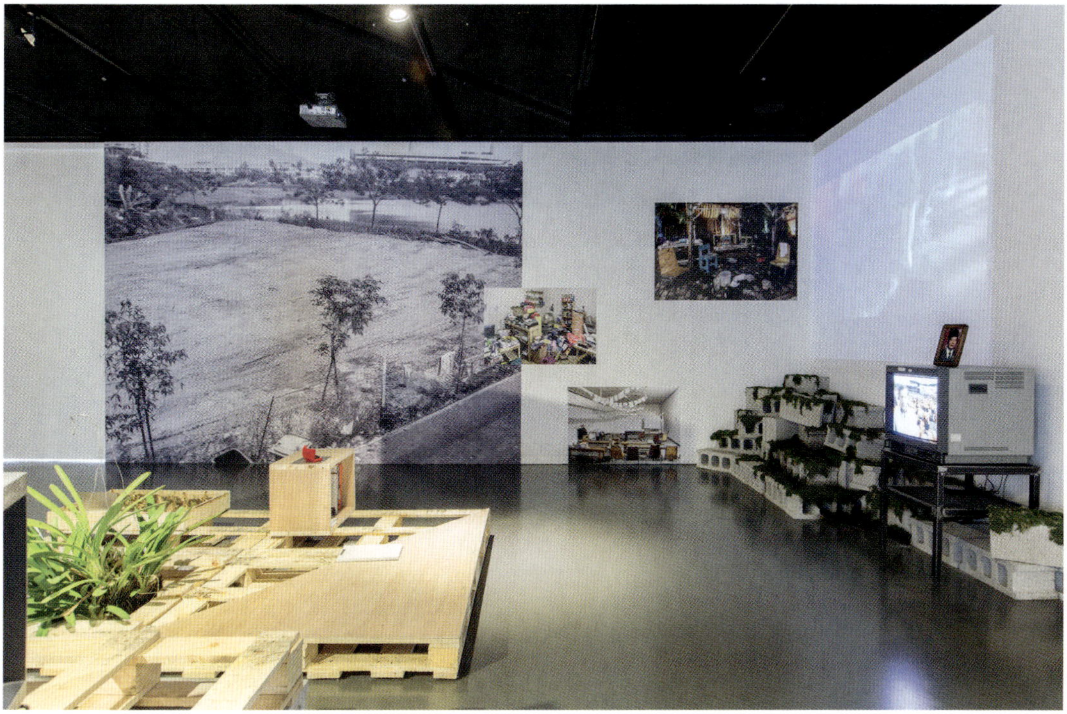

Participation in ‘The Growing Manual’, Seoul Museum of Art, Seoul, Korea, 18 March – 20 April 2014

818

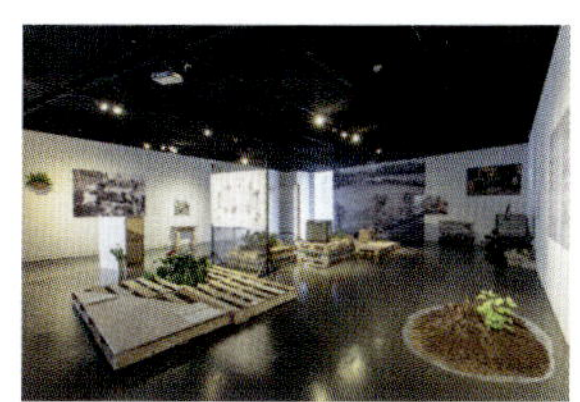

819

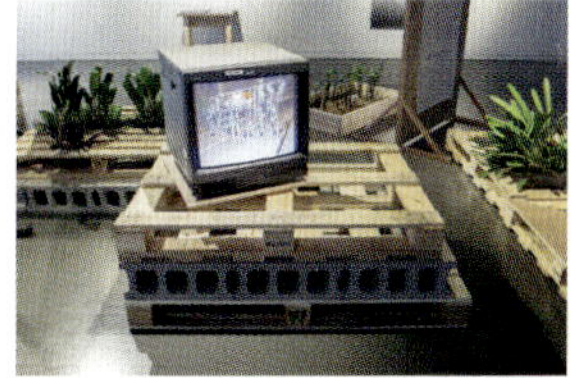

820

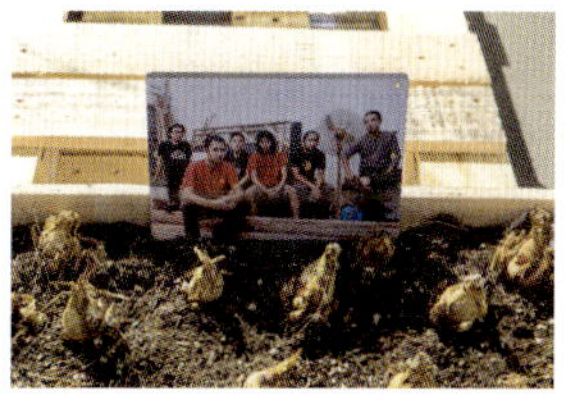

821

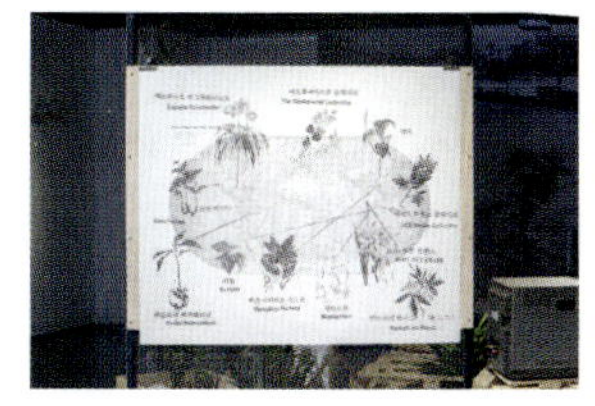

822

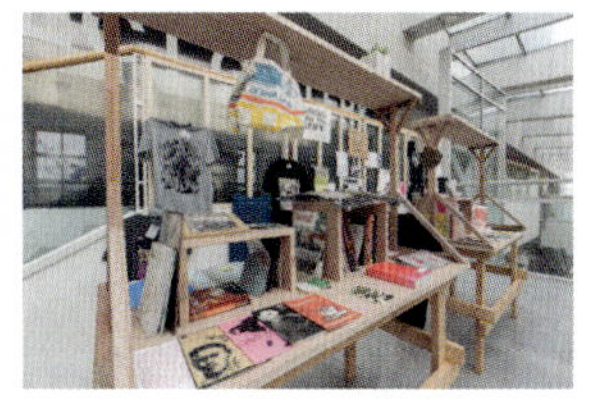

823

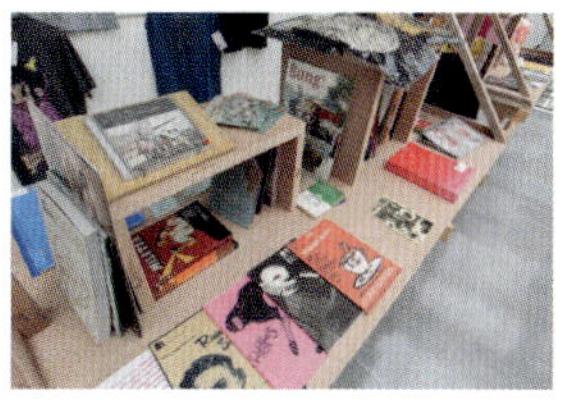

824

In a condition of non-physical emergency/force majeur, such as economic crisis, no funding, no money, bankruptcy, for the worst, can be back to the most basic infrastructure in order to survive [see the Infrastructure section: Models & Programs/No Budget] or just forget about art, if you only carry yourself to survive.

'Swatata', RURU Gallery, 24 April – 7 May 2014

with Arie Syarifudin, Ismal Muntaha and Muhammad Fatchurofi; curated by Mitha Budhyarto

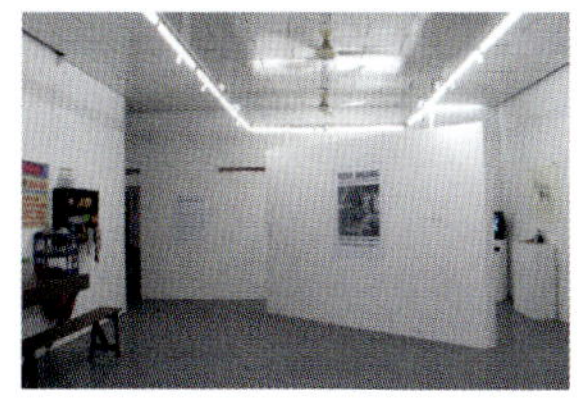

825

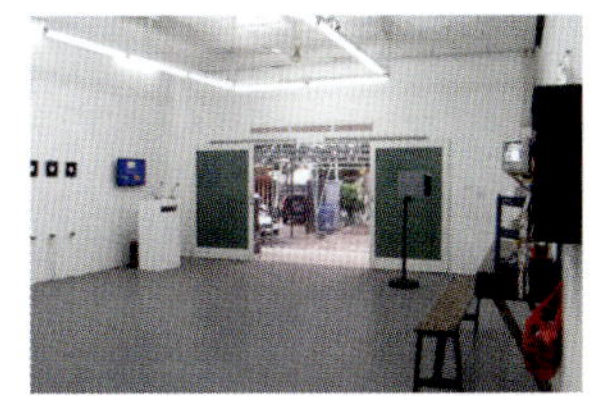

826

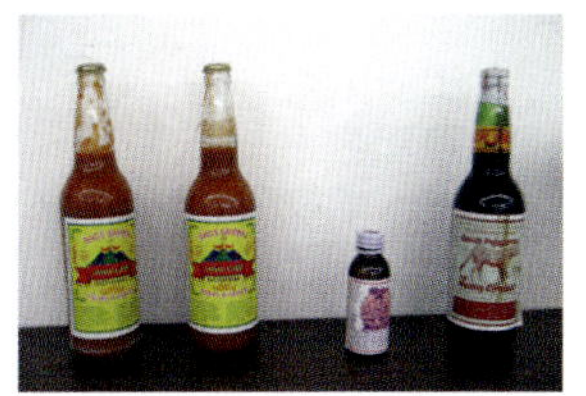

827

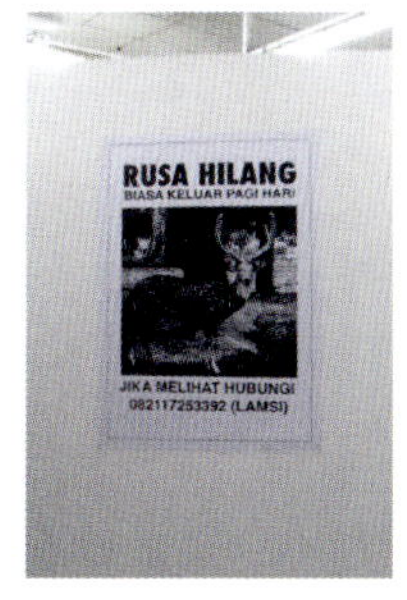

828

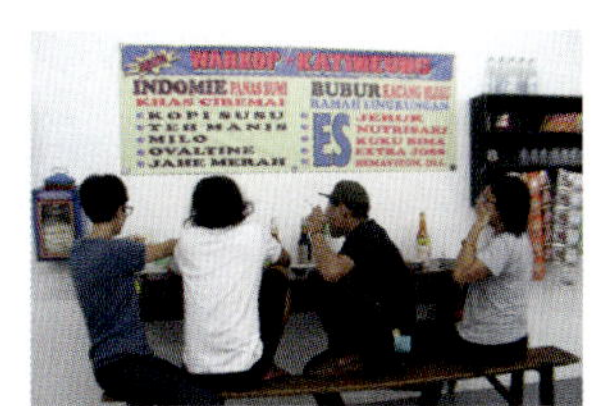

829

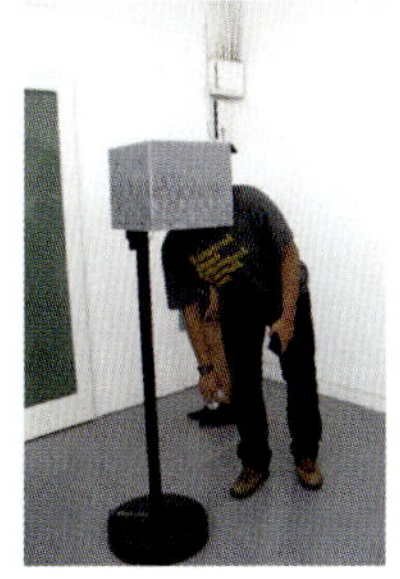

830

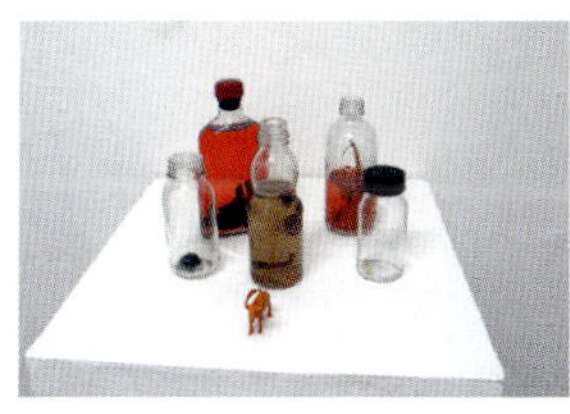

831

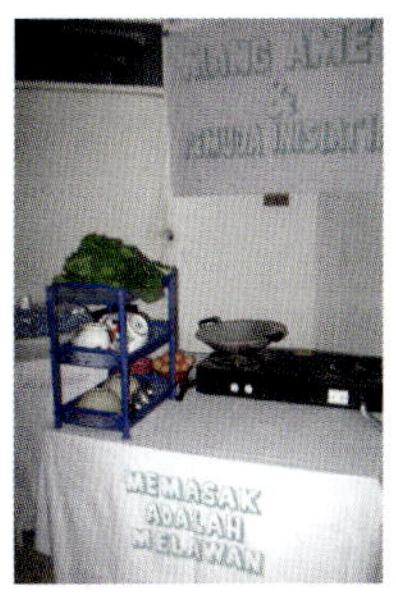

832

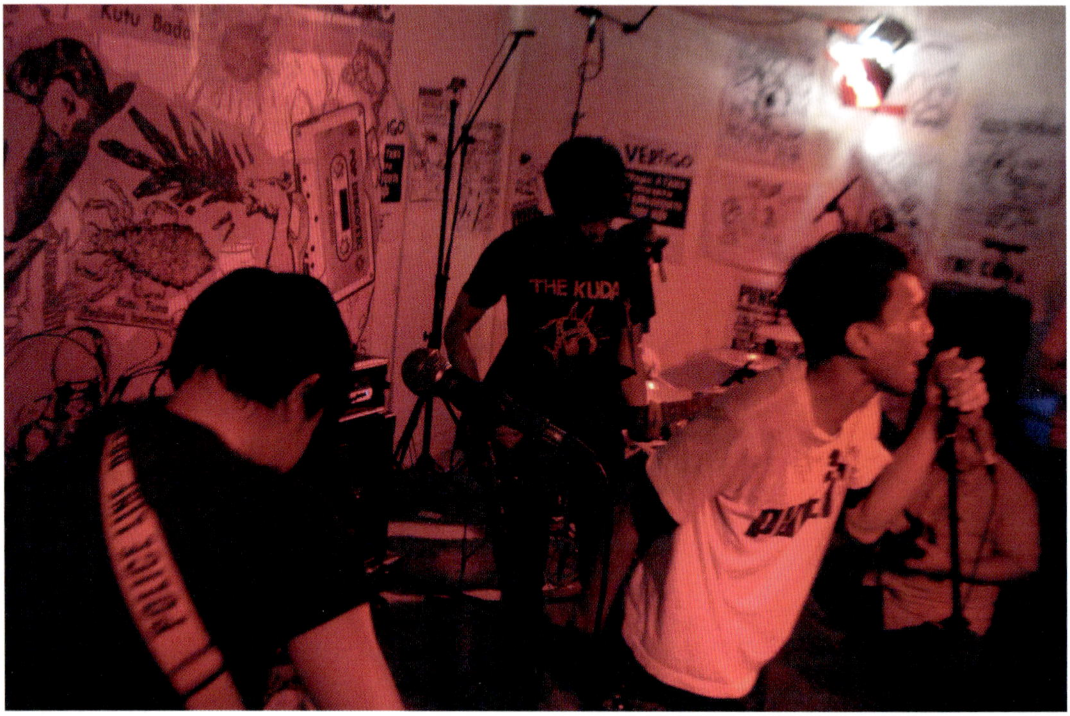

833

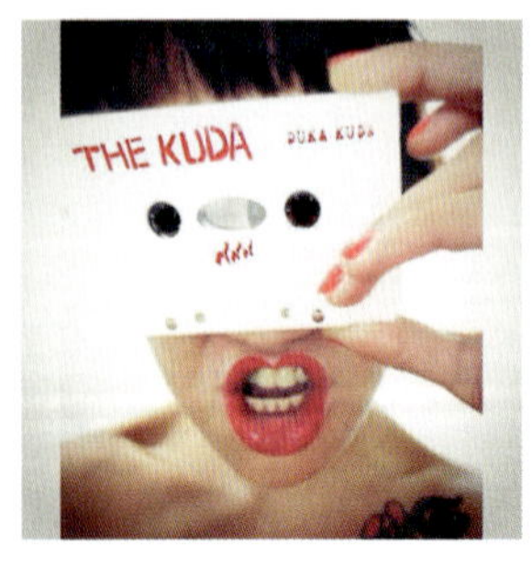

834

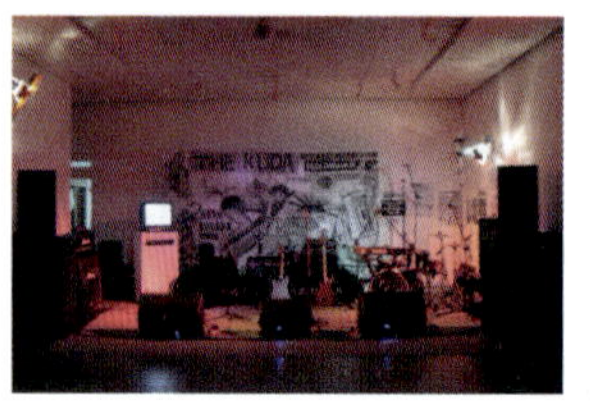

835

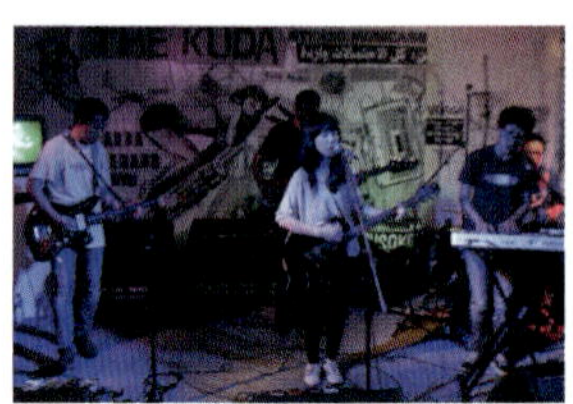

836

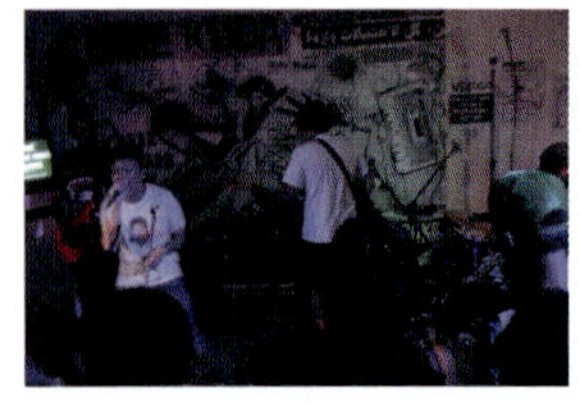

837

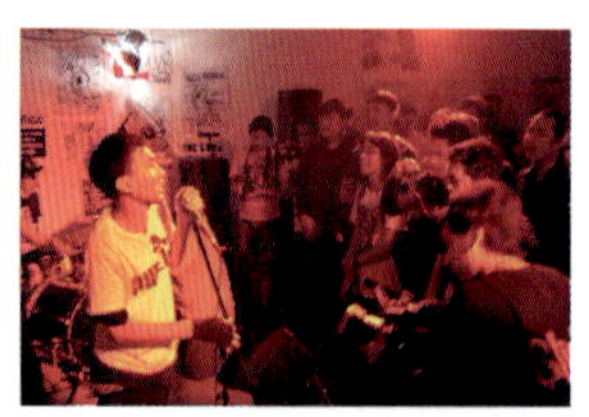

838

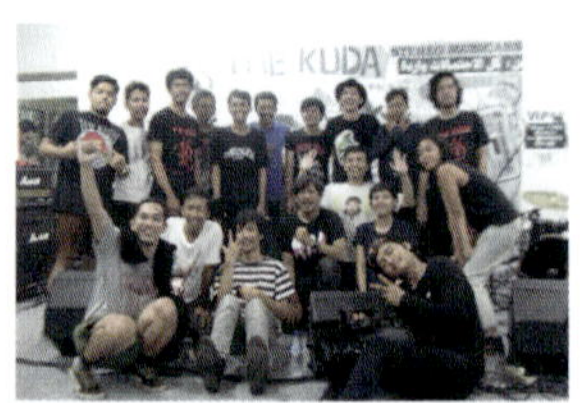

839

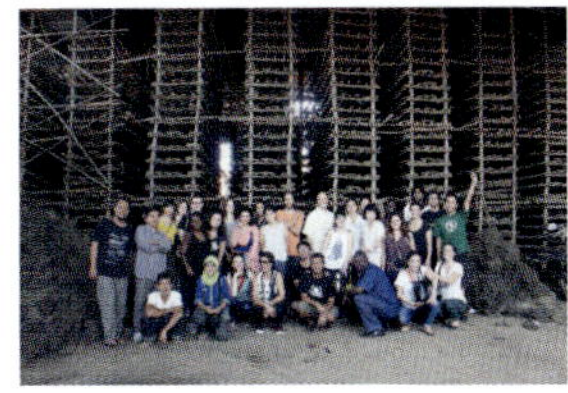

840

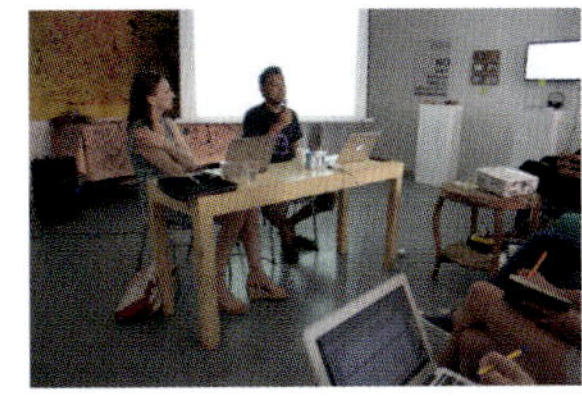

841

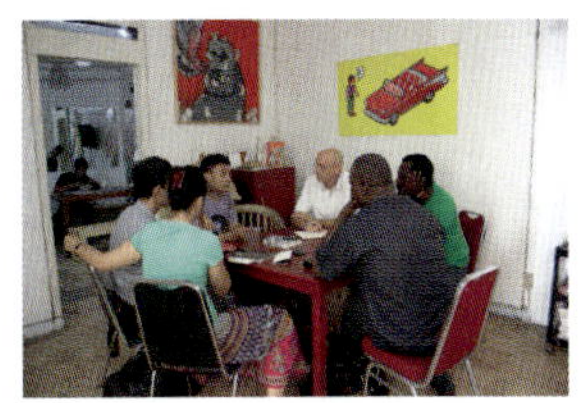

842

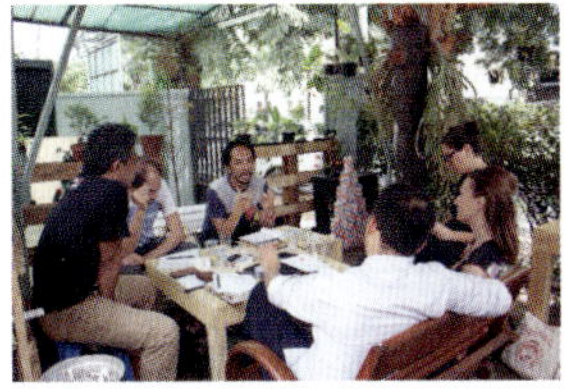

843

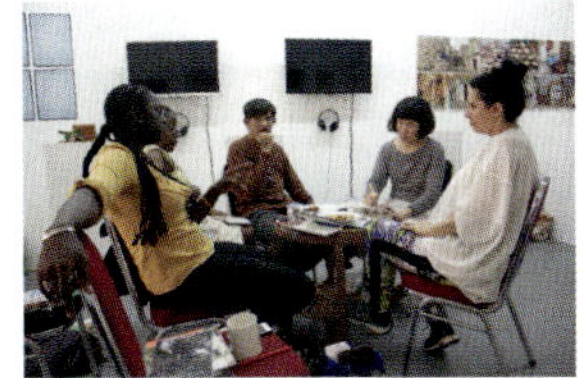

844

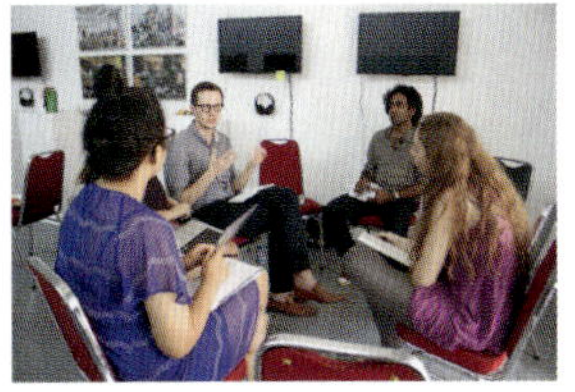

845

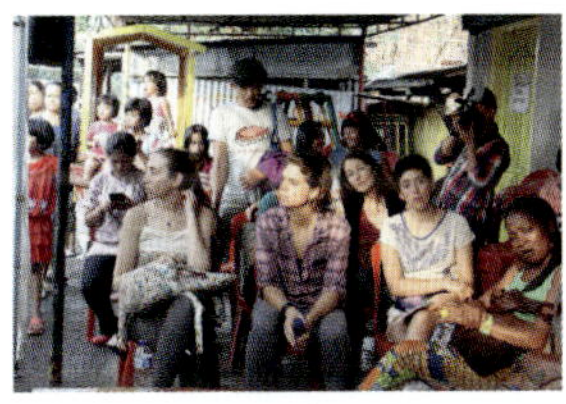

846

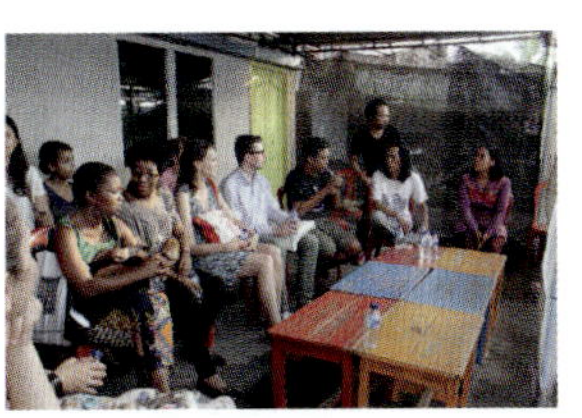

847

ruangrupa got seed money from RAIN (Rijksakademie Artist Initiatives Network). Very early on, Rijksakademie had a strategy to make it possible for artists from Mali, Indonesia etc, to be residents, but often these artists stayed in Amsterdam or Europe after the residency because of resources – you know, the question of resources is a politics for artist groups like ruru. So RAIN supported residents to start something back in their home countries. It was interesting how the initial network of RAIN became much bigger and fuelled the Arts Collaboratory international network that was then brought to documenta [in 2022]. It's astonishing how many people from these initial networks are still exchanging and travelling to each other after these earlier initiatives, often supported by Prince Claus funds, Stichting DOEN etc, to create a south-south connection.

Philippe Pirotte

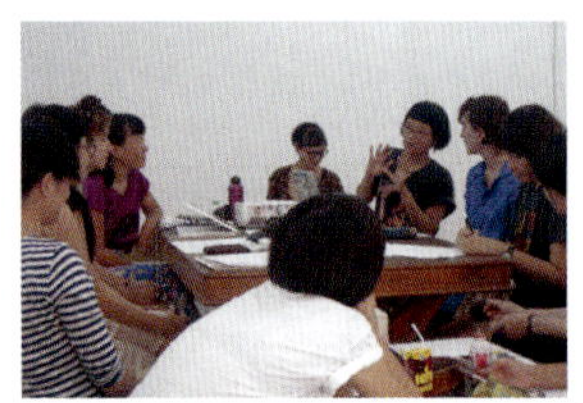
848

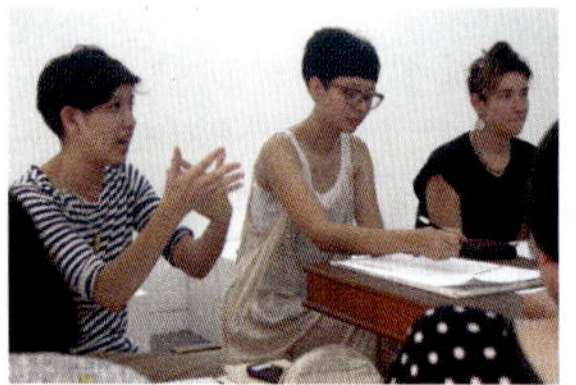
849

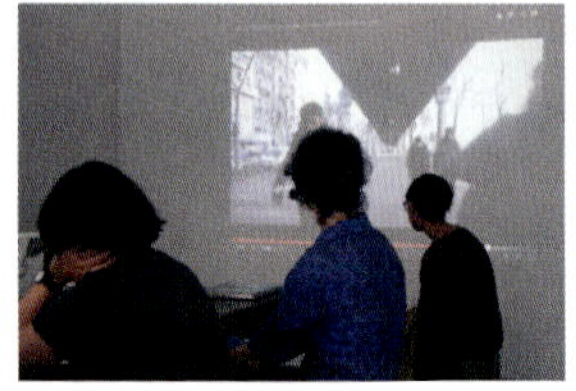
850

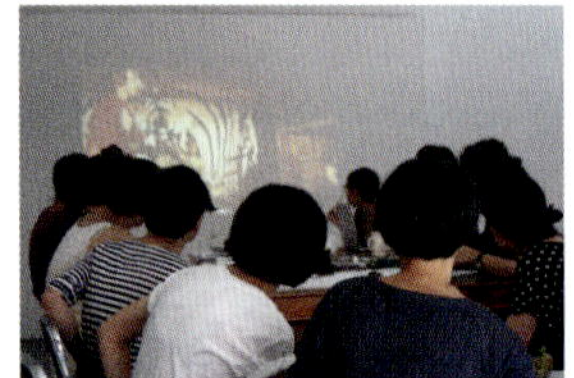
851

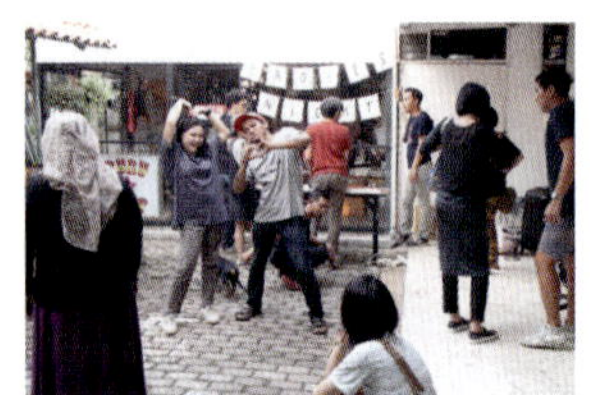
852

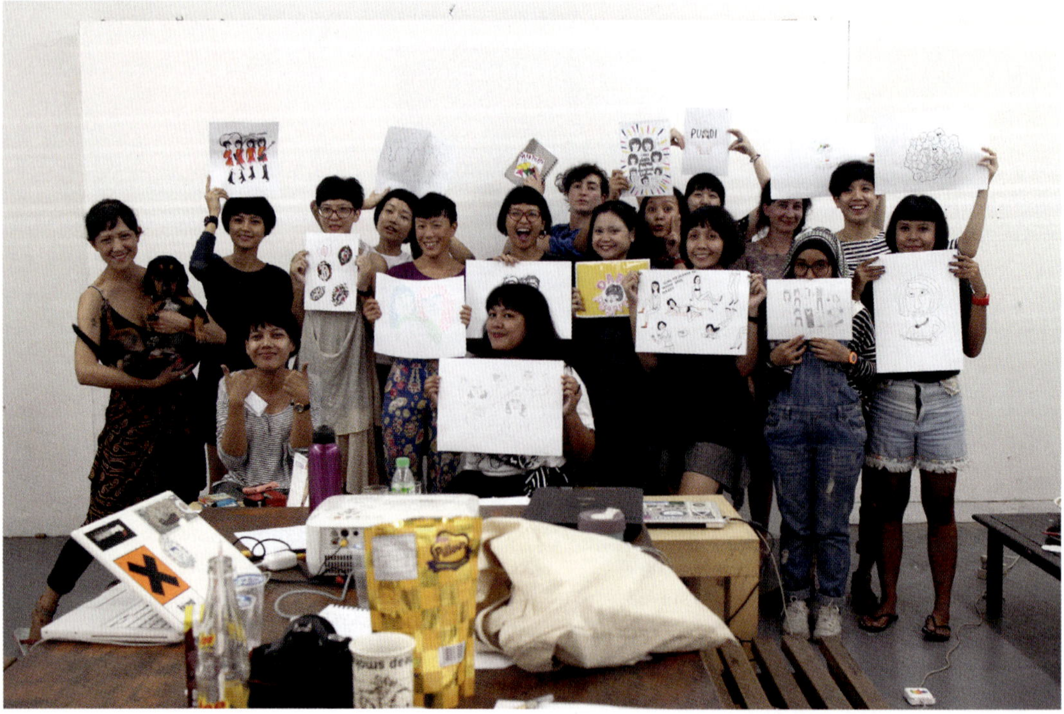

853

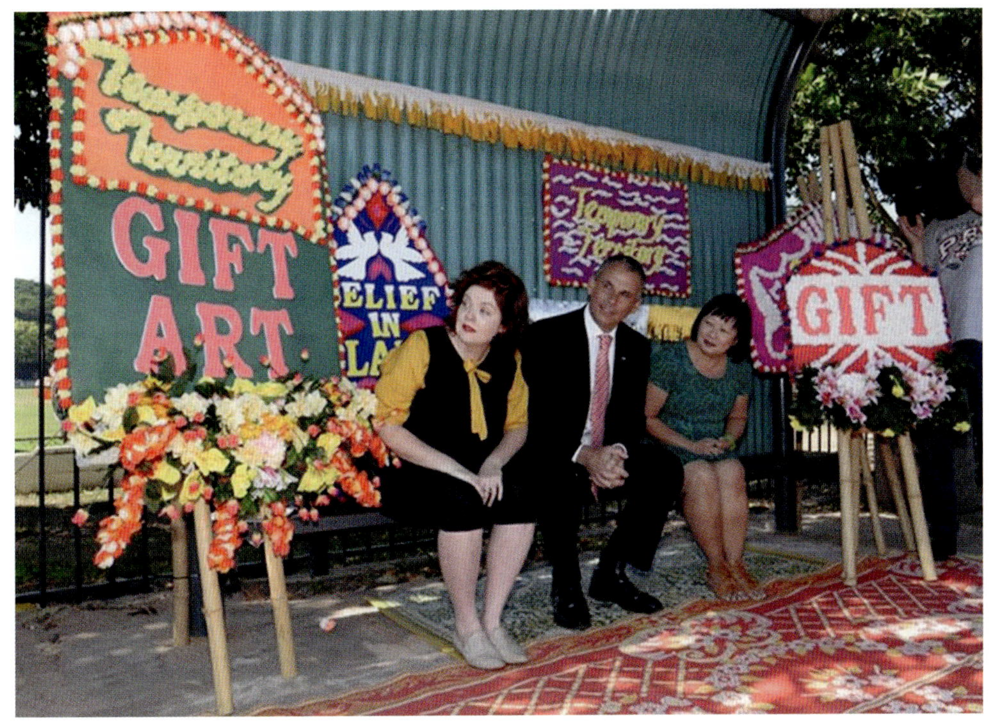

854

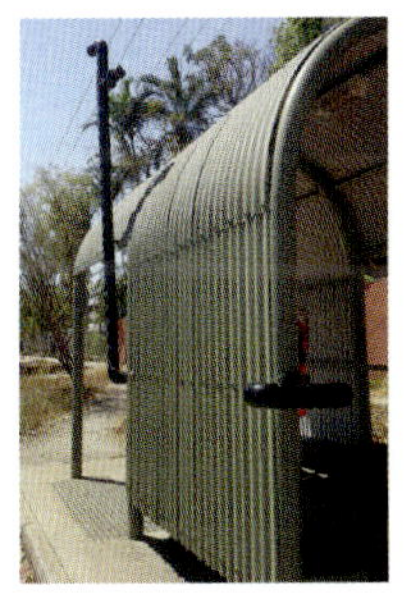

855

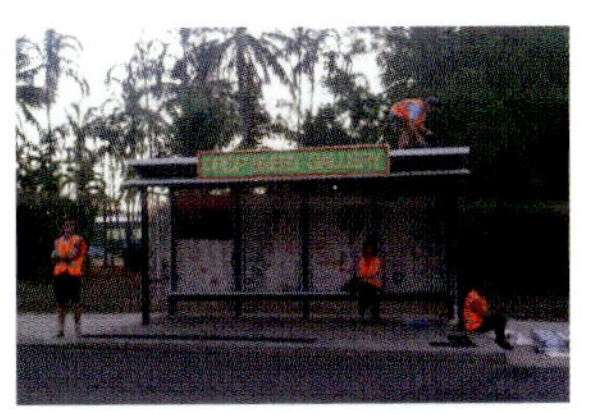

856

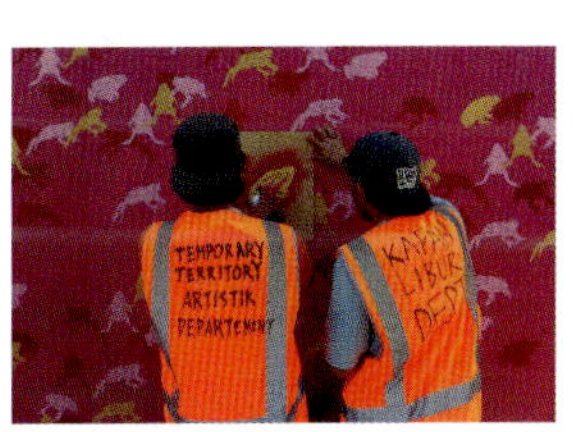

857

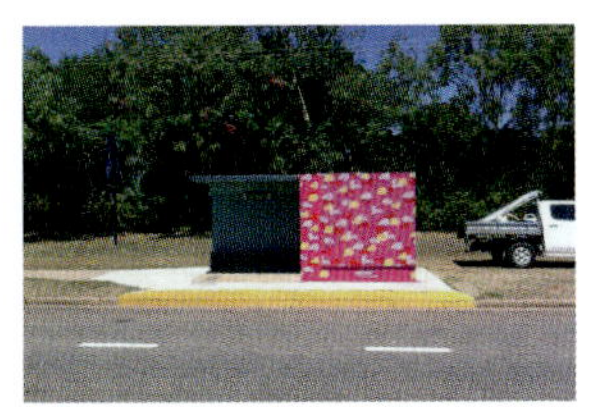

858

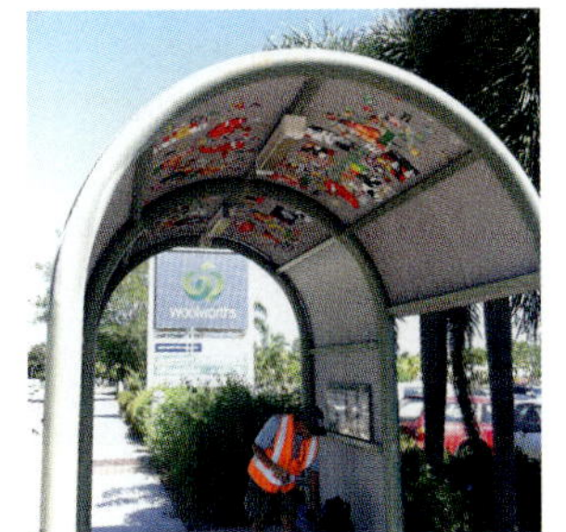

859

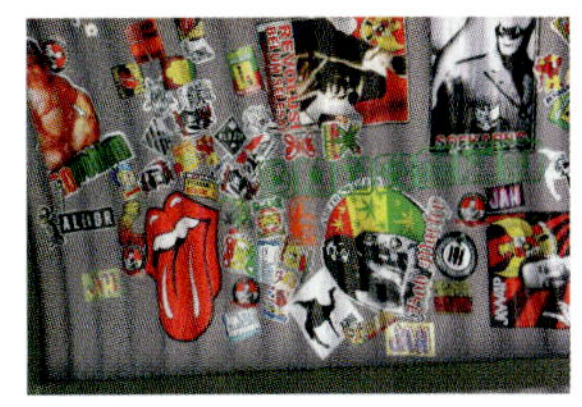

860

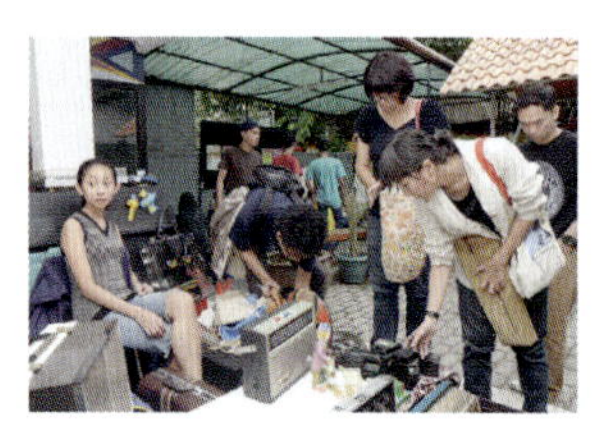
861

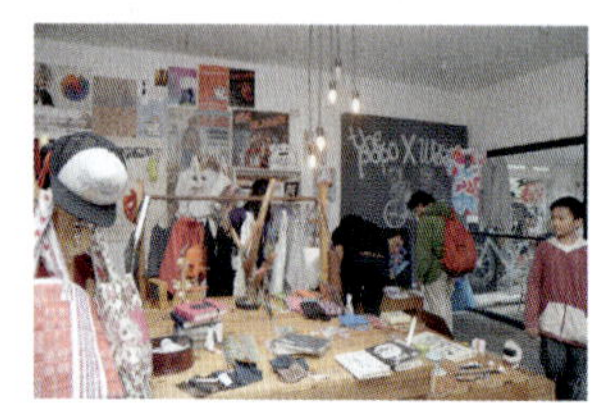
862

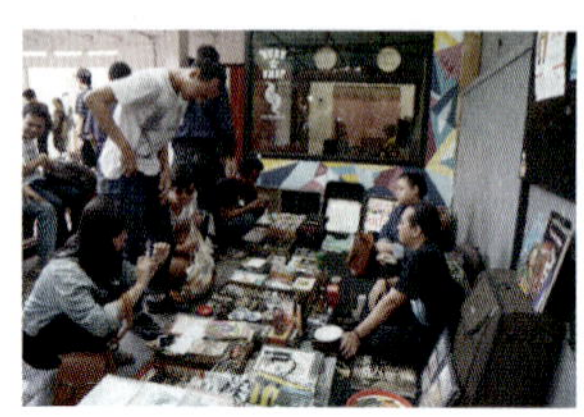
863

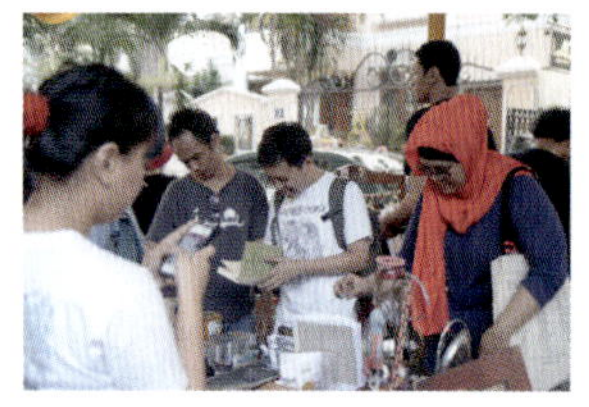
864

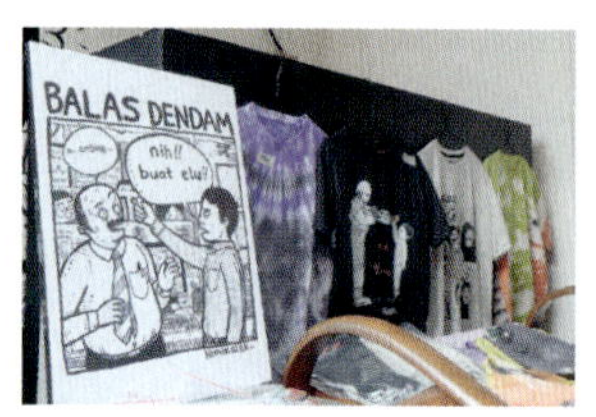

865

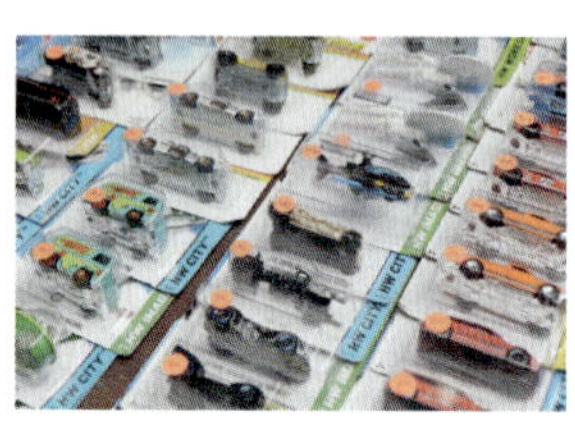
866

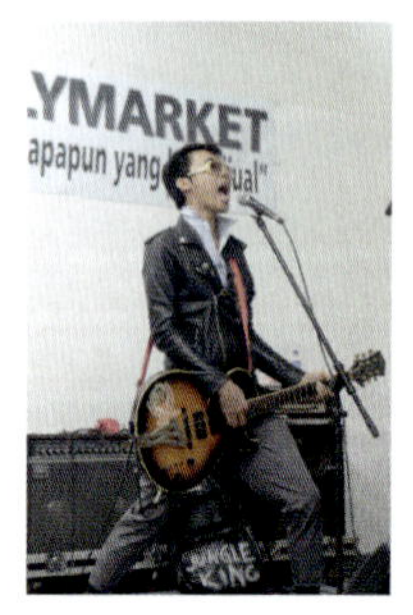
867

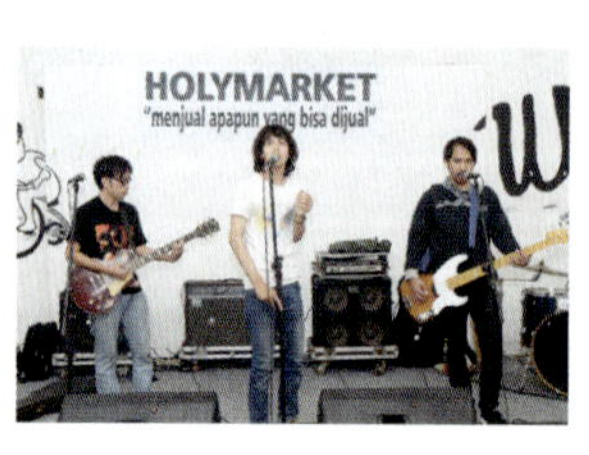

868

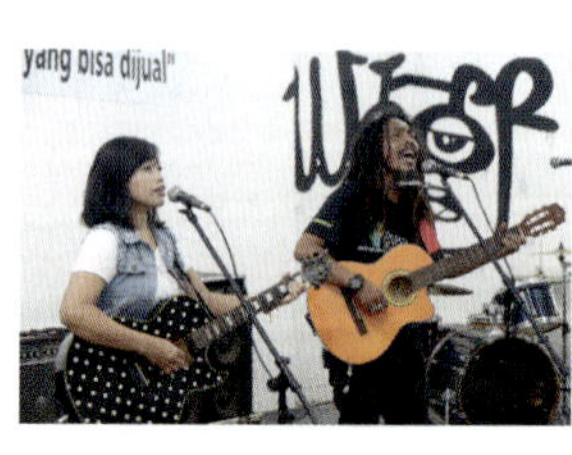

869

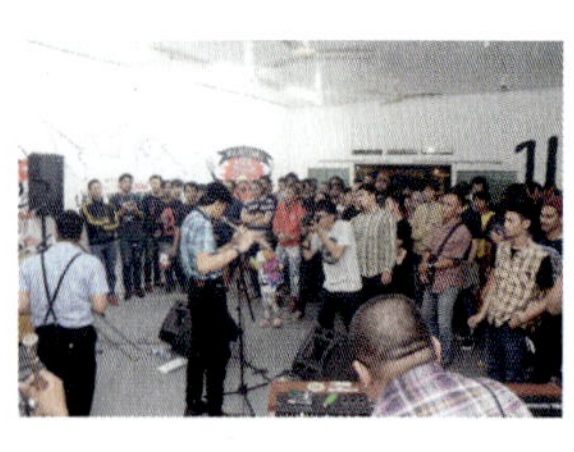
870

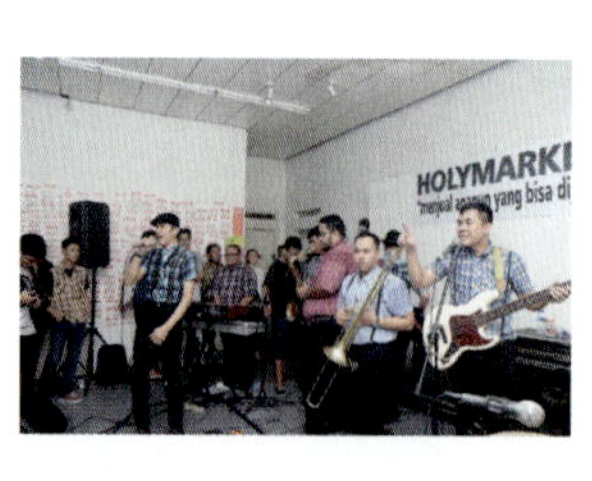
871

RRREC FEST #4, Tanakita Camping Ground, Sukabumi, 31 October – 2 November 2014 281

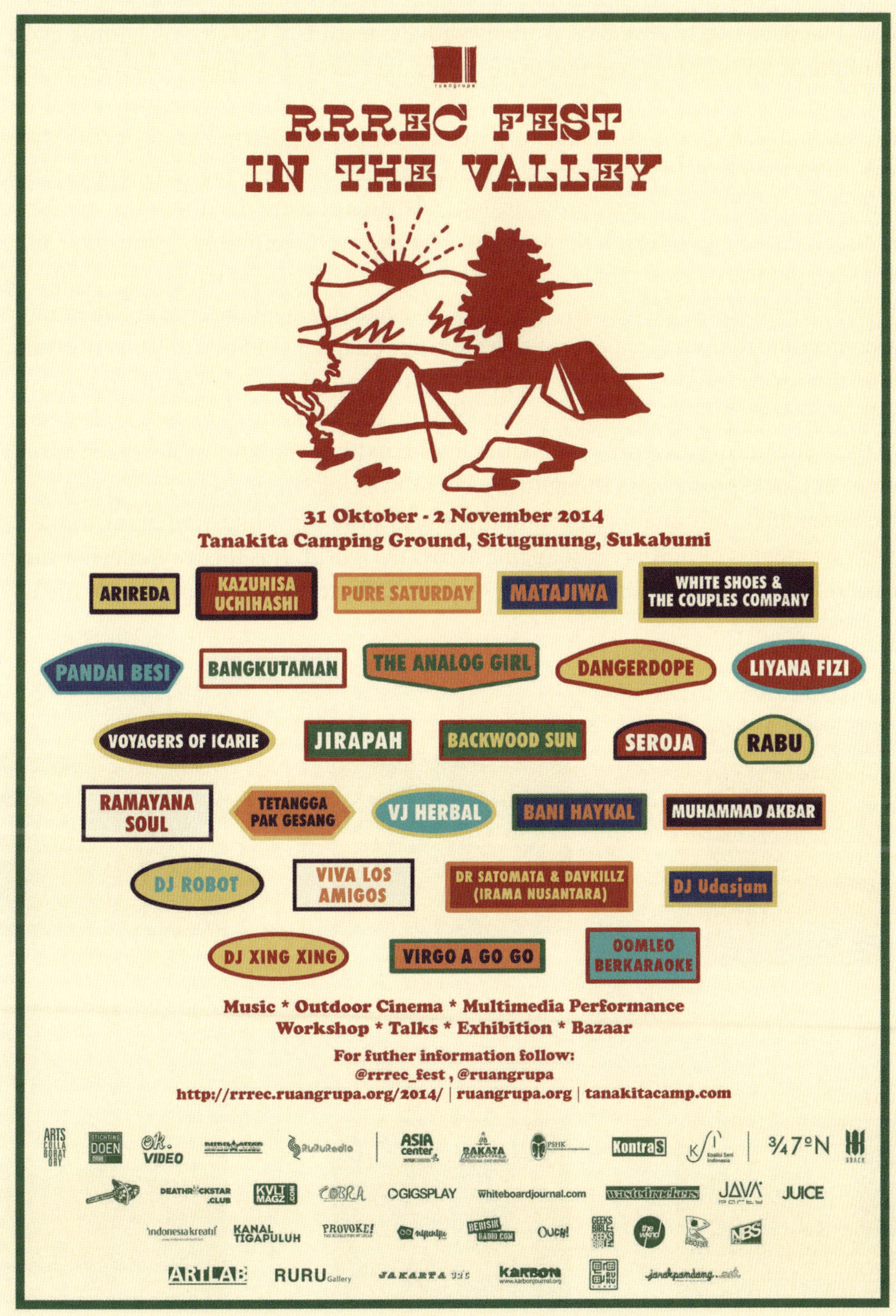

Participation in 31st Bienal de São Paulo, Brazil, 6 September – 7 December 2014

Jakarta is a sprawling city, not unlike São Paulo, divided into a series of neighbourhoods characterised by diversity. Working with the texture of the city, ruangrupa make use of the opportunities that emerge from existing cultural dynamics – responding to what goes on around them. This may mean promoting a band, curating an exhibition or developing an international network that can connect Jakarta's artists to the wider world. The members of ruangrupa therefore work across many fields including music, education, video, community projects, festivals, architecture and their own artistic practices. For the 31st Bienal, they present a hybrid architectural/sculptural structure. This vertiginous environment presents the different activities of the group as reflected through the meetings and experiences they have had during their time in São Paulo. By connecting to diverse aspects of this city, they create a kind of trans-city portrait – one that projects São Paulo back onto itself through the eyes of Jakartan artists, in dialogue with how local initiatives understand the meaning of being a collective. All the elements of ruangrupa's activities found in this installation reflect their spontaneous, entangled yet always thoughtful ways of working. In this way, ruangrupa is able to remain firmly anchored within their local situation while developing a collective awareness of how art is changing across the world. It is this awareness of the possibilities of art today that the group wants to offer to the public of the 31st Bienal.

31st Bienal de São Paulo

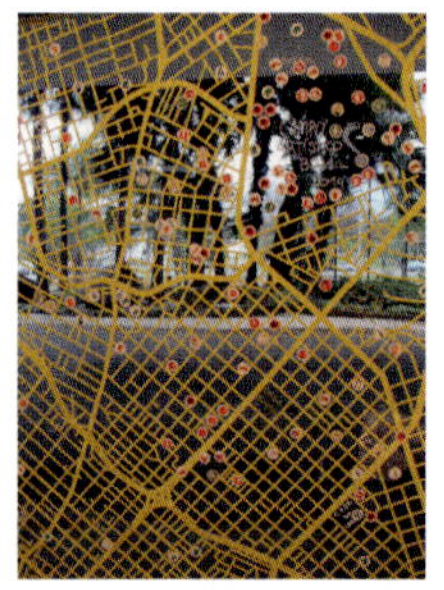

873

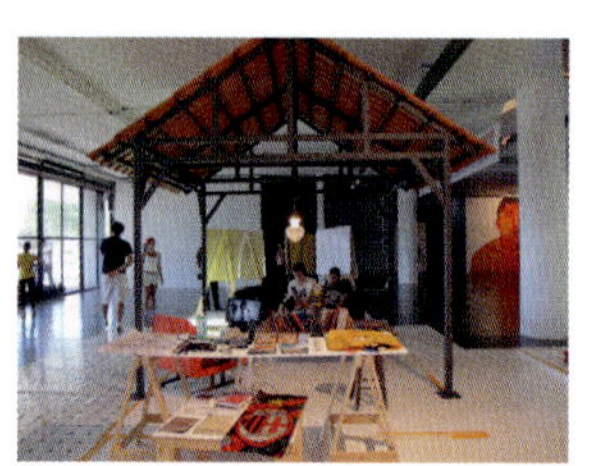

874

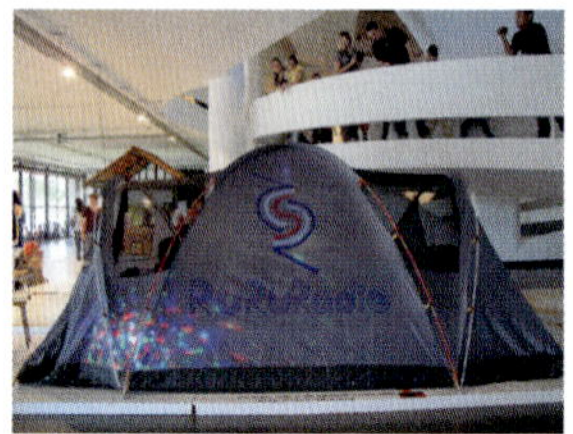

875

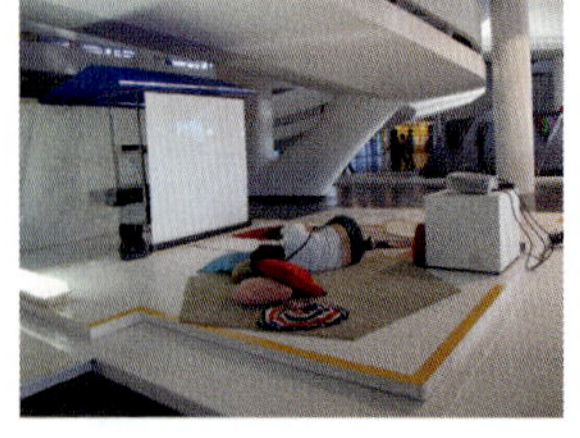

876

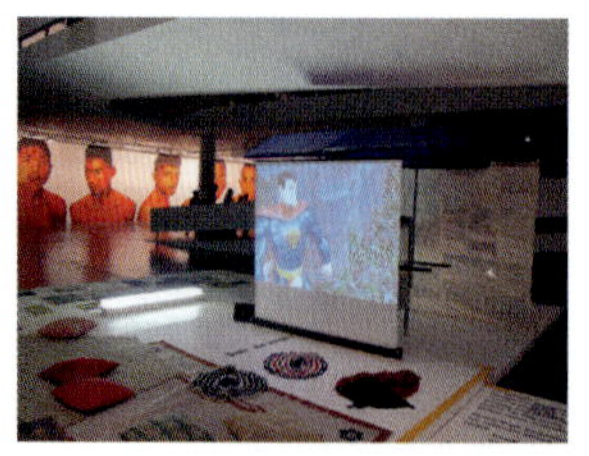

877

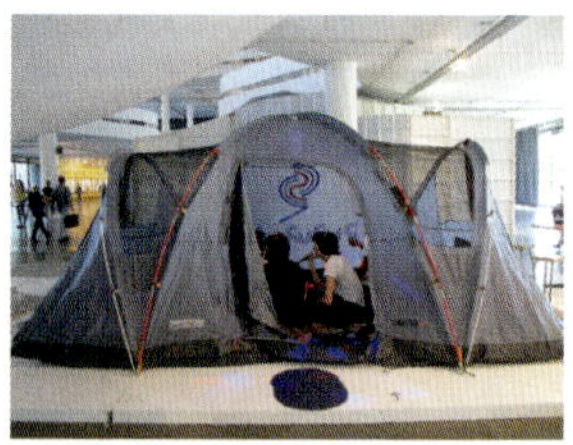

878

Participation in 31st Bienal de São Paulo, Brazil, 6 September – 7 December 2014

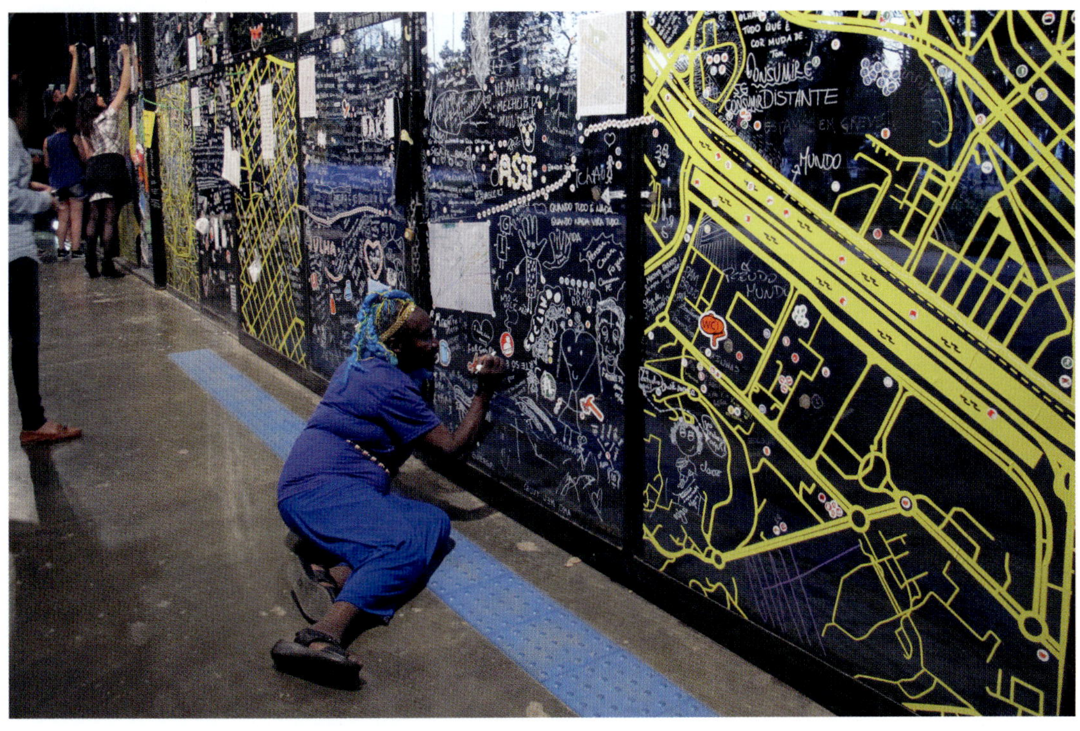

879

The project utilizes the space to 'build' a temporal branch of ruangrupa inside the museum. A translation of ruangrupa's 2011 anniversary project titled 'Siasat'. There's no finished or established work of art, ruangrupa's piece on this biennale is a replica of their headquarters, recreating every room inside the museum. They even recreated their coffee outlet 'Kopi Paste' with clay roof-tile. Furthermore, this temporal branch of ruangrupa also simulates ruangrupa Jakarta's activities. Every room resembles the function of the original room they were modeled after, including a space for an exhibition, a theatre room, a 'RURUshop Radio' tent broadcasting the programs of ruangrupa radio, as well as a karaoke machine operated by the one and only, Oomleo. ... On the set of this project, the public was asked to respond to the piece by making doodles on the museum's wall, or to sing their lungs out in the karaoke room. 'The response from the public was astonishing. Most of them were really excited to get involved with our piece, they are thrilled to finally have the opportunity to doodle and even, scream inside one of the most important buildings in Brazil. Mostly because of the exclusivity of the building – usually Biennales are always related to formal protocols with high profiled artists, where there are restrictions for the public to make a contact with the art piece itself. This Biennale, especially our piece, is an exception to that', Farid Rakun, one of the ruangrupa team explains. ... Reza Afisina, a part of the second group that went to São Paulo said, 'We intentionally invited the public to take no distance from our project, we want our piece to be unexclusive. We engaged with the public from the start, where we collaborated with young local artists, we even did a project with the security team. We asked the public to mess around with our room, more than that, we encouraged them to make programmes/workshops inside our platform.'

Ken Jenie, *Whiteboard Journal*

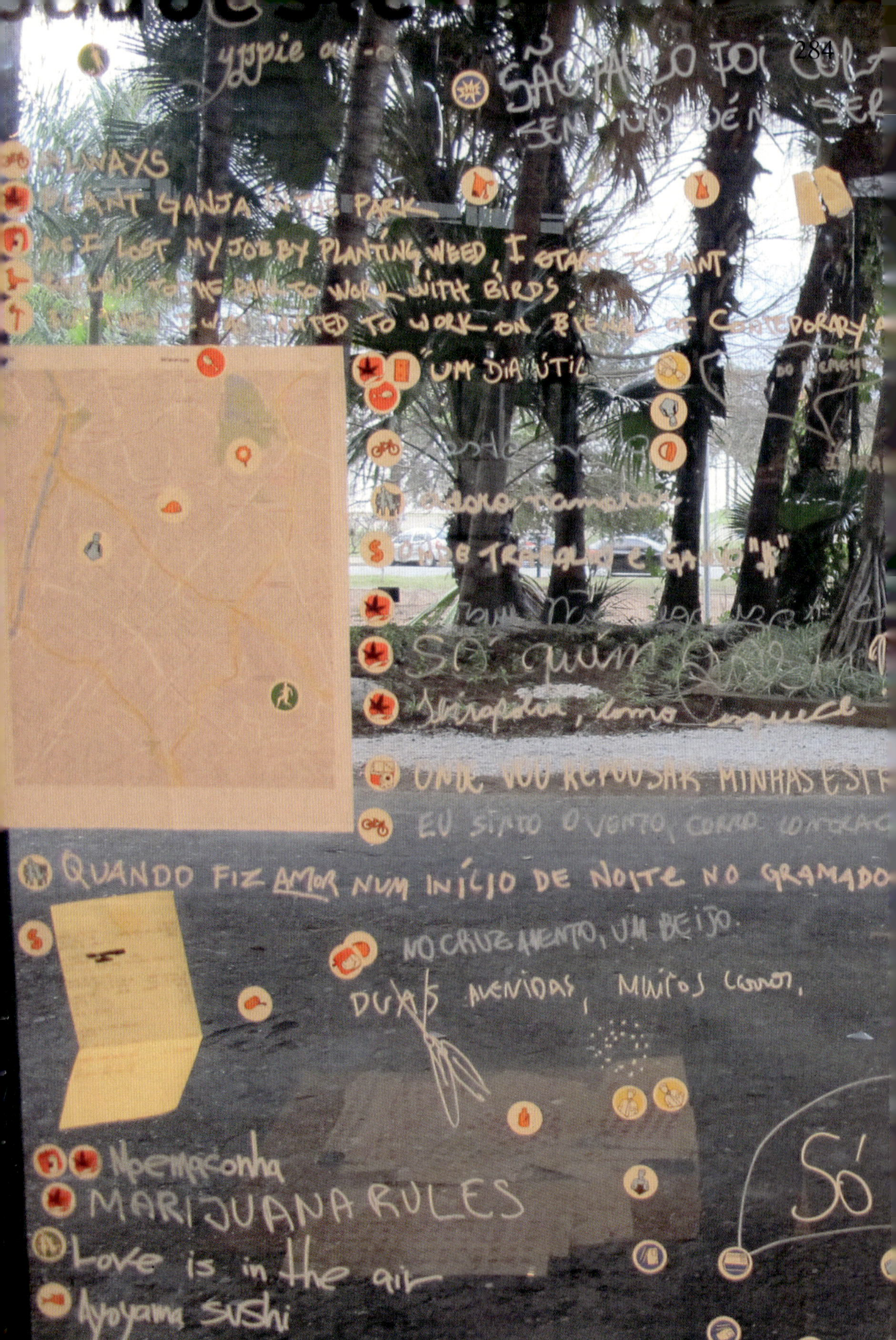
AS I LOST MY JOB BY PLANTING WEED, I START TO PAINT
"UM DIA ÚTIL
Só quem
QUANDO FIZ AMOR NUM INÍCIO DE NOITE NO GRAMADO
NO CRUZAMENTO, UM BEIJO.
DUAS AVENIDAS, MUITOS CARROS.
MARIJUANA RULES
Love is in the air
Ayoyama sushi
Só

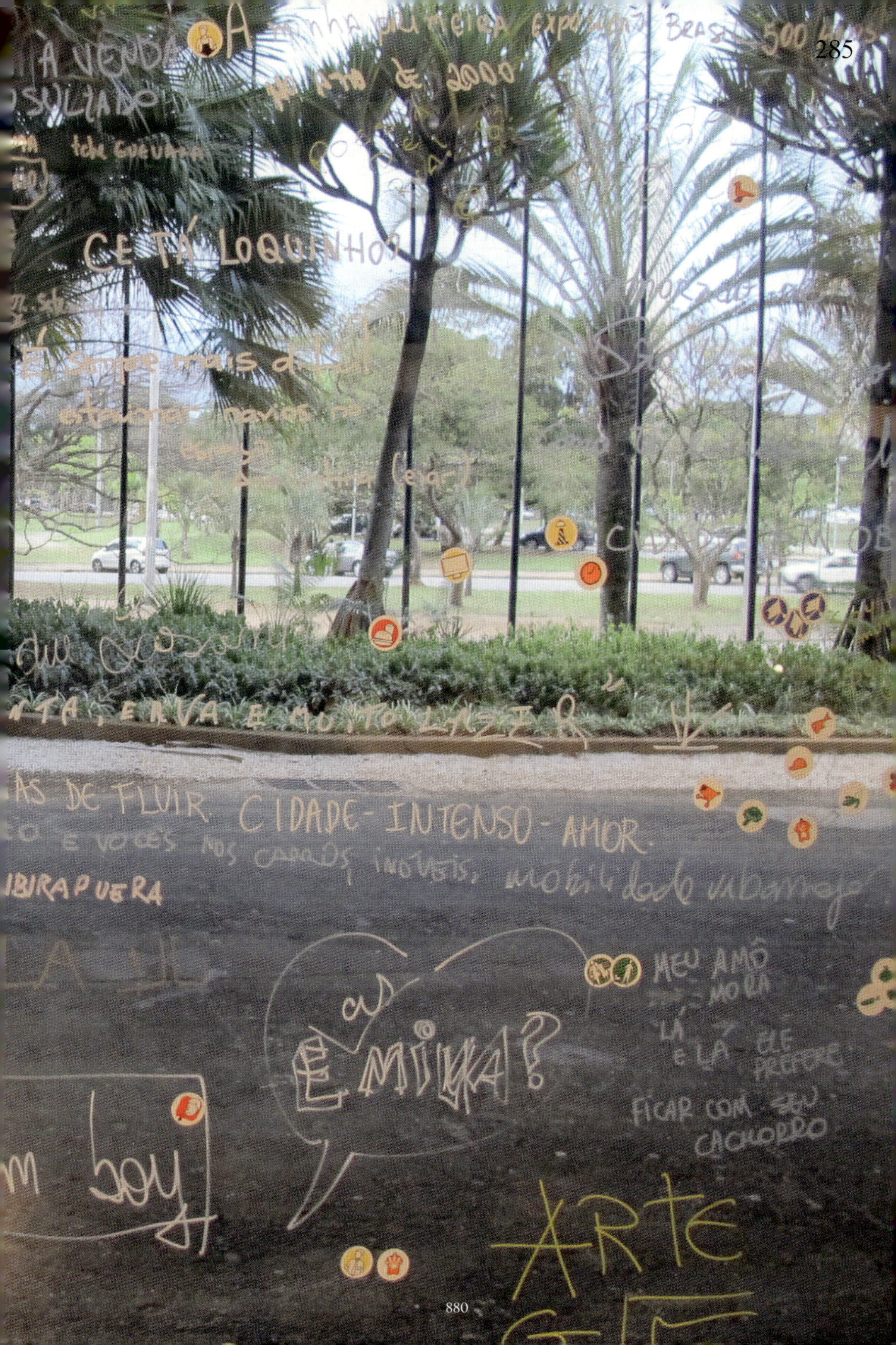
CE TÁ LOQUINHO
CIDADE-INTENSO-AMOR.
MEU AMÔ
MORA
LÁ
E LÁ ELE
PREFERE
FICAR COM SEU
CACHORRO
ARTE

Jakarta 32°C, various venues around Kota Tua Jakarta (Jakarta Old Town), 13–21 December 2014

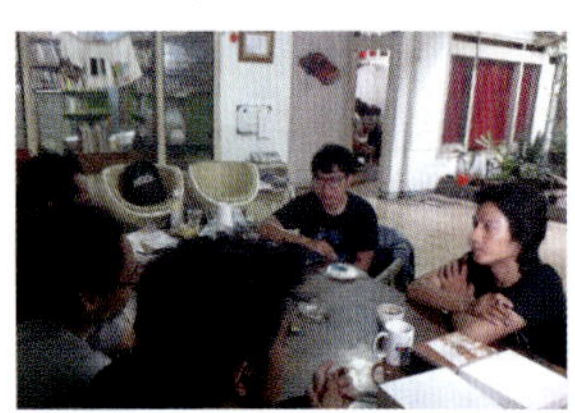

881

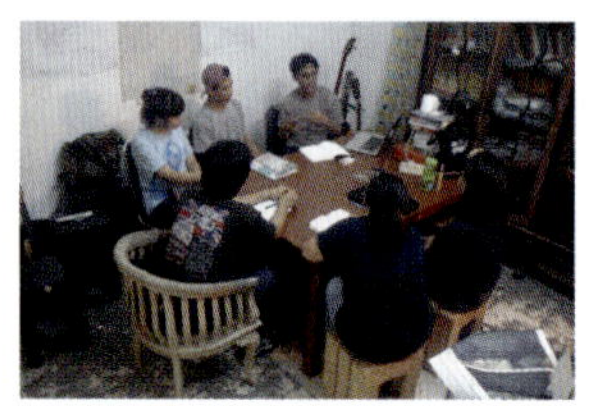

882

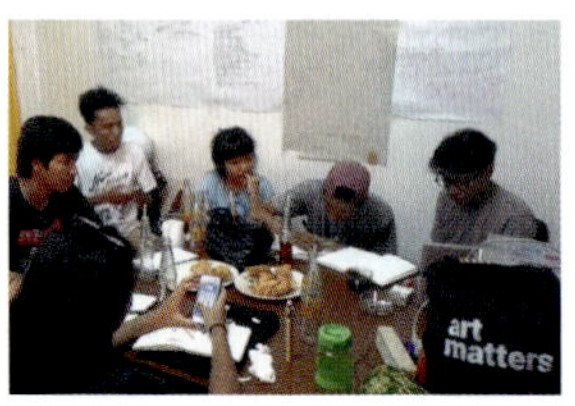

883

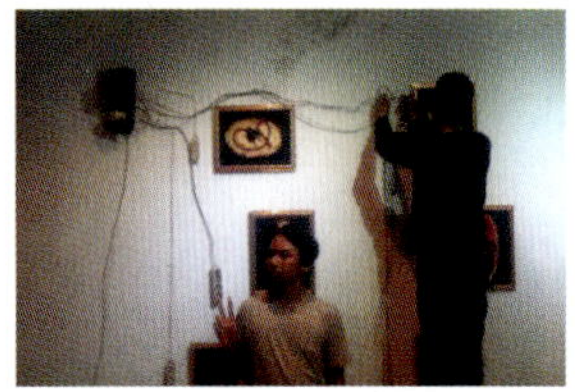

884

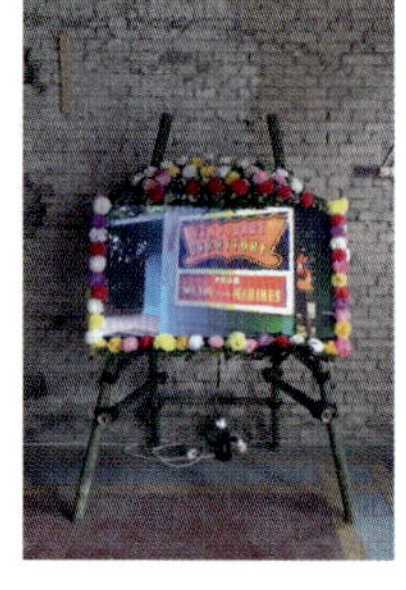

885

see also pp.410–19

'Prototipe' ('Prototype'), exhibition by Benny Wicaksono, RURU Gallery, 28 January – 7 February 2015

in collaboration with Klub Karya Bulutangkis, Uncletwis and Kasetan; curated by Mahardika Yudha

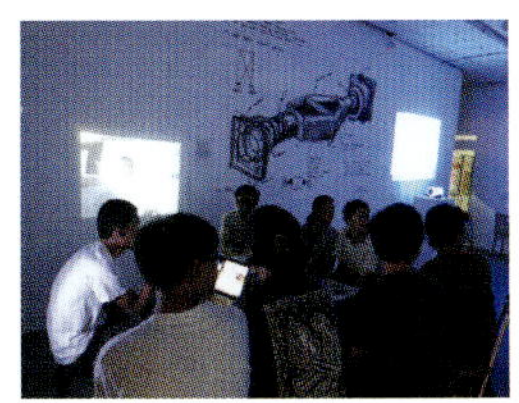

886

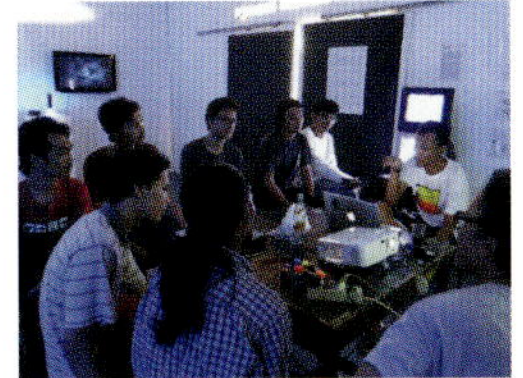

887

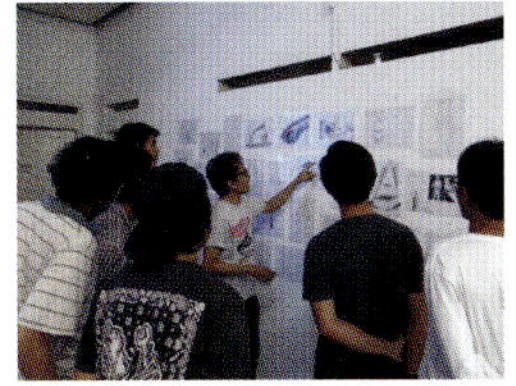

888

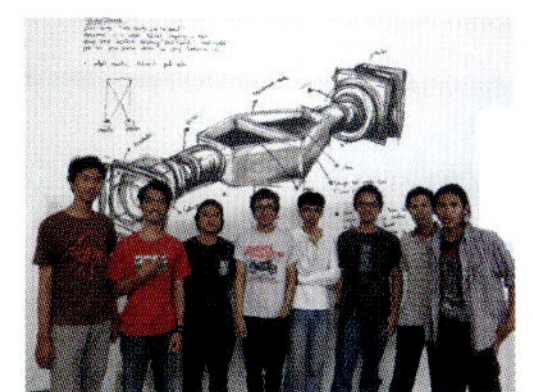

889

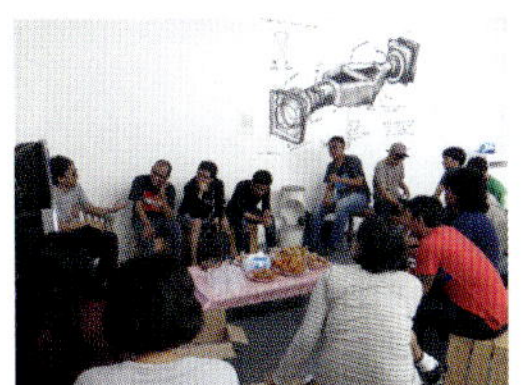

890

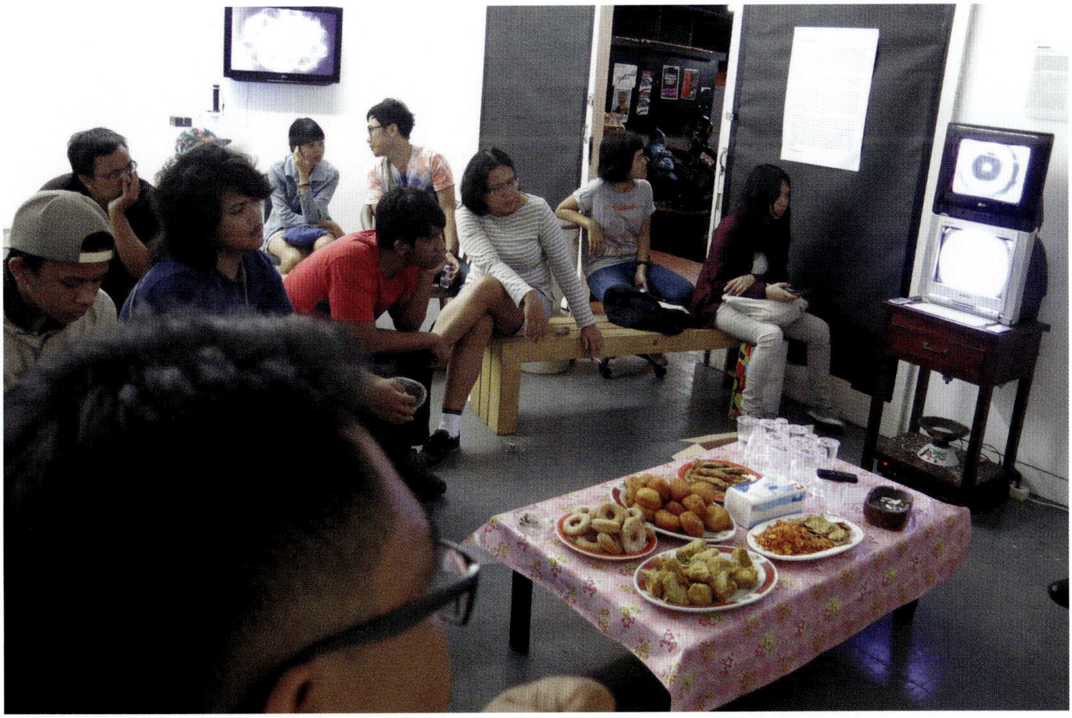

891

'M's Wonderful Drawer', artist-in-residence presentation by Viviana Cardenas, ruru house, February 2015

in collaboration with the Ministry of Culture of Colombia and Arts Collaboratory; featuring also Cut and Rescue, Enomonsta, Ike Vantiani and Junk Not Dead; Viviana Cardenas experimented with toys as tools for engagement and storytelling

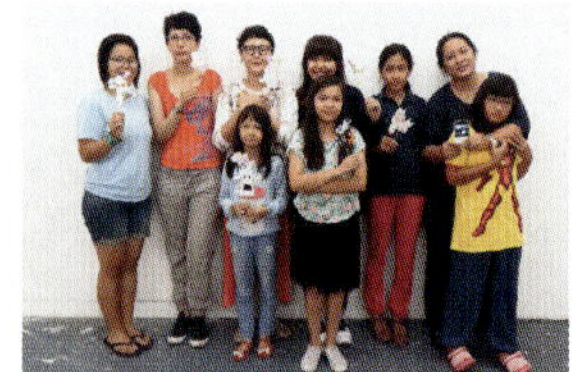

892

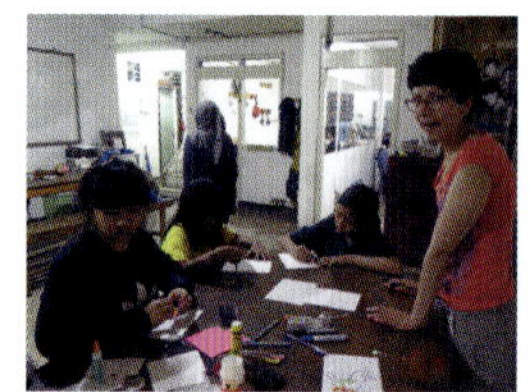

893

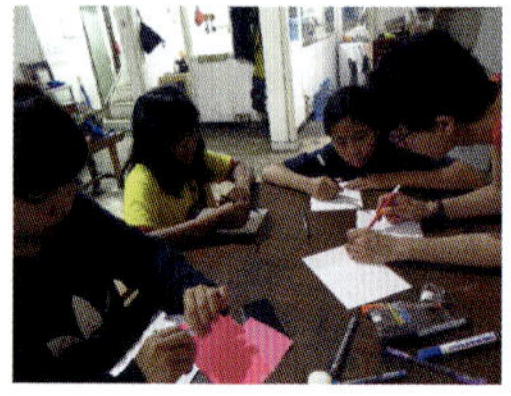

894

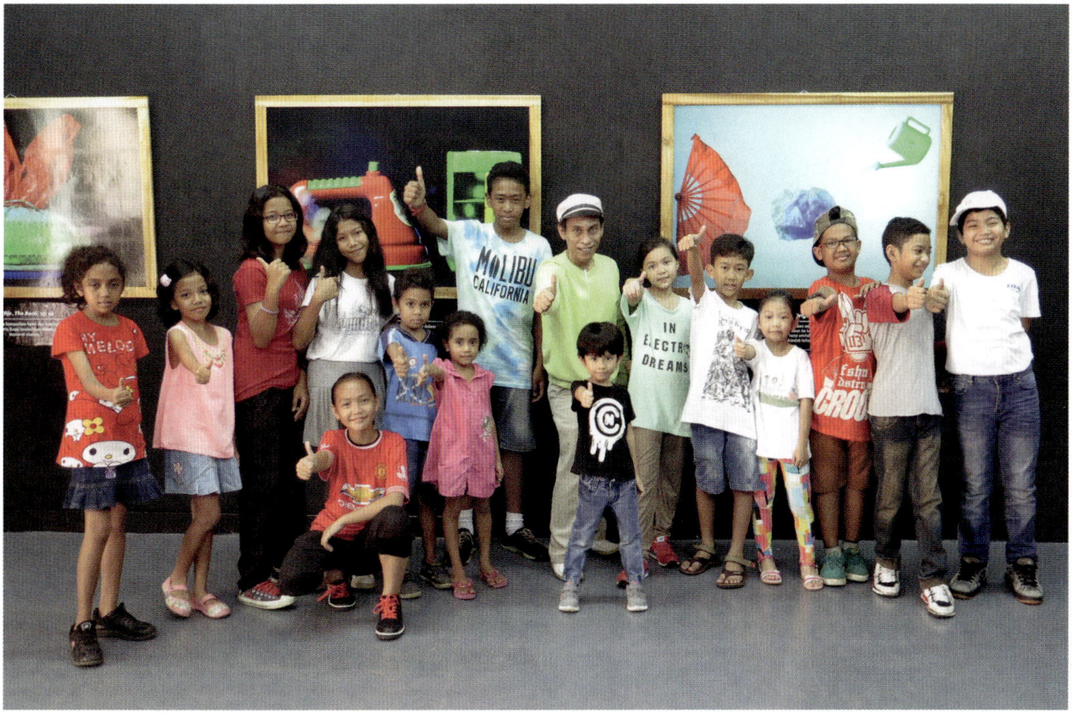

'Hidangan Dari Langit' ('Food from the Skies'), exhibition by PM Toh, RURU Gallery, 14–25 March 2015

895

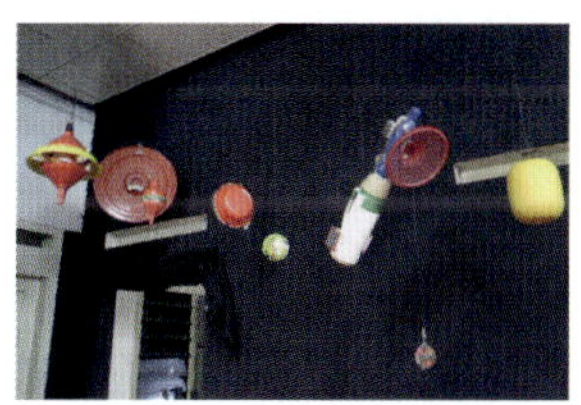

896

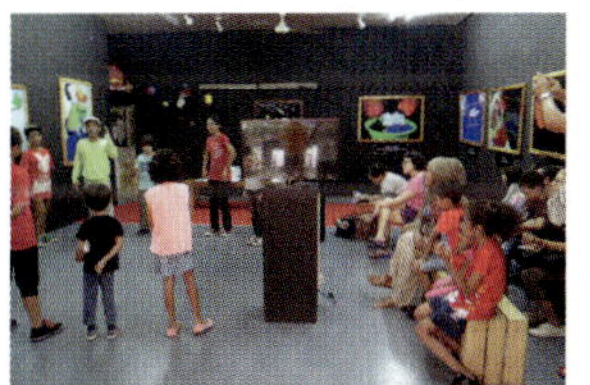

897

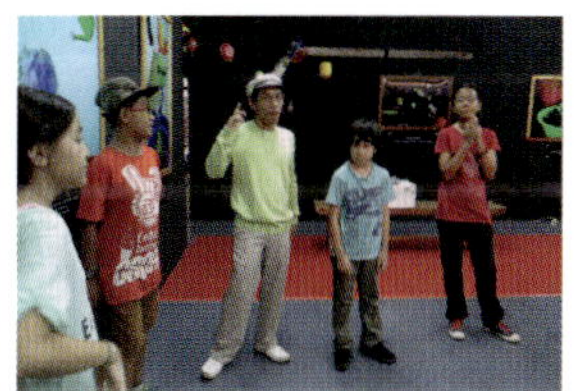

898

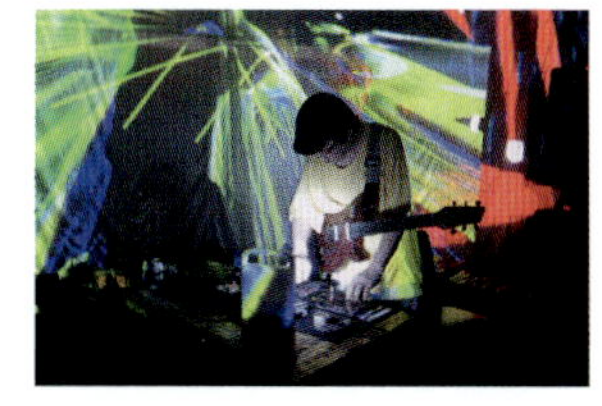

899

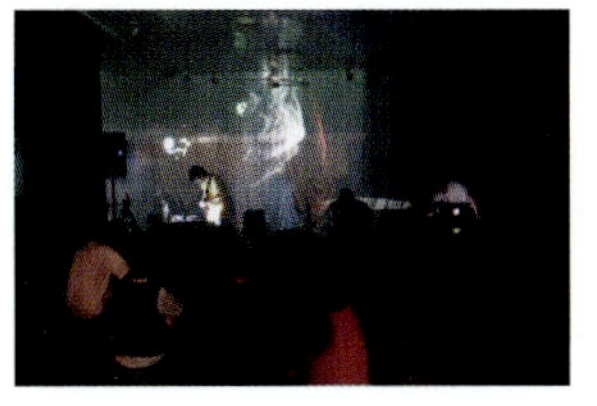

900

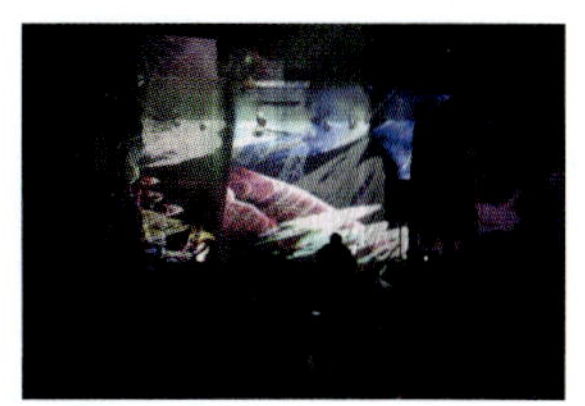

901

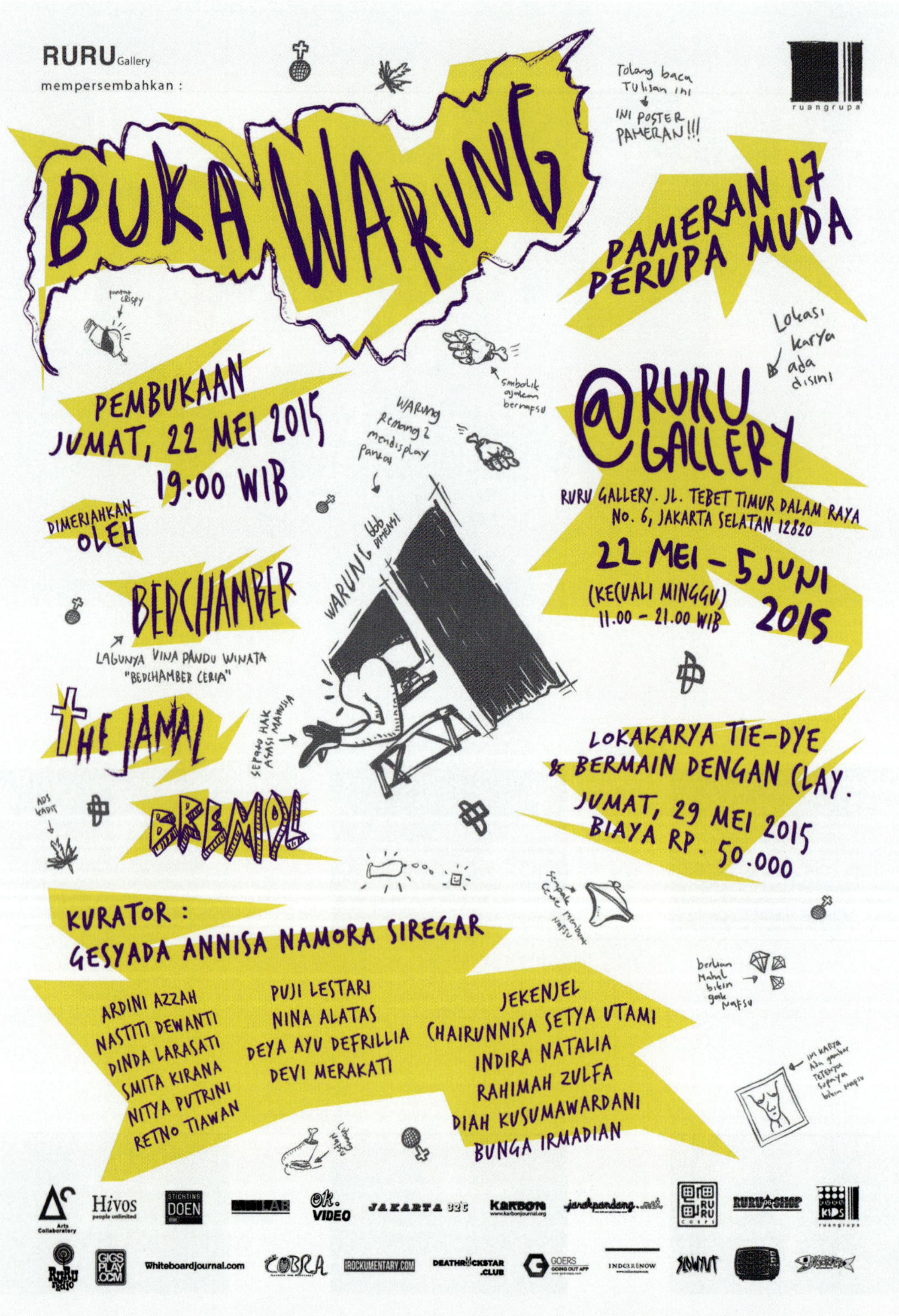
RURU Gallery
mempersembahkan :
ruangrupa
Tolong baca Tulisan ini
INI POSTER PAMERAN!!!
BUKA WARUNG
PAMERAN 17 PERUPA MUDA
Lokasi karya ada disini
PEMBUKAAN
JUMAT, 22 MEI 2015
19:00 WIB
@RURU GALLERY
RURU GALLERY. JL. TEBET TIMUR DALAM RAYA No. 6, JAKARTA SELATAN 12820
22 MEI – 5 JUNI 2015
(KECUALI MINGGU)
11.00 – 21.00 WIB
DIMERIAHKAN OLEH
BEDCHAMBER
LAGUNYA VINA PANDU WINATA "BEDCHAMBER CERIA"
WARUNG 666 DIMENSI
SEPATU HAK ASASI MANUSIA
THE JAMAL
BREMOL
LOKAKARYA TIE-DYE & BERMAIN DENGAN CLAY.
JUMAT, 29 MEI 2015
BIAYA RP. 50.000
KURATOR :
GESYADA ANNISA NAMORA SIREGAR
ARDINI AZZAH
NASTITI DEWANTI
DINDA LARASATI
SMITA KIRANA
NITYA PUTRINI
RETNO TIAWAN
PUJI LESTARI
NINA ALATAS
DEYA AYU DEFRILLIA
DEVI MERAKATI
JEKENJEL
CHAIRUNNISA SETYA UTAMI
INDIRA NATALIA
RAHIMAH ZULFA
DIAH KUSUMAWARDANI
BUNGA IRMADIAN
Arts Collaboratory
Hivos people unlimited
STICHTING DOEN
ok. VIDEO
JAKARTA 32°C
KARBON
jarakpandang.net
RURU CORPS
RURU SHOP
KIDS ruangrupa
RURU Radio
GIGS PLAY.COM
Whiteboardjournal.com
COBRA
IROCKUMENTARY.COM
DEATHROCKSTAR.CLUB
GOERS GOING OUT APP
INDOARTNOW

OK.Video 'Orde Baru' – Indonesia Media Arts Festival, Galeri Nasional Indonesia, Jakarta, 15–28 June 2015

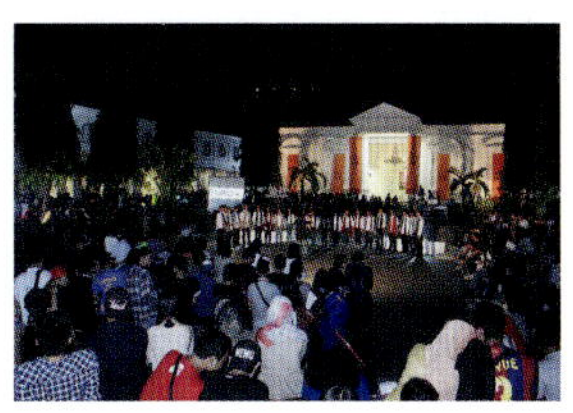

903

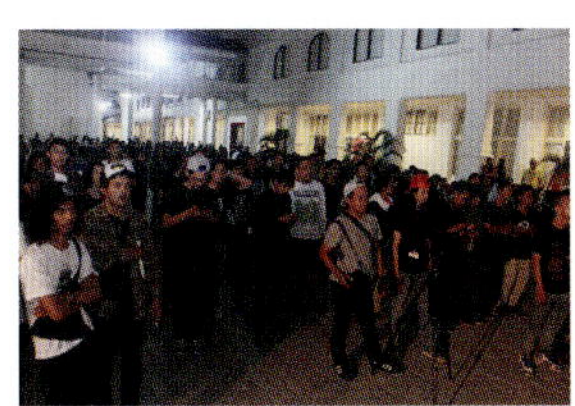

904

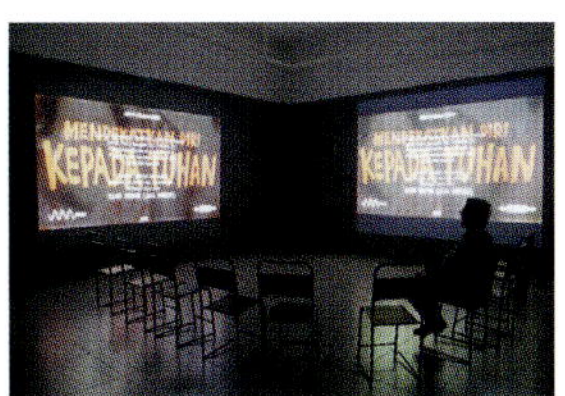

905

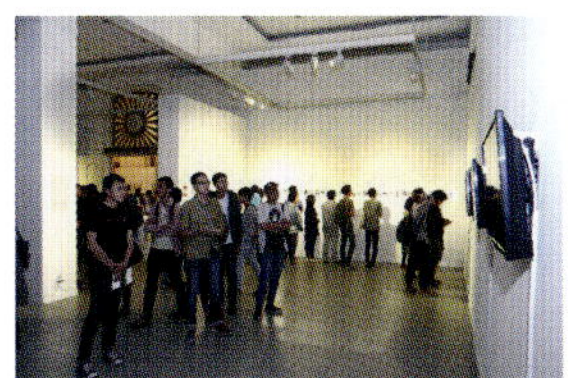

906

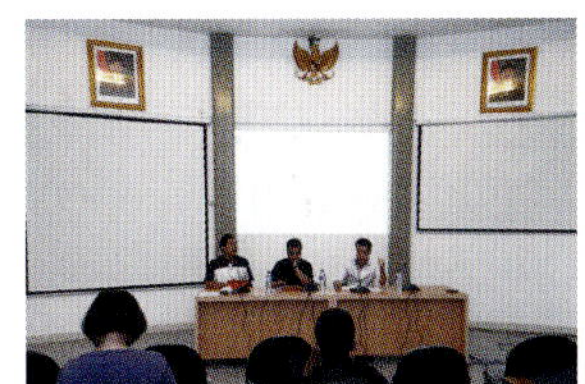

907

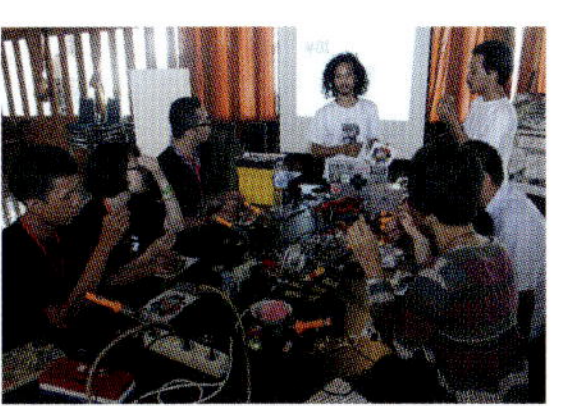

908

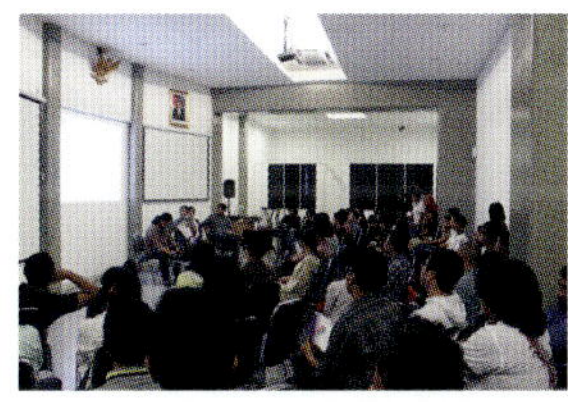

909

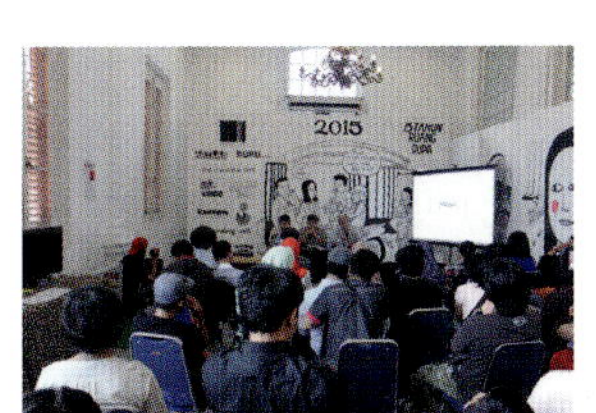

910

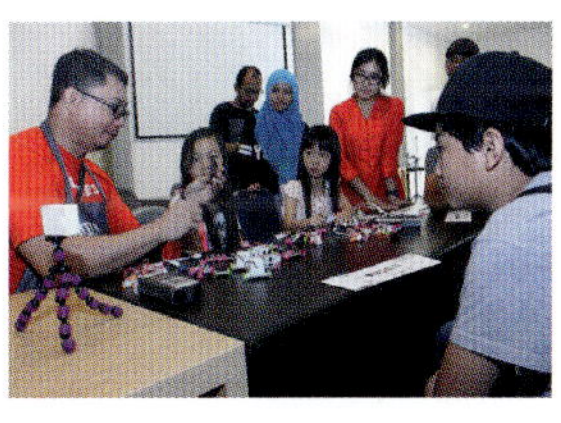

911

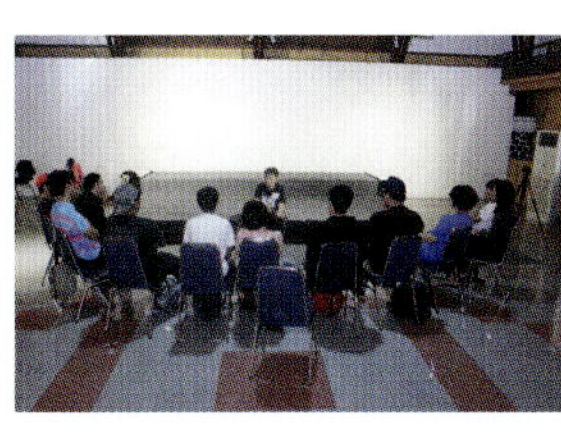

912

WHAT

We are an art and cultural platform founded in 2015 by a group of artists' collectives in Jakarta, located at Gudang Sarinah warehouse, Pancoran, South Jakarta. It is a cross-disciplinary space that aims to maintain, cultivate and establish an integrated support system for creative talents, communities and various institutions. It also aspires to be able to make connections and collaborate, to exchange knowledge and ideas, as well as to encourage critical thinking, creativity and innovations. The results of these joint collaborations will be open for public access – and presented with various exhibitions, festivals, workshops, discussions, film screenings, music concerts and publications of journals.

WHY

In the midst of increasingly contested areas in Jakarta, the physical space for creative potentials to gather and grow is increasingly scarce. This is the main reason why we are setting up this platform. A place that connects dialogues and multidisciplinary co-operation, where citizens and creators gather – driven by the desire to work, to learn together and to create amazing things!

WHO

RURU Corps is a communication bureau founded in 2011 by three arts organisations in Jakarta, namely ruangrupa (ruangrupa.org), Forum Lenteng (forumlenteng.org) and SERRUM (serrum.id).

Gudang Sarinah Ekosistem

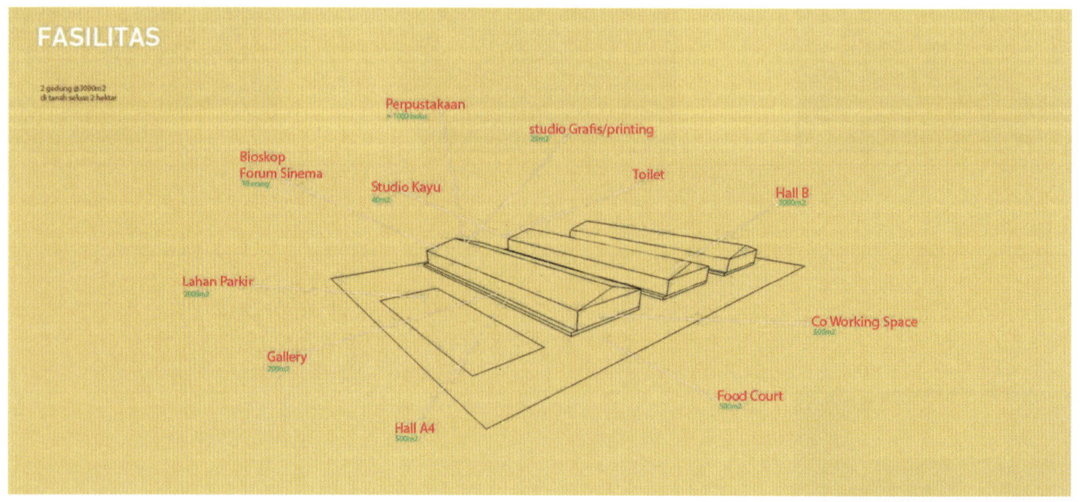

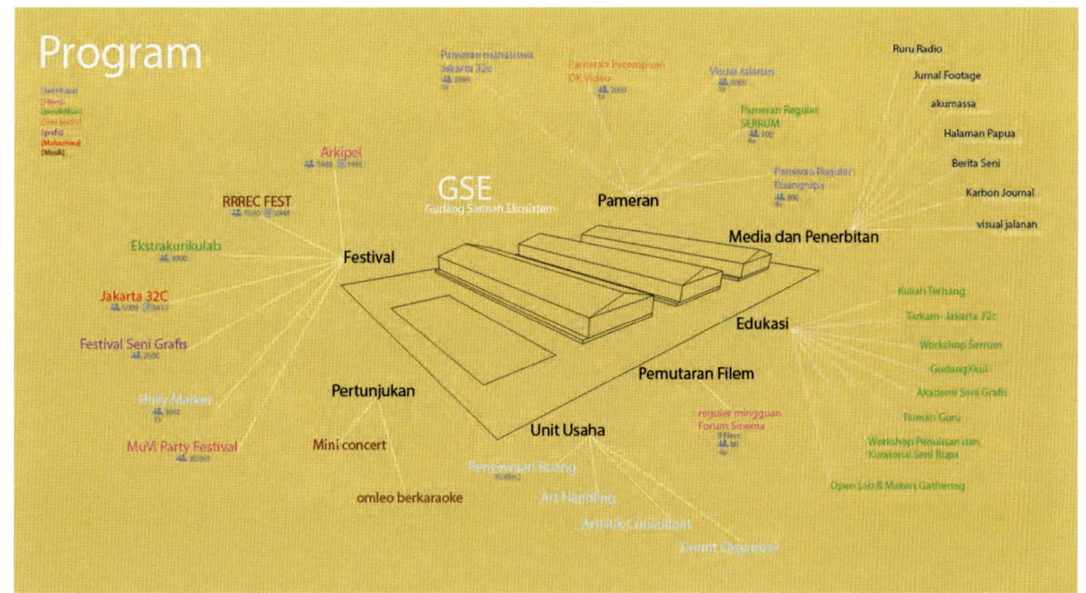

914

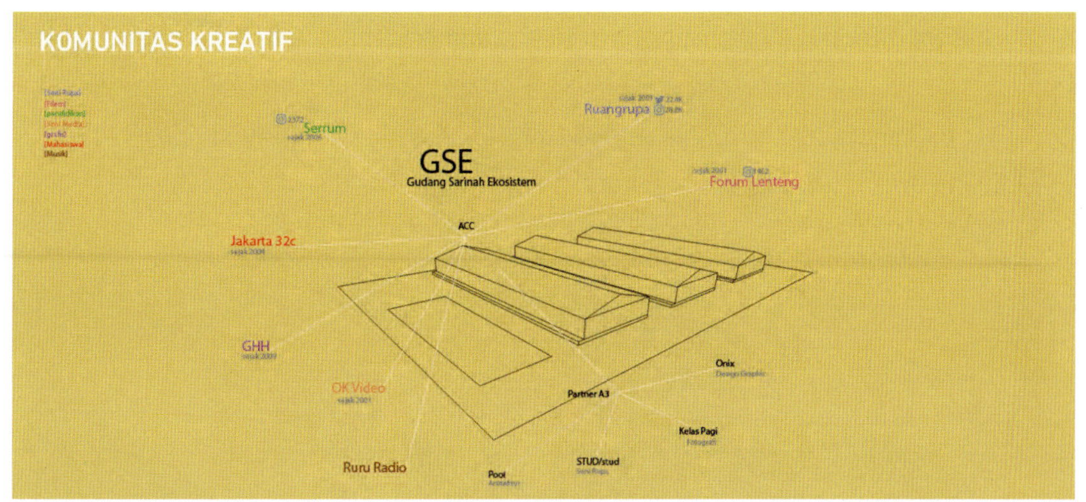

915

see also pp.410–19

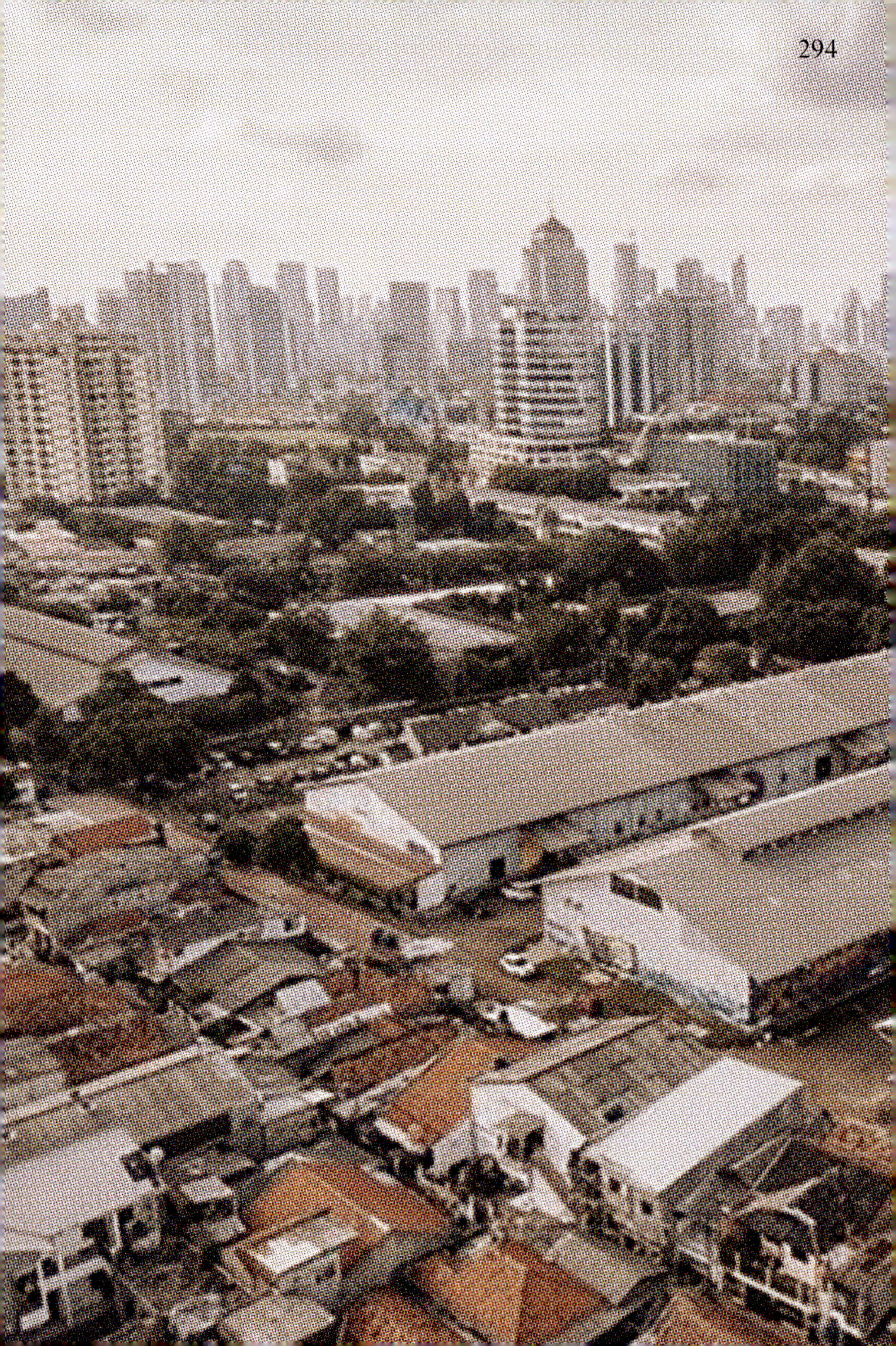

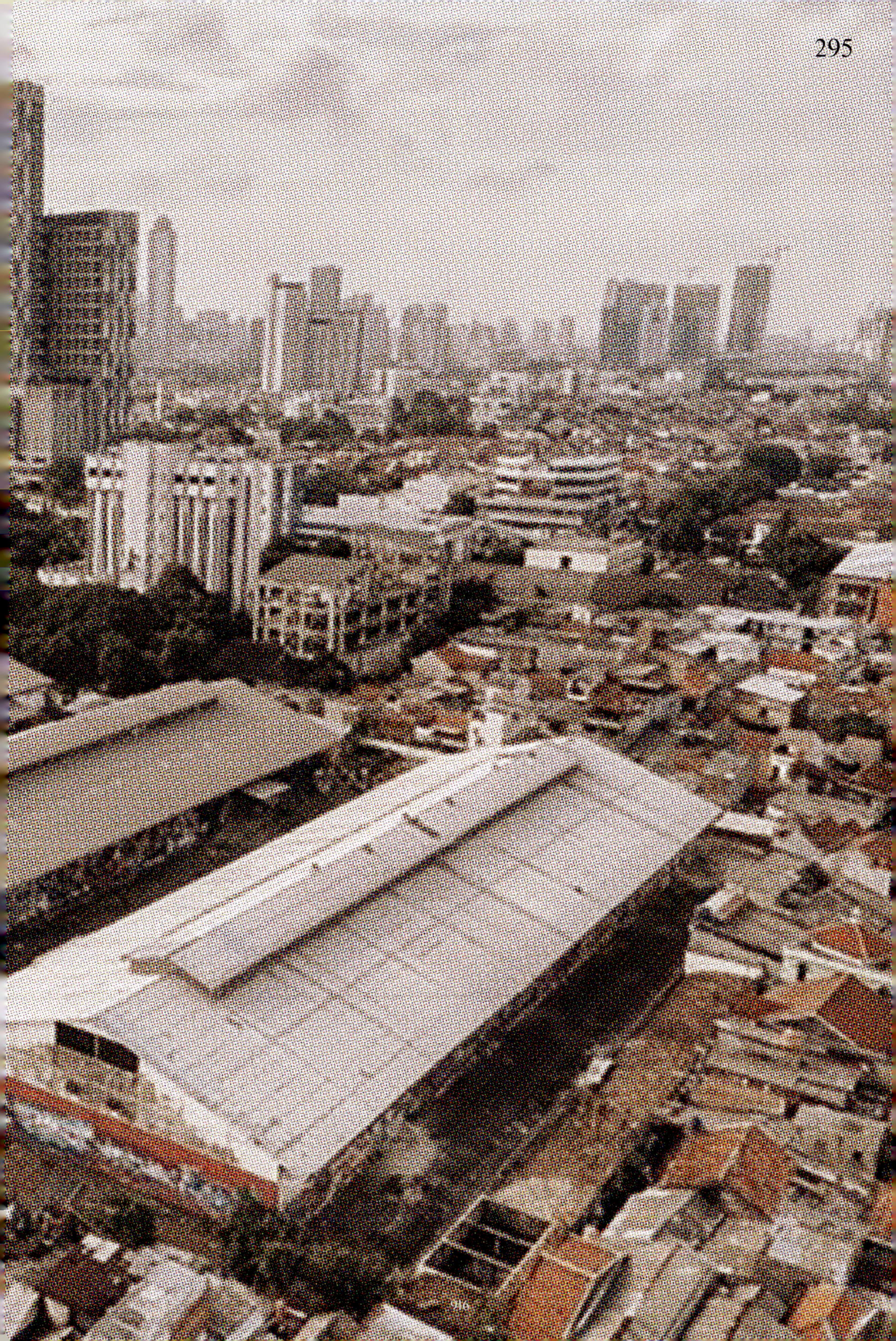

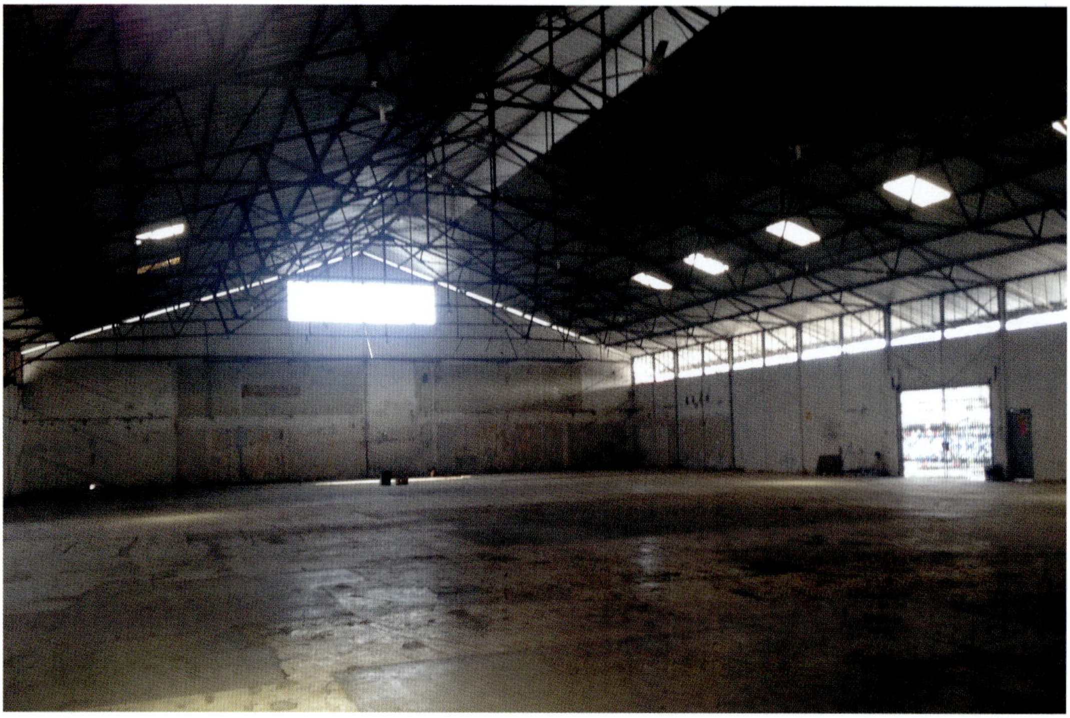

917

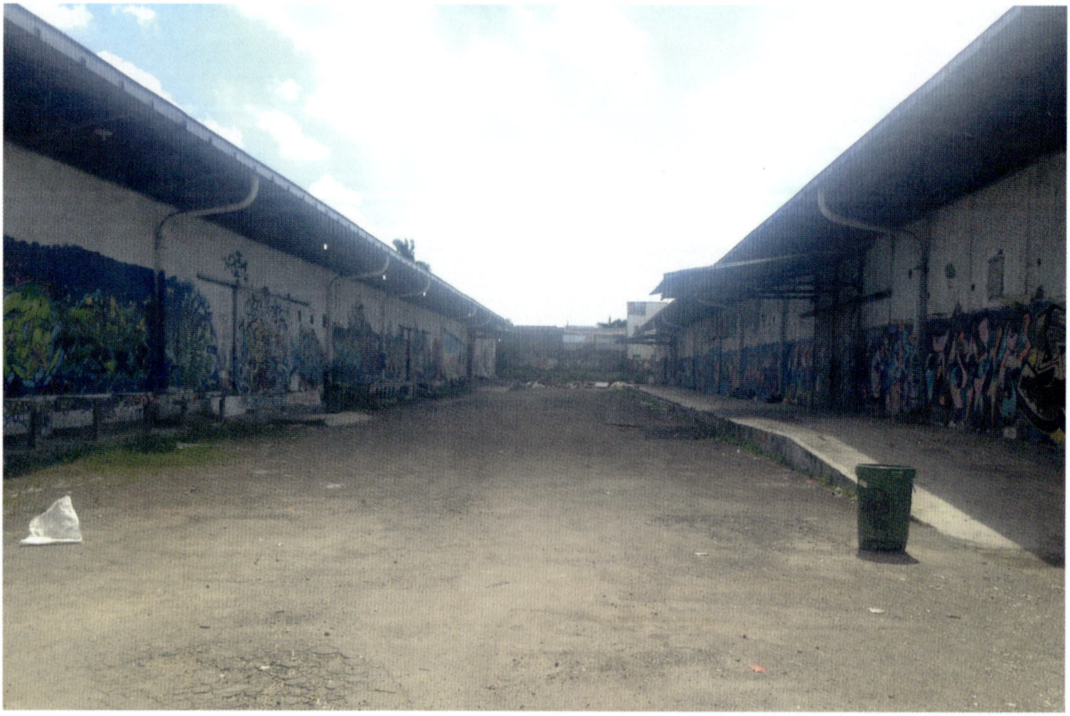

918

After I returned to Japan, I received an email which gives us the latest updates. In 2016, ruangrupa moved their base to a bigger space called Gudang Sarinah. The building used to be a warehouse, which was used as a venue for Jakarta Biennale 2015. They are now occupying two spaces, 3000m2 each, so huge! They are going to stay there at least for three years, from 2016. To split the cost of rent, and to build up a stronger community through 'sharing', they have invited five other organisations to use the warehouse. So the space will soon to be filled with many activities such as exhibitions, educational programmes, music events and movie screenings etc. They are now planning to start a visual communication agency, RURU Corps, with other organisations to manage all the profitable works for Gudang and the local community. This movement will not only influence their workstyle but also bring changes to their ways of thinking. As for ruangrupa as an organisation, it is shrinking in the number of members. Now, only four have remained to take care of administrative matters. This some kid of 'dissolution' somehow enables them to focus on more experimental projects in some specific fields. They also mentioned Gudang Sarinah Ekosistem, as a great community to explore the new and unique way to experiment with collective works.

Nozomu Ogawa

There was a necessity to move [to Gudang Sarinah]. The house could not hold the programmes anymore. It was too full with old people and their things, the younger generation needed more space to grow. Gudang Sarinah was run in a different way compared to the Tebet houses. It's difficult because it required high maintenance and was really expensive. We were artists, we managed activities and were experimenting with our business unit at that time, so we ran the space as commercial space. That meant we had to work harder (*laughs*). We also experienced more complicated collectivity, because there were many more people. What I like during Gudang Sarinah and also in Gudskul is that ruru disappears. You cannot really see us or you rarely meet us there. It's good for the new generations to initiate things in this way.

Indra Ameng

When we moved to Gudang Sarinah, it was crazy – especially financially. I still remember one moment clearly: we were in the finance room back in Tebet, in a discussion with Ade and our auditors. The auditor said, 'Ade, this is absolutely impossible. This is the monthly rent, and we also have to manage all the people working with us.' It was something like that. But Ade was always optimistic. He just said, 'We'll be okay.' At the time, our idea was to collaborate with other collectives – to create events together, earn money together and work together. 'If you can be together, why do you have to be alone?' Ade said. I always imagine Ade as someone sitting high up in a tree, able to see the whole picture. He had everything planned – briefly, but clearly. Then came the financial challenges. We were two or three months behind on rent, and we kept wondering how we would find the money, even though we had already tried so many strategies. At some point, during one of our many *nongkrong* sessions, an opportunity opened up to propose a long-term plan to the Ford Foundation. Part of that plan included collectively buying land – because we knew that owning a space would reduce our operational costs for all collectives involved in the long run. The support we received allowed us to clear the remaining rent at Gudang Sarinah, purchase the land and start building what would become Gudskul. Gudang Sarinah was an important turning point – a real example of how a space could be collectively managed, activated and transformed. It wasn't just about using space; it was about building ecosystems through it. We were incredibly fortunate, and we didn't take it for granted. In Gudskul, we've made many efforts – like building RUX, our creative business space/unit. It's our commercial wing. We've invited freelance marketers to collaborate, organised events both big and small, secured sponsorships and funding, and rented out spaces for exhibitions, meetings and artist studios.

Daniella F. Praptono

At one point – before we moved to and around Gudang Sarinah time – some people 'resigned' from ruru. Because the structurelessness didn't work. It was also hard to tell whether there was a tendency to underestimate how to distribute the work, or how much consciousness there was of the unequal power relations within it. Some of us renewed our relationship with ruru after giving it some distance, which is healthy. There's a feeling of affection attached to it. So breaking with it or growing apart also feels like a heartbreak. Loving affection aside, there were also critical perspectives that ruru needed to work on, particularly on how work is distributed and to whom. This is not only ruru, it concerns the Indonesian art scene in general.

Riksa Afiaty

With Gudang Sarinah, we learned how to 'monetise' space – not just in terms of money, but in broader ways: through knowledge, shared spaces, resources, networks, trust and friendships. It was the first time, for ruangrupa, Serrum and Grafis Huru Hara, that we shared our space and other resources. I remember, just three months after we moved in and started running activities, *Kompas* newspaper published a half-page article about how we were activating idle spaces. Not long after, two large commercial space operators in Jakarta approached us and offered their spaces for us to manage. It was a strange kind of offer – unusual, unexpected. For us, Gudang Sarinah wasn't about chasing profit. It brought far more in terms of relationships and long-term value. Many networks formed there and still continue today. Selarasa Food Lab's Majelis Sayur (vegetable *majelis*) Jagakarsa, for instance, began in the urban farmer market of GS. Many other social and artistic ecosystems also grew from that space – even though, financially, we were bleeding and struggling all the way through. But eventually, we found our way. That model opened up other kinds of support. Without GS, there would be no Gudskul.

Ade Darmawan

Around the time of Gudang Sarinah, with other collectives we built shared resources, including from so-called 'business units' – and in that time ruangrupa could access project based funding from three directions: the state, the private sector and international sources. Up until then, we had worked with many other collectives and organisations. We never grew alone, and we never worked alone. That meant we had to share what we had – including funding. And from there, the practice of *lumbung* began to take shape. With Serrum, for example, the exchange was mutual from early on. If you ask them, they'd humbly say they learned a lot from us – but in reality, we also learned so much from working with them. Forum Lenteng preferred a strict financial split, which reflected a different principle. For us, it was never just about dividing money, we are not a private company – it was about building trust and long-term cooperative financial models, what we called *lumbung*. In ruangrupa, decisions are made collectively, grounded in trust among us. We've set clear boundaries too: no centered figure is involved in strategic decisions, to avoid the concentration of influence and ensure transparency. With FL, trust issues emerged – not just about money, but also about differing values, working cultures and ethics. Especially when the Ford Foundation entered, these tensions – financial, personal and ethical – surfaced more clearly and became harder to ignore.

Ade Darmawan

Since the early 2000s, we (Serrum) already worked with ruru and ruru members as friends, which means the trust was already developed. When the idea of a collective of collectives was put on the table for Gudang Sarinah, it was quite easy for us to adapt. As Serrum, we have always been thinking about how to benefit all of us (ourselves, ruru and Gudang Sarinah Ekosistem). Then it continued at Gudskul. In the same roof, we have time to meet each other and build intimate relationships and discussion. For me, I consider ruru as older brothers. Many of them are five or ten years older than myself. We knew each other for twenty years. Because of the compound, when we have more members to think for all of us, we feel safe actually. Because my friends will also think of me, and vice versa. It's like building a security net.

JJ Adibrata

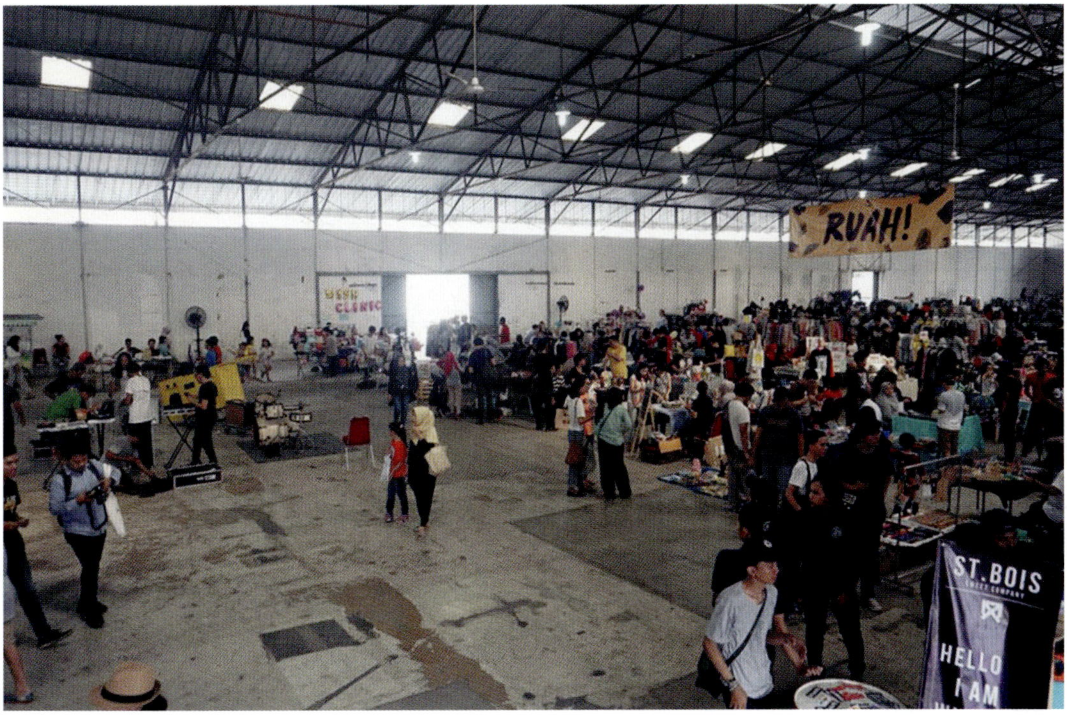

919

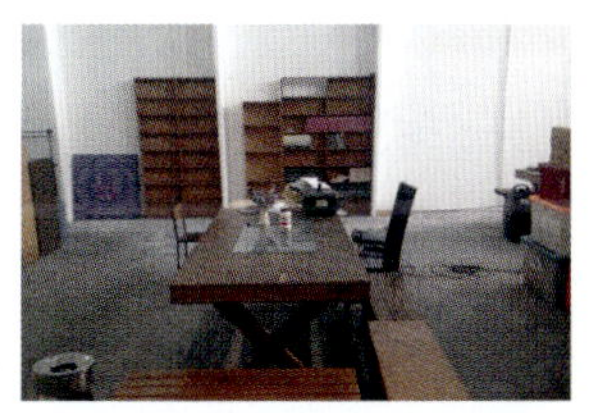

920

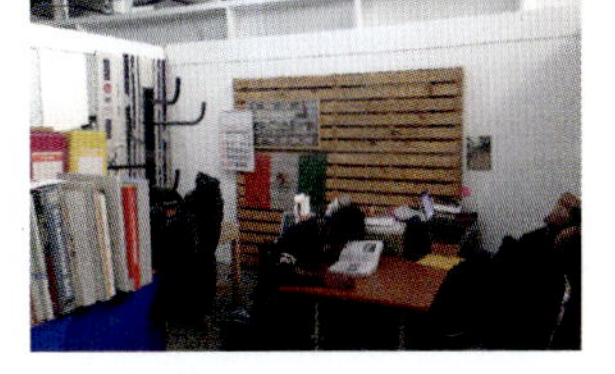

921

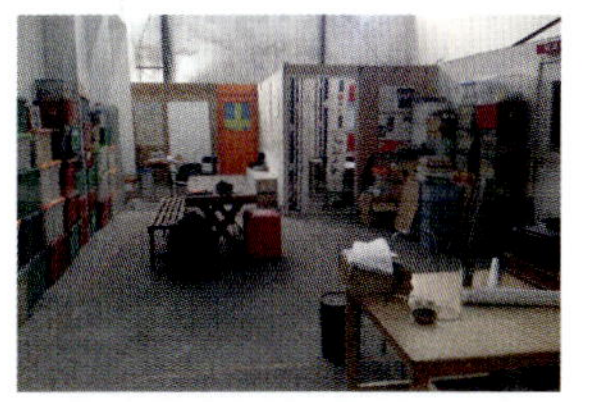

922

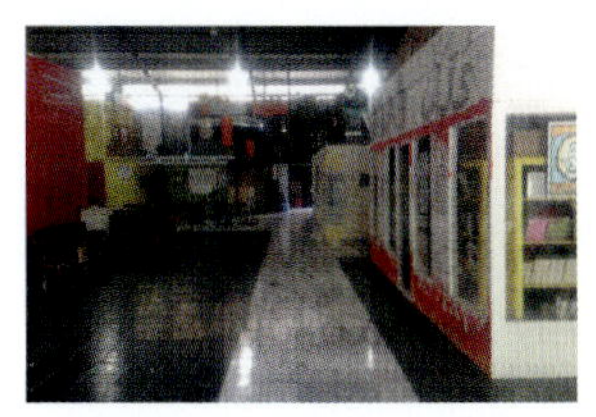

923

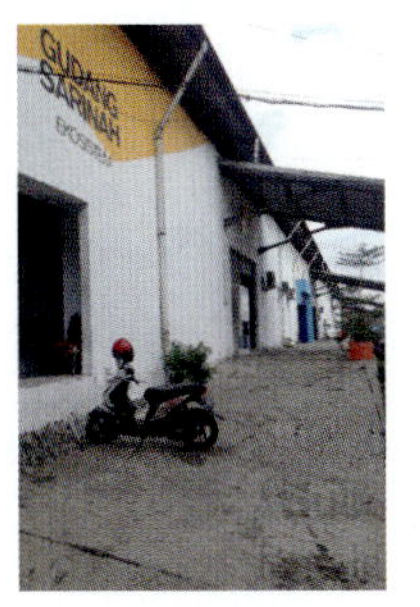

924

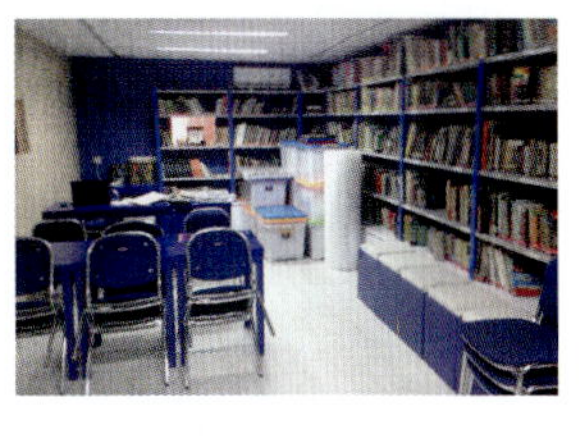

925

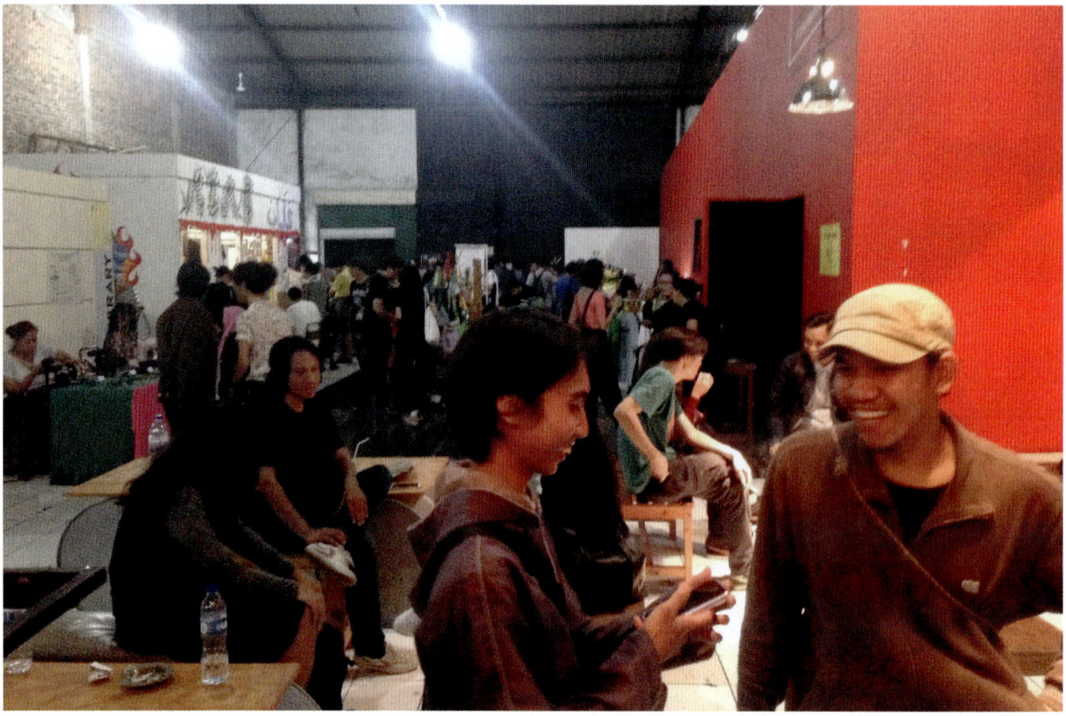

926

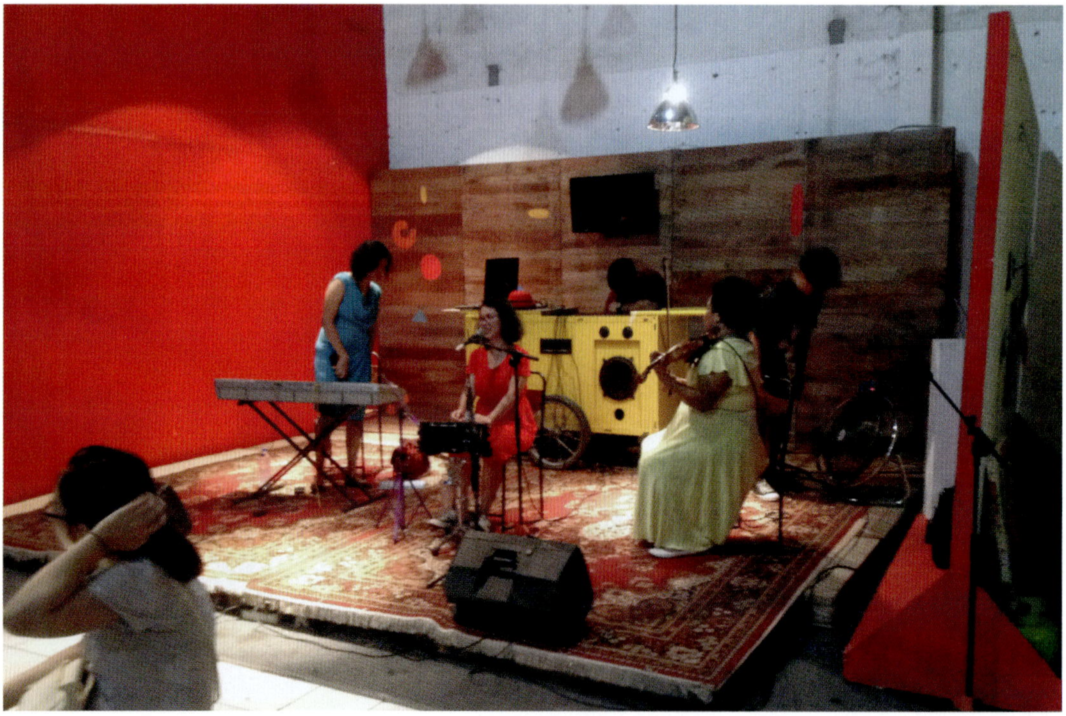

927

I always wonder why ruangrupa stays until now, because it's really difficult. If I meet someone who says we want to be like ruru, I would say, 'No, no you don't you would regret your life forever' (*laughs*). I think the house is very important. That's what I missed when we moved to Gudang Sarinah, which became a working place. When you live with someone intimately as a family in the house, you always have this resistance attitude to keep things going no matter how bad a certain person is, because you cannot push away a family member. That's the feeling I had in the house, for being part of ruru. At Gudang Sarinah, it's a bit overwhelming not just in terms of cost but psychologically as well. Somehow we became a bit institutionalised, even though there's a resistance to be so from the beginning.

Leonhard Bartolomeus

Gudang Sarinah phase, following the 2015 Jakarta Biennale, seeing how ruru federated with other initiatives, such as Grafis Huru Hara and Serrum, was a very interesting thing to witness. ruangrupa were like cultural entrepreneurs for the government in a certain sense because the Sarinah building needed to be lifted up. It became huge and also took away their attention for things that they really wanted to do. ruru did two biennales there and many fairs and gigs. Then in Gudskul phase, ruangrupa was no longer the 'head', they moved under Gudskul. By then, ruru became very powerful, because the government started to ask them to organise things and they had the know-how and competence. It's very interesting how ruru rethought these moments of being too powerful.

Philippe Pirotte

When they were moving to Gudang Sarinah, they were also doing Sonsbeek 16. That's a bit of a mesmerising thing for me, like how can you do two things at the same time. That's a lot of work. I have to say I've never understood Gudang Sarinah, because it exhausted so many people, demanding so much from your network, promising so many things to people as well. This scaling up came with a lot of costs that I didn't want to see to happen. Sometimes we have to remind each other of getting out of touch I would say. I don't know if that was healthy. But on the contrary other people say Gudang Sarinah was a nice artwork in that it shows what scaling up would entail. For sure if they haven't done Gudang Sarinah, they would not have been able to do documenta [fifteen]. Gudang Sarinah was not an ambition to move towards a certain end, it was more of a strengthening of muscle and letting loose again.

reinaart vanhoe

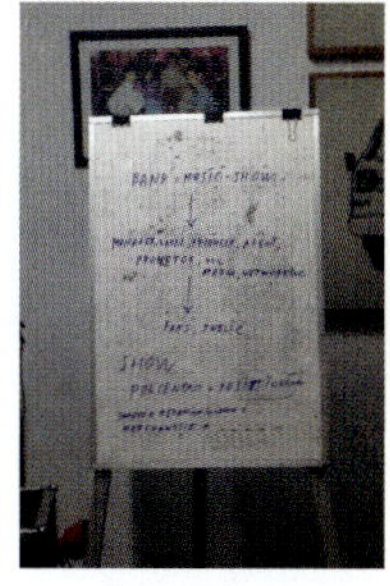

928

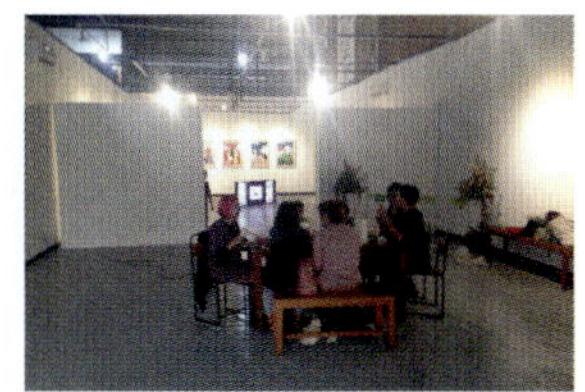

929

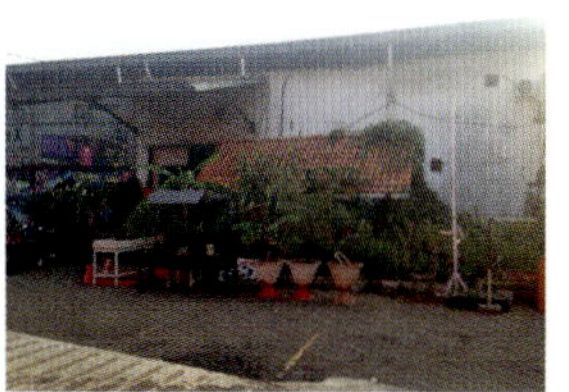

930

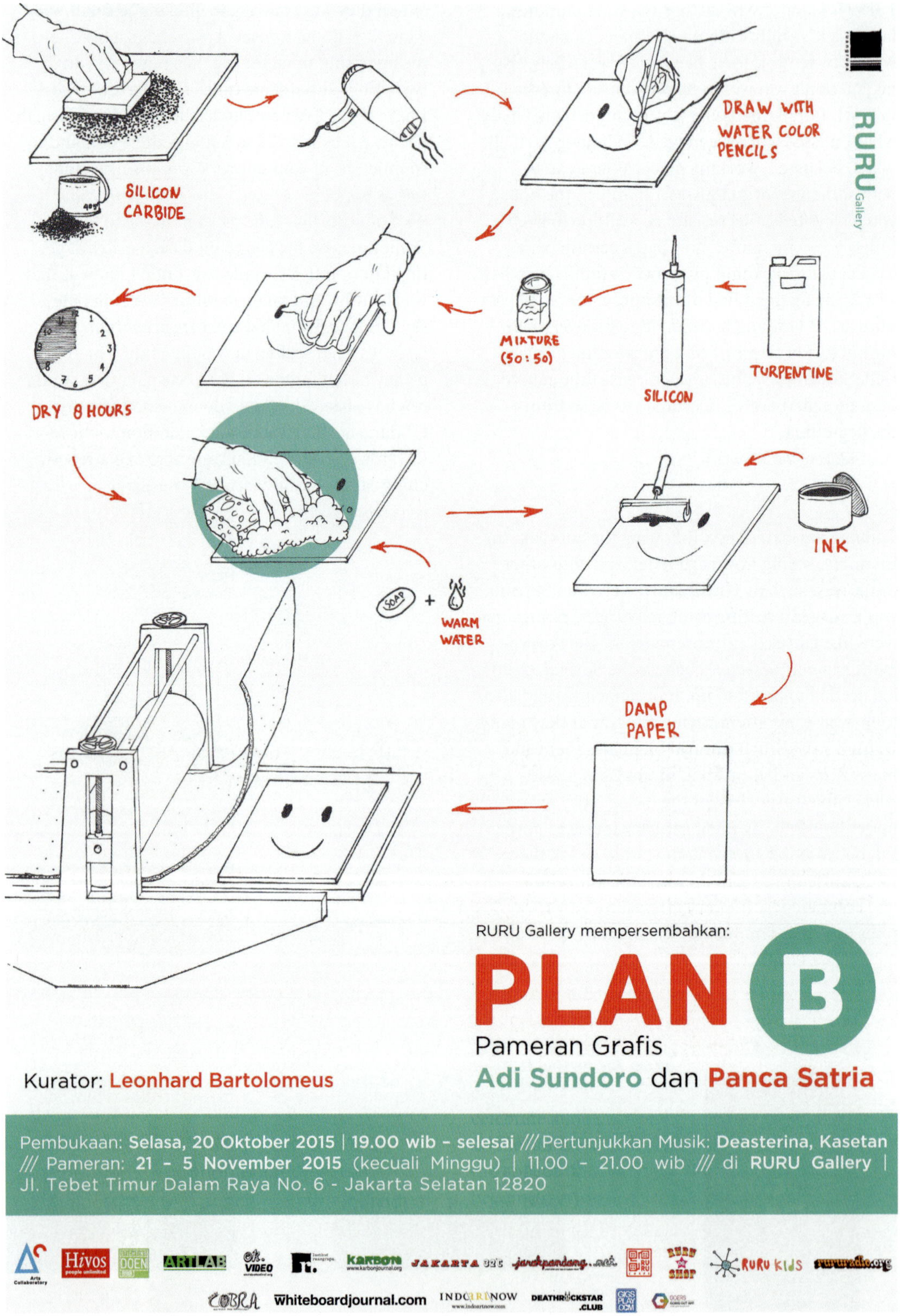

SILICON CARBIDE

DRAW WITH WATER COLOR PENCILS

RURU Gallery

TURPENTINE

SILICON

MIXTURE (50:50)

DRY 8 HOURS

INK

SOAP + WARM WATER

DAMP PAPER

RURU Gallery mempersembahkan:

PLAN B

Pameran Grafis

Adi Sundoro dan **Panca Satria**

Kurator: **Leonhard Bartolomeus**

Pembukaan: **Selasa, 20 Oktober 2015 | 19.00 wib - selesai** /// Pertunjukkan Musik: **Deasterina, Kasetan** /// Pameran: **21 - 5 November 2015** (kecuali Minggu) | 11.00 - 21.00 wib /// di **RURU Gallery** | Jl. Tebet Timur Dalam Raya No. 6 - Jakarta Selatan 12820

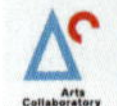
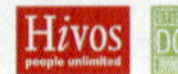

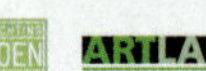
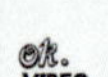
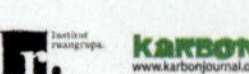
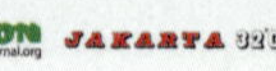
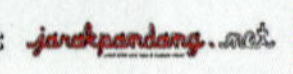
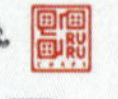
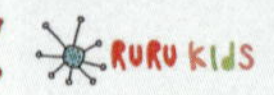
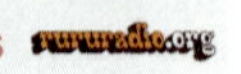
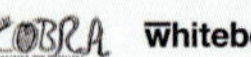

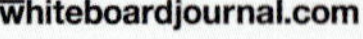

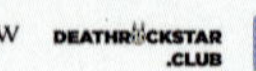

Sonsbeek 16: 'transACTION', Arnhem, The Netherlands, 4 June – 18 September 2016 303

In 2016, curatorial collective ruangrupa presents Sonsbeek 16: transACTION. This edition is characterized by its connections with the city, engagement with communities, interactions with residents and visitors, and many local partners. This starts in July 2015, a year before the official opening of the exhibition, with the opening of the 'ruruhuis' in a vacant shop in the center of Arnhem. It becomes a lively meeting place with a programme of discussions, workshops, lectures, culinary activities, performances, pop-up markets and karaoke nights, where curators and the people of Arnhem meet each other.

Thanks to several open calls, the artworks in the park could literally be used by the public, for instance for weddings, performances and cooking. Throughout the city, different artworks are on display, including striking murals.

Sonsbeek 16

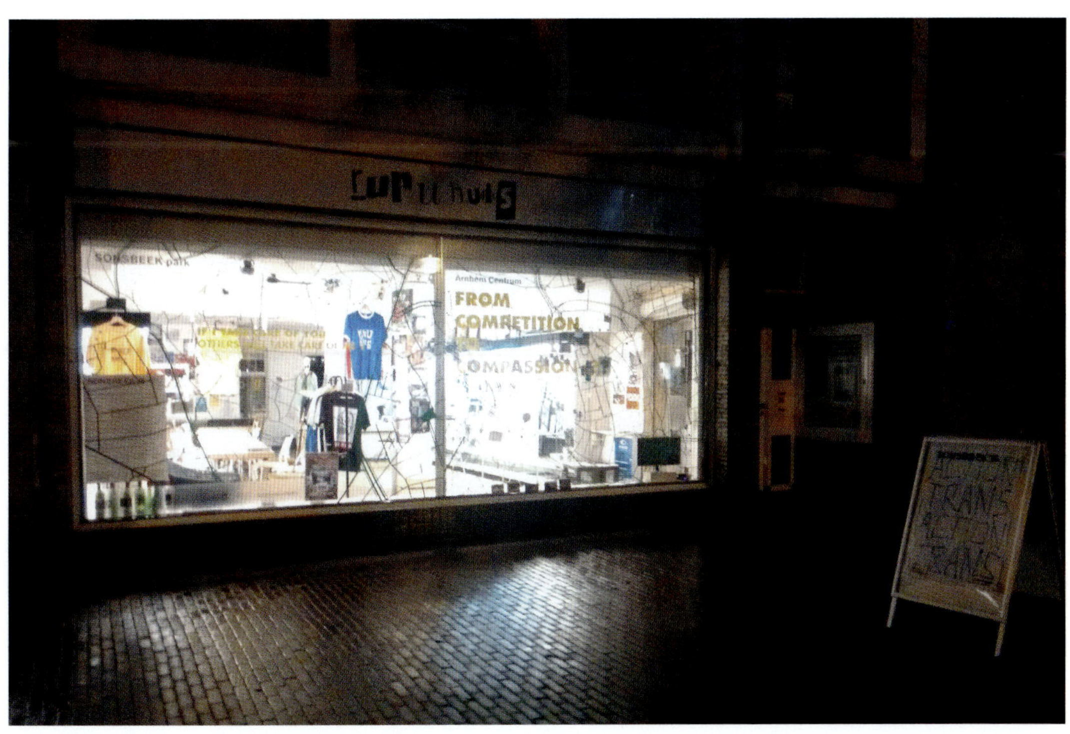

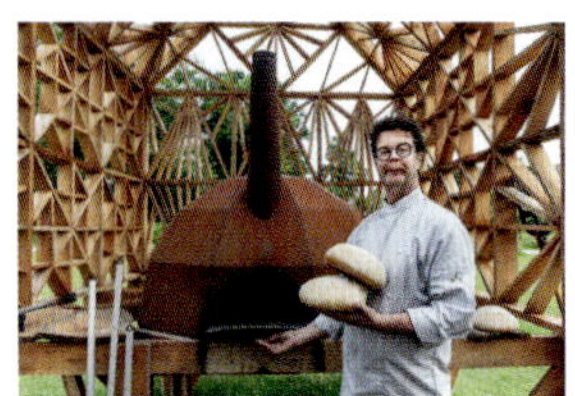

933

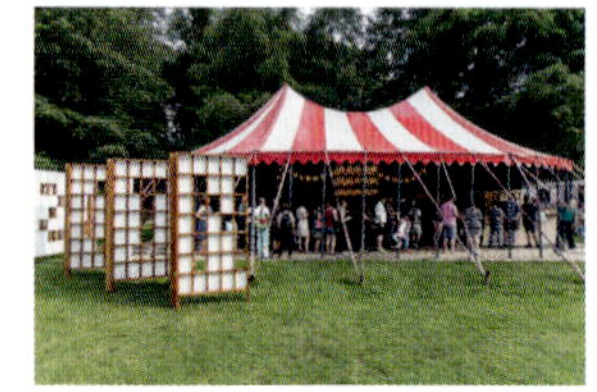

934

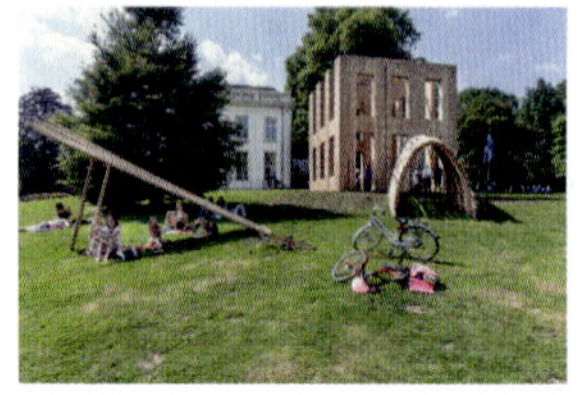

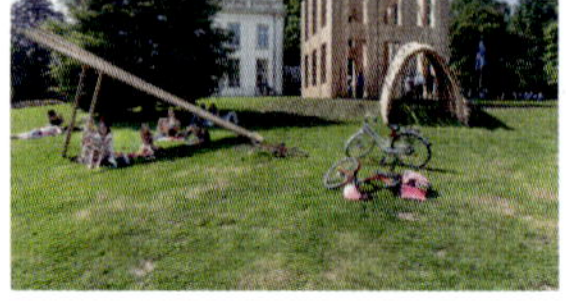

935

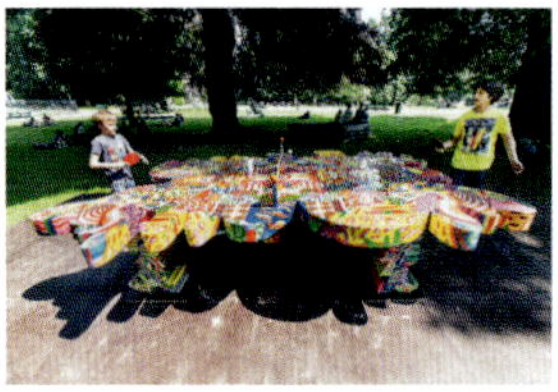

936

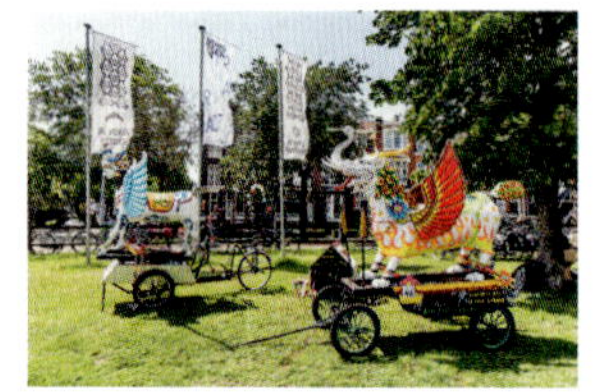

937

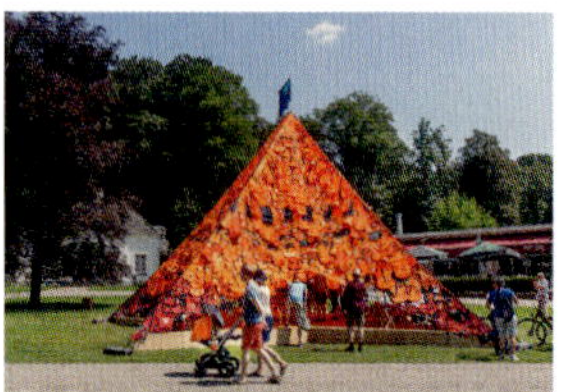

938

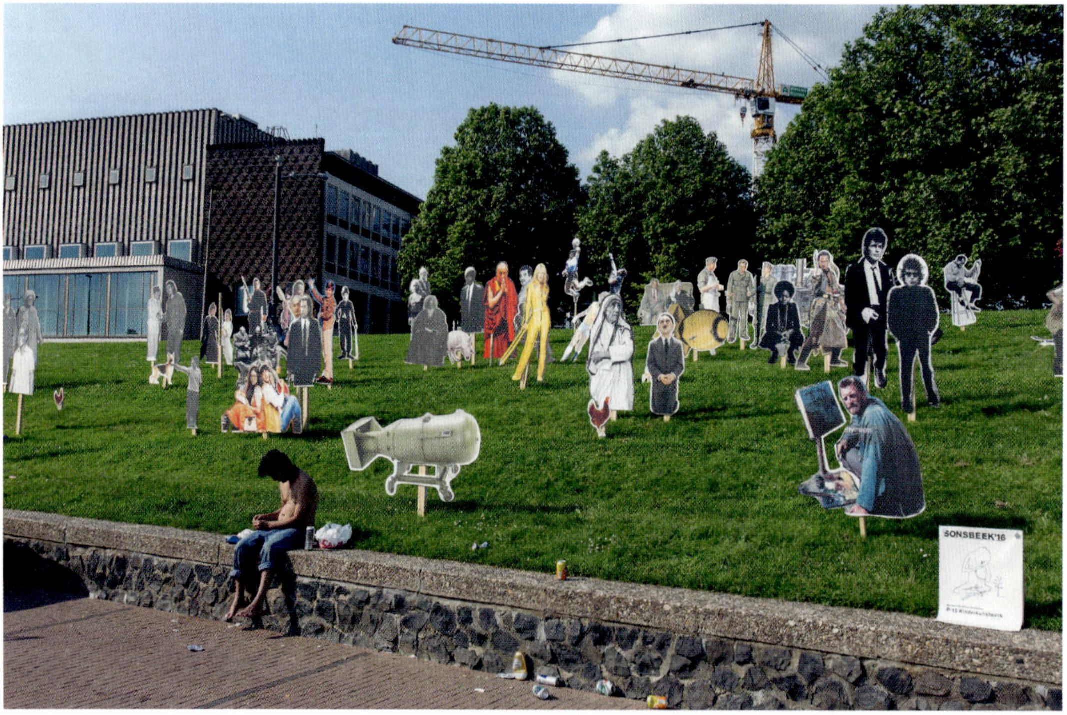

939

Sonsbeek 16: 'transACTION', Arnhem, The Netherlands, 4 June – 18 September 2016

[Sonsbeek] was initiated in 1949 by Arnhem's leaders in an effort to rejuvenate the city, about an hour's drive from Amsterdam, and to bring some of the joy back to its war-torn park. The first edition of Sonsbeek featured more than 200 sculptures along the park's pathways and was attended by more than 100,000 visitors. Many of the works tried, in one way or another, to process or commemorate The Netherlands' traumatic wartime experience. ... This year's Sonsbeek, with 45 artworks by artists from 22 countries in the world, is guest curated by the Jakarta-based artist collective ruangrupa, which chose as this year's theme the concept of 'transACTION.' Members of ruangrupa, a group of artists who are all concerned with urban spaces and social engagement, arrived in Arnhem in July 2015 and set up an open-door workshop called ruru house, which allowed them to interact with people from the city and to get to know Arnhem better. 'We are trying to use it as a space for people to transact,' explained Ade Darmawan, a member of the collective. 'We invite artists to create the space, rather than just to create objects.' ... Entering Sonsbeek Park, past a little white windmill and restaurant with a paddling pool for children, the visitor comes upon a large wooden structure, by the artist Alphons der Avest, designed with patterns from five major world religions. Inside the structure, bakers from various backgrounds will make a range of goods – Turkish bread, Dutch rolls, Italian pizza – that are meant to be shared with the public. As time goes by, the wood that made the house will be fed into the oven, so the house will consume itself, Mr. Darmawan said. Down the hill and along the stream, the Dutch artist Rob Voerman has created another house-like installation over and around an existing waterfall. The artist modeled the design on the idea of a bank, with an open foyer and high ceilings, to explore the notion of economic and natural transactions. From the outside it looks more like a Frank Gehry or Zaha Hadid structure, with its glossy aluminium exterior and small, eye-like stained glass windows in the facade. Other artists have chosen less trafficked areas of the park for more quiet contemplation. Shilpa Gupta, from Mumbai, has selected a clearing in the woods to create a space for meditation. 'We've got a bank, a church, a workshop and a playground,' said Mr. Darmawan, guiding a visitor through the park as works were still being built in mid-May. 'The idea is to create a kind of city inside the city with new versions of institutional structures.'

Nina Siegal, *The New York Times*

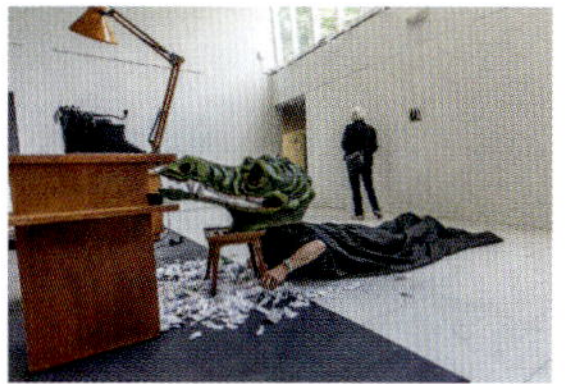

940

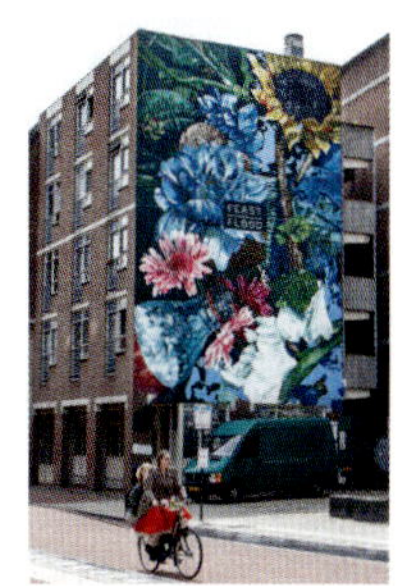

941

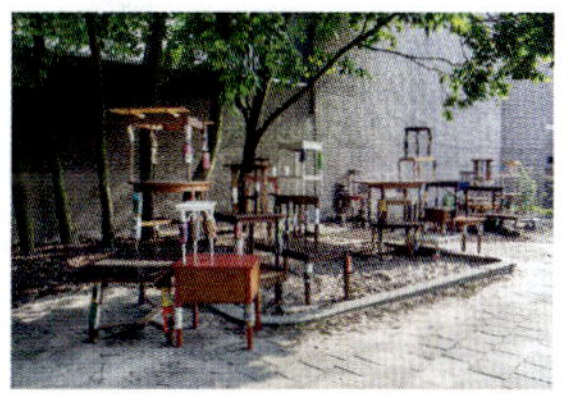

942

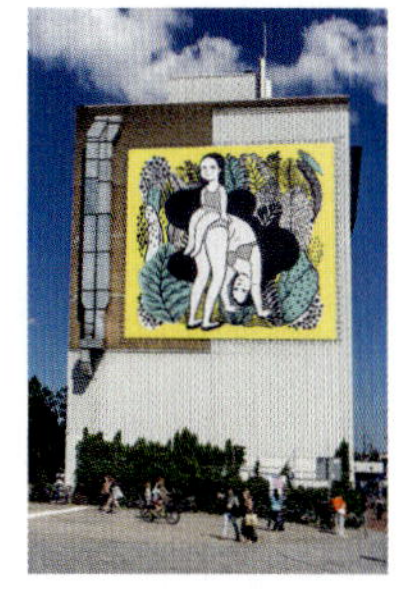

943

what exactly is ruru huis?

Is this serious, is this Art?

what is this?

It's being present

It's Nongkrong

chit chat - building - exchange - platform

It's not just an event platform

Hang around, initiate, connect, make, learn, laugh, ..

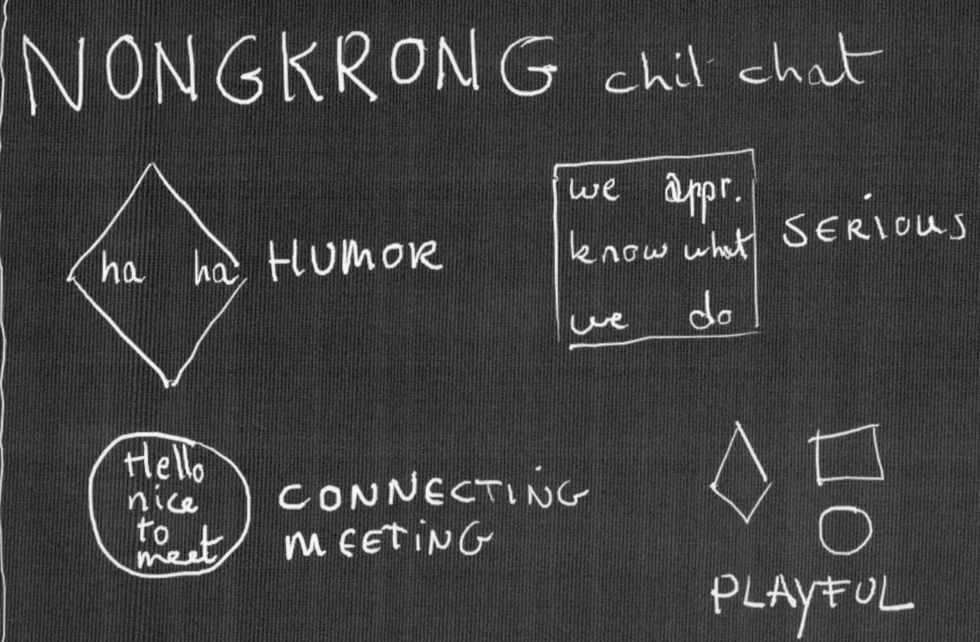

Sonsbeek 16: 'transACTION', Arnhem, The Netherlands, 4 June – 18 September 2016

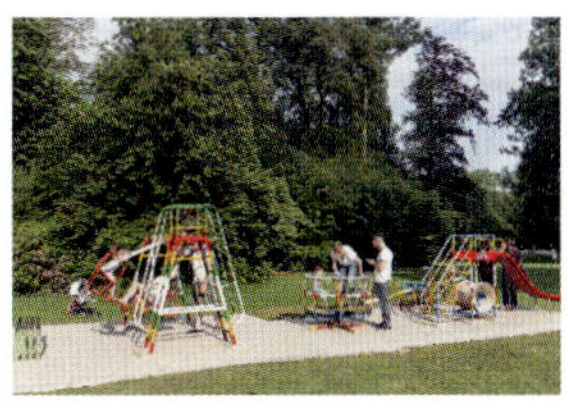

945

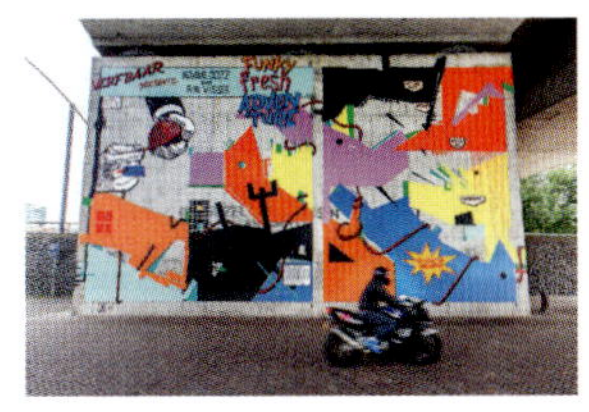

946

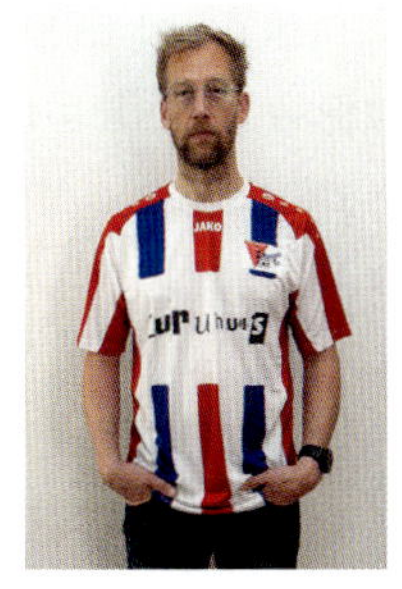

947

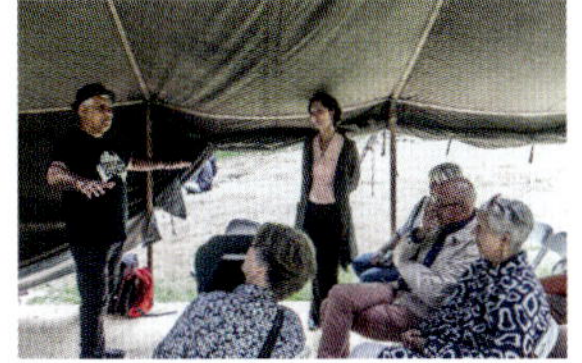

948

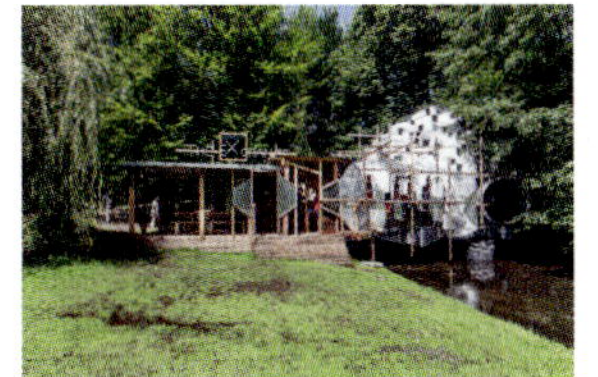

949

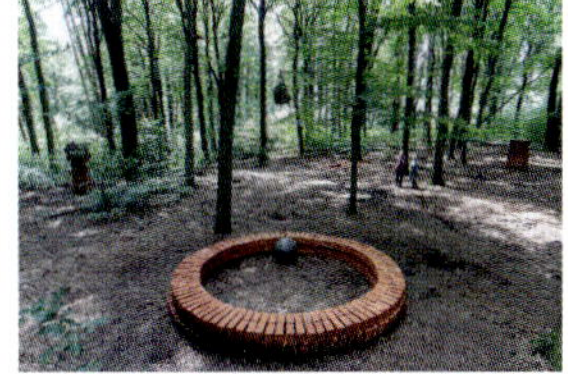

950

Since its establishment in 2000, ruangrupa has given attention to encouraging progress the idea of art in the context of the urban and broad scope of culture. This intention is manifested through a variety of programmes, exhibitions, festivals, Visual Arts laboratories, workshops, research, as well as publishing books, magazines and online journal. In 2015, this effort was expanded by presenting Institut ruru (Ir.) to conquer new challenges in the realm of education.

Institut ruangrupa (Ir.) is our version of an ideal school: unaccredited, non-degree-granting educational wing with no fixed curriculum. After establishing ourselves as a house for cultural and artistic production, the Institut is ruangrupa's latest effort to conquer the next frontier: an examination of our existing artists' collective mode of operation as both tool and method for knowledge production. Our ever-changing educational model is a nod towards the constant incongruities of everyday life: between our deteriorating urban condition with our insistence to keep it that way, between our inadequate public school system with our inability to replace it, between being an independent individual with becoming a part of the collective, up to the tension between the private and the public.

For Aichi Triennale 2016, Ir. would like to implement the method and practice that has been done by ruangrupa before. As a project, Ir. were functioning as a shelter of knowledge and 'human manufacturing' process, especially build a special context with Japan young artist and the local resident at Choja-machi. In Japanese culture, we see Ir. as a style of Dojo, a place to learn, to specifically train or learn something. In corresponding with the event theme, Ir. is a model of ruangrupa's way of thinking as a collective space.

In detail, will facilitate a short course of study followed by the selected participants, after going through the stages of proposal selection and interview. The participants can choose subjects/classes to suit your needs. In practice, the learning activities inside and outside the classroom will be recorded and shown as Ir. archive. Participants will also have the support material to complete the projects at the end of their study. This programme will also open opportunities for scholars/practitioners from Japan to be involved as a guest lecturer and spread his knowledge to the public for free.

ruangrupa

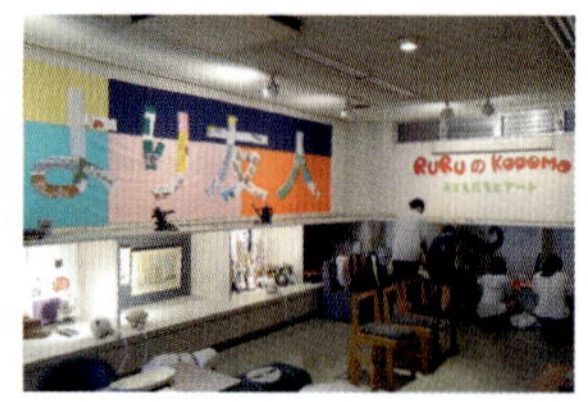

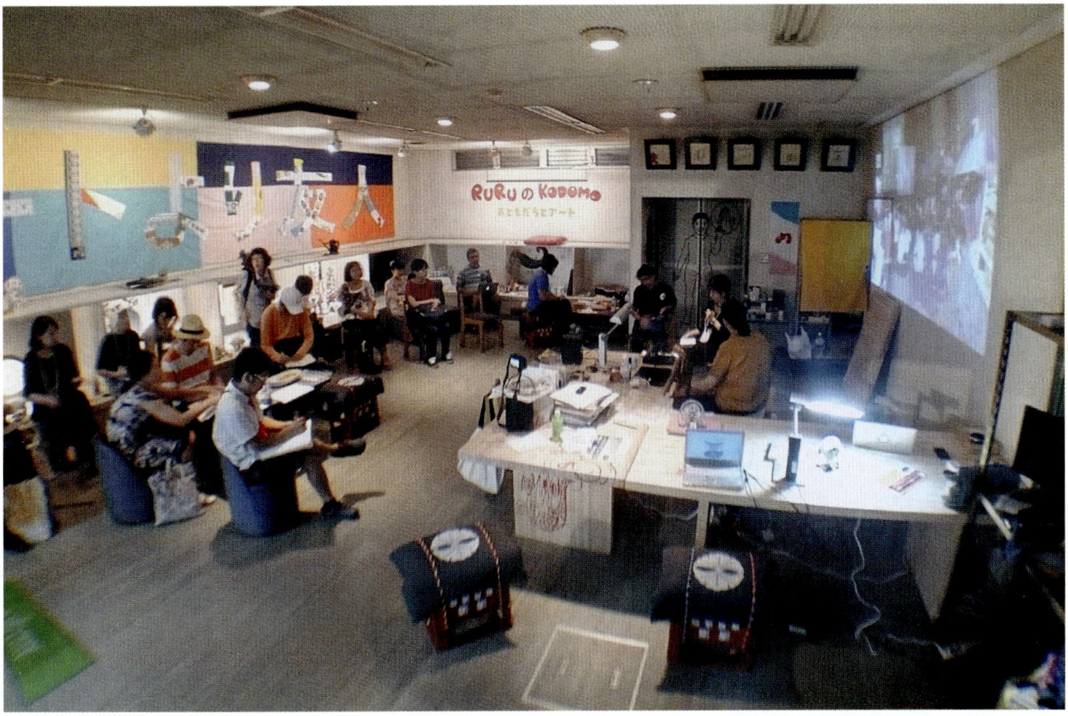

952

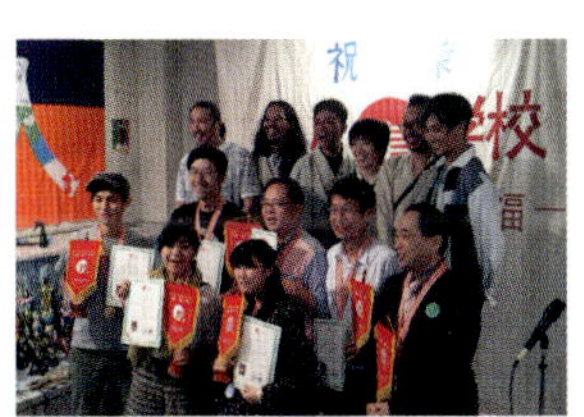

953

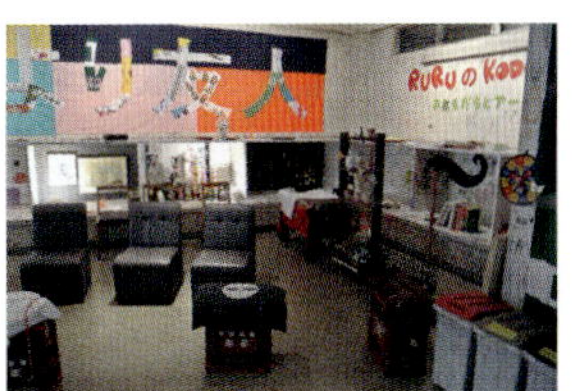

954

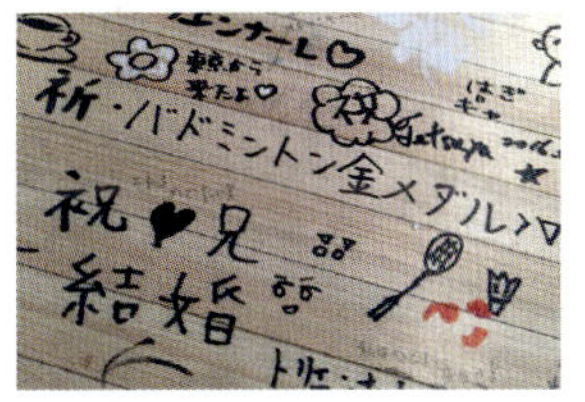

955

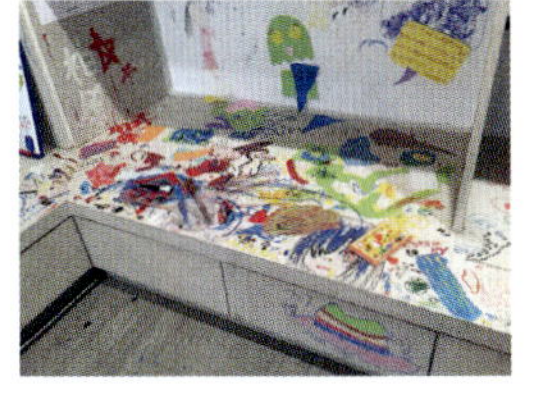

956

see also pp.428–30

RRREC Fest at the Museum, Museum Nasional Indonesia, Jakarta, 18–24 May 2017 310

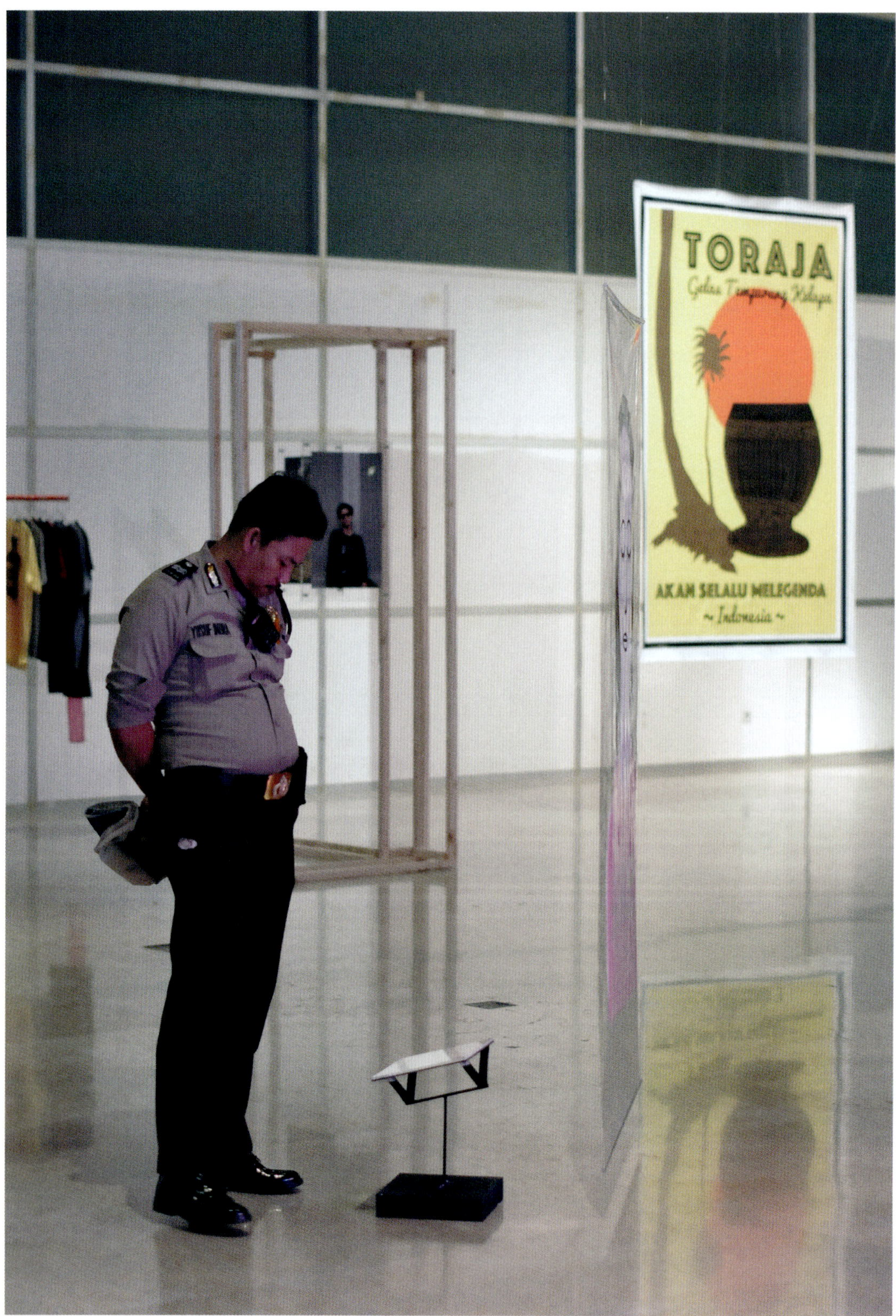

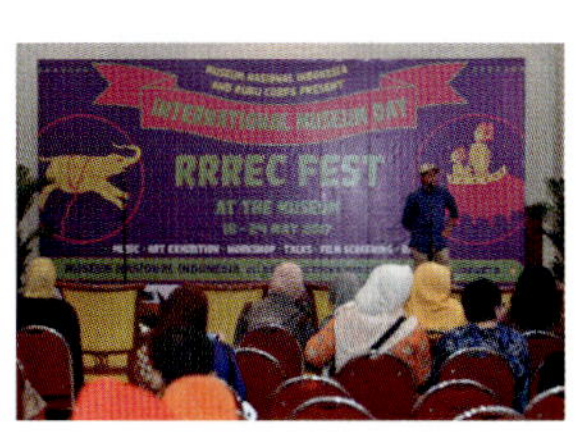

958

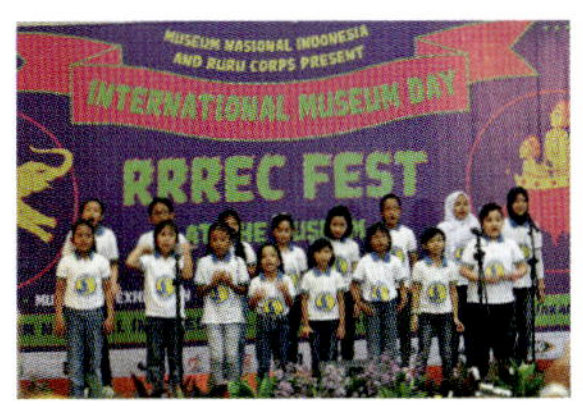

959

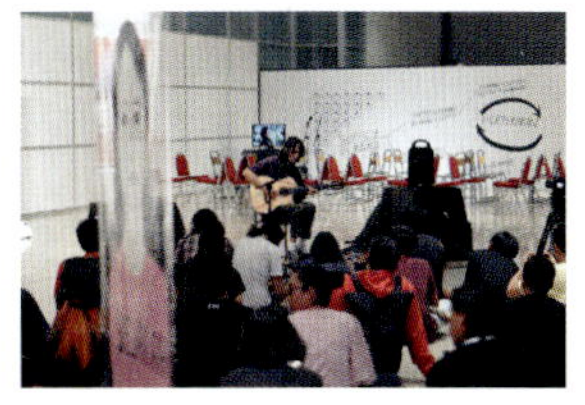

960

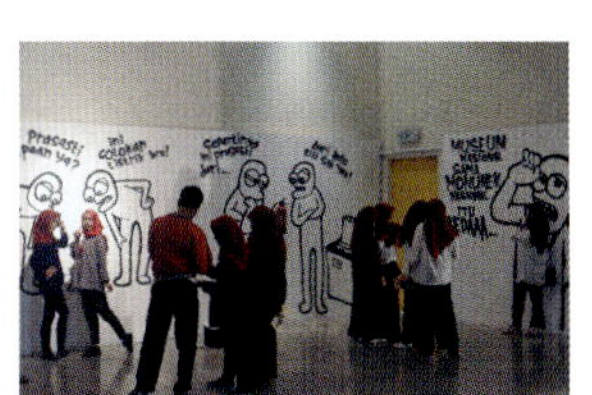

961

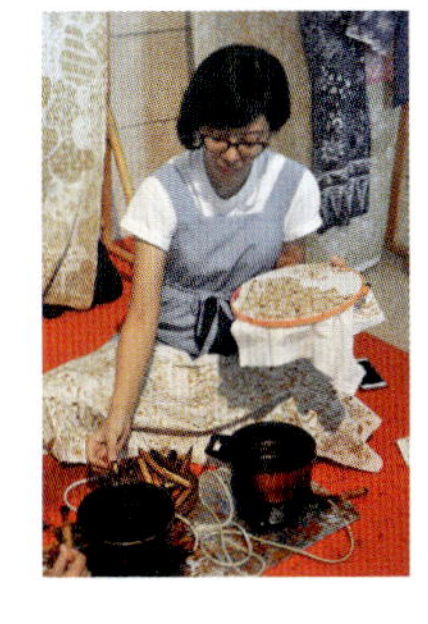

962

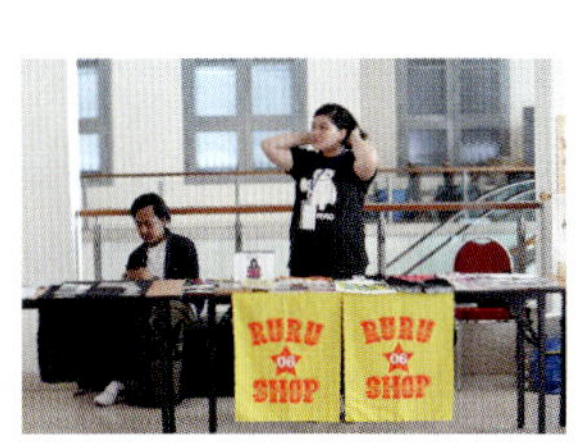

963

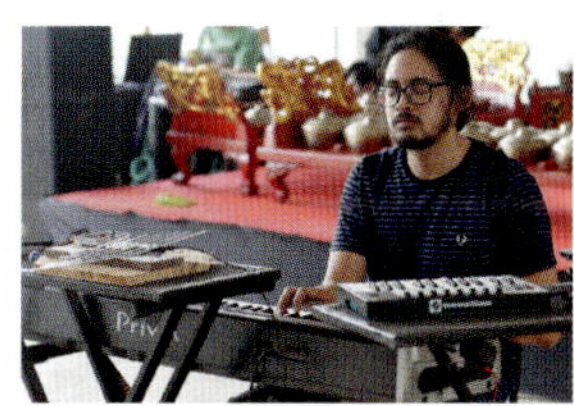

964

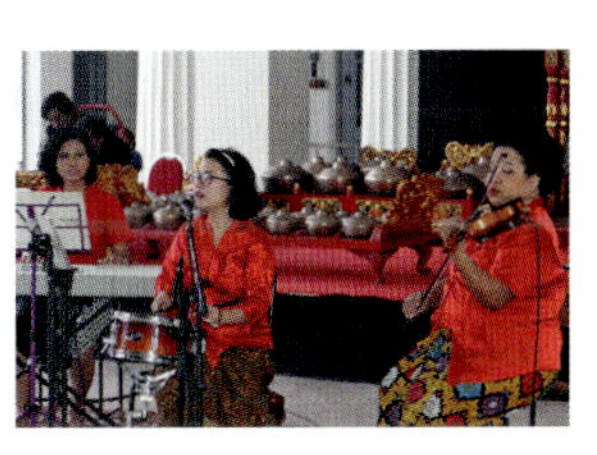

965

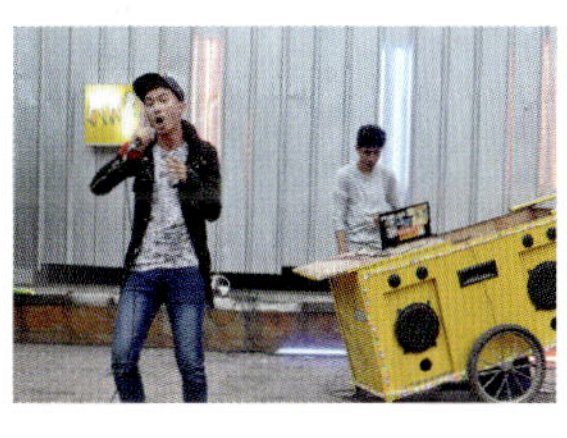

966

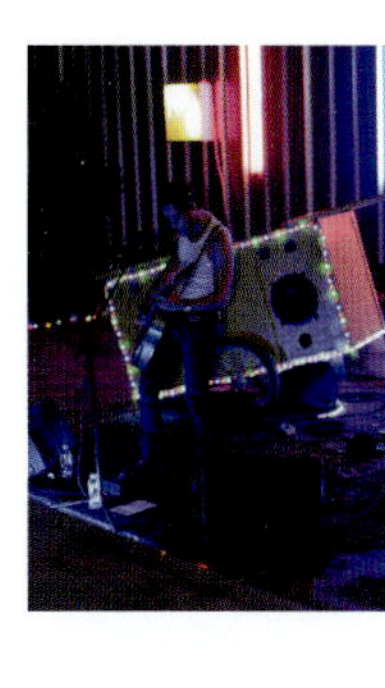

967

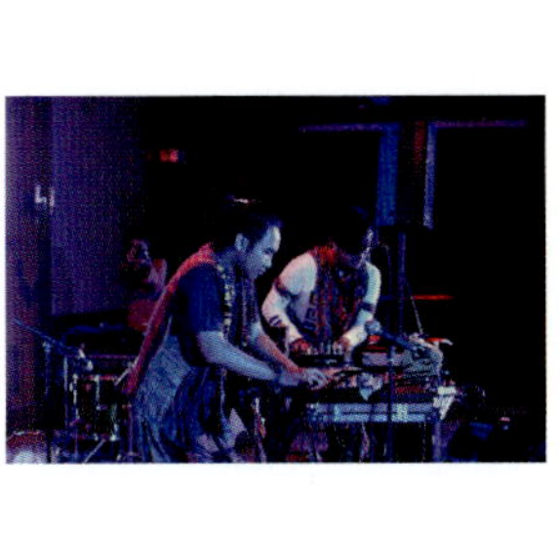

968

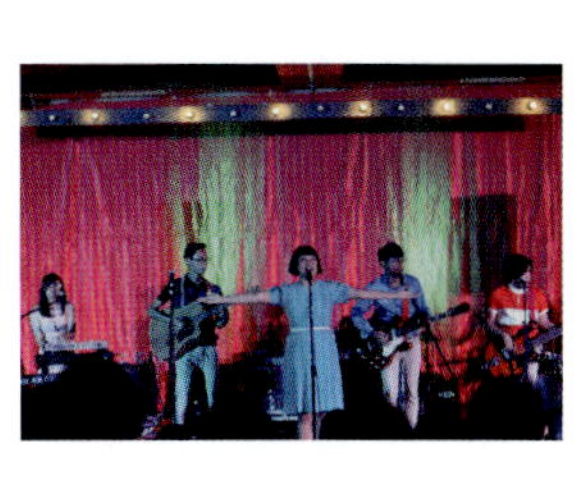

969

ruru.zip: New Edition, installation for 'SUNSHOWER: Contemporary Art from Southeast Asia 1980s to Now', Mori Art Museum, Tokyo, 5 July – 23 October 2017

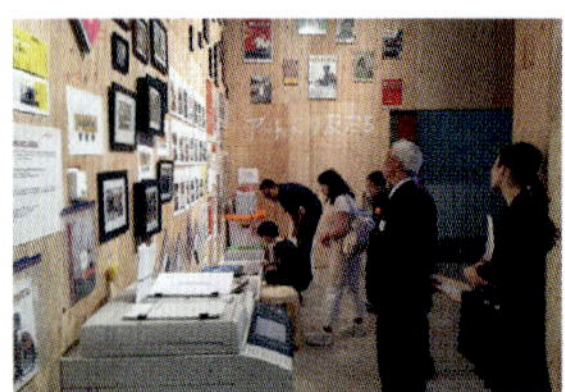

970

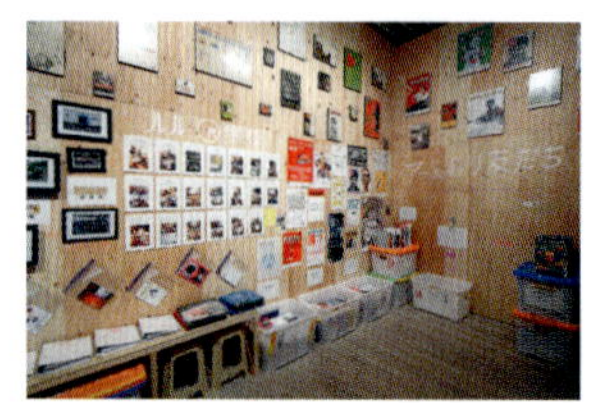

971

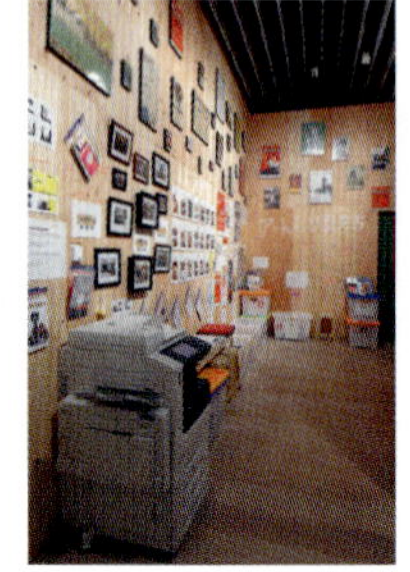

972

OK.Video 'OK.PANGAN' – 8th Indonesia Media Arts Festival, Gudang Sarinah Ekosistem, Jakarta and Pusat Perpustakaan dan Penyebaran Teknologi Pertanian, Bogor, 22 July – 16 August 2017

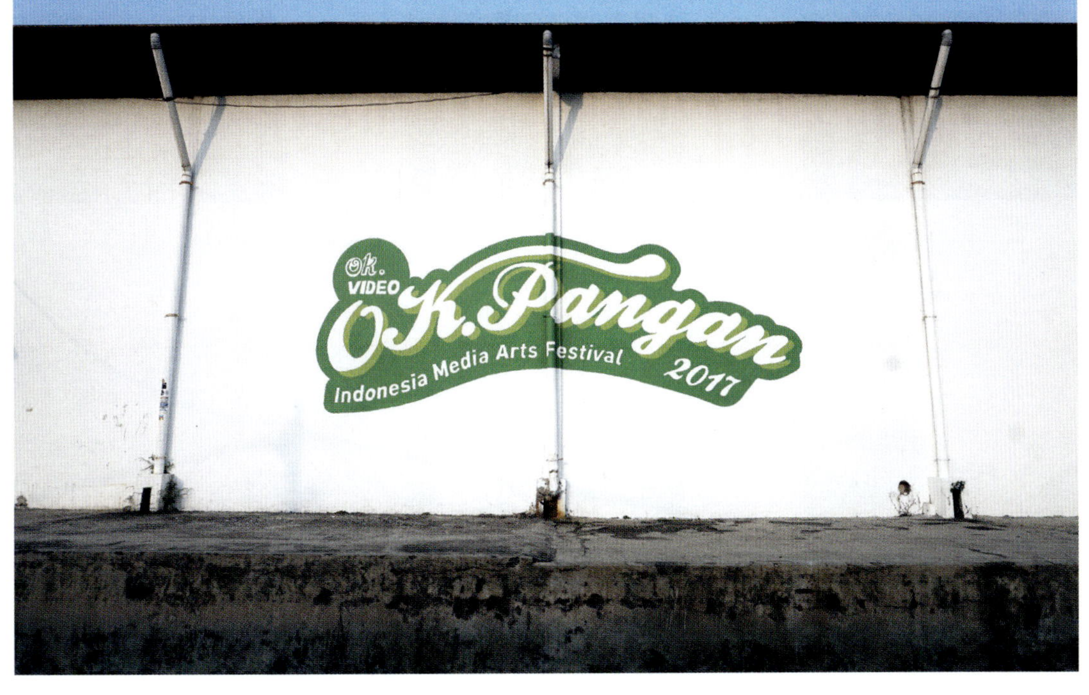

973

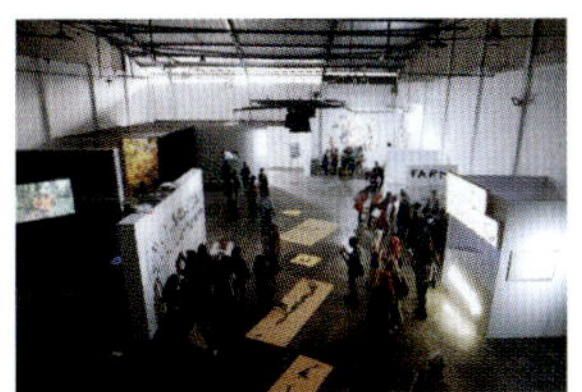

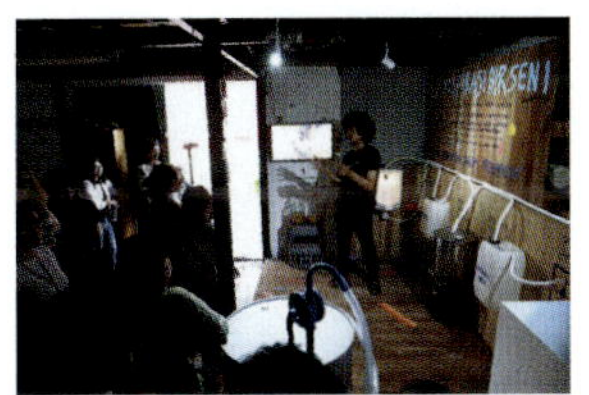

974

975

976

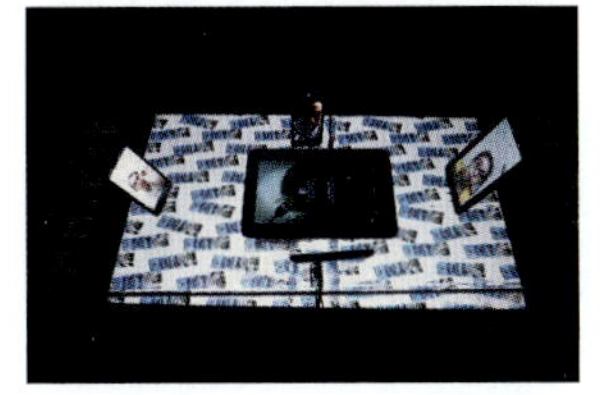

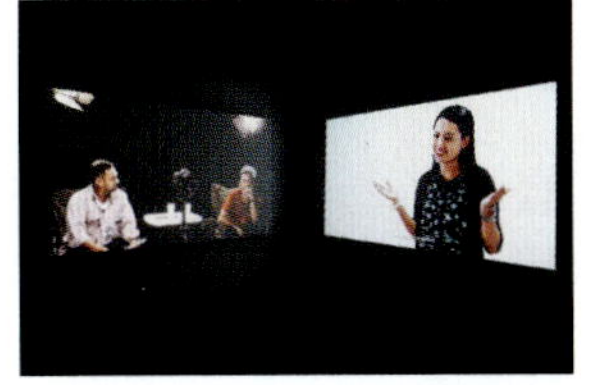

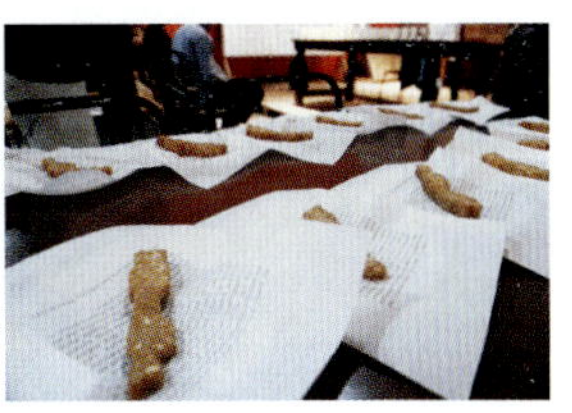

977

978

979

OK.Video 'OK.PANGAN' – 8th Indonesia Media Arts Festival, Gudang Sarinah Ekosistem, Jakarta and Pusat Perpustakaan dan Penyebaran Teknologi Pertanian, Bogor, 22 July – 16 August 2017

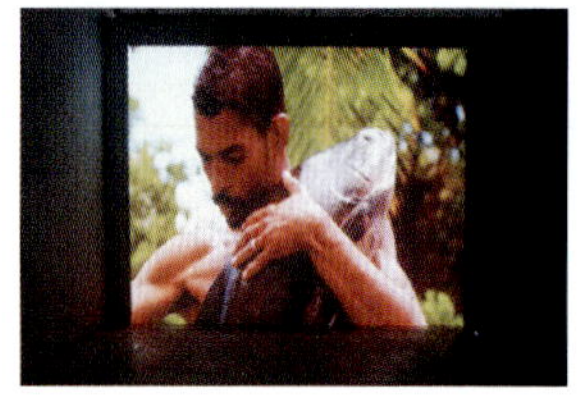

980

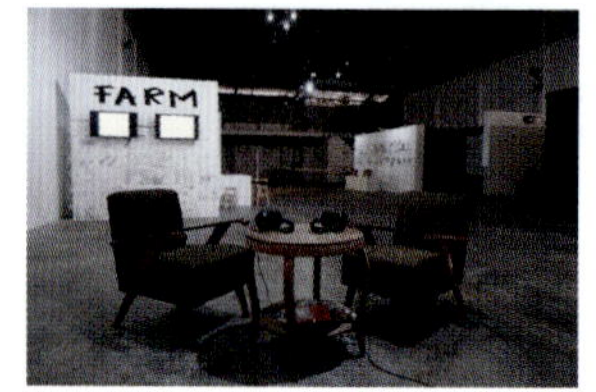

981

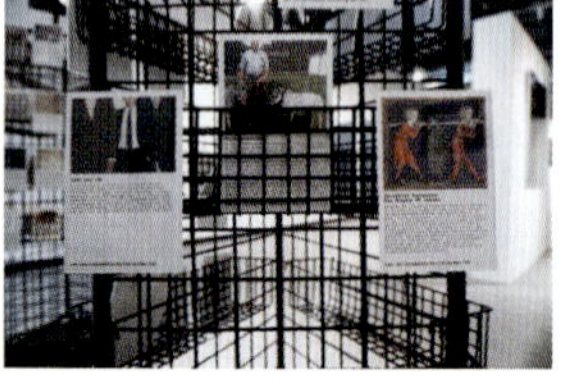

982

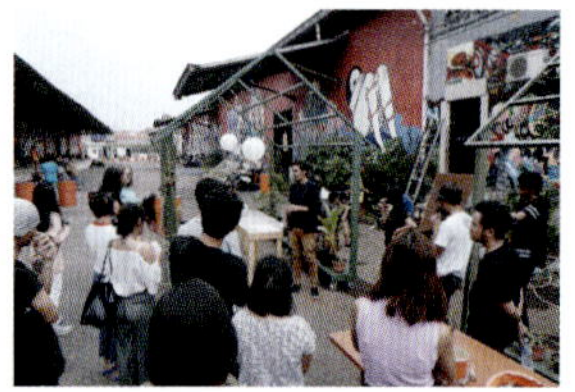

983

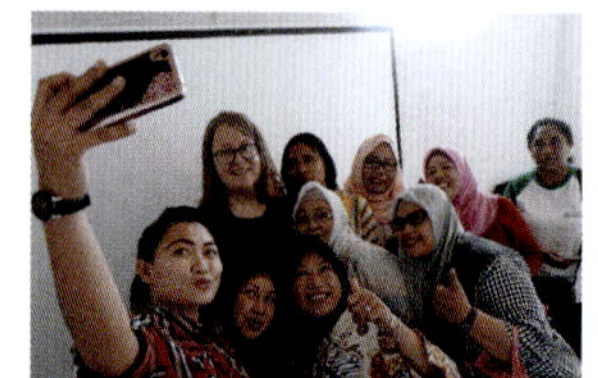

984

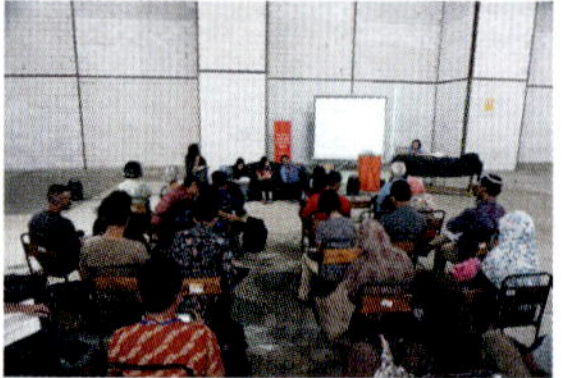

985

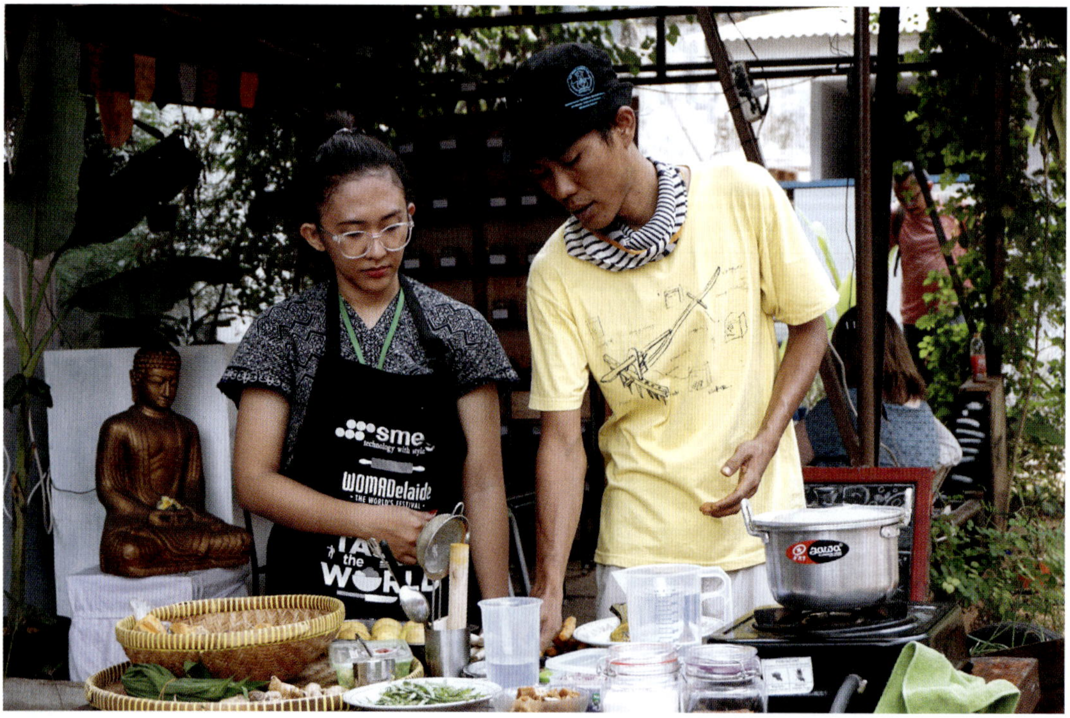

986

ruangruparasite, installation for 'Cosmopolis #1 Collective Intelligence', Centre Pompidou, Paris, 18 October – 18 December 2017

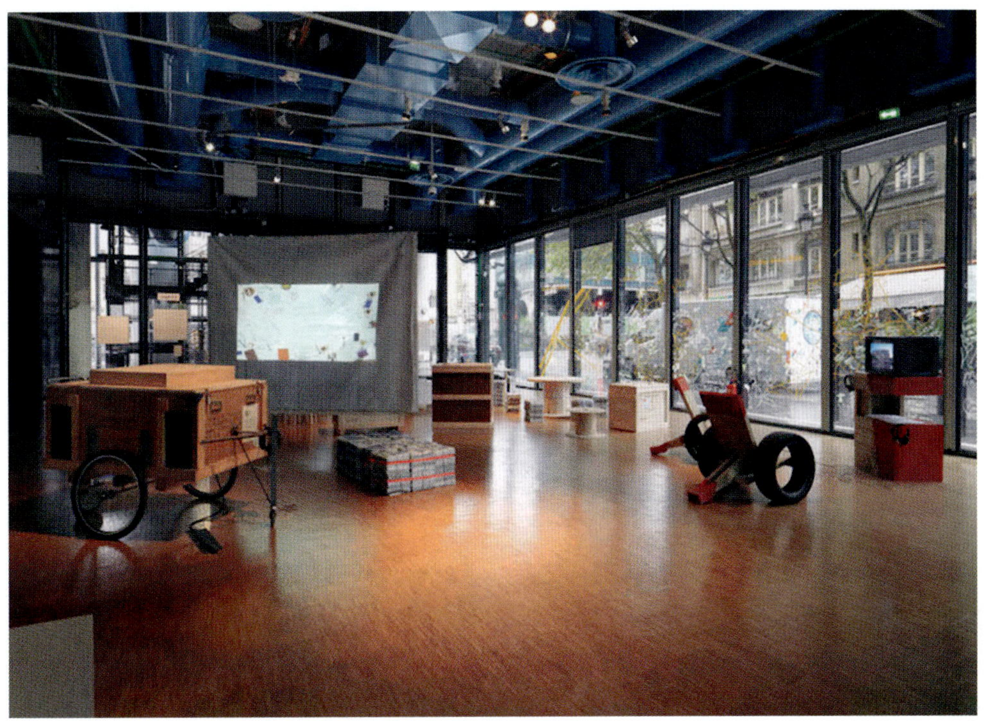

987

During ruru's participation in São Paulo Biennale, Sonsbeek in Arnhem, Pompidou in Paris, I spent most time somewhere else outside of Indonesia – which I enjoyed at that time (and which is not the case at all today). I learned how to manage a lot of things and how ruangrupa as curators make artistic decisions (meaning, how to curate in the ruangrupa way). I speculated that that's how I could be useful and contribute to the collective. In my opinion, compared to other ruru members I'm less visible inside the country itself (which I deem to be a valuable quality), but with the English-speaking realm and the, for want of a better word, West, I can help push ruru's agenda so that more things can happen. Maybe, it's both because I'm more comfortable with it, plus it seems that no one else likes to do that. Sometimes, people joked that I was ruru's foreign minister, the diplomat (*laughs*).

farid rakun

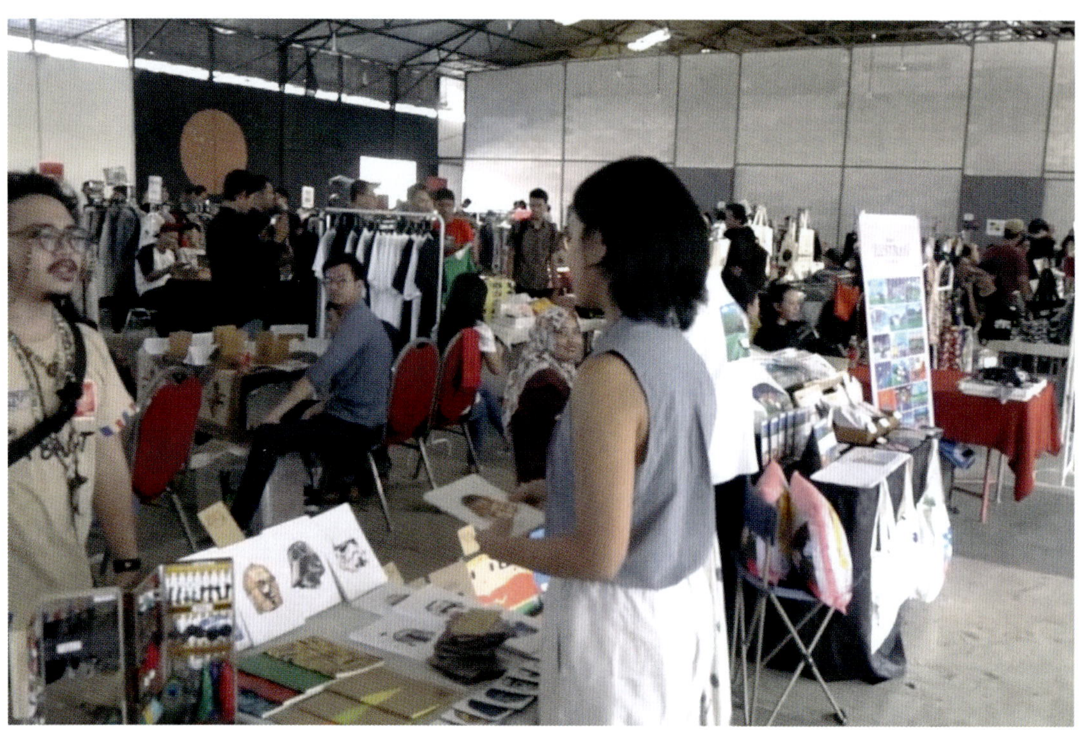

988

If you asked us before 2016, we would say that no institution is doing good enough work. Right now, because of where we are at, we should not deny the fact that we've become an institution ourselves. We're not as young as we were when we started. When we can accept that we can be an institution, the question becomes: an institution like what?

farid rakun

There were some gigs that people in ruru didn't talk about, because they were money-making things, like music events and youth workshops for different cigarette companies – cigarette companies cannot do regular advertising. It was actually me and Sari [Julia Sarisetiati] who were cold enough to deal with that. We needed the money, that's it. Also, Sari and I were doing lots of report writing. ... No one would talk about the commercial work that they do, but there are times you do that to pay your rent. And you cannot pay your rent from ruangrupa salary. Everyone has surviving skills that they don't even talk about. People just know. If someone is not around, then they must be working, individually. It's like an untold secret.

Grace Samboh

Due to the lack or even absence of a supporting structure, ruangrupa feels the need to act, to organise, and not only to provide a space but more importantly to create an infrastructure, in order to generate critical mass, to connect with and support kindred spirits, to learn and to exchange, to register and generate fictions in order to link one's own insights to related activities, to make alternative forces visible. This provides an opportunity to apply our ideas in a more useful way. Also, ruangrupa currently finds itself in a phase of operating increasingly on an institutional level, of being in a position to negotiate on a political level. This transition costs a great deal of time and energy, and is not without some serious learning obstacles. Sometime around 2005, ruangrupa survived a serious internal financial crisis; ten years later, let us hope that ruangrupa also manages to pull through this organisational crisis. The organisation is in a state of transition, there are many new people, the individual career of several members is flourishing; there is more than enough work to be done.

reinaart vanhoe

Back when I was in college (1996–97), I helped manage the finances for the student union at IKJ (Jakarta Art Institute). Because of that experience, my friends at ruru trusted me to help manage ruru finances too. At that time, ruru's financial situation was unstable – up and down, constantly fluctuating. We often only had enough to survive the next two or three months. If we had funding, we got paid for our projects. If not, we simply didn't. That was the reality. Thankfully, even though it wasn't easy, we eventually gained support from several institutions – both government and private organisations like Parekraf, Kemendikbud, the Ford Foundation, DOEN and other commercial partners began accepting and supporting our proposals. But it's based on project support. Around 2004, we established a finance team at ruru. Mr. Lory joined us – he was our finance guy, and he was incredibly helpful. He organised everything so we could properly manage audits. Now, with Gudskul Ekosistem, our finance team has grown. We now have Leni and Putri, both with accounting backgrounds. I noticed the difference right away. As an artist, I sometimes treat finances like I were a magician – juggling money creatively to make things work. But that kind of intuition doesn't always come naturally to professional accountants. And yes, it can be risky. In the beginning, we encouraged them to try being flexible. Often, we start a project that requires upfront costs, but we only receive the funding after the event is done. That's when we need to get creative – find strategies, do a bit of juggling. Over time, we learned from each other. Now, Leni and Putri have adapted to our way of working – and we, in turn, have adapted to theirs. It's not always easy working with artists – and the same goes for working with accountants. It can be stressful on both sides. But we're fortunate to live and work collectively. We support one another, financially and otherwise. Every entity in the ecosystem contributes. We practice openness, transparency and trust – these are values we continue to nurture and protect. Even now, we're still thinking, still trying, still figuring out how to make money together. But maybe that's part of the art too – the art of thinking, of strategising. We just keep going.

Daniella F. Praptono

We are setting off from a contemporary art ecosystem developed from a not-for-profit work model. A large part of our operational support comes from our constitutive collective, which in turn were given by donor institution, sponsors and independent funding from our business unit, apart from the funds given from our member out of their own volition. When we decided to work together as an ecosystem, we tried to set a system of co-storehouse where every resource we have is collected and shared in proportion to every collective need. The various resources from every collective come in many forms: money, programme, equipment or even books. We pooled those assets for easier access and sharing for every member of the collective.

Gudskul Ekosistem consists of many elements: artists, curators, art writers, managers, researchers, musicians, directors, architects, cooks, artistic designers, designers, fashion designers, street artists and individuals with various other expertise. This variety makes Gudskul an affluent and dynamic ecosystem. Gudskul also houses a multitude of collectives with differing practices and artistic mediums: installation, archive, video, sound, performance, media art, public participation, printmaking, graphic design, education, etc. This variegated bunch also enriches the issues and involved parties in many collaborative projects, socially, politically, culturally, economically, environmentally and even educationally.

Gudskul Ekosistem

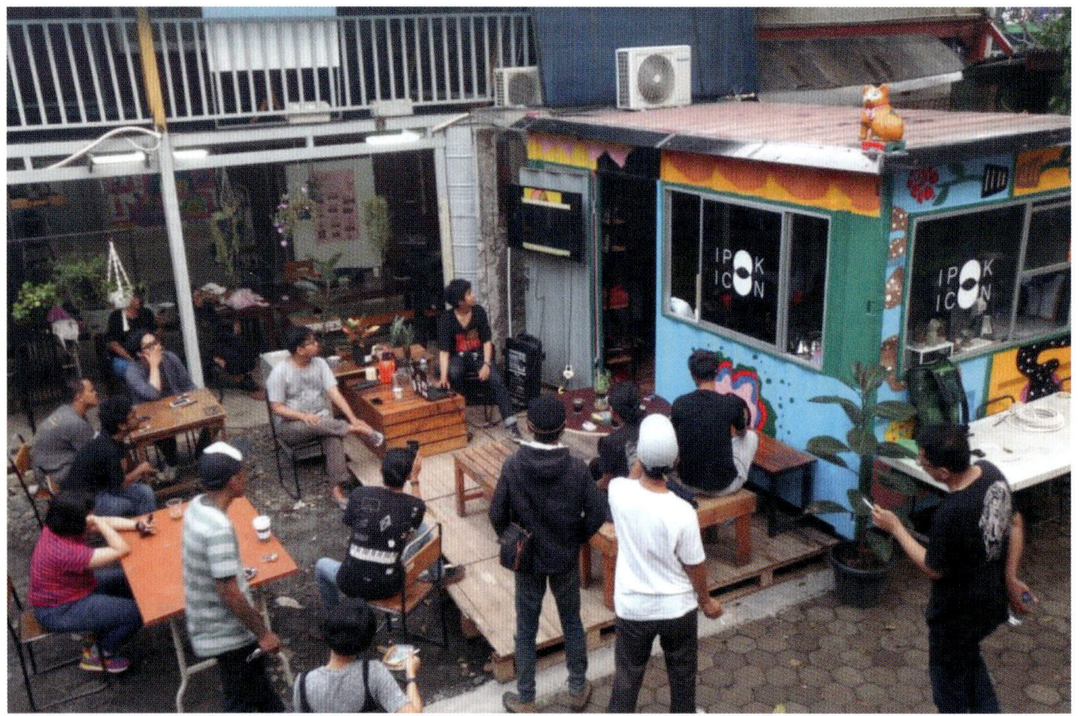

How little I know about you[1]

or *PASANGKAN TALI KELEDAR KESELAMATAN SEMASA DUDUK*[2]

An attempt to start a list to assist differing bodies to work together[3]

In no particular order:

1. Us for you, you for us. You use us, we use you.
2. Let us realize fully and address one vital exciting challenge: that between us, we have different backgrounds and sensibilities. Therefore, we understand history and responsibility, clearly, differently.
3. We deem differences as treasured spaces, where interventions, explorations, experimentations and opportunities are staged within.
4. Generosity is key. Humility is as much so. Compare your titling with mine, as an example.
5. "Our kind" don't function well in meetings.
6. Embrace slowness—a different slowness, not bureaucratic but the self-caring kind—once in a while.
7. We like to challenge Marx by rarely separating work against leisure. Precarious, they said. We just simply do not want to be alienated, we reply.
8. We operate in different time-scales. We understand, and therefore experience, age differently. Relationships, too.
9. Hang out with us. Let's waste time on each other.
10. As tempting as it might sound, let us not keep producing a one-off like we often did. Like human relationships, our biggest work lies in how to (continue) work(ing) with each other.
11. Dance with us. We don't struggle, we hustle. We dance, therefore we revolt.
12. Eat, drink and socialize with us. Get to know each other better. It will take time. Let's take it.
13. We are curious beings. We do not dismiss. Not even you.
14. Our question is always, what good could working together with someone, or something, bring to each of our particular contexts? How can we continuously assist each other in a more sustained way, in space and in time?
15. Should we build "bridges", or actually "platforms" is a much useful allegory? Really?

16. Our public is different than yours. That is why we were interested in working together in the first place, no?
17 Utilize us to help you reach out to your forgotten next-door neighbors. Let us do what we're best at—engage with the locals. Assist us.
18. We are trained to be networkers, therefore we struggle to be non-representational. We are never stand-ins. Not for our contexts, cities, nations, countries.
19. We deem social skills as important as, if not more vital than, artistic merits.
20. Let us teach each other what flexibility means. We are good for each other that way.
21. As you put your gaze to the global sky, we know it's difficult to keep in touch with what's happening on the ground. We are ground specialists. It's nice to be working with you.
22. We exist as a sign of the certain failures in the nation-state system. Do not expect us to act as a United Colors of Benetton signage in your public programmes.
23. For some, there's no "identity politics" There is just simple, plain politics. Like there are no "women artists" or "outsider artists", there are just artists.
24. We challenge individuality. We challenge the very notion of genius. Your existence is to identify, mystify and guard them.
25. CVs, bios and list of achievements we deem to be superfluous. If I coule be allowed to use the words of the great Richard Bell, "How do you even write a collective CV?"[4]
26. There's a reason why "pigeonhole" is a term. Who the pigeon is and who the hole is between us, you decide.

---

[1] This is a pun from the title "How little you know about me", an exhibition staged in MMCA, Seoul, Korea. The title can be seen as an attempt to render the term more generous, mature and humble. It is an awareness, which is not about you not knowing enough about me, like what teenagers shouted to their parents, but more the humility brought by the fact that I don't know enough about you.

It is good to state that although written for the occasion, this text is not specifically about our experience of participating in the exhibition. It is a culmination our previous experiences collaborations, while at the same time addressing our speculative future collaborators.

[2] As the picture conveyed, the term is the Malay translation of "fasten your seatbelt while seated" As an Indonesian, reading this term is uncanny—familiar in their unfamiliarity. This term also reminds me of the well-known stunt by the Malaysian artist Roslisham 'Ise' Ismail, where he likes to wear a t-shirt by the budget airline AirAsia to art openings, as to say that the airline has contributed a lot to (at least Southeast) Asian art scenes just by making flying to each other's respective locations affordable.

[3] The idea to undertake this attempt comes from ruangrupa's past and current experiences working with more traditional and established institutions outside of Indonesia. It might be useful to retell here that ruangrupa was born as a reaction against the visual art infrastructures, existing in Jakarta, or even Indonesia, in the end of 90s/beginning of 00s. With very few exceptions, either commercial or government funded institutions at that time were top-down in their hierarchies. Fast-forward 18 years after, to today, ruangrupa finds ourselves existing in parallel these type of institutions. No longer against. The differences in perspectives and approaches, nevertheless, remain.

Another push that gave birth for this attempt also came from conversations with several participants of "How little you know about me", during the installation week. Special shoutout to Marika B. Constantino, from our fellow exhibition participant, Manila-based 98B COLLABoratory, who extended the conversation several days after in Roxas City, the Philippines, during South East Asia Art Residencies Meeting 2018. I assume she would not realize this fact, but it's credit where credit's due.

[4] Richard Bell, "Bell's Theorem: Aboriginal Art—It's a White Thing!" in The Koori History Website (November 2002). [http://www.kooriweb.org/foley/resources/art/bellessay.html, last accessed 3 May 2018] The word in italics is mine.

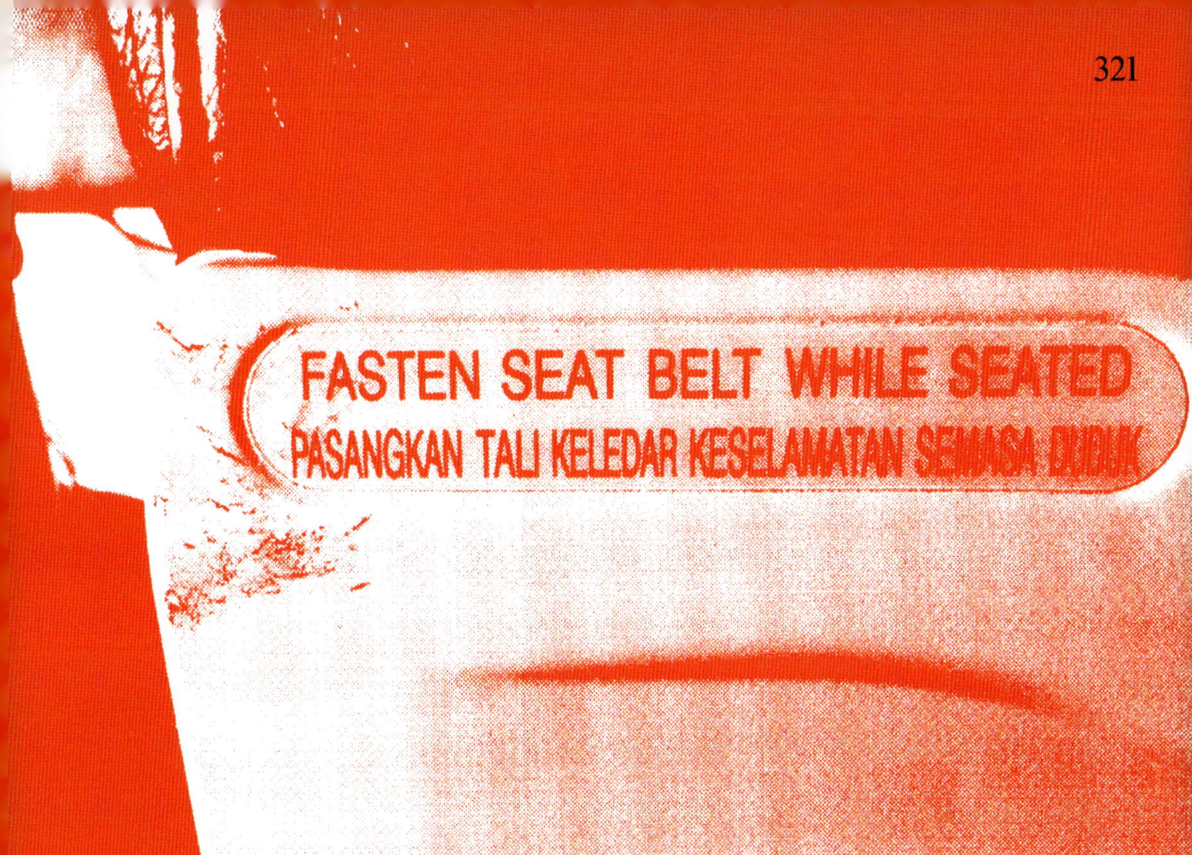

27 When there's a need to label us, refrain. We don't fit neatly to categories, while it's your job to produce them.

28. We are a product of certain (non) bureaucracy. You are built upon it as foundation.

29. In order to build and maintain our cool products, we also built factories to sustain their very production.

30. Adapt a "can-do" attitude. Always.

31. Adapt a "can-do" attitude. Always.

32. Adapt a "can-do" attitude. Always.

33. Remember economy, of scale. We are not those artists whose practice fit in with your business model, which in turns were founded to support certain art forms. Again, not our forms.

34. We simply cannot work first, get paid later. Most of our budget goes straight to humans. Some people cannot wait.

35. Unlike what's known now as gig-economy, for us cash often still works best.

36. Conflict is overrated, so don't shy away from it. We strive from and within it.

37 Horizontality is so much so. It's a useful myth, but nevertheless still a myth.

38. We are not a product of politically correctness. As a consequence, we will never be correct politically.

39. Asia is, indeed, a method. The usefulness of any method lies on the hand of its beholder. Our advice: don't be afraid to let it slip from your hand.
40. Having said all the above, be assured that we will never stop trying to surprise you, as we know you do not appreciate surprises.
41. When you think you know us, we know you better.
42. Relax.
43. Last but not least, enjoy the bumpy ride, as we know we will!
44. Don't worry… as you can always flee and do business-as-usual.
JAKET KESELAMATAN DI BAWAH TEMPAT DUDUK.

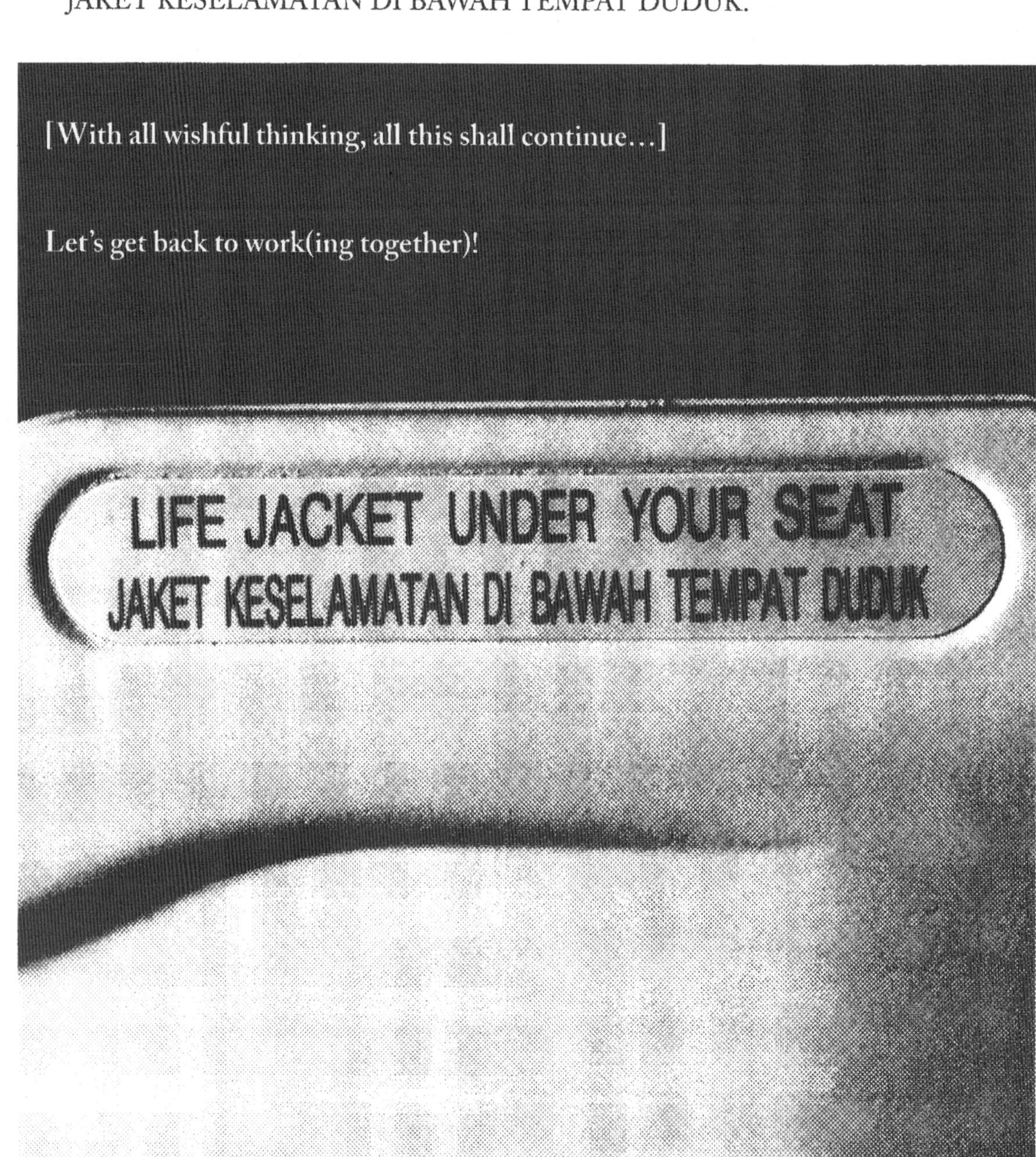

We [ruangrupa] no longer have our own space. If you go to Gudskul now, you can find Grafis Huru Hara's space and Serrum's space. You can no longer find ruangrupa's space. I would say we are more dissolved since Gudang Sarinah, from 2015 onwards, after fifteen years of being together. Whether we have a ruangrupa office is not important any more. I mean instead all of us were ready to soak into the collective [Gudskul Ekosistem]. At the moment, we only exist online, on the website.

Iswanto Hartono

There were lots of discussions before we became Gudskul – an informal education platform. When Gudskul started, we had to write proposals to generate income. A lot of ruru come from Sundanese and Javanese backgrounds. Because of that, it's always about politeness and harmony. Compared to them – maybe because I'm half Javanese half Batak – I'm not as 'nice', haha. Perhaps that's why potential foreign funders are warmer towards me?

farid rakun

There were some moments which we would have potential conflicts in interests, as we are all organisations in Indonesia. Yet, through Gudskul, we were trained to think beyond our own organisation's ego and think for the umbrella (Gudskul Ekosistem), to be more supportive. Rather than getting all the benefits, we were trained to think how to give to everyone. It would be implemented in the majelis, our monthly organisational meetings.

JJ Adibrata

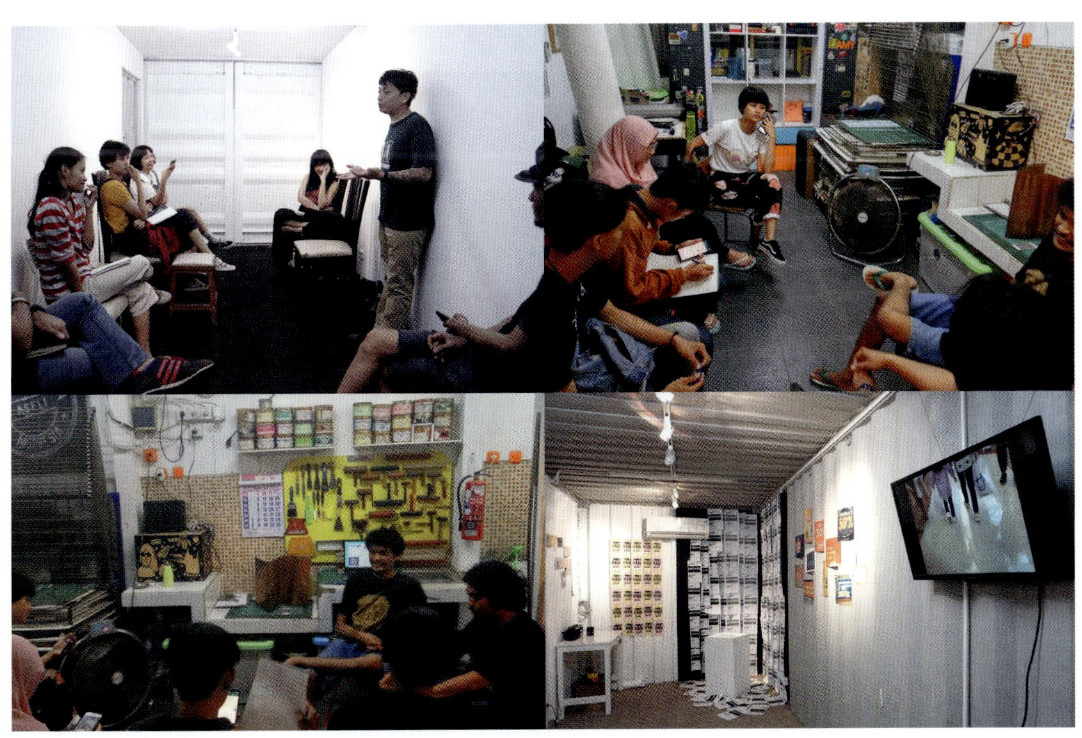

 see also pp.410–19, 428–29

'Pemandangan', exhibition by Dwi 'Ube' Wicaksono Suryasumirat, RURU Gallery, 27 January – 18 February 2018

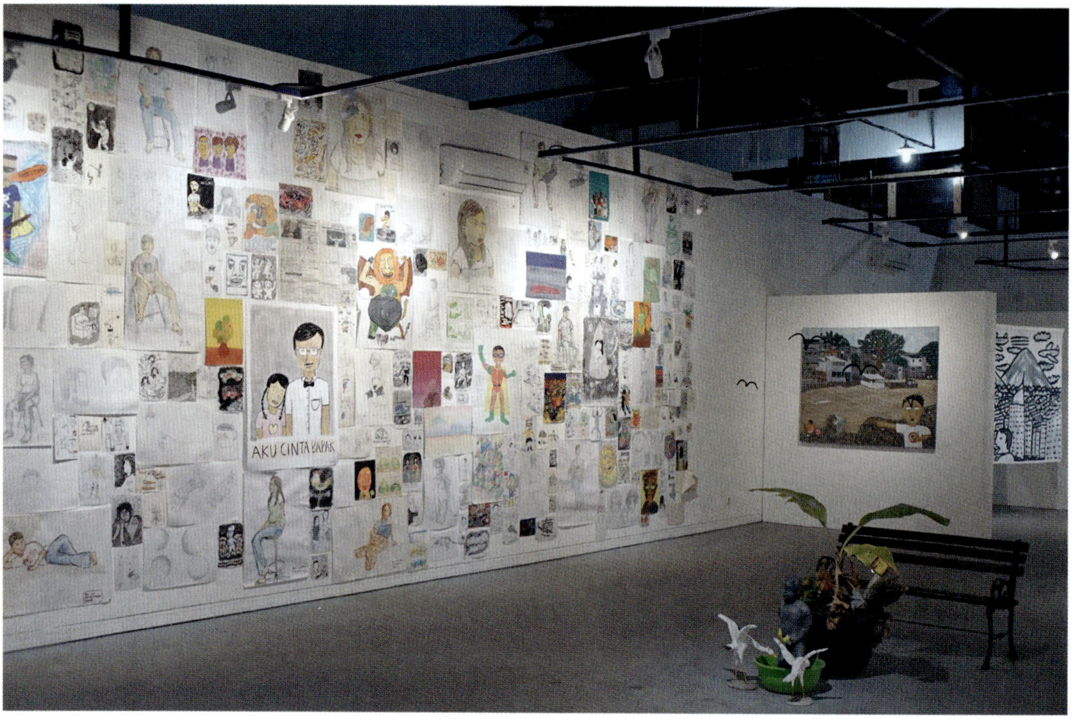

991

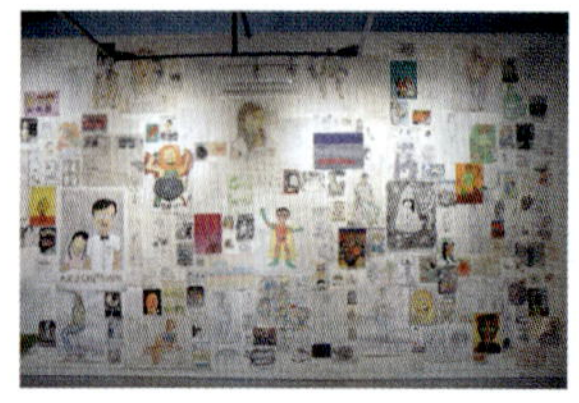

992

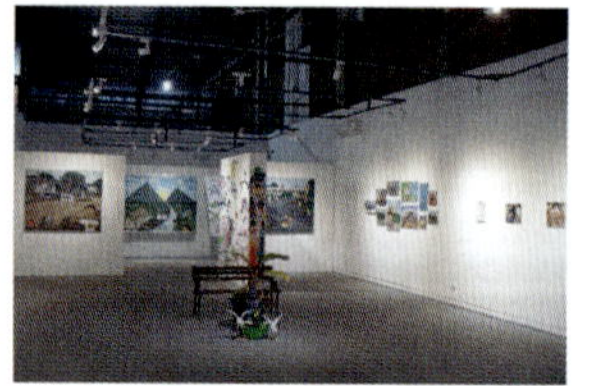

993

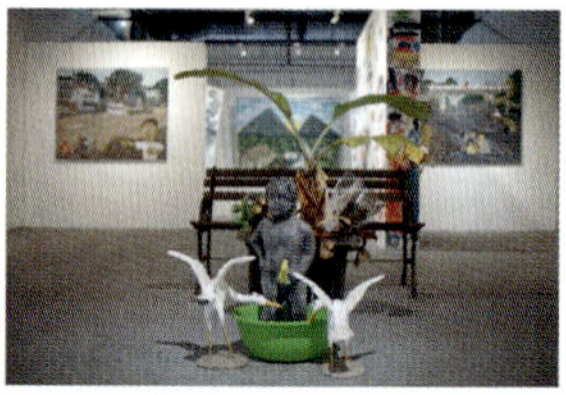

994

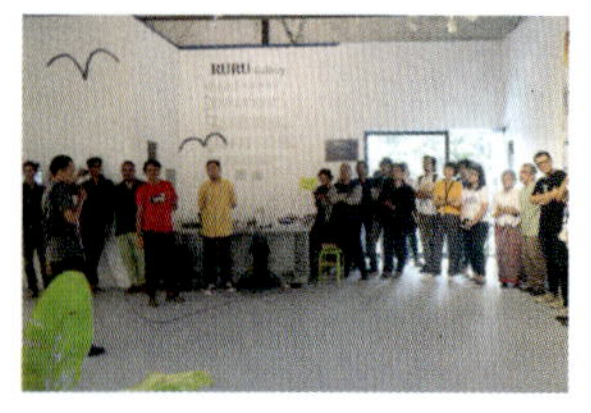

995

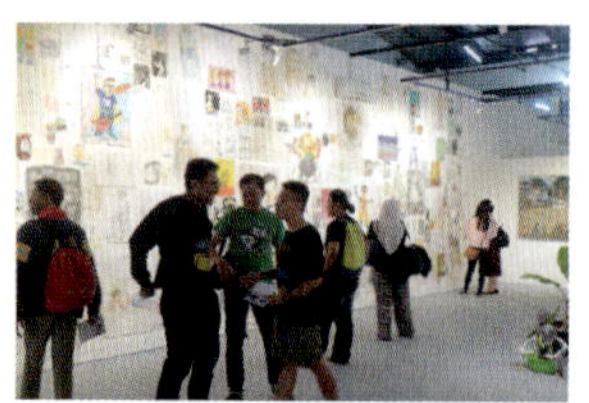

996

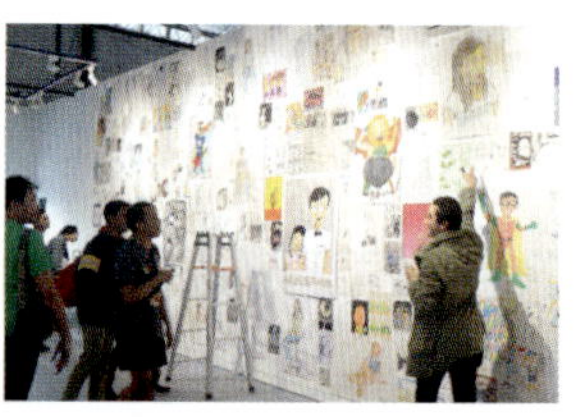

997

THE KUDA: *The Untold Story of Indonesian Underground Music in the 70s*, installation for 'Songs for the People: Music and Politics in Indonesia', Art Sonje Center, Seoul, 3 March – 8 April 2018

ruangrupa restaged *THE KUDA*, first exhibited in the 2013 edition of Asia Pacific Triennale; curated by Alia Swastika

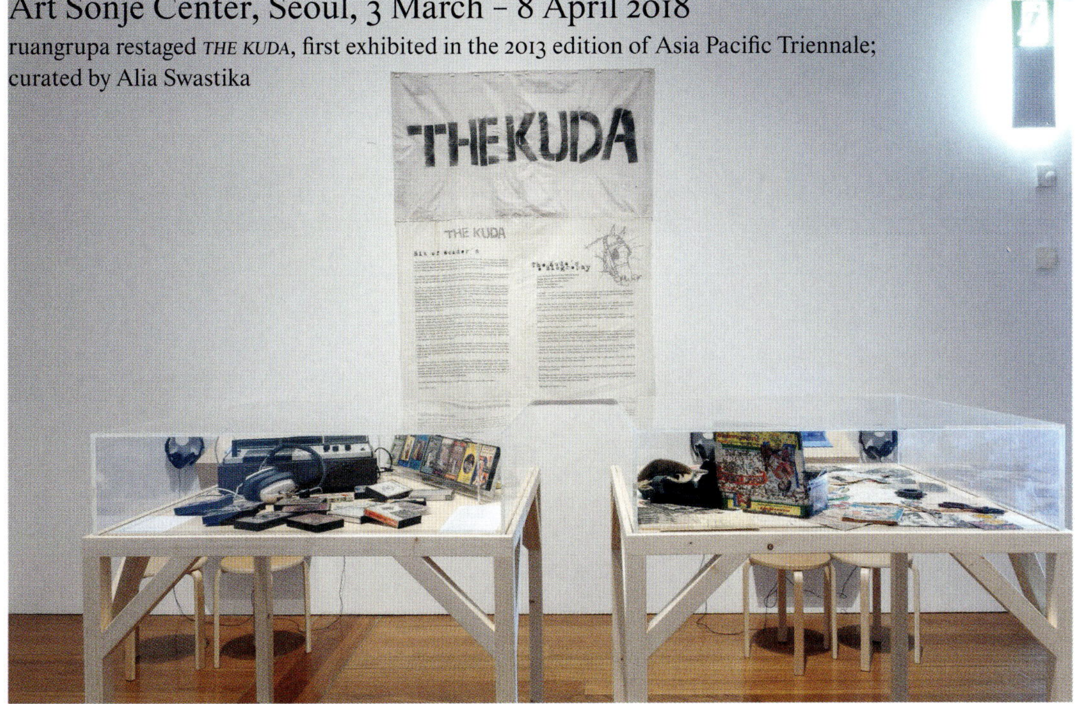

998

'Efek Rumah Tangga?', exhibition by Arman Arief Rachman, RURU Gallery, 24 March – 15 April 2018

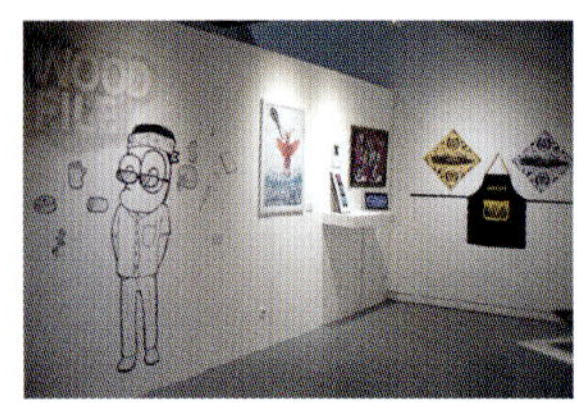

999

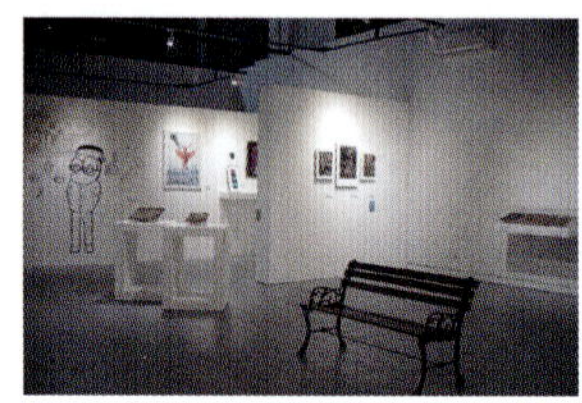

1000

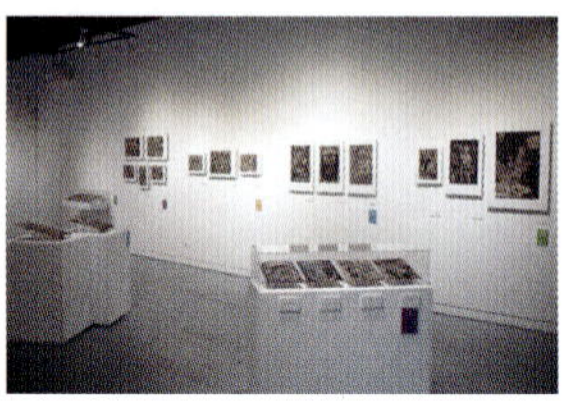

1001

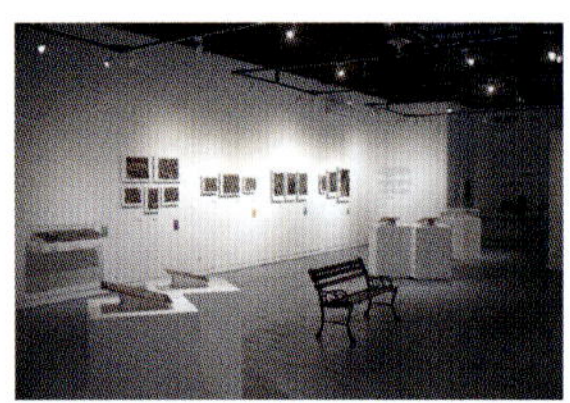

1002

Participation in 'Food Today: Indonesian Food, Society and Media Art', Asia Culture Center, Gwangju, 21 December 2018 – 24 February 2019 327

ruangrupa presented major works and archival materials from OK.Video 'OK.PANGAN' – 8th Indonesia Media Arts Festival (2017)

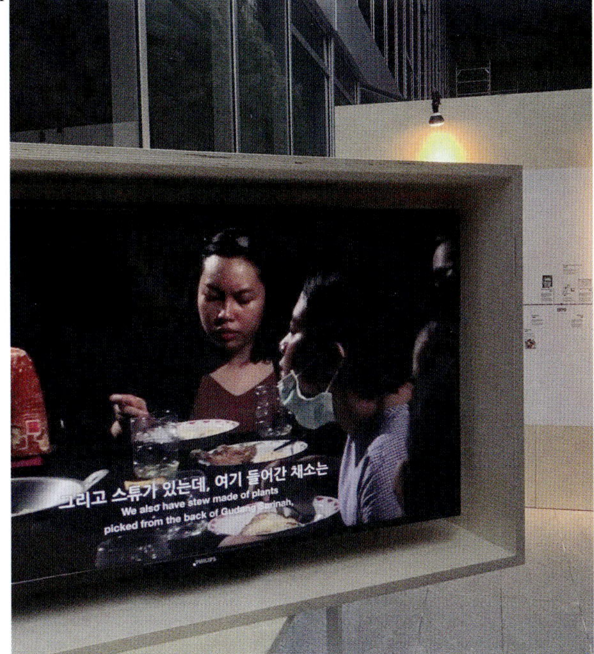

1004

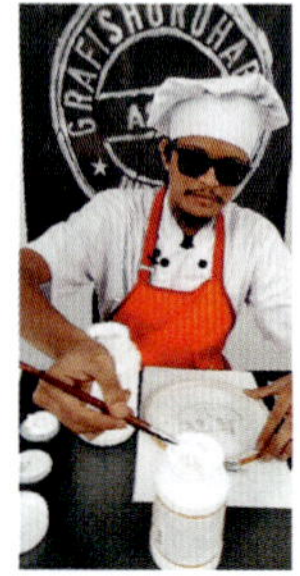

1005

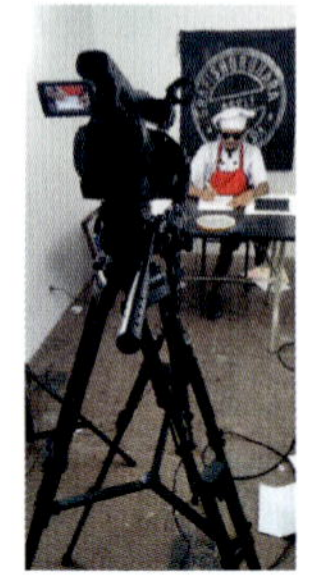

1006

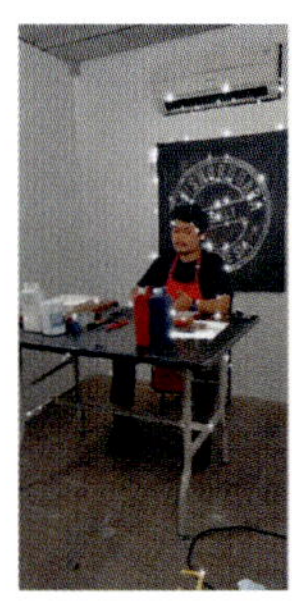

1007

'Knowledge Garden Festival', exhibition project by Gudskul, Art Gallery of York University, Toronto, Canada, 22–30 October 2021

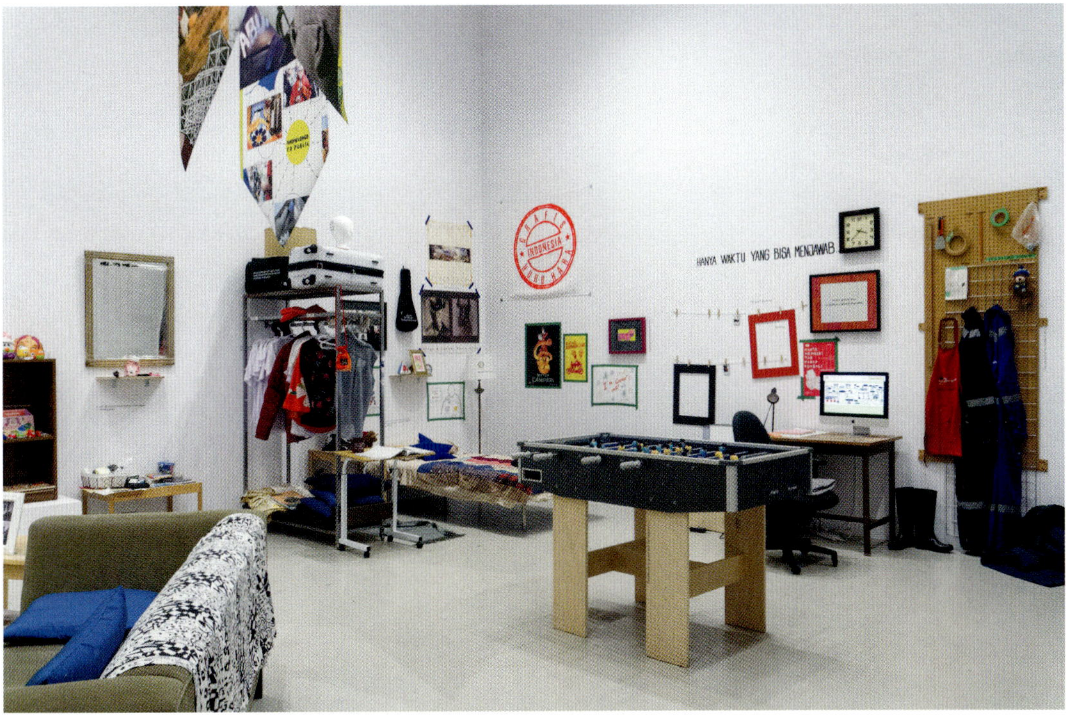

1008

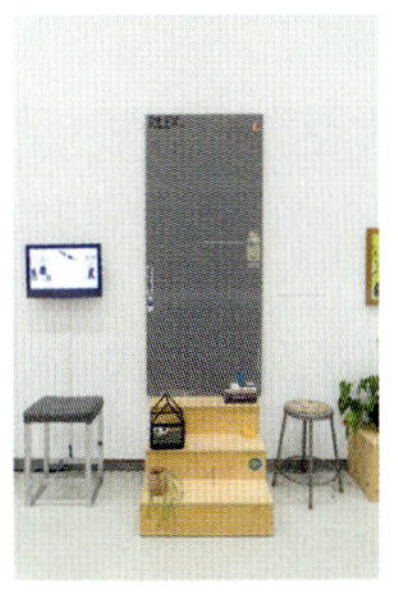

1009

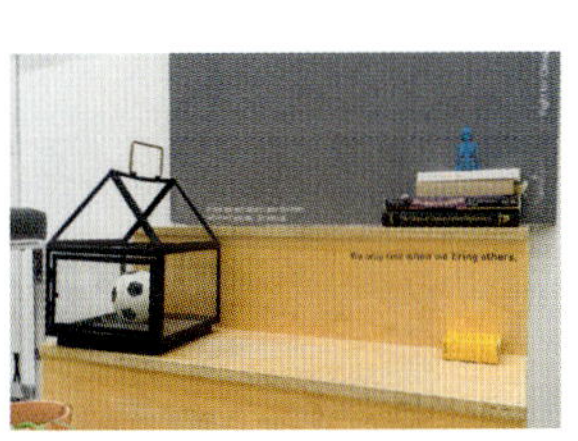

1010

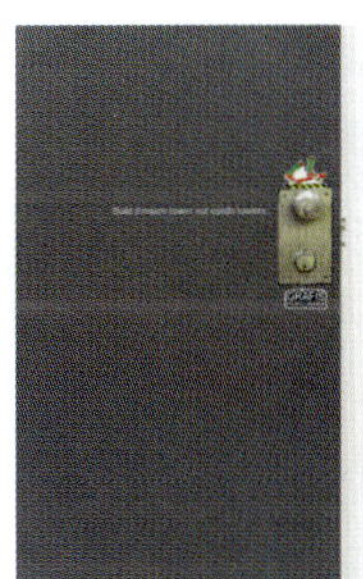

1011

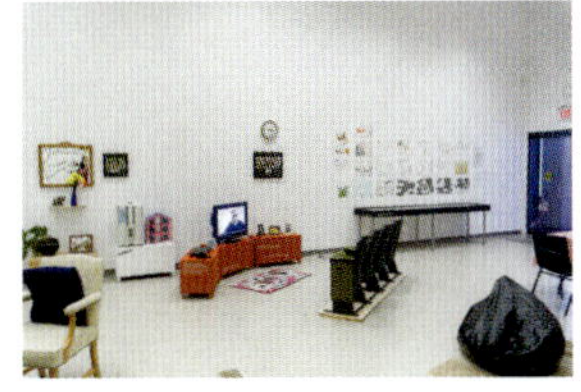

1012

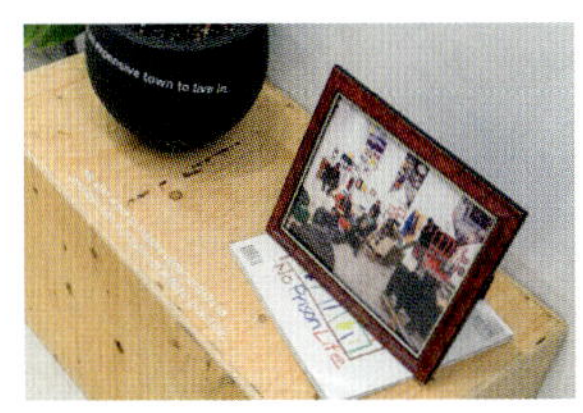

1013

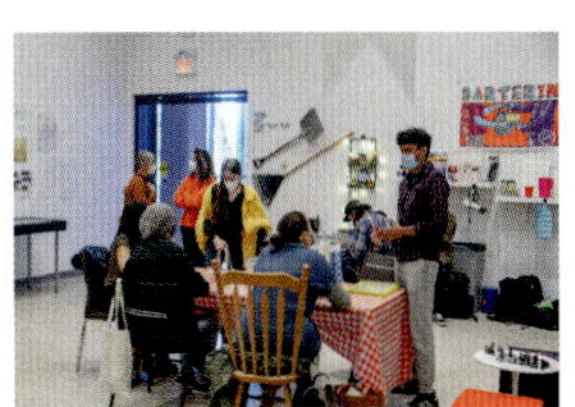

1014

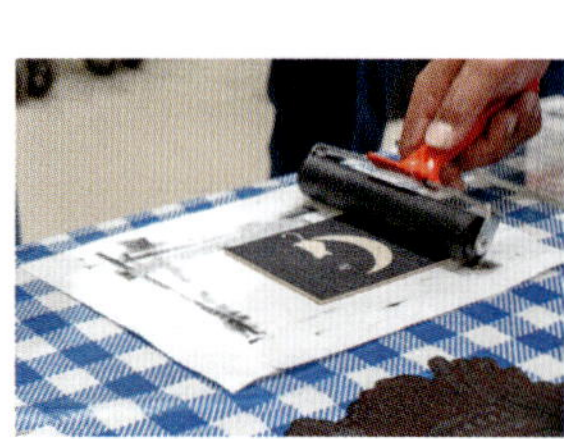

1015

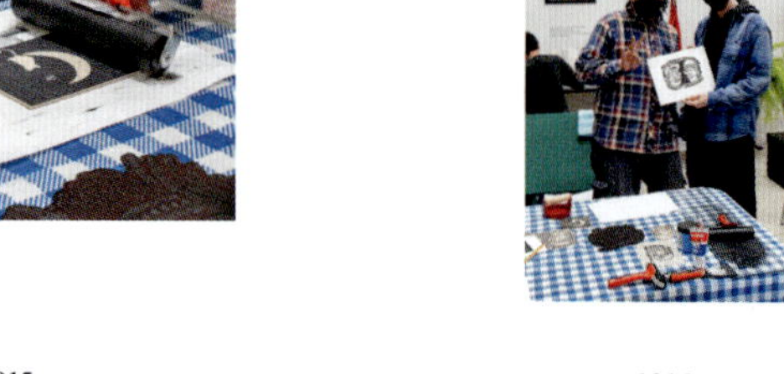

1016

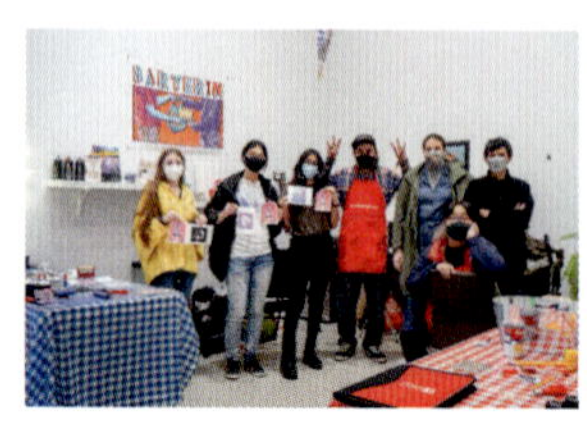

1017

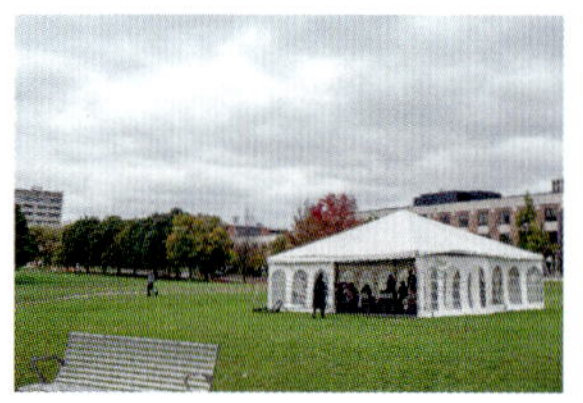

1018

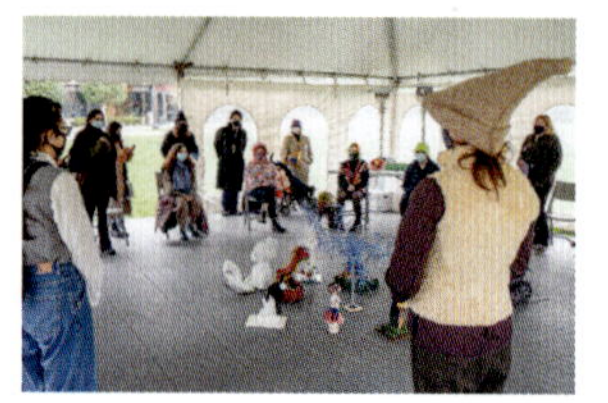

1019

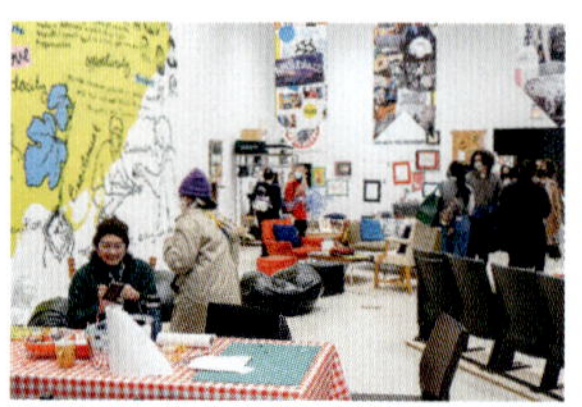

1020

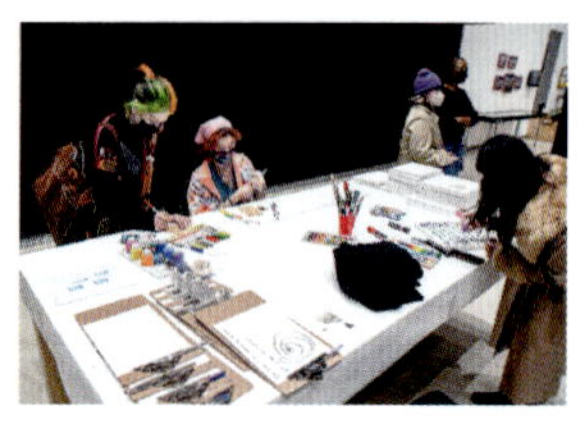

1021

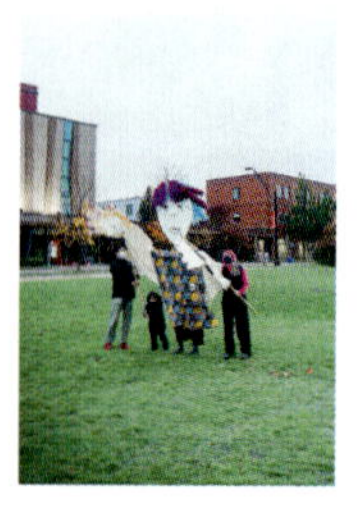

1022

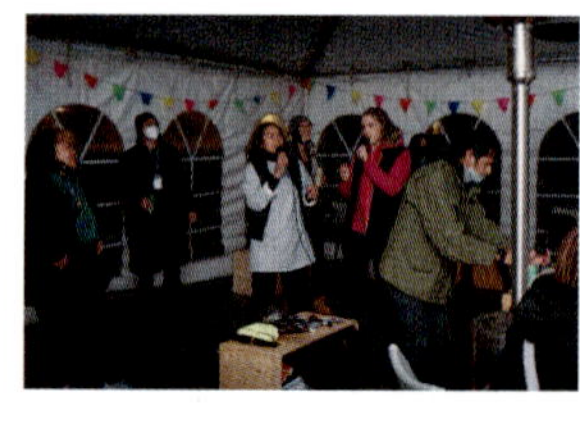

1023

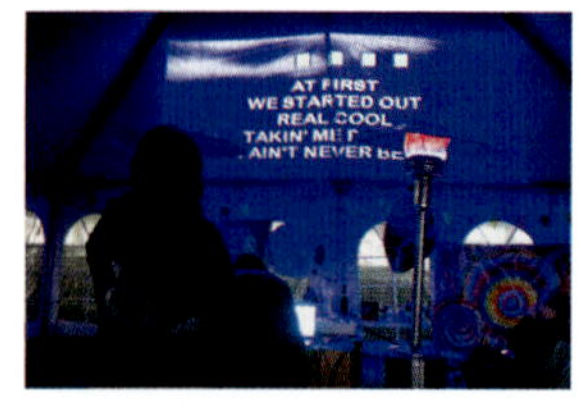

1024

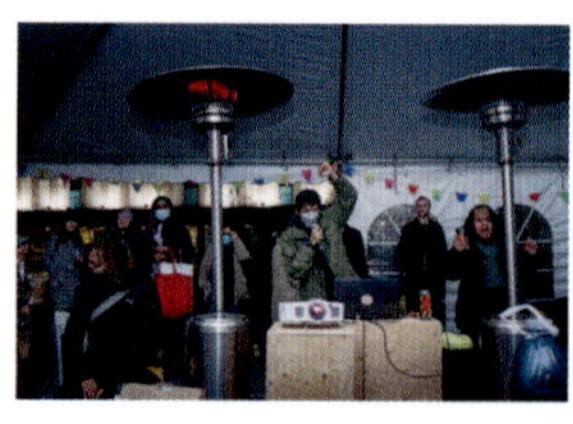

1025

'Drawing Drawings', exhibition by Abi Rama, RURU Gallery, 6 November 2021

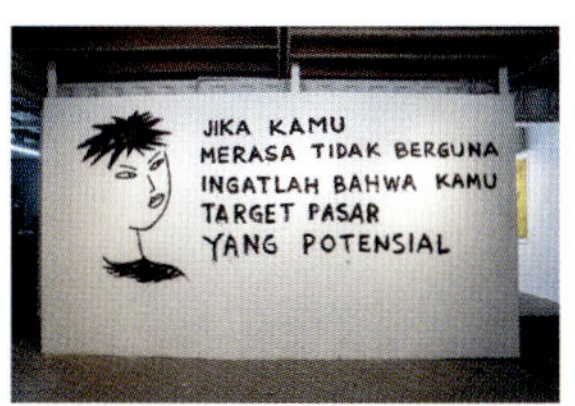

1026

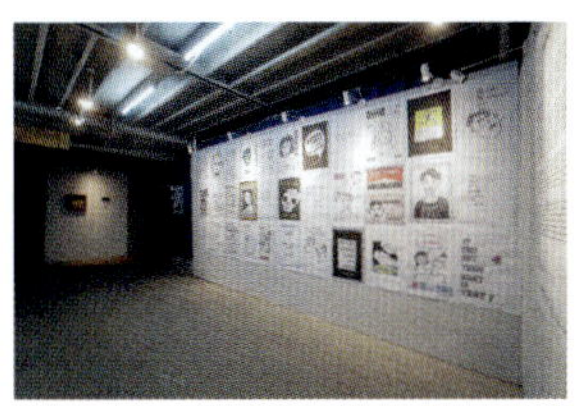

1027

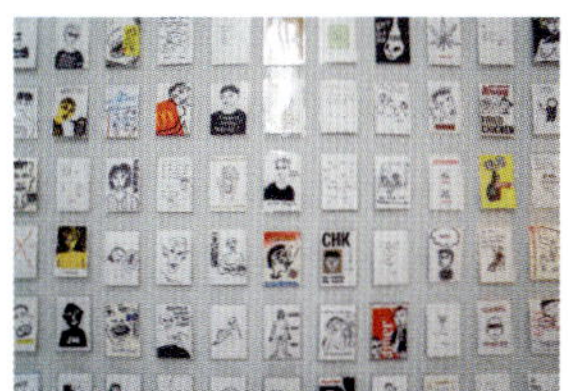

1028

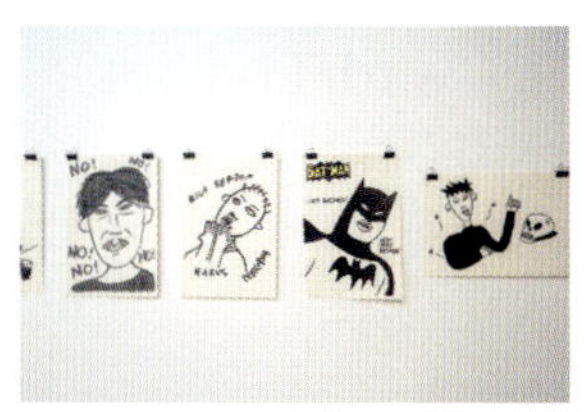

1029

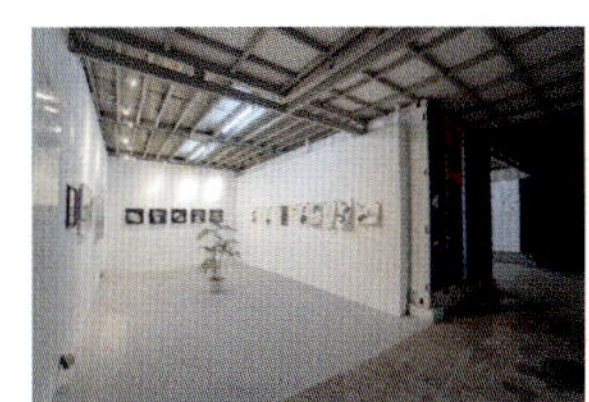

1030

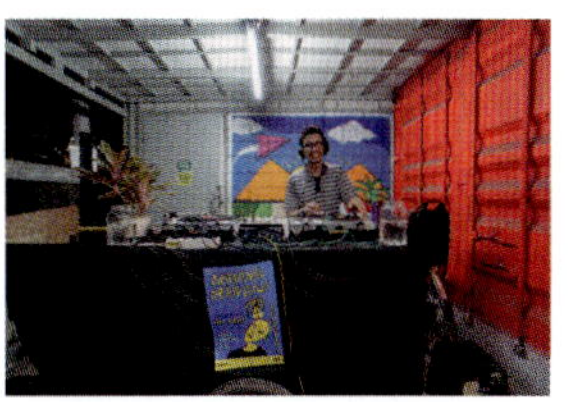

1031

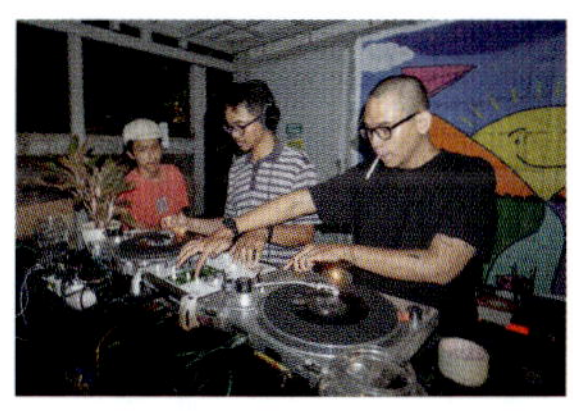

1032

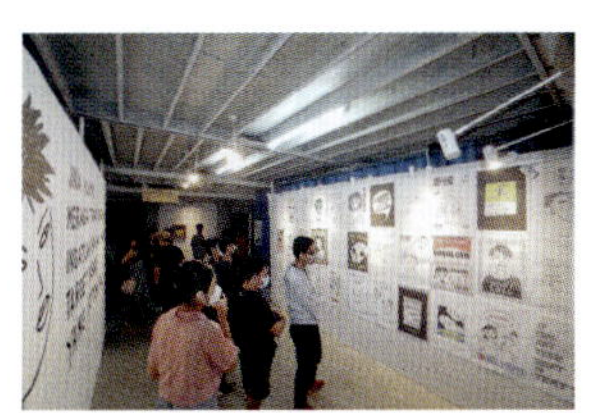

1033

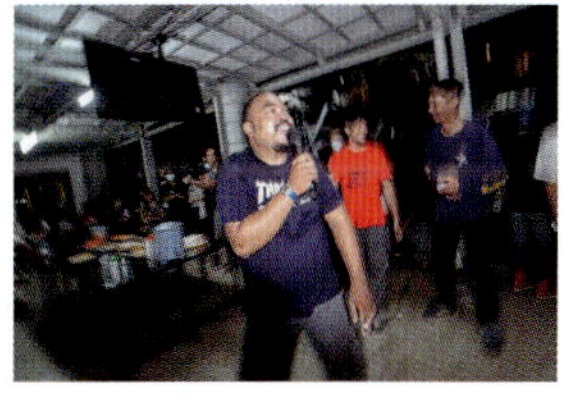

1034

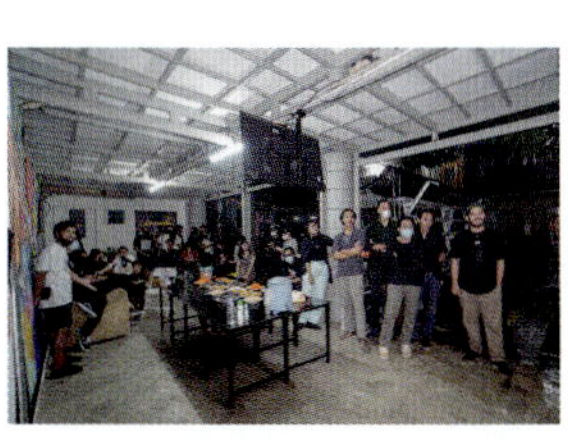

1035

At the end of 2021, twelve art collectives across regions all over Indonesia agreed to create an experimental network called lumbung Indonesia. This initiative was projected as a forum for mutual support and resource sharing among the art collectives involved. ... Another thing that lumbung Indonesia wants to achieve in the future is a just form of economy incorporated into effective artistic practices through an imagination and an adoption of a new way of life, ecosystem, and organisation that are more just, human and comprehensive. Therefore, lumbung Indonesia focusses its artistic practice on experimentation of collective activism, economics, education, ecology and spatial imagination – in urban, rural and public spaces. ... Our deepest gratitude goes to Gudskul Ekosistem for their assistance, providing the meeting space for the participating collectives of lumbung Indonesia: Forum Sudut Pandang (Palu), Gelanggang Olah Rasa (Bandung), Gubuak Kopi (Solok), Hysteria (Semarang), Ketjil Bergerak (Yogyakarta), Komunitas KAHE (Maumere), Pasirputih (North Lombok), Rumah Budaya Sikukeluang (Pekanbaru), Serbuk Kayu (Surabaya), SIKU Ruang Terpadu (Makassar), Sinau Art (Cirebon), and TROTOARt (Jakarta).

Doni Ahmad and Eka Putra Nggalu

After documenta accepted our invitation to join our journey and to become part of our ekosistem, we decided – with their opportunities and support – to keep on extending invitations to different people. ... The first fourteen initiatives we invited committed to becoming part of *lumbung*-building processes before and beyond documenta fifteen. These initiatives became known as lumbung inter-lokal members. More than fifty other artistic practices, both individual and collective in nature, joined afterwards, forming what has become known as lumbung artists. Besides these invitations, our own existence in our current localities had to be carved out more deeply in Indonesia, more broadly in our international circles and newly in Kassel. Thus, together, lumbung Indonesia, lumbung inter-lokal and lumbung Kassel were formed, with the aim of their members identifying what resources were in their power and deciding how to use them.

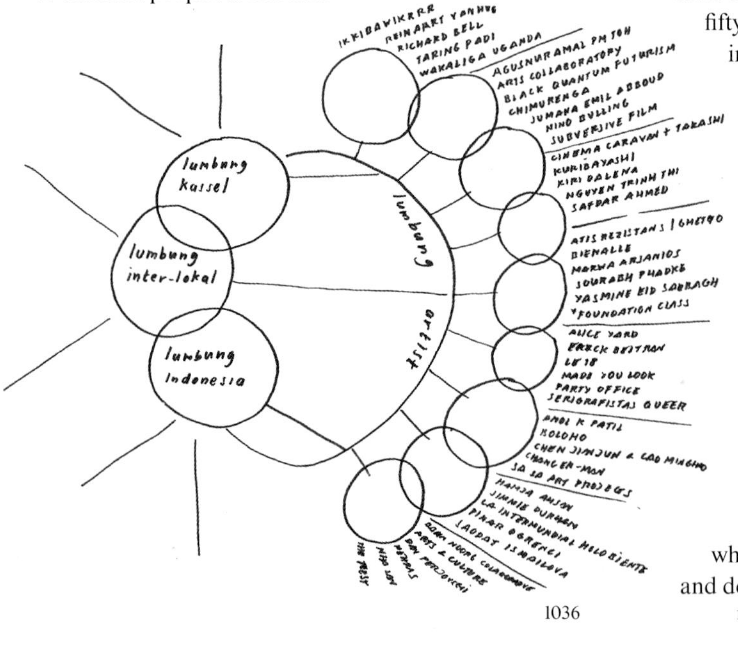

1036 ruangrupa

documenta fifteen (artistic direction), Kassel, Germany, 18 June – 25 September 2022

'We want to create a globally oriented, collaborative and interdisciplinary art and culture platform that will remain effective beyond the 100 days of documenta fifteen. Our curatorial approach strives for a different kind of collaborative model of resource use – in economic terms but also with regard to ideas, knowledge, programmes and innovations.'

ruangrupa has based documenta fifteen upon the values and ideas of *lumbung*. *lumbung*, which directly translates as 'rice barn', refers to a communal building in rural Indonesia where a community's harvest is gathered, stored and distributed according to jointly determined criteria as a pooled resource for the future. As a concrete practice, *lumbung* is the starting point of documenta fifteen: principles of collectivity, resource building and equitable distribution are pivotal to the curatorial work and impact the entire process – the structure, self-image and appearance of documenta fifteen.

ruangrupa / documenta fifteen

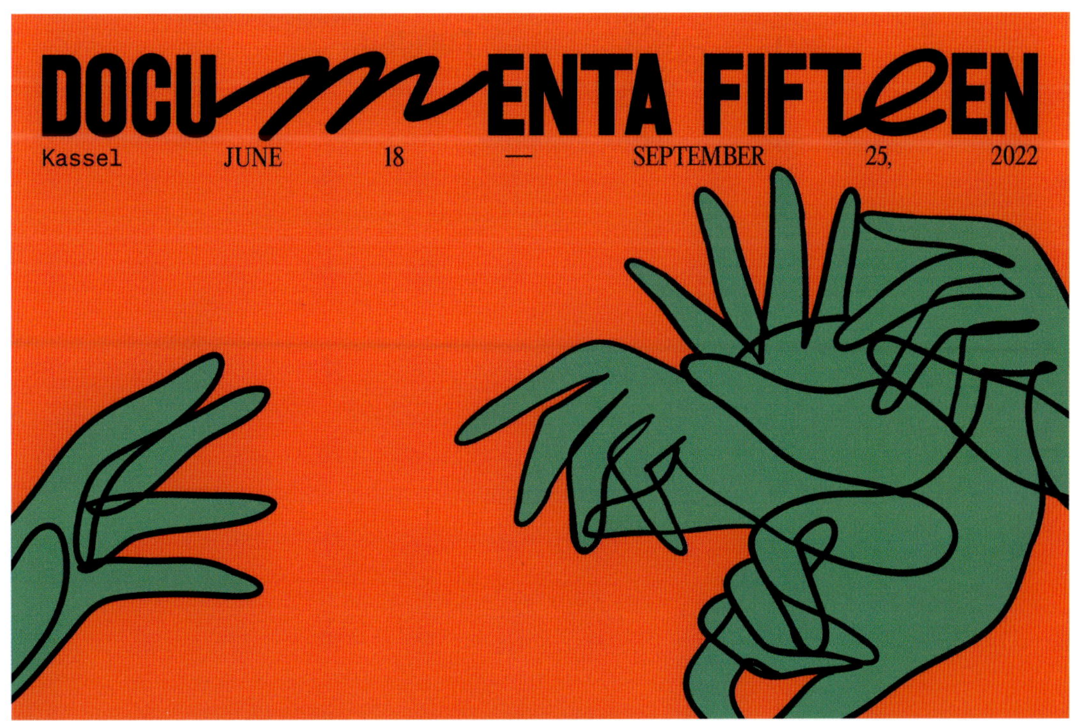

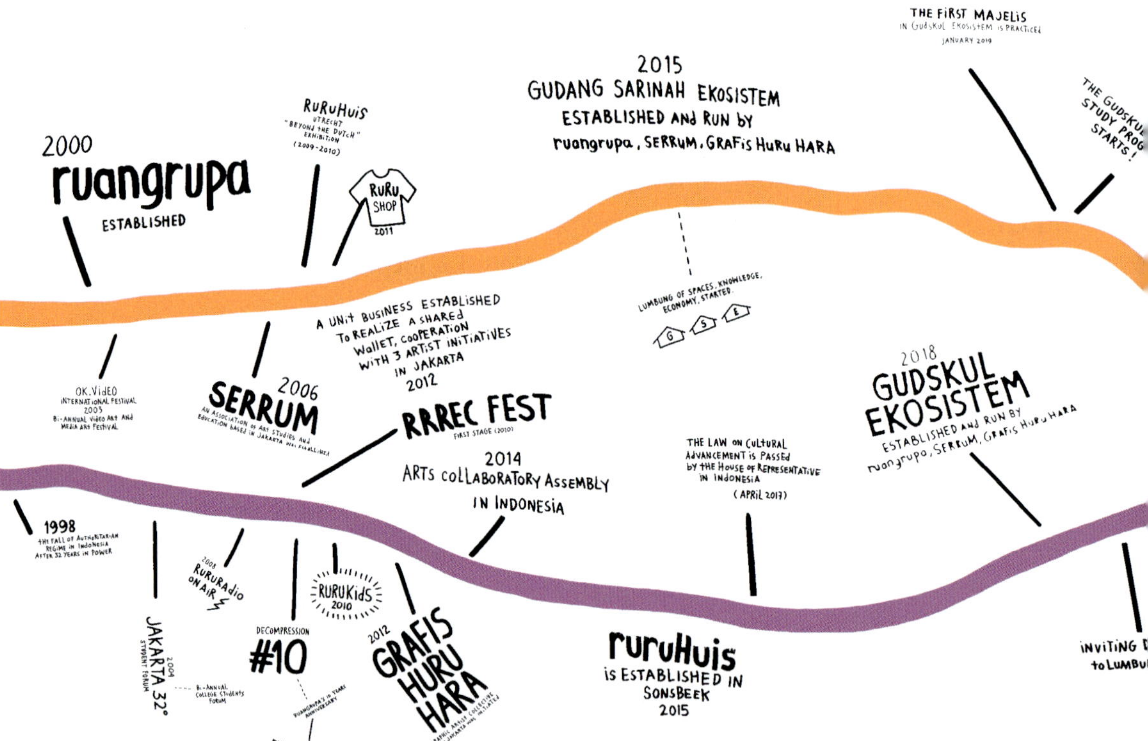
2000
ruangrupa
ESTABLISHED
RuRuHuis
UTRECHT
"BEYOND THE DUTCH"
EXHIBITION
(2009-2010)
RURU SHOP
2011
2015
GUDANG SARINAH EKOSISTEM
ESTABLISHED AND RUN BY
ruangrupa, SERRUM, GRAFIS HURU HARA
THE FIRST MAJELIS
IN GUDSKUL EKOSISTEM IS PRACTICED
JANUARY 2019
A UNIT BUSINESS ESTABLISHED
TO REALIZE A SHARED
WALLET, COOPERATION
WITH 3 ARTIST INITIATIVES
IN JAKARTA
2012
LUMBUNG OF SPACES, KNOWLEDGE, ECONOMY, STARTED
G S E
OK.VIDEO
INTERNATIONAL FESTIVAL
2003
BI-ANNUAL VIDEO ART AND MEDIA ART FESTIVAL
2006
SERRUM
RRREC FEST
FIRST STAGE (2010)
2014
ARTS COLLABORATORY ASSEMBLY
IN INDONESIA
THE LAW ON CULTURAL
ADVANCEMENT IS PASSED
BY THE HOUSE OF REPRESENTATIVE
IN INDONESIA
(APRIL 2017)
2018
GUDSKUL
EKOSISTEM
ESTABLISHED AND RUN BY
ruangrupa, SERRUM, GRAFIS HURU HARA
1998
THE FALL OF AUTHORITARIAN REGIME IN INDONESIA AFTER 32 YEARS IN POWER
2003
RURURADIO
ON AIR
JAKARTA 32°
2004
STUDENT FORUM
BI-ANNUAL COLLEGE STUDENTS FORUM
DECOMPRESSION
#10
RUANGRUPA'S 10 YEARS ANNIVERSARY
EXPANDING SPACES
AND PUBLIC
RURUKIDS
2010
2012
GRAFIS
HURU
HARA
ruruHuis
is ESTABLISHED IN
SONSBEEK
2015

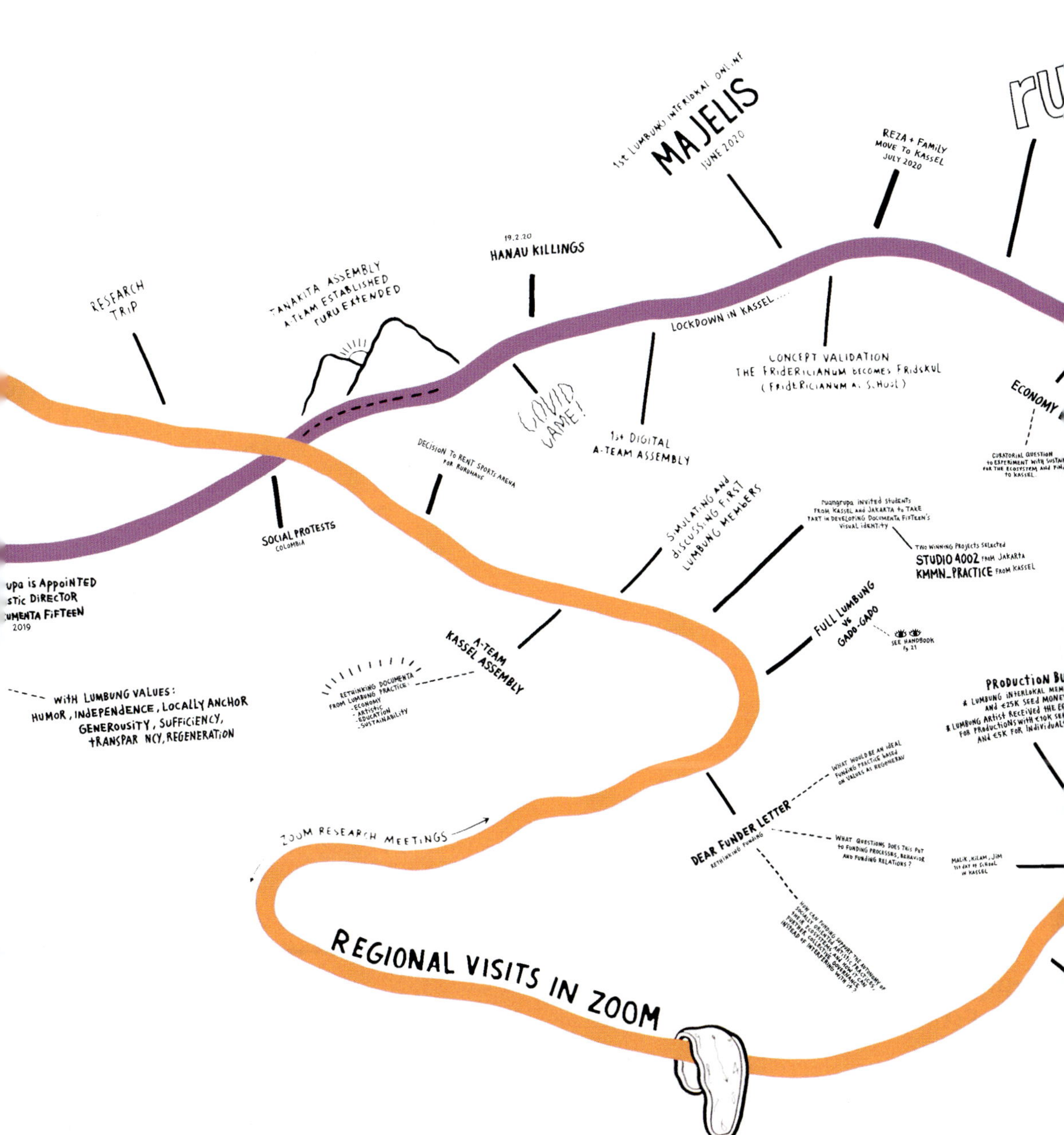
1st LUMBUNG INTERLOKAL ONLINE
MAJELIS
JUNE 2020
REZA + FAMILY MOVE TO KASSEL JULY 2020
19.2.20
HANAU KILLINGS
RESEARCH TRIP
TANAKITA ASSEMBLY
A-TEAM ESTABLISHED
RURU EXTENDED
LOCKDOWN IN KASSEL....
CONCEPT VALIDATION
THE FRIDERICIANUM BECOMES FRIDSKUL
(FRIDERICIANUM AS SCHOOL)
ECONOMY
CURATORIAL QUESTION
COVID CAME!
1st DIGITAL A-TEAM ASSEMBLY
DECISION TO RENT SPORTS ARENA FOR RURUHAUS
SOCIAL PROTESTS
COLOMBIA
SIMULATING AND DISCUSSING FIRST LUMBUNG MEMBERS
ruangrupa invited students from Kassel and Jakarta to take part in developing documenta fifteen's visual identity
TWO WINNING PROJECTS SELECTED
STUDIO 4002 FROM JAKARTA
KMMN_PRACTICE FROM KASSEL
2019
A-TEAM KASSEL ASSEMBLY
FULL LUMBUNG VS GADO-GADO
SEE HANDBOOK Pg. 21
WITH LUMBUNG VALUES:
HUMOR, INDEPENDENCE, LOCALLY ANCHOR
GENEROUSITY, SUFFICIENCY,
TRANSPAR NCY, REGENERATION
RETHINKING DOCUMENTA FROM LUMBUNG PRACTICE:
- ECONOMY
- ARTISTIC
- EDUCATION
- SUSTAINABILITY
PRODUCTION
WHAT WOULD BE AN IDEAL FUNDING PRACTICE BASED ON VALUES AS REGENERAU
ZOOM RESEARCH MEETINGS
DEAR FUNDER LETTER
RETHINKING FUNDING
WHAT QUESTIONS DOES THIS PUT TO FUNDING PROCESSES, BEHAVIOR AND FUNDING RELATIONS?
MALIK, KILAM, JIM
1st DAY OF SCHOOL IN KASSEL
HOW CAN FUNDING SUPPORT THE AUTONOMY OF SOCIALLY ORIENTED ARTISTIC PRACTICES, THEIR ECOSYSTEMS, AND HOW IT CAN FURTHER COLLECTIVE GOVERNANCE INSTEAD OF INTERFERING WITH IT?
REGIONAL VISITS IN ZOOM

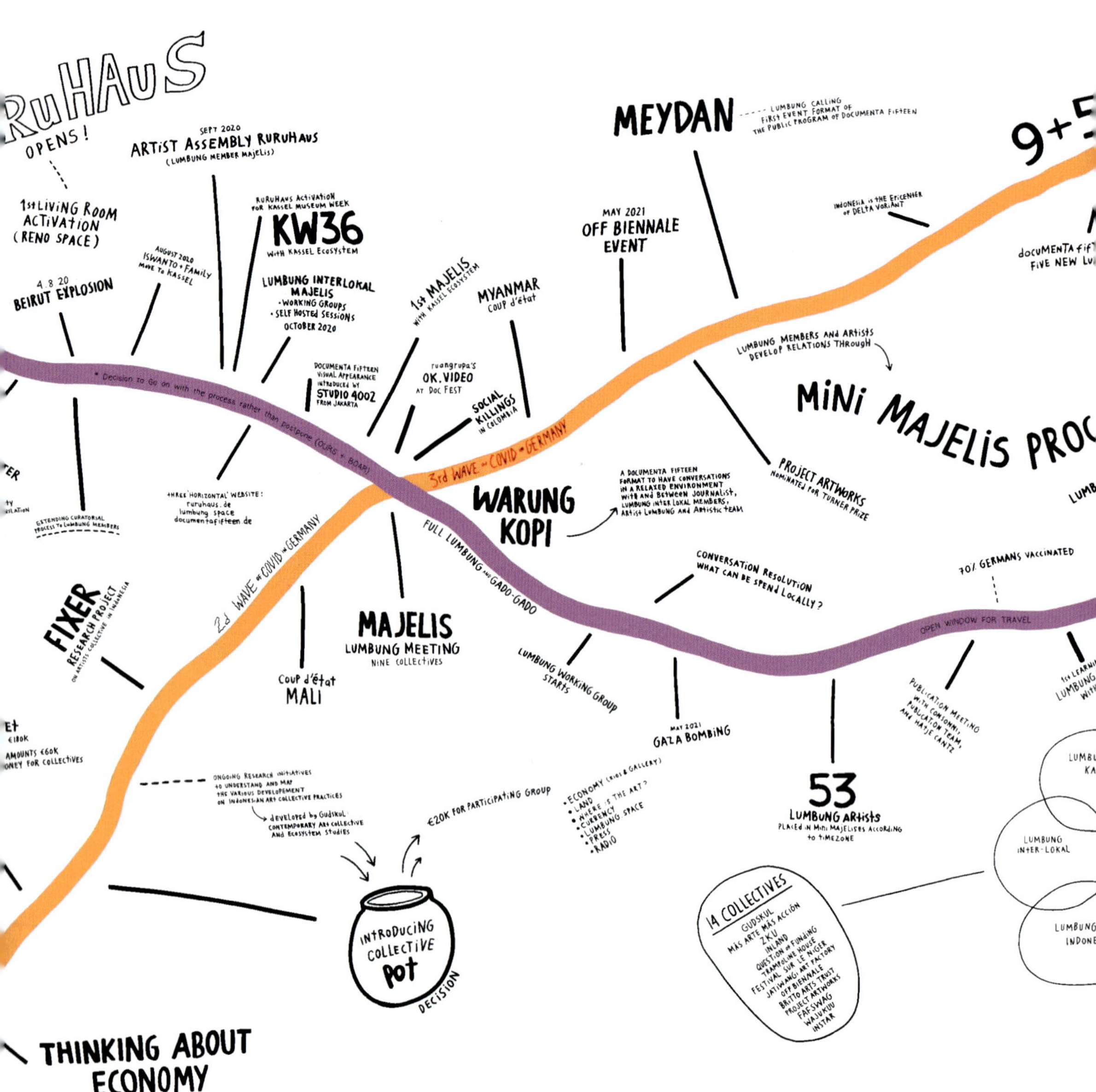
RuHAuS
OPENS!
SEPT 2020
ARTiST ASSEMBLY RURUHAUS
(LUMBUNG MEMBER MAJELIS)
1st LiViNG ROOM ACTiVATiON (RENO SPACE)
RURUHAUS ACTIVATION FOR KASSEL MUSEUM WEEK
KW36
WITH KASSEL ECOSYSTEM
AUGUST 2020 ISWANTO + FAMILY MOVE TO KASSEL
4.8.20
BEIRUT EXPLOSION
LUMBUNG INTERLOKAL MAJELIS
• WORKING GROUPS
• SELF HOSTED SESSIONS
OCTOBER 2020
1st MAJELIS WITH KASSEL ECOSYSTEM
MYANMAR COUP d'état
MAY 2021
OFF BIENNALE EVENT
MEYDAN
LUMBUNG CALLING FIRST EVENT FORMAT OF THE PUBLIC PROGRAM OF DOCUMENTA FIFTEEN
9+5
INDONESIA IS THE EPICENTER OF DELTA VARIANT
DOCUMENTA FIFTEEN VISUAL APPEARANCE INTRODUCED BY STUDIO 4002 FROM JAKARTA
ruangrupa's OK. VIDEO AT DOC FEST
SOCIAL KILLINGS IN COLOMBIA
Decision to Go on with the process rather than postpone (OURS + BOARD)
3rd WAVE OF COVID • GERMANY
LUMBUNG MEMBERS AND ARTISTS DEVELOP RELATIONS THROUGH
MiNi MAJELIS PROC
PROJECT ARTWORKS NOMINATED FOR TURNER PRIZE
WARUNG KOPI
A DOCUMENTA FIFTEEN FORMAT TO HAVE CONVERSATIONS IN A RELAXED ENVIRONMENT WITH AND BETWEEN JOURNALIST, LUMBUNG INTERLOKAL MEMBERS, ARTIST LUMBUNG AND ARTISTIC TEAM
THREE 'HORIZONTAL' WEBSITE: ruruhaus.de lumbung space documentafifteen.de
EXTENDING CURATORIAL PROCESS TO LUMBUNG MEMBERS
FULL LUMBUNG AND GADO-GADO
2nd WAVE OF COVID • GERMANY
FIXER
RESEARCH PROJECT ON ARTISTS COLLECTIVE IN INDONESIA
MAJELIS
LUMBUNG MEETING
NINE COLLECTIVES
COUP d'état MALI
CONVERSATION RESOLUTION WHAT CAN BE SPEND LOCALLY?
70% GERMANS VACCINATED
OPEN WINDOW FOR TRAVEL
LUMBUNG WORKING GROUP STARTS
MAY 2021
GAZA BOMBiNG
PUBLICATION MEETING WITH COMSONNI, PUBLICATION TEAM, AND HATJE CANTZ
53
LUMBUNG ARtists
PLACED IN MINI MAJELISES ACCORDING TO TIMEZONE
AMOUNTS €60K
MONEY FOR COLLECTIVES
ONGOING RESEARCH INITIATIVES TO UNDERSTAND AND MAP THE VARIOUS DEVELOPEMENT ON INDONESIAN ART COLLECTIVE PRACTICES
DEVELOPED BY Gudskul: CONTEMPORARY ART COLLECTIVE AND ECOSYSTEM STUDIES
€20K FOR PARTICIPATING GROUP
• ECONOMY (KIOS & GALLERY)
• LAND
• WHERE IS THE ART?
• CURRENCY
• LUMBUNG SPACE
• PRESS
• RADIO
INTRODUCING COLLECTIVE POT
DECISION
14 COLLECTIVES
GUDSKUL
MÁS ARTE MÁS ACCIÓN
ZKU
INLAND
QUESTION OF FUNDING
TRAMPOLINE HOUSE
FESTIVAL SUR LE NIGER
JATIWANGI ART FACTORY
OFF BIENNALE
BRITTO ARTS TRUST
PROJECT ARTWORKS
FAFSWAG
WAJUKUU
INSTAR
LUMBUNG INTER-LOKAL
THINKING ABOUT ECONOMY
WORKING GROUP

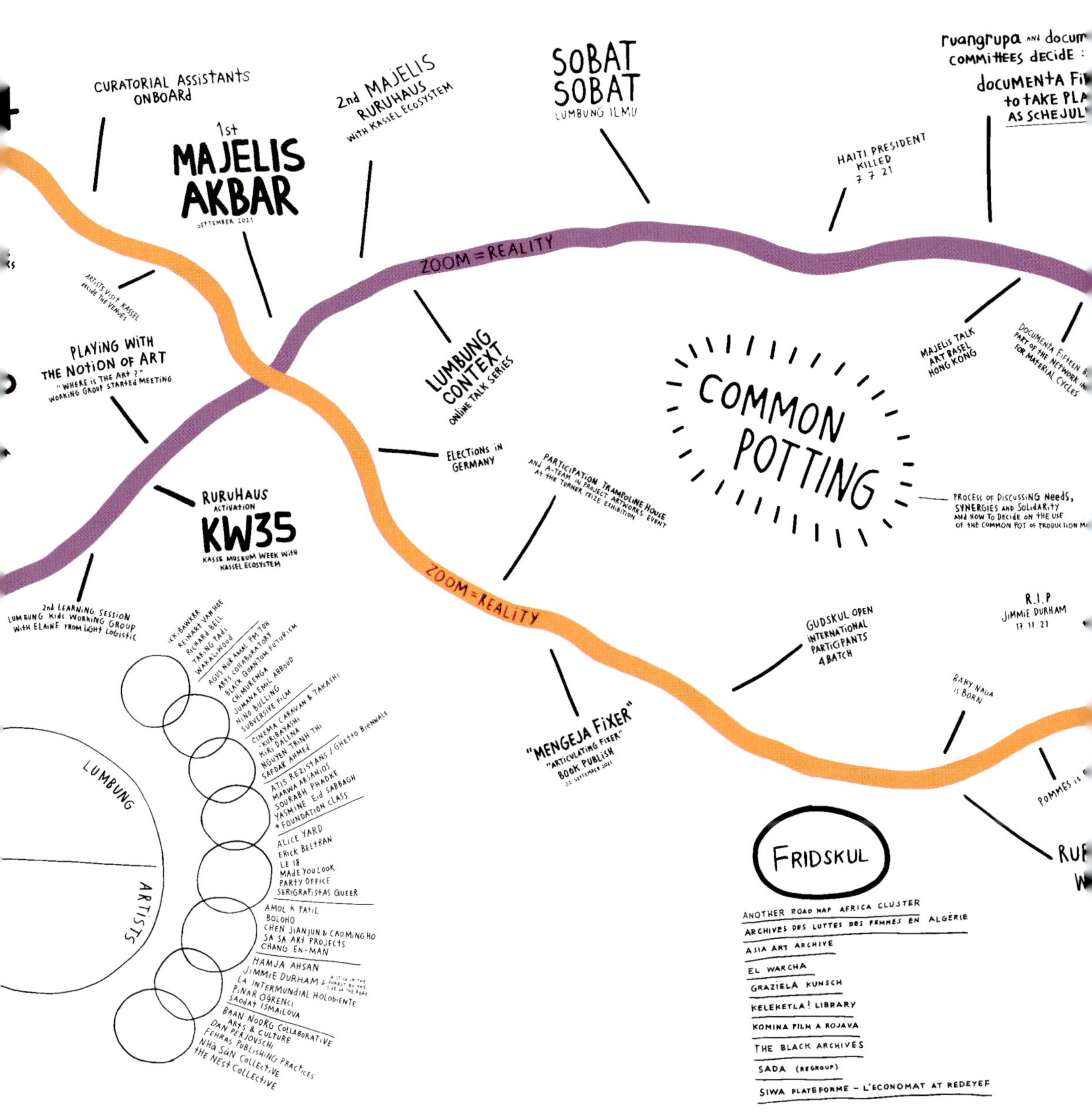

When we started hanging out in conversation with the artists it was shortly after Covid-19 was declared a pandemic. We thought we had two years to build and fill the *lumbung* with resources for both the everyday and crises alike. With Covid, the collapse came much earlier and with such brute force that it pressured us to consider how we could speed up the start of sharing resources straight away. At the same time, we insisted on going slow, meeting several times and building up trust.

ruangrupa

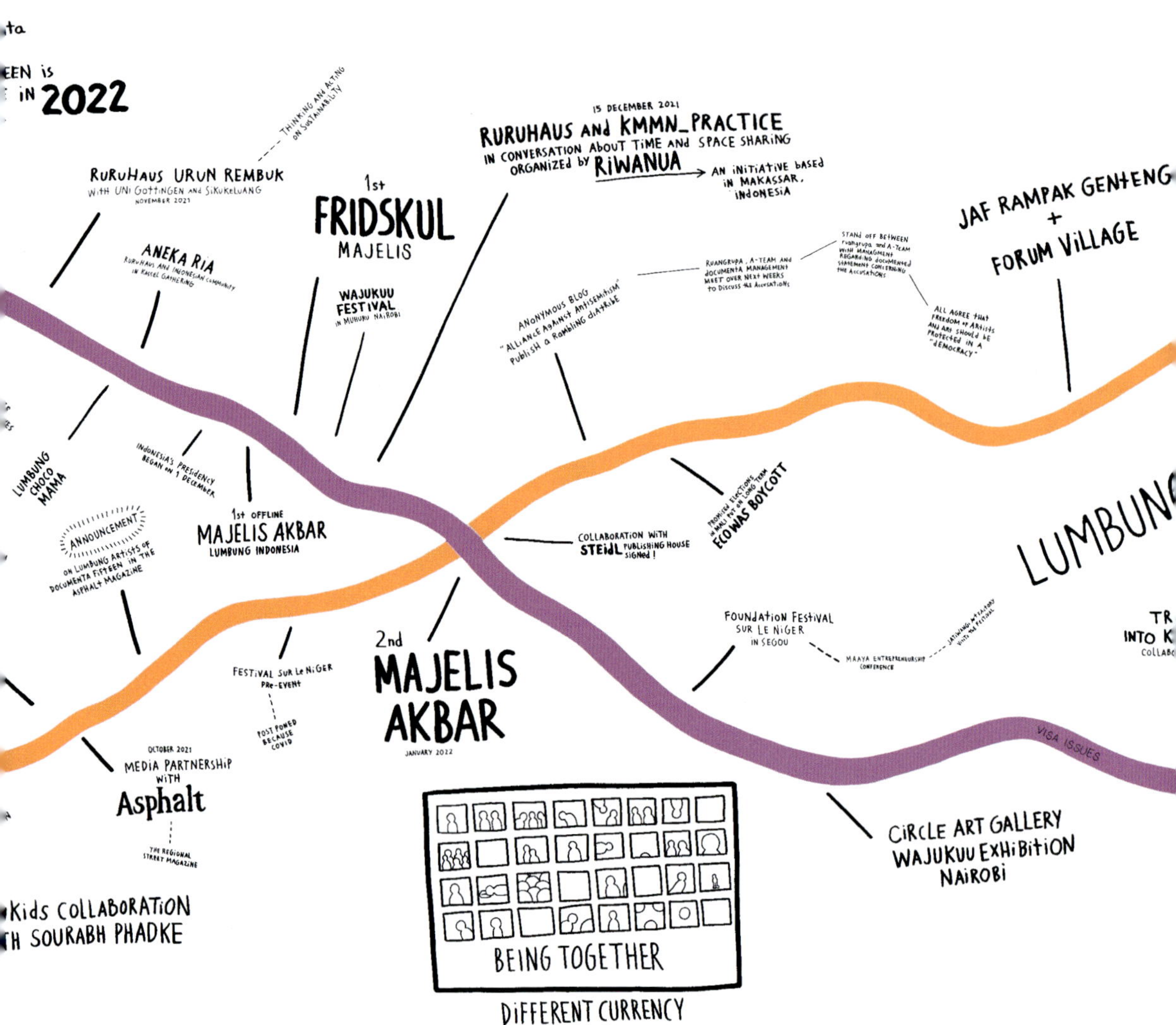

ta
EEN is
IN 2022
THINKING AND ACTING ON SUSTAINABILITY
RURUHAUS URUN REMBUK
WITH UNI GOTTINGEN AND SIKUKELUANG
NOVEMBER 2021
ANEKA RIA
RURUHAUS AND INDONESIAN COMMUNITY IN KASSEL GATHERING
1st
FRIDSKUL
MAJELIS
WAJUKUU FESTIVAL
IN MUHURU NAIROBI
15 DECEMBER 2021
RURUHAUS AND KMMN_PRACTICE
IN CONVERSATION ABOUT TIME AND SPACE SHARING
ORGANIZED BY RIWANUA
AN INITIATIVE BASED IN MAKASSAR, INDONESIA
ANONYMOUS BLOG "ALLIANCE AGAINST ANTISEMITISM" PUBLISH A RAMBLING DIATRIBE
RUANGRUPA, A-TEAM AND DOCUMENTA MANAGEMENT MEET OVER NEXT WEEKS TO DISCUSS THE ACCUSATIONS
STAND OFF BETWEEN RUANGRUPA AND A-TEAM WITH MANAGMENT REGARDING DOCUMENTED STATEMENT CONCERNING THE ACCUSATIONS
ALL AGREE THAT FREEDOM OF ARTISTS AND ART SHOULD BE PROTECTED IN A "DEMOCRACY"
JAF RAMPAK GENTENG
+
FORUM VILLAGE
LUMBUNG CHOCO MAMA
INDONESIA'S PRESIDENCY BEGAN ON 1 DECEMBER
ANNOUNCEMENT
ON LUMBUNG ARTISTS OF DOCUMENTA FIFTEEN IN THE ASPHALT MAGAZINE
1st OFFLINE
MAJELIS AKBAR
LUMBUNG INDONESIA
COLLABORATION WITH STEIDL PUBLISHING HOUSE SIGNED!
PROMISED ELECTIONS IN MALI PUT ON LONG TERM
ECOWAS BOYCOTT
LUMBUN
FESTIVAL SUR LE NIGER PRE-EVENT
POSTPONED BECAUSE COVID
2nd
MAJELIS AKBAR
JANUARY 2022
FOUNDATION FESTIVAL SUR LE NIGER IN SEGOU
MAAYA ENTREPRENEURSHIP CONFERENCE
TR
INTO K
COLLAB
OCTOBER 2021
MEDIA PARTNERSHIP WITH
Asphalt
THE REGIONAL STREET MAGAZINE
VISA ISSUES
CIRCLE ART GALLERY
WAJUKUU EXHIBITION
NAIROBI
Kids COLLABORATION
TH SOURABH PHADKE
BEING TOGETHER
DIFFERENT CURRENCY

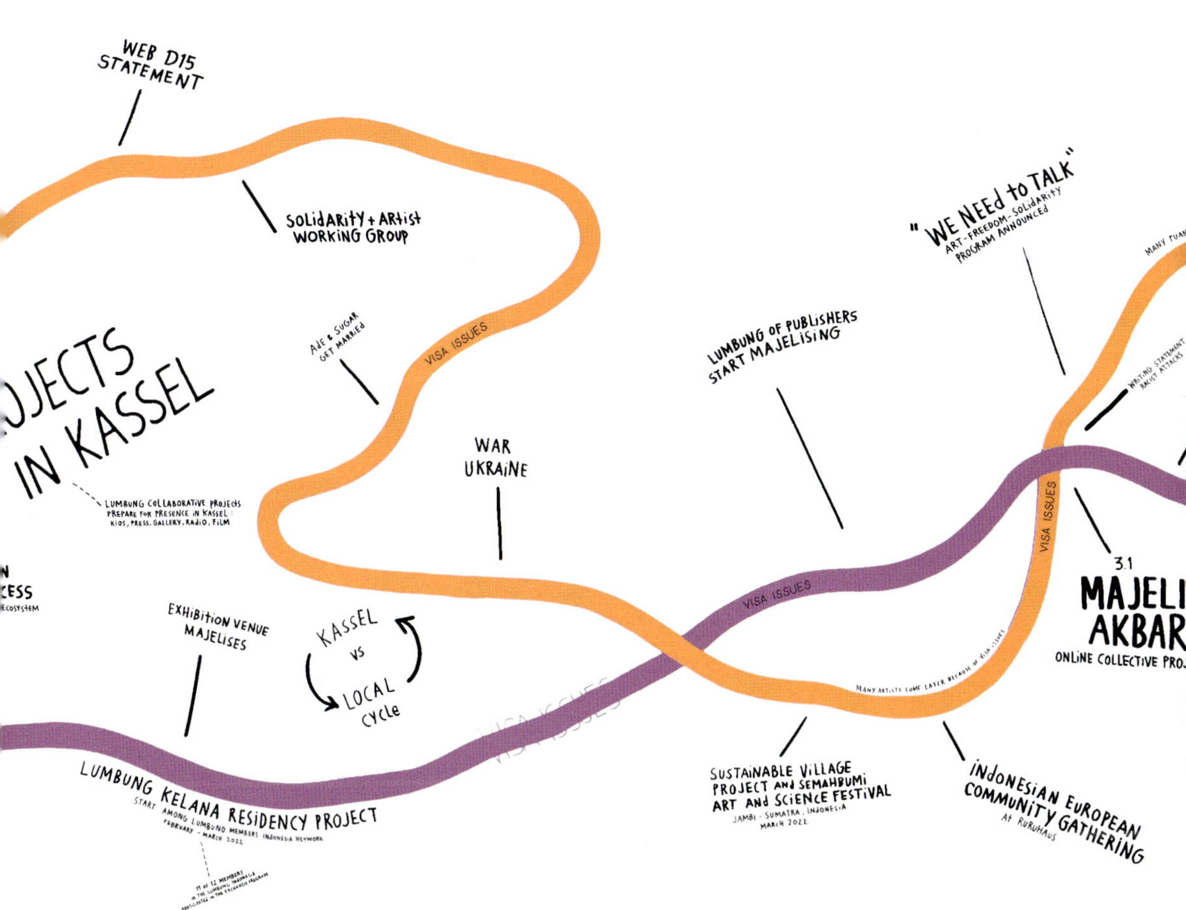
WEB D15 STATEMENT
SOLIDARITY + ARTIST WORKING GROUP
…JECTS IN KASSEL
LUMBUNG COLLABORATIVE PROJECTS PREPARE FOR PRESENCE IN KASSEL: KIOS, PRESS. GALLERY, RADIO, FILM
AJE & SUGAR GET MARRIED
VISA ISSUES
WAR UKRAINE
LUMBUNG OF PUBLISHERS START MAJELISING
"WE NEED TO TALK"
ART-FREEDOM-SOLIDARITY PROGRAM ANNOUNCED
WRITING STATEMENT RACIST ATTACKS
3.1
MAJELI
AKBAR
ONLINE COLLECTIVE PROJ
…N
…CESS
…ECOSYSTEM
EXHIBITION VENUE MAJELISES
KASSEL VS LOCAL CYCLE
VISA ISSUES
MANY ARTISTS COME LATER BECAUSE OF VISA ISSUES
LUMBUNG KELANA RESIDENCY PROJECT
START AMONG LUMBUNG MEMBERS INDONESIA NETWORK
FEBRUARY – MARCH 2022
SUSTAINABLE VILLAGE PROJECT AND SEMAHBUMI ART AND SCIENCE FESTIVAL
JAMBI - SUMATRA, INDONESIA
MARCH 2022
INDONESIAN EUROPEAN COMMUNITY GATHERING
AT RURUHAUS

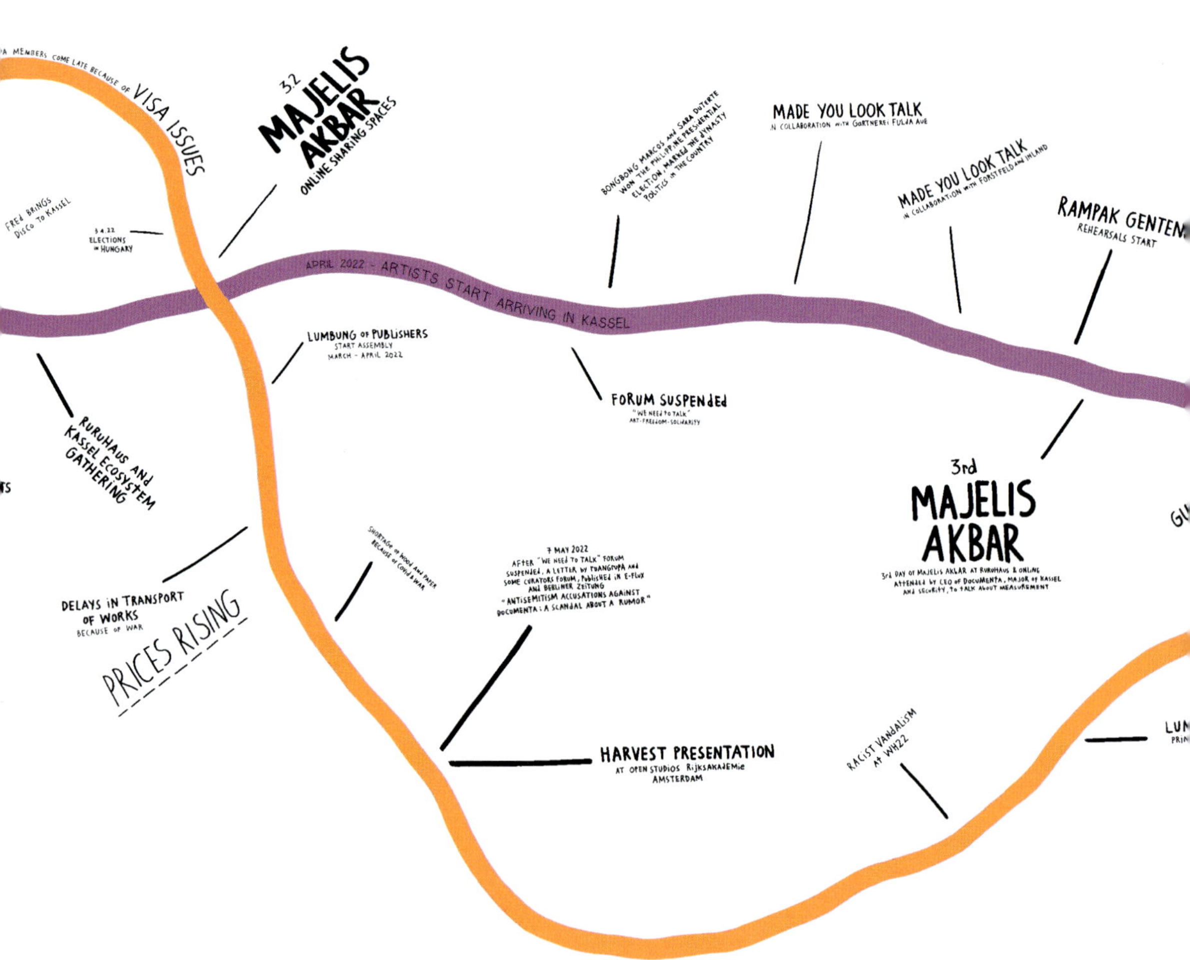
MEMBERS COME LATE BECAUSE OF VISA ISSUES
3.2 MAJELIS AKBAR
ONLINE SHARING SPACES
FRED BRINGS DISCO TO KASSEL
3.4.22 ELECTIONS IN HUNGARY
BONGBONG MARCOS AND SARA DUTERTE WON THE PHILIPPINE PRESIDENTIAL ELECTION, MARKED THE DYNASTY POLITICS IN THE COUNTRY
MADE YOU LOOK TALK
IN COLLABORATION WITH GÄRTNEREI FULDA AUE
MADE YOU LOOK TALK
IN COLLABORATION WITH FORSTFELD AND IMLAND
RAMPAK GENTEN
REHEARSALS START
APRIL 2022 - ARTISTS START ARRIVING IN KASSEL
LUMBUNG OF PUBLISHERS
START ASSEMBLY
MARCH - APRIL 2022
FORUM SUSPENDED
"WE NEED TO TALK"
ART-FREEDOM-SOLIDARITY
RURUHAUS AND KASSEL ECOSYSTEM GATHERING
3rd
MAJELIS AKBAR
3rd DAY OF MAJELIS AKBAR AT RURUHAUS & ONLINE ATTENDED BY CEO OF DOCUMENTA, MAJOR OF KASSEL AND SECURITY, TO TALK ABOUT MEASUREMENT
SHORTAGE OF WOOD AND PAPER BECAUSE OF COVID & WAR
7 MAY 2022
AFTER "WE NEED TO TALK" FORUM SUSPENDED, A LETTER BY RUANGRUPA AND SOME CURATORS FORUM, PUBLISHED IN E-FLUX AND BERLINER ZEITUNG
"ANTISEMITISM ACCUSATIONS AGAINST DOCUMENTA: A SCANDAL ABOUT A RUMOR"
DELAYS IN TRANSPORT OF WORKS
BECAUSE OF WAR
PRICES RISING
HARVEST PRESENTATION
AT OPEN STUDIOS RIJKSAKADEMIE AMSTERDAM
RACIST VANDALISM AT WH22

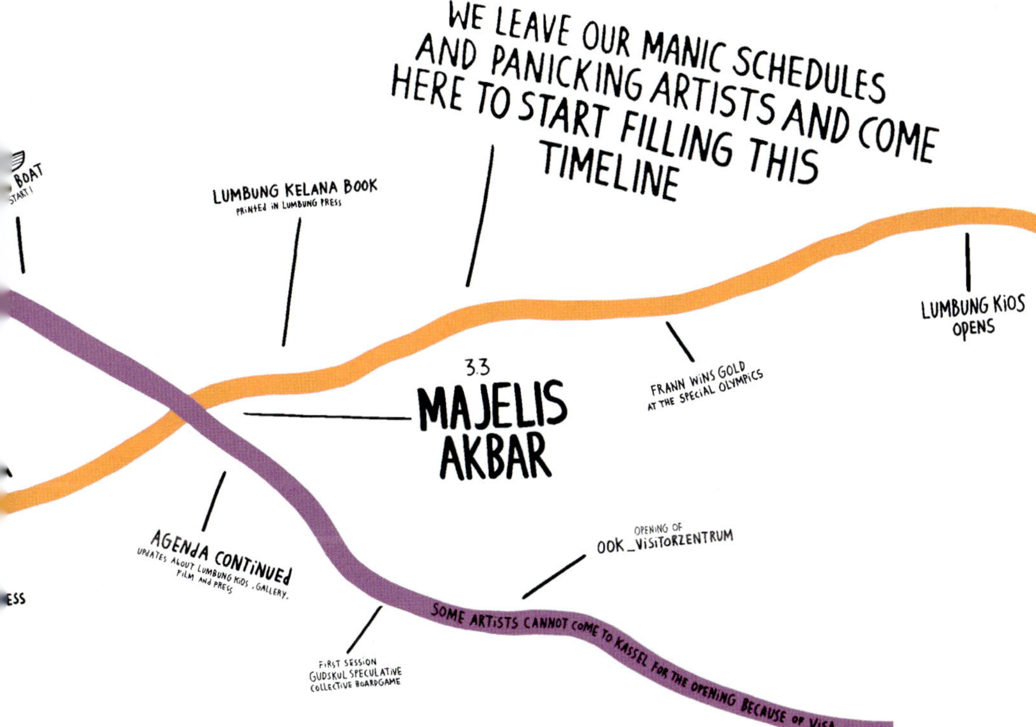
WE LEAVE OUR MANIC SCHEDULES AND PANICKING ARTISTS AND COME HERE TO START FILLING THIS TIMELINE
BOAT
START!
LUMBUNG KELANA BOOK
PRINTED IN LUMBUNG PRESS
LUMBUNG KIOS OPENS
FRANN WINS GOLD AT THE SPECIAL OLYMPICS
3.3
MAJELIS AKBAR
AGENDA CONTINUED
UPDATES ABOUT LUMBUNG KIOS, GALLERY, FILM AND PRESS
ESS
OPENING OF
OOK_VISITORZENTRUM
SOME ARTISTS CANNOT COME TO KASSEL FOR THE OPENING BECAUSE OF VISA ...
FIRST SESSION
GUDSKUL SPECULATIVE
COLLECTIVE BOARDGAME

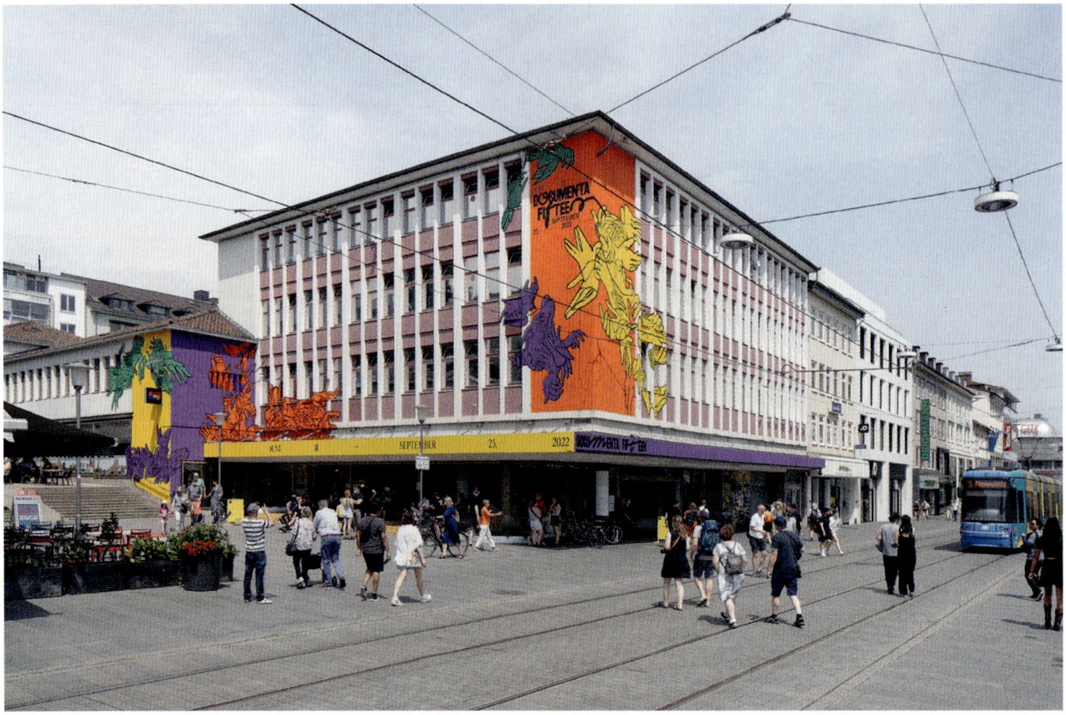

1039

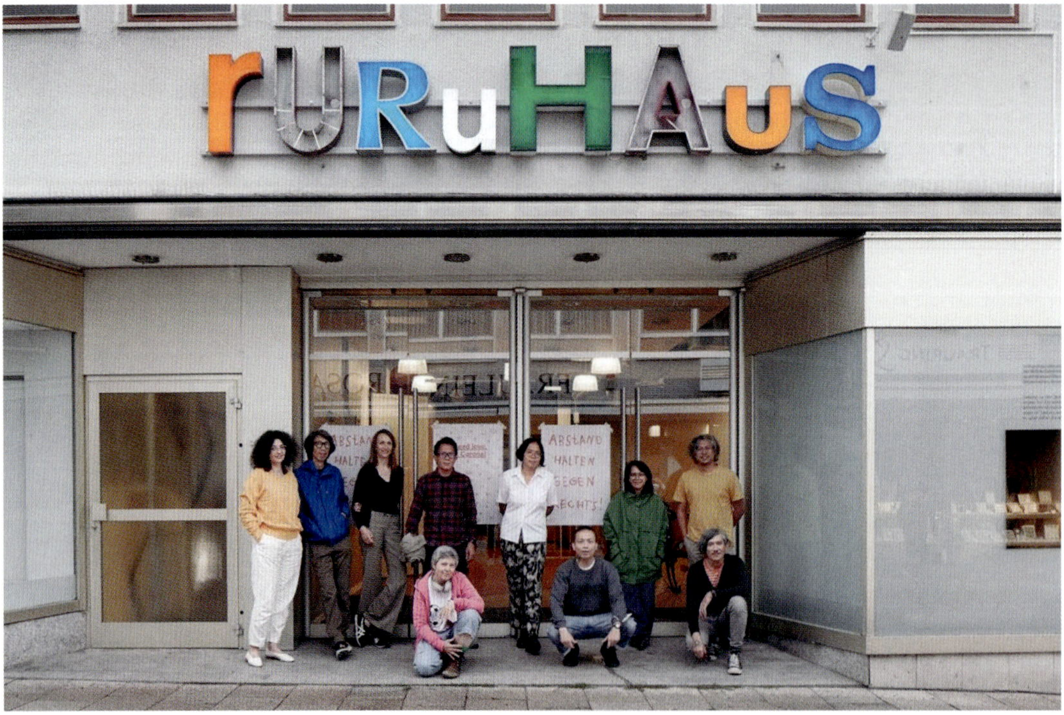

1040

documenta fifteen (artistic direction), Kassel, Germany, 18 June – 25 September 2022

documenta fifteen is practice and not theme based. It is not about *lumbung* or the commons, or any such notion. When we started, we realised that making a 'showcase' of collective practices, done by many art centres, would be a trap. Instead, this exhibition and journey are with collectives and artists who have long-standing experience with practicing and not preaching (much) – walking the talk – and who would like to learn new tricks, strategies and approaches from one another to enrich their local communities. So, in a way it is a study of many models.

ruangrupa

For me it feels like we grew up together, and ruangrupa is one of the 'persons' that are most influential to how I have developed my further life and career. Our relationship is first of all being friends, but I think we have been inspiring each other throughout the next twenty years of working life, sometimes more intensively, sometimes more at a distance. ruangrupa's way of working and its values have been guiding also a lot of other work I have been doing amongst others in funding practice. When I entered the artistic team of documenta fifteen, for the first time I became part of the collective. Now we are discussing how to build on the *lumbung* experience and are developing some new projects while keeping the *lumbung* going in a slow pace.

Gertrude Flentge

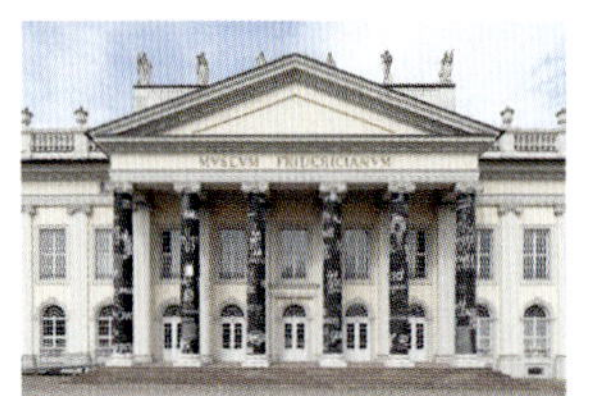

1041

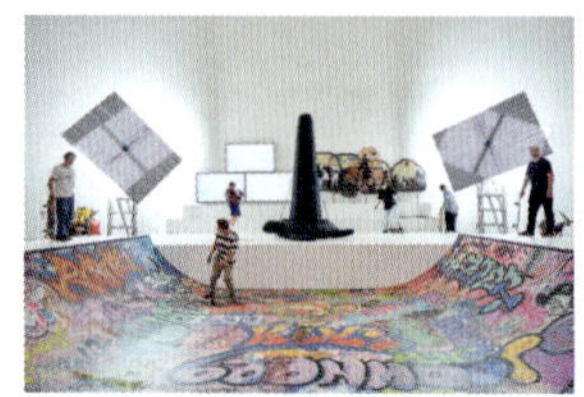

1042

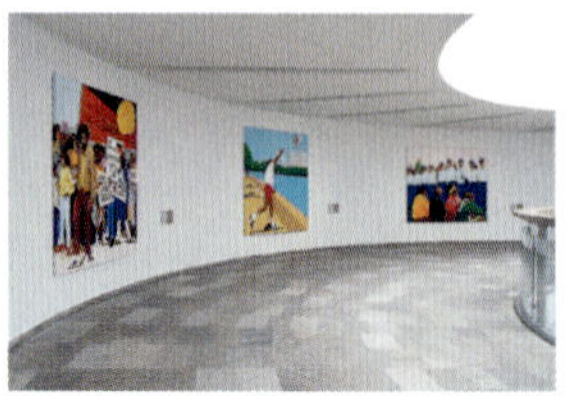

1043

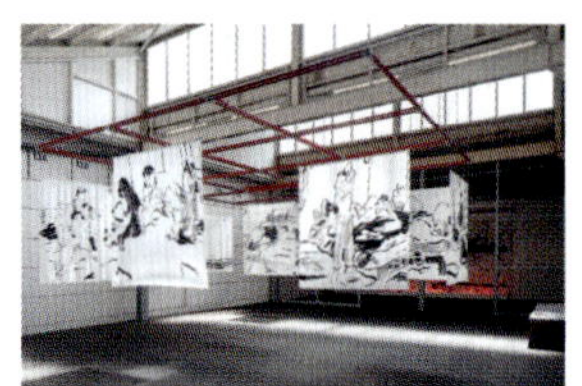

1044

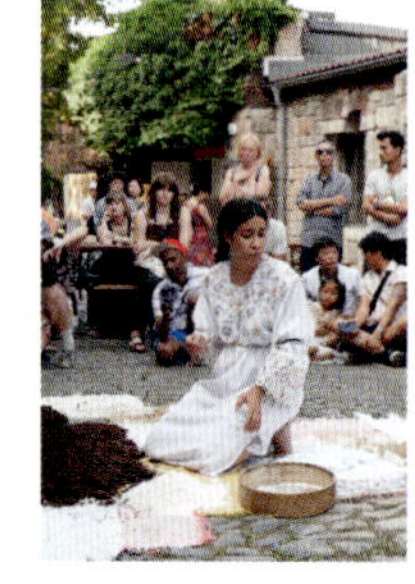

1045

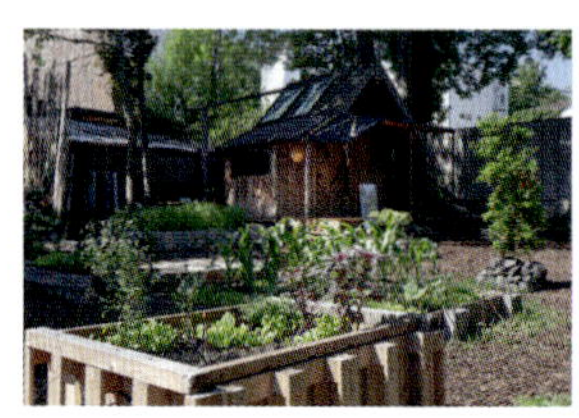

1046

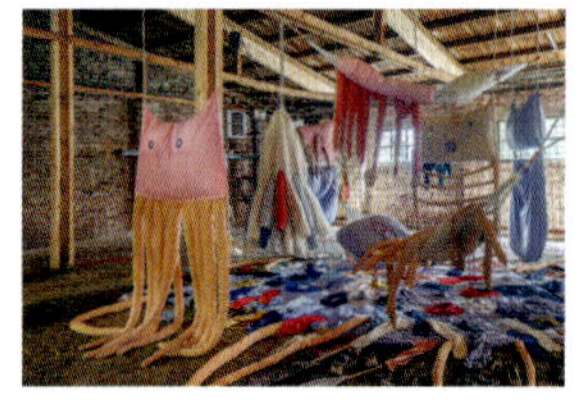

1047

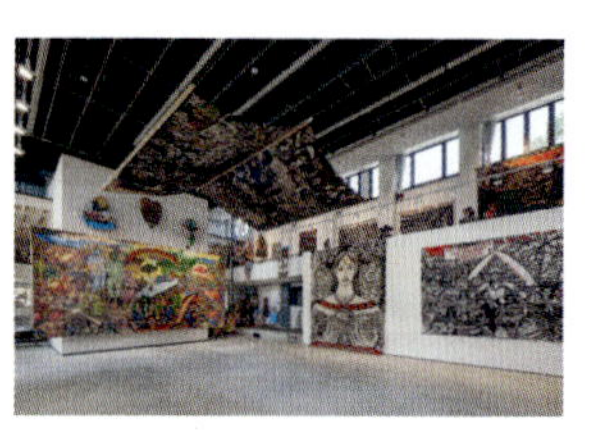

1048

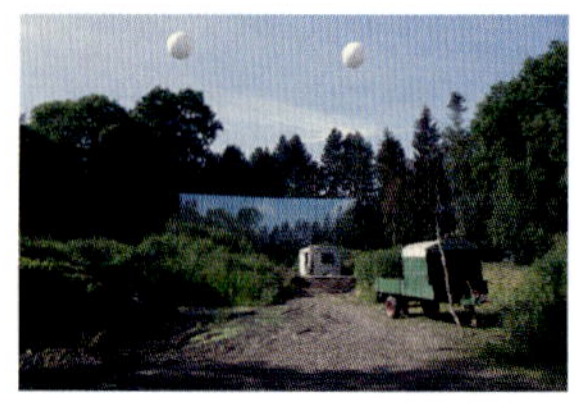

1049

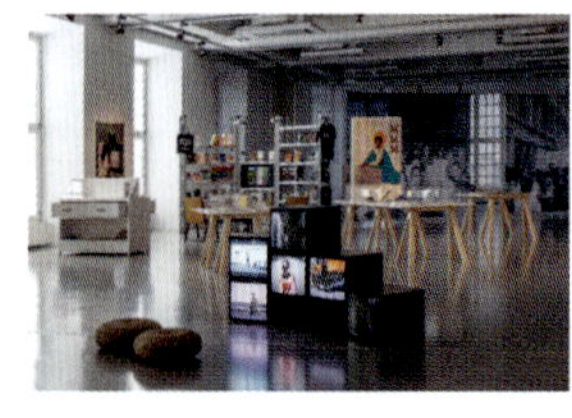

1050

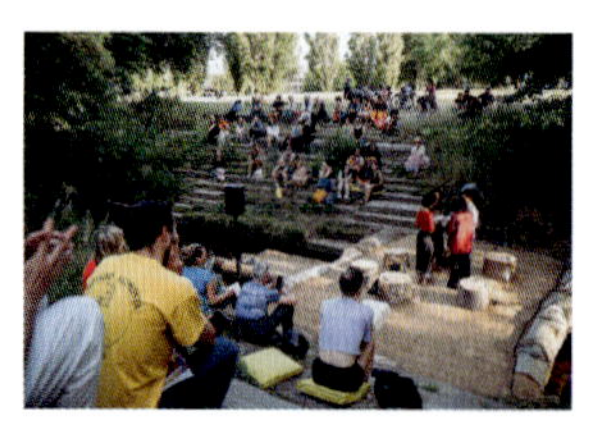

1051

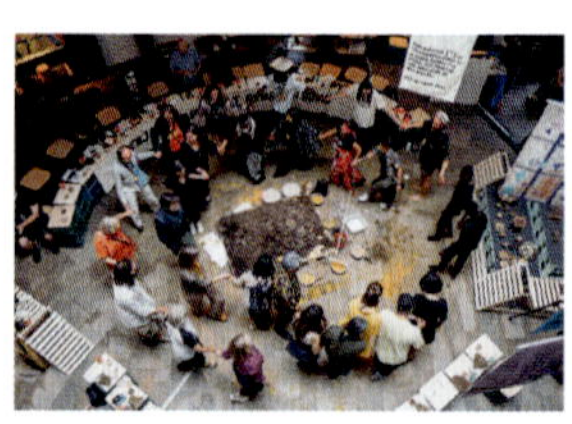

1052

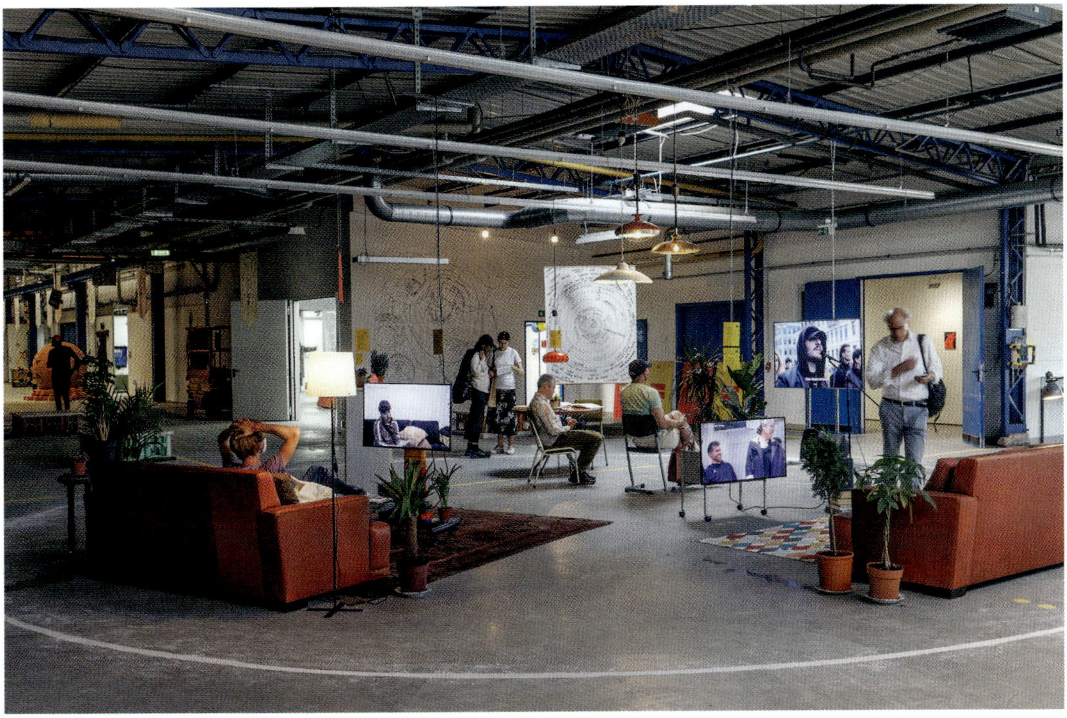

1053

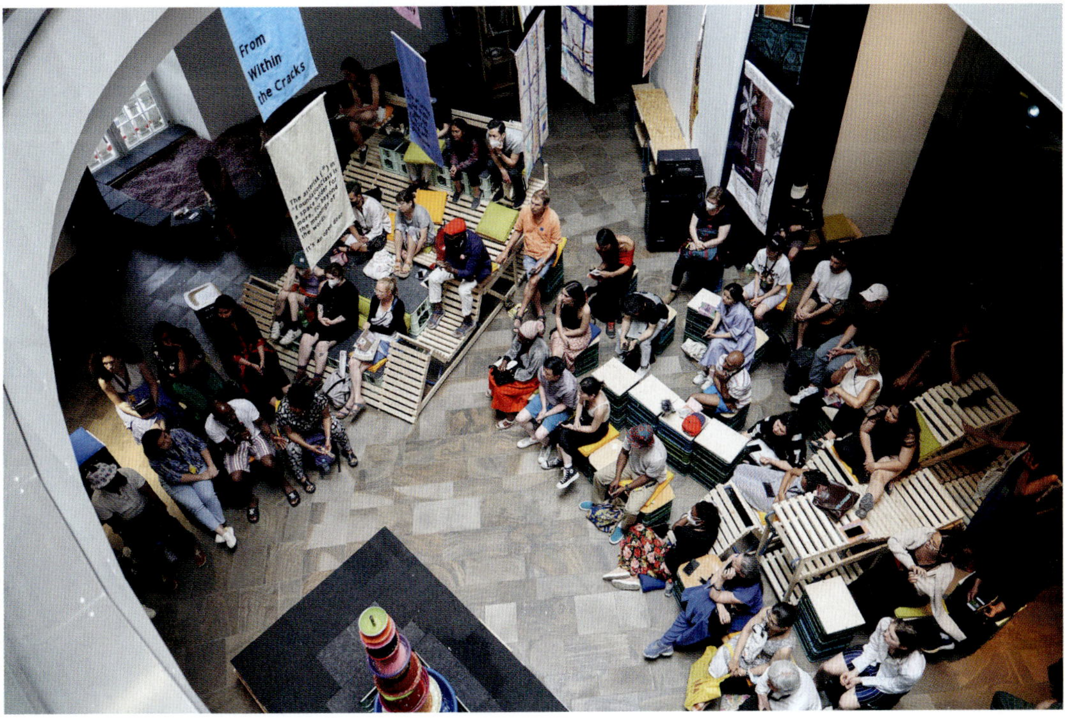

1054

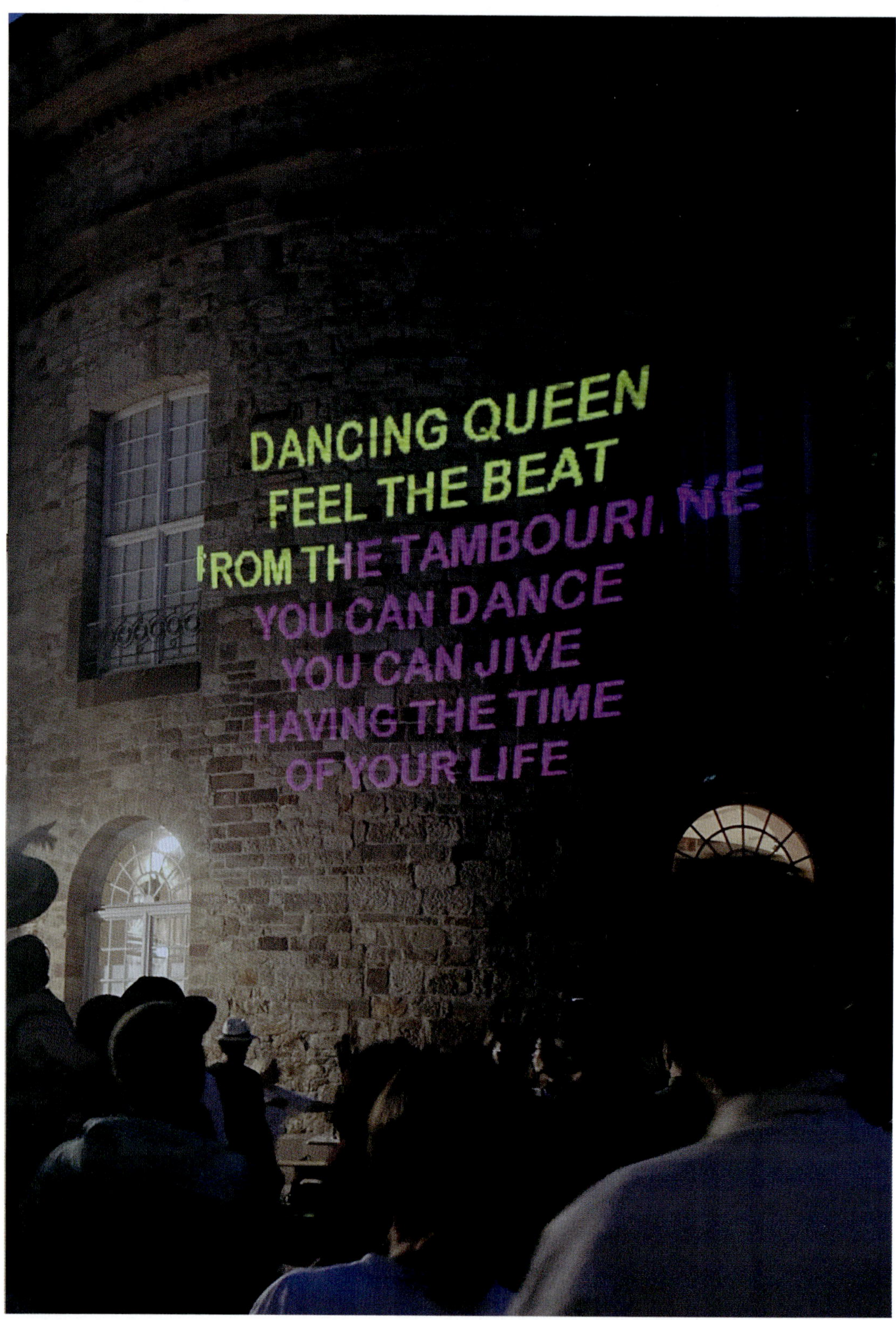
DANCING QUEEN
FEEL THE BEAT
FROM THE TAMBOURI NE
YOU CAN DANCE
YOU CAN JIVE
HAVING THE TIME
OF YOUR LIFE

documenta fifteen (artistic direction), Kassel, Germany, 18 June – 25 September 2022

documenta fifteen was held for 100 days, with tons of various exhibitions, performances, festivals, workshops, movie screenings, radio programmes and discussions each day – so it was a challenge for me to fully 'sweep' the whole thing before leaving. One of the most memorable music festivals was 'Meydan', which presented bands and electronic music performances from all over the world. Various documenta artists also organised independent events in their own venues, ranging from discussions to cooking and karaoke parties. Among those that I visited were the venues of Gudskul, Jatiwangi Art Factory, Party Office, Bannorg and Cinema Caravan. All of the events were open to the public. ... Kassel was full of visitors – both local and from all over the world – throughout documenta fifteen. Trams were packed, restaurants were crowded and the city felt so much more alive. Notable for me was that throughout the exhibition I had the chance to taste various kinds of unique dishes from all over the world, made by the artists of documenta fifteen. Cooking and eating together with them – which usually just happened organically outside of the formal agendas – were moments to get to know each other in a relaxed and warm atmosphere.

Ary Sendy

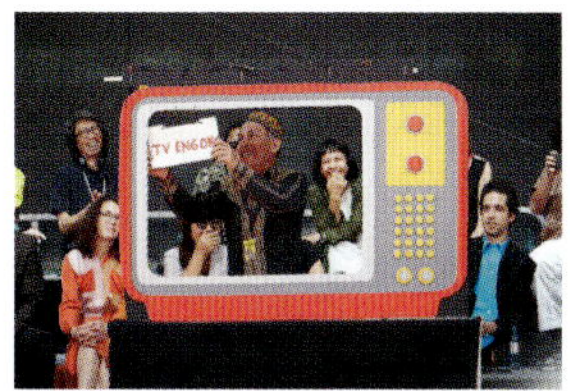

1056

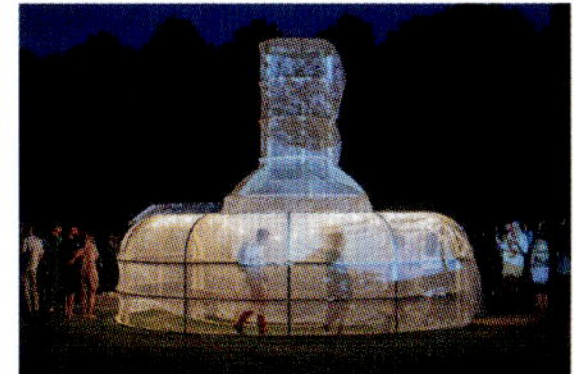

1057

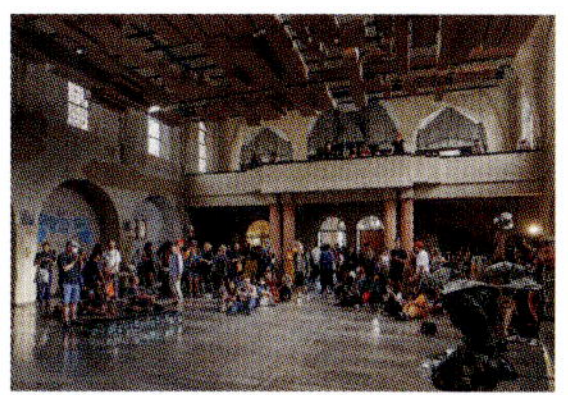

1058

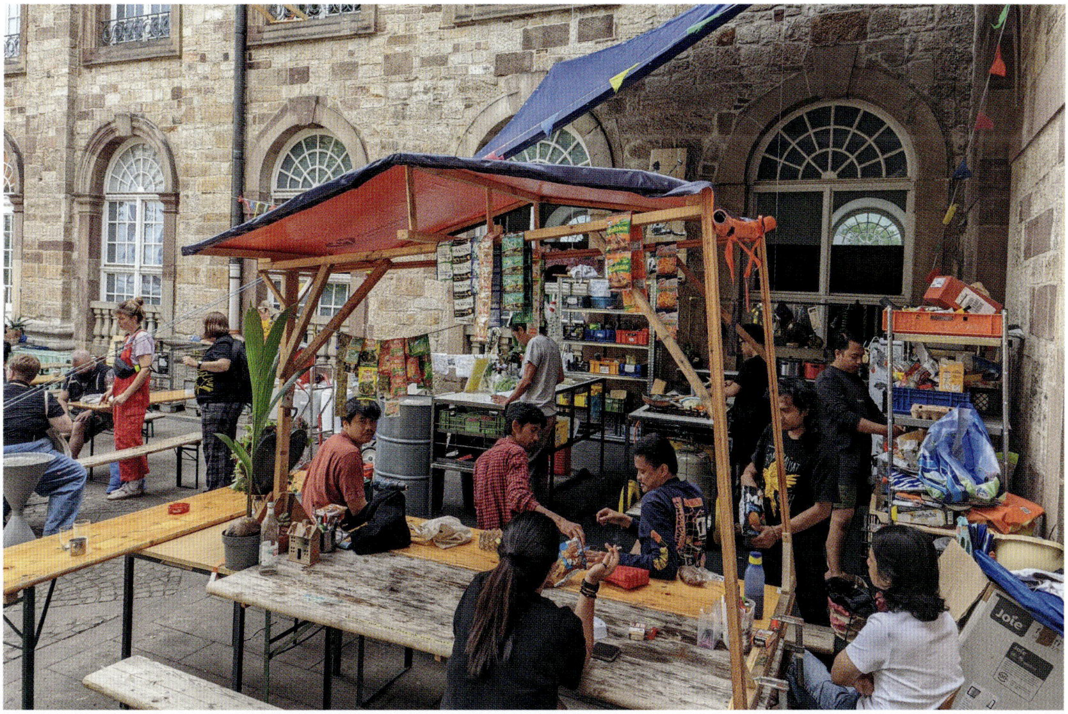

1059

see also pp.12–38

Since the *lumbung* is working towards a circular and sustainable economy the resources could be shared within it and go to the local and global communities of the artworks, causes, artists and lumbung interlokal. Lumbung members and artists can share the cost of the infrastructure of the gallery. The resources accumulated, can be then divided in different percentages. The distribution of the resources can be different for each member and artist (going towards the community of the artwork, causes, lumbung interlokal...) or we could agree on certain fixed percentages, or a combination for both. The context of *lumbung* can be used as a practice of questioning the commercial aspect of the gallery space. The lumbung Gallery could be a way for thinking towards a fair distribution amongst the artists themselves as well. It could contribute to the sustainability of the *lumbung* at large, since it will function as an instigator for the economy of the *lumbung* that survives after, whilst posing a cultural question about economy, as one of the income-generating projects in the *lumbung*.

lumbung Gallery working group

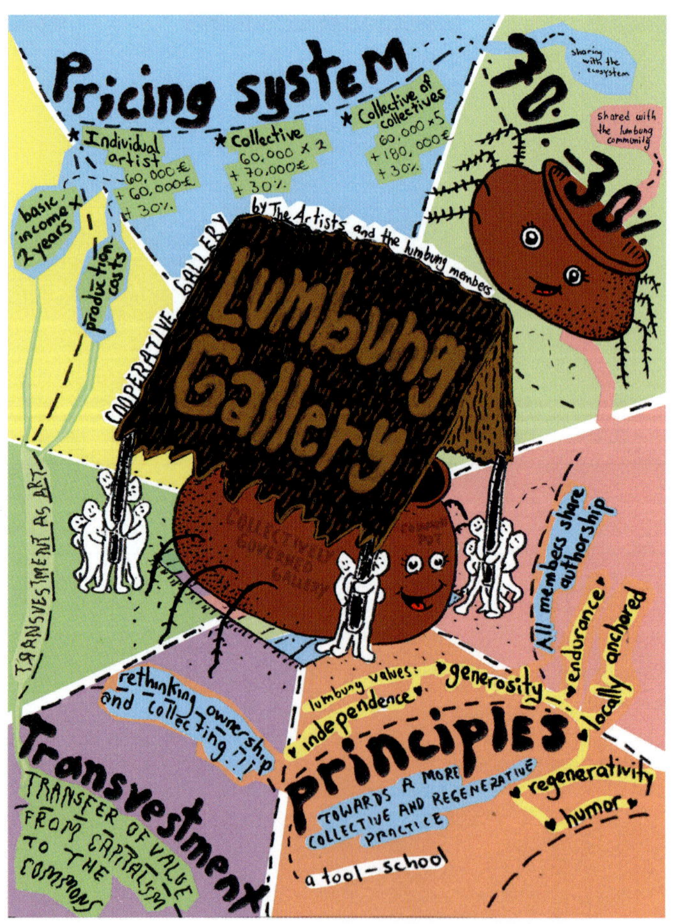

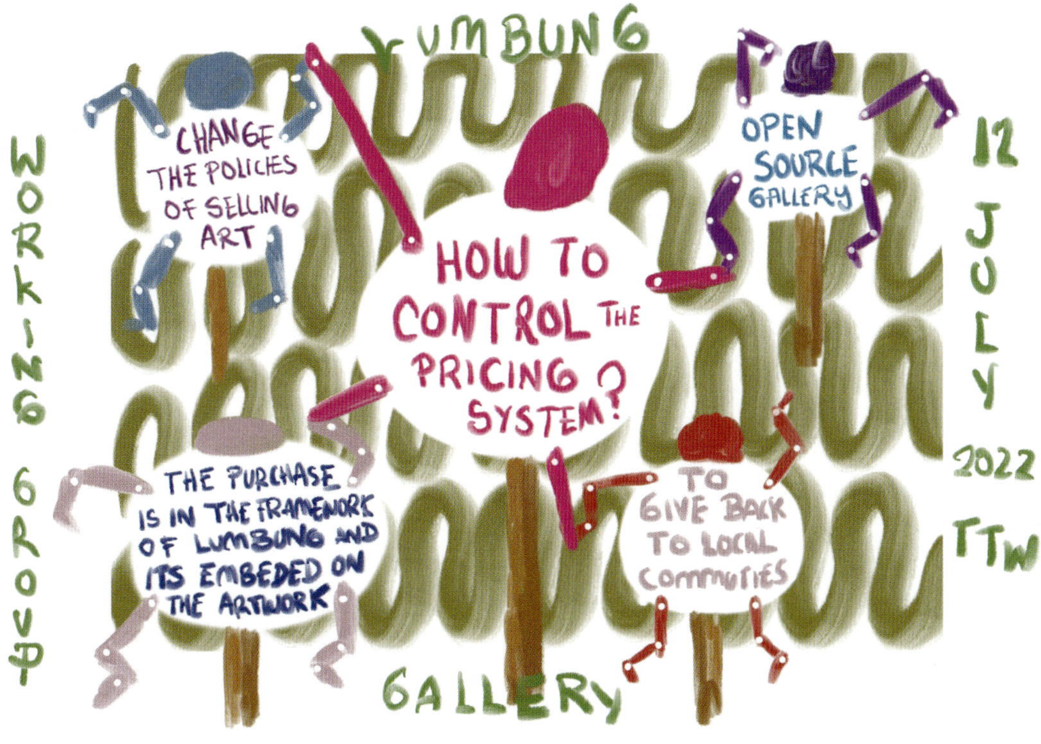

1061

In practice, what *lumbung* means is a repurposing of a part of the considerable resources made available to the exhibition for building up the resilience of the invited Lumbung 1 partners in their home bases. In doing so, ruangrupa partially switched the responsibility from themselves as curators making a world exhibition in Germany to the documenta gGmbH's responsibility for compensating the communities whose creativity they were inevitably going to extract in order to present them in Kassel. The line between this approach and the demand for restitution and re-existence articulated by decolonial theory is a short one. It anticipates what decolonial scholars critique and seeks to already address the imbalance in power and resources between the colonising and colonised worlds before any engagement is initiated. As I have said, this discourse was never named decolonial by ruangrupa – perhaps to avoid such a trigger word for the political right; perhaps to refuse an intellectual framework they had not shaped. But the decolonial as I understand it is written all over their project. The challenge or even paradigm shift that *lumbung* does represent to the Western art institutional system is to decolonise itself of its modes of extraction and cultural superiority. Even more crucially, it offers forms of self-management and models of financial sustainability that would compete with the economic system of commercial galleries and auction houses. This varies from asking Western museums and art institutions to concern themselves with the long-term health of invited art and activist communities, to the way it invented a self-managed art sales and distribution system through the proposal of the lumbung Gallery as a profit-recycling, artist-managed gallery structure.

Charles Esche

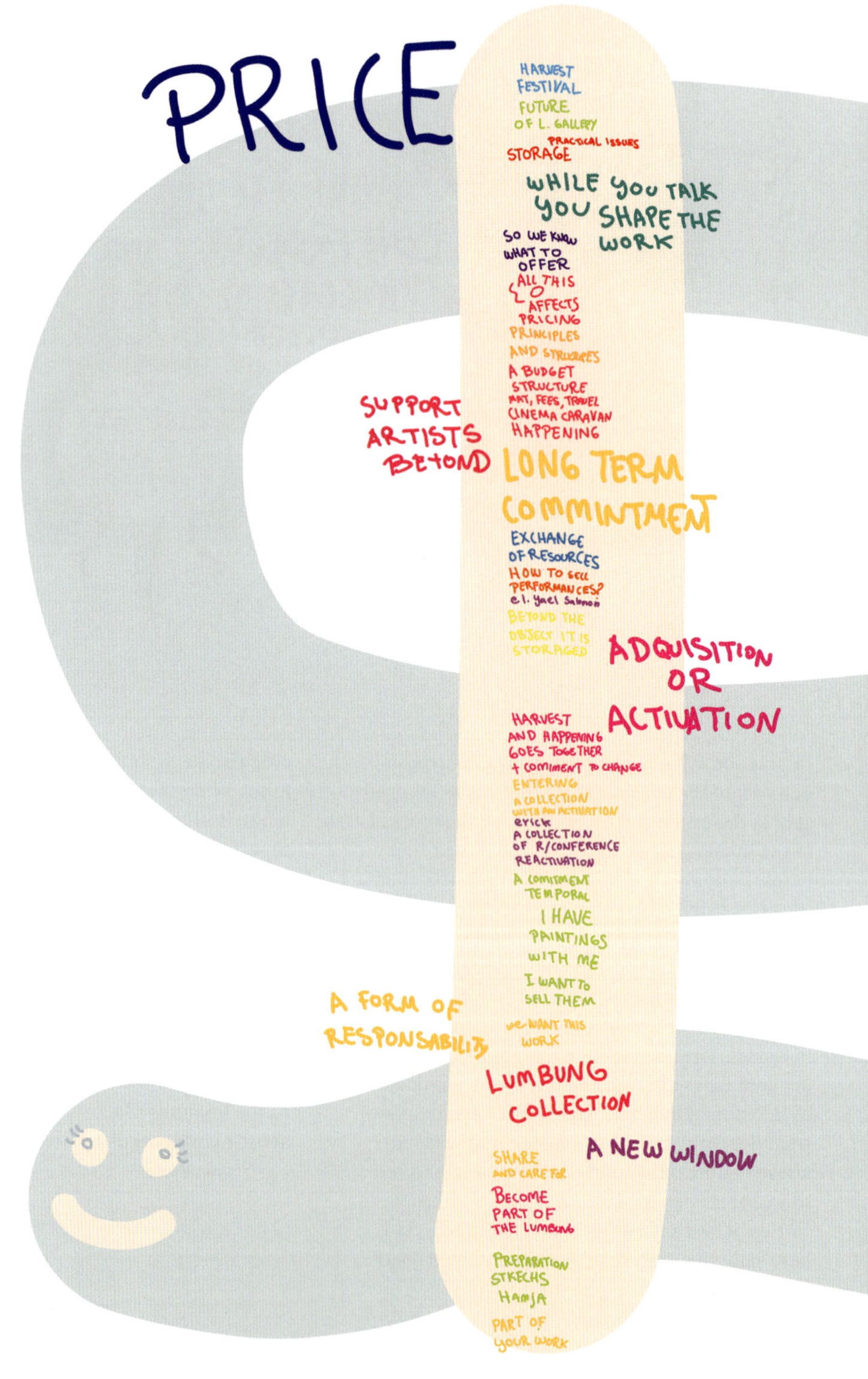
PRICE
HARVEST FESTIVAL
FUTURE OF L. GALLERY
PRACTICAL ISSUES
STORAGE
WHILE YOU TALK YOU SHAPE THE WORK
SO WE KNOW WHAT TO OFFER
ALL THIS AFFECTS PRICING
PRINCIPLES AND STRUCTURES
A BUDGET STRUCTURE
MAT, FEES, TRAVEL
CINEMA CARAVAN
HAPPENING
SUPPORT ARTISTS BEYOND
LONG TERM COMMINTMENT
EXCHANGE OF RESOURCES
HOW TO SELL PERFORMANCES?
e.l. Yael Salomon
BEYOND THE OBJECT IT IS STORAGED
ADQUISITION OR ACTIVATION
HARVEST AND HAPPENING GOES TOGETHER
+ COMIMENT TO CHANGE
ENTERING A COLLECTION WITH AN ACTIVATION
ERICK
A COLLECTION OF R/CONFERENCE
REACTIVATION
A COMITMENT TEMPORAL
I HAVE PAINTINGS WITH ME
I WANT TO SELL THEM
WE WANT THIS WORK
A FORM OF RESPONSABILITY
LUMBUNG COLLECTION
A NEW WINDOW
SHARE AND CARE FOR
BECOME PART OF THE LUMBUNG
PREPARATION STKECHS
HAMJA
PART OF YOUR WORK

CO-OWNERSHIP
IN EDITIONS

TAYLORED MADE
MODELS FOR
EACH WORK

HOW IT WORKS WITH
NON-PHYSICAL WORKS

CONCEPTUAL LENGUAGE
TO UNDERSTAND WHAT
WE ARE PROPOSING

THE COLLECTIVE
ENGAGES WITH
THE LUMBUNG GALLERY

SOME PEOPLE WILL
CONTRIBUTE TO THE POT
BUT NOT BE PART OF
THE GALLERY

WE ARE STILL
WAITING FOR
PRICES

TO EXPLAIN
THE WORKING PROCESS
WITH THE BUYERS

SLOW PROCESS
WILL TAKE SOME TIME

COLLECTIVE
PRICING
AND SOME PEOPLE
WOULDNT LIKE IT

WE NEED
FEEDBACK
FROM ARTIST

LUMBUNG
GALLERY CAN
BE IN ANOTHER SPACE

ACTIVATION BEYOND DOCUMENTA

BRING IDEAS
TO LUMBUNG AFTERMATH

LUMBUNG GALLERY
IN THE INTERNET
ON THE WEBSITE
IMAGES, INTERVIES,
ART WORKS RADIO TEXT

WHAT WE
WANT TO COMUNICATE?
IT IS GOING TO BE
SLOW,

A PLAN TO
COMUNICATION

WHAT ARE THE
STEPS NEED IT?

MEETING WITH
OTHER MINIMAJELIS

HOW TO COMUNICATE
THE PRICING?

LENGUAGES BARRIERS
DIFFERENT
UNDERSTANDINGS

BRING IDEAS
FOR THE FUTURE OF
LUMBUNG GALLERY

FUTURE

lumbung Kios is a network of decentralised and self-run kiosks, to trade goods over the distributed social and cultural network in different locales. Its mission is to create a sustaining model to raise income through the sales of goods produced by lumbung members, lumbung artists and their local ecosystem. As the sustainability principle is not only about the economy, it's very important to consider the environmental pressure and impacts if the trading process would happen amongst the many different locales. To also think of sustainability in the green sense: lumbung Kios experiments with the Feral Trade model as a mechanism to distribute the products it sells. This is a slow distribution/trade mechanism that was established by artist Kate Rich; to trade goods using the active-physical mobility resources of lumbung Kios's existing social network, which then allows the distribution process to occur.

lumbung Kios working group

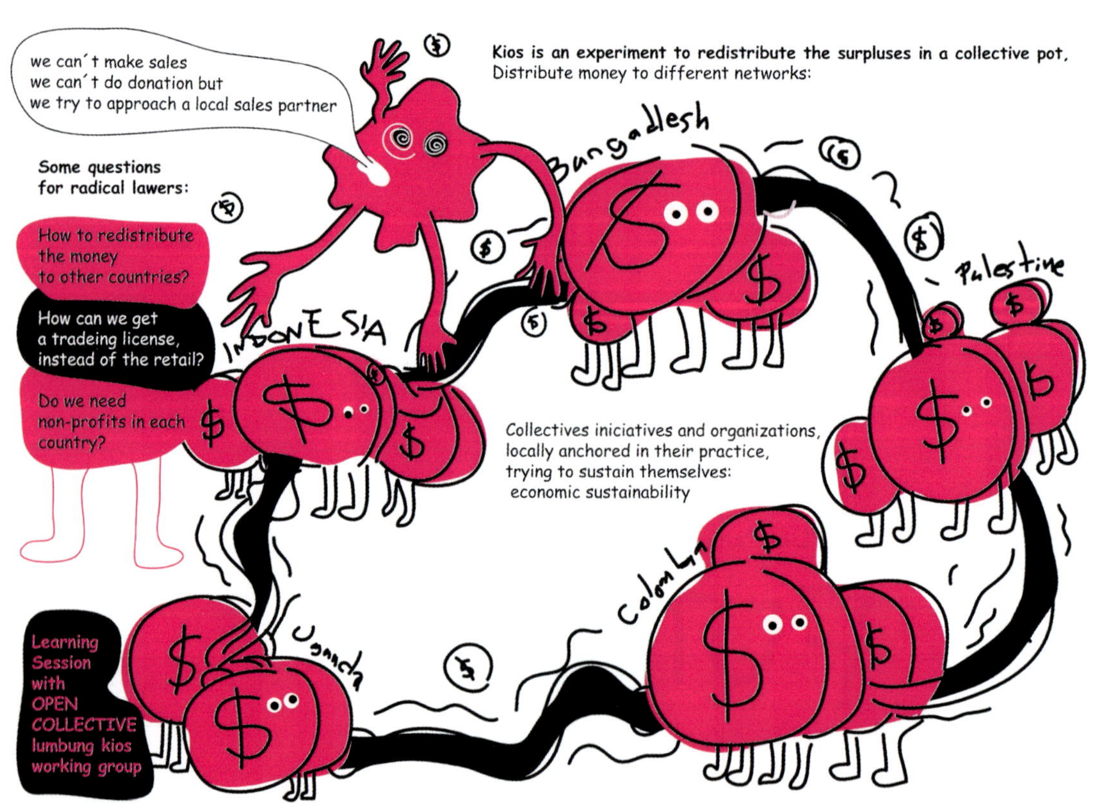

Before Reformasi, the society was suppressed. Everything that resembled *lumbung* practice was considered to be leftist and looked at with suspicion. After Reformasi, ruangrupa tapped into the spirit of creating critical awareness against whatever structure was around them. They tried to fill in the urban space that was being completely segregated and colonised by the neoliberal paradigm. These were valuable interventions, I think. But on the other hand, the reformation itself was filled with lots of problems. It was not a linear progression towards openness nor democratisation. It was hijacked by so many interests and very convoluted. In this kind of atmosphere, we cannot idealise a total freedom in society or a complete transformation of the structure. If we cannot be completely free outside the system, we have to infiltrate the system and try to capture any kind of leftover space that we can occupy. Whether it's the structure given by the New Order, or today's structure, we need to negotiate with them to create the space. I think the *lumbung* practice that ruru offers is definitely that. It also coincides with other *lumbung* practices that the *kampungs* have been doing, for example. Although they are not fully attached to each other, they are going on at the same time. The right wing is getting very strong, so the challenge is bigger now. Different *lumbung* practices are not systematic or massive, in a structural sense, but they emerge here and there and everybody starts to connect with one another. We hope that it can somehow make changes. ruru is facing lots of challenge after documenta – and not only in Germany, where they were criticised and marginalised. Of course, within the 'microcosm' of interpersonal interaction in Kassel, you could feel the affirmative atmosphere. But outside that it was completely not working. Even in Indonesia, *lumbung* practice has not gathered enough attention, and the discussion is not as significant as it should have been.

Melani Budianta

There is an increasing demand for more accountability in the organising practices of arts and culture, especially in terms of gender, race/ethnicity and class. This intersectionality of politics was not much visible or being discussed in the first ten years after Reformasi when I started to work in the arts. So there's a change in the ecosystem. The younger generation of arts practitioners in Indonesia was born during Reformasi and after. In international lingo, they are the 'Generation Z', but I guess in the Indonesian context, they are more suitably called the 'Reformasi Babies'. The Reformasi Babies are now starting their careers in the arts as artists, curators, managers, with the awareness of broken promises of democracy from Reformasi. I've met many of them who relentlessly demand fair working conditions and are critical towards the invisible power structures in the arts. I am often wondering how this generational wave of change is being navigated in daily organising practices within arts organisations, especially in ruru with such a large scale of work.

Syafiatudina

lumbung.space and lumbung Press are mediums for lumbung artists and members to communicate with each other and the larger public. lumbung.space is an experimental social and publishing platform for sharing harvests by all the members online. It is non-extractive, co-governed by the users and built on open platforms. It functions as a *lumbung* with a members-only backend for artists to store, discuss and organise content and a frontend where users can see and interact with the published content.

ruangrupa

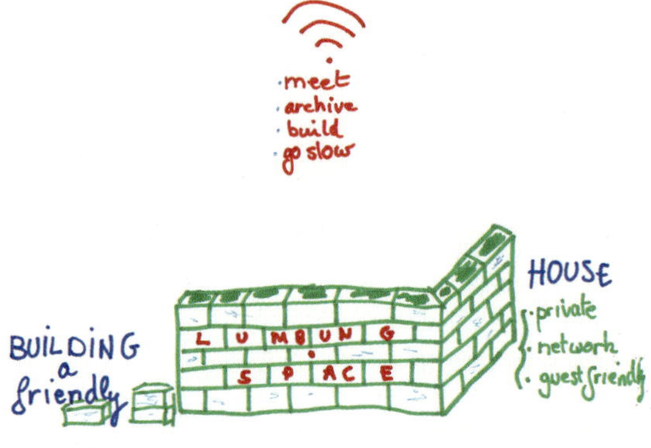

1064

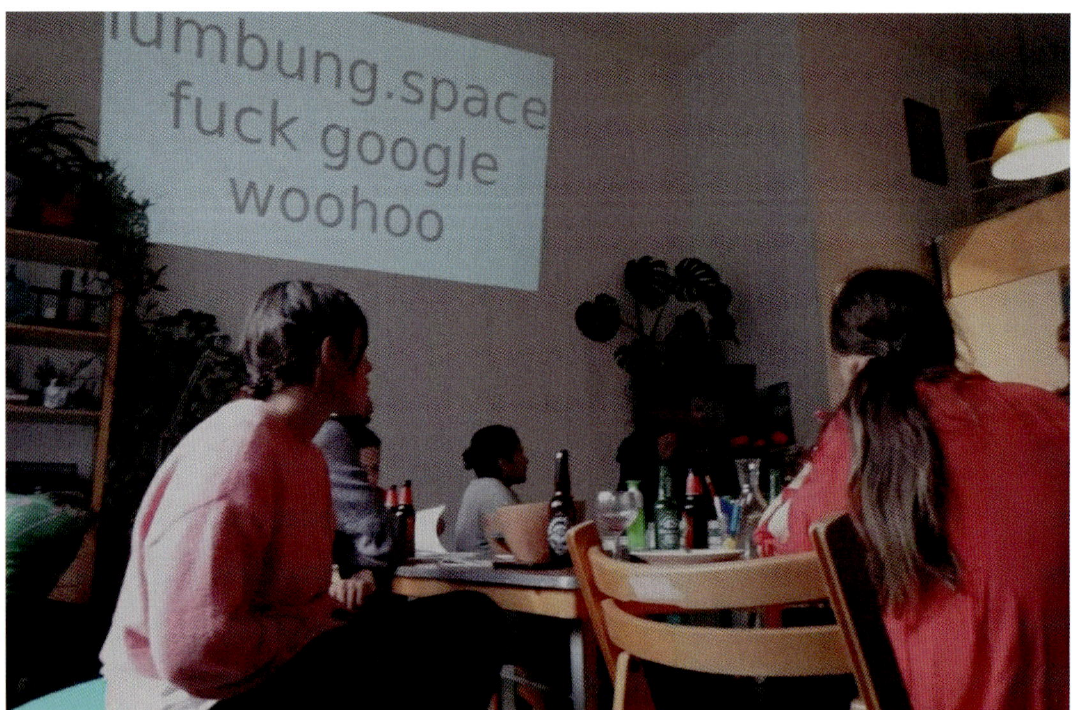

1065

It is not difficult to notice that a lot of lumbung artists carry a lot of stories and want to publish material in many forms, from many sources, in many languages and with varied objectives. We want to create a tool that may be used for everyone and which can visualise that energy in the form of a series of process publications. We want to keep a collective approach but without losing multiplicity. Many projects are articulated in many parts and different times, so it is crucial to have as much direct information from the artist as possible. We are interested in creators explaining, without mediation, their projects within their own strategies and logic. This press will favour energy and flow of information. Two inks (duo tone).

lumbung Press working group

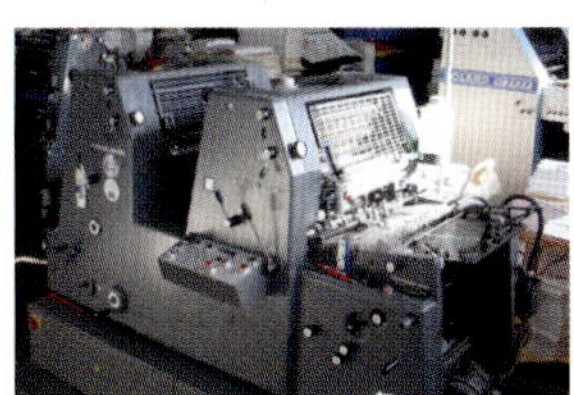

1066

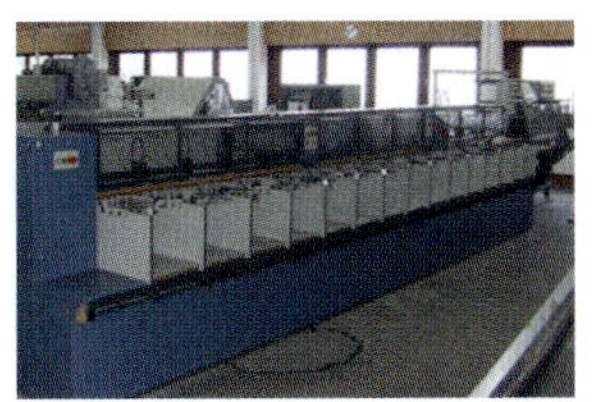

1067

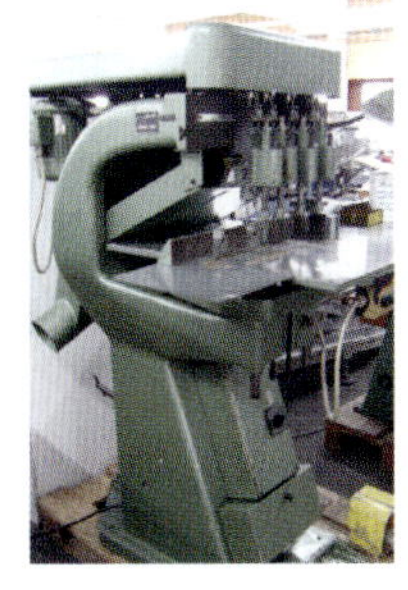

1068

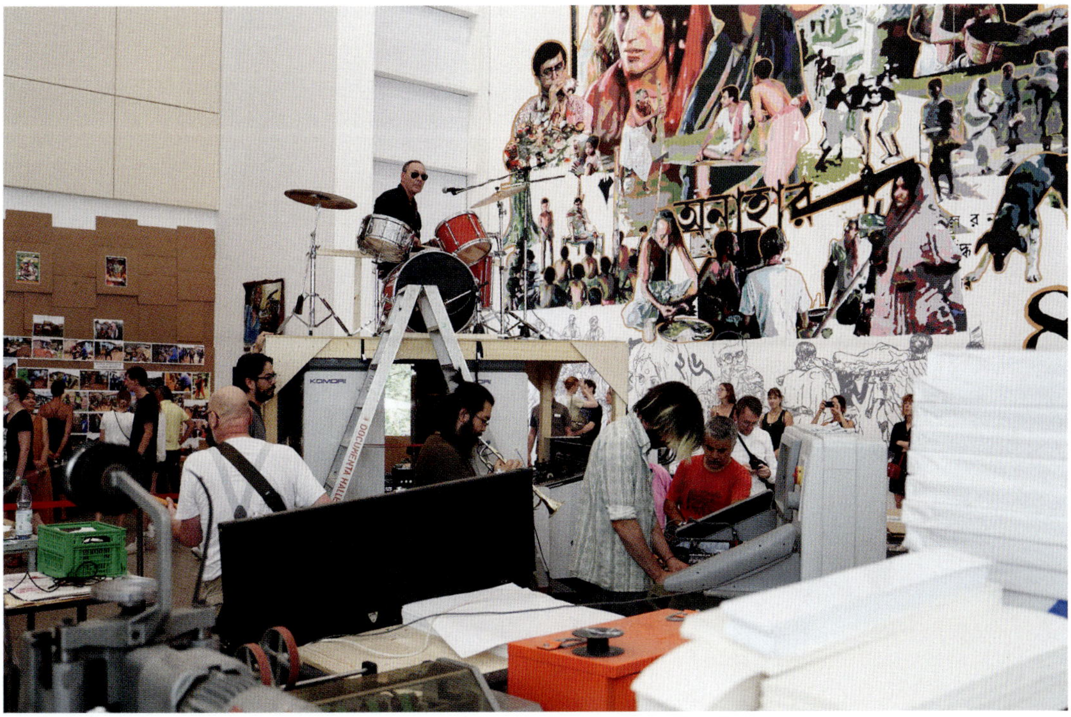

1069

The lumbung of Publishers emerges within the framework of the international contemporary art fair documenta fifteen, held in Kassel every five years. This effort brings together over twenty independent artists and projects whose editorial practices and philosophies resonate with the principle of collective work, in tune with the community-driven proposal that characterises this year's edition of documenta under the artistic direction of the ruangrupa curatorial collective.

Since March 2022, the editors, organisers and harvesters have gathered together through a series of virtual assemblies to create an international network, sharing practices, strategies and tools. Also, they have been collaborating in the creation of a programme of workshops, presentations, site-specific activations, readings and exhibitions open to the public at documenta fifteen.

lumbung of Publishers working group

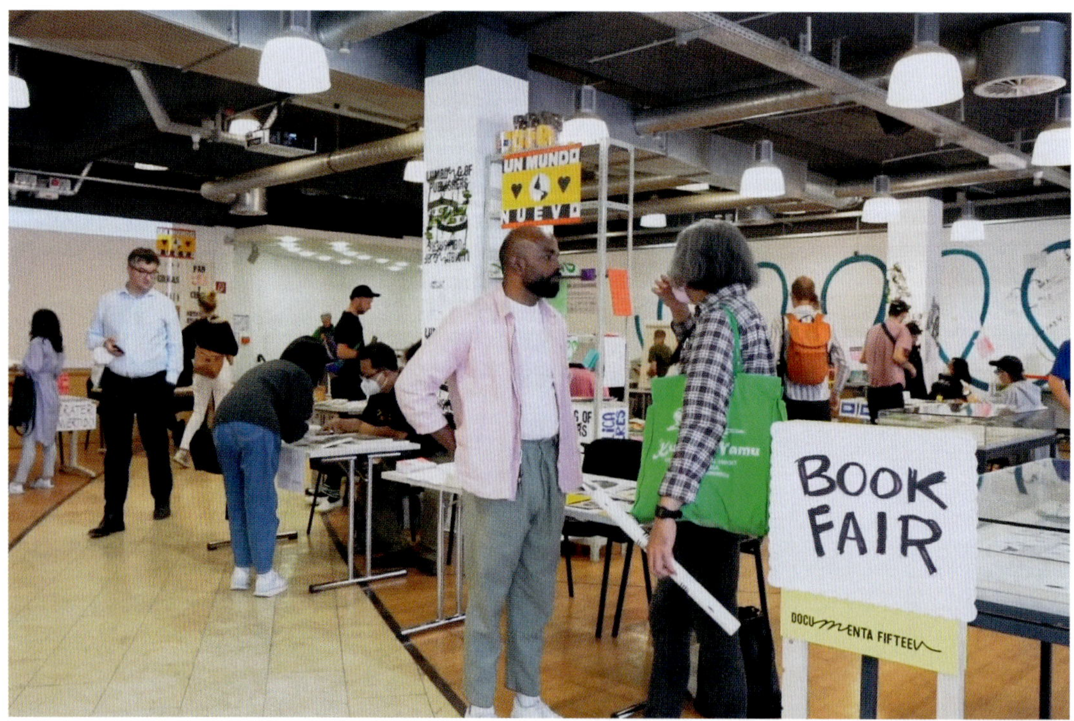

The lumbung Land working group, on the other hand, has been discussing developing a way of 'investing' by using the collective pot in specific land projects run by members – projects that question ownership of land, that start from community needs and collective use and governance, and that combine agriculture, biodiversity, culture and the spiritual. Combining experimentation on land with experimentation on currencies and decentralised autonomous organisations would be a start towards building a true, interlocally connected and collectively governed economy.

ruangrupa

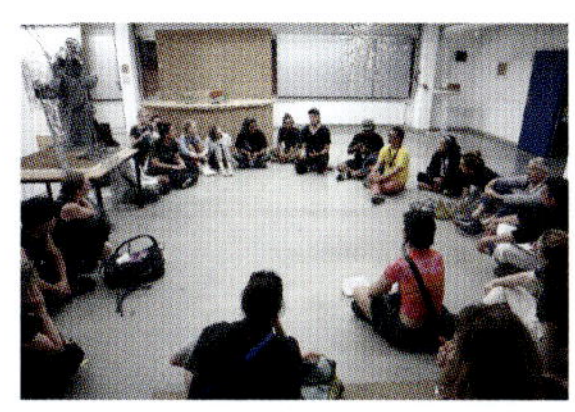

1071

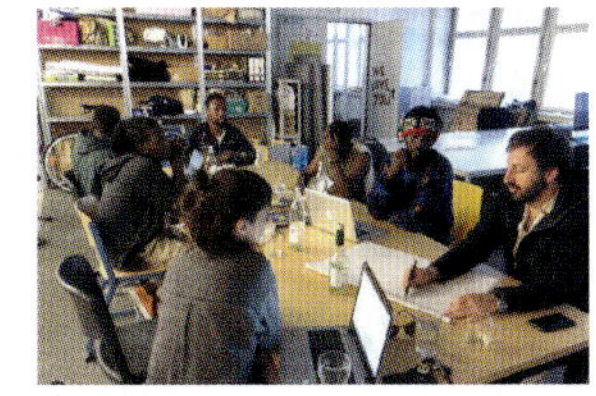

1072

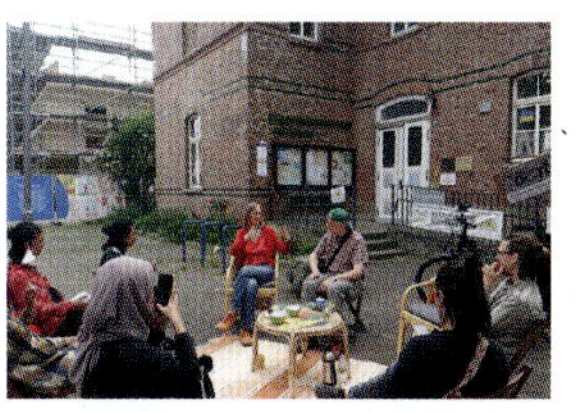

1073

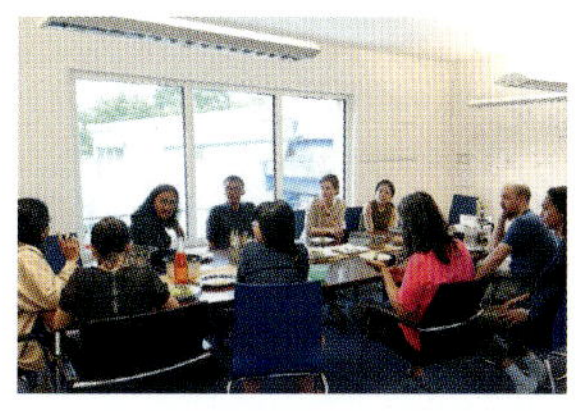

1074

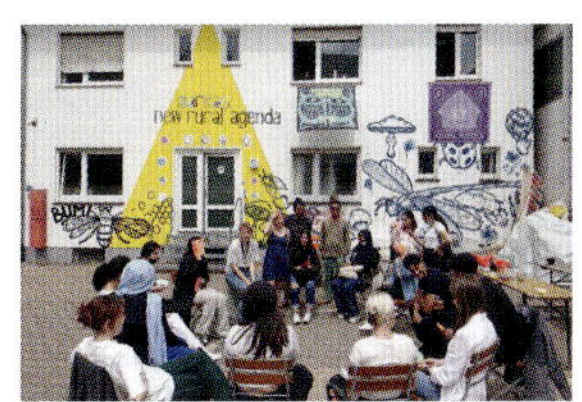

1075

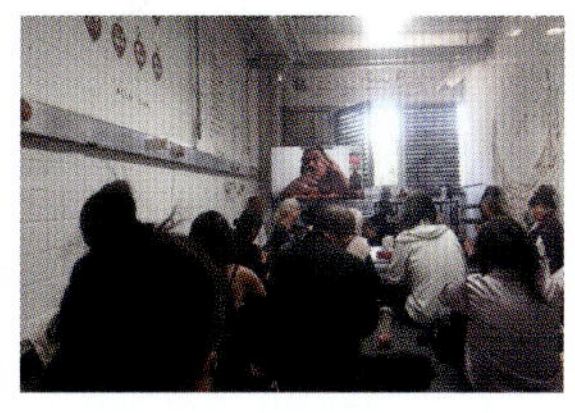

1076

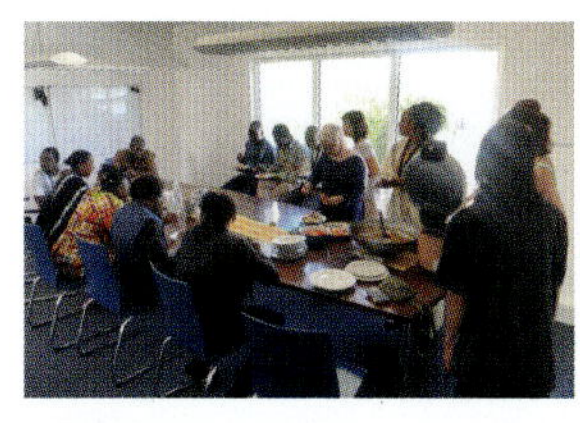

1077

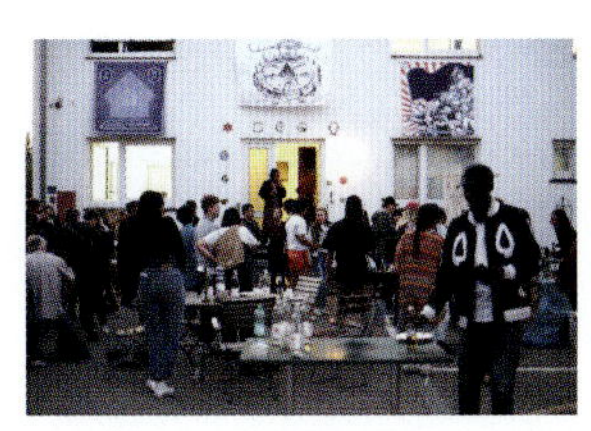

1078

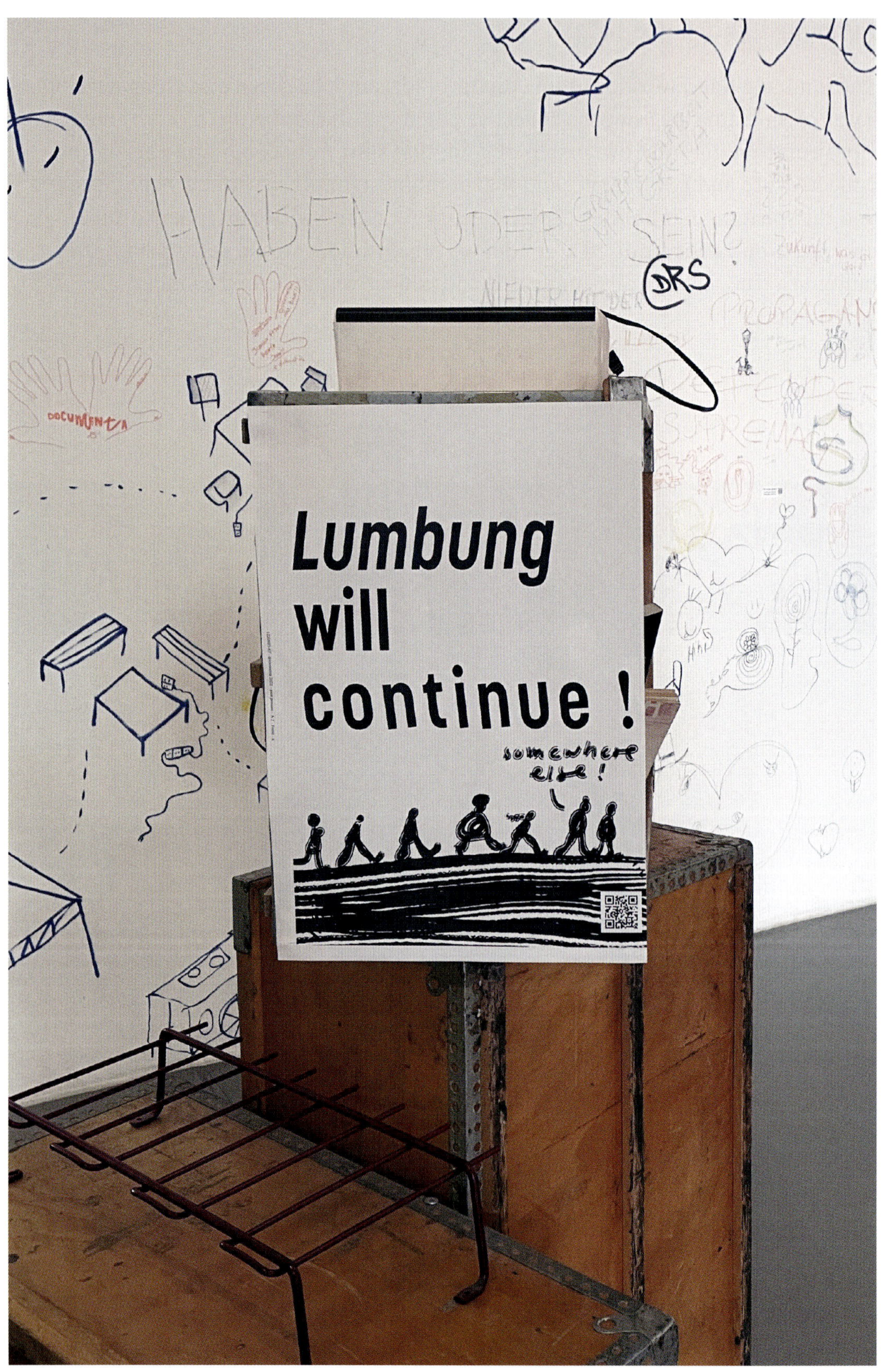
Lumbung
will
continue !
somewhere
else !
HABEN ODER SEIN?
documenta
DRS

Many of us were involved with ruangrupa for a shorter or longer period. Because if you are in Jakarta, there is no where else to go where you can just hang out and be yourself. And when you find other people that agree to you being you, then you can make something happen. There are also many non-members who are always around ruangrupa; their positions are very interesting.

Grace Samboh

Some consider the fluidity and flexibility of the work style in ruangrupa as an alternative space, which is different from the disciplinary routine of office work in a multinational company, government office or in the professional world. Some, however, cannot cope with it. A meeting in ruangrupa can last from late afternoon to midnight. The long duration is caused by the digression in the discussion, from the topic of the meeting to the culinary world, the flora and fauna, or something to laugh about.

Mirwan Andan

I'm curious about how ruangrupa deal with criticism. ruru has become the generation that gets to decide a lot – and how do they see that? Of course, they have their own younger generation within the collective, but they are some sort of institution now. They also never said they were anti-institution. It's very interesting. As they've become very powerful in Indonesia thanks to their achievements in the international art world and locally, what is the kind of responsibility they would like to take on? To be very blunt, why wouldn't they occupy the role of Minister of Culture, for example? They are very close to that in a sense. Of course I understand why not, but they need an ally there, because otherwise it's not going to function. It also depends on who's going to be the minister. I wonder also how different political climates might shift their strategy. But ruru reinvent themselves all over again time and again too. They have now so much information collected from mapping the work of collectives across the whole country. It's not that they own that material, but they created data. This information would become an asset in cultural policy. Imagine all the resources that they assemble through the strategy of friendships.

Philippe Pirotte

It is at the core an artists' initiative with a mix of an open collaborative creative lab and a rock'n'roll band. But the strength of ruru is the ability and consistency of challenging norms about contemporary society, capitalism and urban lives in its own authentic ways (again, especially among the post-Reformasi Indonesian art scene but also relevant globally), while retaining and making the best of the Jakartan 'happy go lucky' solidarity, sense of humour and relaxed attitude against all odds. As ruru evolves, *lumbung* is a proposal of a sustainability platform which stems from the heart and lifeblood of an art scene with the best qualities above, though how it continues to challenge the current social-political landscape in mainstream society remains to be seen.

Farah Wardani

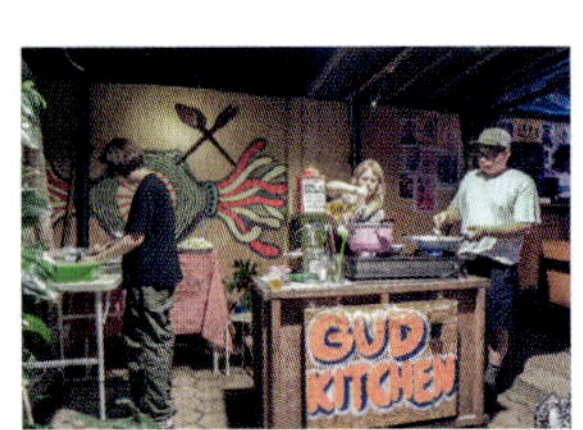

1080

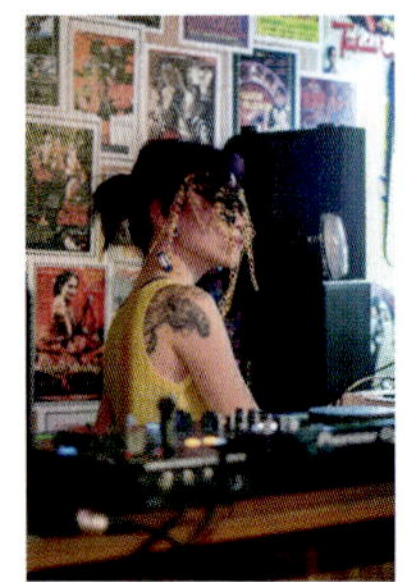

1081

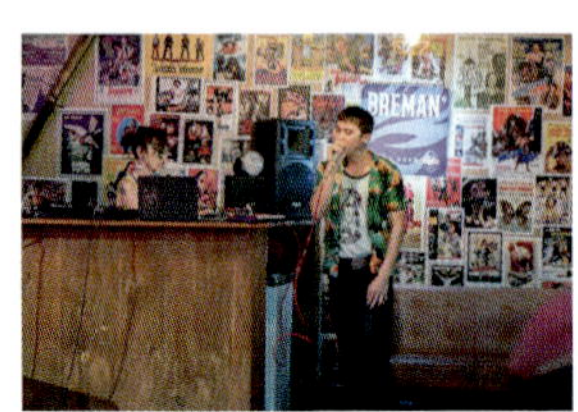

1082

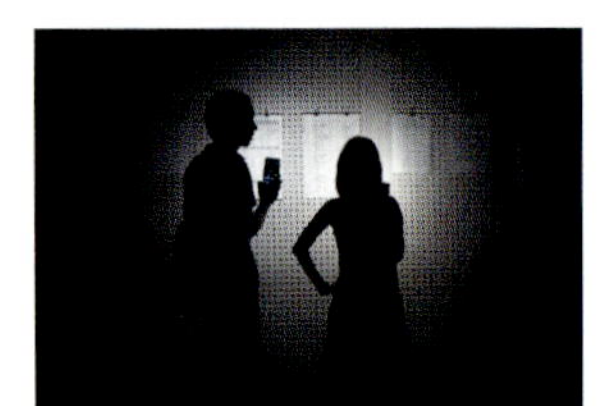

1083

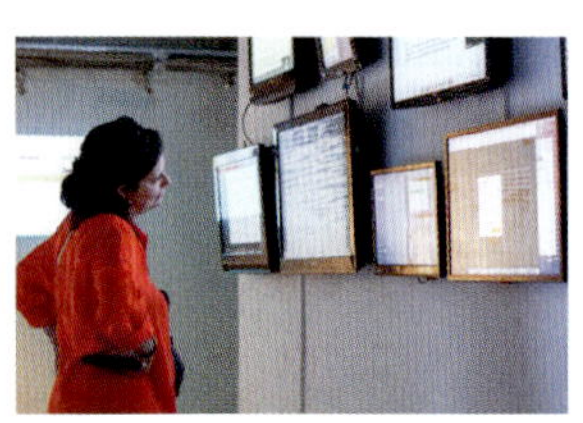

1084

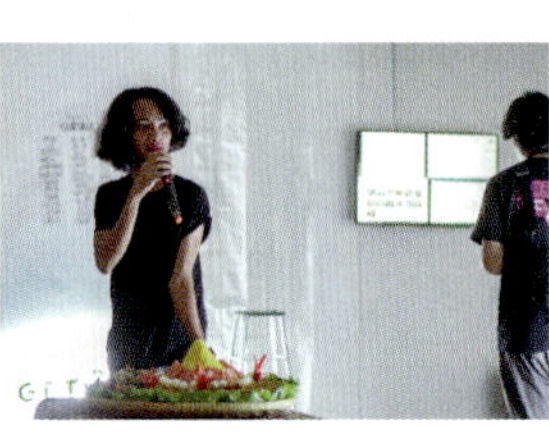

1085

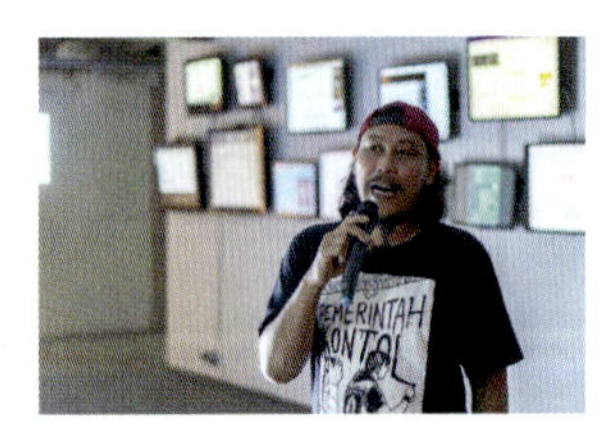

1086

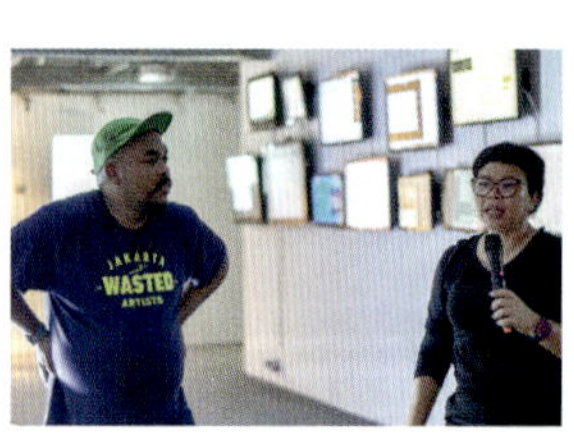

1087

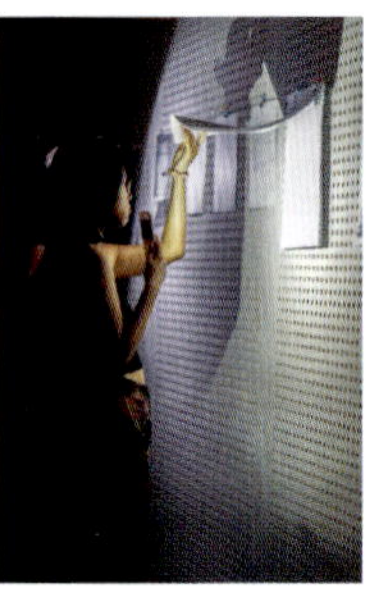

1088

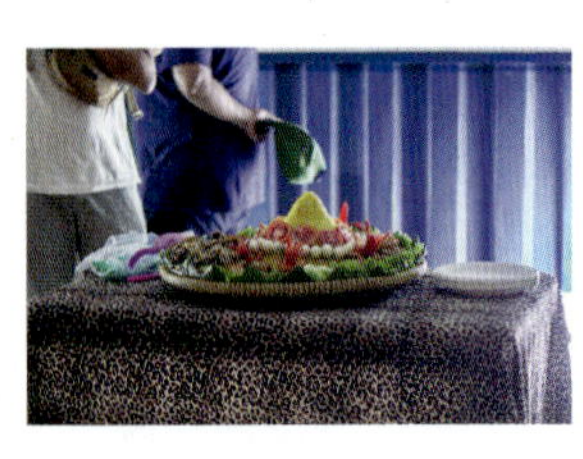

1089

1090

1091

How to work with government support

- Becareful of the corruption and manipulation. They are the experts
- As small as they give you, make sure the programs directly engage with public.
- Trust no one

BALIKPAPAN
Legenda
Rute Jauh
Rute Pendek
1 Gedung Parkir Klandasan | Bioskop Gelora
2 Taman Bekapai
3 Novotel
4 Gereja Katolik Santa Theresia
5 Rumah Panggung Cagar Budaya
6 Tugu Australia dan Lapangan Merdeka
7 Komp Banua Patra | Kedai Kangkung
8 Nissen Hut (Rumah Lengkung)
9 MONPERA
10 Kantor Pos
11 Masjid At-Taqwa
12 Toko Kaset Mickey
13 Rumah Jengki Wisma Kuang
14 Banua Patra
15 Balikpapan War Cemetery
16 Goa Volker
17 Sumur Mathilda
18 Kantor Pertamina
19 Meriam Askit
20 Lapangan Foni
21 Nammin
22 Rumah Dahor
AUSTRALIAN WAR MEMORIAL
RCDIG1024281

1092

Legenda
Rute Jauh
Rute Pendek
1 Gedung Parkir Klandasan | Bioskop Gelora
2 Taman Bekapai
3 Novotel
4 Gereja Katolik Santa Theresia
5 Rumah Panggung Cagar Budaya
6 Tugu Australia dan Lapangan Merdeka
7 Komp Banua Patra | Kedai Kangkung
8 Nissen Hut (Rumah Lengkung)
9 MONPERA
10 Kantor Pos
11 Masjid At-Taqwa
12 Toko Kaset Mickey
13 Rumah Jengki Wisma Kuang
14 Banua Patra
15 Balikpapan War Cemetery
16 Goa Volker
17 Sumur Mathilda
18 Kantor Pertamina
19 Meriam Askit
20 Lapangan Foni
21 Nammin
22 Rumah Dahor
AUSTRALIAN WAR MEMORIAL
RCDIG1024281

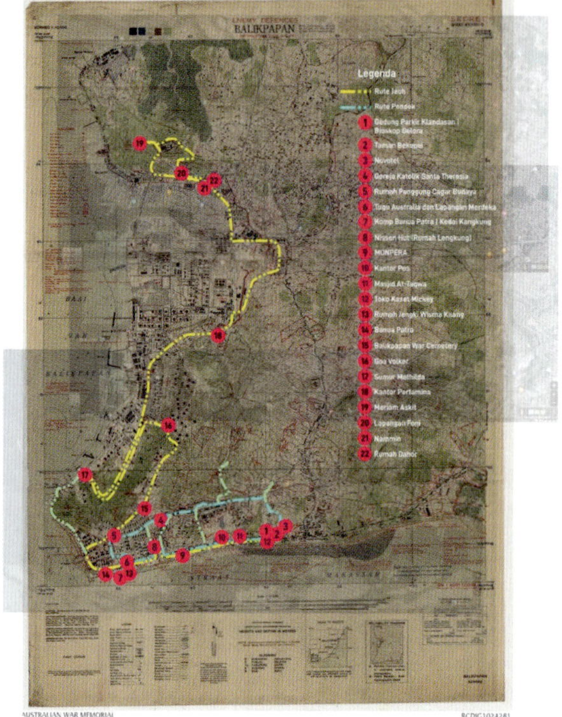

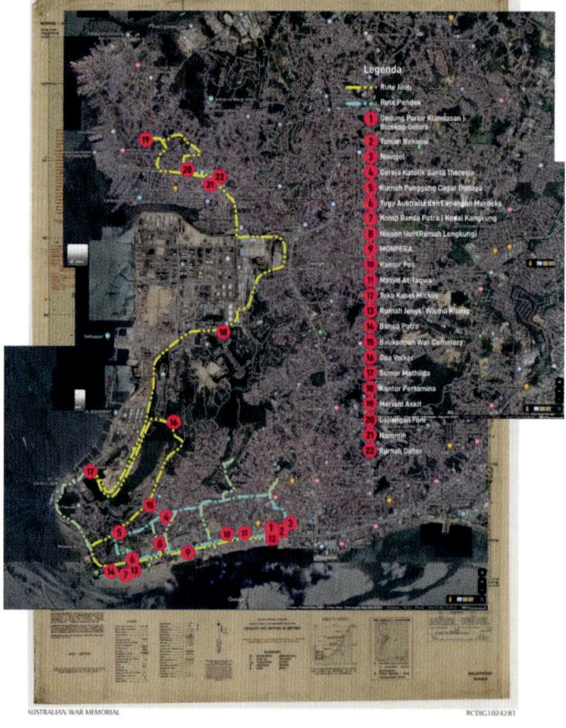

1093

SYNCHRONIZEFESTIVAL.COM
BERSAMA, LET'S GO!
SYNCHRONIZE
FEST
BE25AMA
2025
3. 4. 5 OKTOBER 2025

1094

SYNCHRONIZE FEST
TOGETHER
Bersama

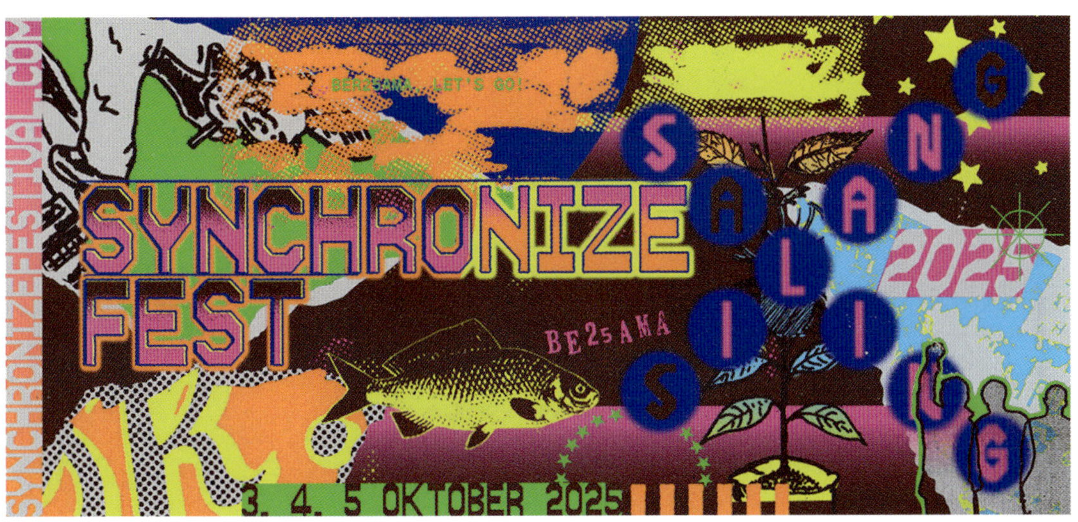

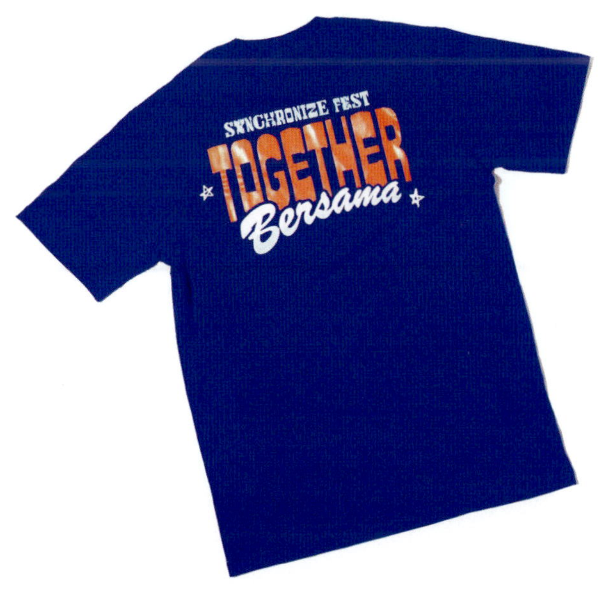

1095

If you don't need to, You don't have to

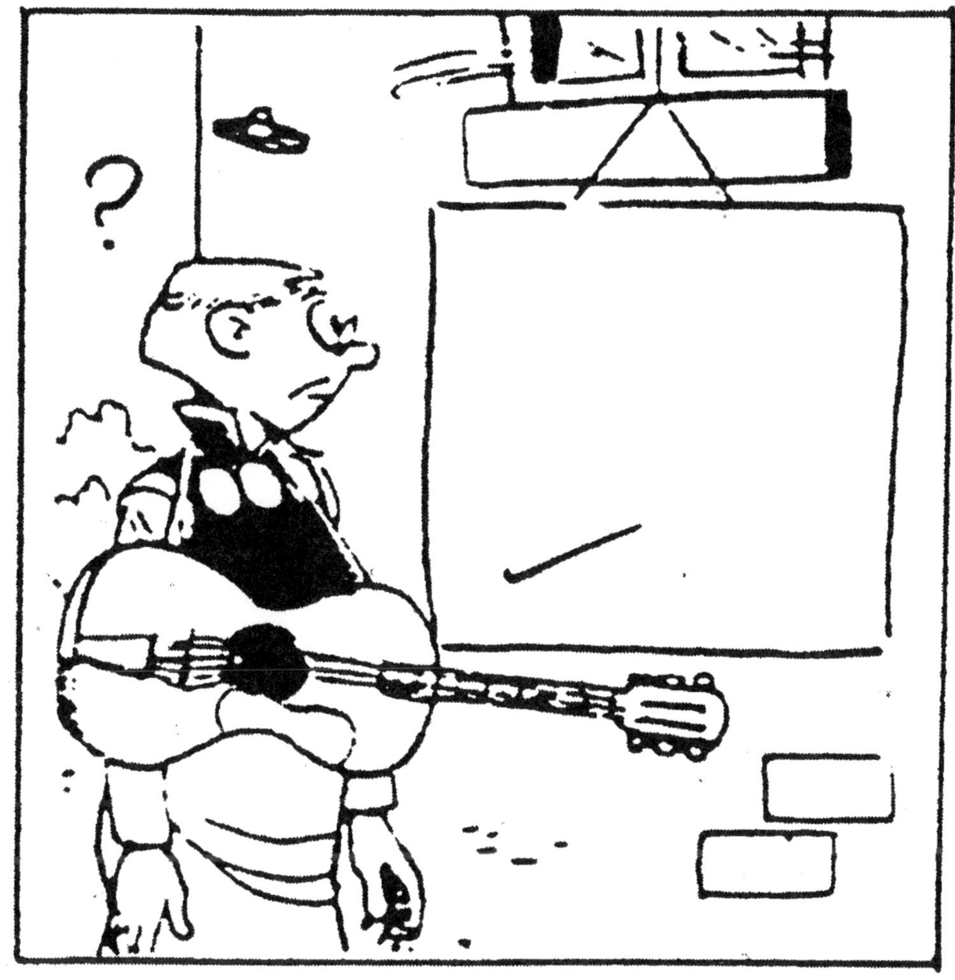

Form is a translation
tool for 1:1
manifestation.

This section features a series of focussed case studies that highlight key aspects of ruangrupa's practice. We explore long-standing projects such as *Karbon* journal and OK.Video alongside one-off exhibition-events such as 'Lekker Eten Zonder Betalen'; and gain insight on the inner workings of ruru as an institution from different generations.

Ardi Yunanto

Translated and edited from Bahasa Indonesia by Ibrahim Soetomo

ruangrupa initiated *Karbon* journal in 2000 to study public space, urban art and visual culture in Indonesia through publishing. When I spoke with Ardi Yunanto, formerly editor in chief at *Karbon*, in July 2024, he detailed its transition from a printed journal (2000–07) to an online platform (2007–15); its ambition to connect art and everyday life; its cross-disciplinary readerships; its operational challenges within ruru; and its editorial shift in responding to urban and socio-political changes in Jakarta in the mid-2010s. Threading through Ardi's history of *Karbon*, transcribed from our conversation and edited for publication here, are anecdotes of his contributions to ruru since 2003 and of how he grew into an established editor by finding his way into supporting authors, commissioning research and writing, and managing *Karbon*'s programme and budget, against all odds. This text exposes the joys and struggles of sustaining a publishing practice in the arts as well as the challenges of meeting individual needs in a collective.

Ardi and I had our first conversation back in 2017, in Jakarta. He had already left ruru, while I found myself wishfully trying to turn ruru's Jakarta 32°C website into a pilot writing platform for university students, despite my limited knowledge of editorial work. I looked to Ardi for guidance. We have rarely met since, but what he shared has stayed with me. In editing his recollections seven years since our very first meeting, I found myself once again attuned to Ardi's deep knowledge.

Ibrahim Soetomo

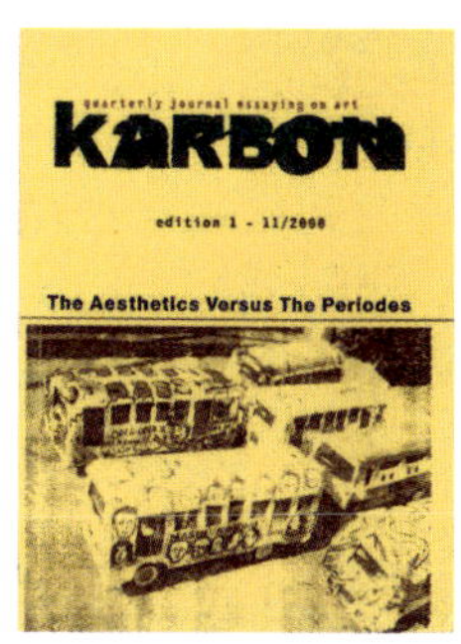

Karbon, issue 1, 2000. Courtesy ruangrupa

Karbon was originally a printed publication. Since around 2000, ruru was doing something new – at least new in Jakarta. They were thinking about public art, video art and performance art. ruru promoted things like screen-printed stickers and other visual culture of the city that they saw as not only commodities but as part of art practice.

ruru was very small back then, so everyone and every project talked about one thing at a time. For example, when ruru worked on art and public space, they organised a discussion and processed the transcript into the first printed journal edition of *Karbon*. Every project had a journal version to cover things that could not be conveyed through the project itself. *Karbon* featured plenty of interviews, because it was easier to hear directly from the practitioners.

At the time, only ruru knew what they were doing. Seeing stickers as art, for example, was considered nonsense. Art institutions like Cemeti Art House in Yogyakarta or Teater Utan Kayu in Jakarta were not focussing on urban art. They focussed on more contemporary or fine art. When ruru came along, they could not expect other people to understand or to help them by writing. They had to write themselves. Those who were actively involved in *Karbon* in the beginning were Ronny Agustinus, Ugeng T. Moetidjo and Hafiz Rancajale.

There was hardly any feedback on *Karbon*. Discourse with practitioners was thrown into place, but it did not generate discussion among critics, maybe because it was new. But I think it did open much conversation about how urban art relates to architecture, to urban space and to all sorts of things. Architects like Marco Kusumawijaya were involved. People outside of art could talk about art of bigger, unexclusive scope, which was something that ruru also hoped for.

In the bigger context, the most distinguishing thing, at least in terms of urban issues, was the discourse on the urban as a political space. Scholarship like Abidin Kusno's writing, about the city as part of political contestation, was novel for everyone, and I happened to read his writings. This was new not just for ruru but for everyone in Indonesia. My eyes were opened when I read Kusno's work. I thought, 'Finally, there is this person who can articulate the city in an academic way, different from what I have encountered so far.' Maybe others had thought the same way but had not been able to express their ideas fluently in words or put them under careful scrutiny.

*

I joined ruru in 2003, casually by *nongkrong-nongkrong*. I already knew of ruru through an interview in *Trolley* magazine, from when I was still living and studying in Malang. Reading that interview, I felt this was the art I was looking for. Maybe it was because I was architecturally trained and did not study fine art. This kind of art talked about things I understood, things outside of art that act as integral parts of it. At the time I was involved in an art association in Malang that comprised several campuses. I used to paint, you know? We organised live drawing in the city square.

A friend of mine brought back several copies of *Karbon* from Jakarta. He mentioned that ruru was planning a small tour of screenings in typical art hubs like Yogyakarta and Bandung, to introduce video art before the inaugural OK.Video festival, in 2003. Malang was not included. When ruru was on tour, I was waiting to graduate and between jobs, so I volunteered by email to organise a venue in Malang. There I met Indra Ameng and Ade Darmawan for the first time.

After OK.Video, I did not know what I wanted to do. I was too lazy to become an architect, but I finished my degree anyway. I went to Jakarta and stopped by ruru. For the first year, I helped ruru with basic research. They were working on the *Apartment Project* (2003), and I used Google to do searches about apartments, houses and so on.

I eventually joined *Karbon* for its fifth edition, published in May 2003, with a focus on 'alternative space'. It included interviews with various art venues, many of which no longer exist. My role included transcription and editing, and I contributed to a subsequent edition about 'audience'. With Farah Wardani, who was already working there, I helped edit the journal's contents. Learning by doing. I was not sure whether my writing or editing was good. I had also only just started reading about art and cities. Farah eventually left to work at *Visual Arts* magazine, if I remember correctly.

*

Working on print media is tiring. We hardly sold anything. If we gave *Karbon* away for free, we also did not get significant responses. *Karbon* was published on a whim. We hoped for it to be a quarterly journal, but it kept getting delayed. I also did not have enough knowledge to discuss art, no matter how

A spread from *Karbon*, issue 6, April 2004, focussing on 'audience'. Courtesy ruangrupa

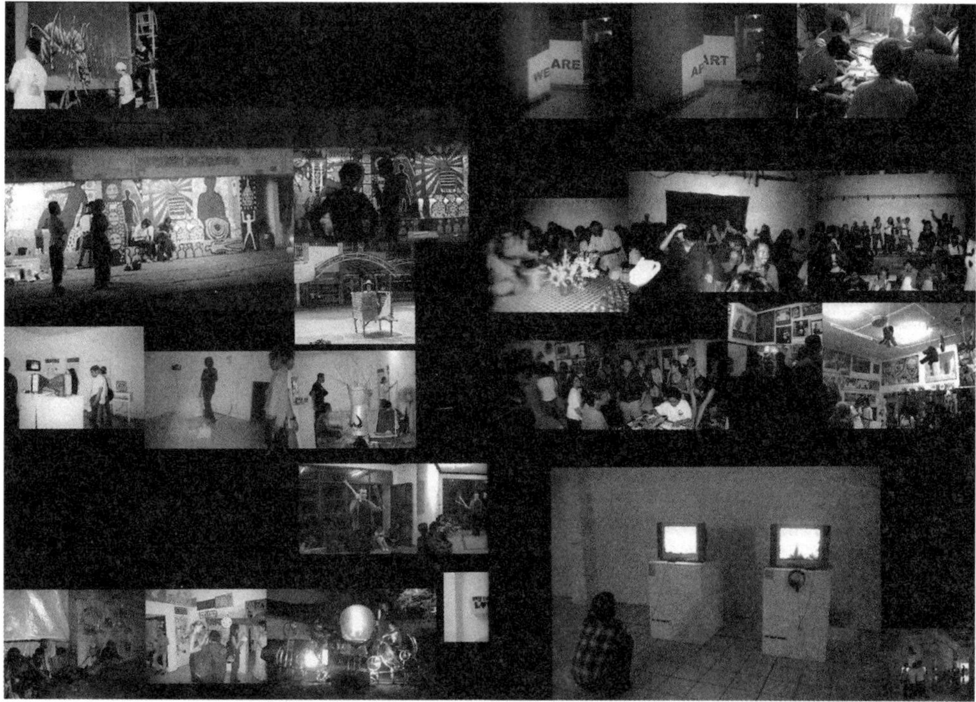

contemporary. It felt like everything we wanted to offer to readers, whether about public, urban, video or performance art, had been done. We needed responses and discourse based on what we were offering. Making physical journals became exhausting when their reception remained unknown.

Karbon eventually went online, in 2007. The approach was different, but the spirit was the same. We still talked about art in a way that was intended to be more accessible and observable from multiple perspectives. We scheduled writing evenly throughout the year for *Karbon* online, and we had to keep updating the website. It acted like a broadsheet. This was the right time, too, because mass media, such as *Kompas*, *Tempo* and *Detik*, was gradually and slowly going online.

Since I had a background in architecture, I liked seeing art as part of city life. I returned to the first and second printed journal editions of *Karbon* on public space and urban art and developed them for *Karbon* online. The theme was basic. If we talked about transportation, we talked about artworks placed at bus stops, and there were even discussions about transportation that had nothing to do with art. Any theme we chose was multifaceted. Like a *gado-gado* (mixed salad).

ENGLISH | BAHASA INDONESIA Login | Register Search Go

KARBON journal.org

jurnal *online* tentang ruang publik, kota, seni visual dan budaya visual di Indonesia

BERANDA FOKUS ARTIKEL SPEKULASI ULASAN KOLOM LAYAR KACA FOTO BIOSKOP KITA ACARA KARBON 2000-2006 TENTANG KAMI JARINGAN

FOKUS 7: DES 2010 - DES 2011

Menyeduh jeda, lincahnya ruang ngopi kita
Rika Febriyani

Taktik dan strategi gerilya untuk arsitektur sekolahan
Kristanti Paramita

Nakal penuh akal demi warga? Dinas Artistik Kota menjawabnya
jurnal Karbon

Ojek menyalip, Go-Jek menyelip
Roy Thaniago

Di kota, semoga tak jemu, Odong-odong kian melaju
Rika Febriyani

Arsitektur komunitas, arsitektur multi-penulis
Anonim

FOKUS 6 | AGUSTUS 2009
FOKUS 5 | FEBRUARI 2009
FOKUS 4 | JANUARI 2008
FOKUS 3 | AGUSTUS 2007
FOKUS 2 | MEI 2007
FOKUS 1 | MARET 2007

FOKUS 7: Des 2010 - Des 2011

Di kota, semoga tak jemu, Odong-odong kian melaju

Rika Febriyani

24 Agustus 2011

"Andong, kereta kuda. Kalau yang ini, jadinya Odong-odong," kata Kohar, seorang perakit Odong-odong di Prumpung Pedati, Jakarta Timur (Gambar 1.a – 1.e). [1] Diusung gerobak beroda dan digerakkan tenaga sepeda, Odong-odong dikenal sebagai wahana permainan keliling. Warga kota sudah tak asing dengan berbagai macam bentuk Odong-odong ini, yang menyediakan tempat duduk bergerak naik-turun seiring irama musik bagi anak-anak, dari yang berbentuk kuda-kudaan ala komidi putar sampai kincir seperti bianglala di Ancol, yang dikayuh 'abang-abang' keluar-masuk kampung.

Ternyata pada sebutan "Odong-odong", ada jejak kata "andong". Andong, kereta kuda masa lampau yang kini "eksotis", agaknya tinggal sebagai bagian dari kenangan warga tentang situasi kota besar saat masih banyak dilalui kereta kuda itu, bebas dari riuh kendaraan bermotor dan padatnya bangunan. Kota juga semakin hari makin kehilangan ruang bermain, sampai setidaknya hadirlah odong-odong. "Dulu, di kampung namanya kuda-kudaan. Masyarakat Jakarta 'aja yang *ngasih* nama Odong-odong," kata Suhendra, juragan Odong-odong di Tegal Parang, Jakarta Selatan (Gambar 2).[2]

Melacak jejak
Empat sekawan di Gang Kabel, Johar Baru, Jakarta Pusat, memulai usaha Odong-odong sejak 2002. Mereka adalah Fahrudin, Nano, Ajit, dan Andi. "Odong-odong dibawa Fahrudin dari Sukabumi," kata Andi (49), saat saya temui dia di kediamannya di Gang Kabel itu (Gambar 3.a & 3.b).[3]

Namun meskipun katanya dibawa dari Sukabumi, ada yang berkata bahwa asal Odong-odong bukan dari sana. "Odong-odong itu asalnya dari Madura. Ide seorang bapak yang ingin menghibur anaknya. Melihat si anak senang dengan mainan buatannya, kenapa nggak dijadikan usaha?" papar Rintis (25), seorang kawan ketika saya tanya tentang asal-usul Odong-odong. Ia sendiri adalah seorang sekretaris yang berkantor di kawasan Menteng, Jakarta Pusat, dan seperti kebanyakan orang yang saya tanyai, Rintis membuktikan bahwa Odong-odong memang populer: wahana permainan itu bisa dibicarakan dengan siapa saja dan di mana saja di Jakarta ini. Jadi meski perempuan asal Situbondo ini tak ingat siapa bapak pencetus ide Odong-odong itu, dan sumber keterangannya, ia bersikeras bahwa Madura adalah tempat asal Odong-odong. "Tapi," lanjutnya, "di Madura, namanya bukan Odong-odong."[4]

"Odong-odong memang asalnya dari kampung, bukan Jakarta," tegas Suhendra, juragan Odong-odong di Tegal Parang yang asli Sukabumi itu. Sebelum ada di Jakarta, Odong-odong sudah ada di Sukabumi. "Orang Sukabumi bawa Odong-odong merantau ke Jakarta buat cari nafkah," lanjutnya. Pernyataan Suhendra mempertegas keterangan Andi tentang asal-usul Odong-odong sampai ke Jakarta. "Odong-odong dibawa untuk dikembangkan di sini," kisahnya. Maksudnya "Odong-odong dikembangkan" adalah selain diperbanyak, juga diperbaiki bentuknya dari versi Sukabumi tersebut. "Pertama dibawa ke sini, nggak ada alasnya. Ngeri, lihat ke bawah kuda-kudaan: langsung rantai sepeda. Nah, di sini, kita beri triplek buat alas di bawah kuda-kudaan, biar lebih cakep." (Gambar 4).

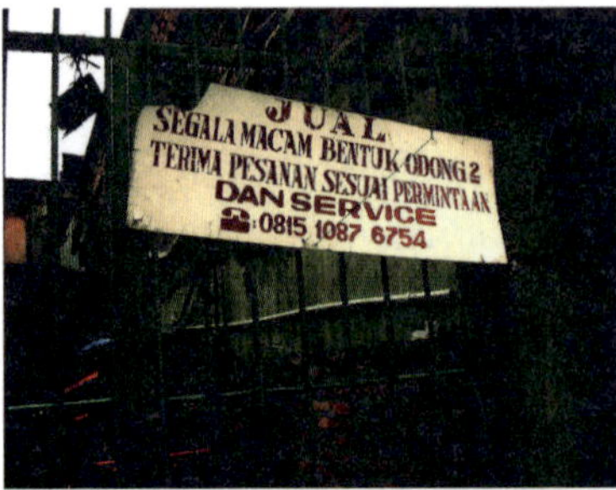

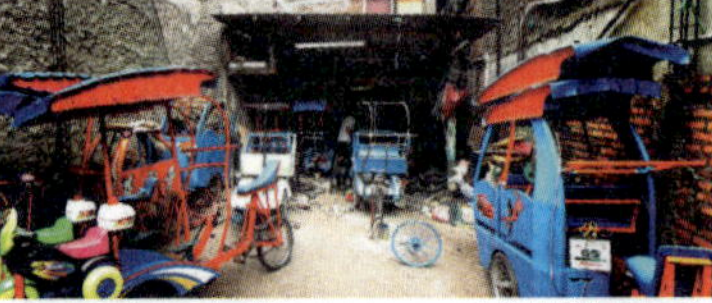

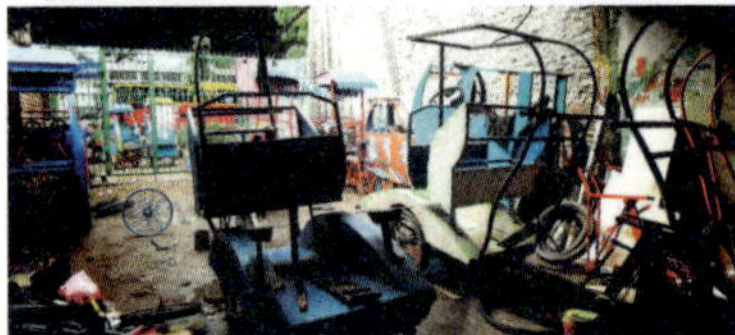

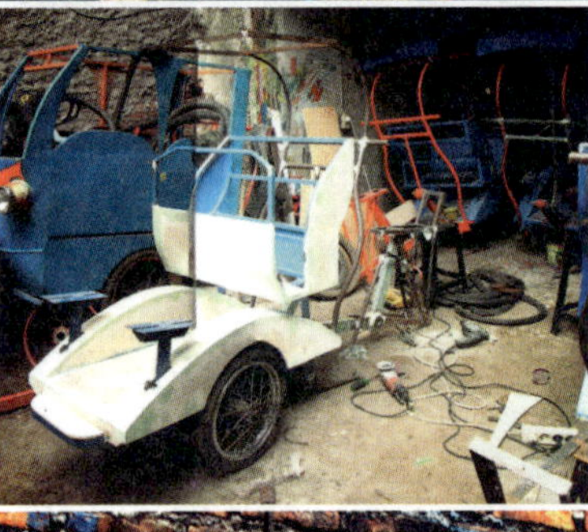

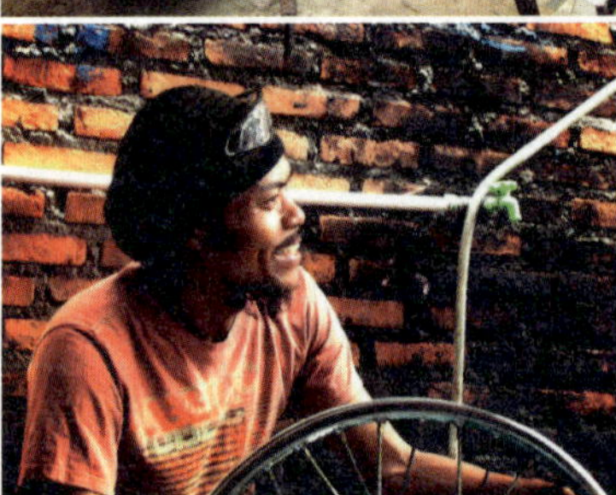

Gambar 1.a-e. Kohar, perakit dan pemilik bengkel Odong-odong Rifky di bengkelnya di Prumpung Pedati, Jakarta Timur, 2011.

We had to show other possible sides of life that intersected with art. I wonder now if I was capable of real intentionality back then, but I think intuitively I wanted to make sure that if we were going to talk about art as part of daily life, we would do more than simply say it was 'related to our lives'. We needed to *demonstrate* that relationship. At that time, the term or discourse about *ekosistem* was yet to come; but if we look at it all now, perhaps we were already talking about a kind of ecosystem – just not of art but more about the city in which visual culture exists.

*

My day-to-day job was to read intensively and extensively about city issues, to look for ideas and for writers, to browse blogs. Because *Karbon* online was a new platform and people were not too familiar with it, I had to actively hunt for writers who would broaden its scope outside the art world.

I searched for writers and I commissioned them to write. Though I would read their previous writing, I did not know if they could write what I was proposing – but I saw their potential and that they would try. My brief was thorough. Sometimes the writer digressed from the brief, as other conversations emerged when we met and talked it over. I can be proud that 80 per cent of the writing in *Karbon* online was new.

Editor and writer divided the work fifty-fifty. I think the people who were invited to write were happy to have someone read and assess their writing, and then offer some direction they had never attempted. If writers have not written about something, it is not because they are unable to see it, but because their attention is not directed there, and because no platform is yet accommodating the writing. Some writers might see this as a challenge, in that is requires writing about topics outside their comfort zone.

I also learnt how to edit from Rani Elsanti, who translated at *Karbon*. Sometimes she would pose questions, returning the translation with a note asking what a certain thing meant – Rani is a good Indonesian editor, too! I also learnt not to make harsh comments and to keep my words respectful. The editing process with the writers I invited went back and forth. It could be six rounds at the most, until finally we thought the text was ready.

I would say that everyone at ruru had no idea how to operate *Karbon* online – including me. So they let me do it by myself. If I made mistakes, that was okay. Now ruru has changed. If there was anything good in that previous era, it was the spirit of experimentation. People were given complete freedom to do whatever they thought was best. Mistakes – no problem. We could argue at the table, but afterwards we would have lunch together. That kind of atmosphere helped. You dared to try.

*

I worked on *Karbon* online often practically by myself. The people I invited were in and out, on and off. Those who joined were farid rakun, Roy Thaniago and Robin Hartanto. In ruru, even though we were full-time workers with a salary below the minimum wage, everyone treated it as a part-time job. Everyone could do other things and use the facilities there. This is where the compensation for not being paid properly lies. I worked on other things alongside *Karbon*, but it was *nongkrong* at ruru almost every day.

Between 2006 and 2016, when ruru's home base was located in Tebet Timur, people outside of ruru – film-makers, activists and comic artists – would come because they wanted to meet other people who had nothing to do with art. They used ruru as a meeting place, sometimes for work meetings, and we were fine with this. Sometimes people came and did not know whom they wanted to meet. ruru was like a hub, and I felt that most strongly between 2007 and 2012. After about two years of running *Karbon* online, I found out that people were reading it. Some of the people who hung out said so, and I was happy – because this was quite useful!

As ruru grew, I told them I could no longer do *Karbon* alone. What I needed was a brainstorming partner. The money for *Karbon* was also not consistent. I once was furious because the money was suddenly cut off, without notice. There were times when the funding had to be used for something else first. I could not prevent the money from being taken away, but it would have been good to know two or three months in advance, especially because I had to commission writers in advance.

All the writers were paid. I insisted on this. The pay was not commensurate with word count, but rather an honorarium. It was decent – IDR750,000 per person – even though we were asking for long articles of 2,000 to 3,000 words. The rate at *Karbon* was on par with *Visual Arts* magazine at the time, which paid around IDR500,000 to 750,000. How many texts were assigned would depend on how much money we had. Form follows budget.

There was a time when I also took care of a ruru writing workshop, when we were collaborating with Dewan Kesenian Jakarta (Jakarta Arts Council). I organised the system and planned for future programmes, but the money was tight. I did not see that others were insistent enough to find money for *Karbon*. In the end, it is much more important to run other programmes first, right? *Karbon* was like an add-on. A nice thing to have. Between 2011 and 2013, along with *Karbon*, I also had to take care of *Bung!* for ruru. It was a short-lived men's lifestyle magazine.

I could not run *Karbon* on my own, with the extent of the problems. I needed a more trained team with a journalistic base that could go in-depth. We could no longer be a platform that relied on contributions and commissions, because the urban issues had gotten so much more complex – too complex to simply sit and write essays.

We needed staff writers, but we could barely afford them. When farid joined, there was Rika Febriyani. She often visited city *kampung* areas and had reporting skills. Although not yet a seasoned journalist, she paid

Meeting at ruangrupa, 2010s. Courtesy ruangrupa

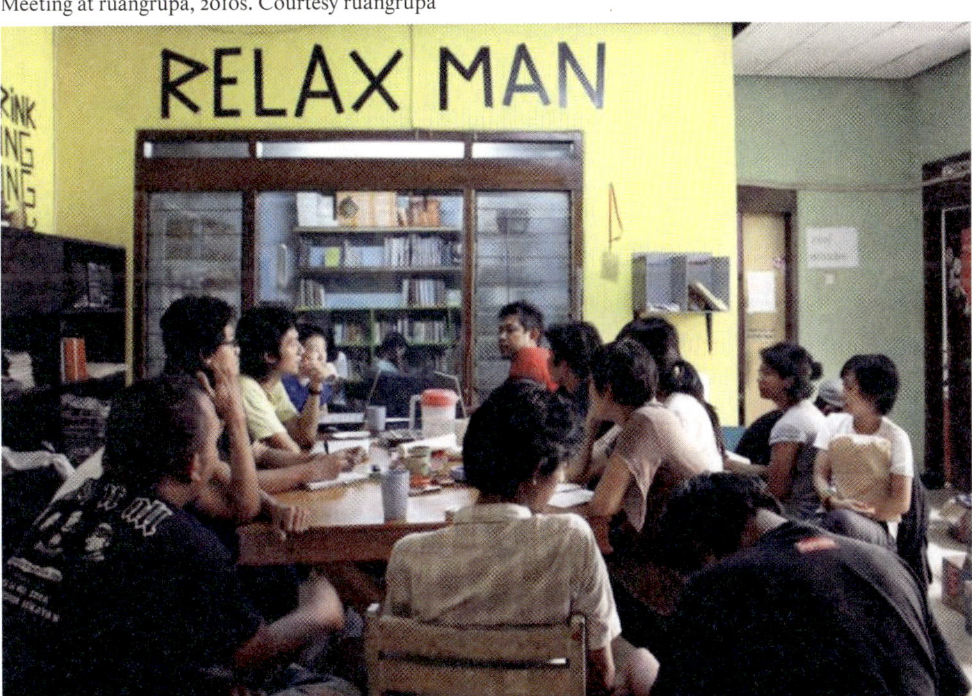

attention to the details. I gave her a special assignment to write in-depth articles about bike-coffee-sellers and *odong-odong* (kiddie rides). Their emergence felt recent, but through research Rika found that they had been around much longer. Both the bike-coffee-sellers and *odong-odong* usually operated in suburbs, and had only just come to *kampung* areas.

I was really proud that we published the first complete articles on those two things. *Karbon* needed more people like Rika, but it was hard, because it involved writing 6,000-word articles. I edited extensively, and did back-and-forth edits, but everyone was happy in the end. When Roy Thaniago was around, we wrote about the ride-hailing company Gojek in their early days, when there were still call centres. This also proved that with staff writers, we could catch new phenomena faster and write about them without relying on others.

I had to look for funding myself. Finally, I applied for funding to do research that eventually became the book *Publik dan Reklame di Ruang Kota Jakarta* (Public and Billboards in Jakarta's Urban Spaces, 2013). I had hoped to save some money to subsidise *Karbon*. There was 300 million IDR a year to cover research to printing. I only saved 10 per cent, which was not enough to run *Karbon*, which needed 100 million IDR per year. The plan to save from a project failed.

In 2013, there was a plan to start Institut ruangrupa. Ade Darmawan offered me the opportunity to take care of it along with farid. Eventually, Berto Tukan and others took care of *Karbon*.

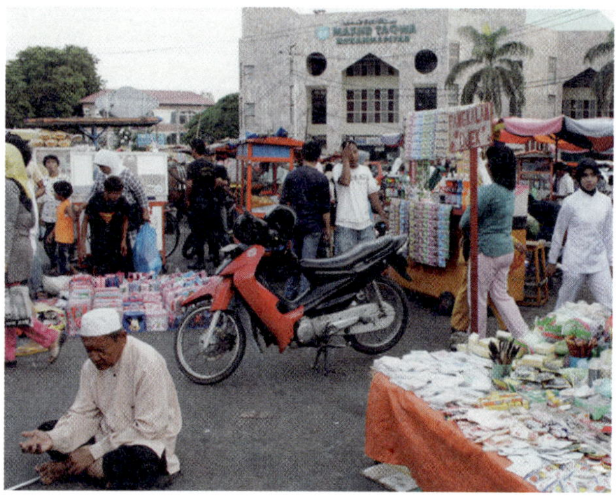

Documentation of Ojek (motor-bike taxi) in a market in Jakarta, published on the 'Photo' page on karbonjournal.org, 3 June 2009. The 'Photo' page was introduced in that year to encourage citizens to actively participate in observing the urban area. Courtesy ruangrupa. Photo: Siska Yuliana

I partially quit in 2014 because I had run out of money. Eventually, I took an office job. Since then, I have not been active in ruru. *Karbon* was left unattended. During the time that Basuki 'Ahok' Tjahaja Purnama was Governor of Jakarta (2014–2017), I think *Karbon* entered a different phase. Jakarta changed a lot. Whereas before we could easily point out issues in the city and blame them on government mismanagement, during Ahok's term this was no longer the case. He made people believe that the government is actually meant to serve the public, and many of his policies were supported by the middle class. However, his harsh approach, inability to accept criticism, sterilised city plans and lack of support for the urban poor eventually led to aggressive evictions targeting the latter. *Karbon* still needed more in-depth, politicised writing and direct interviews with people on the ground – like what Rika did. The essay format we had been using was no longer sufficient.

In the end, everything was interconnected. On the one hand, we could not provide enough funding and resources for *Karbon* to grow and provide fresh perspectives, and I could not keep running it alone in the same way, without responding to the immediate socio-political changes going on. Or maybe *Karbon* needed to adapt – not by forcing itself to be more critical as journalism, but by taking advantage of emerging digital developments. On the other hand, ruru's focus was shifting to developing the Gudang Sarinah Ekosistem as a new space. This required more professional management and, of course, much funding. Institut ruangrupa was also still being developed, and its direction was not entirely clear.

So, by 2015, I felt it was the right time for me to resign. I needed more time to earn extra income to support my parents. I also had the ambition to write fiction, which, within a few years, I achieved: I have published a novella, and I am working on my next book. I believe that all my experiences working at ruru and on *Karbon* shaped me into who I am today, and I hope *Karbon* was useful for those who had the chance to read it in its time.

Arianna Mercado

'Lekker Eten Zonder Betalen' was an event and exhibition that took place between 2–30 March 2003 at Cemeti Art House, Yogyakarta. Invited by Cemeti to inaugurate their new space, the project began with an innocuous dinner celebration, which, for one reason or another, morphed into an intense rave and dance party. The remnants of the evening – stacked dirty plates, scribbled walls, muddy floors – remained untouched for nearly a month and became a breeding ground of mold, maggots and questionable odours.

It was an early ruangrupa project and marked by an overtly irreverent attitude and approach to art-making reflective of the youthful spirit of the collective. It was also one of the first times ruangrupa was commissioned to develop an exhibition as artists. In catalogues, interviews and articles, the collective still uses images of the dancing guests and the party's aftermath as self-portraiture emblematic of their work. Observers have followed suit: in a 2022 *New York Times* profile, 'Lekker Eten' was described as 'a shining example of ruangrupa's sensibility and purpose'.[1] Yet in the 25-year history of the collective, it is something of a blip compared to the long-term initiatives OK.Video, Jakarta 32°C and Gudskul. It is even, in a sense, unremarkable, given that convivial gatherings and parties are a well-known feature of the collective's activities. Thus, in this text I will try to make sense of this 'blip': Why does 'Lekker Eten' have such prominence in ruangrupa's collective memory?

The aftermath of 'Lekker Eten Zonder Betalen'. Courtesy ruangrupa

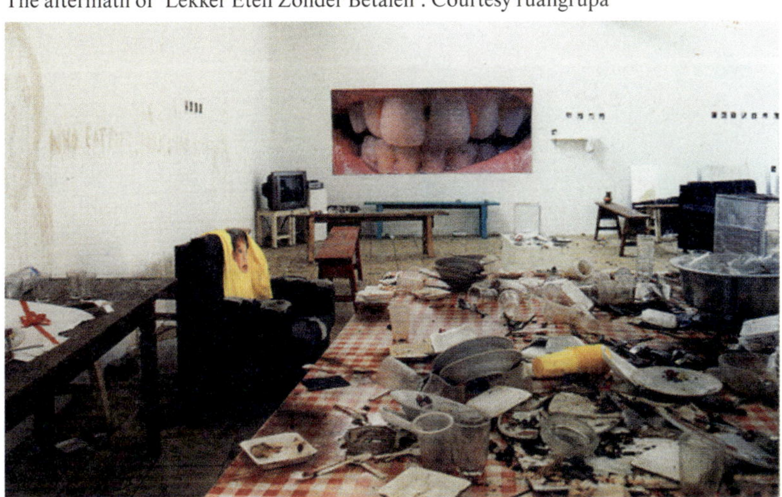

1 Samanth Subramanian, 'A Radical Collective Takes Over One of the World's Biggest Art Show', *The New York Times*, 9 June 2022.

'Lekker eten zonder betalen' is a Dutch phrase adapted by Indonesians as a call to enjoy happiness together through food. It is roughly translatable as 'Tasty meal without paying'. Often said after one has been paid, the phrase is commonly used as joyful encouragement nudging someone to treat everyone to a meal. As an exhibition, 'Lekker Eten Zonder Betalen' reflected experiments into venues of art and circumstance. It asked: What is the role of an artist and how do they manipulate space? How will people behave when artists are able to elicit conditions conducive to celebration? How does the environment of a gallery shift when food and drinks flow freely?

Attempting to trace the history of 'Lekker Eten' feels like trying to find the origins of an urban legend. Many of the photographs in ruangrupa's archive show only the set-up and its results, without formal records of each 'work' or their placement in the space, whether before or after the party. It is similarly uncertain how many artists participated. Were they the sixteen indicated on the poster, the fourteen in ruangrupa's programme or the ten listed on RAIN's official website?[2]

Central to the exhibition was a banquet, which took its staging from large-scale festivities in Indonesia, especially those at five-star hotels,[3] whether weddings, extravagant birthdays or state events. 'Lekker Eten' leaned in on kitsch decor: it was adorned with a buffet, ice sculptures of chickens and horses, and *bunga papan* (flower signage) that read 'Selamat Menikmati Mbak & Mas / P.S. SALAMANISDARISAYA' (Have a good time ladies and gentlemen / P.S. Sweet greetings from me).

Henry 'Batman' Foundation in front of *bunga papan*. Courtesy ruangrupa

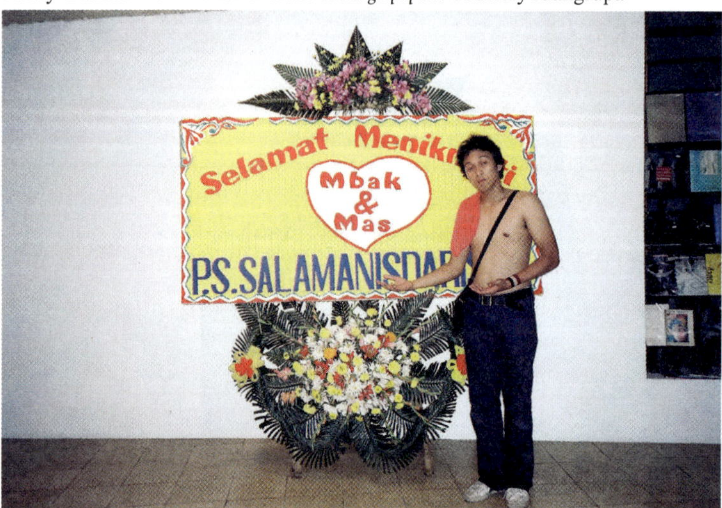

2 Rain Artists' Initiative Network (RAIN), 'Ruangrupa', http://www.r-a-i-n.net/projects/ruangrupa.

3 Yos Supranto, 'Nostalgia Boyong dan Makan Tanpa Bayar', *KOMPAS*, 14 March 2003.

Polaroid by Indra Ameng. Courtesy the artist

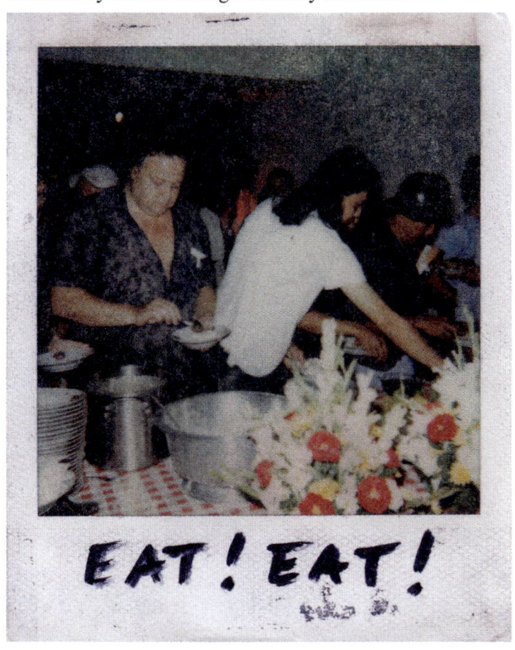

ruangrupa has approached food as pivotal to art exhibitions, hospitality and celebration. To throw a party, one *must* have food. Apart from the exhibition title's focus around eating, the research ruangrupa conducted in the lead-up to 'Lekker Eten' detailed that 60 per cent of the Yogyakarta art community went to openings for free food while only 10 per cent were there to exclusively appreciate art.[4] Surveys were given to the audience during the opening that asked guests about their relationship to food. The buffet itself, which was provided by a catering service that otherwise supplied weddings and such, followed the usual dinner conventions: entrée, main course, dessert. The menu was a mix of Indonesian-Chinese dishes, and it most likely followed the standard set for buffet spreads in Indonesia.[5]

In an email invitation for 'Lekker Eten', ruangrupa wrote: 'All happenings and recordings will be left behind/left in place as objects that have used or given energy throughout the exhibition.'[6] New Wave post-punk Jakarta-based band The Upstairs performed to kick off the opening. Video documentation,

4 '30% of attendees are loyalists to the artists.' The sample size is unknown. *Ibid.*

5 Indra Ameng, correspondence with the author, 7 May 2024. The menu was: *sup kimlo* (kimlo soup); *ayam goreng mentega* (fried butter chicken); *ikan kakap asam manis* (sweet and sour snapper fish); *mie goreng* (fried noodles); *capcay* (mixed vegetables); pudding; and fruit (watermelon, melon, papaya).

6 Susan Ingham, 'Cemeti – the alternative', *Indonesian Contemporary Art: Reformasi,* 18 November 2019.

later installed in the space, depicts the partygoers' range of emotions. The first video records them quietly serving themselves refreshments from the drinks table. Another features shaky footage of The Upstairs playing in front of a seated audience. Allegedly, once their song 'Anarki' (Anarchy) started playing, things went haywire. Countless guests shuffled into the space, smearing the walls with food and tearing down the entrance signage. The final video is of a shirtless man singing and dancing in the dark, packed room. Shouting into the camera, he is singing Alphaville's 1984 synth-pop hit 'Forever Young'. The camera pans to show the whole crowd singing together – some shirtless, others smoking, almost all with arms outstretched.

Written and confirmed first-hand historicisation of the spirit and energy of 'Lekker Eten' can be heard and read in 'Disko Darurat' (Emergency Disco) by The Upstairs, a song inspired by the events of the exhibition.[7] 'Disko Darurat' speaks to the seemingly unplanned, underprepared, explosive nature of the exhibition while also referencing events left up to the imagination:

Double discman, double A batteries	*Double discman, baterai dua A*
Brand new active speakers	*Speaker aktif jaman sekarang*
Second-hand green mixer	*Mixer hijau second hand*
Lighting arrangements for Independence Day	*Tata lampu tujuh belasan*
Dancing	*Berdansa*
Diligently downloading, CD-R	*Tekun download,* CD-R
3 by 4 narrow room	*Ruang sempit tiga kali empat*
Classroom hallway at night	*Lorong kelas di kala malam*
To the exhibition opening	*Hingga pembukaan pameran*
No house music hey na-na na	*Tanpa house music hey na-na na*
(sya-lala-sya-la-la)	*(sya-lala-sya-la-la)*
No breakbeat fa fa-fa-fa	*Bukan breakbeat fa fa-fa-fa*
(sya-lala-sya-la-la)	*(sya-lala-sya-la-la)*
Only eccentric beats	*Hanya sekedar hentakan eksentrik*
For the old souls, dancing[8]	*Dan para orang-orang yang antik, berdansa*

ruangrupa apparently never intended to create such a mess in the gallery, and had initially toyed with the idea of bringing paintings in as a way to subvert expectations of the collective and their projects.[9] They instead decided that each artist was responsible for contributing something to the celebration – ashtrays, a sink, couches, oxygen canisters, DJ sets. At the exhibition's opening, nothing hung on the walls, which left partygoers to

7 Angga Cipta, conversation with Wing Chan and Arianna Mercado, 2 July 2024.
8 Special thanks to Ibrahim Soetomo for assistance in translation.
9 S. Subramanian, 'A Radical Collective', *op. cit.*

Party time, horse ice sculpture on the right. Courtesy ruangrupa

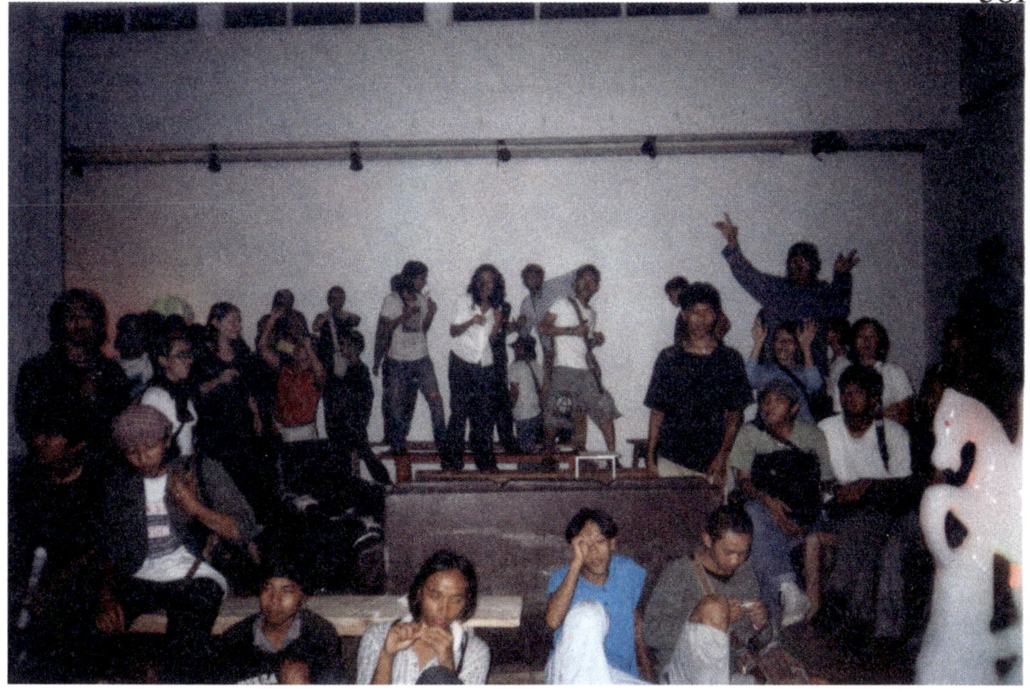

Polaroids taken by Indra Ameng
Left: The Upstairs; Right: Asung (Reza Afisina) as DJ with double discman

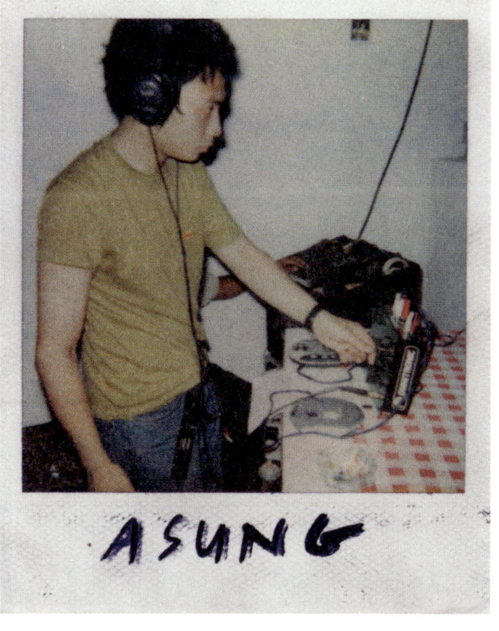

Polaroids by Indra Ameng of attendees and artists. Courtesy the artist

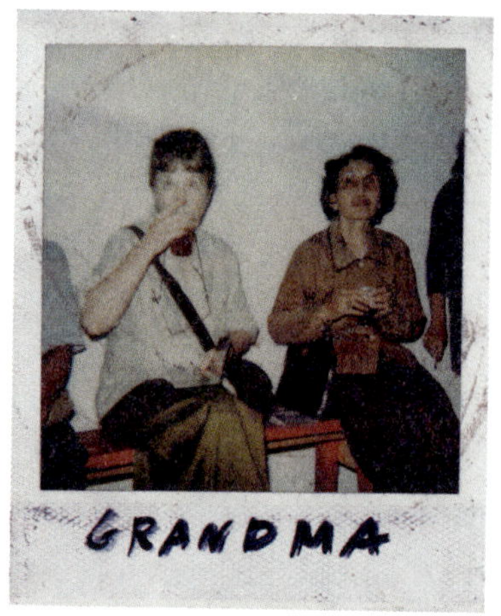

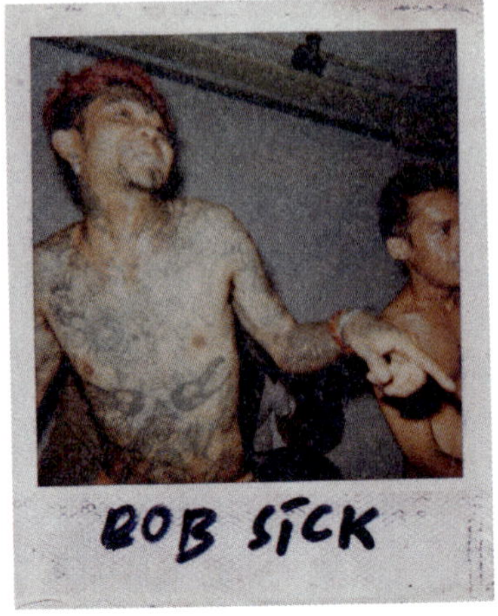

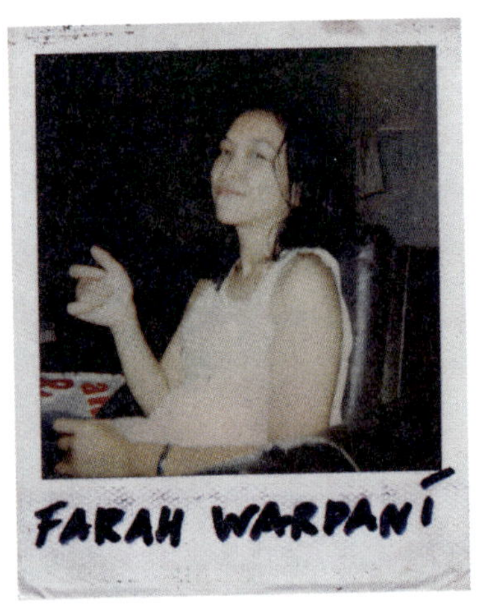

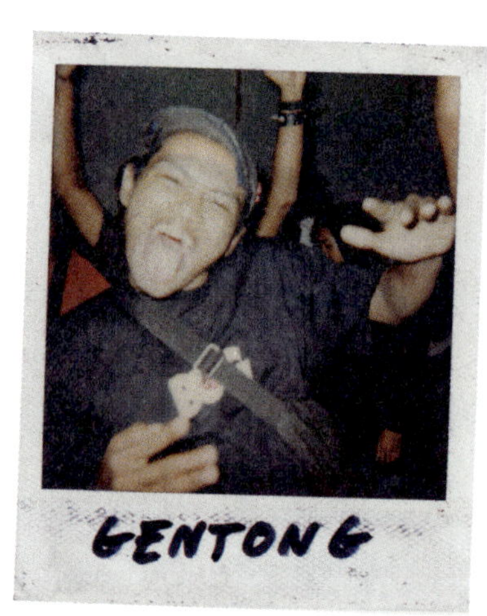

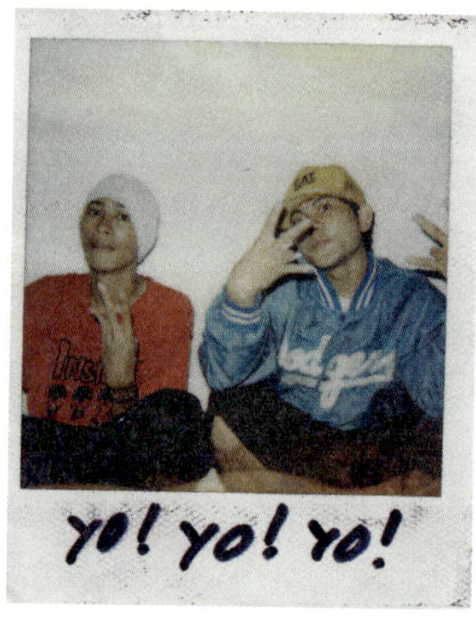

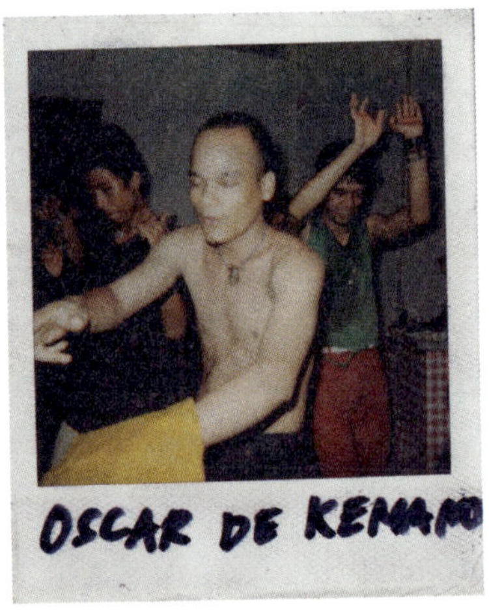

wonder where the art was.[10] As the night unfolded, Cemeti co-founders Nindityo Adipurnomo and Mella Jaarsma exchanged a distressed email: 'Now I am confused what to do because Ruang Rupa wants to leave the mess rotting in the space for the whole month, lots of rats and maggots will appear, and it will be smelly! Don't be mad at me!'[11] A widely circulated image of 'Lekker Eten' signals an odd semblance of 'art' on the gallery's walls: a close-up enlargement of a smiling mouth with particles lodged between teeth. However, this work was brought by Irwan Ahmett and hung only after the party finished.[12]

Nearly two hundred people are said to have attended the opening, yet 'Lekker Eten' was, unsurprisingly, met with mixed feelings from the public. While reviews seemed to approach the exhibition generously, some guests lamented the state of contemporary art and the idea of detritus as art.[13] Each rotting dish, maggot and cigarette butt served as a pungent record of the energy mediated by ruangrupa and their friends. Yogyakarta, dubbed as the art capital of Indonesia and home to a prestigious art school, had more traditional and intellectual dispositions on life and art-making; and perhaps due its history as a centre for revolutionary thought, it was known for a more laid-back atmosphere, plus cheaper studio spaces.[14] ruangrupa confidently played into the stereotypes of Jakarta: fast, aggressive, shallow, amoral, self-righteous, individualistic and sado-masochistic.[15] 'Lekker Eten' seemed to cement ruangrupa as 'bad artists' – the messy, mischievous and unserious collective arriving from the chaotic capital to deface the respected and culturally significant white cube of Cemeti Art House.

10 I. Ameng, conversation with W. Chan and A. Mercado, 16 May 2024.

11 Cemeti Art House, *Exploring Vacuum: 15 Years of Cemeti Art House*, Yogyakarta: Cemeti Art House, 2004, p.6.

12 Indra Ameng recalls that Ahmett's work missed the opening. It was transported via Jimi Multhazam (frontman of The Upstairs) on a public bus. Multhazam accidentally left Ahmett's piece at a restaurant in a rest stop en route to Yogyakarta. I. Ameng, conversation with W. Chan and A. Mercado, 16 May 2024.

13 Y. Supranto, 'Nostalgia Boyong dan Makan Tanpa Bayar', *op. cit.*; S. Subramanian, 'A Radical Collective', *op. cit.*

14 Yogyakarta's history as a centre for revolutionary thought and as the location of ISI Yogyakarta has attracted generations of artists. The city is said to produce and encourage 'serious artists' thanks to the privilege of a slow pace of life, large studio spaces and a vibrant art community. Nuraini Juliastuti, conversation with W. Chan and A. Mercado, 12 April 2024.

15 ruangrupa, 'Lekker Eten Zonder Betalen' planning document, 2003, archive of ruangrupa.

I was initially drawn to 'Lekker Eten' for how its story has surprisingly wormed its way through articles, interviews and conversations with and around ruangrupa. Despite the exhibition being a mere one-off project without any plans of longevity, it continues to be lovingly referenced even by people who were not present at the party. I found myself wondering: Why does ruangrupa still circulate these images? What do the images signify and represent? What can 'Lekker Eten' tell us about ruangrupa's practice today?

ruangrupa's early work was concerned with reacting to the bureaucratisation and commercialisation of the art institution and art itself, posing questions on the sacredness of the gallery as a site for art.[16] I consider 'Lekker Eten' to be one of ruangrupa's most important works – certainly in the eyes of the collective themselves, given the way the trashed banquet's documentation has circulated and been rehashed through the years. The frequent retellings of 'Lekker Eten' speak of ruangrupa in its utopic essence: ludic, spontaneous, approachable and relatable as artists with infectious energies and without overt concern for perfection or neatness.

Though this was not fully articulated in the early 2000s, I see 'Lekker Eten' as a preliminary example of ruangrupa's long-term stance on exhibition-making as merely an 'alibi to learn something together, to experience something together, and to build certain type[s] of ecosystems'.[17] Through 'Lekker Eten', they brought together a wide range of audiences in celebratory co-existence, and, however explosively, were responding to the confines of

After the party: exhibiting remnants of the buffet. Courtesy Indonesian Visual Art Archive

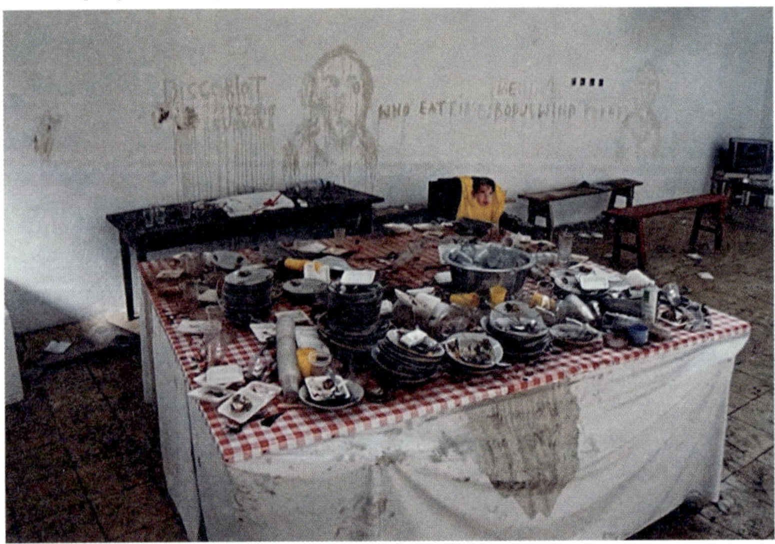

16 Ade Darmawan, conversation with W. Chan and A. Mercado, 28 May 2024.

17 Franz Thalmair, 'ruangrupa: "Our exhibitions are an alibi"', *documenta fifteen: Platform6*.

a gallery as an institution. Perhaps in recirculating these stories and images, ruangrupa seeks to transmit visual manifestos of their past and future work, speaking to an imagination of their magnum opus, their practice par excellence: as mediators of energies, movement and openness that has touched different kinds of otherwise conflicting bodies in space.

I am reminded of Michel Foucault's 'Des Espace Autres' ('Of Other Spaces', 1967), where he conceives of the *heterotopia* to describe disruptive, transformative and contradictory spaces that can be likened to physical approximations of utopias which allow us to contest and subvert the social fabric and norms.[18] Heterotopias suspend time and space, allowing for the co-existence of normally conflicting bodies and spaces.[19] As a party, 'Lekker Eten' opened up reflections on Indonesian society and its decay.[20] Specifically thinking through celebratory experiences as heterotopias, Marie Fraser writes:

> If it marks a passage from order to chaos, this is because it ... renegotiates space to give shape to new realities. ... Festive spaces such as parades, processions or demonstrations not only invite people's involvement, but also urge them to change behaviour, to adopt a festive attitude, a frame of mind shared by all participants. That is to say, we are affected, changed, displaced. Celebration creates a new cohesion within a reality.[21]

I see 'Lekker Eten' within this same frame. Over the course of the evening, ruangrupa was able to create a transformative space bridging friends and strangers, a space of celebration within a gallery that also challenged the gallery as cultural infrastructure. In Ade Tanesia's review of 'Lekker Eten', she briefly mentions the differences between Jakartans and Yogyakartans. Tanesia posits that ruangrupa, coming from the cold and alienating capital, was seeking to create situations to prompt social experiences:

> Still, it was interesting to observe how the exhibition developed, observing how the visitors showed their true colors. In Yogyakarta, where people prefer to be modest and the very opposite of arrogant, some took their chance to show their true colors when the opportunity knocked.[22]

18 Michel Foucault, 'Of Other Spaces: Utopias and Heterotopias' (trans. Jay Miskowiec), *Architecture / Mouvement / Continuité*, October 1984.
19 Anthony Vidler, 'Troubles in Theory VI: from Utopia to Heterotopia', *The Architectural Review*, 3 October 2014.
20 Y. Supranto, 'Nostalgia Boyong dan Makan Tanpa Bayar', *op. cit.*
21 Marie Fraser, 'Let the Festivities Begin: Processions, Parades, and Other Forms of Collective Celebration in Contemporary Art', *esse*, issue 67, 2009.
22 Ade Tanesia, 'Ruang Rupa Exhibition Invites Unique Participation', *The Jakarta Post*, 22 March 2003.

During the party: attendees and artists enjoying the buffet. Courtesy ruangrupa

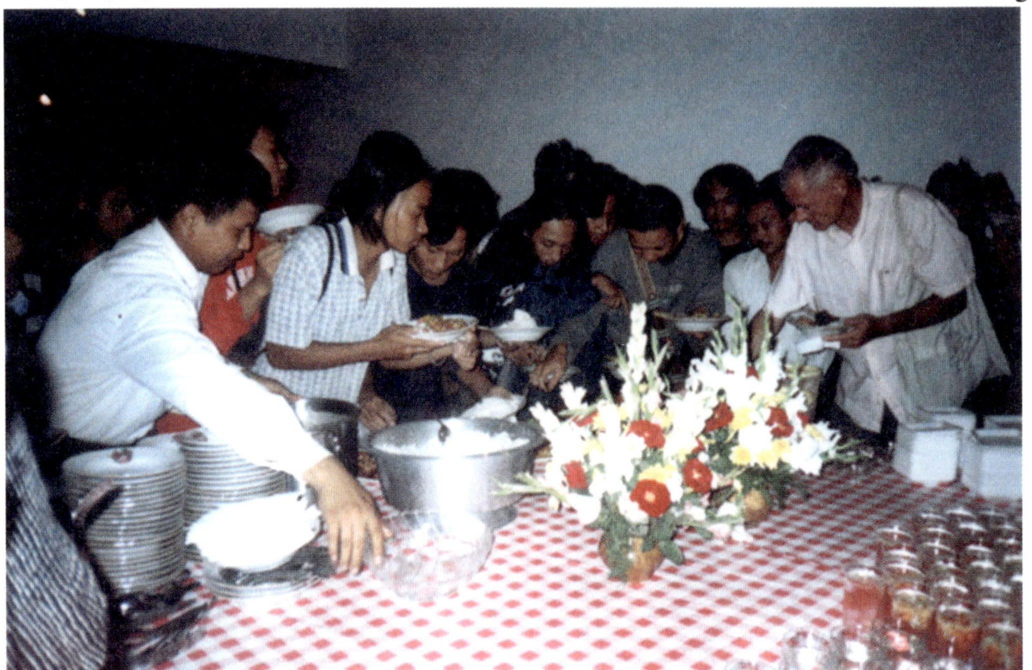

Tanesia reveals a distinct quality to ruangrupa's work as artists: their ability to enable others to reveal their 'true colors'. Extending the concept of heterotopia, the events of 'Lekker Eten' can certainly be read collectively as a happening that mediated an unruly space while also mirroring a utopian vision of human connection. In this utopia, five-star sustenance is free, cultural differences are set aside and 'true colors' can be freely revealed.

'Lekker Eten' demonstrated an organic passage, from order to chaos, within the confines of a gallery. Eating free food and enjoying music was a vehicle for these energies to pass and transform. The later-displayed remnants of the evening, including video documentation, gave viewers a window into what a physical approximation of momentary utopia might have felt like. Images of 'Lekker Eten' might superficially feel like nostalgic remnants of ruangrupa as the 'bad artists', who come out only to make a mess, but the reality feels so distant from this projection. In the two decades since 'Lekker Eten', ruangrupa has organised and orchestrated large-scale international exhibitions, held partnerships with the Indonesian government and sustained long-term arts infrastructure that supports young practitioners. ruangrupa take their work seriously, with genuine and lasting efforts to share and create resources for others.

Heterotopias have been understood as passageways of experimentation, as 'spaces and times of emergent process'.[23] Viewing 'Lekker Eten' as a visual manifesto and projection for how ruangrupa would like to mediate energies and build relationships, I can see how they hope to translate these processes into their current work outside of Jakarta and the island of Java. It's funny seeing images of 'Lekker Eten' within the breadth and scale of work that ruangrupa does now. Their overtly irreverent attitude in the early 2000s has since evolved into ambitious efforts towards arts infrastructure-building on local and national levels in Indonesia. Memories of 'Lekker Eten' still snake their way through. In continuing to represent themselves through images of 'Lekker Eten', ruangrupa crafts a depiction of their practice and practice-to-be as grounded and accessible, where audiences and practitioners across varied ranges of interests, educational backgrounds and social statuses might engage and participate.

23 Claire Champenois, Sarah Drakopoulou Dodd, Daniel Hjorth and Sarah Jack, 'The Other Organization: Heterotopia, Management, and Entrepreneurship', *Journal of Management Inquiry,* vol.34, no.1, pp.41–56.

Between Art and Media Technologies in Indonesia: Genealogy of OK.Video

Umi Lestari and Mahardika Yudha

In July 2003, five years after the overthrow of the Suharto dictatorship, the imperial architecture of the Galeri Nasional Indonesia (National Gallery of Indonesia, GNI) shook with the energy of a new generation. Leading up to this moment, GNI had felt haunted for young artists. The building is located in a strategic area marking the emergence of the anti-communist movement in 1965 and the birth of Suharto's New Order regime, and GNI has played a significant role in the development of modern and contemporary art in Indonesia all the while. It hosted national and international exhibitions for established artists, as well as showcasing its collection of works dating back to colonial times.[1]

The normal functioning of GNI turned upside down on 7 July 2003. The atmosphere became fluid, friendly, warm and egalitarian – crowded with voices. The youngsters were using the building to showcase contemporary art of their generation, especially video art. The Buggles' hit song 'Video Killed the Radio Star' snuck in. By evening time, the GNI evolved into a gig arena, full of young people. It didn't matter that the building stood near the Army Military Police Centre Commander, the Army Strategic Reserve Command, the United States Embassy, the Vatican Embassy and the Istana Merdeka (State Palace). Like a magnet, the museum attracted hundreds of young people to the frenzied party that marked the inauguration of OK.Video, the international video and media arts biennial. Since 2003, OK.Video has not only introduced video and media arts to new contexts and audiences in Indonesia, but has become a lab to support the development of these arts for new generations internationally.

The first part of this co-authored essay will trace the chronological development of OK.Video from 2003 to 2017, examining its position in the Indonesian arts scene, its relevance to society in post-Reformasi times and the experiments it encouraged between art and technology. The second part will reveal co-author Mahardika Yudha's personal, behind-the-scenes journey as a participant in OK.Video between 2007 and 2017. We conclude with a consideration of what can be learned from this history; the importance of decentralisation, archiving and autonomy; and how OK.Video's legacy may continue to help build resources into the future.

1 ruangrupa has a tradition of using site-specific methods. These involve intervening in buildings with specific historical associations. One of their early art projects that utilised this was 'Jakarta Habitus Publik' in 2001. When the National Gallery of Indonesia was selected as the venue for the first OK.Video festival, it was understood that the gallery had a history dating back to the colonial period and the New Order. GNI is located in one of the 'ring one' areas, important to the power struggle that took place from the 30 September to 1 October 1965 and led to the authoritarian government. At the turn of this century, ruangrupa saw an opportunity to bring new value to this building, the largest 'white cube' in Jakarta.

Developments in Media Technology in the 1990s

Around the turn of the 1990s, global perspectives were being transformed by geo-political events such as the Tiananmen Square massacre, the fall of the Berlin Wall, the Gulf War and the dissolution of the Soviet Union. Indonesians witnessed these changes on the newly developed satellite and commercial television stations RCTI (1989), SCTV (1990) and TPI (1991) – channels that broke the New Order government's monopoly on broadcasting via the national public television organisation TVRI. With the dawn of the commercial television era, viewers were accessing diverse programming, including news, films and advertisements from abroad, that reflected a shift from the old ruling system to new corporations and oligarchies. Being able to choose what to watch using their newly discovered remote controls imparted a sense of 'utopia' to viewers, and this intensified as the decade progressed with the rise of digital media technologies such as laser discs and the affordability of accessing VCDs and MP3s. Installations featuring VCDs, montaged advertising sequences and pirated films appeared in train stations, markets and malls; years before the advent of LED videotrons and video walls, this shared experience of public viewing was a familiar part of Indonesian culture.

Pirated computer hardware and software formed enlivening societal traditions. Versions of the video editing software Adobe Premiere, for instance, and the availability of cheap and affordable IEEE 1394 (or FireWire) cables enabled non-specialists to transfer and edit video on their personal computers. The popularisation of wedding video production services, for example, was amongst the first signs of creative video practices in Indonesia. Those services mushroomed following the emergence of early digital technology such as MiniDV and DV in the 90s; whereas in the 80s, the practice was dominated by only a handful of people when the production technology was limited to cassette tapes such as VHS and Betacam. As for video games: if, in the 80s, there were very few home console choices, in the 90s, many and varied options came from Atari, Spica, Sega, Nintendo and Sony, enriching social interactions and facilitating growing vernacular cultures.

This period culminated with the arrival of Web 1.0, which resulted in a proliferation of internet cafes towards the end of the decade. The advent of first-generation websites opened up new avenues of interactive engagement between society and media technology. Web 1.0 also served as an alternative communication and information-distribution channel, particularly for Reformasi activists. They utilised the web to build awareness and solidarity across geographies, ultimately forming a united front against the authoritarian government. As old and new media technologies gave birth to fresh habits and experiences, the Reformasi generation came together in the spectre of the MTV generation – so to speak.

Connecting Art and Technology (2003–05)

The national art discourse in Indonesia has long been dominated by traditional media, even as the relationship between art and technology has sparked considerable debate. For example, at Expo '70 in Osaka, Japan – presented as an occasion for national and corporate pavilions to compete through sophisticated works of art and technology – the Indonesian pavilion showcased painting.[2] A few years later, however, in the mid-1970s, artists Hardi and Gendut Riyanto of the Gerakan Seni Rupa Baru (Indonesian New Art Movement) were seeding the development of media arts in their home country through works utilising television and radio technology. As highlighted by the art historian Sanento Yuliman, the 1986 Computer and Graphic Arts Festival at Taman Ismail Marzuki (TIM) in Jakarta featured artist Djoni Djauhari's 'computer art' – yet, this concept did not evolve into a broader discussion.[3]

In the late 90s, Jim Supangkat and Asmudjo Jono Irianto, both artists, critics and curators, identified, in considering works of video art within a discussion of installation art practice, how limited any larger discussion in this area was at the time.[4] The knowledge gap had notable impact on the early positioning of Indonesian video art pioneer Krisna Murti. When Murti created the project *12 Jam Dalam Kehidupan Penari Agung Rai* (*12 Hours in the Life of Dancer Agung Rai*, 1993), featuring hundreds of photographs alongside three video installations, artist peers and critics considered it 'installation art'.[5] Murti gradually adopted a more positive stance, labelling his work *Belajar Antri Kepada Semut* (*Learning Queue from the Ants*, 1999) a 'performance video installation', and another, *Nenek Moyangku Orang Sangiran* (*My Ancestors are Sangiran Men*, 1999), 'video art'. It should be noted that the

2 Amongst the projects presented at Expo '70 were *Space Projection Ako*, an expanded cinema work by Toshio Matsumoto, and *Pepsi Pavilion*, a conceptual media work by E.A.T. (Experiments in Art and Technology).

3 Sanento Yuliman, 'Seni Komputer. Hidup Komputer!', *Tempo*, 25 October 1986.

4 Jim Supangkat and Asmudjo Jono, Irianto, *Media Dalam Media: Pameran Seni Rupa Instalasi*, Jakarta: Galeri Nasional Indonesia, 1999.

5 Krisna Murti used an 8mm camcorder, tape recorder and camera-made photographs.

impetus to discuss video art in Indonesia emerged during a period of regime change that was influenced by changes in technology's consumption. Advancements in digital technology not only accelerated the distribution of entertainment and information but enriched the cinematic landscape by encouraging the art community to embrace the term 'video' in their work.

OK.Video thus emerged at a pivotal moment in the evolution of digital media. The era witnessed remarkable growth in the festival scene in particular, from the Bandung Video, Film and New Media Art Forum (banf-NAF#1, 2002) to other events that celebrated moving images, such as the Jakarta International Film Festival (1999), the Indonesian Independent Film-Video Festival (1999) and Festival Film Dokumenter (Documentary Film Festival, 2002). OK.Video, initiated by ruangrupa, embraced this dynamic landscape by boldly positioning itself within the realm of video art, underlining its commitment in adopting the name Jakarta Video Art Festival. Interviewed in 2002, Ade Darmawan expanded on ruangrupa's developing plans by stating that 'there will be no MTV-style images; It is not narrative and is not a work that features easy computer graphics. Although anyone can participate, participants must be able to distinguish the work area of art videos from "ordinary" videos.'[6] In the same year, Ugeng T. Moetidjo, who was then involved in ruangrupa, penned an assessment of video as both art and ideological resistance that was published in the collective's journal, *Karbon*.[7]

At GNI in 2003, the first edition of OK.Video gathered a range of video works via ruangrupa's already characteristic (informal and fun-loving) style of presentation. It faced immediate criticism within Indonesia – reflective

Installation view, OK.Video – Jakarta Video Art Festival, Galeri Nasional Indonesia, Jakarta, 7–20 July 2003. Courtesy ruangrupa

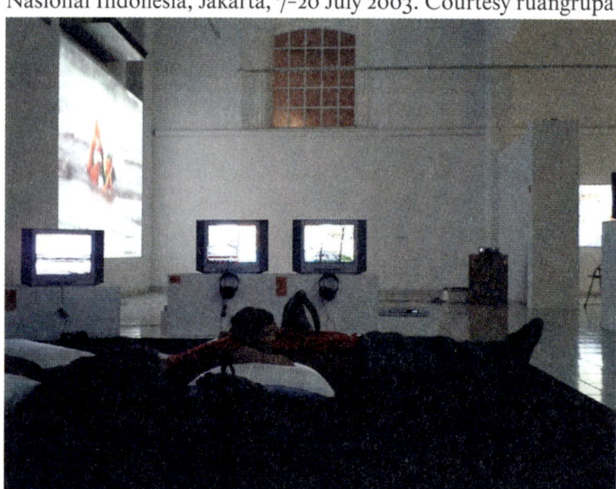

6 Seno Joko Suyono and Bobby Gunawan, 'Dari Lantai Diskotek Dan Besi-Besi Tua', *Tempo*, August 2002.

7 Ugeng T. Moetidjo, 'Praktek Penyaksian: Representasi Dalam Beban Sang Pelihat', *Karbon*, February 2002.

of the aforementioned dominance of traditional media in art discourse. Ronny Agustinus, one of ruangrupa's founders, criticised such rejection by emphasising that the art community should not be surprised by the links being made between art and technology. He highlighted the significant quantity of the artworks selected for OK.Video, which followed from ruangrupa's provocation that post-Reformasi artists had the opportunity to rethink the idea of art itself. With this first event, OK.Video assertively established video art's place in the development of contemporary art in Indonesia.[8]

For its second edition, in 2005, OK.Video removed the term 'Art' from the festival title, in line with ruangrupa's efforts to deconstruct the understanding of art in Indonesia. For ruangrupa, art is a process which includes production modes, precipitation modes, artistic working methods, methodologies, experimentation and collaboration.[9] They insist that art is an act, not an end. Therefore the removal of the word 'art' was another provocation – to destroy the distance between art and non-art, between artists and non-artists, between creators and audiences. This assertion was further underscored by the use of 'Sub/Version' as the festival theme, reflective of the festival's commitment to subversive, subordinate and diverse activities, as well as the forms of duplication and 'versioning' characteristic of new media.[10] The second festival featured a more complex variety of works compared to the first, which showcased single-channel works for the most part. The installation, multichannel and interactive video pieces presented in 2005 addressed provocative ideas related to the main theme, such as subversion, hijacking and manipulation, and aimed at countering norms to promote alternatives. Consequently, the second festival was more focussed on igniting action. While it sought to engage a more general public, its primary audience was the contemporary art community.

One significant takeaway from the 2005 festival was the examination of two contrasting perspectives on technology, the consumer's and the producer's. In Indonesia, consumers often adopt strategies of *mengakali* (outsmarting, or playfully deceiving) technology to survive in the face of limited access and high cost – behaviours that might be perceived as subversive from the producer's viewpoint. OK.Video 2005 highlighted the discourse surrounding 'prosumers' – that is, the relation of producers and consumers where both parties occupy similar positions – at a time where this figure was becoming the target of innovative-technology marketing.

8 Ronny Agustinus, 'Video: Not All Correct', in OK.VIDEO *Post_event_*, Jakarta: ruangrupa, 2004.

9 See David Teh, 'Who Cares a Lot? ruangrupa as Curatorship', *Afterall*, issue 30, 2012, pp.108–17, and reprinted in this volume.

10 *OK.Video SUB/VERSION – 2nd Jakarta Video Art Festival*, Jakarta: ruangrupa, 2005.

Poster of OK.Video 'Sub/Version' - 2nd Jakarta Video Festival, Galeri Nasional Indonesia, Jakarta, 17–31 July 2005. Courtesy ruangrupa

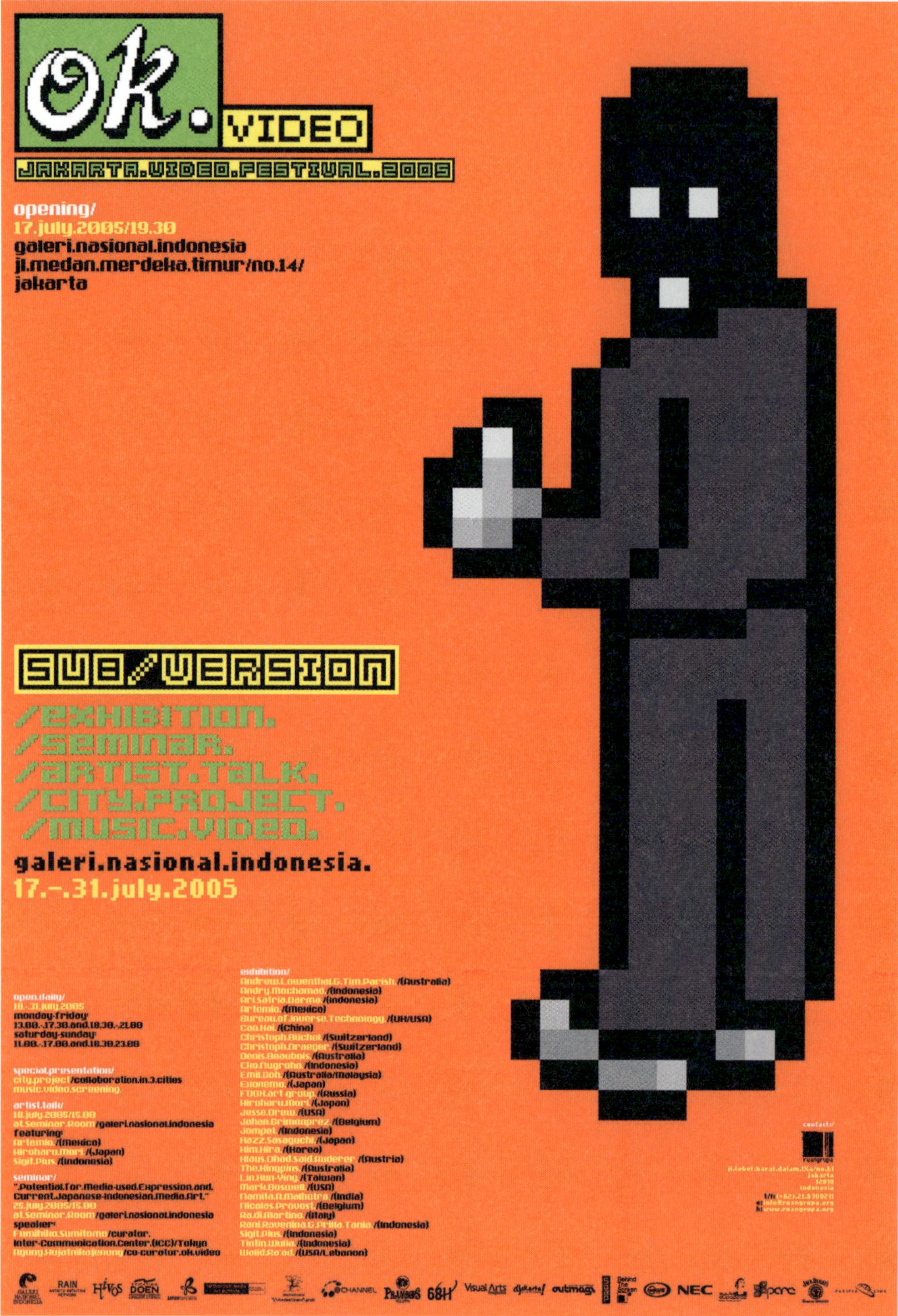

The early editions of OK.Video coincided with the popularisation of networked, peer-to-peer media platforms – most notably YouTube, launched in 2005 – that enabled users to upload and share videos to more directly reach a wide audience. Such increased contact between individuals worldwide, without state mediation, was – and is – much celebrated. By the mid-2000s, several mobile phone models had emerged that included video recording capabilities. From its beginnings, OK.Video tried to deconstruct the idea that only exclusive groups or artists could produce creative media or video works, an ethos that grew in increasing dialogue with the exploding global phenomenon of video-making.

'Militia', OK.Video's Third Jakarta International Video Festival, engendered new audience and video-makers. It introduced the word 'international' into the festival's full title, reflecting the mood of global interconnectivity, and broadened its audiences by entering into public spaces such as bookstores, foreign cultural centres, restaurants, galleries, train stations and government buildings. It also incorporated non-artists into the celebration, its egalitarian approach emphasising that anyone could make videos. This edition involved the collaborative projects of around one hundred participants in twelve cities across Sumatra, Sulawesi and Java.[11] Around half of these participants were students, teachers, civil servants, cultural activists and radio presenters, amongst others. Participants who came from art schools or with an art background tended to make videos that are more abstract and closer to personal expression. In contrast, the non-artists used video more as a documentation or critical medium; they were not burdened by the technical aspect and instead, they flexibly merged various recording tools, methods and practices into a mixed aesthetic that was surprising and refreshing. Over 120 videos made by non-artists and artists were grouped into various themes, motifs and aesthetic languages. The collaborative projects showed that similar experiences were shared by communities despite their various geographies and cultures. In other words, they hinted at the potential of building networks and visions across localities for community survival. A year after 'Militia', Forum Lenteng – most of its members had been the facilitators of these collaborative projects – launched *akumassa* (Eye Public), a media empowering project working with more than ten communities from Sumatra, Java and Nusa Tenggara Barat. Additionally, 'Militia' celebrated artist collectives that emerged in Jakarta, Yogyakarta and Bandung after the 1998 Reformasi. It screened video works by Etnoreflika,

11 Hafiz Rancajale, 'Militia! It's Time to Move', in *OK.Video Militia – 3rd Jakarta International Video Festival*, ed. Ardi Yunanto, Mahardika Yudha and Rani Elsanti, Jakarta: ruangrupa, 2007, pp.13–18.

Poster of OK.Video 'Militia' – 3rd Jakarta International Video Festival, Galeri Nasional Indonesia, Jakarta and other venues across Sumatra, Sulawesi and Java, 10–27 July 2007. Courtesy ruangrupa

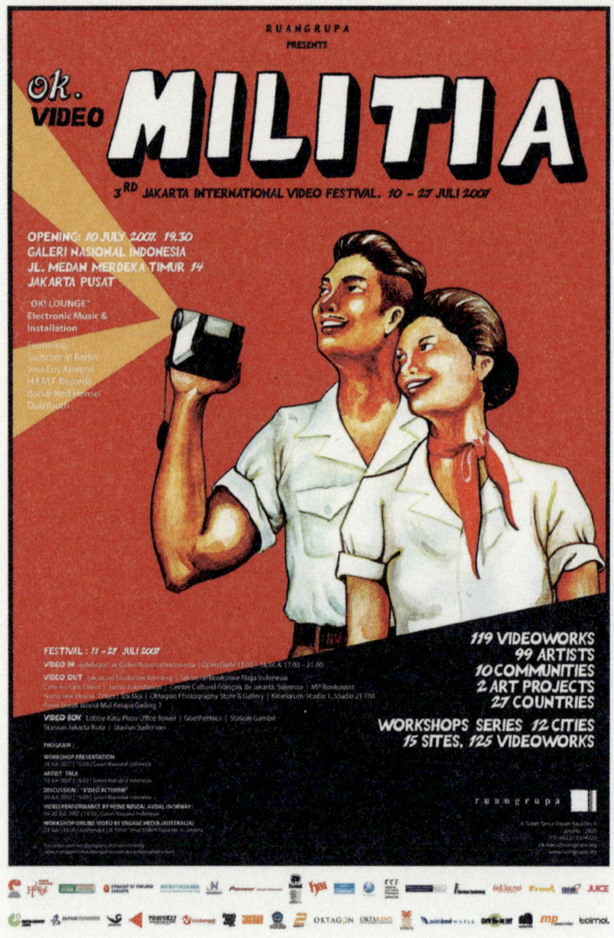

Yogyakarta; Forum Lenteng, Jakarta; Kampung Halaman, Yogyakarta; Urban Poor Consortium, Jakarta; Video Report, Yogyakarta; and Videolab, Bandung.[12] One can speculate that this edition of OK.Video was significant not only in breaking the exclusiveness of video art but also as a forerunner of the birth of *lumbung* practice.

By this time, OK.Video was a barometer for the development of contemporary art, especially video art, in Indonesia. When the festival's fourth edition took place, its theme, 'Comedy', served as an ironic comment on the political situation in Indonesia in 2009 – an election year. The theme was also meant to critique the recent evolution of art in Indonesia, in particular the increased influence of the market. The mid-2000s had seen a resurgence in the Indonesian art market, often referred to as the second

12 A comparable ruru initiative from this time is 'Fixer: Exhibition of Alternative Spaces & Art Collectives in Indonesia' (2010), surveying the working methods of artist collectives across Indonesia in the past decade.

art boom.[13] Realised inside a GNI building painted with red polka dots, 'Comedy' was more modest in scale than 'Militia' and marked a consolidation for the festival, as curator Aminuddin T.H. Siregar summarised:

> Militantly, OK.Video has not only managed to create an open attitude in comprehending a new arena for art practices, but it is also able to accommodate the art genre that in the late nineties to the beginning of the 2000s had been rarely encountered in galleries. Amid the thunders generated by the painting exhibitions that take place every month, OK.Video seems to gather comprehensively video art works that might have been absent for the intervening period of two years.[14]

'Comedy' also engaged, pointedly, with international histories of video art. The special presentation 'Digital Heritage: Video Art in Germany From 1963 to the Present (40 Years Video Arts)' was a collaboration with the Goethe-Institut Jakarta that presented ten key works of German video art, including Joseph Beuys's *Fliz TV* (1970) and Jochen Gerz's *Rufen bis zur Erschöpfung* (*To Cry until Exhaustion*, 1972). 'Digital Heritage' brought exposure amongst the Indonesian public to canonical German video art and marked the entrance of these works into the OK.Video archive for further dissemination; in so doing, it demonstrated how video art and its various support structures, such as archives, developed at a global scale, and exemplified how OK.Video could create conditions to bring Indonesia into the timeline of global video art.

The 2011 edition's theme of 'Flesh' served as a metaphor to discuss the evolution of video art within the art historical landscape, from the merging of video and film art to the ways video was still a new medium for image production and distribution.[15] 'Flesh' developed these ideas in sections, for example, 'How They Did Art Then', conceived by Enin Supriyanto and Grace Samboh.[16] Revered bodies of works by Nam June Paik and Jud Yalkut

13 The first art boom happened in the late 80s and the early 90s. Art historian Sanento Yuliman proposed the term 'Indonesia art boom' for the first time in 1990. For details see 'Antara Seni dan Harta: Boom Seni Lukis' (Between Art Discourse and the Art Market: Art Boom), *Pikiran Rakyat*, 17 July 1990 and 'Ke Mana Seni Lukis Kita-Boom Seni Lukis: Kemelut Medan' (Where is Art Going? – Art Boom: The Turmoil of Art Discourse), *Pikiran Rakyat*, 31 July 1990.

14 See Aminuddin T.H. Siregar, 'In the spirit of OK.Video Comedy, let's laugh at life ... and especially art!', in *OK.Video Comedy – 4th Jakarta International Video Festival*, Jakarta: ruangrupa, 2009.

15 Hafiz Rancajale, 'Menghadirkan Daging Di Hadapan Pemirsa', in *OK.Video Flesh – 5th Jakarta International Video Festival*, Jakarta: ruangrupa, 2011, p.14

16 See D. Teh, 'Who Cares a Lot?', *op. cit.*

(*Video Synthesizer and 'TV Cello' Collectibles*, 1965–71) and Bill Viola (*Memory Surfaces and Mental* Prayers, 1977), for example, were juxtaposed with, say, a funny video from the Ogleng Banyu Biru channel (a lip-sync version of the B.o.B. song 'Nothin' on You' featuring Bruno Mars) and the video 'Udin Sedunia.3gp', an impromptu singing performance by a young person called Udin, who became an Indonesian comedian, actor and TV host after the video went viral in 2010 (it has been viewed 1,352,402 times and counting).[17] The latter videos were made by the public and selected for the 'Digital Viral' section, conceived by Farah Wardani and Ibnu Rizal and distributed across all parts of the festival to promote the combination of high- and lowbrow tastes.[18] Beyond making the strong statement that 'we are all curators', 'Digital Viral' reflected the influence of Web 2.0 media technology on video production in Indonesia, with reference to the curatorial work carried out by the public in the virtual universe, especially on video networks such as YouTube, Vimeo, Metacafe, Dailymotion, etc. Dozens of video links selected from hundreds sent by 25 respondent curators represented a radical act in uprooting video from the internet to bring it into the white cube tradition. It suggested that if anyone can be a curator, curators can curate curators, and curating might no longer recognised as a profession so much as a knowledge-production practice.

Outsmarting Technology as a Survival Strategy (2013–15)

As the idea of the prosumer gained popularity, OK.Video stepped back to examine the forces driving the significant shift in video production and internet-based distribution. They considered the ways in which Indonesia is a country of technology consumers as well as innovators practicing in parallel to devise solutions at the local level that often bridge the gap between material- and idea-based histories. Such commonplace resourcefulness was already deeply rooted in the Dutch East Indies period. During the international economic downturn of the 1930s, for example, the high cost of analogue cameras and newly emerging sound equipment led the film director The Teng Chun to develop a camera capable of recording visuals and sound.[19] The phenomenon evolved into a unique blend of modern and traditional elements that became more widespread during the heyday of New Order in the 1970s

17 These works are available at https://www.youtube.com/watch?v=88xeQa5EyRQ and https://www.youtube.com/watch?v=-_FIwePYdjE respectively.

18 Farah Wardani and Ibnu Rizal, 'Digital Viral: Sebuah Diagnosa Singkat', in *OK.Video Flesh – 5th Jakarta International Video Festival*, Jakarta: ruangrupa, 2011, pp.135–36.

19 See Misbach Yusa Biran, *Sejarah Film 1900–1950: Bikin Film Di Jawa*, Depok: Komunitas Bambu, 2009.

and 80s, when the door to foreign investment was opened wide. In the early 2010s, significant examples included Muhammad Kusrin making his own television, called the Maxreen (inspired by his nickname, Mas Srin).[20] At a distance of many decades, The's and Kusrin's achievements indicate that economic limitations do not necessarily rule out creative developments.

While media technology has the potential to foster countercultures, it benefits corporations as producers of technology. In such conditions, *mengakali* (outsmarting, or playfully deceiving) technology can be viewed as a subversive act, particularly against the framework of media technology itself. This raises the question of how the nature of media technology can be diverted, manipulated, altered or even eliminated. When the underlying systems, structures and laws patented by corporations are dismantled or integrated with other technologies – sometimes even with materials unrelated to the original technology – the action challenges governing principles and regulations. In other words, 'outsmarting' exposes a gap in power that can be seized – even as such actions may not stem from a desire to break the law or from a heroic motivation. They are often driven by a sense of playfulness, boredom or economic necessity. Ultimately, these actions have inspired consumer societies worldwide – video tutorials and how-to videos are amongst the most popular genres on social media platforms today.

Engaging with these dynamics, the 2013 edition of OK.Video, 'Muslihat' (meaning 'deception'), was inspired in part by the cultural strategy of the People's Republic of China in developing their own technology and in part by a 1945 writing of the Indonesian philosopher Tan Malaka in recognising

Installation view, OK.Video 'Muslihat' – 6th Jakarta International Video Festival, Nasional Galeri Indonesia and other venues, Jakarta, 4–15 September 2013. Courtesy ruangrupa

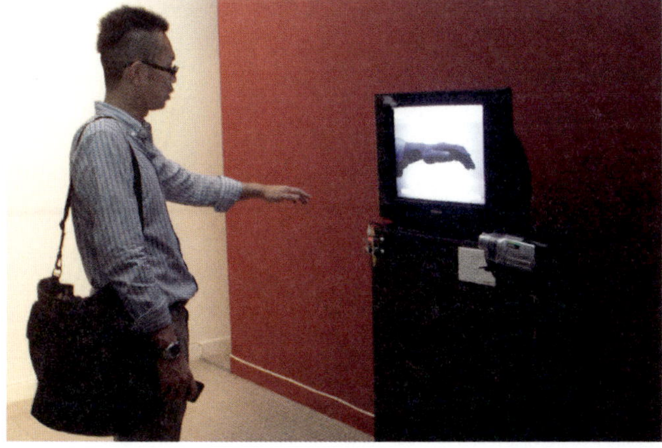

20 Muhammad Kusrin invented his television in 2011. A few years later, the police raided his manufacturing location and his televisions, deemed illegal, was confiscated and burned. In 2016, the government of Jokowi gave official certification to Muhammad Kusrin's television, after the issue of destroying televisions went viral.

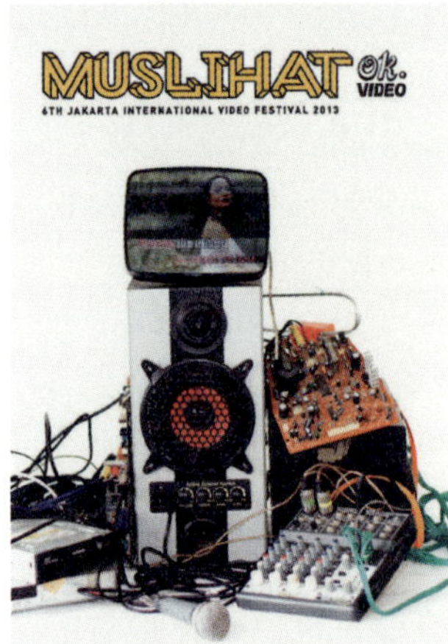

Catalogue of OK.Video 'Muslihat' - 6th Jakarta International Video Festival, Nasional Galeri Indonesia and other venues, Jakarta, 4–15 September 2013. Courtesy ruangrupa

the strategies for survival, learning and self-development in local innovators' sporadic technological developments.[21] 'Muslihat' also returned to the ideas addressed in 'Sub/Version' (2005 edition), with the difference that 'Muslihat' more closely examined, or deconstructed, the production tools responsible for the emergence of video art – cameras, computers, software and hardware. Forty-eight works from sixteen countries were presented in the main exhibition in single channel, multichannel and installation forms. These works were articulated in terms of five 'motives': works as deception themselves; as questions about reality; as a commentary on art institutions and their conventions; as a reflection of consumer deception; and works that tinker with technology.[22] The 2013 festival raised fundamental questions about the dual nature of power inherent in prosumer terminology by showcasing the patterns and methods through which machines create illusions on-screen.

Expanding the Medium (2015–17)

The last two editions of OK.Video further expanded the festival's focus and activities. The 2015 festival theme was 'Orde Baru', to commemorate the humanitarian tragedy that had, fifty years previously, established the path of the New Order government; it also served as a marker for the expanded OK.Video strategy, broadening the festival's scope to include media arts – reflected in the updated subtitle 'Indonesia Media Arts Festival'.[23] 'Media arts' here not only refers to analogue media technology, but also digital and

21 See Tan Malaka, 'Muslihat' (1945), in *Merdeka 100%: Tiga Percakapan Ekonomi-Politik*, Jakarta: Marjin Kiri, 2005.

22 See Irma Chantily, Rizki Lazuardi and Julia Sarisetiati, 'Curatorial Story at a Glance', in *Muslihat OK.Video – 6th Jakarta International Video Festival 2013*, Jakarta: ruangrupa, 2013, pp.32–39.

23 A. Rosdianahangka, *Orde Baru OK.Video – Indonesia Media Arts Festival 2015*, Jakarta: ruangrupa, 2015.

post-digital media technology, as well as emergent disciplines of new media arts and post-new media arts, reflecting concerns of ruangrupa that predate the establishment of OK.Video.

Certainly, media arts are in ruangrupa's DNA,[24] yet the festival's expansion into media arts was indicative of timely developments in video art discourse and the expansion of various strands of practice based in technology – whether sound art, internet art, bio-art, multimedia performance or conceptualist practices. A historical line is thus traced which is not only focussed on the development of video but extends to older mediums such as film and radio. In embracing 'media arts' as a concept, OK.Video was opening up to new possibilities explored through different methodological approaches to evolving creative practice, art and technology.

Another expansion in this era was ruangrupa's creation of Gudang Sarinah Ekosistem in 2016, an early implementation of their practice of *lumbung*, a shared platform for artistic production, knowledge dissemination and activism. While familiar from ruangrupa's project for documenta fifteen

Catalogue of OK.Video 'Orde Baru' – Indonesia Media Arts Festival, Galeri Nasional Indonesia, Jakarta, 15–28 June 2015. Courtesy ruangrupa

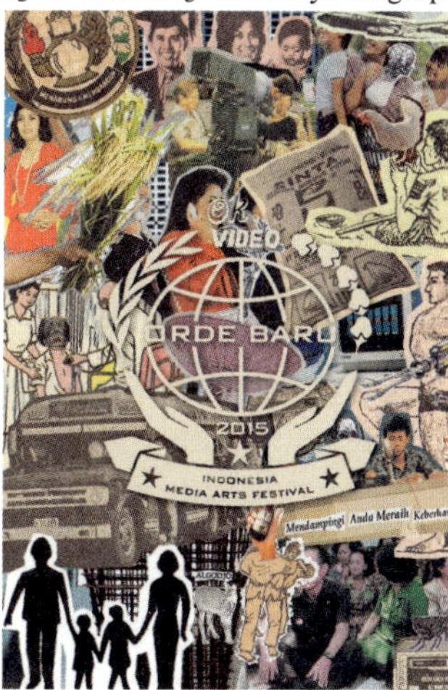

24 From its beginnings, ruangrupa organised plenty of media arts related programmes. Some early examples include the short film workshop *Psychogeography and 'Derive'* with Nina Fischer and Maroan El Sani (Germany) in 2001; artist residency with Michael Blum (Germany/France), who made the film project *My Sneakers* in 2001; the *Silent Forces* workshop in 2001, in which artists Sebastian Diaz Morales (Argentina), Anne Mie van Kerckhoven (Belgium), Aditya Satria (Indonesia) and Adrianto Sinaga (Indonesia) created several multimedia and video art works; *The Swarm Project* in 2001, featuring multimedia-based works by Tero Nauha (Finland) and Ade Darmawan (Indonesia); an exhibition of the *SMS (Short Message System)* art project created collaboratively by Darmawan, Oscar Firdaus (Indonesia), Jimmi Multhazam (Indonesia) and Tina Gillen (USA) in 2002; multimedia performance *Ultra Output Project* by Venza Christ and Jompet, *Polygame* performance by Asbestos, and *Music Video* workshop with Oliver Husain and Michel Klofkorn (Germany), all in 2002; the exhibition *What Do You Mean by Using Another* which presented sound, objects, installations and video art works involving Yunawantyo, Aditya Satria and Ernest Wang in 2002; launching the *Rabu Video Club* (Wednesday Video Club) programme in 2002; publishing the *Karbon* journal which specifically talked about video art (February 2002) and performance art (September 2002). ruangrupa was also active in art events such as the Bandung Video, Film and New Media Art Forum 2002 (bavf-NAF#1), in which they collaborated with the Bio Sampler collective to create a live multi-media performance entitled *Digital Manifesto* (2002); for details see Seno Joko Suyono and Bobby Gunawan, 'Dari Lantai Diskotek dan Besi-besi Tua' (From Disco Floors and Scrap Metal), *Tempo magazine*, 1 September 2002.

in Kassel, Germany, in 2022, the term *lumbung* goes back much further in their collective work. For the Gudang Sarinah initiative, ruangrupa rebranded an old warehouse in southern Jakarta to use it as a testing space for the planned and measured implementation of *lumbung*. OK.Video followed this shift as a vehicle to support an effort to decentralise art – to create an art scene and exhibition space not in the centre of Jakarta.

The transition to Gudang Sarinah presented many obstacles. For instance, OK.Video had to adapt to limited infrastructure, essentially building from scratch. Besides that, the resources were minimal. Only five people were in charge of the festival management at the time. The shift provided opportunities, however, for experimentation, including OK.Video's collaboration with many collectives sharing similar interests in media arts. One of the strategies implemented was to pursue a festival theme reflective of social and political needs in local and global contexts. After moving to Gudang Sarinah, OK.Video made plans for three festivals within six years, on themes of food, water and energy – embodying *lumbung* as a practice. In identifying themes related to people's welfare, *lumbung* forced OK.Video into a further politicisation.

The 2017 festival, 'OK.Pangan' ('OK. Food'), addressed food sovereignty and politics.[25] Co-curators Julia Sarisetiati and Renan Laru-an and the extended curatorial team worked to reveal the relationships between media arts and food. Several young researchers with expertise on food politics were invited onto the curatorial team; nine 'open labs' were conducted to activate the Gudang Sarinah Ekosistem and other ecosystems in Jakarta;

Programme book of OK.Video 'OK.PANGAN' – 8th Indonesia Media Arts Festival, Gudang Sarinah Ekosistem, Jakarta and Pusat Perpustakaan dan Penyebaran Teknologi Pertanian, Bogor, 22 July – 16 August 2017 . Courtesy ruangrupa

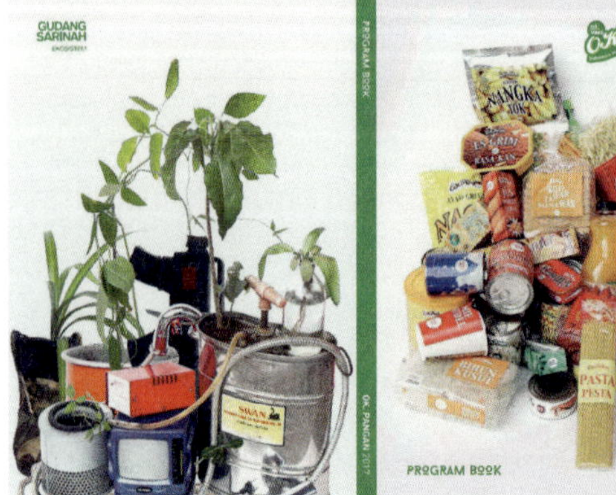

25 Laila Achmad, *OK.Pangan – OK Video Indonesia Media Arts Festival 2017*, Jakarta: ruangrupa, 2017.

and a diverse group of artists engaged directly with the discursive environment. In tandem with these face-to-face open labs, OK.Video launched a virtual residency that embraced a similar artistic vision but operated within a distinct context. This combination produced unique artistic contributions and rich interpretations of related subjects, such as land 'harvesting' (in real and virtual spaces). Additionally, the initiative included a groundbreaking video outreach programme that brought together collectives from across the archipelago to collaboratively screen films on food politics simultaneously. Participating groups included Gubuak Kopi (Solok), Mes56 (Yogyakarta), Pasirputih (North Lombok), Platform61 (Medan), Rel Air (Padang), Sayurankita (Pekanbaru), Serbuk Kayu (Surabaya), Serrupa and Sudutpandang Forum (Palu), SimpaSio Institute (Larantuka), Sinema Kolekan (Jakarta) and Yoikatra (Timika). In an era of widely accessible media technology, this initiative harnessed the power of media to connect audiences across geographic locations, indicative of its immense potential.

'OK.Pangan' would turn out to be the last OK.Video festival to date. The reason why it stopped – or at least, why the festival hit 'pause' in 2017 – reflects a combination of familiar factors, particularly limitations in energies, time and resources. (OK.Video continues to exist as an archive and occasional project platform, of which more below.) The period of organising the biennial, from 2003 to 2017, vividly demonstrates OK.Video's significant role in shaping the Indonesian art scene.[26] Dale Hudson and Patricia R. Zimmermann note that the video art scene in Jakarta diverges from comparable experimental media scenes in East Asia, Europe and North America, which often emphasise avant-garde elitism. Instead, the Jakarta scene has aimed to foster inclusive discussions with broader audiences.[27] Observing the evolution of OK.Video is akin to grasping the insights of Indonesian film theorist David Albert Peransi regarding the unique development of artistic methods and aesthetics in the Global South. Peransi asserts: 'We, who hail from the Global South, are often referred to as the Third World. This carries no sense of inferiority. Our perceived backwardness is, in fact, a privilege, allowing us to explore paths not taken by Europe.'[28]

26 Edwin Jurriëns, *Visual Media in Indonesia: Video Vanguard*, London: Routledge, 2017.

27 Dale Hudson and Patricia Zimmermann, *Thinking Through Digital Media Transnational Environments and Locative Places*, New York: Palgrave Macmillan, 2015.

28 David Albert Peransi's statement is from the discussion 'Contemporary Indonesian Painting', held on 21 December 1974 at Taman Ismail Marzuki on the occasion of 'Pameran Senilukis Indonesia 1974 (Exhibition of Painting 1974)', later known as the first Jakarta Biennale. My (Mahardika Yudha's) transcription is from an audio recording held in the archive of the Jakarta Arts Council.

The Name is OK.Video

At ruangrupa's last house in the Tebet neighborhood of South Jakarta, before they moved to Gudang Sarinah, the atmosphere was friendly, informal and buzzing with different people and activities. In 2013, on the house's first floor, not far from the living room (which served as a gallery), the media editing room was enclosed by one chaotic office space and a more ordered library. The library's DVD collection included all the works presented at OK.Video since its beginning, as well as video works produced by other ruangrupa projects. Visitors who wanted to view videos unavailable in the library were directed to the editing room, which was also a storage area for hard copies of various archival materials: CDs, VCDs and DVDs; VHS, MiniDV and Hi-8 tapes; various hard drives and other digital storage containers in all shapes and sizes. Some lucky visitors found what they came looking for, perhaps via a handwritten note or signature.[29] I would spend hours in this room every day, absorbing everything I could.

I did not become involved with ruangrupa through their art events, nor by feeling inspired at an exhibition held at the space, nor by becoming interested in the contemporary-art-urban-youth-lifestyle their activities projected. I was curious about their collection of video art. I first visited ruangrupa in 2002, while I was still a journalism student at the Institute of Social and Political Science Jakarta (IISIP). This was when I saw video art for the very first time, and I did not understand it. While commercial television and video technologies had been well established for decades, the opportunity to encounter alternative media such as video art was rare in Indonesia. One of the works I saw, which left a lasting impression on me, was *Trembling Time* (2001) by Yael Bartana. The film documents a moment of silence observed by Israeli people. It sparked my curiosity; like a journalist, I traced and collected information about the work until I finally understood what the artist was trying to convey.

My curiosity was again fuelled when I saw ruangrupa's impact on the art scene, and their foregrounding of video art practice, culminating in the inaugural OK.Video event, Jakarta Video Art Festival 2003. What I saw in OK.Video at that time was a very open public space: an invitation to the

29 In 2010, when ruangrupa had its tenth anniversary, there were at least 900 MiniDV cassettes containing video documentation of their activities. Assuming that at least 50 video works were presented at each edition of the festival, there would have been a total of at least 250 video works presented from all over the world by 2011 (not including works sent to open submissions or works from ruangrupa's regular programmes and art projects).

public, especially young people, to do anything connected to video art at all. At the festival's opening, I met Ade Darmawan, ruangrupa's director, and Hafiz Rancajale, artistic director of OK.Video from 2007 to 2011. A few days later, Hafiz, Otty Widasari, several other friends and I formed Forum Lenteng, a collective focussing on technology, media and art activism.

I started working with OK.Video in 2007. I was tasked with reaching out to communities outside Jakarta, for example, Jatiwangi Art Factory (then only two years old and deeply rooted in its locality). The following year, ruru formed its Video Art Development Division to manage its growing artist databases, video collections and video documentation. This was where I worked officially and full-time at ruru – in the morning and early afternoon I'd be at Forum Lenteng, and late afternoon and evening I'd be at ruangrupa (or sometimes this schedule was switched). Our videos were made not only to document OK.Video's activities, but also to serve the needs of promoting and recording other ruru programmes. In 2010, to conclude the early years of ruru and OK.Video's work, the Division published the book and DVD compilation *10 Years of Indonesian Video Art 2000–2010*, which serves as a testament to the resurgence of video art in Indonesia.[30]

In 2011, I had the opportunity to participate in curating OK.Video 'Flesh'. I collaborated with Rizky Lazuardi in organising videos under the sub-theme 'Surveillance & Self Portrait'. I subsequently organised more media arts exhibitions at RURU Gallery and elsewhere.[31] From 2007 to 2016, the management team of OK.Video never grew to more than two people.[32] The team worked on routine programmes, involving archiving, documentation, video libraries, production and education, as well as the festivals' organisation. When organising a festival, we usually enlisted other ruru members or hired workers from other collectives. But almost inevitably, the OK.Video team took on the majority of the research, curation and art handling work because of limited funding.

30 Mirza Jaka Suryana, *10 Tahun Seni Video Indonesia (2000–2010)*, Jakarta: ruangrupa, 2010.

31 For instance, Benny Wicaksono's solo exhibition 'Prototype' (2015), which investigated CCTV, and a project involving several young female artists in Jakarta who created video works from photo archives about sugar factories in the Dutch colonial era. The latter became one of the programmes in the project 'The Sweet and Sour Story of Sugar', a collaboration between ruangrupa and Noorderlicht in 2012.

32 The author (Mahardika Yudha) managed OK.Video from 2007 onwards. When the author quit at the end of 2017, people working at OK.Video included Simon Danang Anggoro aka Gentong, Bellina Erby and Afra Suci Ramadhon. Deasy Elsara (2012–15) and Natasha Abigail (2015–16) were also involved in the management of OK.Video.

Opening of 'Get.Raw Lab: 20 Years of OK.Video', Gudskul Ekosistem, Jakarta, 18 March 2023.
Courtesy ruangrupa

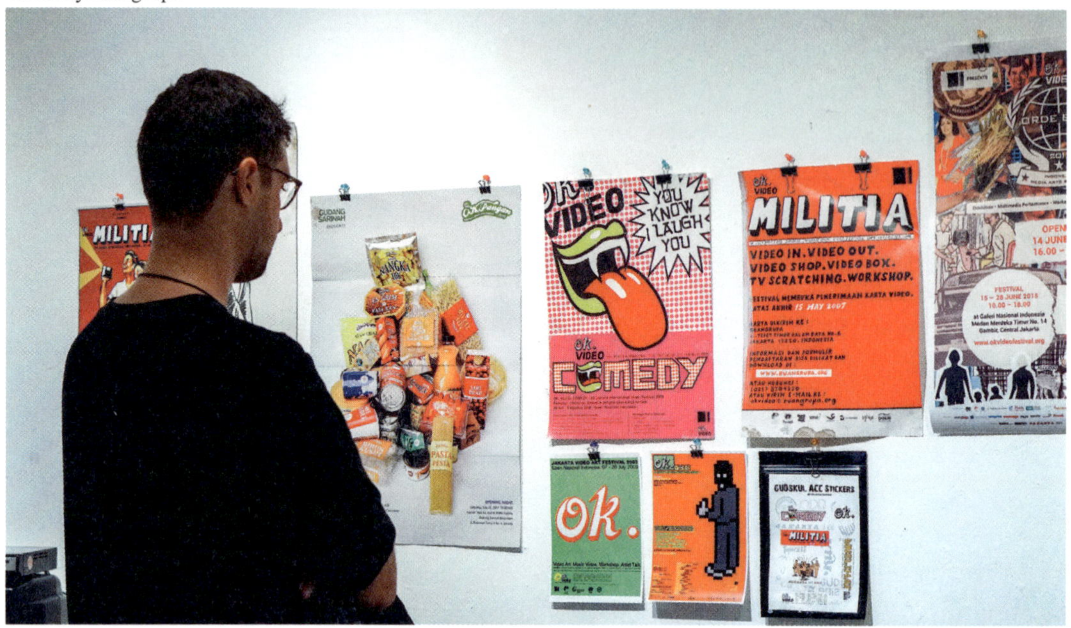

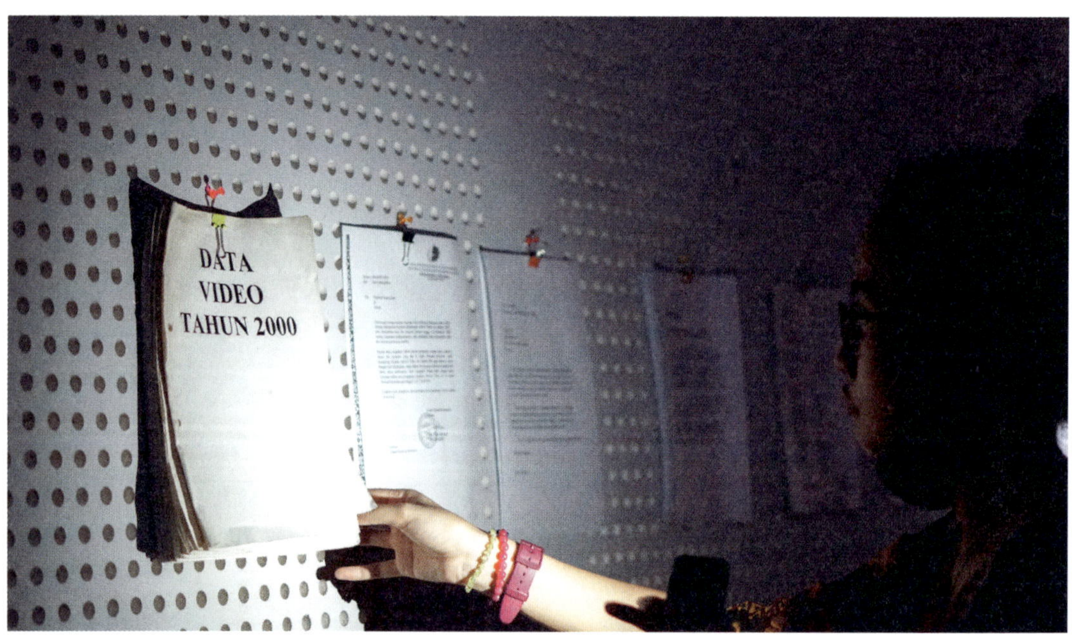

In hindsight, 2013 was a critical moment of change. In addition to expanding the focus of the festival beyond the medium of video, we aspired to build OK.Video as an institution operating independently from ruangrupa. We imagined an OK.Video Centre for Media and Technology that could work more freely in developing programmes, finances, employment and networks. By that time, OK.Video had built various tools for the development of media arts in Indonesia, from archiving and documenting media arts to creating educational programmes, writing criticism, performing curatorial work and encouraging and facilitating the production of new works, and then beyond that, developing opportunities to work with practitioners from wider disciplines, such as local scientists, hackers and activists. OK.Video developed its own resources and infrastructure, which were also used by other divisions in ruru or by friends in other collectives. More precisely, during its first ten years, OK.Video acquired an archive and documentation collection assets, as well as technologies including projectors, televisions, media players, computers, sound systems and so on, which were often borrowed or rented at low prices by other collectives and artists. In terms of human resources, OK.Video helped at various events showcasing video works and media arts, such as the 2015 Jakarta Biennale. In all of these ways, OK.Video established itself as a resource for the future.

What is the status of OK.Video today? In 2023, OK.Video celebrated its twentieth anniversary with the exhibition '20 Years OK.Video' at Gudskul Ekosistem in South Jakarta, which highlighted its role as the most comprehensive public institution for media arts archives in Indonesia. The exhibition included a note I often placed on screens: 'Copying data. Can be used as long as it is not turned off. 14 hours of processing. Thank you.' A new edition of the festival has not taken place since 2017, but OK.Video continues to exist as a media archive (currently based at Gudskul Ekosistem) and as a platform for various related activities. In 2024, for instance, OK.Video collaborated with collectives such as the Makmoer Djaja and Cut and Rescue to document the *Peringatan Darurat* (Emergency Warning) movement, which saw social media memes as a major factor in mobilising mass protests. Also in 2024, OK.Video participated in an art project to archive the work of Indonesian media arts pioneer Krisna Murti, an endeavor that aims to enrich OK.Video's media arts archives as well as sustain long-standing legacies of media arts in Indonesia.

We would like to speculate on some of the possibilities raised by the history of OK.Video. In particular, we would like to suggest three priorities that any equivalent organisation needs to address: decentralisation, media art archiving and collective autonomous organisation.

Art decentralisation encompasses two pivotal aspects: first, the decentralisation of infrastructure for art development, including writing, education and archiving; second, and perhaps most crucial, the redirection of discourse away from Java to ensure that all voices and perspectives across Indonesia are heard and valued. To this day, the development of contemporary and media arts, including OK.Video, has remained centralised on the island of Java. With Indonesia's expansive area, diverse cultures and the growth of contemporary art production and distribution, this cannot adequately serve the needs of the entire country, from Sabang to Merauke. The next important task is therefore to continue the decentralisation of contemporary art, as pioneered by OK.Video with 'Militia' in 2007. As an egalitarian, democratic and popular art medium, media art has a special potential to give birth to art decentralisation.

Preserving media arts in Indonesia is another urgent matter. Video art emerged in the 90s in Indonesia and is now over thirty years old; the challenge of archiving and documenting video works has become increasingly complex due to the diverse and intricate nature of media technology and materials. When we consider existing infrastructure for art archiving, it invariably leads us to the Indonesian Visual Art Archive in Yogjakarta; for film archiving, to Sinematek Indonesia in Jakarta; and for video art and media arts archiving, to OK.Video. However, these art archiving centres have limited resources and infrastructure and are managed by non-governmental organisations that are ill-equipped to cover the vast expanse of Indonesia. The only viable solution is to establish at least one art archiving centre on each island in Indonesia, to ensure that the rich and diverse artistic heritage of the nation is preserved and accessible to all. OK.Video was envisioned to support ruangrupa's vision to create a module-based infrastructure for building and developing media arts. The experiences and methods formulated can be used as a basis for application and development by other collectives throughout Indonesia.

Finally, we would like to consider the potentials that might be created if OK.Video were to be independent from ruangrupa – as was envisioned by its organisers in 2013 – as a publicly organised entity. While this is a more speculative idea, it follows in the *lumbung* spirit because it imagines how OK.Video might work as an organisation managed by multiple collectives, and as a way to realise the aforementioned priorities of decentralisation and building archiving infrastructure. Just as 'Militia' aimed to raise a collective awareness of video as a political medium – whether as a work of art or as a tool for activism – an independent, collectively organised and decentralised OK.Video endeavor would raise awareness of building media arts infrastructure in each region of Indonesia as a political act. As a collective organisation in its own right, rather than a sub-organisation of ruangrupa, its function would be to guide, provide space and act as a support system for the continuing development of media arts in Indonesia. We believe that by combining the priorities of decentralisation, archiving and autonomy, the 'data' of OK.Video's legacy can be secured for future generations.

Gesyada Siregar

OK.Video 'OK.PANGAN' – 8th Indonesia Media Arts Festival, Gudang Sarinah Ekosistem, Jakarta, 22 July – 16 August 2017. Courtesy ruangrupa

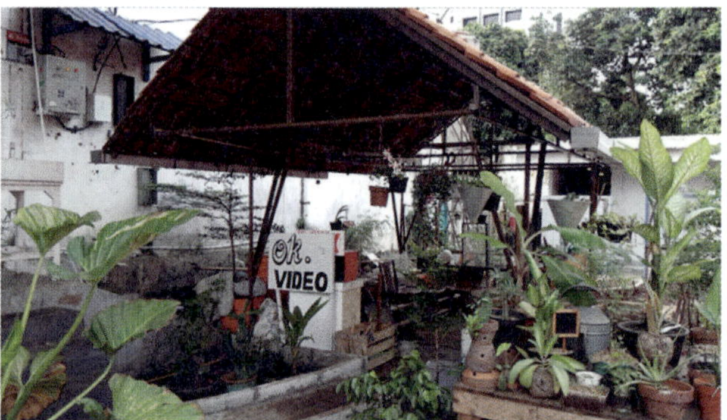

'I know that you have been travelling here and there, but actually I don't really know what your job is', said my sister. She and her family were picking me up from the Soekarno-Hatta International Airport in Jakarta. I was coming back from a work trip to Maumere on Flores Island in 2024, where I had been doing fieldwork for the project 'Ekstrakurikulab: Collective as a School', led by Serrum. The research involved inferring how an artist collective runs their educational programme to societally function in the local ecosystem. But my explanation was not in layman's terms. Also, my recent Instagram stories were video reposts of me doing karaoke and partying with members of artist collective Komunitas KAHE, who hosted us. That didn't help. *How do I convince my sister that what I have been doing is research?* I wondered.

We were in the car. I was in the back seat with my baby niece and my bulky backpack. My sister was in the front seat, multitasking, holding my sleepy oldest niece while co-piloting the car with her driver-husband. I thought of our shared multitasking skills, but I also realised how much my little sister and I had grown apart. I said, 'Hahaha, *bingung, ya, dek*?' ('You must be so confused, eh, sis?') I was startled to realise that if a curator's role is to relate an understanding of things to the general public, and if this field of work is about contemporary art education for different community levels, I was still failing to articulate to my own family, in simple language, what I actually do.

'Did you figure it out now?'

In 2017, I found myself in a similar situation, when my maternal aunt came along with me to Gudang Sarinah Ekosistem. She said, 'I want to know what your workplace looks like.' Perhaps she was pondering what 'this thing' was that had been my recurring excuse for being absent at family gatherings. I took my aunt around to see what was happening in Gudang Sarinah, and to be exact, in the afternoon, before the nocturnal art life began.

Grafis Huru Hara members were lying on gigantic prints on the floor, their clothes permanently stained with ink, their baggy eyes evidencing an all-nighter. On the other side of the warehouse, the media art festival 'OK. Pangan' (OK. Food) was happening. A friend from Yogyakarta was sweeping the floor of his 'Kombucha Hotel' project – a backyard cafe with ponds, plants and stepping stones. My aunt expressed her confusion facially when I introduced him as an artist. They shook hands. The artist was wearing a worn t-shirt, a *sarung*[1] and a pair of dirty flip-flops, and he held a broom

1 A piece of long tubular fabric with a printed pattern, worn by wrapping and tying the fabric around the waist, a *sarung* is like a long flowy skirt. It is usually worn by men in Indonesia.

in one hand. As the tour commenced, my aunt got to see an array of unreadable yet colourful gigantic graffiti and heaps of unidentifiable post-exhibition objects next to drums and wooden pallets, all scattered across Gudang Sarinah's 6,000-square-metre interior.

If all that was still confusing my aunt in terms of what kind of work I do, let's turn to her encounter with Ade Darmawan, whom I was meeting with that day to plan upcoming Jakarta 32°C and RURU Gallery projects. I struggled to find the right 'workplace title' for Ade, given the nature of our artist collective's dynamic. I said 'Tante, this is my *boss*, hehehe', adding that awkward laugh as a hint to Ade.[2] *Well*, I thought, *he is technically the director of ruangrupa, so there is some truth to that.* Ade was wearing a polo shirt, khaki shorts and hiking sandals – too chill to be a boss in any corporate setting. But his short grey hair signified a stereotype that my aunt could buy into.

'Yeah, I am always curious about what Gesya is doing, so I came here to figure it out', my aunt said to Ade in her thick Medan accent.

'I see. Did you figure it out now?' Ade responded, politely.

'Well', she said, her eyebrows raised, 'I am still confused!'

We laughed.

'Well, my family is still confused, too – to this day', said Ade, grinning while scratching his grey head.

We all laughed even more.

I knew Ade personally didn't like to be addressed in terms of hierarchy, but he caught that my awkward laugh was a signal and intuitively played his part in this 'auntie random inspection' situation. They shook hands and nodded, performing an Indonesian non-verbal form of respect.

Shattered Assumptions

ruru was founded when I was still in kindergarten. I was not in Jakarta back then, I was in my birthplace: Medan, North Sumatra. To those who are unaware of Indonesia's geography, Medan is on a different island from Java or Bali. It is closer to Malaysia than it is to Jakarta. When I was ten years old, I moved to Jakarta with my mom and sister. That was in 2004, the same year that ruru's Jakarta 32°C was founded as a division to focus on university student networking and forums in contemporary art. It developed into a biennial for students across disciplines and campuses in Jakarta. Ten years later, I would become involved in coordinating the Jakarta 32°C database and its students' forum. Yet another decade later, here I am, writing my

2 I recalled Ajeng Nurul Aini, as ruru's manager, introduced Ade as her 'boss' to her family when the collective members visited her father's funeral.

reflections to be published in a book about how ruru, Serrum, Grafis Huru Hara, Gudang Sarinah Ekosistem and Gudskul Ekosistem shaped my adulthood and my present perspective as a 30-year-old woman.

The confusion of my sister and aunt was reasonable. I, too, was confused the first time I visited ruru, in 2012, when I was a first-year art student. 'It is a gallery', said an alumnus of Institut Kesenian Jakarta (Jakarta Arts Institute, IKJ), Leonhard Bartolomeus, who would start managing RURU Gallery in 2014. When I arrived in the ruru house, all the assumptions I had about an art space – big, shiny, multi-storey, with glass walls – were shattered.

Dancing Rice or Clay Sculpture

I got to know more about what was inside the ruru house when I was selected to participate in its Young Curator Workshop in 2013, co-organised with Jakarta Arts Council. When I submitted an official letter from ruru manager Ajeng Nurul Aini, requesting my absence from school, some of my Fine Arts teachers at IKJ looked concerned. For two weeks, I attended the workshop at ruru in the morning and went back to the IKJ campus at night to continue my painting and clay sculpture assignments.

Every day was surreal. I clearly remember having an existential crisis on campus. *Knowing that an 'out there' artist can throw rice on top of a speaker to make it dance as an artwork,*[3] *why am I still doing this clay sculpture from scratch at art school? If I am so frustrated and sleep-deprived, why do I still want to finish this assignment on time?* I was torn between being a good student versus a rebellious explorer of this contemporary art world that the curation workshop had revealed to me.

At nineteen years old, I was the youngest participant in the workshop. It was very awkward for me that many ruru members and other participants, mostly between four and twenty years older than me, did not want to be addressed with typical Indonesian honorifics. Some even asked me to call them by name! This was against the customs of my upbringing. In every introduction, I had to figure out which Indonesian language honorifics to use to not make our age gap obvious and yet still show respect. I was curious, excited, fascinated, frustrated, perplexed and stressed, juggling life between workshops, adjusting myself to the new cultural mix of collective and art student lives.

After the workshop, I was drawn to ruru's programmes and people. My early 'jobs' with them included translating exhibition catalogues and assisting international artists on projects. The ruru members knew that I spoke

3 A work by Benny Wicaksono, one of the key speakers in the Young Curator Workshop 2013. Years later, I had the chance to curate his work in a media art exhibition.

English and that I seemed okay with short-notice requests. My time was flexible as an art student. For two years, I became a gig economy worker.

If I were to not aim for a certain job title or position, I thought to myself, *and if were to instead choose what kind of people I work with, it would be these people in ruru.* They were nocturnal, utterly casual and liked to discuss anything, even if it *ngalor-ngidul* (strayed away) from the original meeting agenda. They wore flip-flops to work, blasted cool music while working on laptops, joked here and there while working, smoked cigarettes indoors and were flexible in schedule. *I don't have to become something that I am not. I can learn from them,* I persuaded myself.

Patrap Triloka

Gestures and physical presence – rather than words – are considered more impactful in our artist collective. What we like are more experiential insights; we learn through observing a set of examples, responding to the nuances and showing up in times of need.

This work dynamic is considered a very Patrap Triloka approach – a concept that fascinates me. It is coinage by Indonesian-Javanese thinker Ki Hadjar Dewantara[4] and involves three principles:

ing ngarso sung tuladha (the one at the front shall lead by example);
ing madya mangun karsa (the one in the middle shall take the initiative);
tut wuri handayani (the one in the back shall provide support).[5]

I cannot help but notice a very Taurean attribute in this action-based pedagogy. It asks for a 'little less conversation, more actions, please', and encourages a hands-on, utterly experiential approach. Every collective member rotates and shifts between the three roles. We make an example of putting in the effort to initiate and to support in any capacity, with or without having our say.

4 Ki Hadjar Dewantara's influence on Indonesian education is so significant that his birthday, 2 May, is commemorated as Indonesian National Education Day. He was among the founders of Indische Partij in 1912, one of the first political parties to promote Indonesian nationalism, before the nation's actual independence 33 years later. In 1913, he was exiled to The Netherlands after publishing a satirical text against colonialisation, titled 'If I Were a Dutchman'. Upon his return to pre-Indonesia, he pioneered Taman Siswa in 1922, a significant school and educational system developed in resistance to the Dutch colonial system.

5 This was even the slogan of the Ministry of Education and Culture in Indonesia.

Jakarta 32°c meetings at Gudang Sarinah Ekosistem, 2016–17.
Courtesy ruangrupa & Gudskul Ekosistem

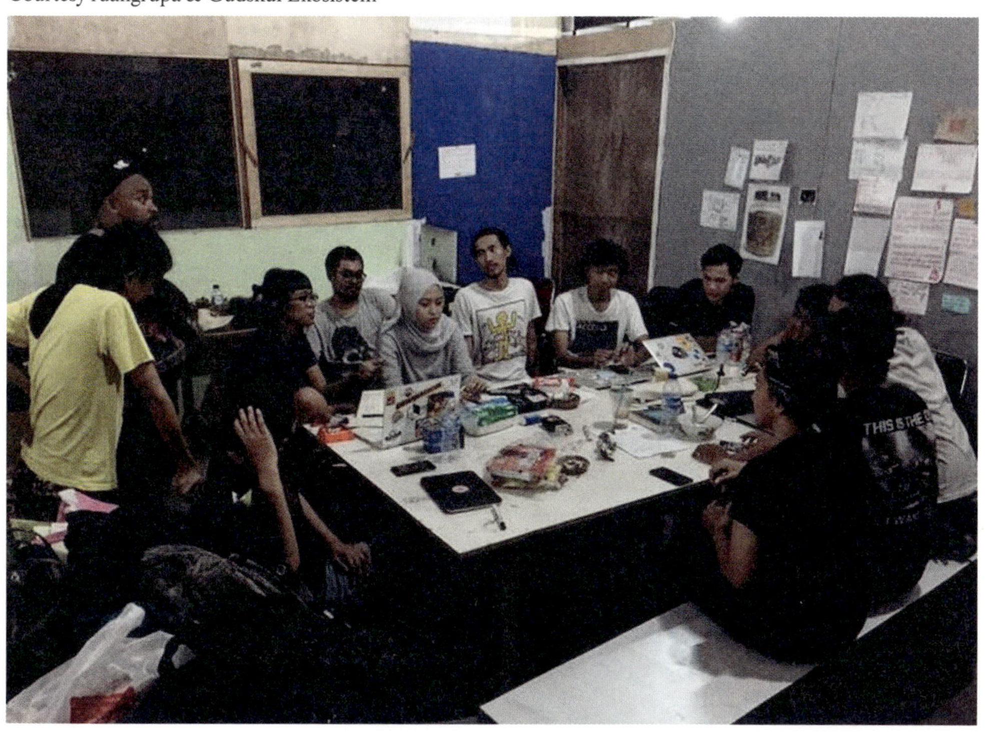

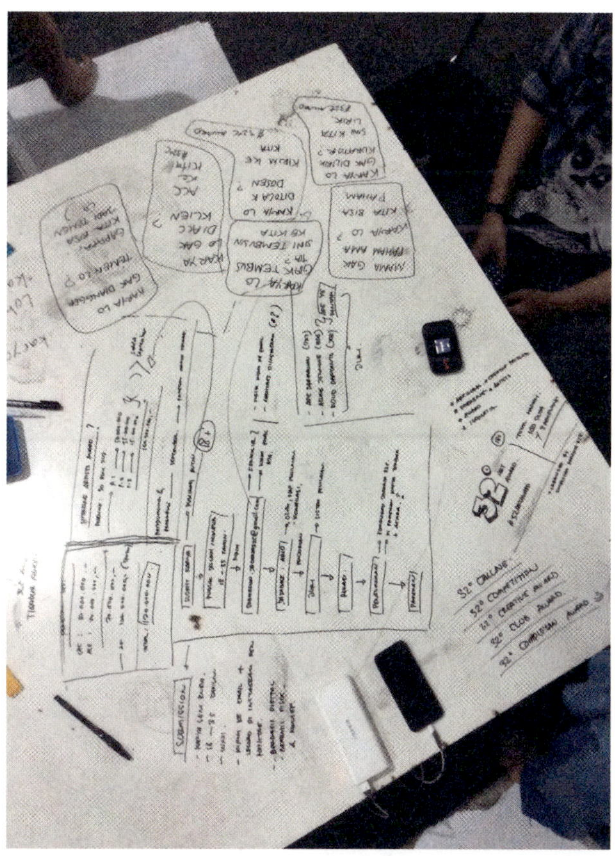

Jakarta 32°c meeting at Gudang Sarinah Ekosistem, 2016–17. Courtesy Gesyada Siregar

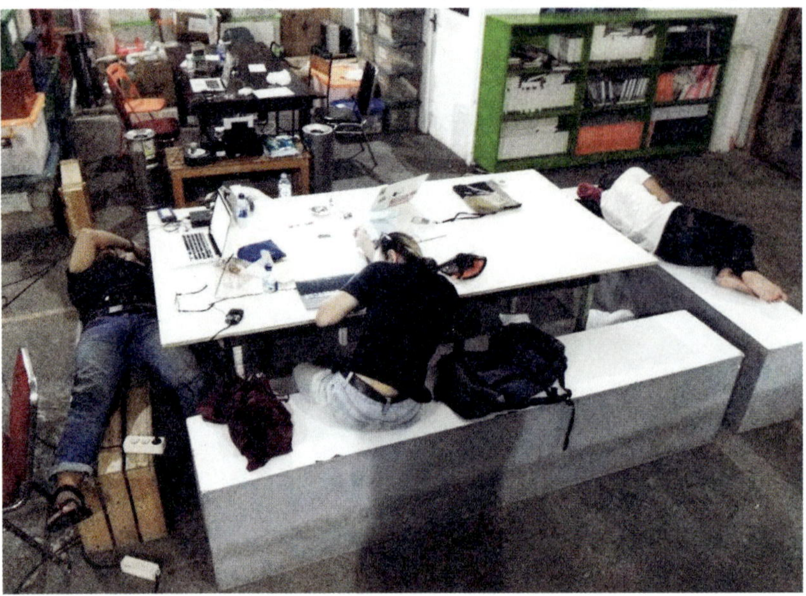

Asking Why and How

In ruru, Serrum, Grafis Huru Hara and, later, Gudskul, the Patrap Triloka principles are practiced in a synchronous or asynchronous mode. I can remember, during my early days working at the Jakarta 32°c festivals, from 2014 to 2018, each year's organising team was comprised of student volunteers. My experience was akin to attending a 'temporary school' and the schooling was driven by processes of self-learning and peer-learning.

The principle of *ing ngarso sung tuladha* (leading by example) was demonstrated not only through members' observable behaviour but also through archiving. The databases of the previous festivals were always passed down to the next generation of organising teams. Going through dusty hard disks was some sort of rite of passage for Jakarta 32°c organisers. My friends and I studied how workshops were formatted by previous facilitators, how proposal decks had been made and how visual identities for promotional materials had come together. We would reuse a formal letter template, adjusting it for various campuses.

ruru members were also very present in our organisational meetings, sharing their insights for us to internalise. The hard disk databases and verbal insights from older generations were presented as nostalgic stories more than as directions, giving us, the new generation, room to think and decide which parts would work for our current context, leading to *ing madya mangun karsa* (taking initiative).

In our organisational meetings and forums, the prompts that our senior members tended to pose were 'Why?' and 'How would you do that?', rather than 'Don't do that.' It took us youngsters quite a while to realise that being asked why and how did not mean disapproval. Our fear of disapproval originated in the 'silent culture' of our educational system. Perhaps this 'delirious 3am political talk' from me, but I believe the 'silent culture' is a legacy from the New Order era. It stems from the misunderstanding that 'critique' is merely an evaluation of what went wrong rather than an inquiry that might shape and test certain hypotheses. Why and how are indeed challenges, intended to make us to understand and feel responsible for our decisions, from the artistic to the managerial.

Being Nakal

Another norm that was fostered through Jakarta 32°C was to praise *nakal* (naughty) works. Of course, in my early days, I found it unsettling. I wondered what the judging limits were, because I thought we were supposed to encourage 'good' artworks. Nobody from the senior members could really elaborate on 'good' *nakal* or 'bad' *nakal*, and the younger generations dared not further probe the definition of *nakal*-ity. The challenge was akin to figuring out grammar of gender articles in many European languages, which can be random and confusing for first-time learners.

Only after reviewing all the artworks by students and wrapping up the festival for the second time did I start to see why encouraging this particular norm made sense. Jakarta 32°C, as an off-campus platform, was a place for Jakartan students to explore mediums and ideas that would be neither received nor accepted in the academic realm. Hence, the *nakal*-ity of the artworks signified their deviation from assignments on campus. It was through encouraging *nakal* that Jakarta 32°C's role fulfilled *tut wuri handayani* (giving support).

The understanding of who, when, where, what to perform of the three Patrap Triloka principles can come tacitly, fluidly and subjectively in an artist collective. Relations in our artist collectives are poetic and multidirectional. At the same time, this can be really confusing and chaotic for people who are not on board yet, because the criteria is so opaque.

Only when we became Gudskul in 2018 did we realise the need to find a system that would be fair and helpful to our members' livelihoods. The cost of living in Jakarta is not cheap. All poetics aside, and however precariously we live as cultural workers, our housing bills continue to run up.

We have experimented with many approaches. We tried distributing monthly fees for all collective members for five years, including through the entire Covid-19 pandemic period. After many changes in our funding system, we have decided it is feasible to have economies run on projects. Committed members sign a pact that they are part of Gudskul's *majelis* (assembly), with all levels of contributions to the ecosystem, which include security, maintenance and finance. As members now have growing families and are well beyond 'post-campus youthful euphoria', we need to develop and test more improvements to our organisational structure, such as borrowing 'office-like' strategies.

Then come the questions again: *Why are we here? Why do these people come together?* Here is an anecdote of how unexplainable this all is. At a monthly *majelis* in our Gudskul – where we talked about everything from financial matters to trivial things to entertain ourselves – I was sharing an astrology app called The Pattern. It has a feature that checks the astrological bond between people based on exact birth data. We ran the function among members who were present. A surprising finding was that all of us have past life connections with one another. Amazed by this finding, we imagined what our collective past life was like.

'Maybe we were running a school or temple', I said.

'Don't be so confident, Gesya', said Berto Tukan, a renowned poet. 'Maybe we did run a temple, or maybe we were just a bunch of catfishes in Hayam Wuruk's pond ... haha', he joked.[6]

We all cackled.

Organisational Behaviour

I am aware of how carefully our members 'formalise' our practices. But again, there are the larger, more complicated questions of 'Why?' and 'How would you do that?' After working for more than ten years, I decided to go back to school. I wanted to take a step back, to see the fuller picture, to find new perspectives, to see where we get stuck and how to find other pathways in the way we work.

In pursuing my master's degree studies in Behavioural and Decision Sciences at the University of Pennsylvania, I have wanted to engage with

6 Hayam Wuruk was a king of Majapahit, a pre-Indonesian kingdom. He reigned over the islands of Java, Sumatra, Kalimantan (Borneo), Bali, Lombok and parts of modern-day Singapore up to southern Thailand.

these questions: What are the practical ways to make collective decisions with numerous cultural workers across differences of experience, age, ambition, extroversion/introversion and attention span? How can we balance the dynamic between taking initiative and following directions when pursuing a common goal? What changes have we intentionally or unintentionally made to our neighbourhood and target communities, and vice versa? How do we streamline decision-making processes within the organisational timeline, given the time needed to build trust with the community? How do we communicate our needs to stakeholders who may not understand the arts?

My degree programme has nothing to do with contemporary art, nor does it ever intersect directly with art collectives. But it feels like a fresh start, and knowledge can be transferable. As I was starting the programme, the roots of my sister's and aunt's confusions became all the more obvious to me. A course on 'Organisational Behaviour' is surprisingly more challenging – and this shakes my 'confirmation bias', causing me another existential crisis. It seems that the artist collective I had been working with over the past decade is nothing like the 'organisations/workplaces' we discuss in class. I have realised that my impediment in explaining my work in layman's term is because members of the artist collective do not operate from generally known corporate lingo. Their version of a groupthink is a mixture of street-smart, verbally agreed-up rules of thumb, created within our small art world.

'Where else can we do that?'

What could be helpful and feasible in planning a healthy future for our artist collectives is uncertain. For now, our 'chaotic' and 'undefinable' organisation relative to the 'corporate' context is, maybe, equivalent to Jakarta 32°C in the midst of art schools. Maybe the messiness and poetic aspects of our organisation are a privilege and a safe space where we can experiment, be 'naughty' with institution-building and art-making, because where else can we do that? Where else, for me at least, can hosting and doing karaoke be part of the research methodology?

My conversations with my sister and aunt about my 'job' are indefinitely resolved. It is humbling to acknowledge that my family members are expressing care. There are things we do not know and that cannot be explained by words but that can be attained through gestures and physical presence, and it is okay this way.

Leonhard Bartolomeus

I miss my partners in crime. The difficulty of thinking by myself only became apparent after I left Jakarta and started working at Yamaguchi Center for Arts and Media (YCAM) in 2019. Thinking independently, which some cultures consider equivalent to thinking critically, seems to be the norm when working in formal institutions. Yet, I feel weird. I am, evidently, uncomfortable in the role of Curator when it involves the expectation that I think and decide solely on everything. I wonder about the origin of my unease, and how I might overcome it in my context outside of Indonesia, as life moves on. Inevitably I return to the realisation that working with ruangrupa for almost a decade – between 2011 and 2019 – changed, for better or for worse, how my brain operates.

*

It took luck and tactics to be part of ruru. In 2011, when I was in my final year of study at Institut Kesenian Jakarta (Jakarta Arts Institute, IKJ), my friend Asep Topan joined ruru's art criticism workshop, and he told me about their curation workshop. I was curious about the curator's role and the knowledge required, but the workshop was cancelled due to a shortage of participants. Not long after, I graduated as an unsuccessful potter, and the curation workshop was cancelled again; so I joined ruru's two-week art criticism workshop with nine other participants, mostly in their mid-twenties. Lectures formed much of the programme, but in-between I got to *nongkrong* with some ruru members and to learn more about what they do. The workshop took place at RURU Gallery – exactly the same place where I first visited ruru, in 2008.

Curatorial workshop with ruangrupa, 2009. Courtesy ruangrupa

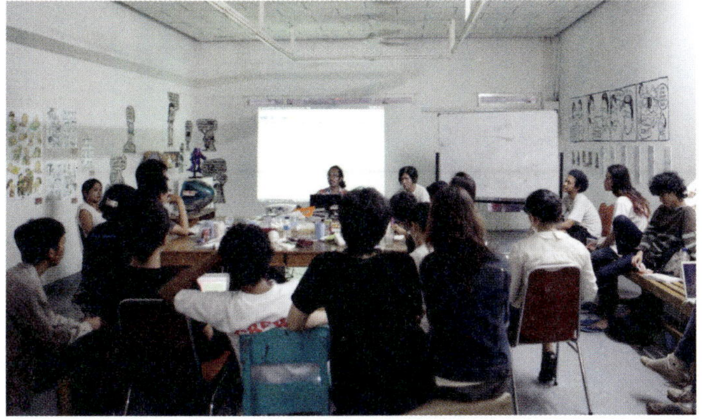

The Bahasa Indonesia term *orang dalam* can be translated as 'insider who can help you get into certain places or get a certain position', and this usually carries negative connotations. Mirwan Andan, who coordinated the workshops, was my *orang dalam* to get into ruru. He helped create my first official work at ruru when he asked me to moderate a discussion for the exhibition 'The Sweet and Sour Story of Sugar' (2012) at Jakarta's Kunstkring Art Gallery. This exhibition focused on photographs of sugar plantations in colonial Indonesia and was a collaboration between ruru and Noorderlicht, an international platform for documentary photography. Not long after, at ruru's year-end celebration, I was introduced to all as 'Andan's funny friend'.

Before these public-facing occasions, the route to gaining access to ruru was not definite. Between the art criticism workshop and the exhibition talk, Ade Darmawan, who would later become my mentor and friend, opened his solo exhibition at ARK Galerie in Jakarta, 'Human Resources Development' (2012). I was tasked with interviewing him for an article online. In our rambling conversation, Ade blurted out, 'Hey Barto, why don't you just work here?' In mild surprise, I replied that I had been working on the second floor of the ruru house, clearing up their archive for a few months already. Ade was pleasantly shocked to hear that. Years later, as I was starting my job at YCAM – entering the institution through official interviews, followed by a formal introduction to the team – ruru's looseness loomed large.

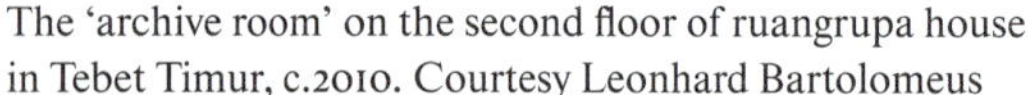
The 'archive room' on the second floor of ruangrupa house in Tebet Timur, c.2010. Courtesy Leonhard Bartolomeus

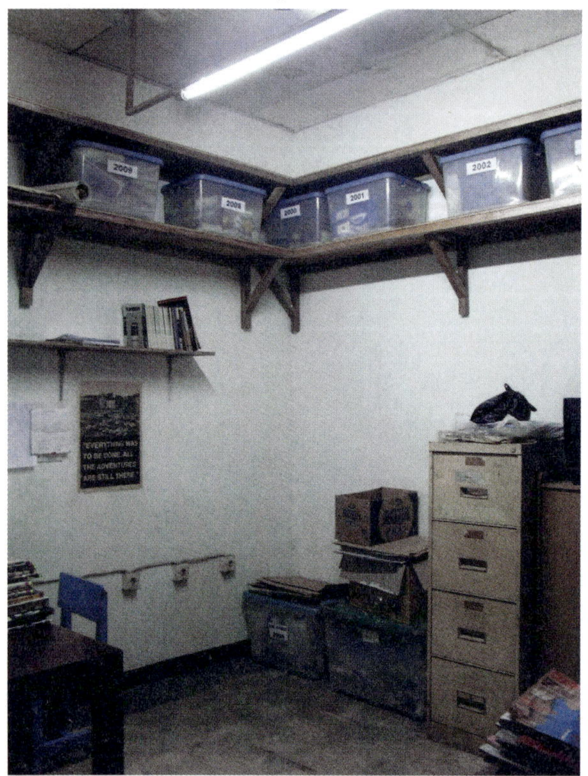

I first heard about ruru when I was a first-year at IKJ. Back then, Jakarta was still recovering from the wounds of Reformasi. In the short period of 2000 to 2005 alone, Indonesia experienced three presidential administrations.

ruru's early projects captured the sense of flux in Jakarta society. I still remember the project posters they pasted on the walls of my art school. Some of my friends would *nongkrong* at ruru's place, because it was a way to be involved with the contemporary art scene in Jakarta. The word 'collective' was too new to register, but ruru's name stood out. From hearsay, the ruru house was as a hub for conversations, for formal and informal gatherings and for the organic development of ideas.

It was not until the solo exhibition 'Happiness' (2008) by Irwan Ahmett (aka Iwang) that I finally set foot in a ruru house. Iwang had been Head of Student Senate at IKJ, but dropped out because he was not satisfied with the education. This made him famous and inspiring – his story resonated with the rebellious spirit of the time and many students were interested in his work. I personally felt his influence, too. I decided to change my major from Graphic Design to Ceramics after participating, with other students and office workers, in Iwang's project 'Change Yourself' (2005), a series of pleasingly designed self-development campaigns.

The ruru house that hosted 'Happiness' was located in the Tebet area, famous among the younger set for its plentitude of street fashion shops, food vendors and cafes. There was nothing special about the house from the outside. Its lightbox with the ruru logo in black-and-white could easily be missed. Only on the days when exhibitions opened would the house would become noticeable – many motorcycles would be parked by the entrance gate (always left unlocked). Years later I would learn that it was ruru's fourth, final and longest-lasting house.

Before 2016, ruru's identity of *ruang* was defined by such occupation, emphasising the importance of social interactions and collective reflections within the designated physical environment of a house. Moreover, I learnt from my own first visit, in 2008, that ruru was coded with multiple degrees of accessibility.

RURU Gallery, where 'Happiness' took place (and where the art criticism workshop would be held), could barely hold thirty visitors – any more risked collisions with the artworks. Judging from the structure and the style of the house, I noticed that the makeshift gallery was formerly the living room.

ruangrupa 'self-portrait', undated. Courtesy ruangrupa

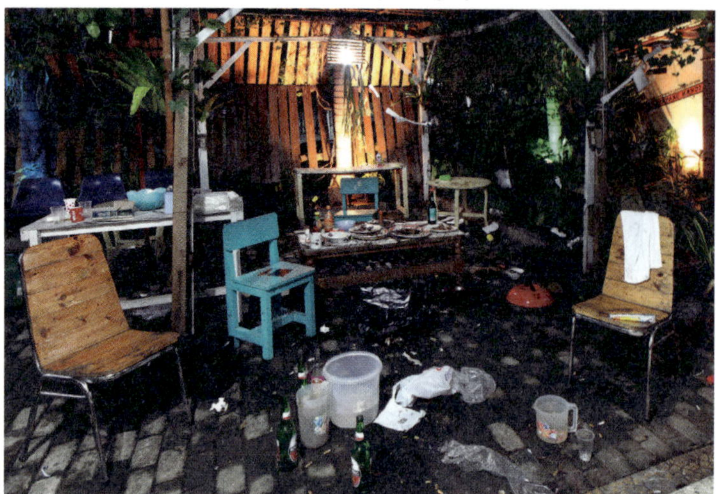

The windows were covered with plywood to create a white cube style of display. What surprised me, however, was that there were people laughing and shouting behind the large wooden partition separating the gallery from the rest of the house. It was a device to limit visitors' access to the ruru living room (originally the house's dining room) and various rooms that functioned as offices or for other specific purposes. Yet, the sign of mild restriction only made me eager to peek over the partition.

The visit left me with a strong impression, but as a semi-introverted art student, I thought ruru's place was too cool, too smart and sometimes too hipster; it was, thus, intimidating. It took me three years from that day to finally want to try some of ruru's programmes. I would find myself working in the even more covert second floor of the house and eventually, in 2014, running the gallery.

*

The physical environment of YCAM, the public art institution where I now work and which I first visited in 2014, during a research trip to Japan, stands in stark contrast to the spaces of ruru. Located on the edge of Honshu, the most prominent island in Japan, the city of Yamaguchi is home to quiet and serene neighbourhoods. The institution started operating in 2003, with the capacity to host 2500 people. Designed by the renowned architect Arata

Isozaki, its horizontal building is covered with glass panels and has a distinct wave roof, mimicking the silhouette of the natural mountain behind it. It looks like an alien spaceship, stranded but accepted, in an area of human settlement. In 2014, it appeared utterly different from anything I had seen in Indonesia, and I was impressed by its magnitude.

I started to wonder which model of art space is more effective in opening access to the public – ruru house, an ordinary residential home with a living room in disguise, or YCAM, whose extraordinary design openly announces 'This is art'? This question lingers for me, though over time I have found that important contributing factors include how the space conveys intimacy (perhaps tied to size) and how such intimacy can be expanded to be felt by non-insiders.

When ruru moved into the 6,000-square-metre Gudang Sarinah warehouse in 2016, the issue of intimacy surfaced with strong tension around whether ruru should grow large or embrace the idea of de-growth, keeping small. The large warehouse offered an increased capacity to work, but it also put more distance between ruru and its friends. In other words, the warehouse permitted ruru to open itself up to a much wider audience, at the expense of close-knit relationships within ruru's circuit. Moving into the warehouse proved a tactical decision to solve some of the challenges ruru had faced for years, such as limited space for public events (especially performance-related ones) and income generation from commercial programmes for sustainability (something ruru had been trying to do with RURU

The Yamaguchi Center for Arts and Media (YCAM), designed by Arata Isozaki. Courtesy YCAM

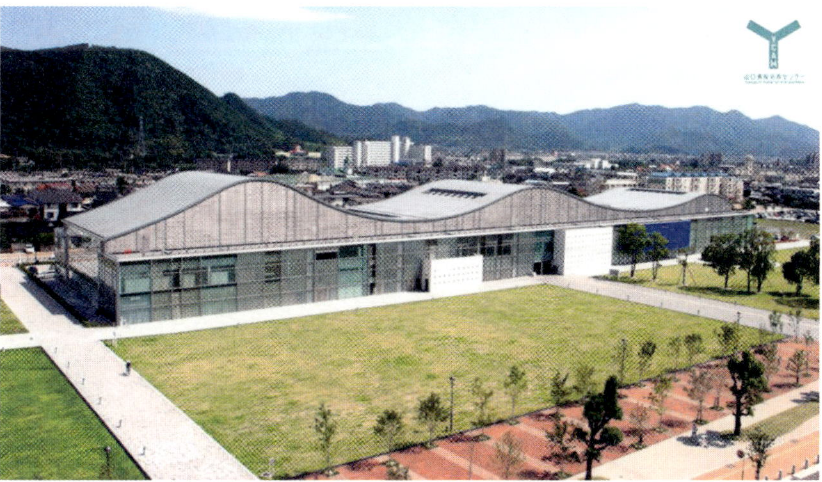

farid rakun's note, taken during a discussion in Copenhagen, 2016. Courtesy Leonhard Bartolomeus

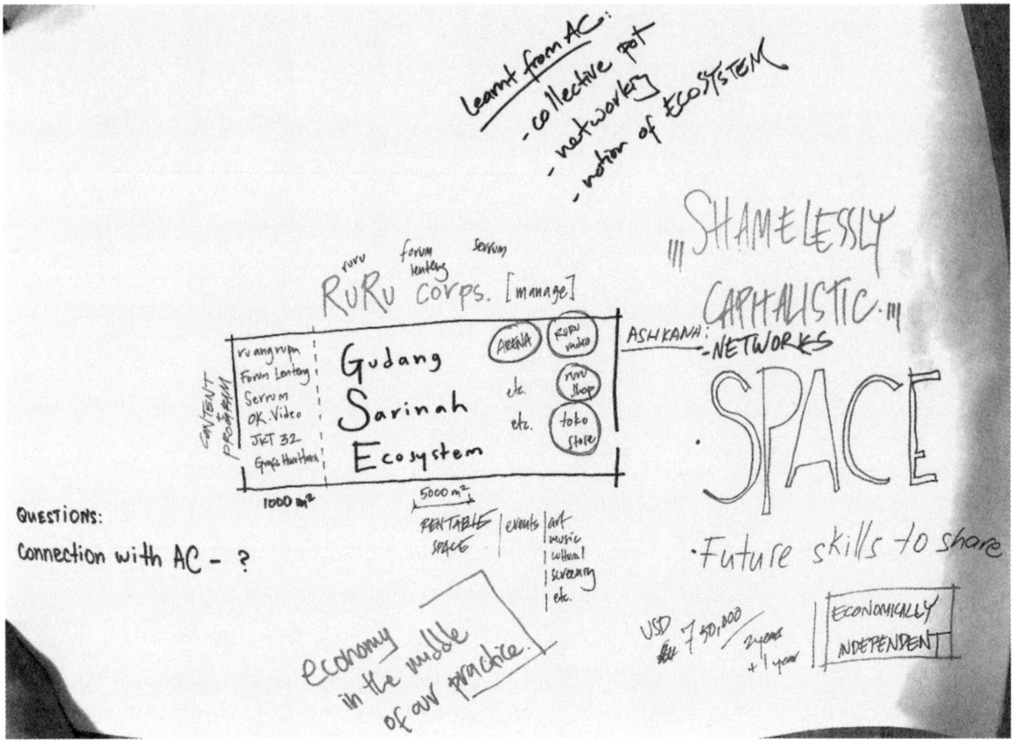

Mindmap showing the transformation from Institute ruangrupa to Gudskul, undated.
Courtesy Leonhard Bartolomeus

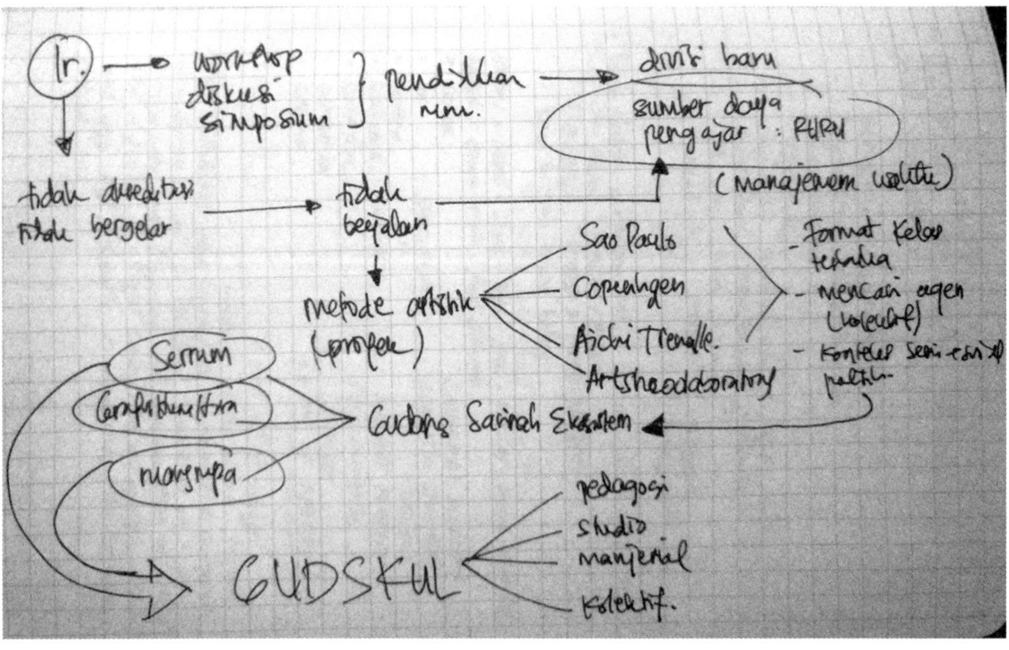

Corps since 2011). I was indeed alright with ruru's decision, though farid rakun joked that ruru was becoming 'shamelessly capitalistic'.

When I met Ade again in 2024, in a workshop for art students in Tokyo, I saw a return to 'home' as a cultural condition for easy access and hospitality. He emphasised the concept of *lembaga seni rumahan*, which I translate freely to 'the aesthetics of home-based art institutions'. Ade had talked about home on an earlier occasion, when he noted:

> Growing up, our home was always open to extended family and friends. We were constantly hosting and welcoming guests. It is a practice deeply ingrained in Indonesian culture, where guests are considered a blessing. This early experience shaped many Indonesians' understandings about home as a space that exists between the private and public realms. In our culture, there is no strict division between these two spheres; they co-exist without conflict.[1]

Central to ruru's identity and practice is the concept of *ruang* (space) as a house with a living room that is by default a home. *Ruang* extends beyond a purely physical understanding to encompass social, ideological and strategic dimensions. The point of articulating 'home-based art institutions' follows this logic, rejecting the idea of a canonical institution and emphasising something more casual, intimate and flexible. In fact, as of 2020, I have brought in ruru friends to try to turn YCAM into a home-based art centre for the public.

*

While the ruru house provided the cultural condition for gathering and hosting, working at ruru for me was not without challenges. These included internal ambiguity and external chaos. ruru did not like to talk about formalities, but I was quite surprised to find out there was an institutional structure within, organised by a director, manager, programmer, accountant and even security guard.

For ruru, a certain degree of ambiguity was not necessarily harmful, as most of the people working inside recognised the value of informal gatherings, open-ended discussions and the unpredictable outcomes that often emerge from collaborative processes. This was followed by an emphasis

1 Ade Darmawan, 'Berakar dan Menjalar: Lumbung Sebagai Model Ekonomi dan Estetika Organisasi Seni' (Taking Root and Spreading Out: Lumbung as an Economic and Aesthetic Model of Art Organisation), Jakarta Arts Council Annual Cultural Speech conference, 10 November 2022.

on process over product, building relationships and fostering a sense of community. It also meant that ruru's management system was often more concerned with creating an environment for creative fermentation and collective learning than with achieving predetermined goals or adhering to strict timelines.

I do not want to categorise the ruru system as 'chaotic' – even though it is really tempting to do so. That everybody and nobody owns ruru became a real challenge once ruru became a bigger institution. To this day, rather than a traditional top-down hierarchy, ruru favours a distributed leadership model wherein decisions are often made collectively. (The introduction of *majelis*, or assembly, in documenta fifteen could be an example of this.) While this promotes a sense of shared ownership and encourages participation, it can also lead to ambiguity, making it difficult to assign clear responsibilities. Only vague conclusions are reached around questions such as who will decide the presentation style or who should deal with administration.

Dealing with chaos from the outside has been hard learning for ruru. The hiring of security services in 2015 followed many cases of theft in the ruru house, due to the casual traffic of people. ruru knew some of the guests visiting the house, but there were also less familiar faces who came just once or twice, or only for music events or movie screenings. Whether to increase the security measures or maintain the chaos became a point of contention. When ruru moved to Gudang Sarinah the following year, chaos control became an even more serious issue.

*

Ruru's ambiguous nature has made it one of the best places for me to learn and unlearn many things: writing, editing, making spreadsheets, drafting funding proposals and working on financial reports; also, Indonesian politics and art history, philosophy, music, film, art display techniques and curatorial work. I think ruru's role as a learning space is something that people have taken for granted, even as its educational platform has extended from Jakarta 32°C and OK.Video to art criticism, curation workshops and various one-off projects.

In 2015, ruru attempted to merge all its learning programmes under a new division called Institut ruangrupa (abbreviated to Ir., a mockery of the colonial-era title for engineers). This non-degree-conferring institute was imagined to foster passion for hands-on learning and knowledge production in the next generation of creatives, including artists, curators, managers and more. Planned to be two-year programme that would turn the city into a living classroom, with participants engaging in practice and discussion while gaining the skills needed to be resilient and thoughtful contributors to the art world, Institut ruangrupa almost never saw the light of day.

It was only when ruru were invited to participate in the 2016 Aichi Triennale that this holistic idea was realised. The idea of Ir. was translated into the three-month ruru Gakkō (ruru school) at the festival, where we learnt much about the potential of our knowledge tools and the many possibilities to educate ourselves as a group.[2] When the project was over, all involved thought that this could be a model to sustain our collective work.

Through ruru Gakkō, ruru indirectly imagined ideas to be done together with friends from other collectives interested in learning through art. ruru later decided to fuse with Serrum and Grafis Huru Hara to create a new identity: we worked together to create the foundation of Gudskul Ekosistem alongside friends and directed the curriculum to offer opportunities for people interested in collective practices. This direction made me interested in exploring various ways of working together with others.

ruru Gakkō (ruru school) at the 2016 Aichi Triennale. Courtesy Leonhard Bartolomeus

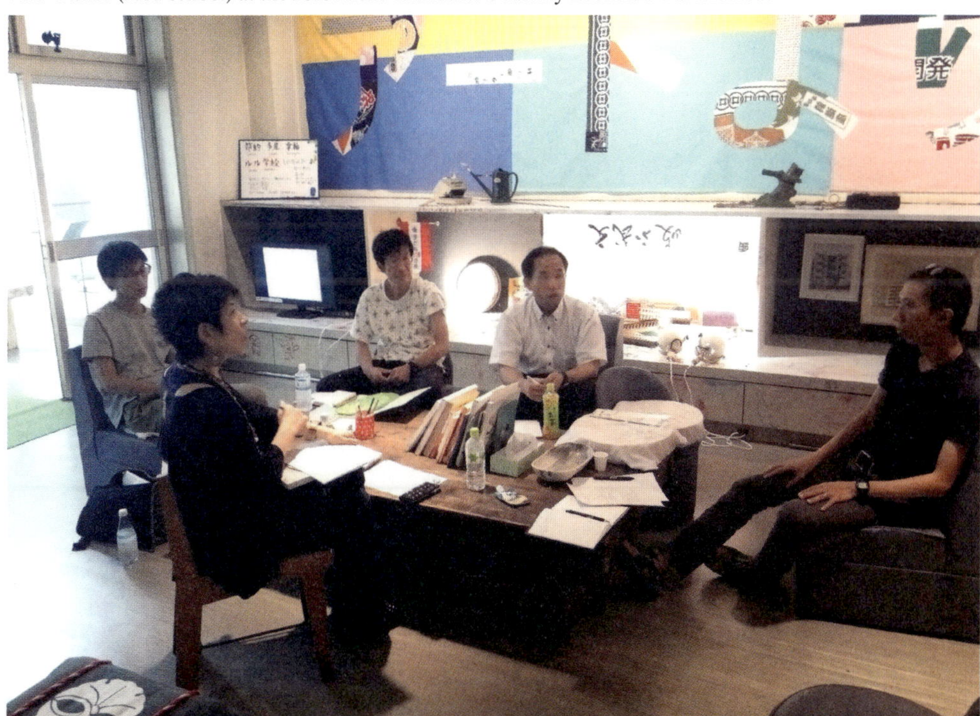

2 The school benefitted from the help of local coordinator Midori Hirota, who has since then published a number of publications in Japan on Indonesian collective art practices.

After Aichi, I was preoccupied with the idea of temporary, formless collectivity. I felt the urge to explore how a 'collective mind' might work without actually forcing others to label themselves as a 'collective'. The prototype of this idea is Kolektif Kurator Kampung (Urban Poor Curators), which I co-founded with seven other curators from Jakarta, Tangerang, Jatiwangi, Semarang and Surabaya during a workshop ruru organised with Jakarta Arts Council in 2017 – which in itself was a mutation from the earlier ruru curatorial workshops. We collaborated with the Urban Poor Consortium (UPC) to create five projects across various *kampungs* in Jakarta, and we released one publication and an unsuccessful YouTube programme. Our group sustained itself for about two years before we failed with good grace. As Gugun Muhammad from UPC shared with us, the collective mindset of people in *kampung* is accelerated by the pursuit of joyous moments. They see art as an escape mechanism; a temporal burst of joy and creativity; a celebration.

My second attempt at a formless collective happened in the context of 'Alternative Education', a three-year project that took place at YCAM from 2020 to 2023. We attempted to open up the institution by using art as a tool for learning, and to create that temporal burst of joy and creativity. The first thing I do in such contexts is find a partner in crime, to counter me in discussions and to balance my mind. And so I approached the Education team at YCAM and asked them to be my co-curators for this project. YCAM in this sense is flexible, offering a similar atmosphere to those I have known in working with ruru and friends. Moreover, the first artist that I invited to work on this project was Serrum, who has been working with art pedagogy in Indonesia for a long time. Unfortunately, they could not come to Japan because of the Covid-19 pandemic, but I continued the project using tools they had prepared.

Serrum, the YCAM Education team and I had an exciting debate about how to interpret 'ease of access'. Based on their experience in the Indonesian art world, Serrum held the view that an exhibition without too many guidelines allows wandering in the exhibition space, putting visitors at ease. The YCAM Education team counter-suggested that, based on their understanding of the common traits of Japanese people, an exhibition with set boundaries allows visitors to understand what they can and cannot do within a space, which puts visitors much more at ease. Attuning to the Education team's observations, Serrum proposed several ideas to work their way around.

'KURIKULAB: Moving Class', exhibition by Serrum, YCAM, 30 October 2021 – 27 February 2022. Courtesy YCAM

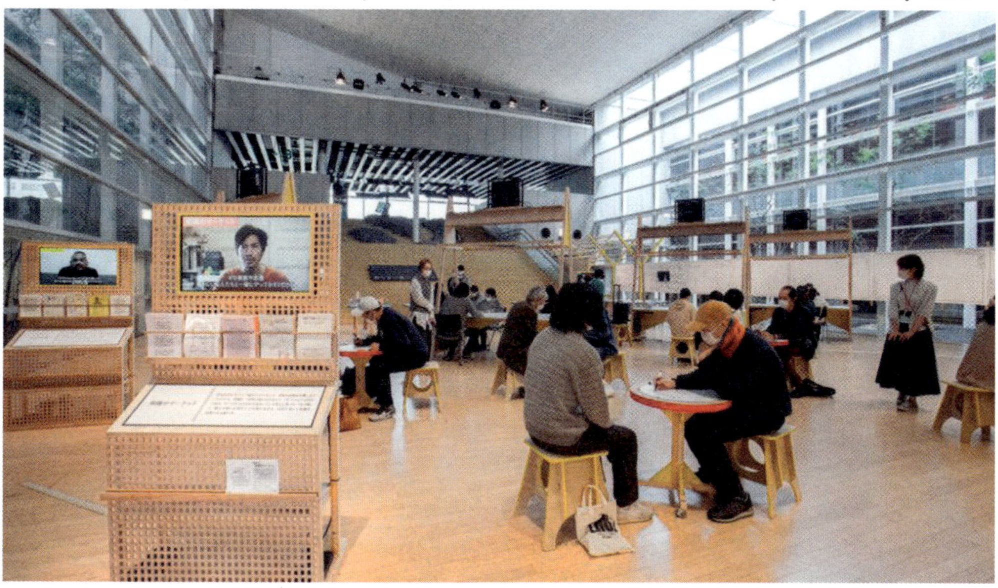

Play Book zine created by Serrum for 'KURIKULAB: Moving Class' exhibition, YCAM, 30 October 2021 – 27 February 2022. Courtesy Serrum & YCAM

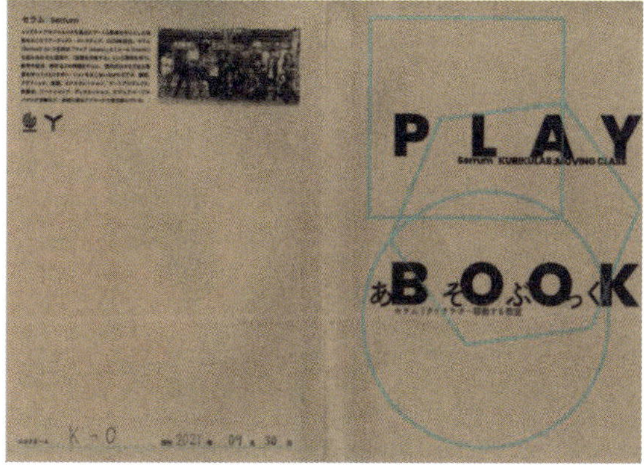

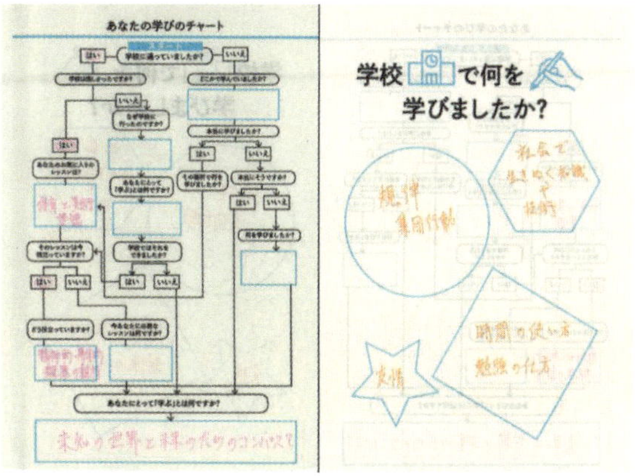

There were many things concerning how collective work might be beneficial for us that needed to be tried and possibly improved upon. Our formless collective ended up creating a simple zine, which became something of an activities book, which could be regarded as delineating 'boundaries' while making room for collaboration between artists and visitors. The project took final form in 2023, at which point I decided to form yet another temporary collective and to create a 'speculative library' inside the institution.

I feel a lot of the elements within these projects resonate with my experiences of ruru. My focus has recently shifted to the idea of 'Arte Util' (Useful Art), a term the Cuban artist Tania Bruguera has popularised. To my knowledge, Bruguera's connection to ruru goes back to a public lecture on art's relation to politics that she gave at Gudskul Ekosistem in 2019.

*

One day in the summer of 2018, during the preparation for Gudskul Ekosistem, I had a conversation with MG Pringotono and Ajeng Nurul Aini about how collectives articulate processes of knowledge transfer. MG said that he felt this process can be like a virus – infectious. Once you get infected, your body becomes a carrier to spread and pay it forward. He used this analogy because of ruru's influence on the development of Serrum, and how Serrum influenced Grafis Huru Hara. Influence thus multiplies, over and over again. Probably this was our intention in creating Gudskul Ekosistem. I personally carry ruru and have spread it in Yamaguchi. I think that with documenta fifteen, ruru spread the virus more widely, and I hope this can be a good thing for the world.

Look for things that can make people around you roll their eyes, things that make them tick.

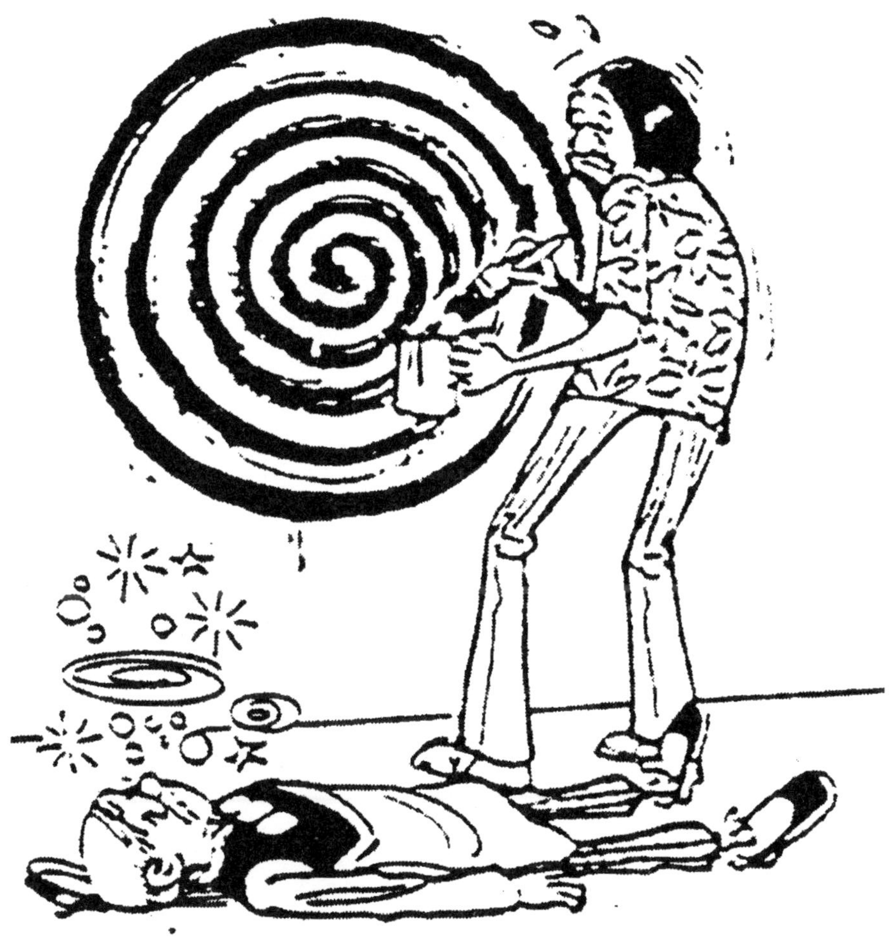

In this section we open up some of the methodological implications of ruru. We highlight questions of theory and practice for researching and archiving ruangrupa, and gather critical reflection on some of the broader ideas – including post-Reformasi narratives, self-organisation and 'collective practice' – through which ruru's histories are told.

Wing Chan & Arianna Mercado

Screenshot taken from ruangrupa website in August 2024, www.ruangrupa.id. Courtesy ruangrupa

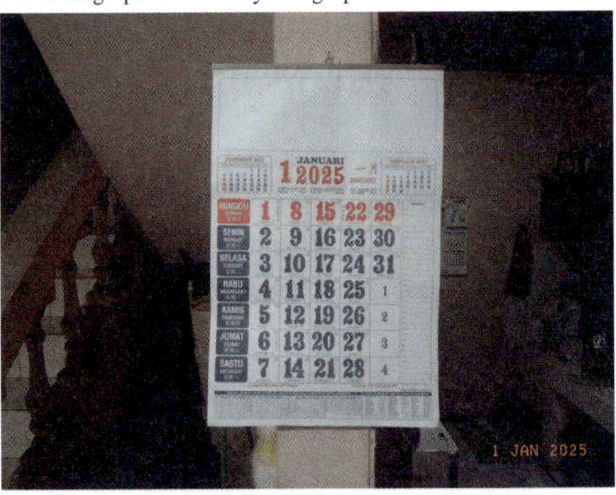

Happy New Year 2023! - ruangrupa

We arrived in Jakarta again in July 2024. The city can tell you a lot about ruangrupa's approaches, methodologies and in-jokes, as we knew from talking with ruru members and friends over recent months, and also years.[1] We had travelled for 23 hours, across 7 time zones, and when we were about to land, the screen on the plane showed 32° Celsius in the city. Outside the airport, the sun was shining. It was the dry season. The crackling sound of cloves burning and a sweet scent synchronised with every long breath we took and held. Our phones automatically directed us to local time GMT+7, but all the physical clocks we encountered that day – at our Airbnb, at the *warung* (street stall), at ruru's quasi-homebase, Gudskul – told different times.

Young Love in the Time of Reformasi

At some earlier point on this research journey, we began imagining ourselves in Jakarta in the early 2000s, after the beginning of Reformasi. We obsessively listened to playlists, read novels and watched films as we scrutinised every detail and easter egg in ruru's visual archive. One of the films we watched was *Ada Apa dengan Cinta?* (What's Up with Cinta?, 2002, directed by Rudy Soedjarwo), a romantic drama that became a cult classic as a story of young love during a time of political change. The film follows Cinta (named for 'love' in Indonesian) as she slowly peels away from her friend group and bourgeois lifestyle to spend time with her crush, Rangga, at second-hand bookshops and gigs, to the confusion of many of her peers. Viewers eventually learn about Rangga's family history and their relationship with left-leaning movements in Indonesia, and these lead Rangga and his father to emigrate at the film's end. *Ada Apa dengan Cinta?* is peppered with sweet scenes of teenage romance and touches of youth culture; it also

1 It is always difficult to pinpoint when a research process begins and ends, but the conversations that led to this book became more concrete around 2018–19, during discussions on ruangrupa's histories and archives between farid rakun, David Morris, Wing Chan and the MRes Art: Exhibition Studies crew at Central Saint Martins. These discussions continued to develop through collaborative student projects exploring the digital ruru archive. Other notable experiences informing the research process were Arianna Mercado's residency at Riwanua library at Gudskul Ekosistem, in 2022; research visits by David Morris to Gudang Sarinah Ekosistem and other art organisations in Jakarta and Yogyakarta, in 2017; experiences of documenta fifteen, in 2022; David and Wing's participation in the Pekan Kebudayaan Nasional (National Cultural Week) in Jakarta, in 2023; and, not least, innumerable discussions with colleagues and friends who have known ruru since their beginnings, as well as with past and present ruru members themselves.

addresses a nation in transition. The film distils the concerns of the Indonesian youth at the turn of the century, their claims to freedom, their rebellion against and attachment to collectivity, their creative exploration and the social milieu of a regime change.[2]

As we consumed English-translated Reformasi-era cult classics, we began to imagine, too, the previous, oppressive regime, which had lasted for over thirty years in Indonesia. Some ruru members were born into it. Once Reformasi came, gatherings were no longer restricted to groups of five people. ruru's birth emerged from a larger group of art students and graduates at the cusp of adulthood, who were pondering what space might enable them to support each other's creative lives in Jakarta – their sprawling, congested and business-oriented home city.[3] ruru was officially born as a *yayasan* (foundation) in 2000 – a term often used for humanitarian or religious affairs. They like to claim the first day of April, April Fools' Day, as their birthday, which may or may not be true.

It would not be a stretch to say that ruru's relationships at this time mirrored young love and forbidden romance, much like what is witnessed in *Ada Apa dengan Cinta?*[4] What is remarkable about the romance of ruru, though, is that it has magically survived for over two and a half decades. Its founding members are no longer young. Life has passed and family duties emerged. In the back of our minds, we wondered how such factors had challenged or fuelled ruru's romance.

2 See Enin Supriyanto's 'Forces of Socio-political Change in Indonesia', in this volume. Along with *Ada Apa dengan Cinta?*, we watched various historical documentaries on the era; read a range of novels including Ayu Utami's *Saman* (1998) and Pramoedya Ananta Toer's *This Earth of Mankind* (1980), and investigative histories such as Vincent Bevins's *The Jakarta Method* (2020); ate meals and talked with women historians and writers at Wisma Siswa Merdeka, a hall for Indonesian international students in northwest London. We have hoped that, through pop culture, literature and conversations (rather than history books), we can better grasp the milieu in which ruru came to be.

3 See Abidin Kusno's 'ruangrupa's Jakarta', in this volume.

4 To our surprise, we encountered copies of Chairil Anwar's existential poetry book *Aku* (1943), a text constantly referenced in *Ada Apa dengan Cinta?*, and the vinyl record of the film's soundtrack in the basement level of Blok M Mall in South Jakarta during our trip. The sound track was sitting next to White Shoes & the Couples Company's *Topstar Collection* (Remastered 2023), below Goodnight Electric's *Love and Turbo Action* (2004) and across from Dara Puspita (Flower Girls)'s *Suara Senja* (2024), all in the same cassette shop that was featured in the music video of C'mon Lennon's hit song *Aku Cinta J.A.K.A.R.T.A.* (2004).

Floorplan of ruangrupa's last house in Tebet, Jakarta, drawn by Indra Ameng. The studios of the indie bands White Shoes & the Couples Company and Goodnight Electric were located on the second floor. Many of the musicians graduated from art school. Courtesy Indra Ameng

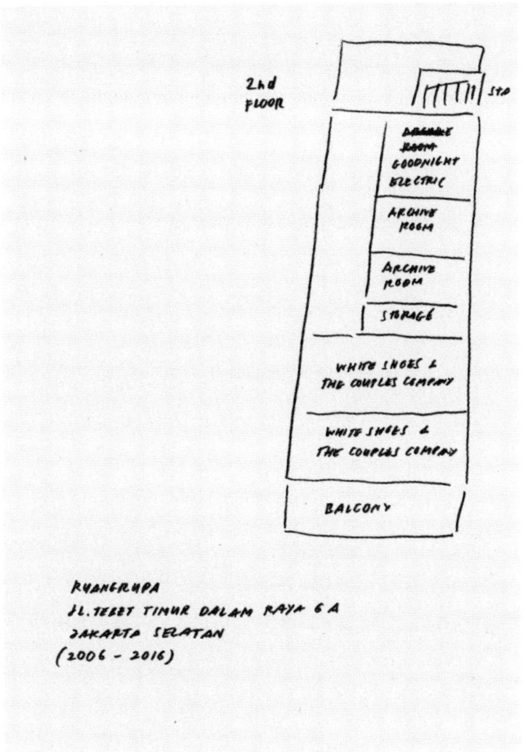

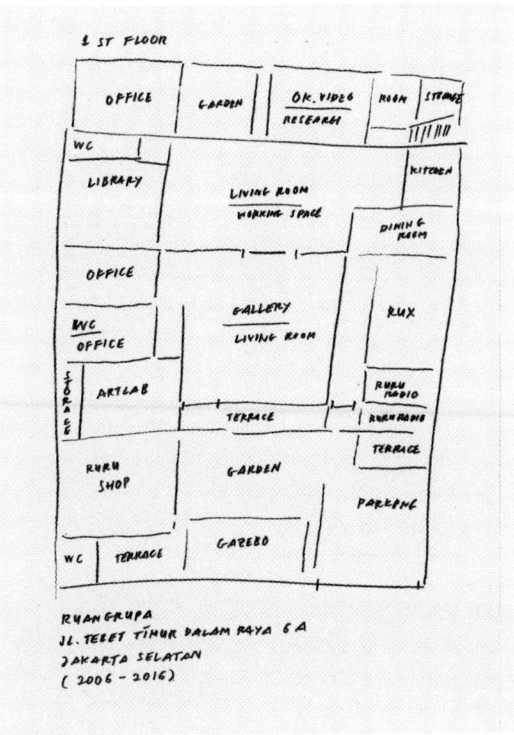

An early task for us was finding ruru members.[5] The list has fluctuated and shifted over the years, and the grey areas are known to be enormous. ruru's website was professionally hacked in September 2024 and remains non-functional at the time of writing, but from memory we can recall the current 'official' members and their rough division of labour: Reza Afisina and Iswanto Hartono oversee ArtLab, from their present base in Europe; Ajeng Nurul Aini manages all of ruru's programmes, having originally joined as a journalism student interested in the OK.Video festival; Indra Ameng manages music-related events and once served as the primary visual documenter of ruru's early activities; Mirwan Andan, Ade Darmawan and farid rakun make the most frequent appearances in interviews and symposia (Andan is a walking dictionary; farid is considered ruru's foreign minister or diplomat; and Ade has a good sense of reading the room and mediating energies, and doesn't hate maths – valuable skills for an organisation's director, which was Ade's 'official' role in ruangrupa, as frequently acknowledged in funding reports for at least the first fifteen years);[6] Narpati Awangga (Oomleo) travels; Daniella F. Praptono (Kunil) oversees RURU Kids and finances; and Julia Sarisetiati (Sari) coordinates Gudskul curriculum, having previously co-initiated RURU Corps and been once a manager at ruru and the first to organise ruru's archives.

Within this group of ten are three generations of practitioners. The group skews male, as it always has – especially in its early years it was known as a 'boys' club'– but the gender dynamic has changed over time and is always more complex than a simple 'head count'.[7] Half of the current members have known each other since the mid-1990s through art school networks between Jakarta and Yogyakarta (Jogja).

Another way to locate ruru members is to follow official documentation as well as promotional ephemera. To look at just the first three years: The founding members listed in ruru's launch and fundraising exhibition were Ronny Agustinus, Ade Darmawan, Oky Arfie Hutabarat, Lilia Nursita, Hafiz Rancajale and Rithmi Widanarko;[8] for ruru's participation in the 2002 Gwangju Biennale, Irwan Ahmett (Iwang) appears too. ruru's exhibition 'print 2000+2 project' (2002) at Taman Ismail Marzuki, Jakarta, provides

5 See chitarum's 'Apa Kabar: Conversations with ruangrupa', in this volume.

6 See Ade Darmawan's 'Big Kiss from Ade Darmawan' (2002) and farid rakun's 'How Little I Know about You' (2018), both reprinted in this volume.

7 For a critique on the gender dynamic at ruru, see Melani Budianta's 'Political Economy and Aesthetics of Space: Genealogy of ruangrupa's *Lumbung* Practice', in this volume.

8 See Ronny Agustinus's 'A Cool Beer Conversation and 3 Years After' (2001), reprinted in this volume.

ruangrupa 'self-portrait', c.2011. Courtesy ruangrupa. Photo: Julia Sarisetiati

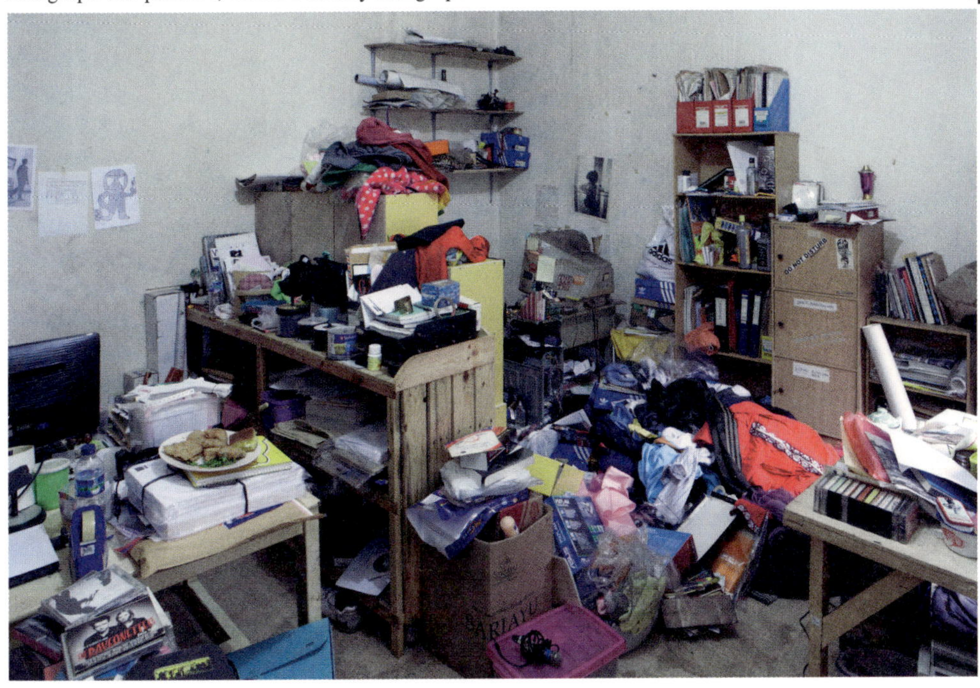

the names of more members: Mahesa Almeida (Dony), Mushowir Bing, Matheus Bondan, Henry Foundation (Batman), Oscar de Kemano (Oca), Anggun Priambodo, Tisna Sanjaya and Teresa Stok. Then, in materials for ruru's legendary exhibition 'Lekker Eten Zonder Betalen' (2003) at Cemeti Art House in Jogja, the names include Aditya Satria, Farah Wardani (Wawah) and Elim Welisangiang, amongst others.[9]

A later group portrait came to us in a series of playful ruru 'character cards', created by Oomleo using an early digital aesthetic. Additional members we noted include: Agus (Samsuga), who has done many things and was born and brought up in the Tebet neighbourhood in South Jakarta, where three ruru houses were based between 2001 and 2016; Laurentius Daniel (Dokter Lory), a professional accountant who has helped Kunil and Ajeng manage auditing processes; Ugeng T. Moetidjo and Ardi Yunanto, editors of ruru's publication *Karbon*;[10] and Mahardika Yudha (Diki), who managed OK.Video and video documentations of ruru activities.[11] In the cards' images, ruru members hold homely 'props': a puppy, a foodstuff, a broom. The superpowers attributed to them on these cards grounded them as diligent cultural practitioners, while filtering ruru's fun-loving spirit.

9 See Arianna Mercado's 'Tasty Meal Without Paying', in this volume.
10 See Ardi Yunanto's 'A Decade at *Karbon*', in this volume.
11 See Umi Lestari and Mahardika Yudha's 'Between Art and Media Technologies in Indonesia: Genealogy of OK.Video', in this volume.

ruangrupa character cards created by Narpati Awangga (aka Oomleo), mid-2000s.
Courtesy the artist & Ade Darmawan

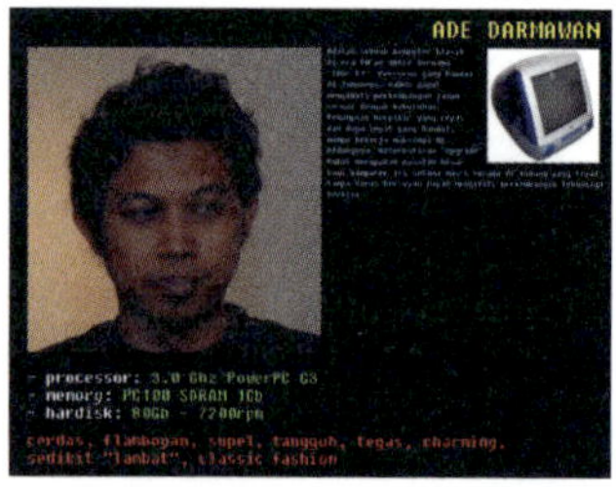

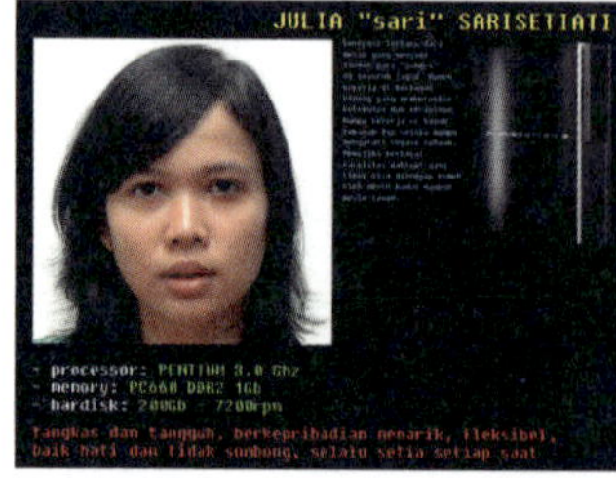

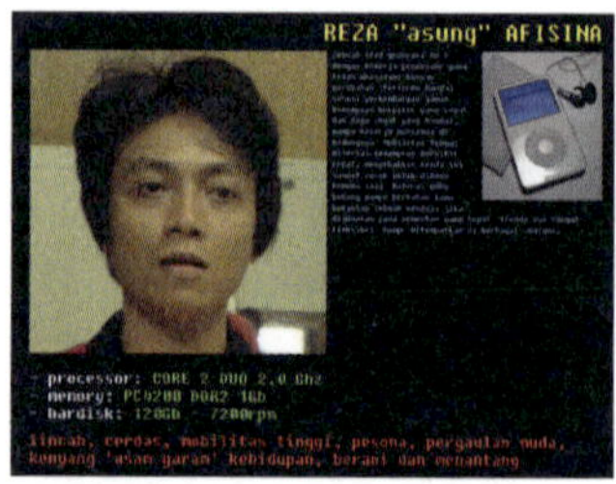

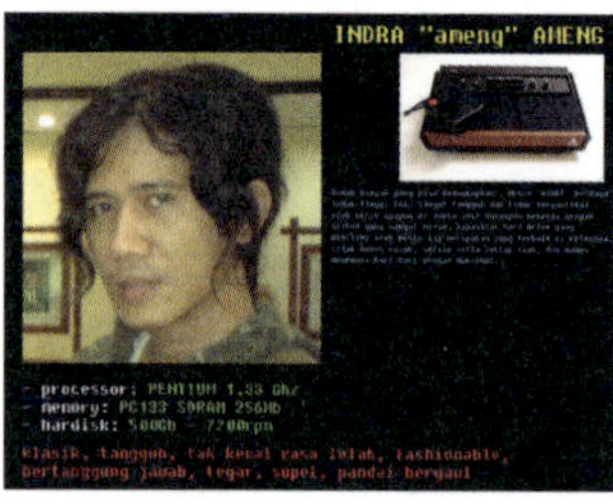

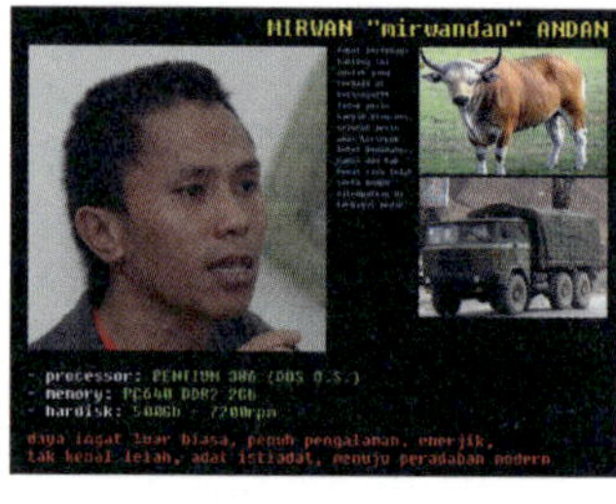

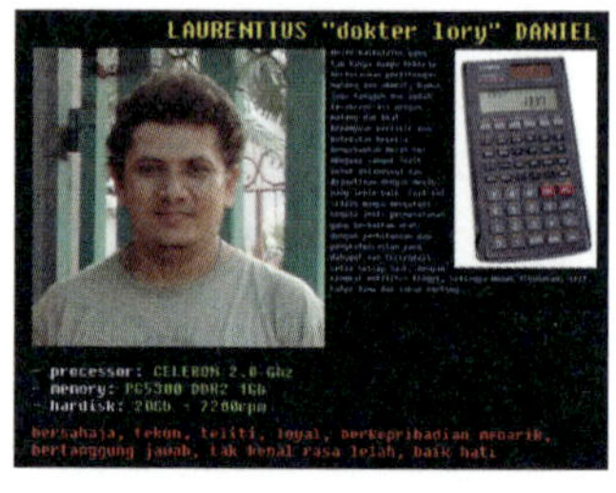

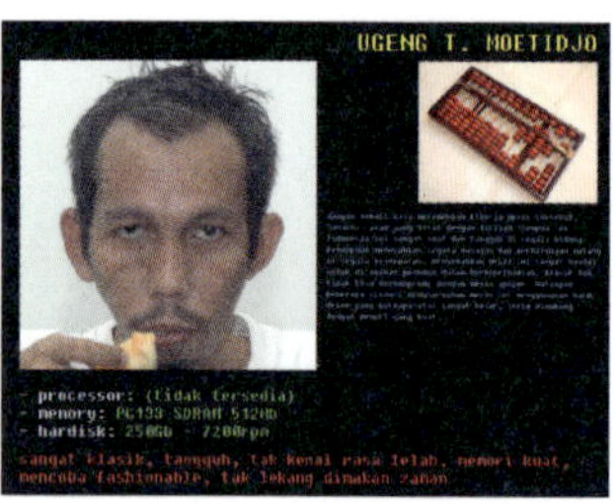

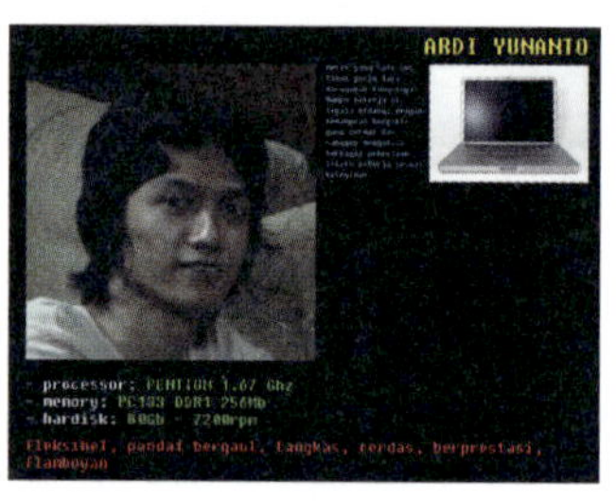

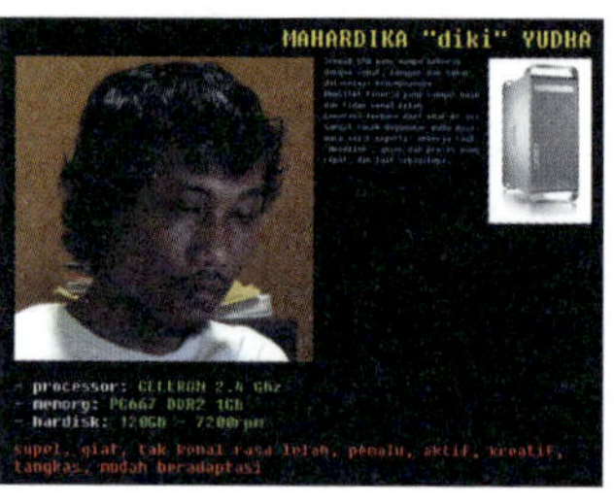

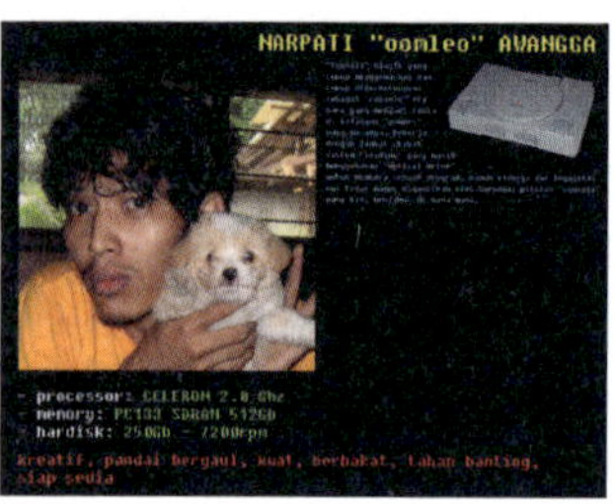

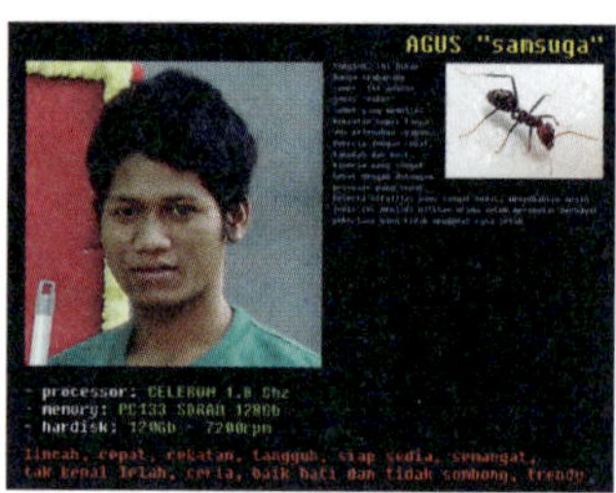

Leafing through RURU Corps booklets, sent by ruru to potential clients of their arts services, we also saw Andang Kelana (then part of Forum Lenteng and the Jakarta 32°C forum of college students), Maya (RURU Corps manager) and MG Pringgotono (part of Serrum Art Handling), in addition to Sari and Reza. These friends represent only a small portion of ruru's large network of support, cultivated over the past 25 years. If ruru's total membership cannot be accounted for, it is due to an abundance, rather than a lack, of documentation. Their digital archive amounts to 49,402 broadly and loosely sorted items, to begin with. Sometimes we joke that our desire to grasp the exact details of ruru is akin to thinking we can spot a handful of confetti through a haze of smoke.

Official members aside, there are also people around ruru who are always present but not necessarily on the record. Simon Danang Anggoro (Gentong), for example, is always around Gudskul, receiving visitors and maintaining ruru's archives.[12] Ary Sendy (Jimged) is also always there, sees ruru as a playground, and once managed the coffee shop Ipok Icon at Gudskul. They each have their own creative practice, like many ruru members. And Leonhard Bartolomeus (Barto) and Gesyada Siregar (Gesya) relate insider stories about growing up in ruru, narratives that escape through the cracks of day-to-day work.[13]

ruru's Resources

The more we have learned about ruru, the more we have marvelled at their flexibility in finding ways to subsidise what they do – an ingenuity they are more likely to claim as simple practical necessity for the context in which they work. ruru's initial funding emerged at a time when Indonesia was becoming increasingly open to international organisations and investors, with foreign NGOs arriving to fund and support various cultural initiatives.

ruru's seed funding came partially from RAIN, a resource and knowledge sharing initiative that formed in 2000 (and in 2007 evolved into the Arts Collaboratory network), supported by Dutch funding from DOEN Foundation, Hivos, Rijksakademie van Beeldende Kunsten and the Dutch Ministry of Foreign Affairs. They have sporadically solicited additional financial support from the Jakarta offices of various European and Asian cultural centres, namely: Japan Foundation Indonesia (from 2000); Goethe Institut Indonesia (from 2001); and French Cultural Centre Indonesia (from 2003), as well as the Ford Foundation, a private American organisation (from 2009). ruru has

12 See Ugeng T. Moetidjo's 'Archives on Space, People and Idea in the Process' (2010), reprinted in this volume.

13 See Leonhard Bartolomeus's 'My Partners in Crime: On Different Institutional Styles' and Gesyada Siregar's 'What I Wish I Had Told My Aunt and Sibling about My "Job"', both in this volume.

also received one-off funding from embassies and international organisations, including an award from UNESCO (2002) and state organisations such as the Jakarta Arts Council.

Over the years, and since the 2010s in particular, ruru has experimented with different ways to self-fund its programme and, occasionally, salaries. They have participated in biennials as artists or as the organiser, including the Aichi Triennale (2016), the Asia Pacific Triennial of Contemporary Art (2012), documenta fifteen (2022), the Gwangju Biennale (2002), the Istanbul Biennial (2005; 2012–13), the Jakarta Biennale (2013, 2015 and 2017), the São Paulo Bienal (2014), the Singapore Biennale (2011) and Sonsbeek (2016). In engaging in these projects, they redirected any artists' or curators' fees to cross-subsidise other ruru interests.

ruru's broad network has been a valuable resource, for both intellectual and material support. Since its beginnings, ruru was endorsed by senior figures in the Jakarta cultural scene, such as poet Toeti Heraty and sculptor and activist Dolorosa Sinaga, and supported by artist peers (artists from Jakarta, Bandung and Jogja – the three cities in Indonesia with historically

ruru house equipped with computers with its seed funding, 2001. Courtesy ruangrupa

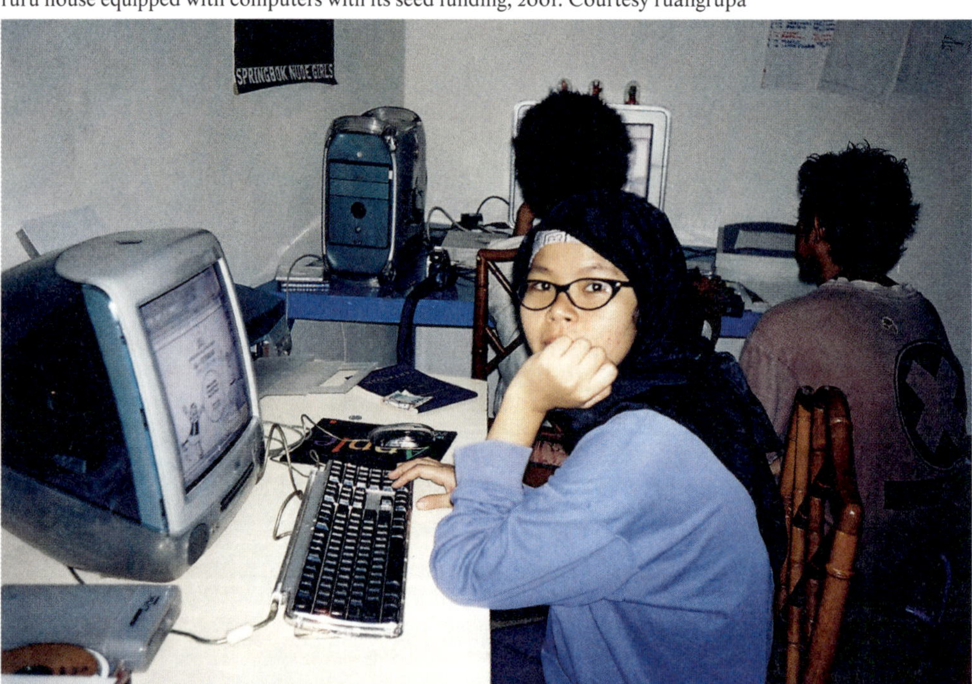

'Garbage Sale' at ruangrupa house, 2003. Courtesy ruangrupa

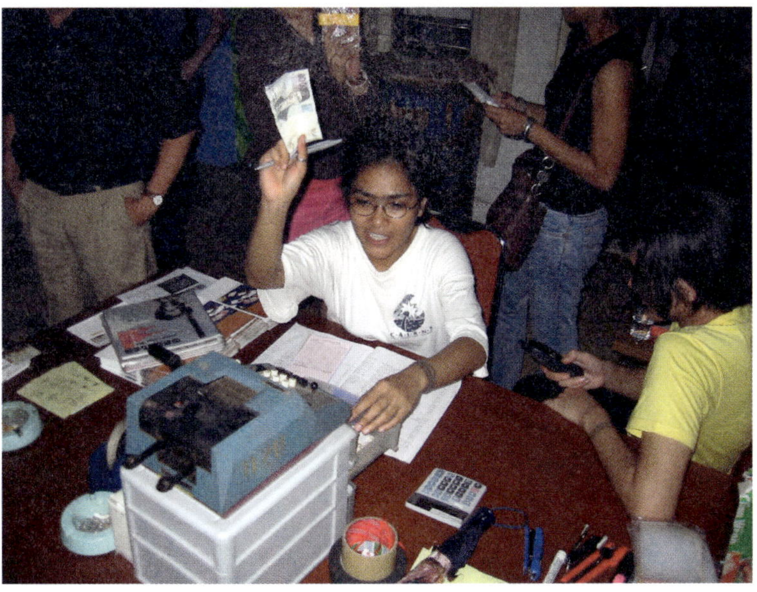

established art schools – contributed a proportion of sales of their work from ruru's inaugural fundraising exhibition). Friends have also helped ruru survive by acting as their suppliers: for instance, Agus operates an antique furniture and woodshop in Tebet and has provided materials for individual ruru members' exhibitions; Lilia Nursita, ruru founding member, runs the printing press Gajah Hidup in South Jakarta, which has printed most of the promotional materials and publications for ruru activities, offering a longer credit period and faster production in cases of urgency. (This press is also the printer for the leftist literature publisher Marjin Kiri, run by founding ruru member Ronny Agustinus and physically located within Gudskul, at Gudside.) To this day, ruru has hosted events such as 'Garbage Sale' (since 2003) and its successor, Holy Market (since 2009, typically held during Ramadan or Christmas), to help artist-friends exhibit work, clear overstock, make some quick cash and build networks. These examples demonstrate the micro-economy supporting and developing adjacent to ruru activities – crucial for ruru's survival and well-being but easily overlooked if we read ruru's resources only through sponsorship logos.[14]

14 See David Teh's 'Who Cares a Lot? ruangrupa as Curatorship' (2012), reprinted in this volume. ruru's programmes additionally received venue and equipment support. For example, OK.Video and Jakarta 32°C received venue support from National Gallery of Indonesia and Taman Ismail Marzuki. They also did not shy away from working with corporations, including the electronics brands NEC and Pioneer to obtain DVD players and monitors as well as the tobacco company Sampoerna to support the college student forum programme Jakarta 32°C in cities outside of Jakarta.

RURU Corps was founded in 2011, at a time when funding from external sources was becoming less available.[15] It is a 'creative bureau' and registered business that provides services such as art direction, book design, conceptual and content development, curatorial consultation, editing, event and exhibition design, art handling, film/video, identity creation and promotional design, product design and website design. While these for-hire services available demonstrate ruru's many talents, they may be seen, more importantly, as resulting from the group's early experimentation in creating alternative economic models to effectively finance their regular activities through external commercial work. The self-funding model of collectively sharing surplus resources to reduce risk was further developed during their Gudang Sarinah Ekosistem era (2015–18) and has continued since via Gudskul Ekosistem (from 2018), which includes the business quarter Gudside, where office and studio spaces can be rented.[16] The collective pot is intended to benefit members equitably – based on need, family commitments and life circumstances.

ruru's Working Process

While it is possible to trace, vaguely, ruru's financial and in-kind support from external parties, it is harder to pin down the labour and time spent to support ruru activities. They sometimes describe their processes as similar to jamming, where different instruments and voices enter and meet on a middle ground to harmonise.[17] Programmes and projects are initially developed based on personal concerns and interests; for instance, Kunil started rurukids in 2010, as she and some of her friends were beginning to have children, while Ameng programmed RRREC Fest as part of his involvement in the Indonesian music scene.

ruru's members talk about themselves as a loose collective, but in reality they are intense, organised and thorough. We were told that the Gudang Sarinah era was difficult and prone to burnout brought on by ruru's massive transitions in size and scope.[18] Learning from the experience of Gudang Sarinah, ruru reduced the scale of its space and projects. Now, as a member of the Gudskul Ekosistem with the collectives Serrum Art Handling and

15 Most notably, the Hivos funding supporting ruangrupa as their partner in Indonesia was about to end, though it lasted a decade (2003–13).
16 See more in-depth analysis in M. Budianta's 'Political Economy and Aesthetics of Space', in this volume.
17 See Nuraini Juliastuti's 'Pedagogical Moments in Jamming', in this volume.
18 See testimonies in this volume's archive section, pp.297, 298, 301.

Grafis Huru Hara, ruru considers their work to be one facet of a bigger project or initiative. As ruru's current 'office' base, the Gudskul complex is well-equipped, with different venues conducive to working and *nongkrong* (hanging out). There is the cafe, other eateries, the library, sleeping areas, childcare facilities, the salon, the kitchen and the classroom. From what we could observe, each ruru member has a different working style and personal time frame (most work happens after lunchtime, from 2pm onwards, with some continuing late into the night, though productivity peaks around 9pm). Despite this looseness, they seem to work well together. ruru members work very hard, with lots of breaks for gossip, laughs, smoking and eating – disruptions that bond. Outsiders working with ruru often have to adapt to their pace and schedule; those who cannot will find things difficult.

Planning, discussions and decisions take place in a *majelis* (assembly) format where concerned members of the collectives are present to discuss projects and issues. We witnessed a *majelis* focussed on the issue of 'hosting' in July 2024. It became a subject in need of urgent address, because there were increasing inquiries about artist residency programmes post-documenta. The meeting we joined lasted a couple of hours, though we had been told it might run up to two full days.

In terms of workplace decor, all tables have snacks. There are different options for seating areas: members can either sit at standard tables or on carpets with low tables. It is a smoking room, of course. Each speaker, attending on site or online, speaks into a mic for at least three minutes, and a designated note taker, called a 'harvester', jots key points onto a big whiteboard visible to all participants. Discussion is done in Bahasa Indonesia. As researchers still learning the language, we deciphered that some people were sharing their experiences of dissatisfaction, including feeling mistreated or exploited as visiting artists or as hosts, and some people (Angga Cipta, aka Acip) shared how they had observed the older generation of ruru hosting artists in their Tebet houses, which left them wondering how to pass down such knowledge.

ruru's major internal restructuring happened in two *majelis* moments – at the end of 2007 and in early 2015 – at the Tanakita forest campsite in Sukabumi, which is also the site for their RRREC Fest in the Valley. The 2015 restructuring took place over a two-night meeting, with 48 people present for the discussions and decision-making.[19] While *majelises* are mostly planned, other meetings and events sometimes happen seemingly spontaneously. Right before we arrived in Jakarta in 2024, Ameng and Indras Oktafia

19 For details, see Ardi Yunanto, Ajeng Nurul Aini, Ade Darmawan and Indra Ameng (eds.), *Ruangrupa 2000–2015*, Jakarta: ruangrupa, 2015, unpaginated.

(Gudskul's librarian) quickly mobilised a Hard Disk Party, which was an occasion to see ruru members' notebooks, Nokia phones, calculators, 'downloads' folders, laptops and external hard discs.[20] It felt like a miracle that so many of the ruru members made themselves available at the time.

Our in-person time with ruru reminded us of the critiques we had heard from long-term friends who honestly assessed ruru's work and processes. These friends discussed which locality and people ruru is accountable to now, in the 2020s; how important (or not) it is for them to work with the government; how different political climates might shift ruru's strategy; how they deal with criticism, especially from younger generations of practitioners; and whether they request too much from their network of friends and co-workers.[21]

On Time and Love, a Post-script

Studying ruru has been a practice in recalibrating ourselves to time differences, both present and past. Much of our experience of Jakarta involved dealing with 'rubber time' (waiting for hours, then being pushed to move quickly); delays during flooding; and the steady marathon of spending time with each other over stretched meals and cigarette breaks. Our body clocks simply changed themselves, quite to our surprise. One of the questions we kept asking ourselves was how ruru has been able to keep it together for this long. Despite all the hardships in funding, and burnout and breakdowns, ruru still manages to survive. As our research continued, we found ourselves moved by the group's openness with us. We unexpectedly received extended invitations to birthday parties, horror metal gigs, family meals and the creation of an English/Bahasa Indonesia bilingual menu at Kuluk Kuluk, the coffee shop at the centre of Gudskul.[22] Perhaps practising kindness and curiosity on a daily basis is one of the answers.

In asking members and outside friends about ruru, a consistent theme emerged: that they love each other very much. It was an intimate and simple sentiment, and one that we were privileged to witness through their actions: members backed up each other when there were concerns of childcare

20 See Özge Ersoy's 'Hard Disk Party, Continued – or, How to Be All Ears', in this volume.

21 See testimonies in this volume's archive section, pp.353 and 359.

22 The translated menu was made by Ube (also an artist) for his friend and co-worker Alif, who had been taking coffee orders from clumsy researcher-visitors like us. It was maybe Alif's second day on the job when we arrived. As the bilingual menu emerged on the last day of our stay, Alif's coffee-making speed also accelerated, from seven minutes to about two and a half on average.

Indra Ameng and Zappa at ruangrupa's library, undated.
Courtesy Indra Ameng

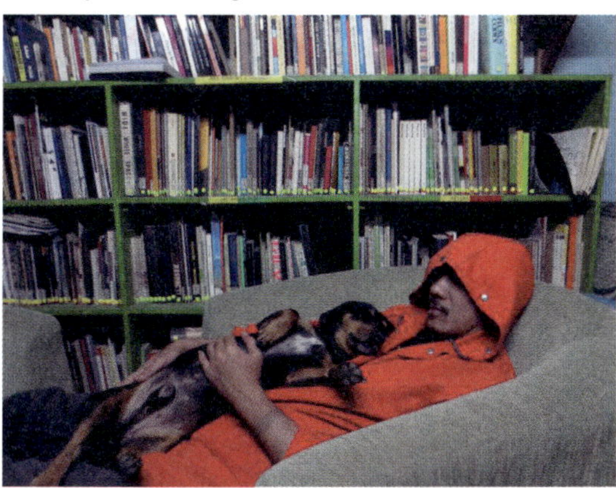

or other family commitments; partners and furry friends (Enad and Zappa, for instance) were involved in ruru activities; in moments of change or grief, members were present in each other's lives, and they were there to cheer for each other's personal achievements; and above all, they genuinely enjoyed each other's company.

Regardless of age, experience and gender, those touched by ruru emphasise the maternal, affectionate and nurturing character of its members. Perhaps more important than art-making, the breadth and longevity of ruru's work and practices teach us about human relationships: how to survive and help peers in times of struggle; how to embrace people for who they are; how to accept mistakes and failure; and how to grow up together.

Özge Ersoy

In his book *How to Disappear*, the writer Haytham El-Wardany lists practice exercises for becoming an 'unseen listener'. Under 'How to join a group,' he writes:

> As you sit in silence, allow your attention to shift randomly between the conversations you hear. [...] Contemplate how the conversations taking place remain adjacent to each other without overpowering one another or cutting each other off. Instead, they enter a relationship similar to that of spatial adjacency; they form a sonic neighbourhood.[1]

As a curator working at Asia Art Archive (AAA) in Hong Kong, I have a particular affinity for 'how to' manuals like El-Wardany's, which reads as both technical and reflective. In organising, digitising and making publicly available the archives of living artists and artist collectives, we at AAA do not refer to a single manual. Instead, we strive to respond to the specific methodologies and artistic sensibilities of the archive under consideration. Often, we ask how an archive can allow space for intuition.

In early 2024, AAA began developing discussions around ruangrupa's archive. We reflected on the implications of collaborating with a collective that has resisted institutionalisation for more than two decades. If ruru's ethos has manifested itself over time – in *nongkrong* (durational exchange), groupthink (a focus on networking and ephemeral working models) and social practice (especially enhanced through music and celebrations) – how might we approach their records? In other words, how does an archive attempt to 'pin down smoke'?

How to Mark Beginnings

ruru and AAA started in the same year, 2000, in Jakarta and Hong Kong respectively. AAA's library had already begun collecting ruru publications in the early 2000s – albeit sporadically – along with CDs and DVDs of their event

1 Haytham El-Wardany, *How to Disappear*, London: Sternberg Press and Cairo/Amman: Kayfa ta, 2018, p.32. The section titles include: 'How to disappear', 'How to reappear', 'How to listen to your inner voice', 'How to find meaning in dead time', 'How to change your frequency', 'How to join a group' and 'How to break with a group'.

photographs and video compilations.[2] In 2016, ruru participated in the AAA series '15 Invitations 15 Years', where they staged pop-up spaces of 'old and new archives' where artists, musicians, designers and cultural initiatives from Jakarta and Hong Kong came together. The idea was for AAA to become an entry point for demonstrating what happens when ruru's sensibilities are applied in Hong Kong. It all kicked off with a celebratory indie music gig in collaboration with a Hong Kong label, echoing how ruru opens exhibitions and programmes for wider groups' enjoyment, for instance at the OK.Video festival in Jakarta.

In 2022, at the invitation of ruru, AAA participated in *lumbung* (resource sharing strategies, or, literally, 'rice barn') for documenta fifteen. We came together with a group of artists, collectives and organisations to form a mini *majelis* (assembly) that met regularly for nearly a year to consider what a temporary school might look like at the Fridericianum in Kassel.[3] Simultaneously, in Hong Kong, AAA was focussed on its own institutional growth and hospitality, as realised in renovations to our library to improve our ability to host gatherings and facilitate artistic exchanges. 'The Collective School' (2022–23), our first exhibition following the reopening of AAA's library, was developed in collaboration with Gudskul, who invited eight artist collectives from across Asia to respond to archival materials related to other collectives in AAA Collections. Following the exhibition, we invited ruru to deliver our annual artist lecture in 2023, exploring ideas of home and collaboration, after years of growing together.

When ruru and the AAA team in Hong Kong began discussing the possibility of collaborating on ruru's archive, the first step was to identify

2 AAA Collections currently hold over 80 records related to ruangrupa, including catalogues, reference books, zines, CDs and DVDs. They include issues of the journal *Karbon* (2000–06); catalogues for OK.Video (2003–11), Jakarta 32°C (2008–16), 'Decompression #10' (2010), 'The Sweet and Sour Story of Sugar' (2012), and '15 Invitations 15 Years: ruangrupa' (2017); zines such as *Bekerja in a Land of Milk and Honey* (2010) and *The Kuda: The Untold Story of Indonesian Underground Music in the 1970s* (2012); publications such as *siasat* (2011), *The Sketchbook Project* (2011), *Search In Flux: Multimedia Art Strategy in Indonesia* (2011), and documenta fifteen magazines and handbooks; photo documentation of selected programmes (2000–05); and more.

3 Other individuals, initiatives and collectives included Another Roadmap Africa Cluster (Kampala, Nyanza, Lubumbashi, Kinshasa, Maseru, Johannesburg, Lagos and Cairo), Archives des luttes des femmes en Algérie (Algiers), Centre d'art Waza (Lubumbashi), El Warcha (Tunis), Graziela Kunsch (São Paulo), Keleketla! Library (Johannesburg), Komîna Fîlm a Rojava (Rojava), Sada [regroup] (Baghdad and other locations), Siwa Plateforme – L'Economat at Redeyef (Redeyef) and the Black Archives (Amsterdam).

Ade Darmawan and farid rakun speaking at Asia Art Archive's Annual Artist's Lecture, 2023, moderated by Christopher K. Ho. Courtesy Asia Art Archive

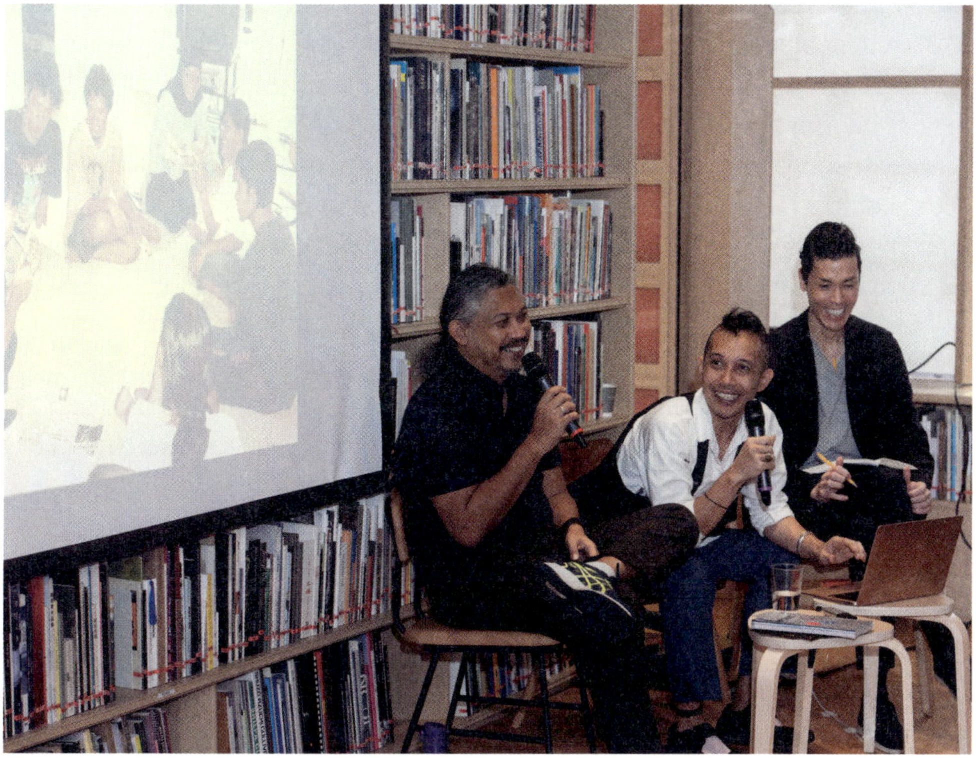

'The Collective School', Asia Art Archive, Hong Kong, 3 October 2022 – 1 April 2023. Courtesy Asia Art Archive

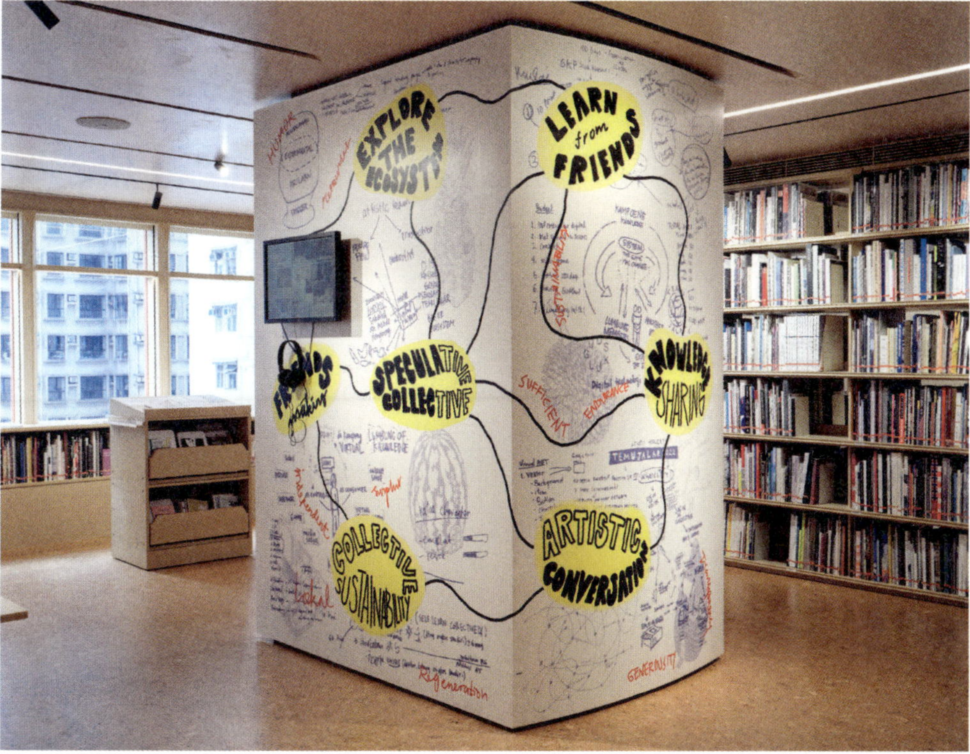

a Jakarta-based project researcher to assess the project's scale and the condition of its materials. Next, we planned a trip to Jakarta to see the archive in person and to continue conversing with ruru members. This trip, in July 2024, would be the first time we at AAA encountered the scale and the depth of the archival records that ruru has kept over the years.

Before our trip, we proposed an in-person workshop where ruru could engage with the standard AAA acquisition reports. Our report template's sections include the biographical details of the archive's owner(s), the condition and storage of the archive, rights and digitisation issues, and the justification for the archive's inclusion in AAA Collections, as well as funding sources, suggested timelines for processing and projected outcomes such as programmes and publications. We anticipated that ruru would bring a creative perspective to this, providing space for members to express personal viewpoints and thoughts in progress, as well as doubts and speculations, illustrated through drawings, diagrams and mind maps. Our aim was to understand which elements of the report various ruru members might want to change or preserve, ultimately challenging our usual standards.

ruru soon suggested replacing the report format with a party. They explained that each member of ruru has their own personal archive and that any narrative or research about the collective would need to call on dispersed digital materials. What became the 'Hard Disk Party' was an unconventional approach for us during the archive's scoping process. AAA more typically begins with the centralised organisational files of an artist collective or independent art space and expands from there. However, we were excited to follow ruru's lead and to see what would emerge. Indeed, this decision was grounded in years of doing things and spending time together – in a kind of long-duration *nongkrong*, so to speak.

How to Throw a Hard Disk Party

On our first day of visit, in July 2024, we gathered at Gudskul Ekosistem in South Jakarta, where we met Indras Oktafia, archivist and librarian at Gudskul, who came on board to lead the scoping process. We started chatting at Kuluk Kuluk, a coffeehouse operated by the artist Ube, which is nestled between double-stacked shipping containers and a more traditional two-storey building. Joining us also were Wing Chan and Arianna Mercado from Afterall. We walked through various rooms designated for RURU Radio, rurukids and RURU Shop, which sold artworks and merchandise by Gudskul

The library at Gudskul Ekosistem, 2024. Photo: Wing Chan

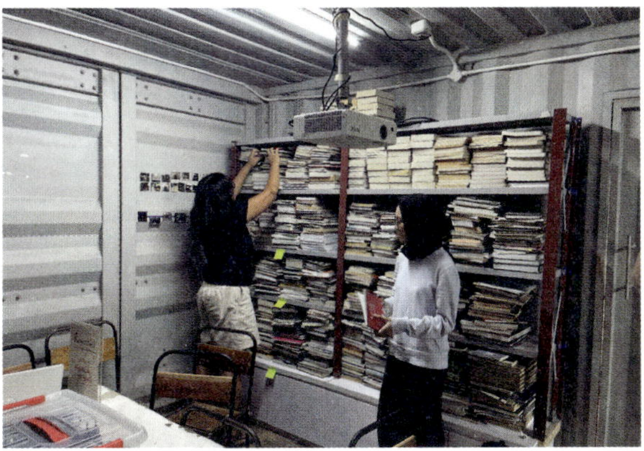

members and their friends. The in-between areas were filled with more artworks, graffiti, chairs, boxes, luggage and musical instruments.

Indras guided us to the library space, located within a shipping container at the centre of the upper floor. The air-conditioned room housed over 5,000 books on metal shelves that lined three walls, along with a meeting table equipped with a projector. We spent much of the next couple of days in this space.

That first afternoon, Indra Ameng shared the poster he had just created for the Hard Disk Party. The invitation called on ruru members to contribute materials: 'This workshop invites all of you to share archives and data related to ruangrupa's journey into one large database that can be accessed together and processed again for the imagination of future goals.' The agenda began with lunch, after which the Party, online meetings and discussions started, punctuated by a coffee break and dinner.

On the poster, a photograph of four ruru members shows them installing their exhibition 'Lekker Eten Zonder Betalen' ('Tasty Meal Without Paying') at Cemeti Art House in Yogyakarta in 2003. Two members sit on benches, one member stands on a ladder to hang ribbons from the ceiling and another

ruangrupa installing 'Lekker Eten Zonder Betalen', Cemeti Art House, Yogyakarta, 2003. Courtesy ruangrupa

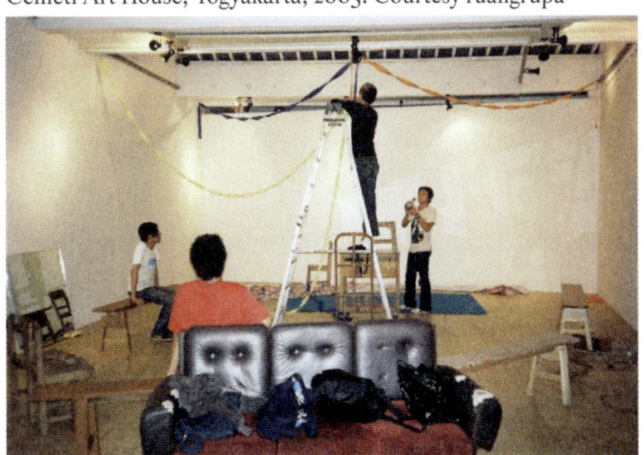

documents the process with a handheld camera. Surrounded by empty furniture, each person gazes in a different direction. The scene is serene, yet something celebratory and unruly is surely going to happen. As we prepared to look at everyone's personal archives before delving into ruru's organisational files, the photograph felt like a prompt to begin our party – and I loved it.

With Indras, we transported over forty external hard drives from the multimedia room to the meeting table in the library. Each heavy, thick, old-style hard drive had a sticky note attached, indicating its size and contents. Earlier in 2024, Indras and Julia Sarisetiati (aka Sari) had checked all of the hard drives and identified that one was malfunctioning. This broken hard drive stored data that Sari had compiled and organised for ruru's tenth anniversary showcase, 'Decompression #10', during 2010 to 2011. Indeed, Sari's own photography and video practice almost always involves digging into archives. Although we did not have the time to go through the entire organisational archive, the forty-plus hard drives on the meeting table stood as calm witnesses, or perhaps listeners, to our discussions over the following days.

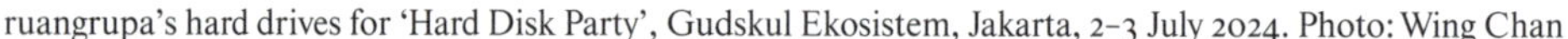

ruangrupa's hard drives for 'Hard Disk Party', Gudskul Ekosistem, Jakarta, 2–3 July 2024. Photo: Wing Chan

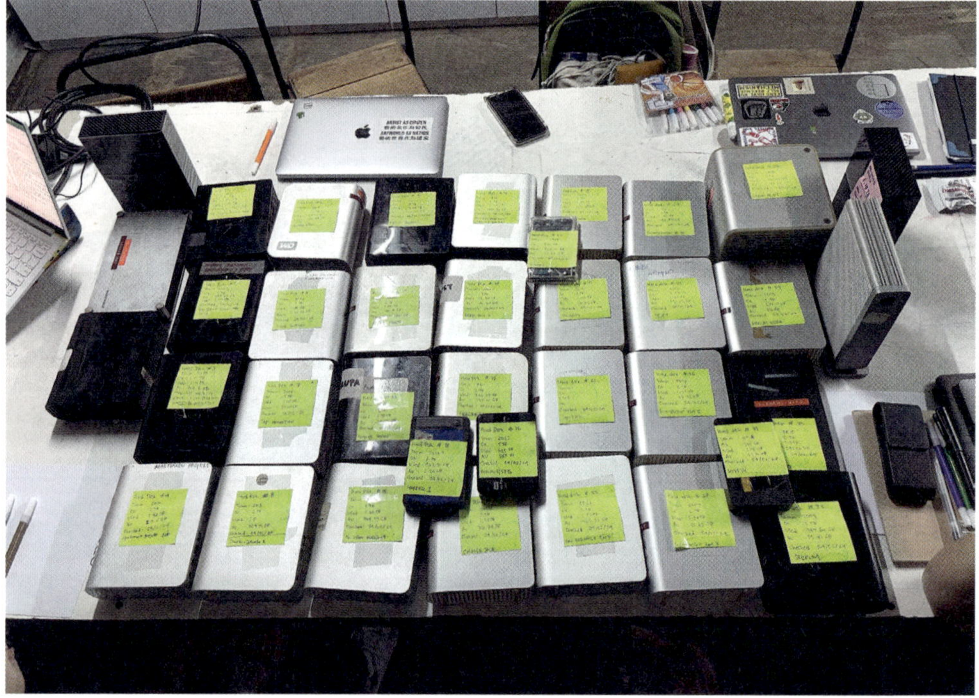

ruangrupa materials at Gudskul Ekosistem, Jakarta, 2024. Photo: Wing Chan

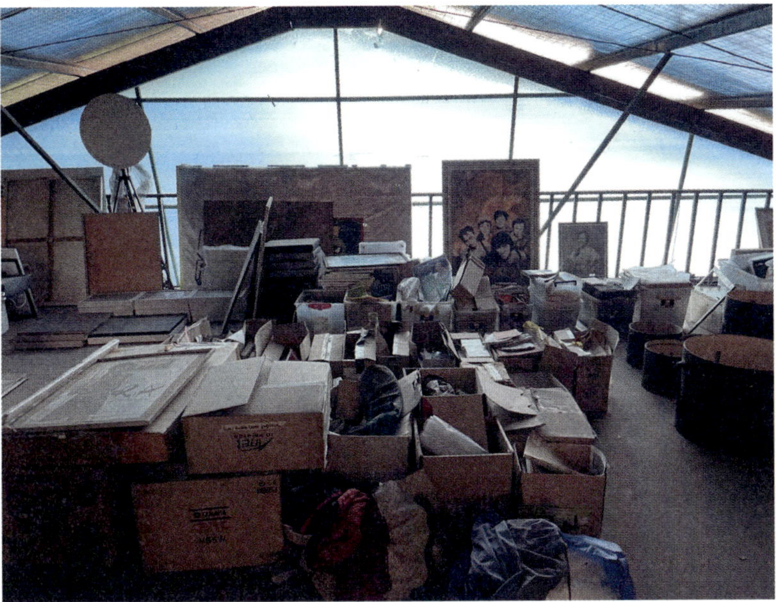

Later, we climbed to the top of the container-turned-library to look at more than fifty plastic and cardboard boxes filled with dusty folders, printed materials and audiovisual recordings. These boxes sat alongside artworks, easels, banners, furniture and old monitors. Simon Danang Anggoro (aka Gentong), who has been part of ruru since the mid-2000s, had helped to physically gather these materials. Indras mentioned that they aimed to sort through everything within the next two months.

How to Embrace a Sprawling Archive

'Many of us are hoarders; I even keep shredded paper.' This was one of the first things Ade Darmawan, a co-founding member of ruru, said to us as he connected his hard drive to the computer we had gathered around. The computer was linked to a projector that enlarged for us Ade's overwhelming number of draft applications, grant proposals, budgets and evaluation reports. Ade proclaimed: 'Every collective should have people who are good at mathematics!' According to him, their evaluation forms evolved from lists of basic information and measurements to compelling

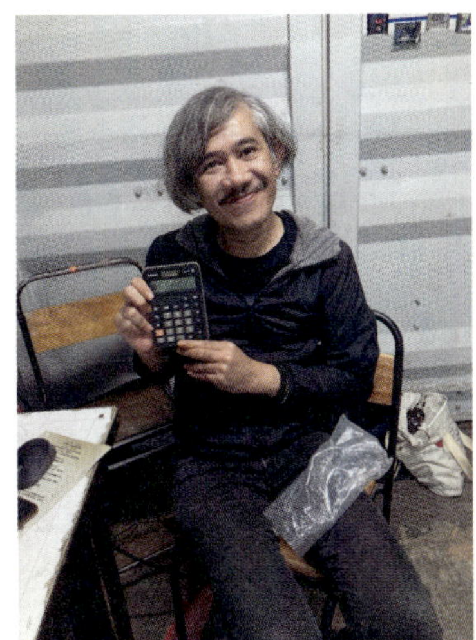

Indra Ameng and his calculator, 'Hard Disk Party', Gudskul Ekosistem, Jakarta, 2 July 2024. Photo: Wing Chan

Indras Oktafia showing the master working timeline for organising ruangrupa's archive (top), Indra Ameng (middle) and Ade Darmawan (bottom) at 'Hard Disk Party', Gudskul Ekosistem, Jakarta, 3 July 2024. Photo: Wing Chan

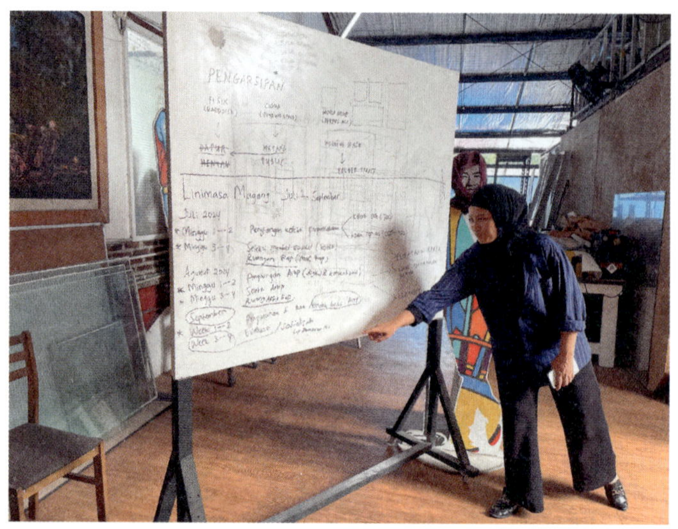

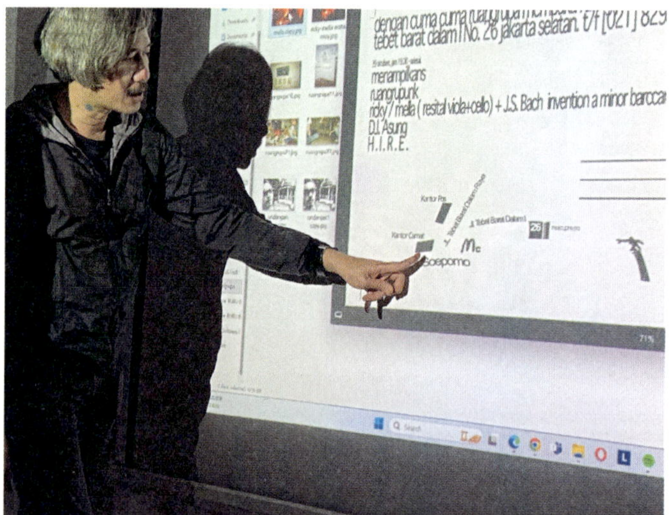

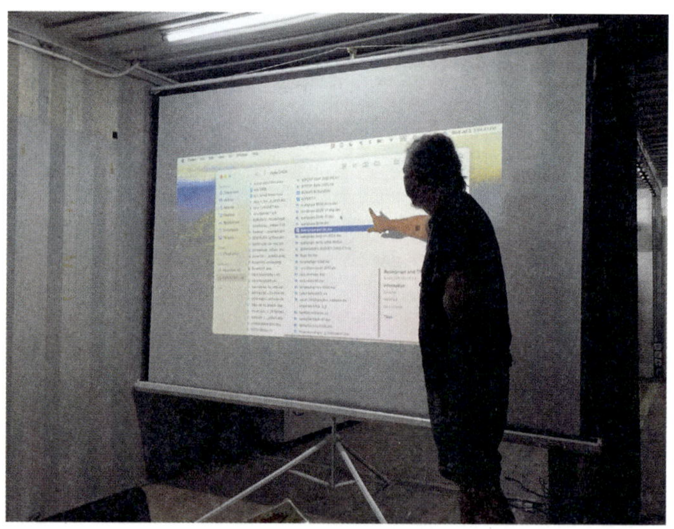

narratives crafted collectively – another example of ruru's capacity to reinvent formats to better suit their processes and, ultimately, persuade funders to adopt their approaches.

Ameng, a photographer and band manager, showed us a collection of photographs featuring people, ruru houses and exhibitions, along with invitation cards, magazine covers, project submissions, open calls, videos from OK.Video and RRREC Fest editions and even tax documents. He mentioned that he had purchased a personal laptop only out of necessity when he travelled to the São Paulo Biennial in 2014, having previously relied solely on one of the seven shared computers at ruru houses. We discussed ruru's long-standing interest in local narratives, as illustrated in materials ranging from an early 2000s photograph of a tree-mounted street sign bearing ruangrupa's name and phone number, to documentation of *Singapura Fiction* (2011), a compilation of photographs, objects, oral accounts and imagined stories about the city-state, as exhibited at the National Museum of Singapore. We also talked about The Kuda, a fictional rock band born out of activism in the 1970s, whose photos were taken by The Secret Agents (Indra Ameng and Keke Tumbuan) and featured in the seventh edition of the Asia Pacific Triennial of Contemporary Art (APT7), at the Queensland Art Gallery and Gallery of Modern Art in 2013.

Certain members not present in Jakarta – namely, Mirwan Andan, Reza Afisina, Ajeng Nurul Aini and Sari – joined the party on Zoom. Through Sari, we learned about the various functions of lumbung.space, a community-governed digital platform and publishing tool for lumbung members. It was on lumbung.space that Sari and Indras began to categorise materials from ruru's 25 years of projects and publications into 15 folders. The first folders addressed ruru's aspirations in terms of functions such as 'living room' and 'school', followed by folders for 'Decompression #10' and recurring festivals including Jakarta 32°C, OK.Video and RRREC Fest, as well as the initiatives rurukids, RURU Radio and ArtLab.

Sari emphasised that the folders serve merely as tools to illustrate connections and relationships and always remain incomplete. Ameng suggested creating a *serbaneka* (miscellaneous) folder for unclassifiable records, and we imagined what these might be. Considering AAA's interconnected databases on the backend of our website, we discussed how we could link these diverse records – of participating individuals, host venues, events and so forth – to one another and to other archival documents about artists and collectives from across Asia and featured in AAA Collections.

‘Hard Disk Party’, Gudskul Ekosistem, Jakarta, 3 July 2024. Photo: Wing Chan

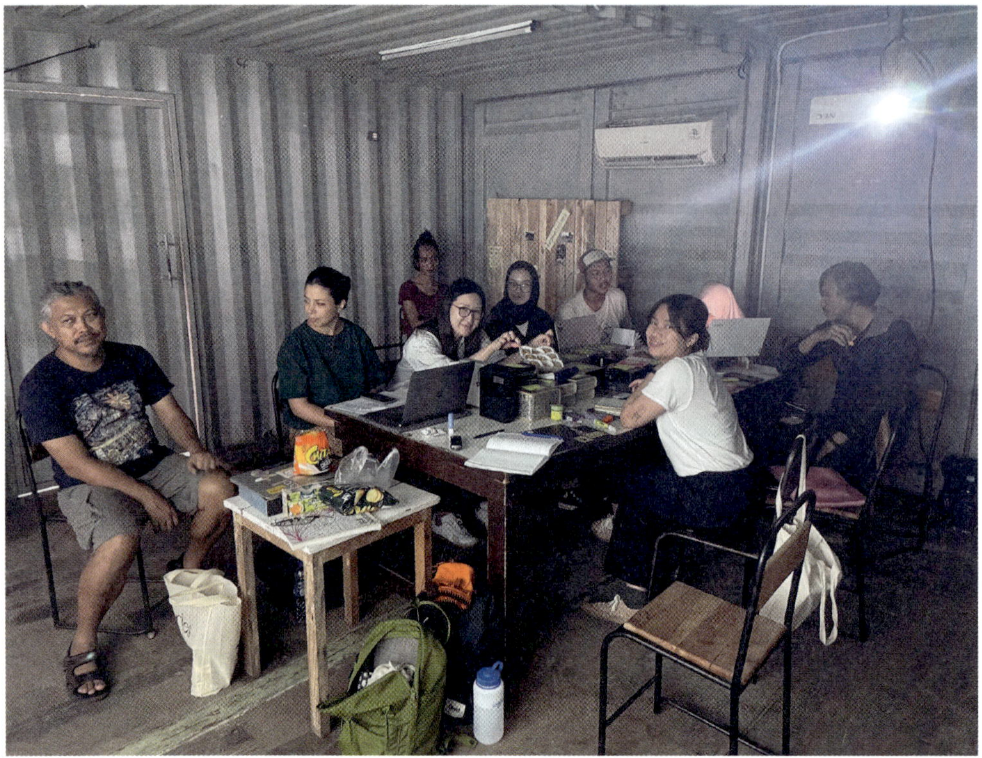

Such an approach would allow users to embark on a ‘research journey’ to uncover connections that might not be immediately visible through the folders alone.

Andan remarked that the archive is a collection of stories he personally holds in his mind. Reza mentioned that he lost a portion of his own memory of ruru when his notebooks were stolen a while back. He added that *Karbon* journal was their first tool for harvesting, and that it helped them to document and reflect on their work. Several members recalled that when ruru participated in the Istanbul Biennial in 2005, they acquired their first digital camera (distinct from Ameng’s much-used analog camera, an Olympus Mju 35mm). Ade noted that in 2007, friends from the University of Indonesia helped ruru establish an organisational system for their library. After the 2007 edition of OK.Video, ruru began developing research and archive sections as part of the ArtLab team, led by Reza and Iswanto Hartono, which later led to ‘Decompression #10’.

Ameng likened the archive to a scattered mind map, requiring further interpretations to connect the dots: ‘We need others’ speculations.’ This led us to discuss the idea of an archive as a form of composting, that is, as an organic process where materials break down and transform, fostering new growth. Ajeng echoed this sentiment: 'I keep getting lost in the archive jungle.' Her words illustrate the overwhelming nature of navigating a vast collection. At times, Ajeng's voice became interlaced with the sound of heavy rains pounding on the roofs while thunderstorms howled – typical phenomena of Jakarta in July. We contemplated this tropical climate as one in which an archive might quickly decompose, and also how this 'jungle' might be cultivated, creating pathways for discovery within its landscape.

In the final part of the four-day party, we discussed what the ruru archive cannot capture, which circled us back to listening – attentively – to ruru's ethos. Andan pointed out that the archive fails to document 'unconditional contributions', referring to acts of generosity and support that may not fit neatly into event records. According to Ade, the archive does not reflect how individual members have grown alongside ruru and the changing landscape of Jakarta over the years; rurukids, for instance, only emerged after Daniella Praptono (aka Kunil) and other members and friends became parents. Reza noted that the archive cannot adequately convey processes of change and decision-making, while Sari emphasised the archive's unsatisfying representation, which risks not only generalising what are in fact a diversity of viewpoints but may also single out only major voices within the collective.

Throughout the week, we revisited ruru's two-part, still-unrealised publishing project *Manual for the Living* and its sequel, *Manual for the Dying*, which ruru began conceptualising with friends in 2022. The first manual, which offers tools and sensibilities for artist collectives, demonstrates 'why we live and work collectively' and was partially realised in 2024 in ruru's revised edition of *siasat*.[4] The second manual addresses collectives that are considering ceasing their activities to envision their afterlives. Ade, Ameng and farid rakun spoke about how ruru has considered ways to dissolve into a collective of collectives, allowing a retreat into the background even as their impact continues in the larger cultural ecosystem.

I asked ruru whether archiving their 25-year history would align more with the first or the second manual – with the living or the dying. We contemplated their legacy, pondering whether the archive could serve as a sort of anti-monument – something that captures ongoing frequencies rather than just loud moments, and that acts as a continuous draft.

4 ruangrupa, *Siasat 2.0*, Jakarta: ruangrupa, 2024.

We wholeheartedly agree with ruru: archives, by their very nature, are never complete. They have inherent limitations, whether due to lost records or data that was never captured in the first place. This is particularly pertinent for artist collectives, where archives often struggle to represent the contradictions and entanglements between individual narratives and the collective identity. The question of completeness becomes even more complex when dealing with the archives of living artists, collectives and independent art spaces that are actively evolving. How can archives fully encapsulate something that is still in flux? This is precisely why AAA conceptualises the archive as a method – a means to cultivate narratives that encourage artists, researchers and cultural workers to reflect, respond and forge connections. And public access is essential for enabling such reflections.

At AAA, we follow a post-custodial archival practice. Our work does not rely on the custody of physical materials; rather, our expertise lies in identifying archives, collaborating with their owners to organise and digitise them, and ensuring open access through our website. Once digitisation is complete, we return the original materials to their owners or assist in finding local custodians. In addition to providing access to archives, we also develop exhibitions, talks and workshops; commission artworks; and produce educational resources. Our team consists of researchers, archivists, librarians, curators, educators and editors, each of whom brings diverse tools and methodologies to the table, while all are dedicated to not only record-keeping but also archive-activating. Our approach, which we call 'preservation through sharing', is grounded in the belief that archives are best maintained when they are actively circulated, utilised, challenged and reinterpreted.

As we prepare to finalise our initial report on the scoping of ruru's archive, we will further investigate how to conceptualise the archive as an emergent site rather than merely a repository. During the Hard Disk Party, we acknowledged the potentials and limitations of the organisational files gathered, and we also created a wealth of new notes, diagrams and audio recordings that embrace the influx of materials, narratives and contradictions related to ruru's various members. For me, this approach mirrors the fractal systems that ruru has cultivated over the past two decades. We want to now explore how the complexity of ruru's practice can enhance, rather than complicate, the archiving process.

This piece of writing is part of a storytelling project that is evolving alongside the formation and sharing of ruru's archive. As an institution housing the archives of many artists and collectives, our role is to be the first unseen listeners and to allow others, in El-Wardany's words, to 'notice the sonic adjacency ... and how each conversation taking place is aurally reliant on the conversation beside it, as though it were seeking company or reassurance in it'.[5] These preliminary stages of working with ruru are our initial attempt to be all ears.

5 H. El-Wardany, *How to Disappear*, *op. cit.*, p.32.

Enin Supriyanto

ruangrupa belongs to the first generation of artist collectives formed in Indonesia during Reformasi, the era of major socio-political change that arrived following economic crisis, youth movements and the end of the New Order government (1966–98). In December 2024, I spoke with Enin Supriyanto, an independent curator and critic with an activist background going back to the 1980s. Enin is not part of ruru but witnessed the art scene from which the collective grew. He described to me changes over the past two decades and looked further back in time to the New Art Movement of the 1970s; to student activism of the 1980s, wherein he found himself bridging leftist theory and direct action; the missed opportunity of civil society after 1998; and the fresh legislation of national cultural policies in 2017. He also considered the potential of collectives in driving social change in Indonesia in the years to come. In transcribing the recollections, his voice became vivid and solid.

My first encounter with Enin was in Jakarta in 2023, outside Produksi Film Negara (PFN), a defunct state-owned film production centre that had been converted for the evening into a playground for a three-hour-long gig by Nayamullah, a band with no fixed members. Overwhelmed by the warmth and togetherness of the gig (and by serious jetlag), I did not start a conversation with Enin until July 2024, when we met outside his gallery in Central Jakarta, Rubanah Underground Hub. Amidst the sweet scent of *kreteks*, Enin passionately commented on the freedom of the press and the doings of Indonesian elite politicians. I was drawn to his insights and continue to wonder at what he has experienced and witnessed.

Wing Chan

The role of student activism has been significant in the political changes of modern Indonesian history. Even the revolution to gain national independence in 1945 was part of a student and youth movement. In the 1960s, students were involved in the toppling of the Sukarno regime. It happened time and again in the 70s. The historical fact that students at Institut Teknologi Bandung (Bandung Institute of Technology, ITB) actively participated in much of this activism was not lost to my generation. Before enrolling in the university, I was already acquainted with several ITB second- and third-year students and I was exposed to the political issues that they discussed. When I was accepted by the Fine Art and Design Department in 1984, I naturally presumed that activism was ingrained in the university environment. Of course, this was not entirely true. Some students really wanted to graduate soon in order to pursue their careers. But one of the extracurricular activities available to students was a study group for the social sciences and political science, where students met regularly to discuss books and essays. Because some of the most active members leaned towards leftist thinkers, I got exposed to the Frankfurt School and the New Left. That's how it all started for me.

I remember academics and scholars were publishing analyses of the leftist movements in Latin America in the social sciences journal *Prisma*,[1] concerning marginalised people under modernisation – be it farmer, labourer or worker, in an urban or rural setting. Studies of developmentalism regimes, by Samir Amin and Andre Gunder Frank amongst others, showed us that theory needed to be revised or adapted to study development in actual contexts. Our study group discussed some of these texts, and this brought our attention to how they related to the case of Indonesia, namely the hidden agenda of the developmental projects proposed by the New Order government. I would say Latin America was the bridge connecting leftist theory and reality, and it forced us to reflect on our own situation.

Direct actions set our generation of student activists apart from the previous generation, who typically were concerned with some very grand or general issues about foreign investment and wealth discrepancy. In the 80s and early 90s in Indonesia, a lot of academics, student activists and NGO activists started to engage directly with land issues. We had a small group of students doing field research and contacting displaced peoples

1 First published in 1971 by a research centre known by its acronym LP3ES (*Lembaga Penelitian, Pendidikan dan Penerangan Ekonomi dan Sosial* – Institute for Social and Economic Research, Education and Information), *Prisma* was very popular amongst my generation of student activists, academics and journalists, as a source of information about current theories and thoughts on social, political and cultural issues.

and communities on the ground. We most definitely researched in Java, but also Sumatra. We started to gather information – with help from activists working in NGOs, we had access to data. Through the study group, we connected with students from different universities in Bandung and started to build networks with students in Yogyakarta (Jogja) and Jakarta, or even Salatiga in central Java. Within this expansive network, much discussion and shared information actually happened. I spent a lot of time with these friends outside of art school. As my active involvement in student activism intensified, I paid little attention to my art studies.

The only possibility for certain political texts to be published and not banned by the government was because of seriousness – indicated by an academic title and writing structure. The government would easily or quickly ban suspicious texts in newspapers or weekly magazines. But *Prisma*, for example, was published by an NGO and the essays were quite academic. Some kind of book publishing also happened during my student years in Bandung; such writings were popular and even available in bookshops (mainly under philosophy), which is surprising if we think about it now! For example, there was a collection of essays on Herbert Marcuse's theory of the 'one-dimensional man', jointly published by a university and a publisher in Jakarta, in Bahasa Indonesia. The government did not associate it with activism. But for my generation, it has given us a more theoretical framework to talk about society. Another publication, also with a cryptic philosophical title, was a study on Max Horkheimer. The exact source was a text compilation prepared by a professor in the Sekolah Tinggi Filsafat Driyarkara (Driyarkara School of Philosophy) in Jakarta. It was a comprehensive beginner's reader on Marxism and Leninism. Officially meant for internal study, it circulated widely in photocopied form. Access could be thought difficult and dangerous, but people always had connections to photocopying services and you could always ask friends to gather some money and make ten copies. I know that the reader also reached students in Jogja and Jakarta, so we had some theoretical references in common.

Several of the primary sources footnoted in the readings – the three volumes of *Das Kapital*, for example – were available in the central library at ITB. Oftentimes I went to the special reference section and looked for names in philosophy or social sciences or political studies, or certain terminologies in the Encyclopedia Americana or Encyclopedia Britannica. Of course, study groups also helped. There were always friends who knew more and were seriously reading certain texts and could lead discussion. Yet another source was friends who somehow could afford to travel abroad, and who brought back books on request. Whenever a book was in our hands, it would be photocopied extensively and distributed amongst study groups alike. There were many other ways to learn. We are talking about pre-internet times!

Students were energetic about absorbing knowledge and information that could give us a firm basis for political thinking and imagination. We thought these changes should happen around us, in Indonesia. Meanwhile, the fear of the oppressive regime, who could do whatever they wanted at any time, was immense. After 1966, any discussion directly related to communism or Marxism in public space was almost impossible. Nobody dared to talk openly about the military in, say, *warung* (street cafes). Most of the time we were afraid of being caught by government intelligence officials. These people circulated in our group as well – they monitored everything. We were very, very, very careful when organising open meetings for our study group, for instance, open discussions with invited academics from other cities. When we had more serious discussions, we needed to be ultra-cautious. We arranged them in remote areas, in a secretive manner. 'Big Brother is watching you' was relatable at that time. The fear was real and very present.

In my student years, I was involved in a big demonstration at the university in August 1989. We never really imagined that the government would take such a serious measure to prosecute protestors, but it happened that way. In the same month, two or three of my friends who were student leaders were caught by the military and disappeared. I was trying to escape and became a fugitive with the help of friends in Bandung, Jakarta and Jogja. But with some agreement amongst the student organisers, I decided to go back to Bandung. The police caught me and handed me over to the military intelligence institution. They put me on trial. After almost a year of detention and then a sentence of three years, I got parole for six months and was released in early 1992. The only job with a decent salary and somehow related to art in the early 90s – for someone who had an unclear background and never finished university – was in the advertising business. With help from friends, I got a job at an advertising and marketing company in Jakarta. Soon, I reconnected with artists and activists and got more involved in the art ecosystem of Indonesia.

The Promises of Reformasi

The political crisis started around 1996. Voices within the elites in the Partai Demokrasi Indonesia Perjuangan (Indonesian Democratic Party of Struggle,

PDIP) coalition started to question the Suharto government and to support the rise of Megawati Sukarnoputri. The government tried to interfere. When the pro-Megawati PDIP camp claimed Megawati had won the internal election to be the next party leader and opened a small office in Jakarta, the government sent paramilitaries to attack the compound. Megawati was supported by student activists. That was July 1996. Once that happened, journalists sympathised with potential change. Soon, students, NGOs, activists, academics and journalists aligned into a bigger group. From July 1997, the Asian Financial Crisis affected Thailand and other part of Asia. A few months later, in September or October 1997, the crisis hit Indonesia and became the most critical and powerful element to shake the Suharto government. The regime tried to maintain power until the end of 1997 and with the re-election of Suharto, but the whole financial crisis was out of control. Meanwhile, student and youth movements started to fill the streets, especially in Jakarta, to express dissatisfaction with the government. The whole financial and socio-political crisis escalated in less than a year. The Indonesian people call this era of change Reformasi.

There are many perspectives to speak about the promises of Reformasi. For myself, the first agenda was to stop Suharto's oppressive New Order rule, which had begun in 1966. This was somewhat achieved when Suharto resigned in May 1998, but the political landscape was still grim. The parliaments and the Majelis Permusyawaratan Rakyat (People's Consultative Assembly) quickly tried to serve the people. With several agendas, they insisted on conducting the general election as soon as 1999, allowing multiple political parties to partake. Yet, the problem was, the student movement and the larger public did not have any say in formulating a new policy or system of general election in Indonesia, even as the elites made almost forty political parties eligible in 1999, compared to three in New Order times. Only five years later, in 2004, the president was elected directly by the people and not only the representative elite politicians. In the beginning years of Reformasi, the government agreed to form the Komisi Pemberantasan Korupsi (Corruption Eradication Commission) and an independent highest judicial court, the Mahkamah Konstitusi Republik Indonesia (Constitutional Court). This was a huge change politically, but in reality it all crumbled and malfunctioned.

I quickly realised that, between 1998 and 2000, rather than amplifying the organisational capacity of the civil society, the whole reform was hijacked and taken over by elite politicians. The long-term effect has been the weakening of civil society. On the one hand, demonstrations could never completely change the regulations ratified by the government. Significant change still relies on the parliaments. The problem is, the majority of political coalitions who control the parliaments are the same ones supporting the government. High-ranking members in coalitions typically work closely with oligarchs' businesses or are oligarchs themselves and thus detached from the common people. On the other hand, people's political apathy is high. The participation rate in many of the provincial elections in November 2024, including Jakarta, was the lowest since Reformasi took place. We are now continuing the trajectory where elites control politics and the civil society is utterly disorganised.

For me personally, the two most important changes to happen after Reformasi are freedom of the press and internet access. Soon after Reformasi, the government lifted their control over newspapers and magazines. Independent investigative journalism and news agencies became possible. A lot of new publications happened at that time, which was very interesting. It correlated with the spread of the internet. Even though the internet was expensive and not many people had it, some people already started to communicate with friends in the country or abroad using the early ListServ channel. Mobile phones were still expensive, but people who could afford to started using them to send text messages. It was the ease of communication, and of escaping control by any governmental bodies, that was a huge inspiration. With free press and internet access, the whole atmosphere changed regarding freedom of expression.

ruangrupa represented one of the earliest expressions amongst young artists forming their own organisations and groups after Reformasi. Under Suharto's New Order, you were not permitted to form this kind of organisation – you needed to go through infinite bureaucracy to assemble whatever group. ruru's engagement in the urban fabric of Jakarta is different from the Bandung generation, for example. It makes sense that one of their earliest programmes focussed much on graffiti and murals made on site in public space. Those activities became a channel and a direct expression to show how you reclaim public space that belongs to the people. I can totally relate.

I knew more of the members who engaged in media and technology through the OK.Video festivals. It was the biggest attempt to use new media for freedom of expression and art-making. Several artists had already started this kind of new media presentation in the Bandung art circle, but ruru came to organise them as a biennial. That a festival so big was consistently held was pioneering. I worked independently and unattached to any institution or academy and so I didn't always have projects with ruru directly; but I followed them, knew individual members and visited ruru's house in Tebet many times, and I met them in forums outside of Indonesia.

ruru probably also looked at me as someone strange, because I was still working with commercial galleries until around 2007. As of 2000, the year ruru formed, several new galleries opened in Jakarta. I consider it meaningful that these commercial galleries accepted the provocative and experimental work I proposed then, either paintings or installation, as long as they were profitable. I felt there was no agenda I had to fulfil to work with them. I would say the whole framework of ruru, or artist collectives alike, and commercial galleries was very different since the beginning, but the individual practices of artists in contemporary art were accepted indeed by the commercial. When the commercial scene was no longer challenging, I spent more time in Jogja and started working extensively with Grace Samboh, most significantly on the Equator Symposium (2010–18), a parallel event to the Jogja Biennale. It was a path for us to explore new models of politics, and to ask about building networks in the country as well as knowledge sharing through south-to-south international connections, or whether we would like to put attention into community activities as initiatives of change, not only in art but in many different forms. A similar approach to the organisation of Equator Symposium was used to curate Pekan Kebudayaan Nasional (National Cultural Week) in Jakarta in October 2023, which was partially as a homecoming of the *lumbung* practice vocalised by ruru and friends in documenta fifteen.

As for larger cultural policies in Indonesia, we experienced them in the past seven years when Hilmar Farid was the Director General of Culture under the Ministry of Education, Culture, Research and Technology. With an activist background himself in the 1990s, and a strong network of artist communities, academics and activists, in April 2017 he implemented the first-ever legislation around cultural development in Indonesia. Because of this legislation, we have clear legal grounds to talk about cultural development and access to the state budget for arts and cultural activities via the Dana Indonesiana (Indonesian Fund) – this is revolutionary. The whole funding procedure is accessible clearly and easily online. For instance, for documenta fifteen, probably sixty or more people could travel internationally because of this grant. This shows that the government has worked in these past years.

In October 2024, the Prabowo Gibran government made a separate, single department of cultural ministry. If the government changes their policy under this new cultural ministry, I still don't see that it will quickly kill or weaken the activities of the many collectives and cultural activities in Indonesia, aside from those that have relied significantly on this funding from the beginning. For those who have survived without this funding for years already, I don't think the funding changes will affect them. Strategically, they will continue. Collectives and practitioners started after 1998 have received foreign funding occasionally, but basically they have founded their own networks and utilised whatever resources were within their reach to survive.

Reclaiming Public Space (1970s)
vs Identifying with Communities and Societies (2020s)

Between 1975 and 1977, the Gerakan Seni Rupa Baru (New Art Movement, GSRB) started to form in art schools in Jogja and Bandung. While the proponents of GSRB neither explained nor provided clear evidence of their direct relationship with student activism in general, the whole activist atmosphere was there. Students instigated big demonstrations in Jakarta in 1975, then in Bandung in 1978. If art students started criticising their own curriculum and embracing new practices and approaches in their art-making, it was probably in a shared spirit with activism on the streets. GSRB died out gradually as student activism also slowed down – I can see the connection. The New Order government's grip on power became stronger in the early and mid-1980s. They got support from global capital and enjoyed more income from international oil petroleum companies with Indonesia as a member of OPEC. The middle class probably considered everything good and, thus, not much conflict happened.

The experiments of GSRB were very much restricted within the arts, and very internal. Nonetheless, the distinction as to whether you expressed criticism on the streets or within a small circle in a small gallery was not that important to me, because either way you put your life at risk in this repressed environment under a super oppressive regime. As a rebel, you had to embrace whatever forms of action as opportunity to reclaim public space. The case would be very different, say, after Reformasi, when you could find many channels to express yourself freely. But in the 70s, there was almost no option. Under the oppressive regime, even your private space was often being intruded upon. Back then, if I could make an exhibition that could spread not so much a political message but an attitude of freedom or deviance, I still considered it fine. It was still meaningful to my own group or community, at the very least. It contributed to the power of spreading an important understanding: yes, you *can* do this, you still have your freedom, and we can reclaim our own space, the public space.

During a recent discussion in Jogja about activism and collectives, I proposed the years to come will constitute our democracy, in the sense that we will see whether the collectives who currently work with communities and societies wherever they are based in Indonesia will become a driving force for genuine socio-political change. I don't see that political parties in Indonesia will change the way they operate or the way they relate to civil society. We have to rely on something completely different.

Collectivity is one of the central agencies in the art ecosystem of Indonesia in post-Reformasi times. But it has definitely evolved and I can see two shifting generations of artist collectives. The first generation emerged between 1999 and about 2007, in the big cities of Java. The second generation spread out geographically to reach Jatiwangi, Madura, Flores, Maumere, Papua, Sulawesi, distant corners of Kalimantan, Sumatra and almost everywhere in Indonesia – which is very interesting and important. Even though several new initiatives have emerged in Java, many others are found in remote areas. If ruru concerned much about urban society setting, the one in Jatiwangi definitely not – instead, they focus on clay, earth, land, forest or social-environmental issues, for instance. Similarly, collectives on small islands in the eastern part of Indonesia have completely different interests in how they identify with the social problems of their neighbourhoods and communities. These collectives are middle or lower-middle class, if we still can use these terms. They live and deal with completely different socio-political contexts in each of their areas.

Their value system is different compared to that of my generation, where a lot of activism started from the art and was embodied in the art scene for justification. Even personally, I try to find a provocative position, but I still need the art world to identify and validate my work. GSRB and the experimental arts of the late 80s and early 90s made an impact not directly on larger society but within the art circle – meaning, within the justification system that existed amongst the practitioners of the art ecosystem. In contrast, what is interesting about this new collective approach is that their identification and validation process does not really need the art ecosystem! It can happen outside of the art. For me, this is very important. The further away these collectives are from the capital, the freer they actually are. Because, historically speaking, the infrastructure involved in establishing our ecosystem only existed in Java's big cities – Jakarta, Bandung and Jogja. Sometimes, in a remote area, a collective doesn't even have a gallery, a national museum or any kind of art institution around to validate them. Instead, they activate themselves because of the relevance or urgency of the project they are doing in direct connection with the community and social groups on the ground. Their direct community and society – not the art ecosystem – are the foundation.

That is the basis of my argument as to why I think collectives could potentially play a significant role in the democracy dynamic of Indonesia in the upcoming years. Even though Indonesia might have a scary future politically, I am still excited to see what will come of these many collectives whom I have been fortunate to meet in the past two or three years in different parts of the country, and to witness what they are doing in their surroundings. I know that the changing agent of the future will no longer be a typical student movement or student protest like those that I experienced decades ago.

Nuraini Juliastuti

This writing emerged from questions: What aspects of jamming provide insights into collective practices? How can jamming allow us to think about self-organising practices differently? And, can jamming disrupt and challenge the formulaic standardisation around the discourse of collective practices?

My understanding of collective practices has been shaped by the dynamics of social and political movements. Elsewhere I have argued that the development of independent arts and culture spaces as well as community-based projects needs to be situated within various 'seasons' to denote changing social and political patterns and times around youth political movements, community history projects, indigenous and agrarian activism.[1] The choice of the word 'season' is intended to suggest certain climatic features of a locality. Its meaning emerged from the 'multiple senses of awakening where futurity might only mean a locus for a new kind of struggle. The past often comes back in the form of unresolved wounds and trauma; its ghosts inhabit the present.'[2]

Feeling and processing all these climatic features teaches a specific lesson: something, or things, will always fall out of a season. Things in and out of this occurrence signal to living beings that our environment in distress. Such temporality is also the intrinsic character of jamming. Can the people who are engaged in a jamming activity be perceived as a kind of collective? Taking jamming as a starting point to talk about collective practices opens up a more sensorial approach to perceiving collectivism. It asks that we identify the different aspects which shape the formation of a collective space. A collective might be formed and shaped by waves of sound, by an ensemble of collective bodily movements or by a room to breathe in and out.

On the other hand, I am aware of how the living room and the kitchen have become standard entry points to talking about collective practice. Within the Indonesian context, a history of independent arts and culture spaces narrates the development of informal spaces, whether the living room, bedroom, garage or kitchen. Stepping into the living room means showing an intention to get to know one another. Going into the kitchen is like taking a step further to learn different, previously undisclosed but resourceful ways to support an institution. The living room and the kitchen gain value through learnt and experiential logics of making things work within global contemporary art settings. They are deployed to perform new vocabularies around collective practices. This leads to the question of whether an arts and culture institution always needs the work of certain artists (mostly from the Global

1 See Nuraini Juliastuti, *Commons Museums: Pedagogies for Taking Ownership of What is Lost*, Berlin: ICI Berlin Press, 2024, pp.20–25.

2 *Ibid.*, p.20.

South) to perform such hospitality.[3] Today, it engenders more reflective questions about the perception of a house. What makes a house a house? This forms an especially pressing question in a time of ongoing genocide and international complicity in the normalised forced dispossession and displacement of Palestinians.

Christopher Small's concept of 'musicking' opens up a fresh way to look at collective practice. Small asserts that 'to music is to take part, in any capacity, in a musical performance, whether by performing, by listening, by rehearsing or practicing by providing material for performance (what is called composing) or dancing'.[4] I take Small's concept as an invitation to study the inner workings of arts and culture production which goes beyond the visibility of the finished work of art. It encourages us to pay attention to the invisible and ongoing efforts and labour which sustain the working process to make *something happen*. These various invisible elements include friendship, kindness, friction and informal supports.[5] Sandra Ruiz and Hypatia Vourloumis's concept of 'formless formation' sheds new light on formlessness as 'a principle of social organising and direct action;

3 The existence of ruangrupa's ruruHaus at documenta fifteen (2022) can be perceived as an attempt to establish the living room as part of a global theory on the making of arts and cultural spaces. Prior to this, ruangrupa had developed ruruhuis to centre their curatorial practices at Sonsbeek 16. The documenta fifteen website's description of ruruHaus reads: 'ruruHaus is the heart of documenta fifteen. Here you can experience the practice of *lumbung*. Even before the opening, a constant coming and going reigned in the building, a sum of many conversations, Zoom meetings, cooking sessions, and brainstorming bouts. ruruHaus is the "living room" of documenta fifteen.' See https://documenta-fifteen.de/en/venues/ruruhaus. Another case in point is the GUD Instituut Living Room, which formed through a collaboration between Gudskul and Het Nieuwe Instituut, Rotterdam. This living room was part of the programme 'Arus Balik – Shifting Currents' (2024), which works to 'bring together architecture and design networks that link the regions and their diasporas, recognising architecture and design as material witnesses and pathways to possible shared futures'. See https://nieuweinstituut.nl/en/projects/arus-balik.

4 Christopher G. Small, *Musicking: The Meanings of Performing and Listening*, Middletown, CT: Wesleyan University Press, 1998, p.9.

5 In previous research ('Commons People: Managing Music and Culture in Contemporary Yogyakarta', doctoral thesis, Leiden University, 2019), I extend Small's concept of 'musicking' to study various dimensions of 'making music'. I use it to study the development of an initiative in internet-based recording, event organising, cassette collection and cassette repair to save a historical record company and establish a record company.

an inherent solidarity; and the method of resonance'.[6] Ruiz and Vourloumis emphasise the state of being formless as 'new planetary practices of social border breakage: the necessary undoing of the political economy and its "terms of order"'.[7] I perceive this as a cue to view jamming as a new mode of building relations across geographical locations, while sensitising us to various forms of formlessness.

Memories of Jamming

During my high school and college years in the 1990s, to jam meant band practice and play music with others. Forming a band defined coolness for me and other local youths back then. Spending hours after school jamming in a rented studio was a way to maintain an identity as an *anak band* (Indonesian for a 'member of a band'). I was never part of a band. But I liked watching the jamming sessions organised by some of my classmates.

In jamming, the other participants are not fixed. The constellation instead depends on context, opportunity and the anticipation of what joy might come from practice. After a jamming session finishes, what remains is the lingering desire to spend more time playing instruments together. Being held up in a 'traffic jam' (also called simply a 'jam'), means being unable to move while on the road. The same word, of course, refers to a situation where papers are stuck in a printer. Jamming can also mean an interference in a soundscape. In all of these situations, jamming creates a temporary disruption in the regularity of everyday life – in other words, short-term chaos. Getting stuck in traffic, or *macet*, has become characteristic of urban life. In Jakarta, for example, enduring traffic for hours on the way from one point to another is thought almost normal. The jam emerged as a kind of shock to the system, to alter the regularity, speed and smoothness of things. To put different meanings of jamming into different contexts is to consider accepting slowness and attunement with one's surroundings.

6 Sandra Ruiz and Hypatia Vourloumis, *Formless Formation: Vignettes for the End of this World*, Colchester, UK: Minor Compositions, 2021, p.20.

7 *Ibid.*, p.15.

Preparation for 'Decolonial Joy Party', 'Amsterdam Assembly', Framer Framed, Amsterdam, 7 October 2021. Photo: Nuraini Juliastuti

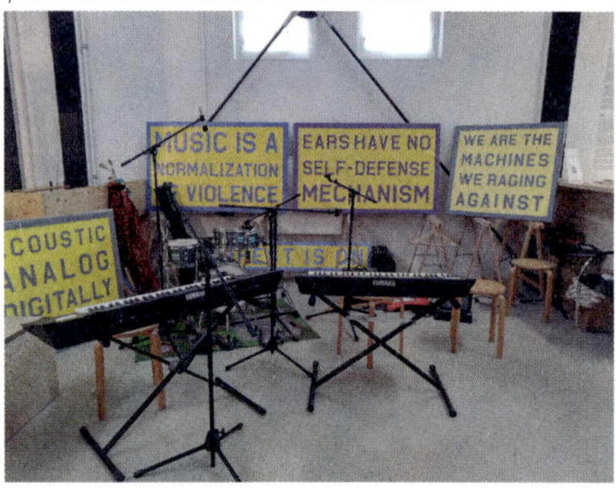

'Amsterdam Assembly: Letting Go of Having to Speak All the Time', Framer Framed, Amsterdam, 8 October 2021. Photo: Nuraini Juliastuti

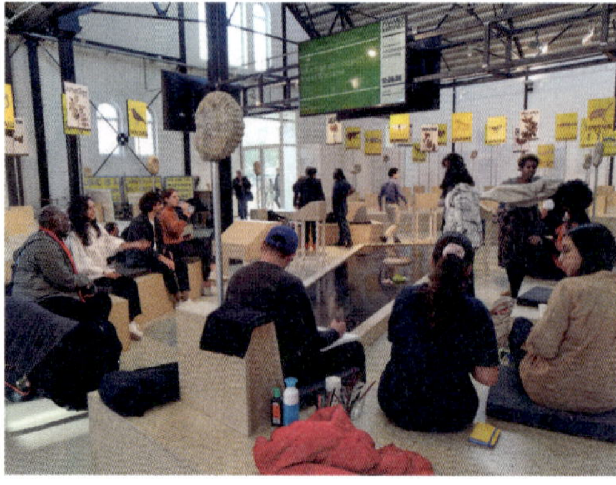

In 2021, I co-organised the event 'Amsterdam Assembly: Letting Go of Having to Speak All the Time' at the Framer Framed, Amsterdam.[8] The second day explored 'listening', for its closure we convened the 'Decolonial Joy Party'. I initially suggested we invite Julian 'Togar' Abraham to DJ and contribute some tunes. As the assembly unfolded, what was initially a simple music activity became a full jamming session, led by Togar at the Rijksakademie, with Diana Cantarey, Daniel Aguilar Ruvalcaba and Sungeun Lee. Here are some of my observations from the assembly's jamming activity: jamming creates a space for gathering; jamming prolongs the duration of the gathering; jamming encourages people to listen to each other; and jamming propels people to do a wide range of joyful activities (which might not happen otherwise). And indeed, the air was filled with so much joy that night.

8 'Amsterdam Assembly: Letting Go of Having to Speak All the Time' was a gathering and thinking space for activists, artists, scholars and other cultural practitioners to discuss topics around decolonisation, pedagogy, racism and the politics of archiving. Organised by Vrije Universiteit Amsterdam, University of Amsterdam and the Research Center for Material Culture at Framer Framed from 7 to 9 October 2021, the event was part of the 'Worlding Public Cultures: The Art and Social Innovation' project. I took part as a researcher affiliated with Amsterdam School for Cultural Analysis, University of Amsterdam. Carine Zaayman, also from the Amsterdam team, and I designed the assembly's plan together. See 'Amsterdam Assembly: Letting Go of Having to Speak All the Time', Framer Framed website; and 'Amsterdam Assembly', Worlding Public Cultures website. The jamming was part of the assembly event 'LISTENING: Building Together Many Voices'.

In 2024, the Indonesia Pavilion at the 15th Gwangju Biennale played around with the concept of jamming in a gathering of the project 'The Broken Hearts are Singing'. The Indonesian Pavilion, dubbed the 'Jamming Pavilion' and curated by Syafiatudina, employed 'brokenheartedness' as a lens to interrogate complex relationships and the sense of belonging – to lands, communities and nations.[9] In one of the project's written musings, jamming is translated into a willingness to perform improvisation as an 'act of playing together, responding while being attuned to each other's sound'.[10] This involves being in tune with the rhythm of histories, including the sounds of those who have been marginalised by greedy, violent power. It runs on the same wavelength as what Tineke E. Jansen refers to as *darimana* in her critical analysis and reflection on the histories of Indonesian-Chinese women living in The Netherlands. The phrase *darimana* means, in Indonesian, 'Where are you from?' This phrase is often uttered to people of colour (Indonesians included) to other and ultimately negate their existence in white-dominated social spaces. Jansen uses *darimana* as 'a shorthand for herstories' (or stories and voices being silenced and suppressed) and also to encourage the act of listening and being attentive through the auditory sensorial system.[11] What kinds of historical moments are encountered by the bodies who move through jamming?

9 This writing provides little space to talk about the Indonesian Pavilion at length, other than to say that it used Julian 'Togar' Abraham's installation work as a space to host gatherings and collaborations with other artists and collectives. See Syafiatudina, 'The Broken Hearts are Singing', curatorial note for Gwangju Biennale Pavilion 2024.

10 'How do you translate "jamming" into Bahasa Indonesia? The act of playing together, responding while being attuned to each other's sound, is not foreign to local cultures in Indonesia. However, finding one word that encapsulates this situation involves asking around and looking for translation suggestions. Literally, "jamming" can be translated as "jammed" or "something is stuck." "Traffic jam" is a common use of this word. Another word for "jamming", which is "improvisation" or "improvisasi", might be able to illustrate the action.' See 'Random Note on Translating Jamming', Broooken Space website, https://broooken.space/. It is interesting to note similarities in the understanding of the etymology of the word *jamming* between the Indonesian Pavilion's musing and mine.

11 Tineke E. Jansen, *Tuning In: Darimana?*, Amsterdam: Archival Textures, 2024, p.22.

Breathing Mobility

I want to situate jamming in the context of contemporary art practices where artists and cultural practitioners work with intensified mobility. Trans-local residencies in different social and political environments have become the characteristic work pattern of contemporary art practice. Since the early 2000s, there has been a rise in the number of artists and cultural practitioners taking positions and residencies at various institutions in the Global North. This corresponds with certain changes governing the field of arts and culture in post-1998 Indonesia, as the field has moved away from being heavily controlled by the state. There is a growing confidence in taking on the role of cultural producer, with more active engagement in seeking partnerships with non-Indonesian local contexts. It expands the scope of exploration in developing various modes of gathering and experimentation to make use of space, time and resources.

The exploration has propelled a vision to reimagine cultural funding. In Indonesia, the availability of funding from international agencies has been vital in enabling knowledge performativity in independent spaces. Recent developments show how independent spaces have practiced autonomy through obtaining and combining community-based entrepreneurship, collective funds, local philanthropy, state funding, the art market and funding and presentation mobility from the global art ecosystem.[12]

The illustrated anthology of writings titled *We Had Plans* (2021), published on the occasion of the Rijksakademie's 150th anniversary, allocated some of its sections to the discussion of jamming as a regular activity at the Rijksakademie between 2020 and 2022.[13] Below is a selection of statements and articulations gleaned from the volume, with their attributions:

> When you rephrase it [jamming] as improvisation, it does become very important to me in terms of letting go of an extreme valuation of preparedness and just agreeing to be present in the moment and pour from what you already have.
>
> Julian 'Togar' Abraham

12 See Nuraini Juliastuti, 'Experimental Survival Strategies for Economic Independence in Alternative Cultural Art Spaces', in *Spelling Fixer 2021: The Reading of Indonesian Art Collectives in the Past 10 Years*, Jakarta: Yayasan Gudskul Studi Kolektif, 2021, pp.294–95.

13 Irene de Craen, Taylor Le Melle and Natasha Soobramanien (ed.), *'We Had Plans': A Book Published on the Occasion of the 150th Year of the Rijksakademie van Beeldende Kunsten in Amsterdam, Which Happened to Coincide with a Global Pandemic, During Which Resident Artists Continued to Work Collaboratively as Well as Individually on Their Respective Practices, Whilst also Navigating What Could be Called Expanded Practice*, Amsterdam: Rijksakademie, 2021.

[Jamming] is not just about playing whatever, but it is also trying to listen what the other people are doing, and trying to do something together in the moment.

Daniel Aguilar Ruvalcaba

[Jamming] is not only hearing the other, but it is allowing the other to influence your own actions and then bring it somehow in some results together.

Aldo Esparza Ramos

The beauty of jamming and the jam, all the jamming, is that it is very out of form. It is something that tries to avoid being categorised into something, or formalised or rationalised into what art practice wants to do with our practice.

Yazan Khalili

The rules [in jamming] are made up while we are playing.

Diana Canterey[14]

Sungeun Lee, an artist who participated in the jamming session at 'Amsterdam Assembly', contributed a drawing followed by a dreamy kind of essay narrating their struggle to let go of the competitive, goal-oriented culture ingrained in the cultural landscape of South Korea, where they were brought up. The drawing and essay serve as a kind of breathing space. In Sungeun's words: 'But I think with jamming we are practicing breathing together.'[15]

Drawing by Sungeun Lee in *We Had Plans*. Courtesy the artist

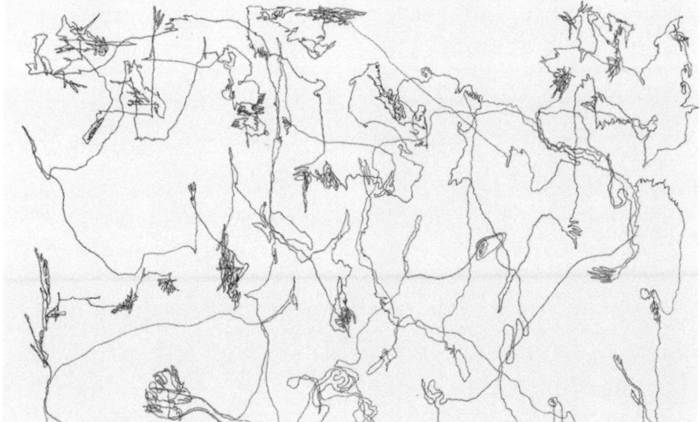

14 'Germination State #04: Continue on Jamming, on Pajamas', in *ibid.*, pp.119–26. This discussion took place on 21 February 2021.

15 Sungeun Lee, *Untitled*, in I. de Craen, *We Had Plans*, pp.115–16.

Indeed, Sungeun's contribution is a gentle reminder of the vitality of breathing together. During the Covid-19 pandemic, breathing took on different levels of meaning. Social isolation was a tool for saving lives, that is, for sustaining the condition for breathing. What kinds of entities might emerge from becoming attuned to each other's breathing?

Alexis Pauline Gumbs's book *Undrowned: Black Feminist Lessons from Marine Mammals* (2022) encourages us to see the intersectionality and solidarity dimensions of breathing practice. It suggests that we extend our breathing to other beings' breathing practices, situating it within a vortex of complex histories. According to Gumbs, the study of marine mammals (narwhals, belugas, bowhead whales, blacktip reef sharks) provides insights into how the vital aspects of breathing are less about the existence of the individual being than collective survival. Gumbs states that 'breath is a practice of presence'.[16] Learning how marine mammals physically transform as they grow (including how they adjust in the ways they breath, move and behave alongside their kin and surroundings) can mean redefining our intentions in terms of living in relation with other beings. Throughout its pages, *Undrowned* echoes breathing as a matter of co-existing, of not being drowned together. In Sungeun's drawing and essay, an even more nuanced, multidirectional interpretation is offered, which sees jamming (breathing together) as a mechanism to move back and forth between solo and group performance.

The Classroom Experiments

Oftentimes I like to refer to collective thinking in a classroom setting as 'jamming'. This is particularly pronounced in 'An Inventory of Sound Heritage', a course I have organised since 2022 at HKU University of the Arts, Utrecht. The students are encouraged to explore the sonic aspect of heritage and archive-making practices, with jamming perceived as a storytelling method to generate objects, collective stories and more conversation. Each session of the course emulates the jamming session wherein everyone contributes thoughts, stories and the sound of one's critical thinking together with others.

I want to return to Sungeun's notion of breathing and their struggle with the strong competitive culture in education and work. I compare it with the testing procedure used as the usual method for examining the performance of students, or learners, in understanding subject study. How would an assessment procedure also function as a learner-based reflection tool

16 Alexis Pauline Gumbs, *Undrowned: Black Feminist Lessons from Marine Mammals*, Chico, CA: AK Press, 2022, p.25.

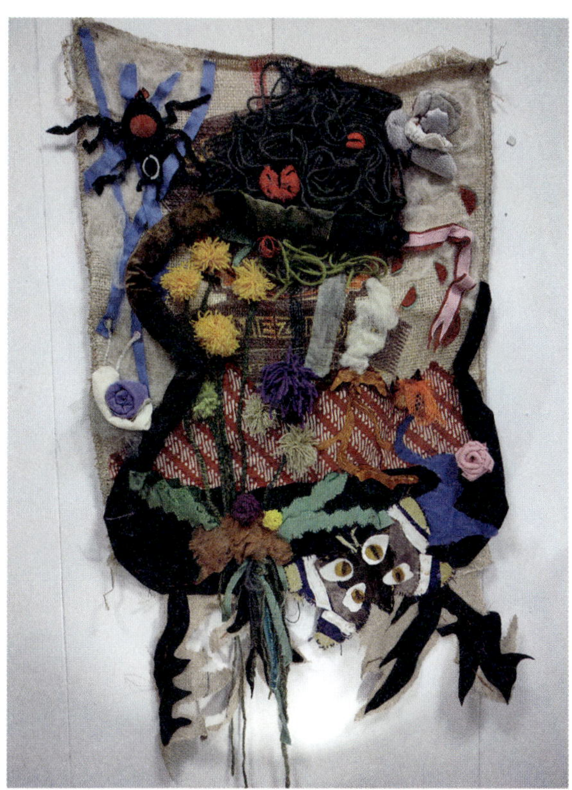

Arpillera created collectively during 'Transdisciplinary Practice: An Inventory of Sound Heritage', 2024. *Arpillera* is a textile craft work that symbolises women's resistance during the Augusto Pinochet dictatorship in Chile, which was introduced by Mirella Moschella to the rest of the class (Changli Luo, Aisha Hachem, Sophia Wang, Hannah Fleischman and Sohrab Kashani). Photo: Nuraini Juliastuti

to become more open to experimentation? I tie this question back to the standardised ways for performing the finished products of artworks.

The shared values between jamming and a class session designed like a jamming session lies in the character of the outcomes. Following the temporality dimension of jamming, each session will produce different kinds of sound. Thinking about the class as jamming means acknowledging different routes of learning within a pedagogical setting. It disrupts conventional ways of learning, where teachers are authoritative figures transmitting knowledge to students within an academic institution. Jamming also contributes a positive disruption to dominant thinking around authorship in contemporary art practices where the artist figure is regarded as the sole source of creative expression.

In the class-as-jamming process, critical thinking emerges from and is situated within the gathering, which instills the idea that the importance of learning lies not in having a fixed goal, but rather in the willingness to articulate thinking through the act of meandering together. Along with this, collective writing offers a route to define the meaning of a concept, which is less dependent on the singular voice.[17] Returning to 'An Inventory of Sound Heritage', I attempted in that course to keep shifting my role as teacher and student, or learning participant, through my participation in the making, thinking and sharing process.

I see a through line connecting collective writing with the mixtape. Both suggest a line of knowledge production where everyone tries to find their own modes of tuning in to each other. Collective writing emerges as a mode where everyone tries to blend in; a mixtape represents a working mode of polyphony where voices stay in their original formats. The blending-in process takes place in the effort to find a suitable framework to structure the multiple voices contained in the mixtape. A mixtape also suggests a different way to deal with scattered resources. Within the context of the 'IMAGINART', a project in which I also take part, some works are materialised (and documented) in the format of the mixtape. We have produced three so far: Mixtape no. 1, 'Radical Institutionalism' (2021); Mixtape no. 2, 'Practi-theorising Counterinstitutions' (2022); and Mixtape no.3 'Artistic Activism and Prefigurative Politics' (2024).[18] Here, the definition of 'mixtape' represents the act of compiling records of conversations; identifying various works by scholars, artists and cultural practitioners which resonate with the work of our project's members; and organising workshops to bring people together. As a method, the mixtape works as a valuation system to measure and identify a wealth of the networks in a certain social environment.

17 It might be worth listing some precedents to collective writing as an inseparable part of class jamming. Carine Zaayman and I were invited to lecture and organise a workshop with BEAR Fine Art (Base for Experiment, Art and Research) students and tutors at the ArtEZ University of the Arts, Arnheim in 2022. During the workshop, collaborative writing was used as a method to encourage exploration around knowledge, the politics of archives, and decolonial thinking and attitudes. The activity was partly inspired by a similar collective writing exercise called 'Writing Companions' at the 'Amsterdam Assembly' in 2021. The writing exercise with the BEAR students was an attempt 'to shift how we think of ourselves as teachers, as students, as artists and as people'. See Nuraini Juliastuti and Carine Zaayman, 'Here We Are', in Clare Butcher (ed.), *We Contain Multitudes: Expanding Spaces and Forms of Mentorship within Art Education and Practices*, Arnhem: ArtEZ Press, pp.25–43. 'Here We Are' also serves as an extended reflection on the 'Amsterdam Assembly' and the 'Decolonial Joy Party'. The title of the assembly, 'Letting Go of Having to Speak All the Time', spoke to the need to disrupt the hierarchical roles of academics (and academic writings) in defining meaning in public spaces.

18 These are all available at https://imaginart.site.

A Magnificent Space Filled with Tempo

In 2024, I saw the multimedia installation *Ruang Elok Sarat Tempo* (A Magnificent Space Filled with Tempo, 2024) by Julian 'Togar' Abraham at the ARTJOG in Yogyakarta. On ARTJOG's website, the 'concept' of the work was described:

> This work is a temporary stopping space in a journey of memory around listening and being heard. It is appropriate for space to share its corners for the circulation of air, voice and sound. Sounds are organised to listen to each other and be heard as a part of everyday life. A kind of space for harmony between what moves and what stays.
>
> Everyday life is used as a way to understand a world full of allusions. Each touch produces a sound. Sounds are recognised until they become voices. Sound is memory. Memories are cherished together. Wherever you go you will take them with you.
>
> Like a moonlit night. Silence is like darkness without artificial light. Using the reflection of moonlight as a source of visual guidance. In harmony with the eyes, the ears require adjustment before they become sensitive again. Blending with the atmosphere, balancing each other between words and sounds, in a temporary time.
>
> Through this work, Togar invites us to feel and understand sound, in an atmosphere full of intimacy. Sound is a medium to be absorbed so that its essence can be known, just like prophecy, which needs to be interpreted continuously according to the conditions of the times.[19]

ARTJOG is an annual art event in Yogyakarta (more familiarly known as Jogja) that started as the Jogja Art Fair in 2008. While the works by other artists on view at ARTJOG were considered finished, Togar's work emerged as a space to enable the making of new works. The producers of these new works were not limited to artist-friends who came by the space at Togar's invitation. Rather, visitors to ARTJOG also became active producers as they made new sounds during their time in the space. As visitors came and went, I noticed that they also tried to play the different musical instruments available. This act of playing was perhaps born out of curiosity or the result of opportunity. Either way, the availability of instruments in the space prompted people to play music or simply produce sound. In this regard, the instruments were not just mere tools to play but active agents informing sound production and

19 This description was copied by the author from ARTJOG's site in 2024; the relevant page is not archived online.

deserving of proper acknowledgement and gratitude. For example, in an Instagram post to mark the launch of a related project, a vinyl by Tropical Tap Water (TTW, more on this ahead), Diana Cantarey wrote the following:

> With gratitudes to a drum set from Takeshi Ikeda, an organ from Simnikiwe Buhlungu, an organ from Özgur Atlagan, an electric guitar from Sungeun Lee, an electric bass from Diana Cantarey, accordion from Daniel Aguilar Ruvalcaba, shaker sculpture from Salim Bayri, painting from Anh Tran, a poster from Pennie Key, electric keyboard from Julian Abraham 'Togar', reel to reel tape player from Simnikiwe Buhlungu, a signage from Togar, flute from Sunken, surd from Togar, fidget tubes from Molly Palmer and more musical instruments, keyboard from Mette Sterre, chimes from Silvia Martes, clay sculptures and a collage from Tropical Tap Water, a sofa from Togar, microphones, mixers, cables, amplifier, microphone and microphone stands from Rijksakademie Medialab.[20]

The arrangement of many things within *Ruang Elok Sarat Tempo* felt familiar. I had seen Togar's signage many times before, including, for the first time, at his studio at the Rijksakademie in 2021. Perhaps the studio was the first iteration of the jamming space at ARTJOG. *Ruang Elok Sarat Tempo* had new signage too: 'From the river to the sea, Palestine will be free', 'Palestina Merdeka' (Independent Palestine). One item of signage appeared in the format of a neon box: 'Ears Have No Self-Defence Mechanism'. The way the sofa, the dresser and the drum set were arranged made me feel like I had seen them before, but I knew that some things were not exactly the same as at the studio. I recognised some small details, such as the photograph of a mother and a child which was placed on top of a cassette player. I also saw the original of the collage used for the cover of the TTW vinyl. One thing is for sure: ARTJOG was the first time I saw Togar's project presented as part of an art exhibition.

As part of an artwork in an exhibition, jamming engenders different experiences and expectations. Probably the most obvious question it raises is whether it is possible to organise jamming without falling into making a work of single authorship. In addition, at ARTJOG jamming was available to the public. It was almost an open opportunity, happening by chance or coincidence. In most cases, visitors to an exhibition are strangers to each other (though certain exhibitions have the capacity to bring in a community of artists, thinkers and cultural practitioners). As the visitors came and went

20 Diana Cantarey (@dianadicealgo), Instagram post, 2 July 2024.

Julian 'Togar' Abraham, *Ruang Elok Sarat Tempo*, ARTJOG, Yogyakarta, 2024. Courtesy Julian 'Togar' Abraham. Photo: Nuraini Juliastuti

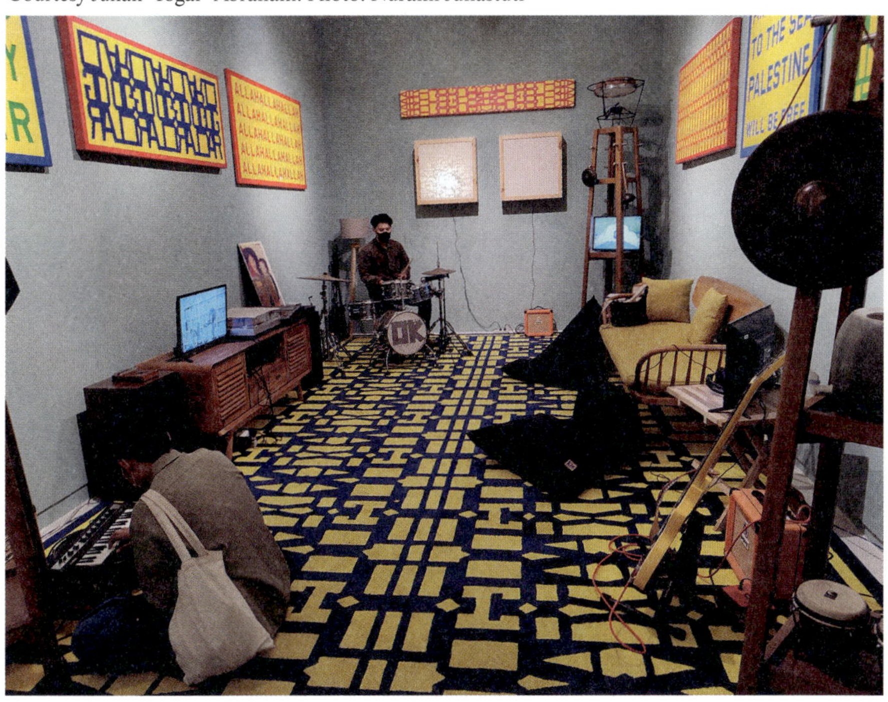

Vinyl LP by Tropical Tap Water, included as part of *Ruang Elok Sarat Tempo*. Courtesy Tropical Tap Water. Photo: Nuraini Juliastuti

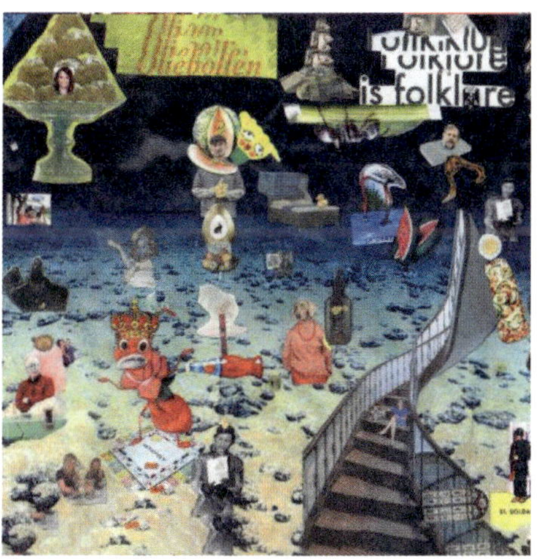

Ruang Elok Sarat Tempo, detail. Courtesy Julian 'Togar' Abraham. Photo: Nuraini Juliastuti

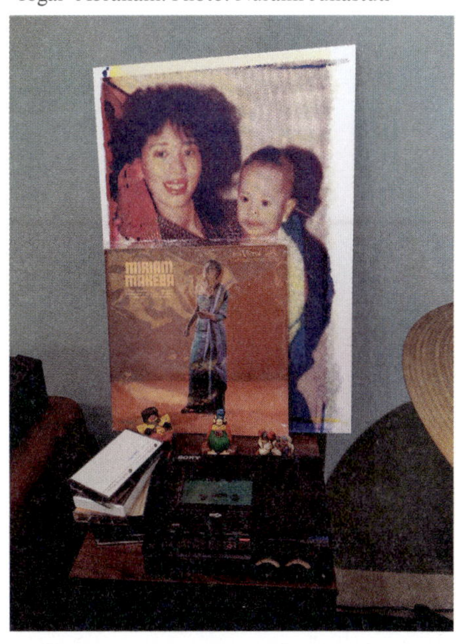

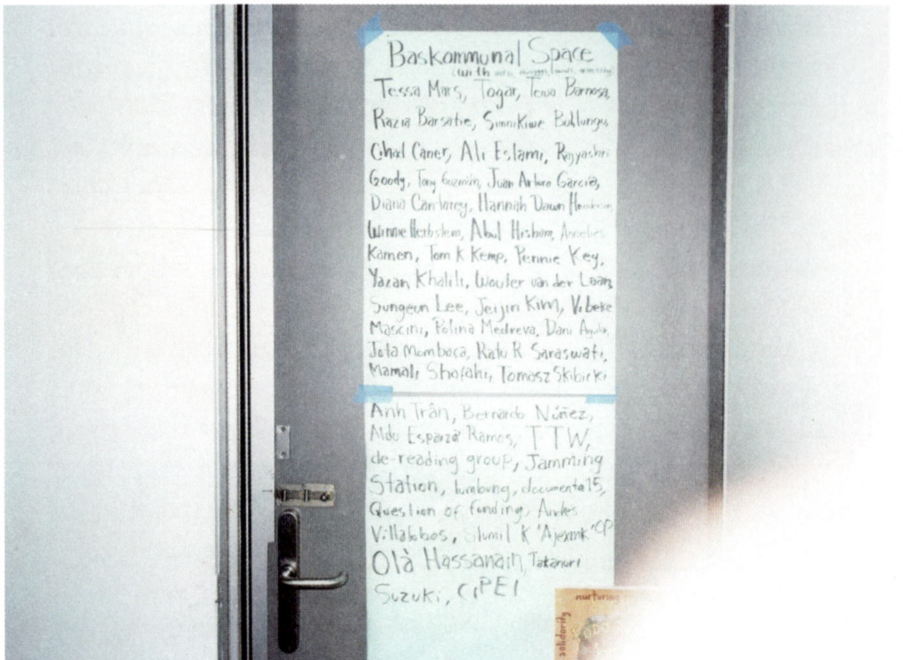
Baskommunal Space
Tessa Mars, Togar,
Razia Barsatie,
Ali Eslami,
Goody, Juan Arturo García,
Hannah Dawn
Abul Hisham,
Kamen, Tom K Kemp, Pennie Key,
Yazan Khalili, Wouter van der Laan
Sungeun Lee, Jeijin Kim,
Mascini, Polina Medveva,
Jota Mombaça, Ratu R Saraswati,
Mamali Shafahi, Tomasz Skibicki
Anh Trân, Bernardo Núñez,
Aldo Esparza Ramos, TTW,
de-reading group, Jamming
Station, lumbung, documenta 15,
Question of funding, Andes
Villalobos,
Olà Hassanain, Takanori
Suzuki, CIPEI
nurturing
solidarity

at ARTJOG, they did not really stay in the room for long. As soon as they were satisfied with playing the instruments, they moved on to the next room to see other artists' works, and new visitors entered Togar's space. There was no arrangement to allow visitors to jam with others at designated times only. What happened was, visitors took turns playing certain instruments and this provided the opportunity to observe different behaviours in the use of the tools and for engagement with others. Could visitors voluntarily initiate their own mechanisms for sharing the musical tools and not taking too much space? How could visitors manage to utilise playing instruments as a means to get to know one another?

Tropical Tap Water and 'Baskommunal Space'

The entity Tropical Tap Water (Julian 'Togar' Abraham, Daniel Aguilar Ruvalcaba, Simnikiwe Buhlungu and Diana Cantarey) was born out of the jamming practices at the Rijksakademie.[21] I see TTW as a new entity which grew from the need to extend conversations and continue various other activities beyond the constraints of the residency programme.

TTW organised 'Baskommunal Space' during a Rijksakademie open studios event in 2022. *Baskommunal* is a playful word that derives from the *baskom* (Javanese and Indonesian for a big bowl made of plastic or aluminium) and *communal*. A *baskom* is a tool commonly used for storing raw materials or cooking meals. Simnikiwe and Togar were familiar with *baskom*'s meaning in their South African and Indonesian contexts respectively. The Dutch word *kom* means a bowl, and is also used in Afrikaans (though in Afrikaans *kom* is considered a little antiquated).[22] In the sharing of particular words and syllables, the initiators of the 'Baskommunal Space' found common ground.

The format of 'Baskommunal Space' is probably best described in terms of mixture: it was a hangout and a learning and market space at the same time. There were chairs, cushions and sofas to sit on. There were tote bags for sale from The Question of Funding (Yazan Khalili, a QoF member, was also an artist-in-residence at the Rijksakademie). A full set of musical instruments

21 'Tropical Tap Water is a band..., planted and watered at the Rijksakademie van Beeldende Kunsten, Amsterdam in 2020. Sometimes we read [very difficult] theoretical texts together, sometimes we go on train ride adventures to see art together, sometimes we don't see one another and sometimes we jam together. We are professional jammers, open for more for birthday parties, weddings, gender reveal parties, exhibitions, mournings, festivals, and what not.' Tropical Tap Water (@tropicaltapwater7661), YouTube channel description.

22 Online conversation with Carine Zaayman, 29 October 2024.

were placed in the middle of the room, inside a blue inflatable swimming pool which indeed looked like a giant *baskom*. People could play the instruments for others to see. And people could just be there, having conversations about stuff for hours on end. The visual harvests from various conversations were pasted on some of the walls, and there were materials available for harvesting new observations.

TTW emerged as an interesting progression, indicative of how jamming fellows evolve into a study group. 'Baskommunal Space' invited all to see the *baskom* figure as a storyteller in the discussion of the politics of cultural funding across geographic realities. In the Indonesian context, it is common to see piles of *baskoms* in a grieving family's house, with various foods contributed by neighbours near and far. In everyday life, a *baskom*'s contents are materials ready to be redistributed (though an object serving as a *baskom* might not have been designed as such). The collaboration of The Question of Funding (Noor Abed, Rayya Badran, Lara Khaldi, Amany Khalifa and Yazan Khalili) at the 'Baskommunal Space' as part of a network strongly suggested how paying attention to funding can reveal local cultural production in the Palestinian context, and the layered, oppressive and restrictive systems that control the lands and the livelihood of the people.[23] Perhaps it is too early to examine the development of the TTW study around funding and resources. The discussion about funding might be used as a starting point to discuss the roots of extraction in a wider sense. The tote bags by The Question of Funding at the 'Baskommunal Space' asked a direct question: What is at stake today in talking about 'sustainability' in the field of art and culture in a time of crisis? The answer to this question, though a bit elusive, is perhaps best described in the lyrics of the TTW song 'baskOm':

> When there is no tap water
> We use the *baskom*
> When they cut our water
> We use the *baskom*
> When we want to collectively own land
> We use the *baskom*
> But meanwhile
> We use the *baskom*
> For misunderstanding
> To artificially know each other

23 'The Question of Funding is a growing collective of cultural producers and community organisers from Palestine. By producing, documenting, accumulating, and disseminating resources, experience, and knowledge with their wider community, it aims to rethink the economy of funding and how it affects cultural production both in Palestine and the world.' A more complete description of the organisation is available on the documenta fifteen website.

'Baskommunal Space', Rijksakademie, Amsterdam, 2022, including tote bags by The Question of Funding (bottom). Photo: Julian 'Togar' Abraham

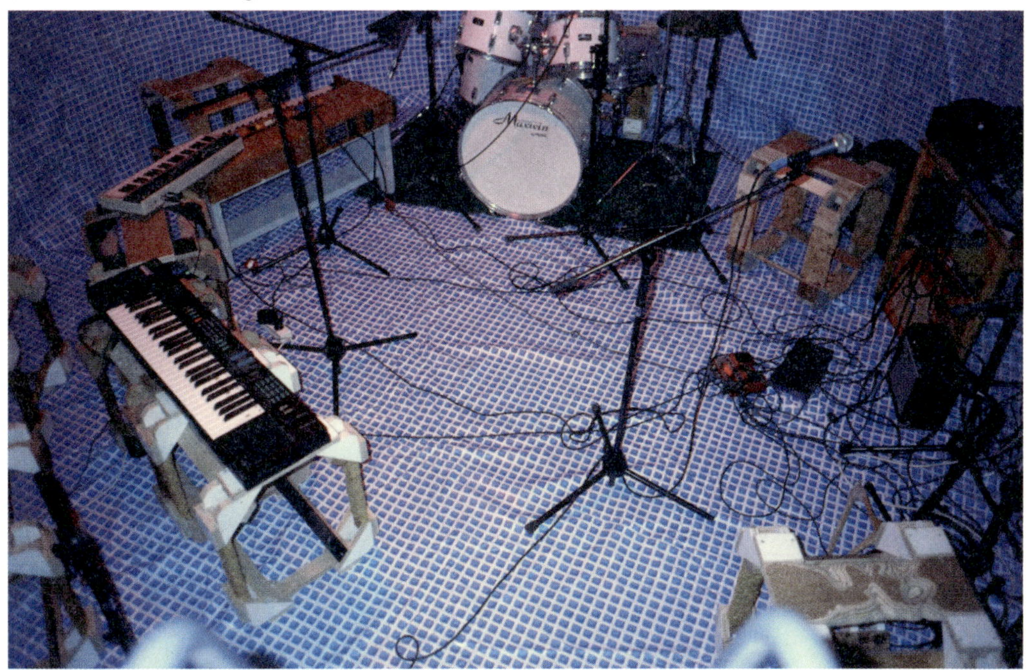

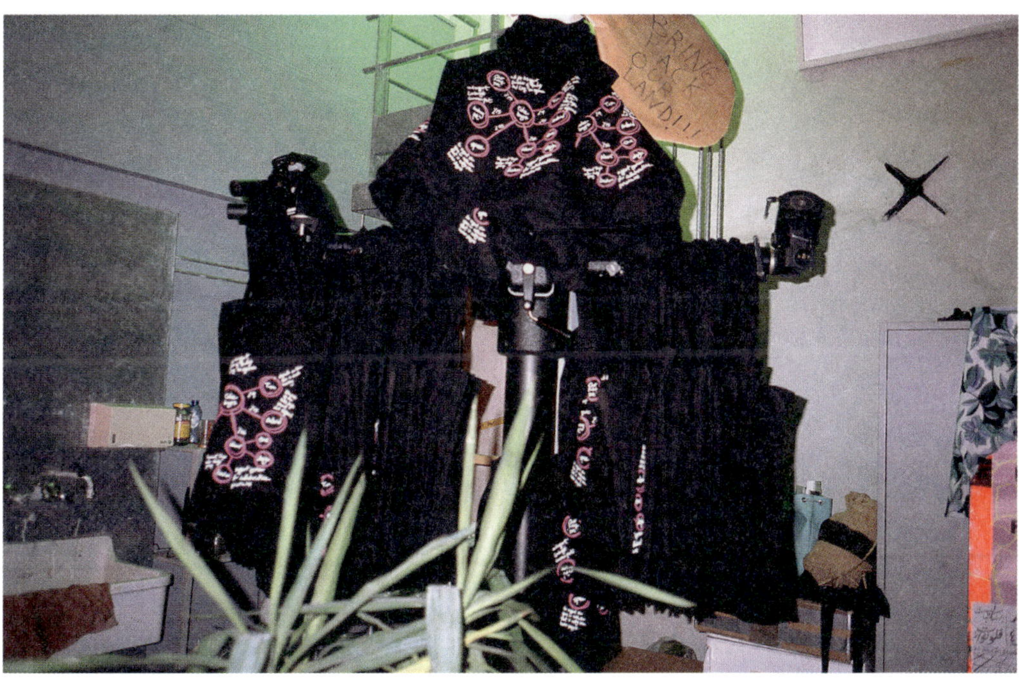

Yes yes yes
We agree
When it is not the first
Either the last
For different struggles
We use the *baskom*
We use the *baskom*
With the more water
Comes the more *baskom*
With the more *baskom*
Comes the more water
With the more water
Comes the more *baskom*
With the more *baskom*
Comes the more good times
With the more good times
Comes the more *lumbung*
With the more *lumbung*
Comes the more Tierra
With the more Tierra
Comes the more flowers
With the more flowers
Comes the more bees
With the more bees
Comes the more sun
With the more sun
Comes the more vaping
With the more vaping
Comes the more cloudys
With the more cloudys
Comes the more rainy
With the more rainy
Comes the more water
With the more water
Comes the more *baskom*
For sure
We use the *baskom*
To decentralise Europe
We use the *baskom*
Something is not yours
We use the *baskom*
Are you able to carry on?
We use the *baskom*?
To know how relevant are the needs
We use the *baskom*
To collectively benefit to everyone
We use the *baskom*
To show solidarity
We use the *baskom*
To liberate money for political long term[24]

24 A music video of the song is available on the TTW YouTube channel.

TTW has also organised a series of International Studies, where they invite people from various collectives and institutions to extend the study group and conversation together.[25] They have also made trips to visit each other in their respective contexts. Togar was in Mexico in early 2023. Diana, Daniel and Simnikiwe were in Jogja in 2024. When I saw Togar's photos documenting his Mexico trip, I wondered what he learnt on that trip. Travelling serves a means (to do something), while it can also be an end at the same time. It might be more apt to see travelling as an avenue to follow objects of curiosity. In essence, curiosity is the main ingredient of learning.

Diana Cantarey, drawing based on a conversation between Nuraini Juliastuti and Cipei – Less Foucault, More Shakira, 2023. Courtesy the artist

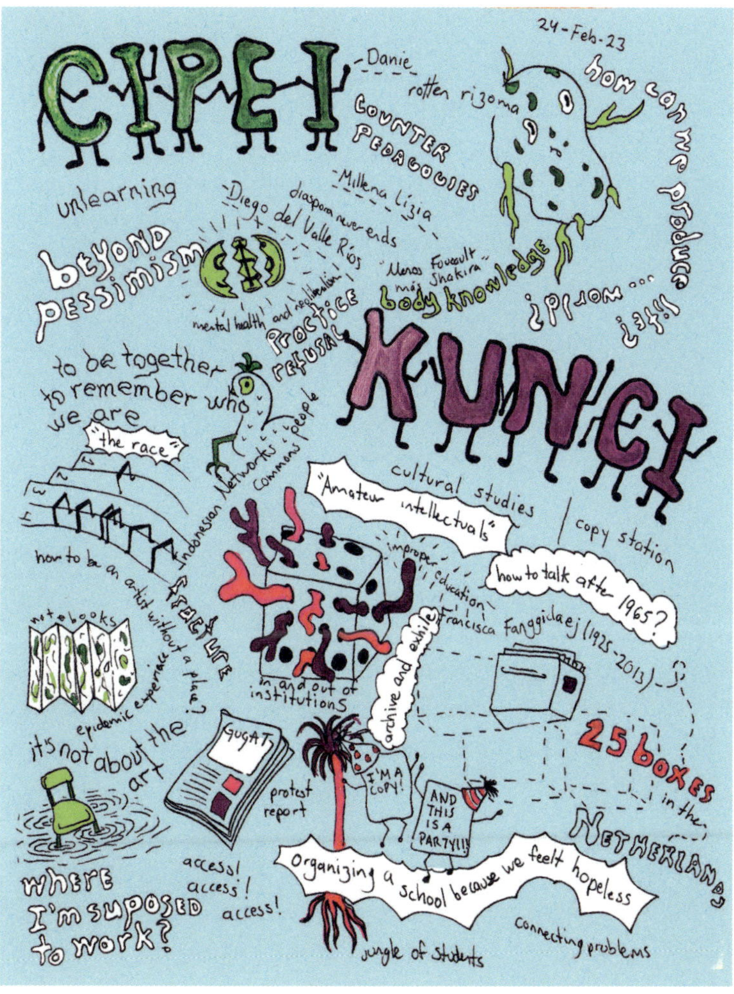

25 In February 2023, TTW invited me to have a conversation with the Mexico-based research platform CIPEI – 'Menos Foucault, Más Shakira' (Less Foucault, More Shakira). The conversation was titled 'Study Group × Study Group' and we talked about access, counter-pedagogy, how to connect our problems and continuing to remember who we are.

Baskom at the Lumbung Practice temporary master's programme space, Sandberg Instituut, 2024.
Photo: Nuraini Juliastuti

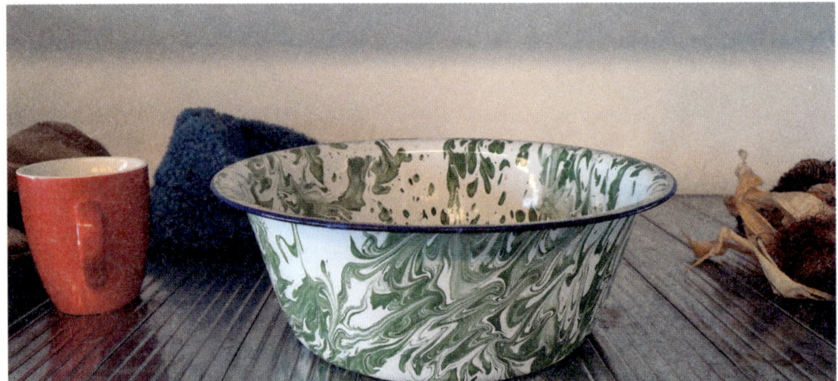

To begin with, jamming emerged as a new way to craft space for bending expectations around music-making practice. Jamming can be put forward as a form with no fixed formation, a practice which produces free-form music. It serves as a means of breathing together. The music serves as an open space where people engaged in it learn to tune in to each other's vibrations, stories and 'herstories'. Jamming offers a pedagogical moment when its formless movement becomes shorthand for resistance to the standardisation of valuation and assessment. Actual experimentation in seeing the classroom as jamming leads to the critical interrogation of hierarchical relations within education institutions.

The present writing develops a vocabulary of the fluid categories around authorship, practiced through a blurring of positions, between teacher and student, collective writing and mixtapes. I contextualise jamming within the global art residency situation to make a point about how mobility plays an important role in reimagining space, time and resources. The development of jamming practice into a long-term International Study group, in the case of Tropical Tap Water, serves as a reminder that travelling, or the ability to be mobile, can also be seen a resource. When I understood that Togar's jamming space was also used as part of the infrastructure to host various gatherings at the Indonesian Pavilion at the recent Gwangju Biennale (2024), I began to see the jamming as shape-shifting. In its ability to shape-shift, jamming offers another shorthand for solidarity-making.

The discussion of *baskom* circles back to the possibility of developing a new vision around resources enabled by trans-local mobility. The question remains: Would it be possible to steadfastly create a pool of resources from water trickling in small streams and irregular travel? In an age of perpetual crises, awareness of the limitations of jamming when it comes to building models for solidarity – whether in terms of scope or scale – might feel hopeless. At the same time, jamming might be the only way to survive.

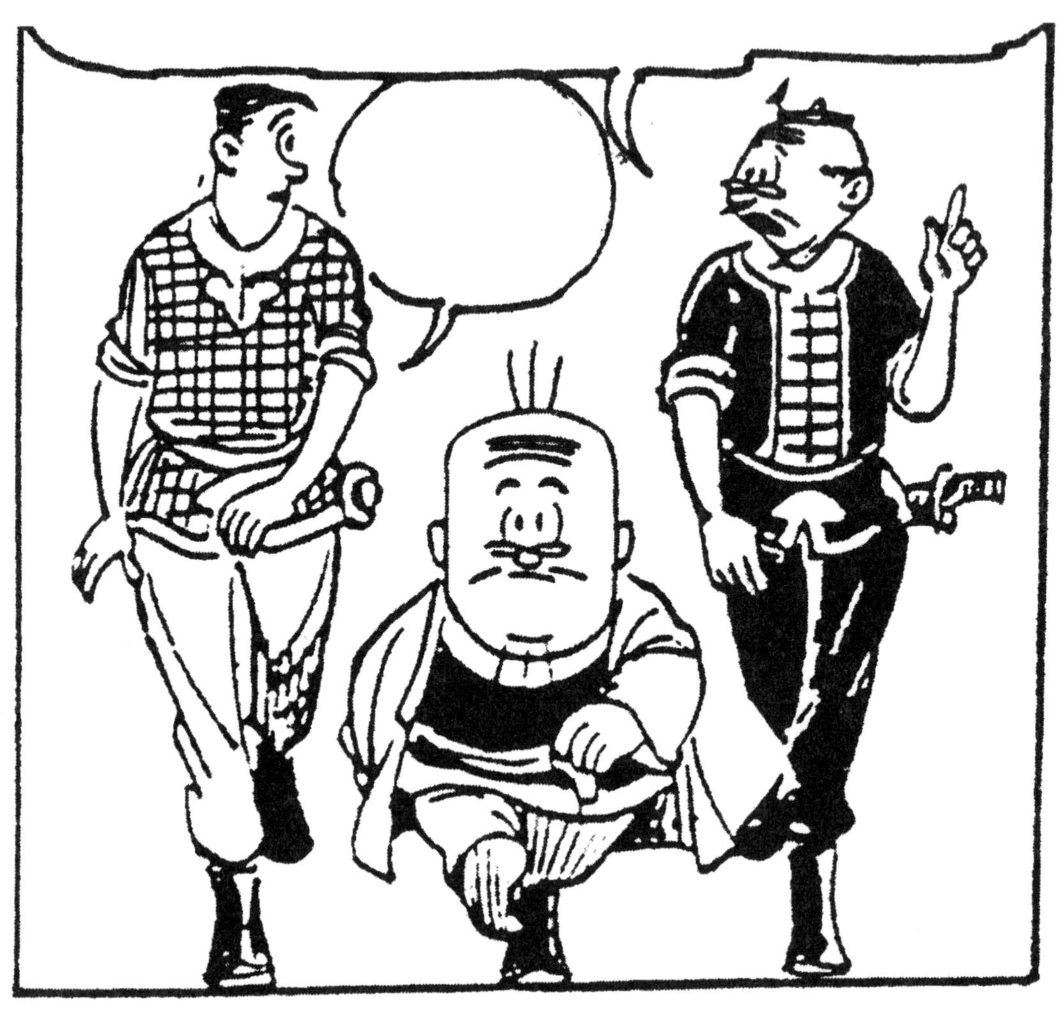

Collectivity is not
only about community.

RONNY AGUSTINUS
is part of ruangrupa. He is the founder and chief editor of Marjin Kiri, an independent publisher dedicated to fostering critical/leftist thinking amongst academia and general readers since 2005. An author and translator specialising in Latin American literature, he authored *Macondo, Para Raksasa, dan Lain-Lain Hal: Seputar Sastra Amerika Latin* (Macondo, the Giants and Other Things: On Latin American Literature; Tanda Baca, 2021).

LEONHARD BARTOLOMEUS
is a curator at the Yamaguchi Center for Arts and Media (YCAM). After graduating, he joined ruangrupa (and later became part of Gudskul Ekosistem). Working with ruangrupa, he developed an interest in the intersection between art, education and community engagement, which then influenced his curatorial projects, such as Kolektif Kurator Kampung (2017–21), 'Kurikulab: Moving Class' in collaboration with Serrum (2021, YCAM), 'The Flavour of Power' in partnership with Bakudapan Food Study Group (2022, YCAM), 'Speculative Library' (2023, YCAM), 'Iida Kaido Kikitori Art Project' (2024) and 'Dance Floor as Study Room' with wendelien van oldenborgh (2024, YCAM).

MELANI BUDIANTA
is an intellectual activist focusing on gender and cultural activism. She taught literature and cultural studies at the Faculty of Humanities, Universitas Indonesia (1983–2024). She serves as an editorial board member for a number of international journals, including *Wacana, Journal of the Humanities of Indonesia* and *Inter-Asia Cultural Studies*.

WING CHAN
is an editor at Afterall Research Centre. She also moonlights as a translator. With David Morris, she co-edited *Precarious Solidarities: Artists for Democracy 1974–77* (Afterall, 2023).

CHITARUM
is a comic artist who lives and works in Yogyakarta. Using a black pen on white paper, she creates comics that explore and question the grey areas of the society we live in today. She shares her comics online via her Instagram page @chitarum. Her comics have also been published by New Naratif, Samandal Comics and Slowork Publishing.

ADE DARMAWAN
is part of ruangrupa. He lives and works in Jakarta as an artist and curator. His work deals with Indonesia, its history and its people, with a particular focus on minor histories that may seem irrelevant but are intrinsic to the DNA of the communities addressed. His presentation of these narratives assumes multiple forms, ranging from installation to objects, drawing, digital print and video.

ÖZGE ERSOY
is senior curator at Asia Art Archive in Hong Kong. Her research interests include expanded ideas of collecting, archiving and exhibition-making. Recent projects include co-curating 'Translations, Expansions' (2022), 'Countering Time' (2024) and 'In Our Own Backyard' (2025). Her writings appear in *The Constituent Museum* (Valiz and L'Internationale, 2018) and *Curating Under Pressure* (Routledge, 2020).

CHARLES ESCHE
is former director of the Van Abbemuseum, Eindhoven. He is an advisor at Jan van Eyck Academie, Maastricht and professor of contemporary art and curating at Central Saint Martins, University of the Arts London. He received the 2012 Princess Margriet Award and the 2014 CCS Bard College Prize for Curatorial Excellence. He is a series editor of Afterall's *Exhibition Histories* series.

NURAINI JULIASTUTI

is a trans-local practicing researcher and writer, focussing on arts organisations, activism, illegality, alternative cultural production, vernacular archiving and contemporary bestiaries. In 1999, Nuraini co-founded Kunci Study Forum & Collective in Yogyakarta. She develops Domestic Notes, a publication-based project that takes domestic and migrant spaces as sites to discuss everyday politics, the organisation of makeshift support systems and women archives. With her family, Nuraini runs a small press, Reading Sideways Press, which publishes works and translations on the intersections of contemporary art, sports culture, literature, sound and other pressing matters. Nuraini teaches at the Master of Fine Art Department, HKU University of the Arts, Utrecht.

ABIDIN KUSNO

is a professor in the Faculty of Environmental and Urban Change at York University, Toronto, and former director of York Centre of Asian Research (YCAR). Formerly, he was the Canada Research Chair in Asian Urbanism and Culture at the Institute for Asian Research at the University of British Columbia. His research focuses on urban politics and cultural history of Indonesia, and Jakarta in particular. His most recent publication is *Jakarta: The City of a Thousand Dimensions* (National University of Singapore Press, 2023).

UMI LESTARI

is a writer and curator. Her research explores Indonesian film history and aesthetics and the potentiality of the act to preserve the archive. She is currently teaching in the film department at Universitas Multimedia Nusantara, Indonesia.

ARIANNA MERCADO

is a cultural worker based in Manila and a senior lecturer at the Department of Theory, College of Fine Arts, University of the Philippines Diliman. She works between exhibitions and publishing and often thinks about learning, land, labour and celebration. Mercado co-founded kiat kiat projects in 2018 and *no exits* in 2022. Formerly, she was a project coordinator and editor at Afterall Research Centre.

UGENG T. MOETIDJO

is an artist and researcher. He conducted media art research (2008–11) and was involved in the ruangrupa collective. In 2023, he researched and wrote the script for the documentary 'Layar Pasti Turun', which is about Indonesia's third female director, Ida Farida, with the Saijah Forum collective. He lives and works in Jakarta.

DAVID MORRIS

is a research fellow and editor at Afterall Research Centre. His work explores different approaches to artistic research, education and exhibition, with a focus on experimental and collective practice. His publications include *Schizo-Culture* (co-edited with Sylvère Lotringer; Semiotext(e)/MIT, 2013), *Artist-to-Artist: Independent Art Festivals in Chiang Mai 1992–98* (co-edited with David Teh, Afterall, 2017) and *Precarious Solidarities: Artists for Democracy 1974–77* (co-edited with Wing Chan; Afterall, 2023). With Helena Vilalta he leads a research masters programme in Exhibition Studies at Central Saint Martins, University of the Arts London, where he is also a trade union organiser.

FARID RAKUN

is part of ruangrupa, with whom he co-curated Sonsbeek 16: 'transACTION' (Arnhem, The Netherlands, 2016) and provided a collective artistic direction for documenta fifteen (Kassel, Germany, 2022). Trained as an architect, rakun wears different hats depending on who is asking.

GESYADA SIREGAR

is a curator, writer and arts organiser based in Jakarta and Philadelphia. At Gudskul Collective Studies programme, she coordinates the 'Articulation and Curation' subject area and works on various interlocal art projects. Currently, she studies behavioural and decision sciences at the University of Pennsylvania, investigating how guesswork, friendship and organisational behaviour affect art ecosystems.

IBRAHIM SOETOMO
is a curator, writer and researcher based in Jakarta. He was previously involved in Jakarta 32°c, managing college student forums and serving as an editor for aspiring student-writers. Now, he writes exhibition reviews and essays, and researches art criticism in Indonesia from the 1950s to the 70s. Blending the criticism tradition with literary and ecological writing, he seeks ways in which art can be written and explored.

ENIN SUPRIYANTO
is an independent curator living and working in Jakarta. Since 1994, he has been curating exhibitions and contributing essays for various publications in Indonesia and abroad. Recent publications include *Indonesian Contemporary Art Now* (with Marc Bollansee; SNP International Publishing, 2007) and *Sesudah Aktivisme: Sepilihan Esai Seni Rupa 1994–2015* (*After Activism: Selected Visual Arts Essays 1994–2015*; Hyphen, 2015).

DAVID TEH
is a writer, curator and assistant professor in the English department at the National University of Singapore. His work spans a variety of topics within the art world, from modern and contemporary Asian art, critical art theory and history, to curatorship and exhibitions.

THE SECRET AGENTS
are Indra Ameng and Keke Tumbuan. A duo working on projects involving conceptual art, good music and other delightful things.

MAHARDIKA YUDHA
is an artist, researcher, curator and writer who lives and works in Tangerang. Yudha studied journalism, and also has experience as a book typist, supermarket manager and worker in an automotive factory.

ARDI YUNANTO
was born in Jakarta. He worked as the editor of the online art and public space journal *Karbon* and the men's lifestyle magazine *Bung!* published by ruangrupa, while also working as an editor, writer, designer and artistic director for various publications and exhibition materials. Currently, in addition to working as a designer and editor in Jakarta, he is a lecturer in Indonesian at the Indonesian Jentera College of Law. *Bermain Rahasia* is his first book of fiction. His essay about *Imung*, Arswendo Atmowiloto's child detective series, was published in the zine *Mancis: Jejak Darah* (baNANA + Studio Batu, 2024).

p.71
ruangrupa, archive note, undated. The ruangrupa digital archive includes various annotations; many of these notes were drafted by Ade Darmawan, as well as other ruru members, and have been edited for this publication
Ade Darmawan, conversation with Wing Chan and Arianna Mercado, 28 May 2024
Agung Jenong, conversation with Wing Chan and David Morris, 2 November 2023

p.73
'Press Release', document from ruangrupa digital archive, 2000; translation by Ibrahim Soetomo

p.74
ruangrupa, archive note, undated

p.76
ruangrupa, archive note, undated
Gertrude Flentge, 'Introduction', in Gertrude Flentge, Els van Odijk and Edith Rijnja (ed.), *Shifting Maps*, Amsterdam: Rijksakademie van beeldende kunsten/Rotterdam: NAi Publishers, 2004, p.10; revised by the author for this publication

p.77
Ade Darmawan, conversation with Wing Chan and Arianna Mercado, 28 May 2024

p.78
Agung Jenong, 'Ruangrupa', in *Singapore Biennale 2011: Open House*, Singapore: Singapore Art Museum, 2011, unpaginated
Patrick Flores, correspondence with Wing Chan and David Morris, 26 July 2023
reinaart vanhoe, correspondence with Wing Chan and David Morris, 7 September 2023
Veronika Kusumaryati, correspondence with Wing Chan and David Morris, 11 August 2023

p.81
Ardi Yunanto, 'karbonjournal.org 2010', document shared with Afterall via Ibrahim Soetomo, 18 October 2024; edited for this publication
ruangrupa, archive note, undated

p.84
ruangrupa, archive note, undated

p.86
ruangrupa, in Gertrude Flentge, Els van Odijk and Edith Rijnja (ed.), *Shifting Maps*, Amsterdam: Rijksakademie van beeldende kunsten/Rotterdam: NAi Publishers, 2004, p.156

p.87
Reza Afisina, conversation with Wing Chan and Arianna Mercado, 23 May 2024

Grace Samboh, conversation with Wing Chan and David Morris, 28 November 2023

p.90
Iswanto Hartono, 'Selatan: Transformation of Urban Cultural Imagery from Melawai to Tebet', in Anthony Gardner (ed.) *Mapping South: Journeys in South-South Cultural Relations*, Victoria: The South Project, 2013, p.232; edited for this publication
Ade Darmawan, conversation with Wing Chan and Arianna Mercado, 28 May 2024
Iswanto Hartono, in 'Taking care of ecosystems through the lumbung process and intangible infrastructures. A conversation with Reza Afisina, Iswanto Hartono and Bellina Erby (from ruangrupa and Gudskul Ecosystem, Jakarta – Indonesia)', *Roots & Routes*, no.42, May–August 2023

p.91
ruangrupa, archive note, undated

p.92
ruangrupa, *Siasat: a Short Tactical Guide for Artist-Run Initiative*, Jakarta: ruangrupa, 2011, p.6

p.93
Gwangju Biennale 2002 – Project 1: PAUSE Realization, Gwangju: Gwangju Biennale Press, 2002, p.275

p.94
Hou Hanru, conversation with Wing Chan and David Morris, 21 November 2023
Reza Afisina, conversation with Wing Chan and Arianna Mercado, 23 May 2024
Gridthiya Gaweewong, from 'Navigating the Zomia Cultural Landscape and Beyond: Independence, Collaboration and Institutional Engagement', The Histories and Archives of Independent Art Spaces of Asia, symposium co-organised by Asia Art Archive and Ministry of Culture, Taiwan Contemporary Cultural Lab, 11 April 2025

pp.95–97
Ade Darmawan, 'Big Kiss from Ade Darmawan', *Karbon: Absolut Versus*, 2002, pp.9–11

pp.99–115
Ronny Agustinus, 'A Cool Beer Conversation and 3 Years After' (trans. Amanda Katherine Rath), *Karbon: Absolut Versus*, 2002, pp.55–71

p.117
Reza Afisina, conversation with Wing Chan and Arianna Mercado, 2 3 May 2024
Sophie Goltz in conversation with Reza Afisina, Ade Darmawan and Iswanto Hartono, 'Collective Crafting in Post-Suharto Indonesia: Journey with Ruangrupa from the Jakarta Institute of the Arts to Documenta Fifteen in Kassel', *Cultural Politics*, vol.18, no.3, 2022
Reza Afisina, in 'Taking care of ecosystems through the lumbung process and intangible infrastructures. A conversation with Reza Afisina, Iswanto Hartono and Bellina Erby (from ruangrupa and Gudskul Ecosystem, Jakarta – Indonesia)', *Roots & Routes*, no.42, May–August 2023
ruangrupa, in response to the statement 'Artist-driven initiatives should be reluctant towards participating in activities coming forth of institutional activism', in Gertrude Flentge, Els van Odijk and Edith Rijnja (ed.), *Shifting Maps*, Amsterdam: Rijksakademie van beeldende kunsten/Rotterdam: NAi Publishers, 2004, p.115

p.119
Gertrude Flentge, correspondence with Wing Chan and David Morris, 27 June 2023

p.121
ruangrupa, archive note, undated

p.122
farid rakun, MRes Art: Exhibition Studies seminar, 23 February 2022
Iswanto Hartono, conversation with Wing Chan and Arianna Mercado, 23 May 2024
Daniella F. Praptono, correspondence with Wing Chan and David Morris, 26 June 2025
Abidin Kusno, correspondence with Wing Chan and Arianna Mercado, 2 July 2024

p.125
ruangrupa, archive note, undated

p.127
Ade Tanesia, 'Ruang Rupa exhibition invites unique participation', *The Jakarta Post*, 22 March 2003

p.130
Farah Wardani and Hafiz Rancajale, introduction to *Karbon*, issue 5, May 2003, p.3; translation revised for this publication

p.131
Laila Achmad (ed.), *OK.Pangan – OK Video Indonesia Media Arts Festival 2017*, Jakarta: ruangrupa, 2017, p.132; edited for this publication

p.133
Indra Ameng, in John Badalu, 'Video Art Festival, the First of Its Kind', *The Jakarta Post*, 7 July 2003
Ade Darmawan, in John Badalu, 'Video Art Festival, the First of Its Kind', *The Jakarta Post*, 7 July 2003

p.134
ruangrupa, archive note, undated

p.137
Sophie Goltz in conversation with Reza Afisina, Ade Darmawan and Iswanto Hartono, 'Collective Crafting in Post-Suharto Indonesia: Journey with Ruangrupa from the Jakarta Institute of the Arts to Documenta Fifteen in Kassel', *Cultural Politics*, vol.18, no.3, 2022; revised by the author for this publication
reinaart vanhoe, conversation with Wing Chan and Arianna Mercado, 10 April 2024
Farah Wardani, correspondence with Wing Chan and David Morris, 3 August 2023

p.138
ruangrupa, *Siasat: a Short Tactical Guide for Artist-Run Initiative*, Jakarta: ruangrupa, 2011, p.7

p.140
Iswanto Hartono, 'Selatan: Transformation of Urban Cultural Imagery from Melawai to Tebet', in Anthony Gardner (ed.), *Mapping South: Journeys in South-South Cultural Relations*, Victoria: The South Project, 2013, p.235
Reza Afisina, in 'Taking care of ecosystems through the lumbung process and intangible infrastructures. A conversation with Reza Afisina, Iswanto Hartono and Bellina Erby (from ruangrupa and Gudskul Ecosystem, Jakarta – Indonesia)', *Roots & Routes*, no.42, May–August 2023
Che Kyongfa, conversation with Wing Chan and David Morris, 11 October 2023

p.143
Farah Wardani and Ardi Yunanto, introduction to *Karbon*, issue 6, April 2004, p.3; translation revised for this publication

p.144
ruangrupa, *Siasat: a Short Tactical Guide for Artist-Run Initiative*, Jakarta: ruangrupa, 2011, p.11

p.147
'Ekosistem – Jakarta 32°C', Gudskul website

p.148
JJ Adibrata, conversation with Wing Chan and Arianna Mercado, 13 June 2024

Ade Darmawan, conversation with Wing Chan and Arianna Mercado, 28 May 2024

p.151
Che Kyongfa, conversation with Wing Chan and David Morris, 11 October 2023

p.152
Esra Sarıgedik Öktem, 'Artist – ruangrupa', 9th International Istanbul Biennale website

p.153
Ardi Yunanto, introduction to *Karbon*, issue 7, January 2006, p.1; translation revised for this publication

p.156
ruangrupa, 'Living (in) the Postcolonial Participating Artists – ruangrupa', Rethinking Nordic Colonialism website
Frederikke Hansen, 'Artistic Team: Fred's Story', documenta fifteen website

p.162
ruangrupa, *Decompression# 10 Expanding the Space and Public: ruangrupa's 10th Anniversary – Programme Book*, Jakarta: ruangrupa, 2010, p.65

p.163
Leonhard Bartolomeus, conversation with Wing Chan and Arianna Mercado, 5 June 2024

p.164
Riksa Afiaty, conversation with Wing Chan and David Morris, 16 November 2023

p.165
ruangrupa, *Siasat: a Short Tactical Guide for Artist-Run Initiative*, Jakarta: ruangrupa, 2011, p.15

p.167
ruangrupa, archive note, 2011

p.171
farid rakun, conversation with Wing Chan and Arianna Mercado, 5 June 2024
Sophie Goltz in conversation with Reza Afisina, Ade Darmawan and Iswanto Hartono, 'Collective Crafting in Post-Suharto Indonesia: Journey with Ruangrupa from the Jakarta Institute of the Arts to Documenta Fifteen in Kassel', *Cultural Politics*, vol.18, no.3, 2022
Farah Wardani, conversation with Wing Chan and Arianna Mercado, 7 March 2024
Tintin Wulia, conversation with Wing Chan, 24 April 2024
Che Kyongfa, conversation with Wing Chan and David Morris, 11 October 2023

p.172
farid rakun, 'Urban Stickers Surfacing in Time', *Inside Indonesia*, 29 September 2014

p.174
Melani Budianta, conversation with Wing Chan and David Morris, 30 October 2023
reinaart vanhoe, 'Generous Structure', in *Also-Space, From Hot to Something Else: How Indonesian Art Initiatives Have Reinvented Networking*, Eindhoven: Onomatopee, 2016, p.34
Gertrude Flentge, correspondence with Wing Chan and David Morris, 27 June 2023
Indra Ameng, conversation with Wing Chan and Arianna Mercado, 16 May 2024
Sophie Goltz in conversation with Reza Afisina, Ade Darmawan and Iswanto Hartono, 'Collective Crafting in Post-Suharto Indonesia: Journey with Ruangrupa from the Jakarta Institute of the Arts to Documenta Fifteen in Kassel', *Cultural Politics*, vol.18, no.3, 2022; revised by the author for this publication

p.177
reinaart vanhoe, 'Generous Structure', in *Also-Space, From Hot to Something Else: How Indonesian Art Initiatives Have Reinvented Networking*, Eindhoven: Onomatopee, 2016, p.34
Ade Darmawan, conversation with Wing Chan and Arianna Mercado, 28 May 2024
Agung Kurniawan, 'The Rebels from the Living Room', in Gertrude Flentge, Els van Odijk and Edith Rijnja (ed.), *Shifting Maps*, Amsterdam: Rijksakademie van beeldende kunsten/Rotterdam: NAi Publishers, 2004, p.152

p.186
Reza Afisina, conversation with Wing Chan and Arianna Mercado, 23 May 2024
Binna Choi, correspondence with Wing Chan, 1 and 8 March 2024

p.187
ruangrupa, 'How to Use This House', in *Grand Domestic Revolution Handbook*, Amsterdam: Valiz, 2014, p.71

p.190
ruangrupa, *Siasat: a Short Tactical Guide for Artist-Run Initiative*, Jakarta: ruangrupa, 2011, p.23

p.197
'RURUKIDS Profile 2023 – English Version', document from ruangrupa digital archive, 2023
Daniella F. Praptono, conversation with Wing Chan and Arianna Mercado, 1 May 2024; correspondence with Wing Chan and David Morris, 26 June 2025

p.199
Grace Samboh, conversation with Wing Chan and David Morris, 28 November 2023

p.200
ruangrupa, 'Introduction', in *Decompression# 10 Expanding the Space and Public: ruangrupa's 10th Anniversary – Programme Book*, Jakarta: ruangrupa, 2010, p.3; translation revised for this publication

pp.201–05
Ugeng T. Moetidjo, 'Archives on Space, People and Idea in the Process', in *Decompression# 10 Expanding the Space and Public: ruangrupa's 10th Anniversary*, Jakarta: ruangrupa, 2010, pp.190–97; the final phrase, missing from the original publication, has been added

p.207
'Ekosistem – RRREC Fest', Gudskul website

p.208
Indra Ameng, conversation with Wing Chan and Arianna Mercado, 16 May 2024
Grace Samboh, conversation with Wing Chan and David Morris, 28 November 2023

p.210
Syafiatudina, correspondence with Wing Chan and David Morris, 25 June 2025
reinaart vanhoe, correspondence with Wing Chan and David Morris, 7 September 2023

p.211
ruangrupa, *Siasat: a Short Tactical Guide for Artist-Run Initiative*, Jakarta: ruangrupa, 2011, p.24

p.212
Agung Kurniawan, 'The Rebels from the Living Room', in Gertrude Flentge, Els van Odijk and Edith Rijnja (ed.), *Shifting Maps*, Amsterdam: Rijksakademie van beeldende kunsten/Rotterdam: NAi Publishers, 2004, p.151
Mirwan Andan, 'All for Jakarta –a note on the tenth anniversary of ruangrupa: Decompression#10, Expanding the Space and Public', *Inter-Asia Cultural Studies*, vol.12, no.4, 2011, p.596
Veronika Kusumaryati, correspondence with Wing Chan and David Morris, 11 August 2023
Simon Danang Anggoro, conversation with Wing Chan and Arianna Mercado, 13 July 2024

p.214
'Singapore Fiction', @ruangrupa-blog Tumblr, 1 March 2011

p.217
Leonhard Bartolomeus, 'Street Art in Indonesian Social and Political Life', *Guggenheim Articles*, 17 October 2012

pp.225–7
ruangrupa, *Siasat: a Short Tactical Guide for Artist-Run Initiative*, Jakarta: ruangrupa, 2011, pp.26–8

p.235
ruangrupa, *Siasat: a Short Tactical Guide for Artist-Run Initiative*, Jakarta: ruangrupa, 2011, p.29

pp.238–45
David Teh, 'Who Cares a Lot? Ruangrupa as Curatorship', *Afterall*, issue 30, Summer 2012, pp.111–17

p.248
Samanth Subramanian, 'The Editing Floor – Outtakes from Indonesia', *multi-storied* substack, 19 June 2022, available online

p.253
Ade Darmawan, in Samanth Subramanian, 'The Editing Floor – Outtakes from Indonesia', *multi-storied* substack, 19 June 2022, available online
Alia Swastika, in reinaart vanhoe, 'Insert #1 to Chapter 2', in *Also-Space, From Hot to Something Else: How Indonesian Art Initiatives Have Reinvented Networking*, Eindhoven: Onomatopee, 2016, p.61

p.271
Gesyada Siregar, conversation with Wing Chan and Arianna Mercado, 19 April 2024
Syafiatudina, correspondence with Wing Chan and David Morris, 25 June 2025
Ajeng Nurul Aini, conversation with Wing Chan and Arianna Mercado, 19 April 2024

p.274
ruangrupa, *Siasat: a Short Tactical Guide for Artist-Run Initiative*, Jakarta: ruangrupa, 2011, p.48

p.277
Philippe Pirotte, conversation with Wing Chan and David Morris, 29 October 2023

p.282
Charles Esche, 'RURU 2000–ongoing', in *Guide of the 31st Bienal de São Paulo: – How to (...) Things that Don't Exist*, São Paulo: Fundação Bienal de São Paulo, 2014, pp.144–45

p.283
Ken Jenie, 'Populist Art: Ruang Rupa at the 31st Biennale of Sao Paolo', *Whiteboard Journal*, 27 October 2014, available online

p.292
Gudang Sarinah Ekosistem, LinkedIn profile

p.297
Nozomu Ogawa, 'ruangrupa', in *Southeast Asia Research Trip: 83 Art Spaces in 9 Countries*, Tokyo: Arts Council Tokyo, 2017, p.115
Indra Ameng, conversation with Wing Chan and Arianna Mercado, 16 May 2024
Daniella F. Praptono, conversation with Wing Chan and Arianna Mercado, 1 May 2024; correspondence with Wing Chan and David Morris, 26 June 2025

p.298
Riksa Afiaty, conversation with Wing Chan and David Morris, 16 November 2023
Ade Darmawan, conversation with Wing Chan and Arianna Mercado, 28 May 2024
Ade Darmawan, correspondence with Wing Chan and David Morris, 25 June 2025
JJ Adibrata, correspondence with Wing Chan and Arianna Mercado, 13 June 2024

p.301
Leonhard Bartolomeus, conversation with Wing Chan and Arianna Mercado, 30 May 2024
Philippe Pirotte, conversation with Wing Chan and David Morris, 29 October 2023
reinaart vanhoe, conversation with Wing Chan and Arianna Mercado, 10 April 2024

p.303
'Sonsbeek 16: transACTION', Sonsbeek website

p.305
Nina Siegal, 'Dutch City Makes the Most of Its Park, and Its History', *The New York Times*, 16 June 2016

p.308
ruangrupa, archive note, undated

p.315
farid rakun, conversation with Wing Chan and Arianna Mercado, 5 June 2024

p.317
farid rakun, MRes Art: Exhibition Studies seminar, 23 February 2022
Grace Samboh, conversation with Wing Chan and David Morris, 28 November 2023
reinaart vanhoe, 'Doing Too Much: Claiming Territory', in *Also-Space, From Hot to Something Else: How Indonesian Art Initiatives Have Reinvented Networking*, Eindhoven: Onomatopee, 2016, p.43
Daniella F. Praptono, conversation with Wing Chan and Arianna Mercado, 1 May 2024; correspondence with Wing Chan and David Morris, 26 June 2025

p.318
Gudskul website

pp.319–22
farid rakun, 'How little I know about you', in *How Little You Know About Me*, Seoul: National Museum of Modern and Contemporary Art, 2018, pp.264–67

p.323
Iswanto Hartono, conversation with Wing Chan and Arianna Mercado, 23 May 2024
farid rakun, conversation with Wing Chan and Arianna Mercado, 5 June 2024
J J Adibrata, correspondence with Wing Chan and Arianna Mercado, 13 June 2024

p.332
Doni Ahmad and Eka Putra Nggalu, 'Introduction', *Kelana Lumbung Indonesia*, Kassel: Lumbung Press, 2022, pp.3–6
ruangrupa et al., 'How to Do Things Differently', in *Documenta Fifteen Handbook*, Berlin and Stuttgart: Hatje Cantz, 2022, p.16

p.333
'About', documenta fifteen website

p.337
ruangrupa et al., '...And Find a Translation to Kassel', in *Documenta Fifteen Handbook*, Berlin and Stuttgart: Hatje Cantz, 2022, p.31

p.343
ruangrupa et al., 'Keep on Doing What You're Doing...', in *Documenta Fifteen Handbook*, Berlin and Stuttgart: Hatje Cantz, 2022, p.30
Gertrude Flentge, correspondence with Wing Chan and David Morris, 27 June 2023

p.347
Ary Sendy, 'Jimged's Stories in Kassel', in *Hundred Days Smell of Rice in Kassel*, Yogyakarta: Kunci Copy Station, 2023, p.91; translation revised for this publication

p.348
'Introduction to a Won't Profile Gallery', document from lumbung.space archive, 2022

p.349
Charles Esche, 'The First Exhibition of the Twenty-First Century – Lumbung 1 (Documenta Fifteen), What Happened, and What It Might Mean Two Years On', *Australian and New Zealand Journal of Art*, 2024, pp.1–10; and T. Heffernan, N. Farro, N. Papastergiadis, D. Butt, T. McDowell and V. Lynn, 'Responses to Charles Esche', *Australian and New Zealand Journal of Art*, 2024, p.8

p.352
'Introduction to Lumbung Kios', document from lumbung.space archive, 2022

p.353
Melani Budianta, conversation with Wing Chan and David Morris, 30 October 2023
Syafiatudina, correspondence with Wing Chan and David Morris, 25 June 2025

p.354
ruangrupa et al., 'From Mini to Akbar: "We Are Not in Documenta Fifteen, We Are in Lumbung One"', in *Documenta Fifteen Handbook*, Berlin and Stuttgart: Hatje Cantz, 2022, p.28; edited for this publication

p.355
'Lumbung Press: Lumbung Members and Lumbung Artists Publications', document from lumbung.space archive, 2022

p.356
'Lumbung of Publishers', document from lumbung.space archive, 2022

p.357
ruangrupa et al., 'From Mini to Akbar: "We Are Not in Documenta Fifteen, We Are in Lumbung One"', in *Documenta Fifteen Handbook*, Berlin & Stuttgart: Hatje Cantz, 2022, p.27

p.359
Grace Samboh, conversation with Wing Chan and David Morris, 28 November 2023
Mirwan Andan, 'All for Jakarta – a note on the tenth anniversary of ruangrupa: Decompression#10, Expanding the Space and Public', *Inter-Asia Cultural Studies*, 12:4, 2011, p.595
Philippe Pirotte, conversation with Wing Chan and David Morris, 29 October 2023
Farah Wardani, correspondence with Wing Chan and David Morris, 3 August 2023

p.361
ruangrupa, *Siasat: a Short Tactical Guide for Artist-Run Initiative*, Jakarta: ruangrupa, 2011, p.68

p.364
ruangrupa, *Siasat: a Short Tactical Guide for Artist-Run Initiative*, Jakarta: ruangrupa, 2011, p.79

inserts
Julia Sarisetiati, correspondence with Reza Afisina, Ajeng Nurul Aini, Indra Ameng, Mirwan Andan, Rahmat Arham, Narpati Awangga, Wing Chan, Ade Darmawan, Charles Esche, Iswanto Hartono, David Morris, Indras Oktafia, Daniella F. Praptono, farid rakun and ruru crew, 8 July 2023
The Secret Agents (Indra Ameng and Keke Tumbuan), correspondence with Wing Chan, 24 September 2024

2000

1 Jakarta map from ruangrupa's collection. Photo: Wing Chan

2 Public art project with Taring Padi and Apotik Komik: bus mural models produced as part of Apotik Komik workshop

3–5 Apotik Komik workshop, with Bambang Toko Witjaksono and Arie Diyanto

6–8 Bus mural models produced as part of Apotik Komik workshop

9–14 Taring Padi mural painting workshop, with people local to the Ciliwung river

15 Interior view of ruangrupa's first house, in the Garuda building complex at Pasar Minggu, Jakarta

16–21 RAIN artist exchange programme, workshop at Centre Soleil d'Afrique

22 'Urban printing workshop', workshop process with participating artist Irwan Ahmett

23 Workshop process, with work by David Tarigan

24–30 Prints, stickers and T-shirts produced as part of the workshop, at ruru house and displayed on Mikrolet vehicles; slogans include 'straight ahead', 'not in a hurry' and 'suicide because bankrupt'

31 From *Karbon* special issue, 'Absolut Versus'

2001

32–39 'Porno', exhibition by Jimmy Multhazam and Henry Irawan, opening and installation views

40 'Porno' poster

41 'Boy Band Only', detail from exhibition by Anggun Priambodo and Mateus Bondan

42 Installation view, 'Boy Band Only'

43 'Boy Band Only' poster

44 *Karbon*, issue 2

45 'Silent Forces': still from work by Anne Mie van Kerckhoven

46 Still from work by Sebastian Diaz Morales

47 Still from work by Adrianto Sinaga

48 Still from work by Ari Satria Darma

49 Still from work by Mahesa 'Doni' Almeida

50 Still from work by Syauqi 'Bimbo'

51 Still from work by Sebastian Diaz Morales

52–56 'Jakarta Habitus Publik', research, preparation and site visits

57 Work by Narpati Awangga aka Oomleo

58 Work by Adi Cumi at Blok M shopping mall

59 Work by S. Teddy D., nearby the National Monument

60–61 Works by Hauritsa

62 Work by Santo Banana, nearby the National Monument

63 Work by Bondi Bondan

64 'Swarm Project', a collaborative project that explored animal society as a possible metaphor for human social structure, discussion

65–66 Tero Nauha presentation/ performance

67 Ade Darmawan presentation

68 Work by Ade Darmawan

69–70 Work by Tina Ward

71 Exhibition party, with Tina Ward and Iin

72 Exhibition party

73 Exhibition party with Bondi Bondan, Anggun Priambodo, Iin and Indra Ameng

74–75 'My Sneakers', exhibition by Michael Blum, process documentation; for this project, the artist attempted to trace his footwear back to the factory in Indonesia where they were produced

76–80 Stills from Michael Blum, *My Sneakers*

81 Exterior view of second ruangrupa house, Tebet Barat, Jakarta

2002

82 *Karbon*, issue 3

83–84 Discussion for *Karbon*, ruru house

85–91 ruangrupa presentation at the 4th Gwangju Biennale, curated by Charles Esche, Hou Hanru and Sung Wan Kyung, installation views

92 *Karbon* special issue, 'Absolut Versus'

93–102 'what do you mean by using another?', installation views

103 'print 2000+2 project', an exhibition exploring ideas and practices of printmaking and print objects; work by Ade Darmawan

104 Installation view with Reza Afisina and work by Irwan Ahmett

105 Work by Indra Ameng

106 Work by Lilia Nursita

107 Work by Bondi Bondan

108 Work by Mushowir Bing

109 Work by Oscar 'Oca'

110 Work by Ronny Agustinus

111 Work by Tisna Sanjaya

112–15 RAIN meeting, Jakarta

116 'Short Message System', exhibition preparation

117 Exhibition preparation, with Ade Darmawan

118 Exhibition preparation, with Ade Darmawan, Azizah Asnawi and Tina Gillen

119 Exhibition opening, with Anggun Priambodho

120 Exhibition opening, with David Tarigan

121–24 Exhibition opening

125 *Karbon*, issue 4
126–29 'Polygame': performance by W. Christiawan
130–31 Performance by Hendrawan Riyanto
132–34 Performance by Mimi Fadmi
135–37 Performance by Rahmat Jabaril

2003

138–47 'Garbage Sale', opening and installation views
148 'Lekker Eten Zonder Betalen' flyer
149 Exhibition preparation, with Ade Darmawan
150–53 Exhibition preparation
154–55 Exhibition opening
156–60 Installation views
161 'Surround' opening, with Mushowir Bing and Reza Afisina
162 Exhibition opening, with Indra Ameng and Henry Foundation
163–67 Exhibition opening
168–72 Installation views
173–75 'Seduction (Boys Don't Cry)': work by Dewi Aditia
176–77 Work by Prilla Tania
178–79 Work by Ferial Affif
180 Installation view
181–82 Work by Puji 'Onet' Siswanti
183 Exhibition opening performance
184 *Karbon*, issue 5
185 OK.Video flyer, front
186–91 OK.Video, opening and installation views
192 OK.Video flyer, back
193–95 OK.Video, installation views
196 'Secrets / No Secrets', exhibition preparation with objects from Farah Wardani
197 Exhibition preparation with objects from Mushowir Bing
198–203 H.I.R.E. presentation and discussion
204–15 Chikako Watanabe and Tomoko Take, workshop and exhibition views

2004

216 Exterior view of third ruangrupa house, Tebet Barat Komp Kejaksaan, Jakarta
217–18 Floor plans, by Indra Ameng
219–20 'Top Collection', a project on the culture of photography in society; work by Irwan Ahmett
221 Work by Dimas Jayasrana
222 Work by Henry Foundation
223 Work by Indra Ameng
224–25 Work by Angki Purbandono
226–29 Work by Wimo A. Bayang
230–35 'the project #25', preparation, opening and installation views
236–37 Work by Rebecca Theodora
238–39 Work by Aprilia Apsari
240 *Karbon*, issue 6
241–45 'Komik Metropolis Gadungan Menyertai Anda', exhibition preparation and opening
246–54 'Zero Eye Lution', installation views
255 Jakarta 32°C logo
256–67 Jakarta 32°C, workshops and installation views
268–76 'Uncensored', opening and installation views

2005

277–78 'We are the generation that wear too many t-shirt', exhibition preparation
279–84 Exhibition views with visitor interaction, including Gandung Bagus Amento, Reza Afisina, Indra Ameng and Julia Sarisetiati
285–88 Works from the exhibition and installation views
289–92 OK.Video 'Sub/Version' installation views
293 'Kaos Project', Istanbul Biennale, curated by Charles Esche and Vasıf Kortun, installation view
294 'Kaos Project', detail

2006

295 *Karbon*, issue 7
296 'MEN AT WORK': work by R.M. Herwibowo, from a series of stickers produced for public spaces
297 Research image for Muhammad Ridwan's project on Padang restaurant signage
298 Work by reinaart vanhoe, from a series of four newsletters including contributions from the other project participants
299 'Pemulung' ('scavenger' or 'waste picker') t-shirt by Godel, from a series intended to support unusual or marginal forms of work
300–04 Installation views
305–09 'PLAYGROUND – LET THE KIDS PLAY', installation views
310–13 'Rethinking Nordic Colonialism Act 3', curated by Kuratorisk Aktion, installation views of ruangrupa's project *You're Welcome*. Courtesy Rethinking Nordic Colonialism
314–17 'PICNIC KIT', installation views
318–19 Work by Sebastian Friedman
320 Installation view
321–24 Interior views of fourth ruangrupa house, Tebet Timur, Jakarta
325 Exterior view
326 Interior view
327–34 'FOR SALE!', installation views

2007

335 OK.Video 'Militia', poster
336–40 Installation views
341 Still from *Bermain* by Melisa Deyatri (Jakarta-Prambors workshop)
342 Still from *Peta Ngombe (Drink Map)* by Seto Hari Wibowo (Malang workshop)
343 Still from *Kaki* by Jefri Hunter, Hauza Syaukani, Oki Helfiska, Madun and Ino Uin (Pekanbaru workshop)
344 Still from *Rob* by Rofikin (Semarang workshop)
345 Still from *Why???* by Uung (Yogyakarta workshop)
346 Still from *Handphone* by Po (Bandung workshop)
347 Installation view
348 Flyer

2008

349–61 'Happiness', exhibition by Irwan Ahmett, opening and installation views
362 Art criticism workshop, with Agung Jenong
363–71 Jakarta 32°C, exhibition preparation, opening and installation views
372–77 'HALOMONO 3', opening and installation views
378–89 'Siklus', curated by Adikara Rachman, discussion, opening and installation views
390–94 'Rayuan Pulau Kelapa', exhibition by Aprilia Apsari, curated by Farah Wardani, preparation
395–99 Opening and installation views
400 *Stiker Kota* research documentation
401 Curating workshop; facilitators included ruangrupa, Enin Supriyanto, Lisabona Rahman, Agung Jenong, Mella Jaarsma, Ade Darmawan, Nuraini Juliastuti, Ariel Yudi, Serrum, Eko Londo and Hikmat Budiman

2009

402–03 Works from *MANDOR*, a publication of work from artists across Indonesia; the artists for the first edition are listed as: 'dias, toro, said, abin, afiz, aiya, tenesa, trina, toto, wahyu, angki, rama, mamat, tumpal, godit, griksa, ryan, bobreng, andre, cumut, alvianda, deka, dimgras, taufik fiki, mira, nabila, prio, sena'
404–11 *MANDOR* launch, exhibition and performances
412–18 Jakarta 32°C Showcase, installation views
419–23 'Jendela PM Toh', curated by Hafiz Rancajale, opening and installation views
424–25 Performance by PM Toh
426–29 Opening and installation views

430–34 'Macro-Micro', curated by Francis Rambert, opening

435 'Femme': work by Stigma Foundation
436–38 Opening and installation views
439–41 Zine workshop with Ika Vantiani

442 'Jimi! Jimi! Jimi!', exhibition by Jimi Multhazam, curated by Ade Darmawan, installation view
443–44 Works by Jimi Multhazam
445–48 Opening, which included performances by Morfem, The Trees and The Wild

449 OK.Video 'Comedy', poster
450 Exhibition opening
451 'Mari Syuting!' ("Let's Shoot!") video workshop with Ari Dina Krestiawan
452 Screening and discussion, Newseum Cafe
453 Artist gathering, ruru house
454–58 Exhibition installation views

459–68 'Lonely Market', documentation

469–74 Stills from works included in 'Footage Jive', exhibition by Mahardika Yudha, curated by Reza Afisina
475–76 Opening performance by Adrian Adioetomo

477 Reza Afisina speaking as part of Thursday Night Supper programme, at apartment 18b, Casco's residency accommodation. Photo: Casco Art Institute: Working for the Commons

478 'copy-paste extraordinaire', exhibition by Henry Foundation, curated by Agung Jenong, installation view
479 Henry Foundation, *Day Off*, 2009
480 Henry Foundation, *Dead End*, 2009
481 Henry Foundation, *Pepsi*, 1997
482 Henry Foundation, *Jurusan Kota*, 1997
483 Exhibition group photograph
484 Indra Ameng, Henry Foundation and Agung Jenong
485–86 Installation views

487–91 'Komik Magnetik', installation views
492 Opening performance

2010

493–97 www.respectastreetartgallery.com, launch presentations

498–504 'Numpang Nampang', exhibition by POPO, curated by Andi Rharharha and Bujangan Urban, installation views and discussion

505 'Ruru Jazz Fest', flyer
506 Performance, with Ricky Surya Virgana on cello

507–12 'Toko Keperluan', exhibition by Anggun Priambodo, installation views
513 Group photograph, with Anggun Priambodo, ruangrupa members and others

514 'Art on Poskart' artwork documentation

515–21 Exhibition opening and installation views

522–23 'Hanya Memberi Tak Harap Kembali' at Galeri Soemardja, Institut Teknologi Bandung, installation views
524 Installation view, Kedai Kebun Forum, Yogyakarta
525 ruangrupa tenth birthday cake, at the opening at Kedai Kebun Forum

526 'Codex Code', sticker
527–32 Installation views, workshops and opening performance

533–40 Holy Market #2, documentation

541 'ruru.zip', installation view. 'Decompression #10: Expanding the Space and Public', organised to mark ruangrupa's tenth anniversary, included three exhibitions at Galeri Nasional Indonesia: 'ruru & friends', curated by Agung Jenong, presented artworks by current and former ruangrupa members alongside artists hosted or supported by them; 'ruru.net', curated by Reza Afisina and Iswanto Hartono, presented ruangrupa's network through 25 invited contributions from collectives and organisations they have collaborated with; and 'ruru.zip', curated by Ugeng T. Moetidjo and Farah Wardani, presented materials from ruangrupa's archive. The 'Decompression #10' programme at Galeri Nasional Indonesia also included a third iteration of 'Hanya Memberi Tak Harap Kembali' ('To Give and Expect Nothing in Return'); the fourth edition of Jakarta 32°C; a programme for children by RURU-kids; 'ruru.mov', a film programme curated by Lisabona Rahman and Anggun Priambodo; and RRREC Fest, a music festival programmed by Henry Foundation and Nasta Sutardjo. 'Decompression #10' also included related presentations at Singapore Night Festival 2010; the exhibition 'Multimedia Arts in Indonesia', curated by Hendro Wiyanto, at Galeri Cipta II, Taman Ismail Marzuki; '10 Years of Indonesian Video Art Compilation', programmed by Hafiz Rancajale, at Goethe Institut Jakarta; a seminar series programmed by Mirwan Andan at Galeri Nasional Indonesia and Taman Ismail Marzuki; and the production of a publication and a feature documentary on ruangrupa

542–46 Jakarta 32°C, installation views
547 Jakarta 32°C, poster
548 Installation view

2011

549 RRREC Fest, performance by The Upstairs

550 Performance by White Shoes & The Couples Company

551–62 'Decompression #10', installation views

563–68 '1001 Doors: Reinterpreting the Tradition', installation views

569–71 *Singapore Fiction*, at the 2011 Singapore Biennale, artistic director Matthew Ngui and curators Russell Storer and Trevor Smith, installation views

572–75 *Mini OK.Video Festival*, installation at Art Dubai, curated by Nav Haq, installation views

576–84 'Berbeda dan Merdeka 100%', documentation

585 'Lonely Market: Artist Artworks Edition', poster

586–87 'Project T70', installation views
588 Work by Irwan Ahmett, presented by himself and Tita Salina
589 Work by Irwan Ahmett
590 Work from 'Kaos Project', 2005
591 Work documentation
592 From *aktuil* (pop music magazine)

593–95 'The Best of the Beast', installation views

596–97 'City_net Asia 2011' installation views

598 OK.Video 'Flesh', poster
599–610 OK.Video 'Flesh', opening and installation views

2012

611–22 'Tanda Mata: Jakarta Merchandise Project', curated by POPO, opening and installation views

623–29 RURUshop Radio launch, documentation

630–41 'Bandung – Jakarta – Singapore: Performance Art Touring', documentation

642–53 'DRIFT: Pameran Seni Multimedia', opening and installation views

654–58 *Bung!* magazine launch, documentation

659 'Top Collection #3': work by Agan Harahap
660 Installation view
661 Work by Nissan Nur Afryansah
662 Work by Reza Mustar
663–67 Exhibition opening and Installation views

668 Ade Darmawan, *Philosophy Football (Match) 3.0*, 2011

669–74 Holy Market, documentation

675–76 ruangrupa participation in the 2012 Busan Biennale, curated by Roger M. Buergel, for which they developed a presentation of their history and archive; installation views

677–87 Jakarta 32°C, opening and installation views

688–96 'Riwayat Saudagar', exhibition by Saleh Husein, curated by M G Pringgotono, opening and installation views

697–704 'The Sweet and Sour Story of Sugar', installation views

2013

705 THE KUDA: *The Untold Story of Indonesian Underground Music in the 70s*, for 'The 7th Asia Pacific Triennial of Contemporary Art': archival photograph of The Kuda

706–12 Exhibition preparation

713–19 Opening and installation views

720 Archival photograph of The Kuda

721 Opening performance by The Family Butcher

722 'Festival Film Musik RURUshop Radio', flyer

723–27 Artist-in-residence talk with Penny Demertzi, documentation

728–34 'Print Process', opening and installation views

735 Flyer

736–42 'Sarimin is Lost in the Market', workshop documentation

743–46 'Visual Mengikat Sejarah', talk with Mitu M. Prie, documentation

747–53 'Body Festival', curated by Ika Vantiani, opening and installation views, including works by Annisa Utami, Natasha Gabriella Tontey and Rega Ayundya Putri; with opening performance by DII and a DJ set by Café Mondo

754–60 Holy Market, documentation

761 'Vertical Villages', installation view. Courtesy 4A Centre for Contemporary Art. Photo: Zan Wimberley

762 OK.Video 'Muslihat', logo

763 Opening talks, with Tadashi Ogawa, director-general of the Japan Foundation in Jakarta

764 Opening talks, with festival curator Mahardika Yudha

765 Opening talks, with (from left) Ade Darmawan, M. Sigit Budi Santoso, Oomleo and opening MC

766 Opening talks, with (from left) Rizki Lazuardi, Irma Chantily, Julia Sarisetiati, Mahardika Yudha, Oomleo and opening MC

767–70 Opening and installation views

771 Opening performance by DJ KRS9TH

772–74 'JAF (Jatiwangi Art Factory) vs KINETIK-WAFT', curated by Alghorie and Benny Wicaksono, opening and installation views

775–81 'Begadang Neng?', opening and installation views

782–85 'Gerobak Bioskop', preparation and installation views

786–87 RRREC Fest #3, flyer

788 'In Delta Flux', presentation by curator Arjon Dunnewind

789–95 Opening and installation views

796–806 Holy Market, documentation

807–812 Pertunjukan Teater Paseban (Paseban Womens' Theatre) performance, documentation. ruangrupa was used as a rehearsal space for the performance, which subsequently toured.

2014

813 *Happy new year!*, elements from an animated GIF circulated by email

814–17 'Untuk Ibnu', documentation

818–24 'The Growing Manual', curated by John Reardon and Hyemin Son, installation views; the exhibition included contributions from ruangrupa and Serrum, among others, including a kiosk with ruangrupa publications

825–32 'Swatata', opening and installation views

833–39 *Duka Kuda* by The Kuda, record launch, documentation; the event included performances by The Kuda, Bequiet, Seaside and DJ Nick Hefner

840–47 The Arts Collaboratory Assembly, a week-long programme with the 24 participating organisations of the network, documentation

848–53 'Ladies Night Market' and Empat Lima workshop, documentation

854 *Temporary Territory*, at the 2014 Darwin Festival, curated by Edwina Lunn, installation view. Photo: Sarah Pirrie

855–60 *Temporary Territory*, installation views

861–71 Holy Market, documentation

872 RRREC Fest #4, flyer

873–80 ruangrupa participation in 31st Bienal de São Paulo, curated by Charles Esche, Galit Eilat, Nuria Enguita Mayo, Pablo Lafuente, Oren Sagiv, Benjamin Seroussi and Luiza Proença, installation views

881–85 Jakarta 32°C, preparatory workshop

2015

886–91 'Prototipe', exhibition by Benny Wicaksono, workshop documentation

892–94 'M's Wonderful Drawer', presentation by Viviana Cardenas, documentation

895–901 'Hidangan Dari Langit', exhibition by PM Toh, installation views

902 'Buka Warung', poster

903–912 OK.Video 'Orde Baru', opening

913–15 Gudang Sarinah Ekosistem, planning documents

916 View of Gudang Sarinah Ekosistem and surrounding area

917–18 Views of Gudang Sarinah Ekosistem, including entrance. Photo: David Morris

919 Holy Market at Gudang Sarinah Ekosistem. Photo: David Morris

920–30 Views of Gudang Sarinah Ekosistem, including RURU Gallery, OK.Video space, RURUshop, office, workspaces and library/archive. Photo: David Morris

931 'Plan B', exhibition by Adi Sundoro and Panca Satria, poster

2016

932 Sonsbeek 16: 'transACTION': ruruhuis in Arnhem. Courtesy reinaart vanhoe

933 Installation view, with work by Alphons ter Avest; for all Sonsbeek 16 documentation (933–50), photography by Maurice Boyer

934 Installation view, with work by Cinema Caravan

935 Installation view, with work by Eko Prawoto

936 Installation view, with work by Louie Cordero

937 Installation view, with work by Jatiwangi Art Factory

938 Installation view, with work by KUNSTrePUBLIK

939 Installation view, with work by Iswanto Hartono

940 Installation view, with work by Eva Koťátková

941 Installation view, with work by Fintan Magee

942 Installation view, with work by Mark Salvatus

943 Installation view, with work by Marishka Soekarna

944 Details from *Karbon* 'Arnhem Files' publication series, edited by Sanne Oorthuizen, with handwritten notes by reinaart vanhoe

945 Installation view, with work by Maze de Boer

946 Installation view, with work by Naamloozz

947 Installation view, with work by reinaart vanhoe

948 Installation view, with work by Richard Bell

949 Installation view, with work by Rob Voerman

950 Installation view, with work by Rossella Biscotti

951–56 ruangrupa pop-up school in Aichi Triennale, documentation

2017

957–69 RRREC Fest at the Museum, documentation

970–72 ruangrupa participation in 'Sunshower', installation views. Courtesy Mori Art Museum, Tokyo. Photo: Kioku Keizo

973–86 OK.Video 'OK.Pangan', installation views

987 ruangrupa participation in 'Cosmopolis #1', installation view

988 Holy Market, documentation

2018

989 Cafe Ipok Icon at Gudskul Ekosistem

990 Interior views of Gudskul Ekosistem, including RURU Gallery and Grafis Huru Hara space

991–97 'Pemandangan', exhibition by Dwi 'Ube' Wicaksono, curated by Saleh Husein, installation views

998 The Kuda showcase in 'Songs for the People', installation view

999–1002 'Efek Rumah Tangga?', exhibition by Arman Arief Rachman, installation views

2019

1003 OK.Video showcase in 'Food Today: Indonesian Food, Society and Media Art', installation view

2021

1004–007 'Oven Studio', flyer and documentation

1008–025 'Gudskul: Knowledge Garden Festival', organised by Callum Schuster, opening, installation views and workshops; the display visualised Gudskul's process of engaging with creative communities across Toronto; the festival included art-making activities, workshops and social gatherings open to audiences

1026–035 'Drawing Drawings', exhibition by Abi Rama, opening and installation views

1036 *lumbung Kassel, lumbung inter-lokal, lumbung Indonesia*, drawing by Indra Ameng, 2022

2022–

1037 documenta fifteen 'key visual', © documenta fifteen 2022

1038 ruangrupa timeline for documenta fifteen

1039 documenta fifteen 'Welcome Centre', exterior view, ruruHaus, Kassel, 19 June 2022. Photo: Nicolas Wefers

1040 documenta fifteen artistic team and ruangrupa members at ruruHaus, Kassel, 2021. From left to right: Lara Khaldi, Iswanto Hartono, Gertrude Flentge, Mirwan Andan, Frederikke Hansen, Julia Sarisetiati, Reza Afisina, Ajeng Nurul Aini, Ade Darmawan, Indra Ameng. Photo: Nicolas Wefers

1041 Dan Perjovschi, *Generosity, Regeneration, Transparency, Independence, Sufficiency, Local Anchor and most of all Humor*, 2022, installation view, Fridericianum. Photo: Nicolas Wefers

1042 Baan Noorg Collaborative Arts and Culture, *The Rituals of Things*, 2022, installation view, documenta Halle. Photo: Nicolas Wefers

1043 Richard Bell, installation view, Fridericianum. Photo: Nicolas Wefers

1044 Nino Bulling, *Sometimes when we kiss, it feels like I am drinking water from your mouth*, 2022, Hafenstrasse 76. Photo: Maja Wirkus

1045 Imane Zoubii, *Is our bread ready yet? (Act I)*, LE 18, WH22, 2022. Photo: Nicolas Wefers

1046 Nhà Sàn Collective, *Tuấn Mami, Vietnamese Immigrating Garden*, 2022, installation view, WH22. Photo: Nils Klinger

1047 OFF-Biennale Budapest, Eva Koťátková, *Daydreaming Workstation*, 2022, installation view (detail), Bootsverleih Ahoi. Photo: Frank Sperling

1048 Taring Padi, *Bara Solidaritas: Sekarang Mereka, Besok Kita / The Flame of Solidarity: First they came or them, then they came for us*, 2022, installation view, Hallenbad Ost. Photo: Frank Sperling

1049 La Intermundial Holobiente, *Theaterschlag*, 2022, installation view, compost heap (Karlsaue). Photo: Nils Klinger

1050 Asia Art Archive and The Black Archives, installation views, Fridericianum. Photo: Frank Sperling

1051 Jumana Emil Abboud, *My Other Half*, 2022, performance, Nordstadtpark. Photo: Martha Friedel

1052 Jatiwangi Art Factory, *New Rural Agenda Summit*, Fridericianum, 21 June 2022. Photo: Martha Friedel

1053 Trampoline House, 2022, installation view, Hübner areal. Photo: Frank Sperling

1054 Keleketla! Library, Asia Art Archive and The Black Archives, 'Conversing', Fridericianum (Fridskul Common Library), Kassel, 19 June 2022. Photo: Nicolas Wefers

1055 Karaoke at GudKitchen/ Fridericianum, 16 June 2022. Photo: David Morris

1056 Press conference performance by Agus Nur Amal (aka PM Toh), Auestadion; 15 June 2022. Photo: Nicolas Wefers

1057 Cinema Caravan and Takashi Kuribayashi, *Screening in Outside of Mosquito Net (Out of the Loop)*, 2022, Karlswiese. Photo: Nils Klinger

1058 Atis Rezistans | Ghetto Biennale, installation view, St. Kunigundis. Photo: Frank Sperling

1059 Gudkitchen (behind Fridericianum). Photo: Tian Zhang

1060–062 lumbung Gallery, harvest drawings by Tropical Tap Water

1063 lumbung Kios, harvest drawing by Tropical Tap Water

1064 lumbung.space, harvest drawing by reinaart vanhoe

1065 lumbung.space workshop at ook_ studio, Rotterdam, 2022

1066–068 lumbung Press, research images

1069 lumbung Press concert with Erick Beltrán, 'Meydan #2', documenta Halle, 13 August 2022. Photo: Nicolas Wefers

1070 Still from 'lumbung of Publishers', documenta fifteen website

1071–078 lumbung Land, documentation of various working group meetings, from the document 'LAND GROUP LUMBUNG INTERLOKAL LAND SCHOOL: Activities report during documenta fifteen'

1079 'Lumbung will continue!' Photo: Khaled Barakeh

1080–091 'Get.Raw Lab: 20 Years of OK.Video', opening

1092–093 'Lumbung Bersambung', maps designed by Enjoy Balikpapan, for ruangrupa's 'From Klandasan via Vasey Highway' tour in Balikpapan facilitated by The Secret Agents and Julia Sarisetiati; the base layer of the design is a map titled 'Enemy Defences – Balikpapan 15 June 1945' produced by Australian Survey Corps

1094–095 Synchronize Festival graphic and t-shirt, 2025. Courtesy Cisarua Creative, Syaiful Ardianto, Bondi Goodboy, Degi Bintoro, haorits and Cycojano

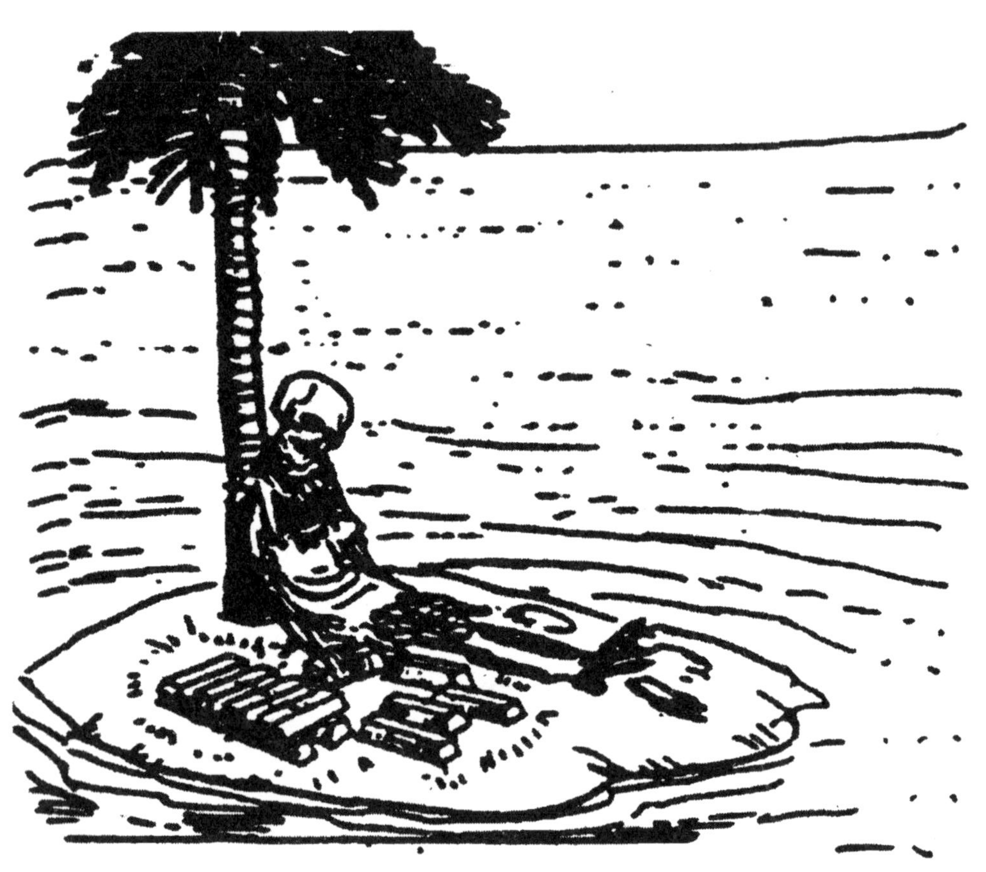

Being bankrupt is
better than being
corrupt.